UNIVERSITY CASEBOOK SERIES®

PROPERTY

PRINCIPLES AND POLICIES

FOURTH EDITION

THOMAS W. MERRILL
Charles Evans Hughes Professor of Law
Columbia Law School

HENRY E. SMITH
Fessenden Professor of Law
Harvard Law School

MAUREEN E. BRADY
Professor of Law
Harvard Law School

FOUNDATION
PRESS

University Casebook Series is a trademark registered in the U.S. Patent and Trademark Office.

© 2007, 2012 THOMSON REUTERS/FOUNDATION PRESS
© 2017 LEG, Inc. d/b/a West Academic
© 2022 LEG, Inc. d/b/a West Academic
  444 Cedar Street, Suite 700
  St. Paul, MN 55101
  1-877-888-1330

Printed in the United States of America

ISBN: 978-1-63659-367-8

To Bob Ellickson and Carol Rose
teachers, colleagues, and friends

PREFACE TO THE FOURTH EDITION

This Fourth Edition preserves the pedagogical approach of the first three, presenting property as cohering around basic notions such as legal things and possession, while successively introducing important qualifications and complications. We continue to organize the subject around important concepts and institutional structures and to provide perspectives from economics, history, and philosophy through the notes and connective discussion. As always, we seek to improve the book, drawing upon our own experience in teaching from it and benefitting from the many helpful comments from other adopters, teaching assistants, and, most importantly, students. With a new co-editor who is a scholar of property law and its history and an experienced user of the book, we have introduced new material and made some further organizational changes designed to make the book a better teaching vehicle.

We have continued to fortify the theme of equity, introducing it in connection with injunctions in Chapter I and going into further depth in Chapter IV. The additional case on injunctions in Chapter I, Pardee v. Camden Lumber Co., allows for the introduction of themes like subjective value, changed conditions, and the like. Chapter II includes new materials on drones and a case on hydraulic fracturing. At various points in the book, we have taken account of recent technological developments, especially in the digital realm. In this and other places in the book, we make reference to the ongoing Restatement (Fourth) of Property, with which all three casebook editors are involved as Reporter and Associate Reporters.

We have also added a full unit on custom and the law in Chapter III, with an emphasis on Native American law. Our new edition adds a landmark case from the Hopi tribal court, Smith v. James. We have brought back United States v. Corrow, about the Native American Graves Protection and Repatriation Act, from the first and second editions into this new unit. Notable changes in Chapter V include a new case on marital property and a greater emphasis on the law of restitution, consistent with our approach throughout the book. We have updated the discussion of land records to reflect increasing use of digital technology, streamlined the material on leasing, revised the discussion of nuisance, and included recent developments in the law of covenants. Chapter X on government forbearance and takings has been reorganized and includes Cedar Point Nursery v. Hassid and a discussion of other recent developments.

For crucial and ongoing input, we continue to be greatly indebted to many friends and colleagues: Shyam Balganesh, Vicki Been, Avi Bell, David Blankfein-Tabachnik, Sam Bray, Yun-chien Chang, Nico Cornell, Richard Briffault, Sara Bronin, Eric Claeys, Steve Eagle, Bob Ellickson, Richard Epstein, Cynthia Estlund, James Grimmelmann, Dan Kelly, Scott Kieff, Brian Lee, Lance Liebman, Jonathan Nash, Shitong Qiao,

Claire Priest, Barak Richman, Carol Rose, Duane Rudolph, Dan Sharfstein, Sun-Joo Shin, Joe Singer, Bruce Smith, Steve Spitz, Joshua Tate, David Waddilove, and Katrina Wyman. For his expert collection of copyright permissions we are again grateful to Brad Conner. We have also profited from and enjoyed our experience using the book to teach our own students, and have benefitted especially from the excellent work of our research assistants at Columbia, Harvard, and Yale. In connection with the preparation of this fourth edition, we would like to express our thanks to Staci Herr and the production team at the Foundation Press. As ever, we would most of all like to thank our families.

THOMAS W. MERRILL
HENRY E. SMITH
MAUREEN E. BRADY

February 10, 2022

PREFACE TO THE FIRST EDITION

This casebook differs from others in that it regards property law as a single subject unified by core principles. There are many important differences between real property (land and buildings), personal property (movable things), intellectual property (original inventions, expressions, and marks), and natural resources (public lands, water, wildlife). Nevertheless, we believe there are certain basic principles that unite these different manifestations of property, and that these principles can and should be the focus of an introductory course.

The most basic principle is that property at its core entails the right to exclude others from some discrete thing. This right gives rise to a general duty on the part of others to abstain from interfering with the thing. This structure of rights and duties leads to characteristic bundles of rights, unites the various institutional forms we call property, and differentiates property rights from personal rights and contract rights. The basic exclusion strategy also serves as the starting point for further elaborations, refinements, exceptions, and overlays, which govern the use of resources with greater particularity. Together these rights to exclude and governance rules collectively make up the law of property and connect property to adjacent areas of contracts, torts, regulation, and public law.

We do not present our foundational principles as dogma. They serve as organizing devices for the casebook. The materials are designed to challenge each student to decide for him or herself whether property is defined by common principles such as the right to exclude others, or whether any such principle is so riddled with qualifications that property can only be regarded as an ad hoc "bundle of rights" without any distinguishing features.

In keeping with our perspective that property law is a unified subject, the casebook does not focus on one type of property such as land, nor does it organize materials into traditional subfields such as real, personal, intellectual, and natural resources. Instead, we draw on cases and materials from each of these areas throughout the book. No attempt is made to provide comprehensive coverage of any subfield; comprehensiveness is not possible, even in real estate law, the traditional focus. Rather our focus is on design principles common to all subfields of property. This reorientation is also appropriate, we believe, given that intellectual property and environmental issues loom much larger in the law school curriculum—and the practice of law—than was true in earlier generations when real estate law was paramount. An introduction to property law should provide a grounding that students can build upon whatever direction their future studies and practice may take.

Although our organizing principles are innovative, the selection of materials is deliberately conventional, as befits a field where stability of expectations plays such a large role. Judicial opinions serve as the primary vehicle for instruction, and we have tried to retain a high proportion of the chestnuts that have traditionally featured in property law materials. The cases are punctuated at intervals with short excerpts from the secondary literature or (in some instances) our own short summary of the secondary literature. These excerpts are designed to supply institutional or historical context, or to raise philosophical or policy questions not expressly addressed by the opinions. The secondary-source excerpts can serve as jumping off points for class discussion, or can be assigned as background reading, as the teacher sees fit.

In editing opinions, we have tried to strike a compromise between, on the one hand, burdening the student with extraneous issues and boilerplate and, on the other hand, reducing opinions to squibs lacking any context. We believe it is important, particularly in an introductory course like property law, to see how the characterization of facts in opinions influences legal conclusions, and how procedural and remedial issues interact with substantive issues. We have tried to leave in enough contextual detail to permit these connections to be explored in class. With respect to secondary materials, the editing is much more drastic, and is designed to capture one or two key points rather than the full nuanced argument. Deletions of text in all materials are indicated by three stars (* * *), but citations have often been omitted without any indication. We have frequently modified the citation form in opinions to conform to modern style. Footnotes have generally been deleted, but where they are retained, we have used their original number. Editor footnotes are indicated by symbols (*, †, etc.).

We have many people to thank for their generous contributions to this book. For their insightful comments on drafts, we would like to thank Richard Briffault, Robert Ellickson, Richard Epstein, Cynthia Estlund, Lance Liebman, Jonathan Nash, Claire Priest, Carol Rose, Sun-Joo Shin, Bruce Smith, Joshua Tate, and the anonymous reviewers for Foundation Press. A special debt of gratitude goes to our students at Columbia, Harvard, and Yale, who participated enthusiastically in our experiments with the earlier versions of this book. For their invaluable assistance tracking down permissions and helping with production, we thank Bradford Connor, P.J. Gach, Monika Piotrowicz, and Sarah Sladen. Our illustrator, Leslie Evans of Seadog Press, provided extensive assistance with illustrations and figures. We have also benefited greatly from the efforts of our research assistants at Columbia and Yale: Mina Farbood, Benjamin Gould, Michael Grisolia, Valerie Jaffee, David Olasky, Matteo Rizzolli, and Mainon Schwartz. Vic Khanna, Alan Schwartz, and the staffs at the Columbia, Harvard, and Yale Law Libraries have also been very kind and helpful in tracking down various materials. We are also deeply appreciative of the many people who assisted us with their advice and permission in connection with the material listed in the acknowledgments. For their excellent work on the book in all stages of its development, we thank John Bloomquist, Jim Coates, Steve Errick,

Tim Payne, and the staff at Foundation Press. Finally, we most of all would like to thank our families for their crucial support in this project.

ACKNOWLEDGMENTS

The authors gratefully acknowledge the permission kindly granted to reproduce the textual excerpts and illustrations indicated below.

Books and Articles

Arruñada, Benito, *Institutional Foundations of Impersonal Exchange: Theory and Policy of Contractual Registries*, Copyright 2012 by the University of Chicago. All rights reserved.

Baird, Douglas, and Thomas Jackson, *Information, Uncertainty and the Transfer of Property*, 13 Journal of Legal Studies 299 (1984). Copyright 1984 by The University of Chicago. All rights reserved.

Beyer, Gerry W., 19A *West's Legal Forms, Real Estate Transactions, Residential* § 48.3 (3d ed. 2002), West Publishing Co. Reprinted with permission.

Calabresi, Guido, and A. Douglas Melamed, *Property Rules, Liability Rules, and Inalienability: One View of the Cathedral*, 85 Harvard Law Review 1089 (1972). Reprinted by permission of the Harvard Law Review Association and William S. Hein Company for The Harvard Law Review, Vol. 85, pages 1089, 1090, 1092, and 1093.

Chafee, Jr., Zechariah, and Sidney Post Simpson, *Cases on Equity, Jurisdiction and Specific Performance* (1934), pages 704–06, 710–11. West Publishing Co. Reprinted with permission.

Coase, Ronald, *The Federal Communications Commission*, 2 Journal of Law & Economics 1 (1959). Copyright © 1959 by the University of Chicago. All rights reserved.

Coase, Ronald, *The Problem of Social Cost*, 3 Journal of Law & Economics 1 (1960). Copyright © 1960 by the University of Chicago. All rights reserved.

Craswell, Richard, *Passing on the Costs of Legal Rules: Efficiency and Distribution in Buyer-Seller Relationships*, 43 Stanford Law Review 361 (1991), pages 378–79. Reprinted with permission.

Demsetz, Harold, *Toward a Theory of Property Rights*, 57 American Economic Review 347–48, 350–58 (1967) (Papers & Proceedings). The American Economic Review. Reprinted with permission.

Ellickson, Robert, *Property in Land*, 102 Yale Law Journal 1315 (1993). Reprinted by permission of The Yale Law Journal Company and William C. Hein Company from *The Yale Law Journal*, Vol. 102, pages 1315–1400.

Grey, Tom, *The Disintegration of Property*, NYU Press. Copyright 1980 by New York University. Reprinted with the permission of New York University Press.

Hansmann, Henry, *Condominium and Cooperative Housing: Transactional Efficiency, Tax Subsidies, and Tenure Choice*, 20 Journal of Legal Studies 25 (1991). Copyright 1991 by the University of Chicago. All rights reserved.

LaFave, Wayne R., *Criminal Law*, West Publishing Co. Reprinted with permission.

Leach, W. Barton, and James K. Logan, *Perpetuities: A Standard Saving Clause to Avoid Violations of the Rule*, 74 Harvard Law Review 1141 (1961). Reprinted by permission of the Harvard Law Review Association and William S. Hein Company from The Harvard Law Review, Vol. 74, pages 1141–42.

Lee, Thomas R., *Stare Decisis in Historical Perspective*, 52 Vanderbilt Law Review 645 (1999). Reprinted with permission.

Mann, Ronald J., *The Concept of Collateral*, in: Commercial Finance: A Transactional Approach 77–83 (Foundation Press 2017).

Ostrom, Elinor, *Governing the Commons: The Evolution of Institutions for Collective Action*. © Cambridge University Press 1990. Reprinted with the permission of Cambridge University Press.

Penner, J.E., *The Idea of Property* (1997), Oxford University Press. Reprinted with permission.

Radin, Margaret, *Property and Personhood*, 34 Stanford Law Review 957 (1982). Reprinted with permission.

Radin, Margaret Jane, *Market-Inalienability*, 100 Harvard Law Review 1849 (1987), pages 1849, 1909–10, 1912–13, 1915–17. Reprinted with permission.

Reich, Charles A., *The New Property*, 73 Yale Law Journal 733 (1964). Reprinted by permission of the Yale Law Journal Company.

Rose, Carol, *The Comedy of the Commons: Custom, Commerce, and Inherently Public Property*, 53 University of Chicago Law Review 711 (1986). Reprinted with permission.

Rose, Carol, *Crystals and Mud in Property Law*, 40 Stanford Law Review 577 (1988). Reprinted with permission.

Rose, Carol, *Energy and Efficiency in the Realignment of Common-Law Water Rights*, 19 Journal of Legal Studies 261 (1990). Reprinted with permission.

Illustrations

Bertaud, Alain, and Bertrand Renaud, graph, Socialist Cities without Land Markets, 41 Journal of Urban Economics 137, 141 (1997).

The Brokaw Mansion, 1 East 79th Street, New York City, photograph, *The Irving Brokaw Mansion Fifth Avenue & 79th Street*. Glass Plate Negative. Undated. Museum of the City of New York. The Underhill Collection. B.1642

The Charles River Bridge, Built in 1785, Courtesy Instructional Resources Corporation.

The Chrisman Sisters in Front of Lizzie Chrisman's Homestead, Custer County, Nebraska, 1886, photograph, Courtesy Nebraska State Historical Society Photograph Collection.

Clifton Terrace, Washington, D.C., photograph, Courtesy Richard Chused.

Craswell, Richard, *Passing on the Costs of Legal Rules: Efficiency and Distribution in Buyer-Seller Relationships*, 43 Stanford Law Review 361 (1991), page 378. Figure 5—Low- and high-valuing marginal customers. Reprinted with permission.

An Egg-Washing Machine, photograph, Courtesy Petaluma Historical Museum.

The Empire Mine and the Town of Palmer, Courtesy Airphoto Jim Wark.

The Fontainebleau and Eden Roc Hotels, Miami Beach, Florida (2 images), Courtesy The Bramson Archive, Miami, FL.

Great Onyx Cave, Postcard published by the Great Onyx Cave Hotel (L.P. Edwards, Proprietor). Courtesy Kentucky Library, Western Kentucky University.

Gwernhaylod House, Overton: West Elevation, 1956, photograph, © Crown copyright: Royal Commission on the Ancient and Historical Monuments of Wales.

Hamidi, left, and a supporter delivering a message to Intel employees on a floppy disk after the Superior Court had enjoined his emails, photograph, Don Preisler.

A Holdout. By MrTinDC, www.flickr.com, licensed under CC BY-ND 2.0.

House in *Shelley v. Kraemer* with Commemorative Marker, Saint Louis Post-Dispatch.

The Howard County Hunt Club, photograph, Courtesy Howard County Historical Society.

An International Harvester 1066 and a Disk Harrow. By Daniel Christensen—Own work, CC BY 3.0, https://commons.wikimedia.org/w/index.php?curid=8336883.

Kelo, Susette in Front of Her House, Photo by Isaac Reese, 2004 © Institute for Justice.

The Kelo House and Its Surroundings, Photograph by Tim Martin. Courtesy The Day Publishing Co., New London, Connecticut.

Klamath Falls City Library, ca. 1960, Courtesy Klamath County Museums.

Lakeside Village, Culver City, California, Courtesy Jack and Ginny Sher.

Lucas's Two Lots, November 1994, Courtesy William A. Fischel, Department of Economics, Dartmouth College.

Map of the Area Involved in Lucas, Douglas R. Porter, The *Lucas Case*, Urban Land, Sept. 1992, at 27, 29.

Map of Land Claims in Johnson v. M'Intosh, From the Law and History Review. Copyright 2001 by the Board of Trustees of the University of Illinois. Used with permission of the University of Illinois Press.

Map of Land at Issue in *Delfino v. Vealencis*, Manel Baucells and Steven A. Lippman, Justice Delayed is Justice Denied: A Cooperative Game Theoretic Analysis of Hold-Up in Co-Ownership, 22 Cardozo L. Rev. 1191, 1222 (2001).

Mayor Ed J. Howard, Ann E. Hodges, and Chief W.D. Ashcraft, the afternoon of the fall, Courtesy Alabama Museum of Natural History, The University of Alabama.

The Mobile Home at Its Final Resting Place after Being Dragged across the Jacques' Field, photograph, Courtesy Patrick A. Dewane, Jr., attorney for Harvey and Lois Jacque.

Myatt, John in His Studio, Photo: Jean-Philippe Defaut/The New York Times/Redux.

One of the Former Lucas Lots after Construction, March 2000, Courtesy William A. Fischel, Department of Economics, Dartmouth College.

Pennsylvania Railroad Station, New York City, Museum of the City of New York.

Professor Longhair, 1977, photograph by Leni Sinclair. Courtesy Leni Sinclair.

Rothko, Mark in his 69th Street Studio, Photograph by Hans Namuth. Courtesy Center for Creative Photography, University of Arizona © 1991 Hans Namuth Estate.

Sanborn Fire Insurance Map of Area in *Sanborn v. McLean*, Source: 9 Sanborn Map Co., Insurance Maps of Detroit, Michigan, No. 12 (1925).

The St. Vrain Creek, photograph by Susan Thomas, Courtesy Susan Thomas.

Timetable for Pacific Air Transport, February 1, 1928, photograph, From the Collection of Craig Morris.

Title Page of the First of the Bamford Manuscripts, Courtesy Princeton University Library.

Uston, Ken, Courtesy Uston Family and www.uston.com.

A View of Navy Pier from the Shoreline in Chicago, photograph, David Bjorgen. This image is licensed under the Creative Commons Attribution ShareAlike License v. 2.5.

Zoning of Properties near the Ambler Realty Tract, Timothy Alan Fluck, Euclid v. Ambler: A Retrospective, 52 J. Am. Planning Ass'n 326, 329, Map 2 (Summer 1986).

SUMMARY OF CONTENTS

TABLE OF CONTENTS

TABLE OF CASES

The principal cases are in bold type.

UNIVERSITY CASEBOOK SERIES®

PROPERTY

PRINCIPLES AND POLICIES

FOURTH EDITION

CHAPTER I

WHAT IS PROPERTY?

A. TWO CONCEPTIONS OF PROPERTY

What is property? There is a surprisingly wide range of answers to this basic question. We start with two conceptions of property. One may be familiar to you already: property as a right to a thing good against the world. In contrast to this traditional everyday view, many theorists adopt a competing conception of property as a collection ("bundle") of rights, with content that varies according to context and policy choices. As a way into these conceptions and the study of property law, we present in this Chapter a series of cases about interferences with legal interests in land. The cases introduce some basic legal concepts important to the study of property, including trespass and nuisance, the use of contracts to resolve property disputes, and the conditions for granting injunctions rather than awarding damages for violations of property rights. We also use the cases to raise more fundamental issues about the nature of property.

1. TRESPASS TO LAND

Jacque v. Steenberg Homes, Inc.
Supreme Court of Wisconsin, 1997.
563 N.W.2d 154.

■ WILLIAM A. BABLITCH, JUSTICE. Steenberg Homes had a mobile home to deliver. Unfortunately for Harvey and Lois Jacque (the Jacques), the easiest route of delivery was across their land. Despite adamant protests by the Jacques, Steenberg plowed a path through the Jacques' snow-covered field and via that path, delivered the mobile home. Consequently, the Jacques sued Steenberg Homes for intentional trespass. At trial, Steenberg Homes conceded the intentional trespass, but argued that no compensatory damages had been proved, and that punitive damages could not be awarded without compensatory damages. Although the jury awarded the Jacques $1 in nominal damages and $100,000 in punitive damages, the circuit court set aside the jury's award of $100,000. The court of appeals affirmed, reluctantly concluding that it could not reinstate the punitive damages because it was bound by precedent establishing that an award of nominal damages will not sustain a punitive damage award. * * *

I.

The relevant facts follow. Plaintiffs, Lois and Harvey Jacques, are an elderly couple, now retired from farming, who own roughly 170 acres near Wilke's Lake in the town of Schleswig. The defendant, Steenberg Homes, Inc. (Steenberg), is in the business of selling mobile homes. In the fall of 1993, a neighbor of the Jacques purchased a mobile home from Steenberg. Delivery of the mobile home was included in the sales price.

Steenberg determined that the easiest route to deliver the mobile home was across the Jacques' land. Steenberg preferred transporting the home across the Jacques' land because the only alternative was a private road which was covered in up to seven feet of snow and contained a sharp curve which would require sets of "rollers" to be used when maneuvering the home around the curve. Steenberg asked the Jacques on several separate occasions whether it could move the home across the Jacques' farm field. The Jacques refused. The Jacques were sensitive about allowing others on their land because they had lost property valued at over $10,000 to other neighbors in an adverse possession action in the mid-1980's. Despite repeated refusals from the Jacques, Steenberg decided to sell the mobile home, which was to be used as a summer cottage, and delivered it on February 15, 1994.

On the morning of delivery, Mr. Jacque observed the mobile home parked on the corner of the town road adjacent to his property. He decided to find out where the movers planned to take the home. The movers, who were Steenberg employees, showed Mr. Jacque the path they planned to take with the mobile home to reach the neighbor's lot. The path cut across the Jacques' land. Mr. Jacque informed the movers that it was the Jacques' land they were planning to cross and that Steenberg did not have permission to cross their land. He told them that Steenberg had been refused permission to cross the Jacques' land.

One of Steenberg's employees called the assistant manager, who then came out to the Jacques' home. In the meantime, the Jacques called and asked some of their neighbors and the town chairman to come over immediately. Once everyone was present, the Jacques showed the assistant manager an aerial map and plat book of the township to prove their ownership of the land, and reiterated their demand that the home not be moved across their land.

At that point, the assistant manager asked Mr. Jacque how much money it would take to get permission. Mr. Jacque responded that it was not a question of money; the Jacques just did not want Steenberg to cross their land. Mr. Jacque testified that he told Steenberg to "[F]ollow the road, that is what the road is for." Steenberg employees left the meeting without permission to cross the land.

At trial, one of Steenberg's employees testified that, upon coming out of the Jacques' home, the assistant manager stated: "I don't give a —— what [Mr. Jacque] said, just get the home in there any way you can." The other Steenberg employee confirmed this testimony and further testified that the assistant manager told him to park the company truck in such a way that no one could get down the town road to see the route the employees were taking with the home. The assistant manager denied giving these instructions, and Steenberg argued that the road was blocked for safety reasons.

The employees, after beginning down the private road, ultimately used a "bobcat" to cut a path through the Jacques' snow-covered field and hauled the home across the Jacques' land to the neighbor's lot. One employee testified that upon returning to the office and informing the assistant manager that they had gone across the field, the assistant manager reacted by giggling and laughing. The other employee confirmed this testimony. The assistant manager disputed this testimony.

When a neighbor informed the Jacques that Steenberg had, in fact, moved the mobile home across the Jacques' land, Mr. Jacque called the Manitowoc County Sheriff's Department. After interviewing the parties and observing the scene, an officer from the sheriff's department issued a $30 citation to Steenberg's assistant manager. * * *

This case presents three issues: (1) whether an award of nominal damages for intentional trespass to land may support a punitive damage award and, if so; (2) whether the law should apply to Steenberg or should only be applied prospectively and, if we apply the law to Steenberg; (3) whether the $100,000 in punitive damages awarded by the jury is excessive. * * *

Figure 1-1
The Mobile Home at Its Final Resting Place after Being Dragged Across the Jacques' Field

Courtesy of Patrick A. Dewane, Jr., attorney for Harvey and Lois Jacque.

II.

* * * Steenberg argues that, as a matter of law, punitive damages could not be awarded by the jury because punitive damages must be supported by an award of compensatory damages and here the jury

awarded only nominal and punitive damages. The Jacques contend that the rationale supporting the compensatory damage award requirement is inapposite when the wrongful act is an intentional trespass to land. We agree with the Jacques. * * *

The general rule was stated in *Barnard v. Cohen*, 162 N.W. 480 (Wis. 1917), where the question presented was: "In an action for libel, can there be a recovery of punitory damages if only nominal compensatory damages are found?" With the bare assertion that authority and better reason supported its conclusion, the *Barnard* court said no. *Barnard* continues to state the general rule of punitive damages in Wisconsin. The rationale for the compensatory damage requirement is that if the individual cannot show actual harm, he or she has but a nominal interest, hence, society has little interest in having the unlawful, but otherwise harmless, conduct deterred, therefore, punitive damages are inappropriate. Jacque v. Steenberg Homes, Inc., 548 N.W.2d 80 (Wis. Ct. App. 1996); Maxwell v. Kennedy, 7 N.W. 657, 658–59 (Wis. 1880).

However, whether nominal damages can support a punitive damage award in the case of an intentional trespass to land has never been squarely addressed by this court. Nonetheless, Wisconsin law is not without reference to this situation. In 1854 the court established punitive damages, allowing the assessment of "damages as a punishment to the defendant for the purpose of making an example." McWilliams v. Bragg, 3 Wis. 424, 425 (1854).[3] The *McWilliams* court related the facts and an illustrative tale from the English case of *Merest v. Harvey,* 128 Eng. Rep. 761 (C.P. 1814), to explain the rationale underlying punitive damages.

In *Merest,* a landowner was shooting birds in his field when he was approached by the local magistrate who wanted to hunt with him. Although the landowner refused, the magistrate proceeded to hunt. When the landowner continued to object, the magistrate threatened to have him jailed and dared him to file suit. Although little actual harm had been caused, the English court upheld damages of 500 pounds, explaining "in a case where a man disregards every principle which actuates the conduct of gentlemen, what is to restrain him except large damages?" McWilliams, 3 Wis. 424 at 428.

To explain the need for punitive damages, even where actual harm is slight, *McWilliams* related the hypothetical tale from *Merest* of an intentional trespasser:

> Suppose a gentleman has a paved walk in his paddock, before his window, and that a man intrudes and walks up and down before the window of his house, and looks in while the owner is at dinner, is the trespasser permitted to say "here is a halfpenny for you which is the full extent of the mischief I have done." Would that be a compensation? I cannot say that it would be. . . .

---

3   Because *McWilliams* was an action of trespass for assault and battery, we cite it not for its precedential value, but for its reasoning.

McWilliams, 3 Wis. at 428. Thus, in the case establishing punitive damages in this state, this court recognized that in certain situations of trespass, the actual harm is not in the damage done to the land, which may be minimal, but in the loss of the individual's right to exclude others from his or her property and, the court implied that this right may be punished by a large damage award despite the lack of measurable harm.

* * * The Jacques argue that both the individual and society have significant interests in deterring intentional trespass to land, regardless of the lack of measurable harm that results. We agree with the Jacques. An examination of the individual interests invaded by an intentional trespass to land, and society's interests in preventing intentional trespass to land, leads us to the conclusion that the *Barnard* rule should not apply when the tort supporting the award is intentional trespass to land.

We turn first to the individual landowner's interest in protecting his or her land from trespass. The United States Supreme Court has recognized that the private landowner's right to exclude others from his or her land is "one of the most essential sticks in the bundle of rights that are commonly characterized as property." Dolan v. City of Tigard, 512 U.S. 374, 384 (1994). This court has long recognized "[e]very person['s] constitutional right to the exclusive enjoyment of his own property for any purpose which does not invade the rights of another person." Diana Shooting Club v. Lamoreaux, 89 N.W. 880, 886 (Wis. 1902) (holding that the victim of an intentional trespass should have been allowed to take judgment for nominal damages and costs). Thus, both this court and the Supreme Court recognize the individual's legal right to exclude others from private property.

Yet a right is hollow if the legal system provides insufficient means to protect it. Felix Cohen offers the following analysis summarizing the relationship between the individual and the state regarding property rights:

[T]hat is property to which the following label can be attached:

> To the world:
>
> Keep off X unless you have my permission, which I may grant or withhold.
>
>> Signed: Private Citizen
>>
>> Endorsed: The state

Felix S. Cohen, Dialogue on Private Property, 9 Rutgers Law Review 357, 374 (1954). Harvey and Lois Jacque have the right to tell Steenberg Homes and any other trespasser, "No, you cannot cross our land." But that right has no practical meaning unless protected by the State. And, as this court recognized as early as 1854, a "halfpenny" award does not constitute state protection.

The nature of the nominal damage award in an intentional trespass to land case further supports an exception to *Barnard*. Because a legal right is involved, the law recognizes that actual harm occurs in every trespass. The action for intentional trespass to land is directed at vindication of the legal right. The law infers some damage from every direct entry upon the land of another. The law recognizes actual harm in every trespass to land whether or not compensatory damages are awarded. Thus, in the case of intentional trespass to land, the nominal damage award represents the recognition that, although immeasurable in mere dollars, actual harm has occurred.

The potential for harm resulting from intentional trespass also supports an exception to *Barnard*. A series of intentional trespasses, as the Jacques had the misfortune to discover in an unrelated action, can threaten the individual's very ownership of the land. The conduct of an intentional trespasser, if repeated, might ripen into prescription or adverse possession and, as a consequence, the individual landowner can lose his or her property rights to the trespasser. See Wis. Stat. § 893.28.

In sum, the individual has a strong interest in excluding trespassers from his or her land. Although only nominal damages were awarded to the Jacques, Steenberg's intentional trespass caused actual harm. We turn next to society's interest in protecting private property from the intentional trespasser.

Society has an interest in punishing and deterring intentional trespassers beyond that of protecting the interests of the individual landowner. Society has an interest in preserving the integrity of the legal system. Private landowners should feel confident that wrongdoers who trespass upon their land will be appropriately punished. When landowners have confidence in the legal system, they are less likely to resort to "self-help" remedies. In *McWilliams,* the court recognized the importance of " 'prevent[ing] the practice of dueling, [by permitting] juries [ ] to *punish* insult by exemplary damages.' " McWilliams, 3 Wis. at 428. Although dueling is rarely a modern form of self-help, one can easily imagine a frustrated landowner taking the law into his or her own hands when faced with a brazen trespasser, like Steenberg, who refuses to heed no trespass warnings.

People expect wrongdoers to be appropriately punished. Punitive damages have the effect of bringing to punishment types of conduct that, though oppressive and hurtful to the individual, almost invariably go unpunished by the public prosecutor. The $30 forfeiture was certainly not an appropriate punishment for Steenberg's egregious trespass in the eyes of the Jacques. It was more akin to Merest's "halfpenny." If punitive damages are not allowed in a situation like this, what punishment will prohibit the intentional trespass to land? Moreover, what is to stop Steenberg Homes from concluding, in the future, that delivering its mobile homes via an intentional trespass and paying the resulting Class B forfeiture, is not more profitable than obeying the law? Steenberg

Homes plowed a path across the Jacques' land and dragged the mobile home across that path, in the face of the Jacques' adamant refusal. A $30 forfeiture and a $1 nominal damage award are unlikely to restrain Steenberg Homes from similar conduct in the future. An appropriate punitive damage award probably will.

In sum, as the court of appeals noted, the *Barnard* rule sends the wrong message to Steenberg Homes and any others who contemplate trespassing on the land of another. It implicitly tells them that they are free to go where they please, regardless of the landowner's wishes. As long as they cause no compensable harm, the only deterrent intentional trespassers face is the nominal damage award of $1, the modern equivalent of *Merest's* halfpenny, and the possibility of a Class B forfeiture under Wis. Stat. § 943.13. We conclude that both the private landowner and society have much more than a nominal interest in excluding others from private land. Intentional trespass to land causes actual harm to the individual, regardless of whether that harm can be measured in mere dollars. Consequently, the *Barnard* rationale will not support a refusal to allow punitive damages when the tort involved is an intentional trespass to land. Accordingly, assuming that the other requirements for punitive damages have been met, we hold that nominal damages may support a punitive damage award in an action for intentional trespass to land. * * *

In conclusion, we hold that when nominal damages are awarded for an intentional trespass to land, punitive damages may, in the discretion of the jury, be awarded. Our decision today shall apply to Steenberg Homes. Finally, we hold that the $100,000 punitive damages awarded by the jury is not excessive. Accordingly, we reverse and remand to the circuit court for reinstatement of the punitive damage award.

NOTES AND QUESTIONS

1.   There is no dispute in this case that Steenberg Homes committed an intentional trespass by moving the mobile home across the Jacques' farm field. The law of intentional trespass is "exceptionally simple and exceptionally rigorous." William L. Prosser, Handbook of the Law of Torts 63 (4th ed. 1971). Any intentional intrusion that deprives another of possession of land, even if only temporarily, is considered a trespass. Restatement (Fourth) of Property, Vol. 2, Div. I, Ch. 1, § 1.1. (Am. L. Inst. Tentative Draft Apr. 7, 2021). The only intent required is to go onto the land; it is not necessary to show that the defendant knew where the boundary was or that the land belonged to someone else. Intentional trespass is sometimes said to be a strict liability tort, because there is no inquiry into the balance of interests between the plaintiff and defendant or whether the intrusion was "unreasonable." Perhaps most strikingly, someone who commits an intentional trespass is subject to liability "irrespective of whether he thereby causes *any* harm to any legally protected interest of the other." Id. (emphasis added). In this sense, trespass to land is like the tort of battery. As one English judge put it: "So if a man gives another a cuff on the ear, though it

cost him nothing, no not so much as a little diachylon, yet he shall have his action, for it is a personal injury. So a man shall have an action against another for riding over his ground, though it do him no damage; for it is an invasion of his property, and the other has no right to come there." Ashby v. White, 92 Eng. Rep. 126, 137 (K.B. 1703) (Holt, C.J.). Does this suggest that a person's land is seen as an extension of her body, and that the law protects both in order to vindicate fundamental rights of personal autonomy? As we will see in Chapter IV, the law is not so protective of personal property (also known as "chattels," "movable things," or "goods"). The *Restatement of Torts* says that a trespass to personal property will result in liability only if it causes harm to the owner of the thing. Restatement (Second) of Torts § 218 cmt. e. What might account for this difference?

2.   One historical explanation for the absence of any harm requirement is that the action for trespass to land was often used to resolve disputes over title to land. Suppose A and B are neighbors and they disagree about the location of the boundary between their properties. Even though neither has done anything to harm the other, A can sue B (or vice versa) for trespass, and the court, in the course of deciding the dispute, will determine where in fact the boundary lies between their two parcels. If a showing of harm were required, then either A or B would have to take some action—like erecting a fence or trampling a flower bed—in order to get the boundary dispute resolved, but it is obviously undesirable to require harmful acts from persons who would not otherwise undertake them, simply in order to resolve their respective rights to land. With the twentieth-century development of so-called quiet title actions (in which any interested person can seek a declaratory judgment resolving a dispute over title to land), however, this rationale has lost most of its force. Does this reform suggest that the action for trespass should now be limited to intrusions that cause actual harm?

3.   Did the Jacques have a sound reason for refusing permission to Steenberg Homes to move the mobile home across their field? The Jacques testified that they were sensitive about intrusions on their land because they had lost some of their property in an adverse possession lawsuit. Adverse possession, which we take up in Chapter II, is in effect a transfer of ownership that takes place when someone occupies land *without permission*, and the statute of limitations runs before the owner challenges the occupation. If the Jacques had given their permission to Steenberg employees to cut across their land, there would have been no basis to assert a claim for adverse possession. In any event, the statute of limitations for challenging trespass to land in Wisconsin is 20 years, Wis. Stat. § 893.25, and the Steenberg moving operation would last only a few hours. So the Jacques' stated reason for objecting to the shortcut had no objective basis in law. Should this make a difference in deciding whether they should be allowed to sue for trespass, or to whether they should be allowed to recover $100,000 in punitive damages?

4.   Even if the Jacques had no sound reason for objecting to Steenberg Homes cutting across their land, why might the legal system want a rule that always (or nearly always) requires permission of the owner before people are allowed to intrude? Most of the Wisconsin Supreme Court's

discussion of this point seems to assume the conclusion: The right to exclude must be enforced because it is an important right. The court suggests two reasons for strictly enforcing such a right: to avoid potential violence and protect privacy rights. But is either concern implicated in the facts of this case? Should that matter in deciding whether to apply the strict rule? Are these arguments ultimately circular? People might not resort to violence to repel intruders if they understood that they did not have the right to exclude trespasses that do no injury to their land. And people might not be so sensitive about their privacy rights if these trespasses were tolerated. Can you think of other reasons for giving owners a near-absolute right to exclude others?

5.   Maneuvering a mobile home around a sharp curve in a country road with seven feet of snow on the ground sounds as if it might be quite dangerous, and could risk bodily injury to Steenberg employees or physical damage to the mobile home. Do you think the court should have taken this into account? Courts in some circumstances have recognized a defense of necessity to an action for trespass (see Chapter IV). It is well established that travelers have a right to deviate from a public road when it is rendered impassable, and, as we will see, this exception to the right to exclude sometimes comes under the heading of "necessity." Dwyer v. Staunton, [1947] 4 D.L.R. 393 (Alberta Dist. Ct.) (holding there to be no trespass in a case of travel on private land where public road was made impassable by snow, despite the objection of the owner). Should Steenberg Homes be able to claim necessity here? If not, why not?

6.   The U.S. Supreme Court has held that "grossly excessive or arbitrary" punitive damages awards violate due process, State Farm Mutual Automobile Ins. Co. v. Campbell, 538 U.S. 408, 416 (2003), and has indicated that ratios of punitive to compensatory damages exceeding nine to one are presumptively suspect as a matter of constitutional law. The punitive damages in *Jacque* are 100,000 times the compensatory damages. The Court also has instructed that one factor in determining whether an award is excessive is the relationship between the award and the maximum civil or criminal penalty the state authorizes for similar conduct. State Farm, 583 U.S. at 428; BMW of North America, Inc. v. Gore, 517 U.S. 559, 583 (1996). According to an omitted portion of the opinion in *Jacque,* the maximum fine under Wisconsin law for misdemeanor trespass was $1,000. The award in *Jacque* is 100 times this amount. On both measures, therefore, the punitive damages award seems suspect. On the other hand, the Court has also noted that an award in excess of nine times compensatory damages "may comport with due process where a particularly egregious act has resulted in only a small amount of economic damages." State Farm, supra, at 426 (internal quotations marks omitted, citing BMW, 517 U.S. at 582) (noting that a higher ratio might be necessary where "the injury is hard to detect or the monetary value of noneconomic harm might have been difficult to determine"). Does this exception apply here? Is the $1,000 ceiling set by the legislature for misdemeanor trespass an accurate benchmark of the social consequences of intentional trespass to unenclosed land? Is it possible that the purpose of the criminal trespass provision is not really to deter

trespasses, so much as to provide a mechanism for the sheriff's department to mediate disputes like the one between the Jacques and Steenberg Homes? See Chapter IV, Part A.

Hinman v. Pacific Air Transport

United States Court of Appeals, Ninth Circuit, 1936.
84 F.2d 755.

■ HANEY, CIRCUIT JUDGE. From decrees sustaining motions to dismiss filed by defendants in two suits, appellants appeal and bring for review by this court the rights of a landowner in connection with the flight of aircraft above his land. Appellant filed one bill against Pacific Air Transport, an Oregon corporation, and another bill against United Air Lines Transport Corporation, a Delaware corporation, in each of which the allegations are nearly identical. Although two appeals are before the court, briefs filed discuss both cases, and therefore we will consider them together. * * *

It is * * * alleged that defendants are engaged in the business of operating a commercial air line, and that at all times "after the month of May, 1929, defendants daily, repeatedly and upon numerous occasions have disturbed, invaded and trespassed upon the ownership and possession of plaintiffs' tract"; that at said times defendants have operated aircraft in, across, and through said airspace at altitudes less than 100 feet above the surface; that plaintiffs notified defendants to desist from trespassing on said airspace; and that defendants have disregarded said notice, unlawfully and against the will of plaintiffs, and continue and threaten to continue such trespasses. * * *

The prayer asks an injunction restraining the operation of the aircraft through the airspace over plaintiffs' property and for $90,000 damages in each of the cases.

Appellees contend that it is settled law in California that the owner of land has no property rights in superjacent airspace, either by code enactments or by judicial decrees and that the ad coelum doctrine* does not apply in California. We have examined the statutes of California, particularly California Civil Code, § 659 and § 829, as well as Grandona v. Lovdal, 21 P. 366 (Cal. 1889); Wood v. Moulton, 80 P. 92 (Cal. 1905); and Kafka v. Bozio, 218 P. 753 (Cal. 1923), but we find nothing therein to negative the ad coelum formula. Furthermore, if we should adopt this formula as being the law, there might be serious doubt as to whether a state statute could change it without running counter to the Fourteenth amendment to the Constitution of the United States. If we could accept and literally construe the ad coelum doctrine, it would simplify the solution of this case; however, we reject that doctrine. We think it is not the law, and that it never was the law.

---

*   [*Ad coelum* is short for *cujus est solum, ejus est usque ad coelum et ad inferos*, which means "whoever owns the soil owns also to the sky and to the depths."—eds.]

Figure 1-2
Timetable for Pacific Air Transport, February 1, 1928

From the Collection of Craig Morris.

This formula "from the center of the earth to the sky" was invented at some remote time in the past when the use of space above land actual or conceivable was confined to narrow limits, and simply meant that the owner of the land could use the overlying space to such an extent as he was able, and that no one could ever interfere with that use.

This formula was never taken literally, but was a figurative phrase to express the full and complete ownership of land and the right to whatever superjacent airspace was necessary or convenient to the enjoyment of the land.

In applying a rule of law, or construing a statute or constitutional provision, we cannot shut our eyes to common knowledge, the progress of civilization, or the experience of mankind. A literal construction of this formula will bring about an absurdity. The sky has no definite location. It is that which presents itself to the eye when looking upward; as we approach it, it recedes. There can be no ownership of infinity, nor can equity prevent a supposed violation of an abstract conception.

The appellants' case, then, rests upon the assumption that as owners of the soil they have an absolute and present title to all the space above the earth's surface, owned by them, to such a height as is, or may become, useful to the enjoyment of their land. This height, the appellants assert in the bill, is of indefinite distance, but not less than 150 feet. * * * This, then, is appellants' premise, and upon this proposition they rest their case. Such an inquiry was never pursued in the history of jurisprudence until the occasion is furnished by the common use of vehicles of the air.

We believe, and hold, that appellants' premise is unsound. The question presented is applied to a new status and little aid can be found in actual precedent. The solution is found in the application of elementary legal principles. The first and foremost of these principles is that the very essence and origin of the legal right of property is dominion over it. Property must have been reclaimed from the general mass of the earth, and it must be capable by its nature of exclusive possession. Without possession, no right in it can be maintained.

The air, like the sea, is by its nature incapable of private ownership, except in so far as one may actually use it. This principle was announced long ago by Justinian. It is in fact the basis upon which practically all of our so-called water codes are based.

We own so much of the space above the ground as we can occupy or make use of, in connection with the enjoyment of our land. This right is not fixed. It varies with our varying needs and is coextensive with them. The owner of land owns as much of the space above him as he uses, but only so long as he uses it. All that lies beyond belongs to the world.

When it is said that man owns, or may own, to the heavens, that merely means that no one can acquire a right to the space above him that will limit him in whatever use he can make of it as a part of his enjoyment of the land. To this extent his title to the air is paramount. No other person can acquire any title or exclusive right to any space above him.

Any use of such air or space by others which is injurious to his land, or which constitutes an actual interference with his possession or his beneficial use thereof, would be a trespass for which he would have remedy. But any claim of the landowner beyond this cannot find a precedent in law, nor support in reason.

It would be, and is, utterly impracticable and would lead to endless confusion, if the law should uphold attempts of landowners to stake out, or assert claims to definite, unused spaces in the air in order to protect some contemplated future use of it. Such a rule, if adopted, would constitute a departure never before attempted by mankind, and utterly at variance with the reason of the law. If such a rule were conceivable, how will courts protect the various landowners in their varying claims of portions of the sky? How enforce a right of ejectment or restitution? Such a rule is not necessary for the protection of the landowner in any right guaranteed him by the Constitution in the enjoyment of his property. If a right like this were recognized and upheld by the courts, it would cause confusion worse confounded. It is opposed to common sense and to all human experience.

We cannot shut our eyes to the practical result of legal recognition of the asserted claims of appellants herein, for it leads to a legal implication to the effect that any use of airspace above the surface owner of land, without his consent would be a trespass either by the operator of an airplane or a radio operator. We will not foist any such chimerical concept of property rights upon the jurisprudence of this country.

We now consider the allegation of the bill that appellees' airplanes, in landing, glide through the air, within a distance of less than 100 feet to the surface of appellants' land, or possibly to a distance within five feet thereof, at one end of his tract. This presents another question for discussion. Whether such close proximity to appellants' land may constitute an impairment of his full enjoyment of the same is a question of fact. If it does, he may be entitled to relief in a proper case.

Appellants are not entitled to injunctive relief upon the bill filed here, because no facts are alleged with respect to circumstances of appellants' use of the premises which will enable this court to infer that any actual or substantial damage will accrue from the acts of the appellees complained of.

The case differs from the usual case of enjoining a trespass. Ordinarily, if a trespass is committed upon land, the plaintiff is entitled to at least nominal damages without proving or alleging any actual damage. In the instant case, traversing the airspace above appellants' land is not, of itself, a trespass at all, but it is a lawful act unless it is done under circumstances which will cause injury to appellants' possession.

Appellants do not, therefore, in their bill state a case of trespass, unless they allege a case of actual and substantial damage. The bill fails to do this. It merely draws a naked conclusion as to damages without facts or circumstances to support it. It follows that the complaint does not state a case for injunctive relief. * * *

The decree of the District Court is affirmed.

■ MATHEWS, CIRCUIT JUDGE, dissents.

NOTES AND QUESTIONS

1.   Some version of the *ad coelum* principle (see n. * supra) is followed in nearly all legal systems for purposes of defining the right to exclude others from land. See Andrea B. Carroll, Examining a Comparative Law Myth: Two Hundred Years of Riparian Misconception, 80 Tul. L. Rev. 901, 912–19 (2006). As Professor Carroll recounts, the rule was extracted from Roman law, and given its Latin name, by medieval monks known as Glossators working in Italy in the twelfth and thirteenth centuries. One of these Glossators, Franciscus, was brought to England by King Edward I in 1273, which led to the introduction of the concept to English law. Lord Coke invoked the concept by its Latin name in some cases in the seventeenth century, and also noted it in his *Institutes*. See 1 Edwardo Coke, The First Part of the Institutes of the Laws of England; Or, A Commentary upon Littleton, § 4a (Francis Hargrave & Charles Butler eds., 16th ed. 1809) (1628). All this, of course, was well before airplanes were invented.

2.   The *ad coelum* principle is fundamental to property in land. Deeds to land nearly always are stated in terms of some measurement of the surface area. But under the *ad coelum* principle, the owner of the surface is also entitled to dig below the surface (for example, to construct a basement for a house) and to build above the surface (for example, to construct a two-story house). Without such an understanding, obviously, the bare right to the surface would be largely worthless. Rights to the column of space above the surface are often referred to as "air rights." Absent some zoning restriction

or covenant restricting the height of buildings, the *ad coelum* principle means that the owner of the surface can construct a building as tall as engineering prowess will allow. Thus, a farmer in an unzoned area of rural Illinois could replicate the Willis Tower (formerly the Sears Tower) on his land, provided he could obtain financing for the project. Height restrictions are common in zoning ordinances, however, and these have been held to be a legitimate exercise of the police power, not requiring any payment of compensation. See Welch v. Swasey, 214 U.S. 91, 106–07 (1909); see also Penn Central Transp. Co. v. City of New York, 438 U.S. 104 (1978), reproduced in Chapter X. We take up some of the issues presented by the *ad coelum* principle's application to subsurface rights in Chapter II.

3.   The question whether airplane overflights are trespasses under the *ad coelum* principle was always more theoretically interesting than practically important. No court (as far as we are aware) has ever concluded that operators of airplanes could be held liable in trespass for flying at cruise altitudes over land below. The injury to each surface owner is small or nonexistent, and the transaction costs of negotiating permissions with each owner would be so large that they would make it impossible to fly airplanes. Courts are far too pragmatic to take such an extreme assertion of rights seriously. The puzzle in *Hinman* (and similar cases involving airplane overflights) is how to carve out an exception for overflights from the *ad coelum* principle without otherwise damaging the rule's general utility. Four different doctrinal moves have been suggested at various times to accomplish this excision.

(1)   The action for trespass is available only to persons who are in possession of land. See Restatement (Second) of Torts § 158(a). One argument, therefore, is that as long as the owner of the surface has not asserted dominion and control over the portion of the column of space in which airplanes fly, the owner cannot sue in trespass. The problem with this argument is that the owner of land is generally regarded as being in "constructive" possession of the land sufficient to maintain trespass, even if the owner is not in actual possession. 87 C.J.S. Trespass § 25 (2000). For example, although the Jacques do not appear to have been in active control of the portion of their farm where Steenberg Homes trespassed, this did not defeat their right to sue for trespass. Similarly, the *ad coelum* principle seems to recognize that the owner of the surface has a kind of exclusive option to build up into the column of space in the future, without regard to whether that space is currently possessed. Thus, it might make more sense to say that owners have an exclusive "right to possess" at least as far up as building technology makes effective possession possible. See Smith v. New England Aircraft Co., 170 N.E. 385, 393 (Mass. 1930). Perhaps the notion of possession itself needs to be better specified than was necessary in earlier times. Restatement (Fourth) of Property, Vol. 1, Div. II, Ch. 1 (Am. L. Inst. Council Draft No. 1, Sept. 13, 2019); Christopher M. Newman, Using Things, Defining Property, in Property Theory 69, 89–98 (James Penner & Michael Otsuka, eds. 2018); Henry E. Smith, The Persistence of System in Property Law, 163 U. Pa. L. Rev. 2055, 2079–80 (2015).

(2) One could argue that airplane overflights are actionable as trespasses only if they cause actual harm to the surface owner. The problem with this argument is, as we have seen, that actual injury or harm is not a traditional element of trespass to land. Again, even though the Jacques did not suffer any actual harm because of the trespass by Steenberg Homes, they were allowed to recover in an action for trespass.

(3) Richard Epstein has argued that airplane overflights are technically trespasses, but the surface owner is not entitled to any damages or other relief because she obtains "implicit in kind compensation" from being able to take advantage of the benefits that airplane travel has to offer—that is, from being able to commit similar trespasses over other people's property. See Richard A. Epstein, *Intel v. Hamidi*: The Role of Self-Help in Cyberspace?, 1 J.L. Econ. & Pol'y 147, 154–55 (2005). In effect, every surface owner has implicitly granted a license to every other person to trespass over her property, since this makes everyone in society better off. In a related argument, Eric Claeys sees the *ad coelum* regime as evolving flexibly because it is ultimately grounded in productive use. Eric R. Claeys, On the Use and Abuse of Overflight Column Doctrine, 2 Brigham-Kanner Prop. Rts. Conf. J. 61 (2013). Do these arguments rest too heavily on hindsight? When airplane travel first developed and challenges were brought based on trespass, no one could be sure air travel would work out to the benefit of all. Today we can say this is undoubtedly true, but it may not have been obvious at the dawn of air travel.

(4) One could reclassify the airspace in which airplanes travel as a type of public property—public navigable airspace—in which no surface owner has any claim of private property rights. The analogy would be to navigable rivers or public highways, which are considered public property open to all. A problem with this theory is that the declaration of public ownership of the navigable airspace might be regarded as a taking of private property, given the previous understanding that the surface owner owns "to the heavens." But even if it were a taking, the compensation might be small or nothing, given the absence of harm and the "implicit compensation" emphasized by Epstein.

For more on the history of the law of airplane overflights, see Stuart Banner, Who Owns the Sky?: The Struggle to Control Airspace from the Wright Brothers On (2008).

4. Which of these legal arguments is embraced by the Court in *Hinman*? The U.S. Supreme Court eventually embraced the fourth theory in *United States v. Causby*, 328 U.S. 256 (1946). The Court concluded that Congress had effectively asserted federal government control over navigable airspace. The Court also concluded that the legislative declaration of federal ownership was not a taking of property, unless the flights come in so low over the property as to destroy the use and enjoyment of the surface area and improvements. For more on *Causby*, see Chapter III. Which solution to the problem of overflights do you find the most appealing?

5. Farmer Hinman and the Burbank airport were not on good terms. A subsequent opinion gives more background. Hinman had tried to get the

airport to purchase or lease his entire 72.5-acre parcel, but the airport refused on the ground that Hinman's asking price was far above fair market value. In response to his loss in the litigation and the holding that he was entitled to only so much airspace as he was actually using, Hinman erected 20-foot poles and a large derrick in the flight path to the airport. The airport offered to pay the cost of removal or of installation of warning lights, and Hinman refused. When the airport sued, the court enjoined the structures as a private and public nuisance. United Airports Co. of California v. Hinman et al., 1940 U.S. Av. Rep. 1 (S.D. Cal. 1939). The Burbank airport was much favored by movie stars and other celebrities and was frequently used to shoot films. Was Hinman a spiteful opportunist? If so, is the law of nuisance (considered in *Hendricks v. Stalnaker* infra) more suited to controlling his behavior than the law of trespass?

6.   Aerial trespass has emerged as a more pressing issue with the advent of unmanned aerial vehicles (UAVs), popularly known as drones. Drones typically fly lower and can hover, potentially coming into more conflict with landowners' uses and invading their privacy. Drones are coming to play an important role in many contexts, from public safety to consumer deliveries. Should landowners have to show substantial harm from a drone overflight to sue in trespass? Even if the drone is one inch above the ground? Even if a drone on a fishing pole dangled over the land would be a per se trespass? Moving upwards from the surface, where does the landowner's possession (or right to possess) stop and the navigation servitude begin, or do they overlap? We will return to the navigation servitude in Chapter II. For more discussion, see Troy A. Rule, Airspace in an Age of Drones, 95 B.U. L. Rev. 155 (2015); Henry E. Smith, Property Beyond Flatland, 10 Brigham-Kanner Prop. Rts. J. 9 (2021).

7.   The problem of airplane overflights also reemerged in debates about the assembly of digital databases. In particular, the Google Books project makes and stores copies of the full text of millions of published books, and allows users to search for and view snippets of the works. Google prevailed on its argument that all this was fair use, Authors Guild v. Google, Inc., 804 F.3d 202 (2d Cir. 2015), but in the course of the controversy, commentators such as Larry Lessig defended the project on the grounds that the problem is essentially the same as that of airplane overflights: The injury to each author is small or nonexistent, and the transaction costs of negotiating consents with each copyright owner would be so large as to make the project of creating such a database infeasible. They argued that just as the courts carved out an exception to the law of trespass for overflights, so they should carve out an exception from copyright law for use of copyrighted books in creating large searchable databases. Claeys, supra, at 99–108. Does Lessig's argument suggest that there may be other circumstances in which exceptions to trespass law should be recognized based on small injury to the landowner and high transaction costs of negotiating permissions? Should the same reasoning apply to the use of fracking technology to extract oil and gas from the ground? Coastal Oil & Gas Corp. v. Garza Energy Tr., 268 S.W.3d 1, 11 (Tex. 2008) (invoking the airplane overflight analogy). See also Briggs v. Southwestern Energy Production Co., excerpted in Chapter II; and see

generally Chapter IV.B (considering various other exceptions to the landowner's right to exclude). If as James Grimmelmann argues, courts give close and exacting scrutiny to uses of copyrighted material by humans but fast-track use through robotic readers, James Grimmelmann, Copyright for Literate Robots, 101 Iowa L. Rev. 657, 667 (2016), where should this leave autonomous drones under the *ad coelum* principle?

2. CONCEPTIONS OF PROPERTY—PHILOSOPHICAL PERSPECTIVES

Scholars who seek to identify the meaning of property tend to fall into two camps. On the one hand, there are the essentialists, who attempt to uncover the single true definition of property as a legal concept. Essentialist efforts can be more or less complex. In an often-quoted passage, William Blackstone, with a bit of self-conscious drama, wrote: "There is nothing which so generally strikes the imagination, and engages the affections of mankind, as the right of property; or that sole and despotic dominion which one man claims and exercises over the external things of the world, in total exclusion of the right of any other individual in the universe." 2 William Blackstone, Commentaries on the Laws of England *2 (1766). This reflects a relatively simple essentialist conception: Property confers a kind of exclusive sovereign control over some "external thing." Others have come up with more complex characterizations of property that are still essentialist, in that they are premised on the understanding that there is one correct meaning of property. For example, Tony Honoré, an English analytical philosopher, has developed a conception of what "full ownership" means in a mature liberal legal system that features no less than eleven elements. See Tony Honoré, Ownership, in Making Law Bind 161 (1987).

On the other hand, there are the skeptics, who believe that it is fruitless to try to come up with a single canonical conception of what property means in a legal system. For the skeptics, "property" is just a word that means nothing until we spell out—using different words— exactly what we are talking about in any given context. The skeptical view is reflected in the common metaphor that property is a "bundle of rights" or "bundle of sticks." The metaphor was apparently first used in a nineteenth century treatise, see John Lewis, Treatise on the Law of Eminent Domain in the United States 43 (1888), and gained wider currency in the 1920s and 1930s. See, e.g., Benjamin N. Cardozo, The Paradoxes of Legal Science 129 (1928). The metaphor implies that one can add to or subtract from the bundle more or less without limit, and still talk about the bundle as property. Many of the Legal Realists who came to the fore in the 1930s shared this view of the plasticity of property. The skeptical perspective is also reflected in the first version of the American Law Institute's *Restatement of Property*. See Restatement of Property § 10 (Am. L. Inst. 1936) ("The word 'owner,' as it is used in this Restatement, means the person who has one or more interests.").

Although the skeptical tradition has the widest following among American law professors today, essentialism is making something of a comeback. We start with an excerpt from James Penner, an English legal philosopher who defends the essentialist view, and then an excerpt from Tom Grey, a law professor who reflects the skeptical tradition that dominates in America.

J.E. Penner, *The Idea of Property in Law*
23, 26–27, 68, 70–71, 75–76 (1997).

A right *in rem* is, roughly, a right in respect of a *res,* a thing. The classic example is a property right. Rights *in rem* are characterized as those rights which bind "all the world," that is, rights which must be respected by all, or virtually all, of the subjects of the legal system; everybody must refrain from trespassing on my land. In contrast, a right *in personam* is a right in the behaviour of some person, such as the right to the performance of a contract. Rights *in personam* bind only specific individuals; only the other party to the contract has any obligations which correlate to one's contractual rights. * * *

One may visualize the holder of a right *in rem* as standing at the hub of a spoked wheel, with the spokes representing relations to a multitude of duty-owers. Yet one may just as easily visualize the ower of a duty not to interfere with property, i.e. the ower of a duty *in rem*, in exactly the position, at the hub, so to speak, except that the spokes will represent relations to all those who hold property. These are lousy pictures, because a moment's notice will confirm that any trace of a *res*, like a bicycle or a pound note, is missing, which is something of a deficiency if we are trying to explain the normative relation which comprises property. * * * But if we pay attention to the fact that rights and duties *in rem* do not refer to persons, not in the sense that the property is not owned by persons, but in the sense that nothing to do with *any particular individual's personality* is involved in the normative guidance they offer, we may get somewhere. * * *

[I]n general, it is completely unknown to us whether any given amount of property is owned by one person or by several or many. * * * We are under one duty to the plurality of property holders however their property is distributed amongst themselves. It is a simple, single duty, and very easy to comply with. * * * As I walk through a car park, my actual, practical duty is only capable of being understood as a duty which applies to the cars there, not to a series of owners. For all I know, the cars are owned by the same person. The content of my duty not to interfere is not structured in any way by the actual ownership relation of the cars' owners to their specific cars. By the same token, if one of the cars has just been sold, so that there is a new owner, or if one of the cars has been lent to the owner's sister-in-law, again, my duty has not changed one whit. Thus transactions between an owner and a specific other do not change the duties of everyone else not to interfere with the property. * * *

The concepts of exclusion and use are more complex than they first appear, because, in general, they are intertwined. One can, of course, have a right to use something without having a right to exclude others, and vice versa. One can have the right to use a library, but no right to exclude others from it. Similarly a guard may have the right to exclude others from the library but no right to use it himself.

Yet rights purely to exclude or purely to use interact naturally, as it were, in the sense that use almost always involves some exclusion of others. As a rightful user of a library, I may not have the right to exclude others, but I would certainly have the right to occupy a desk, or take a book from a shelf. In this sense I have a right *not to be excluded* from the library, since use implies non-exclusion. * * *

How do the right to use and the right to exclude explain the right to property? The right to property is grounded by the interest we have in using things in the broader sense. No one has any interest in merely excluding others from things, for any reason and no reason at all. The interest that underpins the right to property is the interest we have in purposefully dealing with things. Because we have long-term interests in respect of things, and interests in using them in many different ways the broad definition of use is the appropriate one. But because we are concerned with the right to property, we must be concerned with the correlative duties imposed on others. Because of the social setting in which we live, we see that any meaningful right to use is the opposite side of the coin to a right to exclude. Secondly, the right to use reflects our practical interest in exclusively using things, which correlates to duties *in rem* on everyone else not to interfere with our uses of things. Their not using the property is framed in terms of their duties to exclude themselves from it.

Thus at a theoretical level we understand the right to property equally as a right of exclusion or a right of use, since they are opposite sides of the same coin. Yet we can equally see that only one of these ways of looking at the right might drive the analysis in understanding the shape of the property norms in the legal system. It is my contention that the law of property is driven by an analysis which takes the perspective of exclusion, rather than one which elaborates a right to use. In other words, in order to understand property, we must look to the way that the law contours the duties it imposes on people to exclude themselves from the property of others, rather than regarding the law as instituting a series of positive liberties or power to use particular things. This can be expressed as follows, in what I will call the *exclusion thesis: the right to property is a right to exclude others from things which is grounded by the interest we have in the use of things.*

On this formulation use serves a justificatory role for the right, while exclusion is seen as the formal essence of the right. It is our interest in the use of property which grounds the right *in rem* to property and the correlative general duty *in rem*; yet exclusion is the practical means by which that interest is protected, and that makes all the difference to our understanding of property. * * *

NOTES AND QUESTIONS

1.   The distinction between rights *in rem* and *in personam* is fundamental to the law of property, and we will encounter it periodically throughout these materials. The distinction concerns who bears the duty to respect the right. An in rem right creates duties in a large and indefinite class of others ("all the world" is the expression often used with some exaggeration) to respect the right. An in personam right creates a duty in only a small and definitely ascertained number of others (e.g., B owes a duty to A). Not all in rem rights (as defined) are property rights. Rights of bodily security, reputation, and privacy are also in rem in the sense that they create duties of noninterference in a large and indefinite class of others. These are basic duties created by tort law. What makes something an in rem right of property is the recognition of duties in a large and indefinite class of others not to interfere with some *thing* (as opposed to a duty not to interfere with a person). Clearly, one can also have in personam rights with respect to things, in the sense of rights that create duties on the part of only a small number of ascertained others. Contract rights are the clear example. Very roughly speaking—and we emphasize the "very"—the law of torts as it applies to persons and the core of the law of property establish in rem rights, whereas the law of contract establishes in personam rights. One interesting implication of this distinction is that in rem rights tend to be simple, easy-to-understand duties of noninterference (like "no hitting" or "no trespassing"). This is because the duty that corresponds to the right has to be observed by such a large and indefinite mass of people. Complicated rights that impose affirmative duties to take particular actions are more likely to be in personam and hence will be more likely to be imposed by contract or government regulation. For further discussion see Thomas W. Merrill & Henry E. Smith, The Property/Contract Interface, 101 Colum. L. Rev. 773 (2001); Wesley Newcomb Hohfeld, Fundamental Legal Conceptions as Applied in Judicial Reasoning, 26 Yale L.J. 710 (1917).

2.   Penner's emphasis on the right to exclude captures the attitude of the Wisconsin Supreme Court about the property rights of Harvey and Lois Jacque. The court justifies the punitive damages award as a way of vindicating the Jacques' right to exclude others from their land, which the court says is central to the understanding that the land is their property. But what about the dispute in *Hinman*? The *Hinman* court seems to view property more as a collection of rights, and the question whether this includes the right to exclude airplane overflights depends on a considerations of competing social interests, not any a priori conception of what ownership entails.

3.   Penner's conception of property as the right to exclude others from things grounded in our interest in the use of the thing seems to fit ownership of land and tangible personal property like cars—for most purposes at least.

It may even fit certain intellectual property rights like patents and copyrights, which are said to create a right to exclude others from using certain inventions or forms of expression. But how does Penner's conception apply to other interests we commonly call property, like stocks or bonds or money? Money started out as a tangible form of personal property—gold and silver coins that have an intrinsic value. Then it turned into pieces of paper which promised to pay the bearer on demand a certain amount of gold or silver. Today it is just "fiat" currency—a piece of paper (or a digital entry in a computer operated by a bank) of no intrinsic value but which society recognizes as a unit of value that can be exchanged for goods and services that have intrinsic value. See James Willard Hurst, A Legal History of Money in the United States, 1774–1970 (1973). We commonly think of money as property. But what exactly is the "thing" that the owner of money is empowered to exclude others from under Penner's exclusion model?

4.   If property rights, being in rem, create duties on the part of all persons in a community to respect owned things, how do these generalized duties get started? Can it be said that everyone has agreed or consented to being bound to respect property? If so, when and where was this consent given? See, e.g., Geraint Parry, John Locke 51 (1978); Jeremy Waldron, The Right to Private Property 126–283 (1988).

5.   For other analyses that emphasize the centrality of the right to exclude others to the understanding of the interests we call property, see J.W. Harris, Property and Justice 13 (1996); Waldron, supra, at 26–61; Shyamkrishna Balganesh, Demystifying the Right to Exclude: Of Property, Inviolability, and Automatic Injunctions, 31 Harv. J.L. & Pub. Pol'y 593 (2008); Thomas W. Merrill, Property and the Right to Exclude, 77 Neb. L. Rev. 730 (1998).

6.   In other parts of the book, Penner develops what he calls the Separation Thesis: Something can only be an object of property if it is contingently associated with an owner. Penner, supra, at 111. Penner builds on Frederick Pollock, who defined a legal "thing" as "some possible matter of rights and duties conceived as a whole and apart from all others, just as, in the world of common experience, whatever can be separately perceived is a thing." Frederick Pollock, What Is a Thing?, 10 L.Q. Rev. 318, 318 (1894). On this account, a "thing" is central to property:

> [O]n the whole perhaps we have good ground for saying that the 'thing' of legal contemplation, even when we have to do with a material object, is not precisely the object as we find it in common experience, but rather the entirety of its possible legal relations to persons. We say entirety, not sum, because the capacity of being conceived as a distinct whole is a necessary attribute of an individual thing. What the relations of a person to a thing can be must depend in fact on the nature of the thing as continuous or discontinuous, corporeal or incorporeal, and in law on the character and the extent of the powers of use and disposal which particular systems of law may recognize.

Id. at 320–21. Many legal systems denominate property as the "law of things." In the materials that follow, consider what role if any the "legal thing" plays. See Henry E. Smith, Property as the Law of Things, 125 Harv. L. Rev. 1691 (2012). Those who are skeptical about the right to exclude tend also to downplay the importance of things to property. Consider the following.

Tom Grey, *The Disintegration of Property*
in NOMOS XXII: PROPERTY 69–71 (J. Pennock & J. Chapman eds., 1980).

In the English-speaking countries today, the conception of property held by the specialist (the lawyer or economist) is quite different from that held by the ordinary person. Most people, including most specialists in their unprofessional moments, conceive of property as *things* that are *owned* by *persons*. To own property is to have exclusive control of something—to be able to use it as one wishes, to sell it, give it away, leave it idle, or destroy it. Legal restraints on the free use of one's property are conceived as departures from an ideal conception of full ownership.

By contrast, the theory of property rights held by the modern specialist tends both to dissolve the notion of ownership and to eliminate any necessary connection between property rights and things. Consider ownership first. The specialist fragments the robust unitary conception of ownership into a more shadowy "bundle of rights." Thus, a thing can be owned by more than one person, in which case it becomes necessary to focus on the particular limited rights each of the co-owners has with respect to the thing. Further, the notion that full ownership includes rights to do as you wish with what you own suggest that you might sell off particular aspects of your control—rights to certain uses, to profits from the thing, and so on. Finally, rights of use, profit, and the like can be parceled out along a temporal dimension as well—you might sell your control over your property for tomorrow to one person, for the next day to another, and so on. * * *

The same point can be made with respect to fragmentation of ownership generally. When a full owner of a thing begins to sell off various of his rights over it—the right to use it for this purpose tomorrow, for that purpose next year, and so on—at what point does he cease to be the owner, and who then owns the thing? You can say that each one of the many rights holders owns it to the extent of the right, or you can say that no one owns it. Or you can say, as we still tend to do, in the vestigial deference to the lay conception of property, that some conventionally designated rights constitute "ownership." The issue is seen as one of terminology: nothing significant turns on it.

What, then, of the idea that property rights must be rights in things? Perhaps we no longer need a notion of ownership, but surely property rights are a distinct category from other legal rights, in that they pertain to things. But this suggestion cannot withstand analysis either; most property in the modern capitalist economy is intangible. Consider the common forms of wealth: shares of stock in corporations, bonds, various kinds of commercial paper, bank accounts, insurance policies—not to mention more arcane intangibles such as trademarks, patents, copyrights, franchises, and business goodwill.

In our everyday language, we tend to speak of these rights as if they were attached to things. Thus we "deposit our money in the bank," as if we were putting a thing in a place; but really we are creating a complex set of abstract claims against an abstract legal institution. We are told that as insurance policy holders we "own a piece of the rock"; but we really have other abstract claims against another abstract institution. We think of our share of stock in Megabucks Corporation as part ownership in the Megabucks factory outside town; but really the Megabucks board of directors could sell the factory and go into another line of business and we would still have the same claims on the same abstract corporation.

Property rights can no longer be characterized as "rights of ownership" or as "rights in things" by specialists in property. What, then, *is* their special characteristic? How do property rights differ from rights generally—from human rights or personal rights or rights to life or liberty, say? Our specialists and theoreticians have no answer; or rather, they have a multiplicity of widely differing answers, related only in that they bear some association or analogy, more or less remote, to the common notion of property as ownership of things. * * *

The conclusion of all this is that discourse about property has fragmented into a set of discontinuous usages. The more fruitful and useful of these usages are those stipulated by theorists; but these depart drastically from each other and from common speech. Conversely, meanings of "property" in law that cling to their origin in the thing-ownership conception are integrated least successfully into the general doctrinal framework of law, legal theory, and economics. It seems fair to conclude from a glance at the range of current usages that the specialists who design and manipulate the legal structures of the advanced capitalist economies could easily do without using the term "property" at all. * * *

The substitution of the bundle-of-rights for a thing-ownership conception of property has the ultimate consequence that property ceases to be an important category in legal and political theory. This in turn has political implications[.] * * * The legal realists who developed the bundle-of-rights notion were on the whole supportive of the regulatory and welfare state, and in the writings that develop the bundle-of-rights conception, a purpose to remove the sanctity that had traditionally attached to the rights of property can often be discerned. * * *

I would want to deny, however, that the account and explanation of the breakdown of the concept of property offered here is in the last analysis ideological, in the pejorative sense of a mystifying or false apologetic. The development of a largely capitalist market economy toward industrialism objectively demands formulation of its emergent system of economic entitlements in something like the bundle-of-rights form, which in turn must lead to the decline of property as a central category of legal and political thought.

NOTES AND QUESTIONS

1.   Grey's characterization of property as a contingent bundle of rights seems to describe the inquiry in *Hinman* fairly accurately. The dispute is over whether property in land does or does not include, as one of the sticks in the bundle, the right to block airplane overflights. Before the suit, there is uncertainty about whether this is one of the features of property in land. After the decision, we know it is not. According to the bundle-of-rights view, this is how we determine what "property" means, by building up or cutting down the number of sticks in the bundle over time. But how does the bundle-of-sticks metaphor account for the great importance that the Wisconsin Supreme Court in *Jacque* and other courts attribute to the right to exclude others from things as a central feature of property?

2.   Part of the appeal of the bundle-of-sticks metaphor is its "brass tacks" aspect. Proponents see it as cutting through verbiage to get at what's really going on, in a scientifically respectable way. Shane Nicholas Glackin, Back to Bundles: Deflating Property Rights Again, 20 Legal Theory 1 (2014). Penner has returned to this question to offer a vigorous defense of the usefulness of higher-level concepts like property. J.E. Penner, Property Rights: A Re-Examination (2020). See also Christopher. M. Newman, Using Things, Defining Property, in Property Theory 69, 89–98 (James Penner & Michael Otsuka, eds. 2018).

3.   Do Penner and Grey fundamentally disagree about the nature of the concept of property, or do they simply emphasize different aspects of a single but complex phenomenon? Penner, in seeking to explicate the meaning of property, takes as his core case individual ownership of land or tangible personal property. When he moves beyond the core case later in his book and takes up questions such as whether stocks, bonds, and money are "property," the analysis becomes more convoluted. Grey, for his part, does not deny that most people, "including most specialists in their unprofessional moments," have an intuitive conception of property as the right to control things. His case for the "disintegration" of property rests on emphasizing specialized discourses that deal with issues at some remove from the core case of individual ownership of things. If this characterization of the two readings is correct, then the question becomes: Which part of the story should we emphasize—the messiness at the perimeter, or the clarity at the core? Can the decisions in *Jacque* and *Hinman* be reconciled the same way—one dealing with the "normal" rule, the other with an "exception"? For another analysis that contrasts the thing-like view of property held by "ordinary observers" with the bundle-of-sticks view employed by "scientific policymakers," see Bruce A. Ackerman, Private Property and the Constitution (1977); see generally Thomas W. Merrill & Henry E. Smith, What Happened to Property in Law and Economics?, 111 Yale L.J. 357

(2001); *Symposium*: Property: A Bundle of Rights?, 8 Econ. J. Watch 193 (2011) (econjwatch.org).

B. THE TRESPASS/NUISANCE DIVIDE

Jacque v. Steenberg Homes and *Hinman v. Pacific Air Transport* represent two different responses to intentional trespasses to land by strangers. Another contrast, which exposes additional questions about the nature of property rights, concerns the distinction between invasions of land by large objects (like house trailers or airplanes) and interferences with the use and enjoyment of land caused by some activity on neighboring land, like generating pollution or making excessive noise. The latter sorts of interferences are governed by a different common-law doctrine—the law of nuisance—which has traits very different from the law of trespass (at least the version applied in *Jacque*).

1. NUISANCE

Hendricks v. Stalnaker
Supreme Court of Appeals of West Virginia, 1989.
380 S.E.2d 198.

■ NEELY, JUSTICE: Walter S. Stalnaker, defendant below, appeals from a decision by the Circuit Court of Lewis County declaring a water well drilled on his property to be a private nuisance to Harry L. Hendricks and Mary Hendricks, plaintiffs below. The Hendrickses, owners of the property adjacent to that of Mr. Stalnaker, were refused a Health Department permit for a septic system located within 100 feet of Mr. Stalnaker's water well. The Circuit Court of Lewis County, based on a jury verdict, found the water well to be a private nuisance and ordered its abatement. On appeal, Mr. Stalnaker argues that because his water well was not an unreasonable use of his land, he is not liable for the effects on the Hendrickses' property. We agree and, therefore, reverse the decision of the circuit court.

Mr. Stalnaker owns approximately 10 acres of land situated on Glady Fork Road, Lewis County. In 1985, Mr. Stalnaker constructed his home on a 2.493 acre portion of the tract, and had two water wells dowsed. One well was located behind his house and the other, near the Hendrickses' property. The rear well was near land disturbed by a former strip mine and, therefore, the well produced poor quality water. Except for a small section of land near the Hendrickses' property—the location of the second "dowsed" well—most of Mr. Stalnaker's home tract had been disturbed by a strip mine. In August 1985, Mr. Stalnaker spent approximately $3,000 in an unsuccessful attempt to treat the water from the rear well.

In 1984, the Hendrickses purchased approximately 2.95 acres adjacent to Mr. Stalnaker's property for a home site or a trailer development. On 31 December 1985, Mr. Hendricks met with the Lewis County sanitarian to determine locations for a water well and a septic system. The Health Department requires a distance of 100 feet between water wells and septic systems before it will issue permits.[2] Because the Hendrickses' land was too hilly or had been disturbed in order to build a pond, the only location for a septic system on the tract was near Mr. Stalnaker's property. On 13 January 1986, the Hendrickses contacted the county sanitarian to visit their property to complete the septic system permit application. The county sanitarian said because of snowy weather he would come out later in the week.

On 13 January 1986, Mr. Stalnaker called the sanitarian and was told about the Hendrickses' proposed septic system. Mr. Stalnaker was also told that the county sanitarian would be unavailable on 14 January 1986 but could meet with him on 15 January 1986. On 14 January 1986, Mr. Stalnaker contacted a well driller, who applied for and received a well drilling permit for the second well from the assistant sanitarian. The well was completed on 25 January 1986 but was not connected to Mr. Stalnaker's home until January 1987.

On 15 January 1986, the county sanitarian informed Mr. Hendricks that no permit for his proposed septic system could be issued because the absorption field for his septic system was within one hundred feet of Mr. Stalnaker's water well. Mr. Hendricks did install a septic system without a permit in January 1987; however, the system was left inoperative pending the outcome of this suit.

The Hendrickses filed suit in the Circuit Court of Lewis County on 29 January 1987 requesting (1) the water well be declared a private nuisance, (2) the nuisance be abated, and (3) damages. In a bifurcated trial, the jury found that the water well was a private nuisance and the trial judge ordered it to be abated. On the issue of damages the jury found for the defendant and awarded no damages.

I

In the past we have broadly described what constitutes a nuisance:

> A nuisance is anything which annoys or disturbs the free use of one's property, or which renders its ordinary use or physical occupation uncomfortable. . . . A nuisance is anything which interferes with the rights of a citizen, either in person, property, the enjoyment of his property, or his comfort. . . . A condition is a nuisance when it clearly appears that enjoyment of property is materially lessened, and physical comfort of persons in their homes is materially interfered with thereby. (Citations omitted).

---

[2]   The county sanitarian testified that the purpose of the distance requirement was to protect not just an individual well but to prevent contamination of the ground streams of the aquifer.

Martin v. Williams, 93 S.E.2d 835, 844 (W. Va. 1956). * * * This definition of nuisance includes acts or conditions that affect either the general public or a limited number of persons. In *Hark v. Mountain Fork Lumber Co.*, 34 S.E.2d 348, 354 (W. Va. 1945) we defined a public nuisance as that which "affects the general public as public, and [a private nuisance as that which] injures one person or a limited number of persons only."

In order clearly to delineate between a public nuisance and a private nuisance, we define a private nuisance as a substantial and unreasonable interference with the private use and enjoyment of another's land. The definition of private nuisance includes conduct that is intentional and unreasonable, negligent or reckless, or that results in an abnormally dangerous conditions or activities in an inappropriate place. See W. Prosser, Handbook of the Law of Torts § 87 at 580, § 89 at 593 (4th ed. 1971); Restatement (Second) of Torts §§ 821D, 821F, 822 (1979); W. Keeton, Prosser and Keeton on the Law of Torts § 87 (5th ed. 1984). Recovery for a private nuisance is limited to plaintiffs who have suffered a significant harm to their property rights or privileges caused by the interference. Restatement (Second) of Torts §§ 821E, 821F (1979).

Early West Virginia cases indicate that the existence of a private nuisance was determined primarily by the harm caused. Medford v. Levy, 8 S.E. 302 (W. Va. 1888) (cooking odors); Flanagan v. Gregory and Poole, Inc., 67 S.E.2d 865 (W. Va. 1951) (inadequate culvert). Gradually the focus included an examination of the reasonableness of the property's use. See McGregor v. Camden, 34 S.E. 936 (W. Va. 1899) (required an examination of the location, capacity and management of oil and gas well); Pope v. Edward M. Rude Carrier Corp., 75 S.E.2d 584 (W. Va. 1953) (transportation of explosives); Martin, supra (used automobile lot); State ex rel. Ammerman v. City of Philippi, 65 S.E.2d 713 (W. Va. 1951) (tire recapping business); Ritz v. Woman's Club of Charleston, 173 S.E. 564 (W. Va. 1934) (noise); Harless v. Workman, 114 S.E.2d 548 (W. Va. 1960) (coal dust).

In the area of public nuisance, we have made explicit that an examination of the "reasonableness or unreasonableness of the use of property in relation to the particular locality" is a fair test to determine the existence of a public nuisance. Similarly, any determination of liability for a private nuisance must include an examination of the private use and enjoyment of the land seeking protection and the nature of the interference.[5]

Because the present case concerns conduct that is not a negligent, reckless, or abnormally dangerous activity, our discussion of private nuisance is limited to conduct that is intentional and unreasonable. An interference is intentional when the actor knows or should know that the conduct is causing a substantial and unreasonable interference. Restatement (Second) of Torts § 825 (1979). The unreasonableness of an intentional interference must be determined by a balancing of the landowners' interests. An interference is unreasonable when the gravity of the harm outweighs the social value of the activity alleged to cause the harm. See W. Prosser, supra § 87, at 581, § 89 at 596; Restatement (Second) of Torts § 826 (1979); W. Keeton, supra § 88, at 629. Restatement (Second) of Torts §§ 827 and 828 (1979) list some of the factors to be considered in determining the gravity of the harm and the social value of the activity alleged to cause the harm.[6] However, this balancing to determine unreasonableness is not absolute. Additional consideration might include the malicious or indecent conduct of the actor. Restatement (Second) of Torts § 829. * * *

In the case before us, the Hendrickses' inability to operate a septic system on their property is clearly a substantial interference with the use and enjoyment of their land. The record indicates that the installation of the water well was intentional, but there was no evidence that the installation was done so as maliciously to deprive the Hendrickses of a septic system. Mr. Stalnaker wanted to insure himself of an adequate water supply and found no alternative to the well he dug.

The critical question is whether the interference, the installation of a water well, was unreasonable. Unreasonableness is determined by balancing the competing landholders' interests. We note that either use,

---

[5]   The *Restatement (Second) of Torts* § 822 (1979) requires a consideration of unreasonableness as part of the determination of liability.

One is subject to liability for a private nuisance if, but only if, his conduct is a legal cause of an invasion of another's interest in the private use and enjoyment of land, and the invasion is either

(a) intentional and unreasonable, or

(b) unintentional and otherwise actionable under the rules controlling liability for negligent or reckless conduct, or for abnormally dangerous conditions or activities.

[6]   The *Restatement (Second) of Torts* § 827 (1979) lists the following "gravity of harm" factors:

(a) The extent of the harm involved;

(b) the character of the harm involved;

(c) the social value that the law attaches to the type of use or enjoyment invaded;

(d) the suitability of the particular use or enjoyment invaded to the character of the locality; and

(e) the burden on the person harmed of avoiding the harm.

The *Restatement (Second) of Torts* § 828 lists the following "utility of conduct" factors:

(a) the social value that the law attaches to the primary purpose of the conduct;

(b) the suitability of the conduct to the character of the locality; and

(c) the impracticability of preventing or avoiding the invasion.

well or septic system, burdens the adjacent property. Under Health Department regulations, a water well merely requires non-interference within 100 feet of its location. In the case of a septic system, however, the 100 foot safety zone, extending from the edge of the absorption field, may intrude on adjacent property. Thus, the septic system, with its potential for drainage, places a more invasive burden on adjacent property.[7] Clearly both uses present similar considerations of gravity of harm and social value of the activity alleged to cause the harm. Both a water well and a septic system are necessary to use this land for housing; together they constitute the in and out of many water systems. Neither party has an inexpensive and practical alternative. The site of the water well means quality water for Mr. Stalnaker, and the Hendrickses have only one location available for their septic system.

In the case before us, we are asked to determine if the water well is a private nuisance. But if the septic system were operational, the same question could be asked about the septic system.[8] Because of the similar competing interests, the balancing of these landowners' interests is at least equal or, perhaps, slightly in favor of the water well. Thus, the Hendrickses have not shown that the balancing of interests favors their septic system. We find that the evidence presented clearly does not demonstrate that the water well is an unreasonable use of land and, therefore, does not constitute a private nuisance. * * *

We find that because the evidence is not disputed and only one [inference] is reasonable, the trial court should have held as a matter of law that the water well was not a private nuisance. * * *

Reversed.

NOTES AND QUESTIONS

1. The law of nuisance, in contrast to the conventional (*Jacque*-style) law of trespass, is neither simple nor rigorous. In fact, commentators have described nuisance doctrine as so complex and uncertain that it amounts to an "impenetrable jungle." William L. Prosser, Handbook of the Law of Torts 571 (4th ed. 1971). The *Restatement of Torts* valiantly seeks to bring some order to this complexity by providing that a nuisance is an interference with the use and enjoyment of land that causes "significant harm" and is "unreasonable." Restatement (Second) of Torts §§ 821F, 822. The primary definition of "unreasonable," according to the *Restatement*, is that "the gravity of the harms outweighs the utility of the actor's conduct." Id. § 826. The *Hendricks* court, which generally follows the *Restatement*, reads this to

---

[7]   Rules and Regulations of the Health Department § 64–9–5.7 [1983] require a recorded easement or authorization for use of or crossing of adjacent property for off lot disposal of sewage or effluent.

[8]   In a factually similar case, the Supreme Court of Oklahoma held that a sewage lagoon created within 100 feet of a neighbor's water well was a "willful" injury to the adjacent property and awarded attorneys' fees. The court reasoned that under an Oklahoma statute the sewage lagoon actively burdened adjacent property whereas the water well was a non-invasive burden. Schaeffer v. Shaeffer, 743 P.2d 1038 (Okla. 1987).

mean that nuisance liability turns on "balancing the competing landowners' interests."

2.   How does the court here arrive at the conclusion of reasonableness? The court says that the value of the competing interests is "similar," or "perhaps" is "slightly in favor of the water well." Does the opinion give any reasons that might support this conclusion? Should the court, following the guidance of the *Restatement*, have conducted a more rigorous (and perhaps quantified) analysis of the costs and benefits of septic tanks and water wells before deciding the reasonableness issue? Why do you suppose the court did not do this? If a rigorous cost-benefit analysis is not required, should the question of reasonableness be regarded as one of fact? If so, why shouldn't the court accept as controlling the jury's determination that the well was a nuisance?

3.   Although the *Restatement* is widely followed—or at least cited—in modern nuisance cases, it is by no means the only possible approach that courts could take to resolving nuisance disputes. We take up nuisance in greater detail in Chapter IX, but for now, consider these possibilities and ask yourself whether any of them may have carried weight with the court in *Hendricks*:

(1)   Instead of balancing the interests of the parties, perhaps courts should simply ask whether the defendant has committed some kind of "invasion" of plaintiff's land that causes harm above a certain threshold level ("significant harm"). Richard Epstein has argued that under the English common law, a nuisance would be found only if the defendant's conduct had caused or threatened to cause some kind of invasion, such as by air pollution particles, sewage added to a stream, or sound waves—a kind of mini-trespass if you will. Richard A. Epstein, Nuisance Law: Corrective Justice and Its Utilitarian Constraints, 8 J. Legal Stud. 49 (1979). Is the outcome in the instant case consistent with this principle? Would Stalnaker's well, which would draw water from an aquifer common to both parcels of land, have caused any "invasion" of the Hendrickses' subsurface land rights? Conversely, would the Hendrickses' septic tank, which would diffuse waste water into the surrounding soil, have caused any "invasion" of Stalnaker's subsurface rights?

(2)   Another possibility would be to decide these disputes by enforcing the general understanding in the relevant community of what constitutes "normal use" of land. See Robert C. Ellickson, Alternatives to Zoning: Covenants, Nuisance Rules, and Fines as Land Use Controls, 40 U. Chi. L. Rev. 681 (1973). Although it is unclear from the facts as stated, it is likely that both water wells and septic tanks are common uses of land in rural West Virginia. Can it be said that either a water well or a septic tank is more "normal" or "natural" than the other? Water wells have been around since the dawn of civilization, whereas septic fields are a more recent contrivance of human ingenuity. Should this matter?

(3)   Some cases and commentators have given weight to temporal priority, in the sense that the first use to be established is given a presumption of validity relative to a later, incompatible use. See Donald

Wittman, First Come, First Served: An Economic Analysis of "Coming to the Nuisance," 9 J. Legal Stud. 557 (1980). Note that Stalnaker rushes to complete his well before the Hendrickses can obtain a permit for their septic system. Is this a legitimate reason to prefer Stalnaker's use to the Hendrickses' use in determining whether the well is a nuisance? Or is this undesirable behavior? Might it be a legitimate consideration in other circumstances?

(4) A final approach that may explain some of the cases is to ask whether the defendant (or the plaintiff) has been acting in a way consonant with general norms of "neighborliness." See Stewart E. Sterk, Neighbors in American Land Law, 87 Colum. L. Rev. 55, 88–103 (1987). For example, many jurisdictions recognize that the erection of a "spite fence," meaning a fence that is built for the sole purpose of irritating a neighbor, is an actionable nuisance. Id. at 62–63. As between Stalnaker and the Hendrickses, who is behaving in the more "neighborly" fashion? Is this judgment too subjective to serve as the basis for a rule of property law?

Given all these theories or themes in nuisance law competing with the *Restatement*'s balancing test and with each other, can you see why Prosser threw up his hands and said it was an "impenetrable jungle?"

4. Consider again the decision in *Hinman v. Pacific Air Transport* in light of *Hendricks* and the brief summary of nuisance law provided here. Does *Hinman* ultimately subject airplane overflights to a mode of analysis more commonly associated with nuisance than trespass? See also Restatement (Second) of Torts § 159(2) (Am. L. Inst. 1965) ("Flight by aircraft in the air space above the land of another is a trespass if, but only if, (a) it enters into the immediate reaches of the air space next to the land, and (b) it interferes substantially with the other's use and enjoyment of his land."). If there is a subset of trespass cases that should be resolved using nuisance principles, how could that subset be defined? Conversely, is there a subset of nuisance cases that should be handled using a simple and rigorous doctrine like trespass? If so, how could this subset of nuisance cases be defined?

5. Given that intentional trespass is typically clear and strict, and nuisance is typically neither clear nor strict, the boundary between interferences governed by trespass and those governed by nuisance would seem to be a matter of some importance. In principle, the boundary between trespass and nuisance is fixed by the nature of the interests these actions are said to protect: Trespass is said to protect the interest in *possession* of land, while nuisance is said to protect the *use and enjoyment* of land. See Restatement (Second) of Torts § 821D, cmt. d. From this, it has generally been assumed that trespass applies when the defendant intrudes upon the land with some object large and solid enough to physically displace the plaintiff from a portion of her land, such as an intrusion by another person, a vehicle, standing water—or a mobile home. Conversely, if the invasion is committed by small objects like particles of gas or sound or light waves, this will be governed by the law of nuisance. Similarly, noninvasive interferences with use and enjoyment of land, like the construction of a spite fence, will be

governed by the law of nuisance rather than trespass. (We take up the distinction between trespass and nuisance further in Chapter IX.)

2.   EXCLUSION AND GOVERNANCE

Another way to consider the distinction between trespass and nuisance is to think of them as exemplifying two different strategies for resolving disputes about how scarce resources are used: exclusion and governance. See Henry E. Smith, Exclusion versus Governance: Two Strategies for Delineating Property Rights, 31 J. Legal Stud. S453 (2002); Henry E. Smith, Exclusion and Property Rules in the Law of Nuisance, 90 Va. L. Rev. 965 (2004). Under an exclusion strategy, decisions about resource use are in a sense delegated to an owner who acts as the manager or gatekeeper of the resource. For example, the owner decides who gets to come onto the property, what it will be used for, and so forth. To implement this delegation of gatekeeper authority, the law allows the owner of the resource to repel any and all intrusions that do not have the owner's consent. A crude signal—whether an object is intruding on the land or not—is a simple basis for finding a violation. Exclusion is likely to be favored where particular resources like land have multiple potential uses, and when we think it desirable to give owners discretion to choose which use is most valuable. The only task of judges and other officials, under this approach, is to backstop the authority of the owner as manager of the resource. In particular, these officials have no need to monitor—or even to identify—the various permissible uses of the resource. The law of trespass, at least as applied in *Jacque v. Steenberg Homes*, appears to reflect this kind of strategy.

A second and different strategy for solving resource use disputes is governance. This strategy focuses on particular uses of resources, and prescribes particular rules about permitted and prohibited uses without regard to the other attributes of the resource. Governance rules can derive from many sources, including social norms, contracts, government regulations, and common-law judgments. Governance tends to be used in situations where the particular uses of property are of heightened significance, either because they are strongly favored or disfavored. Thus, in *Hendricks v. Stalnaker*, the parties perceive that their land can either be used for groundwater extraction or sewage disposal—but quite likely cannot be used for both. The answer to the question of which use has priority will have very substantial implications for the use and enjoyment of their respective parcels. Under a governance strategy, courts or other officials may determine directly how the property will be used along one or more dimensions singled out as critical. The law of nuisance, at least as applied in *Hendricks v. Stalnaker*, appears to reflect this kind of strategy.

At various points in these materials we will see property law shifting from an exclusion strategy to a governance strategy (or somewhere in between), particularly as disputes over conflicting uses of property become more intense, or more persons are affected by decisions as to how property is used, or both. The distinction between trespass and nuisance is one of the clearest examples of this, and serves to some extent as a model for similar shifts that occur elsewhere in property law.

3.   THE COASE THEOREM

Nuisance law has given rise to a rich literature about the role of private agreements—contracts—that reassign property rights in ways different from how they are originally assigned as a matter of law. Ronald Coase was an economist who was awarded the Nobel Memorial Prize in Economics in 1991 for his identification of the importance of transaction costs in assessing the economic effects of alternative institutional arrangements. His most famous article, part of which is excerpted below, contains an elaborate discussion of English nuisance cases and the role of private agreements in reassigning the rights established by nuisance law. This is also the article that lays out what has subsequently come to be known as the "Coase theorem," which plays an important role in the economic analysis of property rights and in law and economics more generally. Although Coase did not have a law degree, this article has become the most frequently cited work in all of legal scholarship.

Ronald H. Coase, *The Problem of Social Cost*
3 J.L. & ECON. 1–3, 6–8, 13–19 (1960).

This paper is concerned with those actions of business firms which have harmful effects on others. * * *

The question is commonly thought of as one in which A inflicts harm on B and what has to be decided is: How should we restrain A? But this is wrong. We are dealing with a problem of a reciprocal nature. To avoid the harm to B would inflict harm on A. The real question that has to be decided is: Should A be allowed to harm B or should B be allowed to harm A? The problem is to avoid the more serious harm. I instanced in my previous article[1] the case of a confectioner the noise and vibrations from whose machinery disturbed a doctor in his work. To avoid harming the doctor would inflict harm on the confectioner. The problem posed by this case was essentially whether it was worth while, as a result of restricting the methods of production which could be used by the confectioner, to secure more doctoring at the cost of a reduced supply of confectionery products. Another example is afforded by the problem of straying cattle which destroy crops on neighboring land. If it is inevitable that some cattle will stray, an increase in the supply of meat can only be obtained at the expense of a decrease in the supply of crops. The nature of the choice is clear: meat or crops. What answer should be given is, of course, not clear unless we know the value of what is obtained as well as the

---

[1]   Coase, The Federal Communications Commission, 2 J.L. & Econ. 26–27 (1959).

value of what is sacrificed to obtain it. * * * It goes almost without saying that this problem has to be looked at in total *and* at the margin.

I propose to start my analysis by examining a case in which most economists would presumably agree that the problem would be solved in a completely satisfactory manner: when the damaging business has to pay for all damage caused and the pricing system works smoothly (strictly this means that the operation of a pricing system is without cost).

A good example of the problem under discussion is afforded by the case of straying cattle which destroy crops growing on neighboring land. Let us suppose that a farmer and a cattle-raiser are operating on neighboring properties. Let us further suppose that, without any fencing between the properties, an increase in the size of the cattle-raiser's herd increases the total damage to the farmer's crops. What happens to the marginal damage as the size of the herd increases is another matter. This depends on whether the cattle tend to follow one another or to roam side by side, on whether they tend to be more or less restless as the size of the herd increases and on other similar factors. For my immediate purpose, it is immaterial what assumption is made about marginal damage as the size of the herd increases.

To simplify the argument, I propose to use an arithmetical example. I shall assume that the annual cost of fencing the farmer's property is $9 and that the price of the crop is $1 per ton. Also, I assume that the relation between the number of cattle in the herd and the annual crop loss is as follows:

Number in Herd (Steers)	Annual Crop Loss (Tons)	Crop Loss per Additional Steer (Tons)
1	1	1
2	3	2
3	6	3
4	10	4

Given that the cattle-raiser is liable for the damage caused, this additional annual cost imposed on the cattle-raiser if he increased his herd from, say, 2 to 3 steers is $3 and in deciding on the size of the herd, he will take this into account along with his other costs. That is, he will not increase the size of the herd unless the value of the additional meat produced (assuming that the cattle-raiser slaughters the cattle), is greater than the additional costs that this will entail, including the value of the additional crops destroyed. Of course, if, by the employment of dogs, herdsmen, aeroplanes, mobile radio and other means, the amount of damage can be reduced, these means will be adopted when their cost is less the value of the crop which they prevent being lost. Given that the annual cost of fencing is $9, the cattle-raiser who wished to have a herd with 4 steers or more would pay for fencing to be erected and maintained, assuming that other means of attaining the same end would not do so more cheaply. When the fence is erected, the marginal cost due to the liability for damage becomes zero, except to the extent that an increase in the size of the herd necessitates a stronger and therefore more expensive fence because more steers are liable to lean against it at the same time. But, of course, it may be cheaper for the cattle-raiser not to fence and to pay for the damaged crops, as in my arithmetical example, with 3 or fewer steers. * * *

I now turn to the case in which, although the pricing system is assumed to work smoothly (that is, costlessly), the damaging business is not liable for any of the damage which it causes. This business does not have to make a payment to those damaged by its actions. I propose to show that the allocation of resources will be the same in this case as it was when the damaging business was liable for damage caused. * * *

I return to the case of the farmer and the cattle-raiser. The farmer would suffer increased damage to his crop as the size of the herd increased. Suppose that the size of the cattle-raiser's herd is 3 steers (and that this is the size of the herd that would be maintained if crop damage was not taken into account). Then the farmer would be willing to pay up to $3 if the cattle-raiser would reduce his herd to 2 steers, up to $5 if the herd were reduced to 1 steer and would pay up to $6 if cattle-raising was abandoned. The cattle-raiser would therefore receive $3 from the farmer if he kept 2 steers instead of 3. This $3 foregone is therefore part of the cost incurred in keeping the third steer. Whether the $3 is a payment which the cattle-raiser has to make if he adds the third steer to his herd (which it would be if the cattle-raiser was liable to the farmer for damage caused to the crop) or whether it is a sum of money which he would have received if he did not keep a third steer (which it would be if the cattle-raiser was not liable to the farmer for damage caused to the crop) does not affect the final result. In both cases $3 is part of the cost of adding a third steer, to be included along with the other costs. If the increase in the value of production in cattle-raising through increasing the size of the herd from 2 to 3 is greater than the additional costs that have to be incurred (including the $3 damage to crops), the size of the herd will be increased. Otherwise, it will not. The size of the herd will be the same whether the cattle-raiser is liable for the damage caused to the crop or not. * * *

It is necessary to know whether the damaging business is liable or not for damage caused since without the establishment of this initial delimitation of rights there can be no market transactions to transfer and recombine them. But the ultimate result (which maximizes the value of production) is independent of the legal position if the pricing system is assumed to work without cost.

Judges have to decide on legal liability but this should not confuse economists about the nature of the economic problem involved. In the case of the cattle and the crops, it is true that there would be no crop damage without the cattle. It is equally true that there would be no crop damage without the crops. The doctor's work would not have been disturbed if the confectioner had not worked his machinery; but the machinery would have disturbed no one if the doctor had not set up his consulting room in that particular place. * * * If we are to discuss the problem in terms of causation, both parties cause the damage. If we are to attain an optimum allocation of resources, it is therefore desirable that both parties should take the harmful effect (the nuisance) into account in deciding on their course of action. It is one of the beauties of a smoothly operating pricing system that, as has already been explained, the fall in the value of production due to the harmful effect would be a cost for both parties. * * *

[I]t has to be remembered that the immediate question faced by the courts is *not* what shall be done by whom *but* who has the legal right to do what. It is always possible to modify by transactions on the market the initial legal delimitation of rights. And, of course, if such market transactions are costless, such a rearrangement of rights will always take place if it would lead to an increase in the value of production.

The argument has proceeded up to this point on the assumption * * * that there were no costs involved in carrying out market transactions. This is, of course, a very unrealistic assumption. In order to carry out a market transaction it is necessary to discover who it is that one wishes to deal with, to inform people that one wishes to deal and on what terms, to conduct negotiations leading up to a bargain, to draw up the contract, to undertake the inspection needed to make sure that the terms of the contract are being observed, and so on. These operations are often extremely costly, sufficiently costly at any rate to prevent many transactions that would be carried out in a world in which the pricing system worked without cost.

In earlier sections, when dealing with the problem of the rearrangement of legal rights through the market, it was argued that such a rearrangement would be made through the market whenever this would lead to an increase in the value of production. But this assumed costless market transactions. Once the costs of carrying out market transactions are taken into account it is clear that such a rearrangement of rights will only be undertaken when the increase in the value of production consequent upon the rearrangement is greater than the costs which would be involved in bringing it about. When it is less, the granting of an injunction (or the knowledge that it would be granted) or the liability to pay damages may result in an activity being discontinued (or may prevent its being started) which would be undertaken if market transactions were costless. In these conditions the initial delimitation of legal rights does have an effect on the efficiency with which the economic system operates. One arrangement of rights may bring about a greater value of production than any other. But unless this is the arrangement of rights established by the legal system, the costs of reaching the same result by altering and combining rights through the market may be so great that this optimal arrangement of rights, and the greater value of production which it would bring, may never be achieved. * * *

The discussion of the problem of harmful effects in this section (when the costs of market transactions are taken into account) is extremely inadequate. But at least it has made clear that the problem is one of choosing the appropriate social arrangement for dealing with the harmful effects. All solutions have costs and there is no reason to suppose that government regulation is called for simply because the problem is not well handled by the market or the firm. Satisfactory views on policy can only come from a study of how, in practice, the market, firms and governments handle the problem of harmful effects. Economists need to study the work of the broker in bringing parties together, the effect of restrictive covenants, the problems of the large-scale real-estate development company, the operation of Government zoning and other regulating activities. It is my belief that economists, and policy-makers generally, have tended to over-estimate the advantages which come from governmental regulation. But this belief, even if justified, does not do more than suggest that government regulation should be curtailed. It does not tell us where the boundary line should be drawn. This, it seems to me, has to come from a detailed investigation of the actual results of handling the problem in different ways. * * *

NOTES AND QUESTIONS

1.   The problem of cattle trampling crops, which Coase takes as his central example in the excerpt reproduced here, is usually thought to be governed by a branch of the law of trespass rather than nuisance law. Interestingly, however, the rules regarding cattle trespass have varied in different parts of the country with respect to who has the duty to put up a fence to prevent livestock from damaging crops. See Robert C. Ellickson Order without Law: How Neighbors Settle Disputes 42–43 (1991). In most parts of the United States, a "fencing in" rule prevails, whereby the owner of the cattle or other livestock has the duty to put up a fence in order to keep the cattle in. If they escape and trample unfenced crops, the owner of the cattle is liable for damages for trespass. In certain parts of the western United States, however, where grazing livestock on the open range was the historical practice, a rule of "fencing out" sometimes prevails, whereby the burden is on the owner of the crops to put up a fence to keep the cattle out. If the crop owner has failed to put up a fence or to keep it maintained, the cattle owner is not liable when cattle wander into the field and trample the crops. Does the Coase theorem provide a basis for explaining why most states would adopt a fencing in rule, but others a rule of fencing out? See Kenneth R. Vogel, The Coase Theorem and California's Animal Trespass Law, 16 J. Legal Stud. 149 (1987). Interestingly, the fencing in/fencing out distinction

only applies to cattle that wander of their own volition without human guidance. If an owner of livestock deliberately induces his animals to graze on land belonging to another, this is regarded as a trespass, whether the land is open range or not. See Light v. United States, 220 U.S. 523 (1911); Musselshell Cattle Co. v. Woolfolk, 85 P. 874 (Mont. 1906). Also, as Ellickson discovered in his empirical study of modern-day Shasta County, California, landowners there follow a norm requiring that cattle be fenced in, without regard to whether the formal rule on the books requires fencing in or fencing out. Ellickson, supra, at 52–64. Can all of this this be explained in terms of the changes in costs and benefits of land use in the West in recent decades? (Ellickson notes that many of the areas governed by fencing-out laws are now populated by small "ranchettes" where people keep some livestock but also commute to jobs in nearby cities.) Would you expect norms to be more or less uniform than formal law? In close cases, would you expect the norm to be fencing in or fencing out? Which accords more with general norms of possession? Can the Coase theorem explain these features of cattle trespass law and norms that appear to carry forward the traditional exclusion model? See generally Thomas W. Merrill & Henry E. Smith, Making Coasean Property More Coasean, 54 J. L. & Econ. S77 (2011).

2.   Work your way carefully through Coase's example about the rancher and the farmer, and make sure you understand the logic behind his argument that if it is costless to enter into contracts (that is, if "transaction costs" are zero), then the same number of cattle will be raised by the rancher, whether or not the rancher is liable to the farmer for cattle trespass. The basic idea is that if contracting is costless, the parties will keep contracting to modify the initial assignment of property rights until they have exhausted all possible deals that would be to their mutual advantage. The final stopping point will always be the use of resources that creates the greatest joint wealth for the parties, because once this point is reached, neither party can offer the other one a deal that would make both of them better off. Of course, this does not mean that the rancher and the farmer will be indifferent to the initial assignment of property rights. If the rancher starts out with the right to let cattle trespass, then the farmer will have to "bribe" the rancher to cut back to the joint-maximizing number. The rancher will be richer because of the initial assignment of rights. Conversely, if the farmer starts out with the right to be free of cattle trespasses, then the rancher will have to "bribe" the farmer to let him increase the number of cattle. The farmer will be richer because of the initial assignment of rights. So you can be sure that the rancher and the farmer (and others similarly situated) will care about the assignment of rights, because it affects the distribution of wealth. Coase's point is that if we ignore the distributional impact, and focus only on the question of how resources in society are used, the result would be the same regardless of the initial allocation of rights, provided transaction costs are zero. A good text providing further introduction to the Coase theorem and some basic economics concepts is Richard A. Ippolito, Economics for Lawyers 228–46 (2005).

3.   What other assumptions are necessary for the invariance outcome of the Coase theorem to apply? Two assumptions that Coase does not make

 bargaining toward an efficient outcome

explicit are that individuals are rational maximizers and that all values are capable of being expressed in monetary terms. The assumption that persons are rational maximizers means that they prefer more rather than less (of whatever it is they happen to prefer), and that, subject to information constraints, when presented with a choice, they will choose the option that yields more rather than less. Nearly all economists would agree, however, that the assumption that people are rational maximizers is at most a generalization about human behavior, not a postulate that all people act rationally in pursuit of their interests all the time. (Before you have finished this book, you will have encountered some people who probably cannot be regarded as rational maximizers.) How much should the possibility of irrational behavior concern someone interested in the design of legal institutions? Most economists would also agree that there are certain values that people hold dear that cannot be readily translated into dollar terms. How much of a concern should this be to someone designing legal institutions? Are there still other assumptions about human behavior lurking behind the Coase theorem? Robert Cooter has suggested that for the Coase theorem to hold, one must also assume that people are natural cooperators rather than ruthless exploiters. See Robert Cooter, The Cost of Coase, 11 J. Legal Stud. 1 (1982) (comparing the Coase Theorem and the "Hobbes Theorem"). For other issues, such as whether the parties' wealth would affect the allocation of resources in the hypothetical world of zero transaction costs, see, e.g., R.H. Coase, The Firm, the Market, and the Law 170–74 (1988); Harold Demsetz, When Does the Rule of Liability Matter?, 1 J. Legal Stud. 13 (1972); Stewart Schwab, Coase Defends Coase: Why Lawyers Listen and Economists Do Not, 87 Mich. L. Rev. 1171, 1178–84 (1989).

4. Coase himself wrote that the assumption that it is costless to engage in contracts is very unrealistic—"as strange as the physical world without friction." R.H. Coase, The Firm, the Market, and the Law 14 (1988). So the Coase theorem should not be taken to be a guide to understanding the real world. Instead, the theorem should be seen as a kind of thought experiment, which is intended to reveal the importance of transaction costs in the design of legal institutions. Coase in later writing expressed frustration that people mistook his thought experiment to mean that markets achieve efficient results when transaction costs are low. "The world of zero transaction costs has often been described as a Coasian world. Nothing could be further from the truth. It is the world of modern economic theory, one which I was hoping to persuade economists to leave." Id. at 174. His point was more nearly the opposite: that transaction costs are always positive, and hence we cannot assume that *any* institutional arrangement will necessarily generate efficient results. Coase thought that it is always important to compare alternative institutional arrangements, and to try to determine which one will deviate the least from the unattainable ideal of the (mythical) world of zero transaction costs. For more about the Coase theorem and its place in legal scholarship, see Steven G. Medema, The Coase Theorem at Sixty, 58 J. Econ. Lit. 1045 (2020).

5.   One of Coase's controversial claims is that any conflict over resource use (like the rancher and farmer, or a nuisance dispute) is a "reciprocal" one, meaning that each party to the dispute is imposing costs on the other party. This is plausible if we consider a dispute like *Hendricks v. Stalnaker*, involving adjacent landowners who make incompatible demands on the use of the land. But is it equally plausible to say that there is a "reciprocal" relationship between a property owner who has an in rem right to exclude others from her land, and the rest of the world which is subject to a duty to desist from interfering with her land? If the rule were that anyone—not just neighbors—would be entitled to trespass on land, with whom would the present owner of the land have to bargain in order to be free of such trespasses? Everyone on the block? In the United States? The world? What about unborn future would-be trespassers? Or do all these cases just point once again to the importance of transaction costs in the real world? See Clifford G. Holderness, The Assignment of Rights, Entry Effects, and the Allocation of Resources, 18 J. Legal Stud. 181 (1989). Further, the default package of rights the law provides is not as symmetrical with respect to invasions as one would expect if causation of harm were fully reciprocal; people have the right to prevent invasions but robust rights to commit invasions must usually be specially added to this package. See Henry E. Smith, Self-Help and the Nature of Property, 1 J.L. Econ. & Pol'y 69, 70–80 (2005), and Chapter IX.

6.   There is also an enormous literature describing various attempts to test the Coase theorem empirically. See generally Steven G. Medema & Richard O. Zerbe, The Coase Theorem, in The Encyclopedia of Law and Economics 836, 858–73 (2000). Although generalizations are hazardous, much of this literature suggests that bargaining over entitlements is influenced not only by joint wealth maximization, but also by a variety of factors, including the initial distributions of rights, the history of interaction between the parties, and perceptions of what outcomes are regarded as fair.

4. RESOLVING PROPERTY DISPUTES BY CONTRACT

What, you may be asking yourself, is the payoff to the law student from studying the Coase theorem? One very important lesson is that, as a lawyer assisting a client in a dispute over the use of property, you should always try to imagine various ways in which contracts might be used to resolve the problem. Litigation to clarify or enforce property rights may ultimately be unavoidable. But contractual modifications of property rights—"Coasean bargains" as they are sometimes called—should be explored as an alternative to litigation. A contractual rearrangement of rights may be cheaper and more satisfactory to all concerned.

Consider again in this light the dispute in *Hendricks v. Stalnaker*. Nothing in the law would have prevented the parties from bargaining, at any stage of the dispute, over the placement of the well and the septic field. For example, the parties could have agreed to build a well on one parcel and a septic field on the other parcel, and could have granted reciprocal rights to each other (easements) so that each would have had access to both facilities. Alternatively, one party could have bought out the other, and then built a single well and septic field for both parcels; they could then have rented half of the land to a tenant (perhaps the other party) with water and septic services included in the rent.

Another dimension of *Hendricks* concerns the role that land-use regulation plays in creating the dispute. Both Stalnaker and the Hendrickses cannot do what they want to do, because the County Health Department regulation requires that there be at least 100 feet of separation between the edge of a septic field and any water well. Perhaps the Health Department would consider a waiver or modification of this rule if other adjustments were agreed upon by the parties. For example, if the Hendrickses agreed to pretreat their waste water before it enters the septic field, or if Stalnaker agreed to extra monitoring of his well water, perhaps the Health Department could be persuaded to relax its 100-foot buffer zone requirement. This type of solution would entail a more complicated set of negotiations among three parties—Stalnaker, the Hendrickses, and the Health Department. And of course, the Health Department may take the position that it has no authority to grant a variance from the rules, and even if it has authority, there may be no (lawful) method of making a side payment to the Department to induce it to be flexible. But a conscientious lawyer looking for a solution to the problem would want to explore the regulatory side of the dispute as well.

Why didn't any of these "Coasean" solutions happen? One possibility is that the parties (or their lawyers) did not think about these kinds of solutions. Another possibility is that they thought about them, but concluded they were too costly or were technically infeasible. A third possibility is that they did not think about them until transaction costs became too high for any kind of Coasean bargain to take place. The last possibility highlights another point taught by the Coase theorem: It is important to be sensitive to the causes of high transaction costs in order to guide clients toward potential Coasean bargains before those options are foreclosed and litigation is the only recourse.

Many factors, some physical, some psychological, enter into creating high transaction costs. We will not make any attempt to catalogue them all here. You will gradually come to have a greater appreciation of the many impediments to contractual solutions to resource disputes as you go through these materials. We will highlight two factors that loom large throughout property law: assembly problems and bilateral monopoly.

Assembly problems arise when someone wants to assemble property rights from a large number of owners in order to undertake some project. This is an instance in a property setting of high transaction costs stemming from large numbers of contracting parties. *Hinman* is an example of an assembly problem. Suppose each surface owner had the power to block airplanes from entering into the airspace above the surface of his or her land, and suppose that some kind of technology (like advanced radar) is available so that both surface owners and airplanes can detect when airplanes enter the column of space above someone's land. Under these circumstances, persons who want to fly would have to assemble permissions from a huge number of surface owners. This would entail major difficulties in identifying all the affected surface owners, and getting them to communicate and agree on a solution. Even if all the affected surface owners could be identified and engaged in negotiations, some owners might hold out for a very generous payment (unless they could be easily avoided by choosing a different route). More mundane assembly problems arise when highways or utility lines are built or when developers want to acquire multiple contiguous parcels for some large-scale project (see Figure 1-3). Each of these projects typically entails the need to assemble a large number of property rights, and each presents high transaction costs as a consequence.

Another cause of high transaction costs is bilateral monopoly. By this, we do not refer to large industrial monopolies, but rather to localized monopolies—situations in which an owner of property needs something that can be provided by only one other person or entity. In *Hendricks*, it would appear that the physical lay of the land caused each party to have only the other as a possible negotiating partner, as long as each wished to use the land for wells and/or septic systems. Similarly, in *Jacque*, Steenberg Homes had only one route to deliver the mobile home that it regarded as reasonable, but access to that route was controlled by the Jacques. Economists call these localized monopoly problems "bilateral monopolies," because there is a monopoly on each side: only one seller and one buyer for the contested resource. See Richard A. Posner, Economic Analysis of Law § 3.9 (9th ed. 2014); Stewart E. Sterk, Neighbors in American Law, 87 Colum. L. Rev. 55, 57–58, 68–88 (1987).

These bilateral monopoly situations are also a source of high transaction costs, because each of the parties has nowhere else to turn in order to engage in an equivalent transaction. Thus, if the parties disagree about the price or terms for an exchange of resources, prolonged haggling can result. Perhaps one or both parties, perceiving that the other party has no good options, will bargain strategically to try to get an especially favorable deal. See Robert Cooter, The Cost of Coase, 11 J. Legal Stud. 1, 17–24 (1982). Or perhaps one party, the Jacques for example, may for whatever reasons be uninterested in entering into any kind of exchange. A further complication, which seems all too common, is that the parties may have gotten off on the wrong foot with each other, which has led to resentments or "bad blood" that make it very difficult to turn the relationship into a cooperative one. For whatever reasons, bilateral monopoly problems are extremely prevalent in property law.

**Figure 1-3
A Holdout**

By MrTinDC, www.flickr.com, licensed under CC BY-ND 2.0. This row house on Massachusetts Avenue in Washington, D.C., was owned by an architect who refused all entreaties to sell to the developer for many times its assessed value. The developer eventually decided to build around the house, at substantial additional expense. The holdout was reported to be planning to use the house to open a pizza parlor, which never opened, and the house was later sold for a small fraction of the developer's offer.

The lesson for the lawyer advising clients is all too clear (but all too often ignored): It is important to look down the road in order to identify potential assembly problems and bilateral monopoly problems *before* the client gets trapped in a situation that precludes any kind of Coasean bargaining. If the client wants to acquire six contiguous parcels of property for a development, and the first five owners agree to sell but the sixth holds out, what will happen then? If the client wants to acquire a home site, but the only means of access for utility lines is across someone else's property, what will happen then? Ideally, someone should have advised Steenberg Homes about the difficult turn in the private road before it agreed to free delivery of the mobile home in the dead of winter. Ideally, someone should have advised the Hendrickses about the Health Department regulation requiring a 100-foot buffer zone around a septic field before they bought their property. Lawyers of course cannot foresee all problems, but they should be alert to the kinds of problems that can arise, and advise their clients to take all appropriate precautions to be able to acquire the resources they need before they fall into a high-transaction-cost trap.

C. EQUITY AND REMEDIES

Bilateral monopoly situations implicate remedies, especially those deriving from what were once separate courts of equity. Holdout power is enhanced when an owner is afforded more than compensatory damages as a remedy, whether this takes the form of punitive damages or an injunction, the quintessential equitable remedy.

As explored in more depth in Part C of Chapter IV ("Property and Equity"), equity has always played a more or less distinct role within the law, especially in the area of remedies. What the nature of equity's contribution to the law—at any given time and over time—forms an important theme in property law. To be sure, the courts of law and equity have long been merged, at least in most jurisdictions, and there are no longer separate courses on equity in law schools. Nevertheless, the body of less formal principles and doctrines developed in equity is still semi-distinct, and whether an issue is legal or equitable matters for purposes such as whether there is a right to a jury (yes at law, no in equity). "Equitable" aspects of the law of property are important in their own right, and it is worthwhile asking whether they possess some distinct character or serve a special function.

Equity emerged in England out of the activities of the Chancellor, a learned royal advisor, one of whose many functions was to dispense justice according to the King's conscience. By the mid-fourteenth century there emerged a court known as the Court of Chancery. The Chancellor heard petitions from persons who were frustrated by the rigidities or limitations of the common-law courts. The Court of Chancery differentiated itself from the common-law courts on a number of dimensions. The procedures were different: Common-law judges traveled about the country and certain kinds of cases were tried by juries; courts of equity sat in London and did not use juries. The style of decision making was different: The common-law courts followed a system of pleading in which the case had to be presented in terms of standardized writs; the Court of Chancery was willing to consider a wider variety of factors bearing on the individual justice of the situation presented by the parties. These considerations of justice eventually coalesced into a series of equitable maxims that guided the discretion of the Chancellor, a list of which gives their general flavor:

1. Equity follows the law.
2. Equity will not suffer a wrong to be without a remedy.
3. Equity acts in personam, not in rem.
4. Equity is equality.
5. Equity regards as done that which ought to be done.
6. Equity regards substance rather than form.
7. She who seeks equity must do equity.

8. He who comes into equity must come with clean hands.

9. Equity aids the vigilant and diligent.

Roger Young & Stephen Spitz, SUEM—Spitz's Ultimate Equitable Maxim: In Equity, Good Guys Should Win and Bad Guys Should Lose, 55 S.C. L. Rev. 175, 177 (2003). (For a couple of humorous takes on the maxims, see Eugene Volokh, Lost Maxims of Equity, 52 J. Legal Educ. 619 (2002); James Grimmelmann, Koans of Equity, 58 J. Legal Educ. 472 (2008).) Equity also invented its characteristic defenses, including "unclean hands" (related to the maxim), which withholds equity's aid to anyone who has acted unfairly in the transaction in question; estoppel, which prevents a party from taking inconsistent positions that would unfairly harm someone who has relied on the earlier position; and laches, which disallows suit after an unreasonably long time that would work an injustice (an equitable analog to the statute of limitations). Notice the theme of avoiding unfairness and injustice in the maxims and defenses. All of the defenses will turn up in this book at various points.

The equitable remedies too were different: The common law offered basically only awards of damages, whereas the Court of Chancery resolved disputes by issuing mandatory decrees directing individuals to perform certain acts. As captured in the third maxim above, these decrees "operated *in personam*; they were binding on the parties in the cause, but they were not judgments of record binding anyone else and they did not alter or contradict the law." John Baker, An Introduction to English Legal History 112 (5th ed. 2019). Eventually, even the substantive law came to diverge: The Court of Chancery, for example, was responsible for inventing the trust (studied in Chapter VI) and the equitable servitude (studied in Chapter IX), both of which were unknown at common law. Equity offered a range of remedies, the most important of which is the injunction (which is also closely related to specific performance in contract). An injunction is backed up by the court's power to hold a litigant in contempt.

In America, the distinction between the common-law courts and courts of equity was never as sharply observed as in England. For example, in a number of colonies the same judges who sat as a court of common law would periodically sit as the court of equity. Lawrence M. Friedman, A History of American Law 47 (1973). Not all colonies were enthusiastic about equity, or at least about separate equity courts, associated as they were with royal prerogative. During the nineteenth century, equity procedures started to converge with those of the common-law courts, even while the two courts, or modes of sitting as courts, were still kept distinct. Stanley N. Katz, The Politics of Law in Colonial America: Controversies over Chancery Courts and Equity Law in the Eighteenth Century, in 5 Perspectives in American History: Law in American History 259 (Donald Fleming & Bernard Bailyn eds., 1971); Amalia D. Kessler, Our Inquisitorial Tradition: Equity, Procedure, Due Process, and the Search for an Alternative to the Adversarial, 90 Cornell

L. Rev. 1181 (2005). Starting in 1848, with the adoption of the Field Code in New York, many states formally abolished the distinction, declaring a "merger" of law and equity. In other states the distinction persisted, with some states preserving within a unitary judicial system a "law division" and an "equity division," and a few states, most prominently perhaps Delaware, preserving a separate "Court of Chancery." The fusion of law and equity in federal courts occurred in stages, culminating in the unitary system of the Federal Rules of Civil Procedure in 1938. England formally abolished the distinction between law and equity courts in the Judicature Act of 1873. See Kellen Funk, The Union of Law and Equity: The United States, 1800–1938, in Equity and Law: Fusion and Fission 46 (John C.P. Goldberg, Henry E. Smith & P.G. Turner eds., 2019); Patricia I. McMahon, Field, Fusion and the 1850s: How an American Law Reformer Influenced the Judicature Act of 1875, in Equity and Administration 424, 424–25 (P.G. Turner ed., 2016).

Notwithstanding the formal elimination (in most places) of the two court systems, the different procedural, intellectual, and substantive traditions associated with the two systems continue to be important, especially in the law of property. Henry E. Smith, Equity as Meta-Law, 130 Yale L.J. 1050 (2021). In fact, one of the traditional maxims of equity is that property rights enjoy special protection in a court of equity. This maxim is reflected in the law in a number of ways, such as in the understanding that a court of equity will generally grant specific performance to enforce a contract for the sale of real property, even though a breach of contract ordinarily results only in an award of damages. In general, however, if a plaintiff seeks an order compelling the defendant to perform a particular act—such as keeping off the plaintiff's land, or abating a nuisance that affects the plaintiff's land, or specifically performing a contract the defendant has entered into with respect to the land—then the plaintiff must satisfy the various traditional requirements associated with equity in order to obtain such relief. These come into play in the following case.

Pardee v. Camden Lumber Co.

Supreme Court of Appeals of West Virginia, 1911.
73 SE. 82.

■ POFFENBARGER, J. [The plaintiff sought an injunction barring the defendant from cutting down trees on what the plaintiff claimed was his land. The lower court dissolved the injunction on the authority of *McMillan v. Ferrell*, 7 W. Va. 223 (1874), which held that the only remedy for a trespass that results in cutting down trees is an action for damages, unless the defendant is insolvent or some other circumstance precludes recovery of monetary compensation. Noting that the *McMillan* decision "seems not to have commanded uniform approval by the public, nor by the members of the legal profession," the West Virginia Supreme Court agreed to consider whether the 1874 decision should be overruled.] * * *

Under these circumstances, we feel it our duty to re–examine the proposition [adopted in *McMillan*] and thoroughly test its soundness by the application of legal and equitable principles. The chief restraint or limitation upon the overruling of decisions is the inexpediency and injustice of disturbing property rights. Hence it has been said that a line of decisions enunciating a principle which has become a rule of property, or under which property rights have vested by reason of its observance and adoption in contracts, will not be overruled. Here there is no such limitation. To abolish the rule or principle under consideration neither destroys nor impairs any property right or incident. On the contrary, the abolition thereof will conserve and protect such rights and incidents, for no man can be said to have a property right in that which amounts to a trespass against his neighbor or a stranger. The effect will be to give the admitted and acknowledged property owner a more complete remedy for the vindication of his property rights. We regard the rule as one pertaining to remedy only as regards the trespasser who is the sole beneficiary thereof. Hence, if the application of the test above mentioned shall disclose its unsoundness, we shall feel entirely free to abrogate it. Having created or ordained it, this court may consistently discard it, without injury to any person and to the great relief of property owners.

Supposed adequacy of the legal remedy for the cutting of timber, regarded as a mere trespass upon land, constitutes the basis of the rule. If the legal remedy is not adequate, the whole doctrine necessarily fails. Whether it is must be determined by reference to the general policy of the law as disclosed by its application in analogous and related cases. In other words, we must see to what extent the remedies afforded by courts of law and equity protect and vindicate the right of an owner of property to keep it in such condition as he desires. If we find the general object to be the maintenance of this right, respecting all other kinds of property, we must necessarily say it ought to extend to the right of an owner of timber to allow it to stand upon his land in its natural state as long as he desires it to do so. Timber cut down and converted into mere logs and lumber is plainly not the same thing as standing timber. It is equally manifest that the legal remedies are wholly inadequate to reconvert logs and lumber into live, standing, growing trees. Our rule permits a mere trespasser to utterly destroy the forest of his neighbor, provided he is solvent and able to respond in damages to the extent of the value thereof. It can neither restore the forest, nor prevent its destruction. It allows the property to be wholly altered in nature and character, or converts it into a mere claim for damages. After the timber has been cut, the owner may recover possession thereof by an action of detinue, or, waiving that, may recover its value, but this does not in either case restore the property to its former state, nor replace it by the return of an equivalent. The general principles of English and American jurisprudence forbid such a result. They guarantee to the owner of property the right, not only to possession thereof and dominion over it, but also its immunity from injury, unless it be of such character that it may be substantially replaced. On the theory of adequacy of the legal remedy an injunction to prevent the sale or destruction of certain kinds of personal property will be refused, but the principles upon which this conclusion stand cannot be extended to all forms of property either real or personal, and the courts do not attempt so to extend it. Compensation in damages is adequate in all those instances in which the property is injured or destroyed may be substantially replaced with the money recovered as its value. For instance, the world is full of horses, cattle, sheep, hogs, lumber, and many other articles. Ordinarily, one of these may be replaced by another just as good. This principle is applied in a proceeding for specific performance of contracts for the sale of corporate stocks. If the stock belongs to a class found generally in the market for sale, equity refuses specific performance of the contract, because other stock of the same kind can be purchased with the money recovered as damages. If, on the other hand, the stock is limited and unobtainable in the market, specific performance will be enforced. Similarly, as no two pieces of land can be regarded as equivalent in value and character in all respects, equity will always enforce specific performance of a valid contract for the sale thereof. If personal property possesses a value peculiar to its owner, or, as it is generally expressed, has a pretium affectionis, equity will vindicate and uphold the right to the possession thereof and immunity from injury by the exercise of its extraordinary powers. We observe, also, that the law gives a remedy for the possession of personal property, however trivial its value or character may be. It does not limit the owner to a claim for damage, unless the property has gone beyond the reach of its process. As equity follows the law, and, as far as possible, supplies omissions therein, so far as may be necessary to the effectuation of substantial justice, it vindicates the right of an owner to enjoy his property without injury or molestation by the exercise of its preventive powers; but, harmonizing with the great divine rule of help to those who help themselves, equity goes no further than is necessary. Therefore, if a man threatens to take away or kill his neighbor's horse, a court of equity will not interfere by injunction, because the owner may recover the value of that horse and buy another in the general market of substantially the same kind or value. For the same reason, it refuses to enforce specific performance of a contract of sale of a horse. But, if a man is about to destroy his neighbor's heirlooms, things having a peculiar value and insusceptible of replacement by purchase in the market, the legal remedy is not adequate, and a court of equity will, therefore, protect the possession and title of the owner by the exercise of its extraordinary powers. * * * In all these cases, the remedy by law is inadequate, because it does not enforce the right of the injured party to the full extent thereof. Such being the general policy of the law, do we not violate it by denying to the owner of standing timber his clear and indisputable legal right to have it remain upon his land until such time as he shall see fit to convert it into a different kind of property? Moreover, standing timber is everywhere regarded as part of the real estate upon which it grows. The cutting thereof converts it into personal property, and wholly changes its legal nature and incidents. Being a part of the land itself, it has no legal equivalent in nature or value, for no two pieces of land are alike in all respects, nor is a piece of land, stripped of its timber, with a right of action for the felled timber or for damages, the equivalent of the same land with the timber on it. Courts universally hold that all contracts relating to real estate are subjects of equitable cognizance, because they relate to real estate. * * * Of course, the legal remedy is adequate, if the trespass amounts to nothing more than the trampling of the grass or throwing down of the fences, acts in no way affecting the substance of the estate, but the adequacy of the remedy in such cases does not argue efficacy in those cases in which part of the real estate is actually severed and carried away, to the injury and detriment of the inheritance.

Upon the principles and considerations here stated, we are of the opinion that the adoption of this rule was a deviation from fundamental principles of our jurisprudence. It is no doubt attributable to a lack of appreciation of the true character of timber, due to its former abundance and comparative worthlessness. In early days it was regarded as an incumbrance and burden upon lands. Having nothing but forests, the chief object or purpose of landowners everywhere was to get rid of the forests, and prepare their lands for agriculture. There was an abundance of timber, and no market for it. The soil was untillable because of the timber. Hence it was a common practice for owners to cut down the finest of timber, faultless oak, poplar, pine, walnut, and hickory, and burn it upon the premises in log heaps, upon the theory of a disposition of an incumbrance and obstacle to the growth and development of agriculture as a pursuit. Anybody who desired to cut a tree on his neighbor's land in the pursuit of wild animals or the search for deposits of honey had a tacit permission to do so. Forest fires were not regarded as evils, unless they happened to destroy fences, buildings, or other improvements or agricultural implements or products. Timber was not regarded as anything more than an ordinary commercial article, and almost worthless because of its abundance. The prevalence of this estimate of its character was naturally calculated subtly to influence the minds of the judiciary, for the judges were men then, as they now are and always have been, mingling with the populace, and insensibly and unconsciously absorbing, to a greater or less extent, the prevailing sentiment of the people. The error, thus born, has been revealed by the great change of conditions. Timber having become scarce and of great value, the layman, lawyer, and judge has in recent years given the subject more careful, critical, and profound consideration, with the result that the error is practically admitted everywhere.

Violative of principle, as we think, the rule is also contrary to the great weight of authority. In the general struggle for relief from it, courts have in some instances based distinctions upon the relative values of the timber and the land, saying the cutting of timber, constituting the chief value of the land, will be enjoined, but we think a clear case of trespass by the cutting of timber should always be enjoined. In one sense a small quantity of timber on land is more indispensable to its enjoyment than a large quantity. * * *

For the reasons here stated, the decree complained of will be reversed, the injunction reinstated, and the cause remanded.

■ [BRANNON, J.'s concurring opinion omitted.]

NOTES AND QUESTIONS

1.   The threshold question for injunctions, as it is in equity generally, is whether the legal remedy is adequate. If law—usually damages—will do, then equity has no role to play. It is only where injury (or sometimes threatened injury) is irreparable, through damages, that a court will even consider an injunction. For example, this hurdle can be overcome by showing that the harm is not susceptible of measurement (e.g. subjective value) or replacement. These considerations sound so broad that some have questioned whether inadequacy of the legal remedy is really much of an obstacle to injunctions at all. See Douglas Laycock, The Death of the Irreparable Injury Rule (1991); but see Samuel L. Bray, The System of Equitable Remedies, 63 UCLA L. Rev. 530, 533 (2016); Smith, Equity as Meta-Law, supra, Yale L.J. at 2021. Damages can also be inadequate if the invasion is repeated or continuing, which would require a multiplicity of suits—an unfair burden on the potential plaintiff. We will encounter such a situation in *Baker v. Howard County Hunt*, excerpted in Chapter IV.

2.   Injunctions are sometimes considered "supracompensatory remedies," in that they can afford a plaintiff more than damages, especially those pegged at market prices. And they can certainly burden defendants more than the requirement to pay a damages award. They are sometimes identified with "property rules" as opposed to liability rules," in the framework of Guido Calabresi and A. Douglas Melamed, which we take up in Chapter IX. This stringency of injunctions is often genuine, but injunctions are more targeted and can be softened or delayed to give the defendant time to comply. Perhaps it is more apt to call an injunction "specific relief," aimed at giving right holders the very thing to which they are entitled. However, as we will see in later chapters, some traditional legal causes of action result in specific relief. Notably ejectment is the action to recover possession of land, and replevin is used to force a wrongful possessor to hand over an item of personal property (Chapter IV).

3.   Corresponding to its potentially severe impact and the need for careful crafting and sometimes on-going supervision, the injunction is a discretionary remedy administered by judges, not juries. This discretion is not unbounded but subject to a variety of presumptions and rules of thumb, as well as more formal defenses, such as unclean hands and disproportionate hardship. (We will see the latter at work in the building encroachment cases in Chapter IV.) How should a judge decide whether an item of personal property or even an aspect of land is so subjectively important or irreplaceable that an injunction is appropriate? Are judges' notions of what

constitutes an "heirloom" or is associated with a "pretium affectionis" likely to be too narrow or elitist? What do you think of Judge Poffenbarger's tour through the history of attitudes towards trees in West Virginia? Given the court's recognition that social values about property change over time, do you agree with the judge's confident claim that a threat "to take away or kill" a neighbor's horse would not warrant an injunction if such a case arose today? Are the problems here more severe than in contracts, where the related remedy of specific performance is reserved for certain kinds of contracts— including those for the sale of land? For that matter, is land always unique or special?

4.   Given the analysis of the irreparable injury principle in *Pardee*, would the Jacques be entitled to an injunction against Steenberg Homes if they could somehow get to court before the delivery of the mobile home took place? In what sense is there any irreparable harm to the Jacques' land from scooping a path through the snow with a bobcat? Or does the *Jacque* decision, awarding $100,000 in punitive damages for an intentional trespass, rest on a different principle about property than the one recognized in *Pardee*?

5.   Much of the opinion in *Pardee* focuses on whether to overrule a long line of cases denying injunctions against threatened tree-cutting. The issue of stare decisis is one that you will encounter in all your courses, and it has special resonance in property (Chapter X). How reluctant should judges be to overturn a precedent? What if people have arranged their affairs in reliance on the old but undesirable precedent? It seems a stretch to say that anyone relied significantly on the no-injunction rule of *McMillan v. Ferrell*. Was that case understandable at the time and became an embarrassment when social values changed, or was it wrong on the day it was decided? Equity courts originally did not adhere to stare decisis, but became more like law courts in this regard long before the merger of law and equity. Is there something special about equitable relief that resists formulation as rules backed up by full-blown stare decisis?

CHAPTER II

ACQUISITION AND CLAIM SCOPE

Where does property come from? The earliest and most widespread kind of property is the general respect for possession that arose before historical records were kept—and that children learn early in their lives. As we will see "possession" has a variety of meanings, from the factual possession of someone in control of a resource, to legal possession and rights to possess, and even the possessory rights of an owner. Indeed, among the ways that ownership can get started is for someone to possess a thing for the first time with the requisite intent. What kinds of events qualify as establishing a root of title, from which a sequence of voluntary conveyances can then unfold? Roots of title can be started in a variety of ways. Other modes of original acquisition include discovery, creation, and accession. Accession involves an owner of one resource being able to claim ownership of a related subordinate resource—as where the owner of a tree owns its fruits. Possession and accession often work in tandem to establish the scope of a property claim. We also examine problems that arise when one or more involuntary acquisition events occur, and when different principles of establishing original acquisition come into conflict.

A. FIRST POSSESSION

Most of the property you own was probably acquired from someone else, by purchase or gift. The person from whom you acquired it probably got it from someone else, also by purchase or gift. That person, in turn, got it from someone else, and so on. But how do these chains of ownership get started? What kinds of events qualify as establishing a root of title, from which a sequence of voluntary conveyances can then unfold? In this Part we consider various modes of original acquisition—ways in which ownership can be established other than through voluntary conveyance from a previous owner.

Perhaps the most familiar principle for establishing a new root of title is simply being the first to possess something that is unclaimed by anyone else. "First in time" is deceptively simple, but what does it mean to "possess" something? What sorts of resources can be said to be "unclaimed" by anyone else? From where do we derive standards for resolving these sorts of issues?

1. WILD ANIMALS

Pierson v. Post

Supreme Court of New York, 1805.
3 Cai. R. 175, 2 Am. Dec. 264.

This was an action of trespass on the case commenced in a justice's court, by the present defendant against the now plaintiff.

The declaration stated that Post, being in possession of certain dogs and hounds under his command, did, "upon a certain wild and uninhabited, unpossessed and waste land, called the beach, find and start one of those noxious beasts called a fox," and whilst there hunting, chasing and pursuing the same with his dogs and hounds, and when in view thereof, Pierson, well knowing the fox was so hunted and pursued, did, in the sight of Post, to prevent his catching the same, kill and carry it off. A verdict having been rendered for the plaintiff below, the defendant there sued out a *certiorari,* and now assigned for error, that the declaration and the matters therein contained were not sufficient in law to maintain an action. * * *

■ TOMPKINS, J. delivered the opinion of the court. This cause comes before us on a return to a *certiorari* directed to one of the justices of Queens county.

The question submitted by the counsel in this cause for our determination is, whether Lodowick Post, by the pursuit with his hounds in the manner alleged in his declaration, acquired such a right to, or property in, the fox, as will sustain an action against Pierson for killing and taking him away?

The cause was argued with much ability by the counsel on both sides, and presents for our decision a novel and nice question. It is admitted that a fox is an animal *ferae naturae,** and that property in such animals is acquired by occupancy only. These admissions narrow the discussion to the simple question of what acts amount to occupancy, applied to acquiring right to wild animals?

If we have recourse to the ancient writers upon general principles of law, the judgment below is obviously erroneous. Justinian's Institutes, lib. 2. tit. 1. s. 13. and Fleta, lib. 3. c. 2. p. 175. adopt the principle, that pursuit alone vests no property or right in the huntsman; and that even pursuit, accompanied with wounding, is equally ineffectual for that purpose, unless the animal be actually taken. The same principle is recognised by Bracton, lib. 2. c. 1. p. 8.

Puffendorf, lib. 4. c. 6. s. 2. and 10. defines occupancy of beasts *ferae naturae,* to be the actual corporal possession of them, and Bynkershoek is cited as coinciding in this definition. It is indeed with hesitation that

---

*   [Wild by nature, as opposed to domestic animals—eds.]

Puffendorf affirms that a wild beast mortally wounded, or greatly maimed, cannot be fairly intercepted by another, whilst the pursuit of the person inflicting the wound continues. The foregoing authorities are decisive to show that mere pursuit gave Post no legal right to the fox, but that he became the property of Pierson, who intercepted and killed him.

It therefore only remains to inquire whether there are any contrary principles, or authorities, to be found in other books, which ought to induce a different decision. Most of the cases which have occurred in England, relating to property in wild animals, have either been discussed and decided upon the principles of their positive statute regulations, or have arisen between the huntsman and the owner of the land upon which beasts *ferae naturae* have been apprehended; the former claiming them by title of occupancy, and the latter *ratione soli*.** Little satisfactory aid can, therefore, be derived from the *English* reporters.

Barbeyrac, in his notes on Puffendorf, does not accede to the definition of occupancy by the latter, but, on the contrary, affirms, that actual bodily seizure is not, in all cases, necessary to constitute possession of wild animals. He does not, however, *describe* the acts which, according to his ideas, will amount to an appropriation of such animals to private use, so as to exclude the claims of all other persons, by title of occupancy, to the same animals; and he is far from averring that pursuit alone is sufficient for that purpose. To a certain extent, and as far as Barbeyrac appears to me to go, his objections to Puffendorf's definition of occupancy are reasonable and correct. That is to say, that actual bodily seizure is not indispensable to acquire right to, or possession of, wild beasts; but that, on the contrary, the mortal wounding of such beasts, by one not abandoning his pursuit, may, with the utmost propriety, be deemed possession of him; since, thereby, the pursuer manifests an unequivocal intention of appropriating the animal to his individual use, has deprived him of his natural liberty, and brought him within his certain control. So also, encompassing and securing such animals with nets and toils, or otherwise intercepting them in such a manner as to deprive them of their natural liberty, and render escape impossible, may justly be deemed to give possession of them to those persons who, by their industry and labour, have used such means of apprehending them. Barbeyrac seems to have adopted, and had in view in his notes, the more accurate opinion of Grotius, with respect to occupancy [requiring more than wounding but allowing possession by instruments such as nets]. * * * The case now under consideration is one of mere pursuit, and presents no circumstances or acts which can bring it within the definition of occupancy by Puffendorf, or Grotius, or the ideas of Barbeyrac upon that subject.

The case cited from 11 Mod. 74–130 [*Keeble v. Hickeringill*], I think clearly distinguishable from the present; inasmuch as there the action

---

**   [By reason of the soil—eds.]

was for maliciously hindering and disturbing the plaintiff in the exercise and enjoyment of a private franchise; and in the report of the same case, 3 Salk. 9 Holt, Ch. J. states, that the ducks were in the plaintiff's decoy pond, and *so in his possession,* from which it is obvious the court laid much stress in their opinion upon the plaintiff's possession of the ducks, *ratione soli.*

We are the more readily inclined to confine possession or occupancy of beasts *ferae naturae,* within the limits prescribed by the learned authors above cited, for the sake of certainty, and preserving peace and order in society. If the first seeing, starting, or pursuing such animals, without having so wounded, circumvented or ensnared them, so as to deprive them of their natural liberty, and subject them to the control of their pursuer, should afford the basis of actions against others for intercepting and killing them, it would prove a fertile source of quarrels and litigation.

However uncourteous or unkind the conduct of Pierson towards Post, in this instance, may have been, yet his act was productive of no injury or damage for which a legal remedy can be applied. We are of opinion the judgment below was erroneous, and ought to be reversed.

■ LIVINGSTON, J. My opinion differs from that of the court. Of six exceptions, taken to the proceedings below, all are abandoned except the third, which reduces the controversy to a single question.

Whether a person who, with his own hounds, starts and hunts a fox on waste and uninhabited ground, and is on the point of seizing his prey, acquires such an interest in the animal, as to have a right of action against another, who in view of the huntsman and his dogs in full pursuit, and with knowledge of the chase, shall kill and carry him away?

This is a knotty point, and should have been submitted to the arbitration of sportsmen, without poring over Justinian, Fleta, Bracton, Puffendorf, Locke, Barbeyrac, or Blackstone, all of whom have been cited; they would have had no difficulty in coming to a prompt and correct conclusion. In a court thus constituted, the skin and carcass of poor *reynard* would have been properly disposed of, and a precedent set, interfering with no usage or custom which the experience of ages has sanctioned, and which must be so well known to every votary of Diana. But the parties have referred the question to our judgment, and we must dispose of it as well as we can, from the partial lights we possess, leaving to a higher tribunal, the correction of any mistake which we may be so unfortunate as to make. By the pleadings it is admitted that a fox is a "wild and noxious beast." Both parties have regarded him, as the law of nations does a pirate, *"hostem humani generis,"** and although *"de mortuis nil nisi bonum,"*** be a maxim of our profession, the memory of the deceased has not been spared. His depredations on farmers and on

---
*   [Enemy of the human race—eds.]
**   [Do not speak ill of the dead—eds.]

barn yards, have not been forgotten; and to put him to death wherever found, is allowed to be meritorious, and of public benefit. Hence it follows, that our decision should have in view the greatest possible encouragement to the destruction of an animal, so cunning and ruthless in his career. But who would keep a pack of hounds; or what gentleman, at the sound of the horn, and at peep of day, would mount his steed, and for hours together, "*sub jove frigido,*" or a vertical sun, pursue the windings of this wily quadruped, if, just as night came on, and his stratagems and strength were nearly exhausted, a saucy intruder, who had not shared in the honours or labours of the chase, were permitted to come in at the death, and bear away in triumph the object of pursuit? Whatever Justinian may have thought of the matter, it must be recollected that his code was compiled many hundred years ago, and it would be very hard indeed, at the distance of so many centuries, not to have a right to establish a rule for ourselves. In his day, we read of no order of men who made it a business, in the language of the declaration in this cause, "with hounds and dogs to find, start, pursue, hunt, and chase," these animals, and that, too, without any other motive than the preservation of Roman poultry; if this diversion had been then in fashion, the lawyers who composed his institutes, would have taken care not to pass it by, without suitable encouragement. If any thing, therefore, in the digests or pandects shall appear to militate against the defendant in error, who, on this occasion, was the foxhunter, we have only to say *tempora mutantur;**** and if men themselves change with the times, why should not laws also undergo an alteration?

It may be expected, however, by the learned counsel, that more particular notice be taken of their authorities. I have examined them all, and feel great difficulty in determining, whether to acquire dominion over a thing, before in common, it be sufficient that we barely see it, or know where it is, or wish for it, or make a declaration of our will respecting it; or whether, in the case of wild beasts, setting a trap, or lying in wait, or starting, or pursuing, be enough; or if an actual wounding, or killing, or bodily tact and occupation be necessary. Writers on general law, who have favoured us with their speculations on these points, differ on them all; but, great as is the diversity of sentiment among them, some conclusion must be adopted on the question immediately before us. After mature deliberation, I embrace that of Barbeyrac, as the most rational, and least liable to objection. If at liberty, we might imitate the courtesy of a certain emperor, who, to avoid giving offence to the advocates of any of these different doctrines, adopted a middle course, and by ingenious distinctions, rendered it difficult to say (as often happens after a fierce and angry contest) to whom the palm of victory belonged. He ordained, that if a beast be followed with *large dogs and hounds*, he shall belong to the hunter, not to the chance occupant; and in like manner, if he be killed or wounded with a lance or sword; but

---

***   [Times change—eds.]

if chased with *beagles only*, then he passed to the captor, not to the first pursuer. If slain with a dart, a sling, or a bow, he fell to the hunter, if still in chase, and not to him who might afterwards find and seize him.

Now, as we are without any municipal regulations of our own, and the pursuit here, for aught that appears on the case, being with dogs and hounds of *imperial stature,* we are at liberty to adopt one of the provisions just cited, which comports also with the learned conclusion of Barbeyrac, that property in animals *ferae naturae* may be acquired without bodily touch or manucaption, provided the pursuer be within reach, or have a *reasonable* prospect (which certainly existed here) of taking, what he has *thus* discovered an intention of converting to his own use.

When we reflect also that the interest of our husbandmen, the most useful of men in any community, will be advanced by the destruction of a beast so pernicious and incorrigible, we cannot greatly err, in saying, that a pursuit like the present, through waste and unoccupied lands, and which must inevitably and speedily have terminated in corporal possession, or bodily *seisin,* confers such a right to the object of it, as to make any one a wrongdoer, who shall interfere and shoulder the spoil. The justice's judgment ought, therefore, in my opinion, to be affirmed.

Judgment of reversal.

NOTES AND QUESTIONS

1.   *Pierson v. Post* is probably the most famous case in property law, but until recently little was known about Jesse Pierson and Lodowick Post, or the background to their dispute over the fox. A recent outpouring of scholarship has now recently added significantly to our knowledge about the case. The episode on which the case is based occurred near Southampton, in eastern Long Island, not in Queens, where it was tried (perhaps for the convenience of the attorneys). According to Bethany Berger, Jesse Pierson, the defendant, was a schoolmaster who was descended from one of the families that founded Southampton. His father, David Pierson, was a farmer and a pillar of the community. As a "proprietor" of the town, David claimed special privileges in the areas treated as commons where the episode with the fox presumably took place. Lodowick Post, the plaintiff who organized the fox hunting party, was the son of Nathan Post, who had made large amounts of money as a privateer in the Revolutionary War and later through commercial ventures following the war. Although poorly educated, Nathan purchased a large home in the center of town, flaunted his wealth in various ways (including, presumably, by supporting fox hunting parties), and contested the rights of the proprietors to their special privileges in the use of the commons. Berger plausibly concludes that the litigation reflected a clash between a traditional elite and new wealth: Both sides perceived in the actions of the other a fundamental challenge to different visions of how the community should be organized and controlled. See Bethany R. Berger, It's Not About the Fox: The Untold History of *Pierson v. Post,* 55 Duke L.J. 1089 (2006).

Andrea McDowell focuses on the customs associated with fox hunting. We learn from her study that organized fox hunting with hounds was a social activity, not an efficient means of destroying foxes as predators. If one wanted to exterminate foxes in a cost-effective manner, trapping was the way to go. One of the conventions of organized fox hunting was that the fox should be killed by the hounds. This was to give the hounds a "taste of blood," which would make them more eager to chase down foxes in the future. So it is unlikely that Post had any expectation of capturing the fox as a trophy or obtaining any value from the fox pelt (which would be worth only a few dollars in any event). In England the principle of *ratione soli* (referred to in passing by Justice Tompkins in his majority opinion) applied only to animals hunted as game, such as deer and rabbits, not to predators like foxes. This principle of *ratione soli* conferred an exclusive privilege on the owner of land to hunt, or to license others to hunt game on his land. However, until 1809, foxes and other beasts of prey were regarded as "outlaws" and could be pursued by any person even on private land owned by another. In *Essex v. Capel* (1809) (reported in: An account of the trial between George Earl of Essex, plaintiff, and the Hon. & Rev. Wm. Capel, defendant . . . at the Summer Assizes holden at Hertford, July 20th, 1809 (London, Luke Hansard & Sons 1810)), this privilege was overturned, and the court held that a landowner could exclude a foxhunting party, although local mores operated to permit foxhunting on private property for many years afterwards. See Andrea McDowell, Legal Fictions in *Pierson v. Post,* 105 Mich. L. Rev. 735, 753 (2007).

From the recent discovery by Angela Fernandez of the long-misplaced trial record in *Pierson*, it appears that there were numerous grounds for reversing the trial court, but both Tompkins's opinion and Livingston's dissent focused on the rule of capture. Angela Fernandez, The Lost Record of *Pierson v. Post*, the Famous Fox Case, 27 L. & Hist. Rev. 149 (2009). Her informed speculation is that Chief Justice James Kent set the problem as a sort of homework assignment for the other judges, leading to the dutiful (and uncharacteristic) citations to foreign treatises in Tomkins's majority opinion and the tone of defiant mockery in the Livingston dissent. Angela Fernandez, *Pierson v. Post*: The Hunt for the Fox 45–140 (2018). Much other lore has built up around the case, much of it rather dubious. See Daniel R. Ernst, *Pierson v. Post*: The New Learning, 13 Green Bag (2d ser.) 31 (2009).

2.   *Pierson* was decided shortly after the American Revolution, and the court declines to follow English regulations and doctrines on capture of wild animals. Not surprisingly, there were no prominent American precedents on point. Faced with a dearth of authority, the judges turned to legal treatises for an answer to the question of who had a better claim to the fox. The treatises cited cover a vast range of time and space. Justinian's *Institutes* is a synthesis of Roman law compiled during the reign of the Emperor Justinian in the sixth century A.D. Bracton and Fleta were English legal writers of the thirteenth century. Grotius, Pufendorf, Bijnkershoek, and Barbeyrac were legal writers from the continent of Europe writing in the seventeenth and eighteenth centuries. Blackstone wrote his influential *Commentaries on the Laws of England* in the eighteenth century. What

assumption about the nature of property rights are the judges making when they consult these types of sources and implicitly give them equal weight in their quest to determine who has the better claim to the fox? When Justice Livingston's dissent suggests, perhaps semi-facetiously, that the dispute should have been submitted to "the arbitration of sportsmen," is he making a different assumption about the nature of property rights? Which premise strikes you as better? By what criteria should we decide which premise is better?

3.   This is a suit between just two individuals, but the outcome will determine who owns the dead fox. If property rights are good against "all the world," or create duties of noninterference in all persons in the relevant legal community, how can such rights be established in a suit between A and B? Is it because the fox is assumed to be an "unowned" thing and hence up for grabs by the first person to "capture" it or reduce it to possession in some other way, such as by killing it? How do we know foxes are unowned things? What if the owner of the land on which the fox was hunted down (or the proprietors of Southampton, see Note 1 above) asserted a claim to the fox? What if the State of New York claimed ownership of all wild animals found within the state? See Geer v. Connecticut, 161 U.S. 519 (1896) (holding that state could prohibit transport of captured wild animals to another state because the state owned such animals before they were captured); Hughes v. Oklahoma, 441 U.S. 322 (1979) (overruling *Geer*).

4.   First possession is a widespread device for establishing claims of ownership in a variety of contexts, not just wild-animal law. Why? One set of answers centers around Locke's famous defense of private property based on labor and individual desert. See John Locke, Two Treatises of Government, Second Treatise, §§ 25–51, at 285–302 (Peter Laslett ed., 1988) (1690). Locke argued that every person owns his own body and his own labor. Hence, when a person mixes his labor with some unclaimed thing (like a wild animal), that person can justly claim also to own the thing. Certainly, Locke argued, the person who has expended labor acquiring the object has a better claim to it than anyone else, as long as he leaves "enough and as good" for others to acquire, and does not overclaim things to the point that they spoil or go to waste. Which of the two opinions in *Pierson v. Post*—Justice Tompkins's opinion for the majority or Justice Livingston's dissent—seems to put the most weight on desert arising from the expenditure of labor, in deciding when possession of a wild animal has been established? Why does mixing labor with a thing make the thing mine rather than constitute an abandonment of my labor—or merely give me the right to demand payment for my services? (See Wetherbee v. Green, infra, and the treatment of the common-law doctrine of accession.) For discussion of these and related questions, see Richard A. Epstein, Possession as the Root of Title, 13 Ga. L. Rev. 1221 (1979). Elsewhere in the same article Epstein also suggests that Livingston's position might have been correct because the custom of hunters would have given the fox to Post. Assuming that was indeed the custom of hunters, do you agree that custom should provide the basis for the legal rule?

5.   One reason custom might play a role in resolving disputes over possession is the need to communicate claims of possession to others. Who

are the others in *Pierson v. Post*? Pierson, of course. But should Post be taken as mainly communicating to other hunters? To the general public? On the communication problem in possession, see Carol M. Rose, Possession as the Origin of Property, 52 U. Chi. L. Rev. 73, 78 (1985); Henry E. Smith, The Language of Property: Form, Context, and Audience, 55 Stan. L. Rev. 1105, 1115–25 (2003).

6.   *Pierson* is often viewed through the lens of incentives. See, e.g., Dhammika Dharmapala & Rohan Pitchford, An Economic Analysis of "Riding to Hounds": *Pierson v. Post* Revisited, 18 J.L. Econ. & Org. 39 (2002). Does the certain control rule provide less incentive for hunting foxes, as Livingston suggests, or does it encourage those in the position of Post to hurry up and catch the fox? Is protection of poultry really the object here? It would seem that huntsmen in England and their imitators in the United States actually paid farmers to tolerate—and sometimes even to raise—foxes in order to have the pleasure of hunting them. See McDowell, supra.

7.   Whatever the incentive effects in the context of fox hunting, a first-in-time rule can lead to wasteful competitions and races to be first. First-in-time seems to work best when a clear winner will emerge quickly because of that person's special skill or relationship to the resource. That person's advantage will forestall wasteful competition to be first. See, e.g., Dean Lueck, First Possession as the Basis of Property, in Terry L. Anderson & Fred S. McChesney, Property Rights: Cooperation, Conflict, and Law 200 (2003). It can also be helpful if some salient feature marks out the clear winner such that potential competitors will recognize the "winner" early and give up the contest. Does anything in the rule of first possession help ensure this result?

Keeble v. Hickeringill

Queen's Bench, 1707.
11 East 574, 103 Eng. Rep. 1127 [report date 1809].

Action upon the case. Plaintiff declares that he was, 8th November in the second year of the Queen [1704], lawfully possessed of a close of land called Minott's Meadow, [in which was] a decoy pond, to which divers wildfowl used to resort and come: and the plaintiff had at his own costs and charges prepared and procured divers decoy ducks, nets, machines and other engines for the decoying and taking of the wildfowl, and enjoyed the benefit in taking them: the defendant, knowing which, and intending to damnify the plaintiff in his vivary, and to fright and drive away the wildfowl used to resort thither, and deprive him of his profit, did, on the 8th of November, resort to the head of the said pond and vivary, and did discharge six guns laden with gunpowder, and with the noise and stink of the gunpowder did drive away the wildfowl then being in the pond: and on the 11th and 12th days of November the defendant, with design to damnify the plaintiff, and fright away the wildfowl, did place himself with a gun near the vivary, and there did discharge the said gun several times that was then charged with the gunpowder against the said decoy pond, whereby the wildfowl were frighted away, and did forsake the said pond. Upon not guilty pleaded, a verdict was found for the plaintiff and 20£ damages.

■ HOLT C.J. I am of opinion that this action doth lie. It seems to be new in its instance, but is not new in the reason or principle of it. For, 1st, this using or making a decoy is lawful. 2dly, this employment of his ground to that use is profitable to the plaintiff, as is the skill and management of that employment. As to the first, every man that hath a property may employ it for his pleasure and profit, as for alluring and procuring decoy ducks to come to his pond. To learn the trade of seducing other ducks to come there in order to be taken is not prohibited either by the law of the land or the moral law; but it is as lawful to use art to seduce them, to catch them, and destroy them for the use of mankind, as to kill and destroy wildfowl or tame cattle. Then when a man useth his art or his skill to take them, to sell and dispose of for his profit; this is his trade; and he that hinders another in his trade or livelihood is liable to an action for so hindering him. * * * [W]here a violent or malicious act is done to a man's occupation, profession, or way of getting a livelihood; there an action lies in all cases. But if a man doth him damage by using the same employment; as if Mr. Hickeringill had set up another decoy on his own ground near the plaintiff's, and that had spoiled the custom of the plaintiff, no action would lie, because he had as much liberty to make and use a decoy as the plaintiff. This is like the case of 11 H. 4, 47. One schoolmaster sets up a new school to the damage of an antient school, and thereby the scholars are allured from the old school to come to his new. (The action was held there not to lie.) But suppose Mr. Hickeringill should lie in the way with his guns, and fright the boys from going to school, and their parents would not let them go thither; sure that schoolmaster might have an action for the loss of his scholars. 29 E. 3, 18. A man hath a market, to which he hath toll for horses sold: a man is bringing his horse to market to sell: a stranger hinders and obstructs him from going thither to the market: an action lies, because it imports damage. Action upon the case lies against one that shall by threats fright away his tenants at will. 9 H. 7, 8. 21 H. 6, 31. 9 H. 7, 7. 14 Ed. 4, 7. Vide Rastal. 662. 2 Cro. 423. * * * Now considering the nature of the case, it is not possible to declare of the number that were frighted away; because the plaintiff had not possession of them, to count them. Where a man brings trespass for taking his goods, he must declare of the quantity, because he, by having had the possession, may know what he had, and therefore must know what he lost. * * * The plaintiff in this case brings his action for the apparent injury done him in the use of that employment of his freehold, his art, and skill, that he uses thereby. * * * And when we do know that of long time in the kingdom these artificial contrivances of decoy ponds and decoy ducks have been used for enticing into those ponds wildfowl, in order to be taken for the profit of the owner of the pond, who is at the expence of servants, engines, and other management, whereby the markets of the nation may be furnished; there is great reason to give encouragement thereunto; that the people who are so instrumental by their skill and industry so to furnish the markets should reap the benefit and have their action. But, in short, that which is the true reason is that this action is not brought to recover damage for the loss of the fowl, but for the disturbance; as 2 Cro. 604, Dawney v Dee. So is the usual and common way of declaring.

Figure 2-1

Drawn by Author.   Vincent.Brooks Day & Son, lith.

ENTRANCE TO A DECOY PIPE, WITH DOG AT WORK AND WILD FOWL
FOLLOWING HIM UP THE PIPE.

Source: Sir Ralph Payne-Gallwey, The book of duck decoys, their construction, management, and history (London, J. Van Voorst, 1886).

NOTES AND QUESTIONS

1.   Samuel Keeble was a yeoman who made a living from catching ducks. A duck decoy is an elaborate system of passages and nets. According to Brian Simpson, both Keeble and his neighbor, Hickeringill, had constructed duck decoys. Keeble's original decoy was far away from his neighbor's, but when Keeble built a new decoy much closer to Hickeringill's, the closeness and the resultant competition provoked a characteristically direct response from the latter. Edmund Hickeringill, for whom the term "eccentric" hardly does justice, has been called a "half crazy minister and controversial pamphleteer." (His last work is apparently "A Burlesque Poem in Praise of Ignorance," in which he has unkind things to say of lawyers.) He was an excommunicated Baptist, then a Quaker, then a Deist. After a military career at the end of the Commonwealth, he was ordained in the Church of England. His troubles and disputes, both inside and outside the courtroom, were epic—particularly with his bishop, who after Hickeringill's death is said to have ordered the complimentary remarks chiseled off Hickeringill's tombstone. Despite all this behavior, Hickeringill would be

considered a gentleman landowner. A.W. Brian Simpson, Leading Cases in the Common Law 58–61 (1995); A.R. Solly, Edmund Hickeringill, Eccentric, 58 Essex Rev. 127 (1949).

2. This case is the subject of multiple, conflicting reports. The others are 11 Mod. 74, 130 (sub nom. Keeble v. Hickringill); 3 Salk. 9 (sub nom. Keeble v. Hickeringhall). The one reproduced here, from the East report and reprinted in the English Reports, was taken from a manuscript by Chief Justice Holt and is thought to be the most reliable. Notice that the version of *Keeble* cited in *Pierson v. Post*, supra, characterizes the grounds of decision quite differently, as resting on *ratione soli*. The East version was not available until after the decision in *Pierson v. Post*. Does this change your view of *Pierson*?

3. The case is brought in trespass on the case rather than plain trespass, because Hickeringill did not physically invade Keeble's land. How would the court in *Hendricks v. Stalnaker* (see Chapter I) have handled this type of dispute? How if at all would the newness of Keeble's second decoy and its proximity to Hickeringill's older decoy affect a balancing of the gravity of the harm versus the utility of the defendant's conduct?

4. The law is often called upon to regulate various forms of competition. Cases like *Pierson v. Post* and other possession cases in the following materials involve competition to capture resources—sometimes but not always wild animals—and make them into private property. *Keeble v. Hickeringill* is about wild animals, but is it about property in animals? Property in land? About competition? Is this competition harmful? How can one tell whether a given type of competition is harmful or beneficial overall? See, e.g., Harold Demsetz, Wealth Distribution and the Ownership of Rights, 1 J. Legal Stud. 223, 231–32 (1972); Benjamin L. Fine, An Analysis of the Formation of Property Rights Underlying Tortious Interference with Contracts and Other Economic Relations, 50 U. Chi. L. Rev. 1116 (1983).

Consider in this regard that the East version of *Keeble* was reported as a note to a similar case from 1809, *Carrington v. Taylor*, 11 East 571, 103 Eng. Rep. 1126 (K.B. 1809). In that case, the defendant had shot at birds from a boat in a public river and drove them from plaintiff's "ancient decoy"— but he did not shoot into the decoy. The court held there was sufficient evidence of "willful disturbance" to support a jury verdict for the plaintiff.

2. OPEN ACCESS AND THE COMMONS

First possession is used to establish ownership when the thing being claimed is regarded as unowned—as being up for grabs. We need to form a clearer understanding of this state of affairs in order to have a better sense of the contexts in which things are eligible for claiming through first possession. That state of affairs is often referred to as a "commons," but this term is fraught with ambiguity.

Elinor Ostrom, *Governing the Commons: The Evolution of Institutions for Collective Action*
2–3, 8–10, 12–16, 18–21 (1990).

The tragedy of the commons

Since Garrett Hardin's challenging article in *Science* (1968), the expression "the tragedy of the commons" has come to symbolize the degradation of the environment to be expected whenever many individuals use a scarce resource in common. To illustrate the logical structure of his model, Hardin asks the reader to envision a pasture "open to all." He then examines the structure of this situation from the perspective of a rational herder. Each herder receives a direct benefit from his own animals and suffers delayed costs from the deterioration of the commons when his and others' cattle overgraze. Each herder is motivated to add more and more animals because he receives the direct benefit of his own animals and bears only a share of the costs resulting from overgrazing. Hardin concludes:

> Therein is the tragedy. Each man is locked into a system that compels him to increase his herd without limit—in a world that is limited. Ruin is the destination toward which all men rush, each pursuing his own best interest in a society that believes in the freedom of the commons.

Hardin was not the first to notice the tragedy of the commons. Aristotle long ago observed that "what is common to the greatest number has the least care bestowed upon it. Everyone thinks chiefly of his own, hardly at all of the common interest" (*Politics*, Book II, ch. 3). Hobbes's parable of man in a state of nature is a prototype of the tragedy of the commons: Men seek their own good and end up fighting one another. In 1833, William Forster Lloyd sketched a theory of the commons that predicted improvident use for property owned in common. More than a decade before Hardin's article, H. Scott Gordon (1954) clearly expounded similar logic in another classic: "The Economic Theory of a Common-Property Research: The Fishery." Gordon described the same dynamic as Hardin:

> There appears then, to be some truth in the conservative dictum that everybody's property is nobody's property. Wealth that is free for all is valued by no one because he who is foolhardy enough to wait for its proper time of use will only find that it has been taken by another. . . . The fish in the sea are valueless to the fisherman, because there is no assurance that they will be there for him tomorrow if they are left behind today.

John H. Dales (1968) noted at the same time the perplexing problems related to resources "owned in common because there is no alternative!" Standard analyses in modern resource economics conclude that where a number of users have access to a common-pool resource, the total of resource units withdrawn from the resource will be greater than the optimal economic level of withdrawal. * * *

CURRENT POLICY PRESCRIPTIONS

Leviathan as the "only" way

Ophuls (1973) argued, for example, that "because of the tragedy of the commons, environmental problems cannot be solved through cooperation . . . and the rationale for government with major coercive powers is overwhelming." Ophuls concluded that "even if we avoid the tragedy of the commons, it will *only* be by recourse to the tragic necessity of Leviathan." Garrett Hardin argued a decade after his earlier article that we are enveloped in a "cloud of ignorance" about "the true nature of the fundamental political systems and the effect of each on the preservation of the environment." The "cloud of ignorance" did not, however, prevent him from presuming that the only alternatives to the commons dilemma were what he called "a private enterprise system," on the one hand, or "socialism," on the other. With the assurance of one convinced that the alternative of the commons is "too horrifying to contemplate", Hardin indicated that change would have to be instituted with "whatever force may be required to make the change stick." In other words, "if ruin is to be avoided in a crowded world, people must be responsive to a coercive force outside their individual psyches, a 'Leviathan,' to use Hobbes's term."

The presumption that an external Leviathan is necessary to avoid tragedies of the commons leads to recommendations that central governments control most natural resource systems. * * *

The optimal equilibrium achieved by following the advice to centralize control, however, is based on assumptions concerning the accuracy of information, monitoring capabilities, sanctioning reliability, and zero costs of administration. Without valid and reliable information, a central agency could make several errors, including setting the carrying capacity or the fine too high or too low, sanctioning herders who cooperate, or not sanctioning defectors. * * *

Privatization as the "only" way

Other policy analysts, influenced by the same models, have used equally strong terms in calling for the imposition of private property rights whenever resources are owned in common (Demsetz 1967; O. Johnson 1972). "Both the economic analysis of common property resources and Hardin's treatment of the tragedy of the commons" led Robert J. Smith (1981) to suggest that "the *only* way to avoid the tragedy of the commons in natural resources and wildlife is to end the common-property system by creating a system of private property rights." Smith stressed that it is "by treating a resource as a common property that we become locked in its inexorable destruction." Welch advocated the creation of full private rights to a commons when he asserted that "the establishment of full property rights is necessary to avoid the inefficiency of overgrazing" (1983). He asserted that privatization of the commons was the optimal solution for all common-pool problems. His major concern was how to impose private ownership when those currently using a commons were unwilling to change to a set of private rights to the commons.

Those recommending the imposition of privatization on the herders would divide the meadow in half and assign half of the meadow to one herder and the other half to the second herder. Now each herder will be playing a *game against nature* in a smaller terrain, rather than a game against another player in a larger terrain. The herders now will need to invest in fences and their maintenance, as well as in monitoring and sanctioning activities to enforce their division of the grazing area. It is presumed that each herder will now choose $X/2$ animals to graze as a result of his own profit incentive. This assumes that the meadow is perfectly homogeneous over time in its distribution of available fodder. If rainfall occurs erratically, one part of the grazing area may be lush with growth one year, whereas another part of the area may be unable to support $X/2$ animals. The rain may fall somewhere else the next year. In any given year, one of the herders may make no profit, and the other may enjoy a considerable return. If the location of lush growth changes dramatically from year to year, dividing the commons may impoverish both herders and lead to overgrazing in those parts where forage is temporarily inadequate. Of course, it will be possible for the herder who has extra fodder in one year to sell it to the other herder. Alternatively, it will be possible for the herders to set up an insurance scheme to share the risk of an uncertain environment. However, the setup costs for a new market or a new insurance scheme would be substantial and will not be needed so long as the herders share fodder and risk by jointly sharing a larger grazing area. * * *

If one recommendation is correct, the other cannot be. Contradictory positions cannot both be right. I do not argue for either of these positions. Rather, I argue that both are too sweeping in their claims. Instead of there being a single solution to a single problem, I argue that many solutions exist to cope with many different problems. Instead of presuming that optimal institutional solutions can be designed easily and imposed at low cost by external authorities, I argue that "getting the institutions right" is a difficult, time-consuming, conflict-invoking process. It is a process that requires reliable information about time and place variables as well as a broad repertoire of culturally acceptable rules. New institutional arrangements do not work in the field as they do in abstract models unless the models are well specified and empirically valid and the participants in a field setting understand how to make the new rules work.

Instead of presuming that the individuals sharing a commons are inevitably caught in a trap from which they cannot escape, I argue that the capacity of individuals to extricate themselves from various types of dilemma situations varies from situation to situation. The cases to be discussed in this book illustrate both successful and unsuccessful efforts to escape tragic outcomes. * * *

An alternative solution

To open up the discussion of institutional options for solving commons dilemmas, I want now to present [another outcome] in which the herders themselves can make a binding contract to commit themselves to a cooperative strategy that they themselves will work out. * * *

The herders * * * must now negotiate prior to placing animals on the meadow. During negotiations, they discuss various strategies for sharing the carrying capacity of the meadow and the costs of enforcing their agreement. Contracts are not enforceable, however, unless agreed to unanimously by the herders. Any proposal made by one herder that did not involve an equal sharing of the carrying capacity and of enforcement costs would be vetoed by the other herder in their negotiations. Consequently, the only feasible agreement—and the equilibrium * * *— is for both herders to share equally the sustainable yield levels of the meadow and the costs of enforcing their agreement so long as each herder's share of the cost of enforcement is less than [that herder's share of the benefits]. * * *

A self-financed contract-enforcement game is no panacea. Such institutional arrangements have many weaknesses in many settings. The herders can overestimate or underestimate the carrying capacity of the meadow. Their own monitoring system may break down. The external enforcer may not be able to enforce ex post, after promising to do so ex ante. A myriad of problems can occur in natural settings, as is also the case with the idealized central-regulation or private-property institutions. * * *

An empirical alternative

* * * Let us now briefly consider a solution devised by participants in a field setting—Alanya, Turkey—that cannot be characterized as either central regulation or privatization. The inshore fishery at Alanya, as described by Fikret Berkes (1986b), is a relatively small operation. Many of the approximately 100 local fishers operate in two- or three-person boats using various types of nets. Half of the fishers belong to a local producers' cooperative. According to Berkes, the early 1970s were the "dark ages" for Alanya. The economic viability of the fishery was threatened by two factors: First, unrestrained use of the fishery had led to hostility and, at times, violent conflict among the users. Second, competition among fishers for the better fishing spots had increased production costs, as well as the level of uncertainty regarding the harvest potential of any particular boat.

Early in the 1970s, members of the local cooperative began experimenting with an ingenious system for allotting fishing sites to local fishers. After more than a decade of trial-and-error efforts, the rules used by the Alanya inshore fishers are as follows:

- Each September, a list of eligible fishers is prepared, consisting of all licensed fishers in Alanya, regardless of co-op membership.

- Within the area normally used by Alanya fishers, all usable fishing locations are named and listed. These sites are spaced so that the nets set in one site will not block the fish that should be available at the adjacent sites.

- These named fishing locations and their assignments are in effect from September to May.

- In September, the eligible fishers draw lots and are assigned to the named fishing locations.

- From September to January, each day each fisher moves east to the next location. After January, the fishers move west. This gives the fishers equal opportunities at the stocks that migrate from east to west between September and January and reverse their migration through the area from January to May.

The system has the effect of spacing the fishers far enough apart on the fishing grounds that the production capabilities at each site are optimized. All fishing boats also have equal chances to fish at the best spots. Resources are not wasted searching for or fighting over a site. No signs of overcapitalization are apparent.

The list of fishing locations is endorsed by each fisher and deposited with the mayor and local gendarme once a year at the time of the lottery. The process of monitoring and enforcing the system is, however, accomplished by the fishers themselves as a by-product of the incentive created by the rotation system. * * * Cheating on the system will be observed by the very fishers who have rights to be in the best spots and will be willing to defend their rights using physical means if necessary. Their rights will be supported by everyone else in the system. The others will want to ensure that their own rights will not be usurped on the days when they are assigned good sites. The few infractions that have occurred have been handled easily by the fishers at the local coffeehouse. (Berkes 1986b, p. 74).

Although this is not a private-property system, rights to use fishing sites and duties to respect these rights are well defined. And though it is not a centralized system, national legislation that has given such cooperatives jurisdiction over "local arrangements" has been used by cooperative officials to legitimize their role in helping to devise a workable set of rules. That local officials accept the signed agreement each year also enhances legitimacy. The actual monitoring and enforcing of the rules, however, are left to the fishers. * * *

Many potential answers spring to mind regarding the question why some individuals do not achieve collective benefits for themselves, whereas others do. However, as long as analysts presume that individuals cannot change such situations themselves, they do not ask what internal or external variables can enhance or impede the efforts of communities of individuals to deal creatively and constructively with perverse problems such as the tragedy of the commons.

NOTES AND QUESTIONS

1.   As Ostrom notes, the potential problems with open access have long been apparent, long before Garrett Hardin coined the immensely influential phrase, "the tragedy of the commons," to describe the problems associated with an open-access resource in which there is an unrestricted privilege to capture some valued feature of the resource. See Garrett Hardin, The Tragedy of the Commons, 162 Science 1243 (1968). H. Scott Gordon's classic analysis, H.S. Gordon, The Economic Theory of a Common Property Resource: The Fishery, 62 J. Pol. Econ. 124 (1954), had been anticipated many years earlier by Jens Warming, writing in Danish. See Om "Grundrente" af Fiskegrunde, 49 Nationalökonomisk Tidsskrift 495 (1911), transl. in P. Anderson, "On Rent of Fishing Grounds": A Translation of Jens Warming's 1911 Article, with an Introduction, 15 Hist. Pol. Econ. 391 (1983). So who gets to claim to be the "first possessor" of the idea of the tragedy of the commons: Aristotle, Warming, Gordon, or Hardin? Does this example provide a clue as to why ideas are not subject to ownership through first possession?

2.   Hardin was a biologist, and his big concern was with overpopulation. His work fits into a neo-Malthusian movement of the 1960s and 1970s that emphasized the finiteness of the earth and predicted imminent depletion of natural resources. That there is a potential tragedy in the use of natural resources is well understood. But in what sense is there an additional tragedy of the commons in "breeding," as Hardin believed?

3.   Hardin's primary example, the traditional grazing commons, was hardly tragic. Grazing commons in traditional agricultural societies such as those of medieval and early modern Europe were not open access. A limited group had grazing rights and exercised the right to exclude noncommoners. Over centuries, those with access to common grazing areas governed their behavior with restrictions on the amount and manner of grazing. Some of these grazing commons survive to this day and do not show obvious signs of tragedy. Elsewhere in Ostrom's book and in the rest of her work, for which she won the Nobel Memorial Prize in Economics in 2009, she analyzes a range of case studies and explores factors leading toward and away from tragedy.

4.   Solutions to the problem of the commons require some form of coercion or cooperation. For example, a group of herders might (as has often happened) institute rules to limit their use of the commons and achieve conservation. But how is such cooperation forthcoming? Isn't the provision of

such rules a commons itself? See James E. Krier, The Tragedy of the Commons, Part Two, 15 Harv. J.L. & Pub. Pol'y 325, 336–38 (1992).

5.   Another possible solution to overuse of an open access resource like fisheries is the creation of a new type of property, individual transferable quotas (ITQs), which restrict the overall level of access to the fishery and yet are transferable, so individuals can exit and enter from the fishing industry. See, e.g., Christopher Costello, Steven D. Gaines, & John Lynham, Can Catch Shares Prevent Fisheries Collapse?, 321 Sci. 1678 (2008); Katrina Wyman, The Recovery in U.S. Fisheries, 31 J. Land Use & Envtl. L. 149 (2016). The relative merits of carbon taxes versus cap-and-trade regulation are considered in William D. Nordhaus, To Tax or Not to Tax: Alternative Approaches to Slowing Global Warming, 1 Rev. Envtl. Econ. & Pol'y 26 (2007); Reuven S. Avi-Yonah & David M. Uhlmann, Combating Global Climate Change: Why a Carbon Tax is a Better Response to Global Warming than Cap and Trade, 28 Stan. Envtl. L.J. 3 (2009).

Commons, Anticommons, and Semicommons

If an open access regime creates the "tragedy of the commons," in which no one has the right to exclude anyone else, is there a mirror image problem, in which everyone has the right to exclude everyone else? From a hypothetical proposed by Frank Michelman, Michael Heller developed the concept of the *anticommons*, where too many have the right to exclude and consequently no one is able to use a resource. Michael Heller, The Tragedy of the Anticommons: Property in the Transition from Marx to Markets, 111 Harv. L. Rev. 621 (1998); see also Michael Heller, The Gridlock Economy: How Too Much Ownership Wrecks Markets, Stops Innovation, and Costs Lives (2008); Frank I. Michelman, Ethics, Economics, and the Law of Property, in NOMOS XXIV: Ethics, Economics, and the Law 3, 15 (1982). Heller's original example was street kiosks in post-Soviet Moscow. Because too many stakeholders had rights in storefronts and could prevent their use, new businesses bypassed empty store buildings and set up shop in metal kiosks on the sidewalks in front of the stores. Traditional holdout problems can sometimes be characterized as an anticommons: If too many permissions are required, rights to a larger resource may never be assembled. Patents on gene fragments are a particular source of anticommons worries because research projects may require the collection of many permissions from many different patent holders. Michael A. Heller & Rebecca S. Eisenberg, Can Patents Deter Innovation? The Anticommons in Biomedical Research, 280 Science 698 (1998). Evidence is hard to come by, but surveys of industry participants have found that patents on research tools have not restricted access as much as anticommons theory might suggest; solutions to the problem of fragmented rights include licensing, inventing around, infringing, public disclosure, and litigation. See generally Jonathan Barnett, The Anti-Commons Revisited, 29 Harv. J. L. & Tech. 127 (2015); Anna B. Laakmann, The New Genomic Semicommons, 5 UC Irvine L. Rev. 1001 (2015).

anticommons — overindexing on right to exclude

Others have argued that in certain specialized contexts, an anticommons can be a good thing. For example, giving many people a veto over development of a resource like a park can help secure the commitment to preserve the park for future generations. Abraham Bell & Gideon Parchomovsky, Of Property and Antiproperty, 102 Mich. L. Rev. 1 (2003). Similarly, there is sometimes virtue to be found in multiple vetoes in the political arena. Political scientists and others have theorized that under some conditions multiple vetoes are beneficial in terms of producing stability (with some sacrifice of decisiveness in decision-making). See, e.g., Josephine T. Andrews & Gabriella R. Montinola, Veto Players and the Rule of Law in Emerging Democracies, 37 Comp. Pol. Stud. 55 (2004); George Tsebelis & Eric C. Chang, Veto Players and the Structure of Budgets in Advanced Industrialized Countries, 43 Eur. J. of Pol. Res. 449 (2004). The Framers of the U.S. Constitution may have had something like this in mind when setting up a system of federalism and separation of powers, which creates many checks and balances on political actors. See The Federalist No. 51 (James Madison).

Note that the underlying dynamic that creates a tragedy of the anticommons is similar to that which gives rise to the tragedy of the commons. For each tragedy, the individual has an incentive to act in a way that imposes costs on others, either by exercising her right of access (to a commons) or her right to exclude others (from an anticommons). For each tragedy, overcoming the problem requires some kind of realignment of rights, and doing this requires dealing with holdouts and freeriders. So are there really mirror image problems, or is there only one underlying tragedy at work? For discussion, see James M. Buchanan & Yong J. Yoon, Symmetric Tragedies: Commons and Anticommons, 43 J.L. & Econ. 1 (2000); Lee Anne Fennell, Common Interest Tragedies, 98 Nw. U. L. Rev. 907 (2004); Francesco Parisi, Norbert Schulz & Ben Depoorter, Duality in Property: Commons and Anticommons, 25 Int'l Rev. L. & Econ. 578 (2006). The commons and anticommons are usually discussed in terms of efficiency and specific interventions. How much do we need to account for basic questions of distributional justice and the foundations of entitlements? Compare David Blankfein-Tabachnick, Intellectual Property and Midlevel Principles, 101 Calif. L. Rev. 1315, 1347–48 (2013) (arguing for essential role for distributional considerations and baselines in justifying IP) with Robert P. Merges, Foundations and Principles Redux: A Reply to Professor Blankfein-Tabachnick, 101 Calif. L. Rev. 1361, 1381 (2013) (defending an approach to justice in IP that focuses on mid-level principles—efficiency, preservation of the public domain, proportionality, and dignity—distinct from foundations that justify why we have an IP system at all).

The commons and the anticommons are not the only common-property regimes in town. Others have identified the *semicommons*, which occurs when a given resource is subject to private exclusion rights in some uses or along other related dimensions, but is a commons or open access for other purposes or along other dimensions. In many traditional grazing commons farmers would have exclusive rights to particular strips of land to grow crops during part of the year, but then the strips would be thrown open for common grazing during other parts of the year. See Henry E. Smith, Semicommon Property Rights and Scattering in the Open Fields, 29 J. Legal Stud. 131 (2000). In such a system, individuals will have an incentive to favor their part of the semicommons (with goods like manure) and to trash other parts of the semicommons (with excessive trampling, etc.); elaborate governance rules and configurations of rights seem to have been developed to contain these problems. Intellectual property rights are particularly likely to be incomplete, leaving room for interaction between exclusion rights and the commons (the public domain). For example, consider the doctrine of fair use in copyright, which permits copying of portions of copyrighted works for certain purposes, such as criticism, reporting, or scholarship. See 17 U.S.C. § 107. This effectively makes a work subject to the owner's exclusive control for some purposes, and yet in the public domain for other purposes. For an argument that the Internet is a semicommons, see James Grimmelmann, The Internet Is a Semicommons, 78 Fordham L. Rev. 2799 (2010); see also Robert A. Heverly, The Information Semicommons, 18 Berkeley Tech. L.J. 1127 (2003). As with the anticommons, a full-blown semicommons with an effective governance structure can be quite stable, but may be hard to change because the interlocking private and commons rights are difficult to disentangle and negotiate over. Even the classic commons mixes common and private. Fish in the ocean are regarded as an open-access resource in their natural state, but once they have been reduced to possession under the rule of capture they are regarded as privately owned.

3. OTHER APPLICATIONS OF FIRST POSSESSION

The principle of first possession applies in contexts besides hunting and fishing. For example, abandoned or lost property is subject to the rule of first possession. Suppose you decide to dispose of your old computer monitor by setting it on the curb where the garbage gets picked up. You have in effect relinquished ownership of the monitor, and implicitly signaled that it can now be claimed by the first person who comes along and decides to take possession of it. Or, suppose you lose a ring that falls out of your pocket on the public sidewalk. Here, you have not relinquished ownership, but (subject to some qualifications considered later in the chapter) the first person who comes along and decides to take possession of the ring can claim a kind of qualified ownership of it: The finder has a superior right to the ring relative to everyone in the world, *except you*, the true owner.

Sunken Vessels. Another area in which possession plays a crucial, and especially complex, role is the law governing sunken vessels. Under

semicommons — sometimes open access, sometimes subject to private exclusion (farming land?)

the common law as developed in the federal admiralty courts, possession of sunken vessels gives rise to rights to ownership under the law of finds, or to rights of salvage under the law of salvage. The law of maritime finds awarded ownership to the first possessor but only if the vessel was abandoned (and not still claimed by its owners or their insurers), and therefore unowned at the time of taking possession. Property is abandoned when an owner manifests an intention to relinquish all future claims of possession or ownership (see Chapter IV).

If the vessel is not abandoned, a successful "salvor" (as such a person is called in this context) has a claim for a generous percentage of the value of the vessel and its cargo, but does not acquire ownership of the vessel or its full value. See generally Grant Gilmore & Charles L. Black, Jr., The Law of Admiralty 532–73 (2d ed. 1975); Thomas J. Schoenbaum, Admiralty and Maritime Law ch. 14 (6th ed. 2018). By gaining and maintaining possession, a salvor would have a right to engage in salvage without interference from other would be salvors, thus preventing yet another instance of the tragedy of the commons. Perhaps not surprisingly, the standard for possession of a salvor is lower than that for finders of abandoned vessels. That is, acts that would be sufficient for salvage-possession might not be sufficient for a finder to establish acquisition-possession. As one court put it:

> To enjoy the continued right to exclusive possession and protection from interference of rival salvors, a salvor must exercise due diligence and must be capable of actually saving the property. The salvor must intend to reduce the property to physical possession by dealing with the entire wreck site in such a manner as to warn other potential salvors of the claimed area.

MDM Salvage, Inc. v. Unidentified, Wrecked and Abandoned Sailing Vessel, 631 F. Supp. 308, 312 (S.D. Fla. 1986). A successful salvor is entitled to a lien to secure payment of the award (see Chapter VII). Salvor-in-possession rights, however, do not extend to preventing others from visiting or photographing the wreck. See R.M.S. Titanic, Inc. v. Haver, 171 F.3d 943, 970 (4th Cir. 1999). The law of salvage has overtones of unjust enrichment (can you see why?), and like unjust enrichment it is equitable in character (see Chapter IV). Because the original owner loses rights if a vessel is deemed abandoned, courts tend to favor applying the law of salvage rather than the law of finds in ambiguous situations. Traditional maritime principles of finds and salvage were similar across seafaring nations, relying to a great extent on custom, thus simplifying the resolution of questions arising from wrecks in international waters. More recently, efforts have been made to bring this area of law under treaties, but it remains unclear whether these treaties codify customary international law. See generally David J. Bederman, Law of the Land, Law of the Sea: The Lost Link between Customary International Law and the General Maritime Law, 51 Va. J. Int'l L. 299 (2011). The most comprehensive such treaty is the United

Nations Convention on the Law of the Sea (UNCLOS), which the United States recognizes as a codification of custom but has not ratified.

To maintain possession over a wreck, one needs both to provide notice and to prove diligence. In the celebrated case of *Eads v. Brazelton*, 79 Am. Dec. 88 (Ark. 1861), Brazelton put blazes on trees on the shore that allowed one to line up the exact site of the wreck of the steamboat America in the Mississippi River, and he floated a buoy over the wreck. In January 1855, Brazelton had his salvage boat in the area, and was all set to begin raising the cargo of lead but he heard of another wreck and went off to try to raise it. By the time he returned, the river was running too high for him to engage in salvage work at the site of the America. Meanwhile Eads moved in. Eads was a clever inventor (and designer of the Eads Bridge in St. Louis) who had developed a dredging boat he called a "submarine" to which a diving bell was attached. When Eads commenced salvage operations, Brazelton sought an injunction, claiming he was the first to find the sunken vessel. The blazes on the trees and the buoy would seem more than adequate to signal Brazelton's intent to all the world. Nevertheless, the court determined that Brazelton had not established possession. Possession requires more than notice, but also due diligence in acting to achieve full dominion and control over a resource. There was no question of Brazelton's intent to appropriate and that he had taken steps in that direction before Eads appeared. But the court decided that in this context one must have the salvage vessel over the site of the wreck before one can be said to be in possession of the wreck. (It is interesting to ask whether Brazelton would have lost if he had only been away for a day or two. Would this be consistent with due diligence?)

The standard for possession may also be evolving with new technology that is able to reach wrecks at greater depths. In *Columbus-America Discovery Group, Inc. v. The Unidentified, Wrecked and Abandoned Sailing Vessel, S.S. Central America*, 1989 A.M.C. 1955, 1958 (E.D. Va. 1989), the court allowed "telepossession," defined as "(1) locating the object searched; (2) real time imaging of the object; (3) placement or capability to place teleoperated or robotic manipulators on or near the object, capable of manipulating it as directed by human beings exercising control from the surface; and (4) present intent to control . . . the location of the object." Should one be able to claim possession of foxes by videotaping them? Why not?

Sunken vessels also often contain valuables, especially old currency and historically significant items. For gold and silver in any form hidden for later discovery (other than as unmined minerals in place) the law of treasure trove may apply. Treasure trove (the term incorporates the Norman French word for "found") applies to caches of gold and silver and sometimes other valuables on land or sea. (Gold and silver as part of burial of the dead was not treasure trove.) In England, treasure trove with no identified owner belonged to the Crown at its option. In the

United States, treasure trove is not treated specially but falls under the general law of finders. Later in this Chapter we take up the competing claims of finders and the owners of the place where objects are found.

Treasure trove often consists of items valuable as both precious metals and as historical artifacts. Concerns about historic preservation have led to major legislation governing sunken vessels. In the Abandoned Shipwreck Act of 1987 (ASA), 43 U.S.C. §§ 2102–2106, Congress declared that all qualifying wrecks in navigable waters are subject to federal ownership, which is immediately to be transferred to the state in whose waters the wreck is found. Id. § 2105. States in turn have passed laws that protect archeological sites (as has the federal government for archeological finds on federal lands, see Archaeological Resources Protection Act of 1979, 16 U.S.C. §§ 470aa–470mm), and these may apply to sunken vessels. Such state laws were formerly preempted to the extent that they were inconsistent with federal maritime law, but the ASA now potentially gives such state preservation statutes greater scope of application. See Lawrence J. Kahn, Sunken Treasures: Conflicts between Historic Preservation Law and the Maritime Law of Finds, 7 Tul. Envtl. L.J. 595, 630 (1993). The ASA also rejects the traditional law of finders and salvors, the idea being that the states will better protect the historic value of sunken vessels. Much of the uncertainty produced by the ASA stems from the criteria for its application in the first place: It applies only to wrecks that are abandoned, located on the submerged land of a state, and either embedded on the sea floor or eligible for listing in the National Register of Historic Places. Id. § 2105 (a).

Consider how this plays out in practice. A salvor wishing to establish rights of find or salvage in a wreck could file an in rem action against the ship—meaning the vessel is fictionally treated as the defendant and the litigation will establish the rights of everyone to that "thing"—in federal district court under its admiralty jurisdiction. But to establish admiralty jurisdiction will often require divulging the site of the wreck, which a salvor may be loath to do, both because of potential marauders and because the state in which the wreck is located may gain full rights, leaving the salvor with nothing. For a dramatic example, see Great Lakes Exploration Group, LLC v. Unidentified Wrecked and (For Salvage-Right Purposes), Abandoned Sailing Vessel, 522 F.3d 682 (6th Cir. 2008). Jockeying over disclosure can also occur in an international context. See, e.g., Sea Hunt, Inc. v. Unidentified Shipwrecked Vessel or Vessels, 221 F.3d 634 (4th Cir. 2000). For these reasons, commentators have sometimes proposed—and salvors have tried (mostly unsuccessfully) to assert—intellectual property rights over their finds. See, e.g., Justin S. Stern, Smart Salvage: Extending Traditional Maritime Law to Include Intellectual Property Rights in Historic Shipwrecks, 68 Fordham L. Rev. 2489 (2000).

Home Run Baseballs. In the late 1990s, major league baseball players, assisted (it now appears) by performance-enhancing drugs, began hitting record numbers of home runs. Milestone home run balls became important collector's items, commanding large sums of money. Not surprisingly, fans inside and sometimes outside the ball parks engaged in intense competitions to snag one of these prize home run baseballs. These competitions, in turn, sometimes generated controversies about who had been the first to capture or reduce to possession a particular ball. The most famous of these controversies resulted in a litigated decision, *Popov v. Hayashi*, 2002 WL 31833731 (Cal. Super. Ct. 2002).

Baseballs used in professional baseball games are considered the property of the home team, but once they leave the playing field are regarded as abandoned property. Like other abandoned property, they can be claimed by the first person to take possession of them. The *Popov* case involved a dispute over who was the first to possess the record-setting 73rd home run ball hit by Barry Bonds of the San Francisco Giants at San Francisco's PacBell Park on October 7, 2001. A videotape recorded at the scene showed that after the ball sailed over the fence, it landed in the webbing of a softball glove worn by Alex Popov. It was unclear from the tape, however, whether Popov had full control of the ball as he fell to the ground. Popov was immediately engulfed by a mob of fans, who grabbed and kicked at him trying to obtain the ball. At some point, the ball came loose from the scrum, and was picked up by Patrick Hayashi (who had also been knocked down by the mob). Hayashi stood up, put the ball in his pocket, and waited until he had the attention of the video camera operator, at which time he held the ball aloft, showing that he had the ball. Popov sued Hayashi, claiming that Popov was the first possessor and hence was entitled to the ball. At the time of trial, it was thought the ball might be worth as much as $1 million, although eventually it was sold for $450,000.

The trial featured, in addition to the videotape and the testimony of numerous eye witnesses, a discussion forum of several law professors about the application of the rule of first possession to home run baseballs. Judge Patrick McCarthy, who presided over the trial, eventually reached a Solomonic judgment: He decreed that the ball should be sold, with half the proceeds given to Popov and half to Hayashi. He reasoned that although Popov could not prove that he had established possession of the baseball, once it landed in his mitt he had an exclusive "pre-possessory interest" in being allowed to complete the catch without interference. The mob had interfered with this interest. Hayashi, for his part, had not been part of the mob, and was the first unambiguously to establish possession of the ball. Judge McCarthy concluded: "Both men have a superior claim to the ball as against all the world. Each man has a claim of equal dignity as to the other. * * * The court therefore declares that both plaintiff and defendant have an equal and undivided interest in the ball. * * * In order to effectuate this ruling, the ball must be sold and the proceeds divided equally between the parties." As authority for ordering the property sold and the proceeds divided, the judge cited a law review article, R.H. Helmholz, Equitable Division and the Law of Finders, 52 Fordham L. Rev. 313 (1983), which in turn built on a student note, Comment, Lost, Mislaid and Abandoned Property, 8 Fordham L. Rev. 222 (1939). See also Gideon Parchomovsky, Peter Siegelman, & Steve Thel, Of Equal Wrongs and Half Rights, 82 N.Y.U. L. Rev. 738 (2007). Nevertheless, decisions that divide an asset between two potential possessors are rare. Splitting entitlements—or their value—has been more popular with commentators than with courts. Why do you suppose division is not used more often? Would you recommend this as a solution to wild animal cases like *Pierson v. Post*? Is there anything about home run baseballs that makes such cases different?

What role should custom play in determining the rules for establishing ownership of home run baseballs? If custom is important, which customs should we look to? The rules of sports like baseball deal with questions about when a player controls a ball sufficiently to be deemed to have caught it. Are these rules relevant to determine whether a fan has possession of a ball hit out of the park? There has been an outpouring of scholarship on the question of ownership of milestone home run baseballs. See, e.g., Peter Adomeit, The Barry Bonds Baseball Case— An Empirical Approach—Is Fleeting Possession Five Tenths of the Ball?, 48 St. Louis U. L.J. 475 (2004); Paul Finkelman, Fugitive Baseballs and Abandoned Property: Who Owns the Home Run Ball?, 23 Cardozo L. Rev. 1609 (2002); Steven Semeraro, An Essay on Property Rights in Milestone Home Run Baseballs, 56 SMU L. Rev. 2281 (2003).

The potential for violence among fans is yet another (vivid) example of wasteful and destructive racing behavior. These problems also face fishers, salvors, and oil drillers. Observers of intellectual property rights have pointed out that too great a reward for being the first to invent can lead to wasteful races. Some scholars have hypothesized that first possession works best when a clear winner is declared at a stage when other competitors are unlikely to be able to compete effectively. Thus, first-in-time rules work best when potential appropriators have heterogeneous knowledge and abilities. Conversely, where multiple actors must share a resource under a governance scheme of rules of proper use, it is helpful if all those sharing the resource have similar abilities and knowledge. Homogeneity of appropriators conduces to well-functioning governance regimes. See Dean Lueck, The Rule of First Possession and the Design of the Law, 38 J.L. & Econ. 393 (1995); David D. Haddock, First Possession Versus Optimal Timing: Limiting the Dissipation of Economic Value, 64 Wash. U. L.Q. 775 (1986). What implications does this hypothesis have for determining how to allocate home run baseballs? Are the potential appropriators here relatively homogeneous in their knowledge and ability, or heterogeneous?

Oil and Gas. Under the common law, oil and gas are subject to the rule of capture, an application of first possession. Surface owners are free to pump oil and gas from the surface of their parcels, as long as the drilling apparatus stays within the "column of space" projected down from the surface. Slant drilling, i.e., drilling down at an angle that intersects a neighbor's column of space, is a form of trespass. In other legal systems, ownership of the surface does not entail ownership of minerals found beneath the surface. Many civil-law countries, including most Latin American countries, follow the rule that minerals below the surface are owned by the government. See Peter Bakewell, Mining, in Colonial Spanish America 203, 232 (Leslie Bethell ed., 1987).

Under the common-law rule of capture, oil and gas are not considered owned by anyone until reduced to possession. But if some curbs are not placed on pumping, a tragedy of the commons will result. Pumping will be too rapid, thereby wasting the natural propulsion from gas located around the oil. The race to pump would also lead to greater surface storage of oil, leading to dangerous fires. In theory, a contract among all surface owners would be mutually beneficial, but most oil and gas fields involve numerous and heterogeneous participants, leading to high transaction costs in private bargaining for mutual forbearance. One solution is for each owner to take shares in a field under unitary management. This solution, called "unitization," can arise by contract, but with more than four participants, it usually only arises late in the life of an oil and gas field. For this reason, statutes sometimes provide for compulsory unitization upon a vote by some supermajority of the owners over the field. See Gary D. Libecap, Contracting for Property Rights 95–107 (1989); Gary D. Libecap & James L. Smith, Regulatory Remedies to the Common Pool: The Limits to Oil Field Unitization, 22 Energy J. 1 (2001). Part of the problem is informational: Surface owners know more about their own claims than others' and cannot credibly convey that information, and after unitization, it is impossible to tell how each participant would have fared in the absence of an agreement.

The severe tendency toward a tragedy of the commons (open access) presents a host of institutional choice questions. In addition to compulsory unitization, statutes and regulations govern well spacing, rates of extraction, and the manner of drilling and extraction. For the vast amounts of oil and gas on federal lands or on the outer-continental shelf, the federal government can act as a unitary owner, and exploitation and development on these lands is governed by the Mineral Leasing Act of 1920, 30 U.S.C. § 181. Although the government as owner can succumb to its own set of inadequacies (as demonstrated in the Deepwater Horizon oil spill and its aftermath), an unconstrained race to exploit the resource is not one of them.

Property scholars tend to focus on the common law of oil and gas, and the common law by itself is not up to the task of solving the tragedy inherent in oil and gas, in the absence of statute or regulations. The baseline common law rule, as mentioned, is the rule of capture. Sometimes in a bit of colorful metaphor, oil and gas are called fugacious or fugitive minerals and analogized to wild animals. The literature excoriating the rule of capture and the wild animal analogy is vast, especially for being insufficiently "pragmatic" and "empirical." See Richard A. Posner, Overcoming Law 399 (1995). Like many others, Posner announces that the "intelligent" answer is not to analogize to wild animals or use the rule of capture. Id. at 520. But the real question is what mixture of action by courts, legislatures, regulators, and the parties themselves is most cost-effective at solving the problem. Looked at in this light, the wild animal analogy is a short hand for the difficulty (especially for courts) of delineating property rights to this resource (given that oil and gas is not owned by the state and the configuration of surface parcels is fragmented for non-oil and gas related reasons such as farming). See, e.g., Rance L. Craft, Of Reservoir Hogs and Pelt Fiction: Defending the *Ferae Naturae* Analogy Between Petroleum and Wildlife, 44 Emory L.J. 697 (1995); Dean Lueck, The Rule of First Possession and the Design of the Law, 38 J.L. & Econ. 393, 425 (1995). Courts have been able to police around the edges, by labeling as a nuisance activities like letting oil burn off. See generally Henry E. Smith, Semicommons in Fluid Resources, 20 Marq. Intell. Prop. L. Rev. 195 (2016).

One interesting perennial problem that involves reconciling the *ad coelum* principle and first possession is the reinjection of gas into underground formations for storage purposes. The most famous common law opinion, *Hammonds v. Central Kentucky Natural Gas Co.*, 75 S.W.2d 204, 206 (Ky. 1934), overruled by Tex. Am. Energy Corp. v. Citizens Fidelity Bank & Trust Co., 736 S.W.2d 25 (Ky. 1987), used the wild-animal analogy and the rule of capture to hold that reinjection of gas into a gasless underground formation lying under a neighbor's land was not a trespass. One rationale for the no-trespass result was that the gas, like a wild animal released into the wild, was now ownerless and so would not give rise to trespass liability for the releasing party. 75 S.W.2d at 206. An implication of the decision (but not the holding) is that the gas, now wild, is again eligible for capture by the first possessor, which could be any surface owner who lives above part of the underground storage reservoir.

Many states did recognize property in oil and gas beneath surface parcels, in an application of the *ad coelum* principle, but held that it disappeared once the minerals left the owner's column of space. Nonetheless, the recognition even of this fleeting ownership formed the predicate for some common law governing extraction, under the heading of "correlative rights." But again, to the frustration of many commentators, the correlative rights doctrine is not very ambitious, only preventing the grossest forms of waste, such as allowing blow-outs and fires. See Elliff v. Texon Drilling Co., 210 S.W.2d 558, 562–63 (Tex. 1948). The main intervention to prevent waste has been legislative and regulatory. See, e.g., Wyo. Stat. Ann. § 30–5–101(a)(ix) (2003) (defining "correlative rights" as "the opportunity afforded the owner of each property in a pool to produce, so far as it is reasonably practicable to do so without waste, his just and equitable share of the oil or gas, or both, in the pool").

How should the reinjection of gas into underground formations be treated if some ownership of gas in the ground is recognized? An interesting scenario was presented by another classic, *Lone Star Gas Co. v. Murchison*, 353 S.W.2d 870 (Tex. Ct. Civ. App. 1962), in which the court considered the claim that a neighboring surface owner had committed a conversion by sinking a well to extract gas that had been reinjected into an underground reservoir by a gas company and that had migrated under the neighbor's land. The court rejected the wild animal analogy, saying that produced natural gas is more like a domestic animal: "[I]f a horse strays over on a neighbor's land, the neighbor may be entitled to his damages, but he does not, by virtue of the trespass, acquire title to the horse." Id. at 877 (quoting William Jarrell Smith). The court held that the gas company had an action for conversion against the neighbor. No issue was presented in *Lone Star Gas* as to whether the neighbor could recover damages for subterranean trespass (or for restitution?) for the value of the storage facility under his land. Logically, if the stored gas remains the personal property of the gas company, it would seem that the neighbor could sue for trespass, and perhaps could even get an injunction. This could lead to a classic bilateral monopoly problem, and perhaps to condemnation of subsurface rights. The court in *Lone Star Gas* in fact mentioned underground storage condemnation statutes, which many oil and gas states had passed. Id. at 878; see also Cornwell v. Central Kentucky Natural Gas, 249 S.W.2d 531 (Ky. 1952) (finding constitutional a statute providing for condemnation of underground storage space when the surface owner is not prevented from drilling). The details of the condemnation statutes and the private agreements reached on storage of natural gas suggest that depleted underground strata are not worthless or de minimis. The question may arise again if technology is developed to capture and sequester carbon dioxide by injecting it into subsurface areas as part of the effort to control greenhouse gases. Keep all these issues in mind when we return to caves and the accession principle, infra Part E.

What does all this say about the status of the *ad coelum* doctrine and the rule of capture? Should natural gas, once captured, remain the personal property of the gas company when reinjected into a storage basin, or should reinjection cause the gas company to lose title?

For more on the difficulties of establishing rights to subsurface deposits of oil and gas, especially in the context of modern recovery technologies using hydraulic fracturing technology, see Briggs v. Southwestern Energy Production Co., infra Part G.

B. DISCOVERY

Closely associated with first possession or capture is the notion that original title to property can be established through discovery. Certainly, both doctrines rely heavily on being the first to claim something. But whereas first possession requires that one be the first *actually to possess* an unclaimed thing, discovery establishes a unique *right to possess* a thing. The most prominent decision to invoke discovery as a basis for ownership was far more controversial than *Pierson v. Post*, and undoubtedly far more consequential.

Johnson v. M'Intosh

Supreme Court of the United States, 1823.
21 U.S. (8 Wheat.) 543.

ERROR to the District Court of Illinois. This was an action of ejectment for lands in the State and District of Illinois, claimed by the plaintiffs under a purchase and conveyance from the Piankeshaw Indians, and by the defendant, under a grant from the United States. It came up on a case stated, upon which there was a judgment below for the defendant. * * *

[The statement of facts begins with an elaborate chronology of the colony of Virginia, founded by royal charter in 1609, which purported to grant to Virginia lands as far west as present day Illinois and Indiana. It traces the history of those lands, from a European perspective, up to the cession by Virginia to the federal government at the end of the Revolutionary War. It notes that, "from time immemorial," the Illinois and Piankeshaw tribes had actually held and inhabited the lands in controversy in what is now central and southern Illinois and western Indiana.

On July 5, 1773, the chiefs of the Illinois sold certain lands inhabited by the tribe to William Murray and others, for the sum of $24,000. On October 18, 1775, the chiefs of the Piankeshaw sold certain lands occupied by the tribe to Louis Viviat and others for $31,000. One of the grantees in this last transaction was Thomas Johnson, who died in 1819, leaving his interest to his son, Joshua Johnson, and his grandson, Thomas Graham, who were plaintiffs in the case.

In 1795, the Illinois and Piankeshaw tribes entered into treaties with the United States, retaining certain lands as reservations, but ceding to the federal government other of the lands they had previously occupied. On July 20, 1818, the United States sold to William M'Intosh, the defendant, some of the same lands granted by the Piankeshaw to Thomas Johnson, and subsequently inherited by Joshua Johnson and Thomas Graham. Johnson and Graham brought an action in ejectment against M'Intosh, in an effort to establish their superior claim of title to the lands in question. The lower courts ruled for the defendant, M'Intosh.]

■ MR. CHIEF JUSTICE MARSHALL delivered the opinion of the Court. The plaintiffs in this cause claim the land, in their declaration mentioned, under two grants, purporting to be made, the first in 1773, and the last in 1775, by the chiefs of certain Indian tribes, constituting the Illinois and the Piankeshaw nations; and the question is, whether this title can be recognised in the Courts of the United States?

The facts, as stated in the case agreed, show the authority of the chiefs who executed this conveyance, so far as it could be given by their own people; and likewise show, that the particular tribes for whom these chiefs acted were in rightful possession of the land they sold. The inquiry, therefore, is, in a great measure, confined to the power of Indians to give, and of private individuals to receive, a title which can be sustained in the Courts of this country.

As the right of society, to prescribe those rules by which property may be acquired and preserved is not, and cannot be drawn into question; as the title to lands, especially, is and must be admitted to depend entirely on the law of the nation in which they lie; it will be necessary, in pursuing this inquiry, to examine, not singly those principles of abstract justice, which the Creator of all things has impressed on the mind of his creature man, and which are admitted to regulate, in a great degree, the rights of civilized nations, whose perfect independence is acknowledged; but those principles also which our own government has adopted in the particular case, and given us as the rule for our decision.

On the discovery of this immense continent, the great nations of Europe were eager to appropriate to themselves so much of it as they could respectively acquire. Its vast extent offered an ample field to the ambition and enterprise of all; and the character and religion of its inhabitants afforded an apology for considering them as a people over whom the superior genius of Europe might claim an ascendency. The potentates of the old world found no difficulty in convincing themselves that they made ample compensation to the inhabitants of the new, by bestowing on them civilization and Christianity, in exchange for unlimited independence. But, as they were all in pursuit of nearly the same object, it was necessary, in order to avoid conflicting settlements, and consequent war with each other, to establish a principle, which all should acknowledge as the law by which the right of acquisition, which they all asserted, should be regulated as between themselves. This principle was, that discovery gave title to the government by whose subjects, or by whose authority, it was made, against all other European governments, which title might be consummated by possession.

The exclusion of all other Europeans, necessarily gave to the nation making the discovery the sole right of acquiring the soil from the natives, and establishing settlements upon it. It was a right with which no Europeans could interfere. It was a right which all asserted for themselves, and to the assertion of which, by others, all assented.

Those relations which were to exist between the discoverer and the natives, were to be regulated by themselves. The rights thus acquired being exclusive, no other power could interpose between them.

In the establishment of these relations, the rights of the original inhabitants were, in no instance, entirely disregarded; but were necessarily, to a considerable extent, impaired. They were admitted to be the rightful occupants of the soil, with a legal as well as just claim to retain possession of it, and to use it according to their own discretion; but their rights to complete sovereignty, as independent nations, were necessarily diminished, and their power to dispose of the soil at their own will, to whomsoever they pleased, was denied by the original fundamental principle, that discovery gave exclusive title to those who made it.

While the different nations of Europe respected the right of the natives, as occupants, they asserted the ultimate dominion to be in themselves; and claimed and exercised, as a consequence of this ultimate dominion, a power to grant the soil, while yet in possession of the natives. These grants have been understood by all, to convey a title to the grantees, subject only to the Indian right of occupancy.

The history of America, from its discovery to the present day, proves, we think, the universal recognition of these principles. * * *

No one of the powers of Europe gave its full assent to this principle, more unequivocally than England. The documents upon this subject are ample and complete. So early as the year 1496, her monarch granted a commission to the Cabots, to discover countries then unknown to *Christian people*, and to take possession of them in the name of the king of England. Two years afterwards, Cabot proceeded on this voyage, and discovered the continent of North America, along which he sailed as far south as Virginia. To this discovery the English trace their title. * * *

Thus has our whole country been granted by the crown while in the occupation of the Indians. These grants purport to convey the soil as well as the right of dominion to the grantees. * * *

[C]onflicting claims produced a long and bloody war, which was terminated by the conquest of the whole country east of the Mississippi. In the treaty of 1763, France ceded and guarantied to Great Britain, all Nova Scotia, or Acadie, and Canada, with their dependencies; and it was agreed, that the boundaries between the territories of the two nations, in America, should be irrevocably fixed by a line drawn from the source of the Mississippi, through the middle of that river and the lakes Maurepas and Ponchartrain, to the sea. This treaty expressly cedes, and has always been understood to cede, the whole country, on the English side of the dividing line, between the two nations, although a great and valuable part of it was occupied by the Indians. Great Britain, on her part, surrendered to France all her pretensions to the country west of the Mississippi. It has never been supposed that she surrendered nothing, although she was not in actual possession of a foot of land. She surrendered all right to acquire the country; and any after attempt to purchase it from the Indians, would have been considered and treated as an invasion of the territories of France.

By the 20th article of the same treaty, Spain ceded Florida, with its dependencies, and all the country she claimed east or southeast of the Mississippi, to Great Britain. Great part of this territory also was in possession of the Indians.

By a secret treaty, which was executed about the same time, France ceded Louisiana to Spain; and Spain has since retroceded the same country to France. At the time both of its cession and retrocession, it was occupied, chiefly, by the Indians.

Thus, all the nations of Europe, who have acquired territory on this continent, have asserted in themselves, and have recognised in others, the exclusive right of the discoverer to appropriate the lands occupied by the Indians. Have the American States rejected or adopted this principle?

By the treaty which concluded the war of our revolution, Great Britain relinquished all claim, not only to the government, but to the "propriety and territorial rights of the United States," whose boundaries were fixed in the second article. By this treaty, the powers of government, and the right to soil, which had previously been in Great Britain, passed definitively to these States. We had before taken possession of them, by declaring independence; but neither the declaration of independence, nor the treaty confirming it, could give us more than that which we before possessed, or to which Great Britain was before entitled. It has never been doubted, that either the United States, or the several States, had a clear title to all the lands within the boundary lines described in the treaty, subject only to the Indian right of occupancy, and that the exclusive power to extinguish that right, was vested in that government which might constitutionally exercise it. * * *

The States, having within their chartered limits different portions of territory covered by Indians, ceded that territory, generally, to the United States, on conditions expressed in their deeds of cession, which demonstrate the opinion, that they ceded the soil as well as jurisdiction, and that in doing so, they granted a productive fund to the government of the Union. The lands in controversy lay within the chartered limits of Virginia, and were ceded with the whole country northwest of the river Ohio. This grant contained reservations and stipulations, which could only be made by the owners of the soil; and concluded with a stipulation, that "all the lands in the ceded territory, not reserved, should be considered as a common fund, for the use and benefit of such of the United States as have become, or shall become, members of the confederation," & c. "according to their usual respective proportions in the general charge and expenditure, and shall be faithfully and *bona fide* disposed of for that purpose, and for no other use or purpose whatsoever."

US has superior ownership

The ceded territory was occupied by numerous and warlike tribes of Indians; but the exclusive right of the United States to extinguish their title, and to grant the soil, has never, we believe, been doubted. * * *

The United States, then, have unequivocally acceded to that great and broad rule by which its civilized inhabitants now hold this country. They hold, and assert in themselves, the title by which it was acquired. They maintain, as all others have maintained, that discovery gave an exclusive right to extinguish the Indian title of occupancy, either by purchase or by conquest; and gave also a right to such a degree of sovereignty, as the circumstances of the people would allow them to exercise.

The power now possessed by the government of the United States to grant lands, resided, while we were colonies, in the crown, or its grantees. The validity of the titles given by either has never been questioned in our Courts. It has been exercised uniformly over territory in possession of the Indians. The existence of this power must negative the existence of any right which may conflict with, and control it. An absolute title to lands cannot exist, at the same time, in different persons, or in different governments. An absolute, must be an exclusive title, or at least a title which excludes all others not compatible with it. All our institutions recognise the absolute title of the crown, subject only to the Indian right of occupancy, and recognise the absolute title of the crown to extinguish that right. This is incompatible with an absolute and complete title in the Indians.

We will not enter into the controversy, whether agriculturists, merchants, and manufacturers, have a right, on abstract principles, to expel hunters from the territory they possess, or to contract their limits. Conquest gives a title which the Courts of the conqueror cannot deny, whatever the private and speculative opinions of individuals may be, respecting the original justice of the claim which has been successfully asserted. The British government, which was then our government, and whose rights have passed to the United States, asserted title to all the lands occupied by Indians, within the chartered limits of the British colonies. It asserted also a limited sovereignty over them, and the exclusive right of extinguishing the title which occupancy gave to them. These claims have been maintained and established as far west as the river Mississippi, by the sword. The title to a vast portion of the lands we now hold, originates in them. It is not for the Courts of this country to question the validity of this title, or to sustain one which is incompatible with it.

Although we do not mean to engage in the defence of those principles which Europeans have applied to Indian title, they may, we think, find some excuse, if not justification, in the character and habits of the people whose rights have been wrested from them.

The title by conquest is acquired and maintained by force. The conqueror prescribes its limits. Humanity, however, acting on public opinion, has established, as a general rule, that the conquered shall not be wantonly oppressed, and that their condition shall remain as eligible as is compatible with the objects of the conquest. Most usually, they are incorporated with the victorious nation, and become subjects or citizens of the government with which they are connected. The new and old members of the society mingle with each other; the distinction between them is gradually lost, and they make one people. Where this incorporation is practicable, humanity demands, and a wise policy requires, that the rights of the conquered to property should remain unimpaired; that the new subjects should be governed as equitably as the old, and that confidence in their security should gradually banish the painful sense of being separated from their ancient connexions, and united by force to strangers.

When the conquest is complete, and the conquered inhabitants can be blended with the conquerors, or safely governed as a distinct people, public opinion, which not even the conqueror can disregard, imposes these restraints upon him; and he cannot neglect them without injury to his fame, and hazard to his power.

But the tribes of Indians inhabiting this country were fierce savages, whose occupation was war, and whose subsistence was drawn chiefly from the forest. To leave them in possession of their country, was to leave the country a wilderness; to govern them as a distinct people, was impossible, because they were as brave and as high spirited as they were fierce, and were ready to repel by arms every attempt on their independence.

What was the inevitable consequence of this state of things? The Europeans were under the necessity either of abandoning the country, and relinquishing their pompous claims to it, or of enforcing those claims by the sword, and by the adoption of principles adapted to the condition of a people with whom it was impossible to mix, and who could not be governed as a distinct society, or of remaining in their neighbourhood, and exposing themselves and their families to the perpetual hazard of being massacred.

Frequent and bloody wars, in which the whites were not always the aggressors, unavoidably ensued. European policy, numbers, and skill, prevailed. As the white population advanced, that of the Indians necessarily receded. The country in the immediate neighbourhood of agriculturists became unfit for them. The game fled into thicker and more unbroken forests, and the Indians followed. The soil, to which the crown originally claimed title, being no longer occupied by its ancient inhabitants, was parcelled out according to the will of the sovereign power, and taken possession of by persons who claimed immediately from the crown, or mediately, through its grantees or deputies.

That law which regulates, and ought to regulate in general, the relations between the conqueror and conquered, was incapable of application to a people under such circumstances. The resort to some new and different rule, better adapted to the actual state of things, was unavoidable. Every rule which can be suggested will be found to be attended with great difficulty.

However extravagant the pretension of converting the discovery of an inhabited country into conquest may appear; if the principle has been asserted in the first instance, and afterwards sustained; if a country has been acquired and held under it; if the property of the great mass of the community originates in it, it becomes the law of the land, and cannot be questioned. So, too, with respect to the concomitant principle, that the Indian inhabitants are to be considered merely as occupants, to be protected, indeed, while in peace, in the possession of their lands, but to be deemed incapable of transferring the absolute title to others. However this restriction may be opposed to natural right, and to the usages of civilized nations, yet, if it be indispensable to that system under which the country has been settled, and be adapted to the actual condition of the two people, it may, perhaps, be supported by reason, and certainly cannot be rejected by Courts of justice. * * *

After bestowing on this subject a degree of attention which was more required by the magnitude of the interest in litigation, and the able and elaborate arguments of the bar, than by its intrinsic difficulty, the Court is decidedly of opinion, that the plaintiffs do not exhibit a title which can be sustained in the Courts of the United States; and that there is no error in the judgment which was rendered against them in the District Court of Illinois. * * *

NOTES AND QUESTIONS

1.   This case illustrates the practice of courts when faced with conflicting claims to a single piece of property: They recreate the "chains of title" underlying the competing claims, in order to determine which of the parties has the stronger claim. Each claim is traced back a link at a time, until we arrive at the "root of title." Often this exercise will lead back to a single common grantor (e.g., the government or the first possessor), in which case the first transferee from the common grantor is deemed to have the better claim to title. If we assume the Illinois and Piankeshaw Tribes are the common grantor, who would prevail here—Joshua Johnson, who claims by inheritance from Thomas Johnson, who was an original grantee from the Piankeshaw in 1775, or M'Intosh, who purchases from the United States in 1818, which acquired the rights from the Illinois and Piankeshaw by treaty in 1795?

2.   In order to displace the conclusion that would be drawn from ordinary principles about transfers from a common grantor, Chief Justice Marshall draws a distinction between sovereign title ("dominion") based on discovery and Indian title ("occupancy") based on possession. He then traces the chain of title back in time, looking now to acts of discovery that establish dominion rather than occupancy. This takes him all the way back to 1609 when Virginia was established, or perhaps even to 1497 when Cabot

discovered North America. Who wins under the tracing-back exercise once we recharacterize the relevant interests in this fashion? Why does this "chain of title" leave out France, which did not have a policy of forbidding transactions with indigenous people and went further than English settlers in recognizing native property rights? What of George III's Proclamation of 1763 confirming native rights, which helped set the stage for the American Revolution?

3.   Eric Kades has called into question whether this case was really about competing chains of title to the same land. According to Kades, this was a fabricated suit based on false stipulated facts: The plaintiffs' and the defendant's land did not even overlap, as reflected in his map, reproduced here as Figure 2-2. Eric Kades, History and Interpretation of the Great Case of *Johnson v. M'Intosh*, 19 Law & Hist. Rev. 67, 68 (2001). The plaintiffs' predecessors (Murray, Viviat, etc.) had tried repeatedly to get the Virginia colonial governor and later Congress to recognize their titles, to no avail. Nor did the plaintiffs get "title" from all the Indians that had some claim to the land. Eric Kades, The Dark Side of Efficiency: *Johnson v. M'Intosh* and the Expropriation of American Indian Lands, 148 U. Pa. L. Rev. 1065, 1067, 1081–90 (2000). Such contrived lawsuits were not as uncommon in those days, though today we assume that "feigned" lawsuits do not satisfy the "case or controversy" requirement of Article III of the Constitution.

4.   Some of the selling tribes in *Johnson v. M'Intosh* were under great pressure because of declining population due to disease and surrounding enemy Indian tribes. The great Illinois confederation could not defend itself against other tribes and settlers. The first two parcels in the case, in South and Central Illinois, were purchased from three remaining Illinois tribes (the Kaskaskia, Peoria, and Cahokia tribes). Their numbers had recently been much reduced (Illinois tribes fell from 10,500 in 1680 to 2,500 in 1736 to 500 in 1800, because of disease and Indian enemies on all sides). The second two parcels, in Southern Illinois and Indiana, came from the Piankeshaw tribe, one of six Miami tribes (Miami population fell from 7,500 in 1682 to some 2,000 in 1736). Kades, supra, at 1081–82.

5.   What is the relationship between dominion and occupancy? How can the Indians have a present possessory interest—title of occupancy—and the United States also have "title"? Is the right of occupancy an interest otherwise unknown to American law, as most believe? For an argument that *Johnson* and the other Marshall Court decisions on the discovery doctrine are better interpreted as recognizing a fee simple in the Indians subject to a restraint on alienation and the federal government's right of preemption (exclusive right to purchase), see Michael C. Blumm, Why Aboriginal Title is a Fee Simple Absolute, 15 Lewis & Clark L. Rev. 975 (2011); see also Mitchel v. United States, 34 U.S. (9 Pet.) 711, 756 (1835) (English king had "ultimate reversion in fee"); see also Oneida Indian Nation of New York v. State of New York, 691 F.2d 1070, 1075 (2d Cir. 1982) ("Thus the concept of fee title in the context of Indian lands does not amount to absolute ownership, but rather is used interchangeably with 'right of preemption,' or the preemptive right over all others to purchase the Indian title or right of occupancy from the inhabitants."), citing Oneida Indian Nation v. County of Oneida, 414 U.S.

661, 670 (1974). On this alternative view, a transferee from the United States prior to the extinguishment of Indian title would have an executory interest, another future interest we will take up in Chapter V. Notice also that here as elsewhere property and sovereignty notions are sometimes hard to pry apart.

Figure 2-2

Map of Land Claims in *Johnson v. M'Intosh*

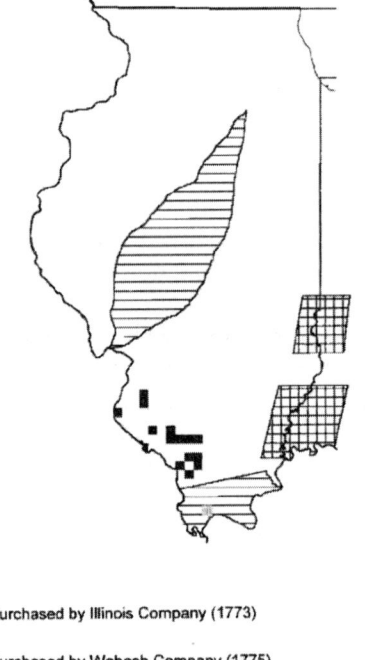

Legend

    Tracts Purchased by Illinois Company (1773)

    Tracts Purchased by Wabash Company (1775)

    Townships Containing McIntosh Purchases of 1815 (at issue in case)

    Township Containing McIntosh Purchase of 1819 (not at issue in case)

From the Law and History Review. Copyright 2001 by the Board of Trustees of the University of Illinois. Used with permission of the University of Illinois Press.

6.   Under either interpretation, how can the Indian right of occupancy be extinguished? Why should "conquest" be regarded as an acceptable method of extinguishing the right of occupancy? Does Marshall think that the result he reaches is consistent with what morality and international law would dictate? What do you make of the line in the opinion, "Conquest gives a title which the Courts of the conqueror cannot deny"? Does this concede too much to raw power? Or is the point rather that too many titles to too much land depend on the validity of discovery and conquest as means of establishing original title to land in North America—that the assumed validity of these methods of original acquisition has too much gravitational force for courts to ignore it? Either way, does this case validate the view that property is theft? Does it at least imply that all property ultimately flows

from the state, with its monopoly on the legitimate use of force and coercion? Note that conquest was later limited by the Court to "defensive" or "just cause" wars. Worcester v. Georgia, 31 U.S. (6 Pet.) 515 (1832); see also Article III of the Northwest Ordinance of 1787. Does this make more palatable the proposition that the Indian right of occupancy can be extinguished by conquest? For a detailed study of the use of the discovery doctrine in *Johnson v. M'Intosh*, see Lindsay G. Robertson, Conquest by Law: How the Discovery of America Dispossessed Indigenous Peoples of their Lands (2005); see also Jedediah Purdy, Property and Empire: The Law of Imperialism in *Johnson v. M'Intosh*, 75 Geo. Wash. L. Rev. 329 (2007). For surveys of the treatment of indigenous peoples' land throughout the English-speaking world, see, e.g., Stuart Banner, How the Indians Lost Their Land: Law and Power on the Frontier (2005); Kent McNeil, Common Law Aboriginal Title (1989); Robert J. Miller et al., Discovering Indigenous Lands: The Doctrine of Discovery in the English Colonies (2010).

7.   One justification for the decision intimated by Chief Justice Marshall is that the Indians had no concept of property in land comparable to the understanding of the white settlers. He describes "the tribes of Indians inhabiting this country" as "fierce savages" "whose subsistence was drawn chiefly from the forest." They were hunter-gatherers, who had left the land "a wilderness." The white settlers, in contrast, were "agriculturists," who parceled out the land in private plots, causing game to flee "into thicker and more unbroken forests" and the Indians to follow. These views, which were standard for the time in which Marshall lived and wrote, have recently been called into question. According to William Cronon, for example, New England Indians recognized the concept of territoriality, in the sense of areas subject to exclusive control and use by particular villages. William Cronon, Changes in the Land: Indians, Colonists, and the Ecology of New England 58–61 (1983). They also recognized individual property rights in utilitarian objects such as baskets, kettles, hoes, bows, arrows, and canoes. Id. at 61. With respect to land, southern New England Indians, who engaged in extensive agriculture, recognized something close to exclusive rights of particular families to fields planted with corn, although these fields were generally abandoned every eight years or so when soil nutrients were exhausted. Id. at 62. Other recognized land rights were similar to what the Romans called usufructs—rights to engage in particular uses of particular parcels of land. Thus, "different groups of people could have different claims on the same tract of land depending on how they used it. Any village member, for instance, had the right to collect edible wild plants, cut birchbark or chestnut for canoes, or gather sedges for mats, wherever these things could be found. . . . The same was not true, on the other hand, of hunting that involved the setting of snares or traps. . . . [Animals that had to be caught by using traps] were best hunted by spreading the village population over as broad a territory as possible, and so usufruct rights had to be designed to hold the overlap of trapped areas to a reasonable minimum." Id. at 63–64. See also Philip P. Frickey, Marshalling Past and Present: Colonialism, Constitutionalism, and Interpretation in Federal Indian Law, 107 Harv. L. Rev. 381 (1993); Charles F. Wilkinson, American Indians, Time, and the Law: Native Societies in a Modern Constitutional Democracy (1987). Similar

conclusions about aboriginal understandings of property have been reached by other scholars. See, e.g., Stuart Banner, Two Properties, One Land: Law and Space in Nineteenth-Century New Zealand, 24 Law & Soc. Inquiry 807, 811–12 (1999); Robert Williams, The American Indian in Western Legal Thought (1990).

8.   One understanding that Indians almost surely did not originally share with the European settlers was that of land as a commercial commodity subject to bargain and sale. The question of the nature of sales by Indians to Europeans and later Americans has been the subject of much research and commentary. Many of the sales were fraught with misunderstanding in the very earliest times in the eastern United States, and with violence in later times in the West when Indians had fewer places to which they could retreat. See Terry L. Anderson & Peter J. Hill, The Not So Wild, Wild West: Property Rights on the Frontier (2004); see also Cronon, supra, at 67–81.

9.   What was the ultimate impact on Native Americans of the doctrine of discovery rationalized in *Johnson v. M'Intosh*? Commentators today tend to take a dim view of the decision. Kades argues that the policy of allowing non-Indians to purchase land from Indians only with the permission of the United States government was disadvantageous to the Indians. Kades, supra, at 1103–31. This policy, recognized in *Johnson v. M'Intosh*, was originally codified in the Indian Trade and Intercourse Act of 1790, ch. 33, 1 Stat. 137 (expired 1793). See also William C. Canby, Jr., The Status of Indian Tribes in American Law Today, 62 Wash. L. Rev. 1, 2–6 (1987). Indians could theoretically remain on the land but could not force potential buyers to compete with each other, thus depressing prices. A more charitable view of the decision might ask whether Indians were likely to get a better deal in the nineteenth century from Congress and the federal judiciary, or from state legislatures and state judiciaries. By distinguishing between dominion and occupancy, and asserting that only the federal government could extinguish native rights of occupancy, Chief Justice Marshall—at least in theory—inserted the federal government and its courts as a buffer between natives and their property interests and the land-hungry European settlers. The federal government, representing a more diffuse set of interests, was arguably more even-handed in its treatment of land disputes between natives and settlers than state governments and state courts would have been. On the other hand, the farther west land sales occurred, the less likely that the federal government could enforce its wishes. Also, Anderson and Hill point out that members of the U.S. Army, both privates and officers, had incentives to drum up business by fomenting conflicts with the Indians.

10.   The potential importance of denying the states any power to divest Indians from their lands and territory is suggested by *McGirt v. Oklahoma*, 140 S. Ct. 2452 (2020). The Supreme Court, in an opinion by Justice Gorsuch, held that Congress by treaties with the Creek Nation in the 1830s had established a Creek Reservation in what is now northeast Oklahoma, including the city of Tulsa. Only Congress, he held, has the authority to abrogate solemn promises made to tribes in the form of a treaty, and no subsequent Act of Congress clearly expressed an intent to eliminate the

reservation. Consequently, the State of Oklahoma had no authority to try enrolled Indians for major crimes allegedly committed in the area. Chief Justice Roberts dissented, arguing that everyone had acted for years as if the reservation no longer existed in its original form. This reality on the ground, he argued, should be controlling on the question of criminal jurisdiction. Which opinion is more consistent with the general approach of Chief Justice Marshall in *Johnson v. M'Intosh*?

11. The history of Indian land ownership after *Johnson v. M'Intosh* has been an unhappy one. As the nineteenth century drew on, Indians were forced into reservations in the West. In the Dawes General Allotment Act of 1887, 24 Stat. 388, Congress allotted land to various tribes and imposed a version of an Anglo-American style property system, all with the purpose of Indian assimilation. Allotted lands were to be held in trust by the United States and then turned over to individual Indian owners, but placed under the jurisdiction of the state in which the land was located. Proponents and opponents of allotment both believed that Indians had only common property and systematically ignored the mix of private and common property and the diversity of Indian property systems and their development over time. After allotment, any changes in Indian property systems had to be effected by federal legislation. Various provisions of the allotment act caused Indian land ownership to decline by 80% by 1934 when Congress passed the Indian Reorganization Act. This statute promoted Indian governments but retained much federal control and proved rigidly bureaucratic. In *Tee-Hit-Ton Indians v. United States*, 348 U.S. 272 (1955), the Supreme Court held that Congress could take Indian land without compensation. The Court again downplayed Indian notions of property and Indian sovereignty. At one point the Court quoted from Justice Jackson in another case: "We agree . . . that no legal rights are today to be recognized in the Shoshones by reason of this treaty. We agree . . . as to their moral deserts. We do not mean to leave the impression that the two have any relation to each other." Northwestern Bands of Shoshone Indians v. United States, 324 U.S. 335, 358 (1945) (Jackson, J., concurring).

Land Grants from the Federal Public Domain*

When the original thirteen colonies broke free from Britain, a number of them—Massachusetts, Connecticut, New York, Virginia, North and South Carolina, and Georgia—had charters that included lands extending from the Atlantic seaboard to the Mississippi River. The remaining colonies had much more limited claims to territories along the Atlantic coast. After much political wrangling, the states with claims to western lands agreed to cede those lands to the newly formed federal government. This was the beginning of the federal public domain, a vast quantity of land held by the federal government for disposition and eventual formation of new states. The original federal public domain,

---

* [The following account is primarily drawn from Paul W. Gates, History of Public Land Law Development (1968), a magisterial study of the history of public lands in the United States.—eds.]

which extended from the Allegheny Mountains to the Mississippi River, was soon enormously expanded. The largest augmentations were the Louisiana Purchase of 1803, in which the United States acquired most of the land from Louisiana to Montana; the Treaty with Spain in 1818, which added Florida and western Louisiana; the annexation of Texas in 1845; the Oregon Compromise with Britain in 1846, which secured what is now Washington, Oregon and Idaho; the concessions wrested from Mexico in 1848 after the Mexican-American War, which included California, Nevada, Utah, Arizona, New Mexico, and western Colorado; and the purchase of Alaska from Russia in 1867. The quantity of resources to be disposed of, once Indian title to the lands was extinguished by treaty or conquest, was staggering—approximately 1.4 billion acres of land.

When the western lands were ceded, the reigning idea was that the federal government would sell the lands at auction in order to raise money to pay off the Revolutionary War debts. To facilitate this process, Congress (during the waning days of the Articles of Confederation) adopted legislation known as the Land Ordinance of 1785. This statute probably had a more profound impact on the physical appearance of America than any other piece of legislation before or since. Influenced by the ideas of a committee headed by Thomas Jefferson, the Ordinance of 1785 mandated a system for surveying and disposing of public domain lands. The Ordinance set up a system of principal meridians (north-south) and geographer's lines (east-west) based on longitude and latitude, creating 36-square mile townships (six miles on a side) that would contain one mile square numbered sections. We return to the details of this system and the less systematic "metes and bounds" method in the states not carved out of the public domain in Chapter VIII.

Another important provision of the Ordinance of 1785 was the reservation of section 16 in every township "for the maintenance of public schools within the said township." The idea was not that all 640 acres in Section 16 would be the playground for a one-room school house (although one can see the remains of one-room school houses on Section 16 in many rural areas today). Rather, the territorial governments, and then the states formed out of the territories, would be able to sell or lease the land in Section 16 in order to raise revenue for the support of public schools. Thus, the federal government, from the very beginning, was committed to heavily subsidizing public education through the disposition of the public lands. This was followed by other measures, most prominently the Morrill Act of 1862, which set aside large tracts of public lands for sales to support the creation of public universities—the so-called "land grant" colleges and universities that form the backbone of much of our system of higher education today.

Following the Ordinance of 1785, the official policy of the federal government continued to emphasize sales of land from the public domain. Once Indian claims were extinguished and the land was surveyed, it would be placed for sale at public auction. Congress set the initial minimum price at $2 an acre, with no limitation on the amount of land that could be purchased. Sales were disappointing, however, apparently because the minimum price was too high, and agitation for more liberal divestment policies quickly mounted. Congress responded by easing the conditions for sales on credit. Widespread defaults and forfeitures followed. Various relief acts were passed by Congress to benefit those who were unable to come up with cash to pay for the lands they had purchased. In 1821 further credit sales were prohibited, and the minimum price was reduced to $1.25 per acre. Forfeitures continued to plague those who had previously purchased on credit, and in 1832 Congress essentially gave up on further attempts to recover amounts still owed. Federal land prices were lowered further by the Graduation Act of 1854, which allowed for progressively lower prices for any land that did not sell at the minimum price.

While official federal policy continued to favor sales of land, the reality on the ground was different. During the colonial era, many states outside New England had seen widespread claims of unsettled land by squatters who moved onto choice parcels without any pretense of legal title. As Paul W. Gates recounts:

> Squatters were a rough and sometimes unruly lot. They were contemptuous of the rights of large owners, contributed no taxes to the support of government, and caused conflicts for colonial administrations by their intrusions into areas claimed by the Indians. James Logan, agent for the Penn holdings, described the Scotch-Irish—the most restless and least law-abiding of the hordes of immigrants coming into Pennsylvania—as "bold and indigent strangers" who, when challenged for their titles, replied that the Penns "had solicited for colonists and they had come accordingly." They took up land in "an audacious manner," alleging that "it was against the laws of God and nature that so much land should be idle while so many Christians wanted it to labor on to raise their bread."

Gates, supra, at 66. These squatters became numerous and vociferous enough that even before the cession of western lands to the federal government, Virginia and North Carolina had enacted laws allowing squatters a right of "preemption," which essentially gave squatters an option to purchase the land they occupied, thereby trumping the rights of purchasers at subsequent public-land sales.

After 1785, the practice of squatting continued, notwithstanding the official policy of disposing of land by sale. Although the practice was frequently condemned, Congress received hundreds of petitions from squatter-settlers seeking preemption rights for their holdings. Often, but not always, Congress responded with ad hoc legislation granting these requests, effectively ratifying acts that had been illegal when the land was taken. As western interests' political representation in Congress increased, preemption acts became broader. The process culminated in the enactment of the Preemption Act of 1841, which granted a general prospective preemption right on federal land, provided Indian title had been extinguished and the land had been surveyed. Settlers could claim up to 160 acres of land before it went to public auction, provided they inhabited and improved the land, constructed some kind of dwelling on it, and agreed to pay the minimum price of $1.25 per acre. There is considerable evidence that the Preemption Act was often abused. For example, logging companies would use dummies, persons appearing independent but actually controlled by the company, to file preemption claims for timber land in Michigan, Wisconsin, and Minnesota, which provided the legal authority to enter the land. The companies would then clear cut the standing timber—often magnificent old-growth white pines—and the preemption claim would be abandoned before any funds were paid to the government. Nevertheless, preemption remained a significant avenue for disposal of public lands until 1891, when the Preemption Act was finally repealed.

Squatter-settlers adopted another tactic for securing legal title to the land they had occupied: They banded together to form claims associations. These were combinations designed to prevent competitive bidding at public land sales, in order to ensure that local settlers could purchase the land of their choosing at the minimum price. Little is known about exactly how these associations operated, since they did not keep written records of their activities. But it is widely surmised that they had an even greater impact on securing land for squatter-settlers than did the preemption laws. Gates relates the following account:

> Sandford C. Cox, an eye-witness of a government sale at the Crawfordsville, Indiana office, wrote of the town being full of strangers when the sales commenced [in 1825]. The eastern and southern portions of the state were strongly represented, as well as Ohio, Kentucky, Tennessee, and Pennsylvania. There was little competitive bidding as "the settlers, or 'squatters' as they are called by speculators, have arranged matters among themselves to their general satisfaction. If, upon comparing numbers, it appears that two are after the same tract of land, one asks the other what he will take not to bid against him. If neither will consent to be bought off, they then retire, and cast lots, and the lucky one enters the tract at Congress' price—$1.25 per acre—and the other enters the second choice on his list." If a speculator "showed a disposition to take a settler's claim from him, he sees the white of a score of eyes snapping at him, and at the first opportunity he crawfishes out of the crowd."

Gates, supra at 152.

The most interesting legislation disposing of federal land, in terms of its impact on the popular imagination, was the Homestead Act of 1862. This legislation grew out of a land reform movement of the 1830s and

1840s, spearheaded by the New York newspaper publisher Horace Greeley. Advocates argued that the government should grant free small homesteads to any citizen who relocated westward, in order to draw surplus labor from the cities in the East. This, they argued, would help raise wages for the poor who remained behind, and would act as a "safety valve" against urban unrest. The original Act of 1862 allowed any citizen to claim 160 acres of unsold surveyed land. If the homesteader inhabited the land and cultivated it for five years, he received title to the land without any payment (other than filing fees). Only one homestead could be acquired per family, but it was possible to obtain 160 acres by homestead and another 160 by preemption—although not at the same time, since actual inhabitation was required for each. Homesteaders could also get title to their homestead land before five years were up, by converting the claim to a preemption claim and paying $1.25 per acre. Congress eventually realized that a parcel of 160 acres was too small to sustain productive agricultural operations in arid areas on the Great Plains, where there is not enough rainfall for crop production. Later homestead acts authorized larger claims of up to 640 acres.

Figure 2-3
The Chrisman Sisters in Front of Lizzie Chrisman's
Homestead, Custer County, Nebraska, 1886

Courtesy of Nebraska State Historical Society Photograph Collections. To help their family accumulate enough acreage in western Nebraska to graze livestock, each of the four Chrisman sisters took homestead, timber, and preemption claims, each having a sod house similar to the one in the picture. Two or more of the sisters would then take turns living with each other, in order to comply with the family-habitation requirements of the laws.

Although granting individual plots of land to settlers was probably the largest single category of federal land disposal, the government granted lands for other purposes as well. Veterans of the Revolutionary War, the War of 1812, the Mexican-American War, and the Civil War were given "scrip" that could be exchanged for federal lands. As previously noted, states were given Section 16 of every township to support public education, and were later given large grants for the support of state colleges. Generous grants of land were also given to companies formed to build turnpikes, canals, and railroads. Finally, special grants of land were made to settlers who agreed to plant trees on the prairies (the Timber Culture Act of 1873) or to irrigate desert areas (the Desert Land Act of 1877).

By the late nineteenth century, public attitudes toward disposition of the public domain began to change. The process of settlement began to run out of gas, as remaining tracts were too arid, mountainous, or remote to attract further private entry. The public also began to perceive that some of the federal land was simply too valuable to sell or give away. The area now occupied by Yellowstone National Park was reserved from further entry or homesteading in 1872, and reservations of Yosemite and other future national parks followed. Huge tracts of forested land in the West were reserved by presidential proclamation, followed by the creation of the National Forest System in 1897 and the National Park System in 1916. Finally, the Taylor Grazing Act of 1934 closed all of the remaining public domain from further private entry (other than entry by prospectors for mineral claims). Public sentiment since then has, if anything, hardened against further private disposition of federal lands. The result is that today almost 30 percent of the land mass of the United States—approximately 662 million acres—is controlled by the federal government. These lands are managed by large federal bureaucracies—the Bureau of Land Management, the Bureau of Indian Affairs, and the National Park Service in the Department of Interior; and the National Forest Service in the Department of Agriculture.

NOTES AND QUESTIONS

1. In retrospect, congressional policy toward disposition of the public domain seems riddled with inconsistencies. Congress was at once too generous (making grants to veterans and railroads and favored insiders) and too stingy (setting the initial minimum price for sale at $2 per acre). Part of the problem was conflicting desires: to tap public lands as a source of revenue in order to pay off war debts; to promote rapid development of the interior of the continent; to avoid sanctioning either "speculators" or "squatters." Two relatively consistent policies, either of which would have promoted rapid development, would have been to auction the land to the highest bidder with no minimums, or to permit unlimited homesteading. Either policy, however, might have reduced federal revenues from initial land sales. And the first (unlimited sales) would have had the appearance of abetting "speculators," while the second (unlimited homesteading) would have appeared to sanction

"squatters." So instead, Congress vacillated back and forth between promoting sales (subject to minimum prices) and promoting homesteading (subject to acreage restrictions and other limitations). Somehow, the country got developed, although the system of disposal produced enormous conflict and litigation along the way.

2.   Economists have pointed out that despite the appearance of free land, homesteading carried with it a steep price paid for by the hardships endured by the settlers and the concomitant premature cultivation of remote tracts. See Terry L. Anderson & P. J. Hill, The Race for Property Rights, 33 J.L. & Econ. 177, 195 (1990). Again, racing behavior if unconstrained can dissipate the value of a natural resource. On the other hand, it has also been argued that from the United States' point of view, homesteading provided collective defense of the frontier areas against Europeans, Mexicans, and Indians. See Douglas W. Allen, Homesteading and Property Rights; or, "How The West Was Really Won," 34 J.L. & Econ. 1, 22–23 (1991).

3.   Are preemption laws and homestead laws additional examples of acquisition of property by first possession? By discovery? Under both systems, claimants would scout around until they spotted a choice parcel of unclaimed land, which they would then occupy and claim for themselves upon payment of a fixed minimum price ($1.25 under the Preemption Act) or minimal filing fees (under the homestead acts). The law on the books—the Ordinance of 1785 and the system of land sales and registrations managed by the Land Office—would suggest that the public domain was divided into well-defined parcels and distributed in a very orderly fashion. But would it be more accurate to characterize the situation on the ground, at least for the first hundred years or so, as a kind of open-access commons? If so, what does this tell us about the conditions that cause a resource to be regarded as a commons?

4.   What accounts for the great resistance today to further privatization of the public domain? Many national forests, for example, could be owned and managed by privately-owned lumber and paper companies, many of which already own and manage large tracts of forest lands. On one estimate, the National Forest System loses 25 cents on every dollar it spends managing the National Forests. Could it be that a variety of interest groups, including lumber and paper companies, are happy having their activities subsidized by federal taxpayers? See James L. Huffman, The Inevitability of Private Rights in Public Lands, 65 U. Colo. L. Rev. 241 (1994). Or have past abuses of federal lands, such as the clear cutting of old-growth forests in the upper Midwest, created pervasive distrust of private stewardship for resources like timber?

C. CREATION

A third principle used to establish original ownership is creation. This principle applies primarily to property in the form of information. Persons who create new information are (sometimes) rewarded with a right to control how others use the information, and this control right is called intellectual property. As technological innovation accelerates and is disseminated more quickly throughout the world, property rights in information are becoming increasingly important to the U.S. and world economies, and are commanding an increasing share of legal attention and resources, compared to tangible property.

Property rights in information are different from property rights in tangible goods in important ways. Perhaps most significantly, although information can be costly to produce, the marginal post-production cost of copying or reproducing it is zero (or close to it). Moreover, use of the information by one consumer does not diminish the use by another; in this sense, information is what economists call a "nonrival" good. Thus, the primary reason for creating property rights in information is to provide incentives for producing and developing it, not to assure that it is allocated efficiently among potential users of it.

Intellectual property rights are today governed primarily by complicated statutory regimes adopted by the U.S. Congress. The principal regimes are patent, which applies to new, useful, and nonobvious inventions; copyright, which applies to original works of authorship; and trademark, which applies to words or symbols that identify commercial enterprises, goods, and services. It would take us too far afield to study any one of these statutory regimes, let alone all three, in any detail in an introductory course in property. Instead, we will include cases and materials that arise out of intellectual property controversies throughout the course where they illustrate or present problems that are characteristic of property rights more generally. In this section, which deals with the principle of establishing title by creation, we will concentrate primarily on rights in information that have a common-law (or equitable) basis.

International News Service v. Associated Press

Supreme Court of the United States, 1918.
248 U.S. 215.

■ MR. JUSTICE PITNEY delivered the opinion of the Court. The parties are competitors in the gathering and distribution of news and its publication for profit in newspapers throughout the United States. The Associated Press, which was complainant in the District Court, is a co-operative organization, incorporated under the Membership Corporations Law of the state of New York, its members being individuals who are either proprietors or representatives of about 950 daily newspapers published in all parts of the United States. * * * Complainant gathers in all parts of the world, by means of various instrumentalities of its own, by exchange with its members, and by other appropriate means, news and intelligence of current and recent events of interest to newspaper readers and distributes it daily, to its members for publication in their newspapers. The cost of the service, amounting approximately to $3,500,000 per annum, is assessed upon the members and becomes a part of their costs of operation, to be recouped, presumably with profit, through the publication of their several newspapers. Under complainant's by-laws each member agrees upon assuming membership that news received through complainant's service is received exclusively for publication in a particular newspaper, language, and place specified in the certificate of membership, that no other use of it shall be permitted, and that no member shall furnish or permit any one in his employ or connected with his newspaper to furnish any of complainant's news in advance of publication to any person not a member. And each member is required to gather the local news of his district and supply it to the Associated Press and to no one else.

member agreement to only use info given by AP for news publication

+ exclusive supplier agreement

Defendant is a corporation organized under the laws of the state of New Jersey, whose business is the gathering and selling of news to its customers and clients, consisting of newspapers published throughout the United States, under contracts by which they pay certain amounts at stated times for defendant's service. It has widespread news-gathering agencies; the cost of its operations amounts, it is said, to more than $2,000,000 per annum; and it serves about 400 newspapers located in the various cities of the United States and abroad, a few of which are represented, also, in the membership of the Associated Press.

INS

The parties are in the keenest competition between themselves in the distribution of news throughout the United States; and so, as a rule, are the newspapers that they serve, in their several districts. * * *

[Complainant's] bill was filed to restrain the pirating of complainant's news by defendant in three ways: First, by bribing employees of newspapers published by complainant's members to furnish Associated Press news to defendant before publication, for transmission by telegraph and telephone to defendant's clients for publication by them; second, by inducing Associated Press members to violate its by-laws and permit defendant to obtain news before publication; and, third, by copying news from bulletin boards and from early editions of complainant's newspapers and selling this, either bodily or after rewriting it, to defendant's customers.

AP piracy claims

The District Court, upon consideration of the bill and answer, with voluminous affidavits on both sides, granted a preliminary injunction under the first and second heads, but refused at that stage to restrain the systematic practice admittedly pursued by defendant, of taking news bodily from the bulletin boards and early editions of complainant's newspapers and selling it as its own. * * *

PP: injunction granted for 1 and 2. denied for 3

The only matter that has been argued before us is whether defendant may lawfully be restrained from appropriating news taken from bulletins issued by complainant or any of its members, or from newspapers published by them, for the purpose of selling it to defendant's clients. Complainant asserts that defendant's admitted course of conduct in this regard both violates complainant's property right in the news and constitutes unfair competition in business. And notwithstanding the case has proceeded only to the stage of a preliminary injunction, we have

Ⓠ here

deemed it proper to consider the underlying questions, since they go to the very merits of the action and are presented upon facts that are not in dispute. As presented in argument, these questions are: 1. Whether there is any property in news; 2. Whether, if there be property in news collected for the purpose of being published, it survives the instant of its publication in the first newspaper to which it is communicated by the news-gatherer; and 3. whether defendant's admitted course of conduct in appropriating for commercial use matter taken from bulletins or early editions of Associated Press publications constitutes unfair competition in trade.

The federal jurisdiction was invoked because of diversity of citizenship, not upon the ground that the suit arose under the copyright or other laws of the United States. Complainant's news matter is not copyrighted. It is said that it could not, in practice, be copyrighted, because of the large number of dispatches that are sent daily; and, according to complainant's contention, news is not within the operation of the copyright act. * * *

In considering the general question of property in news matter, it is necessary to recognize its dual character, distinguishing between the substance of the information and the particular form or collocation of words in which the writer has communicated it.

No doubt news articles often possess a literary quality, and are the subject of literary property at the common law; nor do we question that such an article, as a literary production, is the subject of copyright by the terms of the act as it now stands. * * *

But the news element—the information respecting current events contained in the literary production—is not the creation of the writer, but is a report of matters that ordinarily are *publici juris*; it is the history of the day. It is not to be supposed that the framers of the Constitution, when they empowered Congress "to promote the progress of science and useful arts, by securing for limited times to authors and inventors the exclusive right to their respective writings and discoveries" (Const. art. 1, § 8, par. 8), intended to confer upon one who might happen to be the first to report a historic event the exclusive right for any period to spread the knowledge of it.

We need spend no time, however, upon the general question of property in news matter at common law, or the application of the copyright act, since it seems to us the case must turn upon the question of unfair competition in business. * * * We are dealing here not with restrictions upon publication but with the very facilities and processes of publication. The peculiar value of news is in the spreading of it while it is fresh; and it is evident that a valuable property interest in the news, as news, cannot be maintained by keeping it secret. Besides, except for matters improperly disclosed, or published in breach of trust or confidence, or in violation of law, none of which is involved in this branch of the case, the news of current events may be regarded as common property. What we are concerned with is the business of making it known to the world, in which both parties to the present suit are engaged. That business consists in maintaining a prompt, sure, steady, and reliable service designed to place the daily events of the world at the breakfast table of the millions at a price that, while of trifling moment to each reader, is sufficient in the aggregate to afford compensation for the cost of gathering and distributing it, with the added profit so necessary as an incentive to effective action in the commercial world. The service thus performed for newspaper readers is not only innocent but extremely useful in itself, and indubitably constitutes a legitimate business. The parties are competitors in this field; and, on fundamental principles, applicable here as elsewhere, when the rights or privileges of the one are liable to conflict with those of the other, each party is under a duty so to conduct its own business as not unnecessarily or unfairly to injure that of the other.

Obviously, the question of what is unfair competition in business must be determined with particular reference to the character and circumstances of the business. The question here is not so much the rights of either party as against the public but their rights as between themselves. And, although we may and do assume that neither party has any remaining property interest as against the public in uncopyrighted news matter after the moment of its first publication, it by no means follows that there is no remaining property interest in it as between themselves. For, to both of them alike, news matter, however little susceptible of ownership or dominion in the absolute sense, is stock in trade, to be gathered at the cost of enterprise, organization, skill, labor, and money, and to be distributed and sold to those who will pay money for it, as for any other merchandise. Regarding the news, therefore, as but the material out of which both parties are seeking to make profits at the same time and in the same field, we hardly can fail to recognize that for this purpose, and as between them, it must be regarded as *quasi* property, irrespective of the rights of either as against the public.

In order to sustain the jurisdiction of equity over the controversy, we need not affirm any general and absolute property in the news as such. The rule that a court of equity concerns itself only in the protection of property rights treats any civil right of a pecuniary nature as a property right (In re Sawyer, 124 U.S. 200, 210 (1888); In re Debs, 158 U.S. 564, 593 (1895)); and the right to acquire property by honest labor or the conduct of a lawful business is as much entitled to protection as the right to guard property already acquired (Truax v. Raich, 239 U.S. 33, 37–38 (1916); Brennan v. United Hatters, 65 Atl. 165, 171–72 (N.J. 1906); Barr v. Essex Trades Council, 30 Atl. 881 (N.J. Ch. 1894)). It is this right that furnishes the basis of the jurisdiction in the ordinary case of unfair competition. * * *

The peculiar features of the case arise from the fact that, while novelty and freshness form so important an element in the success of the business, the very processes of distribution and publication necessarily occupy a good deal of time. Complainant's service, as well as defendant's, is a daily service to daily newspapers; most of the foreign news reaches this country at the Atlantic seaboard, principally at the city of New York, and because of this, and of time differentials due to the earth's rotation, the distribution of news matter throughout the country is principally from east to west; and, since in speed the telegraph and telephone easily outstrip the rotation of the earth, it is a simple matter for defendant to take complainant's news from bulletins or early editions of complainant's members in the eastern cities and at the mere cost of telegraphic transmission cause it to be published in western papers issued at least as early as those served by complainant. Besides this, and irrespective of time differentials, irregularities in telegraphic transmission on different lines, and the normal consumption of time in printing and distributing the newspaper, result in permitting pirated news to be placed in the hands of defendant's readers sometimes simultaneously with the service of competing Associated Press papers, occasionally even earlier.

Defendant insists that when, with the sanction and approval of complainant, and as the result of the use of its news for the very purpose for which it is distributed, a portion of complainant's members communicate it to the general public by posting it upon bulletin boards so that all may read, or by issuing it to newspapers and distributing it indiscriminately, complainant no longer has the right to control the use to be made of it; that when it thus reaches the light of day it becomes the common possession of all to whom it is accessible; and that any purchaser of a newspaper has the right to communicate the intelligence which it contains to anybody and for any purpose, even for the purpose of selling it for profit to newspapers published for profit in competition with complainant's members.

The fault in the reasoning lies in applying as a test the right of the complainant as against the public, instead of considering the rights of complainant and defendant, competitors in business, as between themselves. The right of the purchaser of a single newspaper to spread knowledge of its contents gratuitously, for any legitimate purpose not unreasonably interfering with complainant's right to make merchandise of it, may be admitted; but to transmit that news for commercial use, in competition with complainant—which is what defendant has done and seeks to justify—is a very different matter. In doing this defendant, by its very act, admits that it is taking material that has been acquired by complainant as the result of organization and the expenditure of labor, skill, and money, and which is salable by complainant for money, and that defendant in appropriating it and selling it as its own is endeavoring to reap where it has not sown, and by disposing of it to newspapers that are competitors of complainant's members is appropriating to itself the harvest of those who have sown. Stripped of all disguises, the process amounts to an unauthorized interference with the normal operation of complainant's legitimate business precisely at the point where the profit is to be reaped, in order to divert a material portion of the profit from those who have earned it to those who have not; with special advantage to defendant in the competition because of the fact that it is not burdened with any part of the expense of gathering the news. The transaction speaks for itself and a court of equity ought not to hesitate long in characterizing it as unfair competition in business. * * *

It is no answer to say that complainant spends its money for that which is too fugitive or evanescent to be the subject of property. That might, and for the purposes of the discussion we are assuming that it would furnish an answer in a common-law controversy. But in a court of equity, where the question is one of unfair competition, if that which complainant has acquired fairly at substantial cost may be sold fairly at substantial profit, a competitor who is misappropriating it for the purpose of disposing of it to his own profit and to the disadvantage of complainant cannot be heard to say that it is too fugitive or evanescent to be regarded as property. It has all the attributes of property necessary for determining that a misappropriation of it by a competitor is unfair competition because contrary to good conscience. * * *

* * * Indeed, it is one of the most obvious results of defendant's theory that, by permitting indiscriminate publication by anybody and everybody for purposes of profit in competition with the news-gatherer, it would render publication profitless, or so little profitable as in effect to cut off the service by rendering the cost prohibitive in comparison with the return. * * *

It is to be observed that the view we adopt does not result in giving to complainant the right to monopolize either the gathering or the distribution of the news, or, without complying with the copyright act, to prevent the reproduction of its news articles, but only postpones participation by complainant's competitor in the processes of distribution and reproduction of news that it has not gathered, and only to the extent necessary to prevent that competitor from reaping the fruits of complainant's efforts and expenditure, to the partial exclusion of complainant, and in violation of the principle that underlies the maxim *sic utere tuo*, etc.

It is said that the elements of unfair competition are lacking because there is no attempt by defendant to palm off its goods as those of the complainant, characteristic of the most familiar, if not the most typical, cases of unfair competition. But we cannot concede that the right to equitable relief is confined to that class of cases. In the present case the fraud upon complainant's rights is more direct and obvious. Regarding news matter as the mere material from which these two competing parties are endeavoring to make money, and treating it, therefore, as *quasi* property for the purposes of their business because they are both selling it as such, defendant's conduct differs from the ordinary case of unfair competition in trade principally in this that, instead of selling its own goods as those of complainant, it substitutes misappropriation in the place of misrepresentation, and sells complainant's goods as its own.

Besides the misappropriation, there are elements of imitation, of false pretense, in defendant's practices. The device of rewriting complainant's news articles, frequently resorted to, carries its own comment. The habitual failure to give credit to complainant for that which is taken is significant. Indeed, the entire system of appropriating complainant's news and transmitting it as a commercial product to defendant's clients and patrons amounts to a false representation to them and to their newspaper readers that the news transmitted is the result of defendant's own investigation in the field. But these elements, although accentuating the wrong, are not the essence of it. It is something more than the advantage of celebrity of which complainant is being deprived. * * *

■ MR. JUSTICE HOLMES, dissenting. When an uncopyrighted combination of words is published there is no general right to forbid other people repeating them—in other words there is no property in the combination or in the thoughts or facts that the words express. Property, a creation of law, does not arise from value, although exchangeable—a matter of fact. Many exchangeable values may be destroyed intentionally without compensation. Property depends upon exclusion by law from interference, and a person is not excluded from using any combination of words merely because some one has used it before, even if it took labor and genius to make it. If a given person is to be prohibited from making the use of words that his neighbors are free to make[,] some other ground must be found. One such ground is vaguely expressed in the phrase fair trade. This means that the words are repeated by a competitor in business in such a way as to convey a misrepresentation that materially injures the person who first used them, by appropriating credit of some kind which the first user has earned. The ordinary case * * * is palming off the defendant's product as the plaintiff's but the same evil may follow from the opposite falsehood—from saying whether in words or by implication that the plaintiff's product is the defendant's, and that, it seems to me, is what has happened here. * * *

[I]n my view, the only ground of complaint that can be recognized without legislation is the implied misstatement[.] [I]t can be corrected by stating the truth; and a suitable acknowledgement of the source is all that the plaintiff can require. I think that within the limits recognized by the decision of the Court the defendant should be enjoined from publishing news obtained from the Associated Press for [___] hours after publication by the plaintiff unless it gives express credit to the Associated Press; the number of hours and the form of acknowledgment to be settled by the District Court.

■ MR. JUSTICE BRANDEIS, dissenting. * * * The sole question for our consideration is this: Was the International News Service properly enjoined from using, or causing to be used gainfully, news of which it acquired knowledge by lawful means (namely, by reading publicly posted bulletins or papers purchased by it in the open market) merely because the news had been originally gathered by the Associated Press and continued to be of value to some of its members, or because it did not reveal the source from which it was acquired? * * *

News is a report of recent occurrences. The business of the news agency is to gather systematically knowledge of such occurrences of interest and to distribute reports thereof. The Associated Press contended that knowledge so acquired is property, because it costs money and labor to produce and because it has value for which those who have it not are ready to pay; that it remains property and is entitled to protection as long as it has commercial value as news; and that to protect it effectively, the defendant must be enjoined from making, or causing to be made, any gainful use of it while it retains such value. An essential element of individual property is the legal right to exclude others from enjoying it. If the property is private, the right of exclusion may be absolute; if the property is affected with a public interest, the right of exclusion is qualified. But the fact that a product of the mind has cost its producer money and labor, and has a value for which others are willing to pay, is not sufficient to ensure to it this legal attribute of property. The general rule of law is, that the noblest of human productions— knowledge, truths ascertained, conceptions, and ideas—became, after voluntary communication to others, free as the air to common use. Upon these incorporeal productions the attribute of property is continued after such communication only in certain classes of cases where public policy has seemed to demand it. These exceptions are confined to productions which, in some degree, involve creation, invention, or discovery. But by no means all such are endowed with this attribute of property. The creations which are recognized as property by the common law are literary, dramatic, musical, and other artistic creations; and these have also protection under the copyright statutes. The inventions and discoveries upon which this attribute of property is conferred only by statute, are the few comprised within the patent law. There are also many other cases in which courts interfere to prevent curtailment of plaintiff's enjoyment of incorporeal productions; and in which the right to relief is often called a property right, but is such only in a special sense. In those cases, the plaintiff has no absolute right to the protection of his production; he has merely the qualified right to be protected as against the defendant's acts, because of the special relation in which the latter stands or the wrongful method or means employed in acquiring the knowledge or the manner in which it is used. Protection of this character is afforded where the suit is based upon breach of contract or of trust or upon unfair competition.

The knowledge for which protection is sought in the case at bar is not of a kind upon which the law has heretofore conferred the attributes of property; nor is the manner of its acquisition or use nor the purpose to which it is applied, such as has heretofore been recognized as entitling a plaintiff to relief. * * *

[T]he plaintiff does not contend that the posting was wrongful or that any papers were wrongfully issued by its subscribers. On the contrary it is conceded that both the bulletins and the papers were issued in accordance with the regulations of the plaintiff. Under such circumstances, for a reader of the papers purchased in the open market, or a reader of the bulletins publicly posted, to procure and use gainfully, information therein contained, does not involve inducing any one to commit a breach either of contract or of trust, or committing or in any way abetting a breach of confidence. * * *

Plaintiff further contended that defendant's practice constitutes unfair competition, because there is "appropriation without cost to itself of values created by" the plaintiff; and it is upon this ground that the decision of this court appears to be based. To appropriate and use for profit, knowledge and ideas produced by other men, without making compensation or even acknowledgment, may be inconsistent with a finer sense of propriety; but, with the exceptions indicated above, the law has heretofore sanctioned the practice. Thus it was held that one may ordinarily make and sell anything in any form, may copy with exactness that which another has produced, or may otherwise use his ideas without his consent and without the payment of compensation, and yet not inflict a legal injury; and that ordinarily one is at perfect liberty to find out, if he can by lawful means, trade secrets of another, however valuable, and then use the knowledge so acquired gainfully, although it cost the original owner much in effort and in money to collect or produce.

Such taking and gainful use of a product of another which, for reasons of public policy, the law has refused to endow with the attributes of property, does not become unlawful because the product happens to have been taken from a rival and is used in competition with him. The unfairness in competition which hitherto has been recognized by the law as a basis for relief, lay in the manner or means of conducting the business; and the manner or means held legally unfair, involves either fraud or force or the doing of acts otherwise prohibited by law. In the "passing off" cases (the typical and most common case of unfair competition), the wrong consists in fraudulently representing by word or act that defendant's goods are those of plaintiff. In the other cases, the diversion of trade was effected through physical or moral coercion, or by inducing breaches of contract or of trust or by enticing away employees. In some others, called cases of simulated competition, relief was granted because defendant's purpose was unlawful; namely, not competition but deliberate and wanton destruction of plaintiff's business.

That competition is not unfair in a legal sense, merely because the profits gained are unearned, even if made at the expense of a rival, is shown by many cases besides those referred to above. He who follows the pioneer into a new market, or who engages in the manufacture of an article newly introduced by another, seeks profits due largely to the labor and expense of the first adventurer; but the law sanctions, indeed encourages, the pursuit. * * *

The great development of agencies now furnishing country-wide distribution of news, the vastness of our territory, and improvements in the means of transmitting intelligence, have made it possible for a news agency or newspapers to obtain, without paying compensation, the fruit of another's efforts and to use news so obtained gainfully in competition with the original collector. The injustice of such action is obvious. But to give relief against it would involve more than the application of existing rules of law to new facts. It would require the making of a new rule in analogy to existing ones. The unwritten law possesses capacity for growth; and has often satisfied new demands for justice by invoking analogies or by expanding a rule or principle. This process has been in the main wisely applied and should not be discontinued. Where the problem is relatively simple, as it is apt to be when private interests only are involved, it generally proves adequate. But with the increasing complexity of society, the public interest tends to become omnipresent; and the problems presented by new demands for justice cease to be simple. Then the creation or recognition by courts of a new private right may work serious injury to the general public, unless the boundaries of the right are definitely established and wisely guarded. In order to reconcile the new private right with the public interest, it may be necessary to prescribe limitations and rules for its enjoyment; and also to provide administrative machinery for enforcing the rules. It is largely for this reason that, in the effort to meet the many new demands for justice incident to a rapidly changing civilization, resort to legislation has latterly been had with increasing frequency.

The rule for which the plaintiff contends would effect an important extension of property rights and a corresponding curtailment of the free use of knowledge and of ideas; and the facts of this case admonish us of the danger involved in recognizing such a property right in news, without imposing upon news-gatherers corresponding obligations. A large majority of the newspapers and perhaps half the newspaper readers of the United States are dependent for their news of general interest upon agencies other than the Associated Press. The channel through which about 400 of these papers received, as the plaintiff alleges, "a large amount of news relating to the European war of the greatest importance and of intense interest to the newspaper reading public" was suddenly closed. The closing to the International News Service of these channels for foreign news (if they were closed) was due not to unwillingness on its part to pay the cost of collecting the news, but to the prohibitions imposed by foreign governments upon its securing news from their respective countries and from using cable or telegraph lines running therefrom. For aught that appears, this prohibition may have been wholly undeserved; and at all events the 400 papers and their readers may be assumed to have been innocent. For aught that appears, the International News Service may have sought then to secure temporarily by arrangement with the Associated Press the latter's foreign news service. For aught that appears, all of the 400 subscribers of the International News Service would gladly have then become members of the Associated Press, if they could have secured election thereto. It is possible, also, that a large part of the readers of these papers were so situated that they could not secure prompt access to papers served by the Associated Press. The prohibition of the foreign governments might as well have been extended to the channels through which news was supplied to the more than a thousand other daily papers in the United States not served by the Associated Press; and a large part of their readers may also be so located that they cannot procure prompt access to papers served by the Associated Press.

A Legislature, urged to enact a law by which one news agency or newspaper may prevent appropriation of the fruits of its labors by another, would consider such facts and possibilities and others which appropriate inquiry might disclose. Legislators might conclude that it was impossible to put an end to the obvious injustice involved in such appropriation of news, without opening the door to other evils, greater than that sought to be remedied. * * *

Courts are ill-equipped to make the investigations which should precede a determination of the limitations which should be set upon any property right in news or of the circumstances under which news gathered by a private agency should be deemed affected with a public interest. Courts would be powerless to prescribe the detailed regulations essential to full enjoyment of the rights conferred or to introduce the machinery required for enforcement of such regulations. Considerations such as these should lead us to decline to establish a new rule of law in the effort to redress a newly disclosed wrong, although the propriety of some remedy appears to be clear.

NOTES AND QUESTIONS

1.   The majority says that in order to sustain the injunction, "we need not affirm any general and absolute property in the news as such." Do you agree? Does the principle that underlies the injunction establish an in personam right running against one entity (International News) in favor of another (Associated Press)? Or is it a more general right in rem that binds all the world? Whatever the Supreme Court thought it was doing, lower courts have relied on the decision to create what amounts to a common-law right to exclude others from time-sensitive information that the plaintiff has produced with some effort. See, e.g., National Basketball Ass'n v. Motorola, Inc., 105 F.3d 841 (2d Cir. 1997); Board of Trade of Chicago v. Dow Jones & Co., 456 N.E.2d 84 (Ill. 1983). Recently, news organizations, including the Associated Press, have sued "aggregators," websites that summarize information from other sites. See, e.g., Barclays Capital v. Theflyonthewall.com, 650 F.3d 876 (2d Cir. 2011) (reversing grant of injunction for news organization claiming misappropriation, because news

aggregator was not "free-riding"); see also Associated Press v. All Headline News Corp., 608 F. Supp. 2d 454 (S.D.N.Y. 2009) (denying motion to dismiss hot news misappropriation claim). How, if at all, should the hot news doctrine or misappropriation apply to Internet news aggregators? To collectors of "hot data"? See Victoria Smith Ekstrand & Christopher Roush, From "Hot News" to "Hot Data": The Rise of "Fintech," the Ownership of Big Data, and the Future of the Hot News Doctrine, 35 Cardozo Arts & Ent. L.J. 303, 304 (2017).

2. *International News* is a leading judicial statement—perhaps *the* leading statement—of the idea that property rights should be based on desert, that one should not be allowed to reap where another has sown. This is generally associated with John Locke's labor theory of property, briefly described in the fourth note after *Pierson v. Post*, as opposed to theories based on utility, autonomy, or personhood. Scholars and judges, however, are deeply divided over the foundational principle of intellectual property rights. Are such rights based on protection of the labor and desert of those who create—artists, inventors, or gatherers of hot news? Or are they grounded in the social utility created by providing incentives designed to stimulate the production of new and valuable works, inventions, and information? Compare Douglas G. Baird, Common Law Intellectual Property and the Legacy of *International News Service v. Associated Press*, 50 U. Chi. L. Rev. 411 (1983) (arguing that the law provides for no general reap-what-you-sow principle) with Wendy J. Gordon, On Owning Information: Intellectual Property and the Restitutionary Impulse, 78 Va. L. Rev. 149 (1992) (arguing that intellectual property is consistent with principles behind the law of restitution).

3. Is *International News* an application of the principle of unfair competition, recognized in *Keeble v. Hickeringill*, supra? What about unfair competition makes it inequitable? See, e.g., Shyamkrishna Balganesh, "Hot News": The Enduring Myth of Property in News, 111 Colum. L. Rev. 419 (2011) (unfair competition and restitution); Henry E. Smith, Equitable Intellectual Property: What's Wrong with Misappropriation?, Intellectual Property and the Common Law 42 (Shyamkrishna Balganesh ed., 2013) (unfair competition and equity). (For further consideration of the idea of restitution for unjust enrichment, see Chapter IV.C.)

4. Why couldn't the Associated Press solve its problem by copyright? Under the 1909 Copyright Act in effect when the *International News* case arose, certain notice-giving formalities were required ("Copyright" or an abbreviation and the name of the copyright holder in prescribed places) as well as registration at the Copyright Office. The Associated Press could not comply with the registration requirements before the newspapers were distributed. Since the March 1, 1989 effective date of the U.S. ratification of the Berne Convention in 1988, no notice is required for protection of original works. Hence, at least insofar as the International News Service was copying the text of AP stories (as opposed to reporting on the information they contained), the problem in *International News* could be solved by copyright protection today. The formalities are still relevant, but only because they confer certain evidentiary advantages. See 17 U.S.C. § 401(d). Registration

is not required but likewise confers certain advantages. Id. § 412. Copyright is also relevant in that a broad version of misappropriation grounded in state law (which is where much of unfair competition law now resides) that started to look too much like copyright law would be preempted by the federal copyright statute. 17 U.S.C. § 106.

5.   Another cluster of issues in the *International News* case centers on the role of custom. What if it were true that news organizations had a custom of respecting each other's claims to hot news? Should a court then enforce this custom? For an argument in the affirmative, see Richard A. Epstein, *International News Service v. Associated Press*: Custom and Law as Sources of Property Rights in News, 78 Va. L. Rev. 85 (1992). There has been an outpouring of studies of customary regimes of intellectual property rights in specialized communities, including French chefs, Emmanuelle Fauchart & Eric von Hippel, Norm-Based Intellectual Property Systems: The Case of French Chefs, 19 Org. Sci. 187 (2008), and stand-up comics, Dotan Oliar & Christopher Sprigman, There's No Free Laugh (Anymore): The Emergence of Intellectual Property Norms and the Transformation of Stand-Up Comedy, 94 Va. L. Rev. 1787 (2008). This literature has generally been fairly upbeat about extra-legal IP norms, except for the potential for violence (among the comics, not the chefs). Others are not as enthusiastic, particularly where custom tends to increase intellectual property protection. Jennifer E. Rothman, The Questionable Use of Custom in Intellectual Property, 93 Va. L. Rev. 1899 (2007).

6.   A final issue of importance concerns which institution in society—the courts or the legislature—should decide whether to provide legal protection against misappropriation of hot news. The issue is especially important for intellectual property, but applies in principle to any question about whether to create a new type of property right. Justice Brandeis gives some reasons for preferring the legislature to make these sorts of decisions. What might be the arguments in favor of allowing courts to make the decision (subject, presumably, to revision by the legislature)? For general discussion of the criteria for choosing between courts and legislatures in resolving social policy questions, see Neil K. Komesar, Imperfect Alternatives: Choosing Institutions in Law, Economics, and Public Policy (1994). For discussion focused on which institution should recognize new property rights, see Thomas W. Merrill & Henry E. Smith, Optimal Standardization in the Law of Property: The *Numerus Clausus* Principle, 110 Yale L.J. 1, 58–68 (2000).

7.   Creation, like discovery, bears a degree of similarity to first possession, in that being *first* is important to all three general principles of original acquisition. In keeping with misappropriation not creating a full-blown property right, the firstness here does not require a showing of much originality, at least beyond news value. Creation often requires more, some kind of novelty. Patent law even requires that inventions be nonobvious in order to be patentable:

> A patent for a claimed invention may not be obtained * * * if the differences between the claimed invention and the prior art are such that the claimed invention as a whole would have been

obvious before the effective filing date of the claimed invention to a person having ordinary skill in the art to which the claimed invention pertains. Patentability shall not be negated by the manner in which the invention was made.

35 U.S.C. § 103.

D. PRIOR POSSESSION

Possession is more than a method of original acquisition. Possession is arguably the most basic property institution. Is possession a fact—control over the resource coupled perhaps with an intent to maintain control? Norms of mutual recognition of possessory claims in household implements, foodstuffs, and other everyday objects probably arose deep in prehistory. And claims to territory on small scales bear some resemblance to animal territoriality. At some point law got involved. As you will see, the law's treatment of possession is quite many-sided, from affording protection to plaintiffs in possession, to vindicating a right to possess, to easing the path for possessors to prove ownership. So keep asking yourself in the cases that follow: What does it mean to "possess" something? When and why will the law intervene to protect this possession?

1. RIGHTS TO POSSESS

We sometimes speak of "rights" of possession. Consider the following case.

Haslem v. Lockwood

Supreme Court of Errors of Connecticut, 1871.
37 Conn. 500, 9 Am. Rep. 350.

Trover, for a quantity of manure[.] * * * On the trial it was proved that the plaintiff employed two men to gather into heaps, on the evening of April 6th, 1869, some manure that lay scattered along the side of a public highway, for several rods, in the borough of Stamford, intending to remove the same to his own land the next evening. The men began to scrape the manure into heaps at six o'clock in the evening, and after gathering eighteen heaps, or about six cart-loads, left the same at eight o'clock in the evening in the street. The heaps consisted chiefly of manure made by horses hitched to the railing of the public park in, and belonging to, the borough of Stamford, and was all gathered between the center of the highway and the park; the rest of the heaps consisting of dirt, straw and the ordinary scrapings of highways. The defendant on the next morning, seeing the heaps, endeavored without success to ascertain who had made them, and inquired of the warden of the borough if he had given permission to any one to remove them, and ascertained from him that he had not. He thereupon, before noon on that day, removed the heaps, and also the rest of the manure scattered along the side of the highway adjacent to the park, to his own land.

The plaintiff and defendant both claimed to have received authority from the warden to remove the manure before the 6th of April, but in fact neither had any legal authority from the warden, or from any officer of the borough or of the town. The borough of Stamford was the sole adjoining proprietor of the land on which the manure lay scattered before it was gathered by the plaintiff. No notice was left on the heaps or near by, by the plaintiff or his workmen, to indicate who had gathered them, nor had the plaintiff or his workmen any actual possession of the heaps after eight o'clock in the evening on the 6th of April.

Neither the plaintiff while gathering, nor the defendant while removing the heaps, was interfered with or opposed by any one. The removal of the manure and scrapings was calculated to improve the appearance and health of the borough. The six loads were worth one dollar per load. The plaintiff, on ascertaining that the defendant had removed the manure, demanded payment for the same, which the defendant refused. Neither the plaintiff nor defendant owned any land adjacent to the place where the manure lay. The highway was kept in repair by the town of Stamford.

On the above facts the plaintiff claimed, and prayed the court to rule, that the manure was personal property which had been abandoned by its owners and became by such abandonment the property of the first person who should take possession of the same, which the plaintiff had done by gathering it into heaps, and that it was not and never had been a part of the real estate of the borough or of any one else who might be regarded as owning the fee of the soil. He further claimed that if it was a part of the real estate, it was taken without committing a trespass, and with the tacit consent of the owners of such real estate, and that thereby it became his personal property of which he was lawfully possessed, and at least that he had acquired such an interest in it as would enable him to hold it against any person except the owner of the land or some person claiming under the owner.

The defendant * * * claimed, as matter of law, that if the manure was always personal estate, or became personal estate after being scraped up into heaps, the plaintiff, by leaving it from eight o'clock in the evening until noon the next day, abandoned all right of possession which he might have had, and could not, therefore, maintain his action.

The court ruled adversely to the claims of the plaintiff and held that on the facts proved the plaintiff had not made out a sufficient interest in, or right of possession to, the subject matter in dispute, to authorize a recovery in the suit, and rendered judgment for the defendant.

The plaintiff moved for a new trial for error in this ruling of the court.

■ PARK, J. * * * The manure originally belonged to the travelers whose animals dropped it, but it being worthless to them was immediately abandoned; and whether it then became the property of the borough of Stamford which owned the fee of the land on which the manure lay, it is unnecessary to determine; for, if it did, * * * the removal of the filth would be an improvement to the borough, and no objection was made by any one to the use that the plaintiff attempted to make of it. Considering the character of such accumulations upon highways in cities and villages, and the light in which they are everywhere regarded in closely settled communities, we cannot believe that the borough in this instance would have had any objection to the act of the plaintiff in removing a nuisance that affected the public health and the appearance of the streets. At all events, we think the facts of the case show a sufficient right in the plaintiff to the immediate possession of the property as against a mere wrong doer.

The defendant appears before the court in no enviable light. He does not pretend that he had a right to the manure, even when scattered upon the highway, superior to that of the plaintiff; but after the plaintiff had changed its original condition and greatly enhanced its value by his labor, he seized and appropriated to his own use the fruits of the plaintiff's outlay, and now seeks immunity from responsibility on the ground that the plaintiff was a wrong doer as well as himself. The conduct of the defendant is in keeping with his claim, and neither commends itself to the favorable consideration of the court. The plaintiff had the peaceable and quiet possession of the property; and we deem this sufficient until the borough of Stamford shall make complaint.

It is further claimed that if the plaintiff had a right to the property by virtue of occupancy, he lost the right when he ceased to retain the actual possession of the manure after scraping it into heaps.

We do not question the general doctrine, that where the right by occupancy exists, it exists no longer than the party retains the actual possession of the property, or till he appropriates it to his own use by removing it to some other place. If he leaves the property at the place where it was discovered, and does nothing whatsoever to enhance its value or change its nature, his right by occupancy is unquestionably gone. But the question is, if a party finds property comparatively worthless, as the plaintiff found the property in question, owing to its scattered condition upon the highway, and greatly increases its value by his labor and expense, does he lose his right if he leaves it a reasonable time to procure the means to take it away, when such means are necessary for its removal?

Suppose a teamster with a load of grain, while traveling the highway, discovers a rent in one of his bags, and finds that his grain is scattered upon the road for the distance of a mile. He considers the labor of collecting his corn of more value than the property itself, and he therefore abandons it, and pursues his way. *A* afterwards finds the grain in this condition and gathers it kernel by kernel into heaps by the side of the road, and leaves it a reasonable time to procure the means necessary for its removal. While he is gone for his bag, *B* discovers the grain thus conveniently collected in heaps and appropriates it to his own use. Has *A* any remedy? If he has not, the law in this instance is open to just reproach. We think under such circumstances *A* would have a reasonable time to remove the property, and during such reasonable time his right to it would be protected. If this is so, then the principle applies to the case under consideration.

A reasonable time for the removal of this manure had not elapsed when the defendant seized and converted it to his own use. The statute regulating the rights of parties in the gathering of sea-weed, gives the party who heaps it upon a public beach twenty-four hours in which to remove it, and that length of time for the removal of the property we think would not be unreasonable in most cases like the present one.

We therefore advise the Court of Common Pleas to grant a new trial.

NOTES AND QUESTIONS

1.   Both the trial court and the appeals court appear to accept that the plaintiff (and his workers) did not have "actual possession" of the manure after 8:00 pm on April 6. What then is the correct description of the plaintiff's relationship to the manure after that, which entitles the plaintiff to judgment against the defendant? Is the plaintiff still in "possession" in some sense, although not in "actual" possession? What additional acts would the plaintiff have to perform to be deemed to be in actual possession of the manure?

2.   Should rights of possession to things be limited to those who maintain actual possession of those things? Suppose the plaintiff is standing guard over the manure, and the defendant takes the manure while the plaintiff is looking the other way. Can the defendant now defeat the plaintiff's claim by pointing out that the defendant is now the one in actual possession? As we will see in Chapter IV, the law of larceny and the tort of conversion protect persons in possession of things, but almost invariably the person in actual possession is the one who had taken the thing without the consent of the person previously deemed to be in possession. Does this suggest that "possession" must mean something other than actual possession?

3.   Does raking the manure into piles make the plaintiff now the "owner" of the manure? Suppose the city of Stamford has a street sweeper who comes along at 9:00 pm and sweeps the manure into a cart to take to the city dump. Would the plaintiff have a claim against the city for taking "his" manure?

4.   How important is it to the court's judgment that the plaintiff (or his workers) expended labor in putting the manure into piles? Should the result be different if the plaintiff expended no labor, for example if a valuable piece of fruit fell off a tree into the plaintiff's wagon, which he left overnight to retrieve the next day? What if the defendant could show that lifting the piles into a conveyance and carrying them to the defendant's property entailed

more labor than that expended by the plaintiff in gathering the manure into piles?

5.   Suppose the plaintiff did not gather the manure into piles but had posted a sign on the fence in front of the street, "I hereby claim the manure lying about in the street as my own and will come tomorrow to collect it." Would the plaintiff be entitled to recover against the defendant on these facts, if the defendant came and collected the manure first?

6.   In a part of the opinion not reproduced here, the court considers and dismisses the possibility that the manure was part of the real estate, in this case the public highway. In other contexts, namely farms, manure was considered part of the realty for the reason that the manure and the land were highly complementary. In other words, manure is part of the land in the one case and not the other, based on practical considerations reflected in accepted customs. Is there any problem signaling to potential appropriators which manure is up for grabs and which isn't?

7.   The character of possession in law reflects its origins in everyday life. What counts as possession draws heavily on customs and social norms. The tendency to gravitate to possession to solve problems of conflict and the ease and quickness of signals of possession are well suited for something that people need to apply on the fly. Possession is also correspondingly a cheap method of assessing claims, unlike elaborate systems of proving title we will see later on. For commentary on these and many other issues, see the volume Law and Economics of Possession (Yun-Chien Chang ed., 2015).

2.   SEQUENTIAL POSSESSION ISSUES

What happens if multiple persons serially claim property on some theory other than purchase or gift from the prior owner? This rarely happens, but when it does, it brings out a fundamental proposition about the system of property rights, sometimes called the relativity of title and sometimes referred to as the rejection of the *jus tertii* defense—a defense based on the rights of third parties. Property rights may be good against all the world, but disputes over property usually take the form A v. B, and courts usually ask only as between A and B who has the superior title.

Armory v. Delamirie
King's Bench, 1722.
1 Strange 505, 93 Eng. Rep. 664.

The plaintiff being a chimney sweeper's boy found a jewel and carried it to the defendant's shop (who was a goldsmith) to know what it was, and delivered it into the hands of the apprentice, who under the pretense of weighing it, took out the stones, and calling to the master to let him know it came to three halfpence, the master offered the boy the money, who refused to take it, and insisted to have the thing again; whereupon the apprentice delivered him back the socket without the stones. And now in trover against the master these points were ruled:

1.   That the finder of a jewel, though he does not by such finding acquire an absolute property or ownership, yet he has such a property as will enable him to keep it against all but the rightful owner, and consequently may maintain trover.

2.   That the action will lay against the master, who gives a credit to his apprentice, and is answerable for his neglect.

3.   As to the value of the jewel several of the trade were examined to prove what a jewel of the finest water that would fit the socket would be worth; and the Chief Justice directed the jury, that unless the defendant did produce the jewel, and show it not to be of the finest water, they should presume the strongest against him, and make the value of the best jewels the measure of the damages; which they accordingly did.

NOTES AND QUESTIONS

1.   Although he sold jewelry, Paul de Lamerie was best known as the greatest silversmith of 18th century England. He also had a history of engaging in ethically dubious business practices and at the height of his success allowed his father to be buried in a pauper's grave. The court's solution of ascribing maximum value to the jewel unless the wrongdoer could produce it is often taken as the fountainhead of the adverse inference courts draw against those who have destroyed evidence.

2.   As we shall see, courts are fond of reciting the rule of law announced in the first numbered paragraph of the opinion in *Armory v. Delamirie*. But notice that this rule of law is much broader than was needed to decide the case. The case was a dispute between someone assumed to be the "finder" of a jewel and the shop owner whose apprentice wrongfully converted the jewel when it was handed to the apprentice for purposes of valuation. So we have sequential possession of an object by a finder and a converter. All the court needed to rule for Armory was "that the finder of a jewel, though he does not by such finding acquire an absolute property or ownership, yet he has such a property as will enable him to keep it against a subsequent converter or thief." This narrower rule of law is easy to justify, isn't it? On what possible theory could one defend a rule that allowed thieves to obtain good title to objects they steal from finders? On the other hand, as we shall see, the broad proposition enunciated by the court in support of its ruling, that the finder obtains "such a property as will enable him to keep it against all but the rightful owner," quickly descends into controversy when applied in other factual circumstances.

3.   Suppose Armory stole the jewel from a dresser in a house in which he was cleaning a chimney. Later, the jewel falls through a hole in a pocket in Armory's trousers. Delamirie spots it on the sidewalk and, recognizing its value, claims it as a found object. In a suit by Armory against Delamirie to recover the value of the jewel, what would be the result under the rule of law announced in the principal case? Is this consistent with the outcome we would want to reach as a matter of policy?

4.   A finder, such as Armory, differs from a pure first possessor, like Pierson in *Pierson v. Post*, in two respects. First, when a finder takes possession of an object, the finder does not thereby become the owner. The object is understood to belong to someone else, the true owner, who cannot be identified or located. Thus, whatever rights a finder like Armory has against a third party like Delamirie, the finder's rights are subordinate to those of the true owner (whoever that may be). Second, because the finder's rights remain subordinate to the true owner's, the finder has certain duties toward the true owner. Courts have frequently said in this context that a finder acts as a bailee for the true owner (see Chapter IV for more on bailments). In theory at least, this means the finder may be under a legal duty not to convert the object to the finder's own use, or not to deliver the object to anyone other than the true owner. In practice, since the true owner is the only one who could enforce these duties, as time passes and the true owner fails to appear, the finder may be able to treat the lost object as if it were not different from the finder's own property. But until the statute of limitations for recovery of personal property runs, and the finder can claim title by adverse possession, the finder's title is a qualified one.

5.   Some commentators have advocated a system of rewards for finders. See, e.g., R.H. Helmholz, Equitable Division and the Law of Finders, 52 Fordham L. Rev. 313 (1983); Gideon Parchomovsky, Peter Siegelman & Steve Thel, Of Equal Wrongs and Half Rights, 82 N.Y.U. L. Rev. 738, 770–74, 782–84 (2007). Japan has such a system in its Law Concerning Lost Articles (Ishitsubutsuhō [Law Concerning Lost Articles], Law no. 40 (1899)). Mark West argues that Japan's reputation for getting lost property back to owners stems in large part from its elaborate legal regime of finders' duties to turn in lost property to the police (or to owners of the establishment at which it is found), and of owners' duties to pay rewards of between 5 and 20% of the value of the lost property; possession is awarded to the finder after six months. Much effort is put into teaching this system to schoolchildren. Mark D. West, Losers: Recovering Lost Property in Japan and the United States, 37 Law & Soc'y Rev. 369 (2003). West also reports on an empirical study in which cell phones and wallets were deliberately left at locations in a mixed business-shopping district of Tokyo, in midtown Manhattan, and in front of a New York grocery store catering to a Japanese expatriate clientele (with return rates highest in Tokyo and lowest in New York, and the New York Japanese location in between). Although less well-known, New York law provides that objects worth more than $20 must be turned into the police, and finders can claim the object after a period ranging from 3 months and 10 days to three years and 10 days, depending on the object's value. New York Personal Property Law §§ 252–253.

Clark v. Maloney

Superior Court of Delaware, 1840.
3 Del. 68.

Action of trover to recover the value of ten white pine logs. The logs in question were found by plaintiff floating in the Delaware bay after a great freshet, were taken up and moored with ropes in the mouth of Mispillion creek. They were afterwards in the possession of defendants, who refused to give them up, alleging that they had found them adrift and floating up the creek.

■ BAYARD, CHIEF JUSTICE, charged the jury.—

The plaintiff must show *first*, that the logs were his property; and *secondly*, that they were converted by the defendants to their own use. In support of his right of property, the plaintiff relies upon the fact of his possession of the logs. They were taken up by him, adrift in the Delaware bay, and secured by a stake at the mouth of Mispillion creek. Possession is certainly prima facie evidence of property. It is called *prima facie* evidence because it may be rebutted by evidence of better title, but in the absence of better title it is as effective a support of title as the most conclusive evidence could be. It is for this reason, that *the finder of a chattel, though he does not acquire an absolute property in it, yet has such a property, as will enable him to keep it against all but the rightful owner*. The defence consists, not in showing that the defendants are the rightful owners, or claim under the rightful owner; but that the logs were found by them adrift in Mispillion creek, having been loosened from their fastening either by accident or design, and they insist that their title is as good as that of the plaintiff. But it is a well settled rule of law that the loss of a chattel does not change the right of property; and for the same reason that the original loss of these logs by the rightful owner, did not change his absolute property in them, but he might have maintained trover against the plaintiff upon refusal to deliver them, so the subsequent loss did not divest the *special* property of the plaintiff. It follows, therefore, that as the plaintiff has shown a special property in these logs, which he never abandoned, and which enabled him to keep them against all the world but the rightful owner, he is entitled to a verdict.

Verdict for the plaintiff.

NOTES AND QUESTIONS

1.   Although the facts are a bit cryptic, it appears that *Clark v. Maloney* involves sequential possession by two finders, Finder 1 (Clark) and Finder 2 (Maloney). The court paraphrases the broad rule of law laid down in *Armory v. Delamirie*, and rules for Finder 1. But couldn't the court cite the very same proposition in support of a ruling for Finder 2? If *Armory* would equally support a ruling for either plaintiff or defendant, obviously we need some other principle of law to decide the case. What is that principle?

2.   Do you think the court in *Clark* may have harbored suspicions about the defendants' claim that that they had found the logs "adrift and floating up the creek?" In general, if the rule in cases of Finder 1 versus Finder 2 were that the property goes to Finder 2, would this indirectly encourage theft? The current possessor (who might be a thief) would always

claim that he was a finder, and the burden would be on the first finder to disprove this claim. This might be difficult to do.

3.   Suppose we want to design the rules in these sequential possession cases so as to maximize the chances that the true owner will be able to recover the property. Which party is more likely to be located by the true owner—Finder 1 or Finder 2?

Anderson v. Gouldberg

Supreme Court of Minnesota, 1892.
53 N.W. 636.

This action was brought by the plaintiff, Sigfrid Anderson, against defendants, partners as Gouldberg & Anderson, to recover the possession of ninety-three pine logs, marked L S X, or the value thereof. Plaintiff claimed to have cut the logs on section 22, township 27, range 15, Isanti County, in the winter of 1889–1890, and to have hauled them to a mill on section 6, from which place defendants took them. The title to section 22 was in strangers, and plaintiff showed no authority from the owners to cut the logs thereon. Defendants claimed that the logs were cut on section 26, in the adjoining township, on land belonging to the Ann River Logging Company, and that they [the defendants] took the logs by direction of the Logging Company, who were the owners. The court charged that even if the plaintiff got possession of the logs as a trespasser, his title would be good as against any one except the real owner or some one who had authority from the owner to take them, and left the case to the jury on the question as to whether the logs were cut on the land of the Logging Company, and taken by defendants under its authority. The jury found a verdict for the plaintiff and assessed his damages at $153.45. From an order denying their motion for a new trial, defendants appeal[.] * * *

■ MITCHELL, J. It is settled by the verdict of the jury that the logs in controversy were not cut upon the land of the defendants, and consequently that they were entire strangers to the property. For the purposes of this appeal, we must also assume the fact to be (as there was evidence from which the jury might have so found) that the plaintiffs obtained possession of the logs in the first instance by trespassing upon the land of some third party. Therefore the only question is whether bare possession of property, though wrongfully obtained, is sufficient title to enable the party enjoying it to maintain replevin against a mere stranger, who takes it from him. We had supposed that this was settled in the affirmative as long ago, at least, as the early case of Armory v. Delamirie, (1722) 1 Strange 504 (K.B.), so often cited on that point. When it is said that to maintain replevin the plaintiff's possession must have been lawful, it means merely that it must have been lawful as against the person who deprived him of it; and possession is good title against all the world except those having a better title. Counsel says that possession only raises a presumption of title, which, however, may be rebutted.

Rightly understood, this is correct; but counsel misapplies it. One who takes property from the possession of another can only rebut this presumption by showing a superior title in himself, or in some way connecting himself with one who has. One who has acquired the possession of property, whether by finding, bailment, or by mere tort, has a right to retain that possession as against a mere wrongdoer who is a stranger to the property. Any other rule would lead to an endless series of unlawful seizures and reprisals in every case where property had once passed out of the possession of the rightful owner.

Order affirmed.

NOTES AND QUESTIONS

1. Given the jury's rejection of the defendants' story that they were acting on the authority of the true owners, *Anderson v. Gouldberg* becomes a case of Converter 1 (Anderson) versus Converter 2 (Gouldberg and partner). The court regards the rule of law in *Armory v. Delamirie* as resolving such a dispute. Do you agree? Doesn't the court substitute an even broader proposition of law for the one announced in *Armory*? Is this broader proposition justifiable as a matter of policy in all circumstances involving persons who acquire possession wrongfully? For example, does this broader proposition mean it would be improper for a Good Samaritan to chase down a purse snatcher who has stolen a purse from a third party?

2. Even if we reject the idea that Converter 1 should prevail against subsequent possessors who do not act wrongfully (say a Good Samaritan who recovers the property or a finder), the question remains: Who should prevail in the case of Converter 1 versus Converter 2? Are you persuaded by the court's statement that Converter 1 should prevail because "[a]ny other rule would lead to an endless series of unlawful seizures and reprisals in every case where property had once passed out of the possession of the rightful owner?" Could it not be argued that a rule of "no property among thieves" would reduce the economic returns to thievery, and thus reduce the incidence of theft?

3. As might be expected, there are relatively few reported decisions involving lawsuits between a Converter 1 and a Converter 2. But there is at least one other reported decision, *Russell v. Hill*, 34 S.E. 640 (N.C. 1899), that reaches the opposite result to the one in *Anderson v. Gouldberg*. This was yet another dispute about logs that had been wrongfully taken by A, and then were taken wrongfully from A by B. The court permitted B to defeat an action in trover by A by showing that the true owner of the logs was C. In support of this outcome, the court stated in part:

> [I]n some of the English books, and in some of the Reports of our sister states, cases might be found to the contrary, but * * * those cases were all founded upon a misapprehension of the principle laid down in the case of Armory v. Delamirie, 1 Strange, 505. There a chimney sweep found a lost jewel. He took it into his possession, as he had a right to do, and was the owner, because of having it in possession, unless the true owner should become known. That

owner was not known, and it was properly decided that trover would lie in favor of the finder against the defendant, to whom he had handed it for inspection. But the court said the case would have been very different if the owner had been known[.] * * *

Id. at 640–41. Is this an accurate reading of *Armory v. Delamirie?*

4.   Suppose we want to design the rules in these sequential possession cases to maximize the chances that the true owner will be able to recover the property. Which party is more likely to be found by the true owner— Converter 1 or Converter 2? Is it easier or harder to answer this question than it is when the choice is between Finder 1 and Finder 2?

Relativity of Title and Rejection of the *Jus Tertii* Defense

Armory v. Delamirie and cases like *Clark v. Maloney* and *Anderson v. Gouldberg* are often cited for the proposition that an action to protect possession of property cannot be defeated by setting up a superior title in a third party (the *jus tertii*). The leading case for this view is often said to be *Jeffries v. The Great Western Railway*, (1856) 119 Eng. Rep. 680 (Q.B.). This was an action in trover to recover damages for wrongful taking of some railroad cars; the defendant sought to defeat the action by proving that title to the cars had been assigned to someone else. In rejecting the defense, Chief Justice Campbell said:

> I am of the opinion that the law is that a person possessed of goods as his property has a good title as against every stranger, and that one who takes them from him, having no title in himself, is a wrongdoer, and cannot defend himself by showing that there was title in some third person; for against a wrongdoer possession is a title. The law is * * * essential for the interests of society, that peaceable possession should not be disturbed by wrongdoers. * * * It is not disputed that the jus tertii cannot be set up as a defense to an action of trespass for disturbing the possession. In this respect I see no difference between trespass and trover; for in truth the presumption of law is that the person who has possession has the property. Can that presumption be rebutted by evidence that the property was in a third person, when offered as a defense by one who admits that he himself had no title and was a wrongdoer when he converted the goods? I am of the opinion that this cannot be done[.] * * *

The proposition that a defendant cannot invoke the *jus tertii* to defeat an action to protect possession can be defended on either a substantive or procedural theory. The excerpt from *Jeffries* invokes the substantive theory: One of the objects of the law is to protect peaceful possession; hence, someone who wrongfully interferes with peaceful possession should not be let off the hook by invoking the superior rights of some third party. The procedural theory invokes the bilateral nature of common-law litigation, and the availability of direct testimony by the two opposing parties in such litigation. A sues B; A testifies to what A knows, B testifies to what B knows; the jury decides which party is the more credible. To allow one of the parties to put in issue the rights of a third party not before the court would present potential difficulties of proof, particularly in a time before title registration acts when the best evidence of title would be deeds in the possession of the true owner.

E. THE PRINCIPLE OF ACCESSION

Related to but distinct from possession is what commonly travels under the heading "accession." In general, accession tells us what goes with what: If someone owns A then that person owns some closely related and in some sense subordinate resource B. In a sense, accession tells us what a legal "thing" is: the owner of land owns the trees, structures, airspace, minerals, etc., associated with the land. Sometimes these designations can be altered by transactions, as where someone owns a house but another owns the land beneath it.

Like possession, accession can also be viewed as an original acquisition principle. Ownership of some unclaimed or contested resource is assigned to the owner of some *other* resource that has a particularly prominent relationship to the unclaimed or contested resource. In each case, the assignment of ownership occurs without regard to any voluntary conveyance of the unclaimed or contested resource, and without regard to whether the existing owner is in possession of the contested resource. See David Hume, A Treatise of Human Nature 327 (David Fate Norton & Mary J. Norton eds., 2000) (1739).

1. CROPS AND VEGETATION

One familiar manifestation of accession involves trees, bushes, crops, and flowers that grow on the land. The law generally distinguishes between perennial vegetation—forms of plant life that rejuvenate from year to year without replanting—sometimes called *fructus naturales*, and annual vegetation—forms of plant life that must be replanted on an annual or other periodic basis—sometimes called *fructus industriales*. The general principle is that perennials are deemed to belong to the owner of the soil on which they grow. Similarly, the owner of the soil also is deemed to own fruits, nuts, berries, and flowers that grow on perennials. In contrast, annuals are deemed to belong to the person *in possession* of the soil on which they grow. Why the difference? Often, of course, the owner will also be the one in possession of the soil. But agricultural land is often leased, in which case the tenant is the one in possession of the land during the term of the lease, not the owner, who is the lessor or landlord. If the tenant plants a crop of wheat, corn, or soybeans during the term of the lease, the law recognizes that under some circumstances the tenant is entitled to harvest and sell the crop, not the landlord. See generally Ray Andrews Brown, The Law of Personal Property § 17.2 (3d ed. 1975).

An interesting wrinkle goes by the name of the doctrine of *emblements*. Suppose a tenant farmer has what is called a tenancy at will, meaning the landlord is free to terminate the lease at any time. While the tenancy lasts, the tenant plants an annual crop of hay or wheat. Then, before the crop can be harvested, the landlord terminates the lease, resumes possession, and claims the crop as his own. In these circumstances, the law declares that the tenant, although no longer legally in possession, has the right to enter the land to cultivate and harvest the crop. The doctrine of emblements is an obvious response to a type of opportunistic behavior by landlords, which as we shall see (Chapter IV) is a familiar theme in the law of equity. It does not appear, however, that the doctrine of emblements required the intervention of a court of equity—the common law judges came up with this exception on their own. The doctrine also shares a commonality with cases involving mistaken improvers of personal property, as in *Wetherbee v. Green*, infra, insofar as tenant, through his or her labor in planting the crop, is regarded as having a more prominent relationship to the crop than the absentee landlord.

NOTE

The understanding that things that sprout from the soil belong to the one who has the superior claim to the soil is perhaps the most intuitive and universal application of the principle of accession. Recall the statement in *International News*, supra, that one is generally entitled to reap what one has sown. Indeed, this understanding can be seen as the paradigmatic example of the most general implication of the principle accession: that improvements which enhance the value of a thing belong to the person with the superior claim to the thing being improved. Thus, if the owner of a suburban home works assiduously to plant attractive bushes and flowers, and nurtures their growth and appearance, the owner is understood to be the one who captures the enhanced value of the home, whether measured in terms of self-satisfaction or resale value. Or, to take another example, if someone buys an old car rusting away in a barn, and works to restore it to its original condition, the owner of the old car is understood to be entitled to the improved version. Of course, the principle also works in reverse: If one neglects the upkeep and appearance of a home, or lets their car collect dents and scratches without repair, the owner of the thing suffers the diminished value of the thing. Viewed from this perspective, the principle of accession is one of the most powerful aspects of a system of property, creating a pervasive incentive to invest in and improve things that are owned.

2. INCREASE

Another example of the principle of accession, mentioned by Hume, is that "the offspring of our cattle . . . [are] esteem'd our property, even before possession." This is known as the doctrine of *increase*. As summarized in one opinion, "The general rule, in the absence of an agreement to the contrary, is that the offspring or increase of tame or domestic animals belongs to the owner of the dam or mother. . . . In this respect the common law follows the civil law and is founded on the maxim, *partus sequitur ventrem* [the offspring follows the mother—eds.]. . . . Furthermore, the increase of the increase, ad infinitum, of domestic animals comes within the rule and belongs to the owner of the original stock." Carruth v. Easterling, 150 So.2d 852, 855 (Miss. 1963) (quoting 4 Am. Jur. 2d Animals § 10).

In *Carruth*, a herd of cattle owned by Easterling wandered onto a farm owned by Carruth. Most were eventually returned, but a dispute arose between the parties as to whether Easterling had promised Carruth that he could keep two cows as compensation for the inconvenience of the trespass. When Easterling sued for the return of the two cows, a further dispute arose about whether Easterling was also entitled to a calf that had been born to one of the cows while being kept in custody by Carruth. The Mississippi Supreme Court held that the calf also belonged to Easterling, even though it had likely been conceived while on Carruth's land.

NOTES AND QUESTIONS

1.   The doctrine of increase is apparently one of those legal rules recognized in every known legal system that addresses the issue. See Felix Cohen, Dialogue on Private Property, 9 Rutgers L. Rev. 357, 366 (1954). Moreover, it is a rule, not a standard: Courts have not carved out exceptions for calves sired by prize-winning bulls, or for calves raised at great expense by someone other than the owner of the mother. Id. One exception in English law was for cygnets or baby swans. The Case of Swans, (1592) 77 Eng. Rep. 435 (K.B.). Noting that, unusually among animals, swans remain monogamous throughout their reproductive years, the court ordered the cygnets divided equally between the owner of the cock and the owner of the hen. Id. at 437.

2.   What is the explanation for the doctrine of increase? Is it because of the evidentiary difficulty in establishing paternity, as suggested by *The Case of Swans*? If so, does the advent of modern genetic testing suggest the doctrine will start to break down? Or is the doctrine grounded in the assumption that young animals are generally dependent on their mothers for nurture and upbringing? On this understanding, assigning ownership of the offspring to the owner of the mother helps ensure that this maternal connection remains unbroken. Are these pragmatic considerations sufficient to explain the universal and deeply entrenched nature of the rule? Does it also rest on a psychological perception of the "closeness" of the relationship between the offspring and the mother? Can it be said that in some sense the mother is "in possession" of the offspring? Is the principle of accession another principle of ownership grounded in intuitions about possession? See 2 Blackstone, Commentaries *404 ("The doctrine of property arising from *accession* is also grounded on the right of occupancy.").

3.   If technology evolves to the point that cloning of animals is widespread, will the doctrine of increase cease to determine the rights to

offspring? If the cloning requires a fertilized egg to be carried to birth by a female animal, arguably many of the rationales for increase will continue to apply. But what if an artificial womb or other technology is devised that allows animals to be generated without any obvious mother?

NOTE ON EXPLAINING THE PRINCIPLE OF ACCESSION

The principle of accession can be regarded as an alternative principle of acquisition, distinct from first possession. Like first possession, accession assigns property rights in unowned things, but instead of picking out someone who has expended labor at bringing the thing under her control (as in first possession), the principle of accession assigns the unowned thing to the owner of some prominent other thing. Thus, as we have seen, crops and vegetation are assigned to the person with superior rights to the soil, and the doctrine of increase allocates the offspring of an animal to the owner of the animal's mother. Both first possession and accession identify a singular "winner" in the potential competition to be the owner of the unowned thing. One advantage of accession is that it typically identifies this winner without her having to do anything, and it does not encourage the wasteful racing behavior often associated with first possession, discovery, or creation. (Except insofar as accession makes ownership of the "prominent" thing even more valuable, which sometimes might make contests over *that* thing more intense.) Especially when a new and unexpected resource becomes valuable, the principle of accession assigns it immediately and without further ado. Accession also enhances the incentives to improve property, insofar as new increments in value (like baby animals born to livestock or crops that sprout up on the land) are automatically assigned to the existing owner of the prominently connected asset. But this strength is also a weakness in that the accession principle, especially if pushed very far, gives rise to unearned windfalls, and makes the rich get richer, as it were. See Thomas W. Merrill, Accession and Original Ownership, 1 J. Legal Analysis 459 (2009). Accession is particularly important when new valued attributes come into focus, such as solar or wind resources. See, e.g., Yael R. Lifshitz, Rethinking Original Ownership, 66 U. Toronto L.J. 513 (2016); Note, Accession on the Frontiers of Property, 133 Harv. L. Rev. 2381 (2020).

How is the prominence relationship between an unowned and an owned thing established? Certainly, one can think of various utilitarian arguments supporting various accession doctrines. But it has also been argued, starting with the philosopher David Hume, that accession is also—and perhaps more importantly—a function of human psychology, or what Hume called "the imagination":

> This source of property can never be explain'd but from the imagination ... [F]rom an object, that is related to us, we acquire a relation to every other object which is related to it, and so on, till the thought loses the chain by too long a progress. However the relation may weaken by each remove, 'tis not immediately destroy'd; but frequently connects two objects by means of an intermediate one, which is related to both. And this principle is of such force as to give rise to the right of *accession*, and causes us to

acquire the property not only of such objects as we are immediately posses'd of, but also of such as are closely connected with them.

David Hume, A Treatise of Human Nature, 327 n.75 (David Fate Norton & Mary J. Norton eds., 2000) (1739). He went on to give examples such as "dominion" over the Orkneys, the Hebrides, the Isle of Man, and the Isle of Wight going with dominion over (much larger) Great Britain, not vice versa, and more generally, "small objects become accessions to great ones, and not great to small." Id. Hume's theory of property generally rests on convention, and the accession principle, like possession, rests on a preference for conforming to a widespread pattern of behavior—such as respecting each other's possession—that could have been otherwise.

In a modern economic account that takes off from Hume, Robert Sugden recasts Hume's account in terms of a division game. His primary example is the major North Sea oil and gas reserves discovered in the 1960s, which gave rise to the question of how to divide the find, which was of an as-yet indeterminate extent, among various nations. The solution adopted was to assign portions of the seabed for purposes of hydrocarbon development to the country whose coastline was nearest, which greatly favored Norway, and to a lesser extent Britain. West Germany with a more distant North Sea coast came out badly. Powerful countries like the United States and the Soviet Union got nothing, as did poor countries around the world, which could have used the extra funds. Sugden sees the closeness relationship as defining "prominence" in this context, rather than the geology of the sea bed itself, country size, population, military might, or even default international law. In an experimental setting (connecting dots, for example) one can demonstrate that closeness is often the relation that is psychologically most prominent. See Robert Sugden, The Economics of Rights, Co-operation and Welfare, 91–92, 101–03 (2d ed. 2004). Significantly, Sugden argues that not only the simplicity but also the very arbitrariness of the closeness relationship recommended it as the basis for the division: Unlike some of the other criteria and procedures (such as "equal division"), the accession-style solution based on closeness of coastline was not open to special pleading and extended argument or, one might add, manipulation.

What more generally is the source of the conventions of accession and possession, or even ideas about what counts as possession? Sugden suggests that it is not simply a matter of might makes right. But how do expectations converge on the proximity rule? Some solutions are said to be "focal" in that people can guess each other's answers without communication. In a famous experiment, people at Yale were asked where they would go and when, if told to meet the next day in New York City a friend who had been given similar instructions but with whom no communication was possible. Despite the enormous number of possibilities, a majority picked Grand Central Station and almost all chose noon, exhibiting a high degree of what Thomas Schelling termed "tacit cooperation." Thomas C. Schelling, The Strategy of Conflict 54–56 (1963). Focal solutions to situations that can be modeled as cooperative games draw on common knowledge, but some have argued that these solutions can arise from hard-wired aspects of mind as well. Can this "focal" behavior based on either source be said to be rational? For a discussion of these issues and their relevance to law, see Richard H. McAdams, A Focal Point Theory of Expressive Law, 86 Va. L. Rev. 1649, 1659–63 (2000). What if possessory behavior were conclusively shown to reflect a hard-wired territorial psychology? See, e.g., Bart J. Wilson, The Property Species: Mine, Yours, and the Human Mind (2020); Jeffrey Evans Stake, The Property "Instinct," 359 Phil. Trans. Royal Soc'y Lond. B 1763 (2004). Animals' territoriality has facilitated property in another way: Dogs can be trained to defend humans' property boundaries making them quite cheap to defend, whereas enforcing norms of good behavior requires judgment that is beyond a dog's capacity. See Robert C. Ellickson, Property in Land, 102 Yale L.J. 1315, 1329 (1993). If property in land is grounded in animal territoriality (people's or dogs') does that make it more legitimate, less legitimate, or neither?

In this part we primarily explore the principle of accession as a principle of acquisition, but accession serves another, more pervasive role in property. Accession can be seen as defining the scope of property claims. When someone engages in acts of first possession, we need to know what is being claimed. How do we know that a hunter is claiming the whole fox and not the tail only? When someone claims the surface of land by an act of first possession (rare these days) or adverse possession, how do we know that the subsurface and the air rights are being claimed? Here the definition of a thing (like a fox) and the *ad coelum* principle, see Section 3 infra, tell us how much and exactly what is being claimed. Even someone as identified with first possession as the philosopher John Locke recognized the need within first possession itself for some principle to tell us what the scope of the claim should be. In an echo of the doctrine of accession, he states that labor should give rise to property in a thing when "labour makes the far greatest part of the value of [the thing]," John Locke, The Second Treatise of Government, in Two Treatises of Government 297 (Peter Laslett ed., Cambridge Univ. Press 1988) (1690). He goes on to discuss in detail how labor forms the overwhelming fraction of the value in all sorts of property from agricultural land, to bread, wine, silk and other familiar examples from accession theory. Id. at 297–98. For a discussion of accession and the scope of claims, see Henry E. Smith, Intellectual Property as Property: Delineating Entitlement in Information, 116 Yale L.J. 1742, 1770–77 (2007); see also Christopher M. Newman, Transformation in Property and Copyright, 56 Vill. L. Rev. 251, 280–88 (2011).

Ask yourself as you go through the materials in this Part how people converge on an answer to the questions posed by accession: What goes with what, or, what is a thing?

3. THE *AD COELUM* PRINCIPLE

"*Ad coelum*" is short for the Latin maxim *cujus est solum, ejus est usque ad coelum et ad inferos*. This has been translated as "To whomever the soil belongs, he owns also to the sky and to the depths." Black's Law Dictionary (6th ed. 1990). We encountered the doctrine in connection with *Hinman v. Pacific Air Transport*, the airplane overflight case in Chapter I. The doctrine also applies to resources discovered beneath the surface, such as minerals, oil and gas deposits, or, as in the next case, caves.

Edwards v. Sims

Court of Appeals of Kentucky, 1929.
232 Ky. 791, 24 S.W.2d 619.

■ Opinion by COMMISSIONER STANLEY. This case presents a novel question.*

[About [thirteen] years ago L. P. Edwards discovered a cave under land belonging to him and his wife, Sally Edwards. The entrance to the cave is on the Edwards land. Edwards named it the "Great Onyx Cave," no doubt because of the rock crystal formations within it which are known as onyx. This cave is located in the cavernous area of Kentucky, and is only about three miles distant from the world-famous Mammoth Cave. Its proximity to Mammoth Cave, which for many years has had an international reputation as an underground wonder, as well as its beautiful formations, led Edwards to embark upon a program of advertising and exploitation for the purpose of bringing visitors to his cave. Circulars were printed and distributed, signs were erected along the roads, persons were employed and stationed along the highways to solicit the patronage of passing travelers, and thus the fame of the Great Onyx Cave spread from year to year, until eventually, and before the beginning of the present litigation, it was a well-known and well-patronized cave. Edwards built a hotel near the mouth of the cave to care for travelers. He improved and widened the footpaths and avenues in the cave, and ultimately secured a stream of tourists who paid entrance fees sufficient not only to cover the cost of operation, but also to yield a substantial revenue in addition thereto. The authorities in charge of the development of the Mammoth Cave area as a national park undertook to secure the Great Onyx Cave through condemnation proceedings, and in that suit the value of the cave was fixed by a jury at $396,000. In April, 1928, F. P. Lee, an adjoining landowner, filed this suit against Edwards and the heirs of Sally Edwards, claiming that a portion of the cave was under his land, and praying for damages, for an accounting of the profits which resulted from the operation of the cave, and for an injunction prohibiting Edwards and his associates from further trespassing upon or exhibiting any part of the cave under Lee's land. At the inception of this litigation, Lee undertook to procure a survey of the cave in order that it might be determined what portion of it was on his land. The chancellor ordered that a survey be made, and Edwards prosecuted an appeal from that order to this court. The appeal was dismissed because it was not from a final judgment. Edwards v. Lee, 19 S.W.2d 992 (Ky. 1929).] It was held that the order was interlocutory and consequently one from which no appeal would lie.

---

*   [The next paragraph is taken from a subsequent opinion on remedies.—eds.]

Figure 2-4

Postcard published by the Great Onyx Cave Hotel (L.P. Edwards, Proprietor). Courtesy Kentucky Library, Western Kentucky University.

Following that decision, this original proceeding was filed in this court by the appellants in that case (who were defendants below) against Hon. N. P. Sims, judge of the Edmonson circuit court, seeking a writ of prohibition to prevent him enforcing the order and punishing the petitioners for contempt for any disobedience of it. It is alleged by the petitioners that the lower court was without jurisdiction or authority to make the order, and that their cave property and their right of possession and privacy will be wrongfully and illegally invaded, and that they will be greatly and irreparably injured and damaged without having an adequate remedy, since the damage will have been suffered before there can be an adjudication of their rights on a final appeal. * * *

There is but little authority of particular and special application to caves and cave rights. In few places, if any, can be found similar works of nature of such grandeur and of such unique and marvelous character as to give to caves a commercial value sufficient to cause litigation as those peculiar to Edmonson and other counties in Kentucky. The reader will find of interest the address on "The Legal Story of Mammoth Cave" by Hon. John B. Rodes, of Bowling Green, before the 1929 Session of the Kentucky State Bar Association, published in its proceedings. In Cox v. Colossal Cavern Co., 276 S.W. 540 (Ky. 1925), the subject of cave rights was considered, and this court held there may be a severance of the estate in the property, that is, that one may own the surface and another the cave rights, the conditions being quite similar to but not exactly like those of mineral lands. But there is no such severance involved in this case, as

not a lot of precedent

it appears that the defendants are the owners of the land and have in it an absolute right.

Cujus est solum, ejus est usque ad coelum [et] ad infernos (to whomsoever the soil belongs, he owns also to the sky and to the depths), is an old maxim and rule. It is that the owner of realty, unless there has been a division of the estate, is entitled to the free and unfettered control of his own land above, upon, and beneath the surface. So whatever is in a direct line between the surface of the land and the center of the earth belongs to the owner of the surface. Ordinarily that ownership cannot be interfered with or infringed by third persons. There are, however, certain limitations on the right of enjoyment of possession of all property, such as its use to the detriment or interference with a neighbor and burdens which it must bear in common with property of a like kind.

With this doctrine of ownership in mind, we approach the question as to whether a court of equity has a transcendent power to invade that right through its agents for the purpose of ascertaining the truth of a matter before it, which fact thus disclosed will determine certainly whether or not the owner is trespassing upon his neighbor's property. Our attention has not been called to any domestic case, nor have we found one, in which the question was determined either directly or by analogy. It seems to the court, however, that there can be little differentiation, so far as the matter now before us is concerned, between caves and mines. And as declared in 40 C. J. 947:

> A court of equity, however, has the inherent power, independent of statute, to compel a mine owner to permit an inspection of his works at the suit of a party who can show reasonable ground for suspicion that his lands are being trespassed upon through them, and may issue an injunction to permit such inspection.

There is some limitation upon this inherent power, such as that the person applying for such an inspection must show a bona fide claim and allege facts showing a necessity for the inspection and examination of the adverse party's property; and, of course, the party whose property is to be inspected must have had an opportunity to be heard in relation thereto. In the instant case it appears that these conditions were met. The respondent cites several cases from other jurisdictions in which this power has been recognized and exercised. * * *

We can see no difference in principle between the invasion of a mine on adjoining property to ascertain whether or not the minerals are being extracted from under the applicant's property and an inspection of this respondent's property through his cave to ascertain whether or not he is trespassing under this applicant's property.

It appears that before making this order the court had before him surveys of the surface of both properties and the conflicting opinions of witnesses as to whether or not the Great Onyx Cave extended under the surface of the plaintiff's land. This opinion evidence was of comparatively little value, and as the chancellor (now respondent) suggested, the controversy can be quickly and accurately settled by surveying the cave; and "if defendants are correct in their contention this survey will establish it beyond all doubt and their title to this cave will be forever quieted. If the survey shows the Great Onyx Cave extends under the lands of plaintiffs, defendants should be glad to know this fact and should be just as glad to cease trespassing upon plaintiff's lands, if they are in fact doing so." The peculiar nature of these conditions, it seems to us, makes it imperative and necessary in the administration of justice that the survey should have been ordered and should be made.

access to survey data will settle dispute — so why should D even be nervous if there is no problem?

It appearing that the circuit court is not exceeding its jurisdiction or proceeding erroneously, the claim of irreparable injury need not be given consideration. It is only when the inferior court is acting erroneously, *and* great or irreparable damage will result, *and* there is no adequate remedy by appeal, that a writ of prohibition will issue restraining the other tribunal, as held by authorities cited above.

The writ of prohibition is therefore denied.

■ LOGAN, J. (dissenting). The majority opinion allows that to be done which will prove of incalculable injury to Edwards without benefiting Lee, who is asking that this injury be done. I must dissent from the majority opinion, confessing that I may not be able to show, by any legal precedent, that the opinion is wrong, yet having an abiding faith in my own judgment that it is wrong.

It deprives Edwards of rights which are valuable, and perhaps destroys the value of his property, upon the motion of one who may have no interest in that which it takes away, and who could not subject it to his dominion or make any use of it, if he should establish that which he seeks to establish in the new suit wherein the survey is sought.

It sounds well in the majority opinion to tritely say that he who owns the surface of real estate, without reservation, owns from the center of the earth to the outmost sentinel of the solar system. The age-old statement, adhered to in the majority opinion as the law, in truth and fact, is not true now and never has been. I can subscribe to no doctrine which makes the owner of the surface also the owner of the atmosphere filling illimitable space. Neither can I subscribe to the doctrine that he who owns the surface is also the owner of the vacant spaces in the bowels of the earth.

no one takes ad coelum literally

The rule should be that he who owns the surface is the owner of everything that may be taken from the earth and used for his profit or happiness. Anything which he may take is thereby subjected to his dominion, and it may be well said that it belongs to him. I concede the soundness of that rule, which is supported by the cases cited in the majority opinion; but they have no application to the question before the court in this case. They relate mainly to mining rights; that is, to substances under the surface which the owner may subject to his dominion. But no man can bring up from the depths of the earth the Stygian darkness and make it serve his purposes; neither can he subject to his dominion the bottom of the ways in the caves on which visitors tread, and for these reasons the owner of the surface has no right in such a cave which the law should, or can, protect because he has nothing of value therein, unless, perchance, he owns an entrance into it and has subjected the subterranean passages to his dominion.

RULE
from dissent

A cave or cavern should belong absolutely to him who owns its entrance, and this ownership should extend even to its utmost reaches if he has explored and connected these reaches with the entrance. When the surface owner has discovered a cave and prepared it for purposes of exhibition, no one ought to be allowed to disturb him in his dominion over that which he has conquered and subjected to his uses.

It is well enough to hang to our theories and ideas, but when there is an effort to apply old principles to present-day conditions, and they will not fit, then it becomes necessary for a readjustment, and principles and facts as they exist in this age must be made conformable. For these reasons the old sophistry that the owner of the surface of land is the owner of everything from zenith to nadir must be reformed, and the reason why a reformation is necessary is because the theory was never true in the past, but no occasion arose that required the testing of it. Man had no dominion over the air until recently, and, prior to his conquering the air, no one had any occasion to question the claim of the surface owner that the air above him was subject to his dominion. Naturally the air above him should be subject to his dominion in so far as the use of the space is necessary for his proper enjoyment of the surface, but further than that he has no right in it separate from that of the public at large. The true principle should be announced to the effect that a man who owns the surface, without reservation, owns not only the land itself, but everything upon, above, or under it which he may use for his profit or pleasure, and which he may subject to his dominion and control. But further than this his ownership cannot extend. It should not be held that he owns that which he cannot use and which is of no benefit to him, and which may be of benefit to others.

Shall a man be allowed to stop airplanes flying above his land because he owns the surface? He cannot subject the atmosphere through which they fly to his profit or pleasure; therefore, so long as airplanes do not injure him, or interfere with the use of his property, he should be helpless to prevent their flying above his dominion. Should the waves that transmit intelligible sound through the atmosphere be allowed to pass over the lands of surface-owners? If they take nothing from him and in no way interfere with his profit or pleasure, he should be powerless to prevent their passage?

If it be a trespass to enter on the premises of the landowner, ownership meaning what the majority opinion holds that it means, the aviator who flies over the land of one who owns the surface, without his consent, is guilty of a trespass as defined by the common law and is subject to fine or imprisonment, or both, in the discretion of a jury.

If he who owns the surface does not own and control the atmosphere above him, he does not own and control vacuity beneath the surface. He owns everything beneath the surface that he can subject to his profit or pleasure, but he owns nothing more. Therefore, let it be written that a man who owns land does, in truth and in fact, own everything from zenith to nadir, but only for the use that he can make of it for his profit or pleasure. He owns nothing which he cannot subject to his dominion.

In the light of these unannounced principles which ought to be the law in this modern age, let us give thought to the petitioner Edwards, his rights and his predicament, if that is done to him which the circuit judge has directed to be done. Edwards owns this cave through right of discovery, exploration, development, advertising, exhibition, and conquest. Men fought their way through the eternal darkness, into the mysterious and abysmal depths of the bowels of a groaning world to discover the theretofore unseen splendors of unknown natural scenic wonders. They were conquerors of fear, although now and then one of them, as did Floyd Collins, paid with his life, for his hardihood in adventuring into the regions where Charon with his boat had never before seen any but the spirits of the departed. They let themselves down by flimsy ropes into pits that seemed bottomless; they clung to scanty handholds as they skirted the brinks of precipices while the flickering flare of their flaming flambeaux disclosed no bottom to the yawning gulf beneath them; they waded through rushing torrents, not knowing what awaited them on the farther side; they climbed slippery steeps to find other levels; they wounded their bodies on stalagmites and stalactites and other curious and weird formations; they found chambers, star-studded and filled with scintillating light reflected by a phantasmagoria revealing fancied phantoms, and tapestry woven by the toiling gods in the dominion of Erebus; hunger and thirst, danger and deprivation could not stop them. Through days, weeks, months, and years—ever linking chamber with chamber, disclosing an underground land of enchantment, they continued their explorations; through the years they toiled connecting these wonders with the outside world through the entrance on the land of Edwards which he had discovered; through the years they toiled finding safe ways for those who might come to view what they had found and placed their seal upon. They knew nothing, and cared less, of who owned the surface above; they were in another world where no law forbade their footsteps. They created an underground kingdom where Gulliver's people may have lived or where Ayesha may have found the revolving column of fire in which to bathe meant eternal youth.

When the wonders were unfolded and the ways were made safe, then Edwards patiently, and again through the years, commenced the advertisement of his cave. First came one to see, then another, then two together, then small groups, then small crowds, then large crowds, and then the multitudes. Edwards had seen his faith justified. The cave was his because he had made it what it was, and without what he had done it was nothing of value. The value is not in the black vacuum that the uninitiated call a cave. That which Edwards owns is something intangible and indefinable. It is his vision translated into a reality.

Then came the horse leach's daughters crying: "Give me," "give me." Then came the "surface men" crying, "I think this cave may run under my lands." They do not know they only "guess," but they seek to discover the secrets of Edwards so that they may harass him and take from him that which he has made his own. They have come to a court of equity and have asked that Edwards be forced to open his doors and his ways to them so that they may go in and despoil him; that they may lay his secrets bare so that others may follow their example and dig into the wonders which Edwards has made his own. What may, be the result if they stop his ways? They destroy the cave, because those who visit it are they who give it value, and none will visit it when the ways are barred so that it may not be exhibited as a whole.

It may be that the law is as stated in the majority opinion of the court, but equity, according to my judgment, should not destroy that which belongs to one man when he at whose behest the destruction is visited, although with some legal right, is not benefited thereby. Any ruling by a court which brings great and irreparable injury to a party is erroneous.

NOTES AND QUESTIONS

1.   The Great Onyx cave is said to have been discovered originally by one Edmund Turner, who approached Edwards in 1915, telling him that he knew of a cave underneath his land. The two developed the cave together, with Turner concentrating on the exploration and Edwards on promoting the tourism business. Turner did his part without profiting from the cave, and Edwards later claimed the discovery as his alone. One legend has it that in revenge Turner blocked up passages that led to the nearby Mammoth Cave, and to this day the Great Onyx Cave is the only major cave not connected up to the main local cave system in the Flint Ridge area, despite persistent effort. See Roger W. Brucker & Richard A. Watson, The Longest Cave 277 (1976). Should Turner have had a legal claim against Edwards? Is self-help (if that is what it was) the only answer here? If Turner had come to you as a lawyer before he revealed his discovery to Edwards, how would you have advised him?

2.   Does the dissent in the principal case disagree with the *ad coelum* principle, or does it argue for a different interpretation of the rule than the one advocated by the majority? Under the dissent's proposed rule, what additional facts might have to be found before determining that Lee has no rights to the cave, assuming it occupies a portion of his column of space underground? Is the dissent grounded in the equitable notion that one should not invoke rights with no prospect of direct benefit (or not to "stand on one's extreme rights"), or is it arguing for an alternative rule that ownership of the cave goes with the ownership of the mouth? For a proposal

along the latter lines and a survey of some of the alternatives, see Richard A. Epstein, Holdouts, Externalities, and the Single Owner: One More Salute to Ronald Coase, 36 J.L. & Econ. 553, 563–67 (1993).

3.   Can you see how the *ad coelum* principle represents another example of the general principle of accession? We start with ownership of the surface. Then, as new increments of value are discovered below the surface (minerals, caves, oil and gas) or above the surface (engineering capabilities to construct very tall buildings), these increments of value are automatically assigned to the owner of the surface—the most prominent pre-assigned property. Does the *ad coelum* principle also represent a generalization about who is assumed to be "in possession" of minerals or caves discovered beneath the surface? Is the problem in the present case that this generalization is difficult to justify on the particular facts presented?

4.   It turned out that roughly one third of the Great Onyx Cave was under Lee's land. In a later opinion the Kentucky high court affirmed the chancellor's award of one third of the net profits from the cave business to Lee. Division was mainly in proportion to surface area with some consideration of the proportion of noteworthy sights in the two parts of the cave. Noting that the Edwardses were conscious wrongdoers, it agreed that restitution for unjust enrichment was appropriate, and required disgorgement one third of the profits. On the one hand this remedy disregards the fact that there would have been no profits at all from that one third of the cave without the Edwardses' efforts, but it also takes account of the fact that the Edwardses were "wrongdoers" knowingly exploiting Lee's portion of the cave. But the court also did not go so far as to award Lee any share of the profits from the related hotel business. Edwards v. Lee's Administrator, 96 S.W.2d 1028, 1029 (Ky. 1936). (An innocent trespasser might be liable only for the rental value of the land, but what is the rental value of a mouthless portion of a noteworthy cave?) In an intriguing concurrence, Justice Thomas wanted to treat the cave as being co-owned by the surface owners in proportion to their ownership of the surface. What's the difference? For one thing, he was worried about parts of the cave being closed off to the public, in what might be termed an anticommons. For more on the rights and duties of co-owners among themselves, see Chapter V. Why don't we see more solutions based on notions of co-ownership in the area of accession? Is some version of co-ownership of airspace in effect the result in the airplane overflight cases—which Justice Thomas saw as supportive of his approach?

5.   Judge Logan's dissent views Lee's behavior as an inequitable exercise of his technical rights. Sounding a similar note, one leading torts treatise states that because the surface owner had no practical access to the caves, either now or in the future, the majority decision was "dog-in-the-manger law, and can only be characterized as . . . [a] very bad one." W. Page Keeton et al., Prosser and Keeton on the Law of Torts § 13 (5th ed. 1984). The reference is to one of Aesop's Fables, in which a dog prevents oxen from eating hay, which the dog cannot eat himself. Should such an assertion of rights be considered an abuse of right or extortion (see Chapter IV)?

6.   During and after the litigation, the effort to create a national park around the Mammoth Cave system consumed the area, and it was one in which none other than dissenting Judge Marvel Mills Logan (later a Senator)

was deeply involved all along. Bruce Ziff, The Great Onyx Cases—A Micro-History, 40 N. Ky. L. Rev. 1 (2013). After the litigation over the Great Onyx Cave, its owners operated it as an inholding within the Mammoth Cave National Park, established in 1941, much to the annoyance of Park Service officials. One reason for their irritation was that "[s]ome private owners—and not just those with inholdings inside the Park—set up official-looking booths along the road outside the Park. Here they stationed 'cappers'—solicitors in khaki uniforms and Smokey Bear hats to direct tourists not to Mammoth Cave, but to other commercial caves in the vicinity." Self-help started getting out of control in the so-called "Kentucky Cave Wars." In 1961, the Cox estate sold the Great Onyx Cave to the federal government and it was integrated into the park. See Brucker & Watson, supra, at 59–60, 297.

4. COMBINATIONS OF PERSONAL PROPERTY

The law of personal property contains several doctrines designed to deal with situations in which the personal property of A is joined with the personal property of B (often called a "mixture"), or the personal property of A is combined with the fungible personal property of a collection of other persons (often called "confusion"), or the personal property of A is mistakenly modified by the labor of another (sometimes called "specification"). If the combination can be reversed at a reasonable cost or if the parties have contributed fungible property (like grains of corn) that can be divided up according to the quantity contributed by each, courts will try to restore the parties to their respective contributions. But if the combination cannot be reversed, the proper analysis is more complicated, as illustrated by the following case.

Wetherbee v. Green
Supreme Court of Michigan, 1871.
22 Mich. 311.

This was an action of replevin, brought by George Green, Charles H. Camp and George Brooks, in the circuit court for the county of Bay, against George Wetherbee, for one hundred and fifty-eight thousand black ash barrel-hoops, alleged to be of the value of eight hundred dollars. * * * [T]he jury found for plaintiffs. The judgment entered upon the verdict comes into this court by writ of error.

■ COOLEY J.: * * * Wetherbee claimed * * * that replevin could not be maintained for the hoops, because he had cut the timber in good faith, relying upon a permission which he supposed proceeded from the parties having lawful right to give it, and had, by the expenditure of his labor and money, converted the trees into chattels immensely more valuable than they were as they stood in the forest, and thereby he had made such chattels his own. And he offered to show that the standing timber was worth twenty-five dollars only, while the hoops replevied were shown by the evidence to be worth near seven hundred dollars * * * The evidence offered to establish these facts was rejected by the court, and the plaintiffs obtained judgment. * * *

The objections to allowing the owner of the trees to reclaim the property under such circumstances are, that it visits the involuntary wrong-doer too severely for his unintentional trespass, and at the same time compensates the owner beyond all reason for the injury he has sustained. In the redress of private injuries the law aims not so much to punish the wrongdoer as to compensate the sufferer for his injuries; and the cases in which it goes farther and inflicts punitory or vindictive penalties are those in which the wrong-doer has committed the wrong recklessly, willfully, or maliciously, and under circumstances presenting elements of aggravation. Where vicious motive or reckless disregard of right are not involved, to inflict upon a person who has taken the property of another, a penalty equal to twenty or thirty times its value, and to compensate the owner in a proportion equally enormous, is so opposed to all legal idea of justice and right and to the rules which regulate the recovery of damages generally, that if permitted by the law at all, it must stand out as an anomaly and must rest upon peculiar reasons.

As a general rule, one whose property has been appropriated by another without authority has a right to follow it and recover the possession from any one who may have received it; and if, in the mean time, it has been increased in value by the addition of labor or money, the owner may, nevertheless, reclaim it, provided there has been no destruction of substantial identity. So far the authorities are agreed. A man cannot generally be deprived of his property except by his own voluntary act or by operation of law; and if unauthorized parties have bestowed expense or labor upon it, that fact cannot constitute a bar to his reclaiming it, so long as identification is not impracticable. But there must, nevertheless, in reason be some limit to the right to follow and reclaim materials which have undergone a process of manufacture. Mr. Justice Blackstone lays down the rule very broadly, that if a thing is changed into a different species, as by making wine out of another's grapes, oil from his olives, or bread from his wheat, the product belongs to the new operator, who is only to make satisfaction to the former proprietor for the materials converted: 2 Bl. Com., 404. We do not understand this to be disputed as a general proposition, though there are some authorities which hold that, in the case of a willful appropriation, no extent of conversion can give to the willful trespasser a title to the property so long as the original materials can be traced in the improved article. The distinction thus made between the case of an appropriation in good faith and one based on intentional wrong, appears to have come from the civil law, which would not suffer a party to acquire a title by accession, founded on his own act, unless he had taken the materials in ignorance of the true owner, and given them a form which precluded their being restored to their original condition. 2 Kent, 363. While many cases have followed the rule as broadly stated by Blackstone, others have adopted the severe rule of the civil law where the conversion was in willful disregard of right. The New York cases of *Betts v. Lee,* 5 Johns. 348 (N.Y. 1810); *Curtis v. Groat,* 6 Johns. 168 (N.Y. 1810), and *Chandler v. Edson,* 9 Johns. 362 (N.Y. 1812), were all cases where the willful trespasser was held to have acquired no property by a very radical conversion * * * But we are not called upon in this case to express any opinion regarding the rule applicable in the case of a willful trespasser, since the authorities agree in holding that, when the wrong had been involuntary, the owner of the original materials is precluded, by the civil law and common law alike, from following and reclaiming the property after it has undergone a transformation which converts it into an article substantially different.

The cases of confusion of goods are closely analogous. It has always been held that he who, without fraud, intentional wrong, or reckless disregard of the rights of others, mingled his goods with those of another person, in such manner that they could not be distinguished, should, nevertheless, be protected in his ownership so far as the circumstances would permit. The question of motive here becomes of the highest importance; for, as Chancellor Kent says, if the commingling of property as willfully made without mutual consent, * * * the common law gave the entire property, without any account, to him whose property "was originally invaded, and its distinct character destroyed. Popham's Rep. 38, Pl. 2. If A will willfully intermix his corn or hay with that of B, or casts his gold into another's crucible, so that it becomes impossible to distinguish what belonged to A from what belonged to B, the whole belongs to B." But this rule only applies to wrongful or fraudulent intermixtures. There may be an intentional intermingling, and yet no wrong intended, as where a man mixes two parcels together, supposing both to be his own; or, that he was about to mingle his with his neighbor's, by agreement, and mistakes the parcel. In such cases, which may be deemed accidental intermixtures, it would be unreasonable and unjust that he should lose his own or be obliged to take and pay for his neighbor's[.] * * * In many cases there will be difficulty in determining precisely how he can be protected with due regard to the rights of the other party; but it is clear that the law will not forfeit his property in consequence of the accident or inadvertence, unless a just measure of redress to the other party renders it inevitable.

The important question on this branch of the case appears to us to be, whether standing trees, when cut and manufactured into hoops, are to be regarded as so far changed in character that their identity can be said to be destroyed within the meaning of the authorities. And as we enter upon a discussion of this question, it is evident at once that it is difficult, if not impossible, to discover any invariable and satisfactory test which can be applied to all the cases which arise in such infinite variety. "If grain be taken and made into malt, or money taken and made into a cup, or timber taken and made into a house, it is held in the old English law that the property is so altered as to change the title." 2 Kent, 363. But cloth made into garments, leather into shoes, trees hewn or sawed into timber, and iron made into bars, it is said may be reclaimed by the owner in their new and original shape. Some of the cases place the right of the former owner to take the thing in its altered condition upon the question whether its identity could be made out by the senses. But this is obviously a very unsatisfactory test, and in many cases would wholly defeat the purpose which the law has in view in recognizing a change of title in any of these cases. That purpose is not to establish any arbitrary distinctions, based upon mere physical reasons, but to adjust the redress afforded to the one party and the penalty inflicted upon the other, as near as circumstances will permit, to the rules of substantial justice.

It may often happen that no difficulty will be experienced in determining the identity of a piece of timber which has been taken and built into a house; but no one disputes that the right of the original owner is gone in such a case. A particular piece of wood might, perhaps, be traced without trouble into a church organ, or other equally valuable article; but no one would defend a rule of law which, because the identity could be determined by the senses, would permit the owner of the wood to appropriate a musical instrument, a hundred or a thousand times the value of his original materials, when the party who, under like circumstances, has doubled the value of another man's corn by converting it into malt, is permitted to retain it, and held liable for the original value only. Such distinctions in the law would be without reason, and could not be tolerated. When the right to the improved article is the point in issue, the question, how much the property or labor of each has contributed to make it what it is, must always be one of first importance. The owner of a beam built into the house of another loses his property in it, because the beam is insignificant in value or importance as compared to that to which it has become attached, and the musical instrument belongs to the maker rather than to the man whose timber was used in making it—not because the timber cannot be identified, but because, in bringing it to its present condition the value of the labor has swallowed up and rendered insignificant the value of the original materials. The labor, in the case of the musical instrument, is just as much the principal thing as the house is in the other case instanced; the timber appropriated is in each case comparatively unimportant.

No test which satisfies the reason of the law can be applied in the adjustment of questions of title to chattels by accession, unless it keeps in view the circumstance of relative values. When we bear in mind the fact that what the law aims at is the accomplishment of substantial equity, we shall readily perceive that the fact of the value of the materials having been increased a hundred-fold, is of more importance in the adjustment than any chemical change or mechanical transformation, which, however radical, neither is expensive to the party making it, nor adds materially to the value. There may be complete changes with so little improvement in value, that there could be no hardship in giving the owner of the original materials the improved article; but in the present case, where the defendant's labor—if he shall succeed in sustaining his offer of testimony—will appear to have given the timber in its present condition nearly all its value, all the grounds of equity exist which influence the courts in recognizing a change of title under any circumstances.

D's labor = big improvement to the wood (handwritten margin note)

We are of opinion that the court erred in rejecting the testimony offered. The defendant, we think, had a right to show that he had manufactured the hoops in good faith, and in the belief that he had the proper authority to do so; and if he should succeed in making that showing, he was entitled to have the jury instructed that the title to the timber was changed by a substantial change of identity, and that the remedy of the plaintiff was an action to recover damages for the unintentional trespass.

* * * For the reasons given the judgment must be reversed, with costs, and a new trial ordered.

NOTES AND QUESTIONS

1.   The law governing specification (as it is sometimes called) is another illustration of the principle of accession, at least if we make the Lockean assumption that every person owns his or her own labor. On this assumption, the question in such cases is which "property right" is more prominent: the original object (the tree, the grapes, the wheat) or the labor expended by the improver in transforming the original object (making hoops, or wine, or bread). If the labor is "insignificant" and the original object "prominent," then title stays with the original owner of the object. If the labor is "prominent" and the original object "insignificant," then title passes to the improver (and the improver pays the original owner damages equal to the value of the original object).

2.   Justice Cooley emphasizes the importance of the good faith/bad faith distinction, and indicates his agreement with cases that refuse to transfer title to the creator/improver who has acted in bad faith, i.e., with knowledge that someone else has superior title to the original object. Do you think that bad faith should be irrelevant (Blackstone's view, apparently), should automatically disqualify someone from obtaining title by accession (Cooley's view), or should be one factor to weigh against other factors, like the degree of transformation and the disparity in value added?

3.   Justice Cooley also seeks to downplay the significance of the degree of transformation of the object, and instead puts greater weight on the disparity in value. He had to do this in order to find title by accession in *Wetherbee*, since although the identity of the original logs could be traced in the hoops, the disparity in value was enormous: $700 for the hoops versus $25 for the trees, or a ratio of 28 to 1. Interestingly, just six years later, in *Isle Royale Mining Co. v. Hertin*, 37 Mich. 332 (1877), Cooley, by then Chief Justice, also wrote for the court in denying a claim seeking restitution for the

value of labor expended in mistakenly cutting trees on land owned by someone else. The value of the cut timber was $2.87½ per cord, of which $1.87½ was attributable to labor of the improver, for a ratio of 1.875 to 1. Perhaps more importantly, the mistaken improver had not really transformed the trees at all, other than to cut them down. The opinion in *Isle Royale* placed considerably more emphasis on the absence of transformation, noting that "[p]erhaps no case has gone further than *Wetherbee v. Green* . . . [where] the identity of trees and hoops was perfectly capable of being traced and established."

4. Why do you suppose the degree of transformation has been an important factor in the law of combinations—perhaps more important than good faith or relative value—from Roman times down to the present? Does extensive transformation suggest that the laborer has taken "possession" of the object?

5. Note that the law of combinations also implicates the principle of restitution, discussed more fully in Chapter IV. If the improver is deemed to be the more prominent contributor of value to the transformed object, the improver gets title to the object, but must pay damages to the owner of the raw materials that have been transformed. The measure of damages is presumably the fair market value of the raw material in its pre-transformation state. Suppose the contrary conclusion is reached—that the owner of the raw materials is the more prominent contributor of final value, and hence gets title to the object. Must the owner of the raw material make restitution to the improver for the increased value to the object caused by the improvements? What if, say, the original owner of the timber did not want the trees cut down, but rather prefers that they remain standing as a forest? (Recall Pardee v. Camden Lumber Co., excerpted in Chapter I.) See Restatement Third, Restitution and Unjust Enrichment §§ 9–10 (2011) (restitution law avoids foisting transactions on unwilling parties but will look to whether that party expressed a willingness to pay, has been spared an otherwise necessary expense, or realizes the conferred benefit in money terms).

6. Most of the cases involving the law of combinations have a quaint quality: hoops being carved from logs, wine being pressed from grapes, and so forth. But issues involving improvements arise with considerable frequency in modern intellectual property law. Suppose A gets a patent on a new invention, and B then makes an improvement on the invention. Or suppose A writes a novel which is copyrighted, and B then turns it into a screenplay for a movie. What are the respective rights of A and B in these situations? Intellectual property law does not use combinations doctrine in resolving these issues. Instead, Mark Lemley, a leading intellectual property scholar, summarizes patent law this way:

> The basic structure of the patent model is * * * quite simple. The treatment of improvements is a function of the value and significance of the improvement in relation to the original invention. Improvements which are minor in relation to the original invention are likely to be found to infringe[.] * * * More significant improvements within the range of the original claims

still infringe the original patent, but in such cases the improver is entitled to a patent of his own. This not only encourages the development of significant improvements, but gives improvers bargaining leverage in licensing negotiations in direct proportion to the relative value of their improvements. Finally, truly radical improvements are exempted from liability to the original patent owner, regardless of whether they fall within the literal scope of the original claims, in order to encourage such improvements and to ensure that they reach the market.

Mark A. Lemley, The Economics of Improvement in Intellectual Property Law, 75 Tex. L. Rev. 989, 1070 (1997). How would you characterize the differences between the intellectual property solution to the problem of improvements, and the law of combinations? Which do you think is better, and why?

5. FIXTURES

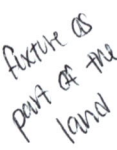

A fixture is defined as "a thing which, although originally a movable chattel, is by reason of its annexation to, or association in use with land, regarded as part of the land." Ray Andrews Brown, The Law of Personal Property § 16.1, at 514 (Walter B. Raushenbush ed., 3d ed. 1975).

Strain v. Green

Supreme Court of Washington, 1946.
172 P.2d 216.

■ ROBINSON, JUSTICE. On August 7, 1943, Jacob Green agreed to sell to William Strain his waterfront home on Mercer Island for thirty-five thousand dollars[.] * * * On August 20, 1943, Green and wife executed a statutory warranty deed to Strain and wife, which they duly acknowledged and delivered to the purchasers on August 27th, receiving the purchase price in full. At some time thereafter, they left the premises, taking with them, from the basement, the hot water tank and enclosed electric heater, the Venetian blinds from the windows, certain lighting fixtures, and three mirrors, two of which were rather firmly attached to the walls. It was also claimed, in the ensuing lawsuit, that they unlawfully carried away a fireplace screen, a tool house, and certain chicken wire, with the posts which supported it. The total value of the articles removed was alleged to be $1,105.

On November 8, 1943, Mr. Hamley, as attorney for the Strains, demanded, in writing, that all of said property be returned to the premises. No part of the demand being complied with, this action was brought in March, 1944. The plaintiffs prayed for a judgment requiring the defendants to return the property, or, in case that that could not be done, for $1,105, and additional sums alleged to have been necessarily expended by the plaintiffs on account of the removal from the property, or which they would be required to expend to reinstall it.

It appears from the evidence that, when the defendants purchased the home, they found the hot water system inadequate, and put in a large, modern insulated tank, with an automatic electric control. When they left the house, they disconnected that tank from the plumbing and electric system, and reconnected the much smaller tank which was serving the house when they bought it. This the plaintiffs found wholly inadequate, and supplemented it, as far as, in view of war time scarcities, they were able to do so, by buying and hooking up two large tanks, and making certain other additions.

When the plaintiffs agreed to buy the house, and up until they had completed the payment on the purchase price, there was a large and beautiful crystal chandelier in the center of the dining room ceiling, and five other matching fixtures in that room and adjoining rooms. The distinctive feature of these articles was their ornamentation by a great number of pendants of imported crystal glass. These fixtures the Greens also disconnected and took with them. Before departing, however, they bought, and installed in place of the fixtures removed, some highly inferior plastic imitations.

When the plaintiffs purchased the house, there was a large plate glass mirror on one of the dining room walls. It had been installed in the following manner: A large piece of three-eighths-inch plywood was firmly nailed to the plastered wall, and the mirror was attached to this backing by screws. The mirror itself was, of course, readily removed. The Greens removed it, and left the plastered wall with the large square of plywood in the middle of it. The mirror having been removed, the plywood had no visible excuse for being there, and the Strains removed it. It still had twenty-six nails in it when introduced in evidence, and holes where there had been a dozen or so more. When the plywood was pried from the wall, each nail brought some of the plaster with it. The mirror over the living room fireplace was attached to the wall in the same manner, although fewer nails were used. This mirror the Greens also removed. The mirror in what was known as the powder room also had a plywood backing, but there is no very convincing testimony that the plywood was nailed, or attached, to the wall, and Mrs. Green's testimony was to the effect that the mirror merely rested upon a table and was held in place by a wire which ran to a hook above it, just as pictures are hung.

As for the other articles, the Venetian blinds were of odd sizes, cut and built especially for the windows of the house. The so-called tool house turned out to be a child's playhouse, and there was no evidence that chicken wire was ever taken from the premises.

The trial court held that the automatic hot water tank was a fixture, and must be returned. The Venetian blinds were also held to be fixtures, and ordered returned. Certain damages were awarded with respect to reinstallations. As the defendants have not cross-appealed, we are not concerned with that portion of the judgment. The court, however, held that the light fixtures and mirrors were personal property, which the defendants had a right to remove, and it is from that holding that this appeal is taken.

We will not undertake to write a treatise on the law of fixtures. Every lawyer knows that cases can be found in this field that will support any position that the facts of his particular case require him to take. As early as 1899, the court said, in *Philadelphia Mortgage & Trust Co. v. Miller*, 56 P. 382 (Wash. 1899): "there is a wilderness of authority on this question of fixtures * * * cases, * * * are so conflicting that it would be profitless to undertake to review or harmonize them."

Throughout the trial, the trial judge repeatedly referred to that case as "the Miller case," and counsel, in his opening brief, refers to it as "the leading case in this jurisdiction." It held that four mantels, a bathtub, and a hot water heater connected with the plumbing were not fixtures. Since much reliance is placed upon that decision, we will quote rather freely from the opinion:

Anciently, mantels were uniformly built as a part of the house, and therefore became a fixture to the realty. * * * But advancing mechanical science and taste have evolved an altogether differently constructed mantel, and mantels such as are described by the testimony in this case are now constructed without reference to any particular house or particular fireplace. They are what are called "stock" mantels, and are sold separately, and made adaptive to any kind of a house. They are, in fact, as much a separate article of merchandise as a bedstead or a table. * * * The same advancement has been made in bath tubs. The old-fashioned bath tub, that was sealed in and actually made a part of the bath room, has largely given place to the more convenient bath tub, that rests upon legs, and can be attached to any heating system that happens to prevail in the house where it is used. And so with heaters or boilers. In this instance the boiler is in no way attached to the building, excepting by its plumbing connections. It could be detached without in any way injuring the realty; * * * . The testimony shows that the building back of the mantels, or that portion of it which was concealed by the mantels, was plastered and kalsomined; that for about three years the mantels were not fastened to the wall in any way, but supported themselves in the position they occupied, and that, after that time, they were fastened to the wall by screws, to render them more stable and keep them from toppling. The boiler and bath tub were not placed in the building for several years after the mortgage was given.

It would seem that the court could not very well have held otherwise than it did, without encroaching upon the province of the jury; for, it is further said:

The question of whether or not the particular piece of furniture or machinery is a chattel or fixture has been held by a majority of the courts to be a mixed question of law and fact. In this case the court instructed the jury. These instructions were not excepted to, and must be presumed to have correctly stated the law; and, the jury having found the facts in favor of the respondent, we would be loath to disturb their findings, unless we were compelled to say that, as a matter of law, the property sued for was a part of the realty.

Respondents also strongly rely on Hall v. Law Guarantee & Trust Society, 60 P. 643 (Wash. 1900). The first headnote to this case reads as follows:

> Gas and electric light fixtures and globes, a windmill, a hot water tank, curtains, window and door screens, when attached to a house, are not fixtures as between a mortgagor and a mortgagee.

Referring to these two cases, the first of which was decided in 1899, and the second in 1900, respondents say, in their brief, that they "have never been overruled in this state and are the law today." Although they may never have been expressly overruled, they at least have been outmoded. We think it highly improbable that it would now be held, even in a case between a mortgagor and a mortgagee, that a mantel, or a bathtub, or an electric hot water heater connected with both the plumbing and the electrical system is not a fixture. The law relating to fixtures has slowly and gradually changed as times have changed. Various household appliances, not formerly held to be fixtures, have become so in this "built-in" era. But the major changes are probably the result of an awareness of the fact that the luxuries of a given generation become the necessities of the next. It seems highly improbable that any present-day court would hold that a foreclosed mortgagor, on surrendering the premises, could lawfully disconnect, and take with him, the household bathtub. * * *

[B]oth Mr. and Mrs. Green categorically testified that they never had any intention that the chandelier, sidelights, and mirrors should ever become fixtures, and that they had removed them, as personal property, from the former houses in which they had lived. Furthermore, their testimony was in no way rebutted.

We do not wish it to be understood that we in any way question the veracity of the respondents, but we are here considering an alleged rule that may be involved in future cases, and, treating the matter wholly impersonally, if a witness testifies that, when he put a chandelier in a house, he intended to take it out if he should ever sell the house, in what possible way can his evidence be disputed? And, passing that, by what ex post facto system of mind reading could a purchaser determine the vendor's state of mind when he installed the chandelier? There is no evidence whatever in the instant case that the respondents told the appellants that they had ever had such an intention until after the appellants had bought, and paid for, the house. If it held in this case that the secret intention of the defendants is determinative of the question whether or not the articles involved are fixtures, that holding will encourage and invite persons less honest than the respondents to attempt to remove from premises sold every at-all-movable article that can be disconnected without breakage.

It has never been the law of this jurisdiction, nor, we think, of any other, that the secret intention of the owner who affixed the disputed article, of itself, determines whether or not it was a fixture or a mere personal chattel.

[In] Ballard v. Alaska Theatre Co., 161 P. 478, 481 (Wash. 1916) [this Court said]:

> The intent is not to be gathered from testimony of the actual state of the mind of the party making the annexation but is to be inferred, when not determined by an express agreement, from the nature of the article affixed, the relation and situation to the freehold of the party making the annexation, the manner of the annexation, and the purpose for which it is made.

The case cited in the above quotation [Washington National Bank v. Smith, 45 P. 736 (Wash. 1896)] was decided fifty years ago, in 1896. Turning to the opinion in the case, we find the following statement, 45 P. on page 739:

> That the intention with which machinery is placed upon the real estate is one of the elements to be taken into consideration in determining whether or not it remains a chattel, or becomes a part of such real estate, is conceded; *but it does not follow that such intention can be shown by testimony as to the actual state of the mind of the person who attached the machinery to the real estate at the time it was attached. On the contrary, his intention must be gathered from circumstances surrounding the transaction, and from what was said and done at the time, and cannot be affected by his state of mind retained as a secret.* (Italics ours.)

It is also said, in Ballard v. Alaska Theatre Co., supra:

> When the annexation is made by a tenant or licensee the presumption is that he did not intend to enrich the freehold, but intended to reserve title to the chattel annexed in himself, while from an annexation by the owner of the property, the presumption is the other way. [Citing cases.] It therefore often happens that the same character of article annexed to the realty in the same way will be held to be a trade fixture and removable when annexed by a tenant, but real property and not removable when annexed by the owner of the property.

The opinion in Hall v. Dare, 252 P. 926, 928 (Wash. 1927), by reference, approves the rule laid down in Filley v. Christopher, 80 P. 834 (Wash. 1905), in which it is said:

> The true criterion of a fixture is the united application of these requisites: (1) Actual annexation to the realty, or something appurtenant thereto; (2) application to the use or purpose to which that part of the realty with which it is connected is appropriated; and (3) the intention of the party making the annexation to make a permanent accession to the freehold.

RULE on fixtures

Respondents in this case were owners when they installed the articles in question. The presumption, then, is (as held in the last of the quotations hitherto made from Ballard v. Alaska Theatre Co., supra) that it was their intention to enrich the freehold. This presumption is not overcome by evidence of secret intention, as is shown by the first of the quotations hitherto made from the same case, and then more plainly by the other quotation to the same effect from Washington National Bank v. Smith. Nor is the fact that the respondents successfully removed the articles from house to house of much, if any, probative value.

on (3) ... presumption = intent to enrich (not overcome by secret intention)

The chandelier and sidelights were actually annexed to the realty, and, clearly, for the use or purpose of that part of the realty (the house) with which they were connected. Their purpose, of course, was to make it livable. The fact that such articles are universally called "light fixtures," is, though not determinative, some evidence that they are fixtures. The fact that, after removing the chandelier and sidelights, the respondents replaced them with others, amounts to an implied admission on their part that a house without light fixtures would not be a complete house. In our opinion, the chandelier and sidelights were fixtures in law and in fact.

lights = fixture

The mirrors—at least two of them—present a much closer question. We are satisfied that there is no adequate proof that the powder room mirror was physically annexed to the realty, and as to that mirror, which seems to have been the most valuable of the three, we need not inquire further. It was not a fixture. The others present a unique situation. Each of them could be taken down from the respective walls by removing a few screws, but in each case that would leave on the wall a large square of plywood which could not be removed, in the one case, without damaging the plaster, and, in the other, without leaving some damage by nail holes, and a portion of the wall of a different shade. We have arrived at the opinion that each of these mirrors and its plywood backing should be regarded as one article, and that in each case that article should be regarded as having been a portion of the house walls, and that, as such, they went with the house to the purchasers by the warranty deed which contained no reservations whatsoever.

mirror 1 = no fixture

will it leave massive dents/ damage in removing? → fixture

mirrors 2/3 = fixture

Except as to the powder room mirror, the judgment, in so far as appealed from, is reversed, and the cause remanded to the trial court for the entry of judgment in accordance herewith.

NOTES AND QUESTIONS

1.   Disputes over whether things are personal property or fixtures arise with some regularity and in several different contexts. One context, represented by the principal case, is when A sells real property to B, and a dispute arises as to whether particular things associated with the property are personal property belonging to A, or fixtures belonging to B. Another context is when C leases an apartment from D, and a dispute arises at the end of the lease over whether particular things C has added to the apartment are personal property belonging to C, or fixtures belonging to the landlord D. A third context is when E takes out a loan secured by a mortgage on real estate with bank F, and a dispute arises over whether certain things E has added to the property are within the scope of F's security interest when E defaults on the loan.

2.   The name "fixtures" implies that only items of personal property that are securely affixed to the land will be regarded as going with the land, but courts have long recognized that other variables are relevant as well. In what is still the most widely cited American case, the court in *Teaff v. Hewitt*, 1 Ohio 511, 1853 WL 54 (1853), held that three factors should be considered: (1) "actual annexation to the realty, or something appurtenant thereto;" (2) "appropriation to the use or purpose of that part of the realty with which it is connected;" and (3) "the intention of the party making the annexation, to make the article a permanent accession to the freehold." 1 Ohio at 10; 1853 WL at 530. Many courts today regard the last factor—the intent of the party making the annexation—as the most importation, although intent is to be determined objectively, by considering other factors such as affixation and the functional importance of the thing in terms of its use on the property.

3.   Although the same doctrine nominally applies in each of the different contexts in which the issue arises, many observers believe that judges lean one way or another in close cases depending on the context. There is a hint of this in *Strain* when the court observes that mantels, bathtubs, and water heaters would most probably be regarded as fixtures "even in a case between a mortgagor and a mortgagee," suggesting that courts would be more likely to consider something as personal property in that context. If true, do you think this is because courts are more sympathetic to some classes of claimants (purchasers, tenants, and borrowers) and less sympathetic to others (sellers, landlords, lenders)? Or can the differences be explained, as the principal case suggests, by different presumptions about the likely intentions of persons in these different contexts?

4.   Is fixtures doctrine just a default rule to be applied in determining the intentions of the parties to a bilateral contract? If so, can it really be said to be a doctrine about the composition of property rights? Or does the doctrine have certain applications that run counter to the parties' intentions, making it an example of how someone—an owner of land—can acquire

objects that originally were personal property belonging to someone else, who had no intention to make a voluntary conveyance?

  5. Although Hume does not mention the law of fixtures, the doctrine can be explained in terms of his theory of the principle of accession. In particular, psychological perceptions seem to play a substantial role in fixtures cases. Consider the different disposition the court reaches in *Strain* with regard to the mirrors in the dining room and living room, and the mirror in the powder room. The same intention and relationship among the parties exists with respect to each of the mirrors. The only difference is that the mirrors in the dining room and living room were attached to the plywood by screws, whereas the mirror in the powder room was hung by wire from a hook. The greater connectedness or proximity between the attached mirrors and the real property causes the court to conclude they are fixtures, i.e., they belong to the owner of the real property, whereas the looser connection between the hung mirror and the realty causes the court to conclude it is personal property.

6. ACCRETION AND AVULSION

Nebraska v. Iowa

Supreme Court of the United States, 1892.
143 U.S. 359.

  This is an original suit, brought in this court by the state of Nebraska against the state of Iowa, the object of which is to have the boundary line between the two states determined. Iowa was admitted into the Union in 1846, and its western boundary, as defined by the act of admission, was the middle of the main channel of the Missouri river. Nebraska was admitted in 1867, and its eastern boundary was likewise the middle of the channel of the Missouri river. Between 1851 and 1877, in the vicinity of Omaha, there were marked changes in the course of this channel, so that in the latter year it occupied a very different bed from that through which it flowed in the former year. Out of these changes has come this litigation, the respective states claiming jurisdiction over the same tract of land. * * *

■ MR. JUSTICE BREWER, after stating the facts in the foregoing language, delivered the opinion of the court. It is settled law that when grants of land border on running water, and the banks are changed by that gradual process known as "accretion," the riparian owner's boundary line still remains the stream, although, during the years, by this accretion, the actual area of his possessions may vary. In *New Orleans v. United States*, 35 U.S. (10 Pet.) 662, 717 (1836), this court said: "The question is well settled at common law, that the person whose land is bounded by a stream of water which changes its course gradually by alluvial formations shall still hold by the same boundary, including the accumulated soil. No other rule can be applied on just principles. Every proprietor whose land is thus bounded is subject to loss by the same means which may add to his territory; and, as he is without remedy for his loss in this way, he cannot be held accountable for his gain."

It is equally well settled that where a stream, which is a boundary, from any cause suddenly abandons its old and seeks a new bed, such change of channel works no change of boundary; and that the boundary remains as it was, in the center of the old channel, although no water may be flowing therein. This sudden and rapid change of channel is termed, in the law, "avulsion." In Gould on Waters, sec. 159, it is said: "But if the change is violent and visible, and arises from a known cause, such as a freshet, or a cut through which a new channel is formed, the original thread of the stream continues to mark the limits of the two estates."

These propositions, which are universally recognized as correct where the boundaries of private property touch on streams, are in like manner recognized where the boundaries between states or nations are, by prescription or treaty, found in running water. Accretion, no matter to which side it adds ground, leaves the boundary still the center of the channel. Avulsion has no effect on boundary, but leaves it in the center of the old channel. * * *

The result of these authorities puts it beyond doubt that accretion on an ordinary river would leave the boundary between two states the varying center of the channel, and that avulsion would establish a fixed boundary, to-wit, the center of the abandoned channel. It is contended, however, that the doctrine of accretion has no application to the Missouri river * * * because of the peculiar character of that stream, and of the soil through which it flows, the course of the river being tortuous, the current rapid, and the soil a soft, sandy loam, not protected from the action of water either by rocks or the roots of trees; the effect being that the river cuts away its banks, sometimes in a large body, and makes for itself a new course, while the earth thus removed is almost simultaneously deposited elsewhere, and new land is formed almost as rapidly as the former bank was carried a way. * * * "The test as to what is gradual and imperceptible in the sense of the rule is that, though the witnesses may see from time to time that progress has been made, they could not perceive it while the process was going on." [quoting Jefferis v. East Omaha Land Co., 134 U.S. 178, 190 (1890), quoting in turn County of St. Clair v. Lovingston, 90 U.S. (23 Wall.) 46, 68 (1874)]. * * *

But what are the facts apparent from [the] testimony? The Missouri river is a winding stream, coursing through a valley of varying width, the substratum of whose soil, a deposit of distant centuries, is largely of quicksand. In building the bridge of the Union Pacific Railway Company across the Missouri river in the vicinity of the tracts in controversy, the builders went down to the solid rock, 65 feet below the surface, and there found a pine log a foot and a half in diameter—of course, a deposit made in the long ago. The current is rapid, far above the average of ordinary rivers; and by reason of the snows in the mountains there are two well-known rises in the volume of its waters, known as the April and June rises. The large volume of water pouring down at the time of these rises, with the rapidity of its current, has great and rapid action upon the loose soil of its banks. Whenever it impinges with direct attack upon the bank at a bend of the stream, and that bank is of the loose sand obtaining in the valley of the Missouri, it is not strange that the abrasion and washing away is rapid and great. Frequently, where above the loose substratum of sand there is a deposit of comparatively solid soil, the washing out of the underlying sand causes an instantaneous fall of quite a length and breadth of the superstratum of soil into the river; so that it may, in one sense of the term, be said, that the diminution of the banks is not gradual and imperceptible, but sudden and visible. Notwithstanding this, two things must be borne in mind, familiar to all dwellers on the banks of the Missouri river, and disclosed by the testimony: that, while there may be an instantaneous and obvious dropping into the river of quite a portion of its banks, such portion is not carried down the stream as a solid and compact mass, but disintegrates and separates into particles of earth borne onward by the flowing water, and giving to the stream that color, which, in the history of the country, has made it known as the "muddy" Missouri; and also that, while the disappearance, by reason of this process, of a mass of bank may be sudden and obvious, there is no transfer of such a solid body of earth to the opposite shore, or anything like an instantaneous and visible creation of a bank on that shore. The accretion, whatever may be the fact in respect to the diminution, is always gradual, and by the imperceptible deposit of floating particles of earth. There is, except in such cases of avulsion as may be noticed hereafter, in all matter of increase of bank, always a mere gradual and imperceptible process. There is no heaping up at an instant, and while the eye rests upon the stream, of acres or rods on the forming side of the river. No engineering skill is sufficient to say where the earth in the bank washed away and disintegrating into the river finds its rest and abiding place. The falling bank has passed into the floating mass of earth and water, and the particles of earth may rest one or fifty miles below, and upon either shore. There is, no matter how rapid the process of subtraction or addition, no detachment of earth from the one side and deposit of the same upon the other. The only thing which distinguishes this river from other streams, in the matter of accretion, is in the rapidity of the change, caused by the velocity of the current, and this in itself, in the very nature of things, works no change in the principle underlying the rule of law in respect thereto.

Our conclusions are that, notwithstanding the rapidity of the changes in the course of the channel, and the washing from the one side and onto the other, the law of accretion controls on the Missouri river as elsewhere; and that not only in respect to the rights of individual landowners, but also in respect to the boundary lines between states. The boundary, therefore, between Iowa and Nebraska is a varying line, so far as affected by these changes of diminution and accretion in the mere washing of the waters of the stream.

It appears, however, from the testimony, that in 1877 the river above Omaha, which had pursued a course in the nature of an ox-bow, suddenly cut through the neck of the bow and made for itself a new channel. This does not come within the law of accretion, but of that of avulsion. By this selection of a new channel the boundary was not changed, and it remained, as it was prior to the avulsion, the center line of the old channel; and that, unless the waters of the river returned to their former bed, became a fixed and unvarying boundary, no matter what might be the changes of the river in its new channel.

We think we have, by these observations, indicated as clearly as is possible the boundary between the two states, and upon these principles the parties may agree to a designation of such boundary, and such designation will pass into a final decree. If no agreement is possible, then the court will appoint a commission to survey and report in accordance with the views herein expressed.

Figure 2-5
Iowa-Nebraska Border

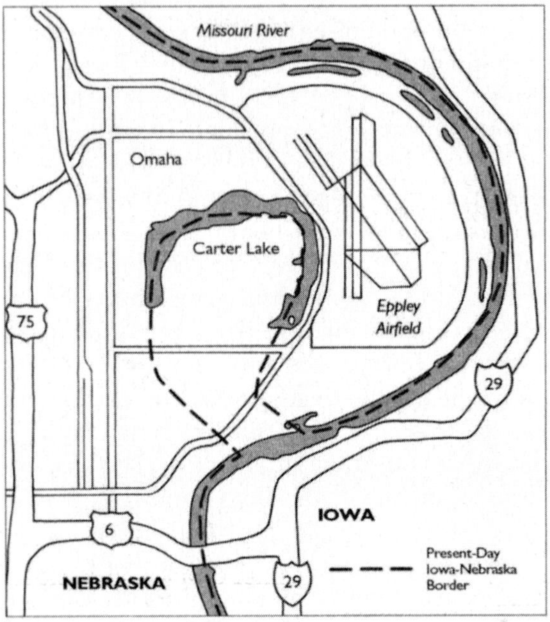

NOTES AND QUESTIONS

1.   As the Court explains, *accretion* refers to the "gradual deposit by water of solid material, whether mud, sand, or sediment, producing dry land which was before covered by water"; and *avulsion* "is the sudden change of the banks of a stream such as occurs when a river forms a new course by going through a bend, the sudden abandonment by a stream of its old

channel and the creation of a new one, or a sudden washing away from one of its banks of a considerable quantity of land and its deposit on the opposite bank." 3 American Law of Property § 15.26, at 855–56 (A. Casner ed., 1952). Other terms sometimes encountered are *reliction*, which refers to "land that has been covered by water, but which has been uncovered by the imperceptible recession of the water;" and *erosion,* which "is the gradual and imperceptible wearing away of land (bordering on water) by the natural action of the elements." Id. Two other terms that arise in this context are *riparian*, which refers to "land bordering on any type of water—rivers, streams, lakes, ponds, and arms of the ocean," and *littoral,* which refers more properly to land bordering the ocean or a major inland sea. Id.

2.   Accretion, reliction, and erosion are all governed by the same rule. Owners of riparian land that is augmented through the operation of accretion or reliction automatically gain title to the new land. Owners of riparian land that is diminished due to erosion automatically lose title to the lost land. This is a rule of law, not just a rule of construction or a default rule. Avulsion, as explained in the principal case, results in no change of boundary lines. What do you suppose happens when the opposite of reliction occurs, that is, when dry land is gradually inundated by a new body of standing water?

3.   Like the rule of increase, the rules of accretion and avulsion are quite universally followed. They date from Roman law, and are apparently followed in virtually all civil-law and common-law jurisdictions. As the principal case suggests, they form part of the international law of boundaries as well as the law of property. The law of accretion and avulsion featured in a recent U.S. Supreme Court case about the possibility of judicial takings. (See Stop the Beach Renourishment, Inc. v. Florida Department of Environmental Protection, excerpted in Chapter X, infra.)

4.   Hume, supra, mentions the rule of accretion as an example of the principle of accession. One can see the logic of this. Deposits of sand and mud imperceptibly added to riparian land are imagined to belong to the riparian landowner, because the deposits are "small" and the existing riparian land is "large," and the deposits are directly attached to the existing land. So the riparian landowner is regarded as the most prominent existing source of property rights to which to assign ownership of the new deposits added by accretion. But can Hume's psychological theory also account for the exception to the rule that governs avulsions? Is avulsion different because it typically involves a change that features a clear winner and loser, whereas accretion, erosion, and reliction have either a winner or a loser but no identifiable party on the opposite side of the ledger?

F. ADVERSE POSSESSION

Our final illustration of the importance of possession is the law of adverse possession. Courts have long held that when an owner sits on her right to exclude, and the statute of limitations for challenging the original unlawful entry expires, not only is the original owner barred from asserting the right to exclude but the adverse possessor now has full title. In effect, the adverse possessor becomes the new true owner, and can now exercise the right to exclude against all the world, including the original owner. Adverse possession applies to both real and personal property, and we provide cases illustrating both applications. If the owner fails to prevent someone from using the property for a particular purpose, as opposed to possessing it, and the statute of limitations runs, then this can give rise to a prescriptive easement. We take up this doctrine in Chapter IX.

Scott v. Anderson-Tully Co.

Court of Appeals of Mississippi, 2015.
154 So.3d 910.

■ BARNES, J. Herman Scott (Scott) filed suit seeking damages after Anderson-Tully Company removed timber from a twenty-acre parcel of land Scott claimed to own. Scott also sought to quiet and confirm title and to enjoin Anderson-Tully from entering the land. The chancellor dismissed Scott's claim, finding that Anderson-Tully had acquired title to the twenty acres through adverse possession. Scott appeals, arguing the chancellor erred. We find no error and affirm.

In 1925, brothers Stewart Scott Jr. and Willie Scott inherited an undivided one-half interest in a 584.6-acre tract of land in Jefferson County, Mississippi. The brothers' respective estates now each own the undivided one-half-interest shares in the property (collectively referred to as "the estate"). Scott, the plaintiff, is the administrator of Stewart Scott Jr.'s estate.

On March 19, 2010, Scott filed suit on behalf of the estate in Jefferson County Chancery Court, alleging that its adjacent landowner to the east, Anderson-Tully, was trespassing on a portion of the estate's property. Scott sought damages for the removal of timber, and he sought an order enjoining Anderson-Tully from entering onto or cutting and removing timber from the property. An amended complaint sought to quiet and confirm title. The disputed property is a somewhat triangular-shaped tract of land located in the northeastern corner of Section 28, Township 10 North, Range 1 East in Jefferson County.[1] Scott claims that the estate owns all property in Section 28, including the disputed acreage east of the wire fence, up to the section line between Sections 28 and 30.

Anderson-Tully answered the complaint and counterclaimed to quiet and confirm its own title. Anderson-Tully claimed that according to its deed, it owned the disputed twenty acres in Section 28 east of the wire fence. Alternatively, Anderson-Tully argued that it acquired title to the

---

[1]   Due to the fact that the property is situated in a non-standard township, a more thorough description of the property would be more of a hindrance than help to the reader. For example, Sections 28 and 30 abut each other for a short distance, and Section 29 lies below them at an angle.

property by adverse possession through its possession and use of the land from 1969 to 2010.

A trial was held, at which Scott presented the testimony of Richard T. Logan of Logan Engineering Company. Scott had hired Logan in 2003 to determine the estate's acreage after Scott became concerned that he was paying taxes on more property than the estate owned. Logan found that the estate owned all of Section 28, including the disputed twenty acres. Logan relied on his personal inspection of the property and a plat prepared in 1944 by B.G. Miller, the county surveyor for Jefferson County at that time. Miller's plat was prepared for a timber deed from the Scotts, and is the only recorded description of the Scotts' land in evidence. Miller's plat reflects difficulty in surveying the area, noting that the southern line of the Scotts' tract "has never been accurately determined but will not vary as much as 5 acres." Miller found that the Scotts' property line on the east ran along the section line between Section 28 and Section 30. He noted the wire fence on the east side of the Scotts' property and found that the "20 1/10 [acres] outside of fence is included in total acreage." However, Miller also made a note on the plat, within the twenty acres, which states that the property is "outside of fence & may be disputed." Logan agreed with Miller's finding that the section line, not the fence line, was the property's border and that the twenty acres belonged to the Scotts. Logan walked the disputed property and stated that the terrain to the east of the fence was "very rough." He found the wire fence was never intended to establish the property's border, but rather was a "convenience fence," or "tree[-]line fence," built to contain livestock. Although other witnesses testified to seeing blue paint along the wire fence that was indicative of Anderson-Tully's ownership, Logan testified that he did not recall seeing any blue paint when he surveyed the property. However, he also testified that he no longer had his field notes and was relying on his memory. Logan examined Anderson-Tully's deed and found no conveyance of any land in Section 28 to Anderson-Tully.

Richard Scott, an heir of Stewart Scott Jr., lived on the Scott property from his birth in 1938 until 1953. He testified he rebuilt the old wire fence on the east side of the property in 1954 because it was in need of repair. When he rebuilt the fence, he moved it a foot or two to the west, along the tree line, because the posts had rotted and he wanted to avoid digging new post holes. According to Richard, the fence was built to contain livestock and was not the property's border. After moving from the property in 1953, he returned every week or two to visit his father. Up until 2010, he would ride horses around the property when he visited, and would sometimes make repairs to the fence. He never saw anyone using the disputed twenty acres.

Anderson-Tully presented the testimony of its company surveyor and forester, E.C. Burkhardt. Burkhardt worked for Anderson-Tully from the early 1950s to 1981. Burkhardt testified that Anderson-Tully came into possession of the disputed tract on February 12, 1969, though quitclaim deed. The deed does not contain a metes-and-bounds description or plat. According to Burkhardt, when Anderson-Tully expressed interest in buying the Jefferson County land in 1969, no one, including the land's owners, knew the acreage. Burkhardt explained that the acreage was unclear because the land in Jefferson County was some of the first land south of Ohio to be surveyed by the United States government in 1805. After complaints about irregularities, the government retraced the original lines to get the correct acreage, and it established the sectional descriptions. After this, the "southwest part of Mississippi more or less reverted to the metes[-]and[-]bounds system." But Burkhardt testified that because the section lines are irregular, determining property lines can be difficult. So, according to Burkhardt, when surveying in the area, the "best evidence is what you find out there on the ground. . . . You've got to pay attention to the lines on the ground, evidence of possession; and quite often that's all you've really got to go by to determine boundary lines." Burkhardt's 1969 survey found that the boundary line between the Scotts' and Anderson-Tully's properties ran along the wire fence, making the disputed twenty acres part of Anderson-Tully's property. Burkhardt placed flags and stakes and used blue paint to mark the boundary line along the fence. Burkhardt's field notes reference conversations with neighboring property owners, including a Scott family member, none of whom objected to his placement of flags and stakes during his survey.

Anderson-Tully admitted Burkhardt's description, which is set out in its deed, does not specifically mention a conveyance of any land in Section 28—the location of the disputed property. But it argues the property "is included in the description . . . by reference" in the "catch-all portion of the description for the Hollywood Tract. . . ." * * *

Anderson-Tully alternatively argued that if the deed did not convey the property, it owned the property through adverse possession. Starting at the time of purchase in 1969, Anderson-Tully marked its perceived boundary line along the wire fence with a particular shade of blue paint—a practice started by the company in the 1920s. The line was repainted in 1986 and 1998. Witnesses testified that the blue line along the fence was visible continuously from 1969 through 2010, when Scott filed suit. Witnesses also testified that the particular shade of blue paint was commonly known in the community as that of Anderson-Tully. From 1969 to 2010, Anderson-Tully maintained the disputed acreage and cut and harvested timber in 1990, 1999, and 2010. The company also issued five hunting licenses to the property. Burkhardt testified that from 1969 until the end of his employment with Anderson-Tully in 1981, no one objected to his survey or interfered with Anderson-Tully's ownership or use of the disputed tract. Burkhardt testified that if someone had regularly crossed the blue line, he would have been notified. He was never notified that the line had been crossed by anyone.

Wilbur Nations, upon whom much of the chancellor's decision relied, testified for Anderson-Tully in regard to its adverse-possession claim. Nations was ninety years old when he testified, and "sharp as a tack," according to the chancellor. Nations, coincidently, was a licensed surveyor in Alabama. Nations testified that he grew up on what he referred to as the Hollywood tract, just east of the Scotts' land. He lived there from 1929 to 1942, and after that would return on weekends to visit through the mid-1950s. According to Nations, the wire fence was recognized by the community as the property line, and Anderson-Tully was the owner of the property to the east of the fence. Nations testified that the Scotts had never used the disputed tract. His family, however, had used the Hollywood tract, including the disputed twenty acres, to run cattle, and they had cut timber on it. Nations recalled that as late as 1993, the Scotts cut timber up to and west of the fence line, but they never cut east of the fence line. He saw blue paint marking the property's boundary along the fence in 1980 and 1985, and again three weeks before trial. He recognized the paint color as that used by Anderson-Tully to mark its borders.

In 1982, Nations joined the Linwood Hunting Club, which leased hunting land from Anderson-Tully beginning in 1972. Nations was present on the property yearly during hunting season (November–January) and throughout the year on the weekends working on roads and deer stands. He testified that the hunting-club members recognized the fence as the boundary line and were aware of the blue paint used by Anderson-Tully to mark its property's borders. From 1995 to 2007, Linwood also leased a portion of the Scotts' property. In 2007, Scott informed Linwood that he would not renew the lease for the 2007–2008 hunting season. A dispute arose between a Linwood member and Scott as to the ownership of the twenty-acre tract to the east of the fence line. Subsequently, in December 2008, Anderson-Tully's attorney sent Scott a letter stating Anderson-Tully was the owner of the disputed tract. Scott consulted an attorney in 2009, but no legal action was taken at that time. Anderson-Tully continued to treat the land as its own, and harvested timber there in early 2010. Scott approached a logger who was on the disputed tract and told him to stop harvesting the timber on the land. The logger replied that he would need something in writing to prove Anderson-Tully was not the owner and then continued harvesting. This led to Scott's complaint filed on March 19, 2010.

After reviewing the parties' property descriptions, the chancellor concluded that neither "accurately describe[s] the disputed tract to any certainty so as to read the various descriptions and know which party is the record title owner of the property." However, the chancellor found that "the evidence overwhelmingly support[ed]" a finding of adverse possession in favor of Anderson-Tully. * * *

This Court "must defer to a chancery court's findings of fact unless they are manifestly wrong or clearly erroneous." Double J Farmlands Inc. v. Paradise Baptist Church, 999 So.2d 826, 829 (¶ 13) (Miss. 2008). * * *

Scott argues Anderson-Tully presented insufficient evidence to prove a claim of adverse possession. Mississippi Code Annotated section 15–1–13(1) (Rev. 2012) states:

> Ten (10) years' actual adverse possession by any person claiming to be the owner for that time of any land, uninterruptedly continued for ten (10) years by occupancy, descent, conveyance, or otherwise, in whatever way such occupancy may have commenced or continued, shall vest in every actual occupant or possessor of such land a full and complete title[.]

"[F]or possession to be adverse[,] it must be (1) under claim of ownership; (2) actual or hostile; (3) open, notorious, and visible; (4) continuous and uninterrupted for a period of ten years; (5) exclusive; and (6) peaceful." Blackburn v. Wong, 904 So.2d 134, 136 (¶ 15) (Miss.2004) (citing Thornhill v. Caroline Hunt Trust Estate, 594 So.2d 1150, 1152–53 (Miss.1992)). The claimant must prove each element by clear and convincing evidence. Id.

1. *Claim of Ownership*

To stake a claim of ownership, the possessor must "fly [his] flag over the property" in such a way as to put the actual owner on notice that the property is "being held under an adverse claim of ownership." Apperson v. White, 950 So.2d 1113, 1117 (¶ 7) (Miss. Ct. App. 2007) (citing Walker v. Murphree, 722 So.2d 1277, 1281 (¶ 16) (Miss. Ct. App. 1998)). The quality, not the quantity, of acts must be considered. Id. at (¶ 8). "The mere presence of a fence, without more, [is not] sufficient to sustain a claim of adverse possession." Double J, 999 So.2d at 829.

After purchasing the Jefferson County property in 1969, Anderson-Tully marked its borders with its recognizable company blue paint. The blue paint ran along the wire fence erected by the Scott family and included the disputed twenty acres in Section 28. Multiple witnesses saw the paint lines between 1969 and 2010, and knew the lines marked the boundary of Anderson-Tully's property. Thomas Middleton, a forester, performed a timber cruise at Scott's request in 2010 to establish damages for Anderson-Tully's removal of trees from the disputed acreage. He testified that the fence line was "distinctly painted" with blue paint. The blue paint was two different shades, indicating to him that the line had been repainted at some point. He was familiar with the blue boundary lines in the area, and he knew that the paint color was the one used by Anderson-Tully to mark its property lines. Anderson-Tully's company records show that it painted the blue line in 1969, and repainted it in 1986 and 1998. Anderson-Tully cut and harvested timber in 1990, 1999, and 2010. It also conducted timber-stand improvements to clear the land of unwanted trees, and granted five hunting licenses to the property. The hunting licenses contained maps, which described the disputed twenty acres as part of the lease.

Scott asserts that regardless of Anderson-Tully's actions, the estate has a possessory claim because he began paying property taxes on the disputed tract in 1993. The chancellor found Scott presented insufficient evidence to support his claim that he paid taxes on the disputed property. Regardless, the payment of taxes alone "is not dispositive of the claim of ownership." Nosser v. Buford, 852 So.2d 57, 61 (¶ 17) (Miss. Ct. App. 2002). Thus, we cannot find the chancellor erred in finding no merit to Scott's argument. We find the evidence sufficient to support the chancellor's finding that Anderson-Tully staked an ownership claim to the property from 1969 to 2010.

2.   *Actual or Hostile*

"Possession is hostile and adverse when the adverse possessor intends to claim title notwithstanding that the claim is made under a mistaken belief that the land is within the calls of the possessor's deed." Wicker v. Harvey, 937 So.2d 983, 994 (¶ 34) (Miss. Ct. App. 2006) (citing Alexander v. Hyland, 58 So.2d 826, 829 (Miss. 1952)). The adverse possessor must possess the property without the owner's permission, because permission defeats any claim of adverse possession.

Anderson-Tully marked, managed, harvested timber, and issued hunting licenses on the disputed property from 1969 to 2010. Anderson-Tully did not seek anyone's permission to use the property. Nations testified that everyone, including the Scotts, treated the wire fence as the dividing line between the properties as early as the 1930s. He recalled that as late as 1993, the Scotts cut timber only to the west of the fence line, but not to its east. The testimony established that after 1969, only Anderson-Tully used the disputed property.

Scott argues Anderson-Tully did not actually or hostilely possess the property because it did not care for or improve the land on a regular basis. "As a general rule, either actual or constructive occupation, cultivation or residence or use is necessary to constitute adverse possession." Kayser v. Dixon, 309 So.2d 526, 528–29 (Miss. 1975). However, "[p]ossessory acts necessary to establish a claim of adverse possession may vary with the characteristics of the land, and adverse possession of 'wild' or unimproved lands may be established by evidence of acts that would be wholly insufficient in the case of improved or developed lands." Apperson, 950 So.2d at 1117 (internal quotation marks and citation omitted). The property in question is undisputedly wild or unimproved land. Thus, "the quantum of proof necessary . . . to establish adverse possession over the disputed parcel is measurably lower than had the property been improved or developed." *Id.* "Possession of such [undeveloped] property may be established by a continued claim evidenced by public acts of ownership." Kayser, 309 So.2d at 529. Anderson-Tully marked the fence line with blue paint in 1969, 1986, and 1998. It cut and harvested timber in 1990, 1999, and 2010. It performed timber-stand improvements, and it issued five hunting licenses. We find the chancellor had substantial support in the evidence to find that these acts were public acts of ownership sufficient to establish an actual or hostile claim of ownership.

3. *Open, Notorious, and Visible*

For possession to be open, notorious, and visible, the possessor "must unfurl his flag on the land, and keep it flying, so that the actual owner may see, and if he will, that an enemy has invaded his domains, and planted the standard of conquest." Roberts v. Young's Creek Inv. Inc., 118 So.3d 665, 670 (Miss.Ct.App.2013) (quoting Wicker, 937 So.2d at 994).

The chancellor found Anderson-Tully openly and notoriously possessed the land from 1969, when it painted its boundary lines blue, until 2010, when Scott filed suit. The possession was visible, as evidenced by eyewitnesses who saw the blue paint along the fence line between 1969 and 2010. The possession was also notorious, as the fence and blue paint were recognized in the community as the dividing line between the properties. In addition to marking its borders with blue paint, Anderson-Tully cut and harvested timber, performed timber-stand improvements, and issued hunting licenses on the property. All of which were open, notorious, and visible to the public. Glynn Brown, Anderson-Tully's regional manager over land in Jefferson County, testified that in 1990 and 1999, when timber was cut, Anderson-Tully accessed the disputed property through the Scotts' property. Each time, the timber-cutting process took approximately a month. No one objected to their entering or cutting timber on the property. Nations testified that when loggers came onto the property, he could hear the timber being cut "a half a mile" away. This evidence supports the chancellor's finding that Anderson-Tully's use was open, notorious, and visible.

4. *Continuous and Uninterrupted for a Period of Ten Years*

Adverse possession requires continuous and uninterrupted possession of a disputed property for at least ten years. Miss. Code Ann. § 15–1–13(1). Even if a party is mistaken as to the calls of his deed, "if he has occupied the land for the statutory period under the claim that it was his own and was embraced within the calls of his deed, he is entitled to recover on the ground of adverse possession[.]" Pittman v. Simmons, 408 So.2d 1384, 1386 (Miss. 1982) (quoting Alexander, 58 So.2d at 829).

Anderson-Tully's possession began upon issuance of its deed in 1969. After marking its perceived boundary lines with blue paint, it proceeded to maintain the property, harvest timber, and issue hunting licenses. Nations testified that everyone, including the Scotts, treated the fence as the dividing line and that the Scotts never used the property east of the fence. Burkhardt testified that during his employment with Anderson-Tully from 1969 to 1981, he was never notified that anyone other than Anderson-Tully crossed the blue line.

Scott argues the possession was not continuous and uninterrupted because he disputed Anderson-Tully's possession in 2003. The chancellor recognized Scott's objection in 2003. The chancellor also noted that at some point, Scott painted an orange line along the fence line, although it was unclear when this was done. Finally, the chancellor found Scott made an indirect claim of ownership in 2007, when he cancelled the Linwood Hunting Club lease. However, the chancellor found these actions of no consequence, as Anderson-Tully's adverse-possession claim had ripened before Scott made the first objection in 2003. The evidence supports the chancellor's finding that Anderson-Tully's possession was continuous and uninterrupted for ten years.

5. *Exclusive*

"Exclusive possession means that the possessor 'evinces an intention to possess and hold land to the exclusion of, and in opposition to, the claims of all others, and the claimant's conduct must afford an unequivocal indication that he is exercising the dominion of a sole owner.'" *Roberts,* 118 So.3d at 671 (quoting *Wicker,* 937 So.2d at 995). Exclusive possession "does not mean that no one else can use the property." *Id.* (citing *Apperson,* 950 So.2d at 1119).

No testimony was presented that the Scotts or anyone other than Anderson-Tully used the property on the east side of the fence after 1969. Scott argues Anderson-Tully "allowed the Scott [family] to lease the disputed 20 acres to [the Linwood Hunting Club]." However, no evidence was presented to support this argument. To the contrary, Anderson-Tully maintained that it leased the twenty acres to the hunting club, and it provided evidence of contracts with plats attached that included the twenty acres. Nations maintained that the Scotts only used the property to the west of the fence line; and Burkhardt testified he would have been notified if anyone had regularly crossed the blue line onto the twenty acres during his employment at Anderson-Tully. No one did. Thus, the evidence supports the chancellor's finding that the possession for the statutory ten-year period was exclusive.

6. *Peaceful*

An adverse possessor's use of a claimed property must be peaceful. Miss. Code Ann. § 15–1–13(1). "[E]xpected disputes associated with the use or ownership of the property are not indicative of the possession not being peaceful." Roberts, 118 So.3d at 671. Burkhardt testified that from 1969 to 1981, no one objected to his survey or interfered with Anderson-Tully's ownership or use of the disputed tract. Scott argues Anderson-Tully's possession was not peaceful because it acted without consent in removing the timber. However, as stated, the first time Scott disputed Anderson-Tully's use of the land was in 2003, well after Anderson-Tully's adverse-possession claim had ripened. Thus, we find sufficient evidence in the record to support the chancellor's finding that Anderson-Tully's possession was peaceful. * * *

Anderson-Tully openly and notoriously possessed the disputed twenty-acre tract in Jefferson County from 1969 until Scott's complaint was filed in 2010. It marked its perceived boundary line with blue paint when it purchased the property in 1969, and repainted the boundary line in 1986 and 1998. It managed timber uninterruptedly from 1969 to 2010 and harvested timber in 1990, 1999, and 2010. No testimony was presented that the Scotts or anyone else used the disputed property after 1969. We find substantial evidence in the record to support the chancellor's finding that Anderson-Tully proved adverse possession by clear and convincing evidence. Therefore, we find the chancellor did not abuse his discretion and affirm.

NOTES AND QUESTIONS

1.   The doctrine of adverse possession evolved from judicial decisions resolving disputes over the application of the statute of limitations for recovery of possession of property. Assume the true owner of property (TO) is for some reason out of possession. She is, say, an absentee owner of land holding it for speculation, or has lost some personal property. Meanwhile, someone else, say a squatter or a finder or other type of adverse possessor (AP), has come into possession of the property. The TO has various causes of action allowing her to recover possession of property from an AP, such as ejectment in the case of land and replevin in the case of personal property (see Chapter IV). But she cannot wait forever to bring such an action. The legislature (Parliament in England or the legislatures of the American states) typically will have enacted statutes of limitations that bar the bringing of such actions after a certain number of years have passed. The time for bringing an action to recover possession of real property varies widely from state to state, from a low of five years to a high of 40 years. See Joseph William Singer, Introduction to Property § 4.2.6 (5th ed. 2017). The time period for bringing an action in replevin to recover personal property is typically shorter (most commonly three to five years).

2.   Of all the "adjectival" requirements for adverse possession—actual, exclusive, open and notorious, continuous, and adverse under a claim of right—which ones are at issue in *Scott v. Anderson-Tully Co.*? Courts often offer variations on the list of adjectival factors, and the list the court provides here is a little unconventional in adding a requirement that the possession be "peaceable" to the list. Does this add anything over and above the other factors? Whatever the exact list of factors one chooses, it can safely be said that the courts seek to assure themselves that the adverse possessor is acting as an owner would.

3.   The "open and notorious" requirement of adverse possession (along with the actual, continuous, and exclusive elements) is generally thought to provide notice to the true owner that someone else is claiming the property. The testimony in the principal case establishes that the much-discussed fence was erected by the Scotts, not by the Anderson-Tully Company. Should a party like Anderson-Tully be able to claim that it has provided notice to the true owner by painting a blue mark—presumably on "its" side—along

the fence erected by the true owners some years earlier for the purpose of containing grazing cattle? Is there any testimony that the Scotts were aware of the blue mark or knew of its significance?

4.   Should cutting timber during three years (out of the statutory 10) and allowing various parties to hunt on the land qualify as "actual" possession? A recent Kentucky case, *Moore v. Stills,* 307 S.W. 2d 71 (2010), concludes that recreational activities like hunting, fishing, and driving over the land in all-terrain vehicles do not qualify as "actual possession." The court was fortified in this conclusion by a recent Kentucky statute, similar to statutes passed in many other states, that provides "[n]o action for the recovery of real property . . . by adverse possession[ ] may be brought by any person whose claim is based on use solely for recreational purposes." Id. at 80, quoting KRS 411.190(8). These statutes are designed to reduce fears of property owners that they may lose their property by tolerating hunters and other recreational users on their land. Is the Mississippi court here bucking the tide by relying on recreational uses to establish "actual use" by the Anderson-Tully Company?

5.   Boundary disputes are a mainstay of adverse possession litigation. In some states, an alternative doctrine, usually called agreed boundaries, is available to resolve such disputes. As stated by a California decision:

> [T]he bases for this doctrine are that when there is uncertainty as to the true boundary between coterminous owners, such owners may, expressly or by implication, fix a boundary line by a fence or otherwise. Acceptance or acquiescence in the line so fixed for a period equal to that prescribed in the applicable statute of limitation . . . establishes the agreed boundary as the actual boundary. The object of this rule is to secure repose, to prevent strife and disputes concerning boundaries and make titles permanent and stable.

Finley v. Yuba County Water District, 99 Cal. App. 3d 691, 699 (1979). Agreed boundaries rests on a state of mind roughly the opposite of adverse possession. Adverse possession requires that the AP has proceeded without the permission of the TO. Agreed boundaries applies when the AP has acted with the permission—at least tacitly—of the TO. One would think that the doctrines are mutually exclusive, but there are any number of cases where APs have invoked both in the alternative. Which doctrine should be preferred as a basis for resolving boundary disputes? How would the principal case be decided under agreed boundaries?

6.   Surveying mistakes can lead to claims of adverse possession, as we will see in *Howard v. Kunto,* infra. Adverse possession often steps in where other systems of establishing ownership are treated as inadequate. Notice that in *Scott,* the area in question was in the U.S. Rectangular Survey, but because of difficult terrain had in effect reverted to metes and bounds (description in terms of lengths, directions, and monuments, see Chapter VIII). Moreover, the company's deed referred to the parcel by name, without even attempting a metes and bounds description. Should this make adverse possession harder or easier to claim? For a dramatic example of conflict

between land records and adverse possession, see Mugaas v. Smith, excerpted in Chapter VIII.

7.   The court here requires that the AP evince a "claim of ownership." Other states require either a "claim of right" or, sometimes, "color of title." "Claim of right" means, roughly, an intent to possess something as one's own. "Color of title" exists when a person has some document—usually a deed, will, or judicial decree—that purports to convey title but does not in fact do so because of some legal defect (e.g., the grantor did not own the land, or the instrument was improperly executed). A few states require "color of title" as an element of adverse possession, but most do not. Still, an adverse possessor with color of title has certain legal advantages. In some states the statute of limitations, which sets the requisite period of adverse possession, is shorter for possessors with color of title. In nearly all states, either by statute or under well-established doctrine, one who actually possesses part of a parcel of land under an instrument giving color of title to the whole parcel is deemed to "constructively possess" the whole. So *actual* adverse possession of part of the parcel described in a defective deed may give rise to *constructive* adverse possession of the whole parcel.

Purposes of Adverse Possession

Why do we permit longstanding adverse possession of property to ripen into a new title good against all the world, including the former owner? The general reasons for having a statute of limitations do not answer this question. There are, to be sure, justifications for having statutes of limitations. As time passes, witnesses die, memories fade, and evidence gets lost or destroyed. The costs of proving or disproving claims invariably increase over time. When these costs get too large, it is unfair to subject defendants to the risk of having to disprove them, and unduly burdensome to force courts to sort them out. But these costs could be avoided simply by interpreting the statute of limitations for actions to recover property to mean that the plaintiff cannot rely on events that happened before the period prescribed by the statute. Suppose the statute of limitations is ten years and the defendant constructed a building on plaintiff's land fifteen years ago. We could interpret the statute to mean that the plaintiff cannot allege or prove events occurring more than ten years ago, such as the original construction of the building. But this would not bar the plaintiff from proving that the building now sits on his land, that it is presently depriving him of possession, and that it should be torn down so as to permit him to recover possession. Such an interpretation would avoid any danger of having to rely on lost evidence or to call witnesses whose memories have faded. In order to justify the doctrine of adverse possession—which treats the passage of the statute not just as a rule that cuts off old claims but as an event that in effect transfers ownership to the adverse possessor—we need some other reason or rationale.

Perhaps the most commonly cited rationale is couched in terms of the reliance interests that the possessor may have developed through longstanding possession of the property. Holmes expressed the idea in typically colorful fashion: "[M]an, like a tree in the cleft of a rock, gradually shapes his roots to his surroundings, and when the roots have grown up to a certain size, can't be displaced without cutting at his life." Letter from Oliver Wendell Holmes to William James (Apr. 1, 1907), in The Mind and Faith of Justice Holmes: His Speeches, Essays, Letters and Judicial Opinions 417, 417–18 (Max Lerner ed., 1943). Modern commentators have recast the argument in terms of loss aversion or the endowment effect. Psychological studies show that people tend to experience losses more acutely than foregone gains. In other words, losing something one already has is relatively more painful than not getting something one does not yet have. If the AP is the person who "has" the property—which makes sense given that the AP is the one in possession—then taking it from the AP may be more demoralizing to the AP than denying it to the TO would be demoralizing to the TO. See Jeffrey Evans Stake, The Uneasy Case for Adverse Possession, 89 Geo. L.J. 2419, 2459–71 (2001). An alternative way to make the point is that the AP may have more of her "personhood" wrapped up in the property than the TO. For the AP, the dispute involves some "thing" which the AP possesses; for the TO, what is at issue is more in the nature of a fungible asset interchangeable with other assets. See Margaret Jane Radin, Time, Possession, and Alienation, 64 Wash. U. L.Q. 739, 748 n.26 (1986).

Another longstanding rationale claims that adverse possession is a penalty designed to discourage TOs from "sleeping on their rights." This has been criticized as privileging active exploitation of land and resources and discouraging passive, preservationist uses. See John C. Sprankling, An Environmental Critique of Adverse Possession, 79 Cornell L. Rev. 816 (1994). But if we recast the point in terms of the gatekeeper idea perhaps it avoids this criticism. Private property can be seen as a system that delegates managerial authority over resources to private individuals who act as gatekeepers. If the gatekeeper falls down on the job, the resource may not be protected against abuse. Indeed, if the resource is a forest or a wetland, a sleeping gatekeeper may result in the resource being looted as an open access commons. Adverse possession can be seen from this perspective as a device for firing gatekeepers guilty of nonfeasance and replacing them with persons who have shown a greater aptitude and eagerness to play the gatekeeper role.

A third rationale is that adverse possession reduces the transaction costs of determining title to assets that last for a long time (like land). Over time, various potential claims to assets can accumulate: Perhaps the property was mortgaged at various times and it is unclear whether those security interests were released; perhaps a married couple owned the property and it is unclear whether both spouses released their claims; perhaps taxes due on the property were not paid in a given year. If all these claims had to be investigated, no matter how old they might be, the costs of establishing clear title to durable assets would be very large—

large enough that they could impair the effective functioning of markets for durable assets. By systematically eliminating these old claims, like a broom that sweeps away old cobwebs, adverse possession reduces the costs of engaging in these transactions, and hence enhances the efficiency of property markets. Sometimes it is said that marketable title acts are equally or more effective in eliminating these old claims. See Stake, supra, at 2443–44. These statutes apply a conclusive presumption that claims not (re)recorded within a certain period of time (e.g., 40 years) can be disregarded in establishing title to property. But marketable title acts can be regarded as a version of adverse possession law—a version with a longer statute of limitations and fewer additional elements. So the existence of these statutes only confirms the need for some mechanism like adverse possession to clear away old claims to property. (For more on marketable title acts and land records generally, see Chapter VIII.)

Adverse Possession Against the Government

At common law one could not obtain title by adverse possession against the crown. This was pursuant to the maxim, *nullum tempus occurrit regi* ("no time runs against the king"). As Blackstone explained, the law presumes "the king is always busied for the public good, and therefore has not leisure to assert his right within the times limited to subjects." 1 Blackstone, Commentaries *240. This assumption carried over to the United States, with the people's elected representatives now enjoying the presumption formerly accorded the king. See, e.g., United States v. Thompson, 98 U.S. 486 (1878); United States v. Hoar, 26 F. Cas. 329 (C.C. Mass. 1821) (Story, J.). The courts concluded that "[i]n a representative government, where the people do not and cannot act in a body, where their power is delegated to others, and must of necessity be exercised by them, if exercised at all, the reason for applying these principles is equally cogent." Thompson, 98 U.S. at 489.

The presumption that adverse possession does not apply to the government took on special significance during the settlement of the United States, given the widespread practice of squatting on the federal public lands, described earlier in this Chapter. Since the courts would not permit adverse possession as a matter of common law, this meant that Congress could determine, in its discretion, the terms and conditions for permitting squatters to obtain title to public land. Congress, through the preemption acts, generally treated the squatters more generously than they would have been treated under the law of adverse possession—but this judgment was for Congress to make. The common-law rule takes on special importance today, given the federal government's retention of millions of acres of National Parks, National Forests, Wilderness Areas, and other uninhabited lands. If adverse possession could be claimed against the federal government, these lands could be at risk, given the very high monitoring costs that would be involved. See Round Table Discussion, Time, Property Rights, and the Common Law, 64 Wash. U.

L.Q. 793, 832–33 (1986) (comments of Robert Ellickson). The presumption that adverse possession does not apply against the government has been retained in some states, modified in others with longer statutes of limitations against the government than against private owners, and has been abolished in still others. See William C. Marra, Adverse Possession, Takings, and the State, 89 U. Det. Mercy L. Rev. 1 (2011).

Carpenter v. Ruperto

Supreme Court of Iowa, 1982.
315 N.W.2d 782.

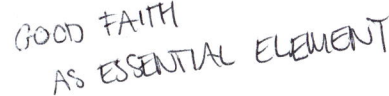

GOOD FAITH AS ESSENTIAL ELEMENT

■ McCORMICK, JUSTICE. Plaintiff Virginia Carpenter appeals from an adverse decree in her action to quiet title to land adjacent to her residential premises based on a theory of adverse possession. * * * We affirm[.] * * *

Plaintiff and her husband moved in 1951 to a home which they purchased in southeast Des Moines. Plaintiff's husband subsequently died, but plaintiff has lived on the premises continuously. Her lot has a frontage of 40 feet and is 125 feet long. * * *

A larger undeveloped lot bounded plaintiff's property to the north. * * *

Defendants and their predecessors have held record title to this lot at all material times.

The property which plaintiff claims to have acquired by adverse possession is the south 60 feet of defendants' lot. Thus, the property in dispute is a 60 by 125 foot parcel adjacent to the north boundary of plaintiff's lot.

When plaintiff and her husband moved into their home in July 1951, the lot north of their property was a cornfield. Although plaintiff was not certain of the location of the northern boundary of her lot, she knew her lot's dimensions, and she knew it did not include the cornfield. In 1952 the corn was not planted as far south on the adjacent lot. Concerned about rats and the threat of fire, and desiring additional yard for their children, plaintiff and her husband cleared several feet of the property to the north, graded it, and planted grass seed on it. Since that time plaintiff has used the land as an extension of her yard. She planted peony bushes on it during the 1950's, installed a propane tank on it approximately 30 feet north of her lot in 1964, constructed a dirt bank on the city right of way to divert water from that parcel in 1965, and put in a driveway infringing five feet onto the land in 1975.

The remainder of defendants' lot was planted in corn until approximately 1957. The lot was owned by Abraham and Beverly Rosenfeld from July 1960 until February 1978. During that period the only use Rosenfelds made of the property was to store junk and debris on it. Except for the strip used by plaintiff, the lot was overgrown with brush and weeds. The Rosenfelds paid all taxes and special assessments on the property. Plaintiff and her husband at one time obtained the Rosenfelds' permission to keep a horse on the lot. On one occasion in the 1960's plaintiff examined the plat of defendants' lot in the courthouse to see if it ran all the way to a street to the north.

When defendant McCormick purchased his interest in the lot in 1978, he was aware of the possibility of a boundary dispute because of the location of plaintiff's propane tank and driveway. He and the other defendants were unsuccessful in their efforts to settle the dispute with plaintiff, who subsequently brought this action.

In seeking to establish her ownership of the disputed parcel, plaintiff alleged she had "for more than thirty (30) years last past been in open, exclusive, hostile, adverse and actual possession under claim of right." The trial court held in part that she did not establish her possession was under a claim of right. The court reasoned that a claim of right must be made in good faith and that plaintiff was not in good faith because she knew someone else had title to the land. Although the court found plaintiff had not proved her claim of adverse possession, it ordered defendants to "do equity" by deeding to her the strip of land her driveway was on and to pay the costs of moving the propane tank to her lot. * * *

The doctrine of adverse possession is based on the ten-year statute of limitations for recovery of real property in section 614.1(5), The Code. One claiming title by adverse possession must establish hostile, actual, open, exclusive and continuous possession, under a claim of right or color of title, for at least ten years, by clear and positive proof. Because the law presumes possession under regular title, the doctrine is strictly construed. These and other governing principles are explained in I–80 Associates, Inc. v. Chicago, Rock Island and Pacific Railroad, 224 N.W.2d 8, 10–11 (Iowa 1974).

As permitted, plaintiff relied on claim of right rather than color of title. In contending the trial court erred in finding she failed in her proof of this element, she attacks the viability of the principal case relied on by the trial court, Goulding v. Shonquist, 141 N.W. 24 (Iowa 1913). Its facts are analogous to those here.

In Goulding the individual also cleared land adjacent to his house. The land was overrun with brush and willows and was frequented by hunters. After clearing it, the individual used the land as a pasture and garden. In finding he did not establish good faith claim of right, the court said:

> When he moved into his present property, the lands in question were objectionable because they were frequented by hunters, and for that reason he and his wife thought they ought to clear them up. He says he supposed they were part of the old river bed or waste land upon which anyone could enter. No other facts

are offered by defendant as a reason for entering into the possession of the land at that time. Whether the title to the land was in the state or some other person, the defendant knew that he had no title and that he had no claim of title, and no right whatever to enter into the possession, and his possession was not in good faith for that reason.

141 N.W. at 25. The court quoted a statement from Litchfield v. Sewell, 66 N.W. 104, 106 (Iowa 1896), * * * "that there can be no such thing as adverse possession where the party knows he has no title, and that, under the law, he can acquire none by his occupation."

Plaintiff argues that it is inconsistent to say ownership can be acquired by claim of right as an alternative to color of title and at the same time say ownership cannot be acquired by a person who knows he does not have title. She also argues that the good faith requirement was eliminated by the court decision in *I–80 Associates, Inc.* Although we agree it is an overstatement to say ownership cannot be acquired by a person who knows he does not have title, plaintiff is incorrect in her argument that good faith is not an essential component of claim of right. Moreover, we agree with the trial court that plaintiff did not prove this element of her adverse possession claim.

good faith IS essential element

The overbreadth of the statement that title cannot be obtained through adverse possession by one who knows he has no title is demonstrated in *Litchfield*, *Goulding* and subsequent decisions. In *Litchfield* the court rejected the adverse possession claim of a person in possession of land under a quitclaim deed from a squatter. In finding an absence of good faith, the court noted the adverse possession doctrine "has no application to one who actually knows that he has no claim, or title, or right to a title." 66 N.W. at 106. Under this holding a mere squatter or one who claims under a squatter cannot have a good faith claim of right to the property, but mere knowledge by the person that he has no title is not preclusive. A claim of right by a squatter is a false claim. To permit a squatter to assert a claim of right would put a premium on dishonesty. See 4 H. Tiffany, Real Property § 1147 at 792 (3d ed. 1975). One of the main purposes of the claim of right requirement is "to bar mere squatters from the benefits of adverse possession." 7 R. Powell, Real Property ¶ 1015 (Rohan ed. 1981).

As in *Litchfield*, the possessor in *Goulding* not only knew that he had no title but that he had no claim of title or any right to enter into possession of the property. He was a mere squatter.

Knowledge of a defect in title is not alone sufficient to preclude proof of good faith:

One is not deprived of the benefit of the statute of limitations merely because his claim of right is unenforceable or his title is known to be defective. The doctrine of adverse possession presupposes a defective title. It is not based on, but is hostile to, the true title. If the statute were to run only in favor of a valid title, it would serve no purpose. The holder of such a title has no need to invoke the statute. Where bad faith is held to negative an alleged claim of right, it is only another way of saying that such claim has been disproved.

Creel v. Hammans, 13 N.W.2d 305, 307 (Iowa 1944).

no title + no basis for claiming interest

Nevertheless, when knowledge of lack of title is accompanied by knowledge of no basis for claiming an interest in the property, a good faith claim of right cannot be established. * * *

We believe plaintiff failed to prove a good faith claim of right in the present case. She knew her lot did not include the cornfield north of it. She knew someone else had title to it and she had no interest in it or claim to it. This is not a case of confusion or mistake. At the time she entered possession of the disputed land, plaintiff knew she had no legal right to do so. To say that one can acquire a claim of right by merely entering possession would recognize squatter's rights. Possession for the statutory period cannot be bootstrapped into a basis for claiming a right to possession.

We hold that the trial court was right in rejecting plaintiff's claim. * * *

Figure 2-6
Land at Issue in *Carpenter v. Ruperto*, June 2006

(Note that the land is now surrounded by a fence.)

NOTES AND QUESTIONS

1. Probably the most contentious issue in the law of adverse possession is what it means to say that the AP's possession must be adverse under a claim of right. (Sometimes courts say "hostile under a claim of right" or just "adverse" or "hostile," and in *Scott*, supra, the court couches it as a "claim of ownership.") Commentators generally distinguish three positions: (1) Adverse under a claim of *right* means that the AP subjectively (but mistakenly) believes he is legally entitled to possession of the property, i.e., the AP is acting in good faith. (2) Adverse under a claim of right means that the AP subjectively believes he is not legally entitled to possession of the property, i.e., the AP is acting in bad faith. (3) The AP's subjective state of mind is irrelevant; all that matters is that the AP has not been given permission by the TO to use the property. The rule (our (2)) requiring bad faith has been called the "Maine Rule," after the convoluted decision in *Preble v. Maine Cent. R. Co.*, 27 A. 149 (Me. 1893). It has always been at best the minority rule; indeed, legislation in Maine now precludes it. See Maine Rev. Stat. § 810–A. Most commentators favor the so-called Connecticut Rule (our (3)), which makes state of mind irrelevant. But disagreement abounds as to whether good faith should be required or all that is required is lack of permission. That adverse possession comes up in squatting, color of title, and boundary mistake cases, has led courts to equivocate and confuse the issue. See, e.g., Lee Anne Fennell, Efficient Trespass: The Case for Bad Faith Adverse Possession, 100 Nw. U. L. Rev. 1037 (2006); Jeffrey Evans Stake, The Uneasy Case for Adverse Possession, 89 Geo. L.J. 2419 (2001); Luke Meier, The Neglected History Behind *Preble v. Maine Central Railroad Company*: Lessons from the "Maine Rule" for Adverse Possession, 44 Hofstra L. Rev. 537 (2016).

2. *Carpenter* is probably in the minority in explicitly requiring good faith as a condition of obtaining title by adverse possession. The English cases and most American legal commentators favor the objective non-permission interpretation of adverse under a claim of right. This position is logical if we think of adverse possession as being grounded in the application of the statute of limitations to a legal action in trespass, ejectment, conversion, or replevin to recover possession of property. None of these actions requires subjective good faith or bad faith on the part of the possessor—lack of permission from the TO is enough—so it stands to reason that the statute of limitations on these actions will run without regard to the subjective state of mind of the adverse possessor. In an important survey of the American appellate case law, however, Professor Helmholz concluded that courts generally grant adverse possession only to possessors who act in good faith. See Richard Helmholz, Adverse Possession and Subjective Intent, 61 Wash. U. L.Q. 65 (1983). His claim is controversial, and elicited a vigorous rejoinder. See Roger Cunningham, Adverse Possession and Subjective Intent: A Reply to Professor Helmholz, 64 Wash. U. L.Q. 1 (1986); Richard Helmholz, More on Subjective Intent: A Response to Professor Cunningham, 64 Wash. U. L.Q. 65 (1986). Helmholz does not contend that most courts actually require good faith; his claim is that, as he reads the recitation of the facts in reported appellate opinions, when courts award title by adverse

possession, the AP almost invariably is portrayed in the opinion as having acted in good faith.

3.   Recent developments in adverse possession law have focused on the role of bad faith. In a notorious (in the nonlegal sense) case in Colorado, a former judge successfully invoked adverse possession in bad faith to acquire one third of his neighbor's land, McLean v. DK Trust, No. 06 CV 982, slip op. at 1 (Dist. Ct. Colo. Oct. 17, 2007). Public protests and death threats ensued, resulting in a successful campaign to amend Colorado law to render bad faith disqualifying in adverse possession cases. Colo. Rev. Stat. § 38–41–101(3)(b)(II). Interestingly, the Colorado statute now gives courts discretion to order compensation to the party losing title in an adverse possession case. Id. § 38–41–108–(5)(a). (For more on compensation in the context of prescriptive easements, see Chapter IX.) Recently, in response to cases that had resulted in the Court of Appeals dropping a good faith requirement for adverse possession, the New York Assembly amended its adverse possession statute to require that adverse possession be asserted under a "claim of right," which in turn requires that an adverse possessor have a reasonable basis to believe she is the true owner. N.Y. Real Prop. Acts. & Proc. Law § 501(3).

4.   Do these developments suggest that the Iowa Supreme Court's position that squatters cannot obtain title to land by adverse possession is the wave of the future? Or does some recent commentary celebrating some instances of squatting suggest the opposite? Eduardo Moisés Peñalver & Sonia K. Katyal, Property Outlaws: How Squatters, Pirates, and Protesters Improve the Law of Ownership (2010); see also Elizabeth M. Glazer, Rule of (Out)law: Property's Contingent Right to Exclude, 156 U. Pa. L. Rev. PENNumbra 331, 342–43 (2008). Or do the recent controversies suggest that limiting adverse possession to good faith possessors accords with widespread moral intuitions, thereby making property norms more secure and easier to communicate? See Thomas W. Merrill & Henry E. Smith, The Morality of Property, 48 Wm. & Mary L. Rev. 1849 (2007).

5.   Is there a limit to how far back we are willing to go to rectify the acquisition of property in bad faith? Should there be a two-tiered statute of limitations (and doctrine of adverse possession)—a relatively short period (say 10 years) for good faith misappropriations, and a much longer period (say 50 years or even 100 years) for bad faith misappropriations? See Richard A. Epstein, Past and Future: The Temporal Dimension in the Law of Property, 64 Wash. U. L.Q. 667, 685–89 (1986). Some countries do have a longer statute of limitations for what amounts to adverse possession in bad faith, and some states have a longer statute of limitations for claims not based on color of title.

6.   Pressure has built to relax adverse possession law in the face of mass injustice. Many courts are reluctant to dismiss on grounds of adverse possession claims by descendants of victims of Nazi persecution seeking to recover artwork and other valuable assets looted by the Nazis many decades before. The Holocaust Expropriated Art Recovery Act of 2016 (codified at 22 U.S.C. § 1621) overrides state statuses of limitations for "artwork or other property that was lost during the covered period" of January 1, 1933 to

December 31, 1945 "because of Nazi persecution" and subjects such claims to a national six-year statute of limitations; the new statute of limitations expires on January 1, 2027 at which time the state statutes will again govern. See Fallon S. Sheridan, The Sunset of the Holocaust Expropriated Art Recovery Act of 2016 and the Rise of the Demand and Refusal Rule, 89 Fordham L. Rev. 2841 (2021). A provision precluding the defense of laches was eliminated from an early version of the bill. Would any application of the doctrine of laches undermine the purpose of the act? See Scott M. Caravello, The Role of the Doctrine of Laches in Undermining the Holocaust Expropriated Art Recovery Act, 106 Va. L. Rev. 1769 (2020).

Howard v. Kunto

Court of Appeals of Washington, 1970.
477 P.2d 210.

■ PEARSON, JUDGE. Land surveying is an ancient art but not one free of the errors that often creep into the affairs of men. In this case, we are presented with the question of what happens when the descriptions in deeds do not fit the land the deed holders are occupying. Defendants appeal from a decree quieting title in the plaintiffs of a tract of land on the shore of Hood Canal in Mason County.

At least as long ago as 1932 the record tells us that one McCall resided in the house now occupied by the appellant-defendants, Kunto. McCall had a deed that described a 50-foot-wide parcel on the shore of Hood Canal. The error that brings this case before us is that the 50 feet described in the deed is not the same 50 feet upon which McCall's house stood. Rather, the described land is an adjacent 50-foot lot directly west of that upon which the house stood. In other words, McCall's house stood on one lot and his deed described the adjacent lot. Several property owners to the west of defendants, not parties to this action, are similarly situated.

Over the years since 1946, several conveyances occurred, using the same legal description and accompanied by a transfer of possession to the succeeding occupants. The Kuntos' immediate predecessors in interest, Millers, desired to build a dock. To this end, they had a survey performed which indicated that the deed description and the physical occupation were in conformity. Several boundary stakes were placed as a result of this survey and the dock was constructed, as well as other improvements. The house as well as the others in the area continued to be used as summer recreational retreats.

The Kuntos then took possession of the disputed property under a deed from the Millers in 1959. In 1960 the respondent-plaintiffs, Howard, who held land east of that of the Kuntos, determined to convey an undivided one-half interest in their land to the Yearlys. To this end, they undertook to have a survey of the entire area made. After expending considerable effort, the surveyor retained by the Howards discovered that according to the government survey, the deed descriptions and the land occupancy of the parties did not coincide. Between the Howards and the Kuntos lay the Moyers' property. When the Howards' survey was completed, they discovered that they were the record owners of the land occupied by the Moyers and that the Moyers held record title to the land occupied by the Kuntos. Howard approached Moyer and in return for a conveyance of the land upon which the Moyers' house stood, Moyer conveyed to the Howards record title to the land upon which the Kunto house stood. Until plaintiffs Howard obtained the conveyance from Moyer in April, 1960, neither Moyer nor any of his predecessors ever asserted any right to ownership of the property actually being possessed by Kunto and his predecessors. This action was then instituted to quiet title in the Howards and Yearlys. The Kuntos appeal from a trial court decision granting this remedy.

At the time this action was commenced on August 19, 1960, defendants had been in occupance of the disputed property less than a year. The trial court's reason for denying their claim of adverse possession is succinctly stated in its memorandum opinion: "In this instance, defendants have failed to prove, by a preponderance of the evidence, a continuity of possession or estate to permit tacking of the adverse possession of defendants to the possession of their predecessors."

Finding of fact 6,[4] which is challenged by defendants, incorporates the above concept and additionally finds defendant's possession not to have been "continuous" because it involved only "summer occupancy."

---

[4] "In the instant case the defendants' building was not simply over the line, but instead was built wholly upon the wrong piece of property, not the property of defendants, described in Paragraph Four (4) of the complaint herein, but on the property of plaintiffs, described in Paragraph Three of the complaint and herein. That the last three deeds in the chain of title, covering and embracing defendants' property, including defendants' deed, were executed in other states, specifically, California and Oregon. And there is no evidence of pointing out to the grantees in said three deeds, aforesaid, including defendants' deed, of any specific property, other than the property of defendants, described in their deed, and in Paragraph Four (4) of the complaint, and herein; nor of any immediate act of the grantees, including defendants, in said Three (3) deeds, aforesaid, of taking possession of any property, other than described in said three (3) deeds, aforesaid; and the testimony of husband, defendant, was unequivocally that he had no intention of possessing or holding anything other than what the deed called for; and, that there is no showing of any continuous possession by defendants or their immediate predecessors in interest, since the evidence indicates the property was in the nature, for [use], as a summer occupancy, and such occupancy and use was for rather limited periods of time during comparatively short portions of the year, and was far from continuous."

Figure 2-7

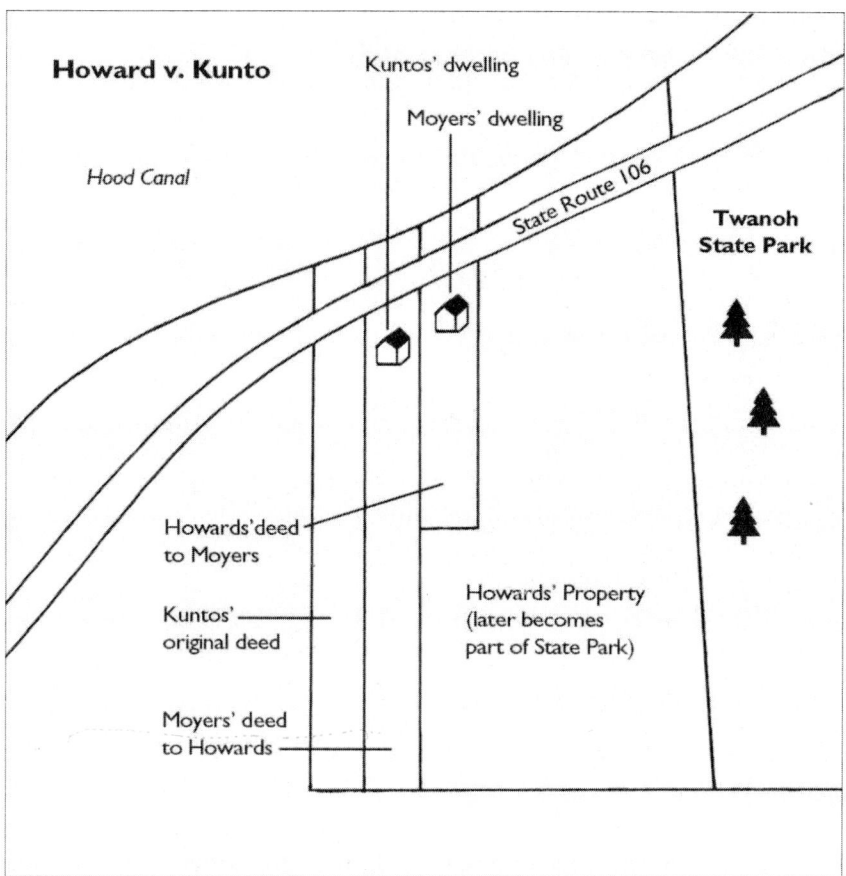

Two issues are presented by this appeal:

(1) Is a claim of adverse possession defeated because the physical use of the premises is restricted to summer occupancy?

(2) May a person who receives record title to tract A under the mistaken belief that he has title to tract B (immediately contiguous to tract A) and who subsequently occupies tract B, for the purpose of establishing title to tract B by adverse possession, use the periods of possession of tract B by his immediate predecessors who also had record title to tract A?

In approaching both of these questions, we point out that the evidence, largely undisputed in any material sense, established that defendant or his immediate predecessors did occupy the premises, which we have called tract B, as though it was their own for far more than the 10 years as prescribed in RCW 4.16.020.[5]

We also point out that finding of fact 6 is not challenged for its factual determinations but for the conclusions contained therein to the effect that the continuity of possession may not be established by summer occupancy, and that a predecessor's possession may not be tacked because a legal "claim of right" did not exist under the circumstances.

We start with the oft-quoted rule that: "To constitute adverse possession, there must be actual possession which is *uninterrupted*, open and notorious, hostile and exclusive, and under a *claim of right* made in good faith for the statutory period." Butler v. Anderson, 426 P.2d 467, 470 (Wash. 1967) (emphasis added).

We reject the conclusion that summer occupancy only of a summer beach home destroys the continuity of possession required by the statute. It has become firmly established that the requisite possession requires such possession and dominion "as ordinarily marks the conduct of owners in general in holding, managing, and caring for property of like nature and condition." Whalen v. Smith, 167 N.W. 646, 647 (Iowa 1918).

We hold that occupancy of tract B during the summer months for more than the 10-year period by defendant and his predecessors, together with the continued existence of the improvements on the land and beach area, constituted "uninterrupted" possession within this rule. To hold otherwise is to completely ignore the nature and condition of the property.

We find such rule fully consonant with the legal writers on the subject. In F. Clark, Law of Surveying and Boundaries, § 561 (3d ed. 1959) at 565: "Continuity of possession may be established although the land is used regularly for only a certain period each year." Further, at 566:

> This rule * * * is one of substance and not of absolute mathematical continuity, provided there is no break so as to sever two possessions. It is not necessary that the occupant should be actually upon the premises continually. If the land is occupied during the period of time during the year it is capable of use, there is sufficient continuity.

We now reach the question of tacking. The precise issue before us is novel in that none of the property occupied by defendant or his

---

[5]   This statute provides:

     4.16.020 Actions to be commenced within ten years. The period prescribed in RCW 4.16.010 for the commencement of actions shall be as follows:

    Within ten years;

    Actions for the recovery of real property, or for the recovery of the possession thereof; and no action shall be maintained for such recovery unless it appears that the plaintiff, his ancestor, predecessor or grantor was seized or possessed of the premises in question within ten years before the commencement of the action.

predecessors coincided with the property described in their deeds, but was contiguous.

In the typical case, which has been subject to much litigation, the party seeking to establish title by adverse possession claims *more* land than that described in the deed. In such cases it is clear that tacking is permitted.

In Buchanan v. Cassell, 335 P.2d 600, 602 (Wash. 1959) the Supreme Court stated: "This state follows the rule that a purchaser may tack the adverse use of its predecessor in interest to that of his own where the land was intended to be included in the deed between them, but was mistakenly omitted from the description." El Cerrito, Inc. v. Ryndak, 376 P.2d 528 (Wash. 1962).

The general statement which appears in many of the cases is that tacking of adverse possession is permitted if the successive occupants are in "privity." See Faubion v. Elder, 301 P.2d 153 (Wash. 1956). The deed running between the parties purporting to transfer the land possessed traditionally furnishes the privity of estate which connects the possession of the successive occupants. Plaintiff contends, and the trial court ruled, that where the deed does not describe *any* of the land which was occupied, the actual transfer of possession is insufficient to establish privity.

To assess the cogency of this argument and ruling, we must turn to the historical reasons for requiring privity as a necessary prerequisite to tacking the possession of several occupants. Very few, if any, of the reasons appear in the cases, nor do the cases analyze the relationships that must exist between successive possessors for tacking to be allowed. See W. Stoebuck, The Law of Adverse Possession In Washington in 35 Wash.L.Rev. 53 (1960).

The requirement of privity had its roots in the notion that a succession of trespasses, even though there was no appreciable interval between them, should not, in equity, be allowed to defeat the record title. The "claim of right," "color of title" requirement of the statutes and cases was probably derived from the early American belief that the squatter should not be able to profit by his trespass.[6]

However, it appears to this court that there is a substantial difference between the squatter or trespasser and the property purchaser, who along with several of his neighbors, as a result of an inaccurate survey or subdivision, occupies and improves property exactly 50 feet to the east of that which a survey some 30 years later demonstrates that they in fact own. It seems to us that there is also a strong public policy favoring early certainty as to the location of land ownership which enters into a proper interpretation of privity.

On the irregular perimeters of Puget Sound exact determination of land locations and boundaries is difficult and expensive. This difficulty is

---

[6]   The English common law does not require privity as a prerequisite for tacking. See F. Clark, Law of Surveying and Boundaries, § 561 (3d ed. 1959) at 568.

convincingly demonstrated in this case by the problems plaintiff's engineer encountered in attempting to locate the corners. It cannot be expected that every purchaser will or should engage a surveyor to ascertain that the beach home he is purchasing lies within the boundaries described in his deed. Such a practice is neither reasonable nor customary. Of course, 50-foot errors in descriptions are [devastating] where a group of adjacent owners each hold 50 feet of waterfront property.

unreasonable

The technical requirement of "privity" should not, we think, be used to upset the long periods of occupancy of those who in good faith received an erroneous deed description. Their "claim of right" is no less persuasive than the purchaser who believes he is purchasing *more* land than his deed described.

In the final analysis, however, we believe the requirement of "privity" is no more than judicial recognition of the need for some reasonable connection between successive occupants of real property so as to raise their claim of right above the status of the wrongdoer or the trespasser. We think such reasonable connection exists in this case.

Where, as here, several successive purchasers received record title to tract A under the mistaken belief that they were acquiring tract B, immediately contiguous thereto, and where possession of tract B is transferred and occupied in a continuous manner for more than 10 years by successive occupants, we hold there is sufficient privity of estate to permit tacking and thus establish adverse possession as a matter of law.

We see no reason in law or in equity for differentiating this case from Faubion v. Elder, 301 P.2d 153 (Wash. 1956) where the appellants were claiming *more* land than their deed described and where successive periods of occupation were allowed to be united to each other to make up the time of adverse holding. This application of the privity requirement should particularly pertain where the holder of record title to tract B acquired the same with knowledge of the discrepancy.

Judgment is reversed with directions to dismiss plaintiffs' action and to enter a decree quieting defendants' title to the disputed tract of land in accordance with the prayer of their cross-complaint.

NOTES AND QUESTIONS

1.   A large number of adverse possession disputes seem to involve seasonal or vacation properties. Why do you suppose this might be the case?

2.   Which of the five standard doctrinal elements is at issue in *Howard v. Kunto*? Why are the other issues ignored?

3.   What is the best characterization of the state of mind of the Kuntos (adverse possessors): good faith, bad faith, or unclear? What state of mind does the State of Washington appear to require in order to establish title by adverse possession?

4.   By limiting tacking to situations in which successive APs are in "privity of estate," the court permits tacking when A enters adversely, and then sells to B, who then sells to C. But tacking would not be permitted where A enters adversely, and then B enters adversely (the very instant A leaves), and the then C enters adversely (the very instant B leaves). Why should these two situations be treated differently?

5.   Note that issues about tacking can arise on both the AP side of the dispute (as discussed in *Howard v. Kunto*) or on the TO side of the dispute. In fact, isn't there a tacking issue on both the AP side and the TO side in *Howard v. Kunto*? The Howards only just recently acquired from the Moyers the deed describing the land on which the Kuntos' house sits. In theory, therefore, the Kuntos must show that the transfer of the deed from the Moyers to the Howards did not start the statute of limitations running anew. Should privity of estate also be required before an AP can tack the current TO's period of ownership onto that of a prior owner in order to show that the period of the statute of limitations has elapsed?

6.   Another wrinkle in the adverse possession timeline is the doctrine of "relation back." Once the AP has satisfied the requirements for acquisition of title by adverse possession, the AP is (now) deemed to have been the owner from the time that the AP first entered into (adverse) possession. Of course, during that time, if the TO had sued the AP in trespass or ejectment or in a quiet title action, the TO would (absent error) be declared the owner. Why might relation back matter? Incidentally, as of what date is the adverse possession complete in this case?

NOTE ON DISABILITIES

Another issue that occasionally arises in determining whether the statute of limitations has run involves whether the TO's circumstances should excuse her from bringing suit or whether they should either slow down or stop the clock running on bringing suit. Typically, state statutes provide that the statute of limitations is tolled for owners suffering from certain narrow classes of disabilities, including being under age, insane, legally incompetent, or (sometimes) in prison, *at the time the AP entered*. Disabilities arising later usually do not affect the running of the statute, and disabilities in the same or successive owners cannot be tacked. Also, other hardships that might hinder the TO from bringing suit, such as poverty, do not affect the running of the statute.

The mechanisms for altering the statutory period vary. Under one common approach, a shorter period of time, say 10 years as opposed to 20 years, is provided as a minimum after the removal of the disability. See, e.g., N.D. Cen. Code §§ 28–01–08 & –14 (providing for special 10-year statute of limitations after removal of disability instead of otherwise applicable 20-year periods in cases of disability); Ohio Rev. Code Ann. § 2305.04 (providing for 10 years after removal of disability if the regular 21-year statute of limitations would already have run). In other states, the disability tolls the statute. See, e.g., Mont. Code § 70–19–413. Usually, a successor of the landowner under the disability benefits from the same provision, but not all states allow for this.

Consider this example. The statutory period for adverse possession is 20 years. When the AP enters, TO is insane. Twenty-five years pass, and then TO regains his sanity. On the first, "additional time," approach, the TO then has 10 years to bring an action to regain possession. (What if the regular statute of limitations is 20 years and the disability is removed in Year 19?) On the second, "tolling," approach, the TO would now have 20 years. If the TO had been a minor at the time of entry by the AP and in the meantime had become insane or gone to prison, the statutory clock would have started ticking again when TO attains the age of majority.

It is easy to see how the disability might make us skeptical that the TO is being truly slothful. Do these rules about disabilities fit in with any of the other rationales for adverse possession? Why should only disabilities existing at the time of the AP's entry affect the length of the statutory period for adverse possession?

Songbyrd, Inc. v. Estate of Grossman

United States District Court, N.D. New York, 1998.
23 F. Supp. 2d 219.

■ HOMER, UNITED STATES MAGISTRATE JUDGE. Plaintiff Songbyrd, Inc. ("Songbyrd") brought this action seeking monetary damages and a declaration of rights in certain recorded music tracks. Presently pending is a motion by defendant Estate of Albert B. Grossman, doing business as Bearsville Records, Inc. ("Bearsville") for summary judgment pursuant to Fed.R.Civ.P. 56 on the ground that the action is barred by the applicable statute of limitations. Songbyrd opposes the motion. For the reasons which follow, the motion is granted.

I.   Facts

This case concerns the possession, ownership, and usage of several master recordings of musical performances made in the early 1970s by New Orleans musician Henry Roeland Byrd, who was professionally known as "Professor Longhair" ("Byrd").[2] The tapes were produced in a Baton Rouge, Louisiana recording studio and soon thereafter came into the possession of a predecessor in interest to Bearsville located in Woodstock, New York. Over time several requests have been made by representatives of Byrd to secure return of the tapes. It is unclear what if any response those requests received, but the tapes have remained in the physical custody of Bearsville continuously since the 1970s.

In August 1986, Bearsville licensed certain of the master recordings to Rounder Records Corporation, which in 1987 released an album of Byrd's music produced from the recordings. In 1991, another recording based on the disputed master recordings was released by Rhino Records.

---

[2]   Songbyrd incorporated in 1993 and conducts business as a successor in interest to Byrd.

That release was made possible by a licensing agreement between Bearsville and the production company.

II.   Procedural Background

Originally filed in Louisiana state court in 1995, this action was removed by Bearsville to the United States District Court for the Eastern District of Louisiana. Bearsville then moved pursuant to Fed.R.Civ.P. 12(b) to dismiss the claim on the ground that the court lacked personal jurisdiction and the claim was barred by Louisiana's period of prescription.[3] The district court held that the action was barred by the applicable prescriptive period and granted the motion without addressing the jurisdictional question. Songbyrd, Inc. v. Bearsville Records, Inc., Civ.A. No. 95–3706, 1996 WL 337259 (E.D.La. June 18, 1996). Songbyrd appealed and the Fifth Circuit Court of Appeals reversed, holding that the claim was not prescribed under Louisiana law. 104 F.3d 773, 779 (5th Cir. 1997). On remand, the district court considered the question of personal jurisdiction, concluded that jurisdiction was lacking, and transferred the action to this district. The present motion followed. * * *

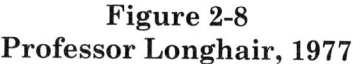

Figure 2-8
Professor Longhair, 1977

Courtesy of Leni Sinclair.

---

[3]   The period of prescription in civil law jurisdictions like Louisiana is roughly synonymous with the common law concept of a statute of limitations. See FDIC v. Barton, 96 F.3d 128, 131 n. 2 (5th Cir. 1996).

IV.   Discussion

A.   Choice of Law

* * * Both parties agree that * * * disposition of this case is governed by New York law.

B.   New York Statute of Limitations

This action is governed by the three year statute of limitations for recovery of chattel provided in N.Y. Civ. Prac. L. & R. § 214(3) (McKinney 1990); Johnson v. Smithsonian Inst., 9 F.Supp.2d 347, 354 (S.D.N.Y. 1998) (New York statute of limitations for conversion and replevin is three years). The issue presented here is when the claim accrued for statute of limitations purposes.

The statute of limitations for conversion begins to run at the time of the conversion. Sporn v. MCA Records, Inc., 448 N.E.2d 1324, 1327 (N.Y. 1983); see also Vigilant Ins. Co. of Am. v. Housing Auth. of the City of El Paso, Tex., 660 N.E.2d 1121, 1126 (N.Y. 1995). In Sporn, New York's Court of Appeals was presented with a case very similar to the case at bar. There, the plaintiff, the successor in interest to the purported owner of rights in certain master recordings, sued the defendant record company for commercially exploiting the master recordings contrary to the plaintiff's interests. Sporn, 448 N.E.2d at 1325–26. The record company defended on the ground that the three year limitations period had begun to run at the time it began using the master recordings contrary to the plaintiff's purported interest and had expired prior to the commencement of the action. Holding that the statute of limitations for conversion begins to run at the time of the conversion, the Court of Appeals affirmed the grant of summary judgment in favor of the record company.

Songbyrd contends that Solomon R. Guggenheim Found. v. Lubell, 569 N.E.2d 426 (N.Y. 1991) ("Guggenheim"), not Sporn, governs this action. In Guggenheim, the New York Court of Appeals held that "a cause of action for replevin against a good-faith purchaser of a stolen chattel accrues when the true owner makes demand for return of the chattel and the person in possession of the chattel refuses to return it." Id. at 429. Songbyrd argues that under Guggenheim the statute of limitations does not begin to run until after a demand for return has been refused, that such a demand has been made but not refused here and as a result the limitations period has not yet begun to run. Guggenheim, however, addresses the different circumstance of possession of a chattel by a bona fide purchaser for value and does not, therefore, provide the controlling rule of law here.

Guggenheim, in fact, recognized that a different rule applies when the stolen chattel remains in the possession of the thief. Citing Sporn, the court stated that in such a circumstance the statute of limitations begins to run from the time of the theft. Guggenheim, 569 N.E.2d at 429. Here, the chattel at issue has remained in the possession of Bearsville, the party alleged to have committed the wrongful taking. There is no evidence that Bearsville was ever a bona fide purchaser for value. Thus, the statute of limitations here began to run at the time Bearsville converted the master recordings. See Vigilant Ins. Co., 660 N.E.2d at 1126 (in a case not involving a bona fide purchaser, a conversion claim accrues at the time of the conversion). Thus, *Guggenheim* is limited to circumstances involving a bona fide purchaser's possession of the chattel.

Having concluded that Songbyrd's conversion claim accrued at the time of the conversion, the question becomes when the master recordings were allegedly converted. "The tort of conversion is established when one who owns and has a right to possession of personal property proves that the property is in the unauthorized possession of another who has acted to exclude the rights of the owner." Key Bank of N.Y. v. Grossi, 642 N.Y.S.2d 403, 405 (App. Div. 3d Dep't 1996). A party acts to the exclusion of the rights of another by exercising dominion and control over the property that is inconsistent with the interests of the true owner. Shaw v. Rolex Watch, U.S.A., Inc., 673 F.Supp. 674, 682 (S.D.N.Y. 1987). Accepting this definition of conversion, the decisive issue is when Bearsville began unauthorized possession of the master recordings.

Bearsville undeniably had lawful and authorized possession of the master tapes when they were first transferred to its predecessor in 1972. In August 1986, the master recordings were licensed by Bearsville to Rounder Records. The result of this agreement was the 1987 release of an album of Byrd's music taken from the master recordings. This licensing agreement clearly demonstrated Bearsville's intent to exercise control over the Byrd recordings to the exclusion of Songbyrd. See Jaywyn Video Productions, Ltd. v. Servicing All Media, Inc., 577 N.Y.S.2d 847, 848 (App. Div. 1st Dep't 1992) (licensing of property rights demonstrates exercise of dominion and control). Any claim for conversion, therefore, accrued no later than August 1986 and was time barred at the time this action was filed in 1995.[4] That Songbyrd may not have known of the conversion at the time it occurred is of no moment. Two Clinton Square Corp. v. Friedler, 459 N.Y.S.2d 179 (App. Div. 4th Dep't 1983); Memorial Hosp. v. McGreevy, 574 N.Y.S.2d 923, 925 (Sup. Ct. 1991) (claim accrues at time of conversion "even though the plaintiff may have been unaware of the occurrence.").

Where, as here, "[t]he conduct of the defendant certainly constituted a denial of both the plaintiff's right to the master recording and a total usurping of plaintiff's right to possess the master recording," the claim is properly stated as one for conversion. Sporn, 448 N.E.2d at 1327. That claim is clearly untimely. The time bar arose in August 1989, three years following the licensing agreement with Rounder Records.[6] Conversion is

---

[4]   Songbyrd has not argued that any tolling provision applies here.

[6]   In the alternative the conversion occurred no later than August 1991 when Bearsville licensed the master recordings to Rhino Records. That agreement resulted in the 1991 Rhino Records release of an album containing seven tracks produced from the master recordings. The exact date of the Rhino Records licensing deal is not clear in the record but necessarily occurred

not a continuing wrong for which every new act that might constitute conversion restarts a new limitations period. Tinker v. Abrams, 640 F.Supp. 229, 232 (S.D.N.Y. 1986) (citing Sporn, 448 N.E.2d at 1326–27). Here, Songbyrd simply failed to commence this action within the applicable statute of limitations. Bearsville's motion must, therefore, be granted.

NOTES AND QUESTIONS

1.   The Fifth Circuit's decision holding that Songbyrd's claim was not subject to prescription under Louisiana law provides some additional details about Professor Longhair:

> The late Henry Roeland Byrd, also known as "Professor Longhair," was an influential New Orleans rhythm-and-blues pianist and composer, and is widely regarded as one of the primary inspirations for the renaissance of New Orleans popular music over the last thirty years. His numerous hits included original compositions such as "Tipitina" and "Go to the Mardi Gras," as well as his famous renditions of Earl King's "Big Chief." After achieving modest commercial success as a local performer and recording artist in the 1940's and 1950's, Byrd fell on hard times during the 1960's. His fortunes began to change for the better in 1970, however, when New Orleans music aficionado Arthur "Quint" Davis, along with others, founded the New Orleans Jazz and Heritage Festival ("JazzFest"). Needing talented performers for JazzFest, Davis located Byrd in 1971 working in an obscure record store in New Orleans and transformed him into a perennial star attraction of the JazzFest and other venues from that time until his death in 1980.

Songbyrd, Inc. v. Bearsville Records, Inc., 104 F.3d 773, 774 (5th Cir. 1997). Albert Grossman, who died in 1986, was one of the founders of the Newport Folk Festival and promoted the careers of a number of musical stars, including Bob Dylan, Janis Joplin, and Gordon Lightfoot. Bearsville, New York, where he lived and worked, is a small town near Woodstock, New York. For more on the background of the case and a comparison of common law adverse possession to Louisiana civilian "acquisitive prescription," see John A. Lovett, Professor Longhair's Legacy: Revendicating Movables under Louisiana Law, in Northern Lights: Essays in Honour of David Carey Miller 31 (Douglas Bain, Roderick Paisley, & Andrew R.C. Simpson eds., 2018).

2.   If one were simply to weigh the equitable claims of the parties, one might expect that courts would give true owners more time to recover property taken by a person in bad faith, like a thief, and less time to recover property taken by someone who has acted in good faith, like a good faith purchaser. Yet New York law regarding adverse possession of personal property appears to do the opposite. Under the time-of-conversion rule applied in the principal case, the statute of limitations begins to run as soon as the property is converted, resulting in a short period to seek recovery.

---

in or before 1991. Thus, with 1991 as the date of conversion, Songbyrd's claim was time barred prior to the commencement of this action in 1995.

Under the demand rule of *Guggenheim*, the statute of limitations does not begin to run until the true owner makes a demand for the return of the property from a good faith purchaser, and the demand is refused. This typically results in a longer period to seek recovery, since the demand and refusal will virtually always occur after the conversion. As a result, New York treats thieves more favorably than good faith purchasers. Is there any justification for this distinction that would explain what otherwise seems quite counterintuitive?

3.   The New Jersey Supreme Court, in *O'Keeffe v. Snyder*, 416 A.2d 862 (N.J. 1980), adopted a third test for determining when the statute of limitations starts to run for purposes of adverse possession of personal property: the discovery rule. Under this rule, "a cause of action will not accrue until the injured party discovers, or by exercise of reasonable diligence and intelligence should have discovered, facts which form the basis of a cause of action." Id. at 869. Generally speaking, the discovery rule would give the TO an intermediate period of time to recover personal property, somewhere in between the conversion rule and the demand rule. The conversion rule applied in *Songbyrd* will generally result in the shortest period because the statute starts to run at the moment of conversion; the discovery rule would provide more time, because it may take a while for a diligent TO to learn about the conversion or discover the whereabouts of the object; the demand rule would provide the longest time, because there is no requirement that the TO show reasonable diligence before asserting the demand for return of the property. What advantages and disadvantages do you see in adopting the discovery rule, as opposed to either the conversion rule or the demand rule?

4.   What is the best characterization of the state of mind of the defendant in *Songbyrd*: good faith, bad faith, or unclear? What state of mind does the Court seem to require for establishing a claim of title by adverse possession?

5.   One oddity of this case is that the parties are really concerned with what is on the tapes—the song recordings—rather than with the physical tapes themselves. Copyright law distinguishes between musical works (sheet music and lyrics) and sound recordings. See 17 U.S.C. § 101. Musical works were brought into federal copyright in 1831, but sound recordings did not receive protection until 1972 and this protection is somewhat different from that for musical works. Can the copyright in a sound recording be adversely possessed? If not, why not?

G. COMPETING PRINCIPLES OF ORIGINAL TITLE

Now that we have seen six principles for establishing original title (first possession, discovery, creation, prior possession, accession, adverse possession), we can also see that some of the more difficult problems of original title in fact involve clashes between parties claiming under competing principles of original acquisition. Since the principles proceed from different premises, it is difficult to say that there is a "right answer" in any of these cases. The cases selected here all involve conflicts between first possession and accession, but in theory similar conflicts could arise between any of the principles.

Briggs v. Southwestern Energy Production Company

Supreme Court of Pennsylvania, 2020.
224 A.3d 334.

■ CHIEF JUSTICE SAYLOR. In this appeal by allowance, we consider whether the rule of capture immunizes an energy developer from liability in trespass, where the developer uses hydraulic fracturing on the property it owns or leases, and such activities allow it to obtain oil or gas that migrates from beneath the surface of another person's land.

I. Background

A. The rule of capture

Oil and gas are minerals, and while in place they are considered part of the land. *See Hamilton v. Foster*, 116 A. 50, 52 (Pa. 1922). They differ from coal and other substances with a fixed situs in that they are fugacious in nature—meaning they tend to seep or flow across property lines beneath the surface of the earth. Such underground movement is known as "drainage." Drainage stems from a physical property of fluids in that they naturally move across a pressure gradient from high to low pressure. Indeed, the extraction of oil or gas by drilling is based, at least in part, on creating a low-pressure pathway from the mineral's subterranean location to the earth's surface.

Oil and gas have thus been described as having a "fugitive and wandering existence," Brown v. Vandergrift, 80 Pa. 142, 147 (Pa. 1875), and have been compared to wild animals which move about from one property to another. See Westmoreland & Cambria Nat. Gas Co. v. DeWitt, 18 A. 724, 725 (Pa. 1889) ("In common with animals, and unlike other minerals, [oil, gas, and water] have the power and the tendency to escape without the volition of the owner."). Accordingly, such minerals are subject to the rule of capture, which is

> [a] fundamental principle of oil-and-gas law holding that there
> is no liability for drainage of oil and gas from under the lands of
> another so long as there has been no trespass . . . .

Black's Law Dictionary 1358 (8th ed. 2004)); accord Brown v. Spilman, 155 U.S. 665, 669–70 (1895). A corollary to this rule is that an aggrieved property owner's remedy for the loss, through drainage, of subsurface oil or gas has traditionally been to offset the effects of the developer's well by drilling his or her own well, often termed an "offset well." See Barnard v. Monongahela Gas Co., 65 A. 801, 803 (Pa. 1907) ("What then can the neighbor do? Nothing; only go and do likewise.").

The reference to "the lands of another" in the above quote does not suggest a developer may invade the subsurface area of a neighboring property by drilling at an angle rather than vertically (referred to as slant drilling or slant wells), or by drilling horizontally beneath the surface. This is because the title holder of a parcel of land generally owns everything directly beneath the surface. Rather, and as suggested by the "no trespass" predicate, it refers to the potential for oil and gas to migrate from the plaintiff's property to the developer's land when extracted from a common pool or reservoir spanning both parcels.

Finally, the rule of capture applies even where devices such as pumps are used to bring the mineral to the surface and thereby reduce the production of neighboring wells.

B.   Hydraulic fracturing

One of the central questions in this matter involves how these principles apply where hydraulic fracturing is used to extract oil or gas from subsurface geological formations. Drillers have enhanced the output of oil and gas wells by fracturing the geological formations for over a century. Initially they used explosives. Hydraulic fracturing was developed in the 1940s, and has been used in Pennsylvania since 1954. Although it would be impractical to set forth a comprehensive description of the technique in the context of the present controversy, there are certain material aspects which are not in dispute. According to the federal government, hydraulic fracturing is

> used in "unconventional" gas production. "Unconventional" reservoirs can cost-effectively produce gas only by using a special stimulation technique, like hydraulic fracturing . . . . This is often because the gas is highly dispersed in the rock, rather than occurring in a concentrated underground location.

United States Environmental Protection Agency (the "EPA"), The Process of Unconventional Natural Gas Production, https://www.epa.gov/uog/process-unconventional-natural-gas-production (viewed Oct. 22, 2019). In terms of how the technique works, the EPA continues:

> Fractures are created by pumping large quantities of fluids at high pressure down a wellbore and into the target rock formation. Hydraulic fracturing fluid commonly consists of water, proppant and chemical additives that open and enlarge fractures within the rock formation. These fractures can extend several hundred feet away from the wellbore. The proppants— sand, ceramic pellets or other small incompressible particles— hold open the newly created fractures.

Id.

After injection, fluid is withdrawn from the well while leaving the proppants in place to hold the fissures open. This enhances the drainage of oil or gas into the wellbore where it can be captured.

C.   Factual and procedural history of this case

(i)   Introduction

This appeal comes to us in a somewhat unusual posture. The parties presently favor essentially the same rule of law: they both, in substance, argue that the traditional rule of capture should apply, subject to the common-law standard for trespass of real property based on physical intrusion onto another's land. See Restatement (Second) of Torts § 158 & cmt. *i* (1965) (indicating liability follows from the defendant's entry onto the plaintiff's property, and noting this includes throwing, propelling, or placing a thing on the land or above or beneath its surface). Each party, moreover, depicts the other as erroneously suggesting that an exception to this framework should pertain where hydraulic fracturing is used to obtain oil or natural gas. In particular, the plaintiffs suggest that Southwestern wishes to convert the rule of capture into a precept whereby energy developers may physically invade the property of others to capture natural gas so long as they are using hydraulic fracturing. For its part, Southwestern portrays the plaintiffs and the Superior Court decision from which it appeals as positing that the rule of capture simply does not apply when hydraulic fracturing is used for energy development on one's own land.

To maintain these positions, the parties proceed from a different understanding of the relevant factual and procedural history. * * *

(ii)   Undisputed facts

Adam, Paula, Joshua, and Sarah Briggs ("Plaintiffs") own a parcel of real estate consisting of approximately eleven acres in Harford Township, Susquehanna County. During all relevant times, Plaintiffs have not leased their property to any entity for natural gas production. Plaintiffs' property is adjacent to a tract of land leased by Appellant Southwestern Energy Production Company for natural gas extraction (the "Production Parcel"). Southwestern maintains wellbores on the Production Parcel and has used hydraulic fracturing to boost natural gas extraction from the Marcellus Shale formation through those wellbores.

(iii)   Proceedings before the Court of Common Pleas

In November 2015, Plaintiffs commenced an action against Southwestern in which they stated two causes of action, trespass and conversion. * * * Notably, Plaintiffs did not expressly allege that Southwestern's activities had caused a physical intrusion into Plaintiffs' property.

Southwestern filed a responsive pleading denying it had extracted gas from Plaintiffs' land and denying it had trespassed upon Plaintiffs' property or converted their natural gas. Southwestern specifically denied it had drilled underneath Plaintiffs' property and stated, further, that it had "only drilled for oil, gas or minerals from under properties for which [Southwestern] has leases."

* * *Southwestern alleged that Plaintiffs' claims were barred by, *inter alia*, the rule of capture. * * *

In their supporting brief, Plaintiffs suggested, for the first time, that Southwestern's hydraulic fracturing activities may have caused a disturbance of the subsurface area of their land in the form of rock fractures propagating horizontally from the wellbore, albeit that, again, they did not expressly contend that Southwestern had injected any material substances into their land. * * *

(v) Southwestern's request for discretionary review

In seeking this Court's review, Southwestern initially mentioned that Plaintiffs had not alleged that Southwestern physically intruded onto their property. * * * As such, Southwestern framed a single issue for our review, as follows:

> Does the rule of capture apply to oil and gas produced from wells that were completed using hydraulic fracturing and preclude trespass liability for allegedly draining oil or gas from under nearby property, where the well is drilled solely on and beneath the driller's own property *and the hydraulic fracturing fluids are injected solely on or beneath the driller's own property*?

* * *

II. Preliminary Discussion

A. Trespass

In Pennsylvania, a trespass occurs when a person who is not privileged to do so intrudes upon land in possession of another, whether willfully or by mistake. * * *

[Southwestern] articulated the issue for this Court's consideration in terms of whether the rule of capture should be applied in the same manner it has always been applied: to allow for the capture of oil and gas which merely drains from an adjacent property after the completion of a well using hydraulic fracturing *solely within the developer's property*. This is an issue, again, on which the parties do not presently diverge: they both answer in the affirmative. Their disagreement is limited to whether any physical intrusion has taken place—a question that is not fairly subsumed within the issue framed for our review.

III. Analysis

The issue as stated by Southwestern should nonetheless be resolved for purposes of this dispute—and to provide guidance to the bench and bar—because at least part of the Superior Court's opinion can reasonably be construed as setting forth a *per se* rule foreclosing application of the rule of capture in hydraulic fracturing scenarios, and that rule rests on faulty assumptions. In particular, and most saliently, the panel appears to have indicated that one litmus for whether the rule of capture applies is whether the defendant's gas extraction methodology relies only on the natural drainage of oil or gas within a conventional pool or reservoir, or whether instead those methods utilize some means of artificial stimulation to induce drainage.

The Superior Court's position in this respect logically rests on one of two grounds: (a) the act of artificially stimulating the cross-boundary flow through the use of hydraulic fracturing solely on the developer's property in and of itself renders the rule of capture inapplicable; or (b) as Plaintiffs argue, any time natural gas migrates across property lines resulting, directly or indirectly, from hydraulic fracturing, a physical intrusion into the plaintiff's property must necessarily have taken place.

As to the first proposition, all drilling for subsurface fugacious minerals involves the artificial stimulation of the flow of that substance. The mere act of drilling interferes with nature and stimulates the flow of the minerals toward artificially-created low pressure areas, most notably, the wellbore. This Court has held that the rule of capture applies although the driller uses further artificial means, such as a pump, to enhance production from a source common to it and the plaintiff—so long as no physical invasion of the plaintiff's land occurs. See Jones v. Forest Oil Co., 44 A. 1074, 1075 (Pa. 1900) (indicating that, absent physical intrusion, a developer may use "all the skill and invention of which a man is capable" to appropriate resources from under his own property). There is no reason why this precept should apply any differently to hydraulic fracturing conducted solely within the driller's property. * * *

The Superior Court may have believed it should impose a different rule because of the added expense associated with hydraulic fracturing as compared to conventional drilling. It expressed its concern that drilling an offset well may not be as affordable to an aggrieved landowner today as it was in the era when conventional drilling was still able profitably to produce oil and natural gas. Southwestern observes, however, that both types of drilling are costly and specialized, and posits that the traditional self-help remedy is still available—as a neighboring landowner may enter into a lease with an energy developer to drill a well and obtain oil or gas through hydraulic fracturing, and be compensated accordingly.

Hydraulic fracturing may be more expensive than conventional drilling and, as a consequence, the feasibility of drilling an offset well may be diminished for some landowners. The judiciary nonetheless lacks institutional tools necessary to investigate the continuing feasibility of self-help remedies under the myriad of circumstances that may present themselves in the context of a dispute such as this one. The legislative branch is not similarly constrained, and if the General Assembly believes that additional measures are needed in favor of small landowners, it is in a better position to ascertain the need for such measures and to articulate their details. Accordingly, we reject as a matter of law the concept that the rule of capture is inapplicable to drilling and hydraulic fracturing that occurs entirely within the developer's property solely because drainage of natural resources takes place as the direct or indirect result of hydraulic fracturing, or that such drainage stems from less "natural" means than conventional drainage.

The second predicate—that drainage from under a plaintiff's parcel can only occur if the driller first physically invades that property—does not lend itself to a purely legal resolution. By design, hydraulic fracturing creates fissures in rock strata which store hydrocarbons within their porous structure. On the state of the present record, this alone does not establish that a physical intrusion into a neighboring property is necessary for such action to result in drainage from that property. We cannot rule out, for example, that a fissure created through the injection of hydraulic fluid entirely within the developer's property may create a sufficient pressure gradient to induce the drainage of hydrocarbons from the relevant stratum of rock underneath an adjacent parcel even absent physical intrusion. Nor can we discount the possibility that a fissure created within the developer's property may communicate with other, pre-existing fissures that reach across property lines. Whether these, or any other non-invasive means of drainage occasioned by hydraulic fracturing, are physically possible in a given case is a factual question to be established through expert evidence. * * *

V.   Summary and Conclusion

In summary, the parties to the appeal are in agreement—and we concur as well—that the rule of capture remains extant in Pennsylvania, and developers who use hydraulic fracturing may rely on pressure differentials to drain oil and gas from under another's property, at least in the absence of a physical invasion. The Superior Court panel erred to the extent it assumed that either (a) the use of hydraulic fracturing alters this rule, or (b) where hydraulic fracturing is utilized, such physical invasion is a necessary precondition in all cases for drainage to occur from underneath another property. More broadly, insofar as the panel's decision may be construed to suggest that a natural-versus-artificially-induced-flow litmus should be employed to determine whether the rule of capture applies in a given situation, that standard rests on a false distinction and is disapproved.

The order of the Superior Court is vacated and the matter is remanded to that court for further proceedings consistent with this opinion.

■ JUSTICE DOUGHERTY (concurring and dissenting). I join the majority's holding that the rule of capture remains effective in Pennsylvania to protect a developer from trespass liability where there has been no physical invasion of another's property. In so holding, the majority correctly recognizes that if there **is** such a physical invasion the rule of capture will **not** insulate a developer engaged in hydraulic fracturing from trespass liability. As I agree with both propositions, I also agree the matter should be remanded for further proceedings involving a specific inquiry into a physical invasion. I respectfully dissent, however, from the notion that this question must be determined by the Superior Court on the present record, and would instead remand to the trial court for completion of the discovery that was forestalled by erroneous summary judgment, and for trial, if necessary. * * *

Finally, I make the following observations relating to the rule of capture in the context of fracking of non-conventional shale deposits. First, although I recognize natural gas has a "fugacious" nature regardless of whether it lies in an open pool or in a sandstone or shale deposit, it is clear that natural gas trapped in shale drains naturally much more slowly than from a pool or from other materials; indeed, this is the very reason developers engage in fracking, to make shale gas development productive faster, that is, more efficient and economically viable. The practice exploits natural shale fractures and creates new ones, and with present technology, much remains mysterious about precisely what happens so far beneath the surface. However, I do not view this uncertainty as a basis to absolve developers from trespass liability if a plaintiff can prove the fluids and proppants they intentionally injected into their wellbores travelled horizontally across property lines and caused drainage of gas previously trapped under the plaintiff's land.

NOTES AND QUESTIONS

1. *Briggs* and other recent decisions that address conflicts between adjacent surface owners over the use of hydraulic fracturing technology, most notably *Coastal Oil & Gas Corp. v. Garza Energy Trust*, 268 S.W. 3d 1 (Tex. 2008), present a conflict between the principle of first possession (the rule of capture as applied to fugacious minerals like oil and gas) and accession (the *ad coelum* principle that says the owner of the surface owns the column of space extending downward vertically for an indefinite distance below the surface). If a jurisdiction is committed to both principles, how should they be reconciled or integrated?

2. *Physical intrusion.* The parties and the court agree that any kind of slant drilling—drilling that starts on surface controlled by the production company that angles as it proceeds underground into the column of space under an adjacent property owner—is barred under the law of trespass. Likewise, the court assumes that a well bore that proceeds downward vertically within the column of space controlled by the production company, which then turns and horizontally enters into the column of space of an adjacent property owner, would be a trespass. (Horizontal drilling is a common feature of "fracking" technology, both for enhanced recovery of natural gas and oil.) What is the rationale for treating as a trespass any intentional use of slant drilling or horizontal drilling that intrudes into the column of space beneath the land of a non-consenting surface owner? Is this carrying the *ad coelum* principle to an unwarranted extreme? After all, one rationale for limiting trespass liability to tangible intrusions is that this puts the landholder on notice that there has been an invasion. Subsurface intrusions by drill bits can be detected only with the aid of sophisticated sonar devices. Or does the *ad coelum* principle in this context provide an

important baseline for negotiations among landowners over various rights to extract valuable minerals?

3. *Trespass by cracks?* The court holds that if there is no physical intrusion by a production company into the column of space of an adjacent property owner, the drainage of natural gas caused by hydraulic fracturing is privileged under the rule of capture. The court does not reach the question whether Southwestern did or did not commit a physical intrusion into the plaintiffs subsurface through the use of fracturing technology. Aside from slant or horizontal drilling, what would constitute a trespassory invasion in this context? If the well bore stops short of the boundary of the plaintiff's subsurface rights, and the defendant injects water, proppants like sand, and chemicals into the area underneath the plaintiff's surface rights, is this a trespass? What if the water, proppants, and chemicals stop short of the boundary, but the pressure exerted by this concoction (colloquially called slickwater) causes cracks to form in the rock underneath the plaintiff's surface rights? As things stand, these questions remain unanswered in oil and gas producing states. Should the answer turn on the state of mind of the production company, i.e., whether the company intended or knew to a high degree of certainty whether the slickwater would enter the subsurface space of another? Should the deliberate creation of cracks in the rock in the subsurface of another be subject to liability as a nuisance but not as a trespass? For discussion, see Keith B. Hall, Hydraulic Facturing: If Fractures Cross Property Lines, Is There an Actionable Subsurface Trespass?, 54 Nat. Res. J. 361 (2014).

4. Ad coelum *and overflights.* In *Garza*, supra, the Texas Supreme Court joined the Pennsylvania court in holding that drainage from the subsurface rights of another landowner caused by the use of fracturing technology is protected under the rule of capture. In contrast to the Pennsylvania Supreme Court, however, the Texas court held that subsurface trespass by fracturing fluids and cracks should be actionable only if this activity can be shown to cause substantial harm to the surface rights of the nonconsenting owner. In support of this conclusion, the Texas court seemingly drew an analogy to airplane overflights, and the provision of the Restatement (Second) of Torts that says overflights are actionable as a trespass only if they cause substantial harm to the surface. 268 S.W. 3d at 11. Is this a better solution than the inquiry apparently contemplated by the Pennsylvania court, into whether fracturing fluids have been injected across a subterranean boundary? For a variety of perspectives, see Owen L. Anderson, Subsurface "Trespass": A Man's Subsurface is Not His Castle, 49 Washburn L. J. 247 (2010); Joseph A. Schremmer, Getting Past Possession: Subsurface Property Disputes as Nuisances, 95 Wash. L. Rev. 315 (2020); John G. Sprankling, Owning the Center of the Earth, 55 U.C.L.A. L. Rev. 979 (2008).

Goddard v. Winchell

Supreme Court of Iowa, 1892.
52 N.W. 1124.

■ GRANGER, J. The district court found the following facts, with some others, not important on this trial: "That the plaintiff, John Goodard, is, and has been since about 1857, the owner in fee simple of the north half of section No. three, in township No. ninety-eight, range No. twenty-five, in Winnebago county, Iowa, and was such owner at the time of the fall of the meteorite hereinafter referred to. (2) That said land was prairie land, and that the grass privilege for the year 1890 was leased to one James Elickson. (3) That on the 2d day of May, 1890, an aerolite passed over northern and northwestern Iowa, and the aerolite, or fragment of the same, in question in this action, weighing, when replevied, and when produced in court on the trial of this cause, about 66 pounds, fell onto plaintiff's land, described above, and buried itself in the ground to a depth of three feet, and became imbedded therein at a point about 20 rods from the section line on the north. (4) That the day after the aerolite in question fell it was dug out of the ground with a spade by one Peter Hoagland, in the presence of the tenant, Elickson; that said Hoagland took it to his house, and claimed to own same, for the reason that he had found same and dug it up. (5) That on May 5, 1890, Hoagland sold the aerolite in suit to the defendant, H. V. Winchell, for $105, and the same was at once taken possession of by said defendant, and that the possession was held by him until same was taken under the writ of replevin herein; that defendant knew at the time of his purchase that it was an aerolite, and that it fell on the prairie south of Hoagland's land. * * * (10) I find the value of said aerolite to be one hundred and one dollars ($101) as verbally stipulated in open court by the parties to this action; that the same weighs about 66 pounds, is of a black, smoky color on the outside, showing the effects of heat, and of a lighter and darkish gray color on the inside; that it is an aerolite, and fell from the heavens on the 2d of May, 1890; that a member of Hoagland's family saw the aerolite fall, and directed him to it."

As conclusions of law, the district court found that the aerolite became a part of the soil on which it fell; that the plaintiff was the owner thereof; and that the act of Hoagland in removing it was wrongful. It is insisted by appellant that the conclusions of law are erroneous; that the enlightened demands of the time in which we live call for, if not a modification, a liberal construction, of the ancient rule, "that whatever is affixed to the soil belongs to the soil," or, the more modern statement of the rule, that "a permanent annexation to the soil, of a thing in itself personal, makes it a part of the realty." In behalf of appellant is invoked a rule alike ancient and of undoubted merit, "that of title by occupancy;" and we are cited to the language of Blackstone, as follows: "Occupancy is the taking possession of those things which before belonged to nobody;" and "whatever movables are found upon the surface of the earth, or in the sea, and are unclaimed by any owner, are supposed to be abandoned by the last proprietor, and as such are returned into the common stock and mass of things; and therefore they belong, as in a state of nature, to the first occupant or finder." * * *

If, from what we have said, we have in mind the facts giving rise to the rules cited, we may well look to the facts of this case to properly distinguish it. The subject of the dispute is an aerolite, of about 66 pounds' weight, that "fell from the heavens" on the land of the plaintiff, and was found three feet below the surface. It came to its position in the earth through natural causes. It was one of nature's deposits, with nothing in its material composition to make it foreign or unnatural to the soil. It was not a movable thing "on the earth." It was in the earth, and in a very significant sense immovable; that is, it was only movable as parts of earth are made movable by the hand of man. Except for the peculiar manner in which it came, its relation to the soil would be beyond dispute. It was in its substance, as we understand, a stone. It was not of a character to be thought of as "unclaimed by any owner," and, because unclaimed, "supposed to be abandoned by the last proprietor," as should be the case under the rule invoked by appellant. In fact, it has none of the characteristics of the property contemplated by such a rule.

We may properly note some of the particular claims of appellant. * * * The general rules of the law, by which the owners of riparian titles are made to lose or gain by the doctrine of accretions, are quite familiar. These rules are not, however, of exclusive application to such owners. Through the action of the elements, wind and water, the soil of one man is taken and deposited in the field of another; and thus all over the country, we may say, changes are constantly going on. By these natural causes the owners of the soil are giving and taking as the wisdom of the controlling forces shall determine. By these operations one may be affected with a substantial gain, and another by a similar loss. These gains are of accretion, and the deposit becomes the property of the owner of the soil on which it is made.

A scientist of note has said that from six to seven hundred of these stones fall to our earth annually. If they are, as indicated in argument, departures from other planets, and if among the planets of the solar system there is this interchange, bearing evidence of their material composition, upon what principle of reason or authority can we say that a deposit thus made shall not be of that class of property that it would be if originally of this planet and in the same situation? * * * It is not easy to understand why stones or balls of metallic iron, deposited as this was, should be governed by a different rule than obtains from the deposit of boulders, stones, and drift upon our prairies by glacier action; and who would contend that these deposits from floating bodies of ice belong, not to the owner of the soil, but to the finder? Their origin or source may be less mysterious, but they, too, are "telltale messengers" from far-off lands, and have value for historic and scientific investigation.

It is said that the aerolite is without adaptation to the soil, and only valuable for scientific purposes. Nothing in the facts of the case will warrant us in saying that it was not as well adapted for use by the owner of the soil as any stone, or, as appellant is pleased to denominate it, "ball of metallic iron." That it may be of greater value for scientific or other purposes may be admitted, but that fact has little weight in determining who should be its owner. We cannot say that the owner of the soil is not as interested in, and would not as readily contribute to, the great cause of scientific advancement, as the finder, by chance or otherwise, of these silent messengers. This aerolite is of the value of $101, and this fact, if no other, would remove it from uses where other and much less valuable materials would answer an equally good purpose, and place it in the sphere of its greater usefulness.

The rule is cited, with cases for its support, that the finder of lost articles, even where they are found on the property, in the building, or with the personal effects of third persons, is the owner thereof against all the world except the true owner. The correctness of the rule may be conceded, but its application to the case at bar is very doubtful. The subject of this controversy was never lost or abandoned. Whence it came is not known, but, under the natural law of its government, it became a part of this earth, and, we think, should be treated as such. * * *

The judgment of the district court is affirmed.

NOTES AND QUESTIONS

1.   Horace Winchell, the defendant in this action, was a geologist with the University of Minnesota and an avid collector of aerolites, or meteorites as they are more commonly called today. When Winchell heard about a large meteorite shower near Forest City, Iowa, he hastened to the site. He arrived at Peter Hoagland's farm at the same time as William Bradford, a local lawyer who evidently sought to acquire the aerolite to resell it for a profit, and a bidding war ensued. Bradford would not pay more than $100, so Winchell won. The lawyer later discovered that the aerolite had fallen on Goddard's land, not Hoagland's, and sued out a writ of replevin in Goddard's name, posting a bond for twice the value of the stone (see Chapter IV for more on replevin). This caused the sheriff to seize the aerolite at the train station, as Winchell was preparing to ship it to Minneapolis. Before the first replevin was tried, Winchell persuaded the University to bring a second replevin action, posting an even higher bond. This caused the sheriff to seize the stone again and turn it back over to Winchell, who spirited it out of the state in a mad dash. The decision reproduced here is the appeal from the first replevin action. Once the Iowa Supreme Court decided the question of title, the only issue in the second action was damages. The jury in this second action fixed the value at $480, which the University paid rather than give up the stone. See Horace V. Winchell, A Meteoric Career, A True Story, 131 Atlantic Monthly 779 (June 1923). According to Professor E. Calvin Alexander, Jr. of the University of Minnesota Department of Geology and Geophysics, the "Forest City Meteorite" remains the property of the

University of Minnesota, although it has been on loan to the Smithsonian Institution in Washington, D.C. for several decades.

2.   The court here may have thought that it had no easy out based on trespass. Goddard, the owner of the pasture where the aerolite fell, had leased the land to Elickson as tenant. A tenant typically exercises full possessory rights over leased property, including the right to determine who may and may not enter the land and on what terms. Since Elickson had granted permission to Hoagland to enter the field and recover the aerolite, it would have been difficult to award the aerolite to Goddard on the simple ground that Hoagland was a trespasser. On the other hand, someone who exceeds the scope of an owner's consent (in the form of a license or easement, see Chapters IV and IX) becomes a trespasser even if his initial entry was lawful. In this case, the tenant Elickson had only the "grass privilege," probably meaning that Elickson had no right to dig for minerals. Would it have exceeded the scope of Elickson's rights if he had dug the aerolite out of the ground himself? If Elickson likewise had no actual authority to authorize digging by Hoagland, does that make Hoagland a trespasser? Would this depend on what Hoagland reasonably believed about the scope of Elickson's rights? How would we expect Hoagland to inform himself about such matters?

3.   How important to the result is it that the aerolite was buried three feet into the ground? Suppose it came down and bounced off a piece of granite, and thus stayed on the surface of the land. Same result? Consider the famous Hodges meteorite. On November 30, 1954, an 8 ½ pound fragment of a meteorite fell through the roof of a house in Sylacauga, Alabama, bounced off a console radio, and struck Ann Hodges who, not feeling well, had been napping on the living-room couch. (See Figure 2-9.) Hodges was painfully but not seriously injured in the arm and hip and was later hospitalized, partly to avoid the clamor of press and curiosity seekers who descended on the Hodges home. Hodges and her husband occupied the house under a lease, and later the Hodges and their landlord, Birdie Guy, got into a legal dispute over who was the owner of the meteorite. Guy's attorney believed that caselaw supported Mrs. Guy's position, based on her ownership of the real property. But public opinion was firmly behind Mrs. Hodges, in part because the meteorite had physically struck her. Should this affect the analysis of the rival claims of ownership? What would Hume and Sugden say? After preliminary sparring (including a threat by Mrs. Hodges to sue Mrs. Guy for her injuries if she was awarded ownership of the meteorite), the case was settled in September 1955, with Mrs. Hodges paying Mrs. Guy $500 to relinquish her claim. Mrs. Hodges donated the meteorite the next year to the Alabama Museum of Natural History, where it is on permanent display. According to John Hall, retired assistant director of the museum, "the only person with a positive experience in the incident was Julius Kempis McKinney, a black farmer," who found a smaller fragment of the same meteorite in the road where he was driving his mules. He brought it home, wound up selling it to the Smithsonian, and purchased a car and a new house from the proceeds of the sale. M.J. Ellington, A Star Fell on

Sylacauga, Decatur Daily (Nov. 30, 2006), http://archive.decaturdaily.com/decaturdaily/news/061130/meteorite.shtml.

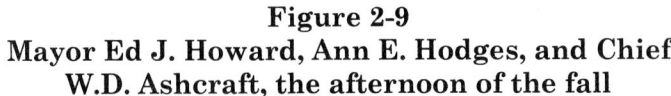

Figure 2-9
Mayor Ed J. Howard, Ann E. Hodges, and Chief
W.D. Ashcraft, the afternoon of the fall

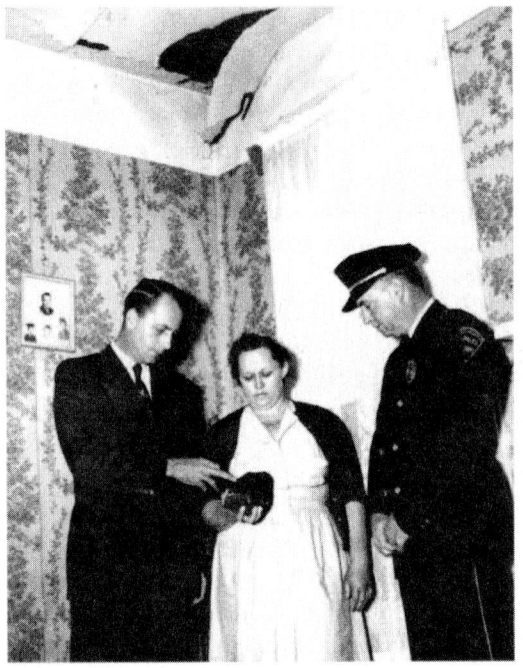

Courtesy of Alabama Museum of Natural History, The University of Alabama. Note the hole in the ceiling and Ann Hodges' swollen hand.

Hannah v. Peel

King's Bench Division, 1945.
[1945] K.B. 509.

On December 13, 1938, the freehold of Gwernhaylod House, Overton-on-Dee, Shropshire, was conveyed to the defendant, Major Hugh Edward Ethelston Peel, who from that time to the end of 1940 never himself occupied the house and it remained unoccupied until October 5, 1939, when it was requisitioned, but after some months was released from requisition. Thereafter it remained unoccupied until July 18, 1940, when it was again requisitioned, the defendant being compensated by a payment at the rate of £250 a year. In August, 1940, the plaintiff, Duncan Hannah, a lance-corporal, serving in a battery of the Royal Artillery, was stationed at the house and on the 21st of that month, when in a bedroom, used as a sick-bay, he was adjusting the black-out curtains when his hand touched something on the top of a window-frame, loose in a crevice, which he thought was a piece of dirt or plaster. The plaintiff grasped it and dropped it on the outside window ledge. On the following morning he saw that it was a brooch covered with cobwebs and dirt. Later, he took it with him when he went home on leave and his wife having told him it might be of value, at the end of October, 1940, he informed his commanding officer of his find and, on his advice, handed it over to the police, receiving a receipt for it. In August, 1942, the owner not having been found the police handed the brooch to the defendant, who sold it in October, 1942, for £66, to Messrs. Spink & Son, Ltd., of London, who resold it in the following month for £88. There was no evidence that the defendant had any knowledge of the existence of the brooch before it was found by the plaintiff. The defendant had offered the plaintiff a reward for the brooch, but the plaintiff refused to accept this and maintained throughout his right to the possession of the brooch as against all persons other than the owner, who was unknown. By a letter, dated October 5, 1942, the plaintiff's solicitors demanded the return of the brooch from the defendant, but it was not returned and on October 21, 1943, the plaintiff issued his writ claiming the return of the brooch, or its value, and damages for its detention. By his defence, the defendant claimed the brooch on the ground that he was the owner of Gwernhaylod House and in possession thereof.

■ BIRKETT J. There is no issue of fact in this case between the parties. As to the issue in law, the rival claims of the parties can be stated in this way: The plaintiff says: "I claim the brooch as its finder and I have a good title against all the world, save only the true owner." The defendant says: "My claim is superior to yours inasmuch as I am the freeholder. The brooch was found on my property, although I was never in occupation, and my title, therefore, ousts yours and in the absence of the true owner I am entitled to the brooch or its value." Unhappily the law on this issue is in a very uncertain state and there is need of an authoritative decision of a higher court. Obviously if it could be said with certainty that this is the law, that the finder of a lost article, wherever found, has a good title against all the world save the true owner, then, of course, all my difficulties would be resolved; or again, if it could be said with equal certainty that this is the law, that the possessor of land is entitled as against the finder to all chattels found on the land, again my difficulties would be resolved. But, unfortunately, the authorities give some support to each of these conflicting propositions.

In the famous case of *Armory v. Delamirie*, 1 Str. 505 (K. B. 1722), the plaintiff, who was a chimney sweeper's boy, found a jewel and carried it to the defendant's shop, who was a goldsmith, in order to know what it was, and he delivered it into the hands of the apprentice in the goldsmith's shop, who made a pretence of weighing it and took out the stones and called to the master to let him know that it came to three-halfpence. The master offered the boy the money who refused to take it and insisted on having the jewel again. Whereupon the apprentice handed him back the socket of the jewel without the stones, and an action was brought in trover against the master, and it was ruled "that the finder of a jewel, though he does not by such finding acquire an absolute property or ownership, yet he has such a property as will enable him to keep it against all but the rightful owner, and consequently may maintain trover." The case of Bridges v. Hawkesworth, 21 L. J.R. 75 (Q. B. 1851) 75, is in process of becoming almost equally as famous because of the disputation which has raged around it. The headnote in the Jurist is as follows: "The place in which a lost article is found does not constitute any exception to the general rule of law, that the finder is entitled to it as against all persons except the owner." * * * The facts appear to have been that in the year 1847 the plaintiff, who was a commercial traveller, called on a firm named Byfield & Hawkesworth on business, as he was in the habit of doing, and as he was leaving the shop he picked up a small parcel which was lying on the floor. He immediately showed it to the shopman, and opened it in his presence, when it was found to consist of a quantity of Bank of England notes, to the amount of £65. The defendant, who was a partner in the firm of Byfield & Hawkesworth, was then called, and the plaintiff told him he had found the notes, and asked the defendant to keep them until the owner appeared to claim them. Then various advertisements were put in the papers asking for the owner, but the true owner was never found. No person having appeared to claim them, and three years having elapsed since they were found, the plaintiff applied to the defendant to have the notes returned to him, and offered to pay the expenses of the advertisements, and to give an indemnity. The defendant refused to deliver them up to the plaintiff, and an action was brought in the county court of Westminster in consequence of that refusal. The county court judge decided that the defendant, the shopkeeper, was entitled to the custody of the notes as against the plaintiff, and gave judgment for the defendant. Thereupon the appeal was brought which came before the court composed of Patteson J. and Wightman J. Patteson J. said: "The notes which are the subject of this action were incidentally dropped, by mere accident, in the shop of the defendant, by the owner of them. The facts do not warrant the supposition that they had been deposited there intentionally, nor has the case been put at all upon that ground. The plaintiff found them on the floor, they being manifestly lost by someone. The general right of the finder to any article which has been lost, as against all the world, except the true owner, was established in the case of Armory v. Delamirie which has never been disputed. This right would clearly have accrued to the plaintiff had the notes been picked up by him outside the shop of the defendant and if he once had the right, the case finds that he did not intend, by delivering the notes to the defendant, to waive the title (if any) which he had to them, but they were handed to the defendant merely for the purpose of delivering them to the owner should he appear." Then a little later: "The case, therefore, resolves itself into the single point on which it appears that the learned judge decided it, namely, whether the circumstance of the notes being found inside the defendant's shop gives him, the defendant, the right to have them as against the plaintiff, who found them." After discussing the cases, and the argument, the learned judge said: "If the discovery had never been communicated to the defendant, could the real owner have had any cause of action against him because they were found in his house? Certainly not. The notes never were in the custody of the defendant, nor within the protection of his house, before they were found, as they would have been had they been intentionally deposited there; and the defendant has come under no responsibility, except from the communication made to him by the plaintiff, the finder, and the steps taken by way of advertisement. . . .We find, therefore, no circumstances in this case to take it out of the general rule of law, that the finder of a lost article is entitled to it as against all persons except the real owner, and we think that that rule must prevail, and that the learned judge was mistaken in holding that the place in which they were found makes any legal difference. Our judgment, therefore, is that the plaintiff is entitled to these notes as against the defendant."

It is to be observed that in Bridges v. Hawkesworth which has been the subject of immense disputation, neither counsel put forward any argument on the fact that the notes were found in a shop. Counsel for the appellant assumed throughout that the position was the same as if the parcel had been found in a private house, and the learned judge spoke of "the protection of his" (the shopkeeper's) "house." The case for the appellant was that the shopkeeper never knew of the notes. Again, what is curious is that there was no suggestion that the place where the notes were found was in any way material; indeed, the judge in giving the judgment of the court expressly repudiates this and said in terms "The learned judge was mistaken in holding that the place in which they were found makes any legal difference." * * *

With regard to South Staffordshire Water Co. v. Sharman, [1896] 2 Q. B. 44 (1896), the first two lines of the headnote are: "The possessor of land is generally entitled, as against the finder, to chattels found on the land." I am not sure that this is accurate. The facts were that the defendant Sharman, while cleaning out, under the orders of the plaintiffs, the South Staffordshire Water Company, a pool of water on their land, found two rings embedded in the mud at the bottom of the pool. He declined to deliver them to the plaintiffs, but failed to discover the real owner. In an action brought by the company against Sharman in detinue it was held that the company were entitled to the rings. Lord Russell of Killowen C.J. said (id. at 46): "The plaintiffs are the freeholders of the locus in quo, and as such they have the right to forbid anybody coming on their land or in any way interfering with it. They had the right to say that their pool should be cleaned out in any way that they thought fit, and to direct what should be done with anything found in the pool in the course of such cleaning out. It is no doubt right, as the counsel for the defendant contended, to say that the plaintiffs must show that they had actual control over the locus in quo and the things in it; but under the circumstances, can it be said that the Minster Pool and whatever might be in that pool were not under the control of the plaintiffs? In my opinion they were. . . . The principle on which this case must be decided, and the distinction which must be drawn between this case and that of Bridges v. Hawkesworth, is to be found in a passage in Pollock and Wright's 'Essay on Possession in the Common Law,' p. 41: 'The possession of land carries with it in general, by our law, possession of everything which is attached to or under that land, and, in the absence of a better title elsewhere, the right to possess it also'." If that is right, it would clearly cover the case of the rings embedded in the mud of the pool, the words used being "attached to or under that land." Lord Russell continued: " 'And it makes no difference that the possessor is not aware of the thing's existence. . . . It is free to anyone who requires a specific intention as part of a de facto possession to treat this as a positive rule of law. But it seems preferable to say that the legal possession rests on a real de facto possession constituted by the occupier's general power and intent to exclude unauthorized interference.' That is the ground on which I prefer to base my judgment. There is a broad distinction between this case and those cited from Blackstone. Those were cases in which a thing was cast into a public place or into the sea—into a place, in fact, of which it could not be said that anyone had a real de facto possession, or a general power and intent to exclude unauthorized interference." Then Lord Russell cited the passage which I read earlier in this judgment and continued: "It is somewhat strange"—I venture to echo those words—"that there is no more direct authority on the question; but the general principle seems to me to be that where a person has possession of house or land, with a manifest intention to exercise control over it and the things which may be upon or in it, then, if something is found on that land, whether by an employee of the owner or by a stranger, the presumption is that the possession of that thing is in the owner of the locus in quo." It is to be observed that Lord Russell there is extending the meaning of the passage he had cited from Pollock and Wright's essay on "Possession in the Common Law," where the learned authors say that the possession of land carries with it possession of everything which is attached to or under that land. Then Lord Russell adds possession of everything which may be on or in that land. South Staffordshire Water Co. v. Sharman, which was relied on by counsel for the defendant, has also been the subject of some discussion. It has been said that it establishes that if a man finds a thing as the servant or agent of another, he finds it not for himself, but for that other, and indeed that seems to afford a sufficient explanation of the case. The rings found at the bottom of the pool were not in the possession of the company, but it seems that though Sharman was the first to obtain possession of them, he obtained them for his employers and could claim no title for himself.

The only other case to which I need refer is Elwes v. Brigg Gas Co., 33 Ch. D. 562 (1886), in which land had been demised to a gas company for ninety-nine years with a reservation to the lessor of all mines and minerals. A pre-historic boat embedded in the soil was discovered by the lessees when they were digging to make a gasholder. It was held that the boat, whether regarded as a mineral or as part of the soil in which it was embedded when discovered, or as a chattel, did not pass to the lessees by the demise, but was the property of the lessor though he was ignorant of its existence at the time of granting the lease. Chitty J. said (id. at 568): "The first question which does actually arise in this case is whether the boat belonged to the plaintiff at the time of the granting of the lease. I hold that it did, whether it ought to be regarded as a mineral, or as part of the soil within the maxim above cited, or as a chattel. If it was a mineral or part of the soil in the sense above indicated, then it clearly belonged to the owners of the inheritance as part of the inheritance itself. But if it ought to be regarded as a chattel, I hold the property in the chattel was vested in the plaintiff, for the following reasons." Then he gave the reasons, and continued: "The plaintiff then being thus in possession of the chattel, it follows that the property in the chattel was vested in him. Obviously the right of the original owner could not be established; it had for centuries been lost or barred, even supposing that the property had not been abandoned when the boat was first left on the spot where it was found. The plaintiff, then, had a lawful possession, good against all the world, and therefore the property in the boat. In my opinion it makes no difference, in these circumstances, that the plaintiff was not aware of the existence of the boat."

A review of these judgments shows that the authorities are in an unsatisfactory state, and I observe that Sir John Salmond in his book on Jurisprudence (9th ed., at p. 383), after referring to the cases of Elwes v. Brigg Gas Co. and South Staffordshire Water Co. v. Sharman, said: "Cases such as these, however, are capable of explanation on other grounds, and do not involve any necessary conflict either with the theory of possession or with the cases already cited, such as Bridges v. Hawkesworth. The general principle is that the first finder of a thing has a good title to it against all but the true owner, even though the thing is found on the property of another person," and he cites Armory v. Delamirie and Bridges v. Hawkesworth in support of that proposition. Then he continues: "This principle, however, is subject to important exceptions, in which, owing to the special circumstances of the case, the better right is in him on whose property the thing is found," and he names three cases as the principal ones: "When he on whose property the thing is found is already in possession not merely of the property, but of the thing itself; as in certain circumstances, even without specific knowledge, he undoubtedly may be." The second limitation Sir John Salmond puts is: "If anyone finds a thing as the servant or agent of another he finds it not for himself, but for his employer." Then: "A third case in which a finder obtains no title is that in which he gets possession only through a trespass or other act of wrongdoing." It is fairly clear from the authorities that a man possesses everything which is attached to or under his land. Secondly, it would appear to be the law from the authorities I have cited, and particularly from Bridges v. Hawkesworth, that a man does not necessarily possess a thing which is lying unattached on the surface of his land even though the thing is not possessed by someone else. A difficulty however, arises, because the rule which governs things an occupier possesses as against those which he does not, has never been very clearly formulated in our law. He may possess everything on the land from which he intends to exclude others, if Mr. Justice Holmes is right; or he may possess those things of which he has a de facto control, if Sir Frederick Pollock is right.

There is no doubt that in this case the brooch was lost in the ordinary meaning of that term, and I should imagine it had been lost for a very considerable time. Indeed, from this correspondence it appears that at one time the predecessors in title of the defendant were considering making some claim. But the moment the plaintiff discovered that the brooch might be of some value, he took the advice of his commanding officer and handed it to the police. His conduct was commendable and meritorious. The defendant was never physically in possession of these premises at any time. It is clear that the brooch was never his, in the ordinary acceptation of the term, in that he had the prior possession. He had no knowledge of it, until it was brought to his notice by the finder. A discussion of the merits does not seem to help, but it is clear on the facts that the brooch was "lost" in the ordinary meaning of that word; that it was "found" by the plaintiff in the ordinary meaning of that word, that its true owner has never been found, that the defendant was the owner of the premises and had his notice drawn to this matter by the plaintiff, who found the brooch. In those circumstances I propose to follow the decision in Bridges v. Hawkesworth, and to give judgment in this case for the plaintiff for £66.

NOTES AND QUESTIONS

1.   According to a local historian, the Peels were the "lords of the manor" of Overton and still live in the village today. The main house of the Peel estate is Bryn y Pys, located nearby; they purchased Gwernhaylod in 1934 primarily to add its farmland and woods to their existing holdings, and they leased the house to tenants. Consider some further history:

> I am afraid [Gwernhaylod] suffered the same fate as many country houses in the U.K. They were requisitioned by the British army 1939–46 and after the war were left in such an awful state by the uncaring and unsupervised soldiers, that they had to be demolished. Windows smashed, lead stolen from roofs, led to the weather getting in and the houses starting to decay and getting into a state that would be too expensive to repair * * * It was also a time when men returning from the war had no desire to go back to be servants and the size of large houses was impractical to run without servants. The final blow was the death of Major Hugh Peel in 1950, leaving his heir, one very young granddaughter. The estate was for a time therefore managed by Trustees on her behalf who

made the decision to demolish the old house. There is still a cottage there created from outbuildings of the old house and this is now lived in by the Peel estate's gamekeeper.

Email communication from Jill Burton, Royal Commission on the Ancient and Historical Monuments of Wales, July 29, 2006.

Figure 2-10
Gwernhaylod House, Overton: West Elevation, 1956

© Crown copyright: Royal Commission on the Ancient and Historical Monuments of Wales.

2.   Again, there is no easy solution here based on trespass. Corporal Hannah had full permission to be where he was when he found the brooch. He was staying at Gwernhaylod on the orders of the British Army, which had requisitioned it during the War.

3.   The court appears to give reduced weight to Major Peel's interest as owner of the house, on the ground that he had never entered into actual possession of the house before the brooch was found. This seems to tilt the court away from accession towards first possession. Major Peel's lack of possession could hardly be a decisive factor, however, given the decision in *Elwes v. Brigg Gas Co.*, cited in the main case, which awarded a pre-historic boat found buried on the land to the landlord rather than the tenant gas company that discovered it while digging. One can hardly be more out of possession than a landlord under a 99-year lease. Would *Hannah v. Peel* have come out the other way if Gwernhaylod had been Major Peel's ancestral home where he had grown up as a boy?

4.   Suppose the brooch had been discovered by Corporal Hannah buried under one inch of soil in the garden. Different result? English law recognizes a special rule for treasure trove, defined to mean gold, silver, bullion, or money concealed in a hidden place. If the treasure trove is buried under ground, it belongs to the Crown. Should the court in *Hannah* have

extended this doctrine to award the brooch to the British government? Absent any Crown and operating in a culture that puts a high premium on individualism, American courts have tended to reject any special rule for treasure trove and generally treat buried treasure like any other kind of lost or abandoned property.

5.   American courts sometimes distinguish between lost and mislaid property in deciding who gets to keep a found object. See, e.g., McAvoy v. Medina, 93 Mass. 548 (1866). An object is said to be mislaid when the owner intentionally places it somewhere and then forgets it (for example, the owner places it on a counter in a store and then leaves without it). An object is said to be lost when the owner is unaware of losing possession of it (for example, it falls out of the owner's pocket). Courts that observe the distinction generally award lost property to the finder, and mislaid property to the owner of the land where it is found. Does this distinction make sense? What policy or objective is being pursued by further subdividing the world of misplaced objects in this fashion? Was the brooch in *Hannah* lost or mislaid?

CONCLUDING NOTE AND QUESTIONS

The idea of possession appears repeatedly in all the material we have covered in this chapter. First possession, obviously, is based on being the first to possess an unclaimed thing. Discovery is based on being the first to discover some thing, and hence having a unique claim to possess it. Creation involves being the first to possess some new or novel thing. Accession is more complicated, but in many of its applications appears to involve the perception that one thing bears such a prominent relationship to another thing that possession of the one thing is also possession of the other thing. And of course adverse possession is based on someone possessing a thing for such a long period of time that the rights of the original owner are extinguished. Moreover, the sequential possession issues seem to suggest that prior possession is privileged in the law, and the cases about competing acquisition principles can be read as turning on which of two rival claims of possession the court finds more compelling in any given context. Does all this suggest that there is only one principle of original acquisition, based on having a stronger claim of possession? Why should possession play such a pivotal role in assigning ownership to things? Can you think of some other principle, unrelated to possession, that might serve as an alternative basis for establishing original claims to ownership of things?

CHAPTER III

VALUES SUBJECT TO OWNERSHIP

What sorts of resources are eligible for claims of property rights? Clearly not every valued thing is or should be property. Human slavery was a system in which one human being claimed ownership of another. A Civil War was fought over this issue, and led to the adoption of the Thirteenth Amendment, which abolished all forms of slavery and involuntary servitude. This gives us one fixed point of reference as to what cannot be included in the system of property rights. Selling babies is also forbidden, although some economists have argued that this policy should be reconsidered. Other resources are thought to belong to the public at large—highways and waterways, and in the more intangible realm, ideas and perhaps the law itself. How do we determine the proper domain of the system of property rights? We start by considering several controversies about interests that may be thought to be too personal or private to be subject to private property rights—human bodies, body parts and fluids, and individuals' unique personality. We then consider certain academic perspectives that inform debates about the proper scope of the system of property rights. This is followed by a consideration of interests that are interwoven in a regime of custom and their relation to law. We then turn to interests that may be thought to be too public to be subject to private property rights—like harbors and beaches. We end with resources that seem to call for some mixture of public and private rights and focus on one prominent such resource—water.

A. PERSONHOOD

One issue that confronts any system of property rights is whether there are certain interests that are inappropriate for treatment as property because they are too closely connected to personhood. There is a universal consensus today that people are not a permissible subject of property rights. Not only is formal slavery abolished, but the Supreme Court has long invalidated schemes that would permit peonage—systems of servitude based on unpaid debts. See, e.g., Bailey v. Alabama, 219 U.S. 219 (1911). The usual justification for this understanding is that people, as autonomous moral agents, should not be regarded as objects or commodities to be bought and sold by other people. But how far does this anti-commodification principle extend? As the cases in this section clearly reveal, modern medical technology is rapidly generating controversial questions about the boundary between persons and property. There is every reason to believe that these issues will multiply and become ever more vexing in the near future. As things presently stand, the law is deeply ambivalent about whether to apply the "property" template in resolving these issues. Controversy also exists about whether it should be possible to claim as property an individual's unique personality or persona.

1. PROPERTY AND THE HUMAN BODY

Moore v. Regents of the University of California

Supreme Court of California, In Bank, 1990.
793 P.2d 479.

I. INTRODUCTION

■ PANELLI, JUSTICE. We granted review in this case to determine whether plaintiff has stated a cause of action against his physician and other defendants for using his cells in potentially lucrative medical research without his permission. Plaintiff alleges that his physician failed to disclose preexisting research and economic interests in the cells before obtaining consent to the medical procedures by which they were extracted. The superior court sustained all defendants' demurrers to the third amended complaint, and the Court of Appeal reversed. We hold that the complaint states a cause of action for breach of the physician's disclosure obligations, but not for conversion.

II. FACTS

[According to the complaint, John Moore, who lived in Seattle, was diagnosed as having hairy-cell leukemia. He traveled to Los Angeles to be treated by Dr. David Golde at the UCLA Medical Center. Golde recommended that Moore's spleen be removed in order to slow down the progress of the disease. Moore signed a written consent form authorizing the operation. Without informing Moore, Dr. Golde and his associates also developed plans to do research on certain white blood cells called T-lymphocytes taken from Moore's spleen. The objective was to produce certain lymphokines, or proteins that regulate the immune system. The genetic code for making these lymphokines is identical in all persons, but it is hard to locate the particular genes responsible for making each lymphokine. Because of his disease, the cells in Moore's spleen had overproduced certain lymphokines, making the process of identification easier.

In order to pursue this research, Dr. Golde and his associates established a new cell line from Moore's T-lymphocytes. They then sought on behalf of themselves and UCLA a patent on the new cell line. The patent was granted, and Golde negotiated a contract with Genetics Institute, Inc., granting the firm exclusive access to the materials and research based on the cell line, in return for $440,000 to be paid to Golde and the Regents over three years, as well as a consultant position and rights to shares of common stock for Golde. It was estimated that the total potential market for products based on lymphokines might eventually reach $3 billion per year.

When Moore learned the use to which his spleen cells had been put, he sued Dr. Golde, his associates, and UCLA. His complaint asserted a number of causes of action including conversion—the taking of property from someone without their consent and converting it to the use of the defendant. He also asserted a number of other causes of action, including lack of informed consent and unjust enrichment. The trial court held that the action for conversion could not be maintained because Moore had no property right in his spleen cells after they had been removed from his body, and that this defect meant that all the other asserted causes of action failed too. Moore appealed.]

III. DISCUSSION

A.   Breach of Fiduciary Duty and Lack of Informed Consent

Moore repeatedly alleges that Golde failed to disclose the extent of his research and economic interests in Moore's cells before obtaining consent to the medical procedures by which the cells were extracted. These allegations, in our view, state a cause of action against Golde for invading a legally protected interest of his patient. This cause of action can properly be characterized either as the breach of a fiduciary duty to disclose facts material to the patient's consent or, alternatively, as the performance of medical procedures without first having obtained the patient's informed consent. * * *

Accordingly, we hold that a physician who is seeking a patient's consent for a medical procedure must, in order to satisfy his fiduciary duty and to obtain the patient's informed consent, disclose personal interests unrelated to the patient's health, whether research or economic, that may affect his medical judgment. * * *

B.   Conversion

Moore also attempts to characterize the invasion of his rights as a conversion—a tort that protects against interference with possessory and ownership interests in personal property. He theorizes that he continued to own his cells following their removal from his body, at least for the purpose of directing their use, and that he never consented to their use in potentially lucrative medical research. Thus, to complete Moore's argument, defendants' unauthorized use of his cells constitutes a conversion. As a result of the alleged conversion, Moore claims a proprietary interest in each of the products that any of the defendants might ever create from his cells or the patented cell line.

No court, however, has ever in a reported decision imposed conversion liability for the use of human cells in medical research. While that fact does not end our inquiry, it raises a flag of caution. In effect, what Moore is asking us to do is to impose a tort duty on scientists to investigate the consensual pedigree of each human cell sample used in research. To impose such a duty, which would affect medical research of

no precedent

importance to all of society, implicates policy concerns far removed from the traditional, two-party ownership disputes in which the law of conversion arose. Invoking a tort theory originally used to determine whether the loser or the finder of a horse had the better title, Moore claims ownership of the results of socially important medical research, including the genetic code for chemicals that regulate the functions of every human being's immune system.

We have recognized that, when the proposed application of a very general theory of liability in a new context raises important policy concerns, it is especially important to face those concerns and address them openly. * * * Moreover, we should be hesitant to "impose [new tort duties] when to do so would involve complex policy decisions" (Nally v. Grace Community Church, 763 P.2d 948, 960 (Cal. 1988)), especially when such decisions are more appropriately the subject of legislative deliberation and resolution. * * *

1.   Moore's Claim Under Existing Law

"To establish a conversion, plaintiff must establish an actual interference with his *ownership* or *right of possession*. . . . Where plaintiff neither has title to the property alleged to have been converted, nor possession thereof, he cannot maintain an action for conversion." (Del E. Webb Corp. v. Structural Materials Co., 176 Cal. Rptr. 824, 833 (Cal. Ct. App. 1981), emphasis added.) * * *

Since Moore clearly did not expect to retain possession of his cells following their removal, to sue for their conversion he must have retained an ownership interest in them. But there are several reasons to doubt that he did retain any such interest. * * *

Neither the Court of Appeal's opinion, the parties' briefs, nor our research discloses a case holding that a person retains a sufficient interest in excised cells to support a cause of action for conversion. We do not find this surprising, since the laws governing such things as human tissues, transplantable organs,[22] blood,[23] fetuses, pituitary glands, corneal tissue,[26] and dead bodies deal with human biological materials as objects sui generis, regulating their disposition to achieve policy goals

---

[22]   See the Uniform Anatomical Gift Act, Health and Safety Code section 7150 et seq. The act permits a competent adult to "give all or part of [his] body" for certain designated purposes, including "transplantation, therapy, medical or dental education, research, or advancement of medical or dental science." (Health & Saf.Code, §§ 7151, 7153.) The act does not, however, permit the donor to receive "valuable consideration" for the transfer. (Health & Saf.Code, § 7155.)

[23]   See Health & Safety Code section 1601 et seq., which regulates the procurement, processing, and distribution of human blood. Health and Safety Code section 1606 declares that "[t]he procurement, processing, distribution, or use of whole blood, plasma, blood products, and blood derivatives for the purpose of injecting or transfusing the same . . . is declared to be, for all purposes whatsoever, the rendition of a service . . . and shall not be construed to be, and is declared not to be, a sale . . . for any purpose or purposes whatsoever."

[26]   See Government Code section 27491.47: "The coroner may, in the course of an autopsy [and subject to specified conditions], remove . . . corneal eye tissue from a body . . ." (id., subd. (a)) for "transplant, therapeutic, or scientific purposes" (id., subd. (a)(5)).

rather than abandoning them to the general law of personal property. It is these specialized statutes, not the law of conversion, to which courts ordinarily should and do look for guidance on the disposition of human biological materials.

Lacking direct authority for importing the law of conversion into this context, Moore relies, as did the Court of Appeal, primarily on decisions addressing privacy rights. One line of cases involves unwanted publicity. (Lugosi v. Universal Pictures, 603 P.2d 425 (Cal. 1979); Motschenbacher v. R.J. Reynolds Tobacco Company, 498 F.2d 821 (9th Cir. 1974) [interpreting Cal. law].) These opinions hold that every person has a proprietary interest in his own likeness and that unauthorized, business use of a likeness is redressible as a tort. But in neither opinion did the authoring court expressly base its holding on property law. Each court stated, following Prosser, that it was "pointless" to debate the proper characterization of the proprietary interest in a likeness. For purposes of determining whether the tort of conversion lies, however, the characterization of the right in question is far from pointless. Only property can be converted.

Not only are the wrongful-publicity cases irrelevant to the issue of conversion, but the analogy to them seriously misconceives the nature of the genetic materials and research involved in this case. * * * [A]s the defendants' patent makes clear—and the complaint, too, if read with an understanding of the scientific terms which it has borrowed from the patent—the goal and result of defendants' efforts has been to manufacture lymphokines. Lymphokines, unlike a name or a face, have the same molecular structure in every human being and the same, important functions in every human being's immune system. Moreover, the particular genetic material which is responsible for the natural production of lymphokines, and which defendants use to manufacture lymphokines in the laboratory, is also the same in every person; it is no more unique to Moore than the number of vertebrae in the spine or the chemical formula of hemoglobin. * * *

* * * [T]he Court of Appeal in this case concluded that "[a] patient must have the ultimate power to control what becomes of his or her tissues. To hold otherwise would open the door to a massive invasion of human privacy and dignity in the name of medical progress." Yet one may earnestly wish to protect privacy and dignity without accepting the extremely problematic conclusion that interference with those interests amounts to a conversion of personal property. Nor is it necessary to force the round pegs of "privacy" and "dignity" into the square hole of "property" in order to protect the patient, since the fiduciary-duty and informed-consent theories protect these interests directly by requiring full disclosure.

The next consideration that makes Moore's claim of ownership problematic is California statutory law, which drastically limits a patient's control over excised cells. Pursuant to Health and Safety Code section 7054.4, "[n]otwithstanding any other provision of law, recognizable anatomical parts, human tissues, anatomical human remains, or infectious waste following conclusion of scientific use shall be disposed of by interment, incineration, or any other method determined by the state department [of health services] to protect the public health and safety." Clearly the Legislature did not specifically intend this statute to resolve the question of whether a patient is entitled to compensation for the nonconsensual use of excised cells. A primary object of the statute is to ensure the safe handling of potentially hazardous biological waste materials. Yet one cannot escape the conclusion that the statute's practical effect is to limit, drastically, a patient's control over excised cells. By restricting how excised cells may be used and requiring their eventual destruction, the statute eliminates so many of the rights ordinarily attached to property that one cannot simply assume that what is left amounts to "property" or "ownership" for purposes of conversion law.

It may be that some limited right to control the use of excised cells does survive the operation of this statute. There is, for example, no need to read the statute to permit "scientific use" contrary to the patient's expressed wish. A fully informed patient may always withhold consent to treatment by a physician whose research plans the patient does not approve. That right, however, as already discussed, is protected by the fiduciary-duty and informed-consent theories.

Finally, the subject matter of the Regents' patent—the patented cell line and the products derived from it—cannot be Moore's property. This is because the patented cell line is both factually and legally distinct from the cells taken from Moore's body. Federal law permits the patenting of organisms that represent the product of "human ingenuity," but not naturally occurring organisms. (Diamond v. Chakrabarty, 447 U.S. 303, 309–310 (1980).) Human cell lines are patentable because "[l]ong-term adaptation and growth of human tissues and cells in culture is difficult— often considered an art . . .," and the probability of success is low. (U.S. Congress, Office of Technology Assessment, New Developments in Biotechnology: Ownership of Human Tissues and Cells (1987) at p. 33 (hereafter OTA Report).) It is this *inventive effort* that patent law rewards, not the discovery of naturally occurring raw materials. Thus, Moore's allegations that he owns the cell line and the products derived from it are inconsistent with the patent, which constitutes an authoritative determination that the cell line is the product of invention. * * *

2.   Should Conversion Liability Be Extended?

* * * Of the relevant policy considerations, two are of overriding importance. The first is protection of a competent patient's right to make autonomous medical decisions. That right, as already discussed, is grounded in well-recognized and long-standing principles of fiduciary duty and informed consent. This policy weighs in favor of providing a

remedy to patients when physicians act with undisclosed motives that may affect their professional judgment. The second important policy consideration is that we not threaten with disabling civil liability innocent parties who are engaged in socially useful activities, such as researchers who have no reason to believe that their use of a particular cell sample is, or may be, against a donor's wishes. * * *

[A]n examination of the relevant policy considerations suggests an appropriate balance: Liability based upon existing disclosure obligations, rather than an unprecedented extension of the conversion theory, protects patients' rights of privacy and autonomy without unnecessarily hindering research.

To be sure, the threat of liability for conversion might help to enforce patients' rights indirectly. This is because physicians might be able to avoid liability by obtaining patients' consent, in the broadest possible terms, to any conceivable subsequent research use of excised cells. Unfortunately, to extend the conversion theory would utterly sacrifice the other goal of protecting innocent parties. Since conversion is a strict liability tort,[38] it would impose liability on all those into whose hands the cells come, whether or not the particular defendant participated in, or knew of, the inadequate disclosures that violated the patient's right to make an informed decision. In contrast to the conversion theory, the fiduciary-duty and informed-consent theories protect the patient directly, without punishing innocent parties or creating disincentives to the conduct of socially beneficial research. * * *

[T]he theory of liability that Moore urges us to endorse threatens to destroy the economic incentive to conduct important medical research. If the use of cells in research is a conversion, then with every cell sample a researcher purchases a ticket in a litigation lottery. Because liability for conversion is predicated on a continuing ownership interest, "companies are unlikely to invest heavily in developing, manufacturing, or marketing a product when uncertainty about clear title exists." (OTA Rep., supra, at p. 27.) * * *[42]

---

[38] " 'The foundation for the action for conversion rests neither in the knowledge nor the intent of the defendant. . . . [Instead,] "the tort consists in the breach of what may be called an absolute duty; the act itself . . . is unlawful and redressible as a tort." ' [Citation.]" (Byer v. Canadian Bank of Commerce, 65 P.2d 67, 68 (Cal. 1937), quoting Poggi v. Scott, 139 P. 815, 816 (Cal. 1914). See also City of Los Angeles v. Superior Court, 149 Cal.Rptr. 320, 323 (Cal. Ct. App. 1978) ["[c]onversion is a species of strict liability in which questions of good faith, lack of knowledge and motive are ordinarily immaterial."].)

[42] In order to make conversion liability seem less of a threat to research, the dissent argues that researchers could avoid liability by using only cell lines accompanied by documentation of the source's consent. (Dis. opn. of Mosk, J., post.) But consent forms do not come with guarantees of validity. As medical malpractice litigation shows, challenges to the validity and sufficiency of consent are not uncommon. Moreover, it is sheer fantasy to hope that waivers might be obtained for the thousands of cell lines and tissue samples presently in cell repositories and, for that reason, already in wide use among researchers. The cell line derived from Moore's T-lymphocytes, for example, has been available since 1984 to any researcher from the American Type Culture Collection. (American Type Culture Collection, Catalogue of Cell Lines and Hybridomas (6th ed. 1988) p. 176.) Other cell lines have been in wide use since as early as 1951. (OTA Rep., supra, at p. 34.)

* * * If the scientific users of human cells are to be held liable for failing to investigate the consensual pedigree of their raw materials, we believe the Legislature should make that decision. Complex policy choices affecting all society are involved, and "[l]egislatures, in making such policy decisions, have the ability to gather empirical evidence, solicit the advice of experts, and hold hearings at which all interested parties present evidence and express their views. . . ." (Foley v. Interactive Data Corp., 765 P.2d 373, 397, fn. 31 (Cal. 1988).) * * *

Finally, there is no pressing need to impose a judicially created rule of strict liability, since enforcement of physicians' disclosure obligations will protect patients against the very type of harm with which Moore was threatened. So long as a physician discloses research and economic interests that may affect his judgment, the patient is protected from conflicts of interest. Aware of any conflicts, the patient can make an informed decision to consent to treatment, or to withhold consent and look elsewhere for medical assistance. As already discussed, enforcement of physicians' disclosure obligations protects patients directly, without hindering the socially useful activities of innocent researchers.

For these reasons, we hold that the allegations of Moore's third amended complaint state a cause of action for breach of fiduciary duty or lack of informed consent, but not conversion. * * *

■ ARABIAN, JUSTICE, concurring. I join in the views cogently expounded by the majority. I write separately to give voice to a concern that I believe informs much of that opinion but finds little or no expression therein. I speak of the moral issue.

Plaintiff has asked us to recognize and enforce a right to sell one's own body tissue *for profit*. He entreats us to regard the human vessel—the single most venerated and protected subject in any civilized society—as equal with the basest commercial commodity. He urges us to commingle the sacred with the profane. He asks much. * * *

It is true, that this court has not often been deterred from deciding difficult legal issues simply because they require a choice between competing social or economic policies. The difference here, however, lies in the nature of the conflicting moral, philosophical and even religious values at stake, and in the profound implications of the position urged. The ramifications of recognizing and enforcing a property interest in body tissues are not known, but are greatly feared—the effect on human dignity of a marketplace in human body parts, the impact on research and development of competitive bidding for such materials, and the exposure of researchers to potentially limitless and uncharted tort liability.

Whether, as plaintiff urges, his cells should be treated as property susceptible to conversion is not, in my view, ours to decide. The question implicates choices which not only reflect, but which ultimately define our essence. A mark of wisdom for us as expositors of the law is the recognition that we cannot cure every ill, mediate every dispute, resolve every conundrum. Sometimes, as Justice Brandeis said, "the most important thing we do, is not doing."[1]

Where then shall a complete resolution be found? Clearly the Legislature, as the majority opinion suggests, is the proper deliberative forum. Indeed, a legislative response creating a licensing scheme, which establishes a fixed rate of profit sharing between researcher and subject, has already been suggested. Such an arrangement would not only avoid the moral and philosophical objections to a free market operation in body tissue, but would also address stated concerns by eliminating the inherently coercive effect of a waiver system and by compensating donors regardless of temporal circumstances. * * *

■ BROUSSARD, JUSTICE, concurring and dissenting [omitted]. * * *

■ MOSK, JUSTICE, dissenting. * * *

The concepts of property and ownership in our law are extremely broad. (See Civ. Code, §§ 654, 655.) A leading decision of this court approved the following definition: " 'The term "property" is sufficiently comprehensive to include every species of estate, real and personal, and everything which one person can own and transfer to another. It extends to every species of right and interest capable of being enjoyed as such upon which it is practicable to place a money value.' " (Yuba River Power Co. v. Nevada Irr. Dist., 279 P. 128, 129 (Cal. 1929).)

Being broad, the concept of property is also abstract: rather than referring directly to a material object such as a parcel of land or the tractor that cultivates it, the concept of property is often said to refer to a "bundle of rights" that may be exercised with respect to that object— principally the rights to possess the property, to use the property, to exclude others from the property, and to dispose of the property by sale or by gift. "Ownership is not a single concrete entity but a bundle of rights and privileges as well as of obligations." (Union Oil Co. v. State Bd. of Equal., 386 P.2d 496, 500 (Cal. 1963).) But the same bundle of rights does not attach to all forms of property. For a variety of policy reasons, the law limits or even forbids the exercise of certain rights over certain forms of property. For example, both law and contract may limit the right of an owner of real property to use his parcel as he sees fit. Owners of various forms of personal property may likewise be subject to restrictions on the time, place, and manner of their use. Limitations on the disposition of real property, while less common, may also be imposed. Finally, some types of personal property may be sold but not given away,[9] while others

---

[1]   Bickel, The Least Dangerous Branch (1962) page 71.

[9]   A person contemplating bankruptcy may sell his property at its "reasonably equivalent value," but he may not make a gift of the same property. (See 11 U.S.C. § 548(a).)

may be given away but not sold,[10] and still others may neither be given away nor sold.[11]

In each of the foregoing instances, the limitation or prohibition diminishes the bundle of rights that would otherwise attach to the property, yet what remains is still deemed in law to be a protectible property interest. "Since property or title is a complex bundle of rights, duties, powers and immunities, the pruning away of some or a great many of these elements does not entirely destroy the title. . . ." (People v. Walker, 90 P.2d 854, 855 (Cal. Dist. Ct. App. 1939) [even the possessor of contraband has certain property rights in it against anyone other than the state].) The same rule applies to Moore's interest in his own body tissue: even if we assume that section 7054.4 limited the use and disposition of his excised tissue in the manner claimed by the majority, Moore nevertheless retained valuable rights in that tissue. Above all, at the time of its excision he at least had *the right to do with his own tissue whatever the defendants did with it:* i.e., he could have contracted with researchers and pharmaceutical companies to develop and exploit the vast commercial potential of his tissue and its products. Defendants certainly believe that *their* right to do the foregoing is not barred by section 7054.4 and is a significant property right, as they have demonstrated by their deliberate concealment from Moore of the true value of his tissue, their efforts to obtain a patent on the Mo cell line, their contractual agreements to exploit this material, their exclusion of Moore from any participation in the profits, and their vigorous defense of this lawsuit. The Court of Appeal summed up the point by observing that "Defendants' position that plaintiff cannot own his tissue, but that they can, is fraught with irony." It is also legally untenable. As noted above, the majority cite no case holding that an individual's right to develop and exploit the commercial potential of his own tissue is *not* a right of sufficient worth or dignity to be deemed a protectible property interest. In the absence of such authority—or of legislation to the same effect— the right falls within the traditionally broad concept of property in our law. * * *

[O]ur society acknowledges a profound ethical imperative to respect the human body as the physical and temporal expression of the unique human persona. One manifestation of that respect is our prohibition against direct abuse of the body by torture or other forms of cruel or unusual punishment. Another is our prohibition against indirect abuse of the body by its economic exploitation for the sole benefit of another person. The most abhorrent form of such exploitation, of course, was the institution of slavery. Lesser forms, such as indentured servitude or even debtor's prison, have also disappeared. Yet their specter haunts the

---

[10]   A sportsman may give away wild fish or game that he has caught or killed pursuant to his license, but he may not sell it. (Fish & Game Code, §§ 3039, 7121.)

The transfer of human organs and blood is a special case that I discuss below (pt. 5).

[11]   E.g., a license to practice a profession, or a prescription drug in the hands of the person for whom it is prescribed.

laboratories and boardrooms of today's biotechnological research-industrial complex. It arises wherever scientists or industrialists claim, as defendants claim here, the right to appropriate and exploit a patient's tissue for their sole economic benefit—the right, in other words, to freely mine or harvest valuable physical properties of the patient's body: "Research with human cells that results in significant economic gain for the researcher and no gain for the patient offends the traditional mores of our society in a manner impossible to quantify. Such research tends to treat the human body as a commodity—a means to a profitable end. The dignity and sanctity with which we regard the human whole, body as well as mind and soul, are absent when we allow researchers to further their own interests without the patient's participation by using a patient's cells as the basis for a marketable product." (Danforth, Cells, Sales, and Royalties: The Patient's Right to a Portion of the Profits, 6 Yale L. & Pol'y Rev. 179, 190 (1988).)

A second policy consideration adds notions of equity to those of ethics. Our society values fundamental fairness in dealings between its members, and condemns the unjust enrichment of any member at the expense of another. This is particularly true when, as here, the parties are not in equal bargaining positions. * * *

There will be * * * equitable sharing if the courts recognize that the patient has a legally protected property interest in his own body and its products: "property rights in one's own tissue would provide a morally acceptable result by giving effect to notions of fairness and preventing unjust enrichment. . . . [¶] Societal notions of equity and fairness demand recognition of property rights. There are bountiful benefits, monetary and otherwise, to be derived from human biologics. To deny the person contributing the raw material a fair share of these ample benefits is both unfair and morally wrong." (Note, Toward the Right of Commerciality: Recognizing Property Rights in the Commercial Value of Human Tissue, 34 UCLA L. Rev. 207, 229 (1986).) * * *

The inference I draw from the current statutory regulation of human biological materials, moreover, is the opposite of that drawn by the majority. By selective quotation of the statutes the majority seem to suggest that human organs and blood cannot legally be sold on the open market—thereby implying that if the Legislature were to act here it would impose a similar ban on monetary compensation for the use of human tissue in biotechnological research and development. But if that is the argument, the premise is unsound: contrary to popular misconception, it is not true that human organs and blood cannot legally be sold.

As to organs, the majority rely on the Uniform Anatomical Gift Act (Health & Saf.Code, § 7150 et seq., hereafter the UAGA) for the proposition that a competent adult may make a post mortem gift of any part of his body but may not receive "valuable consideration" for the transfer. But the prohibition of the UAGA against the sale of a body part is much more limited than the majority recognize: by its terms (Health & Saf.Code, § 7155, subd. (a)) the prohibition applies only to sales for "transplantation" or "therapy." Yet a different section of the UAGA authorizes the transfer and receipt of body parts for such additional purposes as "medical or dental education, research, or advancement of medical or dental science." (Health & Saf.Code, § 7153, subd. (a)(1).) No section of the UAGA prohibits anyone from selling body parts for any of those additional purposes; by clear implication, therefore, such sales are legal.[23] Indeed, the fact that the UAGA prohibits *no* sales of organs other than sales for "transportation" or "therapy" raises a further implication that it is also legal for anyone to sell human tissue to a biotechnology company for research and development purposes. * * *

It follows that the statutes regulating the transfers of human organs and blood do not support the majority's refusal to recognize a conversion cause of action for commercial exploitation of human blood cells without consent. On the contrary, because such statutes treat both organs and blood as property that can legally be sold in a variety of circumstances, they impliedly support Moore's contention that his blood cells are likewise property for which he can and should receive compensation, and hence are protected by the law of conversion. * * *

NOTES AND QUESTIONS

1.   What is the holding of this case? That body parts and fluids removed from a person's body are not property? That body parts and fluids removed from a person's body may not be sold in a commercial transaction, and hence cannot provide the foundation for an action for damages based on conversion? That medical researchers have a public-policy based immunity from liability for conversion when taking body parts and fluids from a person without their consent?

2.   Does the California Supreme Court's decision in fact deny persons compensation for taking their body parts or fluids? A fully informed patient could condition the doctors' right to perform the operation on sharing the fruits of the spleen cells with him. If the UCLA doctors refuse, could Moore shop his proposal to USC and other hospitals? Or should this be illegal? If so, why? Does the right to refuse consent mean that a patient has some right to determine the use of the severed body part? Would that make it property?

3.   Why hasn't Moore abandoned any interest in his spleen cells? If you go to a salon to get a haircut, isn't the usual assumption that you have abandoned your hair cuttings, and the salon can dispose of them as it sees fit? What happens if you learn later that your hair is commercially valuable?

---

[23]   "By their terms . . . the statutes in question forbid only sales for transplantation and therapy. In light of the rather clear authorization for donation for research and education, one could conclude that sales for these non-therapeutic purposes are permitted. Scientists in practice have been buying and selling human tissues for research apparently without interference from these statutes." (Note, "She's Got Bette Davis['s] Eyes": Assessing the Nonconsensual Removal of Cadaver Organs Under the Takings and Due Process Clauses, 90 Colum.L.Rev. 528, 544, fn. 75. (1990).)

Consider the threat by Neil Armstrong, the first man to walk on the moon, to sue his barber for gathering some of Armstrong's hair off the shop floor and selling it for $3,000. (In case you're wondering, the buyer was a Connecticut collector listed by Guinness World Records as having the world's largest collection of celebrity hair.) Terry Kinney, Neil Armstrong Threatens To Sue Barber Who Sold Hair, Akron Beacon J., June 1, 2005, at B1. Or is hair less personal than other body parts? Incidentally, if Armstrong claimed a violation of his right of publicity (see infra Part A.2), how would he likely fare? How should he?

4.   One concern motivating both the majority opinion and some of the dissents relates to the in rem aspect of property. If Moore has property in his cells and can sue for conversion, the set of duty bearers is not limited to the doctors who operated on him (as it is with fiduciary duties). This is beneficial to Moore, but it puts scientists at risk of violating rights about which they may have difficulty investigating. Would a registry of cell lines with provenances help here? What about existing cell lines?

5.   The concern about imposing liability for conversion on remote researchers is made vivid by the story of Henrietta Lacks, as recounted in Rebecca Skloot, The Immortal Life of Henrietta Lacks (2010). Lacks was diagnosed with cervical cancer in 1951, and cancer cells taken from her body by physicians at Johns Hopkins Hospital in Baltimore eventually became an "immortal" cell line known as HeLa cells. Today, it is believed that scientists have grown 20 tons of cells from the HeLa line, which has been used in research generating some 11,000 patents. Lacks died shortly after her cells were removed, almost certainly without being informed of the removal. Her family had no clue that her cells had become an important tool of scientific research until many decades later. If her cells were private property (contrary to *Moore*), would any claim by her descendants for conversion now be barred by adverse possession? Or would the clock not start running until they knew or should have known that the cells were taken, or until they had made a demand for their return (see Chapter II supra)?

6.   As the majority points out, patent law is clear about who is and is not a joint inventor and hence the initial owner of a patent. But the patenting of living organisms has been controversial. Section 101 of the Patent Act, echoing language of Thomas Jefferson in the 1793 Patent Act, provides that "[w]hoever invents or discovers any new and useful process, machine, manufacture, or composition of matter, or any new and useful improvement thereof, may obtain a patent therefor, subject to the conditions and requirements of this title." 35 U.S.C. § 101. In the case of *Diamond v. Chakrabarty*, 447 U.S. 303, 309 (1980), mentioned in the *Moore* opinion, the Supreme Court held that patentable subject matter "include[s] everything under the sun that is made by man," a phrase used by the drafters in the legislative history of the 1952 Act. Ideas and laws of nature are still not patentable subject matter, see Bilski v. Kappos, 561 U.S. 593, 603, 610–11 (2010), but this exception has fluctuated in scope over time. To be patentable, a living organism should be altered from any naturally existing form; merely being distilled in a way not occurring in nature is not enough, Association for

Molecular Pathology v. Myriad Genetics, 569 U.S. 576 (2013). Does this exhaust concerns one might have? How if at all is patenting a gene sequence different from patenting a life-saving pharmaceutical?

7.   How would Moore fare under the law of accession (see Chapter II.D)? Could one say that the good doctors combined their labor with Moore's spleen cells to create a new asset? But didn't they do so in "bad faith"? Should the court have considered whether Moore was entitled to an award of restitution? Could the court have awarded restitution without determining that Moore had a property right in his spleen cells?

Body Parts After *Moore*

Subsequent decisions applying California law have tended to read *Moore* narrowly. In one decision, *Hecht v. Superior Court*, 20 Cal. Rptr. 2d 275, 283 (Cal. Ct. App. 1993), the court held that frozen sperm cells left in a commercial cryogenic laboratory by a man who committed suicide were subject to the jurisdiction and control of the probate court. The decedent's children wanted the sperm destroyed; his girlfriend wanted to take custody of the sperm for possible future use in bearing a child with the decedent's genetic material. The court clearly perceived that some orderly basis for resolving the dispute was required, which meant giving the probate court jurisdiction over the sperm cells. Under California law, however, the power of the probate court extends only to the "property" of a deceased person. So the sperm cells were deemed to be property, at least for these purposes. The court distinguished *Moore* on the ground that it did not involve "gametic" material that can be used for human reproduction, something in which persons from whom the material is taken have a particularly strong interest. Does the decision mean that if Moore had died during the operation, and his heirs had sued to recover the spleen cells, the dispute would have been subject to the jurisdiction of the probate court? Does this mean body parts must be regarded as "property" at least for these purposes? See also In re Estate of Kievernagel, 83 Cal.Rptr.3d 311 (Cal. Ct. App. 2008) (proper disposition of gametic material depends on intent of donor); Yearworth v. North Bristol NHS Trust, [2009] EWCA (Civ) 37 (appeal taken from Eng.) (English Court of Appeal decision concluding that gametic material is common law property).

In another decision, *Newman v. Sathyavaglswaran*, 287 F.3d 786 (9th Cir. 2002), the court was confronted with a constitutional challenge to a California statute that allowed coroners to remove corneas from bodies being autopsied, in order to make them available to persons who need corneal transplants. Parents whose deceased children had had their corneas removed without parental notice sued, claiming they had been deprived of property without due process of law. The court agreed that the parents had a property right in their deceased children's bodies, and hence in corneas taken from their bodies, sufficient to trigger due process protection. It reasoned from California and common law authorities that impose a duty on the next of kin to make arrangements for the burial or other disposal of human bodies (with an accompanying "quasi-property" right of the next of kin in the body of the deceased). *Moore* was not mentioned. Does the decision mean that if Moore had died during the operation and the doctors had then taken his spleen cells for research purposes, Moore's relatives could have sued the doctors for a "taking" of their property? Does it make sense that body parts and fluids removed from a dead body are property, but those removed from a live body are not?

Whether *Newman* will be followed in the future is unclear. In *Conroy v. Regents of the University of California*, 203 P.3d 1127 (Cal. 2009), the California Supreme Court rejected the claim that institutions receiving bodies through donations have a duty to dispose of the remains in a manner that would not shock the sensibilities of family members. A lower court decision involving a coroner's disposal of body parts which had disagreed with *Newman* was vacated and remanded for further consideration in light of this decision. See Perryman v. County of Los Angeles, 63 Cal. Rptr. 3d 732 (Cal. Ct. App. 2007), vacated, 208 P.3d 622 (Cal. 2009). More broadly, courts have generally rejected claims based on alleged mishandling of dead bodies by the government, concluding that the next of kin have insufficient property rights in the body of the deceased to support such actions. See, e.g., Albrecht v. Treon, 889 N.E.2d 120, 129 (Ohio 2008); Evanston Ins. Co. v. Legacy of life, Inc., 370 S.W. 3d 377, 385 (Tex. 2012) (noting that "next of kin have no right to exclude, other than to seek damages in certain circumstances for acts done beyond their consent"); Shelley v. San Joaquin, 996 F. Supp. 2d 921 (E.D. Cal. 2014) (applying California law and relying in part on *Moore*).

NOTES AND QUESTIONS

1.   In light of these further precedents, how would you characterize the status of the *Moore* decision today? Is it tenable to say that body parts and fluids removed from a person's body are "not property"?

2.   Another source of controversy, analogous to the dispute in *Hecht* over frozen sperm, concerns frozen embryos. In *Davis v. Davis*, 842 S.W.2d 588 (Tenn. 1992), a married couple attempting to have children using in vitro fertilization techniques produced a number of fertilized embryos which were then cryogenically frozen. Before the embryos were implanted, the couple divorced. The wife remarried, but the parties could not agree on the disposition of the frozen embryos. The wife wanted them donated for use by childless couples; the husband wanted them destroyed. The Tennessee Supreme Court, after balancing the interests of the parties, ruled for the husband. Would the same result follow if the wife wanted the embryos to attempt a pregnancy herself? Might a husband in a bitter divorce wish to see frozen embryos destroyed knowing that this would be the wife's last chance (but not his) to be a biological parent? If there is any theme in the embryo cases, it is that either party can back out and veto the use of the embryos at any time before implantation. Is this equality? In light of all this, is the

embryo property? What if both biological contributors agree to sell the frozen embryos? For an overview of the extensive literature, see Shirley Darby Howell, The Frozen Embryo: Scholarly Theories, Case Law, and Proposed State Regulation, 14 DePaul J. Health Care L. 407 (2013).

3.   James E. Penner, whom we encountered in Chapter I, has also advanced what he calls the "separation thesis": Only items that are thought of as separate from their owners can be "things" and hence objects of property—the right to a thing. Thus, if someone cuts a lock of your hair while you are sleeping, this would be a violation of your person—a battery. But if someone took a lock of your hair after you had cut it off, this would be a theft. Does this accord with the treatment in the decided cases involving body parts and fluids? With your intuitions? See J.E. Penner, The Idea of Property in Law 111–27 (1997). Consider the case of *R. v. Bentham*, [2005] UKHL 18, in which the House of Lords overturned a conviction for possessing an imitation firearm in the course of a robbery, where the defendant had used his hand to puff out a zipped up jacket to give the impression of a gun. Relying on the premise that "[o]ne cannot possess something which is not separate and distinct from oneself," the court found that, although the defendant's behavior was "reprehensible" (and subject to other criminal liability), the defendant's unsevered finger or hand could not be "possessed." Does this make sense?

Flynn v. Holder
U.S. Court of Appeals, Ninth Circuit, 2012.
684 F.3d 852.

■ KLEINFELD, SENIOR CIRCUIT JUDGE: * * * The complaint challenges the constitutionality of the ban on compensation for human organs in the National Organ Transplant Act [42 U.S.C. § 274e], as applied to bone marrow transplants. * * * [Plaintiffs include parents of sick children, physicians, and parents of mixed race children and African Americans for whom no perfect blood marrow matches have been donated. Plaintiffs also include] a California nonprofit corporation that seeks to operate a program incentivizing bone marrow donations. The corporation proposes to offer $3,000 awards in the form of scholarships, housing allowances, or gifts to charities selected by donors, initially to minority and mixed race donors of bone marrow cells, who are likely to have the rarest marrow type. The corporation, MoreMarrowDonors.org, alleges that it cannot launch this program because the National Organ Transplant Act criminalizes payment of compensation for organs, and classifies bone marrow as an organ.

We generally use the word "marrow" to refer to the soft, fatty material in the central cavities of big bones, what some people suck out of beef bones. Bone marrow is the body's blood manufacturing factory. Bone marrow transplants enable sick patients, whose own blood cells need to be killed to save their lives, to produce new blood cells. For example, patients with leukemia, which is cancer of the blood or bone marrow, may need chemotherapy or radiation to kill the cancer cells in their blood. The treatments kill the white blood cells essential to their immune systems. The patients will die if the killed cells are not quickly replaced with healthy cells. And they cannot be replaced without the stem cells, which we describe below, that can mature into white blood cells. These stem cells can only be obtained through bone marrow transplants.

Until about twenty years ago, bone marrow was extracted from donors' bones by "aspiration." Long needles, thick enough to suck out the soft, fatty marrow, were inserted into the cavities of the anesthetized donor's hip bones. These are large bones with big central cavities full of marrow. Aspiration is a painful, unpleasant procedure for the donor. It requires hospitalization and general or local anesthesia, and involves commensurate risks.

The complaint explains that a new technology has superseded this technique during the last twenty years, after enactment of the National Organ Transplant Act. With this new technique, now used for at least two-thirds of bone marrow transplants, none of the soft, fatty marrow is actually donated. Patients who need bone marrow transplants do not need everything that the soft, fatty substance from bone cavities contains, just some of the marrow's "hematopoietic stem cells." These stem cells are seeds from which white blood cells, red blood cells, and platelets grow. These are not the embryonic stem cells often the subject of controversy. Those stem cells, taken from human embryos, are "pluripotent," that is, they can turn into any kind of cell—brain, blood, retina, toenail, whatever. The stem cells at issue in this case are "hematopoietic stem cells." "Hema" refers to blood, and "poietic" means "pertaining to production." Hematopoietic stem cells turn into blood cells and nothing else. Humans and other large mammals produce these blood stem cells constantly in vast numbers, because our blood cells die within a few months and need continual replacement. The dead blood cells are flushed out in the spleen, the body's garbage disposal for used-up blood cells, and new ones are made in the bone marrow, as long as we live.

Most blood stem cells stay in the bone marrow cavity and grow into mature blood cells there, before passing into the blood vessels. But some blood stem cells flow into and circulate in the bloodstream before they mature. These are called "peripheral" blood stem cells, "peripheral" meaning outside the central area of the body. The new bone marrow donation technique, developed during the past twenty years, is called "peripheral blood stem cell apheresis." "Apheresis" means the removal or separation of something. This procedure begins with five days of injections of a medication called a "granulocyte colony-stimulating factor" into the donor's blood. The medication accelerates blood stem cell production in the marrow, so that more stem cells go into the bloodstream. Then, with no need for sedatives or anesthesia, a needle is inserted into the donor's vein. Blood is withdrawn from the vein and filtered through an apheresis machine to extract the blood stem cells. The remaining components of the blood are returned to the donor's vein. The blood stem cells extracted in the apheresis method are replaced by the donor's bone marrow in three to six weeks. Complications for the donor are exceedingly rare.

The main difference between an ordinary blood donation and apheresis is that instead of just filling up a plastic bag with whole blood, the donor sits for some hours in a recliner while the blood passes through the apheresis machine. This same apheresis technique is sometimes used for purposes other than bone marrow donations, such as when the machine is set up to collect plasma or platelets, rather than stem cells, from a donor's blood. When it is used for these other purposes, the identical technique is called a "blood donation" or "blood plasma donation." When used to separate out and collect hematopoietic stem cells from the donor's bloodstream, apheresis is called "peripheral blood stem cell apheresis" or a "bone marrow donation."

Though the new process makes bone marrow donations much like ordinary blood donations, the matching problem remains. Deep genetic compatibility is critical in bone marrow transplants, because our bodies are xenophobic: white blood cells produced from a donor's imperfectly matched blood stem cells treat the recipient patient's body as foreign, attacking it. This is graft-versus-host disease, which can be fatal or can result in lifelong medical problems for the transplant recipient. All donations from another person, except for one's identical twin, produce at least some graft-versus-host disease in the recipient, but the closer the genetic match, the less disease. Matching is easy in ordinary blood transfusions, because there are only four basic blood types. But there are millions of marrow cell types, so good matches are hard to find. The more diverse the patient's genetic heritage, the rarer the match. For example, African-Americans have especially great difficulty finding a compatible unrelated donor, as they tend to have a mix of African, Caucasian, and Native-American genes, and fewer potential donors are registered in the national civilian registry. * * *

The plaintiff nonprofit proposes to mitigate this matching problem by using a financial incentive. The idea is that the financial incentive will induce more potential donors to sign up, stay in touch so that they can be located when necessary, and go through with the donations. The nonprofit plans to focus its attention initially on minority and mixed race donors, because their marrow cell types are rarer. The financial incentives would be $3,000 in scholarships, housing allowances, or gifts to charities of the donor's choice, which the nonprofit acknowledges would be "valuable consideration" under the statutory prohibition.

Plaintiffs argue that the National Organ Transplant Act, as applied to the MoreMarrowDonors.org's planned pilot program, violates the Equal Protection Clause. They claim that blood stem cell harvesting is not materially different from blood, sperm, and egg harvesting, which are not included under the statutory or regulatory definitions of "human organ." Like donors of blood and sperm, a bone marrow donor undergoing apheresis suffers no permanent harm, experiences no significant risk, and quickly regenerates what is donated. Plaintiffs also argue that any rational basis that Congress had when it passed the statute no longer exists with respect to the pilot program, because of the subsequent development of the apheresis method. Plaintiffs seek declaratory and injunctive relief so that MoreMarrowDonors.org can proceed with the initiative. * * *

As for whether the distinction between the organs or other body substances for which compensation is permitted and those for which it is prohibited has a rational basis, there are two classes of rational basis here: policy concerns and philosophical concerns. The policy concerns are obvious. Some are mentioned in the legislative history, though they need not be. Congress may have been concerned that if donors could be paid, rich patients or the medical industry might induce poor people to sell their organs, even when the transplant would create excessive medical risk, pain, or disability for the donor. Or, looking from the other end, Congress might have been concerned that every last cent could be extracted from sick patients needful of transplants, by well-matched potential donors making "your money or your life" offers. The existing commerce in organs extracted by force or fraud by organ thieves might be stimulated by paying for donations. Compensation to donors might also degrade the quality of the organ supply, by inducing potential donors to lie about their medical histories in order to make their organs marketable. Plaintiffs argue that a $3,000 housing subsidy, scholarship, or charitable donation is too small an amount to create a risk of any of these evils, but for a lot of people that could amount to three to six months' rent.

Congress may have had philosophical as well as policy reasons for prohibiting compensation. People tend to have an instinctive revulsion at denial of bodily integrity, particularly removal of flesh from a human being for use by another, and most particularly "commodification" of such conduct, that is, the sale of one's bodily tissue. While there is reportedly a large international market for the buying and selling of human organs, in the United States, such a market is criminal and the commerce is generally seen as revolting. Leon Kass examines the philosophical issue of commodification[.] * * * To account for why most of us are revolted by the notion of a poor person selling a kidney to feed his family, Kass cites the taboos we have against cannibalism, defilement of corpses, and necrophilia. Kass points to the idea of "psychophysical unity, a position that regards a human being as largely, if not wholly, self-identical with his enlivened body," so that, as Kant put it, to " 'dispose of oneself as a mere means to some end of one's own liking is to degrade the humanity in one's person.' " In this view, "organ transplantation . . . is—once we strip away the trappings of the sterile operating rooms and their astonishing technologies—simply a noble form of cannibalism."

These reasons are in some respects vague, in some speculative, and in some arguably misplaced. There are strong arguments for contrary views. But these policy and philosophical choices are for Congress to make, not us. The distinctions made by Congress must have a rational basis, but do not need to fit perfectly with that rational basis, and the basis need merely be rational, not persuasive to all. Here, Congress made a distinction between body material that is compensable and body material that is not. The distinction has a rational basis, so the prohibition on compensation for bone marrow donations by the aspiration method does not violate the Equal Protection Clause.

The focus, though, of plaintiffs' arguments is compensation for "bone marrow donations" by the peripheral blood stem cell apheresis method. For this, we need not answer any constitutional question, because the statute contains no prohibition. Such donations of cells drawn from blood flowing through the veins may sometimes anachronistically be called "bone marrow donations," but none of the soft, fatty marrow is donated, just cells found outside the marrow, outside the bones, flowing through the veins.

Congress could not have had an intent to address the apheresis method when it passed the statute, because the method did not exist at that time. We must construe the words of the statute to see what they imply about extraction of hematopoietic stem cells by this method. This issue has not been addressed by any of our sister circuits.

Since payment for blood donations has long been common, the silence in the National Organ Transplant Act on compensating blood donors is loud. "Blood" is omitted from the list of examples of "human organs" in the statute and the regulation. The statute says "human organ" is defined as a human "kidney, liver, heart, lung, pancreas, bone marrow, cornea, eye, bone, and skin or any subpart thereof and any other human organ . . . specified by the Secretary of Health and Human Services by regulation." 42 U.S.C. § 274e(c)(1). The regulation adds intestines and the rest of the gastrointestinal tract to the list: "kidney, liver, heart, lung, pancreas, bone marrow, cornea, eye, bone, skin, and intestine, including the esophagus, stomach, small and/or large intestine, or any portion of the gastrointestinal tract." 42 C.F.R. § 121.13 (2010). Neither the statute nor the regulation defines "human organ" to include "blood." The government concedes that the common practice of compensating blood donors is not prohibited by the statute.

The government argues that hematopoietic stem cells in the veins should be treated as "bone marrow" because "bone marrow" is a statutory organ, and the statute prohibits compensation not only for donation of an organ, but also "any subpart thereof." Hematopoietic stem cells are formed in the bone marrow, and most are found there because they generally mature into blood cells and platelets in the marrow. Therefore, the government argues, they should be viewed as "subparts" of the bone marrow, even when these stem cells are obtained through apheresis, which is to say, from blood flowing through veins.

We reject this argument, because it proves too much, and because it construes words to mean something different from ordinary usage. If the government's argument that what comes from the marrow is a subpart of the marrow were correct, then the statute would prohibit compensating blood donors. The red and white blood cells that flow through the veins come from the bone marrow, just like hematopoietic stem cells. But the government implicitly concedes that these red and white blood cells are not "subparts" of bone marrow under the statute, because it explicitly concedes that the statute does not prohibit compensation for blood donations.

As for ordinary usage, the bloodstream consists of plasma containing red cells, white cells, platelets, stem cells that will mature into one of these, and other material. We call this liquid as a whole "blood." No one calls it "bone marrow," even though these cells come from the marrow. There is no reason to think that Congress intended "bone marrow" to mean something so different from ordinary usage. Also, the blood contains not only blood cells and stem cells, but also other substances that come from elsewhere in the body. For example, the blood contains vitamin B12, which enters the bloodstream after binding with intrinsic factor and being absorbed from the small intestine. The government's argument would treat vitamin B12 as a "subpart" of the intestines, and the regulation prohibits paying donors for their intestines or subparts thereof. But every blood draw contains some vitamin B12, and we still call the red liquid "blood," not "guts."

Likewise, every blood draw includes some hematopoietic stem cells. All that differentiates the blood drawn in peripheral blood stem cell apheresis from the blood drawn from a compensated blood donor, other than the filtration process, is the medicine given to donors in the days before the blood draw to increase hematopoietic stem cell secretion. Once the stem cells are in the bloodstream, they are a "subpart" of the blood, not the bone marrow. The word "subpart" refers to the organ from which the material is taken, not the organ in which it was created. Taking part of the liver for a liver donation would violate the statute because of the "subpart thereof" language. But taking something from the blood that is created in the marrow takes only a subpart of the blood. * * *

We construe "bone marrow" to mean the soft, fatty substance in bone cavities, as opposed to blood, which means the red liquid that flows through the blood vessels. The statute does not prohibit compensation for donations of blood and the substances in it, which include peripheral blood stem cells. The Secretary of Health and Human Services has not exercised regulatory authority to define blood or peripheral blood stem cells as organs. We therefore need not decide whether prohibiting compensation for such donations would be unconstitutional.

It may be that "bone marrow transplant" is an anachronism that will soon fade away, as peripheral blood stem cell apheresis replaces aspiration as the transplant technique, much as "dial the phone" is fading away now that telephones do not have dials. Or it may live on, as "brief" does, even though "briefs" are now lengthy arguments rather than, as they used to be, brief summaries of authorities. Either way, when the "peripheral blood stem cell apheresis" method of "bone marrow transplantation" is used, it is not a transfer of a "human organ" or a "subpart thereof" as defined by the statute and regulation, so the statute does not criminalize compensating the donor.

REVERSED.

NOTES AND QUESTIONS

1.   Why is it rational for Congress to decide that compensation can be paid for the transfer of blood, sperm, and eggs, but not bone marrow, when the effect of this is to condemn significant numbers of persons to premature death? Can this distinction be sustained by the argument that many persons find organ sales to be similar to cannibalism?

2.   If blood, sperm, and eggs can be sold, but other body organs and fluids can only be donated (gifted), does this mean that blood, sperm and eggs are "property," whereas other body parts and fluids are not? Or is it more accurate to say that any body part or fluid that can be transferred, by sale or gift, is property, with the possibility of sale going only to the details of what one can do with this property? If Mr. Moore could donate his spleen cells, why are they not his property? For that matter, what is the court doing when it construes the term "subpart"? Is there a requirement here that thinghood is required for there to be property and that we need to know which thing is which? Could Congress redefine terms like "part" and "subpart" in any fashion it chooses?

3.   Given that racial minorities and mixed race persons have more difficulty obtaining donated bone marrow, because of the rarity of the composition of their bone marrow type, should the prohibition on paying compensation for bone marrow be subject to more than "rational basis" scrutiny under the Equal Protection Clause? Note that the Supreme Court has held that disparities in the treatment of persons based on race are subject to heightened scrutiny under the Equal Protection Clause only if the disparities are "intentional." Washington v. Davis, 426 U.S. 229 (1976). In contrast, employment restrictions and housing policies are prohibited by the Civil Rights Acts if they have a "disparate impact" on racial minorities. Should something more than the most minimal scrutiny be required under the Equal Protection Clause when statutes are shown to have a disparate impact on minorities, especially if that disparity can mean the difference between life and death?

4.   Thousands of persons in the United States die each year waiting for a kidney transplant. Kidneys, under the statute, can only be donated; it is unlawful to pay compensation to a person for giving up a kidney to be used for transplant purposes, even though there is comparatively little risk to a

healthy person in giving up one of their two kidneys for these purposes. Taking different and approaches, Spain and Iran are the only countries in which there is currently no shortage of kidneys for transplant. Spain employs presumed consent and a unique program of systematically approaching family members at the time of the death of a loved one. Iran provides for a system of donor compensation by the public and (predominantly) the recipient. See Emily Steeb, The Gift of Life: Can the Organ Procurement Philosophies from Spain and Iran Help Eliminate the Organ Shortage in the United States?, 25 Ind. Int'l & Comp. L. Rev. 311 (2015).

5.   By construing the statute to apply only to the traditional form of bone marrow aspiration, but not to peripheral blood stem cell apheresis, has the court in effect given a near-complete victory to the plaintiffs? As the court indicates, few if any donors would choose the painful form of needle extraction over the newer method, which is more like a prolonged blood donation. Given the policy concerns and the philosophical concerns that the court attributes to Congress, should the court give the plaintiffs a complete victory by statutory interpretation when it is unwilling to do the same by constitutional interpretation? Or is this in fact a desirable way to proceed, given that the statutory interpretation route can be overridden by Congress?

6.   For a variety of perspectives on the shortage of organs for transplantation and suggestions for reform, see Organs and Inducements, 77 Law & Contemp. Probs. No. 3 (2014); see also Julia D. Mahoney, Altruism, Markets, and Organ Procurement, 72 Law & Contemp. Probs. 17 (Summer 2009). For a proposal to increase supply by fostering trust in paired kidney donations, see Nathan B. Oman, Beyond Gift and Bargain: Some Suggestions for Increasing Kidney Exchanges, 81 Law & Contemp. Prob. 37 (2018).

2.   THE RIGHT OF PUBLICITY

Although courts like *Moore* and legislatures like the U.S. Congress that adopted the National Organ Transplant Act are wary of characterizing body parts and fluids as property, courts and legislatures have been more receptive to the idea that an individual's unique persona or personality can be regarded as property. The jurisprudence here began with an extension of tort law to protect privacy, but the law has evolved in ways that make clear the "right of publicity" has most of the attributes of property.

Midler v. Ford Motor Company

United States Court of Appeals for the Ninth Circuit, 1988.
849 F.2d 460.

■ NOONAN, CIRCUIT JUDGE: This case centers on the protectibility of the voice of a celebrated chanteuse from commercial exploitation without her consent. Ford Motor Company and its advertising agency, Young & Rubicam, Inc., in 1985 advertised the Ford Lincoln Mercury with a series of nineteen 30 or 60 second television commercials in what the agency called "The Yuppie Campaign." The aim was to make an emotional connection with Yuppies, bringing back memories of when they were in college. Different popular songs of the seventies were sung on each commercial. The agency tried to get "the original people," that is, the singers who had popularized the songs, to sing them. Failing in that endeavor in ten cases the agency had the songs sung by "sound alikes." Bette Midler, the plaintiff and appellant here, was done by a sound alike.

Midler is a nationally known actress and singer. She won a Grammy as early as 1973 as the Best New Artist of that year. Records made by her since then have gone Platinum and Gold. She was nominated in 1979 for an Academy award for Best Female Actress in The Rose, in which she portrayed a pop singer. Newsweek in its June 30, 1986 issue described her as an "outrageously original singer/comedian." Time hailed her in its March 2, 1987 issue as "a legend" and "the most dynamic and poignant singer-actress of her time."

When Young & Rubicam was preparing the Yuppie Campaign it presented the commercial to its client by playing an edited version of Midler singing "Do You Want To Dance," taken from the 1973 Midler album, "The Divine Miss M." After the client accepted the idea and form of the commercial, the agency contacted Midler's manager, Jerry Edelstein. The conversation went as follows: "Hello, I am Craig Hazen from Young and Rubicam. I am calling you to find out if Bette Midler would be interested in doing . . .?" Edelstein: "Is it a commercial?" "Yes." "We are not interested."

Undeterred, Young & Rubicam sought out Ula Hedwig whom it knew to have been one of "the Harlettes" a backup singer for Midler for ten years. Hedwig was told by Young & Rubicam that "they wanted someone who could sound like Bette Midler's recording of [Do You Want To Dance]." She was asked to make a "demo" tape of the song if she was interested. She made an a capella demo and got the job.

At the direction of Young & Rubicam, Hedwig then made a record for the commercial. The Midler record of "Do You Want To Dance" was first played to her. She was told to "sound as much as possible like the Bette Midler record," leaving out only a few "aahs" unsuitable for the commercial. Hedwig imitated Midler to the best of her ability.

After the commercial was aired Midler was told by "a number of people" that it "sounded exactly" like her record of "Do You Want To Dance." Hedwig was told by "many personal friends" that they thought it was Midler singing the commercial. Ken Fritz, a personal manager in the entertainment business not associated with Midler, declares by affidavit that he heard the commercial on more than one occasion and thought Midler was doing the singing.

Neither the name nor the picture of Midler was used in the commercial; Young & Rubicam had a license from the copyright holder to use the song. At issue in this case is only the protection of Midler's voice.

The district court described the defendants' conduct as that "of the average thief." They decided, "If we can't buy it, we'll take it." The court nonetheless believed there was no legal principle preventing imitation of Midler's voice and so gave summary judgment for the defendants. Midler appeals.

The First Amendment protects much of what the media do in the reproduction of likenesses or sounds. A primary value is freedom of speech and press. Time, Inc. v. Hill, 385 U.S. 374, 388 (1967). The purpose of the media use of a person's identity is central. If the purpose is "informative or cultural" the use is immune; "if it serves no such function but merely exploits the individual portrayed, immunity will not be granted." Felcher and Rubin, Privacy, Publicity and the Portrayal of Real People by the Media, 88 Yale L.J. 1577, 1596 (1979). Moreover, federal copyright law preempts much of the area. "Mere imitation of a recorded performance would not constitute a copyright infringement even where one performer deliberately sets out to simulate another's performance as exactly as possible." Notes of Committee on the Judiciary, 17 U.S.C.A. § 114(b). It is in the context of these First Amendment and federal copyright distinctions that we address the present appeal.

Nancy Sinatra once sued Goodyear Tire and Rubber Company on the basis of an advertising campaign by Young & Rubicam featuring "These Boots Are Made For Walkin'," a song closely identified with her; the female singers of the commercial were alleged to have imitated her voice and style and to have dressed and looked like her. The basis of Nancy Sinatra's complaint was unfair competition; she claimed that the song and the arrangement had acquired "a secondary meaning" which, under California law, was protectible. This court noted that the defendants "had paid a very substantial sum to the copyright proprietor to obtain the license for the use of the song and all of its arrangements." To give Sinatra damages for their use of the song would clash with federal copyright law. Summary judgment for the defendants was affirmed. Sinatra v. Goodyear Tire & Rubber Co., 435 F.2d 711, 717–718 (9th Cir. 1970). If Midler were claiming a secondary meaning to "Do You Want To Dance," or seeking to prevent the defendants from using that song, she would fail like Sinatra. But that is not this case. Midler does not seek damages for Ford's use of "Do You Want To Dance," and thus her claim is not preempted by federal copyright law. Copyright protects "original works of authorship fixed in any tangible medium of expression." 17 U.S.C. § 102(a). A voice is not copyrightable. The sounds are not "fixed." What is put forward as protectible here is more personal than any work of authorship.

Bert Lahr once sued Adell Chemical Co. for selling Lestoil by means of a commercial in which an imitation of Lahr's voice accompanied a cartoon of a duck. Lahr alleged that his style of vocal delivery was distinctive in pitch, accent, inflection, and sounds. The First Circuit held that Lahr had stated a cause of action for unfair competition, that it could be found "that defendant's conduct saturated plaintiff's audience, curtailing his market." Lahr v. Adell Chemical Co., 300 F.2d 256, 259 (1st Cir. 1962). That case is more like this one. But we do not find unfair competition here. One-minute commercials of the sort the defendants put on would not have saturated Midler's audience and curtailed her market. Midler did not do television commercials. The defendants were not in competition with her. See Halicki v. United Artists Communications, Inc., 812 F.2d 1213 (9th Cir. 1987).

California Civil Code section 3344 is also of no aid to Midler. The statute affords damages to a person injured by another who uses the person's "name, voice, signature, photograph or likeness, in any manner." The defendants did not use Midler's name or anything else whose use is prohibited by the statute. The voice they used was Hedwig's, not hers. The term "likeness" refers to a visual image not a vocal imitation. The statute, however, does not preclude Midler from pursuing any cause of action she may have at common law; the statute itself implies that such common law causes of action do exist because it says its remedies are merely "cumulative." Id. § 3344(g).

The companion statute protecting the use of a deceased person's name, voice, signature, photograph or likeness states that the rights it recognizes are "property rights." Id. § 990(b). By analogy the common law rights are also property rights. Appropriation of such common law rights is a tort in California. Motschenbacher v. R.J. Reynolds Tobacco Co., 498 F.2d 821 (9th Cir. 1974). In that case what the defendants used in their television commercial for Winston cigarettes was a photograph of a famous professional racing driver's racing car. The number of the car was changed and a wing-like device known as a "spoiler" was attached to the car; the car's features of white pinpointing, an oval medallion, and solid red coloring were retained. The driver, Lothar Motschenbacher, was in the car but his features were not visible. Some persons, viewing the commercial, correctly inferred that the car was his and that he was in the car and was therefore endorsing the product. The defendants were held to have invaded a "proprietary interest" of Motschenbacher in his own identity. Id. at 825.

Midler's case is different from Motschenbacher's. He and his car were physically used by the tobacco company's ad; he made part of his living out of giving commercial endorsements. But, as Judge Koelsch expressed it in *Motschenbacher*, California will recognize an injury from "an appropriation of the attributes of one's identity." Id. at 824. It was irrelevant that Motschenbacher could not be identified in the ad. The ad suggested that it was he. The ad did so by emphasizing signs or symbols associated with him. In the same way the defendants here used an imitation to convey the impression that Midler was singing for them.

Why did the defendants ask Midler to sing if her voice was not of value to them? Why did they studiously acquire the services of a sound-alike and instruct her to imitate Midler if Midler's voice was not of value to them? What they sought was an attribute of Midler's identity. Its value was what the market would have paid for Midler to have sung the commercial in person.

A voice is more distinctive and more personal than the automobile accouterments protected in *Motschenbacher*. A voice is as distinctive and personal as a face. The human voice is one of the most palpable ways identity is manifested. We are all aware that a friend is at once known by a few words on the phone. At a philosophical level it has been observed that with the sound of a voice, "the other stands before me." D. Ihde, Listening and Voice 77 (1976). A fortiori, these observations hold true of singing, especially singing by a singer of renown. The singer manifests herself in the song. To impersonate her voice is to pirate her identity. See W. Keeton, D. Dobbs, R. Keeton, D. Owen, Prosser & Keeton on Torts 852 (5th ed. 1984).

We need not and do not go so far as to hold that every imitation of a voice to advertise merchandise is actionable. We hold only that when a distinctive voice of a professional singer is widely known and is deliberately imitated in order to sell a product, the sellers have appropriated what is not theirs and have committed a tort in California. Midler has made a showing, sufficient to defeat summary judgment, that the defendants here for their own profit in selling their product did appropriate part of her identity.

Reversed and remanded for trial.

NOTES AND QUESTIONS

1. Slightly more than half of the 27 states that recognize the right of publicity have done so at least initially as a matter of judicial lawmaking. For new types of property, this is unusual; legislatures typically take the lead in adding to, subtracting from, and making major modifications to the basic set of property rights under law. Which institution, legislatures or courts, is the better arena for deciding whether and to what extent to recognize rights of publicity?

2. Many have decried the expansive sweep of some states' right of publicity. In one notable example the Ninth Circuit overturned a grant of summary judgment against Vanna White, who had claimed that an ad based on attempted humor, which included a robot in a dress turning letters on a board made up to resemble the one in the television show *Wheel of Fortune*, violated her common-law right of publicity. In a vigorous dissent from a denial of rehearing *en banc*, Judge Kozinski had this to say:

> * * * The majority isn't, in fact, preventing the "evisceration" of Vanna White's existing rights; it's creating a new and much broader property right, a right unknown in California law. It's replacing the existing balance between the interests of the celebrity and those of the public by a different balance, one substantially more favorable to the celebrity. Instead of having an exclusive right in her name, likeness, signature or voice, every famous person now

has an exclusive right to anything that reminds the viewer of her. After all, that's all Samsung did: It used an inanimate object to remind people of White, to "evoke [her identity]." 971 F.2d at 1399.

Consider how sweeping this new right is. What is it about the ad that makes people think of White? It's not the robot's wig, clothes or jewelry; there must be ten million blond women (many of them quasi-famous) who wear dresses and jewelry like White's. It's that the robot is posed near the "Wheel of Fortune" game board. Remove the game board from the ad, and no one would think of Vanna White. But once you include the game board, anybody standing beside it—a brunette woman, a man wearing women's clothes, a monkey in a wig and gown—would evoke White's image, precisely the way the robot did. It's the "Wheel of Fortune" set, not the robot's face or dress or jewelry that evokes White's image. The panel is giving White an exclusive right not in what she looks like or who she is, but in what she does for a living.

This is entirely the wrong place to strike the balance. Intellectual property rights aren't free: They're imposed at the expense of future creators and of the public at large. Where would we be if Charles Lindbergh had an exclusive right in the concept of a heroic solo aviator? If Arthur Conan Doyle had gotten a copyright in the idea of the detective story, or Albert Einstein had patented the theory of relativity? If every author and celebrity had been given the right to keep people from mocking them or their work? Surely this would have made the world poorer, not richer, culturally as well as economically.

This is why intellectual property law is full of careful balances between what's set aside for the owner and what's left in the public domain for the rest of us: The relatively short life of patents; the longer, but finite, life of copyrights; copyright's idea-expression dichotomy; the fair use doctrine; the prohibition on copyrighting facts; the compulsory license of television broadcasts and musical compositions; federal preemption of overbroad state intellectual property laws; the nominative use doctrine in trademark law; the right to make soundalike recordings. All of these diminish an intellectual property owner's rights. All let the public use something created by someone else. But all are necessary to maintain a free environment in which creative genius can flourish.

The intellectual property right created by the panel here has none of these essential limitations: No fair use exception; no right to parody; no idea-expression dichotomy. It impoverishes the public domain, to the detriment of future creators and the public at large. Instead of well-defined, limited characteristics such as name, likeness or voice, advertisers will now have to cope with vague claims of "appropriation of identity," claims often made by people with a wholly exaggerated sense of their own fame and significance. Future Vanna Whites might not get the chance to create their personae, because their employers may fear some celebrity will claim the persona is too similar to her own. The public will be robbed of parodies of celebrities, and our culture will be deprived of the valuable safety valve that parody and mockery create.

Moreover, consider the moral dimension, about which the panel majority seems to have gotten so exercised. Saying Samsung "appropriated" something of White's begs the question: Should White have the exclusive right to something as broad and amorphous as her "identity"? Samsung's ad didn't simply copy White's schtick—like all parody, it created something new. True, Samsung did it to make money, but White does whatever she does to make money, too; the majority talks of "the difference between fun and profit," 971 F.2d at 1401, but in the entertainment industry fun is profit. Why is Vanna White's right to exclusive for-profit use of her persona—a persona that might not even be her own creation, but that of a writer, director or producer—superior to Samsung's right to profit by creating its own inventions? Why should she have such absolute rights to control the conduct of others, unlimited by the idea-expression dichotomy or by the fair use doctrine?

To paraphrase only slightly *Feist Publications, Inc. v. Rural Telephone Service Co.*, 499 U.S. 340 (1991), it may seem unfair that much of the fruit of a creator's labor may be used by others without compensation. But this is not some unforeseen byproduct of our intellectual property system; it is the system's very essence. Intellectual property law assures authors the right to their original expression, but encourages others to build freely on the ideas that underlie it. This result is neither unfair nor unfortunate: It is the means by which intellectual property law advances the progress of science and art. We give authors certain exclusive rights, but in exchange we get a richer public domain. The majority ignores this wise teaching, and all of us are the poorer for it.

White v. Samsung Electronics America, Inc., 989 F.2d 1512, 1515–17 (9th Cir. 1993) (Kozinski, J., dissenting).

3.   Has Midler appropriated anything in a Lockean sense? If so, has she left "enough and as good" for others? Did Midler labor to produce the unique sound of her voice, and make it familiar to millions of listeners (especially Yuppies, or young upwardly mobile professionals)? Or is the sound of her voice primarily a natural attribute and accident of birth? Incidentally, she recently did a car commercial (for Acura).

4.   Recent controversies provide mixed signals about the trajectory of the right of publicity. Tending in the direction of lesser protection is the opinion in a case in which Tiger Woods sued a company that had marketed copies of a painting by Rick Rush, "Masters of Augusta," commemorating the 1997 Masters golf tournament in Augusta, Georgia, at which Tiger Woods became the youngest player ever to win a Masters tournament. The painting featured a scene containing *inter alia* three large likenesses of Woods in the foreground, with pictures of the clubhouse and past masters in the background. The Sixth Circuit held that the artistic aspect of the painting

gave it First Amendment protection against Woods's right of publicity claim. See ETW Corp. v. Jireh Pub., Inc., 332 F.3d 915 (6th Cir. 2003). A more mixed message is provided by a controversy over the use of images invoking college football players in a video game called "NCAA Football." Keller v. Electronics Arts, Inc., 2010 WL 530108 (N.D. Cal. 2010). The quarterback in the game shared many features with the plaintiff, a former starting quarterback for Arizona State University and the University of Nebraska, including jersey number, height, weight, and home state. The court dismissed the Indiana right of publicity claim but not the California claim, based on Section 3344(a). The court also rejected the argument that the depictions were sufficiently transformative to permit dismissal of the claims as a matter of law. The Ninth Circuit affirmed. In re NCAA Student-Athlete Name & Likeness Licensing Litig., 724 F.3d 1268 (9th Cir. 2013). Should any player be able to require his permission for such uses of his likeness? Should the NCAA, also a defendant in the suit, require participating schools to obtain waivers from players before they join the team?

5. Consider the distributional implications of the right of publicity. The right comes into play only when the invocation of a particular person—his or her likeness, voice, or occupation—has some commercial value, as in advertising. Some who have invoked the right—like the Martin Luther King estate and Bette Midler during the period covered by this decision—have done so to prevent commercialization of an image. But most of the litigation over the right has been by persons who wish to control the use of their image in order to maximize its value in commercial ventures. This represents a very tiny slice of society, consisting for the most part of highly-paid celebrities. In contrast, the restrictions on selling body parts probably has adverse distributional effects for the poorest strata of society, either because poor citizens might want to sell a kidney to augment their income or because the poor are likely to be disadvantaged in gaming the system in order to obtain "free" body parts when they are in need of a transplantation.

6. What does the right of publicity tell us about the "separation thesis" mentioned in the notes after the material on Body Parts After *Moore*? Can a person's image be regarded as a "thing" separate from the person herself? Or does the emergence of the right of publicity call into question the validity of the proposition that property exists only in things separable from persons?

7. There is a division among the states that recognize a right of publicity as to whether the right can be inherited after the celebrity is deceased. What are the competing arguments here? Even if the publicity right is inheritable, should some time limit be placed on the duration of the right? Is the publicity right more like copyright, which has a finite (albeit long) duration? Or is it more like trademark, which can last potentially forever as long as it is continually used?

B. ACADEMIC PERSPECTIVES ON THE DOMAIN OF PROPERTY

Before moving from personhood to customary and public rights, we offer some academic perspectives on the general question of what values should be subject to ownership. The first excerpt, by a leading law-and-economics pioneer, offers a positive theory of the evolution of property rights. Harold Demsetz attempts to explain, in economic terms, when and why property rights emerge in resources that previously were regarded as not being subject to ownership. Margaret Jane Radin, our second author (with excerpts from two different articles), is concerned with normative rather than positive theory. In other words, she attempts to outline a moral basis for regarding certain things as inappropriate subjects for treatment as property.

Harold Demsetz, *Toward a Theory of Property Rights*

57 AM. ECON. REV. 347–48, 350–58 (1967) (Papers & Proceedings).

* * * The Concept and Role of Property Rights

In the world of Robinson Crusoe property rights play no role. Property rights are an instrument of society and derive their significance from the fact that they help a man form those expectations which he can reasonably hold in his dealings with others. These expectations find expression in the laws, customs, and mores of a society. An owner of property rights possesses the consent of fellowmen to allow him to act in particular ways. An owner expects the community to prevent others from interfering with his actions, provided that these actions are not prohibited in the specifications of his rights.

value of prop. in dealings

It is important to note that property rights convey the right to benefit or harm oneself or others. Harming a competitor by producing superior products may be permitted, while shooting him may not. A man may be permitted to benefit himself by shooting an intruder but be prohibited from selling below a price floor. It is clear, then, that property rights specify how persons may be benefited and harmed, and, therefore, who must pay whom to modify the actions taken by persons. The recognition of this leads easily to the close relationship between property rights and externalities.

property + externalities

Externality is an ambiguous concept. For the purposes of this paper, the concept includes external costs, external benefits, and pecuniary as well as nonpecuniary externalities. No harmful or beneficial effect is external to the world. Some person or persons always suffer or enjoy these effects. What converts a harmful or beneficial effect into an externality is that the cost of bringing the effect to bear on the decisions of one or more of the interacting persons is too high to make it worthwhile, and this is what the term shall mean here. "Internalizing" such effects refers to a process, usually a change in property rights, that enables these effects to bear (in greater degree) on all interacting persons.

property as incentive for internalizing ext. costs

A primary function of property rights is that of guiding incentives to achieve a greater internalization of externalities. Every cost and benefit associated with social interdependencies is a potential externality. One condition is necessary to make costs and benefits externalities. The cost of a transaction in the rights between the parties (internalization) must exceed the gains from internalization. In general, transacting cost can be large relative to gains because of "natural" difficulties in trading or they can be large because of legal reasons. In a lawful society the prohibition of voluntary negotiations makes the cost of transacting infinite. Some costs and benefits are not taken into account by users of resources whenever externalities exist, but allowing transactions increases the degree to which internalization takes place. * * *

The Emergence of Property Rights

If the main allocative function of property rights is the internalization of beneficial and harmful effects, then the emergence of property rights can be understood best by their association with the emergence of new or different beneficial and harmful effects.

Changes in knowledge result in changes in production functions, market values, and aspirations. New techniques, new ways of doing the same things, and doing new things—all invoke harmful and beneficial effects to which society has not been accustomed. It is my thesis in this part of the paper that the emergence of new property rights takes place in response to the desires of the interacting persons for adjustment to new benefit-cost possibilities.

The thesis can be restated in a slightly different fashion: property rights develop to internalize externalities when the gains of internalization become larger than the cost of internalization. Increased internalization, in the main, results from changes in economic values, changes which stem from the development of new technology and the opening of new markets, changes to which old property rights are poorly attuned. A proper interpretation of this assertion requires that account be taken of a community's preferences for private ownership. Some communities will have less well-developed private ownership systems and more highly developed state ownership systems. But, given a community's tastes in this regard, the emergence of new private or state owned property rights will be in response to changes in technology and relative prices.

I do not mean to assert or to deny that the adjustments in property rights which take place need be the result of a conscious endeavor to cope with new externality problems. These adjustments have arisen in Western societies largely as a result of gradual changes in social mores and in common law precedents. At each step of this adjustment process, it is unlikely that externalities per se were consciously related to the issue being resolved. These legal and moral experiments may be hit-and-miss procedures to some extent but in a society that weights the achievement of efficiency heavily, their viability in the long run will depend on how well they modify behavior to accommodate to the externalities associated with important changes in technology or market values.

A rigorous test of this assertion will require extensive and detailed empirical work. A broad range of examples can be cited that are consistent with it: the development of air rights, renters' rights, rules for liability in automobile accidents, etc. In this part of the discussion, I shall present one group of such examples in some detail. They deal with the development of private property rights in land among American Indians. These examples are broad ranging and come fairly close to what can be called convincing evidence in the field of anthropology.

The question of private ownership of land among aboriginals has held a fascination for anthropologists. It has been one of the intellectual battlegrounds in the attempt to assess the "true nature" of man unconstrained by the "artificialities" of civilization. In the process of carrying on this debate, information has been uncovered that bears directly on the thesis with which we are now concerned. What appears to be accepted as a classic treatment and a high point of this debate is Eleanor Leacock's memoir on *The Montagnais "Hunting Territory" and the Fur Trade*.[3] Leacock's research followed that of Frank G. Speck[4] who had discovered that the Indians of the Labrador Peninsula had a long-established tradition of property in land. This finding was at odds with what was known about the Indians of the American Southwest and it prompted Leacock's study of the Montagnes who inhabited large regions around Quebec.

Leacock clearly established the fact that a close relationship existed, both historically and geographically, between the development of private rights in land and the development of the commercial fur trade. The factual basis of this correlation has gone unchallenged. However, to my knowledge, no theory relating privacy of land to the fur trade has yet been articulated. The factual material uncovered by Speck and Leacock fits the thesis of this paper well, and in doing so, it reveals clearly the role played by property right adjustments in taking account of what economists have often cited as an example of an externality—the overhunting of game.

Because of the lack of control over hunting by others, it is in no person's interest to invest in increasing or [maintaining] the stock of game. Overly intensive hunting takes place. Thus a successful hunt is viewed as imposing external costs on subsequent hunters—costs that are not taken into account fully in the determination of the extent of hunting and of animal husbandry.

Before the fur trade became established, hunting was carried on primarily for purposes of food and the relatively few furs that were

---

[3]   Eleanor Leacock, American Anthropologist (American Anthropological Asso.), Vol. 56, No. 5, Part 2, Memoir No. 78.

[4]   Cf., Frank G. Speck, "The Basis of American Indian Ownership of Land," Old Penn Weekly Rev. (Univ. of Pennsylvania), Jan. 16, 1915, pp. 491–95.

required for the hunter's family. The externality was clearly present. Hunting could be practiced freely and was carried on without assessing its impact on other hunters. But these external effects were of such small significance that it did not pay for anyone to take them into account. There did not exist anything resembling private ownership in land. And in the *Jesuit Relations*, particularly Le Jeune's record of the winter he spent with the Montagnes in 1633–34 and in the brief account given by Father Druilletes in 1647–48, Leacock finds no evidence of private land holdings. Both accounts indicate a socioeconomic organization in which private rights to land are not well developed.

We may safely surmise that the advent of the fur trade had two immediate consequences. First, the value of furs to the Indians was increased considerably. Second, and as a result, the scale of hunting activity rose sharply. Both consequences must have increased considerably the importance of the externalities associated with free hunting. The property right system began to change, and it changed specifically in the direction required to take account of the economic effects made important by the fur trade. The geographical or distributional evidence collected by Leacock indicates an unmistakable correlation between early centers of fur trade and the oldest and most complete development of the private hunting territory.

> By the beginning of the eighteenth century, we begin to have clear evidence that territorial hunting and trapping arrangements by individual families were developing in the area around Quebec.... The earliest references to such arrangements in this region indicates a purely temporary allotment of hunting territories. They [Algonkians and Iroquois] divide themselves into several bands in order to hunt more efficiently. It was their custom to appropriate pieces of land about two leagues square for each group to hunt exclusively. Ownership of beaver houses, however, had already become established, and when discovered, they were marked. A starving Indian could kill and eat another's beaver if he left the fur and the tail.[5]

The next step toward the hunting territory was probably a seasonal allotment system. An anonymous account written in 1723 states that the "principle of the Indians is to mark off the hunting ground selected by them by blazing the trees with their crests so that they may never encroach on each other. . . . By the middle of the century these allotted territories were relatively stabilized."[6]

The principle that associates property right changes with the emergence of new and reevaluation of old harmful and beneficial effects suggests in this instance that the fur trade made it economic to encourage

---

[5]   Eleanor Leacock, op. cit., p. 15.
[6]   Eleanor Leacock, op. cit., p. 15.

the husbanding of fur-bearing animals. Husbanding requires the ability to prevent poaching and this, in turn, suggests that socioeconomic changes in property in hunting land will take place. The chain of reasoning is consistent with the evidence cited above. Is it inconsistent with the absence of similar rights in property among the southwestern Indians?

Two factors suggest that the thesis is consistent with the absence of similar rights among the Indians of the southwestern plains. The first of these is that there were no plains animals of commercial importance comparable to the fur-bearing animals of the forest, at least not until cattle arrived with Europeans. The second factor is that animals of the plains are primarily grazing species whose habit is to wander over wide tracts of land. The value of establishing boundaries to private hunting territories is thus reduced by the relatively high cost of preventing the animals from moving to adjacent parcels. Hence both the value and cost of establishing private hunting lands in the Southwest are such that we would expect little development along these lines. The externality was just not worth taking into account.

The lands of the Labrador Peninsula shelter forest animals whose habits are considerably different from those of the plains. Forest animals confine their territories to relatively small areas, so that the cost of internalizing the effects of husbanding these animals is considerably reduced. This reduced cost, together with the higher commercial value of fur-bearing forest animals, made it productive to establish private hunting lands. Frank G. Speck finds that family proprietorship among the Indians of the Peninsula included retaliation against trespass. Animal resources were husbanded. Sometimes conservation practices were carried on extensively. Family hunting territories were divided into quarters. Each year the family hunted in a different quarter in rotation, leaving a tract in the center as a sort of bank, not to be hunted over unless forced to do so by a shortage in the regular tract. * * *

NOTES AND QUESTIONS

1.   Demsetz's theory is built around the costs and benefits of property rights. One such cost is the cost of excluding others—marking boundary lines, putting up fences, suing trespassers. Robert Ellickson points out that one reason private ownership based on exclusion is cheaper than communal ownership and mutual monitoring is that the technologies for monitoring are cheaper in the case of exclusion:

> Because private property in land necessitates the policing of boundaries, advances in surveying and fencing techniques may enhance the comparative efficiency of the institution. Preliterate societies developed many simple technologies that a landowner could use to detect and deter trespassers. During Hammurabi's reign around 1750 B.C., pegs were used to mark borders. Cairns, dikes, and stone walls are even more graphic and immovable. In

social environments in which neighbors are inclined to cooperate, physically marked boundaries, if uncontroversially placed, are largely self-enforcing. A four-year old can understand the convention that one does not cross a marked boundary. By contrast, the internal work rules that govern behavior within group-owned land are not nearly as plain to observers.

For millennia, absentee owners have employed simple technologies such as hedges, moats, and impregnable fencing to keep out persons and animals that do not respect boundaries. In addition, domesticated dogs, especially ones that instinctively bark at or attack strangers, are superb boundary defenders. By contrast, dogs are quite useless in enforcing a group's internal rules of conduct. Can a dog be trained to bark when a familiar person has shirked or pilfered? A modern-day landowner intent on detecting boundary violations can resort, in lieu of a dog, to an inexpensive electronic motion detector. "Shirking detectors"—devices that would sound an alarm when a worker was simply going through the motions—have yet to be invented.

Robert C. Ellickson, Property in Land, 102 Yale L.J. 1315, 1328–29 (1993) (footnotes omitted). Is excluding others always cheaper than policing the behavior of those with permitted access? Ellickson notes that things tend to become less clear when the externalities involve larger rather than smaller events. Also, many (most?) assets are best used by more than one person. Such multi-party use typically requires more than a simple exclusionary regime.

2.   If an increase in the value of an asset (and hence the stakes of a resource conflict) can lead to the emergence of property rights, the reverse should also be true: If an asset becomes less valuable, will less effort be expended on protecting property rights in the asset, resulting in the abandonment of the asset into the public domain in extreme situations? Such cases have been documented. In an interesting study of property rights in the nineteenth-century American West, Anderson and Hill show that as land and animals increased and then decreased in value, property rights to them became correspondingly more and then less articulated. Terry L. Anderson & P.J. Hill, The Evolution of Property Rights: A Study of the American West, 18 J.L. & Econ. 163, 170–76 (1975). Interestingly, Demsetz's example of property rights in beavers shows a similar pattern; as prices for beaver pelts have decreased in recent years, unclaimed beavers in Manitoba are proliferating to the point where they are often considered pests, with a government bounty on their heads. See Beavers' Dual Role: National Icon and Huge Pest, N.Y. Times, Mar. 31, 2001, at A4.

3.   Notwithstanding the confident tone of discussion in this article, the nature of property rights in beavers among the Naskapi and Montagne tribes in Labrador actually presents some interesting complexities. Although barely mentioned in Demsetz's article, the rights to beaver hunting territories were subject to important qualifications. Individuals had a right to take anyone's beavers as long as it was for the individual's own consumption. This may have served as an institutionalized kind of insurance

against famine. But this reintroduces some of the common-pool incentives to overuse beavers, and the rule about leaving the pelt is not easy to enforce. According to John C. McManus, An Economic Analysis of Indian Behavior in the North American Fur Trade, 32 J. Econ. Hist. 36 (1972), the beaver population decreased after the rise of the fur trade, whereas with exclusive rights one would expect a stable or growing population. In addition, the Hudson's Bay Company had to incur costs to conserve the beavers, which should not have been necessary according to Demsetz's model. In a sense, the own-consumption exception made the beavers into a semicommons—a regime combining common and private property and in which the two elements interact. Here communal rights for use as food impacted the beavers as private property in the fur trade. Henry E. Smith, Semicommon Property Rights and Scattering in the Open Fields, 29 J. Legal Stud. 131, 143 (2000). For a more systematic study of property rights in traditional societies, see Martin J. Bailey, Approximate Optimality of Aboriginal Property Rights, 35 J.L. & Econ. 183 (1992).

4.   How did the property rights among the Native Americans "evolve?" How do property rights ever evolve? Demsetz abstracts away from the processes that supply property rights and focuses only on the demand side: Where there is a need for property, something emerges. Others have tried to explore the supply of property rights. Some of these accounts emphasize that property starts out as a social norm among the relevant actors, and then is embodied in a more official rule. Consider in this connection the materials later in this Chapter about the possible efficiency of custom and its role in common-law adjudication. Other accounts suggest that certain key players or entrepreneurs who stand to gain disproportionately will lobby for the recognition of property rights. But if property comes into existence only if those who stand to benefit disproportionately seek it, what reason do we have for being optimistic that property will serve to internalize externalities? Why won't those seeking to establish property rights simply grab assets and impose costs on others? For some discussion of these issues, see Gary D. Libecap, Contracting for Property Rights (1989); Stuart Banner, Transitions between Property Regimes, 31 J. Legal Stud. S359 (2002); Saul Levmore, Two Stories About the Evolution of Property Rights, 31 J. Legal Stud. S421 (2002); Katrina Miriam Wyman, From Fur to Fish: Reconsidering the Evolution of Private Property, 80 N.Y.U. L. Rev. 117 (2005).

5.   The Demsetzian approach would lead one to expect property rights to emerge as new resource conflicts arise. How if at all would Demsetz explain the decisions in Part A of this Chapter dealing with property rights in body parts and fluids and the right of publicity? Do these decisions, taken as a whole, suggest that property rights in aspects of the person are gradually emerging as technology develops new and more valuable uses for these things?

6.   Are measurable costs and benefits all that the law of property responds to? Consider the following for a very different perspective.

Margaret Jane Radin, *Property and Personhood*

34 STAN. L. REV. 957, 959–61, 965–66, 968–70, 986–87 (1982).

* * * Most people possess certain objects they feel are almost part of themselves. These objects are closely bound up with personhood because they are part of the way we constitute ourselves as continuing personal entities in the world. They may be as different as people are different, but some common examples might be a wedding ring, a portrait, an heirloom, or a house.

One may gauge the strength or significance of someone's relationship with an object by the kind of pain that would be occasioned by its loss. On this view, an object is closely related to one's personhood if its loss causes pain that cannot be relieved by the object's replacement. If so, that particular object is bound up with the holder. For instance, if a wedding ring is stolen from a jeweler, insurance proceeds can reimburse the jeweler, but if a wedding ring is stolen from a loving wearer, the price of a replacement will not restore the status quo— perhaps no amount of money can do so.

The opposite of holding an object that has become a part of oneself is holding an object that is perfectly replaceable with other goods of equal market value. One holds such an object for purely instrumental reasons. The archetype of such a good is, of course, money, which is almost always held only to buy other things. A dollar is worth no more than what one chooses to buy with it, and one dollar bill is as good as another. Other examples are the wedding ring in the hands of the jeweler, the automobile in the hands of the dealer, the land in the hands of the developer, or the apartment in the hands of the commercial landlord. I shall call these theoretical opposites—property that is bound up with a person and property that is held purely instrumentally—personal property and fungible property respectively. * * *

Once we admit that a person can be bound up with an external "thing" in some constitutive sense, we can argue that by virtue of this connection the person should be accorded broad liberty with respect to control over that "thing." But here liberty follows from property for personhood; personhood is the basic concept, not liberty. Of course, if liberty is viewed not as freedom from interference, or "negative freedom," but rather as some positive will that by acting on the external world is constitutive of the person, then liberty comes closer to capturing the idea of the self being intimately bound up with things in the external world.

It intuitively appears that there is such a thing as property for personhood because people become bound up with "things." But this intuitive view does not compel the conclusion that property for personhood deserves moral recognition or legal protection, because arguably there is bad as well as good in being bound up with external objects. If there is a traditional understanding that a well-developed person must invest herself to some extent in external objects, there is no less a traditional understanding that one should not invest oneself in the wrong way or to too great an extent in external objects. Property is damnation as well as salvation, object-fetishism as well as moral groundwork. In this view, the relationship between the shoe fetishist and his shoe will not be respected like that between the spouse and her wedding ring. At the extreme, anyone who lives only for material objects is considered not to be a well-developed person, but rather to be lacking some important attribute of humanity.

* * * [L]et us begin with the person conceived as bodily continuity. Locke says that "every Man has a Property in his own Person," from which it immediately follows that "[t]he Labour of his Body, and the Work of his hands . . . are properly his."[28] Though * * * Locke elsewhere considers the person as reflective consciousness and memory, he may well mean here that one literally owns one's limbs and hence must own their product. If not, perhaps property in one's person should be understood to mean simply that an individual has an entitlement to be a person or to be treated as a person. This would probably include the right to self-preservation on which Locke bases the right to appropriate.

Locke

If it makes sense to say that one owns one's body, then, on the embodiment theory of personhood, the body is quintessentially personal property because it is literally constitutive of one's personhood. If the body is property, then objectively it is property for personhood. This line of thinking leads to a property theory for the tort of assault and battery: Interference with my body is interference with my personal property. Certain external things, for example, the shirt off my back, may also be considered personal property if they are closely enough connected with the body.

The idea of property in one's body presents some interesting paradoxes. In some cases, bodily parts can become fungible commodities, just as other personal property can become fungible with a change in its relationship with the owner: Blood can be withdrawn and used in a transfusion; hair can be cut off and used by a wigmaker; organs can be transplanted. On the other hand, bodily parts may be too "personal" to be property at all. We have an intuition that property necessarily refers to something in the outside world, separate from oneself. Though the general idea of property for personhood means that the boundary between person and thing cannot be a bright line, still the idea of property seems to require some perceptible boundary, at least insofar as property requires the notion of thing, and the notion of thing requires separation from self. This intuition makes it seem appropriate to call parts of the body property only after they have been removed from the system. * * *

like the cell case

---

[28]   John Locke, *Second Treatise of Government* (New York 1952) (6th ed. London 1764), ch. V, § 27.

Finally, let us consider the view that what is important in personhood is a continuing character structure encompassing future projects or plans, as well as past events and feelings. The general idea of expressing one's character through property is quite familiar. It is frequently remarked that dogs resemble their masters; the attributes of many material goods, such as cars and clothes, can proclaim character traits of their owners. Of course, many would say that becoming too enthralled with property takes away time and energy needed to develop other faculties constitutive of personhood. But, for example, if you express your generosity by giving away fruits that grow in your orchard, then if the orchard ceases to be your property, you are no longer able to express your character. This at least suggests that property may have an important relationship to certain character traits that partly constitute a person.

This view of personhood also gives us insight into why protecting people's "expectations" of continuing control over objects seems so important. If an object you now control is bound up in your future plans or in your anticipation of your future self, and it is partly these plans for your own continuity that make you a person, then your personhood depends on the realization of these expectations. * * *

We must construct sufficiently objective criteria to identify close object relations that should be excluded from recognition as personal property because the particular nature of the relationship works to hinder rather than to support healthy self-constitution. A key to distinguishing these cases is "healthy." We can tell the difference between personal property and fetishism the same way we can tell the difference between a healthy person and a sick person, or between a sane person and an insane person. In fact, the concepts of sanity and personhood are intertwined: At some point we question whether the insane person is a person at all. Using the word "we" here, however, implies that a consensus exists and can be discerned. Because I seek a source of objective judgments about property for personhood, but do not wish to rely on natural law or simple moral realism, consensus must be a sufficient source of objective moral criteria—and I believe it can be, sometimes, without destroying the meaning of objectivity. In the context of property for personhood, then, a "thing" that someone claims to be bound up with nevertheless should not be treated as personal vis-à-vis other people's claimed rights and interests when there is an objective moral consensus that to be bound up with that category of "thing" is inconsistent with personhood or healthy self-constitution.

Judgments of insanity or fetishism are both made on the basis of the minimum indicia it takes to recognize an individual as one of us. There does not seem to be the same reason to restrain a private fetishist as there would be to restrain an insane person prone to violence against others. But the restraint of denying the fetishist's property special recognition as personal is less severe than that imposed on someone deemed violently insane. To refuse on moral grounds to call fetishist property personal is not to refuse to call it property at all. The immediate consequence of denying personal status to something is merely to treat that thing as fungible property, and hence to deny only those claims that might rely on a preferred status of personal property. * * *

The personhood dichotomy comes about in the following way: A general justification of property entitlements in terms of their relationship to personhood could hold that the rights that come within the general justification form a continuum from fungible to personal. It then might hold that those rights near one end of the continuum—fungible property rights—can be overridden in some cases in which those near the other—personal property rights—cannot be. This is to argue not that fungible property rights are unrelated to personhood, but simply that distinctions are sometimes warranted depending upon the character or strength of the connection. Thus, the personhood perspective generates a hierarchy of entitlements: The more closely connected with personhood, the stronger the entitlement.

Does it make sense to speak of two levels of property, personal and fungible? I think the answer is yes in many situations, no in many others. Since the personhood perspective depends partly on the subjective nature of the relationships between person and thing, it makes more sense to think of a continuum that ranges from a thing indispensable to someone's being to a thing wholly interchangeable with money. Many relationships between persons and things will fall somewhere in the middle of this continuum. Perhaps the entrepreneur factory owner has ownership of a particular factory and its machines bound up with her being to some degree. If a dichotomy telescoping this continuum to two end points is to be useful, it must be because within a given social context certain types of person-thing relationships are understood to fall close to one end or the other of the continuum, so that decisionmakers within that social context can use the dichotomy as a guide to determine which property is worthier of protection. For example, in our social context a house that is owned by someone who resides there is generally understood to be toward the personal end of the continuum. There is both a positive sense that people are bound up with their homes and a normative sense that this is not fetishistic. * * *

[handwritten margin note: property as a continuum of importance to person's being]

NOTES AND QUESTIONS

1.   Radin introduces the distinction between property for personhood and fungible property in order to distinguish between the degrees of protection property should receive in different contexts. For example, she argues that the government should have a higher burden of justification to take an occupied home by eminent domain (see Chapter X, Part C) than to take industrial, commercial, or agricultural property. But as she briefly suggests, the personhood perspective can also be used to argue that certain

kinds of objects that are intensely connected to personhood should not be considered property at all.

2.   Radin distinguishes good personhood relations from bad ones based on the idea of fetishism. Is this notion very clear? How much of a consensus on these matters is there? Is Radin right that denying strong property protection is not coercive to those whose property relations are deemed to be fetishistic? What would Radin make of the PBS program "Antiques Roadshow," in which people typically bring in various family heirlooms, patiently endure a longwinded mini-lecture on the object's origins and significance, and then rejoice if the expert gives a higher-than-expected price estimate? There is no suggestion that the participants intend to sell the heirlooms. But does their intense interest in the monetary valuation of the objects at least suggest that the interplay between "personhood" values and "fungible" values is more complex than Radin's account implies?

3.   Which of the various things at issue in the cases in Part A, supra, should be regarded as property for personhood as opposed to being either fungible or fetishistic property: cells taken from one's spleen; frozen sperm cells belonging to one's father; corneas taken from one's deceased children; the commercial value of a person's image? Even if all these things are plausibly regarded as closely linked to personhood, is it clear that personhood concerns are advanced by denying them some or all of the traditional attributes of ownership? Could one argue that the persons for whom these items are personally important are more likely to find their interests disregarded or abused if these things are *not* regarded as property?

4.   Radin has more recently disclaimed the use of the terms "objective consensus" and "health" as a basis for evaluating appropriate property relationships, and has written that "it will advance the argument much better to speak directly about human flourishing." Margaret Jane Radin, Reinterpreting Property 4–5 (1993).

Anti-Commodification and Inalienability Rules

One way to think about the restrictions on commercial sales of body parts, as reflected in statutes like the National Organ Transplant Act, is that they do not deny that body parts and organs have certain attributes of property, but rather they protect these things with what can be called an "inalienability rule." See Guido Calabresi & A. Douglas Melamed, Property Rules, Liability Rules, and Inalienability: One View of the Cathedral, 85 Harv. L. Rev. 1089, 1111–15, 1123–24 (1972). Calabresi and Melamed define inalienability rules as rules that prohibit the transfer of an entitlement. More precisely, the rules regarding body parts and fluids reflect a rule of market-inalienability, meaning that transfers between a willing buyer and willing seller are prohibited, in some or all circumstances.

Why might it make sense to recognize property in certain things but make them inalienable in this sense? Calabresi and Melamed suggest that such an approach might be justified by a variety of rationales. Such a rule might reduce externalities in some contexts, for example if the transferee would likely use the thing in such a way as to impose harms on third parties. They also suggest that inalienability might be justified by what they called "moralisms": "If Taney is allowed to sell himself into slavery, or to take undue risks of becoming penniless, or to sell a kidney, Marshall may be harmed, simply because Marshall is a sensitive man who is made unhappy by seeing slaves, paupers or persons die because they have sold a kidney." Id. at 1112. Finally, they suggest that inalienability rules may be justified by paternalism, if we conclude that "a person may be better off if he is prohibited from bargaining." Id. at 1113–14.

Subsequent commentators have offered other rationales for inalienability rules. Susan Rose-Ackerman argues that such rules may be justified by imperfect information. For example, a rule that blood may be donated but not sold may generate better information about the quality of the blood supply. "If it is difficult for hospitals to judge whether blood contains the dangerous hepatitis virus, while individuals know their own health history, then ideally one would design a collection system that gives contributors an incentive to reveal any past cases of hepatitis." Susan Rose-Ackerman, Inalienability and the Theory of Property Rights, 85 Colum. L. Rev. 931, 946 (1985); see also Richard Titmuss, The Gift Relationship: From Human Body to Social Policy (1971). Richard Epstein emphasizes that inalienability rules may be a response to common-pool problems—"those contexts in which one person is not the exclusive owner of a single resource, but shares it in indefinite proportions with other claimants." Richard A. Epstein. Why Restrain Alienation?, 85 Colum. L. Rev. 970, 978 (1985). These sorts of situations create a danger of overconsumption or excessive withdrawal of resources from the common pool—often termed the "Tragedy of the Commons" (see Chapter II). Restraints on alienation can be one tool for minimizing these dangers and can be used to influence decisions to acquire a resource in the first place. See Lee Anne Fennell, Adjusting Alienability, 122 Harv. L. Rev. 1403 (2009).

Margaret Jane Radin, whom you encountered immediately above in the excerpt on "Property and Personhood," has also turned her sights more specifically on the problem of inalienability rules.

Margaret Jane Radin, *Market-Inalienability*
100 HARV. L. REV. 1849, 1909–10, 1912, 1915–17 (1987).

* * * If some people wish to sell something that is identifiably personal, why not let them? In a market society, whatever some people wish to buy and others wish to sell is deemed alienable. Under these circumstances, we must formulate an affirmative case for market-inalienability, so that no one may choose to make fungible—commodify—a personal attribute, right, or thing. In this Section, I propose and evaluate three possible methods of justifying market-inalienability based

prerogative

on personhood: a prophylactic argument, assimilation to prohibition, and a domino theory.

The method of justification that correlates most readily with traditional liberal pluralism is a prophylactic argument. For the liberal it makes sense to countenance both selling and sharing of personal things as the holder freely chooses. If an item of property is personal, however, sometimes the circumstances under which the holder places it on the market might arouse suspicion that her act is coerced. Given that we cannot know whether anyone really intends to cut herself off from something personal by commodifying it, our suspicions might sometimes justify banning sales. The risk of harm to the seller's personhood in cases in which coerced transactions are permitted (especially if the thing sought to be commodified is normally very important to personhood), and the great difficulties involved in trying to scrutinize every transaction closely, may sometimes outweigh the harm that a ban would impose on would-be sellers who are in fact uncoerced. A prophylactic rule aims to ensure free choice—negative liberty—by the best possible coercion-avoidance mechanism under conditions of uncertainty. This prophylactic argument is one way for a liberal to justify, for example, the ban on selling oneself into slavery. We normally view such commodification as so destructive of personhood that we would readily presume all instances of it to be coerced. We would not wish, therefore, to have a rule creating a rebuttable presumption that such transactions are uncoerced (as with ordinary contracts), nor even a rule that would scrutinize such transactions case-by-case for voluntariness, because the risk of harm to personhood in the coerced transactions we might mistakenly see as voluntary is so great that we would rather risk constraining the exercise of choice by those (if any) who really wish to enslave themselves.

① prerogative

A liberal pluralist might use a prophylactic justification to prevent poor people from selling their children, sexual services, or body parts. The liberal would argue that an appropriate conception of coercion should, with respect to selling these things, include the desperation of poverty. Poor people should not be forced to give up personal things because the relinquishment diminishes them as persons, contrary to the liberal regime of respect for persons. We should presume that such transactions are not the result of free choice. * * *

② Prohibition

A second method of justifying market-inalienability assimilates it to prohibition. If we accept that the commodified object is different from the "same" thing noncommodified and embedded in personal relationships, then market-inalienability is a prohibition of the commodified version, resting on some moral requirement that it not exist. What might be the basis of such a moral requirement? Something might be prohibited in its market form because it both creates and exposes wealth-and class-based contingencies for obtaining things that are critical to life itself—for example, health care—and thus undermines a commitment to the sanctity of life. Another reason for prohibition might be that the use of market rhetoric, in conceiving of the "good" and understanding the interactions of people respecting it, creates and fosters an inferior conception of human flourishing. For example, we accept an inferior conception of personhood (one allied to the extreme view of negative freedom) if we suppose people may freely choose to commodify themselves. * * *

A third method of justifying market-inalienability, the domino theory, envisions a slippery slope leading to market domination. The domino theory assumes that for some things, the noncommodified version is morally preferable; it also assumes that the commodified and noncommodified versions of some interactions cannot coexist. To commodify some things is simply to preclude their noncommodified analogues from existing. Under this theory, the existence of some commodified sexual interactions will contaminate or infiltrate everyone's sexuality so that all sexual relationships will become commodified. If it is morally required that noncommodified sex be possible, market-inalienability of sexuality would be justified. This result can be conceived of as the opposite of a prohibition: there is assumed to exist some moral requirement that a certain "good" be socially available. The domino theory thus supplies an answer (as the prohibition theory does not) to the liberal question why people should not be permitted to choose both market and nonmarket interactions: the noncommodified version is morally preferable when we cannot have both.

We can now see how the prohibition and domino theories are connected. The prohibition theory focuses on the importance of excluding from social life commodified versions of certain "goods"—such as love, friendship, and sexuality—whereas the domino theory focuses on the importance for social life of maintaining the noncommodified versions. The prohibition theory stresses the wrongness of commodification—its alienation and degradation of the person—and the domino theory stresses the rightness of noncommodification in creating the social context for the proper expression and fostering of personhood. If one explicitly adopts both prongs of this commitment to personhood, the prohibition and domino theories merge. * * *

Often commodification is put forward as a solution to powerlessness or oppression, as in the suggestion that women be permitted to sell sexual and reproductive services. * * * The argument that commodification empowers women is that recognition of these alienable entitlements will enable a needy group—poor women—to improve their relatively powerless, oppressed condition, an improvement that would be beneficial to personhood. * * *

The rejoinder is that, on the contrary, commodification will harm personhood by powerfully symbolizing, legitimating, and enforcing class division and gender oppression. * * *

These conflicting arguments illuminate the problem with the prophylactic argument for market-inalienability. If we now permit

[margin handwriting: (3) moral preference for noncommodified version of some things]

commodification, we may exacerbate the oppression of women—the suppliers. If we now disallow commodification—without what I have called the welfare-rights corollary, or large-scale redistribution of social wealth and power—we force women to remain in circumstances that they themselves believe are worse than becoming sexual commodity-suppliers. Thus, the alternatives seem subsumed by a need for social progress, yet we must choose some regime now in order to make progress. This dilemma of transition is the double bind.

The double bind has two main consequences. First, if we cannot respect personhood either by permitting sales or by banning sales, justice requires that we consider changing the circumstances that create the dilemma. We must consider wealth and power redistribution. Second, we still must choose a regime for the meantime, the transition, in nonideal circumstances. To resolve the double bind, we have to investigate particular problems separately; decisions must be made (and remade) for each thing that some people desire to sell.

If we have reason to believe with respect to a particular thing that the domino theory might hold—commodification for some means commodification for all—we would have reason to choose market-inalienability. But the double bind means that if we choose market-inalienability, we might deprive a class of poor and oppressed people of the opportunity to have more money with which to buy adequate food, shelter, and health care in the market, and hence deprive them of a better chance to lead a humane life. Those who gain from the market-inalienability, on the other hand, might be primarily people whose wealth and power make them comfortable enough to be concerned about the inroads on the general quality of life that commodification would make. Yet, taking a slightly longer view, commodification threatens the personhood of everyone, not just those who can now afford to concern themselves about it. Whether this elitism in market-inalienability should make us risk the dangers of commodification will depend upon the dangers of each case.

NOTES AND QUESTIONS

1.   Consider again the various things at issue in the cases in Part A of this Chapter: cells taken from one's spleen; frozen sperm belonging to one's father; corneas taken from one's deceased children; the right of publicity. How would Radin, applying her personhood theory, resolve the questions about whether these items should be alienable? In which cases is the prophylactic theory most relevant? The prohibition theory? The domino theory? In the end, does the personhood perspective help decide whether to adopt an inalienability rule in each of the foregoing situations?

2.   The one clear conclusion that seems to follow from Radin's article on market-inalienability is that minimum welfare rights are necessary to prevent people from being treated like commodities. Do we need the personhood theory in order to reach this conclusion?

3.   To date, those concerned with freedom of contract and economic efficiency often tend to favor expanding the domain of property rights in contested areas ("commodification" if you will), whereas those who give priority to other values such as equality and community often oppose treating body parts, intimate relations, and personal identity like property ("anti-commodification"). More recently, however, some feminists have argued that anti-commodification sometimes promotes subordination, especially in the context of the division of marital property on divorce. See Chapter V. More generally, many have argued that the boundary between market and nonmarket spheres is not fixed or sharply demarcated: Nonmarket relations often have market aspects and vice versa. For discussion of these and related issues, see Rethinking Commodification: Cases and Readings in Law and Culture (Martha M. Ertman & Joan C. Williams eds., 2005).

C. COMMUNITY AND CUSTOM

Custom plays an important role within and outside the law, and nowhere more so than when it comes to property law and institutions. Some believe that property law grew out of earlier customs of mutual forbearance, use rights, and the like. Custom often grows out of a community in order to solve a problem facing that community. If so, what stance should the law take?

1.   CUSTOM AS COMMON LAW

Ghen v. Rich

United States District Court, District of Massachusetts, 1881.
8 F. 159.

■ NELSON, D.J. This is a libel to recover the value of a fin-back whale. The libellant lives in Provincetown and the respondent in Wellfleet. The facts, as they appeared at the hearing, are as follows:

> In the early spring months the easterly part of Massachusetts bay is frequented by the species of whale known as the fin-back whale. Fishermen from Provincetown pursue them in open boats from the shore, and shoot them with bomb-lances fired from guns made expressly for the purpose. When killed they sink at once to the bottom, but in the course of from one to three days they rise and float on the surface. Some of them are picked up by vessels and towed into Provincetown. Some float ashore at high water and are left stranded on the beach as the tide recedes. Others float out to sea and are never recovered. The person who happens to find them on the beach usually sends word to Provincetown, and the owner comes to the spot and removes the blubber. The finder usually receives a small salvage for his services. Try-works are established in Provincetown for trying out the oil. The business is of

considerable extent, but, since it requires skill and experience, as well as some outlay of capital, and is attended with great exposure and hardship, few persons engage in it. The average yield of oil is about 20 barrels to a whale. It swims with great swiftness, and for that reason cannot be taken by the harpoon and line. Each boat's crew engaged in the business has its peculiar mark or device on its lances, and in this way it is known by whom a whale is killed.

killer owns the whale

The usage on Cape Cod, for many years, has been that the person who kills a whale in the manner and under the circumstances described, owns it, and this right has never been disputed until this case. The libellant has been engaged in this business for ten years past. On the morning of April 9, 1880, in Massachusetts bay, near the end of Cape Cod, he shot and instantly killed with a bomb-lance the whale in question. It sunk immediately, and on the morning of the 12th was found stranded on the beach in Brewster, within the ebb and flow of the tide, by one Ellis, 17 Miles from the spot where it was killed. Instead of sending word to Provincetown, as is customary, Ellis advertised the whale for sale at auction, and sold it to the respondent, who shipped off the blubber and tried out the oil. The libellant heard of the finding of the whale on the morning of the 15th, and immediately sent one of his boat's crew to the place and claimed it. Neither the respondent nor Ellis knew the whale had been killed by the libellant, but they knew or might have known, if they had wished, that it had been shot and killed with a bomb-lance, by some person engaged in this species of business.

breach of custom

The libellant claims title to the whale under this usage. The respondent insists that this usage is invalid. It was decided by Judge Sprague, in Taber v. Jenny, 1 Sprague, 315, 23 F. Cas. 605 (D. Mass. 1856), that when a whale has been killed, and is anchored and left with marks of appropriation, it is the property of the captors; and if it is afterwards found, still anchored, by another ship, there is no usage or principle of law by which the property of the original captors is diverted, even though the whale may have dragged from its anchorage. The learned judge says:

> When the whale had been killed and taken possession of by the boat of the Hillman, (the first taker,) it became the property of the owners of that ship, and all was done which was then practicable in order to secure it. They left it anchored, with unequivocal marks of appropriation.

In Bartlett v. Budd, 1 Low. 223, 2 F. Cas. 966 (D. Mass. 1868), the facts were these: The first officer of the libellant's ship killed a whale in the Okhotsk sea, anchored it, attached a waif to the body, and then left it and went ashore at some distance for the night. The next morning the boats of the respondent's ship found the whale adrift, the anchor not holding, the cable coiled round the body, and no waif or irons attached to it. Judge Lowell held that, as the libellants had killed and taken actual possession of the whale, the ownership vested in them. In his opinion the learned judge says:

> A whale, being ferae naturae, does not become property until a firm possession has been established by the taker. But when such possession has become firm and complete, the right of property is clear, and has all the characteristics of property.

He doubted whether a usage set up but not proved by the respondents, that a whale found adrift in the ocean is the property of the finder, unless the first taker should appear and claim it before it is cut in, would be valid, and remarked that "there would be great difficulty in upholding a custom that should take the property of A. and give it to B., under so very short and uncertain a substitute for the statute of limitations, and one so open to fraud and deceit." Both the cases cited were decided without reference to usage, upon the ground that the property had been acquired by the first taker by actual possession and appropriation.

In Swift v. Gifford, 2 Low. 110, 23 F. Cas. 558 (D. Mass. 1872), Judge Lowell decided that a custom among whalemen in the Arctic seas, that the iron holds the whale was reasonable and valid. In that case a boat's crew from the respondent's ship pursued and struck a whale in the Arctic ocean, and the harpoon and the line attached to it remained in the whale, but did not remain fast to the boat. A boat's crew from the libellant's ship continued the pursuit and captured the whale, and the master of the respondent's ship claimed it on the spot. It was held by the learned judge that the whale belonged to the respondents. It was said by Judge Sprague, in Bourne v. Ashley, an unprinted case referred to by Judge Lowell in Swift v. Gifford, that the usage for the first iron, whether attached to the boat or not, to hold the whale was fully established; and he added that, although local usages of a particular port ought not to be allowed to set aside the general maritime law, this objection did not apply to a custom which embraced an entire business, and had been concurred in for a long time by every one engaged in the trade.

In Swift v. Gifford, Judge Lowell also said:

> The rule of law invoked in this case is one of very limited application. The whale fishery is the only branch of industry of any importance in which it is likely to be much used, and if a usage is found to prevail generally in that business, it will not be open to the objection that it is likely to disturb the general understanding of mankind by the interposition of an arbitrary exception.

I see no reason why the usage proved in this case is not as reasonable as that sustained in the cases cited. Its application must necessarily be extremely limited, and can affect but a few persons. It has been recognized and acquiesced in for many years. It requires in the first taker the only act of appropriation that is possible in the nature of the case. Unless it is sustained, this branch of industry must necessarily cease, for no person would engage in it if the fruits of his labor could be appropriated by any chance finder. It gives reasonable salvage for securing or reporting the property. That the rule works well in practice is shown by the extent of the industry which has grown up under it, and the general acquiescence of a whole community interested to dispute it. It is by no means clear that without regard to usage the common law would not reach the same result. That seems to be the effect of the decisions in Taber v. Jenny and Bartlett v. Budd. If the fisherman does all that is possible to do to make the animal his own, that would seem to be sufficient. Such a rule might well be applied in the interest of trade, there being no usage or custom to the contrary. Holmes, Com. Law, 217. But be that as it may, I hold the usage to be valid, and that the property in the whale was in the libellant.

The rule of damages is the market value of the oil obtained from the whale, less the cost of trying it out and preparing it for the market, with interest on the amount so ascertained from the date of conversion. As the question is new and important, and the suit is contested on both sides, more for the purpose of having it settled than for the amount involved, I shall give no costs.

Decree for libellant for $71.05, without costs.

NOTES AND QUESTIONS

1. Most customary whaling rules are variants on first-in-time. As described by Robert Ellickson, the two major rules were the "fast-fish-loose-fish" rule and the "iron-holds-the-whale" rule. Under the fast-fish-loose-fish rule, a whale belonged to the first harpooner as long as it was attached to his boat, in which case he got to keep the whole whale. This rule applied in particular to right whales, which are relatively slow-moving. Under the iron-holds-the-whale rule, the first harpooner would get exclusive rights to the whale as long as he was in fresh pursuit. The iron-holds-the-whale rule tended to be adopted where sperm whales were predominant. Sperm whales were the most valuable and the most dangerous. Ellickson argues that these customs and the custom for finback whales in the *Ghen* case make sense in light of the different resources—types of whales—to which they applied. He also argues that their efficiency (from the point of view of whalers) confirms the hypothesis that close-knit groups will devise and enforce norms among themselves that maximize their wealth (but may cause uncompensated harm to those outside the group—or outgroup externalities). See Robert C. Ellickson, A Hypothesis of Wealth-Maximizing Norms: Evidence from the Whaling Industry, 5 J.L. Econ. & Org. 83 (1989). For a famous discussion of the concept of fast fish versus loose fish, see Herman Melville, Moby Dick, Chapter 89 (1851).

2.   The finder in *Ghen* was not a whaler. But was he part of a close-knit whaling community? Was he likely to have known of the custom of notifying the owner? If not, should he have known that someone was making a claim to the whale? Does that matter? Norms and customs are more easily known within a community than to outsiders, and enforcing a custom against outsiders may cause unfair surprise and wasteful efforts at avoiding such surprises. See Henry E. Smith, Community and Custom in Property, 10 Theoretical Inquiries L. 5 (2009). Moreover, a custom can be good for insiders but bad for society. Where did the customs of whalers leave conservation values?

3.   Interestingly, the fast-fish-loose-fish rule seems to have been the "default" custom and the iron-holds-the-whale rule a departure from it only in those areas where sperm whales predominated. The fast-fish-loose-fish rule accords with the general norms of possession. Might this have made it easier to communicate to others?

4.   What is the difference between a social norm and a custom? Although there is overlap, the idea of a social norm includes informality and being "beyond the law" (even sometimes against the law). Robert C. Ellickson, Order without Law: How Neighbors Settle Disputes (1991). Custom is closer to the law in that it is usually more articulated, and its normative force is close to being "legal" and sometimes winds up actually becoming part of the law. Eugen Ehrlich, Fundamental Principles of the Sociology of Law (Walter L. Moll trans., 1936). Indeed, there was a time when the common law was regarded as the general custom, distinct from the customs pertaining to localities. See David Callies, How Custom Becomes Law in England, in Peter Ørebech et al., The Role of Customary Law in Sustainable Development 158 (2005). In many countries the extent of official recognition of customary rights is an important political issue. For example, in sub-Saharan Africa there has even a movement to register "customary land rights." This has, however, proven difficult, and where it has been implemented, it has shifted decision-making authority away from families and communities to the state and its officials. See Mekonnen Firew Ayano, Rural Land Registration in Ethiopia: Myths and Realities, 52 Law & Soc'y Rev. 1060 (2018).

5.   As we will see in Chapter V, property law is more standardized in many respects than contract law: one can tailor one's contract, but the basic forms of ownership come in a small and closed menu. One effect is that people who have to deal with this or similar property—third parties—need not understand much idiosyncratic detail about property arrangements. Does the recognition of custom as law threaten to upend this balance? Community members may be well informed, but what about binding third parties? Is that coercive? When is community itself a coercive institution? The mining camps from which customs arose that were later adapted into federal law? The "lobster gangs" of Maine, and some (but not all) of the communities discussed by Ostrom in her book (excerpted in Chapter II) employed coercion, sometimes violent, and their exclusion of outsiders could be highly discriminatory. See Carol M. Rose, Left Brain, Right Brain and History in the New Law and Economics of Property, 79 Or. L. Rev. 479, 487–88 (2000).

For an exploration of the tension between personal autonomy and community norms through a textured account of 1950s Chicago, see Alan Ehrenhalt, The Lost City: The Forgotten Virtues of Community in America (1995); see also Robert D. Putnam, Bowling Alone: The Collapse and Revival of American Community (2001).

2. CULTURAL PATRIMONY

Personhood and community interests are also implicated when cultural artifacts are taken from the communities in which they have particular significance. One notable effort to address this problem is reflected in the Native American Graves Protection and Repatriation Act, considered in the following case.

United States v. Corrow

United States Court of Appeals, Tenth Circuit, 1997.
119 F.3d 796.

■ JOHN C. PORFILIO, CIRCUIT JUDGE. This appeal raises issues of first impression in this Circuit under the Native American Graves Protection and Repatriation Act, 25 U.S.C. §§ 3001–3013 (NAGPRA) * * *. Richard Nelson Corrow challenges the constitutionality of 25 U.S.C. § 3001(3)(D) of NAGPRA which defines "cultural patrimony," the basis for his conviction of trafficking in protected Native American cultural items in violation of 18 U.S.C. § 1170(b). [He] contends the definition is unconstitutionally vague, an argument the district court rejected in denying his motion to dismiss that count of the indictment and to reverse his conviction. * * * We affirm.

I. Background

Until his death in 1991, Ray Winnie was a *hataali,* a Navajo religious singer. For more than twenty-five years Mr. Winnie chanted the Nightway and other Navajo ceremonies wearing Yei B'Chei originally owned by Hosteen Hataali Walker. Yei B'Chei or Yei B'Chei *jish* are ceremonial adornments, Native American artifacts whose English label, "masks," fails to connote the Navajo perception these cultural items embody living gods. Traditionally, a *hataali* passes the Yei B'Chei to a family or clan member who has studied the ceremonies or loans the Yei B'Chei to another Navajo clan, Mr. Winnie having acquired his Yei B'Chei from a different clan during his *hataali* apprenticeship. When Mr. Winnie died, he left no provision for the disposition of his Yei B'Chei, and no family or clan member requested them.

Richard Corrow, the owner of Artifacts Display Stands in Scottsdale, Arizona, is an afficionado of Navajo culture and religion, having, on occasion, participated in Navajo religious ceremonies. Some time after Mr. Winnie's death, Mr. Corrow traveled to Lukachukai, Arizona, to visit Mrs. Fannie Winnie, Mr. Winnie's 81–year–old widow, chatting with her; her granddaughter, Rose Bia; and other family members: a great granddaughter, Harriette Keyonnie; and a son-in-law. During one visit, Mrs. Winnie displayed some Navajo screens and robes, and Mr. Corrow inquired about the Yei B'Chei. By his third visit in August 1993, the Winnie family revealed the Yei B'Chei, twenty-two ceremonial masks, and permitted Mr. Corrow to photograph them. Mr. Corrow told Mrs. Winnie he wanted to buy them, suggesting he planned to deliver the Yei B'Chei to a young Navajo chanter in Utah to keep them sacred. Although Mr. Corrow initially offered $5,000, he readily agreed to the family's price of $10,000 for the Yei B'Chei, five headdresses, and other artifacts. Mr. Corrow drafted a receipt,[1] and Mrs. Winnie, who spoke no English, placed her thumbprint on the document after Ms. Bia read it to her in Navajo.

In November 1994, the owners of the East–West Trading Company in Santa Fe, New Mexico, contacted Mr. Corrow telling him that a wealthy Chicago surgeon was interested in purchasing a set of Yei B'Chei. In fact, the purported buyer was James Tanner, a National Park Service ranger operating undercover on information he had received about questionable trade at East–West. When Agent Tanner visited the business, its owners showed him photographs of seventeen of the twenty-two Yei B'Chei that Mr. Corrow purchased from Mrs. Winnie. In the photos, he noticed eagle and owl feathers in several of the large headdresses and ceremonial sticks bundled with small eagle feathers. After negotiations, Agent Tanner agreed to a purchase price of $70,000 for the Yei B'Chei, $50,000 for Mr. Corrow and a $20,000 commission to East–West's co-owners.

"sells" the YBC to undercover NPS agent

On December 9, 1994, Mr. Corrow arrived at the Albuquerque airport en route to Santa Fe carrying one large suitcase, one small suitcase, and a cardboard box. Yet once he was in Santa Fe, F.B.I. agents became worried East–West's owners had been alerted and abandoned their script for the planned buy, instead directly executing the search warrant. Agents found the two suitcases Mr. Corrow had carried to East–West, one holding Navajo religious objects, small bundles, herbs, mini prayer sticks, and other artifacts adorned with eagle feathers. Another suitcase contained eagle feathers rolled inside several cloth bundles, Yei B'Chei dance aprons, and five headdress pieces made of eagle and owl feathers. In the cardboard box was the set of twenty-two Yei B'Chei.

The government subsequently charged Mr. Corrow in a two-count indictment, Count one for trafficking in Native American cultural items in violation of 18 U.S.C. § 1170, 25 U.S.C. §§ 3001(3)(D), 3002(c), and 18 U.S.C. § 2; and Count two for selling Golden Eagle, Great Horned Owl,

---

[1] The receipt stated:

Sold to Richard N. Corrow on this date for cash paid in full, all of the medicine bundles for yei be chai [sic] and fire dance including masks owned by Hosteen Ray Winnie of Lukachucki [sic], AZ.

Selling these medicine bundles or jish is the wife of the late Mr. Winnie, Fanny [sic], and his granddaughter Rose, and his great granddaughter, Harriet, whose signatures are below.

The selling price is in cash of $10,000. Received by below this date.

and Buteoine Hawk feathers protected by the [Migratory Bird Treaty Act, 16 U.S.C. §§ 701–712,] in violation of 16 U.S.C. § 703, 16 U.S.C. § 707(b)(2), and 18 U.S.C. § 2. The court rejected Mr. Corrow's pretrial motion to dismiss Count one based on its purported unconstitutional vagueness, and the trial proceeded comprised predominantly of the testimony of expert witnesses clashing over whether the Yei B'Chei constitute "cultural patrimony" protected by NAGPRA. Having concluded they do, the jury convicted Mr. Corrow of illegal trafficking in cultural items, Count one, but acquitted him of Count two, selling protected feathers, instead finding him guilty of committing the lesser included offense, possession of protected feathers. * * * The district court * * * sentenced him to two concurrent five-year probationary terms and one hundred hours of community service.

II.   NAGPRA

Congress enacted NAGPRA in 1990 to achieve two [principal] objectives: to protect Native American human remains, funerary objects, sacred objects and objects of cultural patrimony presently on Federal or tribal lands; and to repatriate Native American human remains, associated funerary objects, sacred objects, and objects of cultural patrimony currently held or controlled by Federal agencies and museums. H.R.Rep. No. 101–877, 101st Cong., 2d Sess.1990, reprinted in 1990 U.S.C.C.A.N. 4367, 4368. The legislation and subsequent regulations, 43 C.F.R. §§ 10.1–10.17, provide a methodology for identifying objects; determining the rights of lineal descendants, Indian tribes and Native Hawaiian organizations; and retrieving and repatriating that property to Native American owners. NAGPRA's reach in protecting against further desecration of burial sites and restoring countless ancestral remains and cultural and sacred items to their tribal homes warrants its aspirational characterization as "human rights legislation." Jack F. Trope & Walter R. Echo–Hawk, The Native American Graves Protection and Repatriation Act: Background and Legislative History, 24 Ariz. St. L.J. 35, 37 (1992). Indeed, a Panel of National Dialogue on Museum–Native American Relations, which was convened to address the divergent interests of the museum and Native American communities, reported to Congress that "[r]espect for Native human rights is the paramount principle that should govern resolution of the issue when a claim is made." 1990 U.S.C.C.A.N. 4369–70.

Nonetheless to give teeth to this statutory mission, 18 U.S.C. § 1170 penalizes trafficking in Native American human remains and cultural items and creates a felony offense for a second or subsequent violation. Subsection 1170(b), the basis for prosecution here, states:

> Whoever knowingly sells, purchases, uses for profit, or transports for sale or profit any Native American cultural items obtained in violation of the Native American Grave Protection and Repatriation Act shall be fined in accordance with this title, imprisoned not more than one year, or both, and in the case of a

second or subsequent violation, be fined in accordance with this title, imprisoned not more than 5 years, or both.

One must look to NAGPRA, 25 U.S.C. § 3001, for the definition of "cultural item." Section 3001(3) states:

"cultural items" means human remains and—

(D) "cultural patrimony" which shall mean an object having ongoing historical, traditional, or cultural importance central to the Native American group or culture itself, rather than property owned by an individual Native American, and which, therefore, cannot be alienated, appropriated, or conveyed by any individual regardless of whether or not the individual is a member of the Indian tribe or Native Hawaiian organization and such object shall have been considered inalienable by such Native American group at the time the object was separated from such group.

Thus, to be judged "cultural patrimony"[4] the object must have (1) ongoing historical, cultural or traditional importance; and (2) be considered inalienable by the tribe by virtue of the object's centrality in tribal culture. That is, the cultural item's essential function within the life and history of the tribe engenders its inalienability such that the property cannot constitute the personal property of an individual tribal member. "The key aspect of this definition is whether the property was of such central importance to the tribe or group that it was owned communally." Francis P. McManamon & Larry V. Nordby, Implementing the Native American Graves Protection and Repatriation Act, 24 Ariz. St. L.J. 217, 233–34 (1992). The regulations mirror this definition * * *

In this prosecution, then, the definition of cultural patrimony divided into its three component parts required the government prove Mr. Corrow trafficked in an object that (1) was not owned by an individual Native American; (2) that could not be alienated, appropriated, or conveyed by an individual; and (3) had an ongoing historical, traditional, or cultural importance central to the Native American group. Mr. Corrow contends the first and second elements are unintelligible. Thus, he argues, relying upon *United States v. Agnew,* 931 F.2d 1397, 1403 (10th Cir. 1991), the definition does not comport with the due process clause of the Fourteenth Amendment because it fails to give ordinary people fair notice about what conduct is prohibited in such a manner that discourages arbitrary and discriminatory law enforcement.

In support, Mr. Corrow arrays the conflicting expert testimony, characterized by the *amicus curiae*[7] as a conflict between orthodox and

---

[4]   Webster's Third New International Dictionary defines "patrimony" as "anything derived from one's father or ancestors: HERITAGE; an inheritance from the past; an estate or property held by ancient right."

[7]   The Antique Tribal Art Dealers Association, a trade organization promoting authenticity and ethical dealing in the sale of Native American artifacts, filed an amicus brief

moderate Navajo religious views. For the government, Alfred Yazzie, an ordained *hataali* and Navajo Nation Historic Preservation representative, testified the Yei B'Chei must remain within the four sacred mountains of the Navajo for they represented the "heartbeat" of the Navajo people. Also for the government, Harry Walters, a Navajo anthropologist, stated there is "no such thing as ownership of medicine bundles and that these are viewed as living entities." He equated ownership with use, knowing the rituals, but acknowledged often cultural items are sold because of economic pressures. For Mr. Corrow, Jackson Gillis, a medicine man from Monument Valley, testified that if no claim is made by a clan relative or other singer, the *jish* pass to the widow who must care for them. If the widow feels uncomfortable keeping the *jish,* Mr. Gillis stated she has the right to sell them. Harrison Begay, another of Mr. Corrow's expert witnesses, agreed, explaining that because the masks themselves are "alive," a widow, uneasy about their remaining unused, may sell them. Billy Yellow, another *hataali* testifying for Mr. Corrow, reiterated the traditional disposition of a *hataali*'s Yei B'Chei to a spouse, the children, and grandchildren, although he stated nobody really owns the *jish* because they are living gods.

Given these conflicting views on the alienability of the Yei B'Chei, Mr. Corrow asks how an individual, even one educated in Navajo culture, indeed, one accepting the responsibility of inquiring further about the status of the item as the district court deduced from its reading of NAGPRA, can "ascertain ownership when the group itself cannot agree on that point?" The shadow cast by this question, he insists, sufficiently clouds the meaning of "cultural patrimony" to render it unconstitutional. Mr. Corrow's invocation of void-for-vagueness review, however, obfuscates both its doctrinal reach and its application to the facts of this case.

"[T]he void-for-vagueness doctrine requires that a penal statute define the criminal offense with sufficient definiteness that ordinary people can understand what conduct is prohibited and in a manner that does not encourage arbitrary and discriminatory enforcement." Kolender v. Lawson, 461 U.S. 352, 357 (1983). Although *Kolender* acknowledged a judicial shift from concern over deciding whether the statute provides actual notice to "the more important aspect of the vagueness doctrine . . . the requirement that a legislature establish minimal guidelines to govern law enforcement," id. at 358, the legality principle, no crime or punishment without law, is the essence of a Fifth Amendment due process challenge. See 1 W. LaFave & A. Scott, Substantive Criminal Law § 3.1, at 271 (1986). That is, given the limitations of language and syntax, a statute must convey to those individuals within its purview what it purports to prohibit and how it will punish an infraction. * * *

---

contending the government in this case "exploited a controversy between orthodox and moderate Navajo religious perspectives."

Mr. Corrow cannot meet that burden. First, deciding whether the statute gave him fair notice, the district court found, after reviewing all of the expert testimony, Mr. Corrow is knowledgeable about Navajo traditions and culture and "would have been aware that various tribal members viewed ownership of property differently." The court cited the testimony of Ms. Charlotte Frisbie, author of *Navajo Medicine Bundles or Jish: Acquisition, Transmission and Disposition in the Past and Present* (1987). Ms. Frisbie related several calls from Mr. Corrow inquiring about the prices of certain Navajo artifacts. Although she stated he did not specifically ask her about these Yei B'Chei, she expressed her objection to dealers and commercial handlers selling Native American cultural objects in the open market. Ms. Frisbie also reminded him both of the Navajo Nation's implementing procedures to return cultural items and of the enactment of NAGPRA. Most damning, Ms. Bia, Mrs. Winnie's granddaughter, recounted Mr. Corrow's representation that he wanted to buy the Yei B'Chei to pass on to another young chanter in Utah. Reasonably, a jury could infer from that representation that Mr. Corrow appreciated some dimension of the Yei B'Chei's inherent inalienability in Navajo culture. Although Mrs. Winnie stated she believed the Yei B'Chei belonged to her, she testified, "[t]here was another man that knew the ways and he had asked of [the Yei B'Chei] but I was the one that was stalling and ended up selling it." Although this man trained with her husband, he had not offered her any money. This is not a case of an unsuspecting tourist happening upon Mrs. Winnie's hogan and innocently purchasing the set of Yei B'Chei. * * *

Surely, this evidence establishes Mr. Corrow had some notice the Yei B'Chei he purchased were powerfully connected to Navajo religion and culture. While it may be true that even the experts in that culture differed in their views on alienability, *no* expert testified it was acceptable to sell Yei B'Chei to non-Navajos who planned to resell them for a profit, the very conduct § 1170(b) penalizes. All experts testified the Yei B'Chei resided within the Four Corners of the Navajo people and acknowledged the ritual cleansing and restoration required were the Yei B'Chei to be defiled in any way. Thus, while the parameters of the designation "cultural patrimony" might be unclear in some of its applications and at its edges, there is no doubt, in this case as applied to Mr. Corrow, the Yei B'Chei were cultural items which could not be purchased for a quick $40,000 turn of profit. * * * Consequently, even if the term cultural patrimony "might reflect some uncertainty as applied to extreme situations, the conduct for which [defendant] was prosecuted and convicted falls squarely within the core of the [Act]." United States v. Amer, 110 F.3d 873, 878 (2d Cir. 1997). * * *

Consequently, we believe Mr. Corrow had fair notice—if not of the precise words of NAGPRA—of their meaning that Native American objects "having ongoing historical, traditional, or cultural importance central to the Native American group . . . rather than property owned by an individual Native American" could not be bought and sold absent criminal consequences. Moreover, contrary to Mr. Corrow's assertion, § 3001(3)(D) is not infirm because it fails to list examples of cultural items. "In short, due process does not require that citizens be provided actual notice of all criminal rules and their meanings. The Constitution is satisfied if the necessary information is reasonably obtainable by the public." United States v. Vasarajs, 908 F.2d 443, 449 (9th Cir. 1990). * * *

While not dispositive, we would add § 1170(b) includes scienter as an element of the offense ("Whoever knowingly sells, purchases, uses for profit. . . ."). "A statutory requirement that an act must be willful or purposeful may not render certain, for all purposes, a statutory definition of the crime which is in some respects uncertain. But it does relieve the statute of the objection that it punishes without warning an offense of which the accused was unaware." Screws v. United States, 325 U.S. 91, 101–02 (1945) (Douglas, J., concurring). Here, the government was required to prove Mr. Corrow knowingly used the Yei B'Chei for profit assuring his understanding of the prohibited zone of conduct. "[A] scienter requirement may mitigate a criminal law's vagueness by ensuring that it punishes only those who are aware their conduct is unlawful." Gaudreau, 860 F.2d at 360. * * *

We therefore AFFIRM the judgment of the district court.

NOTES AND QUESTIONS

1. The prohibition on individual ownership or sale of "cultural patrimony" in the Native American Graves Protection and Repatriation Act (NAGPRA) appears only in the definitional section of the Act, under the definition of "cultural patrimony" (quoted in the court's opinion). There is no separate prohibition, in the operative sections of the Act, of alienation, appropriation, or conveyance of cultural patrimony. Corrow was prosecuted under a separate provision of the federal criminal code making it a criminal offense to obtain any "cultural items" "in violation of the Native American Grave Protection and Repatriation Act." 18 U.S.C. § 1170. Putting the two provisions together, federal law appears to require, first, a determination that items cannot be subject to private ownership or sale *as a matter of tribal law or tradition*, and then, second, a determination that someone has attempted to acquire such an item in a manner prohibited by tribal law or tradition. Does this strike you as an overly cryptic way to establish, as a matter of federal law, that cultural patrimony cannot be bought and sold? For more on the Navajo Yébîchai healing ceremony, see Harold Carey Jr, Yei Bi Chei (Yebichai) Night Chant-First Day, Navajo People (Sept. 28, 2012), https://navajopeople.org/blog/yei-bi-chei-night-chant-first-day/.

2. Under the interpretation of NAGPRA approved in the principal case, could Mrs. Fannie Winnie also be prosecuted for violating the Act? If one of the purposes of the Act is to prevent commodification of culturally significant objects, should federal prosecutors concentrate only on the demand for such objects from dealers and collectors, or should they also try to suppress the supply?

3. One purpose of NAGPRA was to rectify the historic disrespect shown to the graves and remains of Native Americans. Perhaps the most high-profile dispute under NAGPRA concerned the status of the skeletal remains known as "Kennewick Man" and "The Ancient One," discovered by some students on the banks of the Columbia River in Washington. Preliminary carbon dating indicated that the remains were 8,340 to 9,200 years old, predating the time when it is believed the ancestors of most of today's Native Americans migrated to the Americas. Some of the features of the skeleton were also thought by some researchers to be inconsistent with most Native American skeletal remains. The Interior Department ordered that the skeletal remains be repatriated to area tribes under NAGPRA. When this decision was challenged by a group of scientists anxious to study the remains, the District Court for the District of Oregon held for the scientists and the Ninth Circuit affirmed. Bonnichsen v. United States, 969 F. Supp. 628 (D. Or. 1997), aff'd, 367 F.3d 864 (9th Cir. 2004). The court held that the Act applies only to remains affiliated with presently existing tribes, peoples, or cultures, and held that there was no evidence that any presently existing tribe could trace its ancestry back 9,000 years. Controversies continued to swirl around the remains, which were housed for many years at the University of Washington under an agreement with the U.S. Army Corps of Engineers. After DNA testing in 2014 showed that the man was more related to current Native-Americans than any other current population group, Congress passed legislation to turn over the remains to a coalition of tribes, who buried them in 2017. Tribes Lay Remains of Kennewick Man to Rest, The Spokesman-Review (Feb. 20, 2017), https://www.spokesman. com/stories/2017/feb/20/tribes-lay-remains-of-kennewick-man-to-rest/. See generally David Hurst Thomas, Skull Wars: Kennewick Man, Archaeology, and the Battle for Native American Identity (2000); see generally Alix Rogers, Owning Geronimo But Not Elmer McCurdy: The Unique Property Status of Native American Remains, 60 B.C. L. Rev. 2447 (2019).

4. The Supreme Court has been unsympathetic to claims seeking protection for culturally significant property as a matter of constitutional law. For example, in *Lyng v. Northwest Indian Cemetery Protective Ass'n*, 485 U.S. 439 (1988), the Court rejected the claim that building a road through an Indian burial ground would violate the Free Exercise rights of Native Americans. Can you explain why a majoritarian institution like Congress would be more solicitous of the rights of cultural minorities than a court, which is supposed to be more sensitive to minority rights? Consider in this regard *Navajo Nation v. U.S. Forest Serv.*, 535 F.3d 1058 (9th Cir. 2008), rejecting a challenge under NAGPRA to the practice of using recycled water containing minute quantities of human remains for snowmaking in ski areas. Relying on *Lyng*, the court observed that expansive interpretations of tribal religious claims could result in " '*de facto* beneficial ownership of some rather spacious tracts of public property.' " Id. at 1072 (quoting *Lyng*, 485 U.S. at 453). For a variety of views, see, e.g., Ellen Adair Page, The Scope of the Free Exercise Clause: *Lyng v. Northwest Indian Cemetery Protective Association*, 68 N.C. L. Rev. 410, 421 (1990) (arguing for a stricter judicial test); Joseph William Singer, Property and Coercion in Federal Indian Law: The Conflict between Critical and Complacent Pragmatism, 63 S. Cal. L.

Rev. 1821 (1990) (criticizing the version of pragmatism in *Lyng* for being too complacent and majority-oriented); Marcia Yablon, Property Rights and Sacred Sites: Federal Regulatory Responses to American Indian Religious Claims on Public Land, 113 Yale L.J. 1623 (2004) (arguing for administrative rather than judicial protection).

5.   Similar issues of protection of indigenous communities and their cultures arise in the intangible realm. Groups across the world have sought protection for traditional knowledge, which can range from cultural practices and art to knowledge of the medicinal properties of plants. Quite often traditional knowledge does not fit into the categories of intellectual property, and such rights and concerns about cultural appropriations in general stand in some tension with policies (sometimes reflected in the law and sometimes not) favoring free use of information not covered by property rights. See, e.g., Trevor G. Reed, Fair Use as Cultural Appropriation, 109 Cal. L. Rev. 1373 (2021). Do museums have a duty not to digitize indigenous cultural materials before returning them to their home communities? See Chad Westmoreland, An Analysis of the Lack of Protection for Intangible Tribal Cultural Property in the Digital Age, 106 Cal. L. Rev. 959 (2018). Might not-quite-property regimes like equity and misappropriation (International News v. Associated Press, Chapter II) or restitution for unjust enrichment (Chapter IV) do a better job of reconciling these perspectives and preventing injustice? See Ruth L. Okediji, Traditional Knowledge and Private Law, in The Oxford Handbook of the New Private Law 427 (Andrew S. Gold et al. eds., 2021). Does the filtering of indigenous people's claims through another legal system disrespect that system? Could law defer to some indigenous custom in a fashion that federal law does with respect to laws protecting cultural patrimony in other countries? See Matthew H. Birkhold, The Indigenous McClain Doctrine: A New Tool to Protect Cultural Patrimony and the Right to Self-Determination, 97 Wash. U. L. Rev. 113 (2019).

6.   Is it inherently paradoxical to deploy property law as a means of protecting indigenous cultural heritage which is often regarded (whether accurately or not) as rejecting Western concepts of property? Compare Naomi Mezey, The Paradoxes of Cultural Property, 107 Colum. L. Rev. 2004 (2007) (arguing that "the idea of property has so colonized the idea of culture that there is not much culture left in cultural property") with Kristen A. Carpenter, Sonia K. Katyal & Angela R. Riley, In Defense of Property, 118 Yale L.J. 1022 (2009) (contending that this critique ignores "major theoretical developments in the broader field of property law" that suggest a "stewardship model" of property as opposed to property as an individual entitlement).

7.   Although NAGPRA is unusual in prohibiting any attempt to treat cultural patrimony as private property, restrictions on the use and development of culturally significant properties are more common. Many cities, for example, have enacted historic preservation laws that limit the ability of owners of properties of cultural or historical significance to make modifications to these properties. We will encounter a famous constitutional challenge to the New York City preservation ordinance in Chapter X.

3. CUSTOM BEYOND THE COMMON LAW

Customary law can constitute a system of law. Consider the following case, in which the court seeks to breathe new life into an indigenous regime of customary law.

Smith v. James

Appellate Court of the Hopi Tribe, 1999.
2 Am. Tribal Law 319.

■ Before SEKAQUAPTEWA, Chief Judge, and LOMAYESVA and ABBEY, Judges. * * * Appellant, Ruth Smith, and Appellees, Joyce James, Darlene Ahownewa, and Lorna Quamahongnewa, are enrolled members of the Hopi Tribe from the Village of Hotevilla. Appellees are the granddaughters of Martha Bolehongna, and the daughters of Mollie Honeyestewa, and currently reside on the Hopi Reservation. (James lives in Kykotsmovi, and Quamahongnewa and Ahownewa live in Hotevilla.) Appellant is the daughter of Martha Bolehongna. Appellant left the Hopi reservation in 1938 and now resides on the Yavapai–Apache Reservation with her husband Ted Smith, the Yavapai–Apache tribal chairman. * * *

[handwritten margin note: mother v. daughter (who left the reservation)]

At issue is a tract of farming land located within the Village of Hotevilla upon which there are orchards and bean fields. The parties disagree about who has exclusive rights to use and occupy the land. Appellant asserts that her father and he gave her the property in 1954 in an oral "will". Appellees claim, however, that pursuant to Hopi tradition, their mother, Mollie, got the land since she remained on the land and cared for her mother in her old age while Ruth Smith was "disowned" by her mother and lost her rights to inherit the land because she married a non-Hopi, moved off the reservation, and failed to participate in Hopi ceremonies. Consequently, Appellees argue that because they have assumed the role of caring for the land, rights to the land transferred to them in accord with Hopi tradition. They further state that their uncle, Stephen Albert, affirmed their rights to the land because he told them that Appellant had no rights.

[handwritten margin note: lots to unpack... claims appellant lost right to the land]

This dispute came to the forefront when, in the summer of 1993, Appellant and her son placed metal fencing stakes on the property and, in May of 1994, planted fruit trees on the property. Appellees allege these modifications interfere with their use of the property and are contrary to the Hopi way. In a letter dated May 30, 1994, addressed to Appellant's husband, Appellees requested that Appellant remove the stakes. In response, Appellant sought advice of counsel who wrote to Appellees stating that Appellant had rights to the land and further informing Appellees that if they "persisted in harassing" Appellant she would be forced to take legal action.

On July 26, 1994, Appellees requested that the Village resolve the dispute between the parties. Concurrently, Appellees filed a Petition for a Preliminary Injunction in the Hopi Tribal Court. On August 2, 1994, the Village Board of Directors requested that the Hopi tribal court resolve the matter. Consequently, Petitioners amended their petition to include a Quiet Title action. Respondent answered with a counterclaim requesting the court issue an order quieting Petitioners' title. After numerous continuances, Petitioners filed their response to the counterclaims.

On April 30, 1995 trial court judge ordered a hearing to be held on the issue of ownership and relinquishment of land by female members of Hotevilla who marry non-Hopis and live outside the reservation for extended period of time. A trial was held on June 25, 1995, in which both parties presented evidence. However the hearing originally scheduled for March 31, 1995 was not held until March 27, 1997 due to numerous requests for continuances. At the hearing in the Village of Hotevilla, the court took testimony concerning the custom and traditions of Hotevilla from witnesses selected by the parties.

On April 17, 1998 trial court entered "Findings and Judgement" in the matter of *James, et al. v. Smith,* 94CIV0000019, finding for the Petitioners. On May 6, 1998, Respondent's counsel filed a Notice of Appeal (hereinafter Notice) with the Hopi Tribal Court. The same day, Respondent's counsel filed her Notice of Withdrawal as Attorney for Record. Two days later, Petitioners' counsel also filed Notice of Withdrawal as Counsel of Record. Both parties now proceed *pro per,* without the assistance of counsel. * * *

Threshold Issue:

I.   **May the appellate court exercise jurisdiction over an appeal where the brief has been filed late?**

Assuming the court does have jurisdiction, the following issues are raised:

II.   **May the trial court hold a fact-finding hearing before ascertaining the applicable substantive law?**

III. **Did the trial court employ the proper procedures for finding the village custom?**

SYNOPSIS

The instant case attempts to resolve a land dispute between family members in the village of Hotevilla. Appellees requested that this court dismiss the pending appeal because Appellant did not file her brief within 30 days of filing notice. However, this court has substantial discretion to accept late briefs under the terms of Rule 37(i). Therefore, we choose to deny Appellees' motion and exercise jurisdiction over the appeal.

The trial court properly sought to incorporate customary law into its decision-making process by holding a hearing on village custom. Although the trial court performed wonderfully in the absence of guidelines for conducting such a hearing, there are two reasons that make this court unable to uphold the trial court's decision. First, and foremost, the court held the fact-finding hearing *before* conducting the hearing at the village to ascertain village practice. This unfortunately may result in unfairness to one or both parties since, without knowing the legal standard, the parties cannot put forth evidence to adequately support their claims. Furthermore, the trial court did not apply procedures appropriate to a hearing to find village customary law. The trial court should have allowed the village an opportunity to propose witnesses for the hearing on village custom, and should have allowed the parties an opportunity to introduce further questions about village custom after the initial testimony.

Therefore, it is the judgement of this court that the case be remanded back to the trial court for two separate procedures: first, to hold a new hearing to ascertain village practice with respect to resolution of disputes about inheritance of farm land and, second, to hold a new trial where parties may present evidence after the establishment of the legal standard. The court acknowledges that this remand will delay a result for both the parties. Thus the tribal court may not be the best forum available for dispute resolution of this nature. The parties are free to seek a settlement by seeking an arbitrator to whom the parties are willing to submit their situation. If they agree to be bound by such a decision, they can then seek certification of that decision from the trial court.

DISCUSSION

* * *

II. The Trial Court Decision Cannot be Upheld because it Contains Procedural Errors that Affected the Outcome.

It was necessary for the trial court to inquire into and apply village customary law and practice in the instant case because of the unique history of the Village of Hotevilla. Hotevilla came to be as a result of the split at Old Oraibi in 1906. The establishment of Hotevilla and other communities on Third Mesa, affected the traditional "clan lands" system in operation at Old Oraibi because the split did not necessarily fall along clan lines. Mischa Titiev, OLD ORABI: A STUDY OF THE HOPI INDIANS OF THIRD MESA (1944): 88–89. Under the clan lands system, inheritance of land was traditionally matrilineal, but after the split at Oraibi, inheritance could sometimes be patriline. See Peter M. Whiteley, RETHINKING HOPI ETHNOGRAPHY (1998): 62. Furthermore, with clan lands the fields were always the woman's but with the establishment of these new villages, men came to have different rights in land. See id. at 62, 65. Because traditional systems of clan lands probably do not govern this dispute, it was necessary for the court to apply Village custom.

The Appellate Court of the Hopi Tribe has subject matter jurisdiction to hear appeals from final judgements and orders of the Hopi Tribal Court. See Ordinance 21, § 1.2.5. In an exercise of this jurisdiction, we have reviewed the trial court record and conclude that the trial court's decision cannot be upheld due to procedural errors.

A. *Because the Trial Court held a Fact–Finding Trial before the Hearing on Village Custom, the Parties Did not Know the Applicable Law and therefore Were Unable to Present Substantial Evidence to Support their Claim.*

In the absence of prior case or statutory law to inform the parties of the legal standard, the court is required to hold a hearing to find the law *before* it holds a trial-type hearing where evidence is presented. Because this was not done in this case, the facts presented at the trial in April 1995 cannot serve as evidence to support a finding on behalf of either party.

The parties presented evidence supporting their claims of right to the land in question at a trial, before the trial judge on June 29, 1995. However, a hearing to determine the customary law pertaining to the parties' rights was not held until nearly two years later, in March 1997. See (F.J., at 1). This was a procedural error on the part of the trial court because, without an established legal principle, parties are unable to construct coherent arguments or select the evidence that will support their case since they are forced to speculate as to what the law is. Forcing this speculation is not in the interest of the tribal courts or the parties. Consequently, a new fact-finding hearing is required.

B. *The Procedures Used at the Hearing Did Not Provide the Proper Forum for Ascertaining Village Custom.*

The trial court properly held a hearing at the village level, and the manner in which it conducted the hearing should be commended. The non-adversarial nature facilitated testimony from witnesses and emphasized the purpose of finding the law, not facts. However, because the village was not involved in the selection of witnesses and the parties were not permitted to submit additional questions following the initial testimony, the hearing at the village did not provide a sufficient forum for ascertaining village custom.

Article VII of the Hopi Constitution states that "[a]ssignment of use of farming lands . . . within the established village holdings of . . . Hotevilla . . . shall be made by each village according to established custom." *Hopi Constitution,* Article VII § 1. Pursuant to Article VII, the trial court properly held a hearing to ascertain the village custom regarding rights to farming land acquired by use and inheritance. However, because the Village of Hotevilla waived its jurisdiction, the Tribal Court should have given the Village an opportunity to propose witnesses for the hearing.

The non-adversarial nature of the hearing was also proper since many elders might be fearful of undergoing cross-examination. An adversarial atmosphere would not foster village participation in these hearings. However, the parties should have been afforded an opportunity to request further questions after the initial testimony in order to ensure there are not substantial gaps in the law being found. These procedural errors necessitate a new hearing to find the law.

III. The Case is Remanded back to the Trial Court for New Findings of Law and Fact.

In light of the procedural and substantive errors, this case should be remanded back to the trial court for a new hearing on village custom and a new opportunity to present evidence at a fact-finding trial.

* * *

B. *This Court will Pronounce Procedures for the Trial Court to Employ when Conducting Hearings to Find the Law of the Village.*

(1) Either Party or the Judge, *Sua Sponte,* May Request a Hearing Where Custom is Relevant and not "Proven"

The rule remains that a party wanting to use village custom as a legal standard must "give notice to the other party and the court through pleadings or other written notice". Hopi Indian Credit Ass'n v. Thomas (HICA), AP–001–84 (1996), at 5–6. *HICA* required that parties "prove" the existence of the custom and state its relevance to the issue before the court by referring to precedent, treatises that are accepted by the community, judicial notice, or affidavits of appropriate persons. Id., at 6. However, "proving" custom presents difficulty where there is great diversity among the practices of each village and there is no precedent in the tribal court. Consequently, judicial notice will not generally be available. See HICA, at 6 ("a court may dispense with proof of the existence of a Hopi custom, tradition or culture if it finds . . . [it] to be generally known and accepted within the Hopi Tribe"); See also (Amend. Petition) and (Answer) (presenting different claims about Hotevilla custom). In these instances, a hearing is the proper way to find the law.

(2) Notice shall be given to the parties and the Village to allow participation in the selection of witnesses.

The first step in the special hearing process is Notice. The Court should notice the village and the parties as to the hearing and its purpose, offer guidance as to the kinds of witnesses it seeks, and explain in detail the narrow purpose of a fact-finding hearing to find customary law. Depending on the specific law sought, the judge should try to provide guidance to the Village and the parties for choosing their witnesses. The parties and the Village should then submit a list of potential witnesses along with explanations of the reason for their inclusion on the list, and the type of testimony they can offer. Although the trial judge should give deference to the village's selection of witnesses, the judge should exercise discretion in approving the final list. * * *

IV. The Parties May Choose to Settle Out of Court and the Tribal Court would Encourages Such a Resolution.

Although these parties have brought this dispute before the court, we acknowledge that there are alternatives for these parties to resolve this complex dispute. Clearly, the tribal courts must resolve these disputes when brought them, but the intersection of law, Hopi tribal court procedure, village authority, and tradition is very complicated.

Settlement between the parties may expedite resolution of this matter. First, a mediator can facilitate compromise but the court can only issue the remedies requested by the parties. Second, mediation may result in a quicker decision since a settlement need only be certified, and hearings and appeals may not repeat over and over as they may in this case. Both of these considerations would benefit the parties in light of the frustrations expressed by Appellant and Appellees as to the lengthy decision-making in this dispute. * * *

■ Concurring Opinion, LOMAYESVA, J.

I write to express my agreement with the opinions in parts II and III, but write to comment on the decision in Part I. Although I concur in result, I am disturbed by the undefined nature of this court's discretion. I believe the nature and the substance of the merits involved in this court raises substantial issues of Hopi law. Further, I believe the *pro per* status of the Appellant suggest some relaxation of rigid procedural rules. I suggest this because legal procedural rules are based upon Western precepts, which often clashes with non-Western Hopi sensibilities. Yet, discretion unbound invites uncertainty and disturbs one's reliance upon established law.

NOTES AND QUESTIONS

1. *Smith v. James* is a landmark in the effort to revitalize Hopi customary law. While there was a time when the common law itself was considered the general custom of all of society, the role of custom in the common law is thought to be more modest than it once was. By contrast, custom is at the core of the Hopi system. For an account of how judges and others are using ancient custom in a new way to create a legal system for the Hopi tribe, see Justin B. Richland, Arguing with Tradition: The Language of Law in Hopi Tribal Court (2008).

2. The land at issue in the case is in Hotevilla, a Hopi village which split from another Hopi village, Old Oraibi, in 1906. Hotevilla allowed for more individual property in men than in Oraibi. In Oraibi property would descend to women, who would in turn be obligated to cook in tribal ceremonies. So the parties are arguing two different sets of customs. If tribal custom makes distinctions (like the gender-based ones in the principle case) that state and federal law would not (or could not) make, how intrusive or deferential should federal law be? For similar tensions in Ethiopian land registration, see Ayano, supra, 52 Law & Soc'y Rev. at 1060.

Figure 3-1
Hotevilla in 1912

Creators: Grace Nicholson & Carroll S. Hartman.

3.   Overt invocations of custom are less common in American property law than they once were. Henry E. Smith, Custom in American Property Law: A Vanishing Act, 48 Tex. Int'l L.J. 507 (2013). As we saw in a previous case, *Ghen v. Rich*, nineteenth-century courts deferred to possessory customs of the whaling industry, except when the customs were unreasonable or might disturb the expectations of non-whalers. In recent times, the most famous and high-stakes invocation of custom has been in cases about the public's access to beaches. We delve into this issue in *State of Oregon ex rel. Thornton v. Hay*, later in this Chapter. The common law featured a set of criteria for judges to use in deciding whether to treat a custom as law— criteria famously expounded by Blackstone. These included specific criteria, like longstandingness and reasonableness, and general ones: the custom can be either society-wide or apply within a defined community. 1 William Blackstone, Commentaries *67. Some see tribal custom as closely fitting this description. Gloria Valencia-Weber, Tribal Courts: Custom and Innovative Law, 24 N.M. L. Rev. 225, 246–47 (1994). Others see great challenges in rescuing what remains of custom for some tribes and see value in avoiding Americanized elements. Christine Zuni, Strengthening What Remains, 7 Kan. J.L. & Pub. Pol'y 17 (1997); see generally Elizabeth A. Reese, The Other American Law, 73 Stan. L. Rev. 555 (2021). Reviving custom raises these and many other questions, such as the role, if any, anthropological theories should play in the process. Pat Sekaquaptewa, Key Concepts in the Finding, Definition and Consideration of Custom Law in Tribal Lawmaking, 32 Am. Indian L. Rev. 319 (2008).

4.   Customs grow out of communities and can be used to build up or reinforce those communities themselves, as in *Smith v. James*. Modern

market societies may seem to have less place for community and correspondingly a diminished reliance on custom. But is that true? New kinds of community are arising online. Are these real or spurious communities? Either way, can you think of customs that have arisen online, to which you may feel yourself bound. Why is it that visiting a website in violation of terms of service, especially clickwrap boilerplate, does not seem like a "trespass," but using a stolen password, systematic guessing of passwords, or other hacking activities definitely does? Orin S. Kerr, Norms of Computer Trespass, 116 Colum. L. Rev. 1143 (2016). As you work through the cases in this book, ask yourself how important a role custom plays. Could one possibly understand how possession works without an understanding of customs of everyday life and of various specialized contexts?

5.   Interestingly, community is important to the success of businesses based on non-fungible tokens (NFTs), digital assets that are verified as authentic by blockchain technology (for instance, demonstrating that the holder owns the original version of some digital artwork). Blockchain is an impersonal digital leger of transactional "blocks" of data, in which the leger incorporates all previous blocks and is cryptographically protected against manipulation. The most obvious applications include cryptocurrencies and secure transfers of assets (for example in connection with land transactions, see Chapter VIII), which benefit from the public and impersonal nature of the technology. However, more elaborate use of NFTs go beyond "virtual deeds" to make NFTs programmable. This makes possible entirely new kinds of assets, from digital "sports moments" trading cards to membership in clubs that have grown up around NFTs (like "Bored Ape"), which require the ongoing interest and engagement of a relevant community. See Steve Kaczynski & Scott Duke Kominers, How NFTs Create Value, Harv. Bus. Rev. (Nov. 19, 2021), https://hbr.org/2021/11/how-nfts-create-value. For a discussion of the difficulties in classifying digital assets under current law—are they commodities, securities, currencies, assets, or something other than property?—and how property law might define such assets for legal purposes, see João Marinotti, Tangibility As Technology, 37 Ga. St. U. L. Rev. 671 (2021).

D. PUBLIC RIGHTS

In the previous sections, we considered whether there are certain things that are too private or person-related, or too connected to community, to be objects of ownership as private property (or as property at all). In this section, we take up something of the opposite question—whether there are certain resources that are too "public" to be parceled out into private ownership. In other words, is there a category of resources that should be regarded as "inherently public," and hence should remain accessible only on equal terms to all members of the society?

1. THE NAVIGATION SERVITUDE

a. NAVIGABLE WATERS

The resource with the longest historical claim to being inherently public is navigable water. Under Roman law, according to Justinian's *Institutes*, "all of these things are by natural law common to all: air, flowing water, the sea and, consequently, the shores of the sea." Institutes 2.1.1–5 (J. Moyle trans., 5th ed. 1913). Bracton, writing in the mid-thirteenth century, borrowed from Justinian's *Institutes* and claimed that at common law the sea and seashore were common to all. Henry de Bracton, On the Laws and Customs of England 39–40 (Samuel E. Thorne trans., 1968). Eventually, English law gave distinct treatment to "navigable waters" in four ways: (1) any member of the public had the right to travel by vessel on a body of water that was navigable; (2) any member of the public had the right to fish in a body of water that was navigable; (3) the land beneath navigable water was presumptively owned by the Crown; and (4) disputes arising out of incidents on navigable water were decided by the Royal Admiralty Courts rather than the common-law courts. See Daniel J. Hulsebosch, Writs to Rights: "Navigability" and the Transformation of the Common Law in the Nineteenth Century, 23 Cardozo L. Rev. 1049, 1055, 1066–67 (2002); James R. Rasband, The Disregarded Common Parentage of the Equal Footing and Public Trust Doctrines, 32 Land & Water L. Rev. 1 (1997).

Thus, under English law the King as sovereign owned and controlled all navigable waters within the realm (as opposed to the high seas, which no one owned), and presumptively owned the land beneath navigable waters. Navigable waters, however, were narrowly defined in English law to mean those waters subject to the ebb and flow of the tides. Consequently, submerged land under rivers and lakes not affected by the tides was subject to private ownership. Absent a grant to the contrary, the owner of land bordering on a nonnavigable body of water owned the submerged land to the thread of the current or center line of the river or lake on which the land abutted. Also, the sovereign's ownership and control of navigable waters was qualified by important public rights (*jus publicum*). All waters, whether tidal or not, were subject to a general public easement of free navigation. The King was powerless to interfere with this right. Moreover, private owners of waters that were nontidal but navigable in fact could not interfere with public navigation, provided those wishing to traverse such waters could obtain access without trespassing. The right to fish was also understood to be a public right that could not be defeated with respect to tidal waters and the beds of tidal waters, although owners of land under non-tidal waters could restrict access for fishing.

Adapting these understandings to the American context was complicated by the division of authority between the federal government and the states. The U.S. Constitution gave Congress authority to "regulate Commerce with foreign nations, and among the several States, and with the Indian Tribes." U.S. Const. art. I, § 8, cl. 3. "Commerce" in 1789 took place largely through vessels plying navigable waterways, and so the Constitution appeared to contemplate a federal role in preserving and enhancing navigation. The Constitution also extended the judicial power of the federal courts to "all Cases of admiralty and maritime Jurisdiction." Id. art. III, § 2. This too suggested that the federal courts were to assume the jurisdiction historically exercised by the Royal Courts of Admiralty over disputes arising on navigable waters.

These expectations were eventually vindicated. Congress conferred admiralty jurisdiction on the federal courts in the Judiciary Act of 1789. At first, this jurisdiction was understood to extend only to disputes arising out of navigable waters as defined by English law—that is, to disputes arising out of waters subject to the ebb and flow of the tides. See The Steam-Boat Thomas Jefferson, 23 U.S. (10 Wheat.) 428 (1825). But in 1851, in a dramatic reversal, the Court overruled this decision and held that the admiralty jurisdiction of the federal courts was not limited to tidal waters but extended to all waters that are navigable in fact. The Propeller Genesee Chief v. Fitzhugh, 53 U.S. (12 How.) 443 (1851). The Court noted that in England, with its long coast line and short rivers, the equation of navigable waters with tidal waters did not do great violence to commercial realities. On the North American continent, by contrast, a large number of waterways are not tidal yet are navigable in fact, including the Great Lakes and rivers like the Ohio and the Mississippi. By 1851 it was clear that these waterways would play a vital role in the development of American commerce, and therefore a broader definition of navigable waters was needed.

The federal role in preserving free navigation under the Commerce Clause emerged more slowly. The first decisive step was the Supreme Court's decision in Gibbons v. Ogden, 22 U.S. (9 Wheat.) 1 (1824), where the Court invalidated a monopoly charter granted by the New York legislature to operate steamboats between New York City and New Jersey. Chief Justice Marshall wrote that the word "commerce" in the Constitution "comprehends, and has been always understood to comprehend, navigation within its meaning; and a power to regulate navigation, is as expressly granted, as if that term had been added to the word 'commerce.'" Id. at 193. Gibbons established that Congress has plenary authority to legislate on the subject of commercial navigation. Soon, the commerce power came to be understood as self-executing, even in the absence of legislation by Congress. Thus, for example, in Pennsylvania v. Wheeling & Belmont Bridge Co., 54 U.S. (13 How.) 518 (1851), the Court held that the federal courts, on the authority of the Commerce Clause and without any implementing legislation, could issue an injunction directing that a low-lying bridge be raised in order to prevent undue interference with navigation on the Ohio River. Although Congress could intercede and revise such decisions (as it did with respect to the Wheeling Bridge, see Pennsylvania v. Wheeling & Belmont Bridge Co., 59 U.S. (18 How.) 421 (1855)), the Court deemed the principle of free navigation too important to await implementing legislation from Congress.

Decisions like those involving the Wheeling Bridge eventually crystallized into the notion that the Commerce Clause, of its own force, imposes a "navigation servitude" on all waters of the United States that are in fact navigable. Under this navigation servitude, no state government, and no individual or corporation acting under the authority of state law, has the power to obstruct or interfere with the public's right to free use of waterways for transportation. See, e.g., United States v. Rands, 389 U.S. 121, 122–23 (1967); FPC v. Niagara Mohawk Power Corp., 347 U.S. 239, 249 (1954); Scranton v. Wheeler, 179 U.S. 141, 156–57 (1900).

The question of who has title to submerged land beneath navigable waters has followed a convoluted path in the United States. With respect to tidal lands, the Supreme Court held in *Martin v. Waddell*, 41 U.S. (16 Pet.) 367 (1842), that the original colonies succeeded to the position of English Crown with respect to the ownership of tidal lands. In *Pollard v. Hagan,* 44 U.S. (3 How.) 212 (1845), this understanding with respect to tidal lands was extended to states later admitted to the Union, based on the "equal footing" language contained in their statehood grants. But with respect to lands beneath waters that were not tidal but navigable in fact, the states carved out a variety of positions. Some followed English law, and recognized private ownership of such lands; others decided that the state government owned such lands; still others split the difference, saying that private ownership applied to land under rivers but state ownership applied to land under lakes (especially large ones). In *Shively v. Bowlby*, 152 U.S. 1 (1894), the Court decided that different states were free to take different positions on the ownership of land beneath navigable but nontidal waters.

Today, it can be said that American law recognizes something similar to the *jus publicum* of English common law, but it is grounded in the Commerce Clause rather than in any conception of inherently public property rights. Congress has consistently endorsed the idea that the navigable waters of the United States shall remain open to public navigation. Perhaps most prominently, the Rivers and Harbors Act of 1890 provided that "the creation of any obstruction, not affirmatively authorized by law, to the navigable capacity of any waters, in respect of which the United States has jurisdiction, is hereby prohibited." 26 Stat. 426, 454 (1890). The Act delegated authority to the U.S. Army, acting through its Corps of Engineers, to take legal action against, and if necessary remove, such obstructions to navigable waters. Similarly, the Submerged Lands Act, which confirmed states' right to determine the title to the submerged lands under navigable waters within their borders, Congress reserved to the federal government "all its navigation servitude and rights in and powers of regulation and control of said lands and navigable waters for the constitutional purposes of commerce, navigation, national defense, and international affairs, all of which shall be paramount to, but shall not be deemed to include, proprietary rights of ownership. . . ." 67 Stat. 32, 43 U.S.C. § 1314 (1953).

This does not mean that the division of authority between the federal government and the states is clear. The concept of "navigable waters" generally defines the scope of the authority of the federal government. This was ambiguously defined in the Clean Water Act to mean "the waters of the United States." 33 U.S.C. § 1362(7). The Supreme Court has struggled (without success) to specify what *that* means. See Rapanos v. United States, 547 U.S. 715, 730–39 (2006) (plurality opinion of Scalia, J.) ("waters" refers to relatively permanent, standing, or continuously flowing bodies of water); id. at 759–87 (Kennedy, J., concurring) ("waters" should be defined in light of the pollution control purposes of the Act); Solid Waste Agency of Northern Cook Cty. v. Army Corps of Engineers, 531 U.S. 159 (2001) ("navigable waters" cannot be defined so broadly as to exceed the power of Congress under the Commerce Clause).

b.   NAVIGABLE AIRSPACE

In *United States v. Causby*, 328 U.S. 256 (1946), the Supreme Court held that the principles of federal control over navigable waterways extend to navigable airspace. Causby, a chicken farmer in Greensboro, North Carolina, had the misfortune of having a military airport built next to his farm during the run up to World War II. The testimony showed that roaring military planes passed as low as 83 feet over his property, which so frightened the chickens that some of them flew into the walls and killed themselves, while others stopped laying eggs. Causby sued the United States, claiming that the overflights were a taking of his air rights under the *ad coelum* doctrine. In an opinion by Justice Douglas, the Court agreed that there had been a taking, but only because the overflights caused a direct injury to Causby's use and enjoyment of the land. The Court took pains to emphasize that the federal government has ample authority to assure that navigable airspace remains a public resource:

> The United States relies on the Air Commerce Act of 1926, 44 Stat. 568, 49 U.S.C. § 171 et seq., as amended by the Civil Aeronautics Act of 1938, 52 Stat. 973, 49 U.S.C. § 401 et seq. Under those statutes the United States has "complete and exclusive national sovereignty in the air space" over this country. 49 U.S.C. § 176(a). They grant any citizen of the United States "a public right of freedom of transit in air commerce through the navigable air space of the United States." 49 U.S.C. § 403. And "navigable air space" is defined as "airspace above the minimum safe altitudes of flight prescribed by the Civil Aeronautics Authority." 49 U.S.C. § 180. And it is provided that

"such navigable airspace shall be subject to a public right of freedom of interstate and foreign air navigation." Id. It is, therefore, argued that since these flights were within the minimum safe altitudes of flight which had been prescribed, they were an exercise of the declared right of travel through the airspace. The United States concludes that when flights are made within the navigable airspace without any physical invasion of the property of the landowners, there has been no taking of property. * * *

It is ancient doctrine that at common law ownership of the land extended to the periphery of the universe—*Cujus est solum ejus est usque ad coelum*. But that doctrine has no place in the modern world. The air is a public highway, as Congress has declared. Were that not true, every transcontinental flight would subject the operator to countless trespass suits. Common sense revolts at the idea. To recognize such private claims to the airspace would clog these highways, seriously interfere with their control and development in the public interest, and transfer into private ownership that to which only the public has a just claim. * * *

The airplane is part of the modern environment of life, and the inconveniences which it causes are normally not compensable under the Fifth Amendment. The airspace, apart from the immediate reaches above the land, is part of the public domain. We need not determine at this time what those precise limits are. Flights over private land are not a taking, unless they are so low and so frequent as to be a direct and immediate interference with the enjoyment and use of the land.

Id. at 260–61, 266 (footnotes omitted). As noted in connection with the *Hinman* case (Chapter I), the Court's characterization of the *ad coelum* doctrine as obsolete is best viewed as a piece of rhetorical excess. But there remain significant questions of how to apply or modify *ad coelum* in light of the relatively recent possibility of overflights by aircraft. See generally Stuart Banner, Who Owns the Sky?: The Struggle to Control Airspace from the Wright Brothers On (2008).

After the *Causby* decision, navigable airspace in the United States has assumed roughly the same status as navigable waterways: Federal law trumps any attempt by the states or private property owners to interfere with free public navigation; federal law plays a paramount role in regulating the use of and access to the navigable airspace; and federal policy has been to encourage public access to navigable airspace.

2. THE PUBLIC TRUST DOCTRINE

Illinois Central Railroad Co. v. Illinois

Supreme Court of the United States, 1892.
146 U.S. 387.

■ MR. JUSTICE FIELD delivered the opinion of the court. This suit was commenced on the 1st of March, 1883, in a circuit court of Illinois, by an information or bill in equity filed by the attorney general of the state, in the name of its people, against the Illinois Central Railroad Company, a corporation created under its laws, and against the city of Chicago. * * *

The object of the suit is to obtain a judicial determination of the title of certain lands on the east or lake front of the city of Chicago, situated between the Chicago river and Sixteenth street, which have been reclaimed from the waters of the lake, and are occupied by the tracks, depots, warehouses, piers, and other structures used by the railroad company in its business, and also of the title claimed by the company to the submerged lands, constituting the bed of the lake, lying east of its tracks, within the corporate limits of the city, for the distance of a mile, and between the south line of the south pier near Chicago river, extended eastwardly, and a line extended in the same direction from the south line of lot 21 near the company's roundhouse and machine shops. The determination of the title of the company will involve a consideration of its right to construct, for its own business, as well as for public convenience, wharves, piers, and docks in the harbor. * * *

The city of Chicago is situated upon the southwestern shore of Lake Michigan * * * For a long time after the organization of the city, its harbor was the Chicago river, a small, narrow stream opening into the lake * * *; and in it the shipping arriving from other ports of the lake and navigable waters was moored or anchored, and along it were docks and wharves. The growth of the city in subsequent years, in population, business, and commerce, required a larger and more convenient harbor * * *

Figure 3-2
Chicago Lakefront, Late 1880s

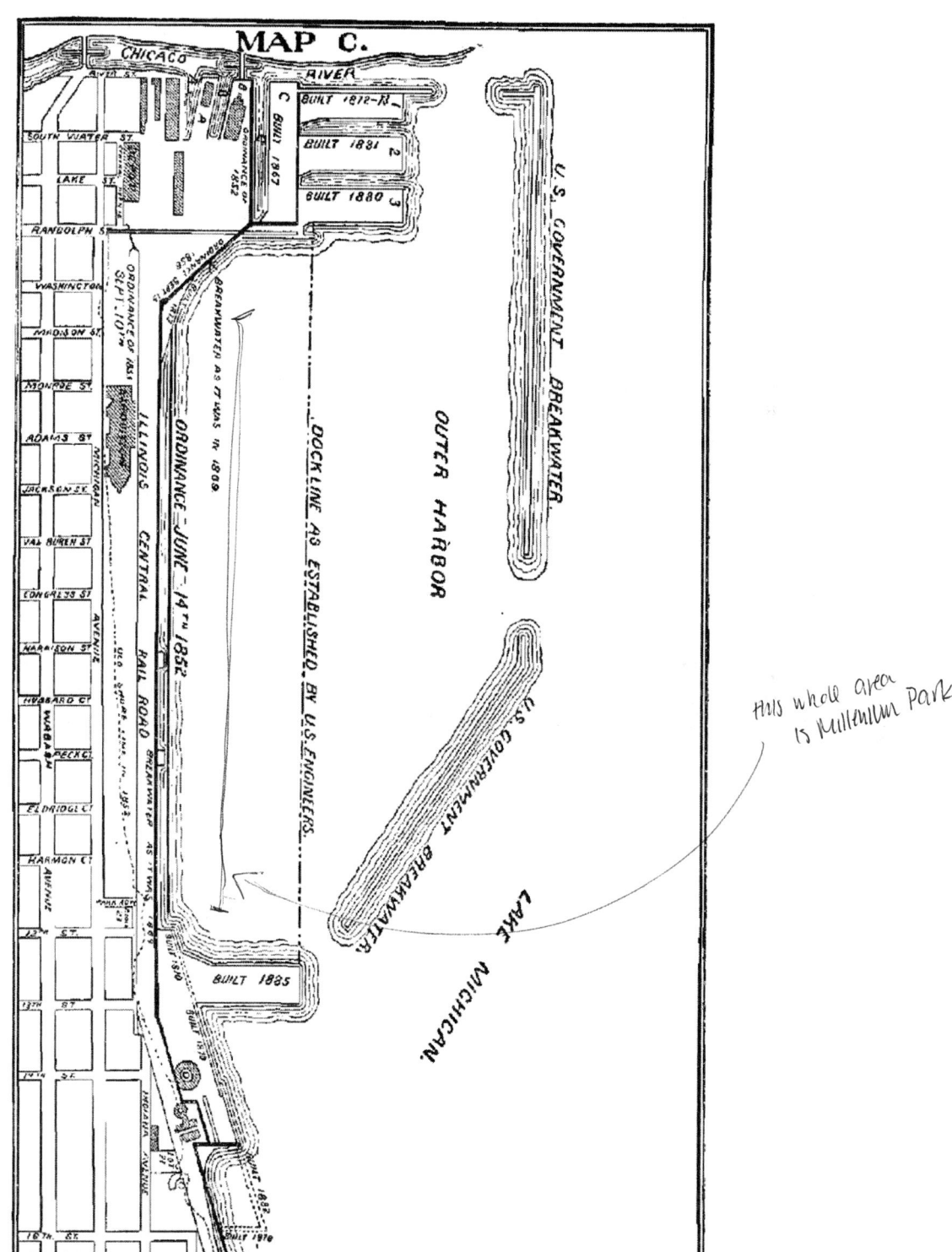

The case proceeds upon the theory and allegation that the defendant the Illinois Central Railroad Company has, without lawful authority, encroached, and continues to encroach, upon the domain of the state, and its original ownership and control of the waters of the harbor and of the lands thereunder, upon a claim of rights acquired under a grant from the state * * *

The state prays a decree establishing and confirming its title to the bed of Lake Michigan, and exclusive right to develop and improve the harbor of Chicago by the construction of docks, wharves, piers, and other improvements, against the claim of the railroad company that it has an absolute title to such submerged lands by the act of 1869 * * *

We proceed to consider the claim of the railroad company to the ownership of submerged lands in the harbor, and the right to construct such wharves, piers, docks, and other works therein as it may deem proper for its interest and business. The claim is founded upon the third section of the act of the legislature of the state passed on the 16th of April, 1869, the material part of which is as follows:

> Sec. 3. * * * [A]ll the right and title of the state of Illinois in and to the submerged lands constituting the bed of Lake Michigan, and lying east of the tracks and breakwater of the Illinois Central Railroad Company, for a distance of one mile, and between the south line of the south pier extended eastwardly and a line extended eastward from the south line of lot twenty-one, south of and near to the roundhouse and machine shops of said company, in the south division of the said city of Chicago, are hereby granted in fee to the said Illinois Central Railroad Company, its successors and assigns: provided, however, that the fee to said lands shall be held by said company in perpetuity, and that the said company shall not have power to grant, sell, or convey the fee to the same, and that all gross receipts from use, profits, leases, or otherwise, of said lands, or the improvements thereon, or that may hereafter be made thereon, shall form a part of the gross proceeds, receipts, and income of the said Illinois Central Railroad Company, upon which said company shall forever pay into the state treasury, semiannually, the per centum provided for in its charter, in accordance with the requirements of said charter: and provided, also, that nothing herein contained shall authorize obstructions to the Chicago harbor, or impair the public right of navigation, nor shall this act be construed to exempt the Illinois Central Railroad Company, its lessees or assigns, from any act of the general assembly which may be hereafter passed, regulating the rates of wharfage and dockage to be charged in said harbor.
>
> * * *

The act, if valid and operative to the extent claimed, placed under the control of the railroad company nearly the whole of the submerged lands of the harbor, subject only to the limitations that it should not authorize obstructions to the harbor, or impair the public right of navigation, or exclude the legislature from regulating the rates of wharfage or dockage to be charged. With these limitations, the act put it in the power of the company to delay indefinitely the improvement of the harbor, or to construct as many docks, piers, and wharves and other works as it might choose, and at such positions in the harbor as might suit its purposes, and permit any kind of business to be conducted thereon, and to lease them out on its own terms for indefinite periods. The inhibition against the technical transfer of the fee of any portion of the submerged lands was of little consequence when it could make a lease for any period, and renew it at its pleasure; and the inhibitions against authorizing obstructions to the harbor and impairing the public right of navigation placed no impediments upon the action of the railroad company which did not previously exist. A corporation created for one purpose, the construction and operation of a railroad between designated points, is by the act converted into a corporation to manage and practically control the harbor of Chicago, not simply for its own purpose as a railroad corporation, but for its own profit generally.

The circumstances attending the passage of the act through the legislature were on the hearing the subject of much criticism. As originally introduced, the purpose of the act was to enable the city of Chicago to enlarge its harbor, and to grant to it the title and interest of the state to certain lands adjacent to the shore of Lake Michigan, on the eastern front of the city, and place the harbor under its control; giving it all the necessary powers for its wise management. But during the passage of the act its purport was changed. Instead of providing for the cession of the submerged lands to the city, it provided for a cession of them to the railroad company. * * *

The question, therefore, to be considered, is whether the legislature was competent to thus deprive the state of its ownership of the submerged lands in the harbor of Chicago, and of the consequent control of its waters; or, in other words, whether the railroad corporation can hold the lands and control the waters by the grant, against any future exercise of power over them by the state.

That the state holds the title to the lands under the navigable waters of Lake Michigan, within its limits, in the same manner that the state holds title to soils under tide water * * * we have already shown; and that title necessarily carries with it control over the waters above them, whenever the lands are subjected to use. But it is a title different in character from that which the state holds in lands intended for sale. It is different from the title which the United States hold in the public lands which are open to pre-emption and sale. It is a title held in trust for the people of the state, that they may enjoy the navigation of the waters, carry on commerce over them, and have liberty of fishing therein, freed from the obstruction or interference of private parties. The interest of the people in the navigation of the waters and in commerce over them may be improved in many instances by the erection of wharves, docks, and piers therein, for which purpose the state may grant parcels of the submerged lands; and, so long as their disposition is made for such purpose, no valid objections can be made to the grants. * * * But that is a very different doctrine from the one which would sanction the abdication of the general control of the state over lands under the navigable waters of an entire harbor or bay, or of a sea or lake. Such abdication is not consistent with the exercise of that trust which requires the government of the state to preserve such waters for the use of the public. The trust devolving upon the state for the public, and which can only be discharged by the management and control of property in which the public has an interest, cannot be relinquished by a transfer of the property. The control of the state for the purposes of the trust can never be lost, except as to such parcels as are used in promoting the interests of the public therein, or can be disposed of without any substantial impairment of the public interest in the lands and waters remaining. * * * A grant of all the lands under the navigable waters of a state has never been adjudged to be within the legislative power; and any attempted grant of the kind would be held, if not absolutely void on its face, as subject to revocation. The state can no more abdicate its trust over property in which the whole people are interested, like navigable waters and soils under them, so as to leave them entirely under the use and control of private parties, except in the instance of parcels mentioned for the improvement of the navigation and use of the waters, or when parcels can be disposed of without impairment of the public interest in what remains, than it can abdicate its police powers in the administration of government and the preservation of the peace. In the administration of government the use of such powers may for a limited period be delegated to a municipality or other body, but there always remains with the state the right to revoke those powers and exercise them in a more direct manner, and one more conformable to its wishes. So with trusts connected with public property, or property of a special character, like lands under navigable waters; they cannot be placed entirely beyond the direction and control of the state.

The harbor of Chicago is of immense value to the people of the state of Illinois, in the facilities it affords to its vast and constantly increasing commerce; and the idea that its legislature can deprive the state of control over its bed and waters, and place the same in the hands of a private corporation, created for a different purpose,—one limited to transportation of passengers and freight between distant points and the city,—is a proposition that cannot be defended.

The area of the submerged lands proposed to be ceded by the act in question to the railroad company embraces something more than 1,000 acres, being, as stated by counsel, more than three times the area of the outer harbor, and not only including all of that harbor, but embracing adjoining submerged lands, which will, in all probability, be hereafter included in the harbor. It is as large as that embraced by all the merchandise docks along the Thames at London; is much larger than that included in the famous docks and basins at Liverpool; is twice that of the port of Marseilles, and nearly, if not quite, equal to the pier area along the water front of the city of New York. And the arrivals and clearings of vessels at the port exceed in number those of New York, and are equal to those of New York and Boston combined. Chicago has nearly 25 per cent. of the lake carrying trade, as compared with the arrivals and clearings of all the leading ports of our great inland seas. In the year ending June 30, 1886, the joint arrivals and clearances of vessels at that port amounted to 22,096, with a tonnage of over 7,000,000; and in 1890 the tonnage of the vessels reached nearly 9,000,000. As stated by counsel, since the passage of the lake front act, in 1869, the population of the city has increased nearly 1,000,000 souls, and the increase of commerce has kept pace with it. It is hardly conceivable that the legislature can divest the state of the control and management of this harbor, and vest it absolutely in a private corporation. Surely an act of the legislature transferring the title to its submerged lands and the power claimed by the railroad company to a foreign state or nation would be repudiated, without hesitation, as a gross perversion of the trust over the property under which it is held. So would a similar transfer to a corporation of another state. It would not be listened to that the control and management of the harbor of that great city—a subject of concern to the whole people of the state—should thus be placed elsewhere than in the state itself. All the objections which can be urged to such attempted transfer may be urged to a transfer to a private corporation like the railroad company in this case.

Any grant of the kind is necessarily revocable, and the exercise of the trust by which the property was held by the state can be resumed at any time. Undoubtedly there may be expenses incurred in improvements made under such a grant, which the state ought to pay; but, be that as it may, the power to resume the trust whenever the state judges best is, we think, incontrovertible. The position advanced by the railroad company in support of its claim to the ownership of the submerged lands, and the right to the erection of wharves, piers, and docks at its pleasure, or for its business in the harbor of Chicago, would place every harbor in the country at the mercy of a majority of the legislature of the state in which the harbor is situated.

We cannot, it is true, cite any authority where a grant of this kind *no precedent* has been held invalid, for we believe that no instance exists where the harbor of a great city and its commerce have been allowed to pass into the control of any private corporation. But the decisions are numerous which declare that such property is held by the state, by virtue of its sovereignty, in trust for the public. The ownership of the navigable waters of the harbor, and of the lands under them, is a subject of public concern to the whole people of the state. The trust with which they are held, therefore, is governmental, and cannot be alienated, except in those instances mentioned, of parcels used in the improvement of the interest thus held, or when parcels can be disposed of without detriment to the public interest in the lands and waters remaining. * * *

■ MR. JUSTICE SHIRAS, with whom concurred MR. JUSTICE GRAY and MR. JUSTICE BROWN, dissenting. * * * [We agree that the State cannot part,] by contract, with her sovereign powers. The railroad company takes and holds these lands subject at all times to the same sovereign powers in the state as obtain in the case of other owners of property. Nor can the grant in this case be regarded as in any way hostile to the powers of the general government in the control of harbors and navigable waters.

The able and interesting statement, in the opinion of the majority, of the rights of the public in the navigable waters, and of the limitation of the powers of the state to part with its control over them, is not dissented from. But its pertinency in the present discussion is not clearly seen. It will be time enough to invoke the doctrine of the inviolability of public rights when and if the railroad company shall attempt to disregard them.

Should the state of Illinois see in the great and unforeseen growth of the city of Chicago and of the lake commerce reason to doubt the prudence of her legislature in entering into the contract created by the passage and acceptance of the act of 1869, she can take the rights and property of the railroad company in these lands by a constitutional condemnation of them. So, freed from the shackles of an undesirable contract, she can make, as she expresses in her bill a desire to do, a "more advantageous sale or disposition to other parties," without offense to the law of the land. * * *

NOTES AND QUESTIONS

1.   Justice Field's opinion seems to imply that the Lake Front Act of 1869 conferred monopoly control over the Chicago harbor on a private railroad company. But this is not true, as is confirmed by Map C reproduced from the record in the case (see Figure 3-2). At the time of the grant, the harbor of Chicago was the Chicago River, which was entered from Lake Michigan in the center of the city. The grant of submerged land to the Illinois Central Railroad began at the south bank of the River and ran from there in a southerly direction. What the Lake Front Act in fact contemplated was that the Illinois Central would construct and operate a new "outer harbor" in the lake south of the river, which would supplement the existing facilities in the Chicago River. To be sure, this supplemental harbor would make the railroad the largest operator of piers and wharfs in the Chicago area, and its facilities would have had a favored position by being nearest the lake. But being the biggest and closest does not make one a monopolist, and it is likely that

plenty of competition would have remained to constrain the pricing of the railroad for its harbor services. Justice Field was an ardent free-marketeer, but he was also a populist who was intensely suspicious of special privileges and charters for corporations. See The Slaughter-House Cases, 83 U.S. (16 Wall.) 36, 83 (1873) (Field, J. dissenting); Paul Kens, Justice Stephen Field: Shaping Liberty from the Gold Rush to the Gilded Age (1997); Charles W. McCurdy, Justice Field and the Jurisprudence of Government-Business Relations: Some Parameters of Laissez-Faire Constitutionalism, 1863–1897, 61 J. Am. Hist. 970, 973 (1975). The argument between Justice Field and Justice Shiras in *Illinois Central* has strong echoes of the debate in *Charles River Bridge v. Warren Bridge*, Chapter X, where Chief Justice Taney argues that corporate charters should be narrowly construed to avoid conferring monopoly privileges and Justice Story, in dissent, says that corporate charters are property that can be modified only by paying just compensation to the owners.

2. Further information about the background of the case may be found in Joseph D. Kearney & Thomas W. Merrill, Lakefront: Public Trust and Private Rights in Chicago chs. 1–2 (2021). Three points are especially noteworthy. First, the railroad's motivations in seeking a grant of the submerged land of the lake in 1869 were largely defensive—to fend off efforts by other groups to obtain a grant of these lands, which would have left the railroad's existing improvements isolated by unfriendly forces. The principal rival consortium was headed up by a Chicago lawyer named Melville Fuller, who by 1892 was Chief Justice of the U.S. Supreme Court. This lends additional significance to his recusal from the case, the stated ground for which was that he had served as counsel to the City of Chicago in the court below. Second, no one in 1869 imagined that the State of Illinois had the resources or expertise to construct an outer harbor for Chicago. Downstate legislators favored a grant to the Illinois Central, which did have the resources and expertise, because the revenues generated by a new harbor operated by the railroad would have been subject to the seven percent gross receipts tax that was then applicable to all of the railroad's in-state operations, and this additional revenue could be spent by the legislature for projects throughout the state. Chicago-based legislators tended to favor a grant to the City of Chicago, which would have allowed the aldermen of the City Council to control construction contracts and leases of harbor facilities, and hence to enrich themselves and their friends. Third, the railroad was accused for many years of using corrupt means to procure the enactment of the Lake Front Act, as is perhaps alluded to in the paragraph in the opinion about alleged irregularities in the passage of the Act. Although there is no hard evidence of bribery of the legislature, the weight of the evidence suggests that some type of corruption did take place in 1869, although, as noted above, the motivation for the graft was largely defensive.

3. The outer harbor contemplated by the Lake Front Act of 1869 was never built. Litigation over the grant and repeal kept the project tied up into the twentieth century, by which time commercial traffic on the Great Lakes had begun to decline. The U.S. Army Corps of Engineers eventually dredged a harbor in the Calumet River and Lake at the southern boundary of

Chicago, which soon supplanted the Chicago River as the area's principal port. The only commercial harbor facility of any significance ever built in Lake Michigan by the government was Navy Pier, which juts into the lake just north of the Chicago River (see Figure 3-3). This was never very successful as a harbor facility; it is today leased out to the commercial operator of a multi-use tourist attraction.

Figure 3-3
A View of Navy Pier from the Shoreline in Chicago

Author: David Bjorgen. This image is licensed under the Creative Commons Attribution ShareAlike License v. 2.5.

4.　What is the source of law for the trust obligation that the Supreme Court identifies as constraining the disposition of public lands under navigable waters? Justice Field never says whether he is applying federal law or state law in *Illinois Central*. In subsequent public trust decisions, the Supreme Court has consistently maintained that the doctrine is grounded in state law. See, e.g., Shively v. Bowlby, 152 U.S. 1 (1894); Appleby v. City of New York, 271 U.S. 364 (1926). This means that the states have been free to adopt various understandings of the public trust doctrine. Some, like Illinois, continue to follow Justice Field's theory that the title to certain resources (like submerged land under navigable waters) is impressed with a governmental trust that can never be abandoned. Others, like New York, treat the public trust as a kind of clear statement rule, requiring that the legislature speak explicitly before privatization of trust resources can take place. Still others, like Wisconsin and Hawaii, have located the public trust in language in the state constitution. These divergent understandings have implications for the resources covered by the trust and how easy or hard it is to modify the trust. See Thomas W. Merrill, The Public Trust Doctrine: Some Jurisprudential Variations and their Implications, 38 Haw. L. Rev. 261 (2016).

5.　One implication of the public trust doctrine, as extended by *Illinois Central* to waters that are nontidal but navigable in fact, is that privately-owned fishing streams such as are found in England and Scotland are difficult, if not impossible, to establish in the U.S. For example, in *Collins v. Gerhardt*, 211 N.W. 115 (Mich. 1926), the defendant was wading and fishing in the Pine River, a fast-moving trout stream accessible by no vessel larger than a canoe. The plaintiff, who owned the land on both sides and the bed of Pine River, sued the defendant for trespass. The court held for the defendant: "From this it follows that the common-law doctrine, viz., that the right of fishing in navigable waters follows the ownership of the soil, does not prevail in this state. It is immaterial who owns the soil in our navigable rivers. The trust remains. From the beginning the title was impressed with this trust for the preservation of the public right of fishing and other public rights which all citizens enjoyed in tidal waters under the common law." Id. at 116. Is this declaration of an inalienable public right of access to fishing streams a blessing or a bane for the protection of fish populations and habitats?

Transformation of the Public Trust Doctrine

The public trust doctrine led a quiet existence until 1970. In that year, Professor Joseph Sax wrote a law review article arguing that the doctrine could be employed as an effective tool for environmental protection. See Joseph Sax, The Public Trust Doctrine in Natural Resource Law: Effective Judicial Intervention, 68 Mich. L. Rev. 471 (1970). Sax did not advocate a rigid rule against privatization of public resources; he was more concerned with developing new forms of public participation and judicial oversight to act as a counterweight to capture of state and local legislatures by developers. The *Illinois Central* decision, which Sax characterized as involving a massive giveaway of public resources with no public interest justification, featured prominently in illustrating the dangers of government capture. The article proved to be enormously influential. It transformed the public trust from a doctrine about public access to commercial navigation, into a doctrine about preservation of natural resources. For example, recent Illinois decisions have applied the public trust doctrine to invalidate proposals to fill a portion of Lake Michigan for expansion of a steel plant, People ex rel. Scott v. Chicago Park Dist., 360 N.E.2d 773 (Ill. 1976), and an expansion of Loyola University's Lake Shore campus, see Lake Michigan Fed'n v. U.S. Army Corps of Engineers, 742 F. Supp. 441 (N.D. Ill. 1990). Controversies continue to arise. In 2016, a federal district court declined to dismiss a public trust lawsuit seeking to block construction on the lakefront of the Lucas Museum of the Narrative Arts, designed to house paraphernalia from the Star Wars movies. The legal impasse caused the project to be cancelled. Most recently, the Obama Presidential Center proposal for Jackson Park survived a number of legal challenges, some based on the public trust. See Protect Our Parks, Inc. v. Chicago Park Dist., 971 F.3d 722 (7th Cir. 2020), cert. denied sub nom. Protect Our Parks, Inc. v. City of Chicago, Illinois, 141 S. Ct. 2583 (2021) (holding that plaintiffs lacked Article III standing on state public trust claim).

One question raised by this reorientation of the public trust doctrine is whether the underlying premise of the doctrine—that title to certain resources must remain in governmental hands—is necessarily well designed to achieve preservationist ends. Although Illinois courts have been willing to block transfers of title to nongovernmental entities like steel plants, private universities, and museums operated by private foundations, they have been much more willing to go along with development projects where title remains in government hands. Thus, for example, the courts have upheld as consistent with the public trust the use of parks for the construction of schools, Paepcke v. Public Building Commission of Chicago, 263 N.E.2d 11 (Ill. 1970); the construction of a massive convention center on landfill in the lake, Fairbank v. Stratton, 152 N.E.2d 569 (Ill. 1958); and the building of a large water filtration plant in the lake, Bowes v. City of Chicago, 120 N.E.2d 15 (Ill. 1954). In its most recent decision, the Illinois Supreme Court rejected a challenge to the radical reconstruction of Soldier Field on public trust land, designed to keep the Chicago Bears football team in Chicago. The court reasoned that the public trust doctrine was not violated because fee simple title to Soldier Field remained in the Chicago Park District, even though the Park District had entered into a 30-year renewable lease with the Bears. See Friends of the Parks v. Chicago Park District, 786 N.E.2d 161 (Ill. 2003).

Cumulatively, these decisions do not suggest that a doctrine focused on legal title will consistently function to preserve natural resources from development. Of course, the relevant question is a comparative one: Is a rule that insists that certain resources remain titled in the name of the government more likely to work to preserve these resources, compared to a rule that permits such resources to be transferred entirely into private hands? Absent the public trust doctrine, would the Chicago lakefront be one long wall of condominiums?

Another question raised by the new preservationist thrust of the public trust doctrine is whether this is consistent with principles of democratic control over state-owned resources. In *Illinois Central*, the public trust doctrine was used to uphold the state legislature's most recent determination of the proper use of the bed of the lake. In 1873, the legislature repealed the 1869 grant to the railroad, restoring title to the lake bed in the State of Illinois; the Supreme Court rejected the railroad's claim of vested rights and upheld the repeal, reasoning that one legislature cannot tie the hands of another in determining the proper disposition of public resources. The decision seems to be a vindication of the principle of democratic control of public resources. In some more recent decisions, however, the public trust doctrine has been used to invalidate projects, despite all relevant publicly accountable governmental bodies having signed off on the project and deemed it to be in the public interest. See, e.g., Lake Michigan Federation, supra. Courts of course invalidate democratically-adopted policies when those policies violate constitutions (though constitutions are also democratically-adopted instruments). But there is no obvious constitutional provision, either in the federal Constitution or in most state constitutions, that authorizes the public trust doctrine. Does the public trust doctrine suffer from a democracy deficit? See William D. Araiza, Democracy, Distrust, and the Public Trust: Process-based Constitutional Theory, the Public Trust Doctrine, and the Search for a Substantive Environmental Value, 45 UCLA L. Rev. 385 (1997); Richard J. Lazarus, Changing Conceptions of Property and Sovereignty in Natural Resources: Questioning the Public Trust Doctrine, 71 Iowa L. Rev. 631, 649–50 (1986).

A third question concerns the scope of the doctrine. Professor Sax and other enthusiasts for the public trust doctrine have envisioned it as applying not just to navigable waterways, but also to inland parks and wilderness areas. Yet, a recent survey indicates that nearly all decisions enforcing the doctrine involve resources that have some connection with navigable water. See Robin Kundis Craig, A Comparative Guide to the Eastern Public Trust Doctrines: Classifications of States, Property Rights, and State Summaries, 16 Pa. St. Envtl. L. Rev. 1 (2007); Robin Kundis Craig, A Comparative Guide to Western States' Public Trust Doctrines, 37 Ecology L.Q. 53 (2010). In one controversial case, the California Supreme Court used the public trust doctrine to abrogate appropriative water rights in nonnavigable streams in order to prevent ecological harms from a decline in the water level of a lake fed by the streams. National Audubon Society v. Superior Court of Alpine County, 658 P.2d 709 (Cal. 1983). But even there, the lake into which the streams flowed, Mono Lake, was a navigable body of water. Although lower court decisions in California have applied the public trust doctrine to wildlife, see Center for Biological Diversity, Inc. v. FPL Group, Inc., 83 Cal.Rptr.3d 588 (Cal. Ct. App. 2008), the California Supreme Court has indicated that outside the context of water, any application of the public trust doctrine must be grounded in statute. See Environmental Protection and Information Center v. California Department of Forestry & Fire Protection, 187 P.3d 888, 926 (Cal. 2008). What accounts for the reluctance of courts to extend the public trust doctrine, at least in its common law incarnation, beyond navigable waterways?

Nearly 30% of the land mass of the United States is owned by the federal government. Much of this land is "leftovers" that no one took during the era when the federal public domain was open to purchase and homestead claims. (With narrow exceptions, the Taylor Grazing Act of 1934 closed the federal public domain to further private appropriation.) But the federal public lands also include spectacular national parks and wilderness areas. The Supreme Court has occasionally spoken of the federal lands as being held by the United States in "trust" for the people. See, e.g., Light v. United States, 220 U.S. 523, 537 (1911) (upholding the creation of the National Forest System). Many states also hold ordinary lands in trust—for example, for support of schools—which are not necessarily subject to the public trust doctrine. Jon A. Souder & Sally K. Fairfax, State Trust Lands: History, Management, and Sustainable Use

(1996). Should the 30% of the national land mass held by the United States be subject to the public trust doctrine, as explicated in *Illinois Central*? Although commentators have occasionally advanced this argument, see, e.g., Charles F. Wilkinson, The Public Trust Doctrine in Public Land Law, 14 U.C. Davis L. Rev. 269 (1980), to our knowledge no federal appeals court has ever endorsed it. Why do you suppose the public trust doctrine has more vitality with respect to state-owned resources than it does with respect to federally-owned resources?

Richard Epstein has suggested that the public trust doctrine should also apply to intellectual property rights whose period of protection has expired, allowing the material to enter the public domain. Richard A. Epstein, Intellectual Property, Congressional Power, and the Constitution: The Dubious Constitutionality of the Copyright Term Extension Act, 36 Loyola L.A. L. Rev. 123, 156–58 (2002). Epstein argues that this would discourage Congress from enacting retroactive extensions of intellectual property right protections, at the behest of interest groups that profit from these rights.

State of Oregon ex rel. Thornton v. Hay

Supreme Court of Oregon, 1969.
462 P.2d 671.

■ GOODWIN, JUSTICE. William and Georgianna Hay, the owners of a tourist facility at Cannon Beach, appeal from a decree which enjoins them from constructing fences or other improvements in the dry-sand area between the sixteen-foot elevation contour line and the ordinary high-tide line of the Pacific Ocean.

The issue is whether the state has the power to prevent the defendant landowners from enclosing the dry-sand area contained within the legal description of their ocean-front property. * * *

The defendant landowners concede that * * * all tideland lying seaward of the ordinary, or mean high-tide line is a state recreation area as defined in ORS 390.720.[1]

From the trial record, applicable statutes, and court decisions, certain terms and definitions have been extracted and will appear in this opinion. A short glossary follows:

ORS 390.720 refers to the "ordinary" high-tide line, while other sources refer to the "mean" high-tide line. For the purposes of this case the two lines will be considered to be the same. * * *

---

[1]   ORS 390.720 provides:

Ownership of the shore of the Pacific Ocean between ordinary high tide and extreme low tide, and from the Oregon and Washington state line on the north to the Oregon and California state line on the south, excepting such portions as may have been disposed of by the state prior to July 5, 1947, is vested in the State of Oregon, and is declared to be a state recreation area. No portion of such ocean shore shall be alienated by any of the agencies of the state except as provided by law.

The land area in dispute will be called the <mark>dry-sand area.</mark> This will be assumed to be the <mark>land lying between the line of mean high tide</mark> and <mark>the visible line of vegetation.</mark>

The vegetation line is the seaward edge of vegetation where the upland supports vegetation. It generally falls in the vicinity of the sixteen foot elevation contour line * * *

The extreme high-tide line and the highwater mark are mentioned in the record, but will be treated as identical with the vegetation line. * * *

Below, or seaward of, the mean high-tide line, is the state-owned foreshore, or wet-sand area, in which the landowners in this case concede the public's paramount right, and concerning which there is no justiciable controversy.

The only issue in this case, as noted, <mark>is the power of the state to limit the record owner's use and enjoyment of the dry-sand area,</mark> by whatever boundaries the area may be described.

The trial court found that <mark>the public had acquired,</mark> over the years, <mark>an easement for recreational purposes</mark> to go upon and enjoy the dry-sand area, and that this easement was appurtenant to the wet-sand portion of the beach which is admittedly owned by the state and designated as a "state recreation area."

[handwritten margin note: Inferred easement]

Because we hold that the trial court correctly found in favor of the state on the rights of the public in the dry-sand area, it follows that the state has an eq<mark>uitable right to protect the public in the enjoyment</mark> of those rights by causing <mark>the removal of fences and other obstacles</mark>. * * *

In order to explain our reasons for affirming the trial court's decree, it is necessary to set out in some detail the historical facts which lead to our conclusion.

The dry-sand area in Oregon has been enjoyed by the general public as a recreational adjunct of the wet-sand or foreshore area since the beginning of the state's political history. The first European settlers on these shores found the aboriginal inhabitants using the foreshore for clam-digging and the dry-sand area for their cooking fires. The newcomers continued these customs after statehood. Thus, from the time of the earliest settlement to the present day, <mark>the general public has assumed that the dry-sand area was a part of the public beach,</mark> and the public has used the dry-sand area for picnics, gathering wood, building warming fires, and generally as a headquarters from which to supervise children or to range out over the foreshore as the tides advance and recede. In the Cannon Beach vicinity, state and local officers have policed the dry sand, and municipal sanitary crews have attempted to keep the area reasonably free from man-made litter.

[handwritten margin note: historic practice of treating beach as public land]

Perhaps one explanation for the evolution of the custom of the public to use the dry-sand area for recreational purposes is that the area could not be used conveniently by its owners for any other purpose. The dry-sand area is unstable in its seaward boundaries, unsafe during winter storms, and for the most part unfit for the construction of permanent structures. While the vegetation line remains relatively fixed, the western edge of the dry-sand area is subject to dramatic moves eastward or westward in response to erosion and accretion. For example, evidence in the trial below indicated that between April 1966 and August 1967 the seaward edge of the dry-sand area involved in this litigation moved westward 180 feet. At other points along the shore, the evidence showed, the seaward edge of the dry-sand area could move an equal distance to the east in a similar period of time.

Until very recently, no question concerning the right of the public to enjoy the dry-sand area appears to have been brought before the courts of this state. The public's assumption that the dry sand as well as the foreshore was "public property" had been reinforced by early judicial decisions. See Shively v. Bowlby, 152 U.S. 1 (1894), which affirmed Bowlby v. Shively, 30 P. 154 (Or. 1892). These cases held that landowners claiming under federal patents owned seaward only to the "high-water" line, a line that was then assumed to be the vegetation line.

In 1935, the United States Supreme Court held that a federal patent conveyed title to land farther seaward, to the mean hightide line. Borax Consolidated, Ltd. v. Los Angeles, 296 U.S. 10 (1935). While this decision may have expanded seaward the record ownership of upland landowners, it was apparently little noticed by Oregonians. In any event, the Borax decision had no discernible effect on the actual practices of Oregon beachgoers and upland property owners.

[handwritten margin note: private property extended in theory but not in practice]

Recently, however, the scarcity of oceanfront building sites has attracted substantial private investments in resort facilities. Resort owners like these defendants now desire to reserve for their paying guests the recreational advantages that accrue to the dry-sand portions of their deeded property. Consequently, in 1967, public debate and political activity resulted in legislative attempts to resolve conflicts between public and private interests in the dry-sand area:

[handwritten margin note: but private business wants to enforce for their guests' benefit]

ORS 390.610

(1) The Legislative Assembly hereby declares it is the public policy of the State of Oregon to forever preserve and maintain the sovereignty of the state heretofore existing over the seashore and ocean beaches of the state from the Columbia River on the North to the Oregon-California line on the South so that the public may have the free and uninterrupted use thereof.

(2) The Legislative Assembly recognizes that over the years the public has made frequent and uninterrupted use of lands abutting, adjacent and contiguous to the public highways and state recreation areas and recognizes, further, that where

such use has been sufficient to create easements in the public through dedication, prescription, grant or otherwise, that it is in the public interest to protect and preserve such public easements as a permanent part of Oregon's recreational resources.

(3) Accordingly, the Legislative Assembly hereby declares that all public rights and easements in those lands described in subsection (2) of this section are confirmed and declared vested exclusively in the State of Oregon and shall be held and administered in the same manner as those lands described in ORS 390.720. * * *

The state concedes that such legislation cannot divest a person of his rights in land, Hughes v. Washington, 389 U.S. 290 (1967), and that the defendants' record title, which includes the dry-sand area, extends seaward to the ordinary or mean high-tide line. Borax Consolidated Ltd. v. Los Angeles, supra.

The landowners likewise concede that since 1899 the public's rights in the foreshore have been confirmed by law as well as by custom and usage. Oregon Laws 1899, p. 3, provided:

That the shore of the Pacific ocean, between ordinary high and extreme low tides, and from the Columbia river on the north to the south boundary line of Clatsop county on the south, is hereby declared a public highway, and shall forever remain open as such to the public.

The disputed area is *sui generis.* While the foreshore is "owned" by the state, and the upland is "owned" by the patentee or record-title holder, neither can be said to "own" the full bundle of rights normally connoted by the term "estate in fee simple." 1 Powell, Real Property § 163, at 661 (1949).

In addition to the *sui generis* nature of the land itself, a multitude of complex and sometimes overlapping precedents in the law confronted the trial court. Several early Oregon decisions generally support the trial court's decision, i.e., that the public can acquire easements in private land by long-continued user that is inconsistent with the owner's exclusive possession and enjoyment of his land. A citation of the cases could end the discussion at this point. But because the early cases do not agree on the legal theories by which the results are reached, and because this is an important case affecting valuable rights in land, it is appropriate to review some of the law applicable to this case.

One group of precedents relied upon in part by the state and by the trial court can be called the "implied-dedication" cases. The doctrine of implied dedication is well known to the law in this state and elsewhere. See cases collected in Parks, The Law of Dedication in Oregon, 20 Or. L. Rev. 111 (1941). Dedication, however, whether express or implied, rests upon an intent to dedicate. In the case at bar, it is unlikely that the landowners thought they had anything to dedicate, until 1967, when the notoriety of legislative debates about the public's rights in the dry-sand area sent a number of ocean-front landowners to the offices of their legal advisers.

A second group of cases relied upon by the state, but rejected by the trial court, deals with the possibility of a landowner's losing the exclusive possession and enjoyment of his land through the development of prescriptive easements in the public.

In Oregon, as in most common-law jurisdictions, an easement can be created in favor of one person in the land of another by uninterrupted use and enjoyment of the land in a particular manner for the statutory period, so long as the user is open, adverse, under claim of right, but without authority of law or consent of the owner. Feldman et ux. v. Knapp et ux., 250 P.2d 92 (Or. 1952); Coventon v. Seufert, 32 P. 508 (Or. 1893). In Oregon, the prescriptive period is ten years. ORS 12.050. The public use of the disputed land in the case at bar is admitted to be continuous for more than sixty years. There is no suggestion in the record that anyone's permission was sought or given; rather, the public used the land under a claim of right. Therefore, if the public can acquire an easement by prescription, the requirements for such an acquisition have been met in connection with the specific tract of land involved in this case.

The owners argue, however, that the general public, not being subject to actions in trespass and ejectment, cannot acquire rights by prescription, because the statute of limitations is irrelevant when an action does not lie.

While it may not be feasible for a landowner to sue the general public, it is nonetheless possible by means of signs and fences to prevent or minimize public invasions of private land for recreational purposes. In Oregon, moreover, the courts and the Legislative Assembly have both recognized that the public can acquire prescriptive easements in private land, at least for roads and highways. See, e.g., Huggett et ux. v. Moran et ux., 266 P.2d 692 (Or. 1954), in which we observed that counties could acquire public roads by prescription. And see ORS 368.405, which provides for the manner in which counties may establish roads. The statute enumerates the formal governmental actions that can be employed, and then concludes: "This section does not preclude acquiring public ways by adverse user."

Another statute codifies a policy favoring the acquisition by prescription of public recreational easements in beach lands. See ORS 390.610. While such a statute cannot create public rights at the expense of a private landowner the statute can, and does, express legislative approval of the common-law doctrine of prescription where the facts justify its application. Consequently, we conclude that the law in Oregon, regardless of the generalizations that may apply elsewhere, does not preclude the creation of prescriptive easements in beach land for public recreational use.

Because many elements of prescription are present in this case, the state has relied upon the doctrine in support of the decree below. We believe, however, that there is a better legal basis for affirming the decree. The most cogent basis for the decision in this case is the English doctrine of custom. Strictly construed, prescription applies only to the specific tract of land before the court, and doubtful prescription cases could fill the courts for years with tract-by-tract litigation. An established custom, on the other hand, can be proven with reference to a larger region. Ocean-front lands from the northern to the southern border of the state ought to be treated uniformly.

The other reason which commends the doctrine of custom over that of prescription as the principal basis for the decision in this case is the unique nature of the lands in question. This case deals solely with the dry-sand area along the Pacific shore, and this land has been used by the public as public recreational land according to an unbroken custom running back in time as long as the land has been inhabited.

A custom is defined in 1 Bouv. Law Dict., Rawle's Third Revision, p. 742 as "such a usage as by common consent and uniform practice has become the law of the place, or of the subject matter to which it relates."

In 1 Blackstone, Commentaries *75–*78, Sir William Blackstone set out the requisites of a particular custom.

Paraphrasing Blackstone, the first requirement of a custom, to be recognized as law, is that it must be ancient. It must have been used so long "that the memory of man runneth not to the contrary." Professor Cooley footnotes his edition of Blackstone with the comment that "long and general" usage is sufficient. In any event, the record in the case at bar satisfies the requirement of antiquity. So long as there has been an institutionalized system of land tenure in Oregon, the public has freely exercised the right to use the dry-sand area up and down the Oregon coast for the recreational purposes noted earlier in this opinion.

The second requirement is that the right be exercised without interruption. A customary right need not be exercised continuously, but it must be exercised without an interruption caused by anyone possessing a paramount right. In the case at bar, there was evidence that the public's use and enjoyment of the dry-sand area had never been interrupted by private landowners.

Blackstone's third requirement, that the customary use be peaceable and free from dispute, is satisfied by the evidence which related to the second requirement.

The fourth requirement, that of reasonableness, is satisfied by the evidence that the public has always made use of the land in a manner appropriate to the land and to the usages of the community. There is evidence in the record that when inappropriate uses have been detected, municipal police officers have intervened to preserve order.

The fifth requirement, certainty, is satisfied by the visible boundaries of the dry-sand area and by the character of the land, which limits the use thereof to recreational uses connected with the foreshore.

The sixth requirement is that a custom must be obligatory; that is, in the case at bar, not left to the option of each landowner whether or not he will recognize the public's right to go upon the dry-sand area for recreational purposes. The record shows that the dry-sand area in question has been used, as of right, uniformly with similarly situated lands elsewhere, and that the public's use has never been questioned by an upland owner so long as the public remained on the dry sand and refrained from trespassing upon the lands above the vegetation line.

Finally, a custom must not be repugnant, or inconsistent, with other customs or with other law. The custom under consideration violates no law, and is not repugnant.

Two arguments have been arrayed against the doctrine of custom as a basis for decision in Oregon. The first argument is that custom is unprecedented in this state, and has only scant adherence elsewhere in the United States. The second argument is that because of the relative brevity of our political history it is inappropriate to rely upon an English doctrine that requires greater antiquity than a newly-settled land can muster. Neither of these arguments is persuasive.

The custom of the people of Oregon to use the dry-sand area of the beaches for public recreational purposes meets every one of Blackstone's requisites. While it is not necessary to rely upon precedent from other states, we are not the first state to recognize custom as a source of law. See Perley et ux'r v. Langley, 7 N.H. 233 (1834).

On the score of the brevity of our political history, it is true that the Anglo-American legal system on this continent is relatively new. Its newness has made it possible for government to provide for many of our institutions by written law rather than by customary law.[6] This truism does not, however, militate against the validity of a custom when the custom does in fact exist. If antiquity were the sole test of validity of a custom, Oregonians could satisfy that requirement by recalling that the European settlers were not the first people to use the dry-sand area as public land.

---

[6]   The English law on customary rights grew up in a small island nation at a time when most inhabitants lived and died without traveling more than a day's walk from their birthplace. Most of the customary rights recorded in English cases are local in scope. The English had many cultural and language groups which eventually merged into a nation. After these groups developed their own unique customs, the unified nation recognized some of them as law. Some American scholars, looking at the vast geography of this continent and the freshness of its civilization, have concluded that there is no need to look to English customary rights as a source of legal rights in this country. See, e.g., 6 Powell, Real Property § 934, note 5, at 362 (1949). Some of the generalizations drawn by the text writers from English cases would tend to limit customary rights to specific usages in English towns and villages. See Gray, The Rule Against Perpetuities §§ 572–588 (1942). But it does not follow that a custom, established in fact, cannot have regional application and be enjoyed by a larger public than the inhabitants of a single village.

Finally, in support of custom, the record shows that the custom of the inhabitants of Oregon and of visitors in the state to use the dry sand as a public recreation area is so notorious that notice of the custom on the part of persons buying land along the shore must be presumed. In the case at bar, the landowners conceded their actual knowledge of the public's long-standing use of the dry-sand area, and argued that the elements of consent present in the relationship between the landowners and the public precluded the application of the law of prescription. As noted, we are not resting this decision on prescription, and we leave open the effect upon prescription of the type of consent that may have been present in this case. Such elements of consent are, however, wholly consistent with the recognition of public rights derived from custom.

suff. presumed (and actual) notice of custom by prop. owners

Because so much of our law is the product of legislation, we sometimes lose sight of the importance of custom as a source of law in our society. It seems particularly appropriate in the case at bar to look to an ancient and accepted custom in this state as the source of a rule of law. The rule in this case, based upon custom, is salutary in confirming a public right, and at the same time it takes from no man anything which he has had a legitimate reason to regard as exclusively his.

For the foregoing reasons, the decree of the trial court is affirmed.

NOTES AND QUESTIONS

1.   The Oregon Supreme Court's invocation of customary rights to resolve the beach access controversy came as quite a surprise. The case had been tried in the lower courts on a public easement theory, not a theory of customary rights. There was no prior invocation of customary rights in Oregon case law, and no one urged the Oregon court to apply the doctrine of customary rights. Note too that the 1967 amendment to the Oregon Beach Bill, quoted by the court, makes no mention of customary rights (it affirms that "easements in the public" have been created "through dedication, prescription, grant or otherwise"). Is the question of customary rights primarily one of fact? Should the court have remanded for a new trial, rather than deciding for itself that the record supported the conclusion that a customary right had been established? In a later decision, *McDonald v. Halvorson*, 780 P.2d 714 (Or. 1989), the Oregon court held that customary rights did not attach to a beach on an inland fresh water cove, because there was no actual proof of customary public use. Does *McDonald's* acknowledgment that the question is one of fact undercut *Thornton's* assertion that customary rights exist along the ocean front all the way from the northern to the southern border of the state?

2.   Ownership of land in Oregon, like that of most other states west of the original thirteen, derives from patents or grants from the federal government. As the court notes in passing, the Supreme Court held in 1935 that federal patents naming the Pacific Ocean as their boundary should be construed as extending to the mean high tide line—that is, as including the dry sand area. Borax Consolidated, Ltd. v. Los Angeles, 296 U.S. 10 (1935). Why weren't property owners in Oregon whose land borders on the Pacific

Ocean entitled to rely on this decision as an authoritative expression of the extent of their property rights? Is it enough to say that the decision "was apparently little noticed by Oregonians" and "had no discernible effect on the actual practices of Oregon beachgoers and upland property owners?"

3.   The court makes much of the fact that most upland property owners do not object when beachgoers use the dry sand area for picnics or supervising children at play. But why isn't this just neighborly behavior? Wouldn't it be reasonable for an upland owner to tacitly consent to such innocuous use, while reserving the right to evict the occasional raucous beer bash?

4.   Beaches are today without doubt the most contested ground for claims that property is inherently public and cannot be subject to private exclusion rights. The issue has been fought out state by state, and sometimes beach by beach. A number of states have used the public trust doctrine to hold that all or part of the dry sand beach is inherently public property. See, e.g., Glass v. Goeckel, 703 N.W.2d 58, 62 (Mich. 2005) (Michigan public trust doctrine protects public right of access to beaches up to the ordinary high water mark); Matthews v. Bay Head Improvement Ass'n, 471 A.2d 355, 363 (N.J. 1984) (New Jersey public trust doctrine protects public access to dry sand areas of a beach controlled by a homeowners' association). Florida, Texas, and Hawaii have joined Oregon in dusting off versions of the customary rights doctrine to declare public rights of access to dry sand beaches. Still others have rejected entreaties to declare beaches public property on any theory. See, e.g., State ex rel. Haman v. Fox, 594 P.2d 1093 (Idaho 1979). Given the plethora of theories and outcomes, it is difficult to say with much confidence in many states exactly what rights the public has to beaches. See, e.g., Sean D. Hamill, No Line in the Sand on Beach Rights: Confusion Reigns in State on Public Access to Shore, Chi. Trib., Aug. 9, 2005, Metro at 1 (surveying various experts and getting conflicting opinions as to the extent of public access to beaches in Illinois).

5.   Notwithstanding the confusion, the overall trend seems to be toward greater public rights or open access to beaches. How, if at all, would Demsetz explain the apparent evolution away from exclusion rights and private property in beaches toward a regime that is more like an open-access commons?

6.   One difference between customary rights and other theories for protecting public rights in beaches and other analogous resources concerns the ability of the legislature to revise the decision. The public trust doctrine may or may not be subject to legislative revision. It depends on how one conceives of the legal source of the doctrine (federal versus state law, constitutional law versus common law), and whether the doctrine is viewed as a rule of construction or a fixed qualification on title. In some states, like Illinois, the public trust doctrine is viewed as a fixed qualification on title and so cannot be revised by the legislature. The doctrine of public prescription probably is subject to legislative revision, although since prescriptive easements are property rights (see Chapter IX), the government might have to condemn these rights and pay just compensation in order to eliminate them. (If the prescriptive easement belongs to the public, who

would receive the compensation?) The doctrine of customary rights is clearly subject to legislative revision. Moreover, since it is unclear that a customary right is a property right, it is at least arguable that the government would not have to pay just compensation to anyone in abrogating customary rights. Customary rights thus are the easiest for the legislature to modify. Do you think this attribute of customary rights provides an additional reason to favor the approach of the Oregon Supreme Court, or does it count against the court's approach?

7.   Did the Oregon Supreme Court, by eliminating the right of private property owners to exclude the public from the dry sand beach, commit a "judicial taking"? In *Stevens v. City of Cannon Beach*, 854 P.2d 449 (Or. 1993), the Oregon court observed that there was no taking in *Thornton* because property owners were on notice when they acquired their land that the public routinely used the dry sand beach for recreational purposes. The U.S. Supreme Court recently rejected a similar claim in *Stop the Beach Renourishment, Inc. v. Florida Department of Environmental Protection*, 560 U.S. 702 (2010) (excerpted in Chapter X, Part D). Two local governments in Florida repaired a storm-damaged beach in such a way as to insert a new public beach between property line of upland owners and the water. The owners claimed this had the effect of taking their right to future accretions (see Chapter II) and their right to have their property touch the water. The Florida Supreme Court rejected the claim, concluding that these rights did not exist under Florida law. The owners then went to the U.S. Supreme Court, arguing that the Florida court had committed a judicial taking. The Court rejected the claim, concluding that the Florida court was right in finding that the claimed rights did not exist. But the Court split 4–4 on the question whether there is such a thing as a judicial taking (only eight Justices participated in the decision). Justice Scalia, writing for four Justices, said it makes no sense to say that the judiciary can accomplish by revisions in property law what would be a taking if attempted directly by the legislative or executive branches. Four other Justices said that the matter was complex and raised a host of practical problems, making it premature to pronounce on the issue.

Carol Rose, *The Comedy of the Commons: Custom, Commerce, and Inherently Public Property*

53 U. CHI. L. REV. 711, 713–21, 749–54, 757–58, 779–81 (1986).

[D]espite the power of the classical economic argument for private property, a curious cross-current has continually washed through American law. Our legal doctrine has strongly suggested that some kinds of property should not be held exclusively in private hands, but should be open to the public or at least subject to what Roman law called the "jus publicum": the "public right."

Moreover, this view is not merely a vestige of premodern thought; there is currently an extensive academic and judicial discussion of the possibility that certain kinds of property ought to be public. In recent years, the most striking version of this "inherent publicness" argument has appeared in a series of cases expanding public access to waterfront property. The land between the low and high tides has traditionally been considered "public property," or at least subject to a public easement for navigational and fishing purposes. But some modern courts have stretched this easement to include a new use—recreation—and have expanded its area from the tidelands to the dry sand areas landward of the high-tide mark.

These new cases extrapolate from older precedents in which the public acquired—or allegedly reasserted—claims to certain types of property, most notably roadways and lands under navigable waters. Like the older precedents, the new beach cases usually employ one of three theoretical bases: (1) a "public trust" theory, to the effect that the public has always rights of access to the property in question, and that any private rights are subordinate to the public's "trust" rights; (2) a prescriptive or dedicatory theory, by which a period of public usage gives rise to an implied grant or gift from private owners; and (3) a theory of "custom," where the public asserts ownership of property under some claim so ancient that it antedates any memory to the contrary.

These theories of increased public access to shores and waterways have garnered a vocal but decidedly mixed reaction. In discussing these theories, some commentators applaud what they regard as a proper recognition of public needs. The public trust idea in particular has spawned an enormous number of cases and articles, some urging extension of a public trust to a much wider range of property where public access or control should be vindicated. But there have also been several very sharp critiques of these cases and articles, and of the expansive doctrines of public control they propound. Some critics deny the underlying public trust and dedicatory theories, and deplore what they see as an unjust and disruptive destruction of private property rights. They argue that if the public wants or needs these waterfront lands so much, it should have to purchase them from the private owners. Moreover, they warn of the consequences of these uncompensated and unpredictable transfers of property rights: frustrated private owners may overreact in trying to protect their property from any implication of "dedication" by installing guard dogs or blowing up access paths to the beach.

More generally, these critics reiterate the basic arguments in favor of private ownership: uncertainty about property rights invites conflicts and squanders resources. The public access cases turn the waterfront into a "commons," where no one has any incentive to purchase the property, invest in it, or care for it, but only to consume as much as possible—all of which leads to deterioration and waste. * * *

Perhaps these doctrines are indeed easily explicable through classical economic thought, and can be subsumed under the well-recognized exceptions to the general principle favoring private and exclusive property rights: "plenteous" goods and "public goods." The first

[handwritten margin note: typical tragedy of commons arg:]

class of exception concerns things that are either so plentiful or so unbounded that it is not worth the effort to create a system of resource management for them, or—stated differently—things for which the difficulty of privatization outweighs the gains in careful resource management. Thus the oceans and air (it used to be said) are at once so plentiful and so difficult to reduce to property that they are left open to the public at large.

The "plenitude" or "boundlessness" exceptions, however, fail to explain the "publicness" of those properties that our traditional doctrines most strongly deemed public property. Roadways, waterways, and submerged lands—not to speak of open squares, which have also sometimes been presumed public—are hardly so copious or so unbounded that they are incapable of privatization. Riverbeds and shorelands can be staked out, roadways can be obstructed, waterways diverted, squares plowed up; in short, they can easily be "reduced to possession" in the classic common law manner of creating proprietary rights out of a "commons." Thus the "public" character of such lands, or even a public easement over them, must have some basis other than our incapacity to reduce them to private possession.

The second exception to the general rule favoring private property may be of more assistance. Since the mid-nineteenth century, economists have told us that there exist predictable instances of "market failure," where Adam Smith's invisible hand fails to guide privately owned resources to their socially optimal uses. These involve "public goods," "natural monopolies," "externalities," and the like. While some of these problems may be solved by collective agreements among the owners of the resources, such agreements are costly and, particularly where a large number of parties must be involved, private collective action is not always possible. Inefficiencies will remain.

Thus a governmental body might be the most useful manager where many persons desire access to or control over a given property, but they are too numerous and their individual stakes too small to express their preferences in market transactions; governmental ownership could broker those preferences. Similarly, a government might be a superior manager (or regulator) of a property whose use involves economies of scale—the railways, bridges, or grain elevators whose monopoly position classically justified governmental ownership or control. Or a government might be a superior manager of those "collective goods" like the broadcast spectrum, wherein some management structure is required to make individual users take account of other users' interests. In a sense, we rely on governmental management of our preeminent system of resource management—private property—and we might view the entire private property regime as a "public property" owned and managed by governmental bodies.

Conventional wisdom instructs that in such cases, the most productive solution would be for government to assume some or all of the rights of ownership and control over the property, and to use its powers to correct the market's misallocation. This conventional conclusion is subject to four conventional caveats: the state must be able correctly to identify instances of market failure; it must be clever enough to exercise its powers so as to reduce the inefficiency; it must avoid errors or political temptations to exercise its powers in ways that create new inefficiencies; and the costs of effective state intervention must not exceed the increase in production it brings about.

 This standard paradigm of neoclassical economics and modern microeconomic theory recognizes only two property regimes: either ownership is vested in private parties or it resides with an organized state. The usual economic approach to property law suggests that productive efficiency will be enhanced when private property is the norm, but government intervenes in recognized instances of market failure.

Thus in the conventional lore, markets are based on private rights or, when markets fail, property may be governmentally managed in the interests of aggregate efficiency. Yet these two options do not logically exhaust all the possible solutions. Neither can they adequately describe all that one finds in the recorded history of property in the Anglo-American universe. In particular, there lies outside purely private property and government-controlled "public property" a distinct class of "inherently public property" which is fully controlled by neither government nor private agents. Since the Middle Ages this category of "inherently public property" has provided each member of some "public" with a bundle of rights, neither entirely alienable by state or other collective action, nor necessarily "managed" in any explicitly organized manner. Aside from individual private property, the nineteenth-century common law of property in both Britain and America, with surprising consistency, recognized two distinguishable types of public property. One of these was property "owned" and actively managed by a governmental body. The other, however, was property collectively "owned" and "managed" by society at large, with claims independent of and indeed superior to the claims of any purported governmental manager. It is this latter type that I call "inherently public property."

Implicit in these older doctrines is the notion that, even if a property should be open to the public, it does not follow that public rights should necessarily vest in an active governmental manager. Despite the well-known problems of unorganized collective access to a resource—the "tragedy of the commons"—equally difficult problems are posed by governmental management: the cost of instituting that management and, perhaps, the temptations of politically motivated redistribution. In some circumstances, then, nineteenth-century common law recognized collective public rights as the optimal alternative whether or not those rights were managed governmentally. * * *

What was so bad about private ownership of "inherently public properties"? * * *

One controversy of particular importance for nineteenth-century roadway prescription concerned the location of purported roads. * * *

As a general rule * * * the exception for roadways applied only to specific passageways, not to open spaces. This exception prevented private holdout against public passage; but it only came into play upon a genuine threat of such behavior. Public meanderings anywhere across an open field suggested that the public had no focused need for a particular path and private owners felt no pronounced temptation for exploitation; therefore such meanderings would not raise a presumption of "dedication."

This anti-holdout rationale is strengthened by its similarity to other nineteenth-century American roadway doctrines. Roadways were the classic subject of eminent domain by the "organized" public. Prescriptive doctrines, by analogy to private law doctrines, assured that the "unorganized" public—which could not exercise eminent domain—was also protected from private holdout. A private party could sometimes own a toll road, but his potential power to capture all "rents" of travel was tempered by treatment as a public utility: the road was open to all members of the public, and the owner could charge tolls reflecting not what the market would bear, but only what would suffice to reimburse his expenses. * * *

Like roadway doctrine, waterway doctrine also reflected an antipathy to the possibility of private monopolization of public passage. This was hardly surprising; it was a commonplace of nineteenth-century jurisprudence that waterways were a "highway" for travel and commerce. Moreover, their location was largely fixed by nature, so that their use was even more subject to holdout than roadways, which are movable. Thus holdout potential explains several cases elevating the public right of water passage above all other uses, even bridges for land roads unless specifically authorized by legislatures. Land traffic might find some other route, whereas ships had no alternative and were especially susceptible to exploitation. * * *

Th[e] rejection of recreation as a public trust purpose, taken together with strong protection of commercial travel on waterways, suggests that the fear of private holdout was central to early nineteenth-century thinking about public access to waterways. * * * The uses of waterways most subject to monopolization or holdout were transportation and commerce, which involved movement from place to place over a relatively narrow "path." As one British court stated, the beach is "not to be regarded as in the full sense of the word a highway," open to recreational uses: no matter how ungenerous the act, beach owners were entitled to treat as trespassers "every bather, every nursemaid with a perambulator, every boy riding a donkey, and every preacher on the shore."[229]

Thus, it is difficult to fit into a "holdout" rationale such public trust uses as swimming, fishing, and hunting. Recreational uses might occur in numerous places, without requiring any great stretch of waterway; moreover, in any normal market, a variety of riparian owners might compete to provide swimming or other recreational facilities. This presents [a] problem * * *: why should we guarantee public access for recreational purposes when there seems to be no threat of private holdout?

[Professor Rose then argues that in addition to holdout prevention, a second rationale supports the publicness of certain spaces, namely increasing returns to scale of the activities practiced there. She notes that the traditional public trust doctrines for roads and waterways overwhelmingly focused on encouraging commerce, and that commerce itself has increasing returns as markets expand; those reasons would support doctrines of open lanes to encourage ever more members of the public to participate. She then returns to the subject of recreation.] * * *

Certainly the role of recreation is a striking example of historic change in public property doctrine. If recreation now seems to support the "publicness" of some property, this undoubtedly reflects a change in our attitudes toward recreation. We might suspect that this changed attitude relates to an increasing perception of recreation as having something analogous to scale returns, and as a socializing institution.

Recreation is often carried on in a social setting, and therefore it clearly improves with scale to some degree: one must have a partner for chess, two teams for baseball, etc. But in the mid-nineteenth century, Frederick Law Olmsted argued that recreation had scale returns in a much more expansive sense: recreation can be a socializing and educative influence, particularly helpful for democratic values.[320] Thus rich and poor would mingle in parks, and learn to treat each other as neighbors. Parks would enhance public mental health, with ultimate benefits to sociability; all could revive from the antisocial characteristics of urban life under the refining influence of the park's soothing landscape. Later recreation and park advocates, though moving away from Olmsted's more contemplative ethic, also stressed the democratic education that comes with sports and team play.

Insofar as recreation educates and socializes us, it acts as a "social glue" for everyone, not just those immediately engaged; and of course, the more people involved in any socializing activity, the better. Like commerce, then, recreation has social and political overtones. The contemplation of nature elevates our minds above the workaday world,

---

[229] Llandudno Urban Dist. Council v. Woods, 2 Ch. 705, 709, [1899] All E.R. 895, 896, 81 L.T.R. 170, 171 (1899).

[320] Frederick Law Olmsted, Civilizing American Cities: A Selection of Frederick Law Olmsted's Writings on City Landscapes 74–81 (S. Sutton ed. 1971).

and thus helps us to cope with that very world; recreational play trains us in the democratic give-and-take that makes our regime function. If these arguments are true, we should not worry that people engage in too much recreation, but too little. This again argues that recreation should be open to all at minimal costs, or at costs to be borne by the general public, since all of us benefit from the greater sociability of our fellow citizens. If we accept these arguments, we might believe that unique recreational sites ought not be private property; their greatest value lies in civilizing and socializing all members of the public, and this value should not be "held up" by private owners.

These arguments support the recent decisions defending public access to the beach. The public's recreational use arguably is the most valuable use of this property and requires an entire expanse of beach (for unobstructed walking, viewing, contemplation) which could otherwise be blocked and "held up" by private owners. But * * * [d]o people using the beach really become more civil, or acquire the mental habits of democracy? And even if they do, is there really a danger of holdout that necessitates inalienable public access?

Attractive as this Olmstedian view may seem, these are not always easy arguments to support, and are extraordinarily difficult to prove. The argument that recreation or the contemplation of nature makes us more civilized and sociable has a very long pedigree in Western thought. Moreover, it may seem particularly attractive as our confidence has waned (perhaps somewhat unjustifiably) in the socializing qualities of commerce. With respect to the holdout problem, one might be skeptical and think that where waterfront owners are numerous, they cannot really siphon off the value of expansive public uses. But whether or not one accepts these arguments in the modern beach debate, older doctrine suggests that the "scale returns" of socialization, taken together with the possibility of private holdout, will underlie any arguments for the inherent publicness of property.

Perhaps the chief lesson from the nineteenth-century doctrines of "inherently public property," then, is that while we may change our minds about which activities are socializing, we always accept that the public requires access to some physical locations for some of these activities. Our law consistently allocates that access to the public, because public access to those locations is as important as the general privatization of property in other spheres of our law. In the absence of the socializing activities that take place on "inherently public property," the public is a shapeless mob, whose members neither trade nor converse nor play, but only fight, in a setting where life is, in Hobbes' all too famous phrase, solitary, poor, nasty, brutish, and short.

NOTES AND QUESTIONS

1. Do you agree with Rose that the movement toward making beaches an open access resource can be explained (or at least justified) on the ground

that this promotes social contact among a large number of persons of mixed backgrounds? What about persons who simply want to take solitary walks on the beach, or quietly contemplate a sunset? If socialization is the objective, wouldn't small crowded beaches be better than long, unobstructed beaches?

2.   Considering the material covered in this section—including that on navigable waters, navigable airspace, the public trust doctrine, customary rights, and the doctrine of public prescriptive rights mentioned in *Thornton* and in the Rose excerpt—do you agree with Rose that there are three categories of property—private, governmental, and inherently public—or just two categories—private and governmental?

3.   One operational distinction between governmental property and inherently public property might be based on who has standing to enforce the property right. Governmental property would be property that can be enforced only by duly appointed officers of the state—such as the state Attorney General's office or the U.S. Department of Justice. Inherently public property would be property that any member of the public can seek to enforce. In this regard, it is interesting to note that many states, including Illinois, have moved toward recognizing very broad "citizen standing" to enforce the public trust doctrine. Illinois traditionally followed the rule that only officers of the state could enforce the trust. See, e.g., People ex rel. Attorney General v. Kirk, 45 N.E. 830 (Ill. 1896). More recently, it overruled this understanding and held that any taxpayer can sue to enforce the trust. See Paepcke v. Public Building Commission of Chicago, 263 N.E.2d 11 (Ill. 1970); see also Friends of the Parks v. Chicago Park District, 786 N.E.2d 161, 169–70 (Ill. 2003) (not questioning private parties' right to enforce the trust).

4.   Another possible category is what has been called "antiproperty," which is in effect a private right to veto nonpublic uses of public property. The public dedication doctrine, mentioned by Rose, is effectively a form of antiproperty, because it allows private property owners who are uniquely affected by a dedication of public property—such as those who own property abutting a street or a park—to sue in equity to enforce the public dedication. Such antiproperty rights can be quite powerful in preserving public spaces, since in effect the government must obtain unanimous consent from abutting owners to eliminate a public use. See Joseph D. Kearney & Thomas W. Merrill, Private Rights in Public Lands: The Chicago Lakefront, Montgomery Ward, and the Public Dedication Doctrine, 105 Nw. U. L. Rev. 1417 (2011); Abraham Bell & Gideon Parchomovsky, Of Property and Antiproperty, 102 Mich. L. Rev. 1 (2003).

5.   If we decide that certain types of resources, like beaches, are "inherently public," and if we confer standing on any member of the public to block privatization or perhaps even development of these resources, does this create a danger of a regulatory "anticommons"? See Chapter II. In other words, do we create too much exclusion? Does "antiproperty," such as the veto rights in abutting private owners recognized by the public dedication doctrine, succumb to the same problem, or does the limited number of private enforcers mitigate this concern, at least to a degree?

E. WATER

Water is a particularly important resource with a wide variety of uses, including drinking and household consumption, farming, raising livestock, irrigation, mining, power, manufacturing, sewage, navigation, wildlife, and recreation. Water can also serve aesthetic and environmental values. These last include what are sometimes called "ecosystem services." Given a growing population with rising demand for water consumption, and the simultaneous rise in demand for the preservation of lakes and streams for recreational and ecological purposes, clashes over water rights will likely intensify in the coming years.

Water is a unique resource different in many respects from land and the typical objects of personal property rights. Water is a fugitive resource with a flow that is only partly predictable. It is also a renewable resource, as a result of the hydrologic cycle. Given its peculiar characteristics, water has always been treated differently from other kinds of resources. Water rights have aspects of both private rights and public rights; they are at once open to individual appropriation and subject to correlative duties to other users. Given the uniqueness of water rights, arguments for greater privatization of water—such as by making water rights freely transferable like other commodities—have long been, and continue to be, controversial.

In the United States, water law consists of a common-law base with statutory and regulatory overlays, at the state and federal levels. In these materials we will concentrate on the common law of water and how it relates to property law's treatment of other resources.

First, some terminology. The law distinguishes water along two axes: *surface* versus *underground*, and *diffuse* versus *in a defined channel (or body)*. We turn first to water in a surface stream, with a look at two different systems, riparian rights and prior appropriation. Diffuse surface water is very different—it is considered undesirable and something to be warded off rather than "used." Next we take a look at groundwater, for which the distinction between diffuse and running in a defined channel has often been important, but also criticized.

1. WATERCOURSES

A riparian owner is one whose land abuts the watercourse, and riparian water rights are appurtenant to the land—the rights to the land and the right to use the water from the surface stream form a package that cannot be split up. (The "littoral" rights of owners whose land abuts a lake, sea, or ocean are similar to riparian rights.) English law developed a conception of riparian rights known as the natural flow theory, whereby each riparian owner could prevent any diversion of the natural flow of a river or stream by an upstream riparian owner. In effect, any disturbance of the natural flow required the consent of each downstream owner. This conception of riparian rights found little favor in the United States, on the grounds that it imposed too great a barrier to the use of water for economic development, such as diverting streams to power water mills. Early on, American courts began to reject the natural flow theory in favor of a more flexible conception of riparian rights that came to be known as the reasonable use theory. The next case is illustrative of the circumstances that gave rise to this American version of riparian rights doctrine.

Evans v. Merriweather

Supreme Court of Illinois, 1842.
4 Ill. 492, 38 Am. Dec. 106.

■ LOCKWOOD, JUSTICE, delivered the opinion of the court: This was an action on the *case*, brought in the Greene Circuit Court, by Merriweather against Evans, for obstructing and diverting a water course. The plaintiff obtained a verdict, and judgment was rendered thereon. On the trial the defendant excepted to the instructions asked for and given, at the instance of the plaintiff. The defendant also excepted, because instructions that were asked by him, were refused. After the cause was brought into this court, the parties agreed upon the following statement of facts, as having been proved on the trial, to wit:

* * * Smith and Baker, in 1834, bought of T. Carlin six acres of land, through which a branch ran, and erected a steam mill thereon. They depended upon a well and the branch for water in running their engine. About one or two years afterwards, John Evans bought of T. Carlin six acres of land, on the same branch, above and immediately adjoining the lot owned by Smith & Baker, and erected theron a steam mill, depending upon a well and the branch for water in running his engine.

Smith & Baker, after the erection of Evans' mill, in 1836 or 1837, sold the mill and appurtenances to Merriweather, for about $8,000. Evans' mill was supposed to be worth $12,000. Ordinarily there was an abundance of water for both mills; but in the fall of 1837, there being a drought, the branch failed, so far that it did not afford water sufficient to run the upper mill continually. Evans directed his hands not to stop, or divert the water, in the branch; but one of them employed about the mill did make a dam across the branch, just below Evans' mill, and thereby diverted all the water in the branch into Evans' well. Evans was at home, half a mile from the mill, and was frequently about his mill, and evidence was introduced conducing to prove that he might have known that the water of the branch was diverted into his well. After the diversion of the water into Evans' well, as aforesaid, the branch went dry below, and Merriweather's mill could not and did not run, in consequence of it, more than one day in a week, and was then supplied with water from his well. Merriweather then brought this suit, in three or four weeks after the putting of the dam across the branch for the diversion of the water, and obtained a verdict for $150. This suit, it is admitted, is the first between the parties litigating the right as to the use of the water. It is further agreed, that the branch afforded usually sufficient water for the supply of both mills, without materially affecting the size of the current, though the branch was not depended upon exclusively for that purpose. Furthermore, that at the time of the grievances complained of by the plaintiff below, the defendant had water hauled in part for the supply of his boilers. That the dam was made below the defendant's well, across the branch, which diverted as well the water hauled and poured out into the branch above the well, as the water of the branch, into the defendant's well. . . .

Upon this state of facts, the question is presented, as to what extent riparian proprietors, upon a stream not navigable, can use the water of such stream? The branch mentioned in the agreed statement of facts, is a small natural stream of water, not furnishing, at all seasons of the year, a supply of water sufficient for both mills. There are no facts in the case showing that the water is wanted for any other than milling purposes, and for those purposes to be converted into steam, and thus entirely consumed. In an early case decided in England,[1] it is laid down that "A water course begins 'ex jure naturae,' and having taken a certain course naturally, can not be diverted." The language of all the authorities is, that water flows in its natural course, and should be permitted thus to flow, so that all through whose land it naturally flows, may enjoy the privilege of using it. The property in the water, therefore, by virtue of the riparian ownership, is in its nature usufructuary, and consists, in general, not so much of the fluid itself, as of the advantage of its impetus.[2] A riparian proprietor, therefore, though he has an undoubted right to use the water for hydraulic or manufacturing purposes, must so use it as to do no injury to any other riparian proprietor. Some decisions, in laying down the rights of riparian proprietors of water courses, have gone so far as to restrict their right in the use of water flowing over their land, so that there shall be no diminution in the quantity of the water, and no obstruction to its course. The decisions last referred to cannot, however, be considered as furnishing the true doctrine on this subject. Mr. Justice Storey, in delivering the opinion of the court, in the case of Tyler v. Wilkinson,[3] says,

I do not mean to be understood as holding the doctrine that there can be no diminution whatever, and no obstruction or

---

[1]   [Shury v. Piggot, 3 Bulstrode 339, 81 Eng. Rep. 280 (K.B. 1625)].

[2]   [Williams v. Morland, 2 Barn. & Cres. 910, 107 Eng. Rep. 620 (K.B. 1824)]; Angell on Water Courses, 11.

[3]   4 Mason 397, 400, 24 F. Cas. 472, 474 (C.C.D.R.I. 1827).

impediment whatever, by a riparian proprietor in the use of water as it flows; for that would be to deny any valuable use of it. There may be, and there must be, of that which is common to all, a reasonable use. The true test of the principle and extent of the use is, whether it is to the injury of the other proprietors or not. There may be diminution in quantity, or a retardation or acceleration of the natural current, indispensable for the general and valuable use of the water, perfectly consistent with the use of the common right. The diminution, retardation, or acceleration, not positively and sensibly injurious, by diminishing the value of the common right, is an implied element in the right of using the stream at all. The law here, as in many other cases, acts with a reasonable reference to public convenience and general good, and is not betrayed into a narrow strictness, subversive of common use, nor into an extravagant looseness, which would destroy private rights.

The same learned judge further says, "That of a thing common by nature, there may be an appropriation by general consent or grant. Mere priority of appropriation of running water, without such consent or grant, confers no exclusive right." * * *

Each riparian proprietor is bound to make such a use of running water as to do as little injury to those below him as is consistent with a valuable benefit to himself. The use must be a reasonable one. Now the question fairly arises, is that a reasonable use of running water by the upper proprietor, by which the fluid itself is entirely consumed? To answer this question satisfactorily, it is proper to consider the wants of man in regard to the element of water. These wants are either natural or artificial. Natural are such as are absolutely necessary * * * to his existence. Artificial, such only as, by supplying them, his comfort and prosperity are increased. To quench thirst, and for household purposes, water is absolutely indispensable. In civilized life, water for cattle is also necessary. These wants must be supplied, or both man and beast will perish.

The supply of man's artificial wants is not essential to his existence; it is not indispensable; he could live if water was not employed in irrigating lands, or in propelling his machinery. In countries differently situated from ours, with a hot and arid climate, water doubtless is absolutely indispensable to the cultivation of the soil, and in them, water for irrigation would be a natural want. Here it might increase the products of the soil, but it is by no means essential, and cannot, therefore, be considered a natural want of man. So of manufactures, they promote the prosperity and comfort of mankind, but cannot be considered absolutely necessary to his existence; nor need the machinery which he employs be set in motion by steam.

From these premises would result this conclusion: that an individual owning a spring on his land, from which water flows in a current through his neighbor's land, would have the right to use the whole of it, if necessary to satisfy his natural wants. He may consume all the water for his domestic purposes, including water for his stock. If he desires to use it for irrigation or manufactures, and there be a lower proprietor to whom its use is essential to supply his natural wants, or for his stock, he must use the water so as to leave enough for such lower proprietor. Where the stream is small, and does not supply water more than sufficient to answer the natural wants of the different proprietors living on it, none of the proprietors can use the water for either irrigation or manufactures. So far, then, as natural wants are concerned, there is no difficulty in furnishing a rule by which riparian proprietors may use flowing water to supply such natural wants. Each proprietor in his turn may, if necessary, consume all the water for these purposes. But where the water is not wanted to supply natural wants and there is not sufficient for each proprietor living on the stream, to carry on his manufacturing purposes, how shall the water be divided? We have seen that, without a contract or grant, neither has a right to use all the water; all have a right to participate in its benefits. Where all have a right to participate in a common benefit, and none can have an exclusive enjoyment, no rule, from the very nature of the case, can be laid down, as to how much each may use without infringing upon the rights of others. In such cases, the question must be left to the judgment of the jury, whether the party complained of has used, under all the circumstances, more than his just proportion.

It appears, from the facts agreed on, that Evans obstructed the water by a dam, and diverted the whole into his well. This diversion, according to all the cases, both English and American, was clearly illegal. For this diversion, an action will lie. * * * Having availed himself of the illegal act of his servant, the law presumes he authorized it. Having arrived at the conclusion that an action will lie in behalf of Merriweather against Evans, for obstructing and diverting the water course mentioned in the plaintiff's declaration, I have not deemed it necessary to examine the instructions given by the court, to see if they accord with the principles above laid down. Having decided that the plaintiff below has a right to recover on the facts, whether the instructions were right or wrong would not vary that result. It is possible that if the true principles which govern this action had been correctly given to the jury, the damages might have been either less or more than the jury have given; but in this case, as the damages are small, the court ought not, where justice has upon the whole been done, to send the case back, to see if a jury, upon another trial, would not give less.

For these reasons I am of opinion that the judgment ought to be affirmed, with costs.

NOTES AND QUESTIONS

1.   The English natural flow theory bears a resemblance to the law of trespass, in the sense that any material interference with downstream riparian rights is forbidden unless the downstream owner consents. The American reasonable use doctrine is more like the law of nuisance, in the sense that a wide variety of contextual factors are relevant in determining whether a diversion is actionable. According to the *Restatement (Second) of Torts* § 850(A) (Am. L. Inst. 1970), a court determining whether a use is reasonable should consider the purpose of the use, its suitability to the water course, the economic and social values at stake, the harm caused, possible accommodation techniques, the protection of existing investments, the ability of adversely affected riparians to bear the loss, and "justice." That would seem to cover just about everything. What accounts for the shift from a strict and predictable doctrine that emphasizes bargaining and consent to one that allows courts to arbitrate disputes among competing riparian claimants? Are the factors that explain the shift similar to the ones that might explain the shift from trespass to nuisance when we move from large invasions of land to small invasions or other interferences with use and enjoyment of land? The emergence of new technologies like water mills is clearly part of the explanation. See Morton J. Horwitz, The Transformation of American Law, 1780–1860, at 34–47 (1977); Carol Rose, Energy and Efficiency in the Realignment of Common-Law Water Rights, 19 J. Legal Stud. 261, 264–96 (1990). Does this suggest that the shift to reasonable use has a broadly Demsetzian explanation? For an argument that water law developed in part according to the internal unfolding of the common law and its own culture, including a reinvigoration of natural-rights-based riparianism in nineteenth-century England, see Joshua Getzler, A History of Water Rights at Common Law (2004).

2.   In at least one critical respect the analogy between the riparian doctrine of reasonable use and the law of nuisance is incomplete. As mentioned earlier, riparian rights run with the land and cannot be severed. Thus, riparian owner A could not sell his rights to nonriparian owner B. Courts have tended to enforce this rule quite strictly. What accounts for this refusal to treat water as a pure commodity that can be severed from use with respect to particular parcels of riparian land? Of course, people inevitably found room to maneuver around the rule against severance. What happens if A subdivides his parcel into two parcels, each with one half of the frontage on the water course? Why stop at two parcels? This is the so-called "bowling alley parcel" problem, in which a riparian landowner sells narrow strips of land to nonriparians, who would then claim rights of reasonable use. Riparian law accordingly developed detailed doctrines to deal with subdivisions of the riparian parcels that threatened to impose too great a burden on other riparian owners.

3.   *Evans v. Merriweather* also draws a sharp distinction between "natural" wants and "artificial" wants. A more common way of drawing the same distinction today is to distinguish between "domestic" and "other" (i.e., nondomestic) uses. The granting of an absolute priority for "natural" or "domestic" uses over "artificial" or "other" uses is also characteristic of

reasonable use doctrine. Domestic uses include household uses (for cleaning and cooking) and small-scale livestock watering—the small farm or homestead is the model for "natural" or "domestic" needs. As employed by the *Evans* court, this distinction comes into play only during periods of drought, when there is too little water to satisfy the natural wants of all riparians. *Evans* seems to suggest that when drought strikes, the upstream riparian can fulfill all his domestic needs, even if this means downstream riparians get little or no water at all. Why privilege the upstream riparian in this fashion? Why not award the water to the first of the competing riparians to have appropriated water for domestic uses? Why not apportion the water among the competing riparians—equally, according to frontage, or on some other basis?

4.   Do principles of adverse possession, considered in Chapter II, apply to riparian water rights? If so, how should adverse use be defined in this context? Is prior appropriation of water enough to establish adversity as against other riparians who seek to appropriate water at a later time? Or must the appropriation be sufficiently great to interfere with what would be classified as "natural" or "domestic" uses by other riparians?

5.   *Evans* suggests that periods of drought will be relatively rare in a state like Illinois, which usually has adequate rainfall to replenish flowing streams. But what happens in a relatively more arid state where drought is more or less the perpetual state of affairs? Consider the following case.

Coffin v. Left Hand Ditch Company

Supreme Court of Colorado, 1882.
6 Colo. 443.

■ HELM, J. Appellee, who was plaintiff below, claimed to be the owner of certain water by virtue of an appropriation thereof from the south fork of the St. Vrain creek. It appears that such water, after its diversion, is carried by means of a ditch to the James creek, and thence along the bed of the same to Left Hand creek, where it is again diverted by lateral ditches and used to irrigate lands adjacent to the last named stream. Appellants are the owners of lands lying on the margin and in the neighborhood of the St. Vrain below the mouth of said south fork thereof, and naturally irrigated therefrom.

In 1879 there was not a sufficient quantity of water in the St. Vrain to supply the ditch of appellee and also irrigate the said lands of appellant. A portion of appellee's dam was torn out, and its diversion of water thereby seriously interfered with by appellants. The action is brought for damages arising from the trespass, and for injunctive relief to prevent repetitions thereof in the future. * * *

It is contended by counsel for appellants that the common law principles of riparian proprietorship prevailed in Colorado until 1876, and that the doctrine of priority of right to water by priority of appropriation thereof was first recognized and adopted in the constitution. But we think the latter doctrine has existed from the date of the earliest appropriations of water within the boundaries of the state. The climate is dry, and the soil, when moistened only by the usual rainfall, is arid and unproductive; except in a few favored sections, artificial irrigation for agriculture is an absolute necessity. Water in the various streams thus acquires a value unknown in moister climates. Instead of being a mere incident to the soil, it rises, when appropriated, to the dignity of a distinct usufructuary estate, or right of property. It has always been the policy of the national, as well as the territorial and state governments, to encourage the diversion and use of water in this country for agriculture; and vast expenditures of time and money have been made in reclaiming and fertilizing by irrigation portions of our unproductive territory. Houses have been built, and permanent improvements made; the soil has been cultivated, and thousands of acres have been rendered immensely valuable, with the understanding that appropriations of water would be protected. Deny the doctrine of priority or superiority of right by priority of appropriation, and a great part of the value of all this property is at once destroyed. * * *

We conclude, then, that the common law doctrine giving the riparian owner a right to the flow of water in its natural channel upon and over his lands, even though he makes no beneficial use thereof, is inapplicable to Colorado. Imperative necessity, unknown to the countries which gave it birth, compels the recognition of another doctrine in conflict therewith. And we hold that, in the absence of express statutes to the contrary, the first appropriator of water from a natural stream for a beneficial purpose has, with the qualifications contained in the constitution, a prior right thereto, to the extent of such appropriation. See Schilling v. Rominger, 4 Colo. 100, 103 (1878).

The territorial legislature in 1864 expressly recognizes the doctrine. It says: "Nor shall the water of any stream be diverted from its original channel to the detriment of any miner, millmen or others along the line of said stream, *who may have a priority of right*, and there shall be at all times left sufficient water in said stream for the use of miners and agriculturists along said stream." Session Laws of 1864, p. 68, § 32.

The priority of right mentioned in this section is acquired by priority of appropriation, and the provision declares that appropriations of water shall be subordinate to the use thereof by prior appropriators. This provision remained in force until the adoption of the constitution; it was repealed in 1868, but the repealing act re-enacted it *verbatim*.

But the rights of appellee were acquired, in the first instance, under the acts of 1861 and 1862, and counsel for appellants urge, with no little skill and plausibility, that these statutes are in conflict with our conclusion that priority of right is acquired by priority of appropriation. The only provision, however, which can be construed as referring to this subject is § 4 on page 68, Session Laws of 1861. This section provides for the appointment of commissioners, in times of scarcity, to apportion the stream "in a just and equitable proportion," to the best interests of all parties, "with a due regard to the legal rights of all." What is meant by the concluding phrases of the foregoing statute? What are the legal rights for which the commissioners are enjoined to have a "due regard?" Why this additional limitation upon the powers of such commissioners?

It seems to us a reasonable inference that these phrases had reference to the rights acquired by priority of appropriation. This view is sustained by the universal respect shown at the time said statute was adopted, and subsequently by each person, for the prior appropriations of others, and the corresponding customs existing among settlers with reference thereto. This construction does not, in our judgment, detract from the force or effect of the statute. It was the duty of the commissioners under it to guard against extravagance and waste, and to so divide and distribute the water as most economically to supply all of the earlier appropriators thereof according to their respective appropriations and necessities, to the extent of the amount remaining in the stream.

It appears from the record that the patent under which appellant George W. Coffin holds title was issued prior to the act of congress of 1866, hereinbefore mentioned. That it contained no reservation or exception of vested water rights, and conveyed to Coffin through his grantor the absolute title in fee simple to his land, together with all incidents and appurtenances thereunto belonging; and it is claimed that therefore the doctrine of priority of right by appropriation cannot, at least, apply to him. We have already declared that water appropriated and diverted for a beneficial purpose is, in this country, not necessarily an appurtenance to the soil through which the stream supplying the same naturally flows. If appropriated by one prior to the patenting of such soil by another, it is a vested right entitled to protection, though not mentioned in the patent. But we are relieved from any extended consideration of this subject by the decision in Broder v. Natoma W. & M. Co., 101 U.S. (11 Otto) 274 (1879).

It is urged, however, that even if the doctrine of priority or superiority of right by priority of appropriation be conceded, appellee in this case is not benefited thereby. Appellants claim that they have a better right to the water because their lands lie along the margin and in the neighborhood of the St. Vrain. They assert that, as against them, appellee's diversion of said water to irrigate lands adjacent to Left Hand creek, though prior in time, is unlawful. In the absence of legislation to the contrary, we think that the right to water acquired by priority of appropriation thereof is not in any way dependent upon the locus of its application to the beneficial use designed. And the disastrous consequences of our adoption of the rule contended for, forbid our giving such a construction to the statutes as will concede the same, if they will properly bear a more reasonable and equitable one.

The doctrine of priority of right by priority of appropriation for agriculture is evoked, as we have seen, by the imperative necessity for artificial irrigation of the soil. And it would be an ungenerous and inequitable rule that would deprive one of its benefit simply because he has, by large expenditure of time and money, carried the water from one stream over an intervening watershed and cultivated land in the valley of another. It might be utterly impossible, owing to the topography of the country, to get water upon his farm from the adjacent stream; or if possible, it might be impracticable on account of the distance from the point where the diversion must take place and the attendant expense; or the quantity of water in such stream might be entirely insufficient to supply his wants. It sometimes happens that the most fertile soil is found along the margin or in the neighborhood of the small rivulet, and sandy and barren land beside the larger stream. To apply the rule contended for would prevent the useful and profitable cultivation of the productive soil, and sanction the waste of water upon the more sterile lands. It would have enabled a party to locate upon a stream in 1875, and destroy the value of thousands of acres, and the improvements thereon, in adjoining valleys, possessed and cultivated for the preceding decade. Under the principle contended for, a party owning land ten miles from the stream, but in the valley thereof, might deprive a prior appropriator of the water diverted therefrom whose lands are within a thousand yards, but just beyond an intervening divide.

We cannot believe that any legislative body within the territory or state of Colorado ever *intended* these consequences to flow from a statute enacted. Yet two sections are relied upon by counsel as practically producing them. These sections are as follows:

> All persons who claim, own or hold a possessory right or title to any land or parcel of land within the boundary of Colorado territory, . . . when those claims are on the bank, margin or neighborhood of any stream of water, creek or river, shall be entitled to the use of the water of said stream, creek or river for the purposes of irrigation, and making said claims available to the full extent of the soil, for agricultural purposes. Session Laws 1861, p. 67, § 1.

> Nor shall the water of any stream be diverted from its original channel to the detriment of any miner, millmen or others along the line of said stream, and there shall be at all times left sufficient water in said stream for the use of miners and farmers along said stream. Latter part of § 13, p. 48, Session Laws 1862.

The two statutory provisions above quoted must, for the purpose of this discussion, be construed together. The phrase "along said stream," in the latter, is equally comprehensive, as to the extent of territory, with the expression "on the bank, margin or neighborhood," used in the former, and both include all lands in the immediate valley of the stream. The latter provision sanctions the diversion of water from one stream to irrigate lands adjacent to another, provided such diversion is not to the "detriment" of parties along the line of the stream from which the water is taken. If there is any conflict between the statutes in this respect, the latter, of course, must prevail. We think that the "use" and "detriment" spoken of are a use existing at the time of the diversion, and a detriment immediately resulting therefrom. We do not believe that the legislature intended to prohibit the diversion of water to the "detriment" of parties who might at some future period conclude to settle upon the stream; nor do we think that they were legislating with a view to preserving in such stream sufficient water for the "use" of settlers who might never come, and consequently never have use therefor.

But "detriment" at the time of diversion could only exist where the water diverted had been previously appropriated or used; if there had been no previous appropriation or use thereof, there could be no present injury or "*detriment.*"

Our conclusion above as to the intent of the legislature is supported by the fact that the succeeding assembly, in 1864, hastened to insert into the latter statute, without other change or amendment, the clause, "*who have a priority of right,*" in connection with the idea of "*detriment*" to adjacent owners. This amendment of the statute was simply the acknowledgment by the legislature of a doctrine already existing, under which rights had accrued that were entitled to protection. In the language of Mr. Justice Miller, above quoted, upon a different branch of the same subject, it "was rather a voluntary recognition of a pre-existing right constituting a valid claim, than the creation of a new one." * * *

But this is an action of trespass; the defendants below were, according to the verdict of the jury, and according to the view herein expressed, wrong-doers * * *

Affirmed.

Figure 3-4
The St. Vrain Creek

Courtesy of Susan Thomas.

NOTES AND QUESTIONS

1.   Is the Colorado Supreme Court's exercise in statutory interpretation convincing? Do the legal principles laid down by the Colorado legislature in 1861 and 1862 sound all that different from those applied as a matter of common law in the *Evans* case? Recall that the Oregon Supreme Court's decision in *Thornton*, supra, which declared a customary public right to use the dry sand beach, was later challenged as a judicial taking. Did the Colorado Supreme Court commit a taking by eliminating the riparian water rights Coffin had under Colorado law when he acquired the property?

2.   The "Colorado doctrine," or prior appropriation, appears to move a long way toward recognizing water as a full-fledged private property right. Water rights are now based on a version of the first-in-time approach that is characteristic of original acquisition of other types of property rights, such as rights to wild animals or abandoned property. Moreover, in contrast to natural flow theory or the reasonable use doctrine, prior appropriation unambiguously permits the first appropriator to take all of the water in the stream. And of course, as *Coffin* holds, prior appropriation permits water to be severed from riparian land and even transported into another watershed. Yet notwithstanding these differences, it would be inaccurate to characterize prior appropriation as treating water like any other commodity. In addition to *de facto* and *de jure* restrictions on sales of water rights (see Note 6 infra), the prior appropriation doctrine incorporates notions of proper use: Generally speaking, only "beneficial uses" of appropriated water are permitted. As in the case of "reasonable use," it is difficult to state with certainty exactly what it means to be a beneficial use. The most famous example cited to show what is not beneficial is using water to flood gophers off one's land. See Tulare Irrigation District v. Lindsay-Strathmore Irrigation District, 45 P.2d 972, 1007 (Cal. 1935). That helps.

3.   In practice, prior appropriation systems are more of a governance regime than an exclusion regime. Henry E. Smith, Governing Water: The Semicommons of Fluid Property Rights, 50 Ariz. L. Rev. 445 (2008). And with increasingly interconnected and regulated water rights, even in riparian states, the governance approach is perhaps becoming even more pronounced. See Eric T. Freyfogle, Context and Accommodation in Modern Property Law, 41 Stan. L. Rev. 1529, 1530 (1989). Traditionally, prior appropriation rights gave a right to use water in a certain way for a certain period of time—rather than a right to a certain volume of water. This helps explain the often-decried doctrine that an appropriator who stops using the water or whose use becomes more efficient has no rights in the excess water. See 2 Waters and Water Rights § 12.03(c)(2) (Robert E. Beck ed., 1991). Given the complexity of the problem and the need to adjust interlocking rights, equity has played an important role in prior appropriation law. Duane Rudolph, Why Prior Appropriation Needs Equity, 18 U. Denver Water L. Rev. 348 (2015).

4.   One limit on well-defined entitlements to water is the measurement technology available. In an earlier era the "miner's inch" was used, which involved forcing water through a one-inch square orifice under conditions that were neither easily controlled nor standardized. See George

A. Gould & Douglas L. Grant, Cases and Materials on Water Law 11–12 (6th ed. 2000). The uncertainty associated with measurement technology probably helps explain the requirement of beneficial use: It was easier to monitor uses than to measure flows of water. Today, the official statutory measure in most western states is the cubic foot per second ("second foot" or "cfs"), which is measured with various meters and registers—and more recently with satellite monitors.

5.   One frequent explanation of the tendency for western states to adopt some variant of prior appropriation is that in the arid West, water is more valuable and hence private property rights in water are more worthwhile. Eastern reasonable use doctrine and western prior appropriation then become a classic Demsetzian story. See, e.g., Terry L. Anderson & P.J. Hill, The Evolution of Property Rights: A Study of the American West, 18 J.L. & Econ. 163, 176–78 (1975). A recent empirical study finds that prior appropriation in Colorado established between 1852 and 2013 was associated with a doubling of infrastructure investment and a substantial increase in agricultural output. Bryan Leonard & Gary D. Libecap, Collective Action by Contract: Prior Appropriation and the Development of Irrigation in the Western United States, 62 J.L. & Econ. 67 (2019).

Additionally, once the potential set of rightholders in the West was no longer limited to riparian owners or even to those whose lands were located in the same watershed, some limiting principle was needed in order to prevent water rights from becoming so finely subdivided as to be of little value. See Benjamin N. Cardozo, The Growth of the Law 117–20 (1924); David B. Schorr, Appropriation as Agrarianism: Distributive Justice in the Creation of Property Rights, 32 Ecology L.Q. 3 (2005). This was also a major concern in mining camps, out of which western water law grew.

On the other hand, as Carol Rose has pointed out, the uses to which water was put in the two areas was different:

> Western water rights evolved from uses of water that were essentially consumptive. Some of these were power uses, such as forced-water hosing of offstream mining slopes, while other uses included such partial consumption as irrigation. * * * [W]estern water uses * * * consumed the water * * * because they took the water away from the stream and did not return it, or at least much of it. * * *

> But eastern riparian rights did not grow up around these consumptive uses of water, even though consumptive uses were sometimes at issue. Eastern riparian rights grew up around the use of water for power—that is—instream power—which is not necessarily a zero-sum game. * * * [I]f I have a mill on the river, and you do too, we can both use the water as it flows by—provided that we do so carefully and do not, for example, alternately interrupt and pour out the water in such a way as to disrupt the millworks downstream. * * *

[T]he point of riparian law was to place boundaries on these necessarily consumptive aspects of water flow use, holding them within "reasonable" and commonly accepted bounds so that the bulk of the water flow would be left intact. What I am suggesting, of course, is that eastern riparian law evolved from an aspect of water use, namely, power, that has aspects of a public good, quite unlike the individually consumptive uses of water that are characteristic of the West. * * *

Carol M. Rose, Energy and Efficiency in the Realignment of Common-Law Water Rights, 19 J. Legal Stud. 261, 290–92 (1990). Which of the foregoing explanations for the emergence of the Colorado doctrine or western appropriation theory is more convincing? Are they incompatible? Consider the conflict in *Evans v. Merriweather* again in light of Rose's account.

6.   One of the most contentious issues these days is the marketing of water rights. Whether water rights can be sold has always been controversial, and the law on the subject has wavered over time. Today, prior appropriation regimes generally allow sales of water rights unless the sale would impose unwanted effects on third parties such as downstream users of the return flow. The fact that water can fetch much higher prices in urban areas than in areas of longstanding agricultural use has led to posturing and bitter political conflict, most notoriously in Los Angeles's purchase of water rights from farmers in the Owens Valley. Compare William L. Kahrl, Water and Power: The Conflict over Los Angeles' Water Supply in the Owens Valley (1982) (arguing that the transfers were coercive and devastated the Owens Valley) with Gary D. Libecap, Owens Valley Revisited: A Reassessment of the West's First Great Water Transfer (2007) (arguing that the transfers benefited Owens Valley owners but they received prices closer to value of land in agricultural rather than municipal use). There is a discernible trend now in the direction of market-alienability. What is the problem with commodifying water in the first place?

7.   Acquiring rights for instream uses, such as rafting or fishing is another live issue in western states today. If water is market-alienable, why not let those who would like to enjoy uninterrupted flow purchase the rights? Traditionally, under prior appropriation, a claim for instream use would not count as an appropriation for beneficial use, perhaps because of a lack of environmental concern or difficulty in delineating instream rights. More recently, western states have been amending their water laws to provide for rights for instream users. In addition, the public trust doctrine (see supra Part D.2) can sometimes unexpectedly cause nonconsumptive uses to trump longstanding appropriative rights. See National Audubon Society v. Superior Court, 658 P.2d 709 (Cal. 1983) (Mono Lake). What is the best way to integrate newfound demand for instream flows into the mosaic of water rights?

8.   Water is not the only resource that is hard to delimit and to specify for purposes of defining rights. (See the material on oil and gas in Chapter II and wind and solar in Chapter IX.) The metaphor of "fugitive" resources has often been criticized, but it may reflect the difficulty that courts as institutions have in addressing problems involving certain resources.

Another perennially difficult resource is the radio spectrum, made famous in law and economics by Ronald Coase. R. H. Coase, The Federal Communications Commission. 2 J.L. & Econ. 1 (1959). The spectrum can be put to many uses, from television, to wireless communication, to GPS, with new uses being devised all the time. Here too, methods of delineation that look like use rights versus others that resemble "parcels"—compare riparianism versus prior appropriation—have been proposed for radio spectrum. Thomas W. Merrill & Henry E. Smith, Making Coasean Property More Coasean, 54 J.L. & Econ. S77, S83–86 (2011). And as with water, the political conflicts over radio spectrum have been epic. See Thomas Winslow Hazlett, The Political Spectrum: The Tumultuous Liberation of Wireless Technology, from Herbert Hoover to the Smartphone (2017).

Diffuse Surface Water

What about surface water that is not in a defined channel, or what is sometimes termed "casual water?" Under the "common enemy" doctrine, first adopted in *Luther v. Winnisimmet Co.*, 63 Mass. (9 Cush.) 171 (1851), each landowner has an absolute right to use self-help to repel inflows of these waters—that is, to combat the "common enemy" of surface water—even if this causes damaging flooding to other landowners. 2 Waters and Water Rights § 10.03(b)(1) (Robert E. Berk ed., 1991 ed., 2000 replacement vol., 2001); 5 Waters and Water Rights § 59.02(b)(2). But if one landowner uses self-help to repel the water and causes the surface water to flow to a second owner's land, the second owner is similarly privileged to try to send the water back. Neither can sue the other. More recently, as conflicts have grown, the common enemy doctrine has been modified (or supplanted) by judicial policing for reasonableness. Again, we can discern a trend from a trespass-like doctrine (absolute privilege to repel invasions) to a more nuisance-like doctrine (arbitrating the rights of the parties under a broad context-sensitive reasonableness standard).

2. GROUNDWATER

Higday v. Nickolaus
Kansas City Court of Appeals, Missouri, 1971.
469 S.W.2d 859.

■ SHANGLER, PRESIDING JUDGE. This appeal is from a judgment dismissing plaintiffs' Petition for Declaratory Judgment and Injunction. The judgment of dismissal was entered upon defendant City's Motion to Dismiss which alleged that plaintiffs' petition failed to plead either a justiciable controversy or any claim upon which relief could be granted. The questions raised on this appeal are: whether the averments of the petition entitle plaintiffs, to a judicial declaration of their rights to the percolating waters underlying their lands, and if so, whether defendant

City's threatened use of the percolating waters is such an infringement of those rights as will be enjoined by equity.

The facts alleged and in substance shown by the petition of plaintiffs, now appellants, are these: Appellants are the several owners of some 6000 acres of farm land overlying an alluvial water basin in Boone County known as the McBaine Bottom. These lands (projected on Exhibit "A" appended hereto [Figure 3-5]) extend from Huntsdale at the north to Easley at the south; they are bordered by a line of limestone bluffs on the east and are enclosed by a sweeping bend of the Missouri River on the west. Underlying this entire plain are strata of porous rock, gravel and soil through which water, without apparent or definite channel, filtrates, oozes and percolates as it falls. This water (much of which has originated far upstream within the Missouri River Valley) has been trapped by an underlying stratum of impervious limestone so that the saturated soil has become a huge aquifer or underground reservoir.

Appellants have devoted the overlying lands to agricultural use with excellent resultant yields. They attribute the fertility of the soil to the continuing presence of a high subterranean water level which has unfailingly and directly supplied the moisture needs of the crops whatever the vagaries of the weather. Appellants also use the underground water for personal consumption, for their livestock, and in the near future will require it for the surface irrigation of their crops.

Respondent City of Columbia is a burgeoning municipality of 50,000 inhabitants which has been, since 1948, in quest of a source of water to replenish a dwindling supply. Following the advice of consulting engineers, it settled on a plan for the withdrawal of water by shallow wells from beneath the McBaine Bottom where appellants' farms are located and thence to transport the water to the City some twelve miles away for sale to customers within and without the City. In December of 1966, the electorate approved a revenue bond issue for the development of a municipal water supply by such a system of shallow wells in the McBaine Bottom. Further scientific analysis and measurement of the basin's water resources followed. With the aid of a test well, it was determined that the underground percolating water table, when undisturbed, rises to an average of ten feet below the soil surface. These waters move laterally through the McBaine alluvium at the rate of two feet per day and in so doing displace 10.5 million gallons of water daily.

Figure 3-5
Exhibit A in *Higday v. Nickolaus*

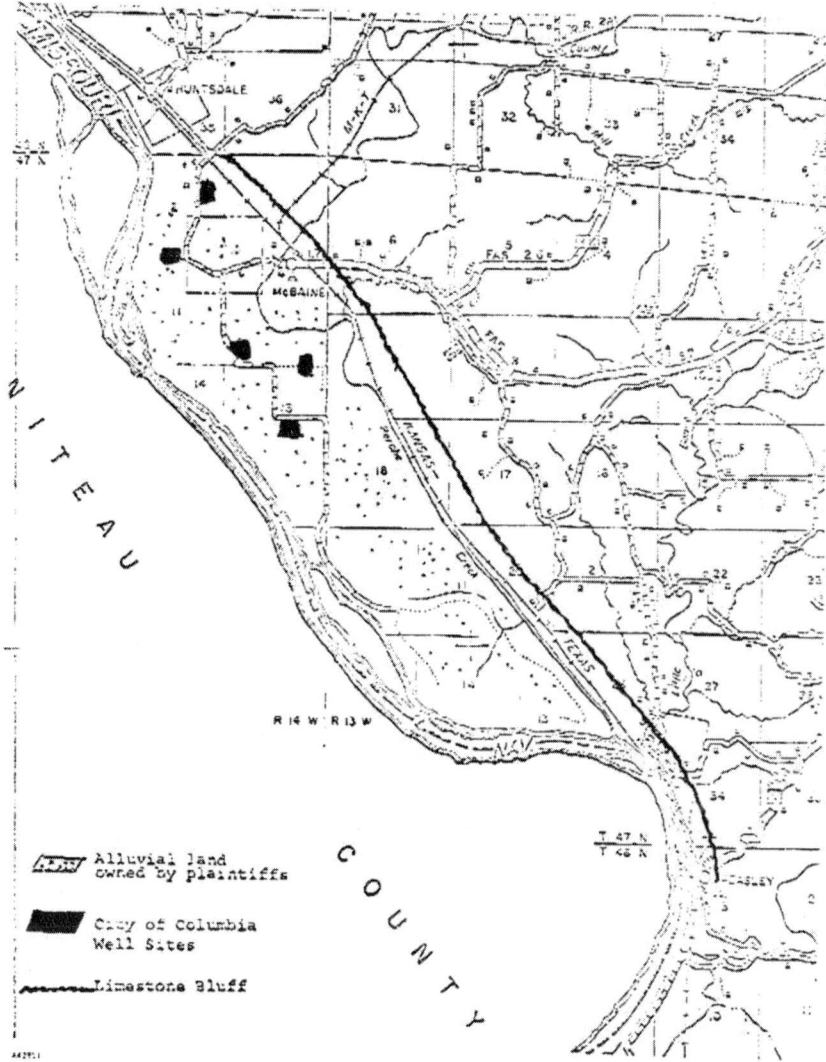

Respondent City, by threat of condemnation, has acquired from some of these appellants five well sites totalling 17.25 acres. The City now threatens to extract the groundwater at the rate of 11.5 million gallons daily for purposes wholly unrelated to any beneficial use of the overlying land, but instead, intends to transport the water to its corporate boundaries some miles away for purposes of sale. The mining of the water as contemplated will reduce the water table throughout the basin from the present average of ten feet to a new subsurface average of twenty feet. Appellants complain that this reduction of the water table will divert percolating waters normally available and enjoyed by appellants for their crops, livestock and their personal use and will eventually turn their land into an arid and sterile surface.

On the basis of these pleaded allegations, plaintiffs sought (1) a judicial declaration that defendant City is without right to extract the percolating waters for sale away from the premises or for other use not related with any beneficial ownership or enjoyment of the land from which they are taken when to do so will deprive them, the owners of the adjacent land, of the reasonable use of the underground water for the beneficial use of their own land, and (2) that defendant City be enjoined from undertaking to do so. * * *

The facts pleaded show the City's design to exploit the McBaine Bottom as the principal source of the municipal water supply has advanced to the point where well sites have been acquired on land adjacent to that held by plaintiffs. (The City acknowledges in its brief that it has committed almost $5,000,000 to this project, that it has acquired the sites for wells and a water treatment plant, and that the laying of water lines is virtually completed.) When the wells become operative, the City claims the right to withdraw groundwater in any quantity at will, for sale, even though damages may result to plaintiffs. * * *

Respondent maintains that since Springfield Waterworks Co. v. Jenkins, 62 Mo.App. 74, was decided by the St. Louis Court of Appeals in 1895, Missouri has recognized the common law rule that a landowner has absolute ownership to the waters under his land and, therefore, may without liability withdraw any quantity of water for any purpose even though the result is to drain all water from beneath his neighbors' lands. Therefore, contends respondent, since the threatened damage plaintiffs plead describes a consequence of the rightful use by respondent of its land, it is *damnum absque injuria* and not actionable. * * *

It is fundamental that injunction will not be granted unless there is some substantial right to be protected. The indispensable basis for injunctive relief is the wrongful and injurious invasion of some legal right existing in plaintiff. The writ will issue also if invasion of that right is threatened by one having the power to do the wrong. Whether plaintiffs' allegations that the defendant municipality threatens to capture the percolating waters from their subjacent lands for purposes of sale in such quantities as will damage them describe an invasion of legal right which equity will enjoin depends upon whether plaintiffs have a right of property in these waters. The answer to that question, in turn, depends upon the rule to be applied to the ownership and use of subterranean percolating waters.

In legal contemplation, subterranean waters fall into two classifications, either underground streams or percolating waters.[2] An

---

[2]   These legal classifications have been roundly criticized by hydrologists and legal commentators as without scientific basis both as to the distinction attempted between percolating waters and underground streams and also because they ignore the essential interrelationship between surface and ground waters. See, e.g., Danielson, Ground Water in Nebraska, 35 Neb.L.Rev. 17 (1955); Clark, Groundwater Management: Law and Local Response, 6 Ariz.Law Rev. 188 (1965); 1 R. Clark, Waters and Water Rights, Sec. 3.1, p. 332

underground stream is defined as water that passes through or under the surface in a definite channel or one that is reasonably ascertainable. Percolating waters include all waters which pass through the ground beneath the surface of the earth without a definite channel and not shown to be supplied by a definite flowing stream. They are waters which ooze, seep, filter and otherwise circulate through the interstices of the subsurface strata without definable channel, or in a course that is not discoverable from surface indications without excavation for that purpose. The rule is that all underground waters are presumed to be percolating and therefore the burden of proof is on the party claiming that a subterranean stream exists. Maricopa County Municipal Water Conservation Dist. No. 1 v. Southwest Cotton Co., 4 P.2d 369, 376 (Ariz. 1931); C & W Coal Corp. v. Salyer, 104 S.E.2d 50, 53 (Va. 1958); Wilkening v. State, 344 P.2d 204, 206 (Wash. 1959).

The law with respect to rights in percolating waters was not developed until a comparatively recent period.[3] Under the English common law rule, percolating waters constitute part and parcel of the land in which they are found and belong absolutely to the owner of such land who may without liability withdraw any quantity of water for any purpose even though the result is to drain all water from beneath the adjoining lands. Under this rule, a municipality [owning] land may collect the underlying percolating waters and use them to supply its inhabitants regardless of the effect on adjoining landowners.

The English rule relating to percolating groundwater was generally followed by American courts through the mid-nineteenth century, although not always with the full rigor of the absolute ownership doctrine. At an early day, the courts expressed dissatisfaction with the English common law rule and began applying what has come to be known variously, as the rule of "reasonable use", or of "correlative rights", or the "American rule."[4] By the turn of the century, a steady trend of decisions was discernible away from the English rule to a rule of reasonable use. The trend continues.[6]

Generally, the rule of reasonable use is an expression of the maxim that one must so use his own property as not to injure another—that each landowner is restricted to a reasonable exercise of his own rights and a reasonable use of his own property, in view of the similar rights of others. As it applies to percolating groundwater, the rule of reasonable use

---

(1967). Also, Restatement, Torts, comment a to Sec. 858 (1939); Lauer, Reflections on Riparianism, 35 Mo.L.Rev. 1, 7 (1970).

[3]   Acton v. Blundell, 12 Mees & W. 324, 152 Eng.Rep. 1223 (Exch. 1843), is generally cited as establishing the doctrine, but an earlier American decision, Greenleaf v. Francis, 35 Mass. (18 Pick) 117 (1836) had reached much the same result. See: Hutchins, Symposium on Water Law, 5 U.Kans.L.Rev. 533, 541 (1957).

[4]   This rule originated in 1862 when the New Hampshire Supreme Court in Bassett v. Salisbury Mfg. Co., 43 N.H. 569, 573 (1862), rejected the doctrine of absolute ownership of percolating waters and adopted a rule of reciprocal reasonable use.

[6]   Rothrauff v. Sinking Spring Water Co., 14 A.2d 87, 90 (Pa. 1940); City of Corpus Christi v. City of Pleasanton, 276 S.W.2d 798, 801 (Tex. 1955).

recognizes that the overlying owner has a proprietary interest in the water under his lands, but his incidents of ownership are restricted. It recognizes that the nature of the property right is usufructuary rather than absolute as under the English rule. Under the rule of reasonable use, the overlying owner may use the subjacent groundwater freely, and without liability to an adjoining owner, but only if his use is for purposes incident to the beneficial enjoyment of the land from which the water was taken. This rule does not prevent the consumption of such groundwater for agriculture, manufacturing, irrigation, mining or any purpose by which a landowner might legitimately use and enjoy his land, even though in doing so he may divert or drain the groundwater of his neighbor.

The principal difficulty in the application of the reasonable use doctrine is in determining what constitutes a reasonable use. What is a reasonable use must depend to a great extent upon many factors, such as the persons involved, their relative positions, the nature of their uses, the comparative value of their uses, the climatic conditions, and all facts and circumstances pertinent to the issues. Bristor v. Cheatham, 255 P.2d 173, 179 (Ariz. 1953); Bollinger v. Henry, 375 S.W.2d 161, 166 (Mo. 1964).[8] However, the modern decisions agree that under the rule of reasonable use *an overlying owner, including a municipality, may not withdraw percolating water and transport it for sale or other use away from the land from which it was taken if the result is to impair the supply of an adjoining landowner to his injury.* Such a use is unreasonable because non-beneficial and "is not for a 'lawful purpose within the general rule concerning percolating waters, but constitutes an actionable wrong for which damages are recoverable' ". Bristor v. Cheatham, supra, 255 P.2d at 178; Canada v. City of Shawnee, 64 P.2d 694 (Okla. 1936); Forbell v. City of New York, 58 N.E. 644, 646 (N.Y. 1900); Rothrauff v. Sinking Spring Water Co., 14 A.2d 87, 90 (Pa. 1940); Meeker v. City of East Orange, 74 A. 379, 385 (N.J. 1909); and cases listed in 55 A.L.R. 1404.

The "reasonable use" rule as developed in the law of ground waters must be distinguished from the "correlative rights" rule. In 1902, the California Supreme Court repudiated the English common law rule in favor of the distinctive correlative rights doctrine which is based on the theory of proportionate sharing of withdrawals among landowners overlying a common basin.[9] Under the doctrine, overlying owners have no proprietary interest in the water under their soil. California remains the only important correlative rights state; Utah has abandoned it, and only Nebraska also applies it to some extent.[10] The administration of such a system of rights has proved extremely difficult in times of water

---

[8]   Bollinger v. Henry, supra, suggests certain factors in the determination of the reasonableness of a use of riparian waters. Secs. 852 and 861 of the Restatement of the Law of Torts (1939) state that the problem of determining a reasonable use is the same whether water is in a water course or lake or under the surface of the earth.

[9]   Katz v. Walkinshaw, 74 P. 766 (Cal. 1903).

[10]   1 R. Clark, Water and Water Rights, Sec. 52.2(B), p. 331.

shortage and has tendered towards an "equalitarian rigidity" which does not take into account the relative value of the competing uses. However suitable this doctrine may be for California—the prime consumer of ground water in the country—or any other state which may follow it, the reasonable use rule offers a more flexible legal standard for the just determination of beneficial uses of ground water, particularly under the climatic conditions of Missouri.

Respondent City contends that the English common law rule of absolute ownership of percolating waters governs in Missouri by virtue of statute and judicial decision. The City seems to suggest that since the Territorial Laws of 1816 adopted the common law as the rule of action and decision in this state and present Sec. 1.010 V.A.M.S. continues that legislative policy, we have no power to change or abrogate it. As we have already noted, Acton v. Blundell (marginal reference 3, supra), which is generally cited as having established the "English common law" rule of percolating waters, was decided in 1843 long after the Territorial Laws of 1816 were enacted. And not until 1860 was it decided that, without liability to an adjoining owner, an overlying owner might exhaust the groundwater to furnish a municipal water supply. Thus, there was no law of any kind on the subject at the time the common law was adopted by statute in this state. The subsequent English decisions declaring the common law on percolating waters are no more binding on us than the decisions of any court of another state. There is no impediment of inherited doctrine to our determination of the question presented according to the justice of the case.

The Missouri law of groundwater rests on a single case, Springfield Waterworks Company v. Jenkins, 62 Mo.App. 74, decided by the St. Louis Court of Appeals in 1895. Respondent City contends the holding in that case "reaffirms the English or Common Law Rule as to percolating waters and (that) this is the final word in Missouri on the subject." * * * We do not share respondent City's confidence that this decision either announces or follows the common law doctrine on the subject. * * *

The intervening three-quarters of a century since Springfield Waterworks Company v. Jenkins, supra, has seen for Missouri a significant urban, industrial and population increase and with it greater demands upon a relatively static water supply. In the past such water disputes as have been brought to our courts usually have arisen "from factual situations pertaining to the existence of too much rather than too little water". Bollinger v. Henry, supra, 375 S.W.2d at 165. The controversy between respondent City and plaintiffs over the McBaine Bottom groundwater, however, is prompted by a scarcity, not an excess, of water to supply the vital needs of both. It is a competition which is destined to recur between other municipalities and landowners as present sources of municipal water supplies diminish and the need for them increases. In such circumstances, appeals to a dogma of absolute ownership of groundwater without consideration of the rights of adjoining landowners seem unpersuasive.

Also, since Springfield Waterworks v. Jenkins, supra, the science of groundwater hydrology has come into existence and has proven the postulates of the common law rule to be unsound. The premise that the owner of the soil owns all that lies beneath the surface so that he may use the percolating water in any way he chooses without liability to an adjoining owner fails to recognize that the supply of groundwater is limited, and that the first inherent limitation on water rights is the availability of the supply.[14] Another postulate of the common law doctrine ascribes to percolating waters a movement so "secret, changeable and uncontrollable", that no attempt to subject them to fixed legal rules could be successfully made. Chatfield v. Wilson, 28 Vt. 49, 53 (1855); Frazier v. Brown, 12 Ohio St. 294 (1861). Modern knowledge and techniques have discredited this premise also. The movement, supply, rate of evaporation and many other physical characteristics of groundwater are now readily determinable. * * *

Recently, in Bollinger v. Henry, supra, 375 S.W.2d at 166, the Supreme Court of Missouri applied the rule of reasonable use to determine the rights of riparian owners. Subterranean streams are governed by the rules applying to natural watercourses on the surface, so the rule of reasonable use is now applicable to them also. 93 C.J.S. Waters § 89; 56 Am.Jur., Waters, Sec. 109; Springfield Waterworks Co. v. Jenkins, supra, 62 Mo.App. at 80. We believe the same rule should apply to subterranean percolating waters. Jones v. Oz-Ark-Val Poultry Company, 306 S.W.2d 111, 113 (Ark. 1957); Wrathall v. Johnson, 40 P.2d 755, 776 (Utah 1935). It is that legal standard, in absence of a statutory expression of a priority of uses, by which existing water resources may be allocated most equitably and beneficially among competing users, private and public. The application of such a uniform legal standard would also give recognition to the established interrelationship between surface and groundwater and would, therefore, bring into one classification all waters over the use of which controversy may arise.

Under the rule of reasonable use as we have stated it, the fundamental measure of the overlying owner's right to use the groundwater is whether it is for purposes incident to the beneficial enjoyment of the land from which it was taken. Thus, a private owner may not withdraw groundwater for purposes of sale if the adjoining landowner is thereby deprived of water necessary for the beneficial enjoyment of his land. Katz v. Walkinshaw, 74 P. 766 (Cal. 1902). Here, the municipality has acquired miniscule plots of earth and by the use of powerful pumps intends to draw into wells on its own land for merchandising groundwater stored in plaintiffs' land, thereby depriving plaintiffs of the beneficial use of the normal water table to their

---

14   1 R. Clark, Waters and Water Rights, Secs. 2.1–2.5; 16 Rocky Mountain Mineral Law Institute 114 (1970); Lauer, Reflections in Riparianism, 35 Mo.L.Rev. 1, 2 (1970).

immediate injury and to the eventual impoverishment of their lands. "There is no apparent reason for saying that, because defendant is a municipal corporation, seeking water for the inhabitants of a city, it may therefore do what a private owner of land may not do. The city is a private owner of this land, and the furnishing of water to its inhabitants is its private business. It is imperative that the people of the city have water; it is not imperative that they secure it at the expense of those owning lands adjoining lands owned by the city." Schenk v. City of Ann Arbor, 163 N.W. 109, 114 (Mich. 1917). Under the rule we apply, however, plaintiffs could have no basis for complaint if the City of Columbia's withdrawals of groundwater for municipal purposes from the McBaine Bottom do not interfere with plaintiffs' beneficial use of such water. Under the facts pleaded, the water table could be maintained at its normal level and damage to plaintiffs avoided if the City were to limit its withdrawals to such quantity as would not exceed the daily recharge rate of 10.5 million gallons. If, on the other hand, the City perseveres in its declared intention to mine the water by at least one million gallons per day, it will become accountable to plaintiffs for [whatever] injury results from such diversion. * * *

This is not to suggest that should proof follow upon the pleadings, perforce injunction will issue. Injunctive relief is a matter of grace, not of right. "The writ of injunction is an extraordinary remedy. It does not issue as a matter of course, but somewhat at the discretion of the chancellor. It is his duty to consider its effect upon all parties in interest, and to issue it only in case it is necessary to protect a substantial right, *and even then not against great public interest*." (Emphasis supplied) Smith v. City of Sedalia, 149 S.W. 597, 601 (Mo. 1912); Johnson v. Independent School Dist. No. 1, 199 S.W.2d 421, 424 (Mo. Ct. App. 1947); 43 C.J.S. Injunctions § 31. It requires the application of the principles of equity under all the circumstances. * * *

The rule of comparative injury suggests that under the facts pleaded and concessions of counsel it may be more equitable to deny injunctive relief than to grant it. * * *

The City has resisted plaintiffs' requested declaratory and injunctive relief on the theory that the common law rule of absolute ownership of percolating waters has governed its relationship with plaintiffs and, therefore, any damage to them could not be a legal injury. It has not sought to exercise its power of eminent domain to acquire the right to withdraw water from beneath plaintiffs' lands doubtless on the premise that it was under no duty to do so. Should the trial court adjudge that plaintiffs are entitled to the declarations they seek, the rule of reasonable use will apply and defendant City will be answerable to plaintiffs for any damage from its unreasonable use of groundwater. Should the trial court adjudge injunctive relief for plaintiffs appropriate, it would be well within its discretion to condition the imposition of that restraint upon the exercise by the City within a reasonable time, of its power of eminent domain to acquire the water rights it has been violating. Failing that, plaintiffs would still have available to them a remedy in the nature of an inverse condemnation for any damage caused by the City's unreasonable use.

The judgment of the trial court is reversed and the cause is remanded for further proceedings consistent with the views we have expressed.

NOTES AND QUESTIONS

1.   The English Rule of *Acton v. Blundell*, also termed the absolute ownership rule, gives the owner of land an absolute right to use as much percolating groundwater as he pleases. The owner is privileged to pump within the space defined by the *ad coelum* rule. The American Rule of reasonable use can be seen as an application of the principle of another famous maxim, *sic utere tuo ut alienum non laedas*, "use your property in such a way as not to injure another's." Under this approach, what constitutes an injury (or conversely what is a proper use) must be defined. How would you characterize these approaches in terms of the distinction between trespass and nuisance, or exclusion and governance (see Chapter I)?

2.   The court here hints strongly that if the City is found to divert groundwater in excess of the natural recharge rate, it will be liable for damages but not an injunction. Would the same conclusion follow in a future case when the applicable rule is clearer? What if the diversion had been for a privately owned manufacturing plant rather than a municipal water system?

3.   The problem of groundwater pumping is somewhat reminiscent of the common pool in oil and gas. Although oil and gas flow somewhat differently, there is still potential for a tragedy of the commons. Solutions to the common-pool problem with oil and gas have typically been late in coming and only partially successful. See Chapter II.A.3.

CHAPTER IV

OWNER SOVEREIGNTY AND ITS LIMITS

As we saw in Chapter I, Blackstone referred to property with some hyperbole as "that sole and despotic dominion which one man claims and exercises over the external things of the world, in total exclusion of the right of any other individual in the universe." 2 William Blackstone, Commentaries on the Laws of England *2. In a famous essay written in the Legal Realist era, Morris Cohen agreed that property is a kind of delegated sovereignty over particular resources. Morris R. Cohen, Property and Sovereignty, 13 Cornell L.Q. 8 (1927). But while Blackstone celebrated owner sovereignty, Cohen warned against conferring too much power on individuals over resources, and argued that the general public, speaking through the sovereign government, should be able to make extensive modifications to owner sovereignty. In this Chapter, we consider in greater detail the extent to which property ownership conveys a type of sovereign authority over things. We start by surveying the various ways in which the law recognizes and protects the right of an owner to exclude others from her "thing." We then consider various limits on owner sovereignty, including necessity, custom, public accommodations laws, public policy, and antidiscrimination laws. This is followed by a consideration of the law of equity, which bears on owner sovereignty in multiple ways, expanding owner powers in some respects and qualifying them in others. Finally, we consider other basic powers that are often associated with owner sovereignty, such as the power to include others (license), the power to transfer possession but not ownership (bailment), and the power to abandon or destroy property.

A. PROTECTING OWNER SOVEREIGNTY

If property entails, at least in its core signification, the right to exclude others from some thing, then it is important to consider the ways in which the law protects this exclusion right. Property owners are in fact given a considerable arsenal of weapons to vindicate their right to exclude others.

1. CRIMINAL LAWS

By convention the criminal laws that protect property are studied in criminal law courses, not property courses, so we will not attempt anything like comprehensive treatment here. Yet it is important not to lose sight of the fact that the criminal law provides extensive protection to property, and that these protections reinforce the civil remedies that traditionally have received attention in property courses. The criminal law "backstopping" of ownership rights is arguably critical to the maintenance of a system of private property. If property owners were left solely to their civil remedies, they might be easily overwhelmed or exhausted by the need to enforce those rights, particularly if violations became numerous or persistent. Another reason for providing criminal law protection of property rights is to utilize the police as an agency for enforcing exclusion rights where self-help (such as trying to evict intruders or chase down thieves) would present a high risk of violence and injury to all concerned (including owners and even third parties).

a.   CRIMINAL LAWS PROTECTING PERSONAL PROPERTY

At common law, personal property was protected by the criminal law of larceny, which prohibited the taking of personal property from the possession of another without legal authority. Possession, as you should be aware by now, can be tricky to define.

A conventional explanation for the "taking from possession" element of larceny is that the law was more concerned with protecting persons than the ownership of things:

> The principal factor which limited the scope of larceny was the requirement that the thief must take it from the victim's possession; larceny requires a "trespass in the taking," as the matter is often stated. The judges who determined the scope of larceny (including its limitations) apparently considered larceny to be a crime designed to prevent breaches of the peace rather than aimed at protecting property from wrongful appropriation. The unauthorized taking of property, even by stealth, from the owner's possession is apt to produce an altercation if the owner discovers the property moving out of his possession in the hands of the thief. But when the wrongdoer already has the owner's property in his possession at the time he misappropriates it (today's embezzlement) or when he obtains the property from the owner by telling him lies (now the crime of false pretenses) there is not the same danger of an immediate breach of the peace. Upon learning how he has been wronged the owner may be as angry at the wrongdoer in these two situations as he is at the thief caught in the act of taking his property by stealth, but the malefactor in these two cases is generally less available for retaliatory measures than when the owner discovers him in the process of taking the property out of his possession.

Wayne R. LaFave, Criminal Law § 19.1(a) (6th ed. 2017) (footnote omitted). Courts and later legislatures kept adding to the inventory of property offenses, often through various "constructive possession" theories. Does this process of evolution tend to undermine the story about the primary concern of the criminal law being the protection of persons rather than ownership of things? At the same time, the law of larceny broadly moved from a focus on taking or asportation to "intent." George

P. Fletcher, The Metamorphosis of Larceny, 89 Harv. L. Rev. 469 (1976). Nevertheless courts still require some physical movement of the property to establish larceny.

Other than larceny and related offenses, personal property is covered by a complex menu of criminal prohibitions. Takings of personal property that directly endanger persons are often punished under the rubric of *robbery*, which is the common-law crime of larceny with the added element that the property is taken from the possession of the victim using force or by putting the victim in fear of immediate serious bodily injury. See Model Penal Code § 222.1. Persons who damage, but do not take, personal property can be charged with the crime of *criminal mischief*. Id. § 220.3.

Controversially, some intentional infringements of intellectual property rights are subject to criminal sanctions; American copyright law includes criminal penalties for copyright infringement, but patent law and trademark law do not. For commentary, see Stuart P. Green, Plagiarism, Norms, and the Limits of Theft Law: Some Observations on the Use of Criminal Sanctions in Enforcing Intellectual Property Rights, 54 Hastings L.J. 167, 209–16 (2002); Cheng Lim Saw, The Case for Criminalizing Primary Infringements of Copyright—Perspectives from Singapore, 18 Int'l J.L. & Info Tech. 95 (2010).

Questions have also been raised recently how if at all theft offenses should cover intangibles more generally. Possession traditionally could only be exercised over tangibles. Some have proposed that possession should be extended to intangibles or that theft offenses should be decoupled from possession. Although special statutes deal with a number of computer-related crimes, trespass-related motions play some role. See Orin S. Kerr, Cybercrime's Scope: Interpreting "Access" and "Authorization" in Computer Misuse Statutes, 78 N.Y.U. L. Rev. 1596, 1640–44 (2003). We will encounter these issues with civil law protection as well.

b. CRIMINAL LAWS PROTECTING REAL PROPERTY

Trespass to land was not a traditional common-law crime, unless the trespass tended to cause a breach of the peace. Only in the second half of the nineteenth century did criminal trespass statutes become common. See People v. Goduto, 174 N.E.2d 385 (Ill. 1961). Some of the early statutes were narrow. Texas's statute covered only hunting, camping, or fishing on enclosed land, and was only amended in 1971 to cover intrusions more generally, requiring notice from the owner (or possessor acting for the owner) immediately before entry that entry is forbidden. (The current version is a little broader as to sources of notice.) Tex. Penal Code Ann. § 30.05(a); see also 720 Ill. Comp. Stat. § 5/21–3(a). Still, even under the modern statutes the penalties for criminal trespass remain quite modest.

The modesty of the penalties for criminal trespass raises questions about the function of these laws. Such penalties cannot be regarded as having any significant deterrent force. (Unless perhaps the social stigma of a misdemeanor trespass conviction is large. Is it?) How then does a landowner protect the right to exclude? One answer would seem to be civil actions (like the civil trespass action at issue in *Jacque v. Steenberg Homes* in Chapter I), but these are rare. Another answer, probably more important historically, is that landowners may use "self-help." In other words, the landowner is privileged to use "reasonable force" to expel unwanted intruders from the land—but not deadly force, at least if the intrusion is onto land or an unoccupied building, see Katko v. Briney, 183 N.W.2d 657 (Iowa 1971) (spring gun cannot be used to defend unoccupied building against trespassers). Self-help has some obvious drawbacks— such as the possibility of violence or injury to the landowner, the intruder, or a bystander—which we consider in greater detail below. This suggests that the principal function of criminal trespass statutes is to create an alternative to landowner self-help. The criminal trespass statutes substitute a police officer for agents of the landowner in enforcing the right to exclude. The police officer is less likely than the landowner to overreact to the situation, and less likely to encounter resistance from the intruder. If there is a genuine dispute between the owner and the intruder over the right of access, it can then be resolved— peacefully—in court.

Given the availability of the police to enforce the landowner's right to exclude in many situations, does this suggest that self-help should be prohibited as a means of enforcing the right when police intervention is feasible? (See *Berg v. Wiley*, infra.)

Many criminal trespass statutes make it a crime to refuse to leave land in possession of another only after being notified to do so. See Tex. Penal Code Ann. § 30.05(a). This imposes a small affirmative burden on the landowner—to notify the intruder to leave before calling the police. Statutes specify in more or less detail what counts as notice. For example, the Texas statute provides for notice by oral or written communication; fencing or enclosure; signs indicating that entry is forbidden; "purple paint marks" on trees or posts that are "vertical lines of not less than eight inches in length and not less than one inch in width" and subject to elaborate spacing requirements; or the presence of standing crops. Tex. Penal Code Ann. § 30.05(b)(2). Why put the burden on the landowner to communicate the intent to exclude rather than put the burden on the intruder to obtain permission to enter? Is this necessary to establish the required scienter (mental state) on the part of the defendant before imposing criminal liability? What implications does the allocation of the burden of communication have for the development of norms of "neighborliness" within a community? Consider also the environmental consequences of notice requirements. These are presumably responsible (at least in significant part) for the proliferation of "No Trespassing,"

"Private Property," and "Do Not Enter" signs one sees on walls, doors, and fences throughout the land. Would rural and urban landscapes be more attractive if the law simply imposed a duty not to trespass on any land enclosed by a fence, wall, or other obvious border, without requiring explicit "notification"?

Real property is protected by criminal laws other than criminal trespass, often with considerably more fire power. Interestingly, however, the heavy artillery of the criminal law, insofar as property in land is concerned, is concentrated almost entirely on offenses that involve buildings or occupied structures. The crime of *arson*, for example, is defined as causing a fire or explosion that destroys "a building or occupied structure of another." Model Penal Code § 220.1(1). Arson is a felony subject to very severe penalties. The crime of *burglary* occurs when a person "enters a building or structure, or separately secured or occupied portion thereof, with purpose to commit a crime therein, unless the premises are at the time open to the public or the actor is licensed or privileged to enter." Id. § 221.1(1). Burglary is also a felony subject to severe penalties. The penalties for criminal trespass are also frequently more severe if the trespass involves a building or occupied structure. Does this overall pattern lend support to the claim that the criminal law is systematically more concerned with protection of persons than protection of property, since occupied structures by definition include persons, and persons are more likely to be found in buildings? In any event, arson and burglary, which are the most severely punished crimes involving land, pose obvious threats to the security of the person.

2.   CIVIL ACTIONS

Civil actions to protect and recover property have a long and complicated history. These actions started out as common-law "writs," which were a kind of standardized pleading that required certain kinds of proof and afforded certain prescribed remedies. Over time, especially with the adoption of the Field Codes in the mid-nineteenth century and then the emergence of modern "notice" or "fact" pleading, the rigidities associated with the writs have been much relaxed. See Rodolfo Batiza, Sources of the Field Civil Code: The Civil Law Influences on a Common Law Code, 60 Tul. L. Rev. 799 (1986).

Nevertheless, the elements associated with the individual writs continue to live on in judicial understandings about what must be proved in order to establish a "cause of action." You may have already noticed this shift in some of the cases covered in this book. Older cases commonly begin with the court reciting the common-law writ that governs the action. See, e.g., Pierson v. Post, Chapter II ("This was an action of trespass on the case . . . "); Wetherbee v. Green, Chapter II ("This was an action in replevin . . . "); Clark v. Maloney, Chapter II ("Action of trover to recover the value of ten white pine logs."). More recent cases no longer follow this format, but they often contain elaborate discussions of whether the defendant's behavior gives rise to a particular cause of action. See, e.g., Moore v. Regents of the University of California, Chapter III (whether defendants' taking of plaintiff's body cells gave rise to an action for conversion). Thus, the features of the common-law writs live on in the law, but in a less direct and noticeable fashion. A good source for those seeking more detail about the common-law writs is Joseph H. Koffler & Alison Reppy, Common Law Pleading (1969). The historical evolution of the writs is discussed in D.J. Ibbetson, A Historical Introduction to the Law of Obligations (1999).

a. CIVIL ACTIONS PROTECTING REAL PROPERTY

We start here with actions to protect real property, which begin somewhat earlier in time than the actions that relate to personal property. By the thirteenth century, English courts would hear claims based on the so-called real actions, such as the writ of novel disseisin and the writ of mort d'ancestor. These actions protected seisin of land, a concept that started out meaning something like possession, but over time became encrusted with technicalities. See A.W.B. Simpson, A History of the Land Law 40–41 (2d ed. 1986). By the end of the sixteenth century, the real actions had fallen into disuse, and had been replaced by writs from the trespass family. Especially prominent were *trespass quare clausum fregit* (trespass "because he broke the close," often called simply "trespass q.c.f."), and trespass *de ejectione firmae*, which became known simply as *ejectment*. Both were originally actions for money damages, but by the sixteenth century, the common-law courts began to give specific recovery of land to certain parties who won an ejectment action. The real actions never were much used in the United States, where the actions of importance in protecting the right to land have always been trespass and ejectment.

Trespass protects possession. Thus, a party must be in possession of land to sue an intruder for trespass q.c.f. There was a longstanding debate, both in England and the United States, as to whether ejectment was an action that protected possession or title or both. See, e.g., Tapscott v. Cobbs, 52 Va. (11 Gratt.) 172 (1854). Whatever ambiguities existed historically, today it is relatively clear that trespass (the q.c.f. is usually dropped these days) is used to vindicate the interest that a person in possession has in exclusive possession of land, and ejectment is used to vindicate the interest of a person who has title to land against a person wrongfully in possession. For example, if land is under lease, and a trespass such as a building encroachment occurs, the tenant in possession is the only one who can bring an action in trespass. The landlord would have to sue in ejectment. See Prosser and Keeton, The Law of Torts § 13, at 78 (5th ed. 1984).

Although the remedy for trespass was originally damages, courts for several centuries have also awarded injunctions against trespasses. See discussion in Baker v. Hunt Club, infra Part C.1. Typically, the plaintiff/

possessor can recover both in a single action: damages for injuries incurred in the past, and an injunction against recurring injury in the future. The plaintiff/owner suing in ejectment can also seek both damages and an in-kind remedy: damages in the form of so-called mesne profits—for example the rental value of the property during the period of wrongful possession—and a process for restoring the owner to possession.

The other civil action of importance to landowners is *nuisance*. A quasi-criminal action known as the assize of nuisance existed as early as the thirteenth century. It was soon replaced by the action on the case for nuisance. Nuisance originally applied to injuries that have their source outside the plaintiff's land, whereas trespass q.c.f. required a breaking of the close, and hence an injury that originated on the land itself. Today, nuisance is understood to protect the interest in use and enjoyment of land, as opposed to trespass, which protects the interest in exclusive possession of land. Damages were the original remedy for a nuisance, but as in the case of trespass q.c.f., injunctive relief became available along the way. (For more on trespass and nuisance, see Chapter IX.)

b. CIVIL ACTIONS PROTECTING PERSONAL PROPERTY

At common law, a number of distinctive writs or rights of action developed to protect owners of personal property. One, which dates from the early fourteenth century and was probably quasi-criminal in its origins, was also a member of the trespass family, in this case the writ of *trespass de bonis asportatis* (or trespass d.b.a.), which applied to the forcible carrying off (asportation) of the plaintiff's goods. It was necessary to allege that the goods had been wrongfully taken from the plaintiff's possession, but was not necessary to allege that they had been converted to the defendant's own use. As with other early trespass actions, an award of money damages was the only remedy available under this writ. The plaintiff could not recover the goods themselves.

Another common-law writ, which emerged in the early fifteenth century and evolved out of the older action for debt, was *detinue*. In contrast to trespass d.b.a., which was based on an unlawful taking, detinue was based on the unlawful detention of goods. Detinue applied when the plaintiff alleged that the defendant had unjustly detained specific goods which remained in the defendant's possession, and which the plaintiff alleged should be returned to him. It was used mainly to recover lost property and in disputes over bailments (temporary rightful possession, see Part D.2 below). If the defendant was found liable, he had the option of either returning the object to the plaintiff or paying its value in damages.

A third common-law writ that became important after the middle of the sixteenth century was *trover*. This action also evolved out of the trespass family, and in particular out of the action for trespass on the case, which was the general action for indirect rather than direct harms. Like detinue, trover did not require that the plaintiff prove an unlawful taking. Trover was used to allege that the defendant had wrongfully converted the plaintiff's goods to his own use, as by consuming it or selling it to a third party. It was not necessary to allege that the goods remained in the defendant's possession as under detinue, only that they had been converted to the defendant's use. Damages were the only remedy until 1854, when Parliament passed a statute authorizing the judge to order return of the goods in appropriate cases.

A fourth common-law writ, and the only one which provided a mechanism for recovering the personal property itself, was *replevin*. Replevin was also an old action, dating from the fourteenth century, and it was originally used in the narrow context where a landlord seized personal property of the plaintiff as a distraint for unpaid rent. Like trespass d.b.a, it was based on a wrongful taking of goods (e.g., because the plaintiff claimed no rent was owed), rather than wrongful detention. Replevin had an unusual procedure. It began with the plaintiff posting a bond, usually for twice the value of the property, whereupon the plaintiff could immediately recover possession of the property. If the plaintiff won, the bond was returned. If the plaintiff lost, then the bond was used to satisfy the defendant's claim (e.g., for unpaid rent).

A fifth common-law writ, which also evolved from the trespass family, was *trespass to chattels* or *trespass to personal property*. This action applied when the defendant had interfered with the plaintiff's possession of personal property, in some manner falling short of conversion. This action was invoked relatively rarely—at least until recently, when it has been dusted off and thrust into the limelight with the emergence of disputes over hacking into computer systems, spamming and other unwanted intrusions into websites and email systems. See Intel Corp. v. Hamidi, infra.

This was the basic menu of options for protecting personal property when the American colonies broke free of England in 1776. The newly independent states eventually adopted laws "receiving" the common law of England, including the writs of trespass d.b.a., detinue, trover, replevin, and trespass to personal property. Ford W. Hall, The Common Law: An Account of Its Reception in the United States, 4 Vand. L. Rev. 791 (1951). But the courts would often modify the common law to accommodate the different circumstances or needs of the fledgling nation.

Replevin was popular in America because it allowed the plaintiff to recover possession of goods rather than simply damages. Over time, the action expanded well beyond its original context of distraint for rent, and came to be used in a variety of circumstances involving the wrongful taking of personal property in which the plaintiff wanted to recover possession. By a variety of fictions and legislative changes, replevin was also expanded to include situations involving wrongful detention, as opposed to takings, of goods. Usually, the state courts retained some version of the original procedure calling for a posting of a bond by the plaintiff and recovery of possession at the outset of the litigation.

Trover became the favored action for plaintiffs seeking relief from wrongful conversion of personal property. Under the influence of the Field Codes popular in the mid-nineteenth century, trover came to be supplanted by the tort of conversion, although in substance it was largely the same. Today, one rarely sees reference to trover. The principal actions for protection of personal property today are replevin, conversion, and trespass to personal property.

Intel Corporation v. Hamidi

Supreme Court of California, 2003.
71 P.3d 296.

■ WERDEGAR, J. [Kourosh Kenneth Hamidi was an engineer formerly employed by the Intel Corporation, a major producer of microchips. Intel maintained a proprietary computer network for its employees. This was connected to the Internet, and Intel employees were allowed to conduct Internet searches and to send and receive messages to persons outside the company using their email addresses, but the full list of internal email addresses was kept confidential. After he was fired, Hamidi and several others formed an organization called Former and Current Employees of Intel (FACE-Intel). Hamidi, who served as the "webmaster" for FACE-Intel, somehow obtained a relatively complete list of Intel's email addresses. Over the course of 21 months, he sent mass emails to these addresses, reaching as many as 35,000 recipients at one time. The messages criticized Intel's employment practices, warned employees of the dangers of those practices, suggested that employees consider leaving Intel and moving to other companies, and urged employees to visit the FACE-Intel website for further information. The messages informed recipients that they could be removed from FACE-Intel's mailing list if they so desired, and FACE-Intel honored these requests.

Intel made various efforts to block the messages from FACE-Intel, but was only partially successful. Hamidi later admitted that he evaded blocking efforts by sending the messages from different computers. Intel sent Hamidi a letter demanding that he stop, but he refused. Intel then sued Hamidi, alleging nuisance and trespass to chattels, and seeking damages and injunctive relief. Intel later dropped the nuisance count and the request for damages. In its court filings, Intel maintained without contradiction that significant staff time was consumed in seeking to block Hamidi's messages. The FACE-Intel website, for its part, claimed that the messages had prompted discussions between "[e]xcited and nervous managers" and the company's human resources department. At no time did Intel claim that the messages had caused any disruption or physical damage to its computer network or its servers.]

civil,
real
(dropped)

civil,
personal   ⟶   interefered w/
                     Intel's possession
                     of its property

On these facts, Intel brought suit, claiming that by communicating with its employees over the company's e-mail system Hamidi committed the tort of trespass to chattels. The trial court granted Intel's motion for summary judgment and enjoined Hamidi from any further mailings. A divided Court of Appeal affirmed.

After reviewing the decisions analyzing unauthorized electronic contact with computer systems as potential trespasses to chattels, we conclude that under California law the tort does not encompass, and should not be extended to encompass, an electronic communication that neither damages the recipient computer system nor impairs its functioning. Such an electronic communication does not constitute an actionable trespass to personal property, i.e., the computer system, because it does not interfere with the possessor's use or possession of, or any other legally protected interest in, the personal property itself. The consequential economic damage Intel claims to have suffered, i.e., loss of productivity caused by employees reading and reacting to Hamidi's messages and company efforts to block the messages, is not an injury to the company's interest in its computers—which worked as intended and were unharmed by the communications—any more than the personal distress caused by reading an unpleasant letter would be an injury to the recipient's mailbox, or the loss of privacy caused by an intrusive telephone call would be an injury to the recipient's telephone equipment.

Our conclusion does not rest on any special immunity for communications by electronic mail; we do not hold that messages transmitted through the Internet are exempt from the ordinary rules of tort liability. To the contrary, e-mail, like other forms of communication, may in some circumstances cause legally cognizable injury to the recipient or to third parties and may be actionable under various common-law or statutory theories [such as interference with contractual relations, intentional infliction of emotional distress, or publication of private facts] * * *

Nor does our holding affect the legal remedies of Internet service providers (ISP's) against senders of unsolicited commercial bulk e-mail (UCE), also known as "spam." A series of federal district court decisions, beginning with *CompuServe, Inc. v. Cyber Promotions, Inc.*, 962 F. Supp. 1015 (S.D.Ohio 1997), has approved the use of trespass to chattels as a theory of spammers' liability to ISP's, based upon evidence that the vast quantities of mail sent by spammers both overburdened the ISP's own computers and made the entire computer system harder to use for recipients, the ISP's customers. In those cases, discussed in greater detail below, the underlying complaint was that the extraordinary *quantity* of UCE impaired the computer system's functioning. In the present case, the claimed injury is located in the disruption or distraction caused to recipients by the *contents* of the e-mail messages, an injury entirely separate from, and not directly affecting, the possession or value of personal property. * * *

Figure 4-1
Hamidi, left, and a supporter delivering a message to Intel employees on a floppy disk after the Superior Court had enjoined his emails

Source: Don Preisler.

DISCUSSION

I.   Current California Tort Law

Dubbed by Prosser the "little brother of conversion," the tort of trespass to chattels allows recovery for interferences with possession of personal property "not sufficiently important to be classed as conversion, and so to compel the defendant to pay the full value of the thing with which he has interfered." (Prosser & Keeton, Torts § 14, pp. 85–86 (5th ed. 1984).)

Though not amounting to conversion, the defendant's interference must, to be actionable, have caused some injury to the chattel or to the plaintiff's rights in it. Under California law, trespass to chattels "lies where an intentional interference with the possession of personal property *has proximately caused injury*." (Thrifty-Tel, Inc. v. Bezenek 54 Cal.Rptr.2d 468 (Cal. Ct. App. 1996), italics added.) * * *

The Restatement, too, makes clear that some actual injury must have occurred in order for a trespass to chattels to be actionable. Under section 218 of the Restatement Second of Torts, dispossession alone, without further damages, is actionable (see id., par. (a) & com. d, pp. 420–421), but other forms of interference require some additional harm to the personal property or the possessor's interests in it. (Id., pars. (b)–(d)). "The interest of a possessor of a chattel in its inviolability, unlike the similar interest of a possessor of land, is not given legal protection by an action for nominal damages for harmless intermeddlings with the

[handwritten margin note: RULE / injury to chattel / or person's rights / to the chattel *]*

chattel. In order that an actor who interferes with another's chattel may be liable, his conduct must affect some other and more important interest of the possessor. *Therefore, one who intentionally intermeddles with another's chattel is subject to liability only if his intermeddling is harmful to the possessor's materially valuable interest in the physical condition, quality, or value of the chattel, or if the possessor is deprived of the use of the chattel for a substantial time, or some other legally protected interest of the possessor is affected as stated in Clause (c).* Sufficient legal protection of the possessor's interest in the mere inviolability of his chattel is afforded by his privilege to use reasonable force to protect his possession against even harmless interference." (Id., com. e, pp. 421–422, italics added.) * * *

In this respect, as Prosser explains, modern day trespass to chattels differs both from the original English writ and from the action for trespass to land: "Another departure from the original rule of the old writ of trespass concerns the necessity of some actual damage to the chattel before the action can be maintained. Where the defendant merely interferes without doing any harm—as where, for example, he merely lays hands upon the plaintiff's horse, or sits in his car—there has been a division of opinion among the writers, and a surprising dearth of authority. *By analogy to trespass to land there might be a technical tort in such a case. . . . . Such scanty authority as there is, however, has considered that the dignitary interest in the inviolability of chattels, unlike that as to land, is not sufficiently important to require any greater defense than the privilege of using reasonable force when necessary to protect them. Accordingly it has been held that nominal damages will not be awarded, and that in the absence of any actual damage the action will not lie.*" (Prosser & Keeton, Torts, supra, § 14, p. 87, italics added, fns. omitted.) * * *

The dispositive issue in this case, therefore, is whether the undisputed facts demonstrate Hamidi's actions caused or threatened to cause damage to Intel's computer system, or injury to its rights in that personal property, such as to entitle Intel to judgment as a matter of law. [T]he undisputed evidence revealed no actual or threatened damage to Intel's computer hardware or software and no interference with its ordinary and intended operation. * * *

Relying on a line of decisions, most from federal district courts, applying the tort of trespass to chattels to various types of unwanted electronic contact between computers, Intel contends that, while its computers were not damaged by receiving Hamidi's messages, its interest in the "physical condition, quality or value" (Rest.2d Torts, § 218, com. e, p. 422) of the computers was harmed. We disagree. The cited line of decisions does not persuade us that the mere sending of electronic communications that assertedly cause injury only because of their contents constitutes an actionable trespass to a computer system through which the messages are transmitted. Rather, the decisions finding electronic contact to be a trespass to computer systems have generally involved some actual or threatened interference with the computers' functioning. * * *

In each of these spamming cases, the plaintiff showed, or was prepared to show, some interference with the efficient functioning of its computer system. In *CompuServe,* the plaintiff ISP's mail equipment monitor stated that mass UCE [unsolicited commercial bulk e-mail] mailings, especially from nonexistent addresses such as those used by the defendant, placed "a tremendous burden" on the ISP's equipment, using "disk space and drain[ing] the processing power," making those resources unavailable to serve subscribers. (CompuServe, supra, 962 F.Supp. at p. 1022.) Similarly, in *Hotmail Corp. v. Van$ Money Pie, Inc.,* 1998 WL 388389, at *7 (N.D. Cal. Apr. 16 1998), the court found the evidence supported a finding that the defendant's mailings "fill[ed] up Hotmail's computer storage space and threaten[ed] to damage Hotmail's ability to service its legitimate customers." *America Online, Inc. v. IMS,* 24 F.Supp.2d 548 (E.D. Va. 1998), decided on summary judgment, was deemed factually indistinguishable from *CompuServe*; the court observed that in both cases the plaintiffs "alleged that processing the bulk e-mail cost them time and money and burdened their equipment." Id. at 550. * * *

Though Hamidi sent thousands of copies of the same message on six occasions over 21 months, that number is minuscule compared to the amounts of mail sent by commercial operations. * * * The functional burden on Intel's computers, or the cost in time to individual recipients, of receiving Hamidi's occasional advocacy messages cannot be compared to the burdens and costs caused ISP's and their customers by the ever-rising deluge of commercial e-mail.

In addition to impairment of system functionality, *CompuServe* and its progeny also refer to the ISP's loss of business reputation and customer goodwill, resulting from the inconvenience and cost that spam causes to its members, as harm to the ISP's legally protected interests in its personal property. Intel argues that its own interest in employee productivity, assertedly disrupted by Hamidi's messages, is a comparable protected interest in its computer system. We disagree. * * *

CompuServe's customers were annoyed because the system was inundated with unsolicited commercial messages, making its use for personal communication more difficult and costly. Their complaint, which allegedly led some to cancel their CompuServe service, was about *the functioning of CompuServe's electronic mail service.* Intel's workers, in contrast, were allegedly distracted from their work not because of the frequency or quantity of Hamidi's messages, but because of assertions and opinions the messages conveyed. Intel's complaint is thus about *the contents of the messages* rather than the functioning of the company's e-mail system. Even accepting *CompuServe's* economic injury rationale, therefore, Intel's position represents a further extension of the trespass to chattels tort, fictionally recharacterizing the allegedly injurious effect of a communication's *contents* on recipients as an impairment to the device which transmitted the message.

This theory of "impairment by content" (Burk, The Trouble with Trespass, [4 J. Small & Emerging Bus.L. 27, 37 (2000)]) threatens to stretch trespass law to cover injuries far afield from the harms to possession the tort evolved to protect. Intel's theory would expand the tort of trespass to chattels to cover virtually any unconsented-to communication that, solely because of its content, is unwelcome to the recipient or intermediate transmitter. * * *

Nor may Intel appropriately assert a *property* interest in its employees' time. "The Restatement test clearly speaks in the first instance to the impairment of the chattel. . . . But employees are not chattels (at least not in the legal sense of the term)." (Burk, The Trouble with Trespass, supra, 4 J. Small & Emerging Bus.L. at p. 36.) Whatever interest Intel may have in preventing its employees from receiving disruptive communications, it is not an interest in personal property, and trespass to chattels is therefore not an action that will lie to protect it. Nor, finally, can the fact Intel staff spent time attempting to block Hamidi's messages be bootstrapped into an injury to Intel's possessory interest in its computers. To quote * * * from the dissenting opinion in the Court of Appeal: "[I]t is circular to premise the damage element of a tort solely upon the steps taken to prevent the damage. Injury can only be established by the completed tort's consequences, not by the cost of the steps taken to avoid the injury and prevent the tort; otherwise, we can create injury for every supposed tort."

Intel connected its e-mail system to the Internet and permitted its employees to make use of this connection both for business and, to a reasonable extent, for their own purposes. In doing so, the company necessarily contemplated the employees' receipt of unsolicited as well as solicited communications from other companies and individuals. That some communications would, because of their contents, be unwelcome to Intel management was virtually inevitable. Hamidi did nothing but use the e-mail system for its intended purpose—to communicate with employees. The system worked as designed, delivering the messages without any physical or functional harm or disruption. These occasional transmissions cannot reasonably be viewed as impairing the quality or value of Intel's computer system. We conclude, therefore, that Intel has not presented undisputed facts demonstrating an injury to its personal property, or to its legal interest in that property, that support, under California tort law, an action for trespass to chattels.

II.   Proposed Extension of California Tort Law

We next consider whether California common law should be *extended* to cover, as a trespass to chattels, an otherwise harmless electronic communication whose contents are objectionable. * * *

Writing on behalf of several industry groups appearing as amici curiae, Professor Richard A. Epstein of the University of Chicago urges us to excuse the required showing of injury to personal property in cases of unauthorized electronic contact between computers, "extending the rules of trespass to real property to all interactive Web sites and servers." The court is thus urged to recognize, for owners of a particular species of personal property, computer servers, the same interest in inviolability as is generally accorded a possessor of land. In effect, Professor Epstein suggests that a company's server should be its castle, upon which any unauthorized intrusion, however harmless, is a trespass.

Epstein's argument derives, in part, from the familiar metaphor of the Internet as a physical space, reflected in much of the language that has been used to describe it: "cyberspace," "the information superhighway," e-mail "addresses," and the like. Of course, the Internet is also frequently called simply the "Net," a term, Hamidi points out, "evoking a fisherman's chattel." A major component of the Internet is the World Wide "Web," a descriptive term suggesting neither personal nor real property, and "cyberspace" itself has come to be known by the oxymoronic phrase "virtual reality," which would suggest that any real property "located" in "cyberspace" must be "virtually real" property. Metaphor is a two-edged sword.

Indeed, the metaphorical application of real property rules would not, by itself, transform a physically harmless electronic intrusion on a computer server into a trespass. That is because, under California law, intangible intrusions on land, including electromagnetic transmissions, are not actionable as trespasses (though they may be as nuisances) unless they cause physical damage to the real property. (San Diego Gas & Electric Co. v. Superior Court, 920 P.2d 669 (Cal. 1996).) Since Intel does not claim Hamidi's electronically transmitted messages physically damaged its servers, it could not prove a trespass to land even were we to treat the computers as a type of real property. Some further extension of the conceit would be required, under which the electronic signals Hamidi sent would be recast as tangible intruders, perhaps as tiny messengers rushing through the "hallways" of Intel's computers and bursting out of employees' computers to read them Hamidi's missives. But such fictions promise more confusion than clarity in the law.

The plain fact is that computers, even those making up the Internet, are—like such older communications equipment as telephones and fax machines—personal property, not realty. Professor Epstein observes that "[a]lthough servers may be moved in real space, they cannot be moved in cyberspace," because an Internet server must, to be useful, be accessible at a known address. But the same is true of the telephone: to be useful for incoming communication, the telephone must remain constantly linked to the same number (or, when the number is changed, the system must include some forwarding or notification capability, a qualification that also applies to computer addresses). Does this suggest that an unwelcome message delivered through a telephone or fax machine should be viewed as a trespass to a type of real property? We think not[.] * * *

More substantively, Professor Epstein argues that a rule of computer server inviolability will, through the formation or extension of a market in computer-to-computer access, create "the right social result." In most circumstances, he predicts, companies with computers on the Internet will continue to authorize transmission of information through e-mail, Web site searching, and page linking because they benefit by that open access. When a Web site owner does deny access to a particular sending, searching, or linking computer, a system of "simple one-on-one negotiations" will arise to provide the necessary individual licenses.

Other scholars are less optimistic about such a complete propertization of the Internet. Professor Mark Lemley of the University of California, Berkeley, writing on behalf of an amici curiae group of professors of intellectual property and computer law, observes that under a property rule of server inviolability, "each of the hundreds of millions of [Internet] users must get permission in advance from anyone with whom they want to communicate and anyone who owns a server through which their message may travel." The consequence for e-mail could be a substantial reduction in the freedom of electronic communication, as the owner of each computer through which an electronic message passes could impose its own limitations on message content or source. As Professor Dan Hunter of the University of Pennsylvania asks rhetorically: "Does this mean that one must read the 'Terms of Acceptable Email Usage' of every email system that one emails in the course of an ordinary day? If the University of Pennsylvania had a policy that sending a joke by email would be an unauthorized use of their system, then under the logic of [the lower court decision in this case], you commit 'trespass' if you emailed me a . . . cartoon." (Hunter, Cyberspace as Place, and the Tragedy of the Digital Anticommons 91 Cal. L. Rev. 439, 508–509 (2003).)

Web site linking, Professor Lemley further observes, "would exist at the sufferance of the linked-to party, because a Web user who followed a 'disapproved' link would be trespassing on the plaintiff's server, just as sending an e-mail is trespass under the [lower] court's theory." Another writer warns that "[c]yber-trespass theory will curtail the free flow of price and product information on the Internet by allowing website owners to tightly control who and what may enter and make use of the information housed on its Internet site." (Chang, Bidding on Trespass: *eBay, Inc. v. Bidder's Edge, Inc.* and the Abuse of Trespass Theory in Cyberspace Law, 29 AIPLA Q.J. 445, 459 (2001).) A leading scholar of Internet law and policy, Professor Lawrence Lessig of Stanford University, has criticized Professor Epstein's theory of the computer server as quasi-real property, previously put forward in the *eBay* case, on the ground that it ignores the costs to society in the loss of network benefits: "eBay benefits greatly from a network that is open and where access is free. It is this general feature of the Net that makes the Net so valuable to users and a source of great innovation. And to the extent that individual sites begin to impose their own rules of exclusion, the value of the network as a network declines. If machines must negotiate before entering any individual site, then the costs of using the network climb." (Lessig, The Future of Ideas: The Fate of the Commons in a Connected World (2001) p. 171; * * *)

We discuss this debate among the amici curiae and academic writers only to note its existence and contours, not to attempt its resolution. Creating an absolute property right to exclude undesired communications from one's e-mail and Web servers might help force spammers to internalize the costs they impose on ISP's and their customers. But such a property rule might also create substantial new costs, to e-mail and e-commerce users and to society generally, in lost ease and openness of communication and in lost network benefits. In light of the unresolved controversy, we would be acting rashly to adopt a rule treating computer servers as real property for purposes of trespass law.* * *

externalities

The judgment of the Court of Appeal is reversed.

■ Concurring Opinion by KENNARD, J. [omitted].

■ Dissenting Opinion of BROWN, J. * * * Intel has invested millions of dollars to develop and maintain a computer system. It did this not to act as a public forum but to enhance the productivity of its employees. Kourosh Kenneth Hamidi sent as many as 200,000 e-mail messages to Intel employees. The time required to review and delete Hamidi's messages diverted employees from productive tasks and undermined the utility of the computer system. "There may . . . be situations in which the value to the owner of a particular type of chattel may be impaired by dealing with it in a manner that does not affect its physical condition." (Rest.2d Torts, § 218, com. h, p. 422.) This is such a case.

The majority repeatedly asserts that Intel objected to the hundreds of thousands of messages solely due to their content, and proposes that Intel seek relief by pleading content-based speech torts. This proposal misses the point that Intel's objection is directed not toward Hamidi's message but his use of Intel's property to display his message. Intel has not sought to prevent Hamidi from expressing his ideas on his Web site, through private mail (paper or electronic) to employees' homes, or through any other means like picketing or billboards. But as counsel for Intel explained during oral argument, the company objects to Hamidi's using Intel's property to advance his message.

not objecting to H's content but to his USE of Intel's computers to spread it

Of course, Intel deserves an injunction even if its objections are based entirely on the e-mail's content. Intel is entitled, for example, to allow employees use of the Internet to check stock market tables or weather forecasts without incurring any concomitant obligation to allow access to pornographic Web sites. (Loving v. Boren 956 F.Supp. 953, 955 (W.D.Okla. 1997).) A private property owner may choose to exclude unwanted mail for any reason, including its content. (Rowan v. U.S. Post Office Dept. 397 U.S. 728, 738 (1970).) * * *

Regardless of whether property is real or personal, it is beyond dispute that an individual has the right to have his personal property free from interference. There is some division among authorities regarding the available remedy, particularly whether a harmless trespass supports a claim for nominal damages. The North Carolina Court of Appeal has found there is no damage requirement for a trespass to chattel. (See Hawkins v. Hawkins, 400 S.E.2d 472, 475 (N.C. 1991).) * * * Several authorities consider a harmless trespass to goods actionable per se only if it is intentional. (Winfield & Jolowicz on Torts, Trespass to Goods 403 (10th ed. 1975); Clerk & Lindsell on Torts ¶ 13–159, p. 703 (17th ed. 1995).) The Restatement Second of Torts, section 218, which is less inclined to favor liability, likewise forbids unauthorized use and recognizes the inviolability of personal property. * * * "The interest of a possessor of a chattel in its inviolability, unlike the similar interest of a possessor of land, is not given legal protection *by an action for nominal damages* for harmless intermeddlings with the chattel. . . . Sufficient legal protection of the possessor's interest in the mere *inviolability of his chattel* is afforded by his *privilege to use reasonable force* to protect his possession against *even harmless interference*." (Rest.2d Torts, § 218, com. e, pp. 421–422, italics added.) Accordingly, the protection of land and chattels may differ on the question of nominal damages unrelated to actual injury. The authorities agree, however, that (1) the chattel is inviolable, (2) the trespassee need not tolerate even harmless interference, and (3) the possessor may use reasonable force to prevent it. Both California law and the Restatement authorize reasonable force regardless of whether the property in question is real or personal. (Civ.Code, § 51; Rest.2d Torts, § 77.) * * *

In 1996, the Appellate Division of the New York Supreme Court considered the claim of plaintiff Tillman, who sought to enjoin the unwanted delivery of a newspaper onto his property. (Tillman v. Distribution Systems of America Inc., 224 A.D.2d 79, 648 N.Y.S.2d 630 (1996).) He offered no specific critique of the newspaper's content, observing only " '[t]here is no reason that we have to clean up [defendant's] mess.' " (Id. at p. 632.) * * * [T]he court rejected the defendants' argument "that there is nothing a homeowner can do to stop the dumping on his or her property of pamphlets or newspapers, no matter how offensive they might be," and instead upheld Tillman's right to prevent the mail's delivery, regardless of whether his objection was due to the quantity (volume) or quality (content) of the messages. (Tillman, at p. 636.) In authorizing injunctive relief, the *Tillman* court found no need to quantify the actual damage created by the delivery; it merely noted that the homeowner should not be forced either "to allow such unwanted newspapers to accumulate, or to expend the time and energy necessary to gather and to dispose of them." (Ibid.) Subsequent courts have extended this policy to the delivery of e-mail as well. * * *

Hamidi concedes Intel's legal entitlement to block the unwanted messages. The problem is that although Intel has resorted to the cyberspace version of reasonable force, it has so far been unsuccessful in determining how to resist the unwanted use of its system. Thus, while Intel has the legal right to exclude Hamidi from its system, it does not have the physical ability. It *may* forbid Hamidi's use, but it *can* not prevent it.

To the majority, Hamidi's ability to outwit Intel's cyber defenses justifies denial of Intel's claim to exclusive use of its property. Under this reasoning, it is not right but might that determines the extent of a party's possessory interest. Although the world often works this way, the legal system should not. * * *

Those who have contempt for grubby commerce and reverence for the rarified heights of intellectual discourse may applaud today's decision, but even the flow of ideas will be curtailed if the right to exclude is denied. As the Napster controversy revealed, creative individuals will be less inclined to develop intellectual property if they cannot limit the terms of its transmission. Similarly, if online newspapers cannot charge for access, they will be unable to pay the journalists and editorialists who generate ideas for public consumption. * * *

The principles of both personal liberty and social utility should counsel us to usher the common law of property into the digital age.

■ Dissenting Opinion by MOSK, J.* * * * The majority fail to distinguish open communication in the public "commons" of the Internet from unauthorized intermeddling on a private, proprietary intranet. Hamidi is not communicating in the equivalent of a town square or of an unsolicited "junk" mailing through the United States Postal Service. His action, in crossing from the public Internet into a private intranet, is more like intruding into a private office mailroom, commandeering the mail cart, and dropping off unwanted broadsides on 30,000 desks. Because Intel's security measures have been circumvented by Hamidi, the majority leave Intel, which has exercised all reasonable self-help efforts, with no recourse unless he causes a malfunction or systems "crash." Hamidi's repeated intrusions did more than merely "prompt[ ] discussions between '[e]xcited and nervous managers' and the company's human resource department" (maj. opn., ante); they also constituted a misappropriation of Intel's private computer system contrary to its intended use and against Intel's wishes.

The law of trespass to chattels has not universally been limited to physical damage. I believe it is entirely consistent to apply that legal theory to these circumstances—that is, when a proprietary computer

---

    *   Associate Justice, Court of Appeal, Second Appellate District, Division Five, assigned by the Chief Justice pursuant to article VI, section 6 of the California Constitution.

system is being used contrary to its owner's purposes and expressed desires, and self-help has been ineffective. Intel correctly expects protection from an intruder who misuses its proprietary system, its nonpublic directories, and its supposedly controlled connection to the Internet to achieve his bulk mailing objectives—incidentally, without even having to pay postage. * * *

Here, Hamidi's deliberate and continued intermeddling, and threatened intermeddling, with Intel's proprietary computer system for his own purposes that were hostile to Intel, certainly impaired the quality and value of the system as an internal business device for Intel and forced Intel to incur costs to try to maintain the security and integrity of its server—efforts that proved ineffective. These included costs incurred to mitigate injuries that had already occurred. It is not a matter of "bootstrapp[ing]" (maj. opn., ante) to consider those costs a damage to Intel. Indeed, part of the value of the proprietary computer system is the ability to exclude intermeddlers from entering it for significant uses that are disruptive to its owner's business operations. * * *

NOTES AND QUESTIONS

1. Recall that in *Jacque v. Steenberg Homes*, the Wisconsin Supreme Court upheld a $100,000 punitive damages award to a couple for a trespass to land that did no injury to the land or any other tangible interest of the owners. Yet according to the majority in *Hamidi*, there is no legal remedy other than self-help for an intentional trespass to personal property that does no physical injury to the property. This means, for example, that if someone repeatedly sits in your car without your permission, and does no damage to it, you have no civil remedy, either for an injunction or damages. Does this strike you as sound? What is the justification for requiring actual injury to establish trespass to personal property but not requiring this to show trespass to land? You may want to reconsider the issue after considering the next set of materials, on self-help.

2. Another way to view *Hamidi* is that it simply limits the available remedies for trespass to personal property to damages, which after all is the general remedy in tort, including for other torts in the trespass family. If the only remedy is damages, then typically one gets no relief unless one can prove actual damages. The unusual thing about trespass to personal property, from this perspective, is that equity will not intervene to issue an injunction in cases of repeated or vexatious invasions of personal property. Compare with Baker v. Howard County Hunt Club, infra Part C.1. What might be the justification for cutting off equitable relief in this context? See Keith N. Hylton, Property Rules, Liability Rules, and Immunity: An Application to Cyberspace, 87 B.U. L. Rev. 1, 16–23 (2007).

3. The majority and dissenting opinions disagree as to whether Intel Corporation has shown that it suffered actual injury because of the unwanted mass emails from Hamidi. Does the majority's conclusion of no injury rest on a presumption that injury based on the content of a

[handwritten margin note: Jacque holding vs. this one]

communication cannot count as injury, at least for trespass purposes? Do the dissents' contrary conclusions rest on a presumption that injury is always present when a proprietor must take measures to exclude an intruder? Which presumption is more appropriate?

4.   Given that Hamidi's invasion of Intel's computer network took the form of electrons, why was trespass to personal property the correct cause of action? If real property were the interest at stake, wouldn't an invasion by electrons be governed by nuisance rather than trespass? (See Chapters I and IX.) Why is there no analogue to nuisance among the actions that protect personal property? Should there be? Should nuisance law be extended to cover intangible invasions into "virtual" space, such as an intranet? See Adam Mossoff, Spam—Oy, What a Nuisance!, 19 Berkeley Tech. L.J. 625 (2004).

5.   Even if one can establish that someone is causing actual harm to an intranet system (or other electronic network), how does one establish a "trespassory invasion" in this context? With physical property, a trespass occurs when the boundary of real property is crossed or when someone touches an item of personal property. But is every form of "unauthorized access" into an electronic network necessarily a trespass?

6.   The most far-reaching issue discussed in *Hamidi* reverts to the question of whether "cyberspace" should be subject to parcelization, with individually-developed segments like intranets and web-sites protected by property-like exclusion rights, or whether it should be regarded as an open-access resource, like navigable waterways and public highways. The debate between the amici curiae summarized by the majority in Part II of its opinion, "Proposed Extension of California Tort Law," poses the question in terms of transaction costs. Richard Epstein argued that parcelization would produce efficient outcomes, because owners of computers linked to the Internet would grant blanket consent to "visitations" by outsiders, and would single out for exclusion only those who are unwanted. Mark Lemley and Larry Lessig argued that parcelization would require some kind of individually negotiated license between the proprietor of the computer network and each outside "visitor," and that these negotiations would unduly burden the flow of information and possibly create a cyber-anticommons. (On the anticommons, see Chapter II.) Who has the better argument? Are spam filters generally an effective device for eliminating unwanted electronic messages?

7.   More disgruntled employees: In *School of Visual Arts v. Kuprewicz*, 771 N.Y.S.2d 804 (N.Y. Sup. 2003), the defendant, a former employee at the School of Visual Arts, posted false job advertisements on Craigslist.com for the job held by SVA's Director of Human Resources, and registered her email address on several pornographic websites, causing her to receive "large volumes" of both applications for her job and pornographic emails. On a motion to dismiss, the court found that the many-headed complaint only stated a cause of action in trespass to personal property. Asserting its agreement with *Hamidi*, the court declared that its decision to sustain the complaint was based on the allegations of physical detriment to the computer system from the volume of mail, not on the intrusive and unwanted character

of the emails. What if the case had involved a smaller volume of emails (or a less vulnerable computer) than was alleged, but the emails were just as disturbing? What if, further, the plaintiff had told the defendant to stop, but the plaintiff refused? Should it matter if self-help had been tried and failed, as in *Hamidi*? See, e.g., Patricia L. Bellia, Defending Cyberproperty, 79 N.Y.U. L. Rev. 2164 (2004); William Hubbard, Communicating Entitlements: Property and the Internet, 22 Yale L. & Pol'y Rev. 401 (2004); Symposium, Property Rights on the Frontier: The Economics and Self-Help and Self-Defense in Cyberspace, 1 J.L. Econ. & Pol'y 1 (2005).

8.   Like many other issues we canvass in this book, the debate between the majority and the dissents is at least in part a debate about the choice of the appropriate institution to resolve an issue. The majority believes that trespass to personal property should be defined narrowly in the context of cyber-invasions, leaving more aggressive regulation up to the legislature. The dissents argue that the courts should step in and provide a remedy based on analogical extension of the common law, leaving it to the legislature to make revisions if necessary. Which approach do you think generally better for adjusting the law to inevitable technological and social changes?

9.   Civil protections of personal property may or may not extend to intangibles. Courts take a wide variety of approaches to whether intangibles (power, wifi-signals, data, assets in online games) can be converted. For an expansive approach to liability, see *Kremen v. Cohen*, 337 F.3d 1024, 1030 (9th Cir. 2003), a decision applying California law in the same year as *Intel v. Hamidi*. Can such assets be possessed? Does that matter? Might such conversion liability vastly expand intellectual property by the back door? See, e.g., João Marinotti, Tangibility as Technology, 37 Ga. St. L. Rev. 671 (2021).

3. SELF-HELP

In addition to formal legal remedies provided by criminal and civil law, property owners are entitled to take a variety of steps to protect or enforce their property rights without the direct involvement of the legal system. These measures, which we collectively call "self-help," may in fact be more important in preserving the general structure of ownership than formal legal remedies; certainly they are utilized far more often. The use of self-help in defending present possession is particularly ubiquitous. Fences, locks on doors, security guards, dogs, burglar alarms, and video cameras are all familiar examples of self-help in the real property context. Ignition locks, safes, indelible serial numbers, and Lojack tracking systems are examples in the personal property realm.

The nature of self-help as a mode of protection for property can be illuminated by considering a distinction introduced by Wesley Newcomb Hohfeld between "rights" and "privileges." See generally Wesley Newcomb Hohfeld, Some Fundamental Legal Conceptions as Applied in Judicial Reasoning, 23 Yale L.J. 16 (1913), reprinted in Wesley Newcomb Hohfeld, Fundamental Legal Conceptions as Applied in Judicial Reasoning and Other Legal Essays, 23–64 (Walter Wheeler Cook ed.,

Yale Univ. Press 1923). A "right" as Hohfeld defined the term, is a claim that one person has against one or more others, which corresponds to a duty that these others have toward the one with the right. Thus, if A owns Blackacre, A has a right to exclude B, C, D, etc. from Blackacre, and B, C, D, etc., have a corresponding duty to keep off Blackacre without A's permission. A "privilege," as Hohfeld used the term, is a freedom to act in certain ways without interference from others, which corresponds to a "no-right" in the others to interfere with the one exercising the privilege. Self-help can be thought of as a type of privilege associated with ownership. If A owns Blackacre, then A has a privilege to engage in a variety of defensive measures to protect Blackacre from invasions or other harms by others, such as B, C, D, etc. The others, B, C, D, etc. have "no-right" to interfere or try to stop A from deploying these defensive measures. Note that a privilege permits but does not compel a person to do certain things. Thus, an owner is permitted to use self-help to protect her interest in possession, but is not required to do so. For example, an owner of an automobile is permitted to lock the doors to discourage theft or joyriding, but if the owner neglects to lock the doors, the owner still has the right, in the Hohfeldian sense, to demand that others not steal the car or engage in joyriding.

Self-help becomes controversial when it involves the use of force, as opposed to passive devices like fences and locks. A person in possession of property can generally use reasonable force when the person "believes that such force is immediately necessary . . . to prevent or terminate an unlawful entry or other trespass upon land or a trespass against or the unlawful carrying away of tangible, movable property." Model Penal Code § 3.06(1)(a). The Model Penal Code takes the position that in the case of burglary, reasonable force does not mean deadly force, unless there is a danger to persons. Id. § 3.06(3)(d). But many jurisdictions disagree, and permit the use of deadly force to avert burglary, whether or not there is proof of a specific threat to persons. See N.Y. Penal Law § 35.20(3).

Even more controversial is the use of self-help to recover possession of property once it has been transferred to another. As the following cases suggest, the current state of the law here diverges between real and personal property.

Berg v. Wiley

Supreme Court of Minnesota, 1978.
264 N.W.2d 145.

■ ROGOSHESKE, JUSTICE. Defendant landlord, Wiley Enterprises, Inc., and defendant Rodney A. Wiley (hereafter collectively referred to as Wiley) appeal from a judgment upon a jury verdict awarding plaintiff tenant, A Family Affair Restaurant, Inc., damages for wrongful eviction from its leased premises. The issues for review are whether the evidence was sufficient to support the jury's finding that the tenant did not abandon or surrender the premises and whether the trial court erred in finding Wiley's reentry forcible and wrongful as a matter of law. We hold that the jury's verdict is supported by sufficient evidence and that the trial court's determination of unlawful entry was correct as a matter of law, and affirm the judgment.

On November 11, 1970, Wiley, as lessor and tenant's predecessor in interest as lessee, executed a written lease agreement letting land and a building in Osseo, Minnesota, for use as a restaurant. The lease provided a 5-year term beginning December 1, 1970, and specified that the tenant agreed to bear all costs of repairs and remodeling, to "make no changes in the building structure" without prior written authorization from Wiley, and to "operate the restaurant in a lawful and prudent manner." Wiley also reserved the right "at (his) option (to) retake possession" of the premises "(s)hould the Lessee fail to meet the conditions of this Lease."[1] In early 1971, plaintiff Kathleen Berg took assignment of the lease from the prior lessee, and on May 1, 1971, she opened "A Family Affair Restaurant" on the premises. In January 1973, Berg incorporated the restaurant and assigned her interest in the lease to "A Family Affair Restaurant, Inc." As sole shareholder of the corporation, she alone continued to act for the tenant.

The present dispute has arisen out of Wiley's objection to Berg's continued remodeling of the restaurant without procuring written permission and her consequent operation of the restaurant in a state of disrepair with alleged health code violations. Strained relations between the parties came to a head in June and July 1973. In a letter dated June 29, 1973, Wiley's attorney charged Berg with having breached lease items 5 and 6 by making changes in the building structure without written authorization and by operating an unclean kitchen in violation of health regulations. The letter demanded that a list of eight remodeling items be completed within 2 weeks from the date of the letter, by Friday, July 13, 1973, or Wiley would retake possession of the premises under lease item 7. Also, a June 13 inspection of the restaurant by the Minnesota Department of Health had produced an order that certain listed changes be completed within specified time limits in order to comply with the health code. The major items on the inspector's list, similar to those listed by Wiley's attorney, were to be completed by July 15, 1973.

---

[1]   The provisions of the lease pertinent to this case provide:

Item #5 The Lessee will make no changes to the building structure without first receiving written authorization from the Lessor. The Lessor will promptly reply in writing to each request and will cooperate with the Lessee on any reasonable request.

Item #6 The Lessee agrees to operate the restaurant in a lawful and prudent manner during the lease period.

Item #7 Should the Lessee fail to meet the conditions of this Lease the Lessor may at their option retake possession of said premises. In any such event such act will not relieve Lessee from liability for payment [of] the rental herein provided or from the conditions or obligations of this lease.

During the 2-week deadline set by both Wiley and the health department, Berg continued to operate the restaurant without closing to complete the required items of remodeling. The evidence is in dispute as to whether she intended to permanently close the restaurant and vacate the premises at the end of the 2 weeks or simply close for about 1 month in order to remodel to comply with the health code. At the close of business on Friday, July 13, 1973, the last day of the 2-week period, Berg dismissed her employees, closed the restaurant, and placed a sign in the window saying "Closed for Remodeling." Earlier that day, Berg testified, Wiley came to the premises in her absence and attempted to change the locks. When she returned and asserted her right to continue in possession, he complied with her request to leave the locks unchanged. Berg also testified that at about 9:30 p. m. that evening, while she and four of her friends were in the restaurant, she observed Wiley hanging from the awning peering into the window. Shortly thereafter, she heard Wiley pounding on the back door demanding admittance. Berg called the county sheriff to come and preserve order. Wiley testified that he observed Berg and a group of her friends in the restaurant removing paneling from a wall. Allegedly fearing destruction of his property, Wiley called the city police, who, with the sheriff, mediated an agreement between the parties to preserve the status quo until each could consult with legal counsel on Monday, July 16, 1973.

Wiley testified that his then attorney advised him to take possession of the premises and lock the tenant out. Accompanied by a police officer and a locksmith, Wiley entered the premises in Berg's absence and without her knowledge on Monday, July 16, 1973, and changed the locks. Later in the day, Berg found herself locked out. The lease term was not due to expire until December 1, 1975. The premises were re-let to another tenant on or about August 1, 1973. Berg brought this damage action against Wiley and three other named defendants, including the new tenant, on July 27, 1973.[2] * * *

The jury * * * awarded Berg $31,000 for lost profits and $3,540 for loss of chattels resulting from the wrongful lockout. The jury also specifically found that Berg neither abandoned nor surrendered the premises. * * *

The first issue before us concerns the sufficiency of evidence to support the jury's finding that Berg had not abandoned or surrendered the leasehold before being locked out by Wiley. Viewing the evidence to support the jury's special verdict in the light most favorable to Berg, as we must, we hold it amply supports the jury's finding of no abandonment

---

[2]   Proceedings in this damage action were suspended for the duration of a separate unlawful detainer action in which Berg sought to recover possession of the premises under Minn.St. c. 566. In that action, this court reversed a judgment awarding possession of the premises to Berg, holding that an unlawful detainer action under Minn.St. c. 566 was not available to a tenant against his landlord. Berg v. Wiley, 226 N.W.2d 904 (1975). An amended complaint in this damage action was served on May 6, 1974. A second amended complaint was served on December 12, 1975, and proceedings were resumed.

or surrender of the premises. While the evidence bearing upon Berg's intent was strongly contradictory, the jury could reasonably have concluded, based on Berg's testimony and supporting circumstantial evidence, that she intended to retain possession, closing temporarily to remodel. Thus, the lockout cannot be excused on ground that Berg abandoned or surrendered the leasehold.

The second and more difficult issue is whether Wiley's self-help repossession of the premises by locking out Berg was correctly held wrongful as a matter of law.

Minnesota has historically followed the common-law rule that a landlord may rightfully use self-help to retake leased premises from a tenant in possession without incurring liability for wrongful eviction provided two conditions are met: (1) The landlord is legally entitled to possession, such as where a tenant holds over after the lease term or where a tenant breaches a lease containing a reentry clause; and (2) the landlord's means of reentry are peaceable. Mercil v. Broulette, 69 N.W. 218 (Minn. 1896). Under the common-law rule, a tenant who is evicted by his landlord may recover damages for wrongful eviction where the landlord either had no right to possession or where the means used to remove the tenant were forcible, or both. See, e.g., Poppen v. Wadleigh, 51 N.W.2d 75 (Minn. 1952); Sweeney v. Meyers, 270 N.W. 906 (Minn. 1937); Lobdell v. Keene, 88 N.W. 426 (Minn. 1901). See, also, Minn.St. 566.01 (statutory cause of action where entry is not "allowed by law" or, if allowed, is not made "in a peaceable manner").

Wiley contends that Berg had breached the provisions of the lease, thereby entitling Wiley, under the terms of the lease, to retake possession, and that his repossession by changing the locks in Berg's absence was accomplished in a peaceful manner. * * * Whether Berg had in fact breached the lease and whether Wiley was hence entitled to possession was not judicially determined. That issue became irrelevant upon the trial court's finding that Wiley's reentry was forcible as a matter of law because even if Berg had breached the lease, this could not excuse Wiley's nonpeaceable reentry. The finding that Wiley's reentry was forcible as a matter of law provided a sufficient ground for damages, and the issue of breach was not submitted to the jury. * * *

It has long been the policy of our law to discourage landlords from taking the law into their own hands, and our decisions and statutory law have looked with disfavor upon any use of self-help to dispossess a tenant in circumstances which are likely to result in breaches of the peace. We gave early recognition to this policy in *Lobdell v. Keene*, 88 N.W. 426, 430 (Minn. 1901), where we said:

> The object and purpose of the legislature in the enactment of the forcible entry and unlawful detainer statute was to prevent those claiming a right of entry or possession of lands from redressing their own wrongs by entering into possession in a violent and forcible manner. All such acts tend to a breach of the

peace, and encourage high-handed oppression. The law does not permit the owner of land, be his title ever so good, to be the judge of his own rights with respect to a possession adversely held, but puts him to his remedy under the statutes.

To facilitate a resort to judicial process, the legislature has provided a summary procedure in Minn.St. 566.02 to 566.17 whereby a landlord may recover possession of leased premises upon proper notice and showing in court in as little as 3 to 10 days. As we recognized in *Mutual Trust Life Ins. Co. v. Berg*, 246 N.W. 9, 10 (Minn. 1932), "(t)he forcible entry and unlawful detainer statutes were intended to prevent parties from taking the law into their own hands when going into possession of lands and tenements * * * ." To further discourage self-help, our legislature has provided treble damages for forcible evictions, §§ 557.08 and 557.09, and has provided additional criminal penalties for intentional and unlawful exclusion of a tenant. § 504.25. In *Sweeney v. Meyers*, supra, we allowed a business tenant not only damages for lost profits but also punitive damages against a landlord who, like Wiley, entered in the tenant's absence and locked the tenant out.

In the present case, as in *Sweeney*, the tenant was in possession, claiming a right to continue in possession adverse to the landlord's claim of breach of the lease, and had neither abandoned nor surrendered the premises. Wiley, well aware that Berg was asserting her right to possession, retook possession in her absence by picking the locks and locking her out. The record shows a history of vigorous dispute and keen animosity between the parties. Upon this record, we can only conclude that the singular reason why actual violence did not erupt at the moment of Wiley's changing of the locks was Berg's absence and her subsequent self-restraint and resort to judicial process. Upon these facts, we cannot find Wiley's means of reentry peaceable under the common-law rule. Our long-standing policy to discourage self-help which tends to cause a breach of the peace compels us to disapprove the means used to dispossess Berg. To approve this lockout, as urged by Wiley, merely because in Berg's absence no actual violence erupted while the locks were being changed, would be to encourage all future tenants, in order to protect their possession, to be vigilant and thereby set the stage for the very kind of public disturbance which it must be our policy to discourage. * * *

We recognize that the growing modern trend departs completely from the common-law rule to hold that self-help is never available to dispossess a tenant who is in possession and has not abandoned or voluntarily surrendered the premises. Annotation, 6 A.L.R.3d 177, 186; 76 Dickinson L.Rev. 215, 227. This growing rule is founded on the recognition that the potential for violent breach of peace inheres in any situation where a landlord attempts by his own means to remove a tenant who is claiming possession adversely to the landlord. Courts adopting the rule reason that there is no cause to sanction such potentially disruptive self-help where adequate and speedy means are provided for removing a tenant peacefully through judicial process. At least 16 states[6] have adopted this modern rule, holding that judicial proceedings, including the summary procedures provided in those states' unlawful detainer statutes, are the exclusive remedy by which a landlord may remove a tenant claiming possession.

While we would be compelled to disapprove the lockout of Berg in her absence under the common-law rule as stated, we approve the trial court's reasoning and adopt as preferable the modern view represented by the cited cases. To make clear our departure from the common-law rule for the benefit of future landlords and tenants, we hold that, subsequent to our decision in this case, the only lawful means to dispossess a tenant who has not abandoned nor voluntarily surrendered but who claims possession adversely to a landlord's claim of breach of a written lease is by resort to judicial process. We find that Minn.St. 566.02 to 566.17 provide the landlord with an adequate remedy for regaining possession in every such case.[8] Where speedier action than provided in §§ 566.02 to 566.17 seems necessary because of threatened destruction of the property or other exigent circumstances, a temporary restraining order under Rule 65, Rules of Civil Procedure, and law enforcement protection are available to the landlord. Considered together, these statutory and judicial remedies provide a complete answer to the landlord. In our modern society, with the availability of prompt and sufficient legal remedies as described, there is no place and no need for self-help against a tenant in claimed lawful possession of leased premises.

Applying our holding to the facts of this case, we conclude, as did the trial court, that because Wiley failed to resort to judicial remedies against Berg's holding possession adversely to Wiley's claim of breach of the lease, his lockout of Berg was wrongful as a matter of law. The rule we adopt in this decision is fairly applied against Wiley, for it is clear that, applying the older common-law rule to the facts and circumstances peculiar to this case, we would be compelled to find the lockout nonpeaceable for the reasons previously stated. The jury found that the lockout caused Berg damage and, as between Berg and Wiley, equity dictates that Wiley, who himself performed the act causing the damage, must bear the loss.

Affirmed.

---

[6]   Annotation, 6 A.L.R.3d 177, 186, Supp. 13, shows this modern rule to have been adopted in California, Connecticut, Delaware, Florida, Georgia, Illinois, Indiana, Louisiana, Nebraska, North Carolina, Ohio, Tennessee, Texas, Utah, Vermont, and Washington.

[8]   Under §§ 566.05 and 566.06, a landlord may regain possession in default proceedings against a tenant personally served with process in as little as 3 to 10 days. Default judgment against a tenant not present and served by posting may be procured in a week to 10 days. §§ 566.05 and 566.06. Trial is by the court unless either party demands a jury trial. § 566.07. Proceedings are stayed on appeal except as against a holdover tenant. § 566.12. Upon execution of a writ of restitution, the tenant is allowed 24 hours to vacate the property.

NOTES AND QUESTIONS

1. Forcible entry and detainer (FED) statutes are used most often in landlord-tenant disputes. The most common type of action, as in the principal case, is one brought by the landlord seeking to regain possession of leased premises from a tenant. In order to bring such an action, the landlord must show that he or she has the right to possession of the premises, which in turn typically requires that the lease contain a clause providing that the tenant forfeits the right of possession or that the landlord has the right to reenter and retake possession upon the happening of certain events (such as nonpayment of rent or holding over after a lease has expired). Can you identify such a clause in the lease in this case? In some states (though not Minnesota), FED statutes can also be invoked by tenants, provided that the tenant wants to be restored to possession following an allegedly wrongful ouster by the landlord. See, e.g., Lees v. Wardall, 554 P.2d 1076 (Wash. Ct. App. 1976). Litigated disputes involving FED statutes also arise in the context of land sale contracts, for example where a seller refuses to turn over possession to a purchaser or where a purchaser enters into possession without having fulfilled all the requirements of the contract. FED statutes are also available in the event that someone with a legal right to possession is forcibly dispossessed by someone without such a right, e.g., a squatter. See generally William Lindsley, Forcible Entry and Detainer, 35A Am. Jur. 2d § 7 (2005). Reported opinions involving the use of FED statutes in such situations are very rare, however. Either these sorts of depredations do not occur very often, or if they do, they are resolved by the police or by criminal trespass charges rather than by civil litigation.

2. Suppose Berg closed the restaurant, put out a sign that said "Closed for Remodeling," disappeared, and failed to pay the rent when it was due at the beginning of the next month. Would Wiley be obliged to file an FED action to regain possession of the premises in these circumstances? If your answer is yes, what if two months have gone by with no Berg and no rent? Is the holding of *Berg v. Wiley* limited to cases where the tenant is still in possession? If so, how do we define "possession" in such situations?

3. *Berg v. Wiley* may have reflected the "growing modern trend" when it was decided in 1978, but it is by no means the unanimous view today. Other courts have more recently held that, at least in the context of commercial landlord-tenant disputes, self-help is still permitted. See, e.g., Northfield Park Associates v. Northeast Ohio Harness, 521 N.E.2d 466 (Ohio Ct. App. 1987); 2 Milton R. Friedman, Friedman on Leases § 18.6 (Patrick A. Randolph, Jr. ed. & rev., 5th ed. 2005). What factors are relevant in deciding whether self-help should be prohibited as a matter of law? For example, would it be relevant if there is a severe backlog of cases in landlord-tenant court or if the sheriff's department is so understaffed that it takes an average of three months to carry out an eviction order?

4. In jurisdictions that still permit self-help, recovery of possession must be accomplished without a breach of the peace. Both the trial court and the state supreme court in *Berg v. Wiley* held that Wiley's actions were not peaceable. What should Wiley have done differently in order to satisfy the

requirement that there be no breach of the peace? Presumably politely asking the party in possession to leave is okay. What about asking the party to leave on threat of litigation? What about demanding that the party leave or else the landlord will cut off utilities or other services? Provided the landlord takes care to ensure that the tenant is not at the premises, what is wrong with changing the locks in the presence of a police officer? Given that Wiley changed the locks in the presence of a police officer, is it plausible to say, as the court does, that "the singular reason why actual violence did not erupt at the moment of Wiley's changing of the locks was Berg's absence and her subsequent self-restraint and resort to judicial process"?

Williams v. Ford Motor Credit Company

United States Court of Appeals, Eighth Circuit, 1982.
674 F.2d 717.

■ BENSON, CHIEF JUDGE. In this diversity action brought by Cathy A. Williams to recover damages for conversion arising out of an alleged wrongful repossession of an automobile, Williams appeals from a judgment notwithstanding the verdict entered on motion of defendant Ford Motor Credit Company (FMCC). * * *

In July, 1975, David Williams, husband of plaintiff Cathy Williams, purchased a Ford Mustang from an Oklahoma Ford dealer. Although David Williams executed the sales contract, security agreement, and loan papers, title to the car was in the name of both David and Cathy Williams. The car was financed through the Ford dealer, who in turn assigned the paper to FMCC. Cathy and David Williams were divorced in 1977. The divorce court granted Cathy title to the automobile and required David to continue to make payments to FMCC for eighteen months. David defaulted on the payments and signed a voluntary repossession authorization for FMCC. Cathy Williams was informed of the delinquency and responded that she was trying to get her former husband David to make the payments. There is no evidence of any agreement between her and FMCC. Pursuant to an agreement with FMCC, S & S was directed to repossess the automobile.

On December 1, 1977, at approximately 4:30 a.m., Cathy Williams was awakened by a noise outside her house trailer in Van Buren, Arkansas.[2] She saw that a wrecker truck with two men in it had hooked up to the Ford Mustang and started to tow it away. She went outside and hollered at them. The truck stopped. She then told them that the car was hers and asked them what they were doing. One of the men, later identified as Don Sappington, president of S & S Recovery, Inc., informed her that he was repossessing the vehicle on behalf of FMCC. Williams explained that she had been attempting to bring the past due payments up to date and informed Sappington that the car contained personal items which did not even belong to her. Sappington got out of the truck,

---

[2]   Cathy Williams testified that the noise sounded like there was a car stuck in her yard.

retrieved the items from the car, and handed them to her. Without further complaint from Williams, Sappington returned to the truck and drove off, car in tow. At trial, Williams testified that Sappington was polite throughout their encounter and did not make any threats toward her or do anything which caused her to fear any physical harm. The automobile had been parked in an unenclosed driveway which plaintiff shared with a neighbor. The neighbor was awakened by the wrecker backing into the driveway, but did not come out. After the wrecker drove off, Williams returned to her house trailer and called the police, reporting her car as stolen. Later, Williams commenced this action.

The case was tried to a jury which awarded her $5,000.00 in damages. * * * The district court entered judgment notwithstanding the verdict for FMCC, and this appeal followed.

Article 9 of the Uniform Commercial Code (UCC), which Arkansas has adopted and codified as Ark.Stat.Ann. § 85–9–503 (Supp. 1981), provides in pertinent part:

> Unless otherwise agreed, a secured party has on default the right to take possession of the collateral. In taking possession, a secured party may proceed without judicial process if this can be done without breach of the peace. . . .[4]

In *Ford Motor Credit Co. v. Herring*, 589 S.W.2d 584, 586 (Ark. 1979), which involved an alleged conversion arising out of a repossession, the Supreme Court of Arkansas cited Section 85–9–503 and referred to its previous holdings as follows:

> In pre-code cases, we have sustained a finding of conversion only where force, or threats of force, or risk of invoking violence, accompanied the repossession. Manhattan Credit Co., Inc. v. Brewer, 341 S.W.2d 765 (Ark. 1961); Kensinger Acceptance Corp. v. Davis, 269 S.W.2d 792 (Ark. 1954).

The thrust of Williams' argument on appeal is that the repossession was accomplished by the risk of invoking violence. The district judge who presided at the trial commented on her theory in his memorandum opinion:

> Mrs. Williams herself admitted that the men who repossessed her automobile were very polite and complied with her requests. The evidence does not reveal that they performed any act which was oppressive, threatening or tended to cause physical violence. Unlike the situation presented in *Manhattan Credit Co. v. Brewer*, supra, it was not shown that Mrs. Williams would

---

[4] It is generally considered that the objectives of this section are (1) to benefit creditors in permitting them to realize collateral without having to resort to judicial process; (2) to benefit debtors in general by making credit available at lower costs, see Griffith v. Valley of the Sun Recovery and Adjustment Bureau, Inc., 613 P.2d 1283 (Ariz. Ct. App. 1980); and (3) to support a public policy discouraging extrajudicial acts by citizens when those acts are fraught with the likelihood of resulting violence, see Morris v. First Nat'l. Bank & Trust Co., 254 N.E.2d 683 (Ohio 1970).

have been forced to resort to physical violence to stop the men from leaving with her automobile.

In the pre-Code case *Manhattan Credit Co. v. Brewer*, 341 S.W.2d 765 (Ark. 1961), the court held that a breach of peace occurred when the debtor and her husband confronted the creditor's agent during the act of repossession and clearly objected to the repossession, 341 S.W.2d at 767–68. In *Manhattan*, the court examined holdings of earlier cases in which repossessions were deemed to have been accomplished without any breach of the peace, id. In particular, the Supreme Court of Arkansas discussed the case of *Rutledge v. Universal C.I.T. Credit Corp.*, 237 S.W.2d 469 (Ark. 1951). In *Rutledge*, the court found no breach of the peace when the repossessor acquired keys to the automobile, confronted the debtor and his wife, informed them he was going to take the car, and immediately proceeded to do so. As the *Rutledge* court explained and the *Manhattan* court reiterated, a breach of the peace did not occur when the "Appellant (debtor-possessor) did not give his permission but he did not object." Manhattan, supra, 341 S.W.2d at 767–68; Rutledge, supra, 237 S.W.2d at 470.

We have read the transcript of the trial. There is no material dispute in the evidence, and the district court has correctly summarized it. Cathy Williams did not raise an objection to the taking, and the repossession was accomplished without any incident which might tend to provoke violence. See also Teeter Motor Co., Inc. v. First Nat'l Bank, 543 S.W.2d 938 (Ark. 1976).

Appellees deserve something less than commendation for the taking during the night time sleeping hours, but it is clear that viewing the facts in the light most favorable to Williams, the taking was a legal repossession under the laws of the State of Arkansas. The evidence does not support the verdict of the jury. FMCC is entitled to judgment notwithstanding the verdict.

The judgment notwithstanding the verdict is affirmed.

■ HEANEY, CIRCUIT JUDGE, dissenting. The only issue is whether the repossession of appellant's automobile constituted a breach of the peace by creating a "risk of invoking violence." See Ford Motor Credit Co. v. Herring, 589 S.W.2d 584, 586 (Ark. 1979). The trial jury found that it did and awarded $5,000 for conversion. Because that determination was in my view a reasonable one, I dissent from the Court's decision to overturn it.

Cathy Williams was a single parent living with her two small children in a trailer home in Van Buren, Arkansas. On December 1, 1977, at approximately 4:30 a. m., she was awakened by noises in her driveway. She went into the night to investigate and discovered a wrecker and its crew in the process of towing away her car. According to the trial court, "she ran outside to stop them * * * but she made no *strenuous* protests to their actions." (Emphasis added.) In fact, the wrecker crew stepped between her and the car when she sought to retrieve personal items from inside it, although the men retrieved some of the items for her. The commotion created by the incident awakened neighbors in the vicinity.

Facing the wrecker crew in the dead of night, Cathy Williams did everything she could to stop them, short of introducing physical force to meet the presence of the crew. The confrontation did not result in violence only because Ms. Williams did not take such steps and was otherwise powerless to stop the crew.

The controlling law is the UCC, which authorizes self-help repossession only when such is done "without breach of the peace * * * ." Ark.Stat.Ann. § 85–9–503 (Supp. 1981). The majority recognizes that one important policy consideration underlying this restriction is to discourage "extrajudicial acts by citizens when those acts are fraught with the likelihood of resulting violence." Despite this, the majority holds that no reasonable jury could find that the confrontation in Cathy Williams' driveway at 4:30 a. m. created a risk of violence. I cannot agree. At a minimum, the largely undisputed facts created a jury question. The jury found a breach of the peace and this Court has no sound, much less compelling, reason to overturn that determination.

Indeed, I would think that sound application of the self-help limitation might require a directed verdict in favor of Ms. Williams, but certainly not against her. If a "night raid" is conducted without detection and confrontation, then, of course, there could be no breach of the peace. But where the invasion is detected and a confrontation ensues, the repossessor should be under a duty to retreat and turn to judicial process. The alternative which the majority embraces is to allow a repossessor to proceed following confrontation unless and until violence results in fact. Such a rule invites tragic consequences which the law should seek to prevent, not to encourage. I would reverse the trial court and reinstate the jury's verdict.

NOTES AND QUESTIONS

1. In a series of decisions in the 1970s, the U.S. Supreme Court wavered back and forth as to whether statutory provisions authorizing summary repossession or disposal of personal property without a prior hearing violate the Due Process Clause. See Fuentes v. Shevin, 407 U.S. 67 (1972) (due process violated by statute authorizing replevin of personal property upon application and posting of bond with no hearing before repossession takes place); Mitchell v. W.T. Grant Co., 416 U.S. 600 (1974) (due process not violated by state statute authorizing "sequestration" of personal property pursuant to ex parte order of judge); North Georgia Finishing, Inc. v. Di-Chem, Inc., 419 U.S. 601 (1975) (due process violated by state statute permitting garnishment of bank account based on conclusory allegations before nonjudicial officer); Flagg Brothers, Inc. v. Brooks, 436 U.S. 149 (1978) (due process not implicated by provision of Uniform Commercial Code authorizing warehouse to sell goods in its custody to

satisfy unpaid debt for warehouse services). Some lower courts interpreted these decisions to mean that self-help repossession that is authorized by Article 9 of the Uniform Commercial Code triggers a due process hearing right. See, e.g., Watson v. Branch County Bank, 380 F. Supp. 945 (W.D. Mich. 1974). But especially after *Flagg Brothers* was decided in 1978, most courts concluded that procedural due process does not apply to self-help repossession under what was then UCC § 9–503 (for the current version, see Revised UCC § 9–609), because such a repossession does not entail any "state action." Given the widespread adoption of the UCC by the states, creditors have tended to rely on the UCC self-help remedy rather than statutory remedies that might trigger due process hearing requirements under *Fuentes* or *Di-Chem*. As a result, persons who own personal property subject to a lien covered by UCC Article 9 have only those rights available under state constitutional law or under interpretations of UCC § 9–609. See Alan R. Madry, State Action and the Due Process of Self-Help; *Flagg Bros.* Redux, 62 U. Pitt. L. Rev. 1 (2000).

2.   There is considerable irony in the fact that the UCC's self-help repossession remedy has generally been held not to trigger due process, whereas replevin actions or garnishment proceedings require due process hearings. Replevin and garnishment statutes typically give owners of personal property significantly *greater* protection than they get in a self-help repossession. But by exempting self-help from due process constraints, the courts have created a powerful incentive for lending companies to use self-help, rather than more protective statutory mechanisms. Contrast the reasoning of decisions like *Berg v. Wiley*, which hold that the creation of summary statutory remedies for recovery of possession of real property eliminates common-law self-help remedies. Few, if any, courts have adopted this line of reasoning with respect to self-help repossession of personal property. As a result, most repossessions of personal property today use self-help.

3.   As a further irony, consider that if S & S Recovery, Inc. had towed away Ms. Williams's car by mistake, when it really intended to repossess her neighbor's car, Ms. Williams might be forced to use a replevin action to get her car back. She could not use Article 9's self-help remedy, because she has no security interest in the car, and Article 9 only covers security interests. If Williams were forced to use replevin to get her car back, S & S Recovery would be entitled to a due process hearing before it could be ordered to return the car to her.

4.   Notwithstanding these ironies, does it make sense as a policy matter to permit self-help repossession of personal property (at least when the owner is in default on a loan secured by the property) but not to permit self-help repossession of commercial real estate (as held in *Berg v. Wiley*)? Which position do you think is best: no self-help repossession of either real or personal property; self-help possession of either real or personal property provided there is no breach of the peace; or self-help repossession of personal property without breach of the peace, but no self-help repossession of real property?

5.   In footnote 6, the court observes that one policy justification for permitting self-help repossession of personal property subject to a security interest is that it benefits "debtors in general by making credit available at lower costs." Can you spell out the argument as to why self-help repossession would have this effect? If self-help repossession would lower the costs of borrowing to finance an automobile or other personal property, would permitting self-help repossession of real property reduce the amount of rent that tenants in general must pay?

6.   Which do you think was probably more unsettling to the individual property holder's sense of personal security and autonomy: Wiley's locking out Berg while her restaurant was closed for remodeling, or S & S Recovery's showing up at 4:30 a.m. to tow Williams's Mustang from her driveway?

B. LIMITS TO OWNER SOVEREIGNTY

Although the property owner has an impressive arsenal of criminal, civil, and self-help remedies to vindicate the right to exclude others, the law has always recognized limits to owner sovereignty. We consider here five categories of exceptions. As always when one has a basic rule (the right to exclude) subject to exceptions, there is a question whether the exceptions should be stated in a rule-like fashion, or whether the whole issue (right to exclude or not) should be resolved in a case-by-case fashion with more attention to the balance of interests in each case. Keep this underlying question of legal design in mind when considering the following materials.

1. NECESSITY

Ploof v. Putnam

Supreme Court of Vermont, 1908.
71 A. 188.

■ MUNSON, J. It is alleged as the ground of recovery that on the 13th day of November 1904, the defendant was the owner of a certain island in Lake Champlain, and of a certain dock attached thereto, which island and dock were then in charge of the defendant's servant; that the plaintiff was then possessed of and sailing upon said lake a certain loaded sloop, on which were the plaintiff and his wife and two minor children; that there then arose a sudden and violent tempest, whereby the sloop and the property and persons therein were placed in great danger of destruction; that, to save these from destruction or injury, the plaintiff was compelled to, and did, moor the sloop to defendant's dock; that the defendant, by his servant, unmoored the sloop, whereupon it was driven upon the shore by the tempest, without the plaintiff's fault; and that the sloop and its contents were thereby destroyed, and the plaintiff and his wife and children cast into the lake and upon the shore, receiving injuries. This claim is set forth in two counts—one in trespass, charging that the defendant by his servant with force and arms willfully and designedly unmoored the sloop; the other in case, alleging that it was the duty of the defendant by his servant to permit the plaintiff to moor his sloop to the dock, and to permit it to remain so moored during the continuance of the tempest, but that the defendant by his servant, in disregard of this duty, negligently, carelessly, and wrongfully unmoored the sloop. Both counts are demurred to generally.

There are many cases in the books which hold that necessity, and an inability to control movements inaugurated in the proper exercise of a strict right, will justify entries upon land and interferences with personal property that would otherwise have been trespasses. A reference to a few of these will be sufficient to illustrate the doctrine. In Mitten v. Faudrye, Popham 161, 79 Eng. Rep. 1259 (K.B. 1626), trespass was brought for chasing sheep, and the defendant pleaded that the sheep were trespassing upon his land, and that he with a little dog chased them out, and that, as soon as the sheep were off his land, he called in the dog. It was argued that, although the defendant might lawfully drive the sheep from his own ground with a dog, he had no right to pursue them into the next ground; but the court considered that the defendant might drive the sheep from his land with a dog, and that the nature of a dog is such that he cannot be withdrawn in an instant, and that, as the defendant had done his best to recall the dog, trespass would not lie. * * * If one have a way over the land of another for his beasts to pass, and the beasts, being properly driven, feed [on] the grass by morsels in passing, or run out of the way and are promptly pursued and brought back, trespass will not lie. See Vin. Ab. Trespass, K. a, pl. 1. A traveler on a highway who finds it obstructed from a sudden and temporary cause may pass upon the adjoining land without becoming a trespasser because of the necessity. Henn's Case, W. Jones, 296 (1632); Campbell v. Race, 61 Mass. (7 Cush.) 408 (1851); Hyde v. Jamaica, 27 Vt. 443, 459 (1855); Morey v. Fitzgerald, 56 Vt. 487 (1884). An entry upon land to save goods which are in danger of being lost or destroyed by water or fire is not a trespass. 21 Hen. VII, 27; Vin. Ab. Trespass, H. a, 4, pl. 24, K. a, pl. 3. In Proctor v. Adams, 113 Mass. 376 (1873), the defendant went upon the plaintiff's beach for the purpose of saving and restoring to the lawful owner a boat which had been driven ashore, and was in danger of being carried off by the sea; and it was held no trespass.

This doctrine of necessity applies with special force to the preservation of human life. One assaulted and in peril of his life may run through the close of another to escape from his assailant. 37 Hen. VII, pl. 26. One may sacrifice the personal property of another to save his life or the lives of his fellows. In Mouse's Case, 12 Co. 63, 77 Eng. Rep. 1341 (K.B. 1609), the defendant was sued for taking and carrying away the plaintiff's casket and its contents. It appeared that the ferryman of Gravesend took 47 passengers into his barge to pass to London, among whom were the plaintiff and defendant; and the barge being upon the water a great tempest happened, and a strong wind, so that the barge and all the passengers were in danger of being lost if certain ponderous things were not cast out, and the defendant thereupon cast out the plaintiff's casket. It was resolved that in case of necessity, to save the lives of the passengers, it was lawful for the defendant, being a passenger, to cast the plaintiff's casket out of the barge; that, if the ferryman surcharge the barge, the owner shall have his remedy upon the surcharge against the ferryman, but that if there be no surcharge, and the danger accrue only by the act of God, as by tempest, without fault of the ferryman, every one ought to bear his loss to safeguard the life of a man.

It is clear that an entry upon the land of another may be justified by necessity, and that the declaration before us discloses a necessity for mooring the sloop. But the defendant questions the sufficiency of the counts because they do not negative the existence of natural objects to which the plaintiff could have moored with equal safety. The allegations are, in substance, that the stress of a sudden and violent tempest compelled the plaintiff to moor to defendant's dock to save his sloop and the people in it. The averment of necessity is complete, for it covers not only the necessity of mooring to the dock; and the details of the situation which created this necessity, whatever the legal requirements regarding them, are matters of proof, and need not be alleged. It is certain that the rule suggested cannot be held applicable irrespective of circumstance, and the question must be left for adjudication upon proceedings had with reference to the evidence [on] the charge. * * *

Judgment affirmed and cause remanded.

NOTES AND QUESTIONS

1.   You may be wondering why the owner's servant cast off the Ploofs. A recent study of the case reveals the background of social conflict in the Lake Champlain area giving rise to the dispute. The Ploofs were a French Canadian family who lived on their boat and transported firewood and other goods on the lake. In keeping with prevailing bigotry against French Canadians at the time, the Ploofs were disliked and were accused of being "pirates" and thieves and even chased away with guns by the genteel residents. Joan Vogel, Cases in Conflict: Lake Champlain Wars, Gentrification and *Ploof v. Putnam*, 45 St. Louis U. L.J. 791, 798–99 (2001). The author contends that this background of conflict is essential to understanding how the dispute arose. Is it relevant to the result? Should it be?

2.   Some of the incidents discussed by the court involve great forces of nature like storms, whereas others involve the behavior of animals like dogs and cattle, and still others involve a response to acts of third parties, like running from an assailant. What are the common elements in these examples that cause courts to treat them as overcoming the owner's right to exclude that otherwise would prevail? Could the mobile home company in *Jacque v. Steenberg Homes*, Chapter I, have raised a defense to trespass

based on necessity? If not, why not? (Consider *Dwyer v. Staunton*, [1947] 4 D.L.R. 393 (Alberta Dist. Ct.), summarized in Note 5 after *Jacque*.)

3.   In another famous necessity case, *Vincent v. Lake Erie Transp. Co.*, 124 N.W. 221 (Minn. 1910), the defendant kept its boat tied to a dock longer than the plaintiff wanted it to remain there, in order to keep the boat from being destroyed by a violent storm arising on Lake Superior. The wind and waves caused the boat to damage the dock. The court held that the defendant was justified in keeping the boat tied to the dock, but that the defendant had to pay the plaintiff for the damage caused to the dock. Is this an application of the principle of restitution, considered more fully infra Part C? Note that both the mistaken improver and the ship-owner tying up to the dock can be viewed as trespassers, and both claim that special circumstances make strict enforcement of exclusion rights by injunction inappropriate. See generally Symposium: *Vincent v. Lake Erie Transportation Co.* and the Doctrine of Necessity, Issues in Legal Scholarship (2005), available at https://www. degruyter.com/journal/key/ils/5/2/html?lang=en.

4.   The exception to the right to exclude recognized in *Ploof* and *Vincent* can be characterized in different ways. One is to say that conditions of necessity shift the right to exclude from the landowner to the person entering under conditions of necessity. Thus, for example, if the intruders are resisted by the landowner, they are now privileged to use self-help— including potentially reasonable force—to enter. The plaintiff "intruders" in *Ploof* did state a cause of action in trespass, which hints that they regarded the repulsion by the defendant's servant to be a violation of their superior rights to occupy the dock. Another characterization would be to say that the landowner still has the right to exclude, but under conditions of necessity can only vindicate that right by seeking a payment of damages for any damage caused by the intruder. Necessity suspends other modes of protection that the landowner can ordinarily invoke, such as the privilege of self-help and the right to obtain an injunction. In effect, the intruder who is subject to forces of necessity can "take" the entitlement without the owner's consent, but when he does so, must pay the owner just compensation. (In the vocabulary introduced by Calabresi and Melamed, which we take up in Chapter IX, the entitlement still belongs to the landowner but is now protected by a "liability rule" rather than a "property rule.") A third characterization would be that the necessity defense negates any liability in tort for trespass, and the damages are a form of restitution for unjust enrichment of the intruder. Which of these characterizations is the best?

5.   Would you apply the rule of compensation recognized in *Vincent v. Lake Erie Transp. Co.* to all cases of necessity? Should it be extended to cases like *Ploof* or *Mouse's Case* (discussed in *Ploof*) where the intrusion is justified by the need to save human life? What about cases involving animals that eat morsels of grass on the side of a designated right of way?

2. CUSTOM

Fisher v. Steward

New Hampshire Supreme Court, 1804.
Smith 60.

Trover for a swarm of bees. There was a second count for two hundred pounds of honey in the comb.

The case was, the plaintiffs found a swarm of bees in a tree on the (defendant's) land in Claremont, marked the tree, and notified the defendant, who cut down the tree, September, 1803, and converted the honey to his own use. * * *

At the trial there was some dispute whether the plaintiffs or one of the defendant's family first discovered the bees, and whether the plaintiffs gave notice of the finding and marking the tree. The other parts of the case were proved.

The Court summed up, and observed that two questions had been made on the trial: first, whether the plaintiffs first discovered the bees; and, secondly, supposing they did, whether the property in the honey was in them.

The first is a question of evidence proper for the consideration of the jury.

The second is a question of law, and one about which the Court entertained no doubt. The plaintiffs do not pretend to have any property in the land or in the tree, nor had they any property in the bees. How then came they by a property in the honey? It must have been by occupancy. But how did they occupy, or appropriate the honey to themselves? They saw the bees enter the tree, they heard them make a noise near the tree, and they marked the tree. The two first gave no right; they do not amount to occupancy. The marking of the tree was a trespass, and consequently can avail the plaintiffs nothing. The doctrine contended for by plaintiffs is injurious to the rights of property. Till the bees occupied the tree in question, it is not pretended that plaintiffs had any right in it. What gave them a right? Having seen a swarm of bees, in which they had no property, occupying it? This circumstance, whether the effect of accident, or the result of labor and skill, cannot lessen the rights of the owner of the soil. Will it be pretended that plaintiffs thereby acquired a right to the tree? If they acquired a title to the honey, they must necessarily have a right to take it away, to cut down the tree, to pass over the defendant's land for the purpose, & c. Admitting the plaintiffs could acquire property in a swarm of bees, or in the honey, by finding, in some cases, they could not do so in the present case, because such right or property interferes with the rights and property clearly vested in defendant; it is inconsistent with it; it lessens its value at least. It is much more consonant to our ideas of property to say, that the bees and honey in the defendant's trees belong to him in the same manner and for the same reasons as all mines and minerals belong to the owner of the soil.

Will it be pretended by the plaintiffs that they could have put, without defendant's permission, a swarm of bees into defendant's tree, and there kept them till they had made honey; and then, in case he cut down the tree, maintained trespass for the cutting, or trover for the honey? One would suppose the present case was not stronger than that; here they had no right to the bees.

It has been said, that, by the usage of this part of the State, the person who finds bees acquires a property in them wherever found. We recognize no such usage. We have no local customs or usages which are binding in one part of the State and not in another. If this be the law here, it must be so in every other part of the State.

Verdict for defendant.

NOTES AND QUESTIONS

1.   Recall the principle that captured wild animals belong to the owner of the land where they are captured, sometimes called *ratione loci* or *ratione soli*, which is alluded to in *Pierson v. Post*, excerpted in Chapter II. Post (the huntsman) alleged in his complaint that the fox had been hunted on a "wild and uninhabited, unpossessed and waste land, called the beach." The court seized on this allegation to sidestep English precedent, observing that the English decisions "have either been discussed and decided upon the principles of their positive statute regulations, or have arisen between the huntsman and the owner of the land upon which beasts *ferae naturae* have been apprehended; the former claiming them by title of occupancy, and the latter *ratione soli*." The *Pierson* court was therefore able to decide the dispute based solely on the principle of first possession, rather than having to sort out the competing claims of first possession and *ratione soli*, a species of accession doctrine. Could the court in *Fisher* have ruled for the defendant on the ground that the plaintiff had not performed acts sufficient to constitute possession of the bees or the hive? Recall in this connection the discussion in *Pierson v. Post* about what acts are required to establish possession. Or is it that the trespass on private land loomed too large for the court?

2.   The tension between first possession and accession in wild animal law is nowhere greater than with respect to bees. Barbeyrac, a natural rights thinker discussed in *Pierson v. Post*, thought that a hive belongs to the first person who discovers the tree where it is located, and marks it as his own. Blackstone equivocated on the subject, noting that there is something to be said for giving the hive to the owner of the soil where it is located, but offering an exception where a swarm "flie from and out of my hive * * * as long as I can keep them in sight, and have the power to pursue them." 2 William Blackstone, Commentaries on the Laws of England *392–93. (How would one prove this?) *Ratione soli*—an instance of the principle of accession—may loom especially large with respect to bees because bees make hives in fixed locations, and the economic value of the bees (i.e., the honey they produce)

inheres in this fixed location. Given this feature, it may be that American courts have been rather more sympathetic to the idea that ownership of bees goes with ownership of land than they have been to the notion that ownership of other types of wild animals killed or captured on private land goes with the land. See Dale D. Goble & Eric T. Freyfogle, Wildlife Law 133–145 (2002) (noting that early American courts were hostile to English doctrines about ownership of land giving rise to control over wildlife on the land, and were sympathetic with the idea of a general privilege to hunt on any unenclosed and uncultivated land). Another wild animal that builds elaborate homes in fixed locations is the beaver—recall in this connection Harold Demsetz's explanation (in Chapter III) of the way private property rights in beaver territories emerged among certain Native American tribes when the value of beaver pelts rose.

3.   As we have also seen, accession depends on some combination of psychological salience and practical utility. Presumably, the proponent of the custom here and perhaps the community creating the custom (if it was one) relied on salience and utility. And yet the court refused legal recognition of the custom because it could not be shown to obtain in all of the state of New Hampshire. Why is this important? Is the court worried about holding non-community members to an in-group custom (see Ghen v. Rich, excerpted in Chapter III).

4.   Perhaps the most famous local, albeit widespread, property custom in the United States limiting a landowner's right to exclude is that of affording hunters a license to hunt over unenclosed unimproved land. Over time, owners became able to opt out of the custom through posting the land. This custom arose in opposition to traditional English law (think Robin Hood and the Sheriff of Nottingham). This custom also made an appearance in a U.S. Supreme Court case. McKee v. Gratz, 260 U.S. 127, 136 (1922) (Holmes, J.) ("[There is a] common understanding with regard to the large expanses of unenclosed and uncultivated land in many parts at least of this country. Over these it is customary to wander, shoot and fish at will until the owner sees fit to prohibit it. A license may be implied from the habits of the country."). Even to this day, a large number of states have so-called "posting laws," which permit anyone to hunt on rural land unless "No Hunting" or "No Trespassing" signs have been prominently posted. See, e.g., Fla. Stat. § 588.10, § 810.09; N.D. Cent. Code § 20.1–01–18 (2002). Mark R. Sigmon, Hunting and Posting on Private Land in America, 54 Duke L.J. 549 (2004) ("Twenty-nine states currently require private landowners to post their land to exclude hunters, twenty-seven of these states by statute."). These laws impose an affirmative burden of notification on the possessor of land for asserting the right to exclude. If the owner does not make the required notification, then the right to exclude is subordinated to the customary right to hunt on unenclosed and uncultivated land owned by another. The trend appears to be moving gradually away from presumed access for hunters unless the land is posted and instead toward a requirement of owner permission to hunt. Posting may soon migrate to a centralized system online. See Richard M. Hynes, Posted: Notice and the Right to Exclude, 45 Ariz. St. L.J. 949 (2013).

5.   In England and some other commonwealth countries like New Zealand, laws have been enacted that codify and extend a customary "right to roam" over rural land. These laws allow persons who like to "ramble" in open countryside to gain access to designated private property without first seeking permission from the owner. See Jerry L. Anderson, Britain's Right to Roam: Redefining the Landowner's Bundle of Sticks, 19 Geo. Int'l Envtl. L. Rev. 375 (2007). The land that may be accessed must first be identified by officials as "mountain, moor, heath or down or registered common land," and mapped after consultation with landowners. Landowners are entitled to designate up to 28 days per year on which the land can be closed to ramblers. Scotland has enacted an even more extensive right to roam, which involves elaborate balancing of the interests of landowners and those who roam. John A. Lovett, Progressive Property in Action: The Land Reform (Scotland) Act 2003, 89 Neb. L. Rev. 301 (2011). A recent empirical study based on differential impact on various areas finds a significant and substantial negative effect on property values from the passage of the Countryside and Rights of Way Act in England and Wales in 2000. Jonathan Klick & Gideon Parchomovsky, The Value of the Right to Exclude: An Empirical Assessment, 165 U. Pa. L. Rev. 917 (2016). What might explain the adoption of right-to-roam laws in the twenty-first century, after a long period in which rural landowners were understood to have the right to exclude such intrusions? Similar issues have arisen in the U.S., where walking is less popular, with respect to outdoor recreational vehicle use on public and private land. See Byron Kahr, The Right to Exclude Meets the Right to Ride: Private Property, Public Recreation, and the Rise of Off-Road Vehicles, 28 Stan. Envtl. L.J. 51 (2009).

3.   PUBLIC ACCOMMODATIONS LAWS

Another important qualification on the right to exclude comes from public accommodations laws. Broadly speaking, the law distinguishes between property not open to the public, like homes, factories, and business offices, and property that offers itself as a "public accommodation." Owners of property not open to the public have long enjoyed broad sovereign authority to exclude others. At common law, subject to the defense of necessity and exceptions based on local custom, the owner of property not open to the public was said to have the right to exclude others for "any reason or no reason at all." Owners of public accommodations, in contrast, have a much more qualified right to exclude. Specifically, they are subject to a general duty of nondiscrimination among customers, meaning they must provide services to customers on a first-come, first-served basis, and they must charge customers only reasonable rates for the services they provide.

The law of public accommodations can be traced to certain implied duties that the common law imposed on persons who held themselves forth to the public as being engaged in one of the "common callings." Thus Blackstone wrote:

There is also in law always an implied contract with a common inn-keeper, to secure his guest's goods in his inn; with a common carrier or bargemaster, to be answerable for the goods he carries; with a common farrier, that he shoes a horse well, without laming him; with a common taylor, or other workman, that he performs his business in a workmanlike manner: in which if they fail, an action on the case lies to recover damages for such breach of their general undertaking. But if I employ a person to transact any of these concerns, whose common profession and business it is not, the law implies no such *general* undertaking; but in order to charge him with damages, a *special* agreement is required. Also if an inn-keeper, or other victualler, hangs out a sign and opens his house for travelers, it is an implied engagement to entertain all persons who travel that way; and upon this universal *assumpsit* an action on the case will lie against him for damages, if he without good reason refuses to admit a traveller.

3 William Blackstone, Commentaries *164.

Over time, these implied duties came to be focused on a narrower list of businesses associated with travel, generally referred to as "inn keepers and common carriers." See, e.g., A.K. Sandoval-Strausz, Travelers, Strangers, and Jim Crow: Law, Public Accommodations, and Civil Rights in America, 23 Law & Hist. Rev. 53 (2005) (arguing that by the mid-nineteenth century the common law imposed special duties to serve only on businesses that served travelers); cf. Joseph William Singer, No Right to Exclude: Public Accommodations and Private Property, 90 Nw. U. L. Rev. 1283 (1996) (contending that before the Civil War, all businesses open to the public were subject to a duty to serve, and arguing that the duty narrowed afterwards).

There has long been a debate over the reasons that led to this narrowing:

In a series of books and articles, [Bruce] Wyman explained this narrowing by arguing that common carrier duties were applied only to those occupations that continued to exhibit effective monopoly. These duties were applicable in earlier times because transportation was very limited and because each town's craftsmen, therefore, had monopolies in their own services. Later the duties of common calling focused on innkeepers and carriers because those occupations entailed legal or economic monopolies. By contrast to Wyman, Charles Burdick, also writing in the early 1900s, challenged this view, noting that common carrier duties were often imposed without a specific finding of monopoly power. Burdick argued that the callings could be identified by a number of indicators that the enterprise was considered "public." First, common carrier duties applied to those activities which historically had been provided by the king or under the king's writ. Second, common carrier duties applied when the public had assisted the enterprise in some manner—through public spending, a grant of eminent domain authority, the use of public property, or the establishment of a legal monopoly. When the legislature had acted in one of these manners, the courts drew on the law of common callings to require that the enterprise serve all.

James B. Speta, A Common Carrier Approach to Internet Connection, 54 Fed. Comm. L.J. 225, 255–56 (2002).

Joseph Singer has advanced a third theory: He argues that the narrowing of public accommodations duties to innkeepers and common carriers was a product of the Jim Crow era of the late nineteenth century when many states, especially in the South, sought to maintain the subordinated position of African-Americans. See Singer, supra, at 1390–1411. In order to achieve this discriminatory objective, the duty to serve was narrowed to innkeepers and common carriers, and the businesses which remained subject to this narrowed duty were deemed to satisfy it by providing "separate but equal" facilities to persons of different races. The Supreme Court facilitated this program by endorsing the narrowed conception of public accommodations in the *Civil Rights Cases*, 109 U.S. 3, 25 (1883), and upholding the separate-but-equal interpretation of the duty against an equal protection challenge in *Plessy v. Ferguson*, 163 U.S. 537 (1896). Notice, however, that Singer's theory that the narrowing was a product of racism presupposes that the common-law duty was significantly broader than innkeepers and common-carriers before the Jim Crow era—a revisionist claim that remains controversial. See, e.g., Sandoval-Strausz, supra; Note, The Antidiscrimination Principle in the Common Law, 102 Harv. L. Rev. 1993, 1996 (1989).

Whatever the underlying reason for restricting the category of public accommodations to innkeepers and common carriers, the duties imposed on these enterprises were relatively limited ones. As summarized by Professor Speta, there were two important duties. Speta, supra, at 257–58. The most fundamental obligation was the duty to serve any person who requested service, provided it was available. Thus, innkeepers and common carriers could not refuse service to persons for "any reason or no reason at all." They would have to have some good reason to refuse service, such as the firm's capacity was exhausted, or the customer would interfere with the quality of service provided to other customers. Second, innkeepers and common carriers had to charge prices that were "reasonable." This did not mean they had to charge exactly the same price to different recipients of the same service. Different customers could be charged different prices, as long as each fell within the zone of reasonable charges.

In a further mutation, the category of enterprises known as innkeepers and common carriers eventually came to be known as public accommodations. Modern public accommodations laws have been influenced by antidiscrimination laws, most prominently Title II of the Civil Rights Act of 1964, 42 U.S.C. § 2000a (2000). This landmark statute provides that all persons are "entitled to the full and equal enjoyment" of places of "public accommodation" without "discrimination or segregation on the ground of race, color, religion or national origin." Id. § 2000a(a). "Public accommodation," in turn, is defined to include (1) "any inn, hotel, motel, or other establishment which provides lodging to transient guests;" (2) "any restaurant, cafeteria, lunchroom, lunch counter, soda fountain, or other facility principally engaged in selling food for consumption on the premises;" and (3) "any motion picture house, theater, concert hall, sports arena, stadium or other place of exhibition or entertainment." Id. § 2000a(b). This definition is broader than the common-law definition (imprecise though it was). The Civil Rights Act only prohibits discrimination based on race or other forbidden categories. But will its broader definition of "public accommodation" filter back and influence the judicial understanding of the types of businesses subject to common-law duties of nondiscrimination and reasonableness?

4. PUBLIC POLICY

The most general exception to the right to exclude—which has been developed primarily by the courts of New Jersey—is that owner sovereignty should give way to considerations of public policy. In this conception, the right to exclude is always subject to a balancing test in which competing social interests must be weighed. The idea was introduced in the following case, and has been elaborated upon and qualified in subsequent decisions.

State v. Shack
Supreme Court of New Jersey, 1971.
277 A.2d 369.

■ WEINTRAUB, C.J. Defendants entered upon private property to aid migrant farmworkers employed and housed there. Having refused to depart upon the demand of the owner, defendants were charged with violating N.J.S.A. 2A:170–31 which provides that "[a]ny person who trespasses on any lands * * * after being forbidden so to trespass by the owner * * * is a disorderly person and shall be punished by a fine of not more than $50." Defendants were convicted in the Municipal Court of Deerfield Township and again on appeal in the County Court of Cumberland County on a trial de novo. We certified their further appeal before argument in the Appellate Division.

Before us, no one seeks to sustain these convictions. The complaints were prosecuted in the Municipal Court and in the County Court by counsel engaged by the complaining landowner, Tedesco. However Tedesco did not respond to this appeal, and the county prosecutor, while defending abstractly the constitutionality of the trespass statute, expressly disclaimed any position as to whether the statute reached the activity of these defendants.

Complainant, Tedesco, a farmer, employs migrant workers for his seasonal needs. As part of their compensation, these workers are housed at a camp on his property.

Defendant Tejeras is a field worker for the Farm Workers Division of the Southwest Citizens Organization for Poverty Elimination, known by the acronym SCOPE, a nonprofit corporation funded by the Office of Economic Opportunity pursuant to an act of Congress, 42 U.S.C.A. §§ 2861–2864. The role of SCOPE includes providing for the "health services of the migrant farm worker."

Defendant Shack is a staff attorney with the Farm Workers Division of Camden Regional Legal Services, Inc., known as "CRLS," also a nonprofit corporation funded by the Office of Economic Opportunity pursuant to an act of Congress, 42 U.S.C.A. § 2809(a)(3). The mission of CRLS includes legal advice and representation for these workers.

Differences had developed between Tedesco and these defendants prior to the events which led to the trespass charges now before us. Hence when defendant Tejeras wanted to go upon Tedesco's farm to find a migrant worker who needed medical aid for the removal of 28 sutures, he called upon defendant Shack for his help with respect to the legalities involved. Shack, too, had a mission to perform on Tedesco's farm; he wanted to discuss a legal problem with another migrant worker there employed and housed. Defendants arranged to go to the farm together. Shack carried literature to inform the migrant farmworkers of the assistance available to them under federal statutes, but no mention seems to have been made of that literature when Shack was later confronted by Tedesco.

Defendants entered upon Tedesco's property and as they neared the camp site where the farmworkers were housed, they were confronted by Tedesco who inquired of their purpose. Tejeras and Shack stated their missions. In response, Tedesco offered to find the injured worker, and as to the worker who needed legal advice, Tedesco also offered to locate the man but insisted that the consultation would have to take place in Tedesco's office and in his presence. Defendants declined, saying they had the right to see the men in the privacy of their living quarters and without Tedesco's [supervision]. Tedesco thereupon summoned a State Trooper who, however, refused to remove defendants except upon Tedesco's written complaint. Tedesco then executed the formal complaints charging violations of the trespass statute.

I.

The constitutionality of the trespass statute, as applied here, is challenged on several scores. * * * These constitutional claims are not established by any definitive holding. We think it unnecessary to explore their validity. The reason is that we are satisfied that under our State law the ownership of real property does not include the right to bar access to governmental services available to migrant workers and hence there was no trespass within the meaning of the penal statute. The policy considerations which underlie that conclusion may be much the same as those which would be weighed with respect to one or more of the constitutional challenges, but a decision in nonconstitutional terms is more satisfactory, because the interests of migrant workers are more expansively served in that way than they would be if they had no more freedom than these constitutional concepts could be found to mandate if indeed they apply at all.

II.

Property rights serve human values. They are recognized to that end, and are limited by it. Title to real property cannot include dominion over the destiny of persons the owner permits to come upon the premises. Their well-being must remain the paramount concern of a system of law. Indeed the needs of the occupants may be so imperative and their strength so weak, that the law will deny the occupants the power to contract away what is deemed essential to their health, welfare, or dignity.

Here we are concerned with a highly disadvantaged segment of our society. We are told that every year farmworkers and their families numbering more than one million leave their home areas to fill the seasonal demand for farm labor in the United States. The Migratory Farm Labor Problem in the United States (1969 Report of Subcommittee on Migratory Labor of the United States Senate Committee on Labor and Public Welfare), p. 1. The migrant farmworkers come to New Jersey in substantial numbers. * * *

The migrant farmworkers are a community within but apart from the local scene. They are rootless and isolated. Although the need for their labors is evident, they are unorganized and without economic or political power. It is their plight alone that summoned government to their aid. In response, Congress provided under Title III–B of the Economic Opportunity Act of 1964 (42 U.S.C.A. § 2701 et seq.) for "assistance for migrant and other seasonally employed farmworkers and their families." Section 2861 states "the purpose of this part is to assist migrant and seasonal farmworkers and their families to improve their living conditions and develop skills necessary for a productive and self-sufficient life in an increasingly complex and technological society." * * *

These ends would not be gained if the intended beneficiaries could be insulated from efforts to reach them. It is in this framework that we must decide whether the camp operator's rights in his lands may stand between the migrant workers and those who would aid them. The key to that aid is communication. Since the migrant workers are outside the mainstream of the communities in which they are housed and are unaware of their rights and opportunities and of the services available to them, they can be reached only by positive efforts tailored to that end.

The Report of the Governor's Task Force on Migrant Farm Labor (1968) noted that "One of the major problems related to seasonal farm labor is the lack of adequate direct information with regard to the availability of public services," and that "there is a dire need to provide the workers with basic educational and informational material in a language and style that can be readily understood by the migrant" (pp. 101–102). The report stressed the problem of access and deplored the notion that property rights may stand as a barrier, saying "In our judgment, 'no trespass' signs represent the last dying remnants of paternalistic behavior" (p. 63).

A man's right in his real property of course is not absolute. It was a maxim of the common law that one should so use his property as not to injure the rights of others. Broom, Legal Maxims (10th ed. Kersley 1939), p. 238; 39 Words and Phrases, "Sic Utere Tuo ut Alienum Non Laedas," p. 335. Although hardly a precise solvent of actual controversies, the maxim does express the inevitable proposition that rights are relative and there must be an accommodation when they meet. Hence it has long been true that necessity, private or public, may justify entry upon the lands of another. * * *

The subject is not static. As pointed out in 5 Powell, Real Property (Rohan 1970) § 745, pp. 493–494, while society will protect the owner in his permissible interests in land, yet

> * * * [s]uch an owner must expect to find the absoluteness of his property rights curtailed by the organs of society, for the promotion of the best interests of others for whom these organs also operate as protective agencies. The necessity for such curtailments is greater in a modern industrialized and urbanized society than it was in the relatively simple American society of fifty, 100, or 200 years ago. The current balance between individualism and dominance of the social interest depends not only upon political and social ideologies, but also upon the physical and social facts of the time and place under discussion.

Professor Powell added in § 746, pp. 494–496:

> As one looks back along the historic road traversed by the law of land in England and in America, one sees a change from the viewpoint that he who owns may do as he pleases with what he owns, to a position which hesitatingly embodies an ingredient of stewardship; which grudgingly, but steadily, broadens the recognized scope of social interests in the utilization of things. * * *

> To one seeing history through the glasses of religion, these changes may seem to evidence increasing embodiments of the golden rule. To one thinking in terms of political and economic ideologies, they are likely to be labeled evidences of "social

enlightenment," or of "creeping socialism" or even of "communistic infiltration," according to the individual's assumed definitions and retained or acquired prejudices. With slight attention to words or labels, time marches on toward new adjustments between individualism and the social interests.

The process involves not only the accommodation between the right of the owner and the interests of the general public in his use of this property, but involves also an accommodation between the right of the owner and the right of individuals who are parties with him in consensual transactions relating to the use of the property. Accordingly substantial alterations have been made as between a landlord and his tenant. See Reste Realty Corp. v. Cooper, 251 A.2d 268 (N.J. 1969); Marini v. Ireland, 265 A.2d 526 (N.J. 1970).

The argument in this case understandably included the question whether the migrant worker should be deemed to be a tenant and thus entitled to the tenant's right to receive visitors, or whether his residence on the employer's property should be deemed to be merely incidental and in aid of his employment, and hence to involve no possessory interest in the realty. * * *

We see no profit in trying to decide upon a conventional category and then forcing the present subject into it. That approach would be artificial and distorting. The quest is for a fair adjustment of the competing needs of the parties, in the light of the realities of the relationship between the migrant worker and the operator of the housing facility.

Thus approaching the case, we find it unthinkable that the farmer-employer can assert a right to isolate the migrant worker in any respect significant for the worker's well-being. The farmer, of course, is entitled to pursue his farming activities without interference, and this defendants readily concede. But we see no legitimate need for a right in the farmer to deny the worker the opportunity for aid available from federal, State, or local services, or from recognized charitable groups seeking to assist him. Hence representatives of these agencies and organizations may enter upon the premises to seek out the worker at his living quarters. So, too, the migrant worker must be allowed to receive visitors there of his own choice, so long as there is no behavior hurtful to others, and members of the press may not be denied reasonable access to workers who do not object to seeing them.

It is not our purpose to open the employer's premises to the general public if in fact the employer himself has not done so. We do not say, for example, that solicitors or peddlers of all kinds may enter on their own; we may assume for the present that the employer may regulate their entry or bar them, at least if the employer's purpose is not to gain a commercial advantage for himself or if the regulation does not deprive the migrant worker of practical access to things he needs.

And we are mindful of the employer's interest in his own and in his employees' security. Hence he may reasonably require a visitor to identify himself, and also to state his general purpose if the migrant worker has not already informed him that the visitor is expected. But the employer may not deny the worker his privacy or interfere with his opportunity to live with dignity and to enjoy associations customary among our citizens. These rights are too fundamental to be denied on the basis of an interest in real property and too fragile to be left to the unequal bargaining strength of the parties. See Henningsen v. Bloomfield Motors, Inc., 161 A.2d 69 (N.J. 1960); Ellsworth Dobbs, Inc. v. Johnson, 236 A.2d 843 (N.J. 1967).

these human rights are more important than property rights

It follows that defendants here invaded no possessory right of the farmer-employer. Their conduct was therefore beyond the reach of the trespass statute. The judgments are accordingly reversed and the matters remanded to the County Court with directions to enter judgments of acquittal.

NOTES AND QUESTIONS

1. Recall that the first case in Chapter I also involved a criminal trespass to real property. In *Jacque v. Steenberg Homes*, the issue was punitive damages, but Steenberg Homes had also been fined $30 for misdemeanor trespass. The *Jacque* court concluded that the criminal fine was insufficient to vindicate the owner's right to exclude. The *Shack* court, in contrast, finds that even a $50 criminal fine results in too much owner sovereignty. What accounts for the difference? The *Shack* court perceives a conflict between the rights of the property owner and the rights of persons. Is there no such conflict in *Jacque*? If not, why not?

2. One important difference between *Shack* and decisions such as *Jacque* is that the court implicitly treats the owner's right to exclude not as a rule but as a standard. Generally speaking, rules are simple decisional devices that take the form: If *x* (a particular fact or condition) then *y* (a particular legal result). For example, this is a rule: If a stranger crosses the boundary of an owner's property without permission, then the owner can have the stranger evicted. Rules generate legal conclusions at low cost and without regard to whether the underlying purposes of the rule are satisfied in any particular case. A standard, in contrast, is a decisional device that directly invokes some conception of the law's purposes or goals. Generally speaking, standards are more complex decisional devices and are more costly to apply, but they hold forth the promise of reaching results that are more consistent with the purposes or goals that the law is seeking to achieve. *Shack* seems to invoke a standard something like this: If a stranger crosses the boundary of an owner's property without permission, then the owner can have the stranger evicted—provided that the owner's interest in protecting his autonomy is sufficiently great and the interests of other persons in abrogating the owner's right to exclude are not more important. Which approach would generate a more satisfactory result in *Shack*? Which approach provides a more practical basis for a system of property rights that

governs the actions of millions of people interacting with millions of parcels of property on a daily basis? The question of rules versus standards pervades the law. See Frederick Schauer, Playing by the Rules 131 (1991). Some locate the key difference between rules and standards in the timing of the decision: Standards, unlike rules, rely on ex post decisionmaking in which the decisionmaker has a greater degree of discretion, whereas rules spell out criteria beforehand. Others stress that rules are more costly to create but cheaper to apply. See Louis Kaplow, Rules Versus Standards: An Economic Analysis, 42 Duke L.J. 557, 608–17 (1992). How do these underlying considerations bear on the situation in *Shack*? On other issues of the extent of owner sovereignty?

3. On facts similar to those in *Shack*, the Maine Supreme Court concluded that farm workers living on housing provided by a farmer are "tenants," and as such "have a right to quiet enjoyment, which includes a right to receive visitors in their homes." State v. DeCoster, 653 A.2d 891, 894 (Me. 1995). In effect, the court added to the rights of farm workers, rather than subtracting from the farmer's right to exclude. Which approach is better? Note that, ordinarily, the rights that tenants have against landlords can be modified by express lease provisions. In some circumstances, however, courts have held that tenants' rights (such as the right to safe and healthy living conditions) are nonwaivable as a matter of public policy (see Chapter VI).

4. Another question raised by *Shack* is: Who has the burden to establish an exception to the right to exclude? Should the owner be free to impose any conditions he wants on the public's right of access, unless and until someone shows that a higher legal authority (like a legislature) has adopted a supervening legal principle that requires him to grant access? For example, Illinois has included in its criminal trespass statute an exception to cover situations like that in *State v. Shack*. 720 Ill. Comp. Stat. § 5/21–3(c) ("This Section does not apply to any person . . . invited by [a] migrant worker or other person so living on such land to visit him at the place he is so living upon the land."). Or, by opening up its land to the migrant workers, should the owner be taken to have relinquished the right to exclude any person the migrant workers might invite? On the approach taken in *Shack*, is this presumption irrebuttable?

5. *Shack* has stimulated much legal commentary, and is often cited by those who regard the "right to exclude" as reflecting an unduly harsh and individualistic conception of property. For a notable recent defense of the New Jersey Supreme Court's doctrine, arguing that it serves important social and moral functions and reminds us that ownership entails certain duties and obligations to society at large, see Gregory S. Alexander, The Social-Obligation Norm in American Property Law, 94 Cornell L. Rev. 745 (2009). The same issue includes a number of responses to Alexander's piece as well as his reply.

6. You may wish to reconsider the issue presented in *Shack* after reviewing the Supreme Court's decision in *Cedar Point Nursery v. Hassid*, 141 S. Ct. 2063 (2021), excerpted in Chapter X. *Cedar Point* holds that a California statute that creates an intermittent right of access to agricultural

land to seek to organize farm workers is an unconstitutional taking of property. Is *Shack* distinguishable because it defines the content of state law as a matter of common law?

Uston v. Resorts International Hotel, Inc.

Supreme Court of New Jersey, 1982.
445 A.2d 370.

■ PASHMAN, J. Since January 30, 1979, appellant Resorts International Hotel, Inc. (Resorts) has excluded respondent, Kenneth Uston, from the blackjack tables in its casino because Uston's strategy increases his chances of winning money. Uston concedes that his strategy of card counting can tilt the odds in his favor under the current blackjack rules promulgated by the Casino Control Commission (Commission). However, Uston contends that Resorts has no common law or statutory right to exclude him because of his strategy for playing blackjack.

We hold that the Casino Control Act, N.J.S.A. 5:12–1 to –152 gives the Commission exclusive authority to set the rules of licensed casino games, which includes the methods for playing those games. The Casino Control Act therefore precludes Resorts from excluding Uston for card counting. Because the Commission has not exercised its exclusive authority to determine whether card counters should be excluded, we do not decide whether such an exclusion would be lawful.

I

Kenneth Uston is a renowned teacher and practitioner of a complex strategy for playing blackjack known as card counting.[1] Card counters keep track of the playing cards as they are dealt and adjust their betting patterns when the odds are in their favor. When used over a period of time, this method allegedly ensures a profitable encounter with the casino.

Uston first played blackjack at Resorts' casino in November 1978. Resorts took no steps to bar Uston at that time, apparently because the Commission's blackjack rules then in operation minimized the advantages of card counting.

On January 5, 1979, however, a new Commission rule took effect that dramatically improved the card counter's odds. The new rule, which remains in effect, restricted the reshuffling of the deck in ways that benefited card counters. Resorts concedes that the Commission could promulgate blackjack rules that virtually eliminate the advantage of card counting. However, such rules would slow the game, diminishing the casino's "take" and consequently its profits from blackjack gaming.

By letter dated January 30, 1979, attorneys for Resorts wrote to Commission Chairman Lordi, asking the Commission's position on the

---

[1]   Uston has described his strategy and his alleged success at Atlantic City blackjack tables on broadcast media and in books. See Uston, Two Books on Blackjack.

legality of summarily removing card counters from its blackjack tables. That same day, Commissioner Lordi responded in writing that no statute or regulation barred Resorts from excluding professional card counters from its casino. Before the day had ended, Resorts terminated Uston's career at its blackjack tables, on the basis that in its opinion he was a professional card counter. Resorts subsequently formulated standards for identification of card counters and adopted a general policy to exclude such players.[2]

The Commission upheld Resorts' decision to exclude Uston. Relying on Garifine v. Monmouth Park Jockey Club, 148 A.2d 1 (N.J. 1959), the Commission held that Resorts enjoys a common law right to exclude anyone it chooses, as long as the exclusion does not violate state and federal civil rights laws. The Appellate Division reversed, 431 A.2d 173 (N.J. Super. 1981). Although we interpret the Casino Control Act somewhat differently than did the Appellate Division, we affirm that court's holding that the Casino Control Act precludes Resorts from excluding Uston. The Commission alone has the authority to exclude patrons based upon their strategies for playing licensed casino games. Any common law right Resorts may have had to exclude Uston for these reasons is abrogated by the act. We therefore need not decide the precise extent of Resorts' common law right to exclude patrons for reasons not covered by the act. Nonetheless, we feel constrained to refute any implication arising from the Commission's opinion that absent supervening statutes, the owners of places open to the public enjoy an absolute right to exclude patrons without good cause. We hold that the common law right to exclude is substantially limited by a competing common law right of reasonable access to public places.

II

This Court has recognized that "[t]he statutory and administrative controls over casino operations established by the [Casino Control] Act are extraordinarily pervasive and intensive." Knight v. Margate, 431 A.2d 833 (N.J. 1981). The almost 200 separate statutory provisions "cover virtually every facet of casino gambling and its potential impact upon the public." Id. at 833. * * *

Pursuant to these statutes, the Commission has promulgated exhaustive rules on the playing of blackjack. These rules cover every conceivable aspect of the game, from determining how the cards are to be shuffled and cut, to providing that certain cards shall not be dealt "until the dealer has first announced 'Dealer's Card' which shall be stated by the dealer in a tone of voice calculated to be heard by each person at the table." It is no exaggeration to state that the Commission's regulation of blackjack is more extensive than the entire administrative regulation of many industries.

---

[2]   Since then an industry-wide policy has developed to ban card counters. Each casino maintains its own list of persons to be barred as card counters.

These exhaustive statutes and regulations make clear that the Commission's control over the rules and conduct of licensed casino games is intended to be comprehensive. The ability of casino operators to determine how the games will be played would undermine this control and subvert the important policy of ensuring the "credibility and integrity of the regulatory process and of casino operations." The Commission has promulgated the blackjack rules that give Uston a comparative advantage, and it has sole authority to change those rules. There is no indication that Uston has violated any Commission rule on the playing of blackjack. Put simply, Uston's gaming is "conducted according to rules promulgated by the Commission." Resorts has no right to exclude Uston on grounds that he successfully plays the game under existing rules.

III

Resorts claimed that it could exclude Uston because it had a common law right to exclude anyone at all for any reason. While we hold that the Casino Control Act precludes Resorts from excluding Uston for the reasons stated, it is important for us to address the asserted common law right for two reasons. First, Resorts' contentions and the Commission's position concerning the common law right are incorrect. Second, the act has not completely divested Resorts of its common law right to exclude.

The right of an amusement place owner to exclude unwanted patrons and the patron's competing right of reasonable access both have deep roots in the common law. See Arterburn, The Origin and First Test of Public Callings, 75 U.Pa.L.Rev. 411 (1927); Wyman, The Law of Public Callings as a Solution of the Trust Problem, 17 Harv.L.Rev. 156 (1904). In this century, however, courts have disregarded the right of reasonable access in the common law of some jurisdictions at the time the Civil War Amendments and Civil Rights Act of 1866 were passed. * * * See, e.g., Ferguson v. Gies, 46 N.W. 718 (Mich. 1890) (after passage of the Fourteenth Amendment, both the civil rights statutes and the common law provided grounds for a non-white plaintiff to recover damages from a restaurant owner's refusal to serve him, because the common law as it existed before passage of the civil rights laws "gave to the white man a remedy against any unjust discrimination to the citizen in all public places"); Donnell v. State, 48 Miss. 661 (1873) (state's common law includes a right of reasonable access to all public places).

The current majority American rule has for many years disregarded the right of reasonable access,[4] granting to proprietors of amusement places an absolute right arbitrarily to eject or exclude any person consistent with state and federal civil rights laws. See Annot., Propriety of exclusion of persons from horseracing tracks for reasons other than

---

[4]   The denial of freedom of reasonable access in some States following passage of the Fourteenth Amendment, and the creation of a common law freedom to arbitrarily exclude following invalidation of segregation statutes, suggest that the current majority rule may have had less than dignified origins. See Bell v. Maryland, [378 U.S. 226 (1964)].

color or race, 90 A.L.R.3d 1361 (1979); Turner & Kennedy, Exclusion, Ejection and Segregation of Theater Patrons, 32 Iowa L.Rev. 625 (1947). See also Garifine v. Monmouth Park Jockey Club, 148 A.2d 1.

At one time, an absolute right of exclusion prevailed in this state, though more for reasons of deference to the noted English precedent of *Wood v. Leadbitter*, 13 M & W 838, 153 Eng.Rep. 351 (Ex. 1845), than for reasons of policy. * * * It hardly bears mention that our common law has evolved in the intervening 70 years. * * * [T]he decisions of this Court have recognized that "the more private property is devoted to public use, the more it must accommodate the rights which inhere in individual members of the general public who use that property." State v. Schmid, 423 A.2d 615 (N.J. 1980).

State v. Schmid involved the constitutional right to distribute literature on a private university campus. The Court's approach in that case balanced individual rights against property rights. It is therefore analogous to a description of the common law right of exclusion. Balancing the university's interest in controlling its property against plaintiff's interest in access to that property to express his views, the Court clearly refused to protect unreasonable exclusions. Justice Handler noted that

> Regulations . . . devoid of reasonable standards designed to protect both the legitimate interests of the University as an institution of higher education and the individual exercise of expressional freedom cannot constitutionally be invoked to prohibit the otherwise noninjurious and reasonable exercise of [First Amendment] freedoms. [Id. at 632]

In *State v. Shack*, 277 A.2d 369 (N.J. 1971), the Court held that although an employer of migrant farm workers "may reasonably require" those visiting his employees to identify themselves, "the employer may not deny the worker his privacy or interfere with his opportunity to live with dignity and to enjoy associations customary among our citizens." Id. at 374. The Court reversed the trespass convictions of an attorney and a social services worker who had entered the property to assist farmworkers there.

Schmid recognizes implicitly that when property owners open their premises to the general public in the pursuit of their own property interests, they have no right to exclude people unreasonably. On the 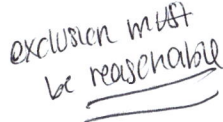 contrary, they have a duty not to act in an arbitrary or discriminatory manner toward persons who come on their premises. That duty applies not only to common carriers, Messenger v. Pennsylvania Railroad Co., 37 N.J.L. 531 (E. & A. 1874), innkeepers, see Garifine, supra, owners of gasoline service stations, Streeter v. Brogan, 274 A.2d 312 (N.J. Ch. Div. 1971), or to private hospitals, Doe v. Bridgeton Hospital Ass'n, Inc., 366 A.2d 641 (N.J. 1976), but to all property owners who open their premises to the public. Property owners have no legitimate interest in unreasonably excluding particular members of the public when they open their premises for public use.

reasonable exclusions

No party in this appeal questions the right of property owners to exclude from their premises those whose actions "disrupt the regular and essential operations of the [premises]," State v. Schmid, 423 A.2d at 631 (quoting Princeton University Regulations on solicitation), or threaten the security of the premises and its occupants, see State v. Shack, 277 A.2d at 374. In some circumstances, proprietors have a duty to remove disorderly or otherwise dangerous persons from the premises. See Holly v. Meyers Hotel and Tavern, Inc., 89 A.2d 6 (N.J. 1952). These common law principles enable the casino to bar from its entire facility, for instance, the disorderly, the intoxicated, and the repetitive petty offender.

Whether a decision to exclude is reasonable must be determined from the facts of each case. Respondent Uston does not threaten the security of any casino occupant. Nor has he disrupted the functioning of any casino operations. Absent a valid contrary rule by the Commission, Uston possesses the usual right of reasonable access to Resorts International's blackjack tables. * * *

V

In sum, absent a valid Commission regulation excluding card counters, respondent Uston will be free to employ his card-counting strategy at Resorts' blackjack tables. There is currently no Commission rule banning Uston, and Resorts has no authority to exclude him for card counting. However, it is not clear whether the Commission would have adopted regulations involving card counters had it known that Resorts could not exclude Uston. The Court therefore continues the temporary order banning Uston from Resorts' blackjack tables for 90 days from the date of this opinion. After that time, respondent is free to play blackjack at Resorts' casino absent a valid Commission rule excluding him.

NOTES AND QUESTIONS

1. Ken Uston was a famous blackjack player. As noted in the opinion he authored leading books on blackjack. His litigation exploits were more controversial. Uston had arrived in New Jersey after having been treated rather roughly and excluded from casinos in Las Vegas. In New Jersey, some people felt he made things worse for card counters and spoiled the game by litigating against the exclusion of card counters, because the measures that casinos would take to counter the counters—such as adding decks and moving up the shuffle point—made the game of blackjack worse. Uston and his team were quite successful at the tables, but Uston claimed that the casinos exaggerated the counters' take by reporting all winning customers as card counters. In addition to writing books about blackjack, in the 1980s he wrote several books about video games such as PAC-MAN and many about a variety of personal computers. He died of a heart attack in 1987 in Paris. See "Ken(neth) (Senzo) Uston," Gale Literature: Contemporary Authors, Gale, 2002. Gale In Context: Biography, https://go.gale.com/ps/i.do ?p=BIC&u=mlin_oweb&id=GALE%7CH1000100927&v=2.1&it=r&sid=book mark-BIC&ugroup=outside.

Figure 4-2
Ken Uston

THE BIG PLAYER

Source: http://www.uston.com.

2. Other courts have reached the opposite conclusion about the continued vitality of the common-law rule giving owners of entertainment venues absolute discretion to exclude persons from the premises. For example, in *Brooks v. Chicago Downs Assn., Inc.*, 791 F.2d 512 (7th Cir. 1986), the court, applying Illinois law, held that a horse racing park could exclude a group of "self-proclaimed expert handicappers" from the park for any reason or no reason at all, as long as there was no discrimination based on "race, color, creed, national origin, or sex." In explaining why it declined to follow *Uston*, the court wrote in part:

> As a policy matter, it is arguably unfair to allow a place of amusement to exclude for any reason or no reason, and to be free of accountability, except in cases of obvious discrimination. In this case, the general public is not only invited but, through advertising, is encouraged to come to the race track and wager on the races' outcome. But the common law allows the race track to exclude patrons, no matter if they come from near or far, or in reasonable reliance on representations of accessibility. We may ultimately believe that market forces would preclude any outrageous excesses—such as excluding anyone who has blond hair, or (like the plaintiffs) who is from Pennsylvania, or (even more outrageous) who has $250,000 to spend in one day of betting. * * * [T]he premise of the consumer protection laws that the New Jersey Supreme Court alluded to in *Uston* * * * recognizes that the reality of an imperfect market allows numerous consumer depredations. Excluding a patron simply because he is named Adam Smith

arguably offends the very precepts of equality and fair dealing expressed in everything from the antitrust statutes to the Illinois Consumer Fraud and Deceptive Business Practice Act.

But the market here is not so demonstrably imperfect that there is a monopoly or any allegation of consumer fraud. Consequently, there is no such explicit legislative directive in the context of patrons attending horse races in Illinois—so the common law rule, relic though it may be, still controls.

Id. at 518–19. See also Donovan v. Grand Victoria Casino & Resort, L.P., 934 N.E.2d, 1111 (Ind. 2010) (declining to follow *Uston* based on the legislative intent behind gaming statutes).

3.   In another case involving horse racing, the New Jersey Supreme Court reaffirmed the common law right of a race track owner to exclude a race horse from the track without regard to its reasons for doing so. Marzocca v. Ferone, 461 A.2d 1133 (N.J. 1983). The New Jersey Court distinguished *Uston* on the ground that it involved the exclusion of a member of the general public, as opposed to those "who wish to perform their vocational activities on racetrack property." Id. at 1137. Is this persuasive? Wasn't Uston a professional card player? Is there something about horse racing that supports giving race track owners a broader discretion to exclude than casino owners enjoy?

4.   How weighty is the casino's interest in *Uston*? At one point the court notes the casino conceded that the Commission could largely eliminate the advantages of card counting through different rules for the game of Blackjack, but that these rules would slow the game and thereby reduce the house's take. Consider in this regard a study by Lawrence Ritter, who has indirectly measured the transaction costs associated with a medium of exchange by showing the amount of advantage Las Vegas casinos forego in order to avoid time-consuming handling of chips in games of dice. Lawrence S. Ritter, On the Fundamental Role of Transactions Costs in Monetary Theory: Two Illustrations from Casino Gambling, 10 J. Money, Credit & Banking 522, 524–28 (1978). The casinos calculate that foregoing the advantage of making more exact change is outweighed by the greater return from faster bets in a context in which the house has a built-in advantage. Who is best at weighing these considerations? Owners of casinos? The Commission? Courts?

5.   The New Jersey Supreme Court has given special consideration to political expression in determining whether to qualify the right to exclude, with mixed results. In *State v. Schmid*, 423 A.2d 615 (N.J. 1980), Princeton University (a private institution) was denied the right to use the law of trespass to prevent a non-student from distributing political literature in an orderly manner on campus. The court noted the speaker's strong interest in disseminating ideas and the University's relatively weak interest in excluding such communications given its traditional open campus policy and its mission of spreading ideas. The case was later dismissed by the U.S. Supreme Court for mootness after Princeton changed its policy. Princeton University v. Schmid, 455 U.S. 100 (1982). In a more recent case, the New

Jersey court considered whether a private homeowners' association could limit the posting of political signs by residents on lawns outside individual residents' units. Committee for a Better Twin Rivers v. Twin Rivers Homeowners' Assn., 929 A.2d 1060 (N.J. 2007). The court acknowledged that only a few states have recognized a constitutional right to engage in free speech on private property. Although it reaffirmed the balancing approach of *Schmid*, it ruled in favor of the homeowners' association. The court noted that the residential community was not open to the general public and that the residents had alternative ways in which they could express their views. Does this decision, coupled with *Marzocca* (reaffirming the common law right of race horse tracks to exclude participants) suggest that New Jersey may be inching back toward the mainstream in its approach to the prerogatives of property owners?

6. Copyright law contains an exception for fair use, which among other things protects a critic quoting from a work. 17 U.S.C. § 107. Should trespass work similarly? Consider *Woolcott v. Shubert*, 111 N.E. 829 (N.Y. 1916), in which the defendants, who operated many theaters had excluded from all its theaters a professional drama critic who in the words of the complaint had "[written] and the *New York Times* [had] published a legitimate and proper criticism of one of the productions controlled by the defendants." Id. at 829. The court did not find the theaters to be public accommodations, and because the critic had not been excluded on the basis of "race, creed, or color," the state's 1895 Civil Rights Act did not apply (see the materials on antidiscrimination in the next Section). The plaintiff lost. Should he have? Should there be a First Amendment defense to trespass for journalists doing undercover work for exposés? For anyone interested in exposing wrongdoing? How would "fair trespass" work? Ben Depoorter, Fair Trespass, 111 Colum. L. Rev. 1090 (2011).

5. ANTIDISCRIMINATION LAWS

Perhaps the most important exception to the general right of a property owner to exclude others is grounded in antidiscrimination laws. As we have seen, owners of public accommodations were subject to antidiscrimination rules at common law. But the Supreme Court, in *Plessy v. Ferguson*, 163 U.S. 537 (1896), held that the Equal Protection Clause was not violated if a state required common carriers to fulfill the antidiscrimination requirement by providing "separate but equal" facilities for persons of different races. After *Plessy* was effectively overruled by *Brown v. Board of Education*, 347 U.S. 483 (1954), separate-but-equal was dismantled in the realm of public accommodations, most decisively under Title II of the Civil Rights Act of 1964. But discrimination in the realm of property not open to the public has presented a more difficult issue. Significant restrictions have been imposed on the right to exclude based on race, gender, religion, national origin, familial status, and disability—and in many jurisdictions, based on marital status and source of income. The statutory category of sex has been variously interpreted, and sexual orientation and gender identity are explicitly mentioned in the law of almost half the states. For example, if you sell your home while using a real estate broker, you cannot exclude potential buyers based on one of these protected categories. But even to this day, there is no legal principle that prohibits a homeowner or tenant from announcing that persons of a particular race or other protected category will be systematically excluded from her home or apartment. To that extent, a significant degree of owner sovereignty remains immune from antidiscrimination duties.

The following case, decided before *Brown v. Board of Education* declared separate-but-equal to be unconstitutional, reflects a notable attempt by the Supreme Court to reconcile the principle of owner sovereignty with the goals of equal protection in the context of housing.

Shelley v. Kraemer

Supreme Court of the United States, 1948.
334 U.S. 1.

■ MR. CHIEF JUSTICE VINSON delivered the opinion of the Court. These cases present for our consideration questions relating to the validity of court enforcement of private agreements, generally described as restrictive covenants, which have as their purpose the exclusion of persons of designated race or color from the ownership or occupancy of real property. Basic constitutional issues of obvious importance have been raised.

The first of these cases comes to this Court on certiorari to the Supreme Court of Missouri. On February 16, 1911, thirty out of a total of thirty-nine owners of property fronting both sides of Labadie Avenue between Taylor Avenue and Cora Avenue in the city of St. Louis, signed an agreement, which was subsequently recorded, providing in part:

> * * * the said property is hereby restricted to the use and occupancy for the term of Fifty (50) years from this date, so that * * * hereafter no part of said property or any portion thereof shall be, for said term of Fifty-years, occupied by any person not of the Caucasian race, it being intended hereby to restrict the use of said property for said period of time against the occupancy as owners or tenants of any portion of said property for resident or other purpose by people of the Negro or Mongolian Race.

The entire district described in the agreement included fifty-seven parcels of land. The thirty owners who signed the agreement held title to forty-seven parcels, including the particular parcel involved in this case. At the time the agreement was signed, five of the parcels in the district were owned by Negroes. * * *

On August 11, 1945, pursuant to a contract of sale, petitioners Shelley, who are Negroes, for valuable consideration received from one Fitzgerald a warranty deed to the parcel in question. The trial court found that petitioners had no actual knowledge of the restrictive agreement at the time of the purchase.

On October 9, 1945, respondents, as owners of other property subject to the terms of the restrictive covenant, brought suit in Circuit Court of the city of St. Louis praying that petitioners Shelley be restrained from taking possession of the property and that judgment be entered divesting title out of petitioners Shelley and revesting title in the immediate grantor or in such other person as the court should direct. The trial court denied the requested relief on the ground that the restrictive agreement, upon which respondents based their action, had never become final and complete because it was the intention of the parties to that agreement that it was not to become effective until signed by all property owners in the district, and signatures of all the owners had never been obtained.

The Supreme Court of Missouri sitting en banc reversed and directed the trial court to grant the relief for which respondents had prayed. That court held the agreement effective and concluded that enforcement of its provisions violated no rights guaranteed to petitioners by the Federal Constitution. At the time the court rendered its decision, petitioners were occupying the property in question. * * *

Figure 4-3
House in *Shelley v. Kraemer* with Commemorative Marker

Source: Saint Louis Post-Dispatch.

Petitioners have placed primary reliance on their contentions, first raised in the state courts, that judicial enforcement of the restrictive agreements in these cases has violated rights guaranteed to petitioners by the Fourteenth Amendment of the Federal Constitution and Acts of

Congress passed pursuant to that Amendment.[4] Specifically, petitioners urge that they have been denied the equal protection of the laws, deprived of property without due process of law, and have been denied privileges and immunities of citizens of the United States. We pass to a consideration of those issues.

I.

Whether the equal protection clause of the Fourteenth Amendment inhibits judicial enforcement by state courts of restrictive covenants based on race or color is a question which this Court has not heretofore been called upon to consider. Only two cases have been decided by this Court which in any way have involved the enforcement of such agreements. The first of these was the case of Corrigan v. Buckley, 271 U.S. 323 (1926). There, * * * [the] only constitutional issue which the appellants had raised in the lower courts, and hence the only constitutional issue before this Court on appeal, was the validity of the covenant agreements as such. This Court concluded that since the inhibitions of the constitutional provisions invoked, apply only to governmental action, as contrasted to action of private individuals, there was no showing that the covenants, which were simply agreements between private property owners, were invalid. Accordingly, the appeal was dismissed for want of a substantial question. Nothing in the opinion of this Court, therefore, may properly be regarded as an adjudication on the merits of the constitutional issues presented by these cases, which raise the question of the validity, not of the private agreements as such, but of the judicial enforcement of those agreements.

The second of the cases involving racial restrictive covenants was Hansberry v. Lee, 311 U.S. 32 (1940). In that case, petitioners, white property owners, were enjoined by the state courts from violating the terms of a restrictive agreement. The state Supreme Court had held petitioners bound by an earlier judicial determination, in litigation in which petitioners were not parties, upholding the validity of the restrictive agreement, although, in fact, the agreement had not been signed by the number of owners necessary to make it effective under state law. This Court reversed the judgment of the state Supreme Court upon the ground that petitioners had been denied due process of law in being held estopped to challenge the validity of the agreement on the theory, accepted by the state court, that the earlier litigation, in which petitioners did not participate, was in the nature of a class suit. In arriving at its result, this Court did not reach the issues presented by the cases now under consideration. * * *

---

[4]   The first section of the Fourteenth Amendment provides: "All persons born or naturalized in the United States, and subject to the jurisdiction thereof, are citizens of the United States and of the State wherein they reside. No State shall make or enforce any law which shall abridge the privileges or immunities of citizens of the United States; nor shall any State deprive any person of life, liberty, or property, without due process of law; nor deny to any person within its jurisdiction the equal protection of the laws."

It cannot be doubted that among the civil rights intended to be protected from discriminatory state action by the Fourteenth Amendment are the rights to acquire, enjoy, own and dispose of property. Equality in the enjoyment of property rights was regarded by the framers of that Amendment as an essential pre-condition to the realization of other basic civil rights and liberties which the Amendment was intended to guarantee. Thus, § 1978 of the Revised Statutes, derived from § 1 of the Civil Rights Act of 1866 which was enacted by Congress while the Fourteenth Amendment was also under consideration, provides:

> All citizens of the United States shall have the same right, in every State and Territory, as is enjoyed by white citizens thereof to inherit, purchase, lease, sell, hold, and convey real and personal property.

This Court has given specific recognition to the same principle. Buchanan v. Warley, 245 U.S. 60 (1917).

It is likewise clear that restrictions on the right of occupancy of the sort sought to be created by the private agreements in these cases could not be squared with the requirements of the Fourteenth Amendment if imposed by state statute or local ordinance. We do not understand respondents to urge the contrary. In the case of Buchanan v. Warley, supra, a unanimous Court declared unconstitutional the provisions of a city ordinance which denied to colored persons the right to occupy houses in blocks in which the greater number of houses were occupied by white persons, and imposed similar restrictions on white persons with respect to blocks in which the greater number of houses were occupied by colored persons. During the course of the opinion in that case, this Court stated: "The Fourteenth Amendment and these statutes enacted in furtherance of its purpose operate to qualify and entitle a colored man to acquire property without state legislation discriminating against him solely because of color."

In Harmon v. Tyler, 273 U.S. 668 (1927), a unanimous court, on the authority of Buchanan v. Warley, supra, declared invalid an ordinance which forbade any Negro to establish a home on any property in a white community or any white person to establish a home in a Negro community, "except on the written consent of a majority of the persons of the opposite race inhabiting such community or portion of the City to be affected."

The precise question before this Court in both the Buchanan and Harmon cases, involved the rights of white sellers to dispose of their properties free from restrictions as to potential purchasers based on considerations of race or color. But that such legislation is also offensive to the rights of those desiring to acquire and occupy property and barred on grounds of race or color, is clear * * * from the language of the opinion in Buchanan v. Warley, supra. * * *

But the present cases, unlike those just discussed, do not involve action by state legislatures or city councils. Here the particular patterns of discrimination and the areas in which the restrictions are to operate, are determined, in the first instance, by the terms of agreements among private individuals. Participation of the State consists in the enforcement of the restrictions so defined. The crucial issue with which we are here confronted is whether this distinction removes these cases from the operation of the prohibitory provisions of the Fourteenth Amendment.

Since the decision of this Court in the Civil Rights Cases, 109 U.S. 3 (1883), the principle has become firmly embedded in our constitutional law that the action inhibited by the first section of the Fourteenth Amendment is only such action as may fairly be said to be that of the States. That Amendment erects no shield against merely private conduct, however discriminatory or wrongful.

We conclude, therefore, that the restrictive agreements standing alone cannot be regarded as a violation of any rights guaranteed to petitioners by the Fourteenth Amendment. So long as the purposes of those agreements are effectuated by voluntary adherence to their terms, it would appear clear that there has been no action by the State and the provisions of the Amendment have not been violated. Cf. Corrigan v. Buckley, supra.

But here there was more. These are cases in which the purposes of the agreements were secured only by judicial enforcement by state courts of the restrictive terms of the agreements. The respondents urge that judicial enforcement of private agreements does not amount to state action; or, in any event, the participation of the State is so attenuated in character as not to amount to state action within the meaning of the Fourteenth Amendment. Finally, it is suggested, even if the States in these cases may be deemed to have acted in the constitutional sense, their action did not deprive petitioners of rights guaranteed by the Fourteenth Amendment. We move to a consideration of these matters.

II.

That the action of state courts and of judicial officers in their official capacities is to be regarded as action of the State within the meaning of the Fourteenth Amendment, is a proposition which has long been established by decisions of this Court. * * *

One of the earliest applications of the prohibitions contained in the Fourteenth Amendment to action of state judicial officials occurred in cases in which Negroes had been excluded from jury service in criminal prosecutions by reason of their race or color. These cases demonstrate, also, the early recognition by this Court that state action in violation of the Amendment's provisions is equally repugnant to the constitutional commands whether directed by state statute or taken by a judicial official in the absence of statute. Thus, in Strauder v. West Virginia, 100 U.S. 303 (1880), this Court declared invalid a state statute restricting jury service to white persons as amounting to a denial of the equal protection of the laws to the colored defendant in that case. In the same volume of the reports, the Court in Ex parte Commonwealth of Virginia, 100 U.S. 339 (1879), held that a similar discrimination imposed by the action of a state judge denied rights protected by the Amendment, despite the fact that the language of the state statute relating to jury service contained no such restrictions. * * *

But the examples of state judicial action which have been held by this Court to violate the Amendment's commands are not restricted to situations in which the judicial proceedings were found in some manner to be procedurally unfair. It has been recognized that the action of state courts in enforcing a substantive common-law rule formulated by those courts, may result in the denial of rights guaranteed by the Fourteenth Amendment, even though the judicial proceedings in such cases may have been in complete accord with the most rigorous conceptions of procedural due process. Thus, in American Federation of Labor v. Swing, 312 U.S. 321 (1941), enforcement by state courts of the common-law policy of the State, which resulted in the restraining of peaceful picketing, was held to be state action of the sort prohibited by the Amendment's guaranties of freedom of discussion. In Cantwell v. Connecticut, 310 U.S. 296 (1940), a conviction in a state court of the common-law crime of breach of the peace was, under the circumstances of the case, found to be a violation of the Amendment's commands relating to freedom of religion. In Bridges v. California, 314 U.S. 252 (1941), enforcement of the state's common-law rule relating to contempts by publication was held to be state action inconsistent with the prohibitions of the Fourteenth Amendment. * * *

III.

Against this background of judicial construction, extending over a period of some three-quarters of a century, we are called upon to consider whether enforcement by state courts of the restrictive agreements in these cases may be deemed to be the acts of those States; and, if so, whether that action has denied these petitioners the equal protection of the laws which the Amendment was intended to insure.

We have no doubt that there has been state action in these cases in the full and complete sense of the phrase. The undisputed facts disclose that petitioners were willing purchasers of properties upon which they desired to establish homes. The owners of the properties were willing sellers; and contracts of sale were accordingly consummated. It is clear that but for the active intervention of the state courts, supported by the full panoply of state power, petitioners would have been free to occupy the properties in question without restraint.

These are not cases, as has been suggested, in which the States have merely abstained from action, leaving private individuals free to impose such discriminations as they see fit. Rather, these are cases in which the States have made available to such individuals the full coercive power of government to deny to petitioners, on the grounds of race or color, the enjoyment of property rights in premises which petitioners are willing and financially able to acquire and which the grantors are willing to sell. The difference between judicial enforcement and nonenforcement of the restrictive covenants is the difference to petitioners between being denied rights of property available to other members of the community and being accorded full enjoyment of those rights on an equal footing.

The enforcement of the restrictive agreements by the state courts in these cases was directed pursuant to the common-law policy of the States as formulated by those courts in earlier decisions. * * * State action, as that phrase is understood for the purposes of the Fourteenth Amendment, refers to exertions of state power in all forms. And when the effect of that action is to deny rights subject to the protection of the Fourteenth Amendment, it is the obligation of this Court to enforce the constitutional commands.

We hold that in granting judicial enforcement of the restrictive agreements in these cases, the States have denied petitioners the equal protection of the laws and that, therefore, the action of the state courts cannot stand. We have noted that freedom from discrimination by the States in the enjoyment of property rights was among the basic objectives sought to be effectuated by the framers of the Fourteenth Amendment. That such discrimination has occurred in these cases is clear. Because of the race or color of these petitioners they have been denied rights of ownership or occupancy enjoyed as a matter of course by other citizens of different race or color. * * *26

Respondents urge, however, that since the state courts stand ready to enforce restrictive covenants excluding white persons from the ownership or occupancy of property covered by such agreements, enforcement of covenants excluding colored persons may not be deemed a denial of equal protection of the laws to the colored persons who are thereby affected. This contention does not bear scrutiny. The parties have directed our attention to no case in which a court, state or federal, has been called upon to enforce a covenant excluding members of the white majority from ownership or occupancy of real property on grounds of race or color. But there are more fundamental considerations. The rights created by the first section of the Fourteenth Amendment are, by its terms, guaranteed to the individual. The rights established are personal rights. It is, therefore, no answer to these petitioners to say that the courts may also be induced to deny white persons rights of ownership and occupancy on grounds of race or color. Equal protection of the laws is not achieved through indiscriminate imposition of inequalities.

---

26   Restrictive agreements of the sort involved in these cases have been used to exclude other than Negroes from the ownership or occupancy of real property. We are informed that such agreements have been directed against Indians, Jews, Chinese, Japanese, Mexicans, Hawaiians, Puerto Ricans, and Filipinos, among others.

Nor do we find merit in the suggestion that property owners who are parties to these agreements are denied equal protection of the laws if denied access to the courts to enforce the terms of restrictive covenants and to assert property rights which the state courts have held to be created by such agreements. The Constitution confers upon no individual the right to demand action by the State which results in the denial of equal protection of the laws to other individuals. And it would appear beyond question that the power of the State to create and enforce property interests must be exercised within the boundaries defined by the Fourteenth Amendment. Cf. Marsh v. Alabama, 326 U.S. 501 (1946). * * *

For the reasons stated, the judgment of the Supreme Court of Missouri * * * must be reversed.

■ MR. JUSTICE REED, MR. JUSTICE JACKSON, and MR. JUSTICE RUTLEDGE took no part in the consideration or decision of these cases.

NOTES AND QUESTIONS

1. For further background on *Shelley*, see Carol Rose, Property Stories: *Shelley v. Kraemer*, in Property Stories 189 (Gerald Korngold & Andrew P. Morriss eds., 2d ed. 2009); see also Richard R.W. Brooks & Carol M. Rose, Saving the Neighborhood: Racially Restrictive Covenants, Law, and Social Norms (2013); Clement E. Vose, Caucasians Only: The Supreme Court, the NAACP, and the Restrictive Covenant Cases (1959). A few years after the decision in *Shelley*, the Court ruled that judicial judgments awarding damages for breach of a racial covenant are also state action forbidden under the Equal Protection Clause. Barrows v. Jackson, 346 U.S. 249 (1953). This eliminated the possible argument that the prohibitory nature of a judicial injunction makes this type of judicial judgment "state action," whereas other types of judicial action such as awarding damages for breach of contract or enforcing a racially discriminatory bequest in a will, are not.

2. We have seen a number of devices or ideas for drawing the line between the sphere of owner sovereignty and the sphere of collective or public sovereignty, including common-law restrictions (e.g., the defense of necessity), custom (e.g., hunting rights), and public accommodations requirements. *Shelley* calls upon yet another device: the state action doctrine. *Shelley* says that a mere "voluntary agreement" among neighbors not to sell to African-Americans would not be state action, and hence is a permissible incidence of owner sovereignty. But if someone calls upon the powers of the courts to enforce such an agreement, any resulting judicial judgment is state action, and hence is subject to the limitations of the Constitution, including the Equal Protection Clause. Recall too that in the context of attempts to recover personal property, the Supreme Court has held that replevin actions and judicial garnishment orders are state action, and hence are subject to the constitutional requirements of the Due Process Clause—but courts have generally assumed that self-help repossessions are not state action, and hence escape due process limitations. Does this suggest

that the sphere of owner sovereignty is limited to efforts to exclude others through informal persuasion based on norms and customs, voluntary compliance with contracts, and self-help? Does this mean that any attempt to invoke the private law of property in a court is automatically transformed into a species of federal constitutional law? Or does this result in too small a sphere for owner sovereignty relative to public sovereignty?

3.   Most (but not all) commentators have concluded that *Shelley* was correctly decided, but they have also been reluctant to endorse the idea that any judicial enforcement of property rights is subject to the various constitutional limitations that apply to government action more generally. Such an understanding might mean, for example, that calling the police to remove a house guest because you find her speech offensive might be subject to challenge under the First Amendment. Trying to identify some limiting principle for *Shelley*'s conclusion that judicial enforcement of racial covenants is state action has nevertheless vexed scholars ever since the decision was handed down. See, e.g., Louis Pollak, Racial Discrimination and Judicial Integrity: A Reply to Professor Wechsler, 108 U. Pa. L. Rev. 1 (1959) (*Shelley* correctly decided because judicial enforcement of the covenant required a person who did not wish to discriminate to engage in discriminatory action); Thomas P. Lewis, The Meaning of State Action, 60 Colum. L. Rev. 1083, 1115 (1960) (*Shelley* correctly decided because racial covenants are functionally equivalent to zoning laws); Louis Henkin, *Shelley v. Kraemer*: Notes for a Revised Opinion, 110 U. Pa. L. Rev. 473 (1962) (*Shelley* justified under a balancing test that compares impact of discrimination on blacks against liberty interest of white property owners); Robert J. Glennon & John E. Nowak, A Functional Analysis of the Fourteenth Amendment "State Action" Requirement, 1976 Sup. Ct. Rev. 221 (*Shelley* properly separated out for invalidation those nongovernmental activities whose existence impairs fundamental constitutional values); Laurence H. Tribe, Constitutional Choices 260 (1985) (*Shelley* correctly decided because enforcement of the covenant was an exception to the general rule followed by the state of prohibiting restraints on alienation); Mark D. Rosen, Was *Shelley v. Kraemer* Incorrectly Decided? Some New Answers, 95 Cal. L. Rev. 451 (2007) (*Shelley* correctly decided but should have been grounded in the Thirteenth Amendment and statutes implementing it rather than the Fourteenth Amendment); but see Lillian BeVier and John Harrison, The State Action Principle and Its Critics, 96 Va. L. Rev. 1767, 1798–1802 (2010) (discussing how *Shelley* is in tension with the general understanding that constitutional restrictions apply to agents of the people but not to the people themselves).

4.   One related but distinct approach to the specter of racially restrictive covenants is to invalidate them on grounds of public policy. For example, in the case of *Re Drummond Wren*, [1945] O.R. 778, 4 D.L.R. 674, the Ontario High Court held that a covenant prohibiting sale of real estate to "Jews or persons of objectionable nationality" was void as against public policy. Courts have traditionally exercised a common-law power to invalidate contracts on grounds of public policy. Indeed, the Supreme Court held, immediately after the decision in *Shelley*, that judicial enforcement of racial

covenants in Washington, D.C. would violate public policy. Hurd v. Hodge, 334 U.S. 24, 34–35 (1948). Why didn't the Court take the same tack in *Shelley* itself? What is the source of law for covenants in Missouri? Might the Supreme Court in *Shelley* have decided that the *failure* of the state courts to apply the public policy exception to racial covenants, when other types of covenants remote from land use regulation are invalidated on these grounds, was the "state action" (or inaction) that violated the federal Constitution?

Use of Trespass Actions to Exclude Persons Based on Race

Shelley v. Kraemer holds that judicial enforcement of a racial covenant to block the sale of a home from a willing seller to a willing African-American buyer is "state action," and hence violates the Equal Protection Clause of the Fourteenth Amendment. What then about judicial enforcement of trespass law at the behest of a property owner to block an African-American from entering property, in circumstances where the owner permits entry by whites? In other words, does *Shelley* require that *any* state enforcement of private property rights is "state action" subject to the constitutional limitations that apply to government, at least when the enforcement action is motivated by racial animus? This issue came to the fore during the civil rights movement of the early 1960s. African-American demonstrators staged numerous sit-ins at segregated lunch counters, restaurants, and public transportation systems, in order to dramatize the injustice of racial segregation at these establishments. White owners, in response, would often call the police to have the demonstrators arrested for trespassing.

In states where segregation was required by law, the Supreme Court held that prosecutions for criminal trespass were state action, without regard to whether the owner's action in calling the police was motivated by a desire to comply with the law or by personal prejudice. Peterson v. Greenville, 373 U.S. 244 (1963). Justice Harlan, concurring in the judgment, thought that state action could be found only where there was individualized proof that the owner was motivated by a desire to comply with the statute. Id. at 252–53. But what if there were no state or local statute requiring segregation, and blacks were excluded from the restaurant or lunch counter because of the personal prejudice of the owner, or because the owner imagined that this was what a majority of his customers wanted?

A number of cases fitting the latter pattern reached the Supreme Court in *Bell v. Maryland*, 378 U.S. 226 (1964). One of the arguments advanced by the demonstrators was that their convictions for trespass were unconstitutional under *Shelley v. Kraemer*. They argued that allowing a restaurant owner who wants to discriminate against blacks to call upon the police and courts to enforce these preferences transforms private discriminatory animus into state action, and is forbidden by the Fourteenth Amendment.

The Court ducked the state action question presented. The lead case involved a sit-in at a restaurant in Baltimore, Maryland. Shortly after the Court granted review, Maryland enacted a statute making racial segregation in public accommodations, including restaurants, unlawful. The majority vacated and remanded for the Maryland courts to determine whether this development would mean that the state courts would "abate" the convictions.

Justice Hugo Black, a former Alabama Senator named to the Court by Franklin Roosevelt, filed a vigorous dissent, joined by Justices Harlan and White. Black struggled without notable success to distinguish *Shelley v. Kraemer*. But he wrote at a time when mounting civil disturbances over race relations had given rise in many quarters to concern about a breakdown in law and order. Black defended trespass law as a necessary ingredient in the maintenance of social order:

> The experience of ages points to the inexorable fact that people are frequently stirred to violence when property which the law recognizes as theirs is forcibly invaded or occupied by others. Trespass laws are born of this experience. They have been, and doubtless still are, important features of any government dedicated, as this country is, to a rule of law. Whatever power it may allow the States or grant to the Congress to regulate the use of private property, the Constitution does not confer upon any group the right to substitute rule by force for rule by law. Force leads to violence, violence to mob conflicts, and these to rule by the strongest groups with control of the most deadly weapons. Our Constitution, noble work of wise men, was designed—all of it—to chart a quite different course: to "establish Justice, insure domestic Tranquility * * * and secure the Blessings of Liberty to ourselves and our Posterity." At times the rule of law seems too slow to some for the settlement of their grievances. But it is the plan our Nation has chosen to preserve both "Liberty" and equality for all. On that plan we have put our trust and staked our future. This constitutional rule of law has served us well. Maryland's trespass law does not depart from it. Nor shall we.

Id. at 346.

Justice Arthur Goldberg, joined by Chief Justice Warren and Justice Douglas, wrote a response to Justice Black's dissent, arguing that the convictions for trespass would have violated the Fourteenth Amendment, provided the state had not amended its law to prohibit segregation in public accommodations. Justice Goldberg did not endorse the theory that the trespass convictions were state action under *Shelley v. Kraemer*. Instead, he advanced an historical argument to the effect that the Framers of the Fourteenth Amendment intended to constitutionalize common-law rights of equal access to inns and common carriers as part of the civil rights enjoyed by all persons. These rights, he further argued, were inconsistent with discrimination by innkeepers or common carriers based on race. Finally, he maintained that these civil rights, as reasonably extrapolated to modern conditions, were broad enough to cover discrimination by restaurants and lunch counters. One virtue Justice Goldberg saw in this alternative theory was that it did not threaten to transform all judicial enforcement of trespass law into state action. His theory only proscribed judicial enforcement of trespass law that would deny African-Americans equal access to public accommodations. Id. at 288–312.

As it turned out, the Court never resolved the question whether enforcement of trespass law motivated by racial prejudice is state action. Shortly after *Bell v. Maryland* was decided, Congress passed the landmark Civil Rights Act of 1964. Title II of that Act prohibited racial discrimination in any public accommodation affected by interstate commerce. 42 U.S.C. § 2000a. The Court quickly held that the Act abated convictions of sit-in protesters under state trespass law. See Jack Greenberg, The Supreme Court, Civil Rights and Civil Dissonance, 77 Yale L.J. 1520, 1532 (1968). The Act effectively ended the era of racial segregation in public accommodations broadly defined, including restaurants, lunch counters, hotels, and common carriers. The fact that the Court had ducked the question whether enforcement of trespass law is state action, without more, meant that owners of property not open to the public can continue to call upon the power of the state to enforce their right to exclude, even when that right is exercised in a discriminatory manner.

A postscript: The named plaintiff in *Bell v. Maryland* was a high school student when he participated in the sit-in at the Baltimore restaurant. He later went on to college and law school. Eventually, he became the Chief Judge of the Maryland Court of Appeals. (Thanks to the late Jack Greenberg, who argued *Bell v. Maryland* in the U.S. Supreme Court, for supplying this information.)

The Fair Housing Act

Congress soon enacted another major piece of civil rights legislation: the Fair Housing Act, as Title VIII of the Civil Rights Act of 1968 is usually known. After declaring "the policy of the United States [to be] to provide within constitutional limitations for fair housing throughout the United States," § 3601, the FHA goes on to prohibit a range of discriminatory behaviors against members of enumerated protected classes in the housing field, with certain exceptions. Over the years the FHA has been amended to add protected classes such as the disabled. Consider the following selected provisions of the FHA.

Fair Housing Act, 42 U.S.C. §§ 3601–3619

§ 3604. Discrimination in the sale or rental of housing and other prohibited practices

As made applicable by section 3603 of this title and except as exempted by sections 3603(b) and 3607 of this title, it shall be unlawful—

(a) To refuse to sell or rent after the making of a bona fide offer, or to refuse to negotiate for the sale or rental of, or otherwise make unavailable or deny, a dwelling to any person because of race, color, religion, sex, familial status, or national origin.

(b) To discriminate against any person in the terms, conditions, or privileges of sale or rental of a dwelling, or in the provision of services or facilities in connection therewith, because of race, color, religion, sex, familial status, or national origin.

(c) To make, print, or publish, or cause to be made, printed, or published any notice, statement, or advertisement, with respect to the sale or rental of a dwelling that indicates any preference, limitation, or discrimination based on race, color, religion, sex, handicap, familial status, or national origin, or an intention to make any such preference, limitation, or discrimination.

(d) To represent to any person because of race, color, religion, sex, handicap, familial status, or national origin that any dwelling is not available for inspection, sale, or rental when such dwelling is in fact so available.

(e) For profit, to induce or attempt to induce any person to sell or rent any dwelling by representations regarding the entry or prospective entry into the neighborhood of a person or persons of a particular race, color, religion, sex, handicap, familial status, or national origin.

(f)(1) To discriminate in the sale or rental, or to otherwise make unavailable or deny, a dwelling to any buyer or renter because of a handicap of—

(A) that buyer or renter,

(B) a person residing in or intending to reside in that dwelling after it is so sold, rented, or made available; or

(C) any person associated with that buyer or renter.

(2) To discriminate against any person in the terms, conditions, or privileges of sale or rental of a dwelling, or in the provision of services or facilities in connection with such dwelling, because of a handicap of—

(A) that person; or

(B) a person residing in or intending to reside in that dwelling after it is so sold, rented, or made available; or

(C) any person associated with that person.

* * *

[handwritten margin note: PROBABLY covers sexual orientation too be Bostock (re: Title VII extension)]

§ 3603(b).   Exemptions

Nothing in section 3604 of this title (other than subsection (c)) shall apply to—

(1)   any single-family house sold or rented by an owner: *Provided*, That such private individual owner does not own more than three such single-family houses at any one time: *Provided further*, That in the case of the sale of any such single-family house by a private individual owner not residing in such house at the time of such sale or who was not the most recent resident of such house prior to such sale, the exemption granted by this subsection shall apply only with respect to one such sale within any twenty-four month period: *Provided further*, That such bona fide private individual owner does not own any interest in, nor is there owned or reserved on his behalf, under any express or voluntary agreement, title to or any right to all or a portion of the proceeds from the sale or rental of, more than three such single-family houses at any one time: *Provided further*, That after December 31, 1969, the sale or rental of any such single-family house shall be excepted from the application of this subchapter only if such house is sold or rented (A) without the use in any manner of the sales or rental facilities or the sales or rental services of any real estate broker, agent, or salesman, or of such facilities or services of any person in the business of selling or renting dwellings, or of any employee or agent of any such broker, agent, salesman, or person and (B) without the publication, posting or mailing, after notice, of any advertisement or written notice in violation of section 3604(c) of this title; but nothing in this proviso shall prohibit the use of attorneys, escrow agents, abstractors, title companies, and other such professional assistance as necessary to perfect or transfer the title, or

(2)   rooms or units in dwellings containing living quarters occupied or intended to be occupied by no more than four families living independently of each other, if the owner actually maintains and occupies one of such living quarters as his residence.

§ 3607.   Religious organization or private club exemption

(a) Nothing in this subchapter shall prohibit a religious organization, association, or society, or any nonprofit institution or organization operated, supervised or controlled by or in conjunction with a religious organization, association, or society, from limiting the sale, rental or occupancy of dwellings which it owns or operates for other than a commercial purpose to persons of the same religion, or from giving preference to such persons, unless membership in such religion is restricted on account of race, color, or national origin. Nor shall anything in this subchapter prohibit a private club not in fact open to the public, which as an incident to its primary purpose or purposes provides lodgings which it owns or operates for other than a commercial purpose, from limiting the rental or occupancy of such lodgings to its members or from giving preference to its members.

(b)(1)   Nothing in this subchapter limits the applicability of any reasonable local, State, or Federal restrictions regarding the maximum number of occupants permitted to occupy a dwelling. Nor does any provision in this subchapter regarding familial status apply with respect to housing for older persons. * * *

NOTES AND QUESTIONS

1.   Suppose an owner denies a single mother with children an apartment and says that he thinks children are too noisy. Does this violate the FHA? What if the discrimination is more subtle? The Supreme Court has recently held that plaintiffs under the FHA need not always show discriminatory intent; namely, discriminatory impact claims are also cognizable under the FHA. Texas Dept. of Housing & Community Affairs v. The Inclusive Communities Project, Inc., 576 U.S. 519 (2015). Justice Kennedy, writing for the majority, noted that disparate impact liability would counteract discriminatory zoning and other systematic exclusion of minorities and was a way of getting at hidden discriminatory intent. To avoid constitutional issues, the opinion goes on to enumerate ways defendants can meet the burden of justifying a policy, such as traffic patterns and historic preservation, and it expresses a preference for race-neutral methods of avoiding disparate impact. Dissents by Justices Alito and Thomas took issue with the majority's invocation of the purpose of the FHA (rather than the text) and developments after the passage of the Act. Should the same standard apply to local governments and to private actors? We return to some of these issues in the materials on exclusionary zoning in Chapter IX.

2.   Section 3603(b)(2) of the FHA is known as the "Mrs. Murphy" exception (presumably the name itself being an example of stereotyping), and is aimed at protecting the associational interests of a landlord living on the premises with three or fewer other apartments. Note that the exception does not apply to advertising. If a live-in owner in a building with four units refuses to rent to a single mother with a young child, is there a violation of the FHA? Suppose the owner places the following advertisement in a newspaper: "For rent: Furnished apartment. No children allowed." Then a single mother with two children applies and is rejected.

3.   What if the landlord places an advertisement saying that the premises would be "rented only to persons speaking Polish, German, or Swedish"? In one case, such an ad was found impermissibly to reflect a preference for certain nationalities even though the landlord contended that it fostered communication. See Holmgren v. Little Village Community Reporter, 342 F. Supp. 512 (N.D. Ill. 1971). Publications are potentially liable for carrying discriminatory advertisements, including those showing only white models in their pictures in such a way as to indicate a racial preference. In Ragin v. New York Times Co., 923 F.2d 995 (2d Cir. 1991), this type of liability under the FHA was held not to violate the First Amendment. What about a recent Korean immigrant landlord who advertises in Korean in a Korean-language newspaper in Los Angeles (but with no stated preference as to type of tenant)? Is there potential liability?

4. At the time the FHA was passed, the predominant vision of antidiscrimination law was an integrationist one, although the statute is framed in terms of individual rights. What if racial quotas are used to maintain integration? In the most famous such situation, Starrett City, a housing development in Brooklyn, used quotas to maintain a strict balance between blacks, Latinos, and whites. In the process black and Latino prospective tenants were turned away from apartments that were later rented to whites. Over a dissent by Judge Newman, the court held that racial ceiling quotas violated the FHA despite the owners' claim that they were being used to maintain integration and prevent "white flight." United States v. Starrett City Associates, 840 F.2d 1096 (2d Cir. 1988).

5. It is important to remember that the Fair Housing Act is not the only antidiscrimination law that might apply to a given discriminatory act in the housing area. Notably, the Civil Rights Act of 1866 provides that "[a]ll citizens of the United States shall have the same right, in every State and Territory, as is enjoyed by white citizens thereof to inherit, purchase, lease, sell, hold, and convey real and personal property." 42 U.S.C. § 1982. This applies to race only, but the Supreme Court has held that the notion of race here is the very broad one prevailing at the time the Act was passed. See Shaare Tefila Congregation v. Cobb, 481 U.S. 615, 617 (1987) (holding that with Civil Rights Act of 1866 Congress "intended to protect from discrimination identifiable classes of persons who are subjected to intentional discrimination solely because of their ancestry or ethnic characteristics" and that Jews are part of protected class) (quotation marks omitted). Based on contemporary Congressional debates, the Court has said that Section 1982 would include groups like Arabs, Chinese, Germans, and Anglo-Saxons. See Saint Francis College v. Al-Khazraji, 481 U.S. 604, 612 (1987). Also, Section 1982 contains no exceptions like those for small landlords and religious organizations in the FHA.

6. The Fair Housing Act does not explicitly ban discrimination based on sexual orientation or transgender status and was long thought not to cover individuals in these categories. But in Bostock v. Clayton County, 140 S. Ct. 1731 (2020), the Supreme Court held that the language in Title VII of the Civil Rights Act prohibiting discrimination in employment "because . . . of sex" logically compels the conclusion that discrimination based on sexual orientation or transgender status is covered by Title VII. Given the parallel language in the FHA, see § 3604 supra, it is likely that a similar conclusion will be reached regarding the coverage of the FHA. For a decision anticipating such a result, see Smith v. Avanti, 249 F. Supp. 3d 1194, 1202–03 (D. Colo. 2017) (interpreting similar language in the Colorado housing discrimination law).

7. Consider the impact of the internet on Section 3604(c)'s ban on discriminatory advertising. If someone posts an ad on a website for the rental of a "whites only" apartment, is the website in violation of the statute? You might think so. But in 1996 Congress enacted the Communications Decency Act, which includes a provision granting immunity from liability to online publishers for the content of user-generated material that appears on their website. 47 U.S.C. § 230(c)(1) (2006). The Seventh Circuit has held that

craigslist.com is immune from liability for discriminatory ads as long as the website does nothing that "induces anyone to post any particular listing or express a preference for discrimination." Chicago Lawyers' Comm. for Civil Rights Under the Law, Inc. v. Craigslist, Inc., 519 F.3d 666, 671 (7th Cir. 2008). Because of the immunity created by the Communications Decency Act (and the difficulty of bringing enforcement actions against large numbers of individuals), a recent article reports that violations of the FHA are rampant on craigslist.com—"roughly several hundred on any given day." Rigel C. Oliveri, Discriminatory Housing Advertisements On-line: Lessons from Craigslist, 43 Ind. L. Rev. 1125, 1127 (2010). In contrast, the Ninth Circuit held that roommate.com could be sued under the FHA, notwithstanding the Communications Decency Act immunity, because the site helped "develop" the content by asking users to create a profile that included characteristics like their sex and sexual orientation (discrimination on this latter basis being prohibited under local law) that was then used to match the user with others with those characteristics. Fair Housing Council of San Fernando Valley v. Roommates.Com, LLC, 521 F.3d 1157, 1166 (9th Cir. 2008) (en banc). This then required the court to consider whether discrimination in the choice of roommates is in fact prohibited by the FHA.

Fair Housing Council of San Fernando Valley v. Roommate.com, LLC

United States Court of Appeals, Ninth Circuit, 2012.
666 F.3d 1216.

■ KOZINSKI, CHIEF JUDGE. There's no place like home. In the privacy of your own home, you can take off your coat, kick off your shoes, let your guard down and be completely yourself. While we usually share our homes only with friends and family, sometimes we need to take in a stranger to help pay the rent. When that happens, can the government limit whom we choose? Specifically, do the anti-discrimination provisions of the Fair Housing Act ("FHA") extend to the selection of roommates?

FACTS

Roommate.com, LLC ("Roommate") operates an internet-based business that helps roommates find each other. Roommate's website receives over 40,000 visits a day and roughly a million new postings for roommates are created each year. When users sign up, they must create a profile by answering a series of questions about their sex, sexual orientation and whether children will be living with them. An open-ended "Additional Comments" section lets users include information not prompted by the questionnaire. Users are asked to list their preferences for roommate characteristics, including sex, sexual orientation and familial status. Based on the profiles and preferences, Roommate matches users and provides them a list of housing-seekers or available rooms meeting their criteria. Users can also search available listings based on roommate characteristics, including sex, sexual orientation and familial status.

The Fair Housing Councils of San Fernando Valley and San Diego ("FHCs") sued Roommate in federal court, alleging that the website's questions requiring disclosure of sex, sexual orientation and familial status, and its sorting, steering and matching of users based on those characteristics, violate the Fair Housing Act ("FHA"), 42 U.S.C. § 3601 et seq. * * *

claim

ANALYSIS

If the FHA extends to shared living situations, it's quite clear that what Roommate does amounts to a violation. The pivotal question is whether the FHA applies to roommates.

I

The FHA prohibits discrimination on the basis of "race, color, religion, sex, familial status, or national origin" in the "sale or rental *of a dwelling*." 42 U.S.C. § 3604(b) (emphasis added). The FHA also makes it illegal to

> make, print, or publish, or cause to be made, printed, or published any notice, statement, or advertisement, with respect to the sale or rental *of a dwelling* that indicates any preference, limitation, or discrimination based on race, color, religion, sex, handicap, familial status, or national origin, or an intention to make any such preference, limitation, or discrimination.

Id. § 3604(c) (emphasis added). The reach of the statute turns on the meaning of "dwelling."

The FHA defines "dwelling" as "any building, structure, or portion thereof which is occupied as, or designed or intended for occupancy as, a residence by one or more families." *Id.* § 3602(b). A dwelling is thus a living unit designed or intended for occupancy by a family, meaning that it ordinarily has the elements generally associated with a family residence: sleeping spaces, bathroom and kitchen facilities, and common areas, such as living rooms, dens and hallways.

dwelling as a living unit

It would be difficult, though not impossible, to divide a single-family house or apartment into separate "dwellings" for purposes of the statute. Is a "dwelling" a bedroom plus a right to access common areas? What if roommates share a bedroom? Could a "dwelling" be a bottom bunk and half an armoire? It makes practical sense to interpret "dwelling" as an independent living unit and stop the FHA at the front door.

There's no indication that Congress intended to interfere with personal relationships *inside* the home. Congress wanted to address the problem of landlords discriminating in the sale and rental of housing, which deprived protected classes of housing opportunities. But a business transaction between a tenant and landlord is quite different from an arrangement between two people sharing the same living space. We seriously doubt Congress meant the FHA to apply to the latter. Consider, for example, the FHA's prohibition against sex discrimination. Could Congress, in the 1960s, really have meant that women must accept men as roommates? Telling women they may not lawfully exclude men from the list of acceptable roommates would be controversial today; it would have been scandalous in the 1960s.

While it's possible to read dwelling to mean sub-parts of a home or an apartment, doing so leads to awkward results. And applying the FHA to the selection of roommates almost certainly leads to results that defy mores prevalent when the statute was passed. Nonetheless, this interpretation is not wholly implausible and we would normally consider adopting it, given that the FHA is a remedial statute that we construe broadly. Therefore, we turn to constitutional concerns, which provide strong countervailing considerations.

II

The Supreme Court has recognized that "the freedom to enter into and carry on certain intimate or private relationships is a fundamental element of liberty protected by the Bill of Rights." Bd. of Dirs. of Rotary Int'l v. Rotary Club of Duarte, 481 U.S. 537, 545 (1987). "[C]hoices to enter into and maintain certain intimate human relationships must be secured against undue intrusion by the State because of the role of such relationships in safeguarding the individual freedom that is central to our constitutional scheme." Roberts v. U.S. Jaycees, 468 U.S. 609, 617–18 (1984). Courts have extended the right of intimate association to marriage, child bearing, child rearing and cohabitation with relatives. Id. While the right protects only "highly personal relationships," the right isn't restricted exclusively to family. The right to association also implies a right *not* to associate.

To determine whether a particular relationship is protected by the right to intimate association we look to "size, purpose, selectivity, and whether others are excluded from critical aspects of the relationship." Bd. of Dirs. of Rotary Int'l, 481 U.S. at 546. The roommate relationship easily qualifies: People generally have very few roommates; they are selective in choosing roommates; and non-roommates are excluded from the critical aspects of the relationship, such as using the living spaces. Aside from immediate family or a romantic partner, it's hard to imagine a relationship more intimate than that between roommates, who share living rooms, dining rooms, kitchens, bathrooms, even bedrooms.

Because of a roommate's unfettered access to the home, choosing a roommate implicates significant privacy and safety considerations. The home is the center of our private lives. Roommates note our comings and goings, observe whom we bring back at night, hear what songs we sing in the shower, see us in various stages of undress and learn intimate details most of us prefer to keep private. Roommates also have access to our physical belongings and to our person. As the Supreme Court recognized, "[w]e are at our most vulnerable when we are asleep because we cannot monitor our own safety or the security of our belongings." Minnesota v. Olson, 495 U.S. 91, 99 (1990). Taking on a roommate means giving him full access to the space where we are most vulnerable.

Equally important, we are fully exposed to a roommate's belongings, activities, habits, proclivities and way of life. This could include matter we find offensive (pornography, religious materials, political propaganda); dangerous (tobacco, drugs, firearms); annoying (jazz, perfume, frequent overnight visitors, furry pets); habits that are incompatible with our lifestyle (early risers, messy cooks, bathroom hogs, clothing borrowers). When you invite others to share your living quarters, you risk becoming a suspect in whatever illegal activities they engage in.

Government regulation of an individual's ability to pick a roommate thus intrudes into the home, which "is entitled to special protection as the center of the private lives of our people." Minnesota v. Carter, 525 U.S. 83, 99 (1998) (Kennedy, J., concurring). "Liberty protects the person from unwarranted government intrusions into a dwelling or other private places. In our tradition the State is not omnipresent in the home." Lawrence v. Texas, 539 U.S. 558, 562 (2003). Holding that the FHA applies inside a home or apartment would allow the government to restrict our ability to choose roommates compatible with our lifestyles. This would be a serious invasion of privacy, autonomy and security.  *normative concerns*

For example, women will often look for female roommates because of modesty or security concerns. As roommates often share bathrooms and common areas, a girl may not want to walk around in her towel in front of a boy. She might also worry about unwanted sexual advances or becoming romantically involved with someone she must count on to pay the rent.

An orthodox Jew may want a roommate with similar beliefs and dietary restrictions, so he won't have to worry about finding honey-baked ham in the refrigerator next to the potato latkes. Non-Jewish roommates may not understand or faithfully follow all of the culinary rules, like the use of different silverware for dairy and meat products, or the prohibition against warming non-kosher food in a kosher microwave. Taking away the ability to choose roommates with similar dietary restrictions and religious convictions will substantially burden the observant Jew's ability to live his life and practice his religion faithfully. The same is true of individuals of other faiths that call for dietary restrictions or rituals inside the home.

The U.S. Department of Housing and Urban Development recently dismissed a complaint against a young woman for advertising, "I am looking for a female christian roommate," on her church bulletin board. In its Determination of No Reasonable Cause, HUD explained that "in light of the facts provided and after assessing the unique context of the advertisement and the roommate relationship involved ... the Department defers to Constitutional considerations in reaching its conclusions." Fair Hous. Ctr. of W. Mich. v. Tricia, No. 05–10–1738–8 (Oct. 28, 2010) (Determination of No Reasonable Cause).

It's a "well-established principle that statutes will be interpreted to avoid constitutional difficulties." Frisby v. Schultz, 487 U.S. 474, 483 (1988). "[W]here an otherwise acceptable construction of a statute would raise serious constitutional problems, the Court will construe the statute to avoid such problems unless such construction is plainly contrary to the intent of Congress." Pub. Citizen v. U.S. Dep't of Justice, 491 U.S. 440, 466 (1989) (internal quotation marks omitted). * * * Reading "dwelling" to mean an independent housing unit is a fair interpretation of the text and consistent with congressional intent. Because the construction of "dwelling" to include shared living units raises substantial constitutional concerns, we adopt the narrower construction that excludes roommate selection from the reach of the FHA. * * *

Because precluding individuals from selecting roommates based on their sex, sexual orientation and familial status raises substantial constitutional concerns, we interpret the FHA * * * as not applying to the sharing of living units. Therefore, we hold that Roommate's prompting, sorting and publishing of information to facilitate roommate selection is not forbidden by the FHA * * *. Accordingly, we vacate the district court's judgment and remand for entry of judgment for defendant. Because the [Fair Housing Councils] are no longer prevailing, we vacate the district court's order for attorney's fees and dismiss the cross-appeals on attorney's fees as moot.

NOTES AND QUESTIONS

1. Laws that prohibit discrimination in private (i.e., non-governmental) housing markets can be said to have three objectives or purposes. First, they are designed to increase housing opportunities for persons in the protected classes. If landlords and sellers are free to discriminate based on race, for example, African-Americans and members of other racial minority groups may find that many of the better-maintained units in more sought-after neighborhoods are foreclosed to them, without regard to their ability to pay. Prohibiting discrimination opens up these additional housing opportunities to members of protected groups. Second, such laws are designed to eliminate the personal harm or indignity suffered by members of protected groups when they are rejected by a landlord or seller on the ground of their status as a member of the group. Third, these laws are designed to eliminate a social message of inferiority or subordination that is communicated to the community at large when landlords and sellers are permitted to discriminate against persons based on their membership in protected groups. Which of the forgoing three purposes is most implicated in the FHA's advertising ban? Is the context of sharing with roommates different?

2. Prior to the enactment of the Fair Housing Act in 1968, regulation of discrimination in housing markets was left largely to state and local

governments. This resulted in considerable variation in antidiscrimination law, enforcement practices, and social norms from one part of the country to another. The 1968 Act represented a major shift in antidiscrimination efforts to the federal level. This meant a movement toward greater uniformity throughout the country in terms of laws, enforcement, and (presumably at least to a degree) social norms. Recent years have seen at least a partial shift back toward more variety in laws and interpretations of laws among states and local governmental units. The opinion in the *Roommate.com* case dealt also with a California statute, treating it in parallel fashion to the FHA (over a dissent on this point). States also differ in the degree to which they have enacted a standard for protecting religious liberty that is stronger than under current federal constitutional case law. See, e.g., Attorney General v. Desilets, 636 N.E. 2d 233 (Mass. 1994).

3.   Technology is blurring the already fuzzy line between the private sphere and the market. Is an Uber car private in a way that a taxicab is not? More to the point for the *Roommate.com* case, how should the FHA apply to Airbnb? A recent empirical study finds "widespread discrimination against guests with distinctly African American names" by Airbnb hosts. Benjamin Edelman, Michael Luca & Dan Svirsky, Racial Discrimination in the Sharing Economy: Evidence from a Field Experiment, 9(2) Am. Econ. J.: Applied Econ. 1, 2 (2017). Should Airbnb be regulated under Title II of the Civil Rights Act, which prohibits discrimination by hotels and motels? See 42 U.S.C. § 2000a(1). Note that Title II contains its own "Mrs. Murphy" exception for an establishment that provides lodging to transient guests in a building "which contains not more than five rooms for rent or hire and which is actually occupied by the proprietor of such establishment as his residence." Id. Or should Airbnb rentals be regarded as temporary selections of roommates, given immunity from liability under Title VIII by the *Roommate.com* decision? How many of Judge Kozinski's reasons for treating space shared by roommates as not being a dwelling apply to a room in a house rented through a service like Airbnb?

4.   Would the case have come out differently if roommate.com invited users to fill out a preference based on race? Religion? (Note that some of Judge Kozinski's examples are based on religious dietary practices.) If racial preferences should lead to a different result than the one here, should questions that have a disparate racial impact, like language or previous involvement with the justice system, be prohibited as well?

C. PROPERTY AND EQUITY

The scope of owner sovereignty is pervasively affected by the law of equity, which we encountered in Chapter I in its role of affording remedies. In some respects, owner sovereignty is enhanced by equity, especially through the development of new remedies like injunctions and some forms of restitution. In other respects, owner sovereignty is limited by equity, based on defenses to the enforcement of legal property rights that apply when owners engage in conduct that is deemed unjust or "inequitable."

Ask yourself as you go through the following materials (and in other chapters and law school courses) what the special province of equity is— or whether there is one. The fusion of law and equity has led some to consider equity to have no special character and to be of historical interest only. Alternatively, equity is regarded as pure ex post fairness-oriented judicial discretion, something to be applauded or decried, depending on one's view of the proper judicial function. The historic suspicion of equity as involving too much discretion has a long pedigree going back at least to the common-law lawyers of the seventeenth century such as Edward Coke and John Selden, the latter of whom complained that because equity was based on the Chancellor's conscience, it was a "roguish thing" and would vary from one Chancellor to another with the length of "the Chancellor's foot." This has animated various attempts to constrain equitable discretion throughout its history. See also Gee v. Pritchard, 36 Eng. Rep. 670, 674 (Ch. 1818); William Holdsworth, Some Makers of English Law 198 (1938). We return to the issue of the structure of equity—its presumptions and shifting burdens—in the cases that follow.

What might be the characteristic function of equity? As reflected in the maxims, equity is traditionally a "law about law," a device to intervene to solve specific problems when the law is grossly out of whack. English and American courts and commentators have often referred to Aristotle's notion of equity, which corrects "law where law is defective because of its generality." Nicomachean Ethics 317 (G.P. Goold ed., H. Rackham trans., Harvard Univ. Press 1982). Legislation can be imperfect simply because it is not detailed enough to cover all possible cases, and perhaps more importantly opportunists are on the lookout for situations in which the law fails to capture its purpose fully, leaving room for exploitation of loopholes. Much of this role for equity came under the heading of "constructive fraud," something that cannot be proven to be fraud but is dangerous enough to warrant a judicial response:

> In this class [of constructive or legal, as opposed to actual, intentional, fraud] may properly be included all cases of unconscientious advantages in bargains, obtained by imposition, circumvention, surprise, and undue influence over persons in general; and in an especial manner, all unconscientious advantages, or bargains obtained over persons, disabled by weakness, infirmity, age, lunacy, idiocy, drunkenness, coverture, or other incapacity, from taking due care of, or protecting their own rights and interests.

Joseph Story, Commentaries on Equity Jurisprudence: as Administered in England and America § 221 (Hillard, Gray & Co. 1836). To deal with constructive fraud, equity must be somewhat open-ended, because as Story notes, "[f]raud is infinite" given the "fertility of man's invention." Id. § 186 (quoting a Letter from Lord Hardwicke to Lord Kaims (June 30, 1759)). There is no doubt that equity is based on morality and judicial discretion, and that it has bad actors in its sight. When it comes to property, equity pays great attention to who knew what when: Violation of rights with notice—in bad faith—is regarded more seriously than inadvertent violations. See generally Henry E. Smith, Equity as Meta-Law, 130 Yale. L.J. 1050 (2021).

We start our exploration of equity with a seemingly straightforward problem. At common law, the only remedy for trespass to land was an action for damages. Not surprisingly, however, landowners who got entangled in disputes over land boundaries or who were threatened with repeated trespasses went to the Court of Chancery, seeking a mandatory order in the form of an injunction against their adversaries. At first the Chancellor refused to grant such relief, stating that equity was not available to enjoin a "mere trespass." But eventually, a variety of exceptions to this rule emerged. American courts of equity adopted these exceptions, which gradually became broader over time. The following decision illustrates the doctrine that eventually emerged.

1. REPEATED TRESPASSES

Baker v. Howard County Hunt

Court of Appeals of Maryland, 1936.
188 A. 223.

■ OFFUTT, JUSTICE. In 1924 Dr. Laurence H. Baker and Rebekah W. Baker, his wife, acquired a small farm of about 65 acres located in the Fifth election district of Howard county on the Clarksville turnpike and the Patuxent river, a few miles from Ellicott City. For a time Dr. Baker used the farm as a "week end escape," but later he and his wife occupied it as a permanent home. From 1926 to 1929 he was the executive secretary of the Johns Hopkins Medical School. In connection with that work he became interested in the effect of well-balanced nutrition on stock, and began a series of experiments on rabbits to determine whether over a long period a well-balanced diet would result in improving the stock. He kept the rabbits used in those experiments on the farm. There he also raised hogs and chickens, kept a garden, and raised buckwheat and other crops. He and his wife lived there intermittently until about 1932, and from that time on he has resided there permanently.

Howard county is, and for many years has been, a foxhunting country, and it is no unusual thing for landowners to keep packs of foxhounds, but it does not appear that prior to 1930, when the Howard County Hunt was formed, there was any organized association of the followers of the sport. That club is an unincorporated association of more than seven persons, which occupies a farm at the junction of the Triadelphia road and the Glenelg road, also in the Fifth election district of Howard county some six or seven miles from the Baker farm. The club itself owns no hounds, but employs as its huntsman Philip Bowen, who furnishes and hunts a pack of hounds for it.

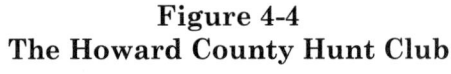

Figure 4-4
The Howard County Hunt Club

Courtesy of Howard County Historical Society.

Weather permitting, the hounds are hunted three days a week throughout the hunting season from early in September to April over a territory which includes the Baker farm. In 1931 Dr. Baker, it was said, noticed foxhounds accompanied by riders in red hunting coats on his farm, and also heard "the horn carried by fox hunters." At that time he paid little attention to them, for he had then no "animals of any great quantity," and it made "very little difference." But by 1933 his stock of rabbits had greatly increased, and on January 14th of that year near sunset, while he was feeding the rabbits, he and his wife heard a great "hue and cry" at the back of the farm, and his wife said, "It looks as though the dogs were at our rabbits again." He "started off to one of the other points," and before he got back to her the dogs were swarming all around the place. Mrs. Baker attempted to drive them off, they "seemed to back right against her," she screamed that she was bitten, he "rushed and hollered at the dogs, and before we knew it they were in the woods." Following that incident, Mr. T. Stockton Matthews, president of the club, wrote Dr. Baker a letter in which in part he said:

> I was shocked to learn of the most unfortunate annoyance and damage caused you and Mrs. Baker last Saturday by hounds of the Howard County Hunt. I immediately got in touch with Mrs. Clark and others whom I thought might know some more of the circumstances, with the concern particularly of the injury to Mrs. Baker and the hope of avoiding the possibility of any serious infection from the wound.

It is distressing to all of us that such an unprecedented and unfortunate accident should have happened. In the conduct of the Hunt and in the control of the hounds, we have endeavored always to merit the good-will and cordial interest of all those in the community who are in sympathy with good sport and with the aims and purposes of the organization to further the best interest of Howard County.

Notwithstanding the assurances in the letter, Dr. Baker complained that no real effort was made to keep the hounds off his property, that they trampled his crops, broke some hot frames, disturbed his rabbits and his chickens, and so annoyed Mrs. Baker that she left the place and that on one occasion in February, 1936, he had been compelled to shoot several of them to get them off his property where they were frightening his chickens. On March 9, 1936, he and Mrs. Baker filed the bill of complaint in this case against the Howard County Hunt and Philip Bowen, in which, after reciting these facts, he prayed: "That the said Howard County Hunt and Philip Bowen, their agents, servants and employees, they and each of them may be enjoined from hunting across your Complainants' property or permitting the pack of Fox Hounds owned by them or in their custody from hunting or overrunning the land of your Complainants or in any manner interfering with your Complainants enjoying the peaceful possession of their property."

In their answer the defendants averred that "members of the Howard County Hunt Club have only ridden through the Complainants' property on one occasion during the past five years; and the said pack of fox hounds have crossed the Complainants' property not more than four times during said period of five years." They further alleged that the injuries to Mrs. Baker "were suffered" more than three years before the suit, and that whatever rights she might have had "by reason" of those injuries "were barred by limitations and laches," and, while they admitted that "their pack of fox hounds" did cross the Baker property in February, 1936, they denied that they terrified the chickens or destroyed "freshly laid eggs," and as to that occasion they further said "that Laurence H. Baker, one of the above named Complainants, did wilfully and without any just cause whatsoever, deliberately shoot into the said pack of fox hounds, as a result of which one of them died shortly thereafter and another is seriously and permanently injured; and these respondents aver that the said pack of fox hounds at the time of the shooting as aforesaid in no way molested the Complainants or their property but were in the act of pursuing a fox."

The case was tried on the issues made by those pleadings, and at the conclusion of the case the court dismissed the bill.

The important questions presented by the appeal are whether equity may afford injunctive relief against a series of trespasses which, while not continuous, are nevertheless part of a single course of conduct which seriously interferes with the right of a landowner to the peaceful enjoyment of his property and, if it may, whether the appellants have made out a case for such relief. * * *

Without further elaboration of the evidence it is sufficient to say that it shows without any substantial doubt that the defendants' hounds have repeatedly overrun the Baker farm, have done substantial injury to their property, that defendants have made no serious effort to prevent the trespasses, and that the resulting damage is of such a character that the Bakers can obtain no adequate relief therefor in an action at law.

Their property is their own; they have an unquestionable right to enjoy it in peace and quiet without molestation or hindrance and to use it for such purpose and pursuits as they will so long as their use of it does not harm others. On the other hand the defendants devote a part of their leisure to the pursuit of an ancient, exhilarating, and healthful sport which is not only lawful, but which for centuries has added to the health and to the pleasure of those who love to combine the freedom and the freshness of the open spaces with the thrills of the chase, the music of the hounds, the rushing air, the creaking of saddle leather, the dash of the thoroughbred, and the sights and sounds of the countryside in the crisp air of the fall and the early winter. They, too, have an unquestionable right to indulge that inclination but only so long as they do not permit it to interfere with the rights of others.

Much interesting learning and some space have been devoted by counsel for the parties to this appeal in tracing the origin, growth, and development of the relative rights of fox hunters and the owners of the land over which they hunt. Indeed, that search has extended from Bacon's Abridgement (1856) to Adkin's Law of Forestry and Law Relating to Trespass and Game (London 1914), but in the end there is no dispute as there can be no doubt that the rights of the fox hunter are subordinate to the rights of the landowner, and that, if the hunter himself goes on the lands of another against the owner's will, he is a trespasser. * * *

In respect to the liability of persons who either send dogs on the land of another in pursuit of game or of a fox which is not ordinarily classified as game, or hunt them in a neighborhood when they have reason to know that the chase will probably take them over land on which they have no right to go, the law is not so certain. It was said by some early commentator seeking a way out of the maze that "dog law is as hard to define as dog latin," Citizens' Rapid-Transit Co. v. Dew, 100 Tenn. 317, 45 S.W. 790 (Tenn. 1898), but since then much of the uncertainty as to the responsibility of the owners of dogs for their trespasses has disappeared. The difficulty of stating with certainty the status of a dog before the law is said to inhere in its nature and is inseparable from its known peculiarities, the difference in breeds, its diverse uses, the diseases to which it is subject, its infirmities of temper, and the impossibility of predicting when or how it will break through the artificial restraints of discipline and revert to its original and instinctive ferocity. 1 R.C.L. 1112.

But as with other branches of the law early doubts have disappeared, and others have succeeded them, in a natural process of evolution in which the law has changed to harmonize with changed conditions.

From [the] cases and the statements of textwriters it may be said that, while the owner of a dog which he has no reason to believe is dangerous or likely to inflict harm upon the persons or property of others is not liable for its trespasses committed of its own volition while roaming abroad, he is liable if he either takes it himself where he knows that, because of its training, nature, and instinct, it will probably damage the property of others, or if with that knowledge he permits it to stray beyond his control.

Applying that rule to the facts of this case the conclusion seems inevitable that, after the defendants in this case had been warned in 1933 that their hounds while hunting in the neighborhood of the appellants' farm were likely to trespass thereon and inflict damage upon his property, they were under a duty to so control their hounds as to prevent further trespass. Nor is there any serious doubt that in violation of that duty they hunted their hounds in the neighborhood of appellants' farm knowing that under the impulse of their instincts and training in following the scent they might and probably would trespass thereon. Nor is there any doubt that, as a result of appellees' indifference to appellants' rights, their negligence in permitting their hounds to be beyond their control in the neighborhood of appellants' farm, appellees' hounds did overrun appellants' farm, disturbed and injured their poultry, rabbits and pigs, and annoyed both Dr. Baker and his wife.

The common law that the owner of a straying reputable dog is not liable for its trespasses because it was not likely to do much damage, 1 R.C.L. 1118, cannot well be applied to a pack or body of fifteen, twenty, or more hounds running as a pack on the same trail, for it is too obvious for comment that such a pack may do substantial damage even to crops.

The notion that a landowner is without remedy for damage or injury suffered as the result of such an invasion of his rights, or that the law affords him no protection against a repetition thereof, lacks substance and reality.

Appellants contend that their remedy is in equity, appellees say that appellants are not entitled to equitable relief, first because they have an adequate remedy at law, and, second, because they do not come into equity with clean hands. The second objection is based upon the fact that Dr. Baker shot several of the appellees' hounds while they were molesting his poultry. It is true that, apart from a statute conferring it, a landowner has no right to kill a dog which is merely trespassing, 3 C. J. 153, but even at common law he may kill it in defense of his person, his property, or of other persons, where circumstances justify a reasonable belief that so extreme and drastic a measure is necessary to protect himself, his family or his property from harm. Id. 153–158. * * * Baker testified that when he shot the hounds they were actually in his chicken yard, "swarming all through the yards," that "some of his" chickens were dead, others were frightened and dashed against the chicken house, and as a "result" he had to kill three of them. That testimony was not contradicted, but, on the other hand, was corroborated by the witness Johnson, who said that when they were shot the hounds were running through the chicken yard. Under such circumstances it cannot be said that Baker's act in shooting the dogs was so tortious as to place him beyond the pale of equitable relief. Assuming that the dogs were not interested in the chickens, but merely ran through or over them in their pursuit of the fox, Dr. Baker could not be expected to calmly analyze their motives in invading his chicken yards, when actually the chickens were flying in all directions before them.

Nor can it be said that appellants had an adequate remedy at law. Assuming that they could have recovered damages in an action at law against the appellees for the repeated invasions of their property, it does not follow that such damages as they might have recovered would have been adequate compensation for the injury done them.

First, because such injuries were in part intangible and incapable of measurement. Dr. Baker was conducting a series of experiments on rabbits. That work was interrupted and its value nullified by the trespassing hounds. The law affords no adequate measure of damages for such an injury. Appellants also attempted to use their farm as a refuge for birds and small animals. The repeated trespasses of the hounds interfered with that plan. The threat of the continued trespasses of the hounds, for those other reasons seriously interfered with their reasonable enjoyment of the property. Even though the hounds were, as appellees contended, "good and kind," that they never acted "mean," and were never known to bite anybody, the Bakers should not be expected to rely with complete confidence upon the mildness of their tempers in view of the fact that they had "scrambled up" on Mrs. Baker, tore her clothes, took the skin off the knuckles of both hands, and bit her in the left hand. For the actual physical injuries there may have been an adequate legal remedy, but for the interference with appellants' enjoyment of their property as affected by the threat of continued recurrences of such incidents the law affords no adequate relief.

Second, where it appears that the defendant manifests an intention of persisting in the perpetration of unlawful acts, the expense, annoyance, and trouble of prosecuting numerous actions at law to recover trifling damages render an action at law an inadequate remedy.

To justify refusal of equitable relief on the ground that the applicant therefor has a remedy at law, the legal remedy must be fully adequate and complete, Miller's Equity, p. 678, for, as stated in Fletcher, Equity Pleading and Practice, p. 246, "The remedy at law which precludes relief in equity must be as practical and efficient to the ends of justice and its prompt administration as the remedy in equity."

Early cases did hold that equity would not relieve against trespasses even though continuing, but it is long since settled that equity will relieve against continuing, Whalen v. Dalashmutt, 59 Md. 250 (1883), or repeated trespasses committed in pursuance of a single plan or purpose, Gilbert v. Arnold, 30 Md. 29 (1869), Georges Creek Coal & Iron Co.'s Lessee v. Detmold, 1 Md. 225 (1851). In Waring v. Stinchcomb, 119 A. 336, 340 (Md. 1922), the court quoted with approval this statement found in Shipley v. Ritter, 7 Md. 408 (1855): "It is the settled law of this state, that although an injunction will not be granted to restrain a trespasser merely because he is a trespasser, yet equity will interfere where the injury is irreparable, or where full and adequate relief cannot be granted at law, or where the trespass goes to the destruction of the property as it had been held and enjoyed, or * * * to prevent multiplicity of suits."

In Spelling on Injunctions, etc. (2d Ed.) § 14 (1893), it is said: "An injunction lies to prevent threatened trespasses, though the damage be susceptible of compensation, where otherwise there is a probability of the wrong being often repeated. * * * "

Pomeroy in his work on Equitable Remedies (section 496) page 4338 et seq., after stating the minority view that equity will not intervene to prevent repeated trespasses by a single defendant, states that: "The jurisdiction of equity to restrain continuous or repeated trespasses rests on the ground of avoiding a repetition of similar actions. * * * When the trespasses complained of are caused by the separate acts of individuals, a multiplicity of suits may be caused to plaintiff either because the defendants are numerous or because a single defendant does the same or similar acts repeatedly. * * * The other view, and the one sustained alike by the weight of authority and by principle, is that if a defendant manifests a purpose to persist in perpetrating his unlawful acts, the vexation, expense and trouble of prosecuting the actions at law make the legal remedy inadequate, and justify a plaintiff in coming into equity for an injunction." * * *

It follows that equity had jurisdiction to grant relief to the appellants; that they made out a case justifying such relief; that the injunction prayed in their bill should have issued; and that there was error in refusing to grant the injunction and in dismissing this bill.

The decree appealed from must therefore be reversed.

NOTES AND QUESTIONS

1.   The issue in *Baker* is not whether the Bakers have the right to exclude foxhunting parties and their dogs from their land—it is assumed they do—but rather whether they can obtain an injunction permanently barring the Howard County Hunt Club from invading their land in the future, or whether they must sue for damages if and when such intrusions occur. Is the mode of reasoning adopted by the court in answering this question similar to that used by the New Jersey Supreme Court in determining whether a public policy exception to the right to exclude applies?

See *State v. Shack* and *Uston v. Resorts International*, Part B.4, supra. Or are there important differences between the inquiry characteristic of equity and the balancing of interests invoked by the New Jersey Supreme Court?

2.   *Baker* illustrates two important maxims of equity: that he who comes into equity must come with clean hands and that equity will intercede only when the remedy at law is inadequate. Are you persuaded by the court's resolution of the clean hands issue? Suppose Dr. Baker did not shoot the dogs in the heat of the moment with chickens flying all about, but instead had lain in wait for them and fired as soon as they crossed the boundary into his farm. Should the court deny an injunction in these circumstances? Does the possibility of seeking punitive damages for intentional trespass, as authorized in *Jacque v. Steenberg Homes* (Chapter I), call into question the conclusion that the Bakers' remedy at law was inadequate? On the facts presented, would the Bakers be entitled to punitive damages had they sued for damages? Do punitive damages and injunctions serve somewhat interchangeable functions here? Which remedy is more likely to protect the Bakers from future harassment by fox hunting parties?

3.   According to the court, the first reason the remedy at law is inadequate is that the injuries sustained to the Bakers' property "were in part intangible and incapable of measurement." Will this be true in every case of threatened trespass to land? When one adds up all the exceptions to the rule that equity will not enjoin a mere trespass—if the injury is irreparable, or if the injury cannot be fully compensated by awards of damages, or if a series of trespasses have been repeated by the same person, or if multiple trespasses are being threatened by different persons—have the exceptions swallowed the rule? Would it be simpler and more accurate to say that equity will always enjoin a threatened trespass, as long as the risk of such an invasion is sufficiently great? (How great? More likely than not to occur?) Or would stating the rule in such an unequivocal fashion be undesirable, because it would deprive equity of its traditional discretion to grant or withhold mandatory relief in light of a wide range of factors that bear on the justice of the situation?

4.   How do you suppose Ronald Coase (Chapter I) would respond to the *Baker* case? Is this just like his example of the rancher and the farmer, or the various nuisance cases he discusses? Should the court have given more consideration to whether the Bakers' farm is more valuable (in terms of the parties' willingness to pay) if used for raising experimental rabbits or as a site for fox hunts? The transaction costs here do not seem to be too great; there are only two parties to the dispute and they have had some communication with each other before the lawsuit is filed. Why do you suppose they did not resolve their differences by contracting for some mutually satisfactory solution?

5.   If the court had denied an injunction to the Bakers, and any damages they received would be inadequate to deter future intrusions by the Hunt Club, would the Bakers have been able to purchase peace and quiet for their rabbits by entering into a contract with the Hunt Club? See Louis Kaplow & Steven Shavell, Property Rules Versus Liability Rules: An Economic Analysis, 109 Harv. L. Rev. 713, 722 (1996): "[E]ven though I

would be willing to pay Jack not to take my car if it were inadequately valued by the courts, there would be no point in paying him to desist—for Jill, or someone else, could come along and take it the next day. Consequently, I would not pay Jack to forbear, and not being paid, he would in fact take my car." Does this consideration provide a justification for awarding either injunctions or punitive damages against repeated trespasses, without regard to whether the trespassing activity is more valuable than the activity of the person trespassed upon?

2.   RESTITUTION

Equity, especially in its role of protecting property rights, is closely associated with restitution and unjust enrichment. The law of restitution joins together older bodies of law, some which traced back to common law and some to equity, but all of which were guided by precepts of equity and the equitable style of decisionmaking. Restitution occupies an important place in the landscape of civil liability. The common law of contracts is broadly concerned with bargained-for benefits and harms. The common law of torts is broadly concerned with non-bargained-for harms. This leaves a category of events unaccounted for: non-bargained-for benefits. Issues involving non-bargained-for benefits are often said to be covered by the law of restitution. There is some ambiguity in the term "restitution," because it can refer to a remedy or to a substantive basis for liability relating to non-bargained-for benefits.

Not just any non-bargained-for benefit will give rise to liability. Often it is said that the characteristic substantive basis for liability in restitution is *unjust enrichment*. Consider a mistaken payment: If A mistakenly pays B a debt she owes to C, can A sue B to undo the transfer and get the payment back? There was no contract between A and B, and B has committed no tort, but B would be unjustly enriched at A's expense if he retained the payment. We have already seen the use of restitution in a case of trespass to land. A later stage of the Great Onyx Cave litigation (Chapter II) dealt with how much of the profits from the cave business the trespasser would have to disgorge. Edwards v. Lee's Administrator, 96 S.W.2d 1028, 1029 (Ky. 1936). This can be regarded as a restitutionary remedy for a wrong. Or, it can be said that it is necessary to reverse the unjust enrichment that would result if the trespasser were to retain the gains from the wrong. Are these views different? Consider the following case.

<h2 style="text-align:center">Olwell v. Nye & Nissen Co.</h2>

Supreme Court of Washington, 1946.
173 P.2d 652.

■ MALLERY, JUSTICE. On May 6, 1940, plaintiff, E. L. Olwell, sold and transferred to the defendant corporation his one-half interest in Puget Sound Egg Packers, a Washington corporation having its principal place of business in Tacoma. By the terms of the agreement, the plaintiff was to retain full ownership in an "Eggsact" egg-washing machine, formerly used by Puget Sound Egg Packers. The defendant promised to make it available for delivery to the plaintiff on or before June 15, 1940. It appears that the plaintiff arranged for and had the machine stored in a space adjacent to the premises occupied by the defendant but not covered by its lease. Due to the scarcity of labor immediately after the outbreak of the war, defendant's treasurer, without the knowledge or consent of the plaintiff, ordered the egg washer taken out of storage. The machine was put into operation by defendant on May 31, 1941, and thereafter for a period of three years was used approximately one day a week in the regular course of the defendant's business. Plaintiff first discovered this use in January or February of 1945 when he happened to be at the plant on business and heard the machine operating. Thereupon plaintiff offered to sell the machine to defendant for $600 or half of its original cost in 1929. A counter offer of $50 was refused and approximately one month later this action was commenced to recover the reasonable value of defendant's use of the machine, and praying for $25 per month from the commencement of the unauthorized use until the time of trial. * * * The court entered judgment for plaintiff in the amount of $10 per week for the period of 156 weeks covered by the statute of limitations, or $1,560, and gave the plaintiff his costs.

Defendant has appealed to this court assigning error upon the judgment, upon the trial of the cause on the theory of unjust enrichment, upon the amount of damages, and upon the court's refusal to make a finding as to the value of the machine and in refusing to consider such value in measuring damages.

The theory of the [plaintiff] was that the tort of conversion could be "waived" and suit brought in quasi-contract, upon a contract implied in law, to recover, as restitution, the profits which inured to [defendant] as a result of its wrongful use of the machine. With this the trial court agreed and in its findings of facts found that the use of the machine "resulted in a benefit to the users, in that said use saves the users approximately $1.43 per hour of use as against the expense which would be incurred were eggs to be washed by hand; that said machine was used by Puget Sound Egg Packers and defendant, on an average of one day per week from May of 1941, until February of 1945 at an average saving of $10.00 per each day of use."

In substance, the argument presented by the assignments of error is that the principle of unjust enrichment, or quasi-contract, is not of universal application, but is imposed only in exceptional cases because of special facts and circumstances and in favor of particular persons; that [plaintiff] had an adequate remedy in an action at law for replevin or claim and delivery; that any damages awarded to the plaintiff should be based upon the use or rental value of the machine and should bear some reasonable relation to its market value. [Defendant] therefore contends that the amount of the judgment is excessive.

It is uniformly held that in cases where the defendant *tort feasor* has benefited by his wrong, the plaintiff may elect to "waive the tort" and bring an action in assumpsit for restitution. Such an action arises out of a duty imposed by law devolving upon the defendant to repay an unjust and unmerited enrichment. Woodward, The Law of Quasi-Contracts, § 272(2), p. 439; Keener on Quasi-Contracts, p. 160. See also Professor Corbin's articles, "'Waiver of Tort and Suit in Assumpsit," 19 Yale Law Journal, p. 221, and "Quasi-Contractual Obligations," 21 Yale Law Journal, p. 533.

It is clear that the saving in labor cost which [defendant] derived from its use of [plaintiff's] machine constituted a benefit.

According to the Restatement of Restitution, § 1(b), p. 12,

> A person confers a benefit upon another if he gives to the other possession of or some other interest in money, land, chattels, or choses in action, performs services beneficial to or at the request of the other, satisfies a debt or a duty of the other, or in any way adds to the other's security or advantage. *He confers a benefit not only where he adds to the property of another, but also where he* saves the other from expense or loss. The word "benefit", therefore denotes any form of advantage.

(Italics ours)

It is also necessary to show that while [defendant] benefited from its use of the egg-washing machine, [plaintiff] thereby incurred a loss. It is argued by [defendant] that since the machine was put into storage by [plaintiff], who had no present use for it, and for a period of almost three years did not know that [defendant] was operating it and since it was not injured by its operation and the [defendant] never adversely claimed any title to it, nor contested [plaintiff's] right of repossession upon the latter's discovery of the wrongful operation, that the [plaintiff] was not damaged because he is as well off as if the machine had not been used by [defendant].

The very essence of the nature of property is the right to its exclusive use. Without it, no beneficial right remains. However plausible, the [defendant] cannot be heard to say that his wrongful invasion of the [plaintiff's] property right to exclusive use is not a loss compensable in law. To hold otherwise would be subversive of all property rights since his use was admittedly wrongful and without claim of right. The theory of unjust enrichment is applicable in such a case.

We agree with [defendant] that [plaintiff] could have elected a "common garden variety of action," as he calls it, for the recovery of damages. It is also true that except where provided for by statute, punitive damages are not allowed, the basic measure for the recovery of damages in this state being compensation. If, then, [plaintiff] had been *limited* to redress *in tort* for damages, as [defendant] contends, the court below would be in error in refusing to make a finding as to the value of the machine. In such case the award of damages must bear a reasonable relation to the value of the property. Hoff v. Lester, 168 P.2d 409 (Wash. 1946).

But [plaintiff] here had an election. He chose rather to waive his right of action *in tort* and to sue *in assumpsit* on the implied contract. Having so elected, he is entitled to the measure of restoration which accompanies the remedy.

> Actions for restitution have for their primary purpose taking from the defendant and restoring to the plaintiff something to which the plaintiff is entitled, or if this is not done, causing the defendant to pay the plaintiff an amount which will restore the plaintiff to the position in which he was before the defendant received the benefit. If the value of what was received and what was lost were always equal, there would be no substantial problem as to the amount of recovery, since actions of restitution are not punitive. In fact, however, the plaintiff frequently had lost more than the defendant has gained, and sometimes the defendant has gained more than the plaintiff has lost.
>
> In such cases the measure of restitution is determined with reference to the tortiousness of the defendant's conduct or the negligence or other fault of one or both of the parties in creating the situation giving rise to the right to restitution. If the defendant was tortious in his acquisition of the benefit he is required to pay for what the other has lost although that is more than the recipient benefited. *If he was consciously tortious in acquiring the benefit, he is also deprived of any profit derived from his subsequent dealing with it.* If he was no more at fault than the claimant, he is not required to pay for losses in excess of benefit received by him and he is permitted to retain gains which result from his dealing with the property.

(Italics ours) Restatement of Restitution, pp. 595, 596.

[Plaintiff] may recover the profit derived by the [defendant] from the use of the machine. [The court then followed Washington caselaw according to which the maximum the plaintiff could receive was the amount prayed for in the complaint, here $25 per month for 36 months, or $900.]

The judgment as modified is affirmed. [Defendant] will recover its costs.

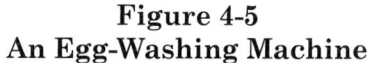

Figure 4-5
An Egg-Washing Machine

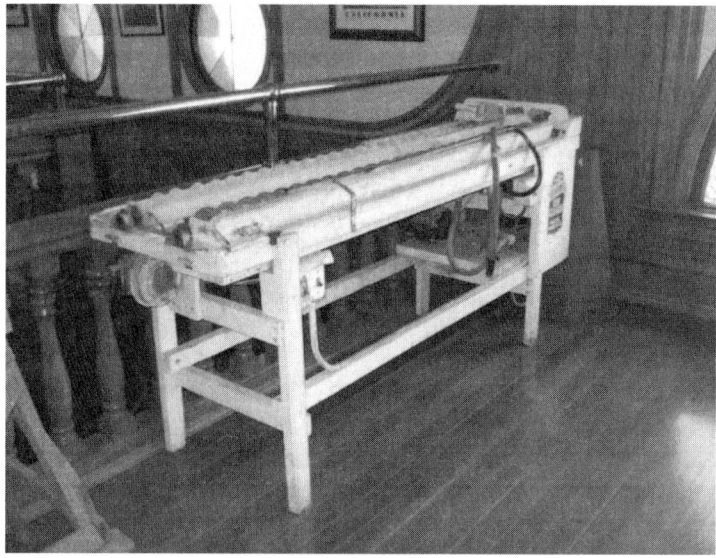

Courtesy of Petaluma Historical Museum.

NOTES AND QUESTIONS

1. The basic elements of an action for restitution are: (1) an "enrichment" of the defendant; (2) at the expense of the plaintiff; (3) under circumstances that are "unjust." See Warren A. Seavey & Austin W. Scott, Restitution, 54 L.Q. Rev. 29, 32 (1938). Note carefully the relational nature of the claim for restitution. There must be a particular defendant who has experienced some kind of windfall, but it must be a windfall "at the expense" of a particular identified plaintiff. Thus, severe misfortune by the plaintiff that does not enrich another particular person will not do. Nor does blind luck on the part of the defendant if this does not come at the expense of someone else. It takes two to make a claim for restitution, and this significantly cabins the scope of the action. In *Olwell*, the violation of the plaintiff's property rights makes for injustice, even if the tort itself is "waived" in order to proceed on the unjust enrichment theory. Still, the general formulation of the principle raises a number of vexing questions— most obviously about what makes an enrichment of the defendant at the expense of the plaintiff "unjust."

2. The court says to deny the plaintiff's right to elect restitution "would be subversive of all property rights since [the defendant's] use was wrongful and without claim of right." Does this make restitution another source of protection for the property owner's right to exclude? The plaintiff Olwell made no attempt to use or rent the machine, and there is no evidence that the defendant's use damaged the machine. Is Olwell's situation analogous to that of Mr. and Mrs. Jacque in *Jacque v. Steenberg Homes*, complaining of an invasion of rights where there has been no injury? There are also overtones here of the distinction between good faith and bad faith

defendants, which looms large in the building encroachment cases considered infra. As the opinion notes, a person who had used the egg-washing machine through a good faith mistake would be liable only for the rental value or the value of the machine, not for the apparently higher amount "saved" by the use of the machine. (Why isn't the rental value the amount "saved"?) Does this give the case a punitive flavor, despite what the court says? Did the defendant's entering the storage area to remove the machine make this worse than if it had misused a machine entrusted to its possession? Should the Washington statute be amended to allow for punitive damages for violations of personal property rights?

3.   The potential robustness of the protection of property through unjust enrichment and restitution can be illustrated with a variant on the scenario in *Olwell*. What if the defendant had simply stolen the machine and sold it to someone else? As we will see in Chapter VIII, in the United States an original owner can get his goods back, even from someone who bought the good from the thief in good faith. But suppose the egg-washing machine is long gone and the plaintiff is able to sue the thief. What should be the measure of damages? Again, the innocent plaintiff has a choice of methods of going after the conscious wrongdoer. The plaintiff could impose a *constructive trust* on the proceeds of the sale. And because the defendant is a wrongdoer, presumptions will work in favor of the plaintiff: If the defendant put the proceeds (say $500) in a bank account that had $800 in it already, and then made a withdrawal of $500, bet the $500 at the racetrack and won an additional $2,000, then the plaintiff would have a claim for the full $2,500. The defendant is said to hold the proceeds as a "constructive" trustee for the plaintiff, reflecting the duty to return "his" money. If, on the other hand, the defendant had lost at the racetrack, the plaintiff could seek $500 from the account. The theory here is that the plaintiff is seeking "his" property and its substitutes over time. This is dramatically illustrated when the wrongdoer is insolvent (as wrongdoers often are in such situations): The plaintiff's other creditors have to share the inadequate assets for pennies on the dollar, but the restitution plaintiff simply asks for his property back in full. State law varies, but the plaintiff's ability to seek the abnormal returns from an asset (the racetrack winnings) is often more limited in the case of a good faith defendant (e.g. the recipient of a mistaken payment), or in cases in which the restitution plaintiff is competing with general creditors. For an argument that the litigation arising out of Bernard Madoff's recent epic Ponzi scheme could have been better handled if more attention had been paid to background principles of restitution, see Andrew Kull, Common-Law Restitution and the Madoff Liquidation, 92 B.U. L. Rev. 939 (2012).

4.   The origins of unjust enrichment and restitution go back to efforts by James Barr Ames and later William Keener at the Harvard Law School to bring together quasi-contract and constructive trust into one body of law dealing with unjust enrichment regardless of the court of origin (constructive trust being in equity and quasi-contract being "at law" although with a heavy equitable flavor). In 1937, two American law professors, Warren A. Seavey and Austin W. Scott, drew on these earlier ideas to bring together a number of situations involving non-bargained-for benefits or unjust enrichment and

gave them a name: the law of restitution. Their efforts were given legitimacy by the American Law Institute, which published their *Restatement (First) of Restitution* in 1937. The first *Restatement* identified equitable considerations as the normative foundation for the law of restitution. See Restatement (First) of Restitution § 42(1). The idea that unjust enrichment is inequitable can in fact be traced back to antiquity. The Roman jurist Pomponius of the second century A.D. is quoted as saying: "For it is by nature fair that nobody should enrich himself at the expense of another." Mark P. Gergen, What Renders Enrichment Unjust?, 79 Tex. L. Rev. 1927, 1927 & n.1 (2001).

In recent years the law of restitution has become a matter of theoretical interest among scholars in England, other commonwealth countries, Israel, and many civil-law countries. Although interest has lagged in the United States, the birthplace of restitution, it appears to be picking up here as well, especially with the recent publication of the *Restatement Third, Restitution and Unjust Enrichment* under the direction of Andrew Kull (the Second Restatement was abandoned in the 1980s before completion). The subject is fascinating, in part because it does not easily fit within the common-law trilogy of contracts-torts-property, and in part because it presents a challenge to explain the doctrine in terms of theoretical frameworks such as economic analysis or corrective justice. See, e.g., Saul Levmore, Explaining Restitution, 71 Va. L. Rev. 65 (1985) (seeking to explain restitution in terms of wealth distribution effects and a desire to encourage participation in markets); Ernest J. Weinrib, Correctively Unjust Enrichment, in Philosophical Foundations of the Law of Unjust Enrichment 31 (Robert Chambers, Charles Mitchell & James Penner, eds. 2009) (justifying unjust enrichment in terms of corrective justice); see generally Ward Farnsworth, Restitution: Civil Liability for Unjust Enrichment (2014); Symposium: A Conference on Restitution and Unjust Enrichment, 92 B.U. L. Rev. 763 (2012).

5.   What is the basis for liability in restitution? Here there is some confusion because "restitution" can refer to a remedy as well as a substantive basis for liability. Many see the substance of restitution in unjust enrichment, but the idea that unjust enrichment can form an independent basis for liability has been criticized on two grounds. One criticism is that the doctrine seems to rest solely on principles of morality, rather than on a more solid foundation in law. See Restatement Third, Restitution and Unjust Enrichment § 1 cmt. b (2011). In an effort to address this criticism, the authors of the new *Restatement* propose to cabin restitution as falling within a set of circumstances they term *unjustified* enrichment—"enrichment that lacks an adequate legal basis" because "it results from a transaction that the law treats as ineffective to work a conclusive alteration in ownership rights." Id. Some examples include a transfer of property to another based on a good faith mistake of fact about the item being transferred or the identity of the transferee; the provision of emergency medical services to a person who is unconscious and cannot give her assent; or profits gained beyond ordinary rental value from intentionally trespassing on someone's land. See also Andrew Kull, Rationalizing Restitution, 83 Cal. L. Rev. 1191 (1995).

Another criticism is that restitution does not embody any unitary principle, but merely reflects a miscellany of circumstances giving rise to the right to restitution. See Peter Birks, Unjust Enrichment and Wrongful Enrichment, 79 Tex. L. Rev. 1767 (2001); Christopher T. Wonnell, Replacing the Unitary Principle of Unjust Enrichment, 45 Emory L.J. 153, 191 (1996). Emily Sherwin, for example, argues that unjust enrichment serves merely a descriptive and organizational function—"a common theme of the various doctrines grouped together as restitution"—rather than being a unified doctrine complementing common-law rules of contract, tort, and property. Emily Sherwin, Restitution and Equity: An Analysis of the Principle of Unjust Enrichment, 79 Tex. L. Rev. 2083, 2108–12 (2001). Hanoch Dagan is less skeptical, and sees unjust enrichment as a loose framework that encompasses benefit-based liabilities that do not fit within the fields of tort, contract, or property law. He advocates using the principle of unjust enrichment as a launching point for a contextual normative analysis that weighs other values such as autonomy, utility, and community. See Hanoch Dagan, The Law and Ethics of Restitution 14–15 (2004). But Dagan also worries that the open-ended nature of this equitable principle may be criticized for allowing judges "unbridled discretion" to fashion remedies.

However these debates are eventually resolved, there is a widespread consensus that restitution is an appropriate remedy in certain circumstances. Be alert throughout these materials for situations in which principles of unjust enrichment or restitution are at work, either in name or in practice.

3. BUILDING ENCROACHMENTS

Minor building encroachments are a recurring issue in property law that presents other dimensions of equity. If an owner knowingly and deliberately builds over the boundary of the parcel on the land of another, a court will have no hesitation in enjoining the structure—ordering it to be torn down. Building such a structure and leaving it there is a trespass, and as we have seen, a repeated or continuing trespass will normally be enjoined. More vexing for courts is the question whether they should enjoin trespasses involving inadvertent and innocent building encroachments. In the typical case, A builds a structure thinking it is on his own land, but it turns out that some portion of the building is actually on B's land. The portion of the building on B's land is a continuing trespass. Does this mean that B is entitled to an injunction that would require—in the extreme case—that the entire building be torn down? Consider the following decisions.

Pile v. Pedrick

Supreme Court of Pennsylvania, 1895.
31 A. 646.

Bill in equity to compel the removal of a wall.

The bill averred that the parties owned adjoining properties, that the defendants had erected a large factory and had in its erection exercised their right to use a portion of the plaintiffs' ground for their party wall; that the defendants were building an additional story to their factory and had inserted some windows in the said wall, and were about to insert others. The bill prayed for an order on defendants to remove the windows already inserted, and an injunction as to the others.

The answer denied that the defendants exercised the right to use a portion of plaintiffs' ground for their party wall, and alleged that the wall erected by them is entirely upon their own ground, as they are advised and verily believe; that they have had the premises surveyed by competent surveyors, and knowing they would want to put windows in their wall they employed competent builders and architects, and instructed them to build the premises wholly upon the land of defendants, and not in any part of said wall to use plaintiffs' premises.

The case was referred to Charles H. Mathews, Esq., as master, who found as a fact that the brick wall of defendants, which is eighteen inches thick, is clear of the property line, from Buttonwood street to Hamilton street, and that it stands its entire length on the defendants' land. That the brick wall rests upon a foundation wall which is two feet thick, and that this foundation wall was clear of the plaintiffs' property from Hamilton street, north, to a point about fifty feet south of Buttonwood street; but, that for the said fifty feet, the said foundation wall encroached on the plaintiffs' property on an average of one and a half inches to one and five eighths inches. * * *

On February 6th, the court entered the following decree: * * *

Order and decree that the defendants by their workmen and pursuant to a permit of the building inspectors have leave to remove so much of their wall mentioned in the master's report, as is upon the ground of the plaintiffs, replacing it by a wall of the existing width to be wholly upon the defendants' ground. But in so doing the said workmen shall not enter upon or dig into the ground of the plaintiffs.

And that the costs of the case shall be paid the respective parties, one half by each.

And it is further ordered that if the permission herein be not exercised within a reasonable time, the plaintiffs have leave to apply to the court for further direction or order.

Errors assigned by plaintiffs were among others, * * * in not directing defendants to remove the windows placed in the wall; * * * [in decreeing] as above, quoting last three paragraphs of decree.

Errors assigned by defendants were among others, * * * in failing to order and decree that the plaintiffs permit the defendants to enter upon the premises of the plaintiffs and remove so much of the wall of the defendants as is upon the ground of the plaintiffs; in decreeing that the costs of the case should be paid by the respective parties, one half by each.

■ WILLIAMS, J. The learned judge of the court below was right in holding that the wall in controversy was not a party wall. It was not intended to be. The defendants were building a factory, and, under the advice of their architect, decided to build within their own lines, in order to avoid the danger of injury to others from vibration which might result from the use of their machinery. They called upon the district surveyor to locate their line, and built within it, as so ascertained. Subsequent surveys by city surveyors have determined that the line was not accurately located at first, but was about 1 1/2 inches over on the plaintiffs'. This leaves the ends of the stones used in the foundation wall projecting into the plaintiffs' lands, below the surface, 1 3/8 inches. This unintentional intrusion into the plaintiffs' close is the narrow foundation on which this bill in equity rests. The wall resting on the stone foundation is conceded to be within the defendants' line. The defendants offered, nevertheless, to make it a party wall, by agreement, and give to plaintiffs the free use of it, as such, on condition that the windows on the third and fourth floors should remain open until the plaintiffs should desire to use the wall. This offer was declined. The trespass was then to be remedied in one of two ways: It could be treated, with the plaintiffs' consent, as a permanent trespass, and compensated for in damages, or the defendants could be compelled to remove the offending ends of the stones to the other side of the line. The plaintiffs insisted upon the latter course, and the court below has, by its decree, ordered that this should be done. The defendants then sought permission to go on the plaintiffs' side of the line and chip off the projecting ends, offering to pay for all inconvenience or injury the plaintiffs or their tenants might suffer by their so doing. This they refused. Nothing remained but to take down and rebuild the entire wall from the defendants' side, and with their building resting on it. This the decree requires, but in view of the course of the litigation the learned judge divided the costs. This is the chief ground of complaint on this appeal. Costs are not of course, in equity. They may be given or withheld as equity and good conscience require. It often happens that a chancellor is constrained to enforce a legal right under circumstances that involve hardship to the defendant, and in such cases it is, as it should be, common to dispose of the costs upon a consideration of all the circumstances, and the position and conduct of the parties. The costs in this case were within the power of the chancellor. They were disposed of in the exercise of his official discretion, and we see no reason to doubt that they were disposed of properly. The decree is affirmed; the costs of this appeal to be paid by the appellants.

Pile v. Pedrick

Supreme Court of Pennsylvania, 1895.
31 A. 647.

■ WILLIAMS, J. This is an appeal from the same decree just considered in *Pile v. Pedrick*, 31 Atl. 646. It is not denied that the foundation wall on which the appellant has built was located under a mistake made by the district surveyor, and does in fact project slightly into the plaintiffs' land. For one inch and three-eighths, the ends of the stones in the wall are said to project beyond the division line. The defendants have no right, at law or in equity, to occupy land that does not belong to them, and we do not see how the court below could have done otherwise than recognize and act upon this principle. They must remove their wall, so that it shall be upon their land. This the court directed should be done within a reasonable time. To avoid further controversy over this subject, we will so far modify the decree as to permit such removal to be made within one year from the date of filing hereof. In all other respects the decree is affirmed; the appellants to pay all costs made by them upon this appeal.

Golden Press, Inc. v. Rylands

Supreme Court of Colorado, 1951.
235 P.2d 592.

■ STONE, JUSTICE. Plaintiffs Rylands and Reid owned a parcel of land fronting on West Colfax Avenue, Jefferson County, upon which were located their residence and garage and some rental cottages. Defendant Golden Press, Inc., constructed a one-story brick and cinder block business building on its property which adjoined plaintiffs' property on the east. According to plaintiffs' survey here unchallenged, the west wall of defendant's building is two inches clear of the lot line at the front or south end, is exactly on the line at the north end, and is approximately 160 feet in length.

In the action here involved, plaintiffs allege that in [constructing] the building defendant caused its foundation and footings to extend from two to three and a half inches upon plaintiffs' land. * * * Plaintiffs prayed for injunction requiring that defendant remove all footings and foundations upon their property * * * Upon issue raised by general denial the case was tried to a jury as to the issue of damages alleged by trespass, the court reserving the determination of the issue of injunction. On the issue of damages the jury returned a verdict in favor of the defendant. The court then found encroachment as alleged and granted mandatory injunction requiring that defendant's projecting footings be removed from plaintiffs' property * * *

Ordinarily, mandatory injunction will issue to compel removal of encroaching structures, but it is not to be issued as a matter of course. On appeal to the court for an equitable remedy, the court must consider the peculiar equities of the case. A study of many decisions discloses no specific and universally-accepted rule as to encroachments. Even in jurisdictions like Massachusetts, in which it has been declared that mandatory injunction for removal of encroachment can only be denied where estoppel or laches is shown, Beaudoin v. Sinodinos, 48 N.E.2d 19 (Mass. 1943), there are numerous cases where injunction has been refused in the absence of those defenses. See cases cited as exceptional in Geragosian v. Un. Realty Co., 193 N.E. 726 (Mass. 1935). Generally in other jurisdictions such harsh rule is not followed. Sometimes a slight and harmless encroachment is held to be within the rule "de minimis," as in Tramonte v. Colarusso, 152 N.E. 90 (Mass. 1926), and McKean v. Alliance Land Co., 253 P. 134 (Cal. 1927), and generally the courts require that he who seeks equity should do equity and come with clean hands. Tramonte v. Colarusso, supra; McKee v. Fields, 210 P.2d 115 (Or. 1949)

Where the encroachment is deliberate and constitutes a willful and intentional taking of another's land, equity may well require its restoration regardless of the expense of removal as compared with damage suffered therefrom; but where the encroachment was in good faith, we think the court should weigh the circumstances so that it shall not act oppressively. 5 Pomeroy' Equity Jurisprudence, page 852, § 508. While the mere balance of convenience is not the proper test, yet relative hardship may properly be considered and the court should not become a party to extortion. Restatement of the Law, Torts, § 941. Where defendant's encroachment is unintentional and slight, plaintiff's use not affected and his damage small and fairly compensable, while the cost of removal is so great as to cause grave hardship or otherwise make its removal unconscionable, mandatory injunction may properly be denied and plaintiff relegated to compensation in damages. Owenson v. Bradley, 197 N.W. 885 (N.D. 1924); Nebel v. Guyer, 221 P.2d 337 (Cal. Dist. Ct. App. 1950); Mary Jane Stevens Co. v. First Nat'l Bldg. Co., 57 P.2d 1099 (Utah 1936).

In the case before us issue was raised in the argument as to whether or not the encroachment was intentional. There was no finding on this issue by the trial court and the decree is not necessarily predicated upon intent. In the absence of proof to the contrary there is a presumption that men act in good faith and that they intend to do what they have the right to do. Prior to the building of the wall, plaintiffs and defendant each employed a surveyor, but neither was called as a witness and the results of their surveys are not disclosed * * *

There is disclosed continued argument by plaintiffs with representatives of defendant during construction of the wall as to trespassing on their lands, but we find no evidence from the record challenging the good faith of defendant's representative in locating the footings.

Again we note that while plaintiffs were continually complaining as to trespass of the workmen on their property, they took no steps for injunction or other legal determination of the disputed line until after both the foundation and upper wall were completed.

Further, we note that the encroachment here complained of is very slight. It is conceded that the wall above the foundation does not project over the property line and that the only encroachment consists of a projection of the footings a distance of two inches at the middle, increasing to three and a half inches at the north end. The top of these footings is about seven feet below the surface of the ground and they go down to nine feet below the surface. They constitute no interference whatever with plaintiffs' present use of the property as a driveway and iris bed, and the only testimony as to future damage was to the effect that if plaintiffs wished to build to their line with a basement, they would have to detour around this slight projection of defendant's footings.

The testimony indicates that the value of plaintiffs' lands is approximately $200 per front foot, so that if defendant had taken the entire strip of three and a half inches both at and below the surface, its value would have been only about $55, and the value of the portions extending from seven to nine feet below the surface and only along the rear eighty feet of wall would appear to be very small. Plaintiffs, at the trial, refused defendant permission to enter upon their property for the purpose of chipping off the encroaching footings with a jack hammer, and demanded that they be removed from defendant's side of the land, if necessary by tearing down the wall. The expense and hardship of such removal would be so great in comparison with any advantage of plaintiffs to be gained thereby that we think it would be unconscionable to require it, and that under all the circumstances disclosed mandatory injunction should have been denied by the trial court, with permission for plaintiffs to proceed, if desired, in damages.

no injunction for removal

Accordingly, the injunctive decree is reversed and the case remanded for further proceedings, if desired, consistent herewith.

NOTES AND QUESTIONS

1.   The encroachments in *Pile* and *Golden Press* were extremely minimal—just a matter of a few inches underneath the soil in both cases. Yet the courts in both cases accept that these intrusions are trespasses, and that some type of rectification is needed to vindicate the property rights of the encroached-upon landowner. This in itself is a testament to the hold of the *ad coelum* rule (discussed in connection with *Hinman* in Chapter I and *Edwards v. Sims* in Chapter II) on the judicial mind. But does rigid enforcement of property boundaries make sense in this context? Another approach, as noted in *Golden Press*, would declare that very small intrusions are "de minimis" and hence would entitle the plaintiff to only nominal

damages. Would you favor this approach over the approaches of *Pile* and *Golden Press*? If so, what would be the point at which "de minimis" is passed, and the intrusion becomes subject to liability?

2.   As the discussion in *Golden Press* suggests, courts in a number of jurisdictions have rejected the absolutist approach of *Pile*. Indeed, counsel for the defendant in *Pile* unsuccessfully argued undue hardship as a reason to withhold the injunction. Exactly how many jurisdictions would award injunctive relief against minor building encroachments is unclear, since some jurisdictions that purport to follow the automatic injunction rule nevertheless have recognized a number of exceptions to the rule (Massachusetts fits this description, see Peters v. Archambault, 278 N.E.2d 729 (Mass. 1972)). A safe generalization would be that, if faced with the facts of *Pile* or *Golden Press*—an unintentional encroachment, only slight damage to the plaintiff's interest, and grave hardship to the defendant if removal of the encroachment were required—most American courts today would probably deny injunctive relief and award only damages.

3.   The doctrinal justification for awarding an injunction is relatively straightforward, although it is interesting that *Pile* sees no need to spell it out. The building encroachment is a trespass (the only intent required is to do the act, even if it as a mistake). And failing to remove the building is a continuing trespass. Restatement (Second) of Torts § 158 ("One is subject to liability to another for trespass . . . if he intentionally . . . (c) fails to remove from the land a thing which he is under a duty to remove"); id. § 161(1) ("A trespass may be committed by the continued presence on the land of a structure . . . which the actor tortiously placed there whether or not the actor has the ability to remove it"). Trespass, as we learned from *Jacque v. Steenberg Homes*, is forbidden without regard to the reasonableness of the intrusion or whether it causes any actual harm.

4.   The doctrinal justification for the outcome in *Golden Press* comes about from viewing the problem from a different angle within the traditions of equity. One of the maxims of equity is that an injunction will issue only if a weighing of interests between the parties—generally called the "balance of the equities"—favors giving the victorious plaintiff the "extraordinary" relief of an injunction rather than damages. What the court looks for is not a deviation from equality of hardship, but rather a court will ask whether a plaintiff who is otherwise eligible to get an injunction should not get it in light of the gross hardship to the defendant in comparison with the benefit to the plaintiff. If the court balances the equities and finds a disproportionate hardship on the defendant, it will deny the injunction. Otherwise, the court will look with favor on the issuance of an injunction. If the injunction is denied, the plaintiff will be limited to the relief it would be entitled to "at law," i.e., damages. This is the doctrinal path followed by *Golden Press* in deciding that the victorious plaintiff (the encroached-upon party) will get only damages, rather than an injunction requiring removal of the encroaching footings.

5.   Note that the court in *Pile* does not seem to disagree with the court in *Golden Press* about the balance of the equities. One contested issue in *Pile* is whether the trial court had authority to divide court costs between the

parties rather than making the losing defendant pay all the costs. In exercising this limited discretion in this fashion, the court seems to signal its displeasure with the plaintiffs' extreme and unreasonable behavior in refusing a license to the defendant to enter onto the plaintiff's land to remove the footings. Why, then, didn't the court use its equitable discretion in light of the relative hardships? It is worth noting that Pennsylvania case law at the time veered between absolutist statements about trespass and more lenient approaches. Henry L. McClintock, Discretion to Deny Injunction against Trespass and Nuisance, 12 Minn. L. Rev. 565, 575–76 (1928); Comment, Injunction—Nuisance—Balance of Convenience, 37 Yale L.J. 96, 97 n.4 (1927). It is also worth asking what the nature of the hardship was. If the encroachers could have avoided the problem by bricking up the windows in the wall they had built, what exactly was the hardship they faced?

6.   It bears emphasis that courts have employed the balancing-of-the-equities approach to deny injunctions against building encroachments only when the original encroachment is innocent—that is, when the encroaching party does not know that the building is encroaching on someone else's property at the time the building is constructed. Courts frequently refer to a person who violates another's property rights without knowing that he or she is doing so as a "good faith" violator. In contrast, someone who knowingly violates another's property rights is called a "bad faith" violator. (Be aware that "good faith" and "bad faith" may have slightly different meanings in other legal contexts, but in property law this is nearly always the meaning of these terms.) When an encroacher acts in bad faith at the time the building is constructed, then the courts universally agree that injunctive relief against the encroachment is appropriate. See, e.g., Warsaw v. Chicago Metallic Ceilings, Chapter IX (upholding injunction requiring destruction of a warehouse built with knowledge of a neighbor's claim that it would block an easement); Mark L. Share, Principles of Equity Will Not Protect Encroachers Who Have Knowingly Invaded Their Neighbors' Property, L.A. Law., Jan. 27, 2005, at 40. Does this exception to *Golden Press* (or perhaps limitation on the *Golden Press* exception to *Pile*) follow from the balancing-of-the-equities maxim, or does it reflect another maxim like the clean hands requirement? If the former, why not treat bad faith at the time the building was constructed as just another factor to weigh in the balance of interests?

7.   Should courts that follow the approach of *Golden Press* focus only on the encroacher's actual knowledge at the time the encroaching structure was built, or should they also ask whether the encroacher acted negligently in failing to avoid the encroachment? California has adopted a Good Faith Improver Act that requires consideration not only of the good faith of the encroacher, but also whether the encroacher was negligent, i.e., failed to procure a survey or ignored obvious warning signs. See Raab v. Casper, 124 Cal.Rptr. 590 (Cal. Ct. App. 1975) (discussing California Good Faith Improver Act as applied to encroaching cabin on adjacent foothill lot). Does this create better incentives for parties to take cost-justified precautions to avoid creating a building encroachment problem? If liability for encroachments is great enough, it can call forth individually worthwhile but socially wasteful efforts at avoiding encroachments through elaborate

surveys. See Stewart W. Sterk, Property Rules, Liability Rules, and Uncertainty about Property Rights, 106 Mich. L. Rev. 1285 (2008).

8.   A dispute analogous to the issue in *Pile* and *Golden Press* reached the U.S. Supreme Court in the context of intellectual property rights (specifically patents). The question was whether the owner of a patent is automatically entitled to a permanent injunction against a defendant who has infringed the patent, or whether courts may sometimes deny an injunction and award only damages. In *eBay Inc. v. MercExchange, L.L.C.*, 547 U.S. 388 (2006), the Court embraced the *Golden Press* position on this issue. Injunctive relief may be granted, the Court said, only if the patent holder can show that such relief is required by "traditional equitable principles." Apparently drawing on the standard for preliminary relief, the Court set forth a four-part test the patent holder must satisfy: "(1) that it has suffered an irreparable injury; (2) that remedies available at law, such as monetary damages, are inadequate to compensate for that injury; (3) that, considering the balance of hardships between the plaintiff and defendant, a remedy in equity is warranted; and (4) that the public interest would not be disserved by a permanent injunction." Id. at 391. The Court did not apply this test, but remanded to the lower courts to determine whether an injunction was appropriate under the circumstances. A concurring opinion by Chief Justice Roberts, joined by two other Justices, emphasized that application of the traditional equitable test will usually result in issuing an injunction, "given the difficulty of protecting a right to *exclude* through monetary remedies that allow an infringer to *use* an invention against the patentee's wishes." Id. at 395. Another concurring opinion by Justice Kennedy, joined by three other Justices, warned that courts should be wary of issuing injunctions in favor of firms that buy up patents to be "employed as a bargaining tool to charge exorbitant fees to companies that seek to buy licenses to practice the patent." Id. at 396. The four-factor test is spreading to other areas of law, see Monsanto Co. v. Geertson Seed Farms, 561 U.S. 139 (2010), and to some state courts. For documentation and an argument that this is undesirable as a matter of history and policy, see Mark Gergen, John M. Golden, & Henry E. Smith, The Supreme Court's Accidental Revolution? The Test for Permanent Injunctions, 112 Colum. L. Rev. 203 (2012). As we have already seen, the traditional approach to injunctions puts great weight on the good or bad faith of the rights violator, unlike the four-factor test in *eBay*.

The Ex Ante/Ex Post Problem

Another important consideration in deciding on a remedy is whether we analyze the situation as it exists *before* the particular conflict over resources arises, or *after* that conflict arises. Economists often speak of "ex ante" analysis and "ex post" analysis (this locution has been picked up by courts in recent years). Ex ante analysis simply refers to an analysis of the situation before some critical event like an accident, or a contract, or a commitment to a particular use of resources, takes place. Ex post analysis refers to an analysis of the situation after such a critical event occurs. In the context of building encroachments, an ex ante analysis would consider the circumstances of two adjacent landowners, one contemplating a building to be placed near the boundary line between their properties, before the building is constructed. Ex post analysis would consider the circumstances of the two landowners after the building is constructed. The analysis of both efficiency and justice may differ dramatically, depending on whether we consider a particular situation from an ex ante or an ex post perspective.

When we consider the question from an ex ante perspective, the solution to building encroachments appears to be easy. The neighboring parties can commission one or more surveys to determine the exact location of the boundary. If it turns out that the building, as designed, will cross the boundary (even if only by a few inches), the building can be re-designed to eliminate the encroachment. Or, perhaps the party who wants to build can strike a deal with the neighbor to buy a bit of the neighbor's land to permit the original design to be maintained without an encroachment. The tough rule in *Pile v. Pedrick* can be seen as maintaining an incentive for anyone contemplating a building close to the boundary line to be extra careful to avoid an encroachment and eliminate any problems before construction starts.

Viewed from an ex post perspective, the problem is much more vexing. Now the cost of maintaining a strong incentive to avoid encroachments comes at a very high price. The two neighbors are trapped in a bilateral monopoly situation (Chapter I). The encroached-upon neighbor can demand that the building be torn down, producing a huge deadweight loss for the encroacher. The encroacher has no one else to turn to who can sell him or her more land to eliminate the encroachment. Bargaining over the sale of more land is likely to break down, unless the encroacher agrees to pay a price that appears to be "extortionate."

Given the bilateral monopoly problem that exists in the ex post situation, and the very real possibility that bargaining will break down over a modification of rights, you can see how courts might be drawn to a solution that limits the encroached-upon party to damages (at least in cases of mistake). If the court shifts from *Pile v. Pedrick* to *Golden Press v. Rylands* what will be the measure of damages? Will the joint wealth of the parties be greater under this solution than it would be under an injunction, assuming no post-injunction modification of rights? Will the outcome be more just than the one that will likely result if the court sticks with *Pile*?

Courts are naturally drawn to ex post analysis because this is how controversies are presented to them. People typically go to court after an accident has happened, a contract has been breached, or a building encroachment has occurred. The court takes the situation as it is presented, and looks for the solution that makes the most sense (is both efficient and fair) given what has transpired and the circumstances in which the parties find themselves. But this does not necessarily mean that the ex post perspective is the correct perspective for thinking about such problems. Ex post analysis tends to focus on fairness and distributional concerns, whereas ex ante analysis is more likely to consider incentives for future conduct. Injunctions might be inefficient from an ex post perspective, and yet still be the more efficient rule in the long run—that is, from an ex ante perspective that stresses incentives for future behavior. We return to this problem in Chapter IX in considering the proper remedy for nuisances like continuing pollution from a plant that has already been built.

NOTE ON MISTAKEN IMPROVERS

Pile v. Pedrick and *Golden Press v. Rylands* involve building encroachments that harm the encroached-upon party—or at least provide no benefit to the encroached-upon party. But what if the encroacher makes a whopping big mistake, and constructs a new building entirely on land belonging to someone else? (This happens from time to time. Henry E. Smith, Law and the Big Oops (May 13, 2015), https://blogs.harvard.edu/nplblog/2015/05/13/law-and-the-big-oops/.) Now the mistake cannot clearly be characterized as causing harm; if anything, it probably confers a benefit on the landowner. Under ordinary rules of property law, the building would be a fixture attached to the land, and hence ownership of the building would automatically pass to the owner of the land by accession. (For more on fixtures, see Chapter II.) Does the mistaken improver nevertheless have any right to recover for the benefit conferred on the true owner? Does the mistaken improver have a privilege to enter the land to remove the building? What if the landowner does not like the building, and was planning to do something else with the land?

These issues presented themselves very colorfully in the case of *Producers Lumber & Supply Co. v. Olney Building Co.*, 333 S.W.2d 619 (Tex. Civ. App. 1960). In that case, H.P. Orts, head of a building company, had mistakenly built a house on land that his company, Olney Building, had already sold to another developer, Producers Lumber, and that was to be used for a house for its manager Montgomery and his wife. When the mistake was discovered—during a title search for financing (see Chapter VIII)—Orts notified Montgomery and negotiations ensued. Montgomery claimed that he didn't like the house and would up making a lowball offer. What happened next was the subject of vivid testimony by Orts:

> Q. Now, you did, on or about April 22, 1958, remove those improvements, did you not? A. That is correct, sir.

> Q. Did you notify Mr. Montgomery or anyone from Producers Lumber and Supply Company that you were going to remove them? A. No, sir.

> Q. How many men do you remember employing on the job of removal? A. Does this have to be exact, or will an approximation do?

> Q. Well, if you know, tell me exactly; otherwise, it has to be approximately. A. I will say—I am going to say ten.

Q. Approximately ten? A. Yes.

Q. Isn't it a fact that you started the removal of these improvements about 2:00 o'clock in the afternoon? A. That is correct, sir.

Q. Isn't it a fact that by 6:00 o'clock in the afternoon, by the use of a bulldozer and a dozen or more men, you had completely removed everything but the slab? A. That's right.

Q. Isn't it a fact that you made no effort to salvage anything on the removal? A. No, sir.

Q. You say that is not true? A. No, sir.

Q. What did you salvage? A. All of the interior partitions, the exterior partitions, the siding, not the siding, but the exterior sheeting, the roof sheeting, electrical and plumbing.

Q. Well, now, actually what happened was that several of your men went out and tore the roof off, isn't that right? A. That's right.

Q. And then you, for lack of a better word I will say "unjointed", the corners and then you hooked on with a dozer and dragged the partitions and framing and roof trusses across the street, is that right? A. Partially, that is correct.

Q. You say that is not true? A. Not all of it.

Q. What is not true? A. The side walls were taken down piece by piece.

Q. The side walls were taken down piece by piece? A. Yes, sir. * * *

Q. You said that you salvaged the electrical? A. Yes. * * *

Q. Now, who did you employ to remove the slab? A. My superintendent.

Q. How did Crea Brothers get on the job? A. I hired their equipment.

Q. What equipment did you hire from Crea Brothers? A. A D-12 tractor, and I believe that slab was so good they couldn't get it up with a D-12 and finally they had to get a crane with a drop hammer, and I told my superintendent if Crea Brothers didn't have the—well, frankly, I don't know where I got the crane with the drop hammer.

Q. Isn't it a fact that they also used a couple of air hammers? A. Oh, yes.

Q. Air hammers, and they had to use torches to cut the steel? A. That is correct. * * *

Q. So the night you tore that house down, $2,768.00 went down the drain; is that right? A. Yes, sir. My money.

Q. Yes, sir. $2,768.00 went up just like that (slapping hands together)? A. That is right.

Q.   As if you had set a match to it, didn't it? A. That is right.

333 S.W.2d at 622–23. The trial court employed special verdicts, and the jury found (i) that Orts built the house in good faith, (ii) that it would cost $600 to restore the land to its pre-building condition, (iii) that Orts acted maliciously in removing the building, and (iv) that Producers should receive $300 in exemplary (punitive) damages. The parties had stipulated that Lot 8 had a value of $5000 and that the house increased the value of the lot by $5000. Verdicts in hand, the trial judge awarded Producers $600 restoration cost. On appeal, the majority held that maliciousness in tearing down the house negated any good faith and that Orts had "unclean hands," making him ineligible to claim restitution for the benefit he had (inadvertently) conferred upon Montgomery. The appeals court awarded not just the $600 restoration cost but also $300 in punitive damages and $5000 for the destroyed house. A vigorous dissent endorsed the traditional idea of self-help to remove structures and stressed that Montgomery was obnoxiously taking advantage of the situation to obtain a windfall. In deciding which of these very different views is more persuasive, consider also that if Orts had not destroyed the building, the remedial scheme would have been rather complex, affording Montgomery a choice: (i) he could ask the court to order the build removed, (ii) he could pay for the building (restitution to prevent his unjust enrichment) or allow the land to be subject to a lien in this amount, see Restatement Third, Restitution and Unjust Enrichment § 10 (2011), (iii) he could require Orts to pay the price for the land in its unimproved state, or (iv) he could ask for partition, with the court selling the land and splitting the proceeds according to the parties' respective interests. (We take up partition in Chapter V.) The basic idea would be for the court to prevent unjust enrichment but not to unduly disadvantage Montgomery, who did not cause the problem in the first place. Of course none of this could happen, because Orts acted to destroy the house. Is that the problem? Or might Montgomery be said to have "abused" his rights—a controversial kind of claim that comes to the fore in the next case.

4.   Abuse of Rights

Sometimes equity will intervene when extreme results reflect what looks to the court like unsavory behavior. In some cases, this will mean not enforcing a transaction if it works a disproportionate hardship on a vulnerable party (see the materials on mortgages in Chapter VII and land transactions in Chapter VIII). Occasionally a court will use its power to deny an injunction where a party might be said to be invoking a right inconsistently with its purpose.

Edwards v. Allouez Mining Co.

Supreme Court of Michigan, 1878.
38 Mich. 46, 31 Am. Rep. 301.

■ COOLEY, J. This is an injunction bill, and the facts are very simple. Defendant at a cost of some sixty thousand dollars erected a stamp mill on the banks of Hill creek in the year 1874, and has since been operating it for copper mining purposes. As a result of its operations large quantities of sand are carried down by the waters of the stream and deposited on the bottom lands below. The evidence leads to the belief that it would be impossible to carry on the mining operations of the defendant with profit unless this is permitted. The year following the erection of defendant's mill, complainant purchased a piece of land through which the creek runs a short distance below the mill, and upon which the mill as operated was depositing sand. The land was not purchased for use or occupation, but as a matter of speculation, and apparently under an expectation of being able to force defendant to buy it at a large advance on the purchase price. It was offered to defendant soon after the purchase, and though no price was named, the valuation which has been put upon it by complainant and his witnesses is from three to five times what it cost him, and this perhaps gives some indication what his expectations were. The real value of the land except as a convenience in the business of defendant would seem to have been small. When defendant declined to purchase, this bill was filed. The prayer is that defendant be restrained from running or depositing its stamp sand on complainant's land, and from polluting the waters of the stream by its operations. This is a short statement of so much of the case as is material to what follows. The circuit judge refused the injunction prayed for, but ordered a reference to a jury for an assessment of damages.

There is no doubt that the operations of defendant, whether they inflict any serious injury on complainant or not, amount in effect to an appropriation of that portion of his property upon which sand is being deposited. It follows and is beyond question that complainant sustains a legal injury for which he is entitled to suitable redress. The only question on this record is, whether he is entitled to the special redress he seeks, namely, an injunction.

An injunction is not a process to be lightly ordered in any case. Where the effect will be to present to the owners of a valuable mill the alternative either to purchase complainant's lands at his own price or to sacrifice their property, any court having the power to order it ought very carefully to scrutinize the case and make sure that equity requires it. In theory its purpose is to prevent irreparable mischief; it stays an evil the consequences of which could not adequately be compensated if it were suffered to go on. The writ "is not *ex debito justitiœ,* for any injury threatened or done to the estate or rights of a person, but the granting of it must always rest in sound discretion, governed by the nature of the case." Enfield Toll Bridge Co. v. Connecticut River Co., 7 Conn. 28, 50 (1828). As is said in another case, "Injunction is not of right but of grace; and to move an upright chancellor to interpose this strongest arm of the law, he must have not a sham case, but a well grounded complaint, the *bona fides* of which is unquestioned, or capable of vindication if questioned." Kenton v. Railway Co., 54 Pa. 401, 454 (1867). "There is no power," says Mr. Justice Baldwin, "the exercise of which is more delicate, which requires greater caution, deliberation and sound discretion, or is more dangerous in a doubtful case than the issuing of an injunction. It is the strong arm of equity, that never ought to be extended unless to cases of great injury, where courts of law cannot afford an adequate or commensurate remedy in damages." Bonaparte v. Camden & A.R. Co., 3 F. Cas. 821, 827 (C.C.D.N.J. 1830). All the cases referred to show that the court looks beyond the actual injury to contemplate the consequences, and however palpable may be the wrong, it will still balance the inconveniences of awarding or denying the writ, and adjudge as these may incline the judicial mind. Even in the case of a palpable violation of a public right to the annoyance of an individual, he must show the equity which requires this summary interference as the only adequate means of obtaining justice.

What is the irreparable injury which is done or threatened in this case? We can see very plainly what it is in the case of many nuisances, and the equity of this particular remedy is then very manifest. If one man creates intolerable smells near his neighbor's homestead, or by excavations threatens to undermine his house, or cuts off his access to the street by buildings or ditches, or in any other way destroys the comfortable, peaceful and quiet occupation of his homestead, he injures him irrevocably. No man holds the comfort of his home for sale, and no man is willing to accept in lieu of it an award of damages. If equity could not enjoin such a nuisance the writ ought to be dispensed with altogether, and the doctrine of irreparable mischief might be dismissed as meaningless. A nuisance which affects one in his business is less in degree, but it may still be irreparable, because it may break up the business, destroy its good will and inflict damages which are incapable of measurement because the elements of reasonable certainty are not to be obtained for their computation. Even in the case of unoccupied land a nuisance may threaten irreparable injury, where it is devoted in its purchase to some special use, or where the person causing the nuisance is irresponsible, and in some other cases which need not here be specially mentioned.

The land injured in this case was bought by the complainant with a preconceived purpose to force a sale of it upon the defendant. He did not want it for a homestead or for business property, but for the money he could compel the defendant to pay for it. It may be said that no one is concerned with the motives of another in making a lawful purchase, or in doing any other lawful act; and this is true as a rule, but it is not true universally. Wherever one keeps within the limits of lawful action, he is certainly entitled to the protection of the law, whether his motives are commendable or not; but if he demands more than the strict rules of law can give him, his motives may become important. In general it must be assumed that the rules of the common law will give adequate redress for any injury; and when the litigant avers that under the circumstances of his particular case they do not, and that therefore the gracious ear of equity should incline to hear his complaint, it may not be amiss to inquire how he came to be placed in such circumstances. If a man invites an injury, he may still have his redress in the courts of law, but his prayer for the special interposition of equity on the ground that what he invited and expected was about irreparably to injure, would not be likely to trouble the judicial conscience very much if it were wholly ignored. * * * We cannot say in this case that complainant had no right to buy, but we can say, as we do, that when he comes demanding strict legal rights, he shall have those, but no more. He is entitled to his rights under the rules of law, but he is entitled to nothing of grace.

The land having been bought to make money from by sale, a legal award of damages for an injury to it, is in furtherance of the purpose of the purchase, and therefore a suitable and a just redress. Defendant is not alleged to be irresponsible, and a jury it is supposed will award all that is reasonable. If complainant wants more than is reasonable, he has a right to obtain it under the rules of law, but he cannot demand the aid of equity in a speculation. If in speculative language he has a corner in real estate, there is no greater reason why he should have the assistance of an injunction to aid his schemes than there would be if on the produce exchange he had effected a corner in grain. Without the writ in either case he may be the sufferer, but he suffers nothing for which damages cannot compensate him. The elements of irreparable injury are entirely wanting to his case.

Our conclusion is that the circuit court gave the complainant all he was entitled to when the case was sent to a jury. The decree must therefore be affirmed with costs.

■ CAMPBELL, C.J. It appears without doubt in this case that defendants, without color or claim of right, are keeping up a continuous series of invasions upon complainant's freehold by using a running stream as a means of transporting sand upon his bottom land in quantities sufficient to bury it. The same course of conduct defiles and silts up the stream, rendering it useless to him for any purpose of business or convenience. It is equivalent in mischief to taking away or destroying his property in the land and his rights in the water.

I cannot concur in the doctrine that any one's rights of this kind are subject to judicial discretion. The rights to equitable relief, where that is the only adequate remedy, are as absolute as to legal relief. The one remedy is no more sacred than the other, and no more capable of lawful denial. If the defendants were to take possession of the land in question by putting a tenant upon it, no power would exist any where to deny complainant his possessory remedy. Where the same sort of wrong is done by indirect assumption of possession so that all the advantages of actual possession are enjoyed by the wrongdoer without going in person upon the soil, there is no reason for denying the only remedy which can secure to complainant the future enjoyment of his own estate, which would not as justly authorize the refusal of a possessory remedy in the other case. And no remedy at law is adequate for such a grievance as is here complained of, because no legal remedy can secure complainant the use of his own property.

It is not claimed, and there is certainly no ground for claiming, that there is any equitable estoppel. Defendants have never acted on any belief that they had a right to do what they are doing. They have always known they were wrong-doers, and have simply presumed on the patience of their neighbors, and neglected to purchase what they could originally have purchased if they had chosen. Neither does the proof show any very serious difficulty in the way of avoiding the mischief, although I do not regard this as at all essential.

It is not denied by complainant that he purchased for speculative purposes. As every one has a right to do this if he chooses, it cannot in any way lessen his claims to protection. It would be, I think, a very dangerous principle to hold that a civil wrong can be lessened by the motives of the party injured, so long as he has done no wrong himself. The property of one man is as much entitled to protection as that of another,—not because he bought it or intends to use it without selfish motives, but because it is property. Any attempt to discriminate would, in my opinion, leave private interests subject to a discretion which no man could calculate upon, and make the judicial conscience the only arbiter of every one's rights. Some courts may have acted on this notion, but it seems to me that such precedents are unjust, and are not consistent with law or equity as we have received them under our constitutional guaranties of protection to person and property.

I think the court below should have granted a perpetual injunction as prayed.

NOTES AND QUESTIONS

1.   The question of whether one's rights can be limited by a wrongful purpose, bad intent, or abuse, is a thorny one in the common law tradition. Civil law systems typically feature a doctrine of abuse of rights, which has many overtones of equity (civil law countries do not have a history of separate equity jurisdiction). See, e.g., Anna di Robilant, Abuse of Rights: The Continental Drug and the Common Law, 61 Hastings L.J. 687 (2010); A.N. Yiannopoulos, Civil Liability for Abuse of Right: Something Old, Something New. . ., 54 La. L. Rev. 1173, 1192–93 (1994). In the common law countries, courts have veered between two poles. On the one hand, courts sometimes make strong absolutist statements, along the lines of the dissent in the excerpted case, that one can exercise a right for any reason whatever. See, e.g., Mayor of Bradford v. Pickles, [1895] A.C. 587 (Eng.) (refusing to enjoin alleged sham mining operation that polluted city's only water supply, and stating that bad motive cannot make unlawful an otherwise lawful act). On the other hand, courts will enjoin as nuisances fences built purely out of spite (Chapter IX) and sometimes intervene in cases like *Allouez Mining*, leading some to see abuse of right as implicit in the common law. Joseph M.

Perillo, Abuse of Rights: A Pervasive Legal Concept, 27 Pac. L.J. 37 (1995); see also Adam J. MacLeod, Property and Practical Reason 146–72 (2015). Is abuse of right the operative notion in *INS v. AP* (Chapter II)? *Hinman* (Chapter I)? How about Judge Logan's dissent in *Edwards v. Sims* (Chapter II)?

2.   Is this case actually an application of established equitable notions? Did the purchaser here have unclean hands? Is there any sense in which there is undue hardship for the defendant company? In another traditional formulation, courts, especially in nuisance cases, would sometimes deny injunctions because a plaintiff should not be allowed to "stand on his extreme rights." Stevens v. Rockport Granite Co., 104 N.E. 371, 373 (Mass. 1914) ("The law of nuisance affords no rigid rule to be applied in all instances. It is elastic. It undertakes to require only that which is fair and reasonable under all the circumstances. In a commonwealth like this, which depends for its material prosperity so largely on the continued growth and enlargement of manufacturing of diverse varieties, 'extreme rights' cannot be enforced."); St. Helen's Smelting Co. v. Tipping, (1865) 11 Eng. Rep. 1483 (H.L.). Is that what is going on here?

3.   Is the problem in cases like *Allouez Mining* that the plaintiff was making an "inefficient threat"? Ian Ayres & Kristin Madison, Threatening Inefficient Performance of Injunctions and Contracts, 148 U. Pa. L. Rev. 45, 50–51 (1999). How should courts identify inefficient threats? Other commentators have argued that injunctions should be refused (and abuse of rights found) when the leverage is illegitimate. Larissa M. Katz, Spite and Extortion: A Jurisdictional Principle of Abuse of Right, 122 Yale L.J. 1444 (2013). How do we define legitimate? If you are tempted to say that the plaintiff here is engaging in blackmail, it is noteworthy that the justification for punishing blackmail has been notoriously difficult to pin down.

4.   The court in *Allouez Mining* sees a problem with using injunctions to support "speculation." Is there a limiting principle here? Should specific performance be unavailable to someone who purchases a Rembrandt at a garage sale or a plot of land over an oilfield of which the current owner is unaware? What if in *Allouez Mining* the previous owner of the downstream land had wanted to negotiate but sold to someone who would be better at playing hardball with the company? Is there any difference if the previous owner had simply hired an aggressive lawyer to press the holdout advantage?

5.   If the lack of development of the damaged tract here is swaying the court, how robust is the court's approach? Will future plaintiffs create a sham investment or occupancy in order to make themselves eligible for the injunction and its holdout potential? See Daniel B. Kelly, Strategic Spillovers, 111 Colum. L. Rev. 1641, 1665–66 (2011). Consider *Van Wagner Advertising Corp. v. S & M Enterprises*, 492 N.E.2d 756 (N.Y. 1986), which involved the lease of outside wall space facing the Midtown Tunnel in New York City. Noting that the new landlord had missed an opportunity to cancel the lease upon the sale and professed to have different plans for the space, the court held that the plaintiff lessee had an adequate remedy in damages and that an injunction would visit disproportionate hardship on the

breaching landlord, and so denied specific performance. The lore is it that after the case was over, the landlord leased to another sign company at a higher rent.

6.   The problem here also has overtones of "coming to the nuisance," which we take up in Chapter IX. Sometimes courts will give defendants a break if the plaintiff moved to the nuisance knowing it was there. Why should this be? Should racing to commit a nuisance first increase one's rights? One would like both parties to act efficiently in light of the other's behavior, which turns out to be a complicated problem. Related is the question of the statute of limitations. Say a court tells the owner of vacant land that there is no injury and so no remedy (damages even?) is appropriate. Then years later the landowner wants to do something with the land that would be impacted by the defendant's activity. Would the landowner lose because of the statute of limitations? Either owners of vacant land should be able to sue or the statute should be tolled. Which is better? See Sturges v. Bridgman, 11 Ch. D. 852 (1879) (Eng.); Richard A. Epstein, Nuisance Law: Corrective Justice and its Utilitarian Constraints, 8 J. Legal Stud. 49, 72–73 (1979).

D. OTHER POWERS OF THE SOVEREIGN OWNER

If one thinks of property as a type of sovereignty over designated things, or perhaps as the power to act as the "gatekeeper" of a thing, then it is important not only to be able to exclude other persons from the thing, but also to be able to include other persons in the use and enjoyment of the thing—and perhaps to be able to exclude oneself from the thing as well. In this Part, we consider a number of basic powers that the sovereign owner or gatekeeper typically can exercise beyond the basic right to exclude others. These include: (1) the power to give permission to someone else to gain access to property, generally called a *license*; (2) the power to transfer temporary custody of property to someone else, known (at least in the context of personal property) as a *bailment*; and (3) the powers to abandon and destroy property. These do not exhaust the elements of owner sovereignty, but we will postpone other attributes, such as the power to determine what happens to property after one's death and the power to transfer, to later chapters.

1. LICENSES

A license can be defined as a permission from an owner of an asset to another person allowing the latter to gain access to the asset on certain terms. It is, simply put, a waiver of the owner's right to exclude. In general, the term "license" refers to a waiver of the exclusion right that is temporary and revocable. A classic example of a license would be the owner's permission to a repair person to enter an apartment to fix a broken dishwasher. If the repair person fails to make the repairs properly, or otherwise misbehaves, the owner can revoke the license and ask him to leave. It is also possible to waive the exclusion right by granting someone an interest of greater permanence and security than a license, the most common examples being easements and leases. These more secure and permanent waivers are often called "property rights," and are distinguished from "mere licenses," but as always one must proceed with care in understanding what exactly is meant by these terms in this context.

Wood v. Leadbitter

Exchequer of Pleas (U.K.), 1845.
153 Eng. Rep. 351, 13 M. & W. 838.

* * *

■ ALDERSON, B. This was an action tried before my Brother Rolfe at the sittings after last Trinity Term. It was an action for an assault and false imprisonment. The plea (on which alone any question arose) was, that at the time of the alleged trespass the plaintiff was in a certain close of Lord Eglintoun, and the defendant, as the servant of Lord Eglintoun, and by his command, laid his hands upon the plaintiff in order to remove him from the said close, using no unnecessary violence. Replication, that, at the time of such removal, the plaintiff was in the said close by the leave and license of Lord Eglintoun. The leave and license was traversed by the defendant, and issue was joined on that traverse. On the trial it appeared that the place from which the plaintiff was removed by the defendant was the inclosure attached to and surrounding the great stand on the Doncaster race-course; that Lord Eglintoun was steward of the races there in the year 1843; that tickets were sold in the town of Doncaster at one guinea each, which were understood to entitle the holders to come into the stand, and the inclosure surrounding it, and to remain there every day during the races. These tickets were not signed by Lord Eglintoun, but it must be assumed that they were issued with his privity. It further appeared, that the plaintiff, having purchased one of these tickets, came to the stand during the races of the year 1843, and was there or in the inclosure while the races were going on, and while there, and during the races, the defendant, by the order of Lord Eglintoun, desired him to depart, and gave him notice that if he did not go away, force would be used to turn him out. It must be assumed that the plaintiff had in no respect misconducted himself, and that, if he had not been required to depart, his coming upon and remaining in the inclosure would have been an act justified by his purchase of the ticket. The plaintiff refused to go, and thereupon the defendant, by order of Lord Eglintoun, forced him out, without returning the guinea, using no unnecessary violence.

My Brother Rolfe, in directing the jury, told them, that, even assuming the ticket to have been sold to the plaintiff under the sanction of Lord Eglintoun, still it was lawful for Lord Eglintoun, without returning the guinea, and without assigning any reason for what he did, to order the plaintiff to quit the inclosure, and that, if the jury were satisfied that notice was given by Lord Eglintoun to the plaintiff, requiring him to quit the ground, and that, before he was forcibly removed by the defendant, a reasonable time had elapsed, during which he might conveniently have gone away, then the plaintiff was not, at the time of the removal, on the place in question by the leave and license of Lord Eglintoun. On this direction the jury found a verdict for the defendant. In last Michaelmas term, Mr. Jervis obtained a rule nisi to set aside the verdict for misdirection, on the ground, that, under the circumstances, Lord Eglintoun must be taken to have given the plaintiff leave to come into and remain in the inclosure during the races; that such leave was not revocable, at all events without returning the guinea; and so that, as [of] the time of the removal, the plaintiff was in the inclosure by the leave and license of Lord Eglintoun. Cause was shewn during last term, and the question was argued before my Brothers Parke and Rolfe and myself; and on account of the conflicting authorities cited in the argument, we took time to consider our judgment, which we are now prepared to deliver. * * *

That no incorporeal inheritance affecting land can either be created or transferred otherwise than by deed, is a proposition so well established, that it would be mere pedantry to cite authorities in its support. All such inheritances are said emphatically to lie in grant, and not in livery [of seisin], and to pass by mere delivering of the deed. In all the authorities and text-books on the subject, a deed is always stated or assumed to be indispensably requisite.

And although the older authorities speak of incorporeal inheritances, there is no doubt but that the principle does not depend on the quality of interest granted or transferred, but on the nature of the subject-matter: a right of common, for instance, which is a profit à prendre, or a right of way, which is an easement, or right in nature of an easement, can no more be granted or conveyed for life or for years without a deed, than in fee simple. Now, in the present case, the right claimed by the plaintiff is a right, during a portion of each day, for a limited number of days, to pass into and through and to remain in a certain close belonging to Lord Eglintoun; to go and remain where if he went and remained, he would, but for the ticket, be a trespasser. This is a right affecting land at least as obviously and extensively as a right of way over the land,—it is a right of way and something more: and if we had to decide this case on general principles only, and independently of authority, it would appear to us perfectly clear that no such right can be created otherwise than by deed. The plaintiff, however, in this case argues, that he is not driven to claim the right in question strictly as grantee. He contends, that, without any grant from Lord Eglintoun, he had license from him to be in the close in question at the time when he was turned out, and that such license was, under the circumstances, irrevocable. * * *

[I]t may be convenient to consider the nature of a license, and what are its legal incidents. And, for this purpose, we cannot do better than refer to Lord C. J. Vaughan's elaborate judgment in the case of *Thomas v. Sorrell*, as it appears in his Reports [(1685) Vaughan 330, 124 Eng. Rep. 1098 (C.P.)]. The question there was as to the right of the Crown to dispense with certain statutes regulating the sale of wine, and to license the Vintners' Company to do certain acts notwithstanding those statutes.

In the course of his judgment the Chief Justice says (Vaughan, 351[, 124 Eng. Rep. at 1109]), "A dispensation or license properly passeth no interest, nor alters or transfers property in anything, but only makes an action lawful, which without it had been unlawful. As a license to go beyond the seas, to hunt in a man's park, to come into his house, are only actions which, without license, had been unlawful. But a license to hunt in a man's park, and carry away the deer killed to his own use; to cut down a tree in a man's ground, and to carry it away the next day after to his own use, are licenses as to the acts of hunting and cutting down the tree, but as to the carrying away of the deer killed and tree cut down, they are grants. So, to license a man to eat my meat, or to fire the wood in my chimney to warm him by, as to the actions of eating, firing my wood, and warming him, they are licenses; but it is consequent necessarily to those actions that my property may be destroyed in the meat eaten, and in the wood burnt. So as in some cases, by consequent and not directly, and as its effect, a dispensation or license may destroy and alter property."

Now, attending to this passage, in conjunction with the title "License" in Brooke's Abridgment, from which, and particularly from paragraph 15, it appears that a license is in its nature revocable, we have before us the whole principle of the law on this subject. A mere license is revocable: but that which is called a license is often something more than a license; it often comprises or is connected with a grant, and then the party who has given it cannot in general revoke it, so as to defeat his grant, to which it was incident.

It may further be observed, that a license under seal (provided it be a mere license) is as revocable as a license by parol; and, on the other hand, a license by parol, coupled with a grant, is as irrevocable as a license by deed, provided only that the grant is of a nature capable of being made by parol. But where there is a license by parol, coupled with a parol grant, or pretended grant, of something which is incapable of being granted otherwise than by deed, there the license is a mere license; it is not an incident to a valid grant, and it is therefore revocable. Thus, a license by A. to hunt in his park, whether given by deed or by parol, is revocable; it merely renders the act of hunting lawful, which, without the license, would have been unlawful. If the license be, as put by Chief Justice Vaughan, a license not only to hunt, but also to take away the deer when killed to his own use, this is in truth a grant of the deer, with a license annexed to come on the land: and supposing the grant of the deer to be good, then the license would be irrevocable by the party who had given it; he would be estopped from defeating his own grant, or act in the nature of a grant. * * *

It was suggested that, in the present case, a distinction might exist, by reason of the plaintiff's having paid a valuable consideration for the privilege of going on the stand. But this fact makes no difference: whether it may give the plaintiff a right of action against those from whom he purchased the ticket, or those who authorized its being issued and sold to him, is a point not necessary to be discussed; any such action would be founded on a breach of contract, and would not be the result of his having acquired by the ticket a right of going upon the stand, in spite of the owner of the soil; and it is sufficient, on this point, to say, that in several of the cases we have cited, * * * the alleged license had been granted for a valuable consideration, but that was not held to make any difference. * * *

In conclusion, we have only to say, that, acting upon the doctrine relative to licenses * * * the direction given to the jury at the trial was correct, and that this rule must be discharged.

Figure 4-6
Plaque in the Sidewalk at Rockefeller
Center, New York City

NOTES AND QUESTIONS

1.   Let us unpack some of the vocabulary in the case. An "incorporeal inheritance" (or "incorporeal hereditament") refers to a nonpossessory property right that descends on death in accordance with the rules for real property. Easements, such as a right to cross another's land, are a principal example. A profit à prendre (or "profit" for short)—a right to gather resources like timber or game on another's land—is another example. "Incorporeal" is a misnomer here, because the rights in question are not intangible (like intellectual property), but are simply use rights in land amounting to something less than full possession. "Livery of seisin" refers to the traditional

ceremony used in feudal times to transfer freehold interests in real property (more on this in Chapter V). Easements and profits were not transferred by livery of seisin, but by deed. A "deed" was traditionally a sealed writing, the seal being a stamp impressed on the paper using melted wax. Today, deeds no longer require hot wax, but often entail formalities like signatures that are witnessed or notarized. The court's point about all this is that a license is typically created orally ("by parol") or by contract, in contrast to property rights like easements and profits, which are created by deed.

2. The rule enunciated by Baron Alderson, that a "mere license" to enter the land of another is always revocable, remains black letter law. The reason for the rule remains elusive in Baron Alderson's opinion. He seems to suggest that the reason is purely formal: property rights to enter the land of another (incorporeal inheritances like easements and profits) must be created by deed, and once created they are irrevocable for their stated term. If there is no deed, however, the interest is a mere license. But this, of course, just tells us how one creates a property right that is irrevocable as opposed to a license. It does not explain why creating a mere license is always revocable. Later in the opinion, Baron Alderson acknowledges that sometimes licenses are in fact also irrevocable. Specifically, a license "coupled with a grant" is irrevocable until such a time as the purpose of the grant is fulfilled. To use his example, if A orally agrees that B can enter A's land to kill and take away a deer, B has an implied license to enter the land for this purpose and the license is irrevocable until the grant is fulfilled or is revoked. Note that neither the license nor the grant in the example is created by deed. So a deed is not always required to create an irrevocable license.

3. In a later U.S. decision, *Marrone v. Washington Jockey Club of the District of Columbia*, 227 U.S. 633, 636 (1913), a patron sued a racetrack for forcibly removing him and for conspiring to ruin his reputation by accusing him of drugging a horse. Because proof of the conspiracy to defame was lacking, Justice Holmes treated the case a matter of revocation of the license. He followed the rule in *Wood v. Leadbitter*, which he described as having established that tickets to enter a race track "do not create a right *in rem.*" He grounded this in the presumed intentions of the parties: "The ticket was not a conveyance of an interest in the race track, not only because it was not under seal, but because by common understanding it did not purport to have that effect. There would be obvious inconveniences if it were construed otherwise." Id. Holmes was clearly right that a ticket to view a single sporting event (or movie or play) is not understood to convey "an interest in the race track." (What about a season ticket or a skybox rental?) Does it follow, however, that the parties do not intend that the license will be irrevocable until the race (or the movie or play) is over? When people purchase a ticket to a horse race, a movie, or a play, don't they usually think they have a right to stay until the performance is over?

4. The result in *Wood v. Leadbitter* has been regarded as unjust by many commentators because Wood entered into a contract with Lord Eglintoun (or his agent) for the right to enter the grounds and watch the races, and he paid a handsome sum of money (a guinea was worth more than a pound sterling) to be allowed to do so. No reason is offered in the opinion

for Lord Eglintoun's subsequent decision to revoke the license and have his servant Leadbitter evict Wood. Recent research reveals, that, as in *Marrone*, problems surrounding the horse betting industry formed the backdrop to *Wood* as well. In the 1840s in England, horse racing had acquired a bad reputation, and Lord Eglintoun was among those trying to clean things up. Leadbitter was an ex-policeman hired to prevent shady activities. Plaintiff Wood was a notoriously crooked bookmaker, who had defaulted on a fraudulent bet. Wood couldn't sue for defamation because he was a defaulter, so he sued for assault and false imprisonment instead. If Wood had won, the racing business faced the prospect of hostile legislation. At the trial, much bad character evidence came in against Wood, after which the trial judge told the jury it was irrelevant. Patrick Polden, A Day at the Races: *Wood v. Leadbitter* in Context, 14 J. Legal Hist. 28 (1993). Does this backstory show that the ability to revoke the license without justification is important for business landowners? Or does it suggest that they should be forced to state their real reasons?

5.   Does the exception recognized in *Wood* for licenses coupled with a grant apply to the ticket to view the Doncaster races? In a later English decision that declined to follow *Wood*—at least with respect to contracts to view a spectacle like a movie—some of the judges suggested that such a contract is in effect a license coupled with a grant, namely, "the right to see." Hurst v. Picture Theatres, Ltd., [1915] 1 K.B. 1 (C.A. 1914) (Buckley, L.J.). A grant is commonly understood to be a conveyance of a property right. *Wood* confirms that permission to hunt deer is a grant of any deer killed in the hunt, and that such a grant entails an implied license to enter the land. A dead deer is personal property. But is the "right to see" a property right? If so, what kind?

6.   Is the understanding that licenses are always revocable (at least "mere licenses") consistent with the idea that property owners have broad sovereign authority to manage and control their thing? The rule means that an owner does not give up the right to exclude by making informal promises to neighbors or friends or even by entering into contracts with service providers or patrons. If things do not work out as anticipated, the owner can reassert the sovereign prerogative to exclude and maintain control over the thing. The owner gives up control over the thing only if a full-fledged property right is transferred to another, such as an easement, a profit, or a lease, and this requires a conveyance accompanied by formalities that impress upon the owner the irrevocable nature of the action being taken. This can also be seen as a manifestation of the idea that exceptions to full-fledged property rights exist only in a limited number of defined forms—the *numerus clausus* idea discussed more fully in Chapter V. If a variety of promises and contracts could give rise to irrevocable licenses, in effect this would permit a proliferation of property forms, which would greatly complicate the system of property rights.

7.   Lawsuits by ticket holders who have been expelled from sporting events or theaters are not common, perhaps because "theater proprietors can be trusted not to expel their patrons unjustifiably." Alfred F. Conard, An Analysis of Licenses in Land, 42 Colum. L. Rev. 809, 823 (1942). More

common are suits by ticket holders who are disgruntled by what they see once they get there. These too generally fail. In one case, a New York Jets fan sued the coach of the New England Patriots for secretly videotaping signals being sent from the sidelines to the Jets' huddle. Mayer v. Belichick, 605 F.3d 223 (3d. Cir. 2010). Citing *Wood v. Leadbitter*, the court held that "a ticket provides a patron with nothing more than a revocable license" id. at 231, and does not guarantee that the ticket holder will "see an 'honest' game played in compliance with the rules of the NFL." Id. at 233.

Equitable Enforcement of Licenses

Can the exceptions to the rule that licenses are always revocable be explained on grounds of equity? Recall that courts of equity will sometimes modify the ordinary rules associated with property in circumstances where they would produce an injustice. For example, although the action for trespass to land originally provided only for damages, courts of equity came to issue injunctions against defendants who commit repeated trespasses (*Baker v. Howard County Hunt*). Similarly, although a permanent trespass in the form of a building encroachment might ordinarily call for an injunction requiring that the encroachment be removed, courts of equity sometimes limit the encroached-upon owner to an award of damages when the mistake is unintentional and harm trivial (*Golden Press v. Rylands*).

The exception to the usual rule of revocability for licenses "coupled with a grant," discussed in *Wood v. Leadbitter*, can also be explained on grounds of equity. If A grants B the right to hunt and kill deer on A's land, and B, acting in reliance on this grant, hunts and kills a deer, it would seem unjust to allow A at that point to revoke the license, in effect depriving B of realizing the purpose of the grant (and depriving B of the fruits of his labor). A court of law, following the understanding that licenses are always revocable, might deny B relief. But if B brought a suit in a court of equity, one might expect the equity court to issue an order enjoining A from revoking the license until B has been given an opportunity to remove the deer. In effect, the equity court would interpose an in personam order directing A to desist from exercising A's ordinary legal right to revoke the license, until the purpose of A's grant to B had been realized. Once the deer is removed, the injunction would lapse and A's ordinary right to exclude would be restored.

Principles of equity can also explain another exception to the ordinary rule that licenses are always revocable, which we consider more fully in Chapter IX. This is where A grants a license to B, and B, acting in reliance on the license and with the knowledge of A, materially changes his position in such a way that it would be inequitable to allow A to revoke the license. To take a classic case, *Rerick v. Kern*, 14 Serg. & Rawle 267 (Pa. 1826), suppose that A gives oral permission to B to change the course of a stream that flows through the land of both A and B. B, in reliance on this permission, builds an expensive water mill on the new watercourse on B's land. A then changes his mind, and demands that the stream be restored to its original course. Allowing A to revoke the permission to divert the stream would impose a very great hardship on B, and courts of equity have issued injunctions in these circumstances barring persons like A from revoking the license for as long as such hardship would result, for example, until the mill is abandoned or can be powered by some other source.

Can principles of equity be used to challenge the result in *Wood v. Leadbitter*? The question was debated at length in the decision by the English Court of Appeal in *Hurst v. Picture Theatres, Ltd.*, [1915] 1 K.B. 1. The plaintiff, Hurst, purchased a ticket to view a motion picture in a theater in London. He gave his ticket to an usher and took his seat, but the management of the theater evidently suspected that he had entered without paying. He was asked to leave and refused, whereupon he was ejected. Hurst sued for assault and false imprisonment. The jury found for Hurst on the question whether he had paid, and he was awarded £150 in damages (a very large sum at the time). The appeals court, over a dissent, declined to follow *Wood v. Leadbitter* and affirmed.

One argument for not following *Wood* was that Parliament in the Judicature Act of 1873 had merged the courts of law and equity, allowing courts of law to rely on principles of equity in resolving disputes. *Wood* had been decided by a court of law before the merger of law and equity, and hence had no choice but to follow the legal rule that licenses are always revocable. Why would a court of equity decide *Wood* differently? The judges in the majority in *Hurst* reasoned that a person who purchases a ticket to see a spectacle (like a movie or a horse race) acquires a contractual right. An implied term of the contract is that the license to enter the venue will not be revoked until the spectacle is over. Because the spectacle is unique (this seems true in the case of a horse race; perhaps not for a movie?), a court of equity would grant specific performance of the contract, in effect enjoining the proprietor from revoking the license until the spectacle is over. Since the proprietor could be enjoined from revoking the license, an attempt by the proprietor to eject the patron is an illegal assault, actionable in tort.

Can you detect the flaw in this reasoning? Judge Phillimore stated in his dissent: "Assume . . . that there was a contract, and assume that the purported revocation was a breach of the contract, and assume that of which I am not certain, that equity would give specific performance of such a contract, still specific performance does not necessarily put the man before he has got specific performance in the legal possession which he gets after he has got specific performance." [1915] 1 K.B. at 18. Remember, equity assesses the equities of the particular case, and if the plaintiff is successful, the equity court issues a personal order directing the defendant to desist or perform particular acts, on pain of contempt. Often it is not possible to predict how the court will rule until it has gathered and considered all the relevant facts. In some contractual disputes, it will still be possible after all the facts have been considered to order specific performance; for example, it may still be possible to order the defendant to complete a sale of land to the plaintiff. But in the case of a dispute over whether a particular patron is entitled to see a particular entertainment, it will be impossible (in virtually every case) to seek and secure an award of specific performance before the spectacle is over. To allow a patron to resist eviction based on a prediction of what would happen if, contrary to fact, a court of equity could hear and resolve the dispute before the performance is over, would seem to invite disorder and possible violence in entertainment venues. As Justice Holmes stated in a similar dispute in a characteristically cryptic fashion: Even if a ticket creates a right enforceable against the proprietor, the ticket holder has "no right to enforce specific performance by self-help." Marrone v. Washington Jockey Club of the District of Columbia, 227 U.S. 633, 636 (1913). Does this help explain why *Wood*, rather than *Hurst*, continues to be regarded as good law by most American jurisdictions?

ProCD, Inc. v. Zeidenberg

United States Court of Appeals, Seventh Circuit, 1996.
86 F.3d 1447.

■ EASTERBROOK, CIRCUIT JUDGE. Must buyers of computer software obey the terms of shrinkwrap licenses? The district court held not, for two reasons: first, they are not contracts because the licenses are inside the box rather than printed on the outside; second, federal law forbids enforcement even if the licenses are contracts. The parties and numerous amici curiae have briefed many other issues, but these are the only two that matter—and we disagree with the district judge's conclusion on each. Shrinkwrap licenses are enforceable unless their terms are objectionable on grounds applicable to contracts in general (for example, if they violate a rule of positive law, or if they are unconscionable). Because no one argues that the terms of the license at issue here are troublesome, we remand with instructions to enter judgment for the plaintiff.

I

ProCD, the plaintiff, has compiled information from more than 3,000 telephone directories into a computer database. We may assume that this database cannot be copyrighted, although it is more complex, contains more information (nine-digit zip codes and census industrial codes), is organized differently, and therefore is more original than the single alphabetical directory at issue in *Feist Publications, Inc. v. Rural Telephone Service Co.*, 499 U.S. 340 (1991). See Paul J. Heald, The Vices of Originality, 1991 Sup.Ct. Rev. 143, 160–68. ProCD sells a version of the database, called SelectPhone (trademark), on CD-ROM discs. (CD-ROM means "compact disc—read only memory." The "shrinkwrap license" gets its name from the fact that retail software packages are covered in plastic or cellophane "shrinkwrap," and some vendors, though not ProCD, have written licenses that become effective as soon as the customer tears the wrapping from the package. Vendors prefer "end user license," but we use the more common term.) A proprietary method of compressing the data serves as effective encryption too. Customers decrypt and use the data with the aid of an application program that ProCD has written. This program, which is copyrighted, searches the database in response to users' criteria (such as "find all people named Tatum in Tennessee, plus all firms with 'Door Systems' in the corporate name"). The resulting lists (or, as ProCD prefers, "listings") can be read and manipulated by other software, such as word processing programs.

The database in SelectPhone (trademark) cost more than $10 million to compile and is expensive to keep current. It is much more valuable to some users than to others. The combination of names, addresses, and SIC [Standard Industrial Classification] codes enables manufacturers to compile lists of potential customers. Manufacturers and retailers pay high prices to specialized information intermediaries for such mailing lists; ProCD offers a potentially cheaper alternative. People with nothing to sell could use the database as a substitute for calling long distance information, or as a way to look up old friends who have moved to unknown towns, or just as an electronic substitute for the local phone book. ProCD decided to engage in price discrimination, selling its database to the general public for personal use at a low price (approximately $150 for the set of five discs) while selling information to the trade for a higher price. It has adopted some intermediate strategies too: access to the SelectPhone (trademark) database is available via the America Online service for the price America Online charges to its clients (approximately $3 per hour), but this service has been tailored to be useful only to the general public.

If ProCD had to recover all of its costs and make a profit by charging a single price—that is, if it could not charge more to commercial users than to the general public—it would have to raise the price substantially over $150. The ensuing reduction in sales would harm consumers who value the information at, say, $200. They get consumer surplus of $50 under the current arrangement but would cease to buy if the price rose substantially. If because of high elasticity of demand in the consumer segment of the market the only way to make a profit turned out to be a price attractive to commercial users alone, then all consumers would lose out—and so would the commercial clients, who would have to pay more for the listings because ProCD could not obtain any contribution toward costs from the consumer market.

To make price discrimination work, however, the seller must be able to control arbitrage. An air carrier sells tickets for less to vacationers than to business travelers, using advance purchase and Saturday-night-stay requirements to distinguish the categories. A producer of movies segments the market by time, releasing first to theaters, then to pay-per-view services, next to the videotape and laserdisc market, and finally to cable and commercial tv. Vendors of computer software have a harder task. Anyone can walk into a retail store and buy a box. Customers do not wear tags saying "commercial user" or "consumer user." Anyway, even a commercial-user-detector at the door would not work, because a consumer could buy the software and resell to a commercial user. That arbitrage would break down the price discrimination and drive up the minimum price at which ProCD would sell to anyone.

Instead of tinkering with the product and letting users sort themselves—for example, furnishing current data at a high price that would be attractive only to commercial customers, and two-year-old data at a low price—ProCD turned to the institution of contract. Every box containing its consumer product declares that the software comes with restrictions stated in an enclosed license. This license, which is encoded on the CD-ROM disks as well as printed in the manual, and which appears on a user's screen every time the software runs, limits use of the application program and listings to non-commercial purposes.

Matthew Zeidenberg bought a consumer package of SelectPhone (trademark) in 1994 from a retail outlet in Madison, Wisconsin, but decided to ignore the license. He formed Silken Mountain Web Services, Inc., to resell the information in the SelectPhone (trademark) database. The corporation makes the database available on the Internet to anyone willing to pay its price—which, needless to say, is less than ProCD charges its commercial customers. Zeidenberg has purchased two additional SelectPhone (trademark) packages, each with an updated version of the database, and made the latest information available over the World Wide Web, for a price, through his corporation. ProCD filed this suit seeking an injunction against further dissemination that exceeds the rights specified in the licenses (identical in each of the three packages Zeidenberg purchased). The district court held the licenses ineffectual because their terms do not appear on the outside of the packages. The court added that the second and third licenses stand no different from the first, even though they are identical, because they might have been different, and a purchaser does not agree to—and cannot be bound by—terms that were secret at the time of purchase.

II

Following the district court, we treat the licenses as ordinary contracts accompanying the sale of products, and therefore as governed by the common law of contracts and the Uniform Commercial Code. Whether there are legal differences between "contracts" and "licenses" (which may matter under the copyright doctrine of first sale) is a subject for another day. See Microsoft Corp. v. Harmony Computers & Electronics, Inc., 846 F.Supp. 208 (E.D.N.Y. 1994). * * * Zeidenberg [argues], and the district court held, that placing the package of software on the shelf is an "offer," which the customer "accepts" by paying the asking price and leaving the store with the goods. Peeters v. State, 142 N.W. 181 (Wis. 1913). In Wisconsin, as elsewhere, a contract includes only the terms on which the parties have agreed. One cannot agree to hidden terms, the judge concluded. So far, so good—but one of the terms to which Zeidenberg agreed by purchasing the software is that the transaction was subject to a license. Zeidenberg's position therefore must be that the printed terms on the outside of a box are the parties' contract—except for printed terms that refer to or incorporate other terms. But why would Wisconsin fetter the parties' choice in this way? Vendors can put the entire terms of a contract on the outside of a box only by using microscopic type, removing other information that buyers might find more useful (such as what the software does, and on which computers it works), or both. The "Read Me" file included with most software, describing system requirements and potential incompatibilities, may be equivalent to ten pages of type; warranties and license restrictions take still more space. Notice on the outside, terms on the inside, and a right to return the software for a refund if the terms are unacceptable (a right that the license expressly extends), may be a means of doing business valuable to buyers and sellers alike. See E. Allan Farnsworth, 1 Farnsworth on Contracts § 4.26 (1990); Restatement (2d) of Contracts § 211 comment a (1981) ("Standardization of agreements serves many of the same functions as standardization of goods and services; both are essential to a system of mass production and distribution. Scarce and costly time and skill can be devoted to a class of transactions rather than the details of individual transactions."). Doubtless a state could forbid the use of standard contracts in the software business, but we do not think that Wisconsin has done so.

Transactions in which the exchange of money precedes the communication of detailed terms are common. * * * [C]onsider the purchase of an airline ticket. The traveler calls the carrier or an agent, is quoted a price, reserves a seat, pays, and gets a ticket, in that order. The ticket contains elaborate terms, which the traveler can reject by canceling the reservation. To use the ticket is to accept the terms, even terms that in retrospect are disadvantageous. See Carnival Cruise Lines, Inc. v. Shute, 499 U.S. 585 (1991). Just so with a ticket to a concert. The back of the ticket states that the patron promises not to record the concert; to attend is to agree. A theater that detects a violation will confiscate the tape and escort the violator to the exit. One could arrange things so that every concertgoer signs this promise before forking over the money, but that cumbersome way of doing things not only would lengthen queues and raise prices but also would scotch the sale of tickets by phone or electronic data service. * * *

III

The district court held that, even if Wisconsin treats shrinkwrap licenses as contracts, § 301(a) of the Copyright Act, 17 U.S.C. § 301(a), prevents their enforcement. The relevant part of § 301(a) preempts any "legal or equitable rights [under state law] that are equivalent to any of the exclusive rights within the general scope of copyright as specified by section 106 in works of authorship that are fixed in a tangible medium of expression and come within the subject matter of copyright as specified by sections 102 and 103." ProCD's software and data are "fixed in a tangible medium of expression", and the district judge held that they are "within the subject matter of copyright". The latter conclusion is plainly right for the copyrighted application program, and the judge thought that the data likewise are "within the subject matter of copyright" even if, after *Feist*, they are not sufficiently original to be copyrighted. One function of § 301(a) is to prevent states from giving special protection to works of authorship that Congress has decided should be in the public domain, which it can accomplish only if "subject matter of copyright" includes all works of a type covered by sections 102 and 103, even if federal law does not afford protection to them. Cf. Bonito Boats, Inc. v. Thunder Craft Boats, Inc., 489 U.S. 141 (1989) (same principle under patent laws).

But are rights created by contract "equivalent to any of the exclusive rights within the general scope of copyright"? Three courts of appeals have answered "no." National Car Rental System, Inc. v. Computer Associates International, Inc., 991 F.2d 426, 433 (8th Cir. 1993); Taquino v. Teledyne Monarch Rubber, 893 F.2d 1488, 1501 (5th Cir. 1990); Acorn Structures, Inc. v. Swantz, 846 F.2d 923, 926 (4th Cir. 1988). The district court disagreed with these decisions, but we think them sound. Rights "equivalent to any of the exclusive rights within the general scope of copyright" are rights established by *law*—rights that restrict the options of persons who are strangers to the author. Copyright law forbids duplication, public performance, and so on, unless the person wishing to copy or perform the work gets permission; silence means a ban on copying. A copyright is a right against the world. Contracts, by contrast, generally affect only their parties; strangers may do as they please, so contracts do not create "exclusive rights." Someone who found a copy of SelectPhone (trademark) on the street would not be affected by the shrinkwrap license—though the federal copyright laws of their own force would limit the finder's ability to copy or transmit the application program.

Think for a moment about * * * everyday transactions in intellectual property. A customer visits a video store and rents a copy of *Night of the Lepus*. The customer's contract with the store limits use of the tape to home viewing and requires its return in two days. May the customer keep the tape, on the ground that § 301(a) makes the promise unenforceable?

A law student uses the LEXIS database, containing public-domain documents, under a contract limiting the results to educational endeavors; may the student resell his access to this database to a law firm from which LEXIS seeks to collect a much higher hourly rate? * * * Everyone remains free to copy and disseminate all 3,000 telephone books that have been incorporated into ProCD's database. Anyone can add SIC codes and zip codes. ProCD's rivals have done so. Enforcement of the shrinkwrap license may even make information more readily available, by reducing the price ProCD charges to consumer buyers. * * * Licenses may have other benefits for consumers: many licenses permit users to make extra copies, to use the software on multiple computers, even to incorporate the software into the user's products. But whether a particular license is generous or restrictive, a simple two-party contract is not "equivalent to any of the exclusive rights within the general scope of copyright" and therefore may be enforced.

REVERSED AND REMANDED.

NOTES AND QUESTIONS

1.   As *ProCD* suggests, license agreements are extremely important in the world of intellectual property. Judge Easterbrook says that there may be some differences between licenses and contracts, but he leaves that for another day, and proceeds to treat a software license exactly like a contract. Indeed many IP licenses are created by contract. And yet despite the tendency to equate licenses and contracts, there are good reasons not to confuse the two. Christopher M. Newman, A License is Not a 'Contract Not to Sue': Disentangling Property and Contract in the Law of Copyright Licenses, 98 Iowa L. Rev. 1101 (2013). Contexts in which seeing a license as a waiver of a property right rather than a contract include licenses enforceable without consideration and licenses to be enforced against a transferee of the copyright.

2.   Courts' acceptance of shrinkwrap licenses has carried over into the more recent clickwrap licenses (under which clicking a button or icon with a mouse constitutes acceptance) and browsewrap licenses (in which browsing past the counterparty's homepage effects acceptance). Woodrow Hartzog, Website Design as Contract, 60 Am. U. L. Rev. 1635, 1642–45 (2011). The use of licenses with intellectual property goes far beyond computer software. Consider, for example, the agreements by which firms like McDonald's or Coca-Cola license franchisees and distributors to use their trademarks and trade names, or by which the producers of commercial movies license the distribution of videos and DVDs made from the movie, or by which the owners of patents license producing firms to use the patented inventions in furnishing various products and services.

3.   Suppose the software is protected by a patent, having a term ending 20 years from the date of the filing of the patent application. The shrinkwrap license, which everyone who buys the software must agree to, provides that the purchaser promises not to allow anyone else to use the software, without the patent owner's express written permission, for 40 years. Has the device of the shrinkwrap license here been used effectively to amend the scope of monopoly protection given by the patent laws? The Supreme Court has made confusing pronouncements on this subject. Compare Brulotte v. Thys Co., 379 U.S. 29 (1964) (holding that the Patent Act preempts enforcement of a contract providing for royalties that continue to accrue after the last of the patents incorporated into the machines in question expired) with Aronson v. Quick Point Pencil Co., 440 U.S. 257 (1979) (no preemption where agreement

provided for reduced royalty in the event that inventor failed to get a patent). What is the difference between a property right to information, which binds the whole world, and a shrinkwrap license, which attempts to bind everyone who uses the information?

4.   Some have expressed dismay at the degree of control that content providers can achieve through contractual restrictions and various technological measures, collectively known as Digital Rights Management, such as built-in software that automatically terminates access after a number of uses or after a set period of time. In what sense do these devices "propertize" information? Compare Julie E. Cohen, DRM and Privacy, 18 Berkeley Tech. L.J. 575 (2003); Dan Burk & Julie Cohen, Fair Use Infrastructure for Rights Management Systems, 15 Harv. J.L. & Tech. 41 (2001) with David Friedman, In Defense of Private Orderings: Comments on Julie Cohen's "Copyright and the Jurisprudence of Self-Help", 13 Berkeley Tech. L.J. 1151 (1998).

5.   What if, in Judge Easterbrook's hypothetical about the software that someone dropped and someone else picked up off the sidewalk, one has to click past an agreement screen every time one launches the program? If consideration is the problem, assume that every time the agreement page is clicked a small payment is transferred via the internet to the software provider. In what sense is the contract right in such a situation different from an in rem property right?

6.   The rise of cyberspace has led to some creative uses of licenses. Consider "virtual worlds," in which people, through online characters called "avatars," can take various actions, interact with others, and acquire "virtual property." Typically, the hosts of the game hold intellectual property rights in the game and claim to be merely licensing use by the game participants. How would you characterize the legal relationship between game hosts and gamers? Should there be limits to what game owners can do with licenses? For the many issues raised by "virtual property" and their implications for actual property, see, e.g., Juliet M. Moringiello, What Virtual Worlds Can Do for Property Law, 62 Fla. L. Rev. 159 (2010); James Grimmelmann, Virtual Worlds as Comparative Law, 49 N.Y.L. Sch. L. Rev. 147, 148–58 (2004); João Marinotti, Tangibility as Technology, 37 Ga. St. L. Rev. 671 (2021). Can one use licenses to in effect create a synthetic bundle of sticks, thereby bypassing all the requirements of property law? See Aaron Perzanowski & Jason Schultz, The End of Ownership (2016).

2. BAILMENTS

A bailment arises when the owner of property (the bailor) temporarily transfers custody of the property to another (the bailee). Usually a bailment is created by a contract, express or implied, and the parties have some special purpose in mind that requires the transfer of possession of particular property; after this purpose is accomplished, it is understood that the property will be returned to the owner (the bailor). Familiar examples of bailments include the transfer of clothing to a dry cleaning shop for cleaning, the transfer of securities to a broker for safekeeping, or the transfer of an automobile to a valet for parking. Because the bailment relationship is usually created by contract, the respective rights and duties of the bailor and bailee have a strong contractual element, and can be modified by agreement of the parties. But because the essence of the bailment contract is the transfer of possession of property, some of the bailor's rights associated with ownership—most notably the right to exclude others from the owned thing—are also transferred to the bailee. Thus, insofar as third parties are concerned, the bailee's rights with respect to the thing are similar to those of an owner. This blending of contractual (in personam) and property (in rem) elements makes for some difficult and interesting complications in bailment law. Restatement (Fourth) of Property, Vol. 3, § 1 (Am. L. Inst. 2021).

Allen v. Hyatt Regency-Nashville Hotel

Supreme Court of Tennessee, 1984.
668 S.W.2d 286.

■ HARBISON, JUSTICE. In this case the Court is asked to consider the nature and extent of the liability of the operator of a commercial parking garage for theft of a vehicle during the absence of the owner. Both courts below, on the basis of prior decisions from this state, held that a bailment was created when the owner parked and locked his vehicle in a modern, indoor, multi-story garage operated by appellant in conjunction with a large hotel in downtown Nashville. We affirm.

There is almost no dispute as to the relevant facts. Appellant is the owner and operator of a modern high-rise hotel in Nashville fronting on the south side of Union Street. Immediately to the rear, or south, of the main hotel building there is a multi-story parking garage with a single entrance and a single exit to the west, on Seventh Avenue, North. As one enters the parking garage at the street level, there is a large sign reading "Welcome to Hyatt Regency-Nashville." There is another Hyatt Regency sign inside the garage at street level, together with a sign marked "Parking." The garage is available for parking by members of the general public as well as guests of the hotel, and the public are invited to utilize it.

On the morning of February 12, 1981, appellee's husband, Edwin Allen, accompanied by two passengers, drove appellee's new 1981 automobile into the parking garage. Neither Mr. Allen nor his passengers intended to register at the hotel as a guest. Mr. Allen had parked in this particular garage on several occasions, however, testifying that he felt that the vehicle would be safer in an attended garage than in an unattended outside lot on the street.

The single entrance was controlled by a ticket machine. The single exit was controlled by an attendant in a booth just opposite to the entrance and in full view thereof. Appellee's husband entered the garage at the street level and took a ticket which was automatically dispensed by the machine. The machine activated a barrier gate which rose and permitted Mr. Allen to enter the garage. He drove to the fourth floor level, parked the vehicle, locked it, retained the ignition key, descended by elevator to the street level and left the garage. When he returned several hours later, the car was gone, and it has never been recovered. Mr. Allen reported the theft to the attendant at the exit booth, who stated, "Well, it didn't come out here." The attendant did not testify at the trial.

Mr. Allen then reported the theft to security personnel employed by appellant, and subsequently reported the loss to the police. Appellant regularly employed a number of security guards, who were dressed in a distinctive uniform, two of whom were on duty most of the time. These guards patrolled the hotel grounds and building as well as the garage and were instructed to make rounds through the garage, although not necessarily at specified intervals. One of the security guards told appellee's husband that earlier in the day he had received the following report:

> He said, "It's a funny thing here. On my report here a lady called me somewhere around nine-thirty or after and said that there was someone messing with a car."

The guard told Mr. Allen that he closed his office and went up into the garage to investigate, but reported that he did not find anything unusual or out of the ordinary.

Customers such as Mr. Allen, upon entering the garage, received a ticket from the dispensing machine. On one side of this ticket are instructions to overnight guests to present the ticket to the front desk of the hotel. The other side contains instructions to the parker to keep the ticket and that the ticket must be presented to the cashier upon leaving the parking area. The ticket states that charges are made for the use of parking space only and that appellant assumes no responsibility for loss through fire, theft, collision or otherwise to the car or its contents. The ticket states that cars are parked at the risk of the owner, and parkers are instructed to lock their vehicles.[1] The record indicates that these tickets are given solely for the purpose of measuring the time during which a vehicle is parked in order that the attendant may collect the proper charge, and that they are not given for the purpose of identifying particular vehicles.

The question of the legal relationship between the operator of a vehicle which is being parked and the operator of parking establishments has been the subject of frequent litigation in this state and elsewhere. The authorities are in conflict, and the results of the cases are varied.[2]

---

[1]   It is not insisted that the language of the ticket is sufficient to exonerate appellant, since the customer is not shown to have read it or to have had it called to his attention. See Savoy Hotel Corp. v. Sparks, 421 S.W.2d 98 (Tenn. Ct. App. 1967).

[2]   See Annot. 13 A.L.R.4th 359 (1982); 7 A.L.R.3d 927 (1966).

It is legally and theoretically possible, of course, for various legal relationships to be created by the parties, ranging from the traditional concepts of lessor-lessee, licensor-licensee, bailor-bailee, to that described in some jurisdictions as a "deposit."[3] Several courts have found difficulty with the traditional criteria of bailment in analyzing park-and-lock cases. One of the leading cases is *McGlynn v. Parking Authority of City of Newark,* 432 A.2d 99 (N.J. 1981). There the Supreme Court of New Jersey reviewed numerous decisions from within its own state and from other jurisdictions, and it concluded that it was more "useful and straightforward" to consider the possession and control elements in defining the duty of care of a garage operator to its customers than to consider them in the context of bailment. That Court concluded that the "realities" of the relationship between the parties gave rise to a duty of reasonable care on the part of operators of parking garages and parking lots. It further found that a garage owner is usually better situated to protect a parked car and to distribute the cost of protection through parking fees. It also emphasized that owners usually expect to receive their vehicles back in the same condition in which they left them and that the imposition of a duty to protect parked vehicles and their contents was consistent with that expectation. The Court went further and stated that since the owner is ordinarily absent when theft or damage occurs, the obligation to come forward with affirmative evidence of negligence could impose a difficult, if not insurmountable, burden upon him. After considering various policy considerations, which it acknowledged to be the same as those recognized by courts holding that a bailment is created, the New Jersey Court indulged or authorized a presumption of negligence from proof of damage to a car parked in an enclosed garage.

Although the New Jersey Court concluded that a more flexible and comprehensive approach could be achieved outside of traditional property concepts, Tennessee courts generally have analyzed cases such as this in terms of sufficiency of the evidence to create a bailment for hire by implication. We believe that this continues to be the majority view and the most satisfactory and realistic approach to the problem, unless the parties clearly by their conduct or by express contract create some other relationship.

The subject has been discussed in numerous previous decisions in this state. One of the leading cases is *Dispeker v. New Southern Hotel Co.,* 373 S.W.2d 904 (Tenn. 1963). In that case the guest at a hotel delivered his vehicle to a bellboy who took possession of it and parked it in a lot adjoining the hotel building. The owner kept the keys, but the car apparently was capable of being started without the ignition key. The owner apparently had told the attendant how to so operate it. Later the employee took the vehicle for his own purposes and damaged it. Under these circumstances the Court held that a bailment for hire had been

---

[3]   See Gauthier v. Allright New Orleans, Inc., 417 So.2d 375 (La. Ct. App. 1982).

created and that upon proof of misdelivery of the vehicle the bailee was liable to the customer.

In the subsequent case of *Scruggs v. Dennis*, 440 S.W.2d 20 (Tenn. 1969), upon facts practically identical to those of the instant case, the Court again held that an implied bailment contract had been created between a customer who parked and locked his vehicle in a garage. Upon entry he received a ticket dispensed by a machine, drove his automobile to the underground third level of the garage and parked. He retained his ignition key, but when he returned to retrieve the automobile in the afternoon it had disappeared. It was recovered more than two weeks later and returned to the owner in a damaged condition.

In that case the operator of the garage had several attendants on duty, but the attendants did not ordinarily operate the parked vehicles, as in the instant case.[5]

Although the Court recognized that there were some factual differences between the *Scruggs* case and that of *Dispeker v. New Southern Hotel Co.*, supra, it concluded that a bailment had been created when the owner parked his vehicle for custody and safe keeping in the parking garage, where there was limited access and where the patron had to present a ticket to an attendant upon leaving the premises. * * *

On the contrary, in the case of *Rhodes v. Pioneer Parking Lot, Inc.*, 501 S.W.2d 569 (Tenn. 1973), a bailment was found not to exist when the owner left his vehicle in an open parking lot which was wholly unattended and where he simply inserted coins into a meter, received a ticket, then parked the vehicle himself and locked it.

Denying recovery, the Court said:

> In the case at bar, however, we find no evidence to justify a finding that the plaintiff delivered his car into the custody of the defendant, nor do we find any act or conduct upon the defendant's part which would justify a reasonable person believing that an obligation of bailment had been assumed by the defendant.

501 S.W.2d at 571.

In the instant case, appellee's vehicle was not driven into an unattended or open parking area. Rather it was driven into an enclosed, indoor, attended commercial garage which not only had an attendant controlling the exit but regular security personnel to patrol the premises for safety.

Under these facts we are of the opinion that the courts below correctly concluded that a bailment for hire had been created, and that upon proof of nondelivery appellee was entitled to the statutory presumption of negligence provided in T.C.A. § 24–5–111.

---

[5] Appellant's employees occasionally parked the vehicles of patrons who were handicapped and under other unusual circumstances.

We recognize that there is always a question as to whether there has been sufficient delivery of possession and control to create a bailment when the owner locks a vehicle and keeps the keys. Nevertheless, the realities of the situation are that the operator of the garage is, in circumstances like those shown in this record, expected to provide attendants and protection. In practicality the operator does assume control and custody of the vehicles parked, limiting access thereto and requiring the presentation of a ticket upon exit. As stated previously, the attendant employed by appellant did not testify, but he told appellee's husband that the vehicle did not come out of the garage through the exit which he controlled. This testimony was not amplified, but the attendant obviously must have been in error or else must have been inattentive or away from his station. The record clearly shows that there was no other exit from which the vehicle could have been driven.

Appellant made no effort to rebut the presumption created by statute in this state (which is similar to presumptions indulged by courts in some other jurisdictions not having such statutes). While the plaintiff did not prove positive acts of negligence on the part of appellant, the record does show that some improper activity or tampering with vehicles had been called to the attention of security personnel earlier in the day of the theft in question, and that appellee's new vehicle had been removed from the garage by some person or persons unknown, either driving past an inattentive attendant or one who had absented himself from his post, there being simply no other way in which the vehicle could have been driven out of the garage.

Under the facts and circumstances of this case, we are not inclined to depart from prior decisions or to place the risk of loss upon the consuming public as against the operators of commercial parking establishments such as that conducted by appellant. We recognize that park-and-lock situations arise under many and varied factual circumstances. It is difficult to lay down one rule of law which will apply to all cases. The expectations of the parties and their conduct can cause differing legal relationships to arise, with consequent different legal results. We do not find the facts of the present case, however, to be at variance with the legal requirements of the traditional concept of a bailment for hire. In our opinion it amounted to more than a mere license or hiring of a space to park a vehicle, unaccompanied by any expectation of protection or other obligation upon the operator of the establishment.

The judgment of the courts below is affirmed at the cost of appellant. The cause will be remanded to the trial court for any further proceedings which may be necessary.

■ DROWOTA, J., dissenting. * * * Even though some courts now suggest that the theory of bailment is an archaic and inappropriate theory upon which to base liability in modern park and lock cases, the majority opinion states that "Tennessee courts generally have analyzed cases such as this in terms of sufficiency of the evidence to create a bailment for hire by implication," and concludes that this is "the most satisfactory and realistic approach to the problem." I do not disagree with the longstanding use of the bailment analysis in this type of case. I do disagree, however, with the majority's conclusion that a bailment for hire has been created in this case.

The record shows that upon entering this parking garage a ticket, showing time of entry, is automatically dispensed by a machine. The ticket states that charges are made for the use of a parking space only and that the garage assumes no responsibility for loss to the car or its contents. The ticket further states that cars are parked at the risk of the owner, and parkers are instructed to lock their vehicles. The majority opinion points out that it is not insisted that this language on the ticket is sufficient to exonerate the garage, since the customer is not shown to have read it or to have had it called to his attention. Savoy Hotel Corp. v. Sparks, 421 S.W.2d 98 (Tenn. Ct. App. 1967). The ticket in no way identifies the vehicle, it is given solely for the purpose of measuring the length of time during which the vehicle is parked in order that a proper charge may be made.

In this case Mr. Allen, without any direction or supervision, parked his car, removed his keys, and locked the car and left the parking garage having retained his ignition key. The presentation of a ticket upon exit is for the sole purpose of allowing the cashier to collect the proper charge. The cashier is not required to be on duty at all times. When no cashier is present, the exit gate is opened and no payment is required.[1] As the majority opinion states, the ticket is "not given for the purpose of identifying particular vehicles." The ticket functioned solely as a source of fee computation, not of vehicle identification.

The majority opinion states: "[W]e do not find the facts of the present case to be at variance with the legal requirements of the concept of a bailment for hire." I must disagree, for I feel the facts of the present case are clearly at variance with what I consider to be the legal requirements of the traditional concept of a bailment for hire.

Bailment has been defined by this Court in the following manner:

> The creation of a bailment in the absence of an express contract requires that possession and control over the subject matter pass from the bailor to the bailee. In order to constitute a sufficient delivery of the subject matter there must be a full transfer, either actual or constructive, of the property to the bailee so as to exclude it from the possession of the owner and all other persons and give to the bailee, for the time being, the sole custody and control thereof. See Jackson v. Metropolitan Government of Nashville, supra, Scruggs v. Dennis, 440 S.W.2d

---

[1] Between one or two in the morning and six or seven a.m., the garage is entirely open without a cashier to collect parking fees. During the day if the cashier leaves his or her post on a break, the exit gate is opened and the vehicle owner may exit without payment.

20 (Tenn. 1969); Old Hickory Parking Corp. v. Alloway, 177 S.W.2d 23 (Tenn. Ct. App. 1944). See generally, 8 Am.Jur.2d 960–61.

In parking lot and parking garage situations, a bailment is created where the operator of the lot or garage has knowingly and voluntarily assumed control, possession, or custody of the motor vehicle; if he has not done so, there may be a mere license to park or a lease of parking space. See, e.g., Lewis v. Ebersole, 12 So.2d 543 (Ala. 1943); Southeastern Fair Association v. Ford, 14 S.E.2d 139 (Ga. Ct. App. 1941).

Rhodes v. Pioneer Parking Lot, Inc., 501 S.W.2d 569, 570 (Tenn. 1973).

From its earliest origins, the most distinguishing factor identifying a bailment has been delivery. Our earliest decisions also recognize acceptance as a necessary factor, requiring that possession and control of the property pass from bailor to bailee, to the exclusion of control by others. The test thus becomes whether the operator of the vehicle has made such a delivery to the operator of the parking facility as to amount to a relinquishment of his exclusive possession, control, and dominion over the vehicle so that the latter can exclude it from the possession of all others. If so, a bailment has been created.

When the automobile began replacing the horse and buggy, our courts allowed bailment law to carry over and govern the parking of vehicles. * * * [C]ases involving parking attendants and personalized service have caused us no problems. The problem arises in this modern era of automated parking, when courts have attempted to expand the limits of existing areas of the law to encompass technological and commercial advances. Such is the case of *Scruggs v. Dennis*, 440 S.W.2d 20 (Tenn. 1969), relied upon in the majority opinion. In *Scruggs*, as in this case, the entire operation is automated, with the exception of payment upon departure. The operation bears little, if any, resemblance to the circumstances found in *Old Hickory Parking Corp.*, *Savoy Hotel*, and *Dispeker*. Yet the Court in *Scruggs*, in quoting extensively from the *Dispeker* opinion, states that "There are some minute differences of fact. . . ." Id., 440 S.W.2d at 22. As pointed out above, the differences of fact in *Dispeker* are not minute or so similar as the *Scruggs* court would suggest. Delivery, custody and control are clearly present in *Dispeker*. I fail to find such delivery, custody and control in *Scruggs* or in the case at bar. In *Dispeker*, the vehicle was actually taken from the owner by an attendant. I believe the *Scruggs* court and the majority opinion today attempt to apply bailment law in situations where there is not a true bailment relationship. * * *

The majority opinion, as did the *Scruggs* court, finds custody and control implied because of the limited access and because "the presentation of a ticket upon exit" is required. I cannot agree with this analysis as creating a bailment situation. I do not believe that based upon the fact that a ticket was required to be presented upon leaving, that this factor created a proper basis upon which to find a bailment relationship. The ticket did not identify the vehicle or the operator of the vehicle, as do most bailment receipts. The cashier was not performing the traditional bailee role or identifying and returning a particular article, but instead was merely computing the amount owed and accepting payment due for use of a parking space. I do not believe the Defendant exercised such possession and control over Plaintiff's automobile as is necessary in an implied bailment. * * *

Plaintiff parked his car, locked it and retained the key. Certainly Defendant cannot be said to have sole custody of Plaintiff's vehicle, for Defendant could not move it, did not know to whom it belonged, and did not know when it would be reclaimed or by whom. Anyone who manually obtained a ticket from the dispenser could drive out with any vehicle he was capable of operating. Also, a cashier was not always on duty. When on duty, so long as the parking fee was paid—by what means could the Defendant reasonably exercise control? The necessary delivery and relinquishment of control by the Plaintiff, the very basis upon which the bailment theory was developed, is missing.

We should realize that the circumstances upon which the principles of bailment law were established and developed are not always applicable to the operation of the modern day automated parking facility. The element of delivery, of sole custody and control are lacking in this case.

NOTES AND QUESTIONS

1. As *Allen* illustrates, many activities in modern life involve more than one category of property relationship—in this case, the Allens and the hotel have entered into both a license agreement and (perhaps) a bailment agreement. As in the present case, selecting the proper category with which to analyze the case can have a pronounced influence on the outcome. There are no fixed rules for deciding which rubric is correct. It is mostly a matter of "fit," which is determined by looking at all the circumstances and the way similar cases have been categorized in the past. Did the court perform the classificatory analysis correctly in this case, based on the prior decisions the opinions discuss?

2. Why not resolve all these disputes by contract? Note that no one seems to take the language printed on the ticket in this case seriously—in contrast to the court in *ProCD*, which upheld the detailed provisions in the shrinkwrap license against various claims that it should not be binding. The problem with using contract to determine the rights and duties associated with various daily events like parking a car, checking a coat, dropping off clothing at the dry cleaners, and so forth is that few people have time to "shop around" and compare the various disclaimers or guarantees that bailees are offering about risk of loss and other potential casualty events. A typical consumer will remain "rationally ignorant" of these details, because the value of the bailed item, discounted by the probability of a theft or accident occurring, does not warrant spending much if any time comparing different standard-form-contract offerings. Of course, consumers may rely on other

clues about the bailee, such as past experience with the bailee, the bailee's reputation in the community, or whether the bailee has a prominent brand name. But even so, there remains a case for imposing a degree of standardization on these relationships through "property" rules that are either nondisclaimable or that can be disclaimed only through very prominent disclosure. If you think standardization makes sense, who should do the standardizing? The courts, through episodic common-law rulings as in the present case? A regulatory agency established for this purpose? A trade association of bailees?

3.   If the Hyatt Regency in Nashville wants to modify the outcome in this case by contract, so that it does not face liability for auto theft in the future, what would you advise it to do?

The Bailee's Duty of Care

One longstanding matter of doctrinal controversy has been the duty of care that the bailee owes to the bailor. Suppose, for example, that the property is lost, stolen, or destroyed while in the custody of the bailee. By what standard do we determine whether the bailee is liable to the bailor for the value of the property that was the subject of the bailment?

The early common law apparently took the position that the bailee's liability to the bailor for lost, stolen, or destroyed goods was absolute. This was perhaps based on the understanding that the contract between the bailor and bailee called for the return of the goods when the purpose of the bailment was realized, and if the bailee failed to return the good, the bailee had violated the parties' understanding. But this rule seemed harsh in many circumstances, and so in *Coggs v. Bernard*, 92 Eng. Rep. 107 (K.B. 1703), Chief Justice Holt undertook to restate the law. His restatement, which was borrowed from the thirteenth-century writer Bracton, who in return borrowed from the Romans, consisted of a complicated six-fold classification of bailments, with different standards of care for each. Few traces of this effort remain today. More influential was Justice Story's effort in his treatise on bailments, which offered a more simplified set of rules:

> When the bailment is for the sole benefit of the bailor, the law requires only slight diligence on the part of the bailee, and of course makes him answerable only for gross neglect. When the bailment is for the sole benefit of the bailee, the law requires great diligence on the part of the bailee, and makes him responsible for slight neglect. When the bailment is reciprocally beneficial to both parties, the law requires ordinary diligence on the part of the bailee, and makes him responsible for ordinary neglect.

Joseph Story, Commentaries on the Law of Bailments § 3, at 27 (9th ed. 1878).

More recently, commentators have urged even greater simplification, advocating a universal standard of "reasonable care" for all bailments. See Kurt Philip Autor, Note, Bailment Liability: Toward a Standard of Reasonable Care, 61 S. Cal. L. Rev. 2117 (1988). In determining whether the bailee exercised reasonable care, such a standard would take into account all the circumstances surrounding the bailment relationship, including whether the bailee received compensation or whether the bailment was for the benefit of the bailee. A survey of modern bailment cases undertaken by Professor Helmholz, however, casts doubt on whether courts in fact apply such a uniform standard of reasonable care. R.H. Helmholz, Bailment Theories and the Liability of Bailees: The Elusive Uniform Standard of Reasonable Care, 41 Kan. L. Rev. 97 (1992). Recent surveys confirm this. See 9 Cal. Jur. 3d Bailments § 28 (updated 2022) (California continues to have a shifting standard of care depending on the type of bailment); 46 Am. Jur. Proof of Facts 3d 361, § 5 (updated 2022) (standard of care depends on the circumstances and varies from slight, to ordinary, to great care).

One complication is that since the relationship between the bailor and bailee is a contractual one, the standard of care can be modified by agreement between the parties before the bailment commences. Attempts to do this are quite common, as when restaurants post signs in coat check rooms disclaiming any liability for items left there, or, as in the *Allen* case, a parking garage prints a disclaimer of liability on the back of the parking ticket dispensed by machine upon entry. Whether these efforts at modifying the standard of care are successful is open to question.

Another complication is that courts seem to be stricter about bailees who misdeliver goods—that is, when they turn the goods over to someone other than the true owner—than they are when the goods are lost, stolen, or destroyed while being held in the custody of the bailee for return to the true owner. Consider, in this light, the following case.

Cowen v. Pressprich
Supreme Court, Appellate Term, New York, 1922.
192 N.Y.S. 242.

■ MULLAN, J. Conversion, for the defendants' alleged wrongful delivery of a bond. The parties on both sides are stock exchange brokers. Plaintiffs had agreed to sell and deliver to defendants a bond of the Oregon Short Line Railroad of the par value of $1,000. To fill that order, plaintiffs ordered the bond from a third bond house, and the latter, by mistake, sent plaintiffs an Oregon & California Railroad bond, and plaintiffs, also by mistake, sent this Oregon & California bond to defendants. There is no controversy as to the manner of the sending. Plaintiffs handed the Oregon & California bond to Goldberg, a youth of 17 years, who was one of plaintiffs' two messengers, or "runners," as they seem to be called. With the bond was a memorandum (also called "slip" or "statement") briefly describing an Oregon Short Line bond. The bond and slip were inclosed together in an envelope. Goldberg took the envelope to defendants' place of business in a Wall Street office building. Defendants' suite of offices had two entrance doors from the office building hall, one for general use, and the other for persons, such as Goldberg, making deliveries. Goldberg entered at the latter door, and was then in a tiny outside room, described as about two feet by six feet. There was no door for passage between this small outside room and an inside, and presumably larger, room. Deliveries were made by dropping papers in a slot in one of the partitions partly forming this small outer room. Above the slot was a window of opaque glass that swung inwards. That window was kept closed unless or until the person acting for defendants at the delivery window should desire to talk to one making a delivery, when he would open the window. Next to the partition containing that slot and window, and in the inner room, was a desk at which was kept seated either a member of defendants' firm or a clerk. At the time here in question there were two persons at that desk, Mr. Quackenbush, of the defendants' firm, and an employee, one Campbell.

Goldberg dropped the envelope through the slot. His testimony was:

I waited until he [the person at the desk] took it in, and then I left. * * * I told him I will call back for a check. Q. Why didn't you ask for the receipt? A. Well, I was in a hurry; I had many deliveries that day, and I had to make them. * * * Q. How long would you say you were in that delivery room in front of that delivery window—from the time you put the bond in until you left? A. It was from a minute to a minute and a half.

Goldberg could not recall whether the person at the other side of the window said anything. He thought, but was not sure, that there was "somebody" else in the little outside room when he was there. It does not appear from Goldberg's testimony whether or not the delivery window was open during any part of his stay while making the delivery. Mr. Quackenbush testified as follows:

Q. Will you tell us what took place at the time of that delivery. A. It was about 10:30 in the morning. Mr. Campbell and myself stood there making up our loans, when a bond shoots through the window like a streak of lightning; it goes right down my desk—that was my desk about the width of this table (indicating stenographer's table)—right down in front of us. As it rolls over, I opened it up; just pulled the bond open that way instantly (indicating). The statement called for an Oregon Short Line five bond; I could see immediately that the bond was an Oregon & California, and we handle thousands of them. Q. What did you do then? A. I immediately opened the window. Q. Where was that; right in front of you? A. Right like that (indicating), and I yelled "Cowen." A young man steps right up, and I says, "Make your statement agree with the bond." The Court: Sir? The Witness: "Make your statement agree with the bond." He mumbled, "Alright," and takes the bond and goes out immediately like that. Q. And he took it? A. He took it. Q. When you say man ___ A. A young boy 19 or 20 years old. Q. What did you do then; close the window? A. Closed the window; went about my work. Q. You were expecting from Cowen & Co. at that time a Short Line bond, were you not? A. Yes; we had purchased one, looking for it. Q. You were looking for it? A. Yes; some day. Q. And you say you instantly found it was not ___ A. It was not more than 15 seconds. Q. And you were under no contract to purchase from Cowen & Co. a California bond? A. No, sir. Q. How long would you say it took between the time that bond came into your slot on to your desk and the time you opened the window and yelled "Cowen"? A. Not a second more than 15. Q. Fifteen seconds? A. Not a second more than that. Q. When you opened the window where did the boy come? A. To my left from the main door. Q. You heard the Goldberg boy testify, did you not, that when he put that bond into your window, he waited about a minute and a half; is that correct? A. I will say no. Q. Did you hear him say anything? A. Nothing. Q. The only thing you know is seeing the bond shoot into the window. A. Exactly. Q. Was there a receipt on that bond to be signed by you? A. No, sir; it was not. Q. It was merely a sale memorandum? A. Exactly. Q. Neither one of them is the young man to whom you delivered the bond? A. No, sir. Q. You delivered the bond to some one else? A. Neither one of those [plaintiffs'] boys.

Mr. Campbell substantially corroborated Mr. Quackenbush's version.

Concededly the boy to whom Quackenbush returned the bond delivered by Goldberg was not Goldberg, but some unidentified boy who made away with the bond. The bond was of the bearer type, fully negotiable.

The defendants have refused to make good the plaintiffs' loss, contending that they were chargeable only with due diligence, and that, accepting the version of the plaintiffs as given by Goldberg, it appears that they exercised all the care required of them. The plaintiffs contend that there was an absolute obligation on the part of the defendants to redeliver the bond to the plaintiffs, and that no question of negligence enters into the case. They also argue that, if the negligence question does enter, there was sufficient evidence to warrant a finding that the defendants did not, in fact, exercise due care. The learned trial judge did not state the ground of his decision in plaintiffs' favor.

A person who has been put, through no act or fault of his own, in such a situation as that in which the defendants were put upon the delivery to them of the wrong bond, has come to be known as "involuntary bailee" * * * or constructive or quasi bailee.

In the field of voluntary bailments, whether they be for hire or be otherwise coupled with an interest on the part of the bailee, or whether they be merely gratuitous, no rule is better settled than that it is the duty of the bailee to deliver the bailed article to the right person, and that delivery to the wrong person is not capable of being excused by any possible showing of care or good faith or innocence.

Such distinctions as have been drawn between the duties of voluntary bailees for compensation and voluntary gratuitous bailees relate solely to the degree of care the bailee should exercise in respect of the custody of the thing bailed. In respect of delivery to the proper person, no such distinction is drawn; the duty in both cases is absolute.

What, then, is the difference, if any, between the duty of a voluntary gratuitous bailee and that of a wholly involuntary bailee? There is an astonishing paucity of decision and text opinion upon the subject. I think, however, that all that can be found upon it points to the conclusion that the involuntary bailee, as long as his lack of volition continues, is not under the slightest duty to care for or guard the subject of the bailment, and cannot be held, in respect of custody, for what would even be the grossest negligence in the case of a voluntary bailment, but that, in case the involuntary bailee shall exercise any dominion over the thing so bailed, he becomes as responsible as if he were a voluntary bailee. * * *

I have reached the conclusion that while, at first blush, it may seem to be imposing upon the defendants an unduly severe rule of conduct to hold them to an absolute liability, the rule is no more severe than the occasion calls for. * * * The defendants could easily have protected themselves by telephoning the plaintiffs that the wrong bond had been delivered, or they could have sent the bond back to the plaintiffs by one of their own messengers. Instead, they chose to take chance of delivering it to the wrong messenger. As the delivery window was closed when the bond was dropped through the slot, and remained closed for an appreciable time, they could not have known what messenger had made the delivery. * * *

The plaintiffs, as has already been mentioned, urge that, if the defendants are not to be held in conversion, they are, at least, liable in negligence. The action, however, was brought in conversion, and both sides insist that it was tried as a conversion action. The judgment therefore may only be sustained, if at all, upon that theory. * * *

Judgment affirmed, with $25 costs, with leave to defendants to appeal to the Appellate Division.

■ BURR, J. (concurring). I concur in the conclusion reached by MR. JUSTICE MULLAN and vote to affirm. I believe that defendants, having received the bond and taken it into their possession, became liable even as gratuitous or involuntary bailees for its proper redelivery to the true owner.

■ LEHMAN, J. (dissenting). I agree in all material particulars with the statement of facts contained in the opinion of MR. JUSTICE MULLAN. * * *

It is unnecessary now to consider whether the complaint sufficiently sets forth any cause of action; for no motion was made by the defendants to dismiss the complaint on the ground of insufficiency, and no such point is raised on this appeal. It is to be noted, however, that the complaint does not allege any negligence on the part of the defendants, and I agree with Mr. Justice MULLAN that no such issue was litigated, and that the judgment can be sustained only if, as a matter of law, the defendants' mistake in returning the bond to the wrong messenger constituted a conversion of the bond or at least a breach of an implied agreement on their part to return the bond only to the plaintiffs.

While the slot in the window constituted an invitation to deliver at that place securities intended for the defendants, it is evident that it constituted an invitation only to deliver securities which the defendants were under some obligation to receive. Obviously no person could by slipping in other securities impose upon the defendants without their consent any affirmative obligation to care for these securities, to pay for them, or even to receive them. The plaintiffs never intended to deliver to the defendants an Oregon & California Railroad bond. By their mistake the plaintiffs divested themselves of possession of the bond, but they did not transfer to the defendants either title or right to possession if they demanded the return of the bond. The defendants had not consented to accept the bond as a deposit, they claimed no title to it, and they were not subject to any trust or obligation as bailees, for a bailment arises only through an express or implied contract. They were put in possession of the bond without any agreement on their part, express or implied, to accept the deposit of the bond; and, though persons who come into possession of the property of others without their consent are sometimes for convenience called "involuntary" or "quasi bailees," they incur no responsibility to the true owner in respect thereof. It is only where they commit some "overt act" of interference with the property that an implied contract of bailment is created. * * *

In the present case the defendants were put in possession of the bond by mistake; they discovered the mistake promptly, and thereafter they committed no "overt act" of interference with the bond except that they attempted to divest themselves of this possession by delivering the bond to a person whom they believed to be the messenger of the plaintiffs. That act was not only consistent with the continued title and right of dominion in the plaintiffs, but was an honest attempt to restore possession to the true owners. It certainly cannot be contended that the defendants were bound at their peril to wait until the plaintiffs came to their office and physically took away their property; they could take proper steps to divest themselves of the possession thrust upon them by mistake without thereby impliedly agreeing, contrary to their clear intention, to accept possession as bailees with the consequent obligations flowing from such relation. It is quite immaterial whether we call these defendants bailees or not if we keep in mind the fact that the possession of these goods was thrust upon them by mistake of the plaintiffs and without their invitation or consent, and that therefore any liability for failure to return the goods to the true owner upon demand must be the result of some act voluntarily done by the defendant thereafter. An attempt to return the bond to the true owner or to the person who delivered it cannot be considered as inconsistent with a recognition of the complete ownership and right of dominion by the true owner, and certainly shows no intent to accept the possession thrust upon the defendants by plaintiffs' mistake, and I fail to see how, in the absence of such elements, any implied contract of bailment can arise. If in making an attempt to return the goods, which was lawful and proper in itself, the defendants used means which were not reasonable and proper, and as a result thereof the goods were lost or misdelivered, then the defendants would be liable for negligence or possibly for conversion, for every man is responsible for his own acts; but, if the defendants had a right to divest themselves of possession and attempt to return the goods, then, in the absence of some obligation resting upon contract to deliver the goods only to the true owner or upon his order, I do not see how the mere fact that through innocent mistake the defendants handed the bond to the wrong messenger could constitute a conversion. The defendants could not properly disregard entirely the mistake in the delivery of the bonds. Common courtesy and prudence, if not the law, certainly placed upon them the duty to take some steps by which the plaintiffs would be apprised of their mistake and enabled to regain their property. The defendants might have placed the bond in a safe and telephoned to the plaintiffs to call for the bond, but they were under the impression that the messenger who delivered the bond was still present, and they gave the bond to him as a means of carrying out their evident duty to apprise the plaintiffs of their error and revest possession in them. * * *

Liability in law must in all cases be founded either on contract or on some wrongful act. The defendants in this case promptly evinced their intention not to accept the possession of the bond thrust upon them by mistake; they merely attempted to divest themselves of this possession, and certainly from such attempt no agreement to accept this possession can be implied. Until that time the defendants were under no obligation either to accept the bond as bailees or return it upon demand to the true owners unless at the time of the demand the bond was still in their possession; and it seems to me anomalous and illogical to say that an absolute obligation to return the bond to the plaintiffs, and not to deliver it to any other person, arises merely from the fact that the defendants did by mistake and through an honest disclaimer of any title or right of possession in the bond physically deliver it to another. They claimed no title and no right to possession in the bond; they attempted to transfer no title or right of possession of their own in the bond; they had physical possession of the bond through plaintiffs' mistake; and they transferred nothing but this physical possession. The plaintiffs could not compel them to retain physical possession, and their act of transferring physical possession even to a stranger under these circumstances shows no exercise of any dominion over the property, for it constitutes no denial of the complete and sole right of dominion in the plaintiffs. In my opinion plaintiffs have therefore no right of action against the defendants unless the means which the defendants used to rid themselves of their possession were not reasonable and proper. * * *

Even if under these pleadings we could consider the question of negligence, I find no evidence upon this question to sustain a judgment in favor of the plaintiffs. There is no doubt that the defendants acted in good faith and in the honest belief that they were handing back the bond to the messenger who delivered it. They had assumed no obligation of any kind to the plaintiffs; any act they performed was for the plaintiffs' benefit, and it was through plaintiffs' mistake that they were called upon to act at all in the premises. Doubtless, if they had foreseen the possibility of mistake, they would not have delivered the bond to the wrong messenger; but it was not unreasonable to suppose that the messenger might be waiting or that, if he had left, no thief would be in the office who would claim to represent the plaintiffs. They probably committed an error of judgment, but for such error they cannot be held liable. Since they owed no obligation to the plaintiffs and acted in good faith under the reasonable belief that they were returning the bond to the messenger who delivered it, I see no ground for imposing upon them liability for the loss of a bond which would never have been lost but for the plaintiffs' mistake, due apparently to the plaintiffs' negligence. * * *

For these reasons, it seems to me that the judgment should be reversed, with costs, and the complaint dismissed, with costs.

Cowen v. Pressprich

Supreme Court, Appellate Division, New York, 1922.
194 N.Y.S. 926.

Determination appealed from and judgment of the Municipal Court reversed, with costs to the appellants in this court and in the Appellate Term, and judgment ordered, for defendants, dismissing the complaint, with costs, upon the dissenting opinion of Lehman, J., at the Appellate Term. Order filed.

NOTES AND QUESTIONS

1. One general issue raised by *Cowen* is whether a bailment can ever be created when there is no contract—no meeting of the minds—between the bailor and the bailee. Esteemed commentators have long disagreed about this. Blackstone and Story both maintained that there could be no bailment without a contract. See 2 William Blackstone, Commentaries on the Laws of England *452–54; Joseph Story, Commentaries on the Law of Bailments § 2, at 5 (James Schouler ed., 9th ed. 1878). But other commentators have argued that bailment relationships can arise in contexts, like the finding of lost

property, where no contract exists between the bailor and bailee. See 9 Samuel Williston, A Treatise on the Law of Contracts § 1030, at 875 (Walter H.E. Jaeger ed., 3d ed. 1967); William King Laidlaw, Principles of Bailment, 16 Cornell L. Q. 286, 287 (1931). To a certain extent this dispute is terminological. If different duties of care attach to someone who is a "true" bailee (based on contract) and an "involuntary" or "constructive" bailee (where there is no contract), then we can speak of Type I and Type II bailments, or of bailments and something else, like "custodial obligations." If some duty of care attaches to a person who takes up custody of property he knows belongs to another, but with whom he has no contractual relationship, what is the source of this duty? Must these duties be grounded in some conception of the nature of property rights? See Christopher Newman, Bailment and the Property/Contract Interface (September 2, 2015), available at http://ssrn.com/abstract=2654988.

2.   In *Cowen*, the court was required to sort out two issues. First, what sort of duty of care attaches to a firm that acquires temporary custody of a bond by mistake? Second, does the rule of strict liability that applies to a bailee who misdelivers a bailed good to a third party, as opposed to losing or damaging a good while it is in its custody, apply to such a firm? The categories the court has to work with—"bailee", "involuntary bailee," "stranger"—do not seem to be nuanced enough to allow the court to come up with a satisfactory resolution.

3.   Does it make sense to treat a securities firm that receives the wrong bond by mistake from a firm with which it has regular dealings as being subject to the same standard of care as someone who finds a ring on the sidewalk? (Finders are typically regarded as "involuntary bailees.") Surely, given the relationship between the firms and their frequent interaction, one would expect the firm that receives the bond by mistake to take reasonable steps to secure the bond and ensure that it makes it back safely to the sending firm. It is not clear that one would expect the same degree of diligence on the part of a mere finder, who has no clue about the identity of the true owner.

4.   Why are bailees subject to strict liability for misdelivery, but only subject to a duty of reasonable care for lost, stolen, or destroyed goods? The doctrinal answer is that bailors sued bailees for conversion in cases of misdelivery, and conversion imposes strict liability on one who converts or permits another to convert property belonging to someone else. Bailors sued bailees for trespass on the case in instances involving lost, stolen, or destroyed goods, and this action came to require proof of negligence. Otherwise, commentators have found the distinction difficult to justify:

> The difference cannot be explained in terms of the degree of harm to the bailor. The bailor loses the property in either case. Indeed, the loss is if anything *less* severe in the case of misdelivery, because there is some chance that the property can be recovered from the third party who has erroneously received it.

> The higher standard of care that traditionally applies to misdelivery begins to make more sense, however, once we realize that misdelivery is a * * * situation that entails * * * the

introduction of the * * * third party. The rule of strict liability seeks to correct for the unequal information between the bailor and the bailee about the risk of transfer to a third party.

Thomas W. Merrill & Henry E. Smith, The Property/Contract Interface, 101 Colum. L. Rev. 773, 816 (2001). The authors also note that "[b]ecause misdelivery confers a benefit on a third party, the bailee may be tempted to connive with a third party to 'misdeliver' the property, and it will be difficult for the bailor to prove that this has happened." Id. at 815.

The Winkfield

Court of Appeal (Eng.), 1901.
[1902] P. 42, [1902–1903] All E.R. 346.

On April 5, 1900, a collision occurred in a fog off Table Bay, on the coast of Cape Colony, South Africa, between the Government transport *Winkfield,* belonging to the Seafield Shipping Company, Limited, outward bound to the Cape with troops for service in South Africa, and the Union mail steam vessel *Mexican* from Cape Town, homeward bound to Southampton with mails, passengers, and cargo. The *Winkfield* was damaged and the *Mexican* sank, but not until all the passengers, crew, and some of the mails and luggage of the *Mexican* had been got on board the other vessel.

The owners, master, and crew of the *Mexican* and the owners of the *Winkfield* commenced cross-actions, which resulted in the owners of the *Winkfield* admitting liability for a moiety of the damage sustained by the *Mexican.* * * *

■ COLLINS, MASTER OF THE ROLLS. This is an appeal from the order of Sir Francis Jeune dismissing a motion made on behalf of the Postmaster-General in the case of the *Winkfield*.

The question arises out of a collision which occurred on April 5, 1900, between the steamship *Mexican* and the steamship *Winkfield*, and which resulted in the loss of the former with a portion of the mails which she was carrying at the time.

The owners of the *Winkfield* under a decree limiting liability to 32,514 £ 17s. 10d. paid that amount into court, and the claim in question was one by the Postmaster-General on behalf of himself and the Postmasters-General of Cape Colony and Natal to recover out of that sum the value of letters, parcels, & c., in his custody as bailee and lost on board the *Mexican*.

The case was dealt with by all parties in the Court below as a claim by a bailee who was under no liability to his bailor for the loss in question, as to which it was admitted that the authority of *Claridge v. South Staffordshire Tramway Co.*, [1892] 1 Q. B. 422, was conclusive, and the President accordingly, without argument and in deference to that authority, dismissed the claim. The Postmaster-General now appeals.

Figure 4-7
The *Mexican*

UNION R.M.S. *MEXICAN*, 1883
Sunk in collision near Capetown, 1900

Source: Marischal Murray, Ships and South Africa (1933).

The question for decision, therefore, is whether *Claridge's Case* was well decided. * * * For the reasons which I am about to state I am of opinion that *Claridge's Case* was wrongly decided, and that the law is that in an action against a stranger for loss of goods caused by his negligence, the bailee in possession can recover the value of the goods, although he would have had a good answer to an action by the bailor for damages for the loss of the thing bailed.

It seems to me that the position, that possession is good against a wrongdoer and that the latter cannot set up the jus tertii unless he claims under it, is well established in our law, and really concludes this case against the respondents. As I shall shew presently, a long series of authorities establishes this in actions of trover and trespass at the suit of a possessor. And the principle being the same, it follows that he can equally recover the whole value of the goods in an action on the case for their loss through the tortious conduct of the defendant. I think it involves this also, that the wrongdoer who is not defending under the title of the bailor is quite unconcerned with what the rights are between the bailor and bailee, and must treat the possessor as the owner of the goods for all purposes quite irrespective of the rights and obligations as between him and the bailor.

I think this position is well established in our law, though it may be that reasons for its existence have been given in some of the cases which are not quite satisfactory. I think also that the obligation of the bailee to the bailor to account for what he has received in respect of the destruction or conversion of the thing bailed has been admitted so often in decided cases that it cannot now be questioned; and, further, I think it can be shewn that the right of the bailee to recover cannot be rested on the ground suggested in some of the cases, namely, that he was liable over to the bailor for the loss of the goods converted or destroyed.

It cannot be denied that since the case of *Armory v. Delamirie*, 1 Stra. 504, not to mention earlier cases from the Year Books onward, a mere finder may recover against a wrongdoer the full value of the thing converted. That decision involves the principle that as between possessor and wrongdoer the presumption of law is, in the words of Lord Campbell in *Jeffries v. Great Western Ry. Co.*, 5 E. & B. 802 [119 Eng. Rep. 680 (Q.B. 1856)], at p. 806, "that the person who has possession has the property." In the same case he says at p. 805: "I am of opinion that the law is that a person possessed of goods as his property has a good title as against every stranger, and that one who takes them from him, having no title in himself, is a wrongdoer, and cannot defend himself by shewing that there was title in some third person, for against a wrongdoer possession is title. * * * " Therefore it is not open to the defendant, being a wrongdoer, to inquire into the nature or limitation of the possessor's right, and unless it is competent for him to do so the question of his relation to, or liability towards, the true owner cannot come into the discussion at all; and, therefore, as between those two parties full damages have to be paid without any further inquiry. The extent of the liability of the finder to the true owner not being relevant to the discussion between him and the wrongdoer, the facts which would ascertain it would not have been admissible in evidence, and therefore the right of the finder to recover full damages cannot be made to depend upon the extent of his liability over to the true owner. To hold otherwise would, it seems to me, be in effect to permit a wrongdoer to set up a jus tertii under which he cannot claim.

But, if this be the fact in the case of a finder, why should it not be equally the fact in the case of a bailee? Why, as against a wrongdoer, should the nature of the plaintiff's interest in the thing converted be any more relevant to the inquiry, and therefore admissible in evidence, than in the case of a finder? It seems to me that neither in one case nor the other ought it to be competent for the defendant to go into evidence on that matter. * * *

The ground of the decision in *Claridge's Case* was that the plaintiff in that case, being under no liability to his bailor, could recover no damages, and though for the reasons I have already given I think this position is untenable, it is necessary to follow it out a little further. There is no doubt that the reason given in *Heydon and Smith's Case*, 13 Co. Rep. 67, 69, 77 Eng. Rep. 1476, 1479–80 (K.B. 1611)—and itself drawn from the Year Books—has been repeated in many subsequent cases. The words are these:

> Clearly, the bailee, or he who hath a special property, shall have a general action of trespass against a stranger, and shall recover all in damages because that he is chargeable over.

It is now well established that the bailee is accountable, as stated in the passage cited and repeated in many subsequent cases. But whether the obligation to account was a condition of his right to sue, or only an incident arising upon his recovery of damages, is a very different question, though it was easy to confound one view with the other.

Holmes C.J. in his admirable lectures on the Common Law, in the chapter devoted to bailments, traces the origin of the bailee's right to sue and recover the whole value of chattels converted, and arrives at the clear conclusion that the bailee's obligation to account arose from the fact that he was originally the only person who could sue, though afterwards by an extension, not perhaps quite logical, the right to sue was conceded to the bailor also. He says at p. 167: "At first the bailee was answerable to the owner because he was the only person who could sue; now it was said he could sue because he was answerable to the owner." * * * This inversion, as he points out, is traceable through the Year Books, and has survived into modern times, though, as he shews, it has not been acted upon. Pollock and Maitland's History of English Law, vol. 2, p. 170, puts the position thus:—"Perhaps we come nearest to historical truth if we say that between the two old rules there was no logical priority. The bailee had the action because he was liable, and was liable because he had the action." It may be that in early times the obligation of the bailee to the bailor was absolute, that is to say, he was an insurer. But long after the decision of *Coggs v. Bernard*, 2 Ld. Raym. 909, 92 Eng. Rep. 107 (Q.B. 1703), which classified the obligations of bailees, the bailee has, nevertheless, been allowed to recover full damages against a wrongdoer, where the facts would have afforded a complete answer for him against his bailor. The cases above cited are instances of this. In each of them the bailee would have had a good answer to an action by his bailor; for in none of them was it suggested that the act of the wrongdoer was traceable to negligence on the part of the bailee. I think, therefore, that the statement drawn, as I have said, from the Year Books may be explained, as Holmes C.J. explains it, but whether that be the true view of it or not, it is clear that it has not been treated as law in our Courts.

Upon this, before the decision in *Claridge's Case*, there was a strong body of opinion in text-books, English and American, in favour of the bailee's unqualified right to sue the wrongdoer * * * The bailee's right to recover has been affirmed in several American cases entirely without reference to the extent of the bailee's liability to the bailor for the tort, though his obligation to account is admitted * * * [T]he root principle of the whole discussion is that, as against a wrongdoer, possession is title. The chattel that has been converted or damaged is deemed to be the chattel of the possessor and of no other, and therefore its loss or deterioration is his loss, and to him, if he demands it, it must be recouped. His obligation to account to the bailor is really not ad rem in the discussion. It only comes in after he has carried his legal position to its logical consequence against a wrongdoer, and serves to soothe a mind disconcerted by the notion that a person who is not himself the complete owner should be entitled to receive back the full value of the chattel converted or destroyed. There is no inconsistency between the two positions; the one is the complement of the other. As between bailee and stranger possession gives title—that is, not a limited interest, but absolute and complete ownership, and he is entitled to receive back a complete equivalent for the whole loss or deterioration of the thing itself. As between bailor and bailee the real interests of each must be inquired into, and, as the bailee has to account for the thing bailed, so he must account for that which has become its equivalent and now represents it. What he has received above his own interest he has received to the use of his bailor. The wrongdoer, having once paid full damages to the bailee, has an answer to any action by the bailor.

The liability by the bailee to account is also well established—see the passage from Lord Coke, and the cases cited in the earlier part of this judgment—and therefore it seems to me that there is no such preponderance of convenience in favour of limiting the right of the bailee as to make it desirable, much less obligatory, upon us to modify the law as it rested upon the authorities antecedent to *Claridge's Case.* * * * *Claridge's Case* was treated as open to question by the late Master of the Rolls in *Meux v. Great Eastern Ry. Co.*, 2 Q. B. 387 (1895), and, with the greatest deference to the eminent judges who decided it, it seems to me that it cannot be supported. It seems to have been argued before them upon very scanty materials. Before us the whole subject has been elaborately discussed, and all, or nearly all, the authorities brought before us in historical sequence.

NOTES AND QUESTIONS

1. *The Winkfield* is significant in rejecting the *jus tertii* defense in the context of a bailment. The owners of the Winkfield are liable in tort. Tort damages are supposed to serve a deterrent as well as a compensatory function. Should the immunity of the Postmaster have any effect on the level of care taken by the operators of the Winkfield? If the crew of the Winkfield had acted recklessly or even willfully, they should presumably be liable for punitive damages. To whom?

2. The court broadly hints that after this case, the Postmaster will hold the funds subject to claims by customers; there will be some way around the Postmaster's immunity. Would the Postmaster be liable to its customers in restitution (see Part C)? What if only 80% of the customers (the bailors) file claims? (In a similar vein, the postal customers theoretically could have sued the Winkfield directly. W. Prosser, Handbook of the Law of Torts § 15, at 96 (4th ed. 1971). There are, however, significant practical obstacles where many customers have a small claim.) If fewer than all customers file claims, leaving some of the damages in the hands of the Postmaster, would such a windfall to the Postmaster call into question the result in the case?

3. What if the bailee is a private shipping company that is liable to the bailor for contract damages? According to the leading case of *Hadley v. Baxendale*, 156 Eng. Rep. 145 (Ex. 1854), the shipper is liable only for foreseeable damages, and if the customer would like damages for an especially valuable package, the customer must reveal the value to the

shipper. Tortfeasors like the Winkfield, on the other hand, are normally liable for any foreseeable damage caused by their negligence. But wasn't damage to the Mexican foreseeable, with the value of the cargo merely going to the size of the damages? So if a particularly valuable package were on the Mexican, would the Winkfield be liable for the full damages even though the shipping company would be liable only for reasonably foreseeable damages, in the contract sense? Should the Winkfield be able to limit its liability under *Hadley*? Assuming that it cannot, should the shipper be able to keep the difference, or should it be liable in restitution to the less-than-forthcoming customer?

3. ABANDONMENT AND DESTRUCTION

Owner sovereignty is also commonly thought to include the right to abandon property (throw it away or relinquish all claim to title) and the right to destroy property (demolish, burn, or otherwise eliminate all or most of its value). This makes sense if we think of property as an individual right important to owner autonomy. If the sovereign owner concludes that the thing is more of a burden than a blessing, why shouldn't she be allowed to get rid of it? But from a broader social welfare perspective, it is not always so clear that abandonment and destruction should be permitted. Consider the following cases.

Pocono Springs Civic Association, Inc. v. MacKenzie

Superior Court of Pennsylvania, 1995.
667 A.2d 233.

■ ROWLEY, PRESIDENT JUDGE. The issue in this appeal is whether real property owned by appellants Joseph W. MacKenzie and Doris C. MacKenzie has been abandoned, as they claim. In an order entered January 5, 1995, the trial court granted summary judgment, in the amount of $1,739.82, in favor of appellee Pocono Springs Civic Association, Inc., which argued successfully to the trial court that appellants had not abandoned their property located in appellee's development, and, therefore appellants were still obligated to pay association fees.[1] * * *

We briefly outline the facts and procedural background of the case as follows: Appellants purchased a vacant lot at Pocono Springs Development, located in Wayne County, on October 14, 1969. In 1987, appellants decided to sell their still-vacant lot. A subsequent offer for the

---

[1]   The covenant upon which appellee relies reads as follows:

An association of all property owners is to be formed by the Grantor and designated by such name as may be deemed appropriate, and when formed, the buyer covenants and agrees that he, his executors, heirs and assigns, shall be bound by the by-laws, rules and regulations as may be duly formulated and adopted by such association and that they shall be subject to the payment of annual dues and assessments of the same.

Deed, Covenant Number 11.

purchase of appellants' lot was conditioned upon the property being suitable for an on-lot sewage system. Upon inspection, the lot was determined to have inadequate soil for proper percolation, and appellants' sale was lost. Believing their investment to be worthless, appellants attempted to abandon their lot at Pocono Springs Development. Appellants claimed that because they successfully abandoned their lot, they are relieved from any duty to pay the association fees sought by appellee. The trial court held, however, that the appellant's abandonment defense is "not a valid defense." We agree with the trial court, and affirm. * * *

Appellants' argument, that they successfully abandoned their lot at Pocono Springs Development, is based upon several actions that they believe disassociate them from the land. First, appellants, after learning that the lot would not meet township sewage requirements, attempted to turn the lot over to appellee. Appellee declined to accept the property. Second, appellants tried to persuade appellee to accept the lot as a gift, to be used as a park-like area for the community. Appellee again declined. Third, in 1986 appellants ceased paying real estate taxes on their lot, and in 1988 the Wayne County Tax Claim Bureau offered the property for sale, due to delinquent tax payments. There were no purchasers. Fourth, in 1990, the lot was again offered for sale by the Tax Claim Bureau. The property again was not sold. The Bureau then placed the lot on its "repository" list. Fifth, appellants signed a notarized statement, mailed to "all interested parties," Brief for Appellants at 9, which expressed their desire to abandon the lot. Sixth, appellants do not accept mail regarding the property. These occurrences, together with appellants having neither visited the lot nor utilized the development's services since 1986, cause appellants to "assert that they do not have 'perfect' title to Lot #20, in Pocono Springs [Development,] [thus] they can and have abandoned said property back to the sovereign." Id. at 11. On the basis of the above, appellants argue that their conduct manifests an intent to abandon, and that their intent to abandon should be a question of fact which precludes summary judgment.

The law of abandonment in Pennsylvania does not support appellants' argument. This Court has held that abandoned property is that:

> ... to which an owner has voluntarily relinquished all right, title, claim and possession with the intention of terminating his ownership, but without vesting it in any other person and with the intention of not reclaiming further possession or resuming ownership, possession or enjoyment.

Commonwealth v. Wetmore, 447 A.2d 1012, 1014 (Pa. Super. 1982) (citations omitted). However, in the instant case, appellants have not relinquished their rights, title, claim and possession of their lots. They remain owners of real property in fee simple, with a recorded deed and "perfect" title. Absent proof to the contrary, possession is presumed to be in the party who has record title. Overly v. Hixson, 82 A.2d 573 (Pa. Super. 1951). As appellants themselves concede, with commendable candor, see Brief for Appellants at 15, no authority exists in Pennsylvania that allows for the abandonment of real property when owned in fee simple with perfect title.[3] Additionally, appellants properly admit that neither refusal to pay taxes nor non use of real property constitutes abandonment. Brief for Appellants at 16; see also Petition of Indiana County, 62 A.2d 3, 5 (Pa. 1948) ("It has frequently been held that abandonment of title is not to be presumed from a mere failure to possess the land or from neglect to pay the taxes thereon; inchoate rights may be abandoned but abandonment is not predictable of perfect titles[.]"). Yet, appellants nonetheless maintain that their non use, refusal to pay taxes, and offers to sell create an abandonment, because of a displayed intent to abandon.

But appellants simply do not accept that the record shows that they have retained "perfect" title to their lot. Neither title nor deed has been sold or transferred. * * * Perfect title, under Pennsylvania law, cannot be abandoned. O'Dwyer v. Ream, 136 A.2d 90 (Pa. 1957). In *O'Dwyer*, our Supreme Court held that once it is determined that good title exists, then the abandonment theory cannot succeed. See also A.D. Graham & Company, Inc. v. Pennsylvania Turnpike Commission, 33 A.2d 22, 29 (Pa. 1943) (which held that the doctrine of abandonment does not apply to perfect titles, only to imperfect titles). Appellants do not cite, and our own research has not discovered, any more recent cases that would cause us to question the authority of the cited decisions. Absent authority to support their argument, therefore, the appeal cannot be successful for appellants. In short, as the trial court held, "[appellant's] 'Abandonment Authorization' [is] not a valid defense." Trial Court Opinion (Conway, P.J.), 1/5/95, at 6.

Appellants further claim that the trial court erred in granting summary judgment because whether they abandoned their lots should be a question of intent, for a jury to determine. * * * In the instant case, appellants' intent is irrelevant. What is controlling is our law, which states that real property cannot be abandoned. The law, therefore, leaves nothing for a jury to decide on this claim, which amounts to a legal impossibility.

* * * [A]ppellee is entitled to judgment as a matter of law.

---

[3]   Most commonly, abandonment involves personal property or railway lines not owned in fee simple. See Quarry Office Park Associates v. Philadelphia Electric Company, 576 A.2d 358 (Pa. Super 1990) (Court reversed order granting summary judgment and remanded the case, holding that whether Conrail abandoned a rail line was a question for the factfinder, because Conrail owned a right of way, rather than a fee simple interest); Commonwealth v. Wetmore, 447 A.2d 1012 (Pa. Super. 1982) (Court affirmed order of trial court that arrested judgment following a jury trial; Court held that abandonment of shotgun occurred when father told chief of police to keep and dispose of weapon); In re Pearlman's Estate, 35 A.2d 418 (Pa. 1944) (fiduciary abandoned interest in life insurance policies).

NOTES AND QUESTIONS

1.   The MacKenzies' property was eventually purchased at a tax foreclosure sale for about $300 and was purchased again, presumably sight unseen, by a California land trust for about $500. The lot remains undeveloped to this day. Pocono Springs Estates is a gated residential community intended as a retreat for residents of New York City, New Jersey, and Philadelphia. To hold down prices, the lots were made narrow, the expectation being that a community sewer system would be installed. But sales of lots were disappointing, assessments lagged, and the sewer system was never installed. Most of the lots remain undeveloped today, and many like the MacKenzies' have been purchased by internet speculators who do not pay their assessments. The association web site long contained the following disclaimer in all capitals: "If you are looking to purchase a lot in Pocono Springs, whether it is from eBay, a private owner, or the county itself, we advise that you do some research prior to purchasing. There are some lots in Pocono Springs that do not pass percolation tests, and cannot be built upon. There are other lots that are not of sufficient size to allow for a building. Not every lot is buildable. No lot is exempt from dues, regardless of suitability for building." Perhaps because of the high rate of tax foreclosures, the community is intensely suspicious of outsiders. One of the editors was denied permission to enter the community to photograph the MacKenzies' lot.

2.   Abandonment of personal property occurs all the time. Every time you take out the garbage, throw something in the waste basket, or haul something to the dump, you are abandoning personal property. Mineral rights are often subject to claims of abandonment when the owners have done nothing to exploit the rights for a period of time. Likewise, easements can be abandoned. Nevertheless, the traditional rule, as the Pennsylvania Supreme Court reports, is that real property cannot be abandoned. See Restatement of Property § 504 cmt. a (1944). The original rationale for this rule probably related to the incidents and services that landowners were supposed to perform in feudal England, which meant that there could be no gap in "seisin" of real property. See Chapter V; Lior J. Strahilevitz, The Right to Abandon, 158 U. Pa. L. Rev. 355, 399 (2010).

3.   This may be an area of the law where formal rules and practice diverge, at least in certain circumstances. During the settlement of the United States, settlers would purchase land (often sight unseen) or file a claim for land under the Homestead Acts; if they discovered once they took up possession of the land that they could not make a go of it, they would simply "pull up stakes" and move on. Usually this happened before a formal title (called a land patent) issued to the settler, so it was not technically abandonment. But functionally speaking it was similar. The recent mortgage crisis in the U.S. also suggests that something similar to abandonment occurs when house prices fall to the point where homeowners owe more in mortgage debt than the house is worth. At least where the homeowner has a "non-recourse" loan, meaning the lender cannot seek to recover the balance due from the homeowner's other assets, many homeowners in these circumstances simply stopped making payments. When this happens, the

lender typically institutes a foreclosure proceeding (see Chapter VII), which results in title and possession being transferred from the homeowner to the lender—in effect the homeowner abandons real property to the lender.

4.   The notion that one cannot abandon real property is also a little odd given other powers (or liabilities) associated with ownership of land. If the owner of real property pays no attention to it, and another person enters onto the property, the owner can lose title to the occupant by adverse possession (see Chapter II). Isn't this a kind of abandonment by inattention or negligence? And of course gifts of real property are perfectly permissible. Isn't a gift of real property a decision by the owner to abandon any claim to the property, combined with designation of someone else as the new owner? Note however that in the adverse possession and gift situations, a new owner takes the place of the owner who has lost or abandoned any claim. The MacKenzies want to relinquish ownership without any substitute owner being designated to take their place.

5.   The MacKenzies' basic problem is that their lot in the Poconos has become a negative-value asset. The liabilities associated with the lot—the annual assessment fee imposed by the homeowners' association plus the property taxes—exceed the positive value anyone can obtain from the lot, given that local land-use regulations prohibit the installation of a septic field. So no one wants it—not the MacKenzies, not any potential purchaser, not the homeowners' association, not even the government (which has the right to take and sell the land because of the unpaid property taxes). But doesn't this describe the condition that leads to abandonment of property in any context? The reason one throws a piece of paper in the waste basket or an empty food container in the garbage is because it has become (for the owner) a negative-value asset. Provided the MacKenzies' action violates no environmental laws, why shouldn't they be allowed to toss the lot in the Poconos in the trash can, so to speak?

6.   Perhaps real property is different because of concern about externalities that might be created by abandonment of real property. The most obvious example would be real property that is a hazardous waste disposal site. Cleaning up the wastes (to protect against future releases affecting neighboring property or exposure of third parties) can often cost more than the property is worth in fair market value terms. Not surprisingly, therefore, environmental statutes like the Comprehensive Environmental Response, Compensation, and Liability Act (CERCLA) impose limits on an owner's ability to escape liability for cleanup costs through abandonment. See 42 U.S.C. § 101(20)(A) (providing that if a state or local government acquires property through abandonment "any person who owned, operated, or otherwise controlled activities at such facility immediately beforehand" is deemed to be the owner).

7.   Come to think of it, aren't there externality problems associated with abandonment of personal property too? What do you think about a strategy of reducing litter, and encouraging recycling, by declaring that personal property cannot be abandoned?

8.   Whether property has been abandoned is a question of intent: The owner must intend to relinquish all claims to the property with no intent that it be acquired by any particular person. The item can then be claimed by the first person who asserts control over it. Strahilevitz, supra at 376. Whether someone intends to abandon property is usually clear from context. An old chair placed just outside the front door is probably being moved in or out; the same chair placed on the curb is probably being abandoned. Nevertheless, problems are encountered. A German art museum discovered that custodial workers had thrown out a work of art by Berlin sculptor Michael Beutler made out of the yellow plastic sheeting used to encase cement. The workers had assumed it was construction rubbish. After the episode, the museum announced that it was instituting monthly "Check Your Art Sense!" classes for the city's sanitation crews.

Eyerman v. Mercantile Trust Co.

Missouri Court of Appeals, St. Louis District, 1975.
524 S.W.2d 210.

■ RENDLEN, JUDGE. Plaintiffs appeal from denial of their petition seeking injunction to prevent demolition of a house at #4 Kingsbury Place in the City of St. Louis. The action is brought by individual neighboring property owners and certain trustees for the Kingsbury Place Subdivision. We reverse.

Louise Woodruff Johnston, owner of the property in question, died January 14, 1973, and by her will directed the executor ". . . to cause our home at 4 Kingsbury Place . . . to be razed and to sell the land upon which it is located . . . and to transfer the proceeds of the sale . . . to the residue of my estate." Plaintiffs assert that razing the home will adversely affect their property rights, violate the terms of the subdivision trust indenture for Kingsbury Place, produce an actionable private nuisance and is contrary to public policy.

The area involved is a "private place" established in 1902 by trust indenture which provides that Kingsbury Place and Kingsbury Terrace will be so maintained, improved, protected and managed as to be desirable for private residences. The trustees are empowered to protect and preserve "Kingsbury Place" from encroachment, trespass, nuisance or injury, and it is "the intention of these presents, forming a general scheme of improving and maintaining said property as desirable residence property of the highest class." The covenants run with the land and the indenture empowers lot owners or the trustees to bring suit to enforce them.

Except for one vacant lot, the subdivision is occupied by handsome, spacious two and three-story homes, and all must be used exclusively as private residences. The indenture generally regulates location, costs and similar features for any structures in the subdivision, and limits construction of subsidiary structures except those that may beautify the property, for example, private stables, flower houses, conservatories, play houses or buildings of similar character.

On trial the temporary restraining order was dissolved and all issues found against the plaintiffs. * * *

The issues, simply stated, involve: (1) Private nuisance; (2) enforcement of restrictive covenants and (3) public policy. * * *

Whether #4 Kingsbury Place should be razed is an issue of public policy involving individual property rights and the community at large. The plaintiffs have pleaded and proved facts sufficient to show a personal, legally protectible interest.

Demolition of the dwelling will result in an unwarranted loss to this estate, the plaintiffs and the public. The uncontradicted testimony was that the current value of the house and land is $40,000.00; yet the estate could expect no more than $5,000.00 for the empty lot, less the cost of demolition at $4,350.00, making a grand loss of $39,350.33 if the unexplained and capricious direction to the executor is effected. Only $650.00 of the $40,000.00 asset would remain.

Kingsbury Place is an area of high architectural significance, representing excellence in urban space utilization. Razing the home will depreciate adjoining property values by an estimated $10,000.00 and effect corresponding losses for other neighborhood homes. The cost of constructing a house of comparable size and architectural exquisiteness would approach $200,000.00.

The importance of this house to its neighborhood and the community is reflected in the action of the St. Louis Commission on Landmarks and Urban Design designating Kingsbury Place as a landmark of the City of St. Louis. This designation, under consideration prior to the institution of this suit, points up the aesthetic and historical qualities of the area and assists in stabilizing Central West End St. Louis. It was testified by the Landmarks Commission chairman that the private place concept, once unique to St. Louis, fosters higher home maintenance standards and is among the most effective methods for stabilizing otherwise deteriorating neighborhoods. The executive director of Heritage St. Louis, an organization operating to preserve the architecture of the city, testified to the importance of preserving Kingsbury Place intact:

> The reasons (sic) for making Kingsbury Place a landmark is that it is a definite piece of urban design and architecture. It starts out with monumental gates on Union. There is a long corridor of space, furnished with a parkway in the center, with houses on either side of the street, ... The existence of this piece of architecture depends on the continuity of the (sic) both sides. Breaks in this continuity would be as holes in this wall, and would detract from the urban design qualities of the streets. And the richness of the street is this belt of green lot on either side, with rich tapestry of the individual houses along the sides.

Many of these houses are landmarks in themselves, but they add up to much more ... I would say Kingsbury Place, as a whole, with its design, with its important houses ... is a most significant piece of urban design by any standard.

To remove #4 Kingsbury from the street was described as having the effect of a missing front tooth. The space created would permit direct access to Kingsbury Place from the adjacent alley, increasing the likelihood the lot will be subject to uses detrimental to the health, safety and beauty of the neighborhood. The mere possibility that a future owner might build a new home with the inherent architectural significance of the present dwelling offers little support to sustain the condition for destruction.

We are constrained to take judicial notice of the pressing need of the community for dwelling units as demonstrated by recent U.S. Census Bureau figures showing a decrease of more than 14% in St. Louis City housing units during the decade of the 60's. This decrease occurs in the face of housing growth in the remainder of the metropolitan area. It becomes apparent that no individual, group of individuals nor the community generally benefits from the senseless destruction of the house; instead, all are harmed and only the caprice of the dead testatrix is served. Destruction of the house harms the neighbors, detrimentally affects the community, causes monetary loss in excess of $39,000.00 to the estate and is without benefit to the dead woman. No reason, good or bad, is suggested by the will or record for the eccentric condition. This is not a living person who seeks to exercise a right to reshape or dispose of her property; instead, it is an attempt by will to confer the power to destroy upon an executor who is given no other interest in the property. To allow an executor to exercise such power stemming from apparent whim and caprice of the testatrix contravenes public policy.

The Missouri Supreme Court held in State ex rel. McClintock v. Guinotte, 204 S.W. 806, 808 (Mo. 1918), that the taking of property by inheritance or will is not an absolute or natural right but one created by the laws of the sovereign power. The court points out the state "may foreclose the right absolutely, or it may grant the right upon conditions precedent, which conditions, if not otherwise violative of our Constitution, will have to be complied with before the right of descent and distribution (whether under the law or by will) can exist." Further, this power of the state is one of inherent sovereignty which allows the state to "say what becomes of the property of a person, when death forecloses his right to control it." McClintock v. Guinotte, supra, at 808, 809. While living, a person may manage, use or dispose of his money or property with fewer restraints than a decedent by will. One is generally restrained from wasteful expenditure or destructive inclinations by the natural desire to enjoy his property or to accumulate it during his lifetime. Such considerations however have not tempered the extravagance or eccentricity of the testamentary disposition here on which there is no check except the courts.

In the early English case of Egerton v. Brownlow, 10 Eng.Rep. 359, 417 (H.L.C. 1853), it is stated: "The owner of an estate may himself do many things which he could not (by a condition) compel his successor to do. One example is sufficient. He may leave his land uncultivated, but he cannot by a condition compel his successor to do so. The law does not interfere with the owner and compel him to cultivate his land, (though it may be for the public good that land should be cultivated) so far the law respects ownership; but when, by a condition, he attempts to compel his successor to do what is against the public good, the law steps in and pronounces the condition void and allows the devisee to enjoy the estate free from the condition." A more recent application of this principle is found in M'Caig's Trustees v. Kirk-Session of the United Free Church of Lismore, et al., 1915 Sess.Cas. 426 (Scot.). There, by codicil to her will, testatrix ordered certain statues erected to honor her family in a tower built in the form of an amphitheater on a hill. Balustrades were to be erected so that even the public would have no access inside the tower. Special provision was made for keeping out the public and the ground enclosed was expressly declared to be a private enclosure. There were no living descendants of any member of the family who might, if so permitted, take pleasure in contemplating the proposed statues. The court states at 434: "If a bequest such as in Miss M'Caig's codicil were held good, money would require to be expended in perpetuity merely gratifying an absurd whim which has neither reason nor public sentiment in its favor." In striking down the provisions of the codicil, the court further notes that there is indeed a "difference between what a man, uncognosed, may do at his own hand, and what the law will support under the provisions of his will . . . therefore, without being illegal in the sense of being contrary to any express rule of the common law or contrary to any statute, the principle of public policy will prevent such post-mortem expenditure. Whether the act is sufficiently contrary to public policy to warrant the court's interference must depend on the degree to which it is against public policy." The court further observed that the erection of the eleven statues "would be of no benefit to anyone except those connected with the carrying out of the work, for whose interest she expresses no concern." M'Caig's Trustees v. Kirk-Session of the United Free Church of Lismore, et al., supra at 438. In the case sub judice, testatrix similarly expressed no such concern; nothing in the will or record indicates an intent to benefit any razing company called upon to destroy her beautiful home.

In the case of In re Scott's Will, Board of Commissioners of Rice County v. Scott et al., 93 N.W. 109 (Minn. 1903), the Supreme Court of Minnesota stated, when considering the provision of a will directing the executor to destroy money belonging to the estate: "We assume, for purpose of this decision, that the direction in the codicil to the executor to destroy all of the residue of the money or cash or evidences of credit belonging to the estate was void." In re Scott's Will, supra at 109. See also Restatement, Second, Trusts § 124, at 267: "Although a person may deal capriciously with his own property, his self interest ordinarily will restrain him from doing so. Where an attempt is made to confer such a power upon a person who is given no other interest in the property, there is no such restraint and it is against public policy to allow him to exercise the power if the purpose is merely capricious." The text is followed by this illustration: "A bequeaths $1,000.00 to B in trust to throw the money into the sea. B holds the money upon a resulting trust for the estate of A and is liable to the estate of A if he throws the money into the sea." Restatement, supra at 267. * * *

It is important to note that the purposes of testatrix's trust will not be defeated by injunction; instead, the proceeds from the sale of the property will pass into the residual estate and thence to the trust estate as intended, and only the capricious destructive condition will be enjoined. * * *

The term "public policy" cannot be comprehensively defined in specific terms but the phrase "against public policy" has been characterized as that which conflicts with the morals of the time and contravenes any established interest of society. Acts are said to be against public policy "when the law refuses to enforce or recognize them, on the ground that they have a mischievous tendency, so as to be injurious to the interests of the state, apart from illegality or immorality." Dille v. St. Luke's Hospital, 196 S.W.2d 615, 620 (Mo. 1946); Brawner v. Brawner, 327 S.W.2d 808, 812 (Mo. banc 1959).

Public policy may be found in the Constitution, statutes and judicial decisions of this state or the nation. In re Rahn's Estate, 291 S.W. 120 (Mo. 1927). But in a case of first impression where there are no guiding statutes, judicial decisions or constitutional provisions, "a judicial determination of the question becomes an expression of public policy provided it is so plainly right as to be supported by the general will." In re Mohler's Estate, 22 A.2d 680, 683 (Pa. 1941). In the absence of guidance from authorities in its own jurisdiction, courts may look to the judicial decisions of sister states for assistance in discovering expressions of public policy.

Although public policy may evade precise, objective definition, it is evident from the authorities cited that this senseless destruction serving no apparent good purpose is to be held in disfavor. A well-ordered society cannot tolerate the waste and destruction of resources when such acts directly affect important interests of other members of that society. It is clear that property owners in the neighborhood of #4 Kingsbury, the St. Louis Community as a whole and the beneficiaries of testatrix's estate will be severely injured should the provisions of the will be followed. No benefits are present to balance against this injury and we hold that to allow the condition in the will would be in violation of the public policy of this state.

Having thus decided, we do not reach the plaintiffs' contentions regarding enforcement of the restrictions in the Kingsbury Place trust indenture and actionable private nuisance, though these contentions may have merit.

The judgment is reversed and the cause remanded to the Circuit Court to enter judgment as prayed.

■ CLEMENS, JUDGE (dissenting). * * * The simple issue in this case is whether the trial court erred by refusing to enjoin a trustee from carrying out an explicit testamentary directive. In an emotional opinion, the majority assumes a psychic knowledge of the testatrix' reasons for directing her home be razed; her testamentary disposition is characterized as "capricious," "unwarranted," "senseless," and "eccentric." But the record is utterly silent as to her motives.

The majority's reversal of the trial court here spawns bizarre and legally untenable results. By its decision, the court officiously confers a "benefit" upon testamentary beneficiaries who have never litigated or protested against the razing. The majority opinion further proclaims that public policy demands we enjoin the razing of this private residence in order to prevent land misuse in the City of St. Louis. But the City, like the beneficiaries, is not a party to this lawsuit. The fact is the majority's holding is based upon wispy, self-proclaimed public policy grounds that were only vaguely pleaded, were not in evidence, and were only sketchily briefed by the plaintiffs. * * *

Kingsbury Place is a "private place" established in 1902 by trust indenture. Except for one well-tended vacant lot (whose existence the majority ignores in saying the street minus #4 Kingsbury Place would be like "a missing front tooth") the trust indenture generally regulates size, constructions and cost of structures to be built on Kingsbury Place. It empowers the trustees to maintain vacant lots and to protect the street from "encroachment, trespass, nuisance and injury." The indenture's acknowledgment that vacant lots did and would exist shows that such lots were not to be considered an "injury." The fact the indenture empowers the trustees to maintain vacant lots is neither an express nor an implied ban against razing residences. The indenture simply recognizes that Kingsbury Place may have vacant lots from time to time—as it now has—and that the trustees may maintain them—as they now do. The indenture itself affords plaintiffs no basis for injunctive relief. * * *

The majority opinion bases its reversal on public policy. But plaintiffs themselves did not substantially rely upon this nebulous concept. Plaintiffs' brief contends merely that an "agency of the City of St. Louis has recently [?] designated Kingsbury Place as a landmark," citing § 24.070, Revised Code of the City of St. Louis. Plaintiffs argue removal of the Johnston home would be "intentional . . . destruction of a landmark of historical interest." Neither the ordinance cited in the brief nor any action taken under it were in evidence. Indeed, the Chairman of the Landmarks and Urban Design Commission testified the Commission did not declare the street a landmark until after Mrs. Johnston died. A month after Mrs. Johnston's death, several residents of the street apparently sensed the impending razing of the Johnston home and applied to have the street declared a landmark. The Commissioner testified it was the Commission's "civic duty to help those people." * * *

The leading Missouri case on public policy as that doctrine applies to a testator's right to dispose of property is In re Rahn's Estate, 291 S.W. 120 (Mo. banc 1927). There, an executor refused to pay a bequest on the ground the beneficiary was an enemy alien, and the bequest was therefore against public policy. The court denied that contention: "We may say, at the outset, that the policy of the law favors freedom in the testamentary disposition of property and that it is the duty of the courts to give effect to the intention of the testator, as expressed in his will, provided such intention does not contravene an established rule of law." And the court wisely added, "it is not the function of the judiciary to create or announce a public policy of its own, but solely to determine and declare what is the public policy of the state or nation as such policy is found to be expressed in the Constitution, statutes, and judicial decisions of the state or nation, . . . not by the varying opinions of laymen, lawyers, or judges as to the demands or the interests of the public." And, in cautioning against judges declaring public policy the court stated: "Judicial tribunals hold themselves bound to the observance of rules of extreme caution when invoked to declare a transaction void on grounds of public policy, and prejudice to the public interest must clearly appear before the court would be warranted in pronouncing a transaction void on this account." In resting its decision on public-policy grounds, the majority opinion has transgressed the limitations declared by our Supreme Court in Rahn's Estate. * * * It requires judicial imagination to hold, as the majority does, that the mere presence of a second vacant lot on Kingsbury Place violates public policy.

As much as our aesthetic sympathies might lie with neighbors near a house to be razed, those sympathies should not so interfere with our considered legal judgment as to create a questionable legal precedent. Mrs. Johnston had the right during her lifetime to have her house razed, and I find nothing which precludes her right to order her executor to raze the house upon her death. It is clear that "the law favors the free and untrammeled use of real property." Gibbs v. Cass, 431 S.W.2d 662 (Mo. Ct. App. 1968). This applies to testamentary dispositions. Mississippi Valley Trust Co. v. Ruhland, 222 S.W.2d 750 (Mo. 1949). An owner has exclusive control over the use of his property subject only to the limitation that such use may not substantially impair another's right to peaceably enjoy his property. City of Fredericktown v. Osborn, 429 S.W.2d 17 (Mo.

Ct. App. 1968), Reutner v. Vouga, 367 S.W.2d 34 (Mo. Ct. App. 1963). Plaintiffs have not shown that such impairment will arise from the mere presence of another vacant lot on Kingsbury Place.

I find no plain error in the trial court's denial of injunctive relief, and on the merits I would affirm the trial court's judgment. * * *

Figure 4-8
#4 Kingsbury Place, Saint Louis, 2006

NOTES AND QUESTIONS

1.   Much speculation has swirled around Louise Woodruff Johnston's motivation in directing "our home" to be razed. Apparently her parents built the house and she lived there all her adult life. Julius K. Hunter, Kingsbury Place: The First Two Hundred Years (1982). Her eight-page original will dated April 1, 1970 and professionally prepared, contains the razing provision in the fourth of seven numbered sections. Three codicils that were added in 1971 and 1972, the last dated a little more than three months before her death, did not amend the provision about razing the house. Thus, Ms. Johnston had multiple opportunities to re-consider her direction to destroy the house, but did not. Does this tend to undermine the suggestion that her decision was ill-considered, capricious, or "eccentric"? In one noted episode from New Haven, Isaphene Hillhouse, who had lived in the family mansion her entire life, gave contingent orders for its destruction in her will. In a letter to a relative, she declared that "there is no more melancholy spectacle than to see a fine old house fall to decay, or pass into the hands of strangers who have no interest in it." Letter from Isaphene Hillhouse to James Hillhouse, March 11, 1897 (Hillhouse Family Papers, Box 50, Folder 338, Sterling Memorial Library, Yale University).

2.   The issue in *Eyerman* is complicated by the (belated) designation of the Johnston home as a historical and aesthetic landmark. Today, historical and architectural preservation laws are much more common than

they were when the principal case was decided. In an important decision reproduced in Chapter X, *Penn Central Transp. Co. v. New York City*, 438 U.S. 104 (1978), the Supreme Court upheld such a historical preservation law against a challenge that it caused a taking of the owner's property. After *Penn Central*, is it clear that St. Louis could prohibit the destruction of an architecturally significant home, before or after the owner's death, so long as the prohibition did not impose unduly harsh financial losses on the owner (or her estate)?

3.   Suppose the owner of the Barry Bonds baseball at issue in *Popov* (discussed in Chapter II) decides for some idiosyncratic reason to destroy the baseball in a public ceremony. This imposes no obvious loss on the community. The actual baseball is a fungible asset indistinguishable from tens of thousands of other baseballs, and is easily reproduced. But because this is understood to be the Barry Bonds record-breaking baseball, the stunt results in the destruction of an asset having at one time a market value among collectors of $450,000. On the authority of *Eyerman*, would a court be justified, perhaps at the instance of a suit brought by other baseball collectors, in enjoining such destruction as contrary to public policy? For another notorious invocation of the right to destroy, see Stephen E. Sachs, Saving Toby: Extortion, Blackmail, and the Right to Destroy, 24 Yale L. Pol'y 251 (2006).

4.   Interestingly, the legal philosopher John Austin uses the type of situation in *Eyerman* to illustrate his conception of ownership: "If I am the absolute owner of my house, I may destroy it if I will. But I must not destroy it in such a manner as would amount to an injury to any of my neighbors." 3 John Austin, Lectures on Jurisprudence 6 (1861–1863). Did that happen here? What if Mrs. Johnston's reason for directing that the house be razed was that she wanted to prevent members of a class protected under antidiscrimination law from ever living there?

5.   *Eyerman* is one of the more aggressive invocations of public policy to stop destruction of property ordered in a will. Courts vary in their approaches to this issue. Lior Strahilevitz, The Right to Destroy, 114 Yale L.J. 781, 789–91 (2005); Abigail Sykas, Waste Not, Want Not: Can the Public Policy Doctrine Prohibit the Destruction of Property by Testamentary Direction?, Vt. L. Rev. 25, 30 (2001). Another area in which the issue arises involves the estates of famous authors and artists who leave instructions that their work or notes be destroyed. If such instructions had been followed, the *Aeneid* and most of the oeuvre of Franz Kafka would have been completely lost. Should the author's wishes be respected, or does an executor have a duty to preserve the work? A duty to whom?

6.   In general, how much can we rely on the owner's incentives as a stand-in for social benefits and costs? On the one hand, an owner who reduces value to future owners thereby reduces the price she might now sell it for, as long as the conditions for capitalization of future values into present market values holds (or, alternatively, the owner can hold the asset long enough for the market price to reflect these values). See, e.g., Harold Demsetz, Toward a Theory of Property Rights, 57 Am. Econ. Rev. 347, 355

(1967) (Papers & Proc.); Strahilevitz, supra. On the other hand, much commentary focuses on the defects in owners' decisionmaking processes and the need for collective intervention to prevent waste. See, e.g., Joseph L. Sax, Playing Darts with a Rembrandt: Public and Private Rights in Cultural Treasures (1999); Edward J. McCaffery, Must We Have the Right to Waste?, in New Essays in the Legal and Political Theory of Property 76 (Stephen R. Munzer ed., 2001); see also Michael Heller, The Boundaries of Private Property, 108 Yale L.J. 1163, 1165–66 (1999). We return to this issue in the materials on dead hand control in Chapters V and VI. Incidentally, according to the website zillow.com, the house at #4 Kingsbury Place is still intact and is estimated to be worth $980,300 as of February 9, 2022 (In previous editions of this casebook, the value was variously placed at over $1.1 million (2016), $711,000 (2011), and over $1.2 million (2007).) Kingsbury Place now maintains a website. http://kingsburyplace.org/.

7.   From a social welfare perspective, is the right to destroy more problematic than the right to abandon? After all, abandonment leaves open the possibility that some other person will take up the property and put it to some productive use. Destruction eliminates any value for all time. But if individual owners are not allowed to make the decision whether to destroy property, who should make this decision? Does the value of the right to destroy depend on whether property is personal as opposed to fungible (see excerpts from Margaret Jane Radin, Chapter III)? Should people be allowed to leave valuable objects like wedding rings in caskets of loved ones when they are buried? Should famous people—political leaders, celebrities, actors and actresses—be allowed to destroy their personal papers and diaries before they die? (A notorious case of second thoughts is that of Dante Gabriel Rossetti, who buried poems with his wife, Lizzie Siddal, and later had his friends exhume the decaying and worm-eaten manuscript. Jan Marsh, Dante Gabriel Rossetti: Painter and Poet 244, 368–69, 374–79 (1999).)

E. OTHER OWNER POWERS

We have not exhausted the list of owner powers in this chapter. Other important powers include the right of succession—to determine who will take property upon one's death; the right to transfer—either by gift, sale, or lease; and the right to employ property as security for a loan—either through a mortgage or a security interest. These other powers are sufficiently important (and complicated) that they will be taken up in later chapters. The right of succession is a major subject of Chapter V; the right of transfer by gift or sale is taken up in Chapter VIII; the right to transfer by lease is considered in Chapter VI; and the power to employ property as security for a loan is the subject of Chapter VII.

CHAPTER V

THE FORMS OF OWNERSHIP

"Out of ould fields must spring and grow the new Corne."
—Sir Edward Coke, Commentaries, Vol. 1, Preface (1600)

A. INTRODUCTION

Property law would hardly exist in a world of Robinson Crusoes, each owning an island and all it contains. Even in our world, if each identified thing had only a single owner, property law would be quite a bit simpler. But resources are often put to best use when they can be shared in some fashion. If A and B can both have access to a resource, they can both bring their special skills to using it and can spread the risk involved in owning it. A more complex property law, with divided ownership, unlocks much more value from things.

Access to resources can be divided along a number of dimensions. We have already seen situations in which an owner's right to exclude gives way to other interests, and this reflects a kind of sharing of assets. We have also seen how ownership can be separated from possession, as in the case of bailments. In this Chapter we focus on divisions that are built into the title of property itself. The law has developed an elaborate menu of forms of ownership, which permit divisions both across time and among multiple persons at any one point in time. We will not consider all forms of ownership in this Chapter. Those covered here are forms of ownership that evolved over time for freehold interests in land (and some extensions to personal property). The forms are less important today than they were when land was the principal form of wealth and prestige in society. But it is still true that one cannot understand the system of property rights we have today without a basic grasp of these forms and the doctrines that govern their interpretation and implementation. Other forms of property that permit more elaborate governance of complexes of assets are covered in Chapter VI, including leaseholds (landlord-tenant), condominiums and cooperatives, and trusts. Security interests, another important type of division, are covered in Chapter VII. Limited use rights, including easements and servitudes, are treated in Chapter IX.

Any time an asset is shared among multiple owners, a collective action problem is created, which can be seen as a kind of miniature "tragedy of the commons" (Chapter II). Consider the situation in which two people share ownership of a common asset, say a house. If they are members of the same household, they could divide the burdens and benefits associated with ownership of the house in a variety of ways. One could own the house and charge the other rent, either monetary or in kind. Or both could own the house and share the responsibilities for taxes, repairs, etc. The house itself might be part of a larger complex of property rights such as a common-interest community. (See the next Chapter.) Problems would arise if one of the owners caused damage to the house or piled too much junk in it, leaving too little space for the other. Another problem, to which we turn momentarily, is presented by successive owners or users. Ownership can be split across time, but current owners do not always have their successors' interests at heart, and vice versa. Another consideration: If people could split ownership of any asset in any way they please, might things start to get too complicated? In part to limit the collective action problems associated with having too many claimants, and in part to keep the information costs associated with complexity from spiraling out of control, the law limits the number and variety of ways in which co-ownership can be organized.

We focus in this Chapter on freehold interests in land, which (for purely historical reasons) exclude leases. The forms of ownership for freehold interests recognized today are the product of historical evolution over many centuries. The aspirations that motivated legal actors to develop certain forms, and to impose certain limitations on their use, have in many instances long since disappeared. Yet the sedimentary residue of their efforts remains. For example, the understanding that someone must "stand seized" of real property at all times is still reflected in contemporary decisions. Still, the original motivation for this rule was to assure that someone was always available to fulfill feudal services and incidents—and these were abolished in 1660!

The good news is that the system of forms devised by common-law lawyers from the seventeenth century onward has a remarkable internal logic to it—more so than most of the common law, and enough so that it is possible to present the system as a body of rules. The reason for the use of highly predictable rules in this context has much to do with the historical aspiration of landowners to direct who would get their land after they died. Obviously, one cannot influence discretionary decisions made by courts or other actors when one is dead. The solution was to constrain the discretion of future actors though a system of rules that any trained lawyer could use to prescribe who would get the property in the future, and that any trained lawyer could interpret in order to advise those having an interest in the matter about who should take the property, thereby assuring that the intentions of the deceased were (mostly) carried out. Thus, although it will be useful to advert to the historical rationale for various rules from time to time, the rules themselves largely stand on their own. The content and the labeling of the rules, at least in this instance, are less important than that they can be manipulated to achieve particular outcomes. But of course in order to participate in this process lawyers must first learn the rules.

B. DIVISIONS BY TIME

When dividing property rights to land over time, the pieces created must conform to a menu of possibilities called estates in land. An *estate* is a type of property right and measures a person's interest in the land in terms of duration. An interest may be either a present possessory estate or one that does not take possession until the happening of some future event—a future interest.

Developments in England and America since the late Middle Ages have had a major impact on the particular forms and vocabulary used in dividing up property rights, and on the system of estates in land in particular. Perhaps more importantly, some of the abiding controversies over this long span of history are at the heart of questions about what function, if any, some of the doctrines surrounding estates and future interests perform.

The estates themselves, or at least the vocabulary in which they are presented, have their roots in the Middle Ages. Under the feudal system, particularly as it emerged in the aftermath of the Norman Conquest of 1066, personal relations were very important. The King would grant tenure—something less than full ownership—over lands to lords who in turn would owe services, chief among them military services, to the King. These lords would then be able to turn around and subinfeudate to their underlings. At the bottom of this feudal property-holding hierarchy were freeholding peasants. Again, the landholding relation between lord and peasants centered around a flow of services in both directions— protection and adjudication in return for labor and other services. The obligations of the tenant were originally centered around military service and farm labor. The "feudal incidents" of the military tenures, for example, ranged from the duty to do the lord and the land no harm ("homage") to the duty to provide funds in exigent circumstances and on the marriage of the lord's daughter ("aids") to the duty to pay to allow the heir of the deceased tenant to assume the tenancy ("relief"). Some peasants would hold land in more informal arrangements called copyhold, which over time became more formalized.

In the feudal relationship, the identity of the one holding beneath made a lot of difference. The emphasis was on ensuring service rather than making land alienable. Alienability threatened the securing of the feudal services. As time went on and the military aspect of feudalism became less important, money transfers replaced some of these services, and land became correspondingly more alienable. The component of services became less important and perhaps more of a notice-giving device, in some cases fancifully so. See A.W.B. Simpson, A History of the Land Law 6 (2d ed. 1986) (noting grant from one William Earl Warren to be held subject to the service of providing one mad bull annually for his lordship's amusement and a grant of lands requiring the tenant each Christmas Day "to make a leap, a whistle and a fart coram domino rege."). Again, it is important to remember that in the more personal world of feudal obligation, the terms of the deal between grantor and grantee were far less standardized than the package of rights afforded to owners today. See Marc Bloch, Feudal Society 115–16, 143–54 (L. A. Manyon trans., 1961).

The conflict over alienation raged with much maneuvering until 1290 when the Statute Quia Emptores (named for its first two words, meaning "because purchasers") made what later became the fee simple fully alienable, without a fine, by permitting substitution of the grantee for the grantor as the lord's new tenant. The medieval land market thus created started out on a small scale, mostly involving odd acres and plots between peasants of the same community. With the upheaval in the wake of the Black Death of the mid-fourteenth century, peasants became more mobile and began moving in and out of villages; land sales became significantly more active. Sir Frederick Pollock & Frederic William Maitland, The History of English Law Before the Time of Edward I (2d ed. 1898); Sir William Holdsworth, An Historical Introduction to the Land Law (1927); D. McCloskey, The Open Fields of England: Rent, Risk and the Rate of Interest, 1300–1815, in Markets in History: Economic Studies of the Past 5, 31–32 (D.W. Galenson ed., 1989).

The problem of occasional payments called feudal incidents—particularly those due on the death of the owner before transfer to an heir—remained, and landowners came to employ a proto-trust device, called a *use* and recognized in Chancery, to avoid the feudal incidents. By having legal title technically reside in a replaceable trustee and equitable title in the effective owner (and later his family successors), one could avoid payments and obligations that were due only on the death of the owner of a corresponding legal estate. In 1535, Henry VIII, in order to deal with various financial and other difficulties, made a deal with the common-law lawyers in Parliament that resulted in the Statute of Uses, effective the next year. The Statute converted many equitable interests into legal interests, thereby restoring feudal incidents and increasing the volume of business for the common-law courts and the lawyers who practiced before them. The use soon returned, in the form of the trust, to which we turn in Chapter VI. A century later, the parliamentary party undid the resurrection of the feudal tenures, which was confirmed by Parliament at the Restoration of the monarchy in 1660. This legislation prohibited the monarch from creating new feudal tenures, reinforcing the move towards a more strictly standardized property system, with legislatures as the main sources of change.

The early state legislatures in the United States carried these developments further, abolishing the remnants of feudal incidents. Notions we have today—such as that a payment of rent is inconsistent with a fee simple—emerged from conflicts between farmers and landowners, especially in states like New York with a history of founding by major proprietors. See Eric Kades, The End of the Hudson Valley's

Peculiar Institution: The Anti-Rent Movement's Politics, Social Relations, and Economics, 27 Law & Soc. Inquiry 941 (2002). As you will see, the simplification of the system of property forms has been carried only so far, and not as far as in England since 1925. American commentators have long called for further simplification. See, e.g., T.P. Gallanis, The Future of Future Interests, 60 Wash. & Lee L. Rev. 513 (2003); Lawrence W. Waggoner, Reformulating the Structure of Estates: A Proposal for Legislative Action, 85 Harv. L. Rev. 729, 732 (1972). And a recent Restatement of Property seeks to implement these ideas. See Restatement (Third) Property: Wills and Other Donative Transfers §§ 24–26 (Am. L. Inst. 2011); see also Restatement (Fourth) of Property, Vol. 4, Div. 1, Chs. 2–3 (Am. L. Inst. Council Draft No. 3, Sept. 29, 2020). One question to ask yourself as you move through these materials is how such simplification could or should occur. Can a court collapse distinctions between estates, or does a step like that require legislation?

Estates in Land

The so-called freehold interests include the undivided fee simple and two types of lesser property rights that leave room for future interests—the life estate and the defeasible fees. Freehold interests originally were those that, as noted above, involved feudal military service obligations, whereas the lease—a nonfreehold estate—did not. This distinction was reflected in the types of actions that could be brought to protect the interest, and in the formalities required to transfer it. In the case of freehold interests, livery of seisin was required to give publicity to the transfer, which was originally effected by a ceremony on the land and could include the handing over of a clod of earth, a twig, or a key to the grantee in front of a crowd of people. (In a less than humane but psychologically insightful procedure, a young child would sometimes be beaten on the spot in order to make the memory of the occasion an indelible and long-lasting one.) Livery of seisin has its echoes in another notice-giving device we will study later: Freehold interests tend to be recorded in land registries, but short-term leases are not.

Note that the holders of a freehold interest, as well as leaseholders, are still sometimes called "tenants."

Figure 5-1
Present Possessory Estates

Freehold

    1. Fee simple absolute

    2. Life estate

    3. Defeasible fees

Nonfreehold

    4. Lease

To understand the system as a whole, it is important to keep in mind which future interests can follow which present possessory interests. As we consider present possessory interests, future interests retained by the grantor, and future interests created in a third party, the diagram in Figure 5-2 may be helpful.

Present Possessory Interests

1. Fee Simple Absolute. The fee simple absolute is the largest package of ownership rights, from which others are carved. It is indefinite in time, or, put differently, it has no natural end. No owner will live forever, but the owner can designate a successor owner, by gift, sale, or will. If the owner dies intestate—without a will—a state intestacy statute will designate certain others, typically spouse, children, or various blood relatives, as the person's heirs, who will then take the property in fee simple.

Example 1: O grants Blackacre "to Marge and her heirs" or "to Marge in fee simple," or "to Marge."

The fee simple is the largest package of rights, and in a transfer, a grantor is presumed to give all that she has, unless she indicates otherwise. Today this is reflected in the fact that if Owner grants Blackacre "to A," this creates a fee simple.

There was a time when to create a fee simple in a deed (but not in a will, where the search for testator's intent has always led to more leniency), one had to use the magic words "to A and his/her heirs." Saying simply "to A" or even "to A in fee simple" would result in a life estate and a reversion (see below). Lawyers tend to be cautious people, and in deeds conveying fees simple they still often use "to A and his/her heirs" or "to A in fee simple" even though strictly speaking these locutions are no longer required.

Figure 5-2
Diagram of Estates

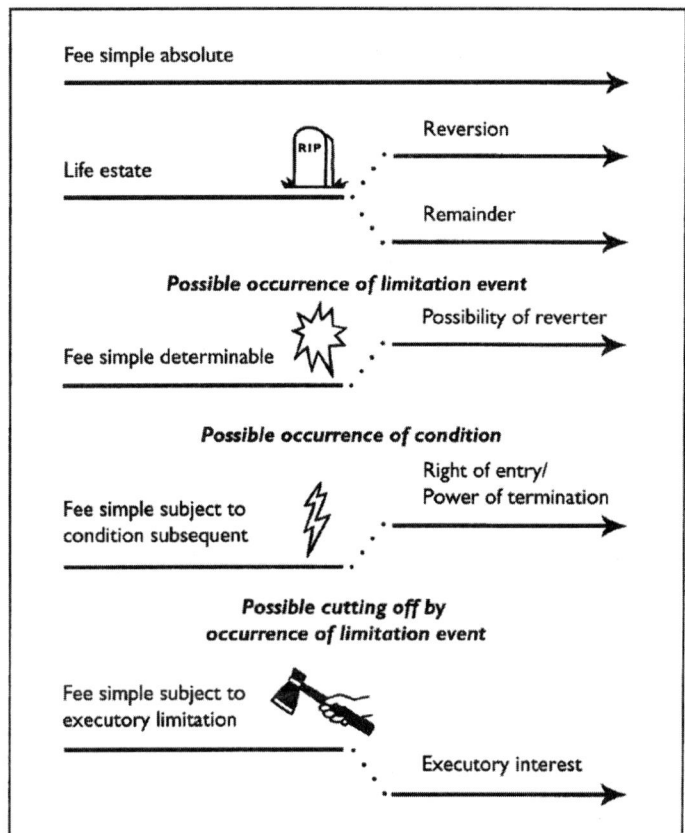

Contrary to popular usage, a person does not have legal heirs until her death (while alive, someone has at most *heirs apparent*). Marge Simpson has no heirs until she dies; her husband Homer, and her children, Bart, Lisa, and Maggie, are only heirs apparent. If a person dies intestate (without a will) and without heirs, then the property will escheat to the state in which the property is located.

Understanding the traditional formulation "and his heirs" is important not just because the phrase is still in common use. It also can be misleading. The phrase does not mean that the heirs receive any interest. Recall that a person does not even have heirs until death. Thus, if Owner grants "to Marge and her heirs," Homer and her children receive nothing. All they have is a "mere expectancy," which is not an interest at all. (Depending on the state's marital laws, Homer might be entitled to something on divorce or at Marge's death, questions to which we return below.) Rather, "and her heirs" are words of *limitation* describing the interest, as opposed to "to Marge," which are words of *purchase*. ("Words of limitation" is something of a misnomer in the case of the fee simple, which is not limited in the sense of the other estates.) Only words of purchase designate someone who is to receive an interest, and a purchaser in this context can be the recipient by sale, gift, or devise (a grant of real estate by will). Here that's Marge (only). Thus, if Marge sells Blackacre, Homer and the children lose their expectancy; they never had an *interest* to lose in the first place.

2.   Life Estate. Unlike the fee simple, which is of unlimited duration, the life estate comes to a natural end with the death of a named person, usually the holder of the estate. Here is an example:

> *Example 2*: O grants Blackacre "to Marge for life, and then to Lisa."

Here Marge has a life estate, followed by a remainder in fee simple in Lisa. We return to remainders and other future interests shortly. Note that the life estate ends with Marge's death; this is built in to the life estate.

The life estate is alienable by gift or sale (but not by will of the named person—can you see why?). What if Marge sells Blackacre during her life? Marge cannot sell more than she has; when Marge dies Lisa will take. If Marge sells, the purchaser will receive a life estate *pur autre vie*— a life estate according to Marge's, not the new owner's, lifespan. So the new owner will lose the property to Lisa when Marge dies. Keep in mind though that the life estate *pur autre vie* involves Marge's mortality risk— the duration of the right depends on when Marge will die—and will be correspondingly less attractive to purchasers in the first place.

3.   Defeasible Fees. The defeasible fees come in three closely related, but for some purposes quite distinct, varieties. These interests are like the fee simple absolute except that they may end on the happening of a named contingency. This leaves room for future interests to become possessory when such a contingency occurs.

a.   Fee Simple Determinable. The fee simple determinable ends automatically upon the occurrence of a named event, whereupon the grantor or the grantor's successor takes the property. This event might never happen, in which case the fee simple determinable acts much like the fee simple absolute, except for the possibility of the contingency happening.

> *Example 3*: O grants Blackacre "to Springfield Law School as long as it is used for instruction in the law, then to O."

The fee simple determinable is created using language of duration, such as "as long as," "so long as," "while," "during," and "until." In traditional parlance, this is a "limitation" rather than a condition. (Here O has a possibility of reverter, to which we return.)

b.   Fee Simple Subject to Condition Subsequent. This defeasible fee continues indefinitely except that, upon happening of the named event—the condition—the interest does *not* automatically end but *can* be ended by action (self-help or lawsuit) by the grantor or the grantor's successor (who, as we will see, holds a future interest called a right of entry or a power of termination).

> *Example 4*: O grants Blackacre "to Springfield Law School, but
> if it is not used for instruction in the law, then O has the right
> to reenter and take the premises."

Here Springfield Law School has a fee simple subject to condition subsequent and O has a right of entry (also called a "power of termination," see infra). If a condo is built on Blackacre instead, then the Law School only loses Blackacre if O (or his successor in interest) takes action to recover the property. With the fee simple subject to condition subsequent, the end of the interest and the transfer to the next interest holder is not automatic, as it was with the fee simple determinable. The fee simple subject to condition subsequent usually employs language of condition such as "but if," "on condition that," "provided that," "provided however," and "if" (as opposed to the language of duration in the determinable fee, e.g., "as long as" as in Example 3), and the condition subsequent is often separated from the description of the interest by a comma. This grammatical separation of the condition into its own clause reflects the treatment of the condition as something separate from the interest that it can cut short.

    c.   Fee Simple Subject to Executory Limitation. If the defeasible fee is followed by an interest not reserved to the grantor—i.e., granted to some third party at the time of conveyance of the present possessory estate—the defeasible fee is called a fee simple subject to executory limitation (and, as we will see, the following future interest is called an executory interest).

> *Example 5A*: O grants Blackacre "to Springfield Law School as
> long as it is used for instruction in the law, then to the
> Springfield Animal Hospital."

> *Example 5B*: O grants Blackacre "to Springfield Law School, but
> if it is not used for instruction in the law, then to the Springfield
> Animal Hospital."

Notice that, here with the fee simple subject to executory limitation, the future interest is in a third party, Springfield Animal Hospital, rather than in the grantor (as was the case with future interests in O in Examples 3 and 4). Notice also that the fee simple subject to executory limitation conflates the nature of the two defeasible fees followed by an interest reserved in the grantor (the fee simple determinable and the fee simple subject to condition subsequent). One can use the "as long as" or "but if" style language interchangeably. The conventional wisdom seems to be that the interest is automatically cut short by the following executory interest upon the happening of the named event, regardless of whether durational or conditional language is used. See Thomas F. Bergin & Paul G. Haskell, Preface to Estates in Land and Future

Interests 52 (1984). At least this is what the commentators say; there seems to be little law on this subject.

Although seldom used, the system of estates allows interests other than the fee simple to be determinable and subject to condition subsequent. For example, "to A for life so long as alcohol is not consumed on the premises" creates and grants a life estate determinable. A lease too can be determinable.

As mentioned earlier, the history of the forms of ownership reflects an attempt by owners both to avoid feudal obligations and to tie up property in their families over the generations. These issues are reflected both in the catalogue of estates and in the doctrines, such as rules on alienability and the Rule against Perpetuities, that constrain the manipulation of estates. In the past this conflict played itself out over another type of fee, the fee tail, which was created by the statute *De Donis Conditionalibus*, 13 Edw., ch. 1, in 1285 and which acquired the feature of long-term inalienability by the fifteenth century. The fee tail has been abolished in most states and has at most a theoretical existence in the others. To create a fee tail, one would use the language "to A and the heirs of his/her body" or "to A and his/her issue." Such an interest would give something like a nontransferable life estate to be followed by a similar interest in the blood descendants (issue) of that person, and so on and on. Only when A's bloodline ends—when A "dies without issue," which can happen hundreds of years after A's death—does the fee tail end. The property would then revert to the grantor (or if the grantor has died, those who have received the grantor's reversion through a chain of transfers by will or under the intestacy statute). The fee tail is a lesser estate than the fee simple absolute; the difference is a reversion in the grantor, even if it is not terribly likely that this reversion will ever become possessory. Keep this in mind when we take up the principle of the conservation of estates. By statute, most states provide today that any attempt to create a fee tail shall be deemed to be another interest or interests, most commonly a fee simple in the immediate grantee.

Future Interests

As we have seen, other than the fee simple absolute, the other estates do not continue indefinitely but may end one way or another. This means that compared with the fee simple absolute, there is "something left," and that is a future interest. These future interests come in a surprisingly large number of varieties. A basic division, reflected in terminology and to a lesser extent in the rules that apply to them, is between interests retained by the grantor and interests created in a third party. These differences are less important than they once were, because interests retained by the grantor are now generally alienable. If they are alienated, though, they do not change their name or character. As we will see when we turn to the Rule against Perpetuities, interests retained by the grantor are treated as already "vested" and so they present no problem under the Rule.

Figure 5-3
Future Interests Retained by Grantors

---

1. Reversion

2. Possiblity of reverter

3. Right of entry (power of termination)

---

1. INTERESTS RETAINED BY THE GRANTOR

Not all interests give their owners a present right to possession. Some interests do not become possessory until sometime in the future, and the circumstances under which this may or may not happen help to define which interest a person has. If a person has a future interest, one also has to ask what present possessory interest one would have if the interest becomes possessory, or in other words what kind of estate is in waiting. For example, if O grants "to A for life, and then to B," A has a present possessory interest in life estate and B has a remainder in fee simple. That is, when A dies, B will have a fee simple. B has something now, but it is a remainder in fee simple, a future interest.

Future interests retained by the grantor are sometimes called "reversionary" interests, even though only one of the three such interests is called a "reversion." One of the pitfalls of the system of classifying estates is the many r-words describing a number of future interests.

a. Reversion. The reversion follows the natural end of a life estate and in other contexts in which an owner has not disposed of the entire fee (such as leaseholds, see Chapter VI).

Example 6: O grants Blackacre "to Marge for life, then to O."

O here retains a reversion. (O could also implicitly retain a reversion if the grant had been simply "to Marge for life.") O had a fee simple and carved out a life estate, retaining the rest of the original fee simple. The "rest" retained is a reversion. Don't call this "rest" a remainder. A reversion is to be contrasted with a remainder, which is the interest (also following a life estate) in someone other than the grantor (to which we return in subsection 2).

As we will see, in the lessor-lessee relationship the lessor retains a reversion, but the lessor also has a present interest—the fee simple subject to the lease—in addition to this reversion.

b. Possibility of Reverter. This is the interest reserved to the grantor that follows a fee simple determinable. That is, O will automatically get the property back if the limitation built into the fee simple determinable occurs (hence the explosion in the diagram, in Figure 5-2, supra). In Example 3 above, repeated here, there is an explicit possibility of reverter:

> *Example 3*: O grants Blackacre "to Springfield Law School as long as it is used for instruction in the law, then to O."

If O has died, then O's successor (by will, intestacy, or by sale, etc.) will take. The possibility of reverter can also be implicit:

> *Example 7*: O grants Blackacre "to Springfield Law School as long as it is used for instruction in the law."

Here O is not mentioned, but because O owned the entire fee simple absolute and granted a fee simple determinable, O must retain a possibility of reverter, here implicitly. In either case, O need not do anything to regain ownership. If the limitation event occurs (here Blackacre ceases to be used for law instruction), then O (or O's successor as holder of the future interest) becomes the fee simple owner again. Notice that if the holder of the fee simple determinable (here the Springfield Law School) does not quit possession, it can start a period of adverse possession. (See Chapter II.) Can you see why?

   c.   Right of Entry/Power of Termination. Like the possibility of reverter, this is an interest retained by the grantor that follows a defeasible fee, but here the preceding defeasible fee must be a fee simple subject to condition subsequent. Consider Example 4 again:

> *Example 4*: O grants Blackacre "to Springfield Law School, but if it is not used for instruction in the law, then O has the right to reenter and take the premises."

O has a right of entry (also called a power of termination). The condition is a condition subsequent for the preceding interest and a condition precedent for the future interest—the right of entry (represented by the lightning bolt in Figure 5-2, supra). If it occurs, nothing happens automatically, but it does give O the right (the power) to change legal relations by ousting the holder of the fee simple subject to condition subsequent. O can either attempt a physical entry (subject to the limits on self-help) or bring an action to recover possession of the land. If O does nothing, then the holder of the fee simple subject to condition subsequent continues on as owner as before. If enough time passes, the right of entry may no longer be exercisable, through the doctrine of laches. Under this doctrine, the right of entry must be exercised within a reasonable time, which some courts take to be the period in the statute of limitations for bringing an action in ejectment. See, e.g., Jeffries v. State ex rel. Woodruff County, 226 S.W.2d 810 (Ark. 1950); Bredell v. Kerr, 147 S.W. 105 (Mo. 1912).

2. INTERESTS CREATED IN A GRANTEE

The present possessory interests need not be followed by an interest in the grantor. Instead the grantor can simultaneously create an interest in a third party. The set of such interests bears different names and has somewhat different features from the otherwise similar set of future interests created in the grantor herself.

Figure 5-4
Future Interests in Grantees

I. Remainder

   Indefeasibly vested

   Contingent

   Vested subject to complete divestment

   Vested subject to partial divestment (or subject to open)

2. Executory interest

---

a.   Remainder. Like the reversion, the remainder follows a life estate, never a fee simple, but unlike the reversion the remainder is in a party other than the grantor.

> *Example 8*: Marge grants Blackacre "to Homer for life, then to Bart, Lisa, and Maggie and their heirs."

Terminology can be confusing, because if instead of granting the "rest" of the fee to a third party, the owner retains it, this "rest" is not a remainder but a reversion. Remainders come in a number of varieties.

The remainder in Example 8 is *indefeasibly vested*, meaning that the identity of the takers—Bart, Lisa, and Maggie—is known and there is no other contingency that has to be fulfilled before the interest is ready to become possessory other than the natural termination of the preceding interest (Homer's death). Further, the remainder in Example 8 is indefeasibly vested because no condition subsequent can cut short the remainder (something to which we return shortly).

Other types of remainder have conditions. One common condition, a condition precedent, makes the remainder a *contingent* remainder. At their creation, remainders can be vested or contingent. These remainders are contingent:

> *Example 8A*: Marge grants Blackacre "to Homer for life, then to his children and their heirs."

> *Example 8B*: Marge grants Blackacre "to Homer for life, then to Bart if he graduates from high school by age 19."

In each of these, some uncertainty remains as to the identity of the class of takers (Example 8A) or the occurrence of the condition (Example 8B, assuming Bart has not graduated yet). When this uncertainty is resolved, the remainders are said to *vest in interest*. We will come back to the distinction between vesting in interest and vesting in possession, but for now note that uncertainty about the identity of the taker or whether a condition for its happening will be fulfilled—vesting in interest—can occur without the person actually coming into possession—vesting in possession. For example, in Example 8B, suppose Homer is alive and Bart has just graduated from high school at an age under 19. Bart's remainder is vested in interest but has not yet vested in possession, which does not happen until Homer dies and his life estate ends. One might ask what would happen in Example 8B if Homer died before Bart had a chance to graduate from high school. It may not be immediately apparent but the life estate and the contingent remainder in Example 8B are supported by an implicit reversion in Marge, which would take after Homer dies and can be divested by Bart's graduation from high school by age 19 (in which case Bart takes). However, if Bart reaches age 19 without having graduated from high school, Marge's reversion vests indefeasibly. Remember, there always has to be someone ready to take, and if the grantor has not given everything away, a (supporting) reversion is retained.

In situations like that in Example 8B, the grantor could also use alternative contingent remainders such that one vests if the other does not and vice versa:

> *Example 8C*: Marge grants Blackacre "to Homer for life, then to Bart if he graduates from high school by age 19, otherwise to Lisa and her heirs."

If alternative contingent remainders appear to cover all the bases, do they add up to a vested remainder? One might think so, but for historical reasons courts held that they do not, and that there is an implied reversion in Marge in these circumstances, even though the chances of the reversion vesting in possession are extremely remote.[1]

Some remainders are vested but not indefeasibly so. A remainder is said to be vested "subject to complete divestment" (or "subject to complete defeasance") if the occurrence of a condition can cause the interest to shift to someone else.

> *Example 8D*: Marge grants Blackacre "to Homer for life, then to Bart; but if Bart fails to graduate from high school by age 19, then to Lisa."

---

[1]   Contingent remainders were historically regarded as "destructible" if the preceding estate terminated for a reason other than its natural termination through death. Thus, if Homer committed treason, and this led to the forfeiture of his life estate, the two alternative contingent remainders would both be destroyed. In this scenario, Blackacre would revert to Marge under her implied reversion.

Unlike the indefeasibly vested remainder in the three named children in Example 8, Bart's remainder here, a remainder subject to complete divestment, can be cut short. But unlike the contingent remainder in Example 8B, the condition here is a condition subsequent not a condition precedent: Bart's remainder vests upon the natural termination of the preceding estate but then can be cut short for reasons other than the natural termination of his own interest. (As we will see, Lisa here has a shifting executory interest.)

As opposed to complete divestment in Example 8D, divestment can be partial. Consider a variant on Example 8A, with a little context added:

> *Example 8E*: Marge grants Blackacre "to Homer for life, then to his children and their heirs." At the time of the grant, Homer is the father of Bart and Lisa (but not yet Maggie).

In such a situation, what, if anything, do Bart and Lisa have? They are part of a class "subject to open" because more members could enter the class (by being born as Homer's children). Thus, Bart and Lisa have vested remainders subject to partial divestment. The remainder is vested because there is no uncertainty as to their status as children of Homer and there is no condition precedent on their remainders. But the remainders in Bart and Lisa are subject to partial divestment because if more children are born to Homer they would diminish the interest of Bart and Lisa (e.g., from one-half to one-third, etc.). So when Maggie is born, the vesting of her remainder partially divests those of Bart and Lisa. Now all three children have remainders subject to partial divestment. When Homer dies, the remainders would vest and, assuming no more children have been born after Maggie, then Bart, Lisa, and Maggie would own Blackacre in fee simple absolute.

The remainder is normally not in the grantee of the life estate—as in "to A for life, then to A" or "to A for life, then to A's heirs"—both because this would normally not be terribly useful and because traditional doctrines would merge the two interests to reassemble a fee simple in A. By contrast, in Example 8 above the language "and their heirs" serves as words of limitation and simply emphasizes that this is a remainder in fee simple; they are words of limitation for the estate-in-waiting. When the interest becomes possessory it will become a fee simple in the three children.

b.   Executory Interest. The executory interest is a future interest in a transferee (not retained by the grantor), but, unlike the remainder following a life estate, which becomes possessory upon the natural end of the preceding interest (death), the executory interest is an interest in a transferee (not retained by the grantor) that divests or cuts short a previous interest (hence the ax in Figure 5-2). That is, the executory interest does not become possessory upon the natural end of the preceding interest (as in the case of a remainder following the death of the holder of a life estate).

Example 9: Marge grants Blackacre "to Bart, but if alcohol is ever consumed on the premises, then to Ned Flanders."

Thus in Example 9, the defeasible fee (fee simple subject to an executory limitation) is cut off early by the happening of the condition subsequent, and the following interest in Ned Flanders is an executory interest. Because the executory interest divests the interest of a third party (here Bart), it is a "shifting" executory interest. If the executory interest divests an interest in the grantor, it is called a "springing" executory interest:

Example 9A: Marge grants Blackacre "to Bart for life, remainder to Lisa 5 years after his death."

Recall that there is a reversion in Marge here that would become possessory in the 5-year period after Bart's death. Lisa has a springing executory interest because it divests the reversion in the grantor (Marge).

An executory interest can cut short—bring to an unnaturally early end—an interest that would otherwise come to a natural end (by death) as in the following example:

Example 10: Homer grants Blackacre "to Marge for life, but if she remarries, then to Lisa."

Incidentally, interests like this were allowed if they could be taken to be motivated by a concern to support a widowed spouse until remarriage, but not if they seemed to be motivated out of a desire to prevent someone's marriage (as in "to Marge for life but if she ever marries Ned Flanders, then to Lisa").

Example 11: Marge grants Blackacre "to Bart as long as the premises are not used for consuming alcohol during his lifetime, then to Ned Flanders."

This is another fee simple subject to an executory limitation (using the "as long as" language) followed by an executory interest. Notice that because the interest in the third-party transferee becomes possessory automatically on the happening of the condition no matter how the triggering event is phrased (as a limitation in the preceding interest or as a condition subsequent to the interest), there is traditionally no future interest in a grantee that works like the right of entry. Again, there is little law dealing with this issue. Keep in mind, though, that even where the preceding interest ends without any affirmative act of the next interest-holder, some action on her part is likely to be necessary for a transfer and, further down the line, in order to avoid the effect of adverse possession.

We can summarize the discussion thus far in the chart in Figure 5-5 (we will return to the Rule against Perpetuities later in the Chapter).

Figure 5-5
Summary of Estates and Future Interests

Present Interest	Examples	Typical Future Interest
Fee Simple Absolute	O grants Blackacre to M. O grants B to M in fee simple. O grants B to M and her heirs.	None None None
Life Estate	O grants B to M for life.	Reversion (in O)
	O grants B to M for life, then to N.	Remainder; *indefeasibly vested*
	O grants B to M for life, then to her adult children.	Remainder; *contingent**
	O grants B to M for life, then to N if Condition (C) occurs.	Remainder; *contingent**
	O grants B to M for life, then to N, but if C occurs, then to K.	Remainder (in N); *vested subject to complete divestment*
	O grants B to M for life, then to her children. [N was the only child at the grant]	Remainder (in N); *vested subject to partial divestment/subject to open**
Fee Simple Determinable	O grants B to M as long as C occurs, (then to O).	Possiblilty of reverter (in O)
Fee Simple Subject to Condition Subsequent	O grants B to M, but if C occurs, then O has the right to reenter and take the premises.	Right of entry/power of termination (in O)
Fee Simple Subject to Executory Limitation	O grants B to M as long as C occurs, then to N. O grants B to M, but if C occurs, then to N.	Executory interest (in N)*

* Subject to the Rule against Perpetuities

Vesting

One source of confusion stems from the multiple senses of "vested." An interest vests *in possession* when the interest becomes a present possessory one. But an interest can vest *in interest* before it vests in possession. Vesting in interest means that various types of uncertainty about the interest have been resolved. This notion of vesting in interest is particularly important in the case of remainders. When created, a remainder is clearly not vested in possession; it is a future interest that will not become possessory until the interests preceding it have terminated. However, a remainder may or may not be vested in interest, and much may turn on this question. In this latter sense, "vested" means that a certain type of uncertainty about whether the interest will ever come to a particular individual has been resolved. This uncertainty can stem from two main sources. First, it may be unclear who will take the interest when it does become possessory.

Example 12: To A for life, then to A's children.

If this is an inter vivos gift (one made while the grantor is still living), there is uncertainty as to who will be a child of A at A's death. (Notice that this is not a problem in the remainder in Example 8, because there the children are listed by name. In Example 8, if more children come along, they do not take.) In Example 12, suppose A has children now. The remainder is vested as to them, but more children may be born. In this situation we would say that the remainder is vested subject to partial divestment (or vested subject to open, as it is sometimes called).

The second type of uncertainty that prevents vesting in interest relates to contingencies.

Example 13: To any of my now living children who pass the bar.

Here there is no uncertainty as to who the children are but there is uncertainty as to whether they will pass the bar (until any such child actually passes it). As children pass the bar, the interest becomes vested as to that child. Now consider this future interest:

Example 14: To A for life, then to the children of A alive at A's death who have by then reached the age of 21.

The contingent remainder here combines elements of uncertainty over both identity and reaching 21. Present children can die and others can be born, and any children under 21 have to reach that age. The supporting reversion in O is considered vested.

In contrast to remainders, other future interests—reversionary interests of various kinds and executory interests—are much simpler as to when they vest in interest. A reversionary interest (a reversion, a possibility of reverter, or a right of entry) is considered vested in interest upon its creation, whether or not the interest ever becomes possessory. (Such an understanding has little to recommend it these days, particularly as interests created in the grantor have become more fully alienable, rendering the family connection to the grantor less distinctive in the case of reversionary interests.) The reality is that it is uncertain whether they will become possessory, and that uncertainty will not be resolved until the contingent event occurs. Nevertheless reversionary interests are considered vested from the moment they are created. Executory interests present the opposite case; normally they must become possessory (vest in possession) in order to vest in interest.[2] As we

---

[2]   The one exception to this generalization is for situations in which an executory interest can change into an indefeasibly vested remainder. For example, O transfers Blackacre "to A for life, remainder to B, but if B fails to survive A, then to C." If B predeceases A, then C's executory interest becomes an indefeasibly vested remainder.

will see, this aspect of executory interests will be very important because executory interests can easily vest too remotely, in violation of the Rule against Perpetuities.

PROBLEMS

What interests are created in the following?

1.   O grants Blackacre "to A for life, then to B and his heirs."

2.   Same as in Question 1. Then C enters adversely. Then thirty years later C is still on Blackacre and A, still alive, has never entered.

3.   O grants Blackacre "to A for life, then to B and her heirs; but if B ever remarries, then to C and her heirs."

4.   O grants Blackacre "to Huxley College as long as it is used for instructional purposes."

5.   O grants Blackacre "to A; but if marijuana is inhaled on the premises, then O shall have the right to reenter and take the premises."

6.   O grants Blackacre "to A; but if marijuana is inhaled on the premises during A's life, then to B and her heirs."

7.   O conveys Blackacre "to A for life, then to B for life, then to C."

8.   O grants Blackacre "to A for life, then to B for life, then to B's children who survive him."

9.   O grants Blackacre "to Springfield Hospital as long as it is used for the care of patients, then to Springfield Animal Clinic."

10.   O grants Blackacre "to A for life, then to A's husband if he survives her."

11.   O grants Blackacre "to A for life, then, if B passes the bar, to B and his heirs as long as he remains a member in good standing of the bar." B is a student in law school.

12.   Bequest (legacy) by O of "$100,000 to A, to be paid when A reaches age twenty-one."

C. MAINTAINING THE SYSTEM

Knowing how to classify estates and interests and even how they combine is just the beginning. Many difficulties arise when property rights are divided, because those with a stake are not guaranteed to agree with each other. And in the case of future interests, the person with the interest may not even be born, and is unavailable for negotiation. In this Section we consider a number of doctrines that are supposed to maintain the system, often by placing limits on what those dividing property rights or enjoying the resulting pieces may do.

1. CONSERVATION OF ESTATES

We have already seen how the system of estates and future interests acts as a sort of "grammar" of property rights. One feature of the system is that when a transfer is made, all of what the grantor had must be accounted for, even if this means implying a reversionary interest. That is, the durational content of the fee simple (or other interest that O starts out with) must be conserved. The principle of conservation of estates ensures that all the pieces of the estate are accounted for.

The principle of conservation applies whenever a grantor might convey something less than her full interest. This usually happens when the grantor starts with a fee simple and conveys away some of that interest. We have already seen numerous examples in which the fee owner grants away a life estate or a defeasible fee and retains a reversionary interest, explicitly or implicitly. But the fee owner may retain something other than the "last" part of the fee simple.

Example: Marge conveys "to Bart when he reaches the age of 21."

Here Marge has conveyed an executory interest to Bart. It is called a springing executory interest because it follows an interest retained by the grantor—as opposed to a shifting executory interest, which takes after another interest created in a third party. Here Marge has retained what's left, but the piece is a present possessory interest, probably a fee simple subject to an executory limitation. The pieces add up to the fee simple Marge started out with. Marge could have retained the "middle" of the timeline as well:

Example: Homer conveys "to Abe for life, then ten years later to Marge and her heirs."

Here Homer has conveyed a life estate to Abe and an executory interest in fee simple to Marge that springs from a reversionary interest retained by Homer. The reversionary interest would be a reversion in fee simple subject to executory limitation. The limitation event here is the tenth anniversary of Abe's death. (Notice that although this interest is for a stated number of years it is a reversion, not a "term of years," which would be a lease.) Again, the interests granted and retained must add up to the fee simple Homer has to begin with.

While the interest retained is either a reversionary or a present possessory interest, notice that in a conveyance, the "last" interest, implicit or explicit, must be a fee simple (absolute) when it becomes possessory. If the last interest is a reversion it must be a reversion in fee simple; if it is a remainder or an executory interest, it must be a remainder in fee simple or an executory interest in fee simple. If not, the chain of interests could come to an end with no one ready to take. Because the whole fee is of unlimited duration, this could never happen. If a holder in fee simple dies without heirs, the property escheats to the state. This is a slight echo of the feudal system, in which all owners ultimately held of the monarch. See In re O'Connor's Estate, 252 N.W. 826 (Neb. 1934).

Williams v. Estate of Williams

Supreme Court of Tennessee, 1993.
865 S.W.2d 3.

■ REID, CHIEF JUSTICE. This suit seeks the construction of the last will and testament of G.A. Williams, deceased, and the declaration of the rights of the parties in a tract of land described in the will.

The record does not contain all the information necessary for the Court to adjudicate the ownership of the land. * * *

The only facts alleged are that G.A. Williams died on November 17, 1944, the instrument attached to the complaint is a copy of his last will and testament, the farm mentioned in the will is located in McMinn County, and, inferentially, the farm was owned by the testator at the time of his death. These allegations are admitted by Rachel Couch, Curtis Williams, and Wayne Williams, the only defendants actually before the Court.

Additional facts, though not proven or stipulated but apparently not disputed by the parties before the Court, are relied upon in the briefs. The will was executed on July 18, 1933, and probated in the Probate Court of McMinn County on November 24, 1944. The testator was survived by nine children, including the three daughters named in the will. The plaintiff, Ethel Williams, who was 92 years of age when the complaint was filed, is the only survivor of the three children named in the will. The defendant Etta Tallent is the only other surviving child of the testator, and the other defendants are lineal descendants of the testator. (There is no statement that the named defendants are all the heirs at law of the testator.) Ethel Williams has maintained possession of the farm since the death of the testator, jointly with Ida Williams and Mallie Williams until their deaths. Apparently none of the three-named daughters ever married, though that fact does not affirmatively appear.

The will is as follows:

I, G.A. WILLIAMS, being of sound mind make this my last will and Testament: At my death I want Ida Williams, Mallie Williams, and Ethel Williams, three of my daughters to have my home farm where I now live, consisting of one hundred and eighty-eight acres, to have and to hold during their lives, and not to be sold during their lifetime. If any of them marry their interest ceases and the ones that remain single have full control of same. I am making this will because they have stayed at home and taken care of the home and cared for their mother during her sickness, and I do not want them sold out of a home. If any one tries to contest this will I want them debarred from any interest in my estate. /s/ G.A. Williams, July the 18, 1933.

The complaint alleged that the interest received by Ethel Williams was a life estate under the will or, in the alternative, a life estate under the will and a "remainder interest" by intestate succession. The latter disposition was adopted by the Chancellor initially, but on rehearing was abandoned for the finding that the devise of a life estate without limitation over indicated an intention that the named daughters have the property in fee simple, which is the position asserted by Ethel Williams on appeal.

The Court of Appeals affirmed the holding of the trial court. It held, on the authority of *White v. Brown,* 559 S.W.2d 938 (Tenn. 1977), that each named daughter owned a one-third undivided interest in fee simple. The record does not support that decision.

The function of a suit to construe a will is to ascertain and effect the intention of the testator. The determinative intention is the predominant purpose expressed by the testator in the will. Statements regarding the means whereby the predominant purpose of the will is to be accomplished will not be given literal effect if they would defeat the predominant intention. * * *

This Court stated the rule more concisely in Moore v. Neely, 370 S.W.2d 537 (Tenn. 1963):

> Another rule of construction is that when a controlling or predominate purpose of the testator is expressed, it is the duty of the court to effectuate that purpose, and to construe all subsidiary clauses so as to bring them into subordination to such purpose. The language of a single sentence is not to control as against the evident purpose and intent shown by the whole will.

Id. 370 S.W.2d at 540.

In the case before the Court, the predominant intention of the testator is clear. Each of the testator's three daughters who had "stayed home" was to have the farm jointly with the other two daughters, so long as they were living and unmarried, as a residence and for their support; after the death or marriage of any of the three daughters, the remaining two daughters would hold jointly until the marriage or death of another; and the remaining unmarried daughter was to hold until she married or died. The statements that the farm was "not to be sold during their lifetime" and "I do not want them sold out of a home" emphasized and reenforced the predominant intention that each of the three daughters have a residence and support during her life or until she should marry. The testator's statement that he was favoring those children above the others because they had "stayed at home and taken care of . . . their mother" implicitly recognized that each had foregone the opportunity to become self-supporting or be supported by a husband, and limiting the duration of the devise to such time as a daughter should marry, indicates that the devise was intended to be a substitute for support that might otherwise have been available.

The intention of the testator was not to make an absolute gift to all or either of the daughters. The first statement in the will limits the devise "during their lives." The next statement limits the devise to the duration of their unmarried state. The testator devised to the daughters an interest not readily alienable and one that could not be defeated by a suit for partition or sale for partition. His reason for selecting the estate devised is indicated by the statements "not to be sold during their lifetime" and "I do not want them sold out of a home." Upon the death or marriage of the named daughters, the testator's purpose as to them would have been accomplished and the testator's heirs would inherit the property by intestate succession.

[handwritten margin note: ref. to heirs = further intent evidence (that the heirs would eventually have interest)]

The testator recognized that his other heirs would acquire some interest in the property upon his death. The primary emphasis was that the daughters' limited interests not be disturbed by the owners of the interest not devised to the daughters. The severity of his admonition is shown by the provision that any person who should "contest" the will would be "debarred" from any interest, not just in the farm but in his estate.

This case is not controlled by *White v. Brown,* relied upon by the Court of Appeals. In that case, the following provision was found to constitute the devise of a fee simple:

> " . . . I wish Evelyn White to have my home to live in and *not* to be *sold.* I also leave my personal property to Sandra White Perry. My house is not to be sold."

559 S.W.2d at 938. The majority in *White* based its decision on that portion of what is now T.C.A. § 32–3–101 (1984) which provides:

[handwritten margin note: White — fee simple unless the will says otherwise via contrary intention expressly stated]

> A will . . . shall convey all the real estate belonging to [the testator], or in which he had any interest at his decease, unless a contrary intention appear by its words in context.

However, in language applicable to the case before the Court, Justice Harbison, dissenting, stated:

> I have serious doubt that the testatrix intended to create any illegal restraint on alienation or to violate any other rules of law. It seems to me that she rather emphatically intended to provide that her sister-in-law was not to be able to sell the house during the lifetime of the latter—a result which is both legal and consistent with the creation of a life estate.

[handwritten margin note: dissent thought intent was clearly for life estate]

Id. at 942. That statute does not control the disposition in the case before the Court because, as discussed above, a contrary intention appears from the will. The provision that each daughter's interest would terminate upon her marriage, as well as upon her death, is a further indication that the testator did not intend for the named daughters to have an absolute estate in the farm. As stated in *Page on Wills,*

[handwritten margin note: here, there IS a contrary intention]

> The gift to A may indicate quite clearly that it is a gift for the life of A, as where the gift is to A for life or until her marriage, or a gift to A for life or during her widowhood. In gifts of this sort, A takes a life estate, since the provision with

reference to marriage or widowhood is, at least, not sufficient to overcome the effect of the provisions of the will which show that testator intends to give to A a life estate only.

. . . .

. . . By what seems to be the weight of authority, a gift to A until her marriage or during widowhood gives a life estate to A. Such life estate would be defeasible or determinable upon the marriage of A.

4 William J. Bowe & Douglas H. Parker, Page on Wills, § 37.22, at 632–634 (4th ed. 1961) (footnotes omitted).

The will as a whole conveys a definite meaning. Though the author obviously was not a skilled legal draftsman, he, also obviously, had a good command of language and was familiar with legal phrases commonly used and understood beyond the legal profession. The testator accurately described the instrument he was writing as his "last will and testament," he asserted that he was "of sound mind," and he employed the traditional words of conveyance—"to have and to hold"—in devising an interest in real estate to the daughters. Even "contest," though perhaps not used accurately in its narrow, technical sense, may indicate an action designed to defeat a testamentary disposition. The conclusion is almost inescapable that, had the testator intended to devise the named beneficiaries an estate in fee, he would have expressed that intention quite clearly. Consequently, the estate devised to the named daughters was less than a fee simple.

Upon the death of the testator, each named daughter held a life estate, defeasible or determinable upon her marriage. See Id. Each daughter also had an executory interest in each of the other two daughters' one-third interest, which would vest in her possession if the other life tenant should die or marry while she remained unmarried. See Lewis M. Simes & Allan F. Smith, The Law of Future Interests, § 285 (2d ed. 1956). The heirs-at-law of the testator held a reversion in fee simple, subject to the determinable life estates and the executory interests in the named daughters, which reversion would vest in possession, at the latest, upon the death of the survivor of the named daughters. See Cornelius J. Moynihan, Introduction to the Law of Real Property, at 94–95 (1962).

The judgment of the Court of Appeals is reversed, and the case is remanded for further proceedings. * * *

NOTES AND QUESTIONS

1.   One principle implicit in the reasoning of both the Tennessee Supreme Court and the appellate court is the *conservation of estates.* Grantors may break up their interests and transfer some or all of the pieces, but the pieces have to add up to what the grantor started out with. Where, as in the *Williams* case, someone is granting a fee simple, all of the pieces have to add up to a fee simple. Can you see why on the Tennessee Supreme

Court's approach, but not on that of the appellate court, a reversion in the heirs is necessary?

2.   The court believes that the will's mention of the heirs (and the possibility of their contesting the will) means that the testator intended that they would take some interest in the property under the will. Does this follow? By definition the heirs are those who would take under the intestacy statute. Wouldn't that furnish sufficient incentive for them to contest the will—and for the testator to worry about this possibility? Do you agree that the testator's use of legal terminology makes the court's conclusion "almost inescapable"? If not, why not?

3.   The will here is apparently a holographic will, i.e., one handwritten by the testator. In some states, statutes provide that some of the requirements (such as witnesses) are dispensed with in the case of holographic wills. Courts also tend to take a less formalistic approach in interpreting holographic wills. The next stage may be video and electronic wills, which are permissible in Arizona, Florida, Indiana, and Nevada. A video will would presumably reduce some of the concerns about fraud and duress associated with holographic wills. But might it introduce new concerns about fraud? Would such wills reduce interpretational problems like the one in *Williams*? Or would the interpretational problems only get worse? See Adam J. Hirsch, Technology Adrift: In Search of a Role for Electronic Wills, 61 B.C. L. Rev. 827 (2020).

4.   In general, will interpretation is a curious blend of formalism and a search for the testator's intent. See, e.g., Bruce H. Mann, Formalities and Formalism in the Uniform Probate Code, 142 U. Pa. L. Rev. 1033 (1994); John H. Langbein, Substantial Compliance with the Wills Act, 88 Harv. L. Rev. 489 (1975). Among the many rules of interpretation that courts employ is one that favors interpretations that avoid intestacy. This canon reflects an assumption that once a testator is expressing an intent to dispose of her property by will, she is unlikely to be expressing a partial intent and deliberately invoking the intestacy laws. (Indeed, the intestacy laws are meant in part to specify a default intent where none is expressed.) Many wills include a residuary clause of this sort: "I give all the rest, residue, and remainder of my estate to. . . ." From the absence of such a clause, do you think the testator wished to create a partial intestacy here?

5.   The court asserts that the set of interests here is inalienable during the lives of the three sisters. Should the testator be able to prevent alienation in this way? (We take up restraints on alienation later in the chapter.) Notice that if the testator had employed a trust, the testator could choose whether to give the trustee the power of alienation.

6.   Most life estates these days are created in trust; they are equitable as opposed to legal life estates. The major source of legal life estates is holographic wills. Such was the case in *Williams*. Lawyers generally avoid legal life estates as cumbersome and litigation-prone, and will instead employ a trust with a lifetime beneficiary coupled with a gift over to the same or to a third party. In a trust arrangement, the various estates and interests serve as methods of carving up the value of the trust assets.

Disclaimer

One of the powers of the owner is to make a gift, but a valid gift requires acceptance by the donee. More generally, it takes two to transfer, and the potential transferee has a veto over the transfer; no one is obligated to accept a property interest. As one court put it, "[t]he law certainly is not so absurd as to force a man to take an estate against his will." Townson v. Tickell, 106 Eng. Rep. 575, 576–77 (K.B. 1819). These principles form the basis of the law of disclaimer, under which a potential recipient can refuse property. Disclaimer has roots in the common law but is now provided for by statute. States vary in terms of whether the statutory disclaimer is the exclusive method. Statutes typically require a clear and unequivocal expression, and accepting any benefit of the asset in question defeats any attempt at disclaimer. Many statutes require certain formalities in order to disclaim interests in real property, such as a writing describing the property. A successful disclaimer results in the one disclaiming being treated as never having owned the disclaimed interest. Why might someone disclaim an interest? In the context of family wealth transmission, a beneficiary might prefer the property to go to the next taker but would like to avoid the tax consequences of a double transfer. A disclaimer may help avoid probate and may prevent the disclaimant's creditors from reaching the property. See Joan B. Ellsworth, On Disclaimers: Let's Renounce I.R.C. Section 2518, 38 Vill. L. Rev. 693 (1993). Recall also the material on abandonment; some property has a negative value because of liabilities such as for environmental clean-up.

2.   THE FLEXIBILITY OF THE ESTATE SYSTEM

As you read through the following materials ask yourself whether the system of estates and future interests can be used to serve the goals of a system of property. Do we have enough devices to achieve the objectives of those wishing to split ownership over time? Or do we, as many argue, have too many interests? As we will see, one of the central features of the estate system is that the menu of forms of ownership is fixed, finite, and closed, a doctrine known (especially in the civil law) as the *numerus clausus* (closed number) of forms of property. One may not create a new form of ownership, in stark contrast to the approach in contract law, in which free customizability (within broad limits) is the norm. Before considering why property takes this very noncontractarian approach, one might ask how a fixed system of estates could possibly be flexible enough to serve people's needs.

One reason that the system is more flexible than appears at first blush is something known in formal language theory as recursiveness. Consider the following example:

Example: O to A for life, then to B for life, then to C for life.

Here in effect what O has done is to carve out a life estate and a reversion and immediately carved out another life estate for B, pushing back the implied reversion still further, and then done so again for C. (If B dies before A or if C dies before either A or B, their respective remainders in life estate are extinguished.) One could think of the owner employing this set of rules (out of a larger set, some of which would correspond to the diagrams in Figure 5-2, supra):

    (i)   Fee simple → Life estate + Reversion

    (ii)   Reversion → Life estate + Reversion

What is special about these rules is that rule (ii) can feed itself. Rules whose output can be fed back into the rule are called *recursive*, as reflected by the fact that Reversion appears on both sides of the arrow in (ii). The owner in the example can be considered to have used Rule (i) and then Rule (ii), and then Rule (ii) again (i.e., twice). In principle there is no limit to how many times O could carve out life estates and push the reversion back yet further. As a result, any set of rules containing a recursive rule like (ii) generates an infinite set of potential outputs. Something similar is typically true in computer programs and in the grammars of natural languages. Among the linguistic phenomena that call for a model including a recursive rule is the complement clause beginning with *that*: "Pat said/believed that Chris is sick," "Leslie said/believed that Pat said/believed that Chris is sick," etc. A sentence can consist of *that* plus another sentence (which can in turn consist of *that* plus another sentence, etc.), with no limit in principle. While it is certainly the case that people can make up new words, one cannot unilaterally make up a rule like the *that* rule. But the *that* rule (and rules like it) permit a finite grammar to capture an infinite set of possible sentences. So too with the basic building blocks of property and the rules for combining them. For a model of the estate system as a formal domain-specific language, see Shrutarshi Basu, Nate Foster & James Grimmelmann, Property Conveyances as a Programming Language, in Proc. 2019 ACM SIGPLAN Int'l Symp. on New Ideas, New Paradigms, & Reflections on Programming and Software (Onward!) 128 (2019).

Using the Estate System for Estate Planning

The system of estates in land was primarily devised with estate planning in mind—determining the distribution of assets that occurs when an individual dies—and this continues to be one of its primary functions today. Estate planning requires predictability, hence the rule-like nature of the system of estates in land and future interests. But flexibility is also important. When the system was getting off the ground, land was all-important, and the family patriarch (land being controlled by the husband as head of the household) would often want to assure that Blackacre would remain in the family to provide a source of support (and social status) for a surviving spouse and children, and he might hope to keep it in the family even longer (in his dreams perhaps forever). Today attitudes are different, but the estate system still provides the building blocks for estate planners. Now, however, rather than leaving Blackacre in a series of legal estates in land, virtually all estate planners will create a trust, either before an owner dies or as part of a will. The corpus of the trust is much more likely to consist of stocks, bonds, partnership interests, and other intangible assets than Blackacre; if there is a Blackacre, its disposition may be regarded as a sideshow. We take up trusts in greater detail in the next Chapter. For now, the important point is that the trust will give legal title to all the assets to a trustee (a trusted family member or friend or a professional financial institution) in fee simple, and will describe various beneficial interests in the earnings from the assets in a surviving spouse, children, etc., understood to be equitable interests, not legal interests. Importantly—and this is a primary reason you are studying these materials—the vocabulary for describing these beneficial equitable interests in trust incorporates the *same* system of estates originally devised for freehold interests in land. Thus, lawyers and other estate planners will employ forms such as the life estate, the remainder, and the executory interest in formulating an estate plan that seeks to realize the goals of the individual for whom such a trust is being set up. Facility with these forms is therefore necessary to be an effective estate planner.

One reason to use a will—with or without a trust—is to avoid the application of the intestacy statute. Each state has an intestacy statute that determines the decedent's heirs and how and when they inherit property. The statute reflects a default presumption about what a decedent would wish if there had been a valid will reflecting his or her intent. Some people's desires diverge very much from these defaults, and such persons have an extra reason to need a will. Even so, studies suggest that many if not most people in the United States die intestate. Thus, intestacy is a blunt instrument and the law does not favor its application. Wills are construed to avoid intestacy. A partially invalid will can lead to partial intestacy.

Under the typical intestacy statute, the intestate's successors are the family, with priority going to the decedent's spouse and issue (lineal descendants). Traditionally, the spouse would get between one third and one half of the estate. The 1990 Uniform Probate Code Section 2–102 would increase this share to 100% under a wide variety of circumstances including no surviving lineal descendants or parents, or no lineal descendants who are not also lineal descendants of the surviving spouse. Studies suggest that this better tracks the preferences of most people. In the absence of any surviving spouse or issue, other relatives are the successors. These are lineal ascendants (parents, grandparents, and so on) and collaterals, who are designated blood relatives who are neither lineal descendants nor ascendants, i.e., siblings, uncles and aunts, nephews and nieces, cousins, and so on. Various systems exist for determining who among these non-spouse, non-issue people succeed.

Generally speaking closer blood relatives take precedence over more distant ones, but states vary as to whether this is based on degrees of *consanguinity* or on the *parentelic* system. Consanguinity counts distance in terms of the number of generations to a common ancestor (e.g., one between parent and child, two between grandparent and grandchild) and if necessary down to the collateral (so degree two for a sibling, i.e., up to the parent and down to the sibling; three for a nephew or niece, etc.). In the parentelic system, priority is given to those close by in terms of sharing a common ancestor even if the deceased and the person in question belong to very different generations. So under the parentelic system grandnieces (related in the fourth degree in terms of consanguinity) have priority over aunts (related in the third degree) because a grandniece is descended from the decedent's parents but an aunt is descended from the grandparents. For details, see Robert H. Sitkoff & Jesse Dukeminier, Wills Trusts, and Estates 79–89 (10th ed. 2017). As you can imagine, these differences and their technical nature can lead to undesired results for the uninformed.

What if a spouse does have a will but leaves the surviving spouse one dollar, or nothing at all? Generally states have a spousal elective share—typically one third, which the surviving spouse may (but need not) elect. Others designated under the will then take proportionately less. Such elective shares replaced earlier special marital property interests in surviving spouses, called dower and curtesy. We return to marital property rights in Part F of this Chapter.

What if a child predeceases a parent who then dies intestate? The child cannot then be an heir. But intestacy statutes differ as to how any surviving descendants of the predeceased child will be treated. Under one system, such children (grandchildren of the intestate) will be allocated shares of the estate *per stirpes*: under the traditional "English" version, the estate is divided into equal shares based on the number of children, alive or deceased, who have descendants living at the intestate's death. Then any share corresponding to a predeceased child is divided in a similar fashion among his descendants. So if O dies with no surviving spouse and has two living children A and B and one predeceased child C who left children C1 and C2, then C1 and C2 each get one-sixth of the estate (A and B each get one-third). In a *per capita* system (and more modern versions of per stirpes) the estate is divided up equally among the members of the generations closest to the intestate with at least one living member (usually the children). In the example, A, B, C1, and C2 all get one fourth. Notice that in each system C is represented by C1 and C2. But any will C may have left generally has nothing to do with how the intestate scheme works with respect to allocating O's assets upon her death. These rules have evolved greatly from earlier notions of primogeniture favoring eldest sons, especially for real estate. Modern intestacy laws, particularly in states using a system based on consanguinity, look more like the traditional system for personal property, which called for equal shares among surviving children.

3.   THE *NUMERUS CLAUSUS*

The catalog of estates is finite and closed, a principle sometimes called the *numerus clausus*. The term *"numerus clausus"* comes from the civil law which, in its various versions, exhibits a strong and explicit principle that property, unlike contract, is not freely customizable by parties but rather is standardized into a closed set of approved forms. In the common law, and U.S. law in particular, the *numerus clausus* is more implicit. Consider the following case.

Charles v. Barzey

Privy Council, United Kingdom, 2002.
[2002] UKPC 68 (Dominica).

■ LORD HOFFMANN. The question in this appeal is the meaning of a devise in the will dated 14 April 1980 of Iris Charles, who died at Elmshall, Dominica on 11 March 1986. At the time of her death she owned several properties. Two were in Cork Street, Roseau. One was No 9, where she was living at the time of her will. The other was No 18, which was a dwelling house together with what was described in her will as an "addition" consisting of a garage and storeroom. The access to these additional premises was directly from the street and they were used by her nephew John Charles as a storeroom for the purposes of the pharmaceutical business of a company controlled by him which occupied the premises next door. Both the house at No 18 and the garage and storeroom were registered in the Register of Titles in Dominica as a single lot and held under the same certificate of title.

She left No 9 Cork Street to John Charles absolutely. The devise of No 18 was in these words:

> I hereby give and bequeath to my niece, Mrs Yvette Barzey my house and lot at 18 Cork Street, Roseau, Dominica. The addition to the house where the garage and storeroom is located I give to my nephew Mr John A. Charles to be used by him as long as he wishes.

Mrs Barzey is the sister of Mr John Charles. She claimed that upon the true construction of the will, she took an unencumbered freehold interest in the whole registered title and that Mr John Charles took nothing. On 11 November 1998 she issued an originating summons in which she sought a declaration to this effect and an order that she be registered with an unencumbered title.

The application came before Einfeld J on 12 March 1999. He held that clause 4 meant that Mrs Barzey was to take the fee simple in No. 18 subject to a life interest in the garage and storeroom given to Mr Charles.

Mrs Barzey appealed to the Court of Appeal, which on 13 September 1999 allowed the appeal. The Court gave a brief judgment:

> In this appeal we see no difference in facts between *Da Costa* [*Da Costa v Warburton* (1971) 17 WIR 334] and this case. The user of the garage and the storeroom is repugnant to the bequest to the appellant.

* * * The interpretation of a will is in principle no different from that of any other communication. The question is what a reasonable person, possessed of all the background knowledge which the testatrix might reasonably have been expected to have, would have understood the testatrix to have meant by the words which she used. Furthermore, as Lord Greene MR said in *In re Potter's Will Trusts* [1944] Ch 70, 77:

> It is a fundamental rule in the interpretation of wills that effect must be given, so far as possible, to the words which the testator has used. It is equally fundamental that apparent inconsistencies must, so far as possible, be reconciled, and that it is only when reconciliation is impossible that a recalcitrant provision must be rejected. Even in that case, of two irreconcilable provisions, it is the later that prevails, but in the present case there is no need to have recourse to this rule of despair.

Their Lordships think, as did Einfeld J, that there cannot really be any doubt about what the testatrix meant. She intended Mrs Barzey to take No 18, subject to the right of Mr Charles to use the garage and storeroom for as long as he wished; an interest which the law will classify as a life interest: compare *Coward v Larkman* (1888) 60 LT 1 (HL). Admittedly she could have made it even clearer by using words like "Except that" before the second sentence of the devise. But that was obviously her intention. It is supported by the background, which was that the garage and storeroom had for many years been used in connection with the pharmacy next door and not with the house.

[One] argument[ ] against giving effect to the evident intention of the testatrix * * * relies upon the doctrine of repugnant conditions, as discussed by the Court of Appeal in *Da Costa v Warburton* (1971) 17 WIR 334. This doctrine is based upon the proposition that there are certain forms of disposition which the law will not allow. For example, a gift which might vest more than 21 years after the death of a life in being was void at common law because it was considered contrary to public policy to allow gifts to take effect at remote dates in the future. A provision for the divesting of property on bankruptcy is void because contrary to the policy of the bankruptcy law. Then there are dispositions which the law of property simply cannot accommodate. There are a limited number of interests which can exist as interests in property and attempts to create interests unknown to the law are ineffectual. Thus a gift of land in fee simple subject to a condition that it shall not be alienated passes an unconditional fee simple. The condition is void because the law does not recognise such an interest as an inalienable fee simple. Another way of making the same point is to say that such a condition is repugnant to the nature of a fee simple.

These rules, of which many other examples could be given, are not rules of construction. They are substantive rules of public policy which prohibit certain kinds of dispositions or the imposition of certain kinds of conditions. In principle, the application of these rules of public policy comes after the question of construction. One first ascertains the intention of the testator and then decides whether it can be given effect. But nowadays the existence of the rules of public policy may influence the question of construction. If the testator's words can be construed in two different ways, one of which is valid and the other void, then unless the testator obviously did not intend to make the kind of gift which would be valid, the court will usually be inclined to construe his will in that sense. The theory of the old rule against perpetuities was that construction was "remorseless": one construed the will as if there was no rule against perpetuities and then, if the gift offended, held it void. See *Gray, The Rules Against Perpetuities* (4th ed 1962 para 629). But that kind of construction is now out of date. * * *

There is absolutely no difficulty about accommodating Iris Charles's intentions within ordinary property concepts. A gift of the fee simple in remainder, subject to a prior life interest in the whole or part of the property in favour of someone else, is an extremely common form of disposition. In their Lordships' opinion the Court of Appeal did not heed the warning of Smith JA in *Da Costa's* case (at p. 339):

> One has to be careful here of arguing in a circle. It seems to me that any direction in a will which has the effect of cutting down a prima facie fee simple estate created by section 23 [of the Jamaican Act, equivalent to section 29 of the Dominican Act, setting up a presumption for a grant in fee simple] can properly be said to be repugnant to that estate. But such a direction is not necessarily void for repugnancy. Take a case where a testator says: 'I give my property at Billy Dunn to my wife'. This is followed by other bequests and devises. Then the will says: 'on the death of my wife my property at Billy Dunn shall go to my son John and his heirs'. Surely, this last devise is repugnant to the prima facie fee simple created by section 23 in the wife's favour! But it nevertheless shows a contrary intention and the wife gets a life interest only . . . In other words, it must first be established that an absolute interest has been created before the question of repugnant conditions can arise.

The present case is even simpler because the reconciliation of the two gifts does not require any revision of the prima facie fee simple given to Mrs Barzey. The gift of a life interest in part of the premises to Mr Charles merely shows that, in respect of that part of the property, her fee simple is to take effect in remainder. That is something which presents no difficulty linguistically, conceptually or as a matter of public policy. Their Lordships accordingly allow the appeal and restore the judgment of Einfeld J. * * *

NOTES AND QUESTIONS

1.   Why does the court hesitate over whether to recognize Mr. Charles's right to remain during his life? In the context of a will, the touchstone is supposed to be the testator's intent. As we will see repeatedly, property law often calls for interpretation of the intent of someone creating a property in terms of a given set of approved options—rather than allowing unfettered tailoring in the way that contractual parties are free to tailor agreements to their particular needs. This pigeonholing exercise is often regarded as an instance of the *numerus clausus* principle. And yet to say that a grantor intended a qualification "repugnant to the fee" sounds rather conclusory, doesn't it? What is it about property that calls for this more standardizing treatment than in contract? We take up the question of justification with the next reading.

2.   If there is a leading case for the *numerus clausus* principle in the United States, it is *Johnson v. Whiton*, 34 N.E. 542 (Mass. 1893), in which the testator's will contained a clause reading "After the decease of all my children, I give, devise, and bequeath to my granddaughter Sarah A. Whiton and her heirs on her father's side one-third part of all my estate, both real and personal, and to my other grandchildren and their heirs, respectively, the remainder, to be divided in equal parts between them." Id. at 542. In a characteristically self-assured and cryptic opinion, Justice Holmes held this to be invalid as intended, because it purported to "create a new kind of inheritance" reminiscent of a recently abolished version of the fee tail. Sarah got a fee simple instead. (Why?) As justification, Holmes pronounced that "[i]t would be most unfortunate and unexpected if it should be discovered at this late day that it was possible to impose such a qualification upon a fee, and to put it out of the power of the owners to give a clear title for generations." Id. Was Holmes right about what Royal Whiton intended—or about the effect on alienability?

3.   The doctrine of fixed estates, an aspect of the *numerus clausus*, is sometimes associated with the feudalism out of which the estate system grew. Often arguments that some feature is "repugnant" to the nature of an estate (often the fee simple) are regarded as not only circular but formalistic and dustily feudal. This type of argument is in fact quite ahistorical. In civil law the *numerus clausus* in its modern form arose in the efforts during and after the French Revolution to abolish the complex feudal property arrangements. In this country, repugnancy to the fee was the doctrinal battle cry of those who wanted to abolish the vestiges of feudalism in nineteenth-century New York, where large landowners had conveyed fees but reserved the right to perpetual ground rents. On rent-related strife in nineteenth-century New York, see Charles W. McCurdy, The Anti-Rent Era in New York Law and Politics, 1839–1865 (2001). These days, the main tension, especially in civil law countries, is between the *numerus clausus* and custom: should customary rights not on the legislatively approved list nevertheless receive

in rem treatment by courts? Yun-chien Chang & Henry E. Smith, The *Numerus Clausus* Principle, Property Customs, and the Emergence of New Property Forms, 100 Iowa L. Rev. 2275 (2015).

As a matter of justification, in both the civil-law and common-law traditions the *numerus clausus* has been something of a puzzle.

Thomas W. Merrill & Henry E. Smith, *Optimal Standardization in the Law of Property: The* Numerus Clausus *Principle*

110 YALE L.J. 1, 24–28, 31–35, 38, 40, 42 (2000).

III. Measurement Costs, Frustration Costs, and the Optimal Standardization of Property Rights

What accounts for the widespread adherence to the *numerus clausus*, not only in the common law but in postfeudal legal systems throughout the world? To the extent that an explanation can be found in the American legal literature, it focuses on a concern with undue restraints on alienation. * * *

The problem with this argument is that the system of estates in land is sufficiently flexible that one can nearly always find a way to effectuate a complicated conveyance. * * *

The leading English case affirming what we call the *numerus clausus* principle, *Keppell v. Bailey*,[102] suggests a different rationale. *Keppell* involved the conveyance of an iron works, in which the purchasers covenanted on behalf of themselves and their successors and assigns to acquire all limestone required by the works from a particular quarry and to ship the limestone to the works on a particular railroad. The Court of Chancery held that this type of agreement, although enforceable as a contract between the original parties, did not fall within the recognized types of servitudes enforceable against subsequent purchasers as a property right running with the land. There was, however, no suggestion in the case that the covenants worked an undue restraint on alienation; indeed, the works had recently been conveyed from the original purchasers to another party. Instead, Lord Chancellor Brougham stressed the more systemic consequences of allowing such "fancies," as they have been called, to be enforced as property rights:

> There can be no harm to allowing the fullest latitude to men in binding themselves and their representatives, that is, their assets real and personal, to answer in damages for breach of their obligations. This tends to no mischief, and is a reasonable liberty to bestow; but great detriment would arise and much confusion of rights if parties were allowed to invent new modes of holding and enjoying real property, and to impress upon their lands and tenements a peculiar character, which should follow

---

[102]   39 Eng. Rep. 1042 (Ch. 1834).

them into all hands, however remote. Every close, every messuage, might thus be held in [a] several fashion; and it would hardly be possible to know what rights the acquisition of any parcel conferred, or what obligations it imposed.[105]

In modern terminology, the Lord Chancellor thought that permitting interests like the covenants in *Keppell* to be established as property rights would create unacceptable information costs to third parties.

In this Part, we develop Lord Chancellor Brougham's germ of an insight by presenting a theory of the *numerus clausus* based on optimal standardization of property rights.

A.   Measurement-Cost Externalities

When individuals encounter property rights, they face a measurement problem. In order to avoid violating another's property rights, they must ascertain what those rights are. In order to acquire property rights, they must measure various attributes, ranging from the physical boundaries of a parcel, to use rights, to the attendant liabilities of the owner to others (such as adjacent owners). Whether the objective is to avoid liability or to acquire rights, an individual will measure the property rights until the marginal costs of additional measurement equal the marginal benefits. When seeking to avoid liability, the actor will seek to minimize the sum of the costs of liability for violations of rights and the costs of avoiding those violations through measurement. In the potential transfer situation, the individual will measure as long as the marginal benefit in reduced error costs exceeds the marginal cost of measurement.

The need for standardization in property law stems from an externality involving measurement costs: Parties who create new property rights will not take into account the full magnitude of the measurement costs they impose on strangers to the title. An example illustrates. Suppose one hundred people own watches. *A* is the sole owner of a watch and wants to transfer some or all of the rights to use the watch to *B*. The law of personal property allows the sale of *A*'s entire interest in the watch, or the sale of a life estate in the watch, or the sale of a joint tenancy or tenancy in common in the watch. But suppose *A* wants to create a "time-share" in the watch, which would allow *B* to use the watch on Mondays but only on Mondays (with *A* retaining for now the rights to the watch on all other days). As a matter of contract law, *A* and *B* are perfectly free to enter into such an idiosyncratic agreement. But *A* and *B* are not permitted by the law of personal property to create a *property right* in the use of the watch on Mondays only and to transfer this property right from *A* to *B*.[110]

[handwritten margin note: costs associated w/ unlimited options of ownership]

---

[105]   Keppell, 39 Eng. Rep. at 1049.

[110]   Time shares are a creation of statute, and the various statutes appear to limit time shares to real estate. Ellen R. Peirce & Richard A. Mann, Time-Share Interests in Real Estate: A Critical Evaluation of the Regulatory Environment, 59 Notre Dame L. Rev. 9, 37–42 (1983).

Why might the law restrict the freedom of *A* and *B* to create such an unusual property right? Suppose, counterfactually, that such idiosyncratic property rights are permitted. Word spreads that someone has sold a Monday right in a watch, but not which of the one hundred owners did so. If *A* now decides to sell his watch, he will have to explain that it does not include Monday rights, and this will reduce the attractiveness of the watch to potential buyers. Presumably, however, A will foresee this when he sells the Monday rights, and is willing to bear the cost of that action in the form of a lower sales price. But consider what will happen now when any of the *other* ninety-nine watch owners try to sell their watches. Given the awareness that someone has created a Monday-only right, anyone else buying a watch must now also investigate whether any particular watch does not include Monday rights. Thus, by allowing even one person to create an idiosyncratic property right, the information processing costs of all persons who have existing or potential interests in this type of property go up. This external cost on other market participants forms the basis of our explanation of the *numerus clausus*.

At this point, it is useful to distinguish three classes of individuals who might be affected by the decision to create idiosyncratic property rights, or fancies, as illustrated by Figure 1. First are the *originating parties*, who are the participants to the transaction creating the fancy; this is *A* and *B* in Figure 1. Second are the *potential successors in interest* to the asset that is being subjected to the fancy. This would be anyone who might purchase A's reserved rights (after the transfer to *B*) as well as anyone who succeeds to the interest acquired by *B*. Potential successors in interest are shown as *C*s and *D*s in Figure 1. Finally, there are the *other market participants*, people who will deal in or with watches other than the one over which *A* and *B* have transacted. Other market participants include those selling and acquiring rights in other watches such as *E* and *F* and *G* and *H* in Figure 1. They also include all who must avoid violating property rights in all watches, rights that are enforced against the world represented by *I* and *J* in Figure 1.[111] In the hypothetical example above, the other market participants are the other ninety-nine watch owners and their successors in title, as well as anyone who potentially might violate a property right in a watch.

The difference between other possible explanations of the *numerus clausus* and our information-cost theory can be understood in terms of this three-way classification. Other explanations focus on the effect of novel property rights on the originating parties and potential successors in interest—the *A*s, *B*s, *C*s, and *D*s of the world. One may say that these classes of individuals fall within the "zone of privity" designated by the box with the dotted line in Figure 1.

---

[111] Thus, other market participants include those whose actual dealings with watches occur by means other than consensual transactions.

Figure 1—The Classes of Affected Parties

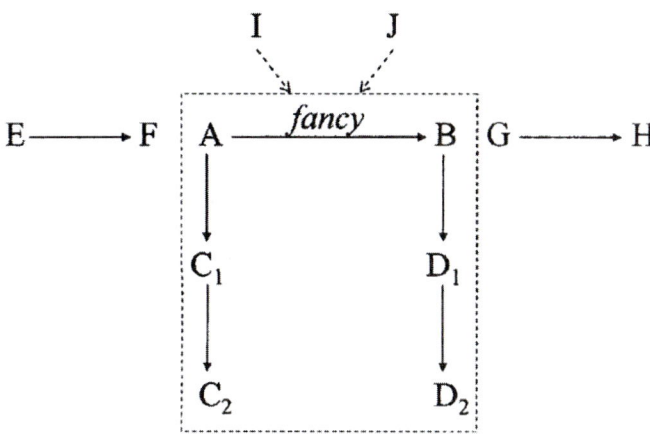

Our explanation, in contrast, focuses on the effect of unusual property rights on other market participants—the Es, Fs, Gs, Hs, Is, and Js of the world—classes of individuals who fall outside the zone of privity. As we argue, explanations based on classes of individuals within the zone of privity have difficulty identifying costs that are not impounded into the price facing those who make the decision whether to create the fancy in the first place. An explanation based on costs incurred by classes of individuals outside the zone of privity does not have this difficulty. * * *

When A creates the Monday right, this can raise the information costs of third parties. If the law allows A to create a Monday interest, individuals wishing to buy watches or bailees asked to repair watches will have to consider the possibility that any given watch is a Monday-only watch (or a watch for any other proper subset of days of the week) rather than a full-week watch. While A and B might be expected to take into account the market-value-lowering effect of undesirable idiosyncratic rights when third parties like C or D consider purchasing property in this watch, they will not take into account the more general effect on processing costs created by the existence of such rights when F is considering a purchase of rights in E's watch, or I and J are worried about violating property rights.

A and B may have subjective reasons for creating property rights based on days of the week. But, the possible existence of such rights will cause information costs for others—such as E, F, G, H, I, and J—to rise. Those considering whether to purchase property rights in watches will have more to investigate: They will have to assure themselves that they are getting all the days of the week that they want. Furthermore, they will have to worry about dimensions of division and elaboration that perhaps no one has yet thought of, making the acquisition of any watch more uncertain as well as riskier. With an indefinite set of types of rights, these costs will be higher than where parties, especially unsophisticated ones, are restricted to the limited menu the law allows. Furthermore, because property rights are in rem, all those who might violate property rights, accidentally or not, must know what they are supposed to respect. An indefinite set of types of rights will raise the cost of preventing violations through investigation of rights.

To return to our hypothetical world of one-hundred watch owners, suppose the value of creating the Monday-only right to *A* is $10, but the existence of this idiosyncrasy increases processing costs by $1 for all watch owners. The net benefit to *A* is $9, but the social cost is $90. As this example suggests, idiosyncratic property rights create a common-pool problem. The marginal benefits of the idiosyncrasy are fully internalized to the owner of the property right, but the owner bears only a fraction of the general measurement costs thereby created. Overall, the creation of external costs associated with this common-pool problem is likely to proceed beyond the optimal level. The problem cannot be resolved by side payments from the remaining ninety-nine to *A*, because the transaction costs are virtually certain to be prohibitive. Consequently, since an individual's interest in creating the nonstandard right—the extra benefit from using it rather than the next best alternative—is less than the additional measurement costs imposed on the other market participants, there is a rationale for the law to prohibit the creation of this kind of idiosyncratic right.

One way to control the external costs of measurement to third parties is through compulsory standardization of property rights. Standardization reduces the costs of measuring the attributes of such rights. Limiting the number of basic property forms allows a market participant or a potential violator to limit his or her inquiry to whether the interest does or does not have the features of the forms on the menu. Fancies not on the closed list need not be considered because they will not be enforced. When it comes to the basic legal dimensions of property, limiting the number of forms thus makes the determination of their nature less costly. The "good" in question here might be considered to be the prevention of error in ascertaining the attributes of property rights. Standardization means less measurement is required to achieve a given amount of error prevention. Alternatively, one can say that standardization increases the productivity of any given level of measurement efforts.

One would expect standardization to have the most value in connection with the dimensions of property rights that are least visible, and hence the most difficult for ordinary observers to measure. The tangible attributes of property, such as its size, shape, color, or texture, are typically readily observable and hence can be relatively easily measured by third parties. In the watch example, the watch can be a Timex or a Rolex and can be any size or color, and so forth. These physical attributes, and of course the price, are relatively easy for third parties to process using their senses, and thus there is less to be gained from standardizing them. The legal dimensions of property are less visible and less easy to comprehend, especially when they deviate from the most familiar forms such as the undivided fee simple. Thus, one would expect the effort to lower third-party information costs through standardization to focus on the legal dimension of ownership.

B.   Frustration Costs and the Language of Property Rights

If the only concern were in reducing third-party measurement costs, then there should be only one mandatory package of property rights, presumably a simple usufruct or an undivided fee simple. But standardization imposes its own costs. Mandatory rules sometimes prevent the parties from achieving a legitimate goal cost-effectively. Enforcing standardization can therefore frustrate the parties' intentions.

potential problems w/ standardization

Although the *numerus clausus* sometimes frustrates parties' objectives, often those objectives can be realized by a more complex combination of the standardized building blocks of property. For example, sophisticated parties with good legal advice can create the equivalent of a lease "for the duration of the war" by entering into a long-term lease determinable if the war ends. The fact that the *numerus clausus* is in this sense "avoidable" does not mean that it is trivial: Even if the standardization effected by the *numerus clausus* principle does not absolutely bar the parties from realizing their ends, this standardization comes at a price. The effect is roughly that of price discrimination: Parties willing to pay a great deal for an objective can achieve it by incurring higher planning and implementation costs. Furthermore, the design and implementation costs imposed by the *numerus clausus* function as a sort of "pollution tax" that should deter parties from insisting on overusing hard-to-process property forms, thereby placing higher processing burdens on market participants and especially courts. * * *

C.   Optimal Standardization and the *Numerus Clausus*

We are now in a position to see how the *numerus clausus* functions to promote the optimal standardization of property rights. From a social point of view, the objective should be to minimize the sum of measurement (and error) costs, frustration costs, and administrative costs. In other words, what we want is not maximal standardization—or no standardization—but optimal standardization. Fortunately, standardization comes in degrees. There is a spectrum of possible approaches to property rights, ranging from total freedom of customization on the one hand to complete regimentation on the other. Neither of these endpoints on the spectrum is likely to minimize social costs. Extreme standardization would frustrate many of the purposes to which property rights are put. On the other hand, total freedom to customize rights would create large third-party measurement and error costs and high administrative costs. Attention should focus on the middle range of the spectrum. Starting from a position of complete regimentation, permitting additional forms of property rights should reduce frustration costs by more than it increases measurement and error costs to third parties and administrative costs. Conversely, if one starts from a position of complete customization of rights, increasing the degree of standardization should lower measurement and error costs and administrative costs by more than the attendant frustration costs will rise. * * *

The *numerus clausus* principle can be seen from this perspective as a device that moves the system of property rights in the direction of the optimal level of standardization * * * By creating a strong presumption against judicial recognition of new forms of property rights, the *numerus clausus* imposes a brake on efforts by parties to proliferate new forms of property rights. On the other hand, by grandfathering in existing forms of property, and permitting legislative creation of new forms, the *numerus clausus* permits some positive level of diversification in the recognized forms of property. We do not argue that any particular number of property forms is in fact optimal. Nor do we argue that the forms currently recognized by the common law are ideal and beyond improvement. We do submit, however, that the *numerus clausus* strikes a rough balance between the extremes of complete regimentation and complete freedom of customization, and thus leads to a system of property rights that is closer to being optimal than that which would be produced by either of the extreme positions.

D.   Information Costs and the Dynamics of Property

Finally, our explanation of the *numerus clausus* generates some general predictions about the way in which property regimes will change over time: As the costs of standardization to the parties and the government shift, we expect the optimal degree of standardization to rise or fall. Consider the rise of registers of interests in real property, that is, recording acts. This device lowers the costs of notice; it is an alternative method of lowering information costs. * * *

Likewise, the more recent move toward increased use of contract principles in areas like electronic commerce fits in well with the information-cost theory of the *numerus clausus*. Notice is arguably easier to furnish (if not to process) when, for example, rights to digital content are being transferred, and notice of restrictions and other features of rights transferred are technologically not difficult to provide. * * * In general, to the extent that technological change allows cheaper notice of relevant interests, the need for standardization by the law will be somewhat diminished. Just as the rise of land registers allowed some loosening of the *numerus clausus*, so too technology that lowers information costs can be expected to weaken the *numerus clausus* further.

NOTES AND QUESTIONS

1. The *numerus clausus* is a mandatory rule that conflicts with the principle of freedom of contract. Why is free customizability of contract rights exempt from the problem of information costs? Do contracts ever present these problems? What makes contracts relevantly different from property? Is it some notion of privity? For one thing the average property right lasts a lot longer. Who is the "audience" for claims of a property sort? Claims under a contract? See, e.g., Thomas W. Merrill & Henry E. Smith, The Property/Contract Interface, 101 Colum. L. Rev. 773 (2001); Carol M. Rose, What Government Can Do for Property (and Vice Versa), in The Fundamental Interrelationships Between Government and Property 214–15 (Nicholas Mercuro & Warren J. Samuels eds. 1999); Bernard Rudden, Economic Theory v. Property Law: The *Numerus Clausus* Problem, in Oxford Essays in Jurisprudence 239, 241 (3d Series, John Eekelaar & John Bell eds., 1987); Henry E. Smith, The Language of Property: Form, Context, and Audience, 55 Stan. L. Rev. 1105 (2003).

2. One alternative explanation for the *numerus clausus* is that it prevents excessive fragmentation. If there are too many veto-wielding co-owners, holdout behavior will cause a resource to be underused. As we saw in Chapter II, this would be a mirror image of the situation with the tragedy of the commons, and has been termed the "tragedy of the anticommons." See Michael A. Heller, The Boundaries of Private Property, 108 Yale L.J. 1163, 1176–78 (1999); see also Francesco Parisi, Entropy in Property, 50 Am. J. Comp. L. 595 (2002). Ask yourself whether the *numerus clausus* and the other maintenance doctrines in this section serve to limit the number of claimants or the number of types of property rights, or both. Focusing only on notice and verification costs tends to lead to skepticism about the *numerus clausus*, compare Merrill & Smith, 110 Yale L.J. at 43–51, 54–58, with Henry Hansmann & Reinier Kraakman, Property, Contract, and Verification: The *Numerus Clausus* Problem and the Divisibility of Rights, 31 J. Legal Stud. S373, S416–17 (2002); see generally Bram Akkermans, The *Numerus Clausus* of Property Rights, in Comparative Property Law: Global Perspectives 100 (Michele Graziadei & Lionel Smith, eds., 2018). Others see the *numerus clausus* as regulating the substance of property interests, see, e.g., Nestor M. Davidson, Standardization and Pluralism in Property Law, 61 Vand. L. Rev. 1597 (2008); Avihay Dorfman, Property and Collective Undertaking: The Principle of *Numerus Clausus*, 61 U. Toronto L.J. 467 (2011); Joseph William Singer, Democratic Estates: Property Law in a Free and Democratic Society, 94 Cornell L. Rev. 1009 (2009).

3. Another aspect of the *numerus clausus* relates to institutional choice. Innovation in property law does occur; for all its antiquarian flavor, even the estate system is quite different from what it was even 100 years ago. The *numerus clausus* directs judges to avoid creating or recognizing private efforts at creating new property forms. But legislatures have the power to do so, and the *numerus clausus* channels innovation into the legislative arena. Consider some examples. The abolition of the fee tail was accomplished by statute, not by judicial decision. As another example, the nineteenth century saw many innovations in marital property. The older

interests were dower, which gave a surviving wife a life estate in one third of the real property held by the husband, and curtesy, which among other things gave a widower a life estate in the wife's land. Eventually, legislatures abolished these forms of property and replaced them with gender-neutral statutes creating a surviving spouse's forced share (usually one third) of the deceased spouse's estate. A surviving spouse of either gender can now elect to take either what the will provides or ownership of one third of the estate. See, e.g., June R. Carbone & Margaret F. Brinig, Rethinking Marriage: Feminist Ideology, Economic Change, and Divorce Reform, 65 Tul. L. Rev. 953, 1010 (1991).

4.   Is it a good idea to give legislatures primary responsibility for creating and destroying forms of property? Elsewhere in the excerpted article, Merrill and Smith argue that making legislatures rather than courts the source of legal change affords the benefits of clarity, universality, comprehensiveness, stability, prospectivity, and implicit compensation. See Merrill & Smith, *Numerus Clausus*, supra, at 58–68. Can you think of contrary arguments that might support giving courts a more active role here? Keep these questions of institutional choice in mind when we discuss developments in landlord-tenant law and condominiums in the next chapter.

5.   The status of the *numerus clausus* as a largely unacknowledged design principle in Anglo-American law has numerous implications for its operation. For example, one of the traditional maxims observed by the courts of equity was that equity will modify property rights less readily than contracts. The implicit approach to the *numerus clausus* also leads courts to downplay or confuse the principle when seeking to streamline doctrine in the name of party intent. As a prominent example, in *Garner v. Gerrish*, 473 N.E.2d 223 (N.Y. 1984), the deceased, Donovan, had signed a lease with Gerrish " 'for and during the term of *quiet enjoyment* from the *first* day of *May,* 1977 which term will end—*Lou Gerrish has the privilege of termination [sic] this agreement at a date of his own choice*' (emphasis added to indicate handwritten and typewritten additions to the printed form)." Id. at 577. Garner, the executor of the estate on behalf of Donovan's widow, argued that the tenancy was at will because traditionally a lease at will on one side was at will on both. With dismissive noises about livery of seisin and dusty feudalism, the court saw no difference between the interest and a life estate and enforced it as written, allowing Gerrish to stay. Unanswered was whether a "lease for life" would carry with it all the tenant protections we will encounter in the next chapter. More generally, what is the harm in creating a "lease for life" if that is not on the menu the law affords? In a fascinating recent article, Bernie Jones unearths more about the relationship between Gerrish and Donovan which suggests, contrary to the court's implicit treatment of the case as one calling for tenant protection against a landlord, that Gerrish may have exercised undue influence as caretaker of a very ill and impaired Donovan. Bernie D. Jones, Garner v. Gerrish and the Renter's Life Estate: Teaching a New Concept of 'Home', 2 Faulkner U. L. Rev. 1 (2010). Would the court have done better to apply the traditional rule and find an at-will tenancy? Should courts try to reach nuanced decisions like the one in *Garner* when many lawyers (like the one

in that case) are not up to the job of showing undue influence or unconscionability in such arrangements?

6.   The more common approach to problems like the lease-for-life is to construe the interest as fitting in the closest of the boxes provided by the estate system through the *numerus clausus*. What would be closest to a lease for life? Compare Thompson v. Baxter, 119 N.W. 797 (Minn. 1909) (life estate) with Kajo Church Square, Inc. v. Walker, 2003 WL 1848555 (Tex. Ct. App.) (tenancy at will); Nitschke v. Doggett, 489 S.W.2d 335 (Tex. Civ. App. 1972), vacated on other grounds, 498 S.W.2d 339 (Tex. 1973) (same). Although it is uncommon for professional drafters—being a cautious lot—to create new estates or fancies, one recurring problem comes from attempts during various wars to create a lease for the duration of the war. As we will see, leases come in four varieties, and a lease for the duration of the war is not one of them. Most courts will deem such leases to be a tenancy at will (a type of lease). See, e.g., National Bellas Hess v. Kalis, 191 F.2d 739 (8th Cir. 1951); Stanmeyer v. Davis, 53 N.E.2d 22 (Ill. App. Ct. 1944); Lace v. Chandler, 1 All E.R. 305 (K.B. 1944). The minority of courts that have upheld such leases as a lease for a term of years have generally done so by changing the definition of a term of years rather than by holding that the parties may freely contract for new types of leases. See, e.g., Smith's Transfer & Storage Co. v. Hawkins, 50 A.2d 267, 268 (D.C. App. 1946). What would be the harm in a lease "for the duration of the war"?

Personal Property

The menu of forms of property for real estate is lengthy—very probably too lengthy. What about personal property? Does the system of estates, developed in the context of land, also apply to personal property? There is surprisingly little authority on the question of how far the system of estates applies to personal property. Some standard reference works state that personal property is subject to the same elaborate structure of forms that applies to estates in land (including future interests). See Restatement (First) of Property § 9 cmt. a, at 23 (1936); 2 William Blackstone, Commentaries *398. But case law does not fully support this broad proposition. One can find decisions upholding future interests in personal property. For example, in *Gruen v. Gruen*, 496 N.E.2d 869 (N.Y. 1986), the court upheld the inter vivos gift of a remainder in a painting following a retained life estate in the donor. But such decisions are rare. See generally John Chipman Gray, Future Interests in Personal Property, 14 Harv. L. Rev. 397 (1901).

In one respect, there is no doubt that the estate system applies to personal property. As has been mentioned, most trusts today consist of assets that would be described as personal rather than real property— stocks, bonds, money markets funds, and other investment vehicles. The beneficial interests in these trusts are described in terms of the estates in land, such as life estates, remainders, and executory interests. So the estate system unquestionably applies to equitable interests in personal property held in trust. To the extent one wishes to create divided ownership in a particularly valuable piece of personal property like a painting or other collectible, it would almost certainly be advisable to use a trust to do this, rather than attempt to create divided legal title using the forms of property recognized for freehold interests.

Why is there not more authority on point with respect future interests in common law personal property? Our knowledge of the early history is limited by the tendency for litigation over items like farm equipment, produce, and animals to take place in local courts with less record keeping. Likewise title in such items typically was less elaborate than in the case of land. Most personal property does not last as long as land does, so there is typically less incentive to specify who will take personal property in future generations. Thus, an additional source of indifference to future interests in personal property probably stemmed from their perishable nature and the high ratio of complication to benefit in such interests.

The analog of the fee simple absolute is "absolute ownership" (also called "full ownership") of personal property. As best we know, the original understanding seems to have been that personal property could not be divided into lesser interests. To get around this rule, people would occasionally use bailments, because the bailor was considered to retain the fee-like ownership during the bailment. Beginning in the fifteenth century, gifts by will of the use and occupancy of personal property for the life of the grantee were allowed. In the nineteenth century some English courts treated such bequests as giving an absolute interest to the intended life recipient and an executory interest to the intended future interest holder. Only later did some courts in England and the United States treat inter vivos gifts with similar accommodation. For a more detailed treatment, see Thomas F. Bergin & Paul G. Haskell, Preface to Estates in Land and Future Interests 121–22 (2d ed. 1984); Lewis M. Simes & Allan F. Smith, The Law of Future Interests (John A. Borron, Jr., ed., 3d ed. 2002).

Even today, courts apply some restrictions on the creation of future interests in personal property. All courts follow the rule that a future interest cannot be created in a "consumable" item. This rule can have real bite when testators are setting up trusts. If the will creates a trust out of all the "rest and residue" of the testator's property, this is likely to include "not only securities or other assets that are appropriate for a trust, but also such egregiously inappropriate items as collar buttons, pet cats, and frying pans. . . ." Ashbel Green Gulliver, Cases and Materials on the Law of Future Interests 68 (1959). Given that one cannot create a future interest in a consumable, this makes for entertaining line-drawing exercises, with food and current crops on one side, diamonds on the other, and conflicting views on farming implements and animals. The solution is to make specific grants of the personal property.

Another limitation involves attempts to create easements or analogous restrictions on the use of items of personal property that would follow ("run with") the item into remote hands. English courts have said this is impermissible, and this seems to be the tendency in the United States. See, e.g., Dr. Miles Medical Co. v. Park, 220 U.S. 373, 404 (1911), overruled by Leegin Creative Leather Products, Inc. v. PSKS, Inc., 551 U.S. 877 (2007); Zechariah Chafee, Jr., Equitable Servitudes on Chattels, 41 Harv. L. Rev. 945, 977–980 (1928); Zechariah Chafee, Jr., The Music Goes Round and Round: Equitable Servitudes and Chattels, 69 Harv. L. Rev. 1250 (1956) (commenting on a decision departing from the general understanding). This has been particularly contentious in the area of software licensing. Compare Glen O. Robinson, Personal Property Servitudes, 71 U. Chi. L. Rev. 1449 (2004) (arguing for enforceability) with Julie E. Cohen, *Lochner* in Cyberspace: The New Economic Orthodoxy of "Rights Management," 97 Mich. L. Rev. 462 (1998) (criticizing tendency to provide legal support for private efforts to enclose information). The informational problems presented by servitudes in intellectual property are sometimes different from those in tangible property; in particular, increasingly popular public licenses—under which a copyright holder will license to anyone on condition that the incorporating work be licensed on the same terms—can potentially conflict with each other, by imposing inconsistent obligations on the creator of the later incorporating work. In another problem particular to IP, consumers in particular may be surprised to know that they have agreed not to engage in what would otherwise be fair use. Molly Shaffer Van Houweling, The New Servitudes, 96 Geo. L.J. 885, 946–47 (2008).

A general concern raised by the possibility of creating nonpossessory property rights in items of personal property is the problem of notice. Such property rights are in rem, but how are dutyholders supposed to know the content of the right? As we will see, in the case of land the notice function is largely served by registries of documents evidencing rights in land. For most types of personal property, such registries are not available, although that may change with the heralded rise of the Internet of Things. Christina M. Mulligan, Personal Property Servitudes on the Internet of Things, 50 Ga. L. Rev. 1121 (2016). The more valuable, durable, and immobile an asset, the more likely there will be a registry. Planes, automobiles, and increasingly valuable art works are subject to registries that one can consult to learn about the various interests of other parties in the assets. But other types of personal property have no registries, making it especially perilous to impose in rem duties on persons with respect to such property when they have no way of knowing which items are restricted and which ones are not.

D. MEDIATING CONFLICTS OVER TIME

1. WASTE

When two or more persons hold interests in a single piece of property there is always potential for conflict. This is certainly true when a grantor divides a fee simple into a life estate and one or more remainders. The holder of the life estate will tend to favor current consumption and investments that produce a quick return. In contrast, the holders of remainders are likely to prefer conservation of the asset and longer-term investments. This conflict may be mitigated somewhat when, as is often the case, the parties are closely related; for example, the life tenant is the grantor's spouse and the holders of the remainders are the couple's children. But intra-familial conflict also occurs, as the following case demonstrates. Here one Isaac V. Brokaw built several adjacent mansions. By will, he left to each of his four children—three sons and a daughter—a life interest in one of four separate dwelling houses. Each life estate was followed by a remainder to the issue of the life tenant. The will provided that if any of the life tenants should die without issue, the remaining heirs of Isaac would get that house. Thus, in the following case, the plaintiff (Isaac's son George) had a life estate, followed by a contingent remainder in George's children, subject in turn to a contingent remainder in the three other children of testator Isaac and their issue living at the time of George's death if George should survive his children. It is these holders of the contingent remainders who object to the razing of the allegedly obsolete mansion.

Brokaw v. Fairchild

Supreme Court, New York County, New York, 1929.
135 Misc. 70, 237 N.Y.S. 6.

■ HAMMER, J. This is an action under section 473 of the Civil Practice Act and Rules of Civil Practice 210 to 212, in which plaintiff asks that it be declared and adjudged that the plaintiff, upon giving such security as the court may direct, has the right and is authorized to remove the present structures and improvements on or affecting the real property No. 1 East Seventy-Ninth street, or any part thereof, except the party wall, and to erect new structures and improvements thereon in accordance with certain proposed plans and specifications. * * *

In the year 1886 the late Isaac V. Brokaw bought for $199,000 a plot of ground in the borough of Manhattan, city of New York, opposite Central Park, having a frontage of 102 feet 2 inches on the easterly side of Fifth avenue and a depth of 150 feet on the northerly side of Seventy-Ninth street. Opposite there is an entrance to the park and Seventy-Ninth street is a wide crosstown street running through the park. Upon the corner portion, a plot of ground 51 feet 2 inches on Fifth avenue and a depth of 110 feet on Seventy-Ninth street, Mr. Brokaw erected in the year 1887, for his own occupancy, a residence known as No. 1 East Seventy-Ninth street, at a cost of over $300,000. That residence and corner plot is the subject-matter of this action. The residence, a three-story, mansard and basement granite front building, occupies the entire width of the lot. The mansard roof is of tile. On the first floor are two large drawing rooms on the Fifth avenue side, and there are also a large hallway running through from south to north, a reception room, dining room, and pantry. The dining room is paneled with carved wood. The hallway is in Italian marble and mosaic. There are murals and ceiling panels. There is a small elevator to the upper portion of the house. On the second floor are a large library, a large bedroom with bath on the Fifth avenue side, and there are also four other bedrooms and baths. The third floor has bedrooms and baths. The fourth floor has servants' quarters, bath, and storage rooms. The building has steam heat installed by the plaintiff, electric light and current, hardwood floors, and all usual conveniences. It is an exceedingly fine house, in construction and general condition as fine as anything in New York. It is contended by plaintiff that the decorations are heavy, not of a type now required by similar residences, and did not appeal to the people to whom it was endeavored to rent the building. It is "a masonry house of the old-fashioned type with very thick walls and heavy reveals in the windows, very high ceilings, monumental staircase and large rooms." "Such as has not been built for probably twenty-five years." "Utterly impractical to remodel for occupancy by more than one family." It "was offered to a great many people for rental at $25,000 with the statement that a lower figure might be considered and no offer of rental was obtained. Mr. Brokaw (the plaintiff) directed that the asking rental be $30,000 to start and finally reduced to $20,000. There is no demand for rental of private houses. There is a sporadic demand for purchase and sale on Fifth avenue for use as private homes. Once in a while somebody will want a private house." The taxes are $16,881, upkeep for repairs $750, and watchman $300. The taxes for 1913 were $8,950.77.

Since 1913, the year of the death of Isaac V. Brokaw and the commencement of the life estate of plaintiff, there has been a change of circumstances and conditions in connection with Fifth avenue properties. Apartments were erected with great rapidity and the building of private residences has practically ceased. Forty-four apartments and only 2 private residences have been erected on Fifth avenue from Fifty-Ninth street to 110th street. There are to-day but 8 of these 51 blocks devoted exclusively to private residences. Plaintiff's expert testified: "It is not possible to get an adequate return on the value of that land by any type of improvement other than an apartment house. The structure proposed in the plans of plaintiff is proper and suitable for the site and show 172 rooms which would rent for $1,000 per room. There is an excellent demand for such apartments. * * * There is no corner in the City of New York as fine for an apartment house as that particular corner."

The plaintiff testified also that his expenses in operating the residence which is unproductive would be at least $70,542 greater than if he resided in an apartment. He claims such difference constitutes a loss and contends that the erected apartment house would change this loss into an income or profit of $30,000. Plaintiff claims that under the facts and changed conditions shown the demolition of the building and erection of the proposed apartment is for the best interests of himself as life tenant, the inheritance, and the remaindermen. The defendants deny these contentions and assert certain affirmative defenses: (1) That the proposed demolition of the residence is waste, which against the objection of the adult defendant remaindermen plaintiff cannot be permitted to accomplish. * * *

Coming, therefore, to plaintiff's claimed right to demolish the present residence and to erect in its place the proposed apartment, I am of the opinion that such demolition would result in such an injury to the inheritance as under the authorities would constitute waste. The life estate given to plaintiff under the terms of the will and codicil is not merely in the corner plot of ground with improvements thereon, but, without question, in the residence of the testator. Four times in the devising clause the testator used the words "my residence." This emphasis makes misunderstanding impossible. The identical building which was erected and occupied by the testator in his lifetime and the plot of ground upon which it was built constitute that residence. By no stretch of the imagination could "my residence" be in existence at the end of the life tenancy were the present building demolished and any other structure, even the proposed 13-story apartment, erected on the site.

It has been generally recognized that any act of the life tenant which does permanent injury to the inheritance is waste. The law intends that the life tenant shall enjoy his estate in such a reasonable manner that the land shall pass to the reversioner or remainderman as nearly as practicable unimpaired in its nature, character, and improvements. The general rule in this country is that the life tenant may do whatever is required for the general use and enjoyment of his estate as he received it. The use of the estate he received is contemplated, and not the exercise of an act of dominion or ownership. What the life tenant may do in the future in the way of improving or adding value to the estate is not the test of what constitutes waste. The act of the tenant in changing the estate, and whether or not such act is lawful or unlawful, *i. e.*, whether the estate is so changed as to be an injury to the inheritance, is the sole question involved. The tenant has no right to exercise an act of ownership. In the instant case the inheritance was the residence of the testator—"my residence"—consisting of the present building on a plot of ground 51 feet 2 inches on Fifth avenue by 110 feet on Seventy-ninth street. "My residence," such is what the plaintiff under the testator's will has the use of for life. He is entitled to use the building and plot reasonably for his own convenience or profit. To demolish that building and erect upon the land another building, even one such as the contemplated 13-story apartment house, would be the exercise of an act of ownership and dominion. It would change the inheritance or thing, the use of which was given to the plaintiff as tenant for life, so that the inheritance or thing could not be delivered to the remaindermen or reversioners at the end of the life estate. The receipt by them at the end of the life estate of a 13-story $900,000 apartment house might be more beneficial to them. Financially, the objecting adults may be unwise in not consenting to the proposed change. They may be selfish and unmindful that in the normal course of time and events they probably will not receive the fee. With motives and purposes the court is not concerned. In Matter of Brokaw's Will, 219 N.Y.S. 734 (N.Y. App. Div. 1927); affd., 157 N. E. 880 (N.Y. 1927), their right to object to a proposed building loan and mortgage for the erection of the proposed apartment was established by decision. They have the same right of objection in this action. To tear down and demolish the present building, which cost at least $300,000 to erect and would cost at least as much to replace, under the facts in this case, is clearly and beyond question an act of waste. In *Winship v. Pitts*, 3 Paige, Ch. 259 (N.Y. Ch. 1832), Chancellor Walworth, although holding that an injunction was properly refused to restrict the erection of a building upon premises where the lease did not specifically limit the use thereof, nevertheless (at page 262 of 3 Paige Ch.) said: "I have no hesitation in saying, that by the law of this state, as now understood, it is not waste for the tenant to erect a new edifice upon the demised premises; *provided it can be done without destroying or materially injuring the buildings or other improvements already existing thereon. I admit he has no right to pull down valuable buildings, or to make improvements or alterations which will materially and permanently change the nature of the property, so as to render it impossible for him to restore the same premises, substantially, at the expiration of the term.*" (Italics mine.)

In Agate v. Lowenbein, 57 N.Y. 604, 607 (1874), the court said: "Had there been no license given to the defendants to do the acts of which the plaintiff complains, the injuries done to the property would have been, apparently, acts of waste, for which the plaintiff could, by the rules of the common law, have brought an action on the case in the nature of waste. *The right which the tenant has is to make use of the property. The power of making an alteration does not arise out of a mere right of user;* it is, therefore, incompatible with his interest for a tenant to make any alteration, unless he is justified by the express permission of his landlord. Holroyd, J., in Farrant v. Thompson (5 B. & Ald., 826, 106 Eng. Rep. 1392 (K.B. 1822)) defines the extent of a lessee's rights. By a lease, *the use, not dominion of the property demised, is conferred.* If a tenant exercises an act of ownership, he is no longer protected by his tenancy."

And at page 614 of 57 N.Y., the court said: "It is, in general, no justification for an act of waste that a party will, at some future time, put the premises in the same condition as they were when the lease was made. The question is, whether the tenant, at the time the wrongful act was done, caused an injury which then affected the plaintiff as to his reversion. * * * The tenant has no right to exercise an act of ownership."

In *Kidd v. Dennison*, 6 Barb. 9, 13 (N.Y. Sup. 1849), the court said: "So if the tenant materially changes the nature and character of the buildings, it is waste, although the value of the property should be enhanced by the alteration. * * * The tenant has no authority to assume the right of judging what may be an improvement to the inheritance. He must confine himself to the conditions of his lease." * * *

The cases given by plaintiff are either cases where a prohibitory injunction against future waste has been sought and the parties have been refused the injunction and relegated to an action for damages for waste, or where, in condemnation proceedings or actions in equity, it appears that the equities between the parties are such that the technical waste committed has been ameliorated. The three cases upon which the plaintiff principally relies are Melms v. Pabst Brewing Co., 79 N. W. 738 (Wis. 1899), and New York, O. & W. R. Co. v. Livingston, 144 N. E. 589 (N.Y. 1924), and Doherty v. Allman, 3 L. R. App. Cas. 709, 717, 721 (H.L. 1878). These are readily distinguishable from the case at bar. In Melms v. Pabst Brewing Co., supra, there was a large expensive brick dwelling house built by one Melms in the year 1864. He also owned the adjoining real estate and a brewery upon part of the premises. He died in 1869. The brewery and dwelling were sold and conveyed to Pabst Brewing Company. The Pabst Company used the brewery part of the premises. About the year 1890 the neighborhood about the dwelling house had so changed in character that it was situated on an isolated lot standing from 20 to 30 feet above the level of the street, the balance of the property having been graded down to fit it for business purposes. It was surrounded by business property, factories, and railroad tracks with no other dwellings in the neighborhood. Pabst Brewing Company, in good faith regarding itself as the owner, tore down the building and graded down the ground for business purposes. Thereafter it was held, in the action of Melms v. Pabst Brewing Co., 66 N. W. 244, that the brewing company had only acquired a life estate in the homestead, although in another action between the same parties (66 N. W. 518 (Wis. 1896)) it was held that as to the other property the brewing company had acquired full title in fee. The action for waste in which the [1899 decision] was delivered was brought and decided after the decisions in the other actions. We find it there said at 79 N. W. 738: "The action was tried before the court without a jury, and the court found, in addition to the facts above stated, that the removal of the building and the grading down of the earth was done by the defendant in 1891 and 1892, believing itself to be the owner in fee simple of the property, and that by the said acts the estate of the plaintiffs in the property was substantially increased, and that the plaintiffs have been in no way injured thereby."

Again, it was stated at 79 N. W. 740: "There are no contract relations in the present case. The defendants are the grantees of a life estate, and their rights may continue for a number of years. The evidence shows that the property became valueless for the purpose of residence property as the result of the growth and development of a great city. Business and manufacturing interests advanced and surrounded the once elegant mansion, until it stood isolated and alone, standing upon just enough ground to support it, and surrounded by factories and railroad tracks, absolutely undesirable as a residence, and incapable of any use as business property. Here was a complete change of conditions, not produced by the tenant, but resulting from causes which none could control. Can it be reasonably or logically said that this entire change of condition is to be completely ignored, and the ironclad rule applied that the tenant can make no change in the uses of the property because he will destroy its identity? Must the tenant stand by, and preserve the useless dwelling house, so that he may at some future time turn it over to the reversioner, equally useless?"

The facts in the above case are clearly not analogous to the facts here. Especially is this recognized from the fact that the plaintiff's dwelling house is far from being "isolated and alone, standing upon just enough ground to support it, surrounded by factories and railroad tracks, absolutely undesirable as a residence." It is located on the northeast corner of Fifth avenue and Seventy-ninth street. Across the avenue to the west is Central Park. To the south across Seventy-ninth street the block Seventy-eighth to Seventy-ninth streets is restricted to private dwellings. The residence itself is surrounded by the three other palatial Brokaw dwellings, forming a magnificent residential layout of the four plots. It may, of course, be that the situation will change in the future. The decision here is concerned only with the present. * * *

The facts, it is seen, in none of the cases cited are analogous to the case at bar. The law and procedure therein also contain no analogy. *Melms v. Pabst Brewing Co.* was a law action for waste claimed to have been committed prior to the action. Upon the existing facts proved at the trial it was found as fact and in equity that the claimed waste was ameliorated and the plaintiff not damaged. * * *

From the foregoing I am of the opinion, and it will accordingly be adjudged and declared, that upon the present facts, circumstances, and conditions as they exist and are shown in this case, regardless of the proposed security and the expressed purpose of erecting the proposed 13-story apartment, or any other structure, the plaintiff has no right and is not authorized to remove the present structures on or affecting the real estate in question. * * *

Figure 5-6
The Brokaw Mansion, 1 East 79th Street, New York City

The Irving Brokaw Mansion Fifth Avenue & 79th Street. Glass Plate Negative. Undated. Museum of the City of New York. The Underhill Collection. B.1642.

Figure 5-7
1 East 79th Street, New York City, in 2006

NOTES AND QUESTIONS

1.   George Brokaw's repeated efforts to persuade the courts to permit him to tear the house down were all rebuffed. He lived in the house until his death in 1935, but neither he nor his wife liked it. The Brokaws divorced in 1929, and Mrs. Brokaw later remarried and went on to greater fame as Clare Boothe Luce. George and Clare had two children, who took ownership of the mansion when George died. One of the children died in 1944, and left her half interest in the mansion to Clare by will. Clare sold this to her second husband, Henry Luce, the publisher of *Time* magazine, and he eventually purchased the other half-interest from George's other child. In 1964, although the house had been designated a landmark by the city, new owners managed to raze the building along with two adjoining mansions, over the objections of the New York City Landmarks Preservation Commission. A large apartment building now stands on the site. Thomas W. Ennis, Landmark Mansion on 79th St. To Be Razed, N.Y. Times (Sept. 17, 1964), at 1.

2.   Who should have standing to bring an action for waste? The original action for waste, following the Statute of Gloucester, 6 Edw. I, ch. 5 (1278), provided for forfeiture of the estate of one guilty of waste, plus the payment of treble damages to those holding affected nonpossessory interests. Perhaps because of the severity of the remedy, courts held that only those holding indefeasibly vested remainders or reversions had standing to bring an action for waste. Later, when the Chancery Court began to issue injunctions against the commission of waste by a tenant-in-possession, the standing rules were relaxed, and holders of contingent remainders, defeasible reversions, or executory interests were allowed to sue, provided they sued on behalf of all nonpossessory interest holders. See Dale A. Whitman et al., The Law of Property 129–32 (4th ed. 2019). This appears to be the understanding that allowed the contingent remaindermen in *Brokaw* to bring an action to enjoin George Brokaw from committing waste. But suppose someone with only a possibility of reverter or an executory interest with a highly remote chance of ever becoming vested seeks to bring an action for waste. Where should the courts draw the line in granting standing to regulate the behavior of the tenant-in-possession?

3.   The action for waste is very old, dating from the twelfth century, and originally had its own writ—the writ of waste. It remains today an important background rule that defines the respective rights of persons who hold possessory and nonpossessory interests in property. The action for waste can be invoked not only by holders of remainders following life estates: It applies in any situation of concurrent or sequential ownership, including lessors objecting to actions by lessees that the lessor claims will damage the lessor's reversion. Increasingly, however, the issues that could be adjudicated by an action for waste are resolved by contract instead. Insofar as property is divided between a life tenant and a remainder, today it will typically be held in trust, and the trust agreement (in a sense a contract between the settlor of the trust and the trustee to manage property in the interests of the beneficiaries) will specify the duties of preservation or rights of modification of the property being managed by the trustee. Generally,

trustees are subject to fiduciary duties relating to management. And nearly all lessors will specify in the lease whether the lessee has a duty to repair or otherwise maintain the property and what degree of latitude the lessee has to make modifications in the property. So the issues covered by the action for waste are usually resolved today by interpreting a trust or a lease, although the duties created by the law of waste can be called upon if there is a gap in these instruments. And the action for waste creates the baseline understanding against which these agreements are negotiated.

4.   Courts over time have developed different categories of waste. The basic distinction is between affirmative waste and permissive waste. *Affirmative waste* is a type of misfeasance. It occurs when the life tenant or lessee undertakes some affirmative act on the property that is unreasonable and causes "excess" damage to the reversionary or remainder interest. The actions that constitute affirmative waste are often defined in terms of what is regarded as "normal" use of the property. Thus, if the property contains minerals or trees, the life tenant or lessee is permitted to engage in normal extraction of minerals and normal tree-cutting, but anything beyond normal would be affirmative waste. One rule of thumb, the "open mines" doctrine, provided that any extraction of minerals was waste unless mining was already occurring on the land at the beginning of the life estate or lease. *Permissive waste* is a type of nonfeasance. It occurs when the life tenant or lessee fails to take some action with regard to the property and the failure to act is unreasonable and causes excess damage to the reversion or remainder. Again, rough conceptions of normal behavior serve to define the baseline against which liability is to be determined. Prominent examples of permissive waste include failing to repair a roof resulting in water damage, not paying taxes as they come due, or allowing an adverse possessor to remain on the land.

5.   A more controversial type of waste—and the type at issue in *Brokaw*—is sometimes called *ameliorative waste*. This is a type of affirmative act by the life tenant or lessee that significantly changes the property, but results in an increase, rather than a diminution, in its market value. The traditional view, which is reflected in *Brokaw*, is that ameliorative waste is just another type of affirmative waste and is not permitted. Under this understanding, the holders of remainder interests are entitled to take possession of the property at the end of the life tenancy or lease in substantially the same form it had when the life tenant or lessee first took possession. Significant change or transformation is ruled out. An opposing view—of which *Melms v. Pabst Brewing Co.*, distinguished in *Brokaw*, is the leading example—permits ameliorative waste, at least when it can be justified by changed circumstances. The *Brokaw* decision was perceived by many as being unduly rigid, in contrast to the more flexible approach of *Melms*, and on the recommendation of a Law Revision Commission the traditional rule enforced in *Brokaw* was repealed in New York in favor of a standard that looks to multiple variables, including changed circumstances in the neighborhood and whether the modification increases the value of the property. See 1937 N.Y. Laws 618, 618–19; N.Y. Real Prop. Acts. Law § 803 (McKinney 2009). A similar approach was endorsed by the Restatement of

Property, which approved of *Melms* and disapproved of *Brokaw*. Restatement (First) of Property § 140 cmt. f (1936). Today, different states take a variety of approaches to waste, and the strict approach of *Brokaw* appears to be followed in only a minority of American jurisdictions. Here as elsewhere in the common law, the law of waste has become more flexible, and generally speaking, the greater one's interest, the more freedom one gets as owner. See generally, John A. Lovett, Doctrines of Waste in a Landscape of Waste, 72 Mo. L. Rev. 1209 (2007); Duane Rudolph, How Equity and Custom Transformed American Waste Law, 2 Charlotte Sch. L. Prop. J. 1 (2015). Civil law systems tend to disallow types of alteration as ameliorative waste rather than balancing interests or evaluating changes in terms of efficiency. See Sally Brown Richardson, Reframing Ameliorative Waste, 65 Am. J. Comp. L. 335 (2017). One approach consistent with the tenor of the law of trusts and wills is to hew closely to the grantor's intent, making an exception only for new beneficial uses not foreseeable at the time of the creation of the interest. Restatement (Fourth) of Property, Vol. 1, Div. 1, Ch. 5, § 5.1 (Am. L. Inst. Council Draft No. 3, Sept. 29, 2020).

6. Are the various rules about waste consistent with economic efficiency? Richard Posner has suggested that courts should apply a simple rule of wealth maximization: If the life tenant's action would maximize the present value of the property (including both the life tenant's interest and the reversion or remainder interests) then it is permissible; conversely, if the life tenant's action would not maximize the present value of the property, it should be condemned as waste. See Richard A. Posner, Economic Analysis of Law § 3.10, at 74–76 (9th ed. 2014). But the legal doctrine does not seem to require maximization of present value by the party in possession. Instead, it enforces "normal" behavior by the party in possession and the preservation of the status quo. Does this suggest the law is more concerned with protecting the autonomy of property owners than with promoting efficiency? Is it relevant here that the law of waste is a default rule, that is, a rule that applies only in the absence of a contrary agreement by the affected parties? Thus, for example, if the life tenant and the holders of remainders in *Brokaw* had all agreed, the mansion could be torn down. (What if Isaac Brokaw's will had stated that the house could be razed in the discretion of the life tenant?) Might concepts like "normal" behavior or use and preserving the status quo provide a better baseline for negotiating contractual modifications than a norm requiring present-value maximization? But what if bargaining breaks down, as in *Brokaw*? Don't the ordinary rules of waste promote inefficient outcomes in these circumstances? For an argument that the strict rule of waste enforced in *Brokaw* promotes efficiency better than a flexible standard or a rule of wealth maximization because it reduces the costs of contracting between possessory and nonpossessory interest holders, see Thomas W. Merrill, *Melms v. Pabst Brewing Co.* and the Doctrine of Waste in American Property Law, 94 Marquette L. Rev. 1055 (2011). Judge Posner has a brief rebuttal in the same issue. Richard A. Posner, Comment on Merrill on the Law of Waste, id. at 1095.

7. Should the law continue to prohibit ameliorative waste? How much should Isaac Brokaw's wishes govern future generations? Why should the

holders of the remainders be able to trump the wishes of the life tenant even when the life tenant is enhancing the value of the remainder? If the remainder holders claim that they attach a high subjective value on preserving the mansion, how do we know whether to believe them? Were the holders of the remainders in *Brokaw* motivated by subjective attachments to the mansion, or by other concerns? Do changed circumstances call for judicial intervention? If so, why didn't the transformation of Fifth Avenue from a boulevard of single-family residences to high-rise apartment buildings qualify as a changed circumstance? Compare the materials on cy pres in Chapter VI.

Valuation of Interests

Whether legal or equitable, courts and others are sometimes called upon to value the various interests that have been carved out of a fee simple. For example, suppose land is divided between a life estate and a remainder, and both tenants decide to sell the property, or the state decides to take the property through eminent domain. The acquiring party will pay for the value of what it obtains—a fee simple—but then we have to decide how to divide the proceeds between the life tenant and the holder of the remainder. In such cases, resort is had to actuarial tables and discount rates.

An example will illustrate how this is done. Suppose Blackacre is worth $100,000 as a fee simple and (to make things less complicated) its value is not expected to change in the foreseeable future. A owns a life estate, and B owns the remainder. A is 98 years old and so has a life expectancy of three years (at least according to the actuarial tables used by the IRS, which does not distinguish male and female life expectancies). Thus, we can assume that A would get the use of the $100,000 asset for the next three years, and B would get the use of the asset thereafter. One way to determine the value of the respective interests is to ask what the remainder to B is worth today, given that B expects to receive Blackacre three years from now. Once we have the value of the remainder, we can then subtract this from $100,000, in order to determine the value of the life estate.

How do we determine the value of the remainder, assumed to be the equivalent of $100,000 received three years from today? If one had $100,000 today one could invest it in a safe investment and would wind up with more than $100,000 three years from now. What we want to find out is the amount today that is equivalent to what one would have to set aside in order to have $100,000 three years from now. To find this out, one would normally use spreadsheet software, but it is important to understand what calculations are actually going on. First we need a discount rate, reflecting the time value of money.[3] Assume this is 7

---

[3]   The discount rate (r), the percentage by which money will change in value over time, is related to the nominal interest rate and the expected rate of inflation:

percent. To have $1 one year from now, the amount P one has to set aside now is roughly 93 cents. $P \times (1 + .07) = \$1.00$ or $P = \$1.00 / (1.07) = \$.93$. That is, to find the present discounted value of a dollar amount one year from now, divide the future amount ($1.00) by the sum of one and the discount rate (here 1.07). One dollar two years from now is like one dollar one year from now, deferred an additional year. It is worth 87 cents now because $P \times (1 + .07) \times (1 + .07) = \$1.00$, or $P = \$1.00 / ((1.07) \times (1.07)) = \$.87$. A dollar deferred three years is worth $\$.82 = \$1.00 / (1.07)^3$, or 81.63 cents. Thus, the remainder that will be worth $100,000 three years from now is worth approximately $81,630 today ($100,000 $/ (1.07)^3$). This can be generalized.[4]

What then is the life estate worth? The property itself is worth $100,000 now and the remainder is worth $81,630 now, leaving $18,370 ($100,000 $81,630) for the life estate.

Another way to reach the same result is to determine what the life estate should be worth in terms of a stream of payments that $100,000 can earn over the three year period. Taking 7 percent to be the rate of return, the $100,000 investment will yield $7,000 each year. The $7,000 earned at the end of the first year is worth $6,542 today (= $7,000 / (1.07)). (This can be thought of as 7,000 times the $.93 present value of each dollar a year from now). Similarly, year two's payment is $6,114 (= $7,000 / $(1.07)^2$), and year three's payment is $5,714 (= $7,000 / $(1.07)^3$). The three payments add to $18,370. If we calculate the value of the life estate this way, we can then subtract this from $100,000 to determine the value of the remainder ($81,630 as before).

The discount factor is crucial here. One interesting feature of the 7% discount rate is that an amount doubles roughly every 10 years at a 7% rate. For comparison, if the discount rate is 4%, the (expected three-year) life estate would be worth $11,100 and the remainder $88,900. But if the discount rate is 10%, then the life estate and remainder are worth $24,869 and $75,131, respectively, in present discounted value terms. The higher the discount rate, the less a future dollar is worth now (and the more valuable the life estate is because it is weighted more towards the present). And at any given discount rate, the further off in the future a dollar is, the less it is worth now. What (if any) discount rate should be applied to benefits obtained in the future from environmental regulation (especially future lives saved) has been the focal point of much controversy in environmental law. See, e.g., Richard L. Revesz, Environmental Regulation, Cost-Benefit Analysis, and the Discounting of Human Lives, 99 Colum. L. Rev. 941 (1999); Arden Rowell,

---

$(1 + i) = (1 + r)(1 + e)$, where i is the nominal interest rate and e is the expected inflation rate.

[4]   More generally, an amount C in the future equals the present value P times the sum of one and the discount factor r, applied for the requisite number n of time periods (here years), i.e., $C = P (1 + r)^n$. We can do this in reverse as well. From a future nominal amount we can calculate the present discounted value using the formula $P = C/(1 + r)^n$.

Quantitative Valuation in Environmental Law, 96 Notre Dame L. Rev. 1539 (2021).

The present values of a life estate and the corresponding remainder also depend on the life expectancy of the life tenant. In our example this was assumed to be three years. Life estates, remainders, and other interests have to be valued for income tax purposes, and the methods there can be taken as illustrative. See I.R.C. § 7520. Using a 7% interest rate, if the life tenant of the $100,000 property is 10 years old, the remainder would have present discounted value of $2,595. If the life tenant is 35, then the remainder is worth $9,155 now. And if the life tenant is 55, 70, or 90, the remainder would be valued at $24,604, $44,456, and $75,748, respectively. Of course, life expectancies are based only on averages over large groups of people. Psychologists have documented that most non-depressed people tend to be optimistic about their own abilities and prospects. (Depressed people are simply realistic in these matters.) Might this affect the negotiation between the holders of the life estate and the remainder?

2. RESTRAINTS ON ALIENATION

One of the normal incidents of owner sovereignty is the ability to alienate or transfer property to another. Consequently, courts have long taken a dim view of attempts to restrain the power of an owner to alienate. Almost any attempt directly to restrain alienation will be held void as contrary to public policy. For example, if O grants Blackacre, which is otherwise generally alienable, "to A in fee simple, on the understanding that A has no power to alienate," the restraint on alienation will be struck down and the conveyance will be interpreted as if it said "to A in fee simple." It did not take courts long similarly to conclude that efforts to use defeasible fees or executory limitations to effectuate complete restraints on alienation are similarly void. For example, if O grants Blackacre "to A in fee simple so long as A does not alienate, then to O," this too will be struck down as an attempt to restrain alienation.

But what about other conditions which have the effect of severely reducing the possibilities of alienation? Suppose alienation is prohibited only to certain categories of transferees? Courts will typically uphold restraints on alienation for a limited period of time if they appear to be reasonably related to some family estate planning objective. Examples would include a restraint on alienation by a minor until he or she reaches the age of majority, or a restraint on a life estate given to a surviving spouse when the property in question (e.g., the family home or farm) is intended ultimately to pass to someone else like surviving children.

Mountain Brow Lodge No. 82, Independent Order of Odd Fellows v. Toscano

Court of Appeal, Fifth District, California, 1967.
257 Cal.App.2d 22, 64 Cal.Rptr. 816.

■ GARGANO, ASSOCIATE JUSTICE. This action was instituted by appellant, a non-profit corporation, to quiet its title to a parcel of real property which it acquired on April 6, 1950, by gift deed from James V. Toscano and Maria Toscano, both deceased. Respondents are the trustees and administrators of the estates of the deceased grantors and appellant sought to quiet its title as to their interest in the land arising from certain conditions contained in the gift deed.

The matter was submitted to the court on stipulated facts and the court rendered judgment in favor of respondents. * * *

The controversy between the parties centers on the language contained in the habendum clause of the deed of conveyance which reads as follows: "Said property is restricted for the use and benefit of the second party, only; and in the event the same fails to be used by the second party or in the event of sale or transfer by the second party of all or any part of said lot, the same is to revert to the first parties herein, their successors, heirs or assigns." Respondents maintain that the language creates a fee simple subject to a condition subsequent and is valid and enforceable. On the other hand, appellant contends that the restrictive language amounts to an absolute restraint on its power of alienation and is void. It apparently asserts that, since the purpose for which the land must be used is not precisely defined, it may be used by appellant for any purpose and hence the restriction is not on the land use but on who uses it. Thus, appellant concludes that it is clear that the reversionary clause was intended by grantors to take effect only if appellant sells or transfers the land.

Admittedly, the condition of the habendum clause which prohibits appellant from selling or transferring the land under penalty of forfeiture is an absolute restraint against alienation and is void. The common law rule prohibiting restraint against alienation is embodied in Civil Code section 711 which provides: "Conditions restraining alienation, when repugnant to the interest created, are void." However, this condition and the condition relating to the use of the land are in the disjunctive and are clearly severable. In other words, under the plain language of the deed the grantors, their successors or assigns may exercise their power of termination "if the land is not used by the second party" or "in the event of sale or transfer by second party." Thus, the invalid restraint against alienation does not necessarily affect or nullify the condition on land use (Los Angeles Investment Company v. Gary, 186 P. 596 (Cal. 1919)).

The remaining question, therefore, is whether the use condition created a defeasible fee as respondents maintain or whether it is also a restraint against alienation and nothing more as appellant alleges.

Significantly, appellant is a non-profit corporation organized for lodge, fraternal and similar purposes. Moreover, decedent, James V. Toscano, was an active member of the lodge at the time of his death. In addition, the term "use" as applied to real property can be construed to mean a "right which a person has to use or enjoy the property of another according to his necessities" (Mulford v. LeFranc, 26 Cal. 88, 102 (1864)). Under these circumstances it is reasonably clear that when the grantors stated that the land was conveyed in consideration of "love and affection" and added that it "is restricted for the *use* and benefit of the second party" they simply meant to say that the land was conveyed upon condition that it would be used for lodge, fraternal and other purposes for which the nonprofit corporation was formed. Thus, we conclude that the portion of the habendum clause relating to the land use, when construed as a whole and in light of the surrounding circumstances, created a fee subject to a condition subsequent with title to revert to the grantors, their successors or assigns if the land ceases to be used for lodge, fraternal and similar purposes for which the appellant is formed.[2] No formal language is necessary to create a fee simple subject to a condition subsequent as long as the intent of the grantor is clear. It is the rule that the object in construing a deed is to ascertain the intention of the grantor from words which have been employed and from surrounding circumstances.

It is of course arguable, as appellant suggests, that the condition in appellant's deed is not a restriction on land use but on who uses it. Be this as it may, the distinction between a covenant which restrains the alienation of a fee simple absolute and a condition which restricts land use and creates a defeasible estate was long recognized at common law and is recognized in this state. Thus, conditions restricting land use have been upheld by the California courts on numerous occasions even though they hamper, and often completely impede, alienation. A few examples follow: Mitchell v. Cheney Slough Irrigation Co., 134 P.2d 34 (Cal. Ct. App. 1943) (irrigation ditch); Aller v. Berkeley Hall School Foundation, 103 P.2d 1052 (Cal. Ct. App. 1940) (exclusively private dwellings); Rosecrans v. Pacific Electric Railway Co., 134 P.2d 245 (Cal. 1943) (to maintain a train schedule); Schultz v. Beers, 245 P.2d 334 (Cal. Ct. App. 1952) (road purposes); Firth v. Marovich, 116 P. 729 (Cal. 1911) (residence only).

Moreover, if appellant's suggestion is carried to its logical conclusion it would mean that real property could not be conveyed to a city to be used only for its own city purposes, or to a school district to be used only for its own school purposes, or to a church to be used only for its own church purposes. Such restrictions would also be restrictions upon who uses the land. And yet we do not understand this to be the rule of this state. For example, in *Los Angeles Investment Company v. Gary*, supra,

---

[2]   It is arguable that the gift deed created a fee simple determinable. However, in doubtful cases the preferred construction is in favor of an estate subject to a condition subsequent.

land had been conveyed upon condition that it was not to be sold, leased, rented or occupied by persons other than those of Caucasian race. The court held that the condition against alienation of the land was void, but upheld the condition restricting the land use. Although a use restriction compelling racial discrimination is no longer consonant with constitutional principles under more recent decisions, the sharp distinction that the court drew between a restriction on land use and a restriction on alienation is still valid. For further example, in the leading and often cited case of Johnston v. City of Los Angeles, 168 P. 1047 (Cal. 1917), the land was conveyed to the City of Los Angeles on the express condition that the city would use it for the erection and maintenance of a dam, the land to revert if the city ceased to use it for such purposes. The Supreme Court held that the condition created a defeasible estate, apparently even though it was by necessity a restriction on who could use the land.

Our independent research indicates that the rule is the same in other jurisdictions. In Regular Predestinarian Baptist Church of Pleasant Grove v. Parker, 27 N.E.2d 522 (Ill. 1940), a condition " 'To have and to hold * * * as long as the same is used by the Regular Predestinarian Baptist Church as a place of meeting * * * ' " was deemed to have created a defeasible estate by the Supreme Court of Illinois. * * *

For the reasons herein stated, the first paragraph of the judgment below is amended and revised to read:

1.   That at the time of the commencement of this action title to the parcel of real property situated in the City of Los Banos, County of Merced, State of California, being described as:

Lot 20 Block 72 according to the Map of the Town of Los Banos was vested in the MOUNTAIN BROW LODGE NO. 82, INDEPENDENT ORDER OF ODD FELLOWS, subject to the condition that said property is restricted for the use and benefit of the second party only; and in the event the same fails to be used by the second party the same is to revert to the first parties herein, their successors, heirs or assigns.

As so modified the judgment is affirmed. Respondents to recover their costs on appeal.

■ STONE, ASSOCIATE JUSTICE. I dissent. I believe the entire habendum clause which purports to restrict the fee simple conveyed is invalid as a restraint upon alienation within the ambit of Civil Code section 711. It reads: "Said property is restricted for the use and benefit of the second party, only; and in the event the same fails to be used by the second party or in the event of sale or transfer by the second party of all or any part of said lot the same is to revert to the first parties herein, their successors, heirs or assigns."

If the words "sale or transfer," which the majority find to be a restraint upon alienation, are expunged, still the property cannot be sold or transferred by the grantee because the property may be used by only the I.O.O.F. Lodge No. 82, upon pain of reverter. This use restriction prevents the grantee from conveying the property just as effectively as the condition against "sale or transfer * * * of all or any part of said lot."

Certainly, if we are to have realism in the law, the effect of language must be judged according to what it does. When two different terms generate the same ultimate legal result, they should be treated alike in relation to that result.

Section 711 of the Civil Code expresses an ancient policy of English common law.* The wisdom of this proscription as applied to situations of this kind is manifest when we note that a number of fraternal, political and similar organizations of a century ago have disappeared, and others have ceased to function in individual communities. Should an organization holding property under a deed similar to the one before us be disbanded one hundred years or so after the conveyance is made, the result may well be a title fragmented into the interests of heirs of the grantors numbering in the hundreds and scattered to the four corners of the earth. * * *

In any event, it seems to me that quite aside from section 782, the entire habendum clause is repugnant to the grant in fee simple that precedes it. I would hold the property free from restrictions, and reverse the judgment.

NOTES AND QUESTIONS

1.   Generally in cases in which an instrument's language is ambiguous as to whether it creates a fee simple determinable or a fee simple subject to condition subsequent, courts tend to favor the latter because it will avoid automatic forfeiture. Does this construction also do more to promote free

----

*   "The conceptual argument is that the law defines the exact nature of every estate in land, that each has certain incidents which are provided by law, and that one of the principal incidents of a fee is alienability. Manning, The Development of Restraints on Alienation Since Gray, 48 Harv. L. Rev. 373 (1935).

"The first of the two reasons most often given for holding restraints void is that a restraint is repugnant to the nature of the fee. Murray v. Green, 28 P. 118 (Cal. 1883); Eastman Marble Co. v. Vermont Marble Co., 128 N.E. 177 (Mass. 1920); Andrews v. Hall, 58 N.W.2d 201 (Neb. 1953); 5 Tiffany, Real Property § 1343 (3d ed. 1939); Manning, supra, at 401. However, Lord Coke believed that restraints were void, not only because they were repugnant to the fee, but because "it is absurd and repugnant to reason" that a tenant in fee simple should be restrained "of all his power to alien." Co. Litt. 223a.

"The second and more practically oriented reason for holding restraints void is that a restraint, by taking land out of the flow of commerce, is detrimental to the economy. Gray, Restraints on Alienation § 21 (2d ed. 1895); 6 Powell, Real Property 1 (1958); 5 Tiffany, op. cit. supra, § 1343. Other reasons have been accepted on occasion by courts: to encourage improvement of property; hampering effect[ive] use of property if the buyer could put it to better use than the seller; removal from trade of increasing amounts of capital; not allowing an individual to appear more prosperous than he is, i.e., a borrower may appear to own property outright, thus able to sell it in payment of a debt, where in reality the property is restrained; balance of dead hand control, i.e., recognizing the right of the individual to control property after death by the proposition that life is for the living and should be controlled by the living and not by the extended hand of the dead. Bernhard, The Minority Doctrine Concerning Direct Restraints on Alienation, 57 Mich. L. Rev. 1173, 1177 (1959)." (12 UCLA L. Rev. No. 3, 956.)

alienation of property? The future interest following both these types of interests can be extinguished if the condition is violated and the grantor (or his successor) fails to reclaim the property within the time established by the statute of limitations. If the interest is a possibility of reverter, and the grantor fails to sue to recover possession in an action in trespass or ejectment before the statute of limitations runs, then the owner of the fee simple determinable gets a fee simple absolute by adverse possession. If the interest is a right of entry, and the grantor fails to assert his right to re-enter within a reasonable period of time, then the owner of the fee simple subject to condition subsequent will be able to obtain an equitable judgment that re-entry is barred by the doctrine of laches, in effect creating a fee simple absolute. In determining what is a reasonable period of time for purposes of laches, courts generally look to the statute of limitations for adverse possession. So there is not a lot of room for distinguishing between the two types of defeasible fees on this ground. Is there some other ground for preferring the fee simple subject to condition subsequent construction on grounds of free alienation?

2.   How far do you suppose the majority would be willing to extend its formal rule that restrictions on use do not violate the prohibition against restraints on alienation? Suppose only one member of the Odd Fellows Lodge, Local No. 82 is still alive, and he is on a respirator in a nursing home. Or, suppose all members of the Lodge have died, and the building stands vacant. Is the restriction still enforceable? How far do you suppose the dissent would be willing to extend its realistic test that would invalidate restrictions on use that have the practical effect of impairing alienation? Suppose it could be shown that any defeasible fee that restricts use to some specific charitable or nonprofit activity will severely impair the market value of the property. Would this be enough to justify a judgment invalidating the condition? Courts generally give greater leeway to restraints on use in gifts for charitable purposes. See Canova Land & Inv. Co. v. Lynn, 856 S.E.2d 581 (Va. 2021); Restatement (Third) of Property (Servitudes) § 3.4 cmt. c (Am. L. Inst. 2000) ("If land is held for conservation, historic preservation, or charitable purposes, very severe restraints on alienation are normally justified to assure that the land continues to be used for the intended purposes.").

3.   What exactly does it mean for property to be restricted to "the use and benefit" of some entity? Suppose there are only three elderly Odd Fellows still alive; they vote unanimously at a formal meeting of the Lodge to sell the building to a real estate developer and to use the proceeds for one final fling in Las Vegas. Is this for the "use and benefit" of the Lodge? Does your answer change if the proceeds are to be used to purchase adjacent rooms in a nursing home, where the three can continue to meet? If these sorts of transactions are permissible, does this significantly alleviate concerns about use restrictions impairing marketability?

4.   What are the reasons for the very strong policy against restraints on alienation? Courts often say that restraints on alienation are "repugnant to the fee," but this just begs the question as to why fee simple ownership (or absolute ownership of personal property) should nearly always include the

power of alienation. Traditional justifications emphasize owner autonomy. Thus, just as owners are generally free to abandon or destroy their property when it no longer suits their needs, see Chapter IV, so it is thought they should be free to dispose of property by sale or gift. Like the powers to abandon or destroy, the power to alienate prevents us from becoming slaves to our property. The principal difference among these powers is that the power to alienate allows the owner to appoint the new owner of the asset— something the owner cannot do if the property is destroyed or abandoned— and this likely makes owners even more willing to part with burdensome ownership obligations. The right to transfer also has powerful efficiency justifications. Free alienability permits things to be reallocated from one person to another so as to allow those who place a higher value on the asset to end up in control of it. If the process of transfer were costless (recall the Coase theorem, Chapter I), all things would end up in the hands of the persons who value them the most. In this happy state of affairs, society would be better off, in terms of the satisfaction of all persons' wants and needs, than it would be under any other allocation of things. Although this state of nirvana is unachievable in practice given positive transaction costs, it is quite likely that society will come closer to achieving such a state if assets are freely transferable, than it will if there are significant restrictions on the transfer of assets. Finally, we can think of free alienation as the primary way in which society changes assignments of responsibility for the management of resources. When one owner-gatekeeper gets tired of performing the role of manager of any asset, he or she can transfer managerial responsibility to someone else who is more eager to take on this role. This method of changing managers taps into local knowledge and probably generates less friction than other methods, such as adverse possession, eminent domain, or having the state decide who gets to be the manager.

5.   All that being said, there are contexts in which free alienation is regarded with suspicion. We have seen in Chapter III that some kinds of things—human beings, body parts, and cultural patrimony—are often regarded as being outside the sphere of interests that can be held as property. What this often means—especially in the context of body parts and genetic material or cultural patrimony—is not that we think persons in possession of such things should have no right to exclude. What it means is that we are uncomfortable allowing such things to be freely transferred from one person to another, especially by sale. Thus, one intermediate solution mentioned in those materials is to afford certain things—like body parts— some of the attributes of property such as the right to exclude while denying these things the feature of full transferability. In other words, sometimes the law *requires* restraints on alienation, rather than prohibiting them.

3.   THE RULE AGAINST PERPETUITIES

The Rule against Perpetuities (RAP) is a crystallization of older doctrines invalidating interests that gave too much remote control to the "dead hand." Notwithstanding its name, the RAP does not prohibit "perpetual" or even very long-lasting interests. After all, the fee simple is an interest of potentially infinite duration, but it is the antithesis of the kind of interests targeted by the RAP. Leases can be very long too—sometimes 99 or even 999 years long—and in some jurisdictions it is possible to create a perpetual lease. Yet these very long leases are also unproblematic under the RAP. Instead, the RAP prohibits the creation of contingent interests that are not certain to vest within a prescribed time period.

Why did courts come to disapprove of contingent rights that might vest too remotely in the future? One reason is that long-lasting contingencies about title can impair alienation. Few people will want to buy property with unresolved contingencies about ownership hanging over it. Another reason relates to concerns about giving the dead too much control over the ownership and use of resources by the living. The RAP basically allows testators to keep ownership contingent for one generation into the future plus the next generation up to the traditional age of majority. The judges who devised the rule thought that these are the only people that a testator can really have any knowledge of or benevolence towards. (Others might disagree.) Beyond that, testators should not be allowed to control the disposition of property. Finally, the RAP is sometimes associated with the objective of breaking up large, potentially overly aristocratic estates. We have seen that in earlier times elite families often regarded keeping property, especially landed property, within the family to be an overriding consideration, and creating various contingent interests that last far into the future (e.g., to account for unborn grandchildren) is one way to do this. The RAP creates a barrier to these kinds of dynastic impulses.

Although informed by these policies, the RAP has evolved into a very formalistic rule, in the sense that it can be applied without direct reference to these policies, or much other contextual information, for that matter. The rule received its canonical (if currently rare) form from Professor John Chipman Gray:

> No interest is good unless it must vest, if at all, not later than twenty-one years after some life in being at the creation of the interest.

John Chipman Gray, Rule Against Perpetuities § 201 (Roland Gray ed., 4th ed. 1942). Gray sought in this formulation the brightest of bright-line rules that would receive "remorseless" application. Id. § 629. What the rule does is define a time period (lives in being plus 21 years) and ask whether within this time period we will know whether or not certain types of questions will be resolved. These questions have to do with uncertainty about vesting in interest, not necessarily vesting in possession. That is, we will be asking whether within the "perpetuities period" contingencies about the identity of the takers and other named events will be removed. Moreover, the RAP is a rule against interests *vesting* (in interest) too remotely, and more precisely against interests *possibly* vesting too remotely, *not* a rule against interests lasting too long. Consider this example:

To Marge for life, then to Bart and his heirs.

The remainder here might last forever (and could remain with Bart forever if he turned out to be immortal), but this would be fine.

Vesting means the elimination of the "suspense" element. This can be of one or more of three types:

> (i)   For a contingent remainder, removing suspense means the ascertainment of the identity of the taker and the satisfaction of all conditions precedent:

> Homer grants Blackacre "to Marge for life and to my first child who shall pass the bar, upon his or her marriage."

Here there is uncertainty as to who Homer's first child to pass the bar will be and whether and when he or she will marry.

> (ii)   For an executory interest eliminating the relevant uncertainty means the taking of possession (the cutting short of the prior interest actually happens);[5]

> Marge grants Blackacre "to Bart as long as no alcohol is ever consumed on the premises during his lifetime, then to Lisa."

Here the uncertainty over whether the condition will occur will not be resolved until Bart dies or consumes alcohol on Blackacre (whichever comes first).

> (iii)   For a remainder subject to open (as in a class gift), it means the closing of the class:

> Abe grants Blackacre "to my children who shall reach the age of 21."

Lack of vesting can happen because the identity of a taker is not determined (for example, heirs are not determined yet) or there is a contingency that has not happened yet. Here we have both.

To summarize: Those future interests potentially subject to the RAP are contingent remainders, executory interests, and vested remainders subject to partial divestment (i.e., subject to open). All other future interests, including those retained by the grantor (reversions, possibilities of reverter, and rights of entry) and other types of vested remainders are not subject to the RAP. Vested remainders subject to complete divestment are not themselves subject to the RAP, although if the interests that divest these vested remainders are executory interests, they of course are subject to the RAP. See Figure 5-5 supra.

Note that for the RAP the measuring lives must exist at the time of the creation of the interest, and then comes the 21-year period (the 21-year period cannot come first). Why 21 years? The idea is that a testator or other grantor can legitimately care about and act paternalistically

---

[5]   Or the conversion of the executory interest into a vested remainder, as in Note 2 of Part B.2.b supra.

toward the next generation plus the next generation after that up to the age at which people become responsible, which courts assumed to be 21.

The RAP is tricky because some very similar sounding interests may fall on opposite sides of the line. Consider some more examples of a generic bequest of personal property:

Example 1: T makes a bequest "to my grandchildren who shall reach the age of 21."

This is valid because all T's grandchildren must be born within the lives of T's children and these lives must be lives in being at T's death. This illustrates a couple of important points. First, a child who is born after T's death is deemed to be in being at conception if the child is later born alive. If the child was later born alive, the common law would add the period of gestation to the perpetuities period. See Thellusson v. Woodford, (1805) 32 Eng. Rep. 1030 (Ch.); W. Barton Leach, Perpetuities in a Nutshell, 51 Harv. L. Rev. 638, 642 (1938). Second, the measuring lives do *not* have to be those of people mentioned in the instrument, need not be holders of previous estates, and need have no special connection to the property. They just need to be people who can affect the vesting (through the condition stated in the instrument or through the identity of the takers).

Example 2: T sets up an inter vivos trust for "my grandchildren who shall reach the age of 21."

This is invalid. It could happen that all the existing children of T may die, and T has more children, one of whom has a grandchild who reaches 21 after the perpetuities period. In this case, no measuring lives can be found that span from the creation of the interest to 21 years before its vesting. Note that this illustrates the importance of considering the perpetuities issue from the standpoint of the time of the *creation of the interest*. This makes all the difference between this example and Example 1, where the interest comes into being when the testator dies, thus preventing the remote vesting scenario with the afterborn child.

Example 3: T makes a bequest "to A's grandchildren who shall reach the age of 21." A is alive at the time of the testator's death.

This is invalid for reasons similar to those in Example 2. Because A can have more children, the children's lives cannot be taken as measuring lives. So the problem is not bequest versus inter vivos transfer but whether there can be more children or not. If so, they cannot be the measuring lives. One might ask what would happen if a bequest is made "to my children for their lives, remainder to my grandchildren who shall reach 21." Again, this is all right even if the testator has a child born several months after his death, because of the extension granted for gestation time.

The RAP has given rise to an enduring sport: Attempting to maximize the perpetuities period by using a larger and younger set of measuring lives. Courts will invalidate such interests when the burden of keeping track of the measuring lives is too great. A time-honored technique is to create an interest that will vest 21 years after the death of the last of a list of a dozen or so healthy babies. Over the line are attempts to similarly use the list of everyone in the New York City phone directory ("to my descendants who shall be living 21 years after the death of everyone listed in the New York City phone book"). See also In re Moore, [1901] 1 Ch. 936, 938 (invalidating as void for uncertainty a gift in trust to endure until "twenty-one years from the death of the last survivor of all persons who shall be living at my death," and noting that "[i]t is impossible to ascertain when the last life will be extinguished. . . . Under these circumstances it is not, I think, necessary for me to consider whether the gift is void as transgressing the rule against perpetuity.") To take the most creative and successful example, in *In re Villar*, [1929] 1 Ch. 243 (C.A.) the court held that the RAP did not invalidate bequests in trust that were to vest "at the expiration of 20 years from the day of the death of the last survivor of all the lineal descendants of Her Late Majesty Queen Victoria who shall be living at the time of my death." [1929] 1 Ch. at 243. At the time of the testator's death in 1926 there were 120 or so such descendants then living. Although it has been suggested that an American court would not uphold such an interest (nor the one employing the city phone book formula), Restatement of Property § 374 cmt. l (1944), why are "royal lives" clauses more likely to be upheld in England than the city phone book approach?

Recall in this connection that future interests retained by the grantor are treated as vested on creation and so satisfy the RAP. Are such interests easier to keep track of than interests created in third parties?

As can be seen in the above examples, the RAP traditionally involved spinning out scenarios of what *might* happen based solely on information available at the time the interest was created. The common law pursued this approach relentlessly, and presumed that anyone, no matter how old, could marry or have children at any time, leading to invalidation on the possibility of "unborn widows" and "fertile octogenarians."

In the unborn widow scenario, a gift is made to A for life and then to A's widow for life, then to A's children then living. This seems fine at first blush, until one spins a story in which A's present wife dies or she and A divorce and A then marries a woman who was born after the creation of the interest. If so the interest in her children could vest outside the perpetuities period. As for the fertile octogenarian, suppose O conveys "to my wife A for life, then to my grandchildren who reach age 21." O and A, both age 80, have a child B, age 45, and B has a child C, age 10. Again this seems fine on cursory examination. But suppose, after the conveyance, that the octogenarian A has another child, D, who then produces a grandchild, E. There is no life in being at the time of the conveyance that can demonstrate, as a matter of what-might-happen logic, that the interest of E will vest or not within the perpetuities period. See Jee v. Audley, 1 Cox 324, 29 Eng. Rep. 1186 (Ch. 1787).

Not surprisingly, such results and the rule that produced them came in for heavy criticism, leading to limited reforms such as a presumption that the fertile octogenarian and unborn widow situations will not arise. Shortly we will take up more sweeping reforms, such as wait-and-see, which would also have saved these sorts of situations from invalidation.

More recently, assisted reproductive techniques have made postmenopausal births possible. More generally, techniques such as cryopreservation of sperm, eggs, and embryos present new challenges for the RAP, where it still exists. Such techniques are sometimes said not to count for the common-law RAP. Can you see the problems posed? For a review of how various reforms do and do not address the challenges to the RAP and inheritance law raised by new reproductive technologies, see Sharona Hoffman & Andrew P. Morriss, Birth After Death: Perpetuities and the New Reproductive Technologies, 38 Ga. L. Rev. 575 (2004).

If you feel uneasy about applying the RAP, you are in good company. The RAP has long been notorious as a trap for the unwary. The California Supreme Court once went so far as to hold it not to be malpractice for a lawyer to miss a subtle perpetuities problem in drafting a will. Lucas v. Hamm, 364 P.2d 685 (Cal. 1961). The Court quoted Professor Gray, the author of the famous formulation of the rule as saying: " 'There is something in the subject which seems to facilitate error. Perhaps it is because the mode of reasoning is unlike that with which lawyers are most familiar. * * * A long list might be formed of the demonstrable blunders with regard to its questions made by eminent men, blunders which they themselves have been sometimes the first to acknowledge; and there are few lawyers of any practice in drawing wills and settlements who have not at some time either fallen into the net which the Rule spreads for the unwary, or at least shuddered to think how narrowly they have escaped it.' Gray, The Rule Against Perpetuities (4th ed. 1942) p. xi." Id. at 690.

A standard solution to the perpetuities problem is to insert a "perpetuities savings clause" into the relevant instrument. Such a clause refers explicitly to the possibility of invalidation under the RAP and specifies a backup plan. Consider the key part of one version of a savings clause:

> If any interest purported to be created in this instrument or in any instrument exercising a power created in this instrument is challenged under the Rule Against Perpetuities or any related rule, I direct the corporate donee (hereafter designated) to appoint the assets which the challenged interest purports to dispose of in such manner as will most closely approximate, within clearly permissible limits, the intention of the person who has executed the instrument purporting to create such interest.

W. Barton Leach & James K. Logan, Perpetuities: A Standard Saving Clause to Avoid Violations of the Rule, 74 Harv. L. Rev. 1141, 1141–42 (1961). Courts have upheld perpetuities savings clauses. See, e.g., Norton v. Georgia R.R. Bank & Trust, 322 S.E.2d 870 (Ga. 1984). The savings clause became a standard practice and made perpetuities problems relatively easy to avoid even before the judicial and statutory reforms discussed below.

Finally, courts have recently started using reinterpretation to save interests from invalidation under the RAP. The method here is in effect to rewrite the instrument so that it conforms with the grantor's intent as closely as possible, but becomes consistent with the RAP. (Courts have had some experience in the doctrine of cy pres, which saves gifts to charity from impossibility, or more recently wastefulness, by substituting another close charity. See Chapter VI.) Even under older RAP doctrine, charities received somewhat favorable treatment. Consider the following example:

> *Example 4*: O grants Blackacre "to Springfield Law School so long as it is used for instruction in the law, but if it is not used for instruction in the law, then to Shelbyville Law School."

The Springfield Law School has a fee simple subject to executory limitation, and the Shelbyville Law School has an executory interest. The executory interest would normally violate the RAP because it is not guaranteed to vest within lives in being plus 21 years. Nevertheless, the executory interest would probably be all right under the rule of two charities: An interest does not violate the RAP if the interest involves a transfer from one charity to another, as here.

PROBLEMS

In the following, identify the interests O is trying to create, and if different, the interests actually created or resulting from the facts given. Assume that the common-law version of the Rule against Perpetuities is in force.

1. O grants Blackacre "to Huxley College, as long as it is used for instructional purposes; then to my son A and his heirs."

2. O grants Blackacre "to A; but if marijuana is inhaled on the premises, then O has the right to reenter and take the premises."

3. O grants Blackacre "to A; but if marijuana is inhaled on the premises, then to B and her heirs."

4. O grants Blackacre "to A for life, then to B's grandchildren who reach the age of 21." Assume that B is dead at the time the interest is created, leaving children but no grandchildren.

5. O grants Blackacre "to A for life, then to my grandchildren who graduate from high school." O has children B and C, but no grandchildren at the time of the grant.

6. As in Problem 5, except the transfer is by devise (a grant of real estate in a will).

Reforms

A growing number of states have significantly reformed or abolished the common-law RAP, or allow parties to opt out of the rule in drafting a will or trust if they chose to do so. Much of the motivation for relaxing the constraints of the RAP comes from the federal tax advantages to dynasty trusts, and there now seems to be a jurisdictional competition to attract trust business by allowing trust settlors to skirt around the RAP (at least among states that do not tax income from trust funds). Max Schanzenbach & Robert Sitkoff, Jurisdictional Competition for Trust Funds: An Empirical Analysis of Perpetuities and Taxes, 115 Yale L.J. 356 (2005). In addition to tax considerations, some testators still want to exercise control over the future. Trust specialists seem to be advertising on that basis. Joshua C. Tate, Perpetual Trusts and the Settlor's Intent, 53 Kan. L. Rev. 595 (2005). Other reforms:

(i) *Wait and See for the Common-Law RAP Period* (or some related period). Under this approach one would, if necessary, wait and see whether the interest vests remotely or not. Thus in Examples 2 and 3 (and in some of the Problems) above, one would wait and see whether additional children were born. If not, the interest would turn out to be valid. But notice that one would typically not know this for quite a while.

(ii) *Wait and See for the Common-Law Period or 90 Years.* This is like wait and see but allows for a 90-year alternative period. Like (i), this approach allows interests to satisfy the RAP the common-law way—ex ante, at the time the interest is created—as well. So if the interest satisfies the common-law RAP one can know it is valid right away. Also, one knows that one won't have to wait more than 90 years to find out either. Some commentators have heavily criticized the 90-year period on the grounds that interests that are only valid because of the 90-year wait-and-see period involve a high degree of uncertainty for this lengthy period of time. Keeping the RAP but adopting wait-and-see in general involves tolerating uncertainty.

(iii) *Interpretation and Implication.* Sometimes drafters and courts will insert a perpetuities savings clause or otherwise reform an interest (as by changing 25 years to 21 years). Courts will sometimes also refuse to invalidate a class gift if it fails to vest for the entire class within the perpetuities period. Thus in a gift to "A's children" the interest is held to vest even if a child might be born too remotely; the interest simply fails with respect to that child only, rejecting the all-or-nothing approach of the common-law RAP. See, e.g., In re Estate of Anderson, 541 So.2d 423 (Miss. 1989).

The Uniform Statutory Rule Against Perpetuities (USRAP) combines approaches (ii) and (iii). Among other things, the USRAP provides for a cy pres-like approach to saving ill-drafted instruments, under which an interested person can petition a court to "reform a disposition in the manner that most closely approximates the transferor's manifested plan of distribution and is within the 90 years allowed" as long as one of a number of conditions holds.

Close to half the states have adopted the USRAP, about a quarter of the states permit trust settlors to opt out of the RAP if they choose, eight states have abolished the RAP outright, and several other states allow courts to reform instruments so as to make them comply with the Rule. Helene Shapo et al., Bogert's Trusts and Trustees § 214, at n.28 (2015); see also Jesse Dukeminier & James E. Krier, The Rise of the Perpetual Trust, 50 UCLA L. Rev. 1303 (2003).

The Problem of Dead Hand Control

The intuition that there is something wrong with dead hand control is a longstanding and fairly robust one. For example, Adam Smith warned that "[t]o give a man power over his property after his death is very considerable, but it is nothing [compared] to an extension of this power to the end of the world." Adam Smith, Lectures on Jurisprudence 467 (R.L. Meek et al. eds., 1978) (ms. 1762–66). As in the case of rules against restraints on alienation, we can ask why we need mandatory rules against dead hand control.

What would testators do if given unlimited discretion? Many testators would like to give freedom to the recipient—often the testator's spouse or children—and here the issue does not arise. But sometimes testators will worry about unwise decisions by the donee, or the testator would like to condition or control the resources into the future. As we saw in Chapter IV, the law gives wide but not unlimited latitude to owners to destroy property, and at first glance controlling property into the future is a less sweeping use of the property. As in the right to destroy, subjecting property to post mortem control is costly to the donee in that she cannot sell it (for a price that would reflect future use) or give it away in some other way. If the present discounted future benefits and liabilities of the property are reflected in current prices (known as "capitalization"), wouldn't the donor take these values into account? What, if anything does capitalization leave out of the picture?

Some have sought to justify the RAP on the ground that dead people cannot experience utility, but even if so, people who are living may derive utility in anticipating such control and might even work harder to create wealth that they can subject to such control. Conversely, some focus on the needs of the members of the future generation who have to live with the dead hand conditions is appropriate. What do we owe future generations? Does the RAP serve these interests?

Others have argued that the future is full of uncertainty and a testator cannot be expected to foresee all the contingencies relevant to the testator's overall plan. We will take up such problems with the cy pres doctrine in Chapter VI. Property rights typically last a long time. Does dead hand control put too much of a burden on future owners and judges to figure out what the creator of the interest wanted? Why don't we have a menu of options for flexibility that the creator of the interest can choose from, ranging from wooden application of the testator's language to letting judges intervene according to their assessment of future needs? If future people reach a consensus that some type of dead hand control is harmful, what is to stop them from simply doing as they wish? For discussion of these issues, see, e.g., Steven Shavell, Foundations of the Economic Analysis of Law 67–72 (2004); Lewis M. Simes, Public Policy and the Dead Hand (1955); Adam J. Hirsch & William K.S. Wang, A Qualitative Theory of the Dead Hand, 68 Ind. L.J. 1 (1992); Jeffrey E. Stake, Darwin, Donations, and the Illusion of Dead Hand Control, 64 Tul. L. Rev. 705 (1990); Symposium, Time, Property, Rights, and the Common Law, 64 Wash. U. L.Q. 661 (1986).

Symphony Space, Inc. v. Pergola Properties, Inc.

Court of Appeals of New York, 1996.
669 N.E.2d 799.

■ KAYE, CHIEF JUDGE. This case presents the novel question whether options to purchase commercial property are exempt from the prohibition against remote vesting embodied in New York's Rule against Perpetuities (EPTL 9–1.1[b]). Because an exception for commercial options finds no support in our law, we decline to exempt all commercial option agreements from the statutory Rule against Perpetuities.

Here, we agree with the trial court and Appellate Division that the option defendants seek to enforce violates the statutory prohibition against remote vesting and is therefore unenforceable.

I. FACTS

The subject of this proceeding is a two-story building situated on the Broadway block between 94th and 95th Streets on Manhattan's Upper West Side. In 1978, Broadwest Realty Corporation owned this building, which housed a theater and commercial space. Broadwest had been unable to secure a permanent tenant for the theater—approximately 58% of the total square footage of the building's floor space. Broadwest also owned two adjacent properties, Pomander Walk (a residential complex) and the Healy Building (a commercial building). Broadwest had been operating its properties at a net loss.

Plaintiff Symphony Space, Inc., a not-for-profit entity devoted to the arts, had previously rented the theater for several one-night engagements. In 1978, Symphony and Broadwest engaged in a transaction whereby Broadwest sold the entire building to Symphony for the below-market price of $10,010 and leased back the income-producing commercial property, excluding the theater, for $1 per year. Broadwest maintained liability for the existing $243,000 mortgage on the property as well as certain maintenance obligations. As a condition of the sale, Symphony, for consideration of $10, also granted Broadwest an option to repurchase the entire building. Notably, the transaction did not involve Pomander Walk or the Healy Building.

The purpose of this arrangement was to enable Symphony, as a not-for-profit corporation, to seek a property tax exemption for the entire building—which constituted a single tax parcel—predicated on its use of the theater. The sale-and-leaseback would thereby reduce Broadwest's real estate taxes by $30,000 per year, while permitting Broadwest to retain the rental income from the leased commercial space in the building, which the trial court found produced $140,000 annually. The arrangement also furthered Broadwest's goal of selling all the properties, by allowing Broadwest to postpone any sale until property values in the area increased and until the commercial leases expired. Symphony, in turn, would have use of the theater at minimal cost, once it received a tax exemption.

Thus, on December 1, 1978, Symphony and Broadwest—both sides represented by counsel—executed a contract for sale of the property from Broadwest to Symphony for the purchase price of $10,010. The contract specified that $10 was to be paid at the closing and $10,000 was to be paid by means of a purchase-money mortgage.

The parties also signed several separate documents, each dated December 31, 1978: (1) a deed for the property from Broadwest to Symphony; (2) a lease from Symphony to Broadwest of the entire building except the theater for rent of $1 per year and for the term January 1, 1979 to May 31, 2003, unless terminated earlier; (3) a 25-year, $10,000 mortgage and mortgage note from Symphony as mortgagor to Broadwest as mortgagee, with full payment due on December 31, 2003; and (4) an option agreement by which Broadwest obtained from Symphony the exclusive right to repurchase all of the property, including the theater.

It is the option agreement that is at the heart of the present dispute. Section 3 of that agreement provides that Broadwest may exercise its option to purchase the property during any of the following "Exercise Periods":

> (a) at any time after July 1, 1979, so long as the Notice of Election specifies that the Closing is to occur during any of the calendar years 1987, 1993, 1998 and 2003;

> (b) at any time following the maturity of the indebtedness evidenced by the Note and secured by the Mortgage, whether by acceleration or otherwise;

> (c) during the ninety days immediately following any termination of the Lease by the lessor thereof other than for nonpayment of rent or any termination of the Lease by the lessee thereof * * *

(d) during the ninety days immediately following the thirtieth day after Broadwest shall have sent Symphony a notice specifying a default by Symphony of any of its covenants or obligations under the Mortgage.

Section 1 states that "Broadwest may exercise its option at any time during any Exercise Period." That section further specifies that the notice of election must be sent at least 180 days prior to the closing date if the option is exercised pursuant to section 3(a) and at least 90 days prior to the closing date if exercised pursuant to any other subdivision.

The following purchase prices of the property, contingent upon the closing date, are set forth in section 4: $15,000 if the closing date is on or before December 31, 1987; $20,000 if on or before December 31, 1993; $24,000 if on or before December 31, 1998; and $28,000 if on or before December 31, 2003.

Importantly, the option agreement specifies in section 5 that "Broadwest's right to exercise the option granted hereby is * * * unconditional and shall not be in any way affected or impaired by Broadwest's performance or nonperformance, actual or asserted, of any obligation to be performed under the Lease or any other agreement or instrument by or between Broadwest and Symphony," other than that Broadwest was required to pay Symphony any unpaid rent on the closing date. Finally, section 6 established that the option constituted "a covenant running with the land, inuring to the benefit of heirs, successors and assigns of Broadwest."

Symphony ultimately obtained a tax exemption for the theater. In the summer of 1981, Broadwest sold and assigned its interest under the lease, option agreement, mortgage and mortgage note, as well as its ownership interest in the contiguous Pomander Walk and Healy Building, to defendants' nominee for $4.8 million. The nominee contemporaneously transferred its rights under these agreements to defendants Pergola Properties, Inc., Bradford N. Swett, Casandium Limited and Darenth Consultants as tenants in common.

Subsequently, defendants initiated a cooperative conversion of Pomander Walk, which was designated a landmark in 1982, and the value of the properties increased substantially. An August 1988 appraisal of the entire blockfront, including the Healy Building and the unused air and other development rights available from Pomander Walk, valued the property at $27 million assuming the enforceability of the option. By contrast, the value of the leasehold interest plus the Healy Building without the option were appraised at $5.5 million.

Due to Symphony's alleged default on the mortgage note, defendant Swett served Symphony with notice in January 1985 that it was exercising the option on behalf of all defendants. The notice set a closing date of May 6, 1985. Symphony, however, disputed both that it was in default and Swett's authority to exercise the option for all of the defendants. According to Symphony, moreover, it then discovered that the option agreement was possibly invalid. Consequently, in March 1985, Symphony initiated this declaratory judgment action against defendants, arguing that the option agreement violated the New York statutory prohibition against remote vesting * * *

Defendant Pergola subsequently served Symphony with separate notice of default dated April 4, 1985, informing Symphony that it was exercising the option on behalf of all defendants pursuant to sections 1, 3(b) and 3(d) of the option agreement and setting the closing date for July 10, 1985. Pergola further notified Symphony that it was alternatively exercising the option under section 3(a) of the option agreement, which was not contingent upon Symphony's default, with the closing date scheduled for January 5, 1987. Symphony did not appear for any of the closing dates contained in Swett's or Pergola's notices. * * *

Thereafter, the parties cross-moved for summary judgment in the instant declaratory judgment proceeding. The trial court granted Symphony's motion while denying that of defendants. In particular, the court concluded that the Rule against Perpetuities applied to the commercial option contained in the parties' agreement, that the option violated the Rule and that Symphony was entitled to exercise its equitable right to redeem the mortgage. The trial court also dismissed defendants' counterclaim for rescission of the agreements underlying the transaction based on the parties' mutual mistake.

In a comprehensive writing by Justice Ellerin, the Appellate Division likewise determined that the commercial option was unenforceable under the Rule against Perpetuities and that rescission was inappropriate. The Appellate Division certified the following question to us: "Was the order of the Supreme Court, as affirmed by this Court, properly made?" We conclude that it was and now affirm.

II. STATUTORY BACKGROUND

The Rule against Perpetuities evolved from judicial efforts during the 17th century to limit control of title to real property by the dead hand of landowners reaching into future generations. Underlying both early and modern rules restricting future dispositions of property is the principle that it is socially undesirable for property to be inalienable for an unreasonable period of time. These rules thus seek "to ensure the productive use and development of property by its current beneficial owners by simplifying ownership, facilitating exchange and freeing property from unknown or embarrassing impediments to alienability" (Metropolitan Transp. Auth. v. Bruken Realty Corp., 492 N.E.2d 379, 381 (N.Y. 1986), citing De Peyster v. Michael, 6 N.Y. 467, 494 (1852)).

The traditional statement of the common-law Rule against Perpetuities was set forth by Professor John Chipman Gray: "No interest is good unless it must vest, if at all, not later than twenty-one years after some life in being at the creation of the interest" (Gray, The Rule Against Perpetuities § 201, at 191 [4th ed. 1942]).

In New York, the rules regarding suspension of the power of alienation and remoteness in vesting—the Rule against Perpetuities—have been statutory since 1830. Prior to 1958, the perpetuities period was two lives in being plus actual periods of minority (see, Real Property Law former § 42). Widely criticized as unduly complex and restrictive, the statutory period was revised in 1958 and 1960, restoring the common-law period of lives in being plus 21 years (see, L.1958, ch. 153; L.1960, ch. 448). * * *

New York's current statutory Rule against Perpetuities is found in EPTL 9–1.1. Subdivision (a) sets forth the suspension of alienation rule and deems void any estate in which the conveying instrument suspends the absolute power of alienation for longer than lives in being at the creation of the estate plus 21 years (see, EPTL 9–1.1[a][2]). The prohibition against remote vesting is contained in subdivision (b), which states that "[n]o estate in property shall be valid unless it must vest, if at all, not later than twenty-one years after one or more lives in being at the creation of the estate and any period of gestation involved" (EPTL 9–1.1[b]). This Court has described subdivision (b) as "a rigid formula that invalidates any interest that may not vest within the prescribed time period" and has "capricious consequences" (Wildenstein & Co. v. Wallis, 595 N.E.2d 828, 831–32 (N.Y. 1992)). Indeed, these rules are predicated upon the public policy of the State and constitute non-waivable, legal prohibitions (see, Metropolitan Transp. Auth. v. Bruken Realty Corp., 492 N.E.2d at 381).

In addition to these statutory formulas, New York also retains the more flexible common-law rule against unreasonable restraints on alienation. Unlike the statutory Rule against Perpetuities, which is measured exclusively by the passage of time, the common-law rule evaluates the reasonableness of the restraint based on its duration, purpose and designated method for fixing the purchase price. (See, Wildenstein & Co. v. Wallis, 595 N.E.2d at 832; Metropolitan Transp. Auth. v. Bruken Realty Corp., 492 N.E.2d at 381–82).

Against this background, we consider the option agreement at issue.

III. VALIDITY OF THE OPTION AGREEMENT

Defendants proffer three grounds for upholding the option: that the statutory prohibition against remote vesting does not apply to commercial options; that the option here cannot be exercised beyond the statutory period; and that this Court should adopt the "wait and see" approach to the Rule against Perpetuities. We consider each in turn.

A. Applicability of the Rule to Commercial Options

Under the common law, options to purchase land are subject to the rule against remote vesting (see, Simes, Future Interests § 132 [2d ed. 1966]; Simes and Smith, Future Interests § 1244 [2d ed.]; Leach,

Perpetuities in a Nutshell, 51 Harv.L.Rev. 638, 660; see also, London & S.W. Ry. Co. v. Gomm, 20 Ch. D. 562 (C.A. 1882)). Such options are specifically enforceable and give the option holder a contingent, equitable interest in the land (Dukeminier, A Modern Guide to Perpetuities, 74 Cal.L.Rev. 1867, 1908; Leach, Perpetuities in Perspective: Ending the Rule's Reign of Terror, 65 Harv.L.Rev. 721, 736–737). This creates a disincentive for the landowner to develop the property and hinders its alienability, thereby defeating the policy objectives underlying the Rule against Perpetuities.

Typically, however, options to purchase are part of a commercial transaction. For this reason, subjecting them to the Rule against Perpetuities has been deemed "a step of doubtful wisdom" (Leach, Perpetuities in Perspective: Ending the Rule's Reign of Terror, 65 Harv.L.Rev. 737). As one vocal critic, Professor W. Barton Leach, has explained,

> [t]he Rule grew up as a limitation on family dispositions; and the period of lives in being plus twenty-one years is adapted to these gift transactions. The pressures which created the Rule do not exist with reference to arms-length contractual transactions, and neither lives in being nor twenty-one years are periods which are relevant to business men and their affairs (Leach, Perpetuities: New Absurdity, Judicial and Statutory Correctives, 73 Harv.L.Rev. 1318, 1321–1322).

Professor Leach, however, went on to acknowledge that, under common law, "due to an overemphasis on concepts derived from the nineteenth century, we are stuck with the application of the Rule to options to purchase," urging that "this should not be extended to other commercial transactions" (id., at 1322).

It is now settled in New York that, generally, EPTL 9–1.1(b) applies to options. In Buffalo Seminary v. McCarthy, 86 A.D.2d 435, 440, 451 N.Y.S.2d 457, 461 (App. Div. 1982), aff'd 447 N.E.2d 76 (N.Y. 1983), the court held that an unlimited option in gross to purchase real property was void under the statutory rule against remote vesting, and we affirmed the Appellate Division decision on the opinion of then-Justice Hancock. Since then, we have reiterated that options in real estate are subject to the statutory rule (see, e.g., Wildenstein & Co. v. Wallis, 595 N.E.2d at 832). * * *

While defendants offer compelling policy reasons—echoing those voiced by Professor Leach—for refusing to apply the traditional rule against remote vesting to these commercial option contracts, such statutory reformation would require legislative action similar to that undertaken by numerous other State lawmakers (see, e.g., Cal.Prob.Code § 21225; Fla.Stat.Annot. ch. 689.225; Ill.Stat.Annot. ch. 765, para. 305/4).

Our decision in *Metropolitan Transp. Auth. v. Bruken Realty Corp.*, 492 N.E.2d 379, supra, is not to the contrary. In *Bruken,* we held that

EPTL 9–1.1(b) did not apply to a preemptive right in a "commercial and governmental transaction" that lasted beyond the statutory perpetuities period. In doing so, we explained that, *unlike options,* preemptive rights (or rights of first refusal) only marginally affect transferability:

> An option grants to the holder the power to compel the owner of property to sell it whether the owner is willing to part with ownership or not. A preemptive right, or right of first refusal, does not give its holder the power to compel an unwilling owner to sell; it merely requires the owner, when and if he decides to sell, to offer the property first to the party holding the preemptive right so that he may meet a third-party offer or buy the property at some other price set by a previously stipulated method (id. at 382).

Enforcement of the preemptive right in the context of the governmental and commercial transaction, moreover, actually encouraged the use and development of the land, outweighing any minor impediment to alienability (id. at 383–84). * * *

Here, the option agreement creates precisely the sort of control over future disposition of the property that we have previously associated with purchase options and that the common-law rule against remote vesting— and thus EPTL 9–1.1(b)—seeks to prevent. As the Appellate Division explained, the option grants its holder absolute power to purchase the property at the holder's whim and at a token price set far below market value. This Sword of Damocles necessarily discourages the property owner from investing in improvements to the property. Furthermore, the option's existence significantly impedes the owner's ability to sell the property to a third party, as a practical matter rendering it inalienable.

That defendants, the holder of this option, are also the lessees of a portion of the premises does not lead to a different conclusion here.

Generally, an option to purchase land that originates in one of the lease provisions, is not exercisable after lease expiration, and is incapable of separation from the lease is valid even though the holder's interest may vest beyond the perpetuities period (see, Berg, Long-Term Options and the Rule Against Perpetuities, 37 Cal.L.Rev. 1, 21; Leach, Perpetuities: New Absurdity, Judicial and Statutory Correctives, 73 Harv.L.Rev. 1320; Simes and Smith, Future Interests § 1244). Such options—known as options "appendant" or "appurtenant" to leases— encourage the possessory holder to invest in maintaining and developing the property by guaranteeing the option holder the ultimate benefit of any such investment. Options appurtenant thus further the policy objectives underlying the rule against remote vesting and are not contemplated by EPTL 9–1.1(b) (see, Metropolitan Transp. Auth. v. Bruken Realty Corp., 492 N.E.2d at 383–84, supra).

To be sure, the option here arose within a larger transaction that included a lease. Nevertheless, not all of the property subject to the purchase option here is even occupied by defendants. The option encompasses the entire building—both the commercial space and the theater—yet defendants are leasing only the commercial space. With regard to the theater space, a disincentive exists for Symphony to improve the property, since it will eventually be claimed by the option holder at the predetermined purchase price. * * *

Put simply, the option here cannot qualify as an option appurtenant and significantly deters development of the property. If the option is exercisable beyond the statutory perpetuities period, refusing to enforce it would thus further the purpose and rationale underlying the statutory prohibition against remote vesting.

B.   Duration of the Option Agreement

1.   Duration Under Section 3(a) of the Agreement

Defendants alternatively claim that section 3(a) of the agreement does not permit exercise of the option after expiration of the statutory perpetuities period. According to defendants, only the possible closing dates fall outside the permissible time frame.

Where, as here, the parties to a transaction are corporations and no measuring lives are stated in the instruments, the perpetuities period is simply 21 years (see, Metropolitan Transp. Auth. v. Bruken Realty Corp., 492 N.E.2d at 381, supra). Section 1 of the parties' agreement allows the option holder to exercise the option "at any time during any Exercise Period" set forth in section three. Section 3(a), moreover, expressly provides that the option may be exercised "*at any time* after July 1, 1979," so long as the closing date is scheduled during 1987, 1993, 1998 or 2003.

Even factoring in the requisite notice, then, the option could potentially be exercised as late as July 2003—more than 24 years after its creation in December 1978. Defendants' contention that section 3(a) does not permit exercise of the option beyond the 21-year period is thus contradicted by the plain language of the instrument.

Nor can EPTL 9–1.3—the "saving statute"—be invoked to shorten the duration of the exercise period under section 3(a) of the agreement. That statute mandates that, "[u]nless a contrary intention appears," certain rules of construction govern with respect to any matter affecting the Rule against Perpetuities (EPTL 9–1.3[a]). The specified canons of construction include that "[i]t shall be presumed that the creator intended the estate to be valid" (EPTL 9–1.3[b]) and "[w]here the duration or vesting of an estate is contingent upon * * * the occurrence of any specified contingency, it shall be presumed that the creator of such estate intended such contingency to occur, if at all, within twenty-one years from the effective date of the instrument creating such estate" (EPTL 9–1.3[d]).

By presuming that the creator intended the estate to be valid, the statute seeks to avoid annulling dispositions due to inadvertent violations of the Rule against Perpetuities. The provisions of EPTL 9–

1.3, however, are merely rules of construction. While the statute obligates reviewing courts, where possible, to avoid constructions that frustrate the parties' intended purposes, it does not authorize courts to rewrite instruments that unequivocally allow interests to vest outside the perpetuities period (compare, EPTL 9–1.2 [reducing age contingency to 21 years, where interest is invalid because contingent on a person reaching an age in excess of 21 years]).

Indeed, by their terms, the rules of construction in EPTL 9–1.3 apply only if "a contrary intention" does not appear in the instrument. * * *

The unambiguous language of the agreement here expresses the parties' intent that the option be exercisable "at any time" during a 24-year period pursuant to section 3(a). The section thus does not permit a construction that the parties intended the option to last only 21 years.

Given the contrary intention manifested in the instrument itself, the saving statute is simply inapplicable. * * *

C.   "Wait and See" Approach

Defendants next urge that we adopt the "wait and see" approach to the Rule against Perpetuities: an interest is valid if it actually vests during the perpetuities period, irrespective of what might have happened (see, Dukeminier, A Modern Guide to Perpetuities, 74 Cal.L.Rev. 1867, 1880). The option here would survive under the "wait and see" approach since it was exercised by 1987, well within the 21-year limitation.

This Court, however, has long refused to "wait and see" whether a perpetuities violation in fact occurs. As explained in *Matter of Fischer*, 120 N.E.2d 688, 692 (N.Y. 1954), "[i]t is settled beyond dispute that in determining whether a will has illegally suspended the power of alienation, the courts will look to what might have happened under the terms of the will rather than to what has actually happened since the death of the testator."

The very language of EPTL 9–1.1, moreover, precludes us from determining the validity of an interest based upon what actually occurs during the perpetuities period. Under the statutory rule against remote vesting, an interest is invalid "unless it *must* vest, if at all, not later than twenty-one years after one or more lives in being" (EPTL 9–1.1[b] [emphasis added]). That is, an interest is void from the outset if it may vest too remotely * * * Because the option here could have vested after expiration of the 21-year perpetuities period, it offends the Rule.

We note that the desirability of the "wait and see" doctrine has been widely debated (see, 5A Powell, Real Property ¶ 827F[1], [3]; see also, Waggoner, Perpetuity Reform, 81 Mich.L.Rev. 1718 [describing "wait and see" as "(t)he most controversial of the reform methods"]). Its incorporation into EPTL 9–1.1, in any event, must be accomplished by the Legislature, not the courts.

We therefore conclude that the option agreement is invalid under EPTL 9–1.1(b). In light of this conclusion, we need not decide whether the option violated Symphony's equitable right to redeem the mortgage.

IV. REMEDY

As a final matter, defendants argue that, if the option fails, the contract of sale conveying the property from Broadwest to Symphony should be rescinded due to the mutual mistake of the parties. We conclude that rescission is inappropriate * * *

A contract entered into under mutual mistake of fact is generally subject to rescission (see, Matter of Gould v. Board of Educ., 616 N.E.2d 142, 145 (N.Y. 1993)). CPLR 3005 provides that when relief against mistake is sought, it shall not be denied merely because the mistake is one of law rather than fact. Relying on this provision, defendants maintain that neither Symphony nor Broadwest realized that the option violated the Rule against Perpetuities at the time they entered into the agreement and that both parties intended the option to be enforceable.

CPLR 3005, however, does not equate all mistakes of law with mistakes of fact * * *

Here, the parties' mistake amounts to nothing more than a misunderstanding as to the applicable law, and CPLR 3005 does not direct undoing of the transaction * * *

The remedy of rescission, moreover, lies in equity and is a matter of discretion (Rudman v. Cowles Communications, 280 N.E.2d 867, 874 (N.Y. 1972)). Defendants' plea that the unenforceability of the option is contrary to the intent of the original parties ignores that the effect of the Rule against Perpetuities—which is a statutory prohibition, not a rule of construction—is always to defeat the intent of parties who create a remotely vesting interest. As explained by the Appellate Division, there is "an irreconcilable conflict in applying a remedy which is designed to void a transaction because it fails to carry out the parties' true intent to a transaction in which the mistake made by the parties was the application of the Rule against Perpetuities, the purpose of which is to defeat the intent of the parties."

The Rule against Perpetuities reflects the public policy of the State. Granting the relief requested by defendants would thus be contrary to public policy, since it would lead to the same result as enforcing the option and tend to compel performance of contracts violative of the Rule. Similarly, damages are not recoverable where options to acquire real property violate the Rule against Perpetuities, since that would amount to giving effect to the option (see, 5A Powell, Real Property ¶ 771[3]).

Accordingly, the order of the Appellate Division should be affirmed, with costs, and the certified question answered in the affirmative.

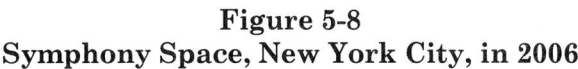

Figure 5-8
Symphony Space, New York City, in 2006

NOTES AND QUESTIONS

1.   Should the RAP apply to commercial transactions like the one in Symphony Space, or should it be limited to contingent interests created in the family wealth transmission context, where the rule originated? If one views the rule as primarily concerned with tempering the desire to create dynastic wealth, then limiting it to the family context would make sense. But are the other policies motivating the RAP—a desire to eliminate restraints on alienation and to limit dead hand control over the ownership and use of resources—limited to the family context? Another issue about the scope of the RAP is whether it should apply to interests that provide only for the future payment of money. Suppose the Perpetual Insurance Company issues a life insurance policy to A in return for a large premium that promises to pay stated sums of money to "such grandchildren of A that reach age 30." Such a promise does not raise any concerns about restraints on alienation, because the Perpetual Insurance Co. can invest the premium payment in a variety of ways unconstrained by the promise to make the future payments. Similarly, it does not seem that the contract involves excessive dead hand control over the future use and disposition of resources. Might it nevertheless be objectionable as a way of creating dynastic wealth? Suppose A (who is very rich) purchases a policy that promises to pay all lineal descendants of A $1

million when they turn 30 in perpetuity? See Holmes v. John Hancock Mutual Life Ins. Co., 41 N.E.2d 909 (N.Y. 1942) (suggesting that the RAP does not apply to life insurance payments, which constitute deferred payments and not income on property).

2.   The RAP traditionally applies to options, and this can be a big problem especially because, as in *Symphony Space*, a corporation is not treated as a measuring life. See also Central Delaware County Authority v. Greyhound Corp., 588 A.2d 485 (Pa. 1991). Some states, especially those following the USRAP approach, exempt options from the Rule. Similarly, section 3.3 of the *Restatement (Third) of Property: Servitudes* would exempt all options from the RAP but subject them to the prohibitions on unreasonable restraints on alienation. In contrast, rights of first refusal such as those retained by a cooperative or condominium board, which apply when a sitting occupant wants to sell, are not subject to the RAP. Likewise, options given to a lessee to renew the lease or purchase the land are not subject to the RAP, because it is thought that they do not inhibit but encourage improvement of the property. Notice that these distinctions—between options in gross on the one hand (as in *Symphony Space*) and options given to lessees and rights of first refusal on the other hand—do not follow from the supposedly "remorseless" logic of the RAP, which would presumably subject all such contingencies to the rule. Rather, the distinctions are grounded in judicial intuitions about the policy consequences of either applying or not applying the RAP. Are courts competent to make these kinds of judgments? Should courts simply follow the logic of the RAP in all cases and wait for the legislature to create exceptions? Or should courts limit the RAP to the family wealth transmission context and wait for the legislature to create extensions?

3.   Courts often interpret ambiguous deeds or even those with contradictory phrases so as to avoid invalidation under the RAP, but some courts will go further than others. The court in *Symphony Space* noted this possibility but saw the New York statute as forbidding the court from engaging in the rewriting of the option agreement that would have been required to make it conform to the RAP. Other courts are far more accommodating. See, e.g., Matter of Estate of Anderson, 541 So.2d 423 (Miss. 1989).

4.   What if the option had been reserved in the grantor Broadwest Realty instead of granted back by Symphony Space after a conveyance of the entire estate from Broadwest to Symphony? Some courts would see the option as an interest that is immediately vested and so presenting no issue with the RAP. Others, like the New York courts, view the exercise of the option as a cutting-off event like that in an executory interest, thus making the RAP applicable even if the option is reserved in the grantor. Which view is better? Does this have anything to do with the wisdom of applying the RAP?

5.   Why did the court strike the entire option under the RAP, rather than just striking the final closing date of 2003? If the option had provided that the last possible closing date was 1998, this would have been less than 21 years after the option contract was created, and hence would not have

violated the rule. The court rejects the argument that the option agreement should be interpreted so as to provide an earlier date of execution of the option. But isn't there also an issue as to how much of the option contract the RAP will be deemed to invalidate?

6. Interestingly, the RAP started out its career as a flexible and equitable standard. This is reflected in Lord Chancellor Nottingham's statement that future interests should be invalidated for remoteness "whereever any visible Inconvenience doth appear; for the just Bounds of a Fee-simple upon a Fee-simple are not yet determined." Duke of Norfolk's Case, 22 Eng. Rep. 931, 960 (Ch. 1682). Only later did the RAP crystallize into a hard rule. Hirsch & Wang, supra, at 55 n.223. Are rules or standards more appropriate here?

7. As mentioned earlier, one of the policies behind the RAP is the limiting of dead hand control. One area in which this concern about rigidity over time has been raised is conservation easements, in which an owner of land grants away (typically for all time) the right to develop the land. (See Chapter IX.) Power to enforce the restriction is typically given to a governmental or nonprofit body. What if it turns out years later that the land could be put to higher use, or that other land is more valuable in an undeveloped state, or even that notions of developed and undeveloped change? See Julia Mahoney, Perpetual Restrictions on Land and the Problem of the Future, 88 Va. L. Rev. 739 (2002).

Vestigial Maintenance Doctrines

There are a number of doctrines that served at one time to clean up conveyances and make them more alienable than they otherwise might have been. In recent times, future interests have been made more fully alienable than they were at common law, thus alleviating some of the problems courts traditionally faced. In addition, as already mentioned, most future interests are now created in trust, where the trustee can be given powers of alienation and appointment, and the entire arrangement, as far as management and distribution of the proceeds are concerned, can be customized to a degree impossible within the catalogue of legal estates and interests.

Four traditional maintenance rules are the Merger Rule, the Rule in Shelley's Case, the Doctrine of Worthier Title, and the Destructibility of Contingent Remainders. Probably only the first remains in full force and effect in most states today. The others have either been abolished, or live on only as rules of construction.

The Merger Rule. Before the feudal incidents were abolished by Parliament in 1660, landowners would attempt various stratagems to avoid them, especially the requirement of paying relief in order to allow property to pass to descendants upon death (an early version of the estate tax). Tenants fearing an early demise also wished to avoid wardship, which allowed the lord to take and keep the full value of the property during the minority of an heir. The common-law courts devised a number of doctrines to block these efforts at evasion of the feudal incidents and wardship. One stratagem would be for O, in one instrument, to convey "to A for life." This of course would create an implied reversion in O. O would then execute a second instrument, conveying his reversion to A. A now held both a life estate and the reversion at the end of the life estate—which together adds up to a fee simple absolute—but A would have acquired these interests by inter vivos conveyances, not by descent. Courts held that when this happened, the two separate conveyances were merged, and A would be treated as having a fee simple absolute. The same rule holds if A receives both a life estate and a vested remainder in fee simple, or if A conveys the life estate back to O who still holds the reversion, or any other combination of transfers that puts in the hands of a single person a series of interests that add up to a larger estate. Whatever its original motivation, the merger rule clearly promotes free alienation of property (can you see why?), and so it is still followed today.

The Rule in Shelley's Case. In another device to avoid having to pay relief, landowners would sometimes attempt to convey property while still alive in such a way that persons would take as purchasers rather than by descent. For example, O might convey in a single instrument "to A for life, then to A's heirs." In a rule first recognized in Abel's Case, Y.B. 18 Edw. II, 577 (1324), and given its definite form in Shelley's Case, 76 Eng. Rep. 206 (K.B. 1581), this stratagem was blocked. Under the rule, if someone uses a single instrument to create a life estate in land in A, and also to create a remainder in persons described as A's heirs (or the heirs of A's body), and the life estate and the remainder are both legal or both equitable, then the interest becomes a fee simple (or fee tail) *in A*. The Rule is a mandatory rule and is not overcome by manifestation of contrary grantor intent. Today, the Rule in Shelley's Case has been abolished in most states, but lives on in a few, primarily on the theory that it promotes alienability of land. (Again, can you see why the application of the rule would make land more alienable?)

Doctrine of Worthier Title. Another scheme to avoid relief would be for a grantor to attempt to create a remainder or executory interest in his own (the grantor's) heirs. Thus, O would grant "to A for life, then to the heirs of O." This was blocked by the Doctrine of Worthier Title, which converted what was in form a remainder in the heirs of O into a reversion in the grantor. Thus, "to A for life, then to the heirs of O," would be treated as if it had said "to A for life, then to O." Again, whatever its original rationale, the rule marginally contributes to alienability. If O could make a grant to "the heirs of O," no one would be in a position to negotiate with anyone else as long as O is alive, because O's heirs have not yet been determined. If the grant is construed as creating a reversion in O, then O can negotiate for a transfer. To the extent the doctrine lives on today, it is as a rule of construction, not a fixed rule of law like the Rule in Shelley's Case. See Doctor v. Hughes, 122 N.E. 221 (N.Y. 1919).

In theory, a grantor could overcome the presumption in the rule by using language exhibiting a contrary intent.

Destructibility of Contingent Remainders. Traditionally, if a (legal, not equitable) contingent remainder in real property failed to take immediately on the termination of all the preceding estates, it would be destroyed. For example, if O conveyed Blackacre "to A for life, then to B if B passes the bar," and A died before B had passed the bar, the rule would destroy the contingent remainder. Who would take? O would, because of the supporting reversion retained by O. The destructibility rule seems to have come about because of a fixation on the definition of a remainder as an interest that takes effect upon the natural termination of a prior estate (death). See Thomas F. Bergin & Paul G. Haskell, Preface to Estates in Land and Future Interests 77–79 (2d ed. 1984). In the example, supposing A dies before B passes the bar, if B were subsequently to take the property this would cut short O's reversion; it would not follow the termination of a life estate like a well-behaved remainder should. Of course, by destroying the contingent remainder, the courts also frustrated O's intentions, all in the name of preserving the correct definition of a remainder. Today, the destructibility rule has largely vanished. Since the grantor could have accomplished the same result by creating an executory interest, courts treat a contingent remainder that does not become possessory upon the natural termination of the previous estate as if it were an executory interest. All states with clear law on the point, except Florida, have abolished the rule, although in a handful of additional states there are older precedents accepting the rule that have not been expressly overruled. In any event, since the doctrine never applied to equitable interests in trusts, and most contingent remainders today are created in trusts, the rule has little effect even in the rare state where it might be enforced.

4. SYSTEMICALLY INTERACTING PRINCIPLES

The various maintenance doctrines and limiting principles work together (or fail to!) as a system. As we saw with the estate system, various rules (like that creating a life estate and a reminder in fee simple out of a fee simple) can feed themselves. Other interactions between principles are possible. Consider how many of the maintenance doctrines and limiting principles come into play in the following case.

City of Klamath Falls v. Bell

Oregon Court of Appeals, 1971.
490 P.2d 515.

■ SCHWAB, CHIEF JUDGE. In 1925, a corporation conveyed certain land to the city of Klamath Falls as a gift for use as the site for a city library. The deed provided, among other things, that the city should hold the land "so long as" it complied with that condition with regard to its use.

In 1969, the city terminated the use of the land for a library, and the question presented by this appeal is, "Does the title to the land remain in the city or did the termination of use as a library cause title to pass to the descendants of the shareholders of the donor-corporation (now dissolved)?"

The issue was presented to the trial court in the form of an agreed narrative statement, pertinent portions of which, in addition to the facts set forth above, are: the donor-corporation was known as the Daggett-Schallock Investment Company; the corporate deed provided that if at any time the city ceased to use the land for library purposes, title to the land should pass to Fred Schallock and Floy R. Daggett, their heirs and assigns; on September 19, 1927, the corporation was voluntarily dissolved, all creditors paid, and all assets (which we interpret as including the rights of the corporation, if any, in the land in question) were distributed in accordance with law to the sole shareholders Schallock and Daggett.

The city of Klamath Falls built a library on the land in 1929 in compliance with the conditions set out in the deed. The library continued in use from that date until July 1, 1969, when the books were moved to the County Library Building. Since that time, the city library services have been provided by Klamath County on a contract basis. The City Library building has not been used for any other purpose and now stands vacant.

After the library closure, the city of Klamath Falls filed a complaint against all the heirs of Schallock and Daggett for declaratory judgment pursuant to ORS ch. 28, asking the court to adjudicate the respective rights of the parties under the deed. The city joined Constance F. Bell, the sole heir of Fred Schallock, and Marijane Flitcraft and Caroline Crapo, the sole heirs of Floy R. Daggett, along with George C. Flitcraft, the husband of Marijane Flitcraft, and Paul Crapo, the husband of Caroline Crapo, as all the necessary parties to the suit.

The defendants Constance F. Bell, Caroline Crapo, and Paul Crapo conveyed their interests in the real property to the defendant Marijane Flitcraft in May and June 1970.

The trial court found that title to the real property was vested in the city of Klamath Falls. Its decision was based on a finding that the gift over to Fred Schallock and Floy R. Daggett was void under the rule against perpetuities.

Figure 5-9
Klamath Falls City Library, ca. 1960

Courtesy of Klamath County Museums. The building is now used as the Klamath Falls City Hall.

The deed, in pertinent part, is as follows:

KNOW ALL MEN BY THESE PRESENTS That Daggett-Schallock Investment Company, a corporation organized and existing under the laws of the State of Oregon, for and as a gift and without any consideration, does hereby give, grant and convey unto the City of Klamath Falls, Oregon, so long as it complies with the conditions hereinafter set forth, and thereafter unto Fred Schallock and Floy R. Daggett, their heirs and assigns, the following described parcel of real estate, in Klamath County Oregon, to-wit * * *

To have and to hold the same unto the said City of Klamath Falls, Oregon (and to any other municipal corporation which may lawfully succeed it) so long as it complies with the conditions above set forth, and thereafter unto Fred Schallock and Floy R. Daggett, their heirs and assigns forever. * * *

I

We conclude that the estate that passed to the city under this deed was a fee simple on a special limitation, which is also known as a fee simple determinable, or a base or qualified fee.* The "magic" words "so long as" have generally been held to create such an estate. Simes and Smith, The Law of Future Interests 345, § 287 (2d ed. 1956), states:

---

*   [This interest would be termed a "fee simple subject to executory limitation" on the more widely used terminology adopted in this book, with fee simple determinable being reserved for an interest followed by an interest reserved by the grantor (a possibility of reverter).—eds.]

* * * The words of duration "so long as" will almost certainly be judicially recognized as the distinctive insignia of such an estate, and, if coupled with a provision which clearly calls for an automatic termination of the estate granted, there is little room for construction. * * *

O'Connell, Estates on Condition Subsequent and Estates on Special Limitation in Oregon, 18 Or.L.Rev. 63, 73 (1939), stresses the use of words:

[T]he creation of an estate on a special limitation is characterized generally by the use of certain words. Typical words are "so long as," "until," or "during." However, any language in the instrument indicating an intent that the estate shall automatically end upon the occurrence of a designated event will be sufficient.

See also Magness v. Kerr, 254 P. 1012 (Or. 1927).

One of the features of the fee simple on a special limitation thus created is that it terminates automatically upon breach of condition.[2] Fremont Lbr. Co. v. Starrell Pet. Co., 364 P.2d 773 (Or. 1961), and cases cited therein.

II

Upon breach of the condition, the deed provided for a gift over to Fred Schallock and Floy R. Daggett or their heirs and assigns. This gift over was an attempt to grant an executory interest since only an executory interest can follow an earlier grant in fee simple.

The rule against perpetuities applies to executory interests; Closset et al. v. Burtchaell et al., 230 P. 554 (Or. 1924).

Gray's classic statement of the rule is as follows:

NO INTEREST IS GOOD UNLESS IT MUST VEST, IF AT ALL, NOT LATER THAN TWENTY-ONE YEARS AFTER SOME LIFE IN BEING AT THE CREATION OF THE INTEREST. Gray, The Rule Against Perpetuities 191, § 201 (4th ed. 1942).

One of the main characteristics of a defeasible fee simple estate is that the first grantee might continue in possession in perpetuity. The city of Klamath Falls could have maintained a library on the site for an indefinite time in the future, or even forever. Therefore, the trial judge correctly found that the gift over to Fred Schallock and Floy R. Daggett, their heirs and assigns, was void ab initio under the rule against perpetuities.

---

[2]   There would be a different result if the interests of the city of Klamath Falls were characterized as a fee simple on a condition subsequent, which is also known as a fee simple conditional. When such an estate is created, there is no forfeiture until the grantor exercises his right of re-entry.

III

The trial court's conclusion does not, however, dispose of the case at bar. Just because the gift over is invalid, it does not follow that the city of Klamath Falls now has an absolute interest in the property in question. There remains the question of whether under the deed a possibility of reverter remained in the grantor corporation.

When a deed reveals an unquestionable intent to limit the interest of the first grantee (here the city of Klamath Falls) to a fee simple on a special limitation, the courts of the United States do not create an indefeasible estate in the first grantee when a subsequent executory interest (here that of Schallock and Daggett) is void under the rule against perpetuities. Instead, the grantor (here the corporation) retains an interest known as a possibility of reverter.[3]

The general rule has been stated to be:

> [W]hen an executory interest, following a fee simple interest in land * * * is void under the rule against perpetuities, the prior interest becomes absolute unless the language of the creating instrument makes it very clear that the prior interest is to terminate whether the executory interest takes effect or not.

Simes and Smith, The Law of Future Interests 316, 318, § 827 (2d ed. 1956).

All the jurisdictions in the United States which have dealt with a determinable fee and an executory interest void under the rule against perpetuities have followed this rule. * * * This conclusion is favored by Restatement, 2 Property, app. 34–47, §§ 228, 229. * * *

IV

However, before this conclusion can be reached, an unusual Oregon rule must be considered. Oregon is one of a small minority of states that holds that a possibility of reverter cannot be alienated, Magness v. Kerr, 254 P. 1012 (Or. 1927); see Annotation, 53 A.L.R.2d 224 (1957), but the Oregon Supreme Court has never held that an attempt to alienate a possibility of reverter destroys it. In the case at bar, the grantor-corporation did attempt to alienate the possibility of reverter with its abortive gift over to Schallock and Daggett.[4] Thus, the question of

---

[3] It is well settled that the rule against perpetuities does not apply to possibilities of reverter. Gray, The Rule Against Perpetuities 46, 348, 349, §§ 41, 313, 314 (4th ed. 1942); Simes and Smith, The Law of Future Interests 311, § 825 (2d ed. 1956); Tiffany, Real Property 167, § 404 (3d ed. 1939). This historical anomaly has been criticized for allowing "dead hand rule" and creating "appalling practical results" when a possibility of reverter does fall in many years after the original grant. Leach, Perpetuities in Perspective: Ending the Rule's Reign of Terror, 65 Harv.L.Rev. 721, 739 (1952); Leach, Perpetuities: The Nutshell Revisited, 78 Harv.L.Rev. 973, 980 (1965). * * * Where the rule against perpetuities has been applied to possibilities of reverter, it has always been done by legislative action. See, 78 Harv.L.Rev. 973, supra, at 989; Sparks, A Decade of Transition in Future Interests, 45 Va.L.Rev. 339, 362 (1959).

[4] ORS 93.120 provides:

whether an attempt to alienate a possibility of reverter destroys it is presented to an Oregon appellate court for the first time. * * *

In Pure Oil Co. v. Miller-McFarland Drilling Co., 34 N.E.2d 854 (Ill. 1941), the Illinois court held that a possibility of reverter is not destroyed when the grantor tries to transfer it, even though the possibility of reverter is not alienable under Illinois law. In Reichard v. Chicago, B. & Q. R. Co., 1 N.W.2d 721 (Iowa 1942), which involved a conveyance after termination of a fee simple subject to a special limitation, the same facts as in Magness v. Kerr, supra, the court said:

> It seems rather fantastic to us, that a conveyance which is ineffective to convey what it attempts to convey is nevertheless an effective means of destroying it.

1 N.W.2d at 729.

We hold that an attempt by a grantor to transfer his possibility of reverter does not destroy it.

V

The remaining issue is the city's contention that upon dissolution of the corporation in 1927, or at the latest, upon the post-dissolution, winding-up period, ORS 57.630(2),[5] the corporation was civilly dead and without a successor to whom the possibility of reverter could descend. As is pointed out in Addy v. Short, 89 A.2d 136, 139 (Del. 1952), the statutory provision for distribution of corporate assets upon dissolution,

> is in effect a statutory expansion of the equitable doctrine that upon dissolution of a corporation its property, notwithstanding the technical rules of the early common law, does not escheat to the sovereign or revert to the original grantor, and will be administered * * * for the purpose of winding up the corporate affairs and distributing the assets to those equitably entitled to them.

In *Addy*, the corporation owning a possibility of reverter was dissolved and five years later the event (the abandonment of the use upon which the deed was conditioned) occurred. Delaware had only a three-

---

* * * Any conveyance of real estate passes all the estate of the grantor, unless the intent to pass a lesser estate appears by express terms, or is necessarily implied in the terms of the grant.

[5]   ORS 57.630(2) provides:

Whenever any such corporation is the owner of real or personal property, or claims any interest or lien whatsoever in any real or personal property, such corporation shall continue to exist during such five-year period for the purpose of conveying, transferring and releasing such real or personal property or interest or lien therein, and such corporation shall continue after the expiration of such five-year period to exist as a body corporate for the purpose of being made a party to, and being sued in any action, suit or proceeding against it involving the title to any such real or personal property or any interest therein, and not otherwise; and any such action, suit or proceeding may be instituted and maintained against any such corporation as might have been had prior to the expiration of said five-year period. This section shall not be construed as affecting or suspending any statute of limitations applicable to any suit, action or proceeding instituted hereunder.

year corporate dissolution winding-up period. The Delaware statutes did contain a provision that even after the three-year period, upon application of creditors or shareholders of a dissolved corporation, the court could appoint a receiver to take charge of the estate of the corporation and to collect debts and property due and belonging to the company. *Addy* held that neither the dissolution of the corporation nor the expiration of the three-year dissolution period worked an extinguishment of the possibility of reverter retained by the deed in question, and that upon the abandonment of the land by the grantee, the possibility of reverter was enlarged to a fee simple title. It further held that as statutory successors to the rights and powers of the corporation the receivers were entitled to the land.

Oregon has no such receivership statute, but the Oregon statutes make it clear that corporate assets no longer escheat or revert to the original grantor upon dissolution. In this case, the parties agree that the corporation was lawfully dissolved, all the creditors paid, and that Daggett and Schallock, the sole shareholders of the corporation, were statutorily entitled to and did receive all of the remaining assets of the corporation. One such asset was the possibility of reverter of the land in question.

The parties further agree that the defendants in this case were all of the heirs of Daggett and Schallock. As is pointed out in 18 Or.L.Rev. 63, supra, there is no Oregon decision on the issue of the descendability of the possibility of reverter. However, the weight of authority recognizes that such an interest is descendable. Restatement, 2 Property 606, Comment A, § 164, and 3 Simes 144–45, § 707 (1936). We discern no sound policy considerations which lead us to a contrary conclusion.[6]

Marijane Flitcraft acquired all rights to the property when the other defendants conveyed their interests to her in 1970.

Reversed.

NOTES AND QUESTIONS

1.   Do you see how this decision involves an application of the principle of conservation of estates? The Daggett-Schallock Investment Company started out with a fee simple absolute having an unlimited duration. It executed a deed that carved this fee simple up into two smaller interests: a fee simple subject to an executory limitation, which was donated to the City, and an executory interest, which was conveyed to the two principal shareholders of the Company, Daggett and Schallock. (The corporation is assumed to have a legal personality separate and distinct from its shareholders; they are, for legal purposes, regarded as separate "persons.") Many years later, the executory interest is declared void under the Rule against Perpetuities. This means that there is now something left over which

---

[6]   It is difficult to understand the reason for the rule that a future interest in the nature of a possibility of reverter should be inalienable.

has not been accounted for—the interest originally occupied by the executory interest—and the difficult question for the court is what sort of legal interest should be implied as a matter of law to fill the void. The perceived imperative that this gap must be filled in order to account for the unlimited duration of the original fee simple is the principle of conservation of estates.

2.   The court discusses two possibilities for filling the gap. First, as argued by the City, the interest originally given to the City—a fee simple subject to an executory limitation—could be expanded into a fee simple absolute. One could say that the City had a fee simple with a forfeiture cloud hanging over its head; the mechanism for enforcing the forfeiture has been declared void; ergo the cloud has now been lifted. Second, as argued by the heirs of Daggett and Shallock, the court invalidating the executory interest can imply a possibility of reverter in the grantor—the Investment Company—and then, given that the corporation has been dissolved, award the possibility of reverter to the shareholders of the corporation (Daggett and Schallock as it happens) and thus to their successors. In a subsequent decision, the court decided that a possibility of reverter is alienable in Oregon. State ex rel. Dept. of Transportation v. Tolke, 586 P.2d 791 (Or. Ct. App. 1978). Does it matter to the result in this case if the possibility of reverter is alienable?

3.   Assuming the legal authorities were sufficiently balanced to permit the court to embrace either the City's view or the heirs' view, why do you suppose the court found the heirs' position more appealing? What was the purpose of imposing the executory limitation in the first place? If invalidated executory interests always result in the expansion of the underlying defeasible fee into a fee simple absolute, what effect might this have on the incentives of persons to make charitable donations of property?

4.   There was a third option for filling the gap in *City of Klamath Falls*: The court could have held that the possibility of reverter escheated to the State of Oregon. Can you articulate the argument that would support this outcome? What advantages and disadvantages would this solution have relative to the two options considered by the court? Should the court have notified the attorney general of Oregon and allowed him or her to enter an appearance to argue in support of escheat? (Note that the State of Oregon and the City of Klamath Falls are different political entities, and might put the land to different uses or spend the proceeds from selling the land in different ways.) Should courts adopt a presumption against escheat? In favor of escheat? Should it depend on the nature of the property? Suppose the corporation dissolved in 1927 and the city stops using the land as a library 100 years later. Suppose further that there are over one hundred descendants of the original shareholders, and, unlike the descendants in the *City of Klamath Falls* case, they cannot agree on a consolidation of their interests. Who is going to take responsibility for notifying all the heirs of their interests, and representing them in court? Will the transaction costs of identifying and adjudicating the claims of the heirs eat up most of the value of the property in dispute?

5.   Interests less than a fee simple can be held void for reasons of public policy or constitutionality. In *Evans v. Newton*, 382 U.S. 296 (1966),

the Supreme Court considered the will of Senator A.O. Bacon of Georgia, who died in 1911. The will left a tract of land, known as Baconsfield, to the city of Macon for use as a park restricted to white persons only. The Court held that Macon could not continue to operate the park on a segregated basis because this would violate the Equal Protection Clause. On remand, the Georgia courts considered whether to revise the will under the cy pres doctrine (see Chapter VI) by striking out the racial restriction, or to declare that the gift to the city had failed. Based on evidence in the will that Senator Bacon was adamant about wanting no mixing of the races in the park, the Georgia courts declared that the gift had failed. Although the will contained no residuary clause, the Georgia courts implied a reversion in the heirs of Senator Bacon. Thus, the park passed by operation of law back into the family's hands. On further review, a divided Supreme Court affirmed. *Evans v. Abney*, 396 U.S. 435 (1970). The Court concluded that the result, although unfortunate, simply reflected a good faith application of state law rules for interpreting and administering wills: Senator Bacon lived and died in a racist era, and the Georgia courts were simply giving effect to his intent. Justices Douglas and Brennan dissented, arguing that the judgment, by perpetuating the discriminatory intentions of Senator Bacon, was state action in violation of the equal protection guarantee. Relying in part on *Shelley v. Kraemer*, Chapter IV, which invalidated judicial enforcement of private racial covenants, they would have reversed.

6.   In considering the effect of an invalid condition in a defeasible fee, might it make a difference whether the grantor used the language of a fee simple determinable or a fee simple subject to condition subsequent? If the executory limitation in *City of Klamath Falls* had been expressed using condition subsequent language ("but if" or "provided that") rather than durational language ("so long as"), the City might well have won. Can you see why? See Restatement of Property § (1936); see also Hermitage Methodist Homes of Virginia, Inc. v. Dominion Trust Co., 387 S.E.2d 740, 745–46 (Va. 1990) (holding that racially restrictive trust interests expressed as a fee simple determinable failed entirely, as opposed to an invalid interest expressed as a fee simple subject to a condition subsequent, which would have avoided forfeiture); Jonathan L. Entin, Defeasible Fees, State Action, and the Legacy of Massive Resistance, 34 Wm. & Mary L. Rev. 769 (1993).

E. CO-OWNERSHIP AND MEDIATING CONFLICTS BETWEEN CO-OWNERS

There are many reasons for multiple people to wish to be co-owners, involving various types of multiple use and relationships based on sharing. But conflicts among co-owners can arise for a variety of reasons. The effects of the use by each co-owner are only partially internalized to that owner. That is why in many situations co-owners need some governance scheme, such as a contract or, more usually, a set of norms of proper use, to regulate their use and care of the property. In addition to these norms, the law itself sometimes provides off-the-rack solutions to problems facing co-owners. These legal solutions tend to take two forms.

One is to afford co-owners exit from the relationship; this is achieved primarily by the action for partition. The other is a set of more detailed governance rules. These rules tend not to be as finegrained as the contractual and norm-based rules that co-owners devise for themselves, and the law's off-the-rack regime tends to protect co-owners mainly in situations of exit. In many American jurisdictions, holders of concurrent interests are quite limited in the remedies available to them, and co-owners in some jurisdictions often wind up seeking an accounting in a partition. 8 Thompson on Real Property § 70.09(h) (1994); 8 Powell on Real Property ch. 56 ¶ 643 (1998).

Concurrent and Marital Estates

Property can be divided and shared among multiple simultaneous owners. This gives rise to divisions in two dimensions: "horizontal" divisions over time and "vertical" divisions at any given moment in time. The two types of division can be combined: Each of the estates in land defined in terms of temporal duration—fee simple, life estate, remainder, etc.—can also be divided among concurrent owners. Thus, one can create concurrent ownership in a fee simple, concurrent life estates (lasting until the last life tenant dies), and concurrent remainders or executory interests.

Some forms of co-ownership shade off into entity law, considered in Chapter VI. At one time, property could be owned by tenancy in partnership, in which the legal title to property was concurrently held by each of the partners. Today, most states provide by statute that the partnership as an entity holds title to the property, much the way corporations as entities hold title to property. Under this entity theory, there is only one owner of the property—the entity (partnership or corporation)—and issues about who manages and controls the property are resolved as a matter of partnership or corporation law, not property law. Nevertheless, keep in mind that forming a trust, partnership, or corporation is an alternative to the co-ownership arrangements considered here. For example, if A, B, and C want to share ownership of a summer cottage, they could either hold title to the cottage as concurrent owners, or they could form a partnership or corporation which would then hold title to the cottage.

The main forms of co-ownership today are the tenancy in common and the joint tenancy. Some states also have an older marital property arrangement, called the tenancy by the entirety, which is like the joint tenancy but more durable. All of the arrangements involve an equal right to possess whenever the interest in question is possessory. Not surprisingly and as we will see, this can lead to conflict.

Tenancy in Common. Each tenant in common has a separate but undivided interest. Each interest is *separate*, in the sense that it is independently descendible, conveyable, and devisable. Since either tenant can unilaterally convey her interest to a third party, property held as tenancy in common can be attached by creditors of each individual tenant. And since each share is independently descendible, there is no right of survivorship (as there would be in a joint tenancy, to which we turn next); the share of each tenant in common passes upon death as part of his or her separate estate. Yet each interest in *undivided*, in the sense that each tenant in common has the right to possess the whole of the property (although they need not exercise that right). Moreover, there is no requirement that each cotenant hold an equal share. One can create a tenancy in common in which A owns a 60 percent interest, B a 30 percent interest, and C a 10 percent interest. Each tenant in such a tenancy in common has an equal right to possess the whole, but their respective share of rents or profits (or their respective obligations to contribute to the payment of taxes or mortgage obligations) will be determined by their respective percentage ownership.

Joint Tenancy. The joint tenancy is exactly like the tenancy in common, except for the treatment of survivorship. As in the tenancy in common, each joint tenant has a separate and undivided interest. Because the interest is undivided, each joint tenant has the right to possess the whole. The principal difference is that in a joint tenancy, a surviving joint tenant automatically acquires the interest of another joint tenant when the other tenant dies. Technically nothing passes; the deceased joint tenant's interest is simply extinguished. The joint tenancy requires four "unities" at the time of creation:

(i)   Time. Each interest must be acquired or vest at the same time.

(ii)   Title. Each must acquire title by the same instrument or by joint adverse possession, never by intestate succession or other operation of law.

(iii)   Interest. Each must have the same legal interest in the property, such as fee simple, life estate, lease, etc., although not necessarily identical fractional shares.

(iv) Possession. Each must have the *right* to possess the whole.

By contrast, the only unity required to create a tenancy in common is that of possession.

Traditionally, if any of the unities is destroyed in a joint tenancy, then we say the joint tenancy is severed and a tenancy in common is created. Each joint tenant while alive has the power unilaterally to transfer his or her interest, and thus each may have his or her interest attached by creditors. When such a transfer or attachment occurs, this may have the effect of severing the unities (which ones?) and may convert the joint tenancy into a tenancy in common. In this sense, a joint tenancy comes with a partial exit right (through the possibility of severance), to supplement the more radical break up that can be achieved through partition. (For more on severance, see *Harms v. Sprague*, infra.) The joint tenancy is only appropriate for an intimate relationship such as a committed relationship or family business.

Tenancy by the Entirety. Roughly half the states have retained the tenancy by the entirety, which is only available for married couples. Like the tenancy in common and the joint tenancy, each co-owner has a separate and undivided interest, and each has the right to possession of the whole. Like the joint tenancy, there is a right of survivorship. But in some states that recognize the tenancy by the entirety, neither spouse can unilaterally transfer or encumber their share of the property without the consent of the other. See United States v. Craft, 535 U.S. 274 (2002) (discussing the law of one such state, Michigan, but declining to insulate property held in tenancy by the entirety from federal taxes owed by one spouse). In all states that recognize this tenancy, there is no *unilateral* exit option as long as the couple stays married. Both spouses can convey to a third person (a "straw") and then have the straw convey back to them as tenants in common, but neither spouse acting unilaterally can sever the tenancy, other than by getting a divorce. Thus, to the four unities required by the joint tenancy, a fifth, marriage, is added.

How do we know which type of concurrent tenancy is created when multiple persons acquire title to property, as when O conveys Blackacre "to A and B" or when O devises Blackacre by will "to my Children, C, D, and E"? At common law, a joint tenancy was presumed in any conveyance that satisfied the four unities (time, title, interest, and possession). A tenancy by the entirety was presumed in any conveyance that satisfied the five unities (time, title, interest, possession, and marriage). Today, a tenancy in common is generally presumed unless there is some other manifestation of intent to create a joint tenancy or a tenancy by the entirety. Thus, if O conveys "to A and B" this will generally be presumed to be a tenancy in common. O would have to say something like "to A and B as joint tenants with right of survivorship and not as tenants in common" to be sure to create a joint tenancy. Similarly one would have to specify "to A and B as tenants by the entirety" (and A and B would have to be married) to create a tenancy by the entirety. Nevertheless, some courts still presume a joint tenancy is intended in the case of an ambiguous transfer to a married couple, and courts in some states that recognize the tenancy by the entirety will presume that this is intended in the case of an ambiguous transfer to a married couple, at least for interests in land.

How do potential co-owners choose which arrangement suits them best? Many factors may influence this decision. First, the survivorship feature in the joint tenancy or the tenancy by the entirety allows a remaining owner to avoid probate (which is costly, cumbersome, and time-consuming). The survivor can sell the property immediately if he or she so chooses. Second, depending on the rules in place in a given state, the joint tenancy (and even more so the tenancy by the entirety) may afford some protection of jointly owned assets from creditors of one of the co-owners. Finally, tax considerations may come into play. However, in the federal income tax, joint filing by married couples generally makes the form of ownership irrelevant for income tax purposes.

As we will see, the types of concurrent ownership arrangements are limited in number and have many mandatory features. Nevertheless, concurrent ownership has become somewhat more customizable in recent times. See, e.g., Jezo v. Jezo, 127 N.W.2d 246 (Wis. 1964) (holding that the presumption that joint tenants own equal shares is subject to rebuttal by evidence of contrary intent). Also, to the extent that partnership and other entity forms are a substitute for direct concurrent ownership of assets, it is worth noting that entity forms have a greater and increasing degree of customizability relative to the traditional forms of concurrent ownership.

Community Property. Some states of the South and West, especially those that have some Spanish or French law in their early histories, feature community property for married couples. Under community property, all property acquired during the marriage (except in some states for gifts and bequests to one spouse) automatically becomes community property. Each spouse has a right to possess community property, but typically any alienation or encumbrance must have the consent of both spouses. Couples can transmute property from separate property to community property and vice versa, but there are often strong presumptions and formalities to overcome in order to prove that what would otherwise be community property is separate. Also, property acquired before the marriage is theoretically separate but may become community property through commingling with community property. On divorce, a spouse arguing that property is separate has the burden of proof and must be able to trace the property, i.e., to document its separate existence from community property, through time and possibly various transactions. Originally, the community property system gave the husband sole management and control of the property during marriage. Now both spouses have such rights, and for certain important transactions to be valid both spouses must consent. This system never considered the wife's legal personality to merge with that of the husband, as was the case at common law (but not in equity). On divorce, community property is subject to equal division. We return below to the problem of defining property for purposes of division on divorce in the common-law (i.e., non-community-property) states.

1. PARTITION

Partition is the most important legal remedy available to concurrent owners. Any cotenant can sue for partition for any reason or no reason at all, and the court will grant the request without further inquiry into the justness or reasonableness of the request. This in effect gives each cotenant an automatic right to terminate the cotenancy at any time. Partition is available to tenants in common and joint tenants. Tenants by the entirety must either convert the property into a tenancy in common or joint tenancy by mutual agreement, or sever the unity of marriage (by divorce), in order to obtain partition.

Delfino v. Vealencis
Supreme Court of Connecticut, 1980.
436 A.2d 27.

■ ARTHUR H. HEALEY, ASSOCIATE JUSTICE. The central issue in this appeal is whether the Superior Court properly ordered the sale, pursuant to General Statutes § 52–500,[1] of property owned by the plaintiffs and the defendant as tenants in common.

The plaintiffs, Angelo and William Delfino, and the defendant, Helen C. Vealencis, own, as tenants in common, real property located in Bristol, Connecticut. The property consists of an approximately 20.5 acre parcel of land and the dwelling of the defendant thereon. The plaintiffs own an undivided 99/144 interest in the property, and the defendant owns a 45/144 interest. The defendant occupies the dwelling and a portion of the land, from which she operates a rubbish and garbage removal business.[3] Apparently, none of the parties is in actual possession of the remainder of the property. The plaintiffs, one of whom is a residential developer, propose to develop the property, upon partition, into forty-five residential building lots.

In 1978, the plaintiffs brought an action in the trial court seeking a partition of the property by sale with a division of the proceeds according to the parties' respective interests. The defendant moved for a judgment of in-kind partition[5] and the appointment of a committee to conduct said

---

[1]   General Statutes § 52–500 states:

Sale of Real or Personal Property Owned by Two or More. Any court of equitable jurisdiction may, upon the complaint of any person interested, order the sale of any estate, real or personal, owned by two or more persons, when, in the opinion of the court, a sale will better promote the interests of the owners. The provisions of this section shall extend to and include land owned by two or more persons, when the whole or a part of such land is vested in any person for life with remainder to his heirs, general or special, or, on failure of such heirs, to any other person, whether the same, or any part thereof, is held in trust or otherwise. A conveyance made in pursuance of a decree ordering a sale of such land shall vest the title in the purchaser thereof, and shall bind the person entitled to the life estate and his legal heirs and any other person having a remainder interest in the lands; but the court passing such decree shall make such order in relation to the investment of the avails of such sale as it deems necessary for the security of all persons having any interest in such land.

[3]   The defendant's business functions on the property consist of the overnight parking, repair and storage of trucks, including refuse trucks, the repair, storage and cleaning of dumpsters, the storage of tools, and general office work. No refuse is actually deposited on the property.

[5]   Such a partition is authorized by General Statutes § 52–495 which states:

Partition of Joint and Common Estates. Courts having jurisdiction of actions for equitable relief may, upon the complaint of any person interested, order partition of any real estate held in joint tenancy, tenancy in common or coparcenary, and may appoint a committee for that purpose, and may in like manner make partition of any real estate held by tenants in tail; and decrees aparting entailed estates shall bind the parties and all persons who thereafter claim title to such estate as heirs of their bodies.

partition. The trial court, after a hearing, concluded that a partition in kind could not be had without "material injury" to the respective rights of the parties, and therefore ordered that the property be sold at auction by a committee and that the proceeds be paid into the court for distribution to the parties.

On appeal, the defendant claims essentially that the trial court's conclusion that the parties' interests would best be served by a partition by sale is not supported by the findings of subordinate facts, and that the court improperly considered certain factors in arriving at that conclusion. In addition, the defendant directs a claim of error to the court's failure to include in its findings of fact a paragraph of her draft findings.

General Statutes § 52–495 authorizes courts of equitable jurisdiction to order, upon the complaint of any interested person, the physical partition of any real estate held by tenants in common, and to appoint a committee for that purpose.[7] When, however, in the opinion of the court a sale of the jointly owned property "will better promote the interests of the owners," the court may order such a sale under § 52–500. See Kaiser v. Second National Bank, 193 A. 761, 764 (Conn. 1937); Johnson v. Olmsted, 49 Conn. 509, 517 (1882).

It has long been the policy of this court, as well as other courts, to favor a partition in kind over a partition by sale. The first Connecticut statute that provided for an absolute right to partition by physical division was enacted in 1720; Statutes, 1796, p. 258; the substance of which remains virtually unchanged today. Due to the possible impracticality of actual division, this state, like others, expanded the right to partition to allow a partition by sale under certain circumstances. See Penfield v. Jarvis, 399 A.2d 1280, 1283 (Conn. 1978); see also Restatement, 2 Property c. 11, pp. 658–61. The early decisions of this court that considered the partition-by-sale statute emphasized that "[t]he statute giving the power of sale introduces . . . no new principles; it provides only for an emergency, when a division cannot be well made, in any other way. The Earl of Clarendon v. Hornby, 1 P.Wms., 446.4 Kent's Com., 365." Richardson v. Monson, 23 Conn. 94, 97 (1854). The court later expressed its reason for preferring partition in kind when it stated: "[A] sale of one's property without his consent is an extreme exercise of power warranted only in clear cases." Ford v. Kirk, 41 Conn. 9, 12 (1874). Although under General Statutes § 52–500 a court is no longer required to order a partition in kind even in cases of extreme difficulty or hardship; see Scovil v. Kennedy, 14 Conn. 349, 360–61 (1841); it is clear that a partition by sale should be ordered only when two conditions are satisfied: (1) the physical attributes of the land are such that a partition in kind is impracticable or inequitable; Johnson v. Olmsted, supra; and (2) the interests of the owners would better be promoted by a partition by

---

[7]   If the physical partition results in unequal shares, a money award can be made from one tenant to another to equalize the shares. 4A Powell, Real Property ¶ 612, pp. 653–54; 2 American Law of Property, Partition § 6.26, p. 113.

sale. Kaiser v. Second National Bank, supra; see Gold v. Rosenfeld, Conn. (41 Conn.L.J., No. 4, p. 18) (1979). Since our law has for many years presumed that a partition in kind would be in the best interests of the owners, the burden is on the party requesting a partition by sale to demonstrate that such a sale would better promote the owners' interests.

The defendant claims in effect that the trial court's conclusion that the rights of the parties would best be promoted by a judicial sale is not supported by the findings of subordinate facts. We agree.

Under the test set out above, the court must first consider the practicability of physically partitioning the property in question. The trial court concluded that due to the situation and location of the parcel of land, the size and area of the property, the physical structure and appurtenances on the property, and other factors,[11] a physical partition of the property would not be feasible. An examination of the subordinate findings of facts and the exhibits, however, demonstrates that the court erred in this respect.

It is undisputed that the property in question consists of one 20.5 acre parcel, basically rectangular in shape, and one dwelling, located at the extreme western end of the property. Two roads, Dino Road and Lucien Court, abut the property and another, Birch Street, provides access through use of a right-of-way. Unlike cases where there are numerous fractional owners of the property to be partitioned, and the practicability of a physical division is therefore drastically reduced * * * in this case there are only two competing ownership interests: the plaintiffs' undivided 99/144 interest and the defendant's 45/144 interest. These facts, taken together, do not support the trial court's conclusion that a physical partition of the property would not be "feasible" in this case. Instead, the above facts demonstrate that the opposite is true: a partition in kind clearly would be practicable under the circumstances of this case.

Although a partition in kind is physically practicable, it remains to be considered whether a partition in kind would also promote the best interests of the parties. In order to resolve this issue, the consequences of a partition in kind must be compared with those of a partition by sale.

The trial court concluded that a partition in kind could not be had without great prejudice to the parties since the continuation of the defendant's business would hinder or preclude the development of the plaintiffs' parcel for residential purposes, which the trial court concluded was the highest and best use of the property. The court's concern over the possible adverse economic effect upon the plaintiffs' interest in the event of a partition in kind was based essentially on four findings: (1) approval by the city planning commission for subdivision of the parcel would be

---

[11]   These other factors included the present use and the expected continued use by the defendant of the property, the property's zoning classification, and the plaintiffs' proposed subdivision plans. We consider these factors later in the opinion.

difficult to obtain if the defendant continued her garbage hauling business; (2) lots in a residential subdivision might not sell, or might sell at a lower price, if the defendant's business continued; (3) if the defendant were granted the one-acre parcel, on which her residence is situated and on which her business now operates, three of the lots proposed in the plaintiffs' plan to subdivide the property would have to be consolidated and would be lost; and (4) the proposed extension of one of the neighboring roads would have to be rerouted through one of the proposed building lots if a partition in kind were ordered. The trial court also found that the defendant's use of the portion of the property that she occupies is in violation of existing zoning regulations. The court presumably inferred from this finding that it is not likely that the defendant will be able to continue her rubbish hauling operations from this property in the future. The court also premised its forecast that the planning commission would reject the plaintiffs' subdivision plan for the remainder of the property on the finding that the defendant's use was invalid. These factors basically led the trial court to conclude that the interests of the parties would best be protected if the land were sold as a unified unit for residential subdivision development and the proceeds of such a sale were distributed to the parties. * * *

[A]ny inference that the defendant would probably be unable to continue her rubbish hauling activity on the property in the future is unfounded. We also conclude that the court erred in concluding that the city's planning commission would probably not approve a subdivision plan relating to the remainder of the property. Any such forecast must be carefully scrutinized as it is difficult to project what a public body will decide in any given matter. See Rushchak v. West Haven, 356 A.2d 104, 107 (Conn. 1975). In this case, there was no substantial evidence to support a conclusion that it was reasonably probable that the planning commission would not approve a subdivision plan for the remainder of the property. Cf. Budney v. Ives, 239 A.2d 482, 485 (Conn. 1968). Moreover, there is no suggestion in the statute relating to subdivision approval; see General Statutes § 8–25; that the undeveloped portion of the parcel in issue, which is located in a residential neighborhood, could not be the subject of an approved subdivision plan notwithstanding the nearby operation of the defendant's business. The court's finding indicates that only garbage trucks and dumpsters are stored on the property; that no garbage is brought there; and that the defendant's business operations involve "mostly containerized ... dumpsters, a contemporary development in technology which has substantially reduced the odors previously associated with the rubbish and garbage hauling industry." These facts do not support the court's speculation that the city's planning commission would not approve a subdivision permit for the undeveloped portion of the parties' property.

The court's remaining observations relating to the effect of the defendant's business on the probable fair market value of the proposed residential lots, the possible loss of building lots to accommodate the defendant's business and the rerouting of a proposed subdivision road, which may have some validity, are not dispositive of the issue. It is the interests of all of the tenants in common that the court must consider; see Lyon v. Wilcox, 119 A. 361, 362–63 (Conn. 1923); 59 Am.Jur.2d, Partition § 118, p. 865; and not merely the economic gain of one tenant, or a group of tenants. The trial court failed to give due consideration to the fact that one of the tenants in common has been in actual and exclusive possession of a portion of the property for a substantial period of time; that the tenant has made her home on the property; and that she derives her livelihood from the operation of a business on this portion of the property, as her family before her has for many years. A partition by sale would force the defendant to surrender her home and, perhaps, would jeopardize her livelihood. It is under just such circumstances, which include the demonstrated practicability of a physical division of the property, that the wisdom of the law's preference for partition in kind is evident.

As this court has many times stated, conclusions that violate "law, logic or reason or are inconsistent with the subordinate facts" cannot stand. Russo v. East Hartford, 425 A.2d 1282, 1284 (Conn. 1979); Connecticut Coke Co. v. New Haven, 364 A.2d 178, 185 (Conn. 1975). Since the property in this case may practically be physically divided, and since the interests of all owners will better be promoted if a partition in kind is ordered, we conclude that the trial court erred in ordering a partition by sale, and that, under the facts as found, the defendant is entitled to a partition of the property in kind.

There is error, the judgment is set aside and the case is remanded for further proceedings not inconsistent with this opinion.

NOTES AND QUESTIONS

1.   On remand, the court awarded Helen Vealencis approximately one acre, including the family homestead and dumpster operation, in the middle of the west end of the 20.5 acre plot (see Figure 5-10). The brothers were awarded the rest of the land, which they sold to a developer for $725,000, laid out in a plat of 42 lots. Based on this price, the market value of the land awarded to Helen was about $72,000. Helen's acreage was separated from the new subdivision by a two-foot strip of land, running from lot 39 down to lot 40, which deprived her of any access to Dino Road in the subdivision. (Her only public access was to Birch Road, via lot 9C.) In addition, the court required Helen to make a payment of $26,000 to the brothers to compensate them for the adverse effect of the garbage dumpster operation on the value of the subdivision. (Such a payment to correct imbalances in a partition in kind is called *owelty*.) So the final value of the award to Helen, in monetary terms, was $46,000; the brothers got $362,500 each. See Manel Baucells & Steven A. Lippman, Justice Delayed is Justice Denied: A Cooperative Game Theoretic Analysis of Hold-Up in Co-Ownership, 22 Cardozo L. Rev. 1191, 1220–43 (2001). Did the trial judge (who had originally ordered a partition sale, only to be reversed by the Connecticut Supreme Court) treat Helen

fairly? Would she have been better off capitulating to the brothers at the outset and foregoing litigation?

Figure 5-10
Plat Showing Land at Issue in *Delfino v. Vealencis*

MAP 1. SUBDIVISION PLOT PLAN FOR THE 20.5 ACRE PARCEL

Source: Manel Baucells & Steven A. Lippman, Justice Delayed is Justice Denied: A Cooperative Game Theoretic Analysis of Hold-Up in Co-Ownership, 22 Cardozo L. Rev. 1191, 1222 (2001).

2. In theory, one co-owner can always buy out the other co-owners. What types of transaction costs are likely to impede some such sales? Why do you think bargaining broke down in *Delfino*, despite the surplus on the table?

3. Not all courts are as seemingly protective of the subjective value of one co-owner as the Connecticut Supreme Court in *Delfino*. Compare Johnson v. Hendrickson, 24 N.W.2d 914 (S.D. 1946) (ordering partition by sale despite some cotenants having a homestead on part of the property and a farm across the road from the homestead). Despite the traditional preference for partition in kind, courts have increasingly favored partition

by sale. In a partition in kind, courts will try if possible to allow a cotenant living on the parcel to keep the portion on which she lives. See, e.g., Anderson v. Anderson, 560 N.W.2d 729 (Minn. Ct. App. 1997).

4.   Partition affords each co-owner an avenue for *exit*, and the threat of exit can help a co-owner protect her interests. Her dealings with the co-owners occur under the shadow of the exit option. Another strategy for exercising leverage without exit is *voice*, expressing dissatisfaction and agitating for change within the group or organization. See Albert O. Hirschman, Exit, Voice, and Loyalty: Responses to Decline in Firms, Organizations and States (1970). A third strategy identified by Hirschman, *loyalty*, leads participants to avoid leaving and to leave quietly when they do. Hirschman explores the complex relationship between exit, voice, and loyalty and the circumstances under which each has advantages and where the two strategies of exit and voice reinforce or undermine each other. Exit places at least one co-owner on the "outside" of the property along with other dutyholders who must respect the exclusion rights of the owner. Voice can be exercised in more or less formal ways within the structure of governance rules over uses of the resource. In the next Chapter we take up condominiums and cooperatives, where these mechanisms are often explicitly incorporated into the bylaws of the relevant community. The notions of exit and voice have been applied to a wide range of public, commercial, and private organizations and groups.

5.   Partition by sale can cause a cash-strapped co-owner to lose subjective value. This is particularly likely in cases in which one of the co-owners is actually living on the property. Some have argued that the law of partition is to blame for the decline in African-American farming since the late nineteenth century, because African-Americans were less likely to have wills and land ownership passing by intestacy became fragmented among an ever-increasing number of descendants of the original owner. From 1920 to 1978, the number of farms operated by African-Americans declined 94%, from 925,710 to 57,271 (in the same period farms operated by whites declined 56%, from about 5.4 million to about 2.4 million). U.S. Comm'n on Civil Rights, The Decline of Black Farming in America 2–3 (1982). For discussion see, e.g., John G. Casagrande Jr., Acquiring Property Through Forced Partitioning Sales: Abuses And Remedies, 27 B.C. L. Rev. 755 (1986); Thomas W. Mitchell, From Reconstruction to Deconstruction: Undermining Black Landownership, Political Independence, and Community Through Partition Sales of Tenancies in Common, 95 Nw. U. L. Rev. 505 (2001); see also Hanoch Dagan & Michael A. Heller, The Liberal Commons, 110 Yale L.J. 549, 602–09 (2001) (presenting partition sales involving African-American farmers as an example to suggest problems with partition). Other possible causes operating at various times include Jim Crow era discrimination in land markets for prime parcels, unequal access to credit and government programs, and the general decline of the family farm (the latter assisted by agricultural subsidies and other programs favoring large farms). For a recapitulation of evidence, see Thomas W. Mitchell et al., Forced Sale Risk: Class, Race, and the "Double Discount", 37 Fla. St. U. L. Rev. 589, 610–19 (2010). In 2010, the Uniform Law Commission adopted a

Uniform Partition of Heirs Property Act, which affords a range of due process protections for heirs to protect them against unfair forced sales in partition. As of late 2021, the UPHPA has been adopted by 18 states.

6.   Would co-owners be better off if exit options were more limited? Some commentators have argued for an approach more like that in civil-law countries, which permit a greater degree of judicial intervention into co-owner relations, with a corresponding de-emphasis on easy partition; this, it has been suggested, might foster more communitarian relations. See Dagan & Heller, supra. But note that cotenants can agree by contract not to partition or can agree to limit the reasons for partition. Such contracts will be enforced, provided they are not an unreasonable restraint on alienation. See, e.g., Michalski v. Michalski, 142 A.2d 645 (N.J. Super. Ct. App. Div. 1958). Also, those who want to provide for a more tailored relationship can form a partnership or a corporation to own the property, with provisions structuring their use of the property incorporated into the partnership agreement or the bylaws of the corporation. Do these sources of flexibility suggest that there is no need to modify the automatic exit right given by the common law?

2.   CONTRIBUTION AND ACCOUNTING

The law does provide some limited regulations of inputs and outputs as between co-owners. The degree to which courts will get involved is low when the parties continue in an ongoing relationship, but increases when one party seeks partition, or, as in the following case, when one party has "ousted" the other from possession.

Gillmor v. Gillmor

Supreme Court of Utah, 1984.
694 P.2d 1037.

■ STEWART, JUSTICE: The defendant Edward Leslie Gillmor appeals from a $29,760 judgment awarded to Florence Gillmor, a cotenant, because defendant obstructed her from exercising her right to occupy land in which she owned an undivided interest with the defendant and C. Frank Gillmor. The property is made up of several large parcels amounting to some 33,000 acres located in Summit, Tooele, and Salt Lake counties.

Two brothers, the parties' fathers, Frank and Edward Lincoln Gillmor, had owned the land and used it for their ranching business. Upon the death of Frank Gillmor, his one-half interest in the property passed in equal shares to his sons, the defendant and C. Frank Gillmor. Edward Lincoln Gillmor continued the ranching business, and for several years grazed cattle and sheep on portions of the common properties. Upon the death of Edward Lincoln Gillmor, his one-half interest passed to his daughter, the plaintiff Florence Gillmor, and she, C. Frank, and the defendant became tenants in common.

In May 1979, the plaintiff filed the instant suit for an accounting and damages for the defendant's exclusive use of the property since January 1, 1979. She also filed a separate suit for partition of the common properties.

The trial was divided into two phases to determine first the damages from January 1, 1979, to May 31, 1980, and second the damages from June 1, 1980, to December 31, 1980. The trial court held that from January 1, 1979, to May 31, 1980, the defendant had grazed livestock on the common properties in such a manner as to constitute exclusive use of the properties and thereby exclude the plaintiff from grazing her livestock on those properties. The trial court awarded a $21,544.91 judgment for one-half the rental value of the properties in favor of Florence Gillmor and against defendant. Defendant did not appeal that decision.

In the second phase of the trial, the trial court found that "[b]etween June 1, 1980 and December 31, 1980, defendant Edward Gillmor continued to graze his sheep and cattle on the common properties in Salt Lake and Summit counties or to use said lands to produce feed for his cattle and sheep, and such use . . . was to the exclusion of the plaintiff."

On appeal, the defendant argues with respect to the second judgment (1) that "there is no evidence or finding on the issue of ouster," and (2) that even if there were an ouster, the damages are excessive.

I.

The law is that a cotenant may sue for his share of rents and profits from common property if he has been ousted from possession of the common property. Roberts v. Roberts, 584 P.2d 378, 380 (Utah 1978). The defendant argues that the trial court did not find that the defendant ousted the plaintiff. The trial court did not specifically use that term in its findings of fact and conclusions of law, but it did find that the defendant had both exercised exclusive use and possession and had also excluded the plaintiff from use of the common properties.

Mere exclusive use of commonly held properties by one cotenant is not sufficient to establish an ouster. A tenant in common has the right to use and occupy the entire property held in cotenancy without liability to other cotenants. Each cotenant has the right to "free and unobstructed possession . . . without liability for rents for the use and occupation thereof." Utah Oil Refining Co. v. Leigh, 96 P.2d 1100, 1102 (Utah 1939).

> That one cotenant is not liable to his cotenant for rents for the occupancy of the common property is elemental. And this is true even though [the cotenant] uses it and derives income therefrom, as where he occupies . . . or farms a piece and takes the crops; or uses it for storage purposes; as long as he does not interfere with the cotenant's right to likewise occupy, use and enjoy.

96 P.2d at 1103 (citations omitted).

However, a cotenant who ousts another cotenant or acts in such a fashion as to necessarily exclude a fellow cotenant, violates the rights of that cotenant. Roberts v. Roberts, 584 P.2d at 380; Utah Oil Refining v. Leigh, 96 P.2d at 1103. To establish a right to share in the rents and profits from the common property, it must be established that a cotenant has used the property so as to "necessarily exclude his cotenant." Utah Oil Refining Co., 96 P.2d at 1103.

Exclusive use means more than one cotenant using the entire property; it requires either an act of exclusion or use of such a nature that it necessarily prevents another cotenant from exercising his rights in the property.[2] Roberts v. Roberts, 584 P.2d at 380–81; Utah Oil Refinery Co. v. Leigh, 96 P.2d at 1103. * * *

The defendant contends that the trial court erred in finding that the defendant had exercised exclusive possession and use of the common properties in such a manner as to exclude the plaintiff from using the land. We disagree. The plaintiff sought to graze livestock on the land to the extent of her interest, but was effectively prevented from doing so. She sent defendant a letter expressing her intent to graze her livestock on the properties in proportion to her ownership and requested that the defendant accommodate her plans by altering his operations accordingly. The defendant refused to respond and continued to graze the lands to their maximum capacity. He even acknowledged that additional grazing would have damaged the range land. The defendant asserts that at various times he or his attorney invited the plaintiff onto the lands, but he never indicated any intention to alter his operations so as to accommodate the plaintiff's use of the land. Had the plaintiff grazed her livestock on the common properties while defendant's livestock was also there, the land would have been overgrazed. Indeed, the defendant admitted that if the plaintiff had attempted to put additional sheep on the land, he would have sought an injunction to prevent damage to the land.

We hold that when a cotenant out of possession makes a clear, unequivocal demand to use land that is in the exclusive possession of another cotenant, and that cotenant refuses to accommodate the other tenant's right to use the land, the tenant out of possession has established a claim for relief. It is not necessary that the out-of-possession cotenant resort to force or to means that would damage the common property to establish a right to legal redress.

II.

The defendant argues that the damage award of $29,760 for seven months of grazing is excessive when contrasted with the award of $21,544.91 in the first phase of trial for seventeen months of grazing. * * * [The court went on to uphold the damages award.]

---

[2] It follows that the burden to establish ouster in a suit to recover rents and profits is less stringent than the burden to establish ouster in an adverse possession action.

The defendant also argues that the damages should not have been awarded for the time when he herded his livestock from one parcel of Gillmor land to another over land owned by a third party pursuant to trail or trespass rights, which include grazing along the way. See generally Anderson v. Osguthorpe, 504 P.2d 1000 (Utah 1972). Since the trail rights are appurtenant to the Gillmor land, there is no sound reason for distinguishing between them and the rights to the fee land. * * *

The defendant also argues that he is entitled to an offset for repairs made on the common property. Sometime after June 1, 1980, he repaired a range fence and a ditch on the common property. He asserts that the fence repairs directly benefited the plaintiff because she now owns land which borders the fence.

Where a cotenant in sole possession makes repairs or improvements to the common property without the consent of his fellow cotenants, he generally has no right of contribution. In *Heiselt v. Heiselt*, 349 P.2d 175, 178–79 (Utah 1960) (quoting 14 Am.Jur. Cotenancy § 49 at 115 (1938)), we stated:

> While contrary doctrines have been enunciated and the question is conceded to be one of great difficulty, it appears to be generally agreed that a cotenant who has made improvements upon the common property without the assent of his cotenants is not ordinarily entitled to contribution and cannot, as a matter of right, charge them with the value or costs thereof or maintain any action that would result in a personal judgment against them. * * * Compensation for improvements is allowed, however, where the other cotenants have stood by and permitted him to proceed to his detriment.

A cotenant may, however, be required to contribute his pro rata share of expenses if the cotenant in possession acted in good faith, with the bona fide belief that he was the sole owner of the property, or when the repairs were essential to preserve or protect the common estate. See Zanzonico v. Zanzonico, 2 A.2d 597 (N.J. Eq. 1938); 20 Am.Jur.2d Cotenancy and Joint Ownership § 62 (1965). Furthermore, where, as here, a cotenant out of possession seeks an accounting or damages, the cotenant in possession, who is held liable for the value of the use, occupancy, or rents collected, is entitled to recover reasonable expenditures made by him for necessary repairs and maintenance.[4] * * *

In the instant case, the evidence indicates that the repairs were a necessary cost of grazing the livestock and should have been deducted from the damages awarded. The case must therefore be remanded for a modification of the judgment. * * *

---

[4] For example, cotenants have recovered their cost of painting buildings to make them suitable for sale or renting, Scott v. Staggs, 276 P.2d 605 (Cal. Ct. App. 1954); completing a partially finished house, Todd v. Stewart, 202 N.W. 844 (Iowa 1925); and making miscellaneous house repairs, Fassitt v. Seip, 95 A. 273 (Pa. 1915).

NOTES AND QUESTIONS

1.   The right of a cotenant to obtain rental payments from another cotenant depends critically on whether the rental payments are based on a rental to a third party or are based on the rental value of the possession to an occupying cotenant. If one cotenant rents to a third party, then the renting cotenant is obliged to share the payments with other cotenants. In these circumstances the non-renting cotenant can bring an action for an accounting, and the court will apportion the rents in accordance with ownership shares. In contrast, there is in general no obligation for one cotenant to pay rent to other cotenants for the value of their possession. The exception is where the cotenant out of possession can prove an ouster. As to what constitutes an ouster, the cases are all over the lot. On the variety of approaches courts have taken, see Evelyn Alicia Lewis, Struggling with Quicksand: The Ins and Outs of Cotenant Possession Value Liability and a Call for Default Rule Reform, 1994 Wis. L. Rev. 331. Acts of physical exclusion from the whole property are sufficient for ouster. But a letter telling a cotenant to vacate or pay rent may or may not be enough. What were the critical facts in *Gillmor* that led the court to find an ouster?

2.   The requirement of complete ouster is sometimes "derived" from the unity of possession (each cotenant has the right to use and possess the whole) that is characteristic of the tenancy in common and other co-ownership arrangements. Is there any other reason? Some contracts scholars have invoked the difference between relatively hard-edged norms appropriate for endgame situations, and more accommodating "relationship preserving" norms often based on reciprocal trust. Enforcing relationship-preserving norms in an endgame scenario might undermine them. See Lisa Bernstein, Merchant Law in a Merchant Court: Rethinking the Code's Search for Immanent Business Norms, 144 U. Pa. L. Rev. 1765 (1996). Might something like this be going on here? As long as the relationship is continuing, should courts adjudicate who washes the car or mops the floor?

3.   Once there is an ouster, the clock may also start ticking on adverse possession. As mentioned in Note 2 in the *Gillmor* case, the standard for ouster in the context of adverse possession is more stringent than for purposes of contribution and accounting. Illustrative of the difficulties is *McAllister v. Norville*, 514 So.2d 1270 (Ala. 1987), in which 14 boat pilots acquired property along Alabama's Gulf coast in 1872 as tenants in common but with an informal right as amongst themselves to "stake a claim" to a portion of the property and build a house on it. Over 100 years later the successors to the original pilots disputed title to parts of "Pilot Town." In a quiet title action, the trial court found an ouster for purposes of adverse possession, but the Supreme Court of Alabama reversed, holding that because the original pilots had wished to establish a selective community in which each owner would have an undivided one-fourteenth interest, the cotenants' acts of possession were permissive.

4.   Whether courts will adjudicate claims by a cotenant for reimbursement from other cotenants also depends on whether the relationship is ongoing or has been terminated. If the relationship is ongoing,

a cotenant can sue for contribution for expenditures that are necessary to preserve the property from being taken through forfeiture, such as the payment of property taxes or mortgage payments. But contribution is unlikely to be awarded for repairs and maintenance expenses, and certainly will not be awarded for improvements. When the relationship is at an end, however, either because one cotenant has sued for partition, or as in *Gillmor* one cotenant has proven ouster by another, courts are more willing to consider offsets for repair and maintenance expenses and may even take expenditures for improvements into account. Reimbursement for these expenditures may be reflected either as offsets from imputed rental payments (as in *Gillmor*) or may be awarded as owelty in a partition action.

3. SEVERANCE

The difference between a joint tenancy and tenancy in common is the right of survivorship. But either joint tenant can unilaterally "sever" the joint tenancy, which destroys the right of survivorship and converts the tenancy into a tenancy in common.

What actions lead to a severance? At common law, severance required the destruction of one of the four unities (time, title, interest, and possession). This was usually achieved through a conveyance to a third party (strawman or straw) who would then reconvey to the grantor. These days one can probably convey to oneself and effect a severance of the joint tenancy. Questions also arise as to whether a unilateral lease by one joint tenant, or as in the following case a unilateral mortgage, severs a joint tenancy.

Harms v. Sprague

Supreme Court of Illinois, 1984.
473 N.E.2d 930.

■ THOMAS J. MORAN, JUSTICE. Plaintiff, William H. Harms, filed a complaint to quiet title and for declaratory judgment in the circuit court of Greene County. Plaintiff had taken title to certain real estate with his brother John R. Harms, as a joint tenant, with full right of survivorship. The plaintiff named, as a defendant, Charles D. Sprague, the executor of the estate of John Harms and the devisee of all the real and personal property of John Harms. Also named as defendants were Carl T. and Mary E. Simmons, alleged mortgagees of the property in question. Defendant Sprague filed a counterclaim against plaintiff, challenging plaintiff's claim of ownership of the entire tract of property and asking the court to recognize his (Sprague's) interest as a tenant in common, subject to a mortgage lien. At issue was the effect the granting of a mortgage by John Harms had on the joint tenancy. Also at issue was whether the mortgage survived the death of John Harms as a lien against the property.

The trial court held that the mortgage given by John Harms to defendants Carl and Mary Simmons severed the joint tenancy. Further, the court found that the mortgage survived the death of John Harms as a lien against the undivided one-half interest in the property which passed to Sprague by and through the will of the deceased. The appellate court reversed, finding that the mortgage given by one joint tenant of his interest in the property does not sever the joint tenancy. Accordingly, the appellate court held that plaintiff, as the surviving joint tenant, owned the property in its entirety, unencumbered by the mortgage lien. * * *

Two issues are raised on appeal: (1) Is a joint tenancy severed when less than all of the joint tenants mortgage their interest in the property? and (2) Does such a mortgage survive the death of the mortgagor as a lien on the property?

A review of the stipulation of facts reveals the following. Plaintiff, William Harms, and his brother John Harms, took title to real estate located in Roodhouse, on June 26, 1973, as joint tenants. The warranty deed memorializing this transaction was recorded on June 29, 1973, in the office of the Greene County recorder of deeds.

Carl and Mary Simmons owned a lot and home in Roodhouse. Charles Sprague entered into an agreement with the Simmons whereby Sprague was to purchase their property for $25,000. Sprague tendered $18,000 in cash and signed a promissory note for the balance of $7,000. Because Sprague had no security for the $7,000, he asked his friend, John Harms, to co-sign the note and give a mortgage on his interest in the joint tenancy property. Harms agreed, and on June 12, 1981, John Harms and Charles Sprague, jointly and severally, executed a promissory note for $7,000 payable to Carl and Mary Simmons. The note states that the principal sum of $7,000 was to be paid from the proceeds of the sale of John Harms' interest in the joint tenancy property, but in any event no later than six months from the date the note was signed. The note reflects that five monthly interest payments had been made, with the last payment recorded November 6, 1981. In addition, John Harms executed a mortgage, in favor of the Simmonses, on his undivided one-half interest in the joint tenancy property, to secure payment of the note. William Harms was unaware of the mortgage given by his brother.

John Harms moved from his joint tenancy property to the Simmons property which had been purchased by Charles Sprague. On December 10, 1981, John Harms died. By the terms of John Harms' will, Charles Sprague was the devisee of his entire estate. The mortgage given by John Harms to the Simmonses was recorded on December 29, 1981.

Prior to the appellate court decision in the instant case no court of this State had directly addressed the principal question we are confronted with herein—the effect of a mortgage, executed by less than all of the joint tenants, on the joint tenancy. Nevertheless, there are numerous cases which have considered the severance issue in relation to other circumstances surrounding a joint tenancy. All have necessarily focused on the four unities which are fundamental to both the creation and the perpetuation of the joint tenancy. These are the unities of interest, title, time, and possession. (Jackson v. O'Connell, 177 N.E.2d 194 (Ill. 1961); Tindall v. Yeats, 64 N.E.2d 903 (Ill. 1946).) The voluntary or involuntary destruction of any of the unities by one of the joint tenants will sever the joint tenancy. Van Antwerp v. Horan, 61 N.E.2d 358 (Ill. 1945).

In a series of cases, this court has considered the effect that judgment liens upon the interest of one joint tenant have on the stability of the joint tenancy. In *Peoples Trust & Savings Bank v. Haas*, 160 N.E. 85 (Ill. 1927), the court found that a judgment lien secured against one joint tenant did not serve to extinguish the joint tenancy. As such, the surviving joint tenant "succeeded to the title in fee to the whole of the land by operation of law." 160 N.E. 85.

Citing to *Haas* for this general proposition, the court in *Van Antwerp v. Horan*, 61 N.E.2d 358 (Ill. 1945), extended the holding in *Haas* to the situation where a levy is made under execution upon the interest of the debtor joint tenant. The court found that the levy was "not such an act as can be said to have the effect of a divestiture of title * * * [so as to destroy the] identity of interest or of any other unity which must occur before * * * the estate of joint tenancy has been severed and destroyed." 61 N.E.2d 358. * * *

Clearly, this court adheres to the rule that a lien on a joint tenant's interest in property will not effectuate a severance of the joint tenancy, absent the conveyance by a deed following the expiration of a redemption period. (See Johnson v. Muntz, 4 N.E.2d 826 (Ill. 1936).) It follows, therefore, that if Illinois perceives a mortgage as merely a lien on the mortgagor's interest in property rather than a conveyance of title from mortgagor to mortgagee, the execution of a mortgage by a joint tenant, on his interest in the property, would not destroy the unity of title and sever the joint tenancy.

Early cases in Illinois, however, followed the title theory of mortgages. In 1900, this court recognized the common law precept that a mortgage was a conveyance of a legal estate vesting title to the property in the mortgagee. (Lightcap v. Bradley, 58 N.E. 221 (Ill. 1900).) Consistent with this title theory of mortgages, therefore, there are many cases which state, in *dicta*, that a joint tenancy is severed by one of the joint tenants mortgaging his interest to a stranger. Yet even the early case of *Lightcap v. Bradley*, cited above, recognized that the title held by the mortgagee was for the limited purpose of protecting his interests. The court went on to say that "the mortgagor is the owner for every other purpose and against every other person. The title of the mortgagee is anomalous, and exists only between him and the mortgagor * * *." Lightcap v. Bradley, 58 N.E. 221.

Because our cases had early recognized the unique and narrow character of the title that passed to a mortgagee under the common law title theory, it was not a drastic departure when this court expressly characterized the execution of a mortgage as a mere lien in *Kling v.*

Ghilarducci, 121 N.E.2d 752 (Ill. 1954). In *Kling,* the court was confronted with the question of when a separation of title, necessary to create an easement by implication, had occurred. The court found that title to the property was not separated with the execution of a trust deed but rather only upon execution and delivery of a master's deed. The court stated:

> In some jurisdictions the execution of a mortgage is a severance, in others, the execution of a mortgage is not a severance. In Illinois the giving of a mortgage is not a separation of title, for the holder of the mortgage takes only a lien thereunder. After foreclosure of a mortgage and until delivery of the master's deed under the foreclosure sale, purchaser acquires no title to the land either legal or equitable. Title to land sold under mortgage foreclosure remains in the mortgagor or his grantee until the expiration of the redemption period and conveyance by the master's deed.

121 N.E.2d 752.

Kling and later cases rejecting the title theory do not involve the severance of joint tenancies. As such, they have not expressly disavowed the *dicta* of joint tenancy cases which have stated that the act of mortgaging by one joint tenant results in the severance of the joint tenancy. We find, however, that implicit in *Kling* and our more recent cases which follow the lien theory of mortgages is the conclusion that a joint tenancy is not severed when one joint tenant executes a mortgage on his interest in the property, since the unity of title has been preserved. As the appellate court in the instant case correctly observed: "If giving a mortgage creates only a lien, then a mortgage should have the same effect on a joint tenancy as a lien created in other ways." Other jurisdictions following the lien theory of mortgages have reached the same result.

A joint tenancy has been defined as "a present estate in all the joint tenants, each being seized of the whole * * * ." (Partridge v. Berliner, 156 N.E. 352 (Ill. 1927).) An inherent feature of the estate of joint tenancy is the right of survivorship, which is the right of the last survivor to take the whole of the estate. Because we find that a mortgage given by one joint tenant of his interest in the property does not sever the joint tenancy, we hold that the plaintiff's right of survivorship became operative upon the death of his brother. As such plaintiff is now the sole owner of the estate, in its entirety.

Further, we find that the mortgage executed by John Harms does not survive as a lien on plaintiff's property. A surviving joint tenant succeeds to the share of the deceased joint tenant by virtue of the conveyance which created the joint tenancy, not as the successor of the deceased. The property right of the mortgaging joint tenant is extinguished at the moment of his death. While John Harms was alive, the mortgage existed as a lien on his interest in the joint tenancy. Upon his death, his interest ceased to exist and along with it the lien of the mortgage. Under the circumstances of this case, we would note that the mortgage given by John Harms to the Simmonses was only valid as between the original parties during the lifetime of John Harms since it was unrecorded. (Ill.Rev.Stat.1981, ch. 30, par. 29; 27 Ill.L. & Prac. Mortgages sec. 65 (1956).) In addition, recording the mortgage subsequent to the death of John Harms was a nullity. As we stated above, John Harms' property rights in the joint tenancy were extinguished when he died. Thus, he no longer had a property interest upon which the mortgage lien could attach.

In their petition to supplement defendant Sprague's petition for leave to appeal, the Simmonses argue that the application of section 20–19 of the Probate Act of 1975 (Ill.Rev.Stat.1981, ch. 110 1/2, par. 20–19) to the facts of this case would mandate a finding that their mortgage on the subject property remains as a valid encumbrance in the hands of the surviving joint tenant. Section 20–19 reads in relevant part:

(a) When any real estate or leasehold estate in real estate subject to an encumbrance, or any beneficial interest under a trust of real estate or leasehold estate in real estate subject to an encumbrance, is specifically bequeathed or passes by joint tenancy with right of survivorship or by the terms of a trust agreement or other nontestamentary instrument, the legatee, surviving tenant or beneficiary to whom the real estate, leasehold estate or beneficial interest is given or passes, takes it subject to the encumbrance and is not entitled to have the indebtedness paid from other real or personal estate of the decedent.

(Ill.Rev.Stat.1981, ch. 110 1/2, par. 20–19.)

While the Simmonses have maintained from the outset that their mortgage followed title to the property, they did not raise the applicability of section 20–19 of the Probate Act of 1975 at the trial level, and thus the issue is deemed waived. Moreover, because we have found that the lien of mortgage no longer exists against the property, section 20–19 is inapplicable, since plaintiff, as the surviving joint tenant, did not take the property subject to an encumbrance.

For the reasons stated herein, the judgment of the appellate court is affirmed.

NOTES AND QUESTIONS

1.   If the Simmonses had dealt with both the Harms brothers, then the lien would have been unaffected by John Harms's death. A financial institution would likely require both of the joint tenants to sign, but the Simmonses were not sophisticated lenders. Should the rule be designed to protect informal lending, or should those involved in real estate sales be expected to hire a lawyer? Community property requires both spouses to

consent for any alienation or encumbrance of land held as community property. See, e.g., La. Civ. Code art. 2347.

2.   Courts are all over the map on the issues raised in *Harms*. One might think that a court applying the title theory of mortgages would find severance. But as the court in Harms notes, the "title" here came to be viewed as given for limited purposes. Some courts still applying the title theory would find no severance by a mortgage given by only one of the joint tenants. With the lien theory, most courts would hold that the lien does not survive the death of the mortgagor joint tenant, but the opposite result under the lien theory can be reached. See Wilken v. Young, 41 N.E. 68, 70 (Ind. 1895). One commentator maintains that the distinction between the "title theory" and the "lien theory" is very largely a formal one, and it becomes increasingly hard to defend it in an era when "the intention of the parties provides the touchstone for deciding most severance cases." R.H. Helmholz, Realism and Formalism in the Severance of Joint Tenancies, 77 Neb. L. Rev. 1, 28–29 (1998) (footnote omitted); see also Wesley A. Sturges & Samuel O. Clark, Legal Theory and Real Property Mortgages, 37 Yale L.J. 691, 709 (1928) (arguing that judges invoke title or lien theory "depending upon [their] sense of convenience and the matters which stimulate them in the particular case."). Should the parties' intent be the touchstone here? Who else has an interest in clarity and simplicity here? Is the Illinois Supreme Court's approach in *Harms v. Sprague* any less formalistic than the approach condemned by Helmholz? Should a court balance the hardship to the mortgagee and the surviving joint tenant on a case-by-case basis?

3.   What if William Harms had died first? If the mortgage lien did not sever the joint tenancy does this mean that the debt is now secured by the entire property?

4.   Although the Simmonses wished to add the argument that Section 20–19 of the Probate Act of 1975 mandates that the lien survive the death of John Harms, the court holds that this argument has been waived. But the court in dictum suggests that the result would be the same even if this provision did apply. Do you agree? How could the statute be clearer? Is the problem that the statute seems to presuppose that an interest "passes" upon the death of a joint tenant, whereas the court sees the survivorship under the joint tenancy as involving no passing of an interest, just the extinguishment of the deceased's interest? Or does the court simply disagree with the policy chosen by the Illinois legislature?

5.   On whether mortgages are liens, the Illinois legislature later adopted the Illinois Mortgage Foreclosure Law, which defines a "mortgage" as:

> any consensual lien created by a written instrument which grants or retains an interest in real estate to secure a debt or other obligation. The term "mortgage" includes, without limitation . . . every deed conveying real estate, although an absolute conveyance in its terms, which shall have been intended only as a security in the nature of a mortgage.

735 ILCS 5/15–1207 (originally enacted on July 1, 1987, as amended). How would parties contract around this, by showing a contrary "intent"? What about parties with mortgages from before 1987, in light of the provision also including within "mortgage" "instruments which would have been deemed instruments in the nature of a mortgage prior to the effective date of this amendatory Act of 1987"? Id. § 15–1207(e).

6.   Another question that arises with some regularity is whether a lease by one joint tenant severs the joint tenancy. Again we find that courts have taken conflicting approaches. Compare Tenhet v. Boswell, 554 P.2d 330 (Cal. 1976) with Alexander v. Boyer, 253 A.2d 359 (Md. 1969). Also, courts will prevent one from profiting, including through inheritance, from one's own act of murder. In *Maine Savings Bank v. Bridges*, 431 A.2d 633 (Me. 1981), the court held that when the husband killed his wife, he severed the joint tenancy and held a one-half interest as a tenant in common with his wife's other heirs.

7.   Not only may the joint tenancy be severed unilaterally, no notice is required. In *Riddle v. Harmon*, 162 Cal. Rptr. 530 (Ct. App. 1980), a married couple, Frances and Jack Riddle, owned real estate as joint tenants. Frances was distressed to learn from her lawyer about the survivorship feature of the joint tenancy and wanted to dispose of her share by will. At common law, to sever the joint tenancy would have required two conveyances, employing a straw: The joint tenant desiring severance would convey to the straw (often someone working in the lawyer's office) who would then reconvey back to the grantor, leaving the erstwhile joint tenants as tenants in common. In *Riddle*, Frances Riddle's attorney prepared a deed in which Frances granted to herself an undivided one-half interest in the property and a will in which she devised her share of the property to another. Twenty days later she died. Reversing the trial court, the appellate court held that a straw is not required to sever a joint tenancy. Do problems remain? Should the joint tenant be able to sever unilaterally without giving notice to anyone? Some statutes (currently including one in California) require recordation to sever a joint tenancy in some circumstances. Would this have helped here? What do you think Frances Riddle would have done with the above-described documents if her husband had suddenly predeceased her?

F. MORE ON MARITAL INTERESTS

Married couples are a special set of co-owners. While a marriage is ongoing the rules of co-ownership are largely the same for married people as for co-owners. (The main exception is the tenancy by the entirety, which is not available to nonmarried co-owners.) Special rules for marital interests emerge primarily in the context of divorce and inheritance. The spousal forced share, see Section C.2 supra, is currently the main constraint on testamentary freedom in the interest of a surviving spouse.

We focus here on the rules for property division on divorce. These are important in their own right, and because they define each spouse's exit option they can be expected to influence relations within an ongoing marriage. In community property states, the rules for division on divorce, as well as those for descent and concurrent use, are tightly connected to the definition of this form of co-ownership. In common-law states (common law for purposes of marital property), division on divorce is governed by principles of equitable division, to the extent they are not displaced by an prenuptial agreement. In recent years, courts have tended to bring equitable division somewhat closer to the approach under community property. One of the central issues in marital property law is how to define "property" for purposes of division on divorce, and in particular how to treat increases in human capital during the marriage. Is it property, and if so in what sense?

Postema v. Postema

Court of Appeals of Michigan, 1991.
471 N.W.2d 912.

■ MAHER, PRESIDING JUDGE. The defendant appeals and the plaintiff cross appeals from the property distribution provisions of a February 3, 1989, judgment of divorce. The primary issue concerns the valuation of defendant's law degree and whether the trial court erred in finding the law degree to be a marital asset. We affirm in part and remand.

Plaintiff and defendant were married on August 11, 1984. At the time of their marriage, defendant was employed as a cost accountant and plaintiff was working as a licensed practical nurse and attending school in pursuit of an associate's degree in nursing so that she could become a registered nurse. It was the plan of the parties when they married that defendant would enroll in law school and that plaintiff would postpone her schooling and work full-time to support them while defendant attended school. Accordingly, shortly after the marriage, the parties moved from Grand Rapids to the Detroit area, where they stayed from September 1984 until May 1987 while defendant attended Wayne State University Law School. In furtherance of the parties' plan, plaintiff obtained a full-time job at an area hospital, earning approximately $53,000 during the period defendant was in law school. Plaintiff also assumed the primary responsibility of maintaining the household, doing all cooking and cleaning, and running all errands. Though defendant did not work at all during his first year in law school, he later worked as a law clerk, full-time during the summers following his first and second years in law school and then part-time during his second and part of his third years. In all, defendant earned approximately $12,000 from clerking. The parties' earnings were used primarily for their support, while defendant's education was financed mostly through student loans totaling $15,000.

Defendant proved to be a successful law student and wrote for the school's law review. After defendant graduated in May 1987, the parties moved back to the Grand Rapids area, where defendant accepted a position as an associate attorney with a local law firm at a starting annual salary of $41,000. The following September, plaintiff resumed classes in pursuit of her associate's degree in nursing. In November 1987, however, the parties separated. Despite the separation, plaintiff continued her classes and eventually received her associate's degree in May 1988, although she had to support herself during that period by working full-time at a local hospital.

Plaintiff testified that marital problems developed early in the marriage. She said defendant would often complain that she was overweight, saying it embarrassed him, and that he would start many verbal fights, usually over things that were insignificant. She claimed the situation got to the point where her whole life revolved around trying not to agitate defendant. Defendant testified that he often asked plaintiff to leave, complained that she was a "fanatic" about cleaning, and admitted that he once presented her with a list of things for her to remember to do so that she wouldn't "irritate" him. Although defendant agreed that he was sometimes difficult to live with and that he treated plaintiff badly from time to time, he blamed it on the stress of law school. According to plaintiff, defendant would often apologize the day after a fight, sometimes verbally and sometimes in a letter. The parties finally separated on November 7, 1987, after defendant informed plaintiff that he had met another woman and had gone out with her a couple of times while plaintiff was working.

The trial court found that the breakdown of the marriage was primarily the fault of defendant, and announced it had considered this fact in its property distribution. After awarding each of the parties their respective automobiles, the trial court awarded plaintiff specific household goods and bank funds totaling $5,000, while awarding defendant specific goods and funds totaling $3,000. Defendant was also held solely responsible for repayment of $14,000 in student loans. Finally, the trial court determined that defendant's law degree was a marital asset subject to distribution. The court valued the degree at $80,000, and awarded plaintiff, as her share of the degree, $32,000 on the basis that this amount would equalize the parties' respective distributive shares. The court ordered this obligation to be paid off in monthly installments of $371.55 or more, at seven percent interest, until fully paid. The court did not award either party alimony.

Defendant now appeals and plaintiff cross appeals as of right. * * * [D]efendant challenges various aspects of the trial court's property distribution, with his primary objection being the court's inclusion of his law degree in the marital estate and the resultant valuation of that degree. On cross appeal, plaintiff also challenges the trial court's valuation of the law degree, contending that it was low.

The goal of a trial court with respect to the division of the marital estate is a fair and equitable distribution under all of the circumstances. The division is not governed by any rigid rules or mathematical formula and need not be equal. The primary question is what is fair. On review, this Court is required to accept the trial court's factual findings unless those findings are clearly erroneous.

I.   THE LAW DEGREE

* * *

In addressing the issue involving defendant's law degree, we will begin by first discussing the rationale behind the recognition that a nonstudent spouse must be compensated whenever a concerted family effort is involved in obtaining an advanced degree, which discussion will include an application of the concept "concerted family effort" to the facts of the instant case. Secondly, we will discuss what we believe to be the appropriate and preferable means of characterizing a claim for compensation involving an advanced degree. Finally, we will address the factors and methods that we believe are relevant in valuing such a claim upon divorce.

A.   *The Concerted Family Effort.*

As indicated above, an award of compensation to a nonstudent spouse is premised upon both general notions of "fairness" and the existence of a "concerted family effort." The relevancy of fairness is that, in Michigan, equitable considerations form the underlying basis for recognizing a claim for compensation involving an advanced degree, and that the ultimate goal in every divorce case is to do what is necessary to accord complete equity under the facts and circumstances of the case.

Second, the concept "concerted family effort" stresses the fact that it is not the existence of an advanced degree itself that gives rise to an equitable claim for compensation, but rather the fact of the degree being the end product of the mutual sacrifice, effort, and contribution of both parties as part of a larger, long-range plan intended to benefit the family as a whole. The concept is premised, in part, on the fact that the attainment of an advanced degree is a prolonged undertaking involving considerable expenditure of time, effort, and money, as well as other sacrifices. Where such an undertaking is pursued as part of a concerted family effort, both spouses expect to be compensated for their respective sacrifices, efforts, and contributions by eventually sharing in the fruits of the degree. Where, however, the parties' relationship ends in divorce, such a sharing is impossible. Although the degree holder will always have the degree to show for the efforts, the nonstudent spouse is left with nothing. Therefore, a remedy consistent with fairness and equity requires that an attempt be made to at least return financially to the nonstudent spouse the value of what that spouse contributed toward attainment of the degree.

Generally, the existence of a concerted family effort will be reflected in many ways. For instance, it is reflected not only through a spouse's tangible efforts and financial contributions associated with working and supporting the mate while the mate pursues the advanced degree, but also through other intangible, nonpecuniary efforts and contributions, such as where a spouse increases the share of the daily tasks, child-rearing responsibilities, or other details of household and family management undertaken in order to provide the mate with the necessary time and energy to study and attend classes. A concerted family effort is also exemplified by the fact that both spouses typically share in the emotional and psychological burdens of the educational experience. For the nonstudent spouse, these burdens may be experienced either directly, such as through the presence of increased tension within the household, or indirectly, such as where the spouse shares vicariously in the stress of the educational experience. Finally, the attainment of an advanced degree during marriage is usually accompanied by considerable sacrifice on the part of both spouses. For the nonstudent spouse, such sacrifice may be reflected by a change in life style during the educational process, the availability of less time to pursue personal interests, or even a decision to either give up or temporarily postpone one's own educational or career pursuits as part of the larger, long-range plan designed to benefit the family as a whole.

Turning now to the instant case, the facts show that plaintiff temporarily postponed her pursuit of an associate's degree in nursing, moved with defendant to the Detroit area so that he could attend law school, and then worked full-time to support herself and defendant while defendant attended classes. This was all done as part of a larger plan to benefit both parties as a whole. Plaintiff, in addition to being the primary financial provider while defendant attended school, wherein she accounted for approximately eighty percent of the parties' total financial support, also bore primary responsibility for the daily household tasks. Moreover, the stress of the law school experience was certainly experienced by both parties, as reflected by the fact that defendant repeatedly blamed his inappropriate behavior toward plaintiff on the stress of law school, and by plaintiff's testimony explaining that her whole life revolved around her trying not to agitate defendant.

We conclude, therefore, that defendant's law degree was clearly the end product of a concerted family effort giving rise to an equitable claim for compensation in favor of plaintiff in recognition of her unrewarded sacrifices, efforts, and contributions toward attainment of the degree.

B.   *Characterization of a Claim for Compensation Involving an Advanced Degree.*

Despite the common recognition among panels of this Court that a spouse who did not obtain an advanced degree should be compensated whenever the degree is the end product of a concerted family effort, panels are in disagreement over the appropriate manner in which a claim for compensation should be considered. While some panels have characterized an advanced degree as a marital asset subject to property division, other panels have held that an advanced degree is more properly considered as a factor in awarding alimony.

After reviewing the various decisions addressing the issue and taking into consideration the underlying principles upon which an award of compensation for an advanced degree is premised, we reject the view holding that an advanced degree is more properly considered as a factor in awarding alimony.

The cases adhering to the alimony view have stated that a degree is simply not "property" for the reasons expressed in Graham v. Graham, 574 P.2d 75, 77 (1978):

> An educational degree such as an M.B.A., is simply not encompassed even by the broad views of the concept of "property." It does not have an exchange value or any objective transferable value on an open market. It is personal to the holder. It terminates on death of the holder and is not inheritable. It cannot be assigned, sold, transferred, conveyed or pledged. An advanced degree is a cumulative product of many years of previous education, combined with diligence and hard work. It may not be acquired by the mere expenditure of money. It is simply an intellectual achievement that may potentially assist in the future acquisition of property. In our view, it has none of the attributes of property in the usual sense of that term.

In rejecting the alimony approach, we first recognize that the basic purpose of paying alimony is to assist in the other spouse's support. Unlike alimony, however, the principles underlying an award of compensation based on the attainment of an advanced degree are neither rooted in nor based on notions of support. Rather, as noted previously, entitlement to compensation stems from the recognition that where a degree is the end product of a concerted family effort, fairness and equity will not permit the degree holder to reap the benefits of the degree without compensating the other spouse for unrewarded sacrifices, efforts, and contributions toward attainment of the degree. Thus, where a concerted family effort is involved, a spouse's entitlement to compensation constitutes a recognized right; it is not dependent upon factors related to the need for support. Therefore, we do not find that an award of alimony is the appropriate means for awarding compensation.
* * *

Finally, contrary to the observations in *Graham, supra,* we do not believe that the consideration of an advanced degree when making the property distribution would be improper merely because a degree cannot be characterized as "property" in the classic sense. Rather, we agree with *Woodworth v. Woodworth,* 337 N.W.2d 332, 335 (Mich. Ct. App. 1983), that "whether or not an advanced degree can physically or metaphysically be defined as 'property' is beside the point [;] [c]ourts must instead focus on the most equitable solution to dissolving the marriage and dividing among the respective parties what they have." Furthermore, as I stated in my concurring opinion in *Olah v. Olah,* 354 N.W.2d 359, 362 (Mich. Ct. App. 1984): "This is an equitable distribution jurisdiction, in which classification of an item as either property or non-property is not decisive in determining the best division of the parties' holdings on divorce." Finally, in *Lewis v. Lewis*, 448 N.W.2d 735, 737–38 (Mich. Ct. App. 1989), this Court added: "[T]he fundamental question in cases involving advanced degrees is not whether a degree is property, but rather 'whether the facts in the case give rise to an *equitable claim* regarding the degree so that a property division can be considered fair and equitable between the parties.'" [Emphasis added.]

We conclude, therefore, that where an advanced degree is the end product of a concerted family effort, involving the mutual sacrifice, effort, and contribution of both spouses, there arises a "marital asset" subject to distribution, wherein the interest of the nonstudent spouse consists of an "equitable claim" regarding the degree.

C. *Valuation.*

Having found that a marital asset giving rise to an "equitable claim" subject to distribution exists where an advanced degree is the end product of a concerted family effort, we will now discuss the appropriate factors and considerations relative to an evaluation of such a claim for purposes of distributing property.

Woodworth, supra, 337 N.W.2d at 337, discussed two methods of compensating a nonstudent spouse for an interest in an advanced degree: (1) awarding a percentage share of the present value of the future earnings attributable to the degree, or (2) restitution. The first method focuses on the degree's present value by attempting to estimate what the person holding the degree is likely to make in a particular job market and subtracting therefrom what that person would probably have earned without the degree. According to *Woodworth*, the nonstudent spouse should then be awarded a percentage share of this value after considering (1) the length of the marriage after the degree was obtained, (2) the sources and extent of financial support given to the degreeholder during the years in school, and (3) the overall division of the parties' marital property. The second method is less involved, because it focuses on the cost of obtaining the degree.

In this case, plaintiff presented an expert who, using the present value method discussed in *Woodworth*, valued defendant's law degree at $230,000. Although defendant did not present his own expert, he took exception to several of the underlying assumptions employed by plaintiff's expert in his valuation of the degree.[3] Using essentially the same formula, but with modifications to the underlying assumptions, defendant presented his own valuations of $15,000, $46,000, and $79,500. The trial court ultimately valued defendant's law degree at $80,000, and then, after determining that the remainder of the property

---

[3]   These underlying assumptions concern annual salary figures, promotions, tax rates, and calculations designed to account for the fact that, over time, earnings are attributable more to the individual degree holder's personal skills and effort, rather than to the degree itself.

distribution resulted in plaintiff receiving a net amount of $5,000, but defendant having a deficit of $11,000, awarded plaintiff $32,000 as her share of the degree, noting that such an award would equalize the parties' respective distributive shares.

It is difficult to tell from the record how the trial court arrived at its initial $80,000 valuation figure. Further, while we certainly agree that plaintiff is entitled to be compensated for her unrewarded sacrifices, efforts, and contributions toward the attainment of defendant's law degree, our review of the record reveals that the trial court's ultimate award of $32,000 failed to account for several relevant and applicable considerations. Accordingly, we conclude that the appropriate remedy in this case is to remand to the trial court for revaluation of plaintiff's "equitable claim" in light of this opinion. On remand, we do not believe that the present value method discussed in *Woodworth*, and purportedly used by plaintiff's expert, is an appropriate means by which to evaluate plaintiff's equitable claim involving the degree. Such a method emphasizes the notion that a nonstudent spouse possesses some sort of pecuniary interest in the degree itself. We believe such a notion misconstrues the underlying premise upon which an award of compensation involving an advanced degree is based. As we have attempted to explain throughout this opinion, an award of compensation is premised upon equitable considerations, wherein the goal is to attempt to financially return to the nonstudent spouse what that spouse contributed toward attainment of the degree. Because such an award is not premised upon the notion that a nonstudent spouse possesses an interest in the degree itself, we do not believe the actual value of the degree is a relevant consideration. In this respect, we agree with the following observations made in Krause v. Krause, 441 N.W.2d 66, 72–73 (1989):

> [W]e believe that defendant is not entitled to any award specifically designed to compensate her for a portion of the 'value' of plaintiff's degree. Rather, we believe that the trial court may consider defendant's assistance to plaintiff in determining an appropriate award . . . .
>
> *   *   *   *   *   *
>
> [T]he trial court must keep in mind that it is compensating defendant for her assistance to plaintiff while he pursued his degree. Thus, the so-called 'value' of the degree or plaintiff's potential income to be earned from having the degree is irrelevant to the analysis. The trial court must focus solely on what is necessary to compensate defendant for the burdens on her or the sacrifices made by her so that plaintiff could pursue his degree.

Among the arguments advanced by defendant in support of his contention that an advanced degree should not be considered when dividing the marital estate are: (1) that marriage is not a commercial venture, (2) that the value of an advanced degree cannot be ascertained with reasonable certainty, and (3) that consideration of a degree as part of the property division would be akin to involuntary servitude. Inherent in each of these arguments, however, is the notion that a nonstudent spouse possesses some type of pecuniary interest in a degree or is entitled to be compensated for a portion of the so-called "value" of the degree, views we specifically reject. Again, we emphasize that the focus of an award involving an advanced degree is not to reimburse the nonstudent spouse for "loss of expectations" over what the degree might potentially have produced, but to reimburse that spouse for unrewarded sacrifices, efforts, and contributions toward attainment of the degree on the ground that it would be equitable to do so *in view of the fact* that that spouse will not be sharing in the fruits of the degree.

This Court, in *Krause*, supra, 441 N.W.2d at 71–72, quoted at length from a portion of an opinion by the Appellate Division of the Superior Court of New Jersey in *Mahoney v. Mahoney*, 442 A.2d 1062 (N.J. App. Div. 1982). Among the observations expressed therein, and with which we find ourselves in agreement, are:

> The termination of the marriage represents, if nothing else, the disappointment of expectations, financial and nonfinancial, which were hoped to be achieved by and during the continuation of the relationship. It does not, however, in our view, represent a commercial investment loss. Recompense for the disappointed expectations resulting from the failure of the marital entity to survive cannot, therefore, be made to the spouses on a strictly commercial basis . . . .

> If the plan fails by reason of the termination of the marriage, we do not regard the supporting spouse's consequent loss of expectations by itself as any more compensable or demanding of solicitude than the loss of expectations of any other spouse who, in the hope and anticipation of the endurance of the relationship and its commitments, has invested a portion of his or her life, youth, energy and labor in a failed marriage. [Krause, supra, 441 N.W.2d at 71–72]

In our view, any valuation of a nonstudent spouse's equitable claim involving an advanced degree involves a two-step analysis. First, an examination of the sacrifices, efforts, and contributions of the nonstudent spouse toward attainment of the degree. Second, given such sacrifices, efforts, and contributions, a determination of what remedy or means of compensation would most equitably compensate the nonstudent spouse under the facts of the case. In this regard, we agree with *Woodworth* that the length of the marriage after the degree was obtained, the sources and extent of financial support given to the degree holder during the years in school, and the overall division of the parties' marital property are all relevant considerations in valuing a nonstudent spouse's equitable claim involving an advanced degree upon divorce.

Where, for instance, the parties remain married for a substantial period of time after an advanced degree is obtained, fairness suggests that the value of an equitable claim would not be as great, inasmuch as the nonstudent spouse will already have been rewarded, in part, for efforts contributed by virtue of having already shared, in part, in the fruits of the degree. Similarly, where the extent of support or assistance provided by the nonstudent spouse, financial or otherwise, is not significant, or where such assistance comes primarily from outside sources for which the nonstudent spouse was not responsible or is not liable, fairness and equity would also suggest that the value of an equitable claim would not be as great.

Furthermore, an equitable remedy may be exemplified in different ways. For example, as this Court recognized in *Krause*, supra, 441 N.W.2d at 72: "[I]f [the nonstudent spouse] wishes to pursue [an] education or take other similar steps to improve . . . employability or income earning potential, it is reasonable and equitable to require the [degree-holding spouse] to assist . . . in those endeavors." Thus, in this type of situation, an award consistent with fairness and equity would be one which requires the degree-earning spouse to provide assistance, in the form of financial support, equivalent to that provided by the nonstudent spouse during the marriage.

Where, however, a nonstudent spouse does not wish to further pursue an education, then perhaps equity would best be served by an award reimbursing the spouse for the amount of financial assistance provided toward attainment of the degree, while also recognizing the other intangible, nonpecuniary sacrifices made and efforts expended.

Ultimately, however, the goal is to arrive at a remedy which, consistent with fairness and equity, will compensate the nonstudent spouse for unrewarded sacrifices, efforts, and contributions toward the degree. Thus, in reviewing such a claim on appeal, the ultimate inquiry is whether the remedy or decision of the trial court was a fair and equitable one under the facts of the case, given the sacrifices, efforts, and contributions of the nonstudent spouse toward the degree.

Affirmed in part and remanded for proceedings consistent with this opinion regarding the valuation of plaintiff's equitable claim involving defendant's law degree. We do not retain jurisdiction.

NOTES AND QUESTIONS

1. The court stops short of calling the law degree a marital asset in the full sense of property. Instead, the court invokes the law of restitution for unjust enrichment (see Chapter IV). In the law of restitution one can have an obligation to hand over property; the source of the obligation can but need not be a property interest. (Restitution for trespass in an underground cave

would be property-based, as would restitution for wrongful use of an egg-washing machine.) But restitution can use other benchmarks, and here it would seem to be the disappointed expectations of the non-degree spouse. The court asserts that the vindication of this expectation requires the return of the contributions she made toward the acquisition of the degree. The award should not include the return on this investment, according to the court, because marriage is not a commercial undertaking. Is that right? Might marriage be both a romantic life commitment and a commercial partnership? Generally, if one spouse is to be compensated for investments made in the other spouse's human capital, what is the nature of the interest or expectation? Is the investment like a loan? Or an equity-like share? See, e.g., Daniel D. Polsby & Martin Zelder, Risk-Adjusted Valuation of Professional Degrees in Divorce, 23 J. Legal Stud. 273 (1994); Lloyd Cohen, Marriage, Divorce, and Quasi Rents; Or, "I Gave Him the Best Years of My Life," 16 J. Legal Stud. 267 (1987).

2.   What role is fault playing in the court's decision? Generally speaking, property division is not used to punish either spouse for behavior during the marriage and the trend has been towards no-fault divorce. (Does no-fault divorce improve or weaken the bargaining position of the more vulnerable spouse?) The court here acknowledges a role for the husband's fault in the property division, which is not typical outside egregious cases. (Was this one?) In the law of restitution, courts tend to engage in more stringent disgorgement in the case of wrongdoing and even trace the product of wrongfully taken assets. If wrongdoing is relevant in *Postema v. Postema*, why wouldn't that furnish a basis for transferring gains to the wife?

3.   The general trend in family law in recent decades has been to prefer a one-time property division upon divorce and to discourage (or prohibit) awards of alimony. Part of the reason for this is to avoid any presumption that one spouse (traditionally the wife) is dependent on the other spouse (traditionally the husband) for support and is incapable of forging a new life on her own. Another part is to avoid the need for ongoing supervision by the court to adjudicate disputes over late or missing alimony payments, requests for modifications in alimony, and the like. The trial court here requires the husband to make monthly payments of $371.55 plus interest in order to pay off the amount owed to the wife for her efforts to support him while he obtained the law degree. The appeals court appears to contemplate a similar award on remand, given that the couple has insufficient assets to make a one-time lump sum settlement. Is this just alimony by another name? In a state that bars all or most alimony awards, can the degree-holding spouse argue that monthly payments are impermissible?

4.   What if the law degree were to be treated as property in some sense? Some states, most notably New York, experimented for a while with treating advanced degrees as marital property subject to equitable division on divorce. See O'Brien v. O'Brien, 489 N.E.2d 712 (N.Y. 1985). Although at one time eight states recognized professional degrees as marital property for at least some purposes, apparently no state currently does so. Even New York in 2016 enacted legislation removing enhanced earning capacity from the category of martial property subject to division, with enhanced earning

capacity to be considered as a factor in equitable division of other assets. N.Y. Dom. Rel. Law § 236(B)(5)(d)(7); Elena Karabatos & Eric A. Tepper, New York's Spousal Maintenance Guidelines, 51 Fam. L.Q. 51, 70 (2017). How does this differ from the approach taken in *Postema v. Postema*? Does the New York legislation do a better job of protecting the non-degree spouse's expectations?

5. How should the role of innate talent and other variables be treated? One older New York appellate court case decided that the increase in the extraordinary earning potential of an opera singer attributable in part to the domestic and voice coaching efforts of her husband was property subject to division. Elkus v. Elkus, 572 N.Y.S.2d 901 (App. Div. 1991). The court held that "the enhanced skills of an artist such as the plaintiff, albeit growing from an innate talent, which have enabled her to become an exceptional earner, may be valued as marital property subject to equitable distribution." 572 N.Y.S.2d at 904. Celebrity status is another form of human capital that can be taken into account in divorce as marital property subject to equitable distribution, and was so treated at one time in New York and New Jersey. See Piscopo v. Piscopo, 555 A.2d 1190, 1191 (N.J. Super. Ch. 1988). Do the unpredictabilities of talent, the ups and downs of life, and evolving career choices make it advisable for courts to retain continuing jurisdiction over property divisions, so that adjustments can be made? What if the husband in *Postema* had decided to ditch law and write poetry in a cabin in Montana? For an argument that today's celebrities are so dependent on the vicissitudes of newer technology like social media that courts' valuations have to be subject to adjustment over time, see Shanice Naidu, What's Love Got to Do with It? The Value of Celebrity Status in Divorce Proceedings, 33 Cardozo Arts & Entertainment L.J. 573 (2015).

6. Does treating the degree as property improperly commodify some aspect of the degree spouse or the nondegree spouse's contribution to the marriage? On commodification, see Chapter III. Is this an arena in which fears of commodification tend to work inequity on the nondegree spouse? Is it possible to avoid such inequity and provide for a "clean break" in divorce? See, e.g., Margaret Jane Radin, Reinterpreting Property 32–24 (1993); Joan Williams, Unbending Gender: Why Family and Work Conflict and What to Do About It 118 (2000).

7. What happens if a couple in a relationship that has not been solemnized by marriage splits up? This was a major issue for same-sex couples before the U.S. Supreme Court held that they are entitled as a matter of constitutional right to marry on the same basis as opposite-sex couples. See Obergefell v. Hodges, 576 U.S. 644 (2015). But marriage is frequently viewed as optional by same-sex and opposite-sex couples alike. When non-formalized relationships break up, courts cannot call upon the marital property statutes as a basis for a division of property. After long not recognizing contracts between unmarried cohabitants, many courts began to apply contract law or restitution at the breakup of such relationships. (The contract approach has been termed "palimony" since the landmark case of Marvin v. Marvin, 557 P.2d 106 (Cal. 1976) (in bank).) See "Palimony" Actions for Support Following Termination of Nonmarital Relationships, 21

A.L.R.6th 351. For discussion, see Ann Laquer Estin, Ordinary Cohabitation, 76 Notre Dame L. Rev. 1381 (2001); Milton C. Regan, Jr., Calibrated Commitment: The Legal Treatment of Marriage and Cohabitation, 76 Notre Dame L. Rev. 1435 (2001); see also Margaret F. Brinig & Steven L. Nock, Marry Me, Bill: Should Cohabitation Be The (Legal) Default Option?, 64 La. L. Rev. 403 (2004); Deborah Zalesne, The Contractual Family: The Role of the Market in Shaping Family Formations and Rights, 36 Cardozo L. Rev. 1027 (2015).

For discussion of how principles of restitution should apply to unmarried cohabitants, see Restatement Third, Restitution and Unjust Enrichment § 28(1) (Am. L. Inst. 2011). The *Restatement* provides for restitution of the value of services rendered but not their traceable product. See id. § 28 cmt. e. Why not, if (again) the expectations of the cohabitants was more like an equity investment than a loan?

8.   Property division can be agreed upon in an antenuptial agreement, but most couples do not take this route. What do you think most couples would agree on if presented ex ante with the question of how to divide assets on divorce? Is this the right question to be asking?

9.   Might cases like *Postema* reflect a fundamentally contractarian view of marriage itself? Many observers, feminist and nonfeminist, treat marriage as a contract, see, e.g., Katherine K. Baker, Comment, Contracting for Security: Paying Married Women What They've Earned, 55 U. Chi. L. Rev. 1193, 1206–13, 1220–27 (1988); Cohen, supra. But other models have their adherents. See Margaret F. Brinig, New Private Law and the Family, in The Oxford Handbook of the New Private Law 377 (Andrew S. Gold et al. eds., 2021) (arguing for covenant rather than contract as the basis for family law). The law traditionally viewed marriage as a status with fixed attributes. Somewhere between status and contract is the partnership model, in which equal sharing and some degree of a partnership "entity" is assumed. Many feminist reformers argue that divorce and marital property law should be brought closer to the sharing ideal implicit in the partnership model. See, e.g., Marjorie E. Kornhauser, Theory Versus Reality: The Partnership Model of Marriage in Family and Income Tax Law, 69 Temp. L. Rev. 1413 (1996); see also Pepper Schwartz, Peer Marriages (1994) (documenting ideal of "peer marriage"—in which resources and responsibilities are shared—and deviation of practice from such ideal); cf. Martha Fineman, The Illusion of Equality: The Rhetoric and Reality of Divorce Reform 2–6, 29 (1991) (arguing that family patterns are currently so unequal that women are entitled to more than an equal share); Ira Mark Ellman, "Contract Thinking" Was *Marvin*'s Fatal Flaw, 76 Notre Dame L. Rev. 1365 (2001) (attacking the contractarian basis of *Marvin*). Others find the notion of an entity separate from the individuals in the marriage to be problematic, with its overtones of the common-law merger of the wife's personality into the "unity" of the marriage. As we noted earlier, entity law, such as that governing partnerships, has become somewhat more contractarian and customizable in recent years. What is most appropriate for marriage? To what extent does marriage rely on informal third-party enforcement (for example, through gossip and the like)? Should it? Depending on your answer to this question,

should marriage be subject to the *numerus clausus* with respect to some of its features? See Elizabeth F. Emens, Regulatory Fictions: On Marriage and Countermarriage, 99 Cal. L. Rev. 235 (2011) (examining other conceptions of marriage and possible regulatory responses).

CHAPTER VI

ENTITY PROPERTY

The forms of property considered in Chapter V are relatively few in number. To revert to a distinction introduced in Chapter I, they largely reflect an exclusion strategy for dealing with resources, rather than a governance strategy. That is, each of the traditional forms like the fee simple, the life estate, and even the tenancy in common operates on the assumption that, at any given point in time, one person or a small number of persons will function as the "gatekeeper" of the resource. The exclusion strategy, however, is too crude to serve as an effective basis for managing the resources used by complex entities like high-rise apartment buildings, business firms, and pension plans. In order to provide for more effective management of resources in these complicated settings, the law has developed certain devices that effectively allow owners to switch to a governance strategy for the management of resources. These devices can be termed "entity property."

The key attribute of these entity property devices is that they permit the management of resources to be separated from their use and enjoyment. This separation allows the managerial or governance function to be concentrated in the hands of specialists, while the use and enjoyment is distributed over a larger and more diffuse group of individuals. Indeed, the principal difference between the traditional legal forms studied in Chapter V, and the entity property devices considered in this Chapter, is that the traditional forms do not permit specialization in the day-to-day management of assets (at least formally), whereas the property devices considered here do permit such specialization. This specialization of functions, more than anything else, explains why entity property devices are so popular.

Although devices for separating management from use and enjoyment of resources can be categorized in different ways, we divide them here broadly in functional terms, based on the nature of the interests of those who use and enjoy the resources. Thus, we distinguish between devices whose function is to govern multiple *possessory* interests in the use of a single complex of assets, and devices whose function is to govern multiple *nonpossessory* interests in the enjoyment of assets (typically interests in the nature of a passive investment). The principal devices in the former category include leases, cooperatives, and condominiums. Each of these devices can be used to separate management of a complex of assets from regular actual use of some portion of the assets by various persons or family units. The principal devices in the latter category include trusts, corporations, nonprofit entities, and partnerships. Here, the organizational form is designed primarily to separate management of a complex of assets from the enjoyment of financial or other intangible returns for various persons or family units.

Another broad distinction among these devices is legal rather than functional. Specifically, one can distinguish between devices that achieve a functional specialization between management and beneficial use of resources at the level of property rights, and devices that achieve this separation at the level of entity law proper. In the former category belong the lease, the condominium, and the trust, which all achieve this division of labor at the level of property rights. With leases, for example, both the lessor and the lessee are regarded as having a type of property right (the leasehold estate and the reversion, respectively), and the nature of these different property rights allows them to specialize their functions. Lease law creates an "entity" for managing property in a functional sense. Other devices that we briefly consider here, including the cooperative, the corporation, and the partnership, achieve a similar division of labor through provisions of entity law—by creating an actual separate legal entity. With corporations, for example, the corporation is regarded as a legal persona that owns property in its own name, much the way individual persons own property, and the specialization of functions among shareholders, corporate managers, and corporate employees is achieved through the law of corporations, not through property law. This explains why we spend little time here on corporations and partnerships—the legal rules for these entities are covered in courses on business associations. But it is important to keep in mind that, functionally speaking, corporations and partnerships can often serve as substitutes for leases or trusts, so it is worth setting forth the full menu of options in managing complex property rights through entity property.

A. SEPARATING MANAGEMENT AND POSSESSORY RIGHTS

We begin with a series of arrangements in which multiple persons have distinct possessory interests in a complex of assets. A preliminary question is why people would ever want to enter into such arrangements. An important part of the answer seems to be that they want to take advantage of the specialized skills of managers of assets, and in particular to concentrate managerial control over common areas or shared facilities that present potential collective action problems or commons tragedies. A key difference among these mechanisms concerns the participants' ability or willingness to commit their own assets to the enterprise. Leases are attractive to those who cannot or do not want to invest their own resources in the larger enterprise; condominiums and cooperatives are more attractive to those who do want to make such an investment (either for tax or other reasons).

1. LEASES

Leases, also known as leaseholds, tenancies, the term of years, or landlord-tenant interests—the terms are basically interchangeable—are probably the second-most commonly encountered form of property after full ownership (the fee simple in the case of land). An astonishing array of things are leased, including both real and personal property. On the real property side, we find leases of agricultural land, commercial office buildings, shopping centers, and of course apartments and houses. On the personal property side, there are leases of heavy construction equipment, computers, autos, tools, and even airplanes. The percentage of real property interests that are leased has held constant or has grown slightly in recent years. The percentage of personal property interests (such as autos, rail cars, and shipping containers) that are leased has exploded in recent decades.

The law that governs leases is very old, having its roots in Roman law. In civil law countries like France that trace their lineage more directly to Roman law, leases are regarded as a specialized form of contract (*contrat de louage*). At common law in England, leases of land gradually emerged as a form of property. Initially, leases were not recognized as a type of freehold interest, and the tenant was not regarded as being seised of the land. Consequently, leases were categorized as a type of personal property ("chattels real"), and passed upon death by rules for personal property. But by the thirteenth century, the common-law courts granted protection to the holder of a term of years. See A.W.B. Simpson, A History of The Land Law 74–75 (2d ed. 1986). Gradually— and with much confusion along the way—leases were assimilated to the system of estates in land created for freehold interests, and were given full protection as an interest in land. Once this assimilation occurred, leases could be thought of as another form of property, like the fee simple, life estate, and defeasible fees we studied in the last chapter.

Whether we categorize leases as a species of contract or a form of property, it is clear that leases have always been regarded as a distinct type of interest in the use and control of things. A key reason for this is that both the lessor and the lessee play an active role in the governance of the underlying asset. During the term of the lease, the lessee is in possession of the asset and as such exercises primary control over it. But the lessor also has a keen interest how the lessee exercises this control. In part this is because the lessor expects to get the asset back once the lease expires; leases always have a duration less than the full useful life of the asset, and the lessor will want to constrain or at least monitor the behavior of the lessee to make sure the asset still has value when it comes back. Lessees also pay the lessor for the use of the asset, nearly always in the form of periodic payments called rent. The lessor will be concerned to make sure the lessee is in a position to continue to make these payments in a timely fashion.

In terms of the evolutionary struggle for survival among different property forms, leases are clearly one of the big winners. Generalizing broadly, the three forms of legal ownership of greatest continuing importance are the fee simple (and full ownership), the lease, and the trust. (As noted earlier, ownership of property by corporations and partnerships, which is also very common, is not regarded as a separate form of property; thus, corporate or partnership property is nearly always held by these entities as a fee simple or lease.) There appear to be three functional aspects of leases that account for the lease's enduring appeal. See generally Thomas W. Merrill, The Economics of Leasing, 12 J. Legal Analysis 1 (2020).

First, leases are a type of de facto financing device. One can think of a lease as an arrangement in which the owner of an asset lends possession to another, in return for periodic payments of money called rent. Indeed, it appears that the original function of leases was to avoid the medieval Church's prohibition of usury: "A capitalist would give to an embarrassed landowner a sum of money down; in return he took a term of years sufficiently long to enable him to recover the capital, together with his profits, out of the revenues of the land." Theodore F.T. Plucknett, A Concise History of the Common Law 572–73 (5th ed. 1956). The close relationship between leases and loans is revealed today by the common practices of entering into a lease with an option to purchase at the end of the lease term (universally used with automobile leases, for example). Given that leases are a type of financing device, it is clear that the rent charge includes an interest component, reflecting the time value of money and the anticipated rate of inflation.

Once we see that leases are a type of financing device, we can understand part of their appeal. Persons who have not accumulated much in the way of assets and/or have poor credit will often prefer to lease assets rather than purchase them. This allows them to acquire shelter to live in, land to farm, or space in which to operate a business like a restaurant, without having to commit their scarce resources to purchasing real estate. Instead, the lessee can concentrate her limited resources on acquiring other inputs—like furniture for the apartment, or equipment to operate the farm, or tables and chairs for the restaurant. If the lessee prospers and accumulates more capital or develops a stronger credit rating, the lessee may eventually decide to own rather than lease the real estate in question. Or maybe not: Leases allow persons to "leverage" their limited resources in roughly the same way that borrowing allows persons to leverage limited resources, and so for any given level of resources some persons will prefer to continue to keep on leasing in order to leverage into larger apartments, bigger farms, more restaurants, etc. than they started out with.

Second, and related to the first point, leases operate as a risk-spreading device. Consider this first from the lessee's perspective. Suppose you move to a new city to take up a new job. You are not sure you will like either the city or the job. You have accumulated enough in savings to purchase a home or apartment in the new city, but you are reluctant to tie up most of your funds in the purchase of one asset, given that you may decide to move elsewhere if things don't work out. Renting is a way of minimizing the risks of investing most of your savings in an asset that you may want to unload in fairly short order (and an asset whose risk may be tightly correlated with one's employment risk). The ability to minimize the risk from a new venture has been a powerful reason for leasing rather than owning over a wide range of activities for as long as leases have been around.

From the lessor's perspective, leasing can be a risk-spreading device as well. If the lessee defaults on the rental obligation, it is usually easier to retake possession of the property than it is to foreclose on a mortgage and retake property held as security for a loan (see Chapter VII). Even greater risk spreading can be achieved if the lessor leases to multiple lessees. Some lessees may fail and default on payment of rent, but it is unlikely that all or even most will, and so the lessor can minimize the risk of nonpayment by spreading this risk over multiple lessees. The built-in security interest provided by leases and the ability to spread risks among multiple leaseholders have long made leasing of property a popular form of investment.

Third, and relevant to the larger themes of this Chapter, leases operate as a mechanism for integrating and managing complexes of assets, and in that sense function as a kind of entity property. Moreover, lessors are often actual legal entities (corporations, partnerships, and the like). In any event, leasing allows owners of resources to switch from a simple exclusion strategy to a governance strategy in overcoming various coordination problems. Not all leases fit this description. Some leases, like a lease of agricultural land, may function primarily as financing and/or risk-spreading devices. Here, simple possession is transferred from the lessor to the lessee, and the property continues to be managed using an exclusion strategy—with the lessee now exercising the right to exclude. Not surprisingly, agricultural leases are frequently oral or, if in writing, are very short. See Douglas W. Allen & Dean Lueck, The "Back Forty" on a Handshake: Specific Assets, Reputation, and the Structure of Farmland Contracts, 8 J.L. Econ. & Org. 366 (1992). But often leasing is used for highly complicated complexes of assets, like high-rise apartment buildings, office buildings, and shopping centers. Leases allow these complexes of assets to be managed using a governance strategy, characterized by a specialization of functions. One party (the lessor) specializes in constructing, maintaining, insuring, and coordinating assets common to the entire complex, while the other parties (the lessees) specialize in possession and operation of discrete units within the larger complex. In a shopping center, for example, the lessor can build, maintain, and insure the parking lot, the utility systems, the common walkways, and can even provide marketing for the complex as a whole.

The lessees are thereby freed up to concentrate on the design, construction, and maintenance of their individual retail spaces. Both the common areas and the individual retail spaces are probably managed more effectively and with lower transaction costs because of this specialization of functions. A similar story can be told about apartment complexes and office buildings.

Although we usually think of leases in the context of interests in land, leasing is also very commonly used to acquire personal property like airplanes and automobiles. To some extent, the use of leasing in these contexts is driven by tax considerations, such as the ease of treating auto lease payments as a business expense. But we can also see the general economic rationale for leasing at work here too. Auto leasing, for example, is clearly a financing device, and functions as a substitute for purchasing an auto with a loan secured by a lien on the auto. Indeed, many banks and financing companies offer both auto leases and loans to consumers. Can you see how automobile leases might also function as risk-spreading devices and as a device allowing specialization of functions between automobile dealers and consumers?

One problem that has long vexed lease law in the real property context is that it does not differentiate between leases in terms of the underlying functional reasons the parties have for entering into a lease. Instead, one body of legal doctrine has been developed that must accommodate both simple leases used as financing or risk-spreading devices, and complex leases used to provide governance structures for complicated enterprises serving multiple persons. To put the matter more concretely, the same law generally applies to long-term (or routinely renewed) leases of agricultural land and to short-term rentals of furnished apartments. Much of the tension in lease law is attributable to this one-size-fits-all aspect. Lease law was formed during an era when leases were simple and were largely used as financing and risk-spreading devices, with the agricultural lease being the central example. Over time, the cases that came before the courts tended increasingly to involve complicated problems of governance, the multi-unit residential apartment building being the central example. The law has responded by moving at least part way from a "property" or exclusion model of leases to a "contract" or governance model, while continuing to strain to encompass both types of situations within a single body of doctrine.

Leases of personal property are governed in every state by Article 2A of the Uniform Commercial Code, originally adopted in 1987. Many of the provisions of Article 2A were borrowed from Article 2 of the Code, which governs sales of personal property. So the law that applies to the growing field of personal property leasing has a relatively contractual flavor and is governed by a statute; in contrast, real property leases are property-like in certain dimensions and are governed by common law principles. It is nevertheless likely that the common law of real property leasing will be invoked to fill certain gaps in Article 2A as they emerge, and that certain features of Article 2A may influence the continuing development of the common law of real property leasing. The coverage of leasing here is limited to real property leases.

a. LEASE TYPES

The common law generally recognized four types of leases: the term of years, the periodic tenancy, the tenancy at will, and the tenancy at sufferance.

Term of Years. This refers to a lease that has a fixed time at which it terminates or ends. Usually this is for one or more years (hence the name), but it can be for a shorter time, like six months or even one day. Some jurisdictions impose an outer limit on the length of a term of years, like 99 years; but others do not, and some leases have been reported to exist that last for as long as 9000 years. Although the original Statute of Frauds (see Chapter VIII) required that leases longer than three years had to be in writing in order to be enforceable, under the version of the Statute in effect in most states, leases for any term longer than one year must be in writing.

The unique legal aspect of the term of years is that neither the lessor nor the lessee is required to give notice to the other before terminating the relationship. On the stated day of termination, the lease simply ends. Usually, of course, the parties will communicate about what will happen upon termination, which in practice means they may negotiate a new term of years (or perhaps a periodic lease) to commence on the termination date. But this is not required. The lessee can just walk away, or the lessor can just reclaim possession, on the designated day of termination.

Periodic Tenancy. This refers to a lease that automatically rolls over for a stated period of time, usually a year or a month. Thus, a lease from year to year is a periodic tenancy that automatically rolls over one year at a time, and a lease from month to month is a periodic tenancy that automatically rolls over one month at a time.

In contrast to the term of years, a periodic tenancy requires that each of the parties give notice to the other if they desire to terminate the lease. Usually, the notice period is the same as the period of recurring rollover. In a lease from month to month, the required notice is one month. In a lease from year to year, the required notice at common law was six months, although this has been modified by statute in many jurisdictions, especially for residential tenancies, with most statutes prescribing one month's notice for termination of a tenancy from year to year.

Tenancy at Will. This refers to a tenancy that lasts only so long as both parties wish it to continue. Either party can terminate at any time for any reason.

At common law, no notice was required for termination of a tenancy at will. This has been changed in many jurisdictions to require notice equal to the period of time at which rent payments are made.

Tenancy at Sufferance. This is sometimes not regarded as a true tenancy and refers to the situation that exists when an individual, who was once in rightful possession of property, holds over after this right has ended. A tenant at sufferance differs from a trespasser in that the tenant's original entry was not wrongful. In many jurisdictions, this difference may limit the lessor's ability to use self-help to evict the tenant at sufferance. See Berg v. Wiley, excerpted in Chapter IV. Otherwise, however, the lessor is free to evict the tenant at sufferance using forcible entry and detainer statutes, or by bringing an action in ejectment.

Suppose a tenant at sufferance mails the lessor a check equal to the rent specified under an expired lease, and the lessor cashes the check? Some courts have construed the lessee's proffer of the check and the lessor's cashing it to be an implied contract to create a new lease (typically a periodic tenancy). See, e.g., Crechale & Polles, Inc. v. Smith, 295 So.2d 275 (Miss. 1974).

PROBLEMS

1.   On January 23, L agrees to rent to T a furnished apartment until February 23 of the same year. What type of tenancy is created?

2.   L agrees to lease a farm to T from year to year, starting on March 1. On November 1, L notifies T that the lease will terminate the following March 1. Under the common law, what type of tenancy does T have come March 1?

3.   T is a defense contractor. War breaks out, and T needs additional warehouse space. L agrees to lease a warehouse to T "for the duration of the war." What type of tenancy is created?

NOTE AND QUESTIONS

The limited menu of lease types (term of years, periodic, at will, at sufferance) is another example of the *numerus clausus* principle, considered in Chapter V. Why do you suppose the common law recognized only four types of leases? The leasehold interest is primarily of significance to two parties—the lessor and the lessee—and they are permitted great flexibility in negotiating various terms and conditions in the written lease that typically governs their relationship (and must govern their relationship for leases of more than one year under the Statute of Frauds). Can one explain the standardization of lease types in terms of third-party interests in acquiring information about lease arrangements? Is it perhaps significant that most of the standardization serves to differentiate among leases that are short-term and often are not governed by a written lease agreement?

b.   THE INDEPENDENT COVENANTS MODEL

It took some time before leases came to be used as an entity property device for managing large real estate complexes. Early leases functioned almost entirely as financing and risk-spreading devices. In that context, the courts developed certain assumptions about the nature of the reciprocal obligations between lessor and lessee. A central assumption was that the lease was at heart a conveyance of a possessory interest in property. The possessory right—including the right to exclude others from the asset—was transferred from the lessor to the lessee for the prescribed term of the lease. This assumption, in turn, led to certain critical conclusions about the allocation of risk of casualty losses as between the lessor and the lessee during the lease term.

Paradine v. Jane

King's Bench, 1647.
Aleyn 27, 82 Eng. Rep. 897.

In debt the plaintiff declares upon a lease for years rendering rent at the four usual feasts; and for rent behind for three years, ending at the Feast of the Annunciation, 21 Car. brings his action; the defendant pleads, that a certain German prince, by name Prince Rupert, an alien born, enemy to the King and kingdom, had invaded the realm with an hostile army of men; and with the same force did enter upon the defendant's possession, and him expelled, and held out of possession from the 19 of July 18 Car. till the Feast of the Annunciation, 21 Car. whereby he could not take the profits; whereupon the plaintiff demurred, and the plea was resolved insufficient * * *

It was resolved, that the matter of the plea was insufficient; for though the whole army had been alien enemies, yet he ought to pay his rent. And this difference was taken, that where the law creates a duty or charge, and the party is disabled to perform it without any default in him, and hath no remedy over, there the law will excuse him. * * * Now the rent is a duty created by the parties upon the reservation, and had there been a covenant to pay it, there had been no questions but the lessee must have made it good, notwithstanding the interruption by enemies, for the law would not protect him beyond his own agreement, no more than in the case of reparations; this reservation then being a covenant in law, and whereupon an action of covenant hath been maintained (as Roll said) it is all one as if there had been an actual covenant. Another reason was added, that as the lessee is to have the advantage of casual profits, so he must run the hazard of casual losses, and not lay the whole burthen of them upon his lessor; and *Dyer* 56.6 was cited for this purpose, that though the land be surrounded, or gained by the sea, or made barren by wildfire, yet the lessor shall have his whole rent: and judgment was given for the plaintiff.

Figure 6-1
Prince Rupert

ILLVSTRISSIMVS PRINCEPS ROBBERTVS, COMES PALATINVS RHENI, EQVES
ORDINIS S° GEORGII HIPPARCHVS SVÆ MAI:⁵ MAGNÆ BRITANNIÆ ETC.

Source: National Archives of Canada.

NOTES AND QUESTIONS

1. *Paradine v. Jane* is an extreme example of the artificiality of common-law pleading. Prince Rupert, described in the case report as "enemy to the King," was in fact King Charles I's nephew and best general. The "alien armies" were the armies for the King, composed almost exclusively of native Englishmen. The apparent explanation for this deliberate fabrication is that England was at Civil War. The courts were under control of Parliament, yet the common-law lawyers "had not yet imagined a basis for traditional common-law rights outside the old framework of royal authority." Hence the false pleading, in which the King's forces are described as "alien armies" and "enemies of the King," meaning, in reality, enemies of Parliament. See Charles M. Haar & Lance Liebman, Property and Law 270–71 (2d ed. 1985).

2. *Paradine* reflects the view that a lease is a conveyance of an interest in land, but it also reflects the view that a lease is a contract—a bundle of covenants or promises, some running from lessor to lessee, others from lessee to lessor. The most important covenant by the lessor was (and is) the covenant of quiet enjoyment, meaning a promise not to interfere with the lessee's possession during the term of the lease. This covenant is critical to

the very conception of a lease—the transfer of possession of property from lessor to lessee—and hence is implied as a matter of law in all leases. The most important covenant by the lessee was (and is) the covenant to pay rent. As *Paradine* suggests, this too was regarded as sufficiently important that it is implied as a matter of law in all leases. Evidently the lease in *Paradine* specified the amount of rent, but did not expressly include a promise by the lessee to pay rent. But the court holds that such a covenant is implied as a matter of law in all leases.

3.   *Paradine* is a leading example of what has been called the independent covenants model of the lessor-lessee relationship. (With one exception: Under this model, failure by the lessor to afford quiet possession *does* excuse the tenant from paying rent.) The assumption of independent covenants provides that all covenants must be performed without regard to whether other covenants have been or can be performed. *Paradine* specifically holds that when Prince Rupert made it impossible for the lessee to plant and harvest crops and hence to enjoy the benefit of the lease, this did not excuse the lessee from performing the covenant to pay rent. Generalizing more broadly, even if the lessor fails to perform a covenant, such as a covenant to repair the premises, the lessee must continue to perform the covenant to pay rent. Alternatively, even if the lessee fails to perform the covenant to pay rent, the lessor must continue to perform the covenant of quiet possession. The remedy in all these events, under the independent covenants model, is for the aggrieved party to sue for damages for breach of covenant. Thus, if the lessor fails to perform a covenant to repair, the lessee must continue to pay rent but may sue the lessor for breach of the covenant to repair. Or if the lessee fails to pay rent, the lessor must continue to perform the covenant of quiet possession, i.e., allow the lessee to stay in possession, but may sue the lessee for breach of the covenant to pay rent.

4.   *Paradine* is also important because of its recognition of the allocation of risk under a lease. The court notes that windfall gains, such as high profits earned from high crop prices, would be captured by the lessee. By parity of reasoning, wipeout losses, such as the seizure of the farm by Prince Rupert, should also be borne by the lessee. The general principle recognized by the court—that the lessee is the "residual claimant" with respect to economic gains and losses associated with the property during the term of the lease—continues to be sound. The typical lease for a fixed rent converts the lessor into a kind of bondholder who earns a fixed periodic payment from the property. The lessee performs a role akin to a shareholder, whose return from the property fluctuates with the vicissitudes of the weather and market conditions—and with the effort and skill the lessee puts into it. See Merrill, Economics of Leasing, supra, 12 J. Legal Analysis at 20–24. This allocation of risk is important to bear in mind and will come up later when we consider certain specific controversies about how gains and losses should be divided under leases.

5.   *Paradine*'s specific application of this understanding of the allocation of risk is that casualty losses associated with the rented property (such as destruction of the premises by fire, earthquake, flood, or war) must

be borne by the lessee during the term of the lease, not the lessor. In other words, when the property that is the subject of the lease is destroyed or damaged, the lessee's obligation to pay rent continues uninterrupted. Over time, this specific application of the allocation of risk has gradually been changed by legislation. For example, if the lease involves residential housing, and the house or apartment burns down, this is deemed today in all jurisdictions to be an event that terminates the lease and hence discharges the lessee from any further obligation to pay rent. The rules with respect to commercial property remain closer to the original understanding of *Paradine*, but have also been modified in various ways in many jurisdictions. See 1 Milton R. Friedman, Friedman on Leases § 9:2 (Andrew R. Berman, ed. & rev., 6th ed. 2017). In a handful of jurisdictions, courts have held that the contract doctrines of impossibility and frustration of purpose may apply to relieve a lessee of further obligations when the premises are destroyed. See, e.g., Albert M. Greenfield & Co. v. Kolea, 380 A.2d 758 (Pa. 1977). Whatever rule is followed, the allocation of risk of casualty loss is generally understood to be a default rule subject to modification by the parties in the lease. Disputes over casualty losses today tend to turn on how to interpret these lease clauses. After Hurricane Katrina, for example, a lessor attempted to terminate all leases in an apartment complex pursuant to a clause that gave the lessor the right to terminate or repair particular apartments or buildings damaged by fire or other events. The court held that this clause did not authorize the termination of leases in buildings that had not been significantly damaged. Horne v. TGM Associates, L.P., 56 So.3d 615, 623–24 (Ala. 2010).

Some Implications of the Independent Covenants Model

The independent covenants model reflected in *Paradine v Jane* had a number of implications for lease law. One was that the lessor made no implicit promises about the fitness of the property for the lessee's purposes. By acquiring possession of the property for the lease term, the lessee assumed all the risks associated with being in possession of an interest in land generally. This was understood to be a default rule: The lessee was free to bargain for a warranty of quality, and if the lessor agreed, this would be enforced by the court. But absent a specific lease clause stipulating that the land would be fit for the lessee's intended purpose, the watchword was *caveat lessee*—let the lessee beware.

A particularly vivid illustration was provided by *Sutton v. Temple*, 12 M & W. 52, 152 Eng. Rep. 1108 (Exch. 1843). Thomas Temple signed a lease to take 24 acres of pasture land from Anne Sutton. After putting his cattle on the pasture, a number of them died. An autopsy by a veterinarian revealed that the animals had been poisoned by eating discarded paint chips concealed in manure that had been spread on the land (presumably by Sutton or a prior lessee) as fertilizer. Temple had little choice but to pasture his cattle elsewhere. But the court refused to excuse him from paying the stipulated rent. It took the rule to be "that if a person contract for the use and occupation of land for a specified time, and at a specified rent, he is bound by that bargain, even though he took it for a particular purpose, and that purpose be not attained."

The rule of caveat lessee was in some tension with the law of contracts as it emerged with respect to sales of personal property, where an implied warranty of fitness for intended purpose came to be recognized. The tension came to a head in cases involving short term rentals of furnished vacation cottages. Here the lease included both reality (the land and the structure) and personal property (the furnishings). Courts in both England and the United States recognized an implied warranty of habitability in such cases. See Smith v. Marrable, 152 Eng. Rep. 693 (Exch. 1843); Ingalls v. Hobbs, 31 N.E. 286 (Mass. 1892). One can imagine how the law might have gradually evolved, with the furnished cottage exception gradually expanding to encompass situations like rentals of apartments in multi-unit urban apartment complexes. But the law did not evolve in this way. Instead, courts tended to continue to assume that rentals of unfurnished apartments were governed by the rule of caveat lessee. Then, in the late 1960s and early 1970s, a sudden avulsion occurred, as one jurisdiction after another recognized an implied warranty of habitability in apartment rentals. See Javins v. First National Realty, infra.

Paradine implies that if the lessee is deprived of possession by some action of the lessor, as opposed to a third party like Prince Rupert, the lessee is off the hook for any further payment of rent to the lessor. In effect, at least one lease covenant—the covenant to pay rent—was regarded as dependent on the lessor's compliance with the covenant of quiet possession. Courts tended to be quite strict about this. Thus, in *Smith v. McEnany*, 48 N.E. 781 (Mass. 1897), the lessor leased a lot with a shed on it to the lessee. Later, the lessor put up a brick wall on an adjoining property, which intruded by one or two feet into the lot behind the shed. The court held that the intrusion was a partial eviction of the lessee that justified the lessee in stopping all rent payments until the intrusion was fixed. Writing for the court, Justice Holmes wrote: "The land is hired as one whole. If by his own fault the landlord withdraws a part of it he cannot recover either on the lease or outside of it for the occupation of the residue."

The most common situation when the covenant of quiet possession came into play was when it turned out that some third party other than the lessor owned the land, and the third party brought an action to evict the lessee. This was universally regarded as a breach of the lessor's covenant of quiet possession that justified the lessee in terminating any further payments of rent. But what if the parties concluded a lease, and on the appointed starting day a holdover tenant was still in possession of the land? Should the holdover tenant be regarded like Prince Rupert— making it the lessee's responsibility to evict the holdover—or should the holdover be regarded like a third party claiming superior title—making it the lessor's responsibility to evict the holdover? Here the authorities were (and still are) divided. Under the so-called "English rule," the lessor is responsible for clearing out any squatters or holdover tenants at the beginning of the lease. Coe v. Clay, 130 Eng. Rep. 1131 (C.P. 1829). Under what has been called the "American rule" (although it is not followed by all American states), the lessee is responsible for getting rid of any squatters or holdover tenants. Hannan v. Dusch, 153 S.E. 824 (Va. 1930). Either way, the parties are free to modify the rule by drafting an appropriate lease clause that allocates responsibility differently.

Whether the lessor has a duty to deliver possession at the onset of the lease illustrates the difficulty of prescribing a single rule that fits all situations. Assuming both parties are fully informed about the relevant variables, the rule they would adopt would plausibly be the one that assigns the duty to the party who is best able to detect the presence of squatters or holdover tenants and to bring an action to have them evicted before the lease starts. In the context of urban apartments, that party is almost surely the lessor. The lessor either lives on the property or has a manager on the property, is familiar with the leasing history, and has some familiarity with eviction procedures (see Chapter IV on forcible entry and detainer (FED) statutes). But in other circumstances, the lessee may be the "cheaper evicter." Consider, for example, a lease of rural agricultural land where the lessee is likely to be a local resident and the lessor is often an absentee owner. In these circumstances, the lessee may be in a better position to monitor for squatters and holdover tenants, and to take action to evict them. Since it is not clear that there is a right answer about the correct default rule that fits all circumstances, it is perhaps not surprising that there is a division of authority as to which rule is better. Perhaps the ideal solution would be to have different default rules for different types of leases. But this is probably best accomplished by legislation, and for whatever reasons, legislatures have not been interested in reform at this level of detail.

c.   EXTENSIONS OF THE INDEPENDENT COVENANTS MODEL

As time marched on, a variety of exceptions and qualifications to the pure independent covenants model emerged. One of the most important was the development of *forfeiture clauses*. These were clauses in leases, invariably insisted upon by lessors, providing that upon the lessee's violation of enumerated covenants in the lease—most crucially the covenant to pay rent—the lessee's interest in the lease would be immediately forfeited.

Forfeiture clauses, which courts have generally upheld, in effect convert the specified tenant covenants covered by the forfeiture clause from independent covenants into dependent covenants. For example, under the model of independent covenants, the lessor's covenant of quiet possession was not extinguished by the tenant's failure to pay rent. The lessor's remedy was periodically to sue the tenant for damages equal to the unpaid rent. With the addition of an enforceable forfeiture clause, the situation is radically changed. Now, the lessee's failure to pay rent means that the lessee's interest in the leasehold estate is subject to forfeiture, in effect releasing the lessor from the covenant of quiet enjoyment. If the lessee remains in possession after forfeiture, he becomes a tenant at sufferance, liable to an action for eviction. If the lessee abandons after forfeiture, the lessor can immediately reenter and retake possession of the premises.

Forfeiture clauses had the effect of tilting the original independent covenants model in favor of the lessor, in that they transformed the lease into a bundle of covenants that were independent insofar as the promises ran to the lessee, and dependent insofar as the promises ran to the lessor. But the legal system responded by developing new doctrines that provided some relief for lessees. We consider here two such doctrines: constructive eviction and surrender.

Blackett v. Olanoff

Supreme Judicial Court of Massachusetts, 1977.
358 N.E.2d 817.

■ WILKINS, JUSTICE. The defendant in each of these consolidated actions for rent successfully raised constructive eviction as a defense against the landlords' claim. The judge found that the tenants were "very substantially deprived" of quiet enjoyment of their leased premises "*for a substantial time*" (emphasis original). He ruled that the tenants' implied warranty of quiet enjoyment was violated by late evening and early morning music and disturbances coming from nearby premises which the landlords leased to others for use as a bar or cocktail lounge (lounge). The judge further found that, although the landlords did not intend to create the conditions, the landlords "had it within their control to correct the conditions which ... amounted to a constructive eviction of each (tenant)." He also found that the landlords promised each tenant to correct the situation, that the landlords made some attempt to remedy the problem, but they were unsuccessful, and that each tenant vacated his apartment within a reasonable time. Judgment was entered for each tenant; the landlords appealed; and we transferred the appeals here. We affirm the judgments.

The landlords argue that they did not violate the tenants' implied covenant of quiet enjoyment because they are not chargeable with the noise from the lounge. The landlords do not challenge the judge's conclusion that the noise emanating from the lounge was sufficient to constitute a constructive eviction, if that noise could be attributed to the landlords.[3] Nor do the landlords seriously argue that a constructive

---

[3]   There was evidence that the lounge had amplified music (electric musical instruments and singing, at various times) which started at 9:30 P.M. and continued until 1:30 A.M. or 2 A.M., generally on Tuesdays through Sundays. The music could be heard through the granite walls of the residential tenants' building, and was described variously as unbelievably loud,

eviction could not be found as matter of law because the lounge was not on the same premises as the tenants' apartments. See 1 American Law of Property § 3.51 at 281 (A. J. Casner ed. 1952). The landlords' principal contention, based on the denial of certain requests for rulings, is that they are not responsible for the conduct of the proprietors, employees, and patrons of the lounge.

Our opinions concerning a constructive eviction by an alleged breach of an implied covenant of quiet enjoyment sometimes have stated that the landlord must perform some act with the intent of depriving the tenant of the enjoyment and occupation of the whole or part of the leased premises. See Katz v. Duffy, 158 N.E. 264 (Mass. 1927), and cases cited. There are occasions, however, where a landlord has not intended to violate a tenant's rights, but there was nevertheless a breach of the landlord's covenant of quiet enjoyment which flowed as the natural and probable consequence of what the landlord did, what he failed to do, or what he permitted to be done. Charles E. Burt, Inc. v. Seven Grand Corp., 163 N.E.2d 4, 6 (Mass. 1959) (failure to supply light, heat, power, and elevator services). Westland Housing Corp. v. Scott, 44 N.E.2d 959, 962–63 (Mass. 1942) (intrusions of smoke and soot over a substantial period of time due to a defective boiler). Shindler v. Milden, 184 N.E. 673, 673–74 (Mass. 1933) (failure to install necessary heating system, as agreed). Case v. Minot, 33 N.E. 700, 701 (Mass. 1893) (landlord authorizing another lessee to obstruct the tenant's light and air, necessary for the beneficial enjoyment of the demised premises). Skally v. Shute, 132 Mass. 367, 370–371 (1882) (undermining of a leased building rendering it unfit for occupancy). Although some of our opinions have spoken of particular action or inaction by a landlord as showing a presumed intention to evict, the landlord's conduct, and not his intentions, is controlling.

The judge was warranted in ruling that the landlords had it within their control to correct the condition which caused the tenants to vacate their apartments. The landlords introduced a commercial activity into an area where they leased premises for residential purposes. The lease for the lounge expressly provided that entertainment in the lounge had to be conducted so that it could not be heard outside the building and would not disturb the residents of the leased apartments. The potential threat to the occupants of the nearby apartments was apparent in the circumstances. The landlords complained to the tenants of the lounge after receiving numerous objections from residential tenants. From time to time, the pervading noise would abate in response to the landlord's complaints. We conclude that, as matter of law, the landlords had a right to control the objectionable noise coming from the lounge and that the judge was warranted in finding as a fact that the landlords could control the objectionable conditions.

---

incessant, raucous, and penetrating. The noise interfered with conversation and prevented sleep. There was also evidence of noise from patrons' yelling and fighting.

This situation is different from the usual annoyance of one residential tenant by another where traditionally the landlord has not been chargeable with the annoyance. See Katz v. Duffy, 158 N.E. 264 (Mass. 1927) (illegal sale of alcoholic beverages); DeWitt v. Pierson, 112 Mass. 8 (1873) (prostitution).[4] Here we have a case more like Case v. Minot, 33 N.E. 700 (Mass. 1893), where the landlord entered into a lease with one tenant which the landlord knew permitted that tenant to engage in activity which would interfere with the rights of another tenant. There, to be sure, the clash of tenants' rights was inevitable, if each pressed those rights. Here, although the clash of tenants' interests was only a known potentiality initially, experience demonstrated that a decibel level for the entertainment at the lounge, acoustically acceptable to its patrons and hence commercially desirable to its proprietors, was intolerable for the residential tenants.

Because the disturbing condition was the natural and probable consequence of the landlords' permitting the lounge to operate where it did and because the landlords could control the actions at the lounge, they should not be entitled to collect rent for residential premises which were not reasonably habitable. Tenants such as these should not be left only with a claim against the proprietors of the noisome lounge. To the extent that our opinions suggest a distinction between nonfeasance by the landlord, which has been said to create no liability (P. Hall, Massachusetts Law of Landlord and Tenant §§ 90–91 (4th ed. 1949)), and malfeasance by the landlord, we decline to perpetuate that distinction where the landlord creates a situation and has the right to control the objectionable conditions.

Judgments affirmed.

NOTES AND QUESTIONS

1. The theory of constructive eviction builds on the exception to independent covenants recognized for actual evictions by the lessor. See

---

[4] The general, but not universal, rule, in this country is that a landlord is not chargeable because one tenant is causing annoyance to another (A. H. Woods Theatre v. North American Union, 246 Ill.App. 521, 526–527 (1927) (music from one commercial tenant annoying another commercial tenant's employees)), even where the annoying conduct would be a breach of the landlord's covenant of quiet enjoyment if the landlord were the miscreant. Contra Kesner v. Consumers Co., 255 Ill.App. 216, 228–229 (1929) (storage of flammables constituting a nuisance); Bruckner v. Helfaer, 222 N.W. 790, 791 (Wis. 1929) (residential tenant not liable for rent where landlord, with ample notice, does not control another tenant's conduct).

The rule in New York appears to be that the landlord may not recover rent if he has had ample notice of the existence of conduct of one tenant which deprives another tenant of the beneficial enjoyment of his premises and the landlord does little or nothing to abate the nuisance. See Cohen v. Werner, 378 N.Y.S.2d 868 (N.Y. App. T. 1975); Rockrose Associates v. Peters, 366 N.Y.S.2d 567, 568 (N.Y. Civ. Ct. 1975) (office lease); Home Life Ins. Co. v. Breslerman, 5 N.Y.S.2d 272, 273 (N.Y. App. T. 1938). But see comments in Trustees of the Sailors' Snug Harbor in the City of New York v. Sugarman, 35 N.Y.S.2d 196, 197–98 (N.Y. App. Div. 1942) (no nuisance).

A tenant with sufficient bargaining power may be able to obtain an agreement from the landlord to insert and to enforce regulatory restrictions in the leases of other, potentially offending, tenants. See E. Schwartz, Lease Drafting in Massachusetts § 6.33 (1961).

Smith v. McEnany, supra. Suppose the lessor commits some act that falls short of an actual eviction but so severely depresses the value of the tenancy that the lessee has no reasonable option but to vacate the premises. In these circumstances, is it not fair to say that the lessor has constructively evicted the lessee? And if the covenant to pay rent is dependent rather than independent when the lessor actually evicts the lessee, shouldn't the covenant to pay rent also be dependent when the lessor constructively evicts the tenant? Upon this reasoning, courts concluded that lessor misfeasance sufficiently serious to cause a reasonable lessee to vacate was a constructive eviction, and excused the lessee from further payment of rent.

2.   *Blackett* involves the considerably trickier issue of lessor nonfeasance rather than misfeasance. The noise from the lounge is being caused by another tenant. The lessor is blamed for not stepping in and forcing the lounge-tenant to hold down the noise. One theory for holding a lessor responsible for constructive eviction based on nonfeasance turns on whether the lessor's inaction violates some specific clause in the lessee's lease. For example, suppose the lessor promises in the lease to provide a "waterproof" basement. The basement leaks, and the lessor does nothing. Courts have held in these circumstances that the lessor's failure to act may constitute a constructive eviction (if the lessor's breach otherwise causes effects that satisfy the severity requirements for constructive eviction and the lessee vacates because of those effects), because the failure to act was the breach of a specific duty outlined in the lease. See Reste Realty Corp. v. Cooper, 251 A.2d 268 (N.J. 1969). Is there a clause in the lessee's lease in *Blackett* that would justify a finding of constructive eviction under the breach-of-lease-clause theory?

3.   How in fact does the court conclude that the lessor is liable for nonfeasance in *Blackett*? Under what circumstances should a lessor's tenant A be regarded as a third-party beneficiary of a clause in the lease between the lessor and tenant B? Many of the earliest constructive eviction cases involved nonfeasance in the form of a lessor who did nothing to evict prostitutes operating in a multi-unit building. See, e.g., Dyett v. Pendleton, 8 Cow. 727 (N.Y. 1826). Does the decision in the instant case rest on a pun on the term "quiet enjoyment"?

4.   How critical is it to the theory of constructive eviction that the lessee actually vacate the premises? On the one hand, since the theory rests on an analogy to actual eviction, one could say that it is necessary that the lessee vacate the premises in order to establish constructive eviction. On the other hand, since the theory is designed to single out lessor breaches that "depriv[e] the tenant of the enjoyment and occupation of the whole or part of the leased premises," one could say that the lessee's decision to vacate is at most only evidence of the severity of the breach, but not a necessary element of the defense. Moreover, the requirement that the lessee vacate puts the lessee at extreme risk if the court agrees with the lessor that the conditions of the premises were not sufficiently dire to justify constructive eviction: The lessee could end up being liable for unpaid rent *and* would have given up whatever value was left in the premises. One possible solution would be to seek a declaratory judgment from a court before vacating, see Charles E.

Burt, Inc. v. Seven Grand Corp., 163 N.E.2d 4 (Mass. 1959), although this would be expensive and usually would take too long. Can you see any functional justification for requiring that the lessee vacate before being allowed to invoke a defense that will eliminate all liability for payment of rent? See Echo Consulting Servs., Inc. v. North Conway Bank, 669 A.2d 227 (N.H. 1995) (adopting the so-far minority position that it is not necessary for lessee to vacate the premises to establish constructive eviction). Compare the discussion in Chapter V about courts being less willing to arbitrate relations between cotenants while the relationship is on-going than they are when one cotenant has been ousted or seeks partition.

5.   In the majority of jurisdictions that continue to require that the lessee vacate in order to claim constructive eviction, disputes often arise over how quickly the tenant must vacate after the offending conditions arise. The general standard is that a lessee must move out in a reasonable time. See Bloch v. Frischholz, 587 F.3d 771, 778 (7th Cir. 2009) (en banc) ("To establish a claim for constructive eviction, a tenant need not move out the minute the landlord's conduct begins to render the dwelling uninhabitable. . . Tenants have a reasonable time to vacate the premises."); Copeland v. Lincoln, 166 P.3d 245, 247 (Colo. Ct. App. 2007) (lessee must quit premises within a reasonable time to establish constructive eviction); R & J Rhodes, LLC v. Finney, 231 S.W.3d 183, 189 (Mo. Ct. App. 2007) (failure by lessee to abandon premises within a reasonable time waives a constructive eviction claim). In most states, the burden is on the lessee to show the reasonableness and speed of her abandonment. See ARE–100/800/801 Capitola, LLC v. Triangle Laboratories, Inc., 550 S.E.2d 31, 35 (N.C. Ct. App. 2001).

6.   *Blackett* alludes to the possibility of proving a partial constructive eviction, meaning, presumably, that the lessee has been constructively evicted from one part of the premises but not from other parts. The law here is unsettled, but there are some precedents upholding claims for partial constructive eviction. See Dennison v. Marlowe, 744 P.2d 906 (N.M. 1987) (holding lessee could claim partial constructive eviction when lessor failed to make the second floor of restaurant habitable); East Haven Associates v. Gurian, 313 N.Y.S.2d 927 (Civ. Ct. 1970) (holding that lessor's failure to eliminate emission of green fluid from air conditioner and ash from incinerator constituted partial constructive eviction from terrace outside apartment). On the reasoning of *Smith v. McEnany*, supra, would a finding of partial constructive eviction authorize the lessee to withhold all of the rent until the partial constructive eviction is corrected?

Gotlieb v. Taco Bell Corporation

United States District Court, Eastern District of New York, 1994.
871 F.Supp. 147.

■ ORENSTEIN, UNITED STATES MAGISTRATE JUDGE: This action involves a dispute arising from an alleged breach of a commercial ground lease, dated August 15, 1991, between the landlord plaintiffs Gotlieb and Blaymore, and tenant defendant Taco Bell Corporation ("Taco Bell").
* * *

The parties entered into a twenty year lease, effective August 15, 1991, for the purpose of establishing a Taco Bell restaurant at 1532–54 86th Street, Brooklyn, New York. The lease provided that the defendant was required to exercise diligence to obtain the necessary permits and administrative approvals to construct and operate the Taco Bell restaurant on the premises. (Lease at ¶¶ 6, 69.) The defendant was entitled to cancel the lease if they were unable to obtain such permits and administrative approval within a six month "permitting period," ending on February 15, 1992. (Lease, at ¶ 6.)

Sometime in September, 1991, local community and religious groups began an organized effort to oppose the construction and operation of the Taco Bell restaurant at the subject location, and against fast-food establishments in the community generally.

This organized opposition included public demonstrations of protest with placards, handbilling, and letter writing, telephone campaigns, and community meetings with local politicians. Taco Bell attempted to assuage this community opposition by attending these meetings, proposing amendments to the design plans and suggesting alternative measures to address the community group's safety and environmental concerns.

During the intervening six month period, the Defendant engaged the services of local attorneys and engineers in an effort to develop plans and a permit application. Nevertheless, defendant did not file its permit application with the appropriate governmental entities until February 14, 1992, one day prior to the expiration of the contractual "permitting period" referred to in paragraph 6 of the lease.

Also on February 14, 1992, defendant served on plaintiffs a written repudiation of the lease pursuant to Lease paragraph 6. Plaintiffs rejected this repudiation also by letter dated February 14, 1992. The plaintiffs initiated the instant action in June, 1992. * * *

A lessor has numerous options when a lessee attempts to repudiate a lease prior to the expiration of its term. See Centurian Development Ltd. v. Kenford Co., Inc., 400 N.Y.S.2d 263, 264 (App. Div. 1977). The landlord may reject the repudiation and do nothing, in which case the tenant continues to remain liable under the terms of the lease, as there is no obligation for a commercial lessor to mitigate damages. See Sage Realty Corp. v. Kenbee Management-New York, Inc., 582 N.Y.S.2d 182 (App. Div. 1992); Mitchell Titus Assocs., Inc. v. Mesh Realty Corp., 554 N.Y.S.2d 136 (App. Div. 1990); Syndicate Bldg. Corp. v. Lorber, 512 N.Y.S.2d 674, 675 (App. Div. 1987) (this duty recently imposed on residential landlords, however the contrary is true in the context of commercial leases). The lessor could also elect to notify the tenant that it was entering the premises and re-letting for the tenant's benefit, in which case the tenant remains liable for any rent deficiency. Underhill v. Collins, 30 N.E. 576 (N.Y. 1892). The lessor also has the option to accept the repudiation, re-enter the premises and re-let for its own benefit. In that event the lessee is generally relieved from any further liability under the lease. See Herter v. Mullen, 53 N.E. 700, 701 (N.Y. 1899); Centurian Development, 400 N.Y.S.2d at 264. No further rent accrues because the landlord-tenant relationship no longer exists. See Hermitage Co. v. Levine, 162 N.E. 97, 98 (N.Y. 1928).

The defendant herein repudiated the lease by letter dated February 14, 1992, sent in response to plaintiff's letter dated February 14, [1992]. Plaintiff's letter rejected defendant's February 10, 1992 request to alter the terms of the lease. The plaintiffs' February 14, 1992 letter explicitly stated that they would reject any attempt by the defendant to repudiate the lease and informed the defendant that they would be held liable under the terms of the lease.

The extent of plaintiffs' entitlement to damages therefore turns upon whether the surrender and repudiation of the lease was accepted, notwithstanding the assertions made in plaintiffs' February 14, 1992 letter.

A. Acceptance of the Repudiation

Termination of an estate by repudiation or surrender may be effected by express agreement or by operation of law, where it is inferred from the conduct of the parties. Riverside Research Inst. v. KMGA, Inc., 497 N.E.2d 669, 670–71 (N.Y. 1986); Gray v. Kaufman Dairy & Ice-Cream Co., 56 N.E. 903 (N.Y. 1900); Tootle Theater Co. v. Shubert Theatrical Co., 162 N.Y.S. 111 (App. Div. 1916).

Acceptance of a surrender is created by operation of law when the parties to a lease do some act so inconsistent with the landlord-tenant relationship which implies "their intent to deem the lease terminated." Riverside, 497 N.E.2d at 670. Such an implied acceptance of surrender has been found in "conduct by the landlord which fell short of an actual re-letting but which indicated the landlord's intent to terminate the lease and use the premises for his own benefit." Centurian Development Ltd. v. Kenford Co., Inc., 400 N.Y.S.2d 263, 264 (App. Div. 1977) ([citations omitted]).

In addition, an outward refusal to accept repudiation of the lease does not bar a finding that the subsequent conduct of the parties creates an acceptance by operation of law. See e.g., Gray, 56 N.E. at 904 (court found acceptance by operation of law where plaintiff refused defendant's offer of surrender yet re-rented in his own name); Tootle Theater, 162 N.Y.S. at 113 ("The fact that plaintiff refused to accept surrender . . . does not establish conclusively the absence of acceptance . . . [it may be] implied from all the circumstances of the case"). Therefore it is of no moment that the plaintiffs rejected the defendant's surrender and repudiation in February of 1992. * * *

Nevertheless, the testimony of plaintiff David Gotlieb at the damages trial revealed that despite the plaintiffs' rejection of the defendant's repudiation and surrender, the plaintiffs negotiated and made a written offer to lease the premises for their sole benefit to a prospective new tenant, Rite-Aid drug stores. Plaintiffs originally referred the representatives of Rite-Aid to Taco Bell for a possible sublet, yet apparently became impatient and initiated this effort to re-rent the property for their sole benefit.

On October 19, 1993, plaintiffs met directly with representatives of the Rite-Aid corporation. At that meeting, the plaintiffs and Rite-Aid representatives discussed renting the subject premises. Plaintiff Gotlieb testified that at that time he decided to deal directly with Rite-Aid, regardless of the consequences. Plaintiff Gotlieb testified:

> A.   After Lee [Blaymore] and I talked about it for a while, I told him I felt that I had to consider negotiating directly with Rite-Aid, let the chips fall where they may. . . . We were paying out considerable expenses month after month and going absolutely nowhere, and I felt it was time to make a decisive move.

A written proposal, dated November 3, 1993, with explicit terms of a proposed lease was then submitted to Rite-Aid representatives.

Mere attempts to re-let are insufficient to establish an acceptance by operation of law. See Levitt v. Zindler, 121 N.Y.S. 483 (App. Div. 1910); Dorrance v. Bonesteel, 64 N.Y.S. 307 (App. Div. 1900). However, the testimony heard by this Court indicates that the plaintiffs' acts are more than a mere attempt to re-let the premises to the general public; plaintiff Gotlieb's testimony, and the letter proposal sent to Rite-Aid representatives, unequivocally demonstrate the plaintiffs' intent to accept the defendant's surrender, re-enter the property and re-let it for their sole benefit. See Centurian Development, 400 N.Y.S.2d at 266. Plaintiffs' actions were inconsistent with the tenant's interest in the property * * * .

The Court finds that as a result of their affirmative conduct, the plaintiffs accepted the defendant's repudiation and surrender of the lease by operation of law between the October 19, 1993, meeting and the November 3, 1993 letter sent to the prospective tenant's agent. Thus the lease was terminated as of November, 1993.

The Court acknowledges that paragraph 62 of the lease contains a boilerplate provision which addresses acceptance of a surrender. The provision acts to shield the landlord vis-a-vis acts by the defendant such as the payment of lesser amounts of rent, or delivery of keys to the premises. Based upon the findings of this Court from the testimony presented, this provision has no effect to shield the plaintiffs from the consequences of their own affirmative conduct to re-rent the property for their sole benefit, which gives rise to an acceptance by operation of law.

B.   Rent

Plaintiffs [contend] they are entitled to all "base rent" both past and future, due under lease paragraph 53(A). Plaintiffs also contend they are entitled to the "additional rent," both past and future, due under lease paragraph 53(D). For the purposes of this discussion the term "rent" refers to both "base rent" and "additional rent" as defined in the lease unless otherwise indicated.

1.   Accrued Rent

Defendant has never paid any rent due under the lease. Although the effective date of the lease was August 15, 1991, the defendant was to commence paying rent on June 15, 1992. (Lease ¶ 52(A)(iv).) The defendant repudiated the lease on February 14, 1992, and therefore never made any rent payments.

A lessee is obligated to pay rent even if the lessee chooses not to occupy the premises. See Darob Holding Co. v. House of Pile Fabrics, Inc., 310 N.Y.S.2d 418 (Civ. Ct. 1970). Based upon the finding that the plaintiffs' implied acceptance of the surrender took place as of November, 1993, and that the lease remained in effect until that time, the defendants are liable for all rent due under the lease up to November, 1993. The defendant was obligated to pay a "base rent" of $10,833.33 per month. *(Lease* at ¶¶ 53(A)(ii), 53(D).) Thus the defendant is liable for base rent for sixteen and one-half (16.5) months, in the sum of $178,749.95.

The defendant was also obligated to pay "additional rent" including, but not limited to, real estate taxes, late charges of one percent with accrued interest, utility services, insurance, and other fixed expenses. *(Lease* at ¶¶ 51, 53(D), 61, 66, 68, 74.) Therefore the defendant is liable for "additional rent" to November 1993, in the amount of $59,815.43, exclusive of interest. * * *

2.   Future Rent

Plaintiffs seek an acceleration of all future rent due under the lease. This Court finds there is no entitlement to rent beyond October, 1993, because the plaintiffs accepted the defendant's repudiation and surrender of the lease. An acceptance of a surrender "operates to discharge the tenant from all liability for rent in the future." Herter v. Mullen, 53 N.E. 700, 701 (N.Y. 1899) ("After the surrender, there could be no recovery of rent, since the landlord could not have the use of the premises and the stipulated rent at the same time.").

Even if the plaintiffs herein merely sat idly by and allowed the defendant to remain in breach, the plaintiffs still could not maintain an action for all future rent because the lease has no acceleration clause. The only lease provision which might be considered an acceleration clause is paragraph 60(c), which provides in pertinent part:

> Tenant . . . shall also pay Landlord as liquidated damages for the failure of Tenant to observe and perform said Tenant's covenants herein contained, any deficiency between the rent hereby and/or covenanted to be paid and the net amount, if any, of the rents collected on account of the Lease or leases of the Demised Premises for each month of the period which would

otherwise have constituted the balance of the term of this Lease. . . . Any such liquidated damages shall be paid in monthly installments by Tenant on the rent day specified in this lease and any suit brought to collect the amount of the deficiency for any month shall not prejudice in any way the rights of Landlord to collect the deficiency of any subsequent month by a similar proceeding.

This is not an acceleration clause but a provision for liquidated damages. See e.g. Anon Realty Assoc., L.P., v. Simmons Stanley Ltd., 583 N.Y.S.2d 778, 780 (Sup. Ct. 1992) (same lease language). In the absence of an acceleration clause no action may be brought for future rent. Maflo Holding Corp. v. S.J. Blume, Inc., 127 N.E.2d 558, 561 (N.Y. 1955) ([citation omitted]).

What remains is an action for liquidated damages. * * * However, plaintiffs have forfeited their right to all future rents as damages because plaintiffs terminated the lease. See Centurian Development, 400 N.Y.S.2d at 266 (finding tenant liable for rent only up to date where surrender accepted by operation of law); Benderson v. Poss, 530 N.Y.S.2d 362, 363 (App. Div. 1988) (limiting landlord's liquidated damage recovery to unpaid charges accrued up to landlord's termination of lease).

Moreover, to recover liquidated damages in the event of a breach, the amount must bear a reasonable relation to the probable loss, and the amount of actual loss must be incapable or difficult of precise estimation. Truck Rent-A-Center v. Puritan Farms 2nd, 361 N.E.2d 1015, 1018 (N.Y. 1977). Here, plaintiffs are negotiating a new lease of the property at a higher rent than that contracted with the defendant. If the plaintiffs are awarded all future rents the result would be "grossly disproportionate to the probable loss." Puritan Farms, 361 N.E.2d at 1018. In fact, a windfall would be the most likely result. Therefore, the plaintiffs are not entitled to future rents under the lease as liquidated damages. * * *

NOTES AND QUESTIONS

1.   The doctrine of surrender, like the doctrine of constructive eviction, is pro-lessee. When a court finds that the lessor has accepted a surrender, the lessee is liable for the full amount of rent owed up to the moment of acceptance, but is off the hook thereafter. The doctrine is based on the idea of a contractual release of liability. The lessor and lessee create a leasehold interest by entering into a lease between themselves. They can extinguish such an interest by agreeing between themselves to release each other from the obligations of the lease. Ordinarily, such a release would require a written contract under the Statute of Frauds (if the lease were for more than one year). The surrender doctrine emerged as courts reasoned that the lessor and lessee could create a mutual release by *implied contract*. This would happen if the lessee vacated the premises with the intention never to return, in effect making an "offer" to surrender the leasehold estate, and the lessor responded by taking action inconsistent with the lessor's continuing right to

the leasehold interest, in effect "accepting" the surrender of the leasehold estate. Although originally grounded in the idea of contractual release, the doctrine of surrender eventually came to be understood as a type of release implied as a matter of law. This means, among other things, that the "offer" and "acceptance" of the surrender do not have to be in writing, notwithstanding the Statute of Frauds.

2.   The doctrine of surrender requires that courts characterize both the actions of the lessor and the lessee as evidencing a particular state of mind. The lessee's state of mind must be to abandon the leasehold. This is usually pretty straightforward, although occasionally it can be disputed (see *Berg v. Wiley* in Chapter IV for an example of a factual dispute over whether the lessee has abandoned). The lessor's state of mind must be to "accept" the abandonment, and reclaim the leasehold interest as an entitlement belonging to the lessor. This gives rise to many more disputes. Reasonably clear cases are when the lessor changes the locks, thereby excluding the lessee from further possession, or relets to a third person who enters into possession. But there is significant litigation over whether more equivocal actions, such as retaining the keys after they have been dropped off by the lessee or entering the premises to put up a "For Rent" sign, constitute an acceptance of surrender. See 2 Milton R. Friedman, Friedman on Leases § 16:3:2 (Andrew R. Berman, ed. & rev., 6th ed. 2017). In *Gotlieb*, the lessors write a letter to Taco Bell explicitly stating that they will not accept a repudiation of the lease. What should they have done differently to avoid the conclusion they had in fact accepted a surrender by the lessee?

3.   The court notes that under New York law a commercial lessor has three options when a lessee abandons: (1) do nothing and sue for accrued rent; (2) relet as the "agent" of the lessee; or (3) accept the lessee's surrender and relet for the lessor's benefit. (New York courts, as the decision indicates, have rejected a duty to mitigate damages in the context of commercial leases.) The *Restatement* is in accord with this statement of landlord options. Restatement (Second) of Property: Landlord and Tenant § 12.1(2). (The *Restatement* also rejects the duty to mitigate—for both residential and commercial leases.) The first option is not very appealing for the lessor if the lessee is struggling financially or has no assets to satisfy a judgment for unpaid rent. Also, if the premises stand empty this may invite vandalism or cause the value of other related property owned by the lessor to deteriorate. The second option is more appealing to lessors. Many leases include clauses that allow the lessor to reenter and relet the premises as the "agent of" the lessee, and New York (like the *Restatement*) gives lessors this option as a matter of law. Under this option the lessor can seek a new lessee and sue the abandoning lessee for damages equal to any benefit of the bargain under the original lease which has been lost. For example, if the lessor reenters and advertises the premises, but three months go by before a suitable substitute lessee is found, the original lessee will remain liable for an additional three months' rent (in addition to any unpaid rent up to the time of abandonment). How does a court tell whether a lessor is reletting for the lessee's account or has accepted the lessee's offer to surrender and is renting for the lessor's account? Should the lessors in *Gotlieb* have written to Taco Bell advising that

they were reletting for Taco Bell's account? Might they have recovered higher damages if they had done so?

4.   Another lease clause lessors sometimes use to protect themselves in the event of a lessee default is a rent acceleration clause, which purports to make all of the rent owing under the lease immediately due. Courts have tended to take a dim view of these clauses, perhaps influenced by the traditional understanding that "the rent issues out of the land." See Smith v. McEnany, supra. This suggests the lease is a conveyance of an interest in land, and that the obligation to pay rent arises from the right to possession of the land, and therefore cannot be treated as a contractual obligation independent of the right of possession. As courts have begun to treat leases more like bilateral contracts, acceleration clauses have been viewed with less hostility, although usually on the understanding that the lessor has a duty to mitigate damages under such a clause. See Aurora Business Park Assoc. v. Michael Albert, Inc., 548 N.W.2d 153 (Iowa 1996) (upholding acceleration clause in conjunction with duty to mitigate as simply assuring that the lessor is made whole). Some jurisdictions, however, continue to refuse to enforce acceleration clauses if they are deemed to be an excessive liquidated damages penalty. See, e.g., NPS, LLC v. Minihane, 886 N.E.2d 670, 675 (Mass. 2008) (upholding an accelerated rent clause as a reasonable form of liquidated damages); Cummings Properties, LLC v. National Communications Corp., 869 N.E.2d 617, 621–22 (Mass. 2007) (upholding an acceleration clause in a commercial lease, so long as it was not a penalty). Do you agree with the court in *Gotlieb* that the clause the lessors assert to be an acceleration clause is really a provision for liquidated damages?

d.   THE MODEL OF DEPENDENT COVENANTS

The 1970s witnessed a "revolution" in lease law, a revolution that was characterized at the time as entailing the repudiation of the "property" conception of leases in favor of a "contract" model of leases. There is reason to be somewhat skeptical of this characterization. As we have seen, lease law has always had a strong contractual flavor, in the sense that leases are regarded as bundles of covenants. Moreover, some of the reforms of the 1970s are difficult to square with ordinary precepts of contract law, insofar as they entailed the adoption of mandatory rules of law rather than default rules (default rules are more typical in the law of contracts). See Roger A. Cunningham, The New and Statutory Warranties of Habitability in Residential Leases: From Contract to Status, 16 Urb. L. Ann. 3 (1979); Mary Ann Glendon, The Transformation of American Landlord-Tenant Law, 23 B.C. L. Rev. 503 (1982); Michael Madison, The Real Properties of Contract Law, 82 B.U. L. Rev. 405, 410–24 (2002); Edward H. Rabin, The Revolution in Residential Landlord-Tenant Law: Causes and Consequences, 69 Cornell L. Rev. 517 (1984). A more accurate characterization might be that the contractual aspect of lease law moved decisively away from the model of independent covenants toward the model of dependent covenants. Although this movement accelerated in the 1970s, it was clearly foreshadowed by earlier decisions, such as the following case, which anticipated in many respects what can be called modern lease law.

Medico-Dental Building Company of Los Angeles v. Horton and Converse

Supreme Court of California, 1942.
132 P.2d 457.

■ CURTIS, J. Plaintiff brought this suit for rent alleged to be due under a lease * * * A trial was had before the court without a jury, and findings were made in favor of the defendant pursuant to its claim that plaintiff's breach of a restrictive covenant in the lease, which violation was not waived by the defendant, prevented the maintenance of this action * * *. From the judgment rendered accordingly for defendant * * * plaintiff has taken this appeal.

On July 1, 1934, defendant, Horton & Converse, as lessee, entered into a written lease covering certain space on the ground floor of the Medico-Dental Building at Eighth and Francisco Streets, Los Angeles, for a term of sixteen years and four months, at a minimum monthly rental of $600 for the part of the term concerned herein, and a fixed percentage of the gross sales. At the time the lease was made, defendant was in possession of the premises, having occupied them since 1925 under a prior lease. As successor in interest by virtue of an assignment of the lease involved herein, plaintiff, Medico-Dental Building Company, stands in the position of the original lessor.

The lease provided that the premises should be "used and occupied by lessee as a drug store and for no other business or purpose, without the written consent of lessor." It also contained the following stipulation: "Lessor agrees not to lease or sublease any part or portion of the Medico-Dental Building to any other person, firm or corporation for the purpose of maintaining a drug store or selling drugs or ampoules, or for the purpose of maintaining a cafe, restaurant or lunch counter therein during the term of this lease."

On December 30, 1937, plaintiff leased the entire ninth floor of the same building to one Dr. Boonshaft, a physician, for a term of three years commencing April 15, 1938. This lease contained the following provisions: "The premises demised hereby are to be used solely as offices for the practice of medicine and dentistry, and lessee agrees that he will not maintain therein or thereon, nor permit to be maintained therein or thereon, a drug store or drug dispensary, nor will lessee compound or dispense, or permit to be compounded or dispensed, drugs or ampoules except in connection with the regular course of treatment of lessee's own patients. Lessee agrees not to display any sign or advertisement on the inside or outside of the demised premises, or the building of which the demised premises are a part embodying the words 'Pharmacy,' 'Drug Store,' 'Dispensary' or words of like import. Lessee understands that lessor has heretofore executed a lease to Horton & Converse granting to said Horton & Converse the exclusive privilege of conducting a drug store business on the ground floor of said Medico-Dental Building, and lessee agrees that he will not do, or permit to be done, anything in connection with the premises demised hereby which would in any way conflict with or constitute a breach by the lessor therein of said Horton & Converse lease."

Dr. Boonshaft went into possession under his lease on April 15, 1938, and occupied the entire ninth floor of the building, where he had from thirty-two to thirty-six treatment rooms and had six to eight doctors associated with him in an organization known as the Boonshaft Medical Group. Independent of this staff but subject to frequent call to the premises in the course of the work of this enterprise were some thirty consultant doctors. The plan of operation of the medical organization was to register groups of employees and lodge members and their families for medical treatment on the basis of a monthly charge per family; registration and payment of the fixed sum entitled the patient to receive, among other things, certain drugs, but additional charges were made for other medicines. Dr. Boonshaft maintained a drug room wherein drugs were sold and prescriptions filled per the order of the regular staff or the consultant doctors in the treatment of patients of the Medical Group. He obtained a pharmacy license on May 10, 1938. Until June 25 of that year he bought his drugs from defendant's store *in the building.* However, he objected to the sales tax charged in connection with such purchases, and on June 25, 1938, he commenced buying wholesale from defendant's wholesale department *at another location,* which source of supply he continued to patronize to the time of trial. * * *

[T]he trial court found that plaintiff by executing the lease with Dr. Boonshaft did demise a part of the Medico-Dental Building to a tenant other than defendant for the purpose of maintaining a drug store and selling drugs on the premises, and that the making of the lease with Dr. Boonshaft was a breach of defendant's lease; that plaintiff in not taking immediate action to abate the drug store on the ninth floor of the building violated its lease with defendant; that plaintiff breached its lease with defendant on August 19, 1938, when it advised defendant that it could make no arrangements with Dr. Boonshaft and could not do anything with him regarding the selling of drugs and the maintaining of the drug store; and that such breaches of the lease were in material respects and were not waived by defendant.

The court also found that a material part of the consideration which induced defendant to enter into the lease with plaintiff was the right to be protected against competition, and that a material part of the consideration failed as the result of plaintiff's execution of the Boonshaft lease. * * *

On this appeal from the judgment rendered for defendant in consequence of the above findings, plaintiff advances the following propositions: (1) Covenants in leases are independent and performance of a covenant by the landlord is not a condition precedent to an action for rent against the tenant; (2) a covenant "not to lease" for a restricted purpose is breached only by actual leasing for such purpose, or by acquiescence in the conduct of the second lessee which is in violation of the restriction, neither of which appears in this case; (3) even if the covenants are dependent and there was a breach of the covenant involved herein, the breach was not so substantial as to go to the whole of the consideration; and (4) there was a waiver by the defendant of the alleged violation. Consideration of the legal aspect of these respective contentions in conjunction with the factual situation which confronted the trial court will demonstrate the propriety of the judgment entered.

The first controversial point is whether the covenants "not to lease" and "to pay rent" are mutually independent or dependent. It is plaintiff's position that a lease is a conveyance as distinguished from a contract, so that any covenant on the part of the lessor is independent of the lessee's obligation to pay rent and each party has his remedy for breach of covenant in an action for damages. While it is true that a lease is primarily a conveyance in that it transfers an estate to the lessee, it also presents the aspect of a contract. (Pollock on Contracts, Third Am. ed., p. 531.) This dual character serves to create two distinct sets of rights and obligations—"one comprising those growing out of the relation of landlord and tenant, and said to be based on the 'privity of estate,' and the other comprising those growing out of the express stipulations of the lease, and so said to be based on 'privity of contract.'" (Samuels v. Ottinger, 146 P. 638, 638–39 (Cal. 1915).) Those features of the lease which are strictly contractual in their nature should be construed according to the rules for the interpretation of contracts generally and in conformity with the fundamental principle that the intentions of the parties should be given effect as far as possible. In line with this concept is the authoritative observation in 32 Am.Jur. § 144, p. 145, that "covenants and stipulations on the part of the lessor and lessee are to be construed to be dependent upon each other or independent of each other, according to the intention of the parties and the good sense of the case, and technical words should give way to such intention."

Noteworthy here are the several provisions of the lease itself plainly indicating the intention and understanding of the parties as to the interbalancing considerations existing between the respective covenants. The agreement by the lessor "not to lease" any other part of the building to any other person for the purpose of its use as a drug store or for the sale of drugs, and the agreement by the lessee "to pay rent" appear in a rider attached to and made a part of the lease, a circumstance of incorporation not to be overlooked in the measure of the parties' comprehension of the reciprocal nature of the specified promises. Moreover, the lessee was limited by the terms of the lease to maintaining a drug store, a restriction emphasizing the import of the lessor's duty in negotiating future demises of other portions of the building. Finally to be noted is the express language of the lease manifesting the conditional character of the stipulations therein contained: "Time is of the essence of this lease and all of the terms and covenants hereof are conditions, and upon the breach by lessee of any of the same lessor may, at lessor's option, terminate this lease. . . ." Thus, the parties recognized in plain terms the essential interdependence of their obligations.

It is an established rule that those covenants which run to the entire consideration of a contract are mutual and dependent. Undoubtedly the restrictive covenant in defendant's lease was of such a nature. The exclusive right to conduct a drug store in the building was vital to defendant's successful operation of its business under the circumstances which prevailed in this case. Defendant's pharmacy was of a distinctive type in that it catered principally to doctors and dentists for reference of prescription work, did not carry the general line of merchandise found in the ordinary drug store, and did not rely upon transient trade. Defendant was and had been maintaining a chain of exclusive prescription pharmacies in Los Angeles for eighteen years. The fact that the Medico-Dental Building was tenanted for the most part by practitioners of the medical and dental professions motivated defendant to select that location for the establishment of one of its retail units. Defendant had occupied the same premises since 1925, and depended upon the tenants of the building and their patients for the major portion of its business. In fact, when vacancies occurred defendant's income from the store suffered to such an extent that the rent was temporarily reduced, and restoration to the former monthly rental level was made contingent upon a material increase in the occupancy of the building. Thus plaintiff knew, as appears from its letter granting the rent concession to defendant, that the "chief source" of defendant's business on the premises was the tenants in the building, and that it was therefore of prime importance that no competitor be rented quarters there. The correlation of these facts with the express provisions of the lease above noted compels the conclusion that the restrictive covenant was not incidental or subordinate to the main object of the lease, but went to the whole of the consideration, and that as such it must be deemed a dependent covenant. * * *

The second question is whether the restrictive covenant was breached by leasing for the prohibited purpose or by the lessor's acquiescence in the conduct of the other lessee amounting to a violation of the restriction.

As to the first part of this question, relative to leasing for the forbidden purpose, the trial court found that plaintiff did lease *a portion of* the Medico-Dental Building to Dr. Boonshaft for the purpose of maintaining a drug store and selling drugs on the premises so demised; that, by executing such lease, plaintiff breached its agreement with defendant; and that, by virtue of one of the provisions of the lease with Dr. Boonshaft, plaintiff intended to and did give such tenant the right and privilege of maintaining a drug store, selling drugs and compounding prescriptions on the premises, and by so doing failed to protect the defendant against competition.

This finding, as to the purpose of plaintiff's demise to Dr. Boonshaft, was based undoubtedly upon inferences drawn from the provisions of that tenant's lease; inferences that plaintiff knew at the time such lease was executed that the Boonshaft Medical Group contemplated the conduct of a type of medical business which would require a large stock of drugs, and that a drug store would be operated in connection therewith; that Dr. Boonshaft regarded the privilege of maintaining a drug store as a material part of the consideration in support of his lease; and inferences drawn from the conduct of plaintiff and Dr. Boonshaft following the latter's entry into possession of the demised premises. * * *

As to the second part of the second question—whether the restrictive covenant was breached by the plaintiff's acquiescence in the conduct of Dr. Boonshaft amounting to a violation of the restriction—the trial court found that the plaintiff in not taking immediate action to abate the drug store on the ninth floor and in advising defendant that it could not do anything with Dr. Boonshaft with respect to the objectionable activity, breached its lease with defendant.

Bearing on this feature of the case is the following evidence. The drug store on the ninth floor was opened in May, 1938. In the latter part of July, 1938, defendant learned that Dr. Boonshaft was maintaining a pharmacy on the premises, and on August 3, 1938, it wrote a letter to plaintiff protesting against the competing activity and demanding that plaintiff immediately put a stop to such objectionable practice. All of the parties concerned met in conference in defendant's office five days later, with the result that plaintiff promised to see what arrangements could be made and to advise defendant. Communications were thereupon had between plaintiff and Dr. Boonshaft, but defendant did not hear further from plaintiff until August 19, 1938, when plaintiff's attorney advised Mr. Horton, defendant's president, by telephone that he had been unable to do anything with Dr. Boonshaft, that "there could not be any arrangements made," and Mr. Horton then said that he thought the premises would be vacated, to which the attorney replied: "Use your own judgment about that."

From this summarization of the pertinent facts it appears that defendant did not precipitately vacate the premises upon learning in the latter part of July, 1938, that the competing drug store was being operated, but followed a reasonable and deliberate course of action designed to afford plaintiff an opportunity to adjust the controversy in a manner consistent with the rights and obligations of the parties. * * *

[T]he findings of the trial court relative to acquiescence have ample support in the evidence, and the conclusion is required that plaintiff concurred in Dr. Boonshaft's maintenance of his drug store in the building.

The third point, that even if there was a breach of the restrictive covenant, it was not so substantial as to go to the whole of the consideration, was discussed in part in connection with the treatment of the first proposition concerning the interdependence of the parties' covenants under the terms of the lease. * * * [I]t is apparent that the exclusive right to engage in a specified business in a particular building was the essence of the consideration for defendant's payment of rent during its many years of occupancy of the premises. * * * [W]here, as here, the covenant of the lessor is of such character that its breach will defeat the entire object of the lessee in entering into the lease, such as rendering his further occupancy of the premises a source of continuing financial loss incapable of satisfactory measurement in damages, it must be held that the covenant goes to the root of the consideration for the lease upon the lessee's part. (University Club v. Deakin, 106 N.E. 790 (Ill. 1914); Hiatt Investment Co. v. Buehler 16 S.W.2d 219 (Mo. App. 1929).) Commensurate with this principle, it is plain that the defendant's loss of potential business on account of the competing drug store was not a matter easily susceptible of monetary estimate, and proof of this element was not required of defendant under its presentation of the rights and duties of the parties in the circumstances of this case. A contrary view would authorize plaintiff to execute instruments similar to the Boonshaft lease for every floor of its building and thus render the restrictive covenant in defendant's lease valueless insofar as the protection of its essential source of income was concerned.

In the case of *Hiatt Investment Co. v. Buehler*, supra, where * * * the lessor's breach of a restrictive covenant similar to the one here involved did not permit its recovery in an action for rent, the court observed at pp. 163–164: "Defendant herein had a choice of several remedies: (1) He could rescind the lease, in which case he would not have been required to pay any further rent; (2) He could have continued under his lease and at the end of the term sued for loss of the profits suffered by reason of the competition of the Crown Drug Company; (3) He could have treated the violation of the covenant by the plaintiff as putting an end to the contract for purposes of the performance and sued for damages." Defendant elected to pursue the first course, and in this case the state of the record showing plaintiff's departure in substance from its contractual obligation establishes the propriety of defendant's position in accord with its choice of available relief. * * *

For the foregoing reasons the judgment is affirmed.

NOTES AND QUESTIONS

1.   *Medico-Dental* is the clearest example we have seen yet of how leases can function as a mechanism for the governance of a complex of assets, as well as a financing or risk-spreading device. The Medico-Dental building is conceived of as a commercial office building devoted exclusively to offices for doctors and dentists. The retail space on the ground floor is rented to a

pharmacy. This arrangement is obviously to the benefit of the pharmacy-tenant, since many patients will stop by to fill prescriptions after leaving the doctors' and dentists' offices. But it is also of benefit to the doctors and dentists, insofar as the pharmacy serves the convenience of their patients and makes it more likely they will continue to patronize doctors and dentists in the building. The arrangement also poses a potential for conflict, as the case reveals. Such conflicts would ordinarily be resolved by the lessor, either through the lessor's drafting of appropriate lease provisions, or its enforcement of these provisions, or its attempt to negotiate compromises or solutions among lessees. When these efforts fail, one or more lessees may walk out, and litigation may result, as in the principal case. Given the complicated collective-governance questions involved, it is probably no accident that the court was drawn to the more flexible precepts of contract law, rather than simple exclusion postulates of property law, in resolving the dispute.

2.   *Medico-Dental* suggests that many disputes that arise under leases can be resolved by applying, in a fairly straightforward fashion, the general rules of contract law that apply to bilateral commercial contracts. A breach by one party, here the lessor, gives rise to a variety of remedial options for the other party, here the lessee. If the breach is sufficiently serious—if it goes to the essence of the consideration under the lease or is sufficiently material—then the options for the promisee (whether it be the lessor or the lessee) include rescission of the lease and termination of further performance by the promisee. If the breach involves a less serious covenant—one that does not go to the essence of the bargain or is not sufficiently material to justify rescission—then the promisee would be entitled to sue for damages only. The result would be, in effect, that major breaches would be treated under a model of dependent covenants, whereas minor breaches would continue to be handled under a model of independent covenants.

3.   Under the dependent covenants model of *Medico-Dental*, does the doctrine of constructive eviction have any continuing role to play? Consider in this regard *Wesson v. Leone Enterprises, Inc.*, 774 N.E.2d 611 (Mass. 2002). The lessee, a financial printing company, complained repeatedly to the lessor about roof leaks. The leaks caused the lessee to cover some of its machinery and supplies with plastic tarps to protect them from water damage, but did not cause any suspension of business activity. The lessee vacated the premises two years before the end of the lease term, citing the roof leaks as the reason. The lessor sued for unpaid rent. The Massachusetts Supreme Judicial Court held on these facts that the roof leaks were not a constructive eviction, because they did not make the property "untenantable for the purposes for which they were used." However, the court also concluded that under the lease, the lessor was responsible to maintain and repair the roof. Adopting the rule of mutually dependent covenants, the court held that the lessor's breach of the covenant to repair deprived the lessee of a "substantial benefit significant to the purpose of the lease" and hence justified the lessee in terminating the lease. The lessee was also awarded relocation costs. After this decision, when if ever would a lessee need to invoke constructive eviction in Massachusetts?

4.   How would the dependent covenants model of *Medico-Dental* apply to a typical month-to-month residential tenancy, perhaps under an oral lease? Would the lessor's duties toward the lessee continue to be defined by the common-law rule of caveat lessee, as reflected in *Sutton v. Temple*? If so, then the new model would offer residential lessees little relief, unless they had the foresight (and the bargaining power) to insist on specific promises in the lease guaranteeing a minimal standard of quality. Perhaps for this reason, courts beginning in the late 1960s began to turn to a different contractual idea—that of the implied warranty of habitability—in addressing conditions of minimal quality standards in residential leases.

Javins v. First National Realty Corp.

United States Court of Appeals, District of Columbia Circuit, 1970.
428 F.2d 1071.

■ J. SKELLY WRIGHT, CIRCUIT JUDGE: These cases present the question whether housing code violations which arise during the term of a lease have any effect upon the tenant's obligation to pay rent. The Landlord and Tenant Branch of the District of Columbia Court of General Sessions ruled proof of such violations inadmissible when proffered as a defense to an eviction action for nonpayment of rent. The District of Columbia Court of Appeals upheld this ruling.

Because of the importance of the question presented, we granted appellants' petitions for leave to appeal. We now reverse and hold that a warranty of habitability, measured by the standards set out in the Housing Regulations for the District of Columbia, is implied by operation of law into leases of urban dwelling units covered by those Regulations and that breach of this warranty gives rise to the usual remedies for breach of contract.

I

The facts revealed by the record are simple. By separate written leases, each of the appellants rented an apartment in a three-building apartment complex in Northwest Washington known as Clifton Terrace. The landlord, First National Realty Corporation, filed separate actions in the Landlord and Tenant Branch of the Court of General Sessions on April 8, 1966, seeking possession on the ground that each of the appellants had defaulted in the payment of rent due for the month of April. The tenants, appellants here, admitted that they had not paid the landlord any rent for April. However, they alleged numerous violations of the Housing Regulations as "an equitable defense or (a) claim by way of recoupment or set-off in an amount equal to the rent claim," as provided in the rules of the Court of General Sessions. They offered to prove

> [t]hat there are approximately 1500 violations of the Housing
> Regulations of the District of Columbia in the building at Clifton
> Terrace, where Defendant resides some affecting the premises

of this Defendant directly, others indirectly, and all tending to establish a course of conduct of violation of the Housing Regulations to the damage of Defendants * * *

Appellants conceded at trial, however, that this offer of proof reached only violations which had arisen since the term of the lease had commenced. The Court of General Sessions refused appellants' offer of proof and entered judgment for the landlord. The District of Columbia Court of Appeals affirmed, rejecting the argument made by appellants that the landlord was under a contractual duty to maintain the premises in compliance with the Housing Regulations.

Figure 6-2
Clifton Terrace, Washington, D.C.

Courtesy of Richard Chused.

II

Since, in traditional analysis, a lease was the conveyance of an interest in land, courts have usually utilized the special rules governing real property transactions to resolve controversies involving leases. However, as the Supreme Court has noted in another context, "the body of private property law * * * , more than almost any other branch of law, has been shaped by distinctions whose validity is largely historical." Courts have a duty to reappraise old doctrines in the light of the facts and values of contemporary life—particularly old common law doctrines which the courts themselves created and developed. As we have said before, "The continued vitality of the common law * * * depends upon its ability to reflect contemporary community values and ethics."

The assumption of landlord-tenant law, derived from feudal property law, that a lease primarily conveyed to the tenant an interest in land may have been reasonable in a rural, agrarian society; it may continue to be reasonable in some leases involving farming or commercial land. In these cases, the value of the lease to the tenant is the land itself. But in the case of the modern apartment dweller, the value of the lease is that it gives him a place to live. The city dweller who seeks to lease an apartment on the third floor of a tenement has little interest in the land 30 or 40 feet below, or even in the bare right to possession within the four walls of his apartment. When American city dwellers, both rich and poor, seek "shelter" today, they seek a well known package of goods and services—a package which includes not merely walls and ceilings, but also adequate heat, light and ventilation, serviceable plumbing facilities, secure windows and doors, proper sanitation, and proper maintenance. * * *

Some courts have realized that certain of the old rules of property law governing leases are inappropriate for today's transactions. In order to reach results more in accord with the legitimate expectations of the parties and the standards of the community, courts have been gradually introducing more modern precepts of contract law in interpreting leases.[11] Proceeding piecemeal has, however, led to confusion where "decisions are frequently conflicting, not because of a healthy disagreement on social policy, but because of the lingering impact of rules whose policies are long since dead."[12]

In our judgment the trend toward treating leases as contracts is wise and well considered. Our holding in this case reflects a belief that leases of urban dwelling units should be interpreted and construed like any other contract.

III

Modern contract law has recognized that the buyer of goods and services in an industrialized society must rely upon the skill and honesty of the supplier to assure that goods and services purchased are of adequate quality. In interpreting most contracts, courts have sought to protect the legitimate expectations of the buyer and have steadily widened the seller's responsibility for the quality of goods and services through implied warranties of fitness and merchantability. * * *

The rigid doctrines of real property law have tended to inhibit the application of implied warranties to transactions involving real estate. Now, however, courts have begun to hold sellers and developers of real property responsible for the quality of their product. For example, builders of new homes have recently been held liable to purchasers for improper construction on the ground that the builders had breached an

---

11   E.g., *Medico-Dental Building Co. v. Horton & Converse*, 132 P.2d 457, 462 (Cal. 1942).

12   Kessler, *The Protection of the Consumer Under Modern Sales Law*, 74 Yale L.J. 262, 263 (1964).

implied warranty of fitness. In other cases courts have held builders of new homes liable for breach of an implied warranty that all local building regulations had been complied with. And following the developments in other areas, very recent decisions and commentary suggest the possible extension of liability to parties other than the immediate seller for improper construction of residential real estate.

Despite this trend in the sale of real estate, many courts have been unwilling to imply warranties of quality, specifically a warranty of habitability, into leases of apartments. Recent decisions have offered no convincing explanation for their refusal; rather they have relied without discussion upon the old common law rule that the lessor is not obligated to repair unless he covenants to do so in the written lease contract. However, the Supreme Courts of at least two states, in recent and well reasoned opinions, have held landlords to implied warranties of quality in housing leases. Lemle v. Breeden, 462 P.2d 470 (Haw. 1969); Reste Realty Corp. v. Cooper, 251 A.2d 268 (N.J. 1969). In our judgment, the old no-repair rule cannot coexist with the obligations imposed on the landlord by a typical modern housing code, and must be abandoned in favor of an implied warranty of habitability. In the District of Columbia, the standards of this warranty are set out in the Housing Regulations.

IV

A.   In our judgment the common law itself must recognize the landlord's obligation to keep his premises in a habitable condition. This conclusion is compelled by three separate considerations. First, we believe that the old rule was based on certain factual assumptions which are no longer true; on its own terms, it can no longer be justified. Second, we believe that the consumer protection cases discussed above require that the old rule be abandoned in order to bring residential landlord-tenant law into harmony with the principles on which those cases rest. Third, we think that the nature of today's urban housing market also dictates abandonment of the old rule.

The common law rule absolving the lessor of all obligation to repair originated in the early Middle Ages.[30] Such a rule was perhaps well suited to an agrarian economy; the land was more important[31] than whatever small living structure was included in the leasehold, and the tenant farmer was fully capable of making repairs himself. These

---

[30]   The rule was "settled" by 1485. 3 W. Holdsworth, A History of English Law 122–123 (6th ed. 1934). The common law rule discussed in text originated in the even older rule prohibiting the tenant from committing waste. The writ of waste expanded as the tenant's right to possession grew stronger. Eventually, in order to protect the landowner's reversionary interest, the tenant became obligated to make repairs and liable to eviction and damages if he failed to do so. Ibid.

[31]   The land was so central to the original common law conception of a leasehold that rent was viewed as "issuing" from the land: "The governing idea is that the land is bound to pay the rent * * * . We may almost go to the length of saying that the land pays it through (the tenant's) hand." 2 F. Pollock & F. Maitland, The History of English Law 131 (2d ed. 1923).

historical facts were the basis on which the common law constructed its rule; they also provided the necessary prerequisites for its application.[33]

Court decisions in the late 1800's began to recognize that the factual assumptions of the common law were no longer accurate in some cases. For example, the common law, since it assumed that the land was the most important part of the leasehold, required a tenant to pay rent even if any building on the land was destroyed.[34] Faced with such a rule and the ludicrous results it produced, in 1863 the New York Court of Appeals declined to hold that an upper story tenant was obliged to continue paying rent after his apartment building burned down. The court simply pointed out that the urban tenant had no interest in the land, only in the attached building. * * *

Another line of cases created an exception to the no-repair rule for short term leases of furnished dwellings. The Massachusetts Supreme Judicial Court, a court not known for its willingness to depart from the common law, supported this exception, pointing out:

> * * * [A] different rule should apply to one who hires a furnished room, or a furnished house, for a few days, or a few weeks or months. Its fitness for immediate use of a particular kind, as indicated by its appointments, is a far more important element entering into the contract than when there is a mere lease of real estate. One who lets for a short term a house provided with all furnishings and appointments for immediate residence may be supposed to contract in reference to a well-understood purpose of the hirer to use it as a habitation. * * * It would be unreasonable to hold, under such circumstances, that the landlord does not impliedly agree that what he is letting is a house suitable for occupation in its condition at the time. * * *[37]

These as well as other similar cases demonstrate that some courts began some time ago to question the common law's assumptions that the land was the most important feature of a leasehold and that the tenant could feasibly make any necessary repairs himself. Where those assumptions no longer reflect contemporary housing patterns, the courts have created exceptions to the general rule that landlords have no duty to keep their premises in repair.

It is overdue for courts to admit that these assumptions are no longer true with regard to all urban housing. Today's urban tenants, the vast

---

[33]   Even the old common law courts responded with a different rule for a landlord-tenant relationship which did not conform to the model of the usual agrarian lease. Much more substantial obligations were placed upon the keepers of inns (the only multiple dwelling houses known to the common law). Their guests were interested solely in shelter and could not be expected to make their own repairs. "The modern apartment dweller more closely resembles the guest in an inn than he resembles an agrarian tenant, but the law has not generally recognized the similarity." J. Levi, P. Hablutzel, L. Rosenberg & J. White, Model Residential Landlord-Tenant Code 6–7 (Tent. Draft 1969).

[34]   Paradine v. Jane, Aleyn 26, 82 Eng.Rep. 897 (K.B. 1647) * * *

[37]   Ingalls v. Hobbs, 31 N.E. 286 (Mass. 1892).

majority of whom live in multiple dwelling houses, are interested, not in the land, but solely in "a house suitable for occupation." Furthermore, today's city dweller usually has a single, specialized skill unrelated to maintenance work; he is unable to make repairs like the "jack-of-all-trades" farmer who was the common law's model of the lessee. Further, unlike his agrarian predecessor who often remained on one piece of land for his entire life, urban tenants today are more mobile than ever before. A tenant's tenure in a specific apartment will often not be sufficient to justify efforts at repairs. In addition, the increasing complexity of today's dwellings renders them much more difficult to repair than the structures of earlier times. In a multiple dwelling repair may require access to equipment and areas in the control of the landlord. Low and middle income tenants, even if they were interested in making repairs, would be unable to obtain any financing for major repairs since they have no long-term interest in the property.

Our approach to the common law of landlord and tenant ought to be aided by principles derived from the consumer protection cases referred to above. In a lease contract, a tenant seeks to purchase from his landlord shelter for a specified period of time. The landlord sells housing as a commercial businessman and has much greater opportunity, incentive and capacity to inspect and maintain the condition of his building. Moreover, the tenant must rely upon the skill and bona fides of his landlord at least as much as a car buyer must rely upon the car manufacturer. In dealing with major problems, such as heating, plumbing, electrical or structural defects, the tenant's position corresponds precisely with "the ordinary consumer who cannot be expected to have the knowledge or capacity or even the opportunity to make adequate inspection of mechanical instrumentalities, like automobiles, and to decide for himself whether they are reasonably fit for the designed purpose." Henningsen v. Bloomfield Motors, Inc., 161 A.2d 69, 78 (N.J. 1960).

Since a lease contract specifies a particular period of time during which the tenant has a right to use his apartment for shelter, he may legitimately expect that the apartment will be fit for habitation for the time period for which it is rented. We point out that in the present cases there is no allegation that appellants' apartments were in poor condition or in violation of the housing code at the commencement of the leases. Since the lessees continue to pay the same rent, they were entitled to expect that the landlord would continue to keep the premises in their beginning condition during the lease term. It is precisely such expectations that the law now recognizes as deserving of formal, legal protection.

Even beyond the rationale of traditional products liability law, the relationship of landlord and tenant suggests further compelling reasons for the law's protection of the tenants' legitimate expectations of quality. The inequality in bargaining power between landlord and tenant has been well documented. Tenants have very little leverage to enforce demands for better housing. Various impediments to competition in the rental housing market, such as racial and class discrimination and standardized form leases, mean that landlords place tenants in a take it or leave it situation. The increasingly severe shortage of adequate housing further increases the landlord's bargaining power and escalates the need for maintaining and improving the existing stock. Finally, the findings by various studies of the social impact of bad housing has led to the realization that poor housing is detrimental to the whole society, not merely to the unlucky ones who must suffer the daily indignity of living in a slum.

Thus we are led by our inspection of the relevant legal principles and precedents to the conclusion that the old common law rule imposing an obligation upon the lessee to repair during the lease term was really never intended to apply to residential urban leaseholds. Contract principles established in other areas of the law provide a more rational framework for the apportionment of landlord-tenant responsibilities; they strongly suggest that a warranty of habitability be implied into all contracts[49] for urban dwellings.

B. We believe, in any event, that the District's housing code requires that a warranty of habitability be implied in the leases of all housing that it covers. The housing code—formally designated the Housing Regulations of the District of Columbia—was established and authorized by the Commissioners of the District of Columbia on August 11, 1955. Since that time, the code has been updated by numerous orders of the Commissioners. The 75 pages of the Regulations provide a comprehensive regulatory scheme setting forth in some detail: (a) the standards which housing in the District of Columbia must meet; (b) which party, the lessor or the lessee, must meet each standard; and (c) a system of inspections, notifications and criminal penalties. The Regulations themselves are silent on the question of private remedies.

Two previous decisions of this court, however, have held that the Housing Regulations create legal rights and duties enforceable in tort by private parties. * * *

The District of Columbia Court of Appeals gave further effect to the Housing Regulations in Brown v. Southall Realty Co., 237 A.2d 834 (D.C. App. 1968). There the landlord knew at the time the lease was signed that housing code violations existed which rendered the apartment "unsafe and unsanitary." Viewing the lease as a contract, the District of Columbia Court of Appeals held that the premises were let in violation of Sections 2304[53] and 2501 of the Regulations and that the lease,

---

[49]   We need not consider the provisions of the written lease governing repairs since this implied warranty of the landlord could not be excluded.

[53]   "No person shall rent or offer to rent any habitation, or the furnishings thereof, unless such habitation and its furnishings are in a clean, safe and sanitary condition, in repair, and free from rodents or vermin."

therefore, was void as an illegal contract. In the light of *Brown*, it is clear * * * that the basic validity of every housing contract depends upon substantial compliance with the housing code at the beginning of the lease term. The *Brown* court relied particularly upon Section 2501 of the Regulations which provides:

> Every premises accommodating one or more habitations shall be maintained and kept in repair so as to provide decent living accommodations for the occupants. This part of this Code contemplates more than mere basic repairs and maintenance to keep out the elements; its purpose is to include repairs and maintenance designed to make a premises or neighborhood healthy and safe.

By its terms, this section applies to maintenance and repair during the lease term. Under the *Brown* holding, serious failure to comply with this section before the lease term begins renders the contract void. We think it untenable to find that this section has no effect on the contract after it has been signed. To the contrary, by signing the lease the landlord has undertaken a continuing obligation to the tenant to maintain the premises in accordance with all applicable law.

This principle of implied warranty is well established. Courts often imply relevant law into contracts to provide a remedy for any damage caused by one party's illegal conduct. * * *

[T]he housing code must be read into housing contracts—a holding also required by the purposes and the structure of the code itself. The duties imposed by the Housing Regulations may not be waived or shifted by agreement if the Regulations specifically place the duty upon the lessor. Criminal penalties are provided if these duties are ignored. This regulatory structure was established by the Commissioners because, in their judgment, the grave conditions in the housing market required serious action. Yet official enforcement of the housing code has been far from uniformly effective. Innumerable studies have documented the desperate condition of rental housing in the District of Columbia and in the nation. * * *

We therefore hold that the Housing Regulations imply a warranty of habitability, measured by the standards which they set out, into leases of all housing that they cover.

V

In the present cases, the landlord sued for possession for nonpayment of rent. Under contract principles,[61] however, the tenant's obligation to pay rent is dependent upon the landlord's performance of his obligations, including his warranty to maintain the premises in habitable condition. In order to determine whether any rent is owed to

---

[61]   In extending all contract remedies for breach to the parties to a lease, we include an action for specific performance of the landlord's implied warranty of habitability.

the landlord, the tenants must be given an opportunity to prove the housing code violations alleged as breach of the landlord's warranty.[62]

At trial, the finder of fact must make two findings: (1) whether the alleged violations[63] existed during the period for which past due rent is claimed, and (2) what portion, if any or all, of the tenant's obligation to pay rent was suspended by the landlord's breach. If no part of the tenant's rental obligation is found to have been suspended, then a judgment for possession may issue forthwith. On the other hand, if the jury determines that the entire rental obligation has been extinguished by the landlord's total breach, then the action for possession on the ground of nonpayment must fail.[64]

The jury may find that part of the tenant's rental obligation has been suspended but that part of the unpaid back rent is indeed owed to the landlord. In these circumstances, no judgment for possession should issue if the tenant agrees to pay the partial rent found to be due. If the tenant refuses to pay the partial amount, a judgment for possession may then be entered.

The judgment of the District of Columbia Court of Appeals is reversed and the cases are remanded for further proceedings consistent with this opinion.[67]

---

[62] To be relevant, of course, the violations must affect the tenant's apartment or common areas which the tenant uses. Moreover, the contract principle that no one may benefit from his own wrong will allow the landlord to defend by proving the damage was caused by the tenant's wrongful action. However, violations resulting from inadequate repairs or materials which disintegrate under normal use would not be assignable to the tenant. Also we agree with the District of Columbia Court of Appeals that the tenant's private rights do not depend on official inspection or official finding of violation by the city government. Diamond Housing Corp. v. Robinson, 257 A.2d 492, 494 (D.C. App. 1969).

[63] The jury should be instructed that one or two minor violations standing alone which do not affect habitability are de minimis and would not entitle the tenant to a reduction in rent.

[64] As soon as the landlord made the necessary repairs rent would again become due. Our holding, of course, affects only eviction for nonpayment of rent. The landlord is free to seek eviction at the termination of the lease or on any other legal ground.

[67] Appellants in the present cases offered to pay rent into the registry of the court during the present action. We think this is an excellent protective procedure. If the tenant defends against an action for possession on the basis of breach of the landlord's warranty of habitability, the trial court may require the tenant to make future rent payments into the registry of the court as they become due; such a procedure would be appropriate only while the tenant remains in possession. The escrowed money will, however, represent rent for the period between the time the landlord files suit and the time the case comes to trial. In the normal course of litigation, the only factual question at trial would be the condition of the apartment during the time the landlord alleged rent was due and not paid.

As a general rule, the escrowed money should be apportioned between the landlord and the tenant after trial on the basis of the finding of rent actually due for the period at issue in the suit. To insure fair apportionment, however, we think either party should be permitted to amend its complaint or answer at any time before trial, to allege a change in the condition of the apartment. In this event, the finder of fact should make a separate finding as to the condition of the apartment at the time at which the amendment was filed. This new finding will have no effect upon the original action; it will only affect the distribution of the escrowed rent paid after the filing of the amendment.

NOTES AND QUESTIONS

1.   For further background on the case, see Richard H. Chused, *Saunders (a.k.a. Javins) v. First National Realty Corporation*, in Property Stories 123 (Gerald Korngold & Andrew P. Morriss eds., 2d ed. 2009). The action began as a lessee rent strike in 1966, organized by a Neighborhood Legal Services Program lawyer, protesting the appalling conditions at Clifton Terrace. By the time the case went to trial, only six protesting lessees remained as defendants. When the case reached the first round of appeals in the local D.C. court of appeals, all protesting lessees had either left the complex or had paid the back rent they owed, making the case technically moot. The D.C. Circuit's decision on further appeal, excerpted here, was issued some four years after the initial rent strike, by which time the building had been taken over by the government and was being extensively renovated. Ironically, Clifton Terrace was listed in the National Register of Historic Places in 2001. The citation reads in part that it is a significant example of a new garden apartment design developed in the 1920s and 1930s, featuring "superior air circulation, more pleasing views, the inclusion of balconies, and enhanced light in each apartment—all at a moderate price." Id. at 126.

2.   The implied warranty of habitability was one of several reforms to residential lease law introduced by courts in the District of Columbia in the late 1960s and early 1970s. Two others of note are the doctrine of retaliatory eviction, see Edwards v. Habib, 397 F.2d 687 (D.C. Cir. 1968), and the illegal lease doctrine, see Brown v. Southall Realty Co., 237 A.2d 834 (D.C. 1968). All three doctrines built on the provisions of the local housing code establishing standards for safe and sanitary residential housing. The doctrine of retaliatory eviction posited that a lessor may not retaliate against a lessee for reporting code violations. Thus, even if the lessee is in a periodic tenancy that the lessor otherwise would be free to terminate at the end of the period (often month-to-month where low-income rental housing is concerned), the lessor cannot give notice to terminate if a court concludes that the termination was motivated by a desire to punish the lessee for asserting her rights under the code. The illegal lease doctrine posited that if the lessor leases property that is subject to one or more code violations, such that the premises are rendered unsafe and unsanitary, then the lease is void and of no legal effect. As a result, the lessor is precluded from suing for unpaid rent based on the lease.

3.   Of the three doctrines, the implied warranty of habitability (IWH) has been the runaway success story. See Mary Ann Glendon, The Transformation of American Landlord-Tenant Law, 23 B.C. L. Rev. 503 (1982); Edward H. Rabin, The Revolution in Residential Landlord-Tenant Law: Causes and Consequences, 69 Cornell L. Rev. 517 (1984). An IWH for residential tenancies or something equivalent is required in most states. See generally 1 Milton R. Friedman, Friedman on Leases § 10:3 (Andrew R. Berman ed. & rev., 6th ed. 2017). Interestingly, however, all but ten states that have adopted the IWH have done so at least in part by legislation, usually by adopting the relevant provisions of the Uniform Residential Landlord Tenant Act, rather than by judicial revision of the common law, as

in *Javins*. Id. The doctrine of retaliatory eviction has been widely adopted to protect lessees who engage in protected activity, such as reporting housing code violations or attempting to organize a tenants' union. But this is a relatively small subset of lessees, relative to those affected by the conditions of the leased premises. The illegal lease doctrine suffers from the fact that if the lease is illegal, then it would seem that the lessee is not only released from the burdens of the lease but cannot claim the benefit of the lease either (such as the covenant of quiet enjoyment). Logically, the tenancy would become a tenancy at will or sufferance, which would allow the lessor to begin immediate eviction proceedings. The IWH, in contrast, gives the lessee additional rights under the lease without subjecting the lessee to immediate eviction. Not surprisingly, law reformers sympathetic to the plight of poor lessees quickly gravitated to the IWH rather than the illegal lease doctrine. Note that the *Javins* court portrays the violations of the housing code as having emerged after the lessees had entered into the leases. This was probably in an attempt to expand lessees' rights beyond the illegal lease doctrine, which requires code violations when the lease is executed. Is it plausible that there were no code violations at Clifton Terrace when the leases were signed, and 1,500 violations shortly thereafter?

4.   The court only addresses the question whether there should be an implied warranty of habitability in leases of "urban residential housing." This leaves open the question whether a similar warranty of fitness for intended purpose should be implied in leases of commercial or agricultural property. To date, only a small minority of states have adopted an implied warranty of fitness in commercial cases. See, e.g., Richard Barton Enters. v. Tsern, 928 P.2d 368 (Utah 1996). More commonly, courts have held, following *Medico-Dental*, that covenants in commercial leases are presumed to be mutually dependent. See, e.g., Teodori v. Werner, 415 A.2d 31 (Pa. 1980). What factors are responsible for courts limiting the implied warranty idea to residential leases?

5.   Should the implied warranty of habitability be a default rule or a mandatory rule of law? The *Restatement* endorses the IWH but provides that it can be waived for consideration (such as reduced rent), provided the agreement is not "unconscionable or significantly against public policy." Restatement (Second) of Property: Landlord and Tenant § 5.6. Most courts, however, have followed *Javins* (see footnote 49), in making the IWH a nonwaivable rule of law. This is seemingly at odds with the court's insistence that leases are contracts, since usually rules of contract law are defaults. The most common rationale for making the IWH a mandatory rule of law, following *Javins*, is the perception that lessees and lessors have "unequal bargaining power." What exactly does this mean in this context? That there is an imbalance between supply and demand in the market for low-income rental properties such that lessors can assume a "take it or leave it" attitude in lease negotiations? That there are asymmetries in the information available to lessors and lessees, such that lessees often would not understand the significance of a waiver of the IWH? That many lessees simply cannot afford the higher rents that lessors would charge for properties protected by a warranty of quality?

6.   The court in *Javins* puts great stress on the provisions of the housing code as defining the content of the IWH. But housing codes vary greatly in terms of the detail with which they regulate rental housing, as well as in the nature of the issues addressed. Should every violation of the housing code be deemed a violation of the IWH? Suppose, for example, that the code requires that all electrical outlets in the kitchen and bathrooms include circuit breakers to prevent shock or electrocution. Is an apartment that has only standard grounded outlets but no circuit breakers in violation of the IWH? Courts sometimes avoid this implication by holding that only those code provisions that implicate "health and safety" define the IWH. But don't circuit breakers implicate health and safety? Alternatively, can the conditions of the apartment violate the IWH even if there is no code violation? Suppose, for example, that the housing code does not require air conditioning. What if the air conditioning system in an apartment building is not working, but the lessor refuses to fix it even though the city is in the midst of a killer heat wave?

7.   Does the doctrine of constructive eviction (considered in *Blackett v. Olanoff*, supra) have any continuing role to play once a jurisdiction has adopted the IWH? The answer is clearly yes, insofar as most jurisdictions have limited the IWH to residential leases and have not adopted an analogous implied warranty of fitness for purpose to commercial leases. Thus, insofar as issues arise about the adequacy of physical conditions and services under commercial leases, they continue to be addressed in most jurisdictions under specific lease provisions or the doctrine of constructive eviction. Constructive eviction may also be of continuing relevance under residential leases, insofar as the jurisdiction relies on its housing code to define the content of the IWH. For example, suppose the housing code does not address the permissible decibel level of noise that may emit from surrounding properties controlled by the lessor. Raucous noise from a bar leased by the lessor might not violate the IWH in these circumstances, requiring that the court turn to the doctrine of *Blackett v. Olanoff*, supra, to provide a remedy.

8.   What are the remedies for violation of the IWH? Courts, following *Medico-Dental* and *Javins*, have tended to say that all remedies are available that would apply in the case of a material breach of a bilateral commercial contract. These include: (1) rescission of the lease by the lessee, thereby allowing the tenant to vacate without further obligation to pay rent; (2) an order directing specific performance of the IWH; (3) an action for damages for breach of the IWH; (4) if the lessor has sued the lessee for unpaid rent, a set-off against rent liability reflecting the lessor's violation of the IWH; and (5) in some jurisdictions, withholding of all or a portion of the rent until the lessor corrects the violation of the IWH or permits the lessee to arrange for repair of the violation.

A particularly vexing question concerns how to determine the damages caused by a breach of the IWH for purposes of remedies (3)–(5) mentioned above—a lessee suit for damages, a setoff from a lessor action for unpaid rent, or rent withholding. The straightforward way to determine damages or set-offs would seem be to take the rent reserved under the lease and subtract the value of the premises in their noncompliant condition. The problem, as tenant advocates and courts quickly discovered, is that rental markets are not that inefficient: The rent reserved under the lease tends to be equal to the value of the premises in their actual (noncompliant) condition. So the standard formula often yields zero damages. This did not seem right to many advocates and courts, so two substitute formulas were developed. One asks, hypothetically, what the fair market rental value would be if the premises were in compliance with the IWH, and then subtracts the value of the premises in their noncompliant condition. This formula is open to the objection that it awards a windfall to the lessee if the rent reserved was less than the fair market value of the premises in compliance with the IWH: The lessee gets, through the damages formula, more than the lessee agreed to pay for. The other, "percentage reduction" formula develops a ratio between (i) the difference between the value of the premises if in compliance with the IWH and the value of the premises if not in compliance with the IWH over (ii) the value of the premises if in compliance with the IWH, and multiplies this ratio times the rent reserved, for the amount of the reduction (damages). Does this alternative avoid the charge of a windfall to the lessee, or is it open to the same objection? See generally Dale A. Whitman et al., The Law of Property § 6.42 (4th ed. 2019).

9.   In a development probably not appreciated at the time, the IWH has had important implications for the scope of the lessor's duty to the lessee and the lessee's guests under tort law. See generally Olin L. Browder, The Taming of a Duty—The Tort Liability of Landlords, 81 Mich. L. Rev. 99 (1982). If we start with the common-law baseline, as reflected in *Paradine v. Jane*, we see that the risk of casualty losses under a lease is originally placed on the lessee. Accordingly, any tort liability for injuries incurred on the premises (slip and fall accidents, assaults by third parties, etc.) would lie with the lessee. This baseline can be modified by particular lease provisions. For example, if the lessor promises to keep the driveways and walkways clear of snow and ice, a slip and fall by a guest of a tenant may plausibly give rise to tort liability for the lessor, based on the lessor's specific undertaking in the lease. This narrow bridgehead of liability becomes potentially huge with the introduction of the implied warranty of habitability. Now, the lessor has a general legal obligation to maintain the premises in a manner consistent with the housing code, and otherwise to insure that it meets minimal standards of public safety and health. This legally-imposed duty can provide the foundation for a broad lessor duty in tort to the lessee and the lessee's guests, including a duty to protect these persons against assaults by intruders who could have been kept at bay with proper security cameras and locks. See, e.g., Sargent v. Ross, 308 A.2d 528 (N.H. 1973) (holding landlord liable for death of four-year-old girl who fell from outdoor stairway not part of a common area).

In California, the courts initially concluded, by analogy to products liability law, that the lessor would be strictly liable for tortious injuries caused by a breach of the IWH. Becker v. IRM Corp., 698 P.2d 116 (Cal. 1985). One decade later, the California Supreme Court changed its mind, overruled *Becker*, and decided that lessors would be liable only for injuries caused by a negligent breach of the IWH. Peterson v. Superior Court, 899 P.2d 905 (Cal. 1995). What do you suppose motivated the retreat? Another source of controversy has been lessor tort liability for crimes and intentional torts by third persons. If a lessor fails to keep the locks on doors in good repair, and a criminal exploits the situation to the injury of a lessee, should the lessor pay? See Kline v. 1500 Mass. Ave. Apartment Corp., 439 F.2d 477 (D.C. Cir. 1970) (holding lessor liable in tort when lessee was criminally assaulted in apartment hallway).

The Consequences of the Implied Warranty of Habitability

Without doubt the most controversial aspect of the IWH has been whether it improves the welfare of low-income lessees. Commentators have addressed this primarily from a theoretical perspective, although there is some empirical evidence bearing on the question.

Theory. In the early years after *Javins*, commentators divided into two camps about whether imposing a mandatory IWH would improve the welfare of low-income lessees. One camp, representing orthodox microeconomic assumptions, argued that the IWH, like any government-mandated minimal product quality standard, would increase both the demand for low-cost housing (because the product would be better) and increase the costs of supplying such housing (because strict code compliance costs money). Consequently, imposing the IWH would cause rents to rise and the supply of low-cost housing to fall. See Richard A. Posner, Economic Analysis of Law § 16.6 (6th ed. 2003); Lawrence Berger, The New Residential Tenancy Law—Are Landlords Public Utilities?, 60 Neb. L. Rev. 707 (1981); Charles J. Meyers, The Covenant of Habitability and the American Law Institute, 27 Stan. L. Rev. 879 (1975). Poor lessees would either have to dig deeper into their pockets to pay for housing or be forced to squeeze more people into smaller units by doubling up.

Another camp, representing legal scholars more sympathetic to the mandatory IWH, argued that the low-income rental market is different from other types of product markets, and that because of these differences, the IWH might improve the quality of housing without any significant increase in rents. Thus, Bruce Ackerman argued that low-income households could not afford to pay more in rent and would refuse to double up. At the same time, lessors, because of their large sunk investment, could not afford to exit from the market, and so the supply of low-income housing was largely fixed. Ackerman accordingly argued that both the demand for and the supply of low-income housing are largely inelastic, at least in the short run, permitting some redistribution from lessors to lessees through a mandatory IWH. Bruce A. Ackerman, Regulating Slum Housing Markets on Behalf of the Poor: Of Housing Codes, Housing Subsidies and Income Redistribution Policy, 80 Yale L.J. 1093 (1971). Duncan Kennedy argued that many slumlords recognize that their property is deteriorating and will have to be abandoned some years in the future; given this realization, such lessors may "milk" the property by forgoing even routine maintenance while continuing to collect as much rent as possible in the period before the end arrives. Imposing a mandatory IWH on such lessors, Kennedy argued, would not change their calculus about how long to remain in the market, but might result in significant improvements in quality for the lessees. Duncan Kennedy, The Effect of the Warranty of Habitability on Low Income Housing: "Milking" and Class Violence, 15 Fla. St. U. L. Rev. 485 (1987).

More recently, "second wave" treatments of the question suggest that the matter is more complex: Some lessees will benefit while others will lose from a mandatory IWH. See Richard Craswell, Passing on the Costs of Legal Rules: Efficiency and Distribution in Buyer-Seller Relationships, 43 Stan. L. Rev. 361 (1991). Craswell, for example, argues that it is critical to distinguish between "marginal" and "infra-marginal" lessees. In a competitive market, the price for a good like housing is determined by the intersection of demand and supply curves. Assuming lessors cannot discriminate among prospective lessees based on their demand for housing, the same rent will be charged to all lessees for housing of equivalent quality. The rent will be determined by the demand of the last or "marginal" lessee who is just willing to pay the price necessary to induce the last or "marginal" lessor to put the housing on the market. But this price does not reflect the value that other lessees place on housing of equivalent quality. The basic postulate of a downward sloping demand curve is that there are other lessees—fewer in number perhaps—who would be willing to pay even more for housing of equivalent quality. Economists refer to these other lessees as "infra-marginal." The marginal lessee pays a price for housing exactly equal to what that lessee is willing to pay. The infra-marginal lessee enjoys a "consumer surplus" equal to the difference between the price she would be willing to pay and the market price, which is determined by what the last or marginal lessee is willing to pay.

Craswell notes that when a mandatory warranty is introduced into a competitive market, the demand curve for the good will shift upward and to the right, because the good is now worth more to consumers than it was before. Similarly, the supply curve for the good will shift upward and to the left, because it is now more expensive to produce the good than it was before. Craswell argues, however, that the demand curve will not necessarily shift up and to the right parallel to the original demand curve. If marginal lessees place a low value on the warranty, perhaps because their budgets are already stretched to maximum and they cannot afford to pay even a few dollars more for housing, then it is possible that the demand curve will shift relatively little for the marginal lessees, but may shift farther for the infra-marginal lessees. Conversely, the opposite might occur. Marginal lessees might place a higher value on the warranty than infra-marginal lessees do. These two possibilities are illustrated by the following graphic, taken from his article, id. at 378:

Figure 6-3
Low- and High-Valuing Marginal Customers

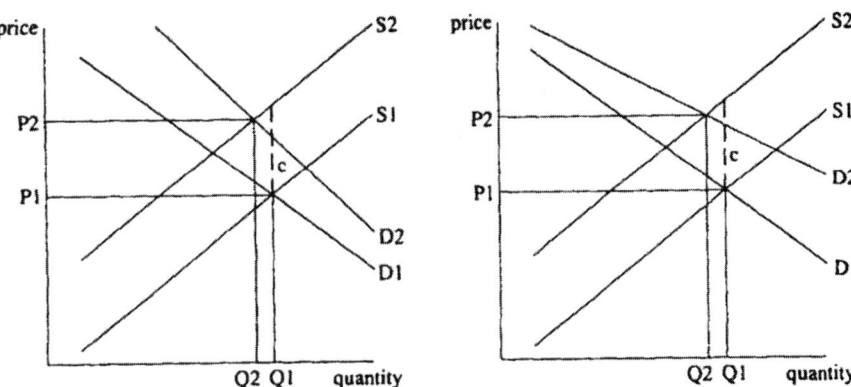

As Craswell explains, in the left-hand side of the graphic:

[T]he vertical shift in the demand curve from *D1* to *D2* exceeds this price increase for most consumers of the product, especially those located toward the left of the graph. This implies that the price increase accompanying the warranty is less than the maximum these consumers are willing to pay for the warranty, so the warranty has made these consumers better off. The only consumers who lose from the introduction of the warranty are those located between the *Q1* and *Q2* lines, whose demand curve shifts upward by less than the price increase from *P1* to *P2*. These consumers are unwilling to buy the product/warranty combination at the higher price. Since these consumers were willing to buy the product before the introduction of the warranty, they are made worse off by having to give up this benefit.

By contrast, the graph on the right in [Figure 6-3] shows a market in which most consumers are made worse off by the warranty because the correlation of consumer preferences has been reversed. In this market, the infra-marginal consumers who are willing to pay the most for the product alone are willing to pay very little extra for the warranty. These consumers are located toward the left of the graph, where the *D1* curve (representing the demand for the product itself) is relatively high, but the *D2* curve (representing the additional demand for the warranty) is only slightly higher. These consumers value the warranty by less than the price increase from *P1* to *P2*, so these consumers will be made worse off by the warranty. Only the consumers located near the *Q1–Q2* margin place a large enough value on the warranty, so these are the only consumers who even come close to benefiting from the warranty.

Id. at 378–79.

Craswell suggests that insofar as the left side graphic is a more plausible depiction of the shift in the demand curve following the introduction of a mandatory warranty, infra-marginal consumers may well benefit from the warranty, whereas marginal consumers may well lose. "[T]he benefit to those consumers who continue to buy the product comes, at least partially, at the expense of the marginal consumers, who now find themselves priced out of the market." Id. at 395.

Craswell is only concerned with determining whether tenant welfare will be improved by imposing a mandatory IWH. What about lessor welfare? Can we presume that lessors will always be worse off, on the ground that if it were in their commercial interest to keep their rental units up to code, they would do so voluntarily? Suppose that in the aggregate the IWH makes infra-marginal lessees better off by, say $1,000, makes marginal lessees worse off by $500, and makes lessors worse off by $750. Are we justified in imposing the IWH on these facts? This outcome is inefficient under an aggregate wealth maximization (Kaldor-Hicks) standard for measuring social utility.

If we reject aggregate wealth maximization as the test, on the ground that it ignores distributional concerns, we still have a dilemma under Craswell's analysis. Suppose lessors are the best-off group affected by the IWH, infra-marginal lessees are the next best-off group, and marginal lessees are the worst-off group. Insofar as the IWH takes from the lessors and transfers to the infra-marginal lessees, it has egalitarian distributional consequences. But how do we weigh the fact that the IWH may also make the worst-off lessees (by assumption here the marginals) even worse off, while benefiting the less-worse-off lessees (here the infra-marginals)? John Rawls suggested in his *Theory of Justice* (1971) that deviations from equal treatment are justifiable only if they can be shown to make the worst-off group in society better off. Does the IWH flunk the Rawlsian test under the hypothetical?

Empirical Evidence. Most studies of the implied warranty of habitability have been theoretical and most of the empirical writing on this issue is casual at best. One early study found a statistically significant effect—an increase of approximately 12 percent—on rent in the early 1970s from receivership laws, in which a noncompliant lessors would lose control over a building to a receiver who would direct repairs. Werner Z. Hirsch, Joel G. Hirsch & Stephen Margolis, Regression Analysis of the Effects of Habitability Laws Upon Rent: An Empirical Observation on the Ackerman-Komesar Debate, 63 Cal. L. Rev. 1098 (1975). Other habitability laws, such as repair-and-deduct and withholding, showed a smaller effect on rents that was not statistically significant. Whether the IWH has an effect on aggregate housing supply is difficult to disentangle from other trends in housing happening at the same time. One reason that the IWH has not had more of an effect is that enforcement levels have been low. A recent overview summarizes the findings of a number of studies based on observations of landlord-tenant courts:

> First, the new substantive regime did not appear to increase the number of eviction cases filed. This suggests that few tenants are withholding rent deliberately to bring the issue of repairs to court.

> Second, the judicial resources applied to the average case are quite modest. Nine-minute trials take the concept of a "rocket docket" to an entirely different level, and the number of jury trials has remained extremely small.

> Third, a huge fraction of eviction cases never reach open court. Landlord-tenant courts have extremely high default rates. * * * Once landlords receive all that they sought—either rent or possession—they voluntarily dismiss their cases. This suggests that tenants are indeed choosing to move rather than litigate. * * *

> Fourth, of the minority of cases that reach court, the overwhelming majority are resolved with no reference to the condition of the premises. * * * Many tenants lack the sophistication to assert the warranty in a written pleading or the presence of mind and assertiveness to do so orally in the momentary window of opportunity presented in open court. Because of very limited legal services funding, tenants are seldom represented by counsel, and without the help of lawyers may not have a clear understanding of their new rights or of court procedures.

David A. Super, The Rise and Fall of the Implied Warranty of Habitability, 99 Cal. L. Rev. 389, 434–36 (2011) (footnotes omitted). The author concludes that "the new regime of landlord-tenant law inaugurated four decades ago has failed at achieving any of its major goals." Id. at 458. (New York City has recently provided for paid legal consultation for low-income lessees complaining about the quality of their housing and for full legal representation in eviction proceedings. It will be instructive to see if this changes the picture painted by Super.)

An alternative to the IWH, which is increasingly the focus of public policy, is to provide direct rental assistance to low-income families, either through housing vouchers or by inducing developers to include rent-subsidized units in new housing developments. For an overview and suggestions for reform, see John J. Infranca, Housing Resource Bundles: Distributive Justice and Federal Law-Income Housing Policies, 49 U. Richmond L. Rev. 1071 (2015).

Sommer v. Kridel

New Jersey Supreme Court, 1977.
378 A.2d 767.

■ PASHMAN, J. We granted certification in these cases to consider whether a landlord seeking damages from a defaulting tenant is under a duty to mitigate damages by making reasonable efforts to re-let an apartment wrongfully vacated by the tenant. Separate parts of the Appellate Division held that, in accordance with their respective leases, the landlords in both cases could recover rents due under the leases regardless of whether they had attempted to re-let the vacated apartments. Although they were of different minds as to the fairness of this result, both parts agreed that it was dictated by *Joyce v. Bauman*, 174 A. 693 (N.J. 1934), a decision by the former Court of Errors and Appeals. We now reverse and hold that a landlord does have an obligation to make a reasonable effort to mitigate damages in such a situation. We therefore overrule *Joyce v. Bauman* to the extent that it is inconsistent with our decision today.

I

* * * This case was tried on stipulated facts. On March 10, 1972 the defendant, James Kridel, entered into a lease with the plaintiff, Abraham Sommer, owner of the "Pierre Apartments" in Hackensack, to rent apartment 6–L in that building.[1] The term of the lease was from May 1, 1972 until April 30, 1974, with a rent concession for the first six weeks, so that the first month's rent was not due until June 15, 1972.

One week after signing the agreement, Kridel paid Sommer $690. Half of that sum was used to satisfy the first month's rent. The remainder was paid under the lease provision requiring a security deposit of $345. Although defendant had expected to begin occupancy around May 1, his plans were changed. He wrote to Sommer on May 19, 1972, explaining

> I was to be married on June 3, 1972. Unhappily the engagement was broken and the wedding plans cancelled. Both parents were to assume responsibility for the rent after our marriage. I was discharged from the U.S. Army in October 1971 and am now a student. I have no funds of my own, and am supported by my stepfather.
>
> In view of the above, I cannot take possession of the apartment and am surrendering all rights to it. Never having received a key, I cannot return same to you.

---

[1]   Among other provisions, the lease prohibited the tenant from assigning or transferring the lease without the consent of the landlord. If the tenant defaulted, the lease gave the landlord the option of re-entering or re-letting, but stipulated that failure to re-let or to recover the full rental would not discharge the tenant's liability for rent.

I beg your understanding and compassion in releasing me from the lease, and will of course, in consideration thereof, forfeit the 2 month's rent already paid.

Please notify me at your earliest convenience.

Plaintiff did not answer the letter.

Subsequently, a third party went to the apartment house and inquired about renting apartment 6–L. Although the parties agreed that she was ready, willing and able to rent the apartment, the person in charge told her that the apartment was not being shown since it was already rented to Kridel. In fact, the landlord did not re-enter the apartment or exhibit it to anyone until August 1, 1973. At that time it was rented to a new tenant for a term beginning on September 1, 1973. The new rental was for $345 per month with a six week concession similar to that granted Kridel.

Prior to re-letting the new premises, plaintiff sued Kridel in August 1972, demanding $7,590, the total amount due for the full two-year term of the lease. Following a mistrial, plaintiff filed an amended complaint asking for $5,865, the amount due between May 1, 1972 and September 1, 1973. The amended complaint included no reduction in the claim to reflect the six week concession provided for in the lease or the $690 payment made to plaintiff after signing the agreement. Defendant filed an amended answer to the complaint, alleging that plaintiff breached the contract, failed to mitigate damages and accepted defendant's surrender of the premises. He also counterclaimed to demand repayment of the $345 paid as a security deposit.

The trial judge ruled in favor of defendant. Despite his conclusion that the lease had been drawn to reflect "the 'settled law' of this state," he found that "justice and fair dealing" imposed upon the landlord the duty to attempt to re-let the premises and thereby mitigate damages. He also held that plaintiff's failure to make any response to defendant's unequivocal offer of surrender was tantamount to an acceptance, thereby terminating the tenancy and any obligation to pay rent. As a result, he dismissed both the complaint and the counterclaim. The Appellate Division reversed in a per curiam opinion, and we granted certification. * * *

II

As the lower courts in both appeals found, the weight of authority in this State supports the rule that a landlord is under no duty to mitigate damages caused by a defaulting tenant. This rule has been followed in a majority of states, Annot. 21 A.L.R.3d 534, § 2(a) at 541 (1968), and has been tentatively adopted in the American Law Institute's Restatement of Property. Restatement (Second) of Property, § 11.1(3) (Tent. Draft No. 3, 1975).

Nevertheless, while there is still a split of authority over this question, the trend among recent cases appears to be in favor of a mitigation requirement.

The majority rule is based on principles of property law which equate a lease with a transfer of a property interest in the owner's estate. Under this rationale the lease conveys to a tenant an interest in the property which forecloses any control by the landlord; thus, it would be anomalous to require the landlord to concern himself with the tenant's abandonment of his own property.

For instance, in *Muller v. Beck*, [110 A. 831 (N.J. 1920)], where essentially the same issue was posed, the court clearly treated the lease as governed by property, as opposed to contract, precepts.[3] The court there observed that the "tenant had an estate for years, but it was an estate qualified by this right of the landlord to prevent its transfer," 110 A. at 832, and that "the tenant has an estate with which the landlord may not interfere." Id. Similarly, in *Heckel v. Griese*, [171 A. 148 (N.J. 1934)], the court noted the absolute nature of the tenant's interest in the property while the lease was in effect, stating that "when the tenant vacated, . . . no one, in the circumstances, had any right to interfere with the defendant's possession of the premises." 171 A. 148, 149. * * *

Yet the distinction between a lease for ordinary residential purposes and an ordinary contract can no longer be considered viable. As Professor Powell observed, evolving "social factors have exerted increasing influence on the law of estates for years." 2 Powell on Real Property (1977 ed.), § 221(1) at 180–81. The result has been that

> [t]he complexities of city life, and the proliferated problems of modern society in general, have created new problems for lessors and lessees and these have been commonly handled by specific clauses in leases. This growth in the number and detail of specific lease covenants has reintroduced into the law of estates for years a predominantly contractual ingredient. (Id. at 181)

Thus in 6 Williston on Contracts (3 ed. 1962), § 890A at 592, it is stated:

> There is a clearly discernible tendency on the part of courts to cast aside technicalities in the interpretation of leases and to concentrate their attention, as in the case of other contracts, on the intention of the parties * * *

See also Javins v. First National Realty Corp., 428 F.2d 1071, 1075 (D.C. Cir. 1970) ("the trend toward treating leases as contracts is wise and well considered") * * *

This Court has taken the lead in requiring that landlords provide housing services to tenants in accordance with implied duties which are

---

[3]   It is well settled that a party claiming damages for a breach of contract has a duty to mitigate his loss.

hardly consistent with the property notions expressed in *Muller v. Beck*, supra, and *Heckel v. Griese*, supra. See Braitman v. Overlook Terrace Corp., 346 A.2d 76 (N.J. 1975) (liability for failure to repair defective apartment door lock); Berzito v. Gambino, 308 A.2d 17 (N.J. 1973) (construing implied warranty of habitability and covenant to pay rent as mutually dependent); Marini v. Ireland, 265 A.2d 526 (N.J. 1970) (implied covenant to repair); Reste Realty Corp. v. Cooper, 251 A.2d 268 (N.J. 1969) (implied warranty of fitness of premises for leased purpose). In fact, in *Reste Realty Corp. v. Cooper*, supra, we specifically noted that the rule which we announced there did not comport with the historical notion of a lease as an estate for years. And in *Marini v. Ireland*, supra, we found that the "guidelines employed to construe contracts have been modernly applied to the construction of leases." 265 A.2d at 532.

Application of the contract rule requiring mitigation of damages to a residential lease may be justified as a matter of basic fairness.[4] Professor McCormick first commented upon the inequity under the majority rule when he predicted in 1925 that eventually

> the logic, inescapable according to the standards of a "jurisprudence of conceptions" which permits the landlord to stand idly by the vacant, abandoned premises and treat them as the property of the tenant and recover full rent, will yield to the more realistic notions of social advantage which in other fields of the law have forbidden a recovery for damages which the plaintiff by reasonable efforts could have avoided. [McCormick, The Rights of the Landlord Upon Abandonment of the Premises by the Tenant, 23 Mich. L. Rev. 211, 221–22 (1925)]

Various courts have adopted this position. See Annot., supra, § 7(a) at 565, and ante at 770–771.

The pre-existing rule cannot be predicated upon the possibility that a landlord may lose the opportunity to rent another empty apartment because he must first rent the apartment vacated by the defaulting tenant. Even where the breach occurs in a multi-dwelling building, each apartment may have unique qualities which make it attractive to certain individuals. Significantly, in *Sommer v. Kridel*, there was a specific request to rent the apartment vacated by the defendant; there is no reason to believe that absent this vacancy the landlord could have succeeded in renting a different apartment to this individual.

We therefore hold that antiquated real property concepts which served as the basis for the pre-existing rule, shall no longer be controlling where there is a claim for damages under a residential lease. Such claims must be governed by more modern notions of fairness and equity. A

---

[4]   We see no distinction between the leases involved in the instant appeals and those which might arise in other types of residential housing. However, we reserve for another day the question of whether a landlord must mitigate damages in a commercial setting.

landlord has a duty to mitigate damages where he seeks to recover rents due from a defaulting tenant.

If the landlord has other vacant apartments besides the one which the tenant has abandoned, the landlord's duty to mitigate consists of making reasonable efforts to re-let the apartment. In such cases he must treat the apartment in question as if it was one of his vacant stock.

As part of his cause of action, the landlord shall be required to carry the burden of proving that he used reasonable diligence in attempting to re-let the premises. We note that there has been a divergence of opinion concerning the allocation of the burden of proof on this issue. See Annot., supra, § 12 at 577. While generally in contract actions the breaching party has the burden of proving that damages are capable of mitigation, here the landlord will be in a better position to demonstrate whether he exercised reasonable diligence in attempting to re-let the premises. Cf. *Kulm v. Coast to Coast Stores Central Org.*, 432 P.2d 1006 (Or. 1967) (burden on lessor in contract to renew a lease).

III

The *Sommer v. Kridel* case presents a classic example of the unfairness which occurs when a landlord has no responsibility to minimize damages. Sommer waited 15 months and allowed $4658.50 in damages to accrue before attempting to re-let the apartment. Despite the availability of a tenant who was ready, willing and able to rent the apartment, the landlord needlessly increased the damages by turning her away. While a tenant will not necessarily be excused from his obligations under a lease simply by finding another person who is willing to rent the vacated premises, see, e.g., *Reget v. Dempsey-Tegler & Co.*, 216 N.E.2d 500 (Ill. App. 1966) (new tenant insisted on leasing the premises under different terms); *Edmands v. Rust & Richardson Drug Co.*, 77 N.E. 713 (Mass. 1906) (landlord need not accept insolvent tenant), here there has been no showing that the new tenant would not have been suitable. We therefore find that plaintiff could have avoided the damages which eventually accrued, and that the defendant was relieved of his duty to continue paying rent. Ordinarily we would require the tenant to bear the cost of any reasonable expenses incurred by a landlord in attempting to re-let the premises, but no such expenses were incurred in this case.[5]
* * *

In assessing whether the landlord has satisfactorily carried his burden, the trial court shall consider, among other factors, whether the landlord, either personally or through an agency, offered or showed the apartment to any prospective tenants, or advertised it in local newspapers. Additionally, the tenant may attempt to rebut such evidence by showing that he proffered suitable tenants who were rejected. However, there is no standard formula for measuring whether the

---

[5]   * * * Because we hold that plaintiff breached his duty to attempt to mitigate damages, we do not address defendant's argument that the landlord accepted a surrender of the premises.

landlord has utilized satisfactory efforts in attempting to mitigate damages, and each case must be judged upon its own facts. Compare Hershorin v. La Vista, Inc., 138 S.E.2d 703 (Ga. App. 1964) ("reasonable effort" of landlord by showing the apartment to all prospective tenants); Carpenter v. Wisniewski, 215 N.E.2d 882 (Ind. App. 1966) (duty satisfied where landlord advertised the premises through a newspaper, placed a sign in the window, and employed a realtor); Re Garment Center Capitol, Inc., 93 F.2d 667 (2d Cir. 1938) (landlord's duty not breached where higher rental was asked since it was known that this was merely a basis for negotiations); Foggia v. Dix, 509 P.2d 412, 414 (Or. 1973) (in mitigating damages, landlord need not accept less than fair market value or "substantially alter his obligations as established in the pre-existing lease"); with Anderson v. Andy Darling Pontiac, Inc., 43 N.W.2d 362 (Wis. 1950) (reasonable diligence not established where newspaper advertisement placed in one issue of local paper by a broker); Scheinfeld v. Muntz T. V., Inc., 214 N.E.2d 506 (Ill. App. 1966) (duty breached where landlord refused to accept suitable subtenant); Consolidated Sun Ray, Inc. v. Oppenstein, 335 F.2d 801, 811 (8th Cir. 1964) (dictum) (demand for rent which is "far greater than the provisions of the lease called for" negates landlord's assertion that he acted in good faith in seeking a new tenant).

IV

The judgment in *Sommer v. Kridel* is reversed. * * *

NOTES AND QUESTIONS

1. Do the facts of *Sommer v. Kridel* stack the question whether the lessor should have a duty to mitigate too much in favor of the lessee? James Kridel has a uniquely sympathetic story, never takes possession of the apartment, and openly communicates with the lessor about his situation. In a companion case decided along with *Sommer*, the lessee abandoned the apartment in the middle of the lease term, apparently made no effort to communicate with the lessor, and offered defenses that the lower court described as "frivolous." Riverview Realty Co. v. Perosio, 350 A.2d 517, 518 (N.J. Super. Ct. 1976), rev'd, 378 A.2d 767 (N.J. 1977). Should these facts make a difference? The New Jersey Supreme Court held they did not, and extended to duty to mitigate to all residential leases.

2. The duty to mitigate damages has been only slightly less successful than the implied warranty of habitability as a reform. One decision reports that 42 states and the District of Columbia have adopted the duty to mitigate damages when the tenant abandons, at least for residential leases. See Austin Hill Country Realty, Inc. v. Palisades Plaza, Inc., 948 S.W.2d 293 (Tex. 1997) (adopting the duty to mitigate under Texas law). A more recent survey article puts the numbers somewhat lower, 33 in favor and 14 against, with other states adopting a standard in between. Stephanie G. Flynn, Duty to Mitigate Damages Upon a Tenant's Abandonment, 34 Real Prop. Prob. & Tr. J. 721, 732 (2000). The *Restatement* rejects an implied duty to mitigate, Restatement (Second) of Property: Landlord and Tenant § 12.1, cmt. i, on the

somewhat curious reasoning that it encourages lessees to abandon leased properties and thus may lead to vandalism. (What does this assume about the financial condition of abandoning lessees?) As in the case of the IWH, the reform effort has focused on residential tenancies, and, as in the case of the IWH, has proceeded more by legislation than by judicial reform. See 2 Milton R. Friedman, Friedman on Leases § 16:3:1 (Andrew R. Berman ed. & rev., 6th ed. 2017) (noting that in the commercial lease context "there has been very little change in the traditional common law rule, and in fact some major jurisdictions, including New York and Pennsylvania, have reiterated their adherence to that rule."). The duty to mitigate, which is a pure contract doctrine, is in fact probably more unambiguously contractual than the IWH. Some decisions, including *Austin Hill*, recognize that the duty to mitigate is a default rule subject to modification by the parties in the lease; the IWH, in contrast, is generally regarded as a mandatory rule of law derived in part from the housing codes which is not subject to waiver.

Figure 6-4
Pierre Apartments, Hackensack, New Jersey

3.   Recall that the common-law courts, working within the framework of the independent covenants model, developed the doctrine of surrender to deal with lessees who abandon the premises. How would *Sommer* be decided under this doctrine? Did Kreidel offer to surrender? Did the lessor accept? Are lessees always better off under the contractual duty to mitigate than they are under surrender? Are lessees free to invoke the old doctrine as an alternative to the duty to mitigate, or should the duty to mitigate override the doctrine of surrender?

4. Should a lessee be required to attempt to sublet or assign the leasehold before the lessor has a duty to mitigate? (See "Transfer of Interests" immediately below.) If the lease requires the lessor's permission to sublet or assign, the lessee could seek the lessor's permission. Even if the lease prohibits subletting or assigning, the lessee could ask the lessor to waive this restriction. Would such a rule encourage communication between lessor and lessee? See David Crump, Should the Commercial Landlord Have a Duty to Mitigate Damages After the Tenant Abandons? A Legal and Economic Analysis, 49 Wake Forest L. Rev. 187 (2014).

e. TRANSFER OF INTERESTS

Before you jump to the conclusion that leases are just a branch of contract law, it is important to consider some issues where property-like notions continue to hold sway. One such issue involves the transfer of possession to the lessee. Under a lease, possession of the property (the land, the apartment, the car) shifts from the lessor to the lessee. Thus, during the term of the lease, the lessee acts as the general gatekeeper of the property, and can exercise the in rem rights of exclusion that we associate with possession of property. In this respect, leases of personal property are a kind of bailment, involving a temporary transfer of possession (but not full ownership). Recall that in *The Winkfield*, in Chapter IV, the court held that a bailee has the right to bring actions against a third-party tortfeasor for interfering with possession of property while in custody of the bailee. Similarly, the lessee has the right to bring actions like trespass or conversion against tortfeasors who interfere with leased land or items of personal property during the term of the lease.

Another set of issues that raise property-like notions involve transfers of either the lessor's reversion or the lessee's leasehold interest to some third party during the term of the lease. The general rule is that when the lessor transfers the reversion, the transferee takes subject to the lessee's leasehold interest, just as someone acquiring property in which another has a life estate would acquire subject to the life estate. But when this happens, is the new lessor bound by all the provisions of the original lease? Consider the following case.

Mullendore Theatres, Inc. v. Growth Realty Investors Co.

Court of Appeals of Washington, 1984.
691 P.2d 970.

■ WORSWICK, JUDGE. Does a landlord's covenant to refund a tenant's security deposit run with the land, thus obligating a successor landlord to refund it? We hold it does not, where the lease permits but does not require that the deposit, if forfeited, be used for the benefit of the leased property.

In 1969, Conner Theatres Corporation became tenant of a part of the Jones Building in Tacoma under a lease that required a deposit of $22,500 as security for performance of the tenant's obligations. The lease provided in part:

> Should the Tenant default in the performance of said lease, the Landlord shall be entitled to apply said deposit on account of any damages which Landlord may sustain by reason of such default by the Tenant. In the event the Tenant shall not be in default under the provisions of said lease, the said deposit shall be returned and paid to the Tenant at the expiration of this lease, to wit, at the close of business on July 31, 1979. . . .

The lease also provided that all covenants in the lease would run with the land.

In 1974, Conner assigned its leasehold interest to Mullendore Theatres, Inc. At that time, the deposit was reduced to $6,000. Sometime before the assignment, the original landlord had transferred the property to North Pacific World Trade Center, Ltd. Growth Realty acquired it when North Pacific defaulted on a note and deed of trust in 1975. Growth ultimately sold it to the City of Tacoma. The City was concerned with the potential $6,000 liability, and wanted to reduce the purchase price by this amount. To avoid this, Growth agreed to indemnify the City for any liability it might have for the security deposit. In 1980, Mullendore negotiated a new lease with the City. To facilitate the transaction, it released any claims it might have against the City for return of the security deposit, but purported to reserve its claims against others who might be liable. Thereafter, it brought this action against Growth.

The trial court held that the covenant to refund the security deposit ran with the land and bound Growth through the indemnification clause in the sales contract between Growth and the City. Growth appeals, contending that the covenant did not run. In the alternative, Growth contends that any obligation it may have assumed was extinguished by Mullendore's release of the City. We agree with Growth's first contention.

A lease covenant does not run with the land unless it touches or concerns the land. To do so, it must be so related to the land as to enhance its value and confer a benefit upon it. Otherwise, it is a collateral and personal obligation of the original lessor.

In order to be a running covenant, a promise to pay money must restrict the use of the funds to the benefit of the property. Rodruck v. Sand Point Maintenance Comm'n, 295 P.2d 714, 722 (Wash. 1956).[1]

There was no such restriction in this covenant. The landlord was not required to spend the money for repairs or maintenance, or in any other way related to the property. He was not even required to transfer it to

---

[1]   In *Rodruck,* the court held a promise to pay assessments for maintenance to be a running covenant. It distinguished that covenant from one which provided for the payment of dues to a property owners association but did not specify how the money was to be spent.

his successors. The covenant was not directly related to, and did not touch and concern, the property.[2]

Since it does not touch and concern the land, this covenant cannot run, despite the language in the lease which says it does. Intent is not enough to make a running covenant out of one which is by its nature personal.

The City had no obligation to return the security deposit. Growth agreed only to indemnify the City against potential liability. That agreement did not create any new liability. We need not consider further arguments concerning the effect of the transactions between the City and Growth or the City and Mullendore.

Reversed.

NOTES AND QUESTIONS

1. Security deposits are (relatively speaking) a modern device for securing the payment of rent and the lessee's performance of other obligations under the lease. At common law, the lessor's main protection was a privilege of self-help known as the "distraint for rent," in which the lessor would seize personal property of the lessee either to coerce the lessee into paying or as a kind of after-the-fact security interest which the lessor could consume or sell in satisfaction of the rent obligation. (As mentioned in Chapter IV, the action for replevin evolved from a writ that allowed lessees to recover distrained property, and then obtain a legal test of whether rent was owed or not.) Today, distraint is rarely encountered, the most prominent exception probably being leases of storage lockers, which are chock full of personal property and have high default rates. But the lessor's right of distraint in this and other contexts is regulated by statutes imposing various notice and waiting period requirements. Security deposits have become far more popular, lessors being more interested in money than in conducting tag sales.

2. When the lessor transfers the reversion and the property is burdened by a lease that is still in effect, the ordinary rule is that new owner of the reversion takes subject to the ongoing leasehold interest. There is authority suggesting that the original parties can contract around this rule and provide in the lease that the leasehold will terminate upon any transfer by the lessor—at least if the termination clause is very prominently disclosed. See Robert S. Schoshinski, American Law of Landlord and Tenant § 8:3 (1980). If a lessor defaults on a loan secured by a mortgage and loses the property in a foreclosure, the new owner is typically not bound by the lease; the lease is regarded as subordinate to the mortgage lien. For more on mortgages, see Chapter VII.

---

[2]   This proposition is supported by the weight of authority from other jurisdictions. Almost all courts that have considered the question have held that a promise to return a security deposit does not run with the land. See Federated Mortgage Investors v. American S & L Ass'n, 121 Cal.Rptr. 137 (Cal. App. 1975); McDonald's Corp. v. Blotnik, 328 N.E.2d 897 (Ill. App. 1975); Mauro v. Alvino, 152 N.Y.S. 963 (Sup. Ct. App. T. 1915); Partington v. Miller, 5 A.2d 468 (N.J. 1939); Tuteur v. P. & F. Enterprises, Inc., 255 N.E.2d 284 (Ohio App. 1970).

3.   However, it is also the ordinary rule that when the reversion is sold the new lessor and the original lessee are not bound by all provisions of the original lease, only by those that "run with the land." In determining whether a lease covenant runs with the land, the ordinary test, applied by the principal case, is to ask (1) whether the parties intended the covenant to run, and (2) whether the covenant "touches and concerns" the land. See Restatement (Second) of Property: Landlord and Tenant § 16.1(2). What is the purpose of imposing this additional requirement beyond intent to run? What does it mean to say that a promise "touches and concerns" the land? The court says that it means the promise must be "so related to the land as to enhance its value and confer a benefit upon it." This is not very helpful, but as we will see more fully when we consider servitudes running with the land in Chapter IX (where the "touch and concern" test also applies), courts have not been able to do much better than this. One would think that if the general rule about continuation of the leasehold when the reversion is sold is subject to modification by contract (i.e., in the original lease), then the rule that only those lease clauses that touch and concern the land would also be subject to modification by contract. (In other words, we would expect "touch and concern" to be only a default rule.) But the court here holds that a provision in the lease stating that all covenants run with the land will not be enforced if the covenant does not in fact touch and concern the land. Can you think of any justification for making the touch and concern test for running covenants nonwaivable?

4.   The court says that in order for a promise to pay money to touch and concern the land, the promise "must restrict the use of the funds to the benefit of the property." Here, the promise is to return a security deposit at the end of the lease. Broadly speaking, a security deposit can be said to have one of two purposes. One is to provide a "damage deposit" that the lessor can tap into to make any necessary repairs for which the outgoing lessee is responsible under the lease. If this is the purpose of the security deposit, why doesn't it touch and concern the land? Is the problem that *keeping* the security deposit would "benefit the property," but *returning* it would not? But isn't the promise to return the deposit necessary in order to get the money and have it on hand if it becomes necessary to keep it? A second purpose is to provide a "security interest" to assure that the lessor receives the final payment of rent. Why doesn't this purpose also touch and concern the land? Consider the matter this way: Surely a covenant to pay rent runs with the land and hence touches and concerns the land. This is of the essence in the bargain between the lessor and the lessee (recall that *Paradine v. Jane* holds that the covenant to pay rent is implied in all leases). If the covenant to pay rent runs with the land, then why doesn't a promise designed to assure that the lessee pays the rent also run with the land? Is the problem again that the security deposit is not being kept (to satisfy unpaid rent) but rather is sought to be returned? But again, isn't the promise to return the deposit necessary to get the money in the first place and hold it as security in the event of nonpayment of rent? However questionable its reasoning might be, the principal case apparently reflects the majority view that a promise to return a security deposit does not run with the land.

5.   Is the problem here that the original lessor, North Pacific World Trade Center, Ltd., very likely put the security deposit in its bank account, and is now bankrupt (and probably dissolved)? North Pacific received a windfall which cannot be recovered. But why, as between the lessee and the successor lessor, should the lessee be stuck with funding the windfall for the predecessor lessor?

Assignment and Sublease

Although lease law was not part of the original scheme of feudalism that gave rise to the system of estates in land studied in Chapter V, it contains analytical elements that are probably closer to feudalism than any other feature of property law. This emerges most clearly with respect to transfers of lessee interests. The law recognizes two types of transfers of lessee interests: sublease and assignment. A sublease operates very much like subinfeudation: The lessor starts with a fee simple; the lessor carves out a lease for the prime lessee from the fee simple; then the prime lessee carves out a sublease for the sublessee from the prime lease; then the sublessee carves out a sub-sublease for the sub-sublessee from the sublease, and so on. Each of the "carving outs" creates an interest of somewhat lesser extent than the interest from which it is taken. An assignment, in contrast, operates very much like alienation: The lessor starts with a fee simple; the lessor carves out a lease for the prime lessee from the fee simple; then the prime lessee alienates the prime lease to a first assignee; then the first assignee alienates the prime lease to a second assignee, and so forth. After the initial creation of the prime lease, there is no "carving out" here; rather the prime lease as a whole is transferred to successive assignees, each of which then steps into the shoes of her assignor. The distinction is illustrated in Figure 6-5.

The distinction between sublease and assignment is important because it affects the identity of the party that the lessor and the lessee in possession must deal with when problems arise in the ongoing relationship under the lease. A sublease is like a feudal hierarchy of lords and tenants; each lord deals with the tenant immediately below in the hierarchy, and each tenant deals with the lord immediately above. Thus, the original landlord/lessor would deal with the prime lessee, and the prime lessee with the sublessee. But the original lessor would not deal with the sublessee, nor the sublessee with the original lessor. At least in theory, each chain in the hierarchy has its own separate lease (sublease, sub-sublease, etc.) that defines the rights and obligations between the particular pair of parties to that instrument. With an assignment, in contrast, the assignee steps into the shoes of the prime lessee, and as such enters into direct relations with the original lessor. After an assignment takes place, the original lessee drops out of the picture, at least insofar as having any direct responsibility for what happens on the property. So after a series of assignments, there are still only two parties who deal with the property: the original lessor and the latest assignee.

Figure 6-5
Sublease and Assignment

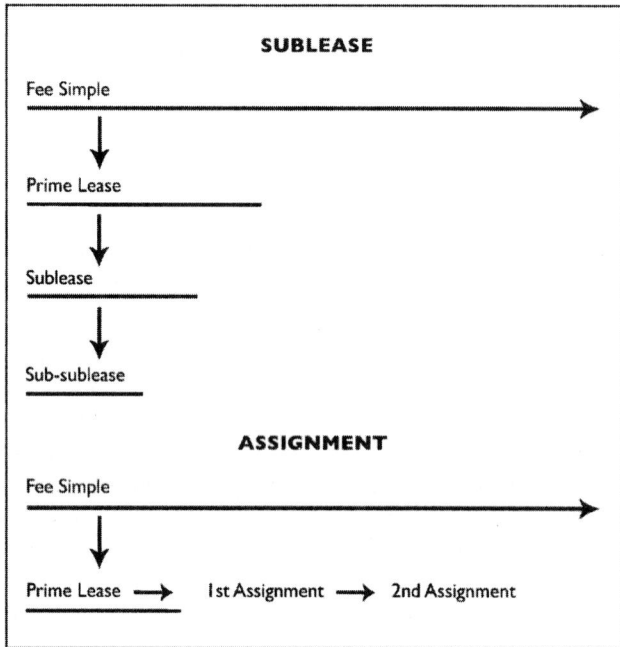

Things are slightly more complicated than this, especially on the assignment side, because lawyers over the years have said that there are two sources of lease obligation: privity of estate and privity of contract. Privity of contract is easier to understand, so let's start there. The obligations that derive from privity of contract are simply the obligations that come from being a party to a binding bilateral contract, in this case, a lease. So if the original lessor and the prime lessee enter into a lease, they are both bound by privity of contract. If the prime lessee and the sublessee enter into a sublease, they are both bound by privity of contract. But if the lessor and the sublessee have not entered into any contractual relationship with each other, they are not bound by privity of contract. One can often identify the parties bound by privity of contract, and who they are bound with, simply by looking at the leases and seeing who has signed which lease.

The source of the obligations that derive from privity of estate is more mystical. Two conditions must be met for privity of estate to apply. First, the parties to be bound must have interests such that one is directly carved out of the interest of the other. One might say that the parties must have interests that are directly "nested" with each other. Second, one of the parties must be in actual possession of the property or have a reversion. If these conditions are satisfied, then the parties are bound by privity of estate in addition to privity of contract. So for example, in the sublease hierarchy, the original lessor is in privity of estate with the prime lessee as long as the prime lessee is in possession of the property, and the prime lessee is in privity of estate with the lessor. If the prime lessee subleases to a sublessee, and the sublessee is in possession, then the prime lessee is in privity of estate with the sublessee, and the sublessee with the prime lessee, but the original lessor is not in privity of estate with the sublessee, nor is the sublessee in privity of estate with the original lessor, because the sublessee's interest is not carved directly out of the lessor's interest.

"So what?," you are probably demanding to know. So far it sounds like privity of contract and privity of estate cover exactly the same people—and they do, on the sublease side of things. But when we get to assignments, we begin to see how the distinction becomes relevant. Suppose the original lessor enters into a lease with the prime lessee. They are in both privity of contract and privity of estate. Then the prime lessee enters into a contract to assign the lease to the first assignee. The assignment does not destroy the contractual relationship between the original lessor and the prime lessee—they are still in privity of contract. But there is no contractual relationship between the original lessor and the first assignee, and so there is no privity of contract between the original lessor and the first assignee. However, the first assignee has now stepped into the shoes of the prime lessee, and holds an interest—the prime leasehold interest—that is directly carved out of (is nested with) the lessor's interest, and the first assignee is now in possession of the property. So the original lessor and the first assignee *are* in privity of estate.

How do we know what sorts of obligations exist between two parties—like the original lessor and the first assignee in our example—who are in privity of estate but not privity of contract? Where is the document, analogous to the written lease we look to in determining the obligations entailed by privity of contract—which tells us what obligations are entailed by privity of estate? Answer: We look to the lease that defines the original leasehold interest, and we impose on the parties those covenants that run with the land. And which covenants run with the land? By now you should have guessed the answer: those covenants that "touch and concern" the land. In other words, we apply the same (rather mysterious) methodology that the *Mullendore Theatres* court used to determine which provisions of the lease bind a successor lessor, in order to determine which provisions of the lease bind a successor lessee in an assignment of the lessee's interest. Perfect symmetry! See Restatement (Second) of Property: Landlord and Tenant § 16.1(2) (same test on both landlord and tenant side for whether transferee is bound by promises in the original lease).

Consider for a moment some of the practical implications of all this. If you are a lessor, and your prime lessee wants to exit from the relationship before the end of the lease, which is better: a sublease or an assignment? To some extent, it depends on how active you are in the management of the property. If you are inactive, you may prefer a sublease, because now the prime lessee will serve as the lessor to the sublessee, collecting rents, answering complaints about broken plumbing, and so forth. But if you are actively involved in management— say you are the lessor of a multi-unit apartment building—an assignment is probably better. With an assignment, the tenant in possession owes a duty to pay rent and perform other obligations that run with the land directly to you under privity of estate. And if for some reason the new lessee defaults, the prime lessee is still on the hook to you under privity of contract. The prime lessee acts as a surety for the performance of obligations by the assignee, as it were. If you are a lessee and you want to exit from the lease before the end of the term, somewhat similar considerations apply. You cannot escape from your obligations to the lessor; you will be stuck with privity of contract and estate under a sublease, and with privity of contract under an assignment. But an assignment may be preferable if you have no intention of returning to the property or otherwise remaining engaged in some aspect of its functioning, since under a sublease the new lessee must deal with you as lessor, whereas under an assignment the new lessee deals with the lessor, leaving you off the hook at least for management responsibilities.

If this were not complicated enough, there are two other concepts that are also relevant in the assignment context: assumption and novation. Assume that a lessor enters into a lease with a prime lessee, who then assigns the lease to the first assignee. An *assumption* would occur if the first assignee expressly agrees as part of an assignment agreement to be bound by the terms of the original lease. In effect, when an assignee makes an assumption, the assignee contractually agrees to be bound by privity of contract as well as by privity of estate. In the event of an assignment with an assumption, the prime tenant is still bound by privity of contract, meaning that there are now two parties bound by privity of contract with the landlord. A *novation* occurs when the parties agree to erase any privity of contract liability on the part of the prime lessee. Thus, if the prime lessee agrees to assign the lease to the first assignee, and the lessor agrees to a novation, then the prime lessee is off the hook altogether. The prime lessee is no longer in privity of estate, and the novation erases the prime lessee's privity of contract. The first assignee is bound by privity of estate, or if the first assignee has agreed to an assumption, by both privity of estate and privity of contract. Assumption and novation operate independently. One can have an assumption without a novation, or a novation without an assumption, or one can have both or neither. Careful drafting is critical to make sure that the right outcome is achieved by the parties involved.

Jaber v. Miller

Supreme Court of Arkansas, 1951.
239 S.W.2d 760.

■ GEORGE ROSE SMITH, JUSTICE. This is a suit brought by Miller to obtain cancellation of fourteen promissory notes, each in the sum of $175, held by the appellant, Jaber. The plaintiff's theory is that these notes represent monthly rent upon a certain business building in Fort Smith for the period beginning January 1, 1950, and ending March 1, 1951. The building was destroyed by fire on December 3, 1949, and the plaintiff contends that his obligation to pay rent then terminated. The defendant contends that the notes were given not for rent but as deferred payments for the assignment of a lease formerly held by Jaber. The chancellor, in an opinion reflecting a careful study of the matter, concluded that the notes were intended to be rental payments and therefore should be canceled.

In 1945 Jaber rented the building from its owner for a five-year term beginning March 1, 1946, and ending March 1, 1951. The lease reserved a monthly rent of $200 and provided that the lease would terminate if the premises were destroyed by fire. Jaber conducted a rug shop in the building until 1949, when he sold his stock of merchandise at public auction and transferred the lease to Norber & Son. Whether this instrument of transfer is an assignment or a sublease is the pivotal issue in this case.

In form the document is an assignment rather than a sublease. It is entitled "Contract and Assignment." After reciting the existence of the five-year lease the instrument provides that Jaber "hereby transfers and assigns" to Norber & Son "the aforesaid lease contract * * * for the remainder of the term of said lease." It also provides that "in consideration of the sale and assignment of said lease contract" Norber & Son have paid Jaber $700 in cash and have executed five promissory notes for $700 each, due serially at specified four-month intervals. Norber & Son agree to pay to the owner of the property the stipulated rental of $200 a month, and Jaber reserves the right to retake possession if Norber & Son fail to pay the rent or the notes. The instrument contains no provision governing the rights of the parties in case the building is destroyed by fire.

Later on the plaintiff, Miller, obtained a transfer of the lease from Norber & Son. Miller, being unable to pay the $700 notes as they came due, arranged with Jaber to divide the payments into monthly installments of $175 each. He and the Norbers accordingly executed the notes now in controversy, which Jaber accepted in substitution for those of the original notes that were still unpaid. When the premises burned Miller contended that Jaber's transfer to Norber & Son had been a sublease rather than an assignment and that the notes therefore represented rent. Miller now argues that, under the rule that a sublease terminates when the primary lease terminates, his sublease ended when the fire had the effect of terminating the original lease.

In most jurisdictions the question of whether an instrument is an assignment or a sublease is determined by principles applicable to feudal tenures. In a line of cases beginning in the year 1371 the English courts worked out the rules for distinguishing between an assignment and a sublease. See Ferrier, Can There be a Sublease for the Entire Term?, 18 Calif.L.Rev. 1. The doctrine established in England is quite simple: If the instrument purports to transfer the lessee's estate for the entire remainder of the term it is an assignment, regardless of its form or of the parties' intention. Conversely, if the instrument purports to transfer the lessee's estate for less than the entire term—even for a day less—it is a sublease, regardless of its form or of the parties' intention.

The arbitrary distinction drawn at common law is manifestly at variance with the usual conception of assignments and subleases. We think of an assignment as the outright transfer of all or part of an existing lease, the assignee stepping into the shoes of the assignor. A sublease, on the other hand, involves the creation of a new tenancy between the sublessor and the sublessee, so that the sublessor is both a tenant and a landlord. The common law distinction is logical only in the light of feudal property law.

In feudal times every one except the king held land by tenure from some one higher in the hierarchy of feudal ownership. "The king himself holds land which is in every sense his own; no one else has any proprietary right in it; but if we leave out of account this royal demesne, then every acre of land is ' held of ' the king. The person whom we may call its owner, the person who has the right to use and abuse the land, to cultivate it or leave it uncultivated, to keep all others off it, holds the land of the king either immediately or mediately. In the simplest case he holds it immediately of the king; only the king and he have rights in it. But it well may happen that between him and the king there stand other persons; Z holds immediately of Y, who holds of X, who holds of V, who holds * * * of A, who holds of the king." Pollock and Maitland, History of English Law (2d Ed.), vol. I, p. 232. In feudal law each person owed duties, such as that of military service or the payment of rent, to his overlord. To enforce these duties the overlord had the remedy of distress, being the seizure of chattels found on the land.

It is evident that in feudal theory a person must himself have an estate in the land in order to maintain his place in the structure of ownership. Hence if a tenant transferred his entire term he parted with his interest in the property. The English courts therefore held that the transferee of the entire term held of the original lessor, that such a transferee was bound by the covenants in the original lease, and that he was entitled to enforce whatever duties that lease imposed upon the landlord. The intention of the parties had nothing to do with the matter;

the sole question was whether the first lessee retained a reversion that enabled him to hold his place in the chain of ownership.

The injustice of these inflexible rules has often been pointed out. Suppose that *A* makes a lease to *B* for a certain rental. *B* then executes to *C* what both parties intend to be a sublease as that term is generally understood, but the sublease is for the entire term. If *C* in good faith pays his rent to *B*, as the contract requires, he does so at his peril. For the courts say that the contract is really an assignment, and therefore *C*'s primary obligation is to *A* if the latter elects to accept *C* as his tenant. Consequently *A* can collect the rent from the subtenant even though the sublessor has already been paid. For a fuller discussion of this possibility of double liability on the part of the subtenant see Darling, Is a Sublease for the Residue of a Lessee's Term in Effect an Assignment?, 16 Amer.L.Rev. 16, 21. * * *

A decided majority of the American courts have adopted the English doctrine in its entirety. Tiffany, Landlord & Tenant, § 151. A minority of our courts have made timid but praiseworthy attempts to soften the harshness of the common law rule. In several jurisdictions the courts follow the intention of the parties in controversies between the sublessor and the sublessee, thus preserving the inequities of feudal times only when the original landlord is concerned. Johnson v. Moxley, 113 So. 656 (Ala. 1927); Saling v. Flesch, 277 P. 612 (Mont. 1929); Mausert v. Feigenspan, 63 A. 610 (N.J. 1906); Hobbs v. Cawley, 299 P. 1073 (N.M. 1931).

In other jurisdictions the courts have gone as far as possible to find something that might be said to constitute a reversion in what the parties intended to be a sublease. In some States, notably Massachusetts, it has been held that if the sublessor reserves a right of re-entry for nonpayment of rent this is a sufficient reversionary estate to make the instrument a sublease. Dunlap v. Bullard, 131 Mass. 161 (1881); Davis v. Vidal, 151 S.W. 290 (Tex. 1912). But even these decisions have been criticized on the ground that at common law a right of re-entry was a mere chose in action instead of a reversionary estate. See, for example, Tiffany, supra, § 151.

The appellee urges us to follow the Massachusetts rule and to hold that since Jaber reserved rights of re-entry his transfer to Norber & Son was a sublease. We are not in sympathy with this view. It may be true that a right of re-entry for condition broken has now attained the status of an estate in Arkansas. See Moore v. Sharpe, 121 S.W. 341 (Ark. 1909); Core, Transmissibility of Certain Contingent Future Interests, 5 Ark.L.Rev. 111. Even so, the Massachusetts rule was adopted to carry out the intention of parties who thought they were making a sublease rather than an assignment. Here the instrument is in form an assignment, and it would be an obvious perversion of the rule to apply it as a means of defeating intention. * * *

In this state of the law we do not feel compelled to adhere to an unjust rule which was logical only in the days of feudalism. The execution of leases is a very practical matter that occurs a hundred times a day without legal assistance. The layman appreciates the common sense distinction between a sublease and an assignment, but he would not even suspect the existence of the common law distinction. As Darling, supra, puts it: "Every one knows that a tenant may in turn let to others, and the latter thereby assumes no obligations to the owner of the property; but who would guess that this could only be done for a time falling short by something—a day or an hour is sufficient—of the whole term? And who, not familiar with the subject of feudal tenures, could give a reason why it is held to be so?" It was of such a situation that Holmes was thinking when he said: "It is revolting to have no better reason for a rule than that so it was laid down in the time of Henry IV. It is still more revolting if the grounds upon which it was laid down have vanished long since, and the rule simply persists from blind imitation of the past." The Path of the Law, 10 Harv.L.Rev. 457, 469. The rule now in question was laid down some years before the reign of Henry IV.

The English distinction between an assignment and a sublease is not a rule of property in the sense that titles or property rights depend upon its continued existence. A lawyer trained in common law technicalities can prepare either instrument without fear that it will be construed to be the other. But for the less skilled lawyer or for the layman the common law rule is simply a trap that leads to hardship and injustice by refusing to permit the parties to accomplish the result they seek.

For these reasons we adopt as the rule in this State the principle that the intention of the parties is to govern in determining whether an instrument is an assignment or a sublease. If, for example, a tenant has leased an apartment for a year and is compelled to move to another city, we know of no reason why he should not be able to sublease it for a higher rent without needlessly retaining a reversion for the last day of the term. The duration of the primary term, as compared to the length of the sublease, may in some instances be a factor in arriving at the parties' intention, but we do not think it should be the sole consideration. The *Bailey* case, to the extent that it is contrary to this opinion, is overruled.

In the case at bar it cannot be doubted that the parties intended an assignment and not a sublease. The document is so entitled. All its language is that of an assignment rather than that of a sublease. The consideration is stated to be in payment for the lease and not in satisfaction of a tenant's debt to his landlord. The deferred payments are evidenced by promissory notes, which are not ordinarily given by one making a lease. From the appellee's point of view it is unfortunate that the assignment makes no provision for the contingency of a fire, but the appellant's position is certainly not without equity. Jaber sold his merchandise at public auction, and doubtless at reduced prices, in order to vacate the premises for his assignees. Whether he would have taken the same course had the contract provided for a cancellation of the deferred payments in case of a fire we have no way of knowing. A decision either way works a hardship on the losing party. In this situation we do not feel called upon to supply a provision in the assignment which might have been, but was not, demanded by the assignees.

Reversed.

NOTES AND QUESTIONS

1. The court makes several assumptions that might be challenged. First, it assumes that *Paradine v. Jane* still describes the risk of casualty loss as between lessor and lessee, unless the lease provides to the contrary. Second, it assumes that the provision in the original lease providing for termination in the event of destruction is not a covenant that runs with the leasehold upon assignment to a new lessee. Third, it assumes that if a prime lease is terminated, a sublease is also terminated. Which if any of these assumptions do you think is questionable? What would be the effect on the result in the case if any of these assumptions was reversed?

2. Although the court announces that it is foreswearing formalism and instead will enforce the intentions of the parties, it appears that the court still assumes that the inquiry into intent will reveal either that the parties intended an assignment or intended a sublease, one or the other. The court does not contemplate the possibility that the analysis of intent might reveal some novel set of rights and duties between transferor and transferee that partake of characteristics different from the standard package of incidents one gets with either an assignment or a sublease. In this sense the anti-formalist inquiry into intentions is still broadly consistent with the *numerus clausus*.

3. The English rule described by the court, which categorizes transfers as being either an assignment or sublease based on whether the prime lessee retains a reversion (even if only of one day at the end of the prime lease), may have been derived from feudalism. But it also has the virtue of being very easy to apply, and hence to comply with. In opposition to the English rule, the court endorses "the common sense distinction between a sublease and an assignment." What is that? That a sublease occurs when the prime tenant acts as a lessor toward the new lessee, and an assignment occurs when the prime lessee just drops out of the picture? But what sorts of facts will be relevant in making this kind of "common sense" determination? An all-things-considered inquiry into the "common sense" of the situation will entail more uncertainty. The prospect of such uncertainty, and litigation caused by uncertainty, could result in much more elaborately drafted leases with lots of redundant declarations of intent superimposed on top of the old formalism. Are these additional drafting costs worth the benefits of avoiding the occasional injustices cited by the *Jaber* court?

4. The court seems to imply that the old formalistic test would be okay if everyone had a competent lawyer; but this cannot be assumed, so we need to allow courts to engage in wide-ranging examinations of party intent. Yet if assignment and subletting occur primarily in commercial lease contexts,

won't the parties nearly always be represented by counsel? Should legal rules be devised on the assumption that some significant percentage of parties advised by counsel will be advised incompetently?

5.   Note that in the event of an assignment without an assumption by the new tenant of the original lease between the lessor and the original lessee, the test for which covenants in the original lease are binding as between the landlord and the new tenant is the same as the test for determining which lease covenants carry over upon the sale of the reversion by the original lessor—those covenants which touch and concern the land. Does this mean, on the reasoning of *Mullendore Theatres*, that the original lessor is not obliged to return a security deposit paid by the original lessee to the new lessee on the termination of the lease?

Kendall v. Ernest Pestana, Inc.

Supreme Court of California, 1985.
709 P.2d 837.

■ BROUSSARD, JUSTICE. This case concerns the effect of a provision in a commercial lease[1] that the lessee may not assign the lease or sublet the premises without the lessor's prior written consent. The question we address is whether, in the absence of a provision that such consent will not be unreasonably withheld, a lessor may unreasonably and arbitrarily withhold his or her consent to an assignment.[2] This is a question of first impression in this court.

I.

* * * The allegations of the complaint may be summarized as follows. The lease at issue is for 14,400 square feet of hangar space at the San Jose Municipal Airport. The City of San Jose, as owner of the property, leased it to Irving and Janice Perlitch, who in turn assigned their interest to respondent Ernest Pestana, Inc. Prior to assigning their interest to respondent, the Perlitches entered into a 25-year sublease with one Robert Bixler commencing on January 1, 1970. The sublease covered an original five-year term plus four 5-year options to renew. The rental rate was to be increased every 10 years in the same proportion as rents increased on the master lease from the City of San Jose. The premises were to be used by Bixler for the purpose of conducting an airplane maintenance business.

Bixler conducted such a business under the name "Flight Services" until, in 1981, he agreed to sell the business to appellants Jack Kendall, Grady O'Hara and Vicki O'Hara. The proposed sale included the business and the equipment, inventory and improvements on the property, together with the existing lease. The proposed assignees had a stronger

---

[1]   We are presented only with a commercial lease and therefore do not address the question whether residential leases are controlled by the principles articulated in this opinion.

[2]   Since the present case involves an assignment rather than a sublease, we will speak primarily in terms of assignments. However, our holding applies equally to subleases. * * *

financial statement and greater net worth than the current lessee, Bixler, and they were willing to be bound by the terms of the lease.

The lease provided that written consent of the lessor was required before the lessee could assign his interest, and that failure to obtain such consent rendered the lease voidable at the option of the lessor.[5] Accordingly, Bixler requested consent from the Perlitches' successor-in-interest, respondent Ernest Pestana, Inc. Respondent refused to consent to the assignment and maintained that it had an absolute right arbitrarily to refuse any such request. The complaint recites that respondent demanded "increased rent and other more onerous terms" as a condition of consenting to Bixler's transfer of interest.

The proposed assignees brought suit for declaratory and injunctive relief and damages seeking, inter alia, a declaration "that the refusal of ERNEST PESTANA, INC. to consent to the assignment of the lease is unreasonable and is an unlawful restraint on the freedom of alienation. . . ." The trial court sustained a demurrer to the complaint without leave to amend and this appeal followed.

II.

The law generally favors free alienability of property, and California follows the common law rule that a leasehold interest is freely alienable. Contractual restrictions on the alienability of leasehold interests are, however, permitted. "Such restrictions are justified as reasonable protection of the interests of the lessor as to who shall possess and manage property in which he has a reversionary interest and from which he is deriving income." (Schoshinski, American Law of Landlord and Tenant § 8:15, at pp. 578–579 (1980)).

The common law's hostility toward restraints on alienation has caused such restraints on leasehold interests to be strictly construed against the lessor. [*Chapman v. Great Western Gypsum Co.*, 14 P.2d 758, 760 (Cal. 1932).] This is particularly true where the restraint in question is a "forfeiture restraint," under which the lessor has the option to terminate the lease if an assignment is made without his or her consent. (See Karbelnig v. Brothwell, 53 Cal.Rptr. 335, 340 (Cal. App. 1966); Civ.Code, § 1442 ["A condition involving a forfeiture must be strictly interpreted against the party for whose benefit it is created."]; 2 Powell on Real Property, ¶ 246[1], at pp. 372.100–372.101.)

---

[5]   Paragraph 13 of the sublease between the Perlitches and Bixler provides: "Lessee shall not assign this lease, or any interest therein, and shall not sublet the said premises or any part thereof, or any right or privilege appurtenant thereto, or suffer any other person (the agents and servants of Lessee excepted) to occupy or use said premises, or any portion thereof, without written consent of Lessor first had and obtained, and a consent to one assignment, subletting, occupation or use by any other person, shall not be deemed to be a consent to any subsequent assignment, subletting, occupation or use by another person. Any such assignment or subletting without this consent shall be void, and shall, at the option of Lessor, terminate this lease. This lease shall not, nor shall any interest therein, be assignable, as to the interest of lessee, by operation of alaw [*sic*], without the written consent of Lessor."

Nevertheless, a majority of jurisdictions have long adhered to the rule that where a lease contains an approval clause (a clause stating that the lease cannot be assigned without the prior consent of the lessor), the lessor may arbitrarily refuse to approve a proposed assignee no matter how suitable the assignee appears to be and no matter how unreasonable the lessor's objection. The harsh consequences of this rule have often been avoided through application of the doctrines of waiver and estoppel, under which the lessor may be found to have waived (or be estopped from asserting) the right to refuse consent to assignment.

The traditional majority rule has come under steady attack in recent years. A growing minority of jurisdictions now hold that where a lease provides for assignment only with the prior consent of the lessor, such consent may be withheld *only where the lessor has a commercially reasonable objection to the assignment,* even in the absence of a provision in the lease stating that consent to assignment will not be unreasonably withheld.

For the reasons discussed below, we conclude that the minority rule is the preferable position. * * *

III.

The impetus for change in the majority rule has come from two directions, reflecting the dual nature of a lease as a conveyance of a leasehold interest and a contract. (See Medico-Dental Bldg. Co. v. Horton & Converse, 132 P.2d 457 (Cal. 1942).) The policy against restraints on alienation pertains to leases in their nature as *conveyances.* Numerous courts and commentators have recognized that "[i]n recent times the necessity of permitting reasonable alienation of commercial space has become paramount in our increasingly urban society." (Schweiso v. Williams, 198 Cal. Rptr. 238, 240 (Cal. App. 1984)). * * *

One commentator explains as follows: "The common-law hostility to restraints on alienation had a large exception with respect to estates for years. A lessor could prohibit the lessee from transferring the estate for years to whatever extent he might desire. It was believed that the objectives served by allowing such restraints outweighed the social evils implicit in the restraints, in that they gave to the lessor a needed control over the person entrusted with the lessor's property and to whom he must look for the performance of the covenants contained in the lease. Whether this reasoning retains full validity can well be doubted. Relationships between lessor and lessee have tended to become more and more impersonal. Courts have considerably lessened the effectiveness of restraint clauses by strict construction and liberal applications of the doctrine of waiver. With the shortage of housing and, in many places, of commercial space as well, the allowance of lease clauses forbidding assignments and subleases is beginning to be curtailed by statutes." (2 Powell, supra, ¶ 246[1], at pp. 372.97–372.98, fns. omitted.) * * *

The second impetus for change in the majority rule comes from the nature of a lease as a *contract*. As the Court of Appeal observed in *Cohen v. Ratinoff*, 195 Cal.Rptr. 84 (Cal. App. 1983), "[s]ince *Richard v. Degan & Brody, Inc.* [espousing the majority rule] was decided, . . . there has been an increased recognition of and emphasis on the duty of good faith and fair dealing inherent in every contract." (Id. at 88.) Thus, "[i]n every contract there is an implied covenant that neither party shall do anything which will have the effect of destroying or injuring the right of the other party to receive the fruits of the contract. . . ." (Universal Sales Corp. v. Cal. Press Mfg. Co., 128 P.2d 665, 677 (Cal. 1942)). * * * Here the lessor retains the discretionary power to approve or disapprove an assignee proposed by the other party to the contract; this discretionary power should therefore be exercised in accordance with commercially reasonable standards. "Where a lessee is entitled to sublet under common law, but has agreed to limit that right by first acquiring the consent of the landlord, we believe the lessee has a right to expect that consent will not be unreasonably withheld." (Fernandez v. Vazquez, 397 So.2d 1171, 1174 (Fla. Ct. App. 1981).)[15]

Under the minority rule, the determination whether a lessor's refusal to consent was reasonable is a question of fact. Some of the factors that the trier of fact may properly consider in applying the standards of good faith and commercial reasonableness are: financial responsibility of the proposed assignee; suitability of the use for the particular property; legality of the proposed use; need for alteration of the premises; and nature of the occupancy, i.e., office, factory, clinic, etc.

Denying consent solely on the basis of personal taste, convenience or sensibility is not commercially reasonable. Nor is it reasonable to deny consent "in order that the landlord may charge a higher rent than originally contracted for." (Schweiso v. Williams, 198 Cal. Rptr. 238, 240 (Cal. App. 1984)). This is because the lessor's desire for a better bargain than contracted for has nothing to do with the permissible purposes of the restraint on alienation—to protect the lessor's interest in the preservation of the property and the performance of the lease covenants. " '[T]he clause is for the protection of the landlord *in its ownership and operation of the particular property*—not for its general economic protection.' " (Ringwood Associates, Ltd. v. Jack's of Route 23, Inc., 379 A.2d 508, 512 (N.J. Super. 1977), quoting Krieger v. Helmsley-Spear, Inc., 302 A.2d 129 (N.J. 1973), italics added.)

In contrast to the policy reasons advanced in favor of the minority rule, the majority rule has traditionally been justified on three grounds.

---

[15]   Some commentators have drawn an analogy between this situation and the duties of good faith and reasonableness implied in all transactions under the Uniform Commercial Code. (U.Com.Code §§ 1–203, 2–103(b); see also U.Com.Code § 1–102, com. 1 [permitting application of the U.Com.Code to matters not expressly within its scope].) See Comment, The Approval Clause in a Lease: Toward a Standard of Reasonableness, [17 U.S.F.L.Rev. 681, 695 (1983)]; see also Levin, Withholding Consent to Assignment: The Changing Rights of the Commercial Landlord, 30 De Paul L.Rev. 109, 136 (1980).

Respondent raises a fourth argument in its favor as well. None of these do we find compelling.

First, it is said that a lease is a conveyance of an interest in real property, and that the lessor, having exercised a personal choice in the selection of a tenant and provided that no substitute shall be acceptable without prior consent, is under no obligation to look to anyone but the lessee for the rent. This argument is based on traditional rules of conveyancing and on concepts of freedom of ownership and control over one's property.

A lessor's freedom at common law to look to no one but the lessee for the rent has, however, been undermined by the adoption in California of a rule that lessors—like all other contracting parties—have a duty to mitigate damages upon the lessee's abandonment of the property by seeking a substitute lessee. (See Civ.Code, § 1951.2.) Furthermore, the values that go into the personal selection of a lessee are preserved under the minority rule in the lessor's right to refuse consent to assignment on any commercially reasonable grounds. Such grounds include not only the obvious objections to an assignee's financial stability or proposed use of the premises, but a variety of other commercially reasonable objections as well. (See, e.g., Arrington v. Walter E. Heller Int'l Corp., 333 N.E.2d 50 (Ill. App. 1975) [desire to have only one "lead tenant" in order to preserve "image of the building" as tenant's international headquarters]; Warmack v. Merchants Nat'l Bank of Fort Smith, 612 S.W.2d 733 (Ark. 1981) [desire for good "tenant mix" in shopping center]; List v. Dahnke 638 P.2d 824 (Colo. App. 1981) [lessor's refusal to consent to assignment of lease by one restaurateur to another was reasonable where lessor believed proposed specialty restaurant would not succeed at that location].) The lessor's interests are further protected by the fact that the original lessee remains a guarantor of the performance of the assignee.

The second justification advanced in support of the majority rule is that an approval clause is an unambiguous reservation of absolute discretion in the lessor over assignments of the lease. The lessee could have bargained for the addition of a reasonableness clause to the lease (i.e., "consent to assignment will not be unreasonably withheld"). The lessee having failed to do so, the law should not rewrite the parties' contract for them.

Numerous authorities have taken a different view of the meaning and effect of an approval clause in a lease, indicating that the clause is not "clear and unambiguous," as respondent suggests. [Citing and quoting Granite Trust Bldg. Corp. v. Great Atlantic & Pacific Tea Co., 36 F.Supp. 77, 78 (D. Mass. 1940); Gamble v. New Orleans Housing Mart, Inc., 154 So.2d 625, 627 (La. App. 1963); In Shaker Bldg. Co. v. Federal Lime and Stone Co., 277 N.E.2d 584, 587 (Ohio Mun. 1971).]

In light of the interpretations given to approval clauses in the cases cited above, and in light of the increasing number of jurisdictions that have adopted the minority rule in the last 15 years, the assertion that an approval clause "clearly and unambiguously" grants the lessor absolute discretion over assignments is untenable. It is not a rewriting of a contract, as respondent suggests, to recognize the obligations imposed by the duty of good faith and fair dealing, which duty is implied by law in every contract.

The third justification advanced in support of the majority rule is essentially based on the doctrine of stare decisis. It is argued that the courts should not depart from the common law majority rule because "many leases now in effect covering a substantial amount of real property and creating valuable property rights were carefully prepared by competent counsel in reliance upon the majority viewpoint." (Gruman v. Investors Diversified Services, 78 N.W.2d 377 (Minn. 1956).) As pointed out above, however, the majority viewpoint has been far from universally held and has never been adopted by this court. Moreover, the trend in favor of the minority rule should come as no surprise to observers of the changing state of real property law in the 20th century. The minority rule is part of an increasing recognition of the contractual nature of leases and the implications in terms of contractual duties that flow therefrom. (See Green v. Superior Court, 517 P.2d 1168, 1172–73 (Cal. 1974).) We would be remiss in our duty if we declined to question a view held by the majority of jurisdictions simply because it is held by a majority. As we stated in *Rodriguez v. Bethlehem Steel Corp.*, 525 P.2d 669 (Cal. 1974), the "vitality [of the common law] can flourish only so long as the courts remain alert to their obligation and opportunity to change the common law when reason and equity demand it." (Id. at 676.)

A final argument in favor of the majority rule is advanced by respondent and stated as follows: "Both tradition and sound public policy dictate that the lessor has a right, under circumstances such as these, to realize the increased value of his property." Respondent essentially argues that any increase in the market value of real property during the term of a lease properly belongs to the lessor, not the lessee. We reject this assertion. One California commentator has written: "[W]hen the lessee executed the lease he acquired the contractual right for the exclusive use of the premises, and all of the benefits and detriment attendant to possession, for the term of the contract. He took the downside risk that he would be paying too much rent if there should be a depression in the rental market. . . . Why should he be deprived of the contractual benefits of the lease because of the fortuitous inflation in the marketplace[?] By reaping the benefits he does not deprive the landlord of anything to which the landlord was otherwise entitled. The landlord agreed to dispose of possession for the limited term and he could not reasonably anticipate any more than what was given to him by the terms of the lease. His reversionary estate will benefit from the increased value from the inflation in any event, at least upon the expiration of the lease." (Miller & Starr, Current Law of Cal. Real Estate 1984 Supp., § 27:92 at p. 321 (1977).)

Respondent here is trying to get *more* than it bargained for in the lease. A lessor is free to build periodic rent increases into a lease, as the lessor did here. Any increased value of the property beyond this "belongs" to the lessor only in the sense, as explained above, that the lessor's reversionary estate will benefit from it upon the expiration of the lease. We must therefore reject respondent's argument in this regard.[17] * * *

IV.

In conclusion, both the policy against restraints on alienation and the implied contractual duty of good faith and fair dealing militate in favor of adoption of the rule that where a commercial lease provides for assignment only with the prior consent of the lessor, such consent may be withheld only where the lessor has a commercially reasonable objection to the assignee or the proposed use. Under this rule, appellants have stated a cause of action against respondent Ernest Pestana, Inc.

■ LUCAS, JUSTICE, dissenting. I respectfully dissent. In my view we should follow the weight of authority which, as acknowledged by the majority herein, allows the commercial lessor to withhold his consent to an assignment or sublease arbitrarily or without reasonable cause. The majority's contrary ruling, requiring a "commercially reasonable objection" to the assignment, can only result in a proliferation of unnecessary litigation. * * *

NOTES AND QUESTIONS

1. The economic reality that underlies the dispute in the principal case is that market rents for hangar space at regional airports in California had undoubtedly risen significantly relative to the rent reserved under the prime lease. Leasing professionals refer to this as the "bonus value" of a lease. It is simply the difference between the rent reserved and the rent obtainable in the leasing market at any given point in time. There are two ways for the original transacting parties to try to capture a positive bonus value. If the lessor is permitted to terminate the original lease and enter into a new lease at market rents, the lessor can capture the bonus. Alternatively, if the lessee is permitted to assign or sublet the original lease, the lessee can assign the lease in return for a lump sum payment or can sublease at a higher rent and thereby capture the bonus. Economically speaking, the issue in the case is which party—lessor or lessee—is entitled to capture the bonus value under the terms of the prime lease. The lessor's position is that the lease entitles the lessor (under established California law) to block the lessee from assigning or subletting for any reason or no reason, so the lessor is entitled to capture the bonus as a condition of giving consent to assignment or subletting. The lessee's position is that as long as the prime lease remains in force, the lessor has no way unilaterally to capture the bonus; only the

---

[17]   Amicus Pillsbury, Madison & Sutro request that we make clear that, "whatever principle governs in the absence of express lease provisions, nothing bars the parties to commercial lease transactions from making their own arrangements respecting the allocation of appreciated rentals if there is a transfer of the leasehold." This principle we affirm; we merely hold that the clause in the instant lease established no such arrangement.

lessee can capture the bonus by assigning or subletting, so the bonus rightly belongs to the lessee. Do you agree with the court's analysis as to how the right to capture the "bonus" is allocated under the lease?

2.   Given that the court is addressing only commercial leases, and that the parties who enter into commercial leases like the one involved in the principal case usually act on advice of counsel, what is the justification for flipping the default rule and awarding the bonus to the lessee (unless the parties have explicitly allowed the lessor to refuse consent for any reason) rather than the lessor (unless the parties constrain the landlord's discretion by requiring a commercially reasonable ground for refusing consent)? Does the Coase theorem (Chapter I) suggest that the parties will bargain around whatever default rule is established to reach the rule that maximizes their joint welfare? If that is the case, does the decision constitute a one-time windfall for lessees under long-term commercial leases negotiated under the assumption that the old default rule would apply?

3.   Recall that leases often function as a mechanism for managing complexes of assets shared by multiple lessees. Does the decision here— requiring that lessors give judicially reviewable reasons for refusing to consent to subleases or assignments unless they expressly reserve the right to act unreasonably—enhance or undermine the lessor's ability to govern a multi-lessee complex?

f. A Form Lease

Form leases may be obtained from a variety of sources. We reproduce below a form obtained from Gerry W. Beyer, 19A West's Legal Forms, Real Estate Transactions, Residential § 48.3 (3d ed. 2002).

Apartment Lease

[READ CAREFULLY]

THIS LEASE CONSTITUTES A BINDING CONTRACT

This *[_____]*, 20__ *[_____]* hereinafter called the ("Lessor") hereby lease to *[_____]*, hereinafter called the ("Lessee") the following premises: Apartment No. *[_____]* ("the Apartment") Building No. *[_____]*, located at *[_____] [_____]*. Rent per month $_____ Security Deposit $_____ TERM *[_____]* Commencement Date *[_____]* Termination Date *[_____]*. Make rent checks payable to: *[_____]* (Tel. No. ___) and remit to: *[_____]*.

1.   **Term.** This lease shall commence at 12 noon on the commencement date indicated above and shall terminate at 12 noon on the termination date indicated above at which time the Lessee shall return possession to the Lessor and return all keys to the Apartment, outside doors and mailbox to the Lessor.

2.   **Rent.** The monthly rental to be paid by the Lessee for the Apartment shall be as indicated above to be paid on the first day of each and every month, in advance, so long as this lease is in force and effect.

3.   Security Deposit. The Lessee will also pay over to the Lessor upon the execution of this lease the sum indicated above to be held by the Lessor during the term of this lease or any extension or renewal thereof, as a SECURITY DEPOSIT for the full, faithful and punctual performance by the Lessee of all lawful covenants and conditions of this lease. It is understood that this security deposit may be applied to damages caused by the Lessee. The Lessor will return the security deposit less the amount applied to damages with interest as required by law and make a full accounting to the Lessee for all damages applied within 30 days after the Apartment is vacated. It is further understood that the security deposit is not to be considered prepaid rent, [nor] shall damages be limited to the amount of this security deposit.

4.   Notices and Complaints. Notices, bills and complaints to the Lessee shall be deemed sufficiently given if deposited in the Lessee's mailbox or sent by mail to the Lessee at his last known address. Notices and complaints by the Lessee to the Lessor shall be mailed to General Investment & Development Co. to the address indicated above or such other address as may be furnished in writing to the Lessee.

5.   Utilities. All electricity charges to the Apartment, including electricity charges for lighting, appliances, heating, ventilating or air conditioning shall be paid for by the Lessee. The Lessor agrees that it will furnish reasonable hot and cold water and reasonable heat during the regular heating season in the Apartment, all in accordance with applicable laws, but the failure of the Lessor to provide any of the foregoing items to any specific degree, quantity, quality, or character due to any causes beyond the reasonable control of the Lessor, such as accident, acts of nature, restriction by City, State or Federal regulations, or during necessary repairs to the apparatus shall not form a basis of any claim for damages against the Lessor.

6.   Mortgages. The Lessor shall have the right to mortgage and the Lessee's rights hereunder shall be subordinate to all mortgages now or hereafter of record affecting the real estate of which the Apartment forms a part.

7.   Nuisance. The Lessee shall not cause any nuisance or act in an unreasonable manner either to the Lessor or to the other Lessees.

8.   Assigning/Subletting. The Lessee will not assign this lease, nor sublet the Apartment, or any part thereof, nor make any alteration in the Apartment without the Lessor's prior consent in writing.

9.   Fire and Casualty. The Lessee will, in the case of fire or other casualty, give immediate notice thereof to the Lessor, who shall thereupon cause the damage to be repaired as soon as it is reasonable and convenient for the Lessor, but if the Apartment be so damaged that the Lessor shall decide neither to rebuild nor to repair, the term of the lease shall cease.

10. Regulations. The Lessee hereby consents to and agrees to, observe any reasonable regulation that may be and as are in effect now or as may be promulgated from time to time. Notice of all current rules and regulations will be given to the Lessee by the Lessor and shall be made a part of this lease. The Lessor shall not, however, be responsible to the Lessee for any non-observance of rules, regulations or conditions on the part of the other Lessees.

11. Insurance. The Lessee understands and agrees that it shall be the Lessee's own obligation to insure his personal property located in the Apartment, and the lessee further understands that the Lessor will not reimburse the Lessee for damage to the Lessee's personal property.

12. Recreational Facilities. The Lessee agrees that he is renting only the Apartment. The monthly rent does not include use of any recreational facilities of the Lessor. The use of any recreational facilities of the Lessor may be allowed or revoked in the Lessor's sole discretion. The Lessor reserves the right to promulgate reasonable rules and regulations governing the use of recreational facilities and to establish and collect fees for the use thereof (and to amend such fees from time to time) and to impose other charges from time to time to cover the costs and expenses of operation, maintenance and ownership of all recreational facilities.

13. Condition of Apartment. It is agreed between the parties that the Apartment has been rented in good order and repair. The Lessee acknowledges that he has inspected the Apartment and the Apartment is in good order except as otherwise noted in writing to the Lessor. The Lessee further agrees that upon vacating the Apartment it will be returned to a similar condition as when it was rented, reasonable wear and tear excepted.

14. Attorney's Fees and Penalties. The Lessee agrees to pay all reasonable attorney's fees and expenses incurred as a result of any breach of this lease. The Lessee further agrees to pay as additional rent a late charge amounting to 10% of his rental obligation for any period of time that the Lessee's rent is more than thirty days late.

15. Complete Agreement. It is agreed, except as herein otherwise provided, that no amendment or change or addition to this lease shall be binding upon the Lessor or Lessee unless reduced to writing and signed by the parties hereto. It is hereby agreed that this is the entire agreement of the parties.

16. Joint and Several Obligations. If this lease is executed by more than one person or entity as Lessee, then and in that event all the obligations incurred by the Lessee under this lease shall be joint and several.

17. Severability. Unenforceability for any reason of any provision(s) of this lease shall not limit or impair the operation or validity of any other provision(s) of this lease.

18. Utility Rate Increases: [omitted]

19. Holdover. If the Lessee remains in possession without the written consent of the Lessor at the expiration of the term hereof or its termination, then the Lessor may recover, in addition to possession, the monthly rental stipulated above for each month, or portion thereof, during the Lessee's holdover plus either one and one-half (½) times the monthly rental or the actual damages sustained by the Lessor, whichever is greater, plus the Lessor's costs of recovering said amounts and possession, including reasonable attorney's fees.

20. Right of Entry. The Lessor may enter the Apartment at any time where such entry is made necessary by an extreme hazard involving the potential loss of life or severe property damage, and between 8:00 A.M. and 8:00 P.M. in order to inspect the Apartment, to make repairs thereto, to show the same to a prospective or actual purchaser or tenant, pursuant to court order, or if the Apartment appears to have been abandoned.

21. Delivery of Lease. The Lessor shall deliver a copy of this lease duly executed by the Lessor or his authorized agent, to the Lessee within thirty (30) days after the Lessee delivers an executed copy of this lease to the Lessor.

22. Renewal. It is understood that the Lessee, having received a renewal lease, shall execute and properly return the same to the Lessor or, alternatively, shall notify the Lessor of his intention not to so renew in either case within the time prescribed by the Lessor.

23. Trustees. No trustee nor any beneficiary of the trust shall be personally liable to anyone under any term, condition, covenant, obligation, or agreement expressed herein or implied hereunder or for any claim of damage arising out of the occupancy of the Apartment.

[signatures]

QUESTIONS

1.   Assume you are advising a client who is interested in renting an apartment and who has been given this form to sign by her prospective lessor. The lease omits to mention certain covenants and provisions that, as we have seen, are critical from a lessee's perspective, such as the covenant of quiet enjoyment, the understanding that material covenants are dependent, a provision calling for termination of the lease upon destruction of the premises, the implied warranty of habitability, and the lessor's duty to mitigate damages. Are any of these omissions matters of serious concern for your client? If so, which ones?

2.   Consider the covenants that are included in the lease. Are there any provisions that you would advise your client to ask the lessor to delete? Many leases contain illegal provisions, which may misinform lessees when a dispute arises. See Meirav Furth-Matzkin, On the Unexpected Use of Unenforceable Contract Terms: Evidence from the Residential Rental

Market, 9 J. Legal Analysis 1 (2017). Are there any provisions that you would advise your client to ask the lessor to modify? If the lessor is willing to consider a short rider to the lease, what is the one thing you would be most anxious to add as an additional provision?

3.   Your client is otherwise happy with the apartment and the proposed rent. The lessor refuses to make any of your suggested deletions, modifications, or additions to the lease. Would you advise your client to go ahead and sign the lease, notwithstanding the reservations you might have about its deficiencies?

g.   RENT CONTROL

The United States is relatively unusual in that rents charged by lessors for both commercial and residential tenancies are today largely free of regulatory oversight by the government. Most other countries have some form of government controls on rents, at least for residential tenancies. Historically, the United States has also experienced significant episodes of rent control, such as during World War I and World War II and again during the period of high inflation in the 1970s and early 1980s. As that inflationary era gave way to a period of prolonged low inflation, rent control regimes were gradually repealed or allowed to lapse, with only New York City and a few cities in California (such as Berkeley and Santa Monica) retaining rent-control regimes. More recently, rent control is on the rise again, primarily in large cities experiencing an influx of new residents and associated housing shortages, which in turn put upward pressure on rents, such as San Francisco, New York, Los Angeles, and Washington, D.C. Another major war or a renewed bout of inflation would predictably give rise to more widespread pressure for a reinstatement of rent controls.

One form of rent control is the rent freeze, which simply prohibits lessors from increasing the rents currently being charged. When rent controls are first imposed, as at the onset of a major war, they typically take the form of a rent freeze. Such regimes are adopted in response to an anticipated surge in demand for rental housing and are designed to prevent unexpected hardships to lessees and windfall profits for lessors. See Franz Hubert, Rent Control: Academic Analysis and Public Sentiment, 10 Swedish Econ. Pol'y Rev. 61, 69 (2003). As time goes by, however, a rent freeze generates inequities and anomalies, especially if prices of inputs for which lessors must pay (such as heating fuel) are not also controlled. Consequently, rent freezes are either suspended after a time, or they evolve into a more permanent form of regulation that allows for adjustments.

Rent control regimes that last for any appreciable period of time seek to stabilize rents rather than freeze them. Rent stabilization takes a variety of forms. Sometimes, as in post-War England up to the Thatcher government or in communist China, a government authority sets a "fair rent" for each apartment. This can be based on a variety of factors, including lessor costs, lessee ability to pay, or the rents charged for comparable uncontrolled units. A more common system is called vacancy decontrol. This restricts rent increases while the lessee remains in possession of a unit, usually permitting annual percentage increases in accordance with some index established by a regulatory body. But when a lessee voluntarily vacates a unit, the lessor is allowed to adjust rents to market levels. Special exceptions may be made for increases in cases of lessor hardship or where a lessor has made significant improvements to the property. New York City has a complicated system in which rents are not decontrolled upon vacancy, but lessors find it much easier to obtain increases from regulators based on claims of hardship and improvements when a tenant vacates—primarily because there is no one to object to the increase. Hence a kind of de facto vacancy decontrol prevails.

Any system of rent stabilization tends to balloon into a system of comprehensive regulation of lessor-lessee relations, turning the rental housing industry into a kind of public utility. The principal reason for this is the vacancy decontrol feature. If lessors could insist that lessees take a one-year term of years, then the lessor could terminate each tenancy at the end of each year and reset rents to market levels. To prevent lessors from doing this, rent stabilization requires that the term of years be abolished, and that lessees be given what are in effect periodic tenancies for an indefinite term. But lessors still have an incentive to induce tenants to vacate, either by withholding services or otherwise engaging in belligerent behavior. To counteract this, so-called landlord-tenant courts must be given authority to scrutinize the level of services lessors provide and to police other types of lessor behavior. Not surprisingly, the housing court in New York City has an enormous docket, much larger (even adjusting for population) than in any other major city without rent controls. Would going to a system in which a regulatory board establishes a fair rent (without regard to the tenure of the lessee) solve this problem? Or would it create other problems of equal or greater magnitude?

Economists have traditionally had nothing good to say about rent control. One survey taken in 1992 found that when economists were asked to respond to 40 statements related to economic policy the greatest recorded degree of consensus (93.5 percent) was to the proposition: "A ceiling on rents reduces the quantity and quality of housing available." Richard Arnott, Time for Revisionism in Rent Control? J. Econ. Perspectives, Winter 1995, at 100. The simple economic critique of rent control is as follows. If rents are fixed at levels below market clearing prices, then demand for rental housing will rise and the supply of rental housing will fall. This creates a gap between the quantity of housing demanded and the quantity supplied. In the short run, the gap will be closed by queuing: There will be waiting lists for housing, or units will be allocated based on favoritism or discrimination. In the long run, the supply will adjust to the controlled price, either because lessors allow the quality of housing to deteriorate, or they convert rental units to condominiums or otherwise take them off the market. So in the end, rent control simply gives lessees less housing or poorer-quality housing than they would have if government did not intervene in setting rents. See generally Edward L. Glaeser & Erzo F.P. Luttmer, The Misallocation of Housing Under Rent Control, 93 Am. Econ. Rev. 1027 (2003).

Defenders of rent control, such as Arnott, supra, point out that this traditional critique applies with greatest force to the rent freeze. A "well designed" rent stabilization program will have a less dramatic impact on lessors, because percentage increases are allowed each year. But even a "well designed" rent stabilization system can have serious distorting effects on the housing market. As other economists have pointed out, vacancy decontrol creates perverse distributional patterns, in which tenants who have lived in the same unit for many years pay substantially lower rents than tenants who have recently moved to the community or have just set up house on their own. See Kaushik Basu & Patrick M. Emerson, The Economics and Law of Rent Control, 110 Econ. J. 939 (2000). The folklore of rent control contains many stories about wealthy dowagers living in spacious apartments at tiny rents, while recent college graduates pay half of their disposable income or more for studio apartments the size of a closet. There is also concern that vacancy decontrol can affect the mobility of the labor market, with workers who have scored a favorable rent control "deal" declining to move to another city to take up a better job because they would lose the subsidy they enjoy from rent control. Basu & Emerson, supra; Glaeser & Luttmer, supra; Robert C. Ellickson, Legal Sources of Residential Lock-ins: Why French Households Move Half as Often as U.S. Households, 2012 U. Ill. L. Rev. 373, 379, 388–89.

Recently economists have offered additional arguments for rent control (of the rent stabilization variety). One argument points out that because each apartment is unique, and because search costs are high, each lessor enjoys a degree of localized monopoly power. Lessors may rationally attempt to exploit this quasi-monopoly by raising rents above levels that would prevail in a competitive market for fungible goods, like bushels of grain or shares of stock. Hence some tempering of rents, through rent stabilization, can improve the efficiency of the market by eliminating the premium lessors can exact from their localized monopoly power. See Aaron S. Edlin, *The New Palgrave*: Surveying Two Waves of Economic Analysis of Law, 2 Am. L. & Econ. Rev. 407, 419–20 (2000). This argument, however, would seem to justify imposing price controls on virtually any nonfungible good. For example, freestanding homes are undoubtedly more unique than apartments, and the search costs of finding the right home are at least as high as those of finding the right apartment, yet few would argue that the prices of freestanding homes should be regulated. As Edlin suggests, the amount and quality of information required to use price controls to combat local monopoly may be too great.

Other commentators who reject the economic perspective have defended rent control on personhood and communitarian grounds. Most notably, Margaret Jane Radin has argued that rent control (of the vacancy decontrol variety) is justified precisely because it tends to lock people in to particular apartments and particular communities. See Margaret Jane Radin, Residential Rent Control, 25 Phil. & Pub. Affairs 350 (1986). People develop subjective attachments to their apartments, which become an important element in their personal identities. And they form networks of relationships in their communities, which would be disrupted if they—or the other members of the community—were continually moving out in response to rent increases. By providing an additional incentive for everyone to stay put, rent control thus enhances these personhood values. Note that this argument presents the flip side of the concerns of Basu & Emerson, supra, about how vacancy decontrol is unfair to newcomers and may create rigidities in labor markets. See generally Stephanie M. Stern, Reassessing the Citizen Virtues of Homeownership, 111 Colum. L. Rev. 890 (2011). This is a theme we see often in property law—how to strike the right balance between stability and change (see Chapter X in particular).

As is often the case, our capacity to theorize about a legal phenomenon, in this case rent control, exceeds our empirical knowledge. Nevertheless, a survey of empirical studies of rent control, drawing upon 27 different studies from around the world (with New York City being the most frequently studied), draws some qualified conclusions. See Bengt Turner & Stephen Malpezzi, A Review of Empirical Evidence on the Costs and Benefits of Rent Control, 10 Swedish Econ. Pol'y Rev. 11 (2003). The studies show that the "transfer efficiency"—the ratio of lessee benefits to lessor costs—is "less than 100 percent," although how much less varies depending on the market. Id. at 47. Translated, rent control reduces the aggregate wealth of society because lessees gain less than lessors lose. The studies also show no consistent redistributive effects from rich to poor. Lessors tend to be somewhat better off than lessee, but not always, and some well-to-do lessees benefit from rent control. Id. Other findings, which are more qualified, are that rent control in one sector of the housing market tends to drive up rents in other uncontrolled sectors, id. at 46, and that the more stringent a country's system of rent controls, "the less housing investment is obtained" from the private sector. Id. A recent study of new controls in San Francisco concludes that lessors subject to rent controls have reduced the quantity of housing they supply by 15%. Rebecca Diamond, Tim McQuade & Franklin Qian, The Effects of Rent Control Expansion on Tenants, Landlords, and Inequality: Evidence from San Francisco, 109 Am. Econ. Rev. 3365 (2019). Do these findings, however qualified, vindicate the traditional hostility of economists to rent control?

The problematic effects of rent control have arguably been magnified by the growth of homesharing through the internet such as Airbnb rentals. Although systematic data are lacking, it appears that significant numbers of lessees who live in rent-controlled apartments in high-growth cities like New York, San Francisco, and Washington, D.C. have "monetized" the implicit subsidy they get from controls by renting out their apartments to tourists and other short-term renters at market rates. See Stephanie M. Stern, Rent Control Sharing, 13 Law & Ethics Hum. Rts. 141, 144 (2019) (arguing that this development further distorts the effect of rent controls on lessee mobility, "entrenches rent control's distributional failings," and further reduces "incentives for landlords to maintain and repair property").

Rent control has been subject to repeated constitutional challenges ever since its initial introduction in the United States during World War I. In *Block v. Hirsh*, 256 U.S. 135 (1921), the Supreme Court rejected a due process challenge to controls established in Washington, D.C. to keep rents from rising with the influx of military and government workers during World War I. Speaking through Justice Holmes, the Court found that the controls satisfied a legitimate public purpose because they were a temporary response to emergency conditions. "A limit in time, to tide over a passing trouble, well may justify a law that could not be upheld as a permanent change." Id. at 157. He noted further that "[m]achinery is provided to secure to the landlord a reasonable rent," and that on the question whether the rent was reasonable "the courts are given the last word." Id. at 157, 158. Justice McKenna, writing for four dissenters, asked: "If such exercise of government be legal, what exercise of government is illegal?" Id. at 161. More recently, the Supreme Court has considered several challenges to rent stabilization schemes but has always upheld the challenged law. See Lingle v. Chevron USA Inc., 544 U.S. 528 (2005); Yee v. City of Escondido, 503 U.S. 519 (1992); Pennell v. City of San Jose, 485 U.S. 1 (1988). Indeed, the Court has never invalidated a rent control scheme on constitutional grounds. When the New York legislature toughened New York City's rent control laws in 2019, a constitutional challenge was quickly dispatched on a motion to dismiss. 335–7 LLC v. New York City, 524 F. Supp. 3d 316 (S.D.N.Y. 2021).

The COVID Pandemic Eviction Moratoria

The COVID-19 pandemic hit the United States with full force in March 2020 and continued in waves of various intensity through the balance of 2020 and all of 2021. The pandemic and various government policies to try to stem the spread of the virus, such as lockdowns, imposed severe economic hardship on many persons and their families. Particularly hard hit were those dependent on work in service industries like restaurants, hotels, and tourism. It was feared that many of these persons and affected business would be unable to continue to meet their rental obligations and would face eviction and possible homelessness. There were two possible government responses. One was to adopt programs providing direct financial support for rental payments, analogous to emergency programs providing expanded unemployment compensation or general financial support to families from the government. The other was to enact a moratorium on evictions for nonpayment of rent. Although some states and local governments experimented with rent support programs, the dominant response was the enactment of moratoria on evictions. One reason for this policy choice was that evictions are ordered by courts—agencies of the government (and themselves significantly shut down)—and thus legislation suspending evictions was relatively easy to describe and enforce. Another reason, presumably, is that the cost of barring evictions would be borne by lessors in the form of lost rental income rather than by the government.

At the federal level, Congress ordered a limited nationwide moratorium on evictions early in the pandemic. Coronavirus Aid, Relief, and Economic Security Act (CARES Act), Pub. L. No. 116–136, § 4024, 134 Stat. 281 (2020). As the expiration of the moratorium approached, the Centers for Disease Control (CDC) issued its own broader moratorium. Temporary Halt in Residential Evictions to Prevent Further the Spread of COVID-19, 85 Fed. Reg. 19,654 (Sept. 4, 2020). As the CDC moratorium was in turn winding down, Congress extended it for another month. But when that month passed with no further action from Congress, the CDC decided to extend the moratorium without additional congressional authority. It justified this move based on a 1944 statute that authorized it to issue orders for fumigation, pest extermination, and "other measures, as in [its] judgment may be necessary" to prevent "sources of dangerous infection to human beings." Public Health Service Act of 1944, codified as amended at 42 U.S.C. § 264(a). Various associations of lessors sued in federal court, arguing that this language did not support a nationwide moratorium on evictions. Acting on applications for stays of injunctive relief in the summer of 2021, the Supreme Court agreed, and lifted a stay of an injunction against the CDC order. Alabama Ass'n of Realtors v. Dep't of Health and Human Servs., 141 S. Ct. 2485 (2021). Some states responded by adopting new statewide eviction moratoria, but in most of the country lessors were again free to pursue eviction proceedings.

Were eviction moratoria a proper response to the Covid pandemic and the economic hardship experienced by a subset of the population? Would direct financial support to lessors, as under Emergency Rental Assistance Programs, have been a better response? What impact will the moratoria have on future investment in new rental properties, already in short supply in many major cities?

2. COMMON-INTEREST COMMUNITIES

Leases are the oldest form of property that facilitates the separation of management from interests in possession of the property, and they remain the most common form of entity property used for these purposes. But recent decades have witnessed a surge in the use of alternative forms of entity property in which multiple persons enjoy individual possessory interests while common areas are subject to specialized management, namely condominiums, cooperatives, and other common-interest communities like gated private residential subdivisions. These common interest communities differ from leases in that, although common areas are owned and managed by some entity that specializes in oversight of these common areas, the persons who obtain individual possessory rights in these complexes have ownership interests that can be described as equivalent to a fee simple. See Restatement (Third) of Property: Servitudes § 1.8 (2000). Approximately 74 million persons in the U.S. now live in some form of common interest community, about 22.5 percent of the population, and the number continues to grow.

Because the individual possessory rights in cooperatives, condominiums, and common-interest communities are functionally equivalent to a fee simple, these property forms are not used as financing or risk-spreading devices the way leases often are. One can find isolated farms, restaurants, and single-family homes that are leased, because the lessee does not want (or is not wealthy enough) to sink significant capital into acquiring the necessary possessory rights in fee simple. But one will not find many isolated farms, restaurants, or single-family homes held as cooperatives, condominiums, or common interest communities. This is because these property forms do not offer any financing or risk-spreading advantages relative to fee simple ownership. They make sense only as a mechanism for separating management functions of common areas from individual possessory units, and so they are only encountered in contexts where this specialization of functions is desired.

The shared feature of all common interest communities is that multiple persons have an undivided interest in certain common assets. The most common example would be an apartment building, in which multiple persons own particular apartments, but all have an undivided common interest in the lobby, the heating plant, the elevators, and so forth. Another example would be a residential gated community, in which multiple persons own free-standing homes, but all share an undivided common interest in a fence, security office, and perhaps other facilities like a swimming pool or recreation room. This division of management authority between individual possessory units and common facilities could equally be achieved by leasing (and often is, at least in apartment buildings). But increasingly one finds cooperatives, condominiums, and common interest communities used for these purposes.

The oldest of these alternative property forms is the cooperative apartment building. The first cooperative apartment building was built in New York City in 1876. The popularity of this form of housing, especially for upper income apartment dwellers, grew in fits and starts throughout the early decades of the twentieth century, and eventually spread to other cities such as Washington, D.C. and Chicago. Today, New York is the only city with a significant number of cooperative apartment buildings. Legally speaking, cooperatives are corporations. The corporation holds fee simple title to the entire complex, including both the individual units—typically apartments—and the common facilities. Individuals who wish to live in the building must purchase shares of stock in the corporation, and the corporation then leases a designated space to them, typically under a long-term renewable lease of 99 years. The common areas—the building shell, lobby, elevators, heating plant, etc.—are owned and managed by the corporation, acting through a board of directors elected by the shareholders. Most cooperative apartments borrow money for construction and improvements, with the loan secured by a mortgage on the entire building. The individual shareholders, as the owners of the corporation, are responsible for paying off this debt. For this reason, cooperative apartments have always been very picky about the creditworthiness of those who seek to buy units in the cooperative—and notoriously snoopy about their financial affairs and general reputations. After all, if one shareholder fails to make payments when due, the other shareholders have to make up the difference. Originally, cooperatives held only a single blanket mortgage on the building held in the name of the corporation. More recently, banks (at least in New York) have been allowed to lend money to individuals secured by their shares in the corporation. Typically, individuals who acquire units are on the hook for both types of financing.

Condominiums are, relatively speaking, a much newer form of property in the United States. They apparently originated in Spanish law, and came to the U.S. indirectly via Latin America and then Puerto Rico. The critical event in leading to their spread in the U.S. was lobbying by Puerto Rican interests to extend mortgage insurance offered by the Federal Housing Administration to condominiums, which happened in 1961. Henry Hansmann, Condominium and Cooperative housing: Transactional Efficiency, Tax Subsidies, and Tenure Choice, 20 J. Legal Studies 25, 61–62 (1991). Real estate developers in other states then lobbied their state legislatures to enact statutes authorizing condominiums in order to tap into this new potential market, and soon the condominium form of ownership spread by statute throughout the country. Condominiums differ from cooperatives in that individual units—typically apartments but increasingly also townhouses—are owned within the walls by individuals in fee simple (rather than being leased as with a cooperative). The common areas—including the outer walls, the heating system, the lobby, and any shared recreational facilities—are owned by the unit owners as tenants in common. This tenancy in common is regulated by a master deed or declaration which is binding on all unit owners. The master deed or declaration typically calls for the creation of a homeowners' association, which manages the common facilities and charges assessments to the unit owners to pay for the upkeep, operating expenses, and taxes associated with the common facilities. Unlike cooperatives, which gained a foothold in only a few cities and today are found predominantly in New York, condominiums have been a much more successful innovation and are today found everywhere in growing numbers.

A third type of common interest community, which we will call an association subdivision, consists of stand-alone units—typically single-family homes—which nevertheless enjoy certain facilities in common with other stand-alone units. Such association subdivisions can be organized as condominiums, or they can be created using servitudes running with the land (see Chapter IX), or may be formed under special statutes that authorize the creation of such subdivisions and set forth the basic outlines of their organization and governance. See Lee Anne Fennell, Contracting Communities, 2004 U. Ill. L. Rev. 829, 837–41. Early forms of association subdivisions were private streets, squares, or gardens accessible only by surrounding homeowners, who paid assessments for upkeep of these common facilities (some of these still exist). (See Tulk v. Moxhay and Neponsit Property Owners' Association v. Emigrant Bank, Chapter IX.) Today, association subdivisions are commonly built around golf courses, lakes, or marinas, but one increasingly encounters gated residential communities in which streets and sidewalks are owned in common (as are other common facilities) and access is limited by private security guards.

Common interest communities all present special problems in terms of management and control of the facilities shared in common by the individual unit holders. In this respect, they can be instructively contrasted to leasing as a device for managing shared facilities. In terms of the governance of common facilities, the lease can be seen as a kind of dictatorship: The lessor rules as "lord" over these aspects of the complex. The lessor is a constrained dictator, of course. The lessor must exercise her powers in such a way as to keep tenants paying their rent, convince tenants to renew their leases, and convince new tenants to enter into leases when old tenants vacate. Cooperatives, condominiums, and common-interest communities, in contrast, represent a kind of democracy. The unit owners must determine some way to organize themselves collectively in order to manage common areas and shared facilities. Usually this is done through some combination of a basic organizing document and an ongoing elected governing body. A number of commentators have observed that this amounts to a kind of "private government," complete with a constitution, a legislature, executive enforcement action, and a method for dispute resolution. See, e.g., Robert

C. Ellickson, Cities and Homeowners Associations, 130 U. Pa. L. Rev. 1519 (1982).

a.   THE TRIBULATIONS OF SHARED GOVERNANCE

Any time a group of people takes on responsibility for governance of common resources, certain tensions and disagreements are likely to arise. The following excerpt describes some of the general difficulties created by collective governance of common facilities in cooperatives and condominiums; its analysis is equally applicable to association subdivisions.

Henry Hansmann, *Condominium and Cooperative Housing: Transactional Efficiency, Tax Subsidies, and Tenure Choice*
20 J. LEGAL STUD. 25, 34–36, 64–65, 68 (1991).

* * * A potentially significant source of costs in residential cooperatives and condominiums, though one that is not often discussed, lies in the collective decision-making mechanisms that these forms require.

a) Inefficient Decisions. If the interests of all members of the cooperative or condominium were identical, the decisions they made collectively would presumably be efficient. In fact, however, their interests often diverge substantially. For one thing, members vary in their preferences: some will be satisfied with wood-grained vinyl for the elevator walls, while others will strongly prefer spending what is necessary to have real wood; some will want better laundry facilities in the basement, while those who take their laundry out or have their own machines will not. In addition, interests will diverge because the members' apartments differ in structure or location: those on the ground floor may be less eager than those on the top floor to refurbish the elevators. As a consequence, there will be substantial room for outcomes that do not maximize the aggregate surplus of the occupants. This might occur, for example, when the preferences of the median member are different from those of the mean, or when an unrepresentative coalition achieves dominance in collective decisions because their opportunity cost of time is low or because they are otherwise strategically positioned to dominate the decision-making process.

In contrast, the landlord of a rental building, in making decisions that affect the occupants of the building as a group, generally has an incentive to select policies that are efficient since that will maximize the aggregate rents she can charge. Moreover, the landlord, in contrast to the owner-occupants of a cooperative or condominium, is generally free to choose efficient outcomes since she contracts separately with each individual occupant, thus depriving them of the special opportunity that a voting mechanism gives them to act strategically. In short, market contracting is likely to be more efficient than voting in aggregating the preferences of a building's occupants.

b)   Transaction Costs of Decision Making. Quite aside from the efficiency of the decisions ultimately made, there may be substantial transaction costs associated with the *process* of making collective decisions in a cooperative or condominium, such as the time that the occupants devote to meetings and other governance activities. A single individual acting as landlord can presumably collect information and make decisions with less expenditure of effort.

Moreover, the costs of collective decision making in a cooperative or condominium may be high even in comparison with *collective* ownership of the same building by a group of nonresident investors acting through a partnership or corporation. To be sure, the members of a cooperative or condominium have some distinct advantages in decision making that nonresident investor-owners lack. The members commonly occupy the building for a number of years and devote a substantial portion of their income to it; consequently, they have both the incentive and the opportunity to invest in information about the building. Moreover, much relevant information about the building is likely to come to the members without extra effort simply because they live there. And, because the members all reside in close proximity to each other, meetings are easy to arrange. In contrast, owners who are merely investors and not occupants will generally be located far from the building and from each other and, consequently, will be in a less advantageous position to exercise effective oversight or make collective decisions. Further, the investors' alternative is to delegate decision-making responsibility to a manager whom they will also have difficulty monitoring and who, lacking full ownership, will have interests that diverge from those of the investors.

On the other hand, investors differ from owner-occupants in having highly homogeneous interests. As a consequence, rental buildings, even when owned collectively by a numerous group of investors, may be spared the high transaction costs of decision making, as well as the potentially inefficient outcomes, that cooperatives and condominiums incur as a consequence of conflicts in preferences and interests among their members. And these savings may outweigh the economies that owner-occupants experience in gathering information and communicating with each other.

c)   How Costly Is Collective Decision Making? Although it is difficult to obtain direct empirical observations on the costs of collective decisionmaking, substantial anecdotal and case-law evidence suggests that conflicts among members are, indeed, a serious problem in the governance of cooperatives and condominiums and that homogeneity of membership is an important aid to viability. Moreover, the success or failure of cooperative enterprise in a variety of industries other than housing seems strongly correlated with the degree of homogeneity of interest among the members. * * *

Even more persuasive evidence that the recent spread of cooperatives and condominiums is primarily a response to tax incentives * * * comes from the remarkable paucity of commercial buildings organized as cooperatives or condominiums. * * *

Twenty years ago, when condominiums were still new, it was widely thought that they would see their greatest growth in the commercial sector. Yet this has not occurred. Commercial cooperatives and condominiums remain a rarity; multiunit commercial buildings are still almost universally organized on a rental basis. In New York City, for example, despite the extensive development of both cooperatives and condominiums in the residential sector, there was evidently only one office building organized as a condominium before 1978, and there were none organized as cooperatives. Since then, the rate of formation (primarily through conversion) of office cooperatives and condominiums has increased; nevertheless, as of December 1984 there were still only sixty such buildings in New York City in total, divided roughly equally between cooperatives and condominiums. And this was true despite the fact that office cooperatives and condominiums escape New York City's commercial rent tax. * * *

One reasonable overall interpretation of the data might be as follows: For all but a small fraction of the occupants of multiunit housing, neither the cooperative nor the condominium form would be competitive with rental in the absence of a tax subsidy. * * * By the mid-1950s, the net tax subsidy to owner-occupancy was sufficiently large to make cooperative housing less expensive than rental for a substantial segment of the population, and this is reflected in the gradually increasing share of the multiunit housing market represented by cooperatives in the 1950s and 1960s. Then, in the early 1960s, the condominium form was made available in the United States, largely fortuitously, though perhaps also in part as a response to the stronger demand for owner-occupied apartments generated by the tax subsidy. It subsequently took nearly a decade—until the early 1970s—to accumulate sufficient experience with the condominium form to make it acceptable to a broad segment of the market. After that, however, the existing tax subsidy sufficed to induce condominiums to spread rapidly through the housing market.

If this interpretation is roughly correct, it follows that, without a tax subsidy, cooperatives and condominiums might compete poorly with rental in the market for residential apartments and, at least outside of jurisdictions with rent control, might today have a relatively insignificant market share. This means, in turn, that the tax subsidy to owner-occupied housing may induce substantial inefficiency in the organization of apartment buildings and that a significant fraction of the value of the subsidy may be lost to this inefficiency. * * *

NOTES AND QUESTIONS

1.   Hansmann views the collective decision-making associated with common interest communities as an additional cost beyond the costs associated with living in rental housing communities. Is this so clear? Is it possible that what Hansmann regards as inefficiencies and transaction costs others regard as a benefit? We all know people who like to join clubs and associations that do little other than hold meetings, elect new members and officers, and sponsor programs. Is it possible that these same sorts of people—call them "civics"—also prefer to participate in collective decision-making about whether there will be real wood or wood-grained vinyl in the elevators in their building, rather than submit to the will of a dictatorial landlord on these matters? If enough civics participate in the housing market, perhaps this helps explain the popularity of living in common interest communities. Providing some support for Hansmann, one type of selling point encountered in advertisements for used condominium units is "No HOA!" [homeowners' association]. This suggests that at least a significant segment of market for common interest communities agrees with Hansmann that collective governance housing is a hassle.

2.   If Hansmann is correct that common interest communities impose costs—or at least what many consumers regard as costs—above and beyond rental communities, then this creates a puzzle: Why have common interest communities proliferated in recent decades? The percentage of Americans living in some type of common interest communities doubled between 1976 and 1999. Michael H. Schill et al., The Condominium Versus Cooperative Puzzle: An Empirical Analysis of Housing in New York City, 36 J. Legal Stud. 275, 279 (2007). Currently, common interest communities represent over 60 percent of new home sales. Clearly, the governance costs associated with this form of living must be outweighed by other benefits. The question is, what are those benefits?

3.   Hansmann argues in the excerpted article that the preference for common interest communities is attributable to tax breaks. He presents historical data comparing the tax benefits of investing in a multiple-unit housing complex (as a lessor) versus owning a unit in a multi-unit housing complex (as a condo owner). Until the Tax Reform Act of 1986, the tax benefits of being an investor (such as accelerated depreciation) exceeded the tax benefits of owning (such as the deduction for property taxes and home mortgage interest payments). After the Reform Act, the benefits of owning became relatively greater. He argues that this switch in relative tax subsidies is roughly coincident with the boom in construction of common interest communities, especially condominiums.

4.   Calculating the tax consequences of owning versus renting is tricky, however. Lessors can deduct taxes and interest payments too (as business expenses) and in addition they can deduct depreciation, something owners cannot do. In a competitive rental market, these tax "savings" should be passed on, at least in part, to renters in the form of lower rents. Also, tax policies are always changing, with the home mortgage interest deduction subject to special limits and the partial phase-out of itemized deductions for

higher-income taxpayers. Perhaps the most decisive objection to the tax benefit theory comes from the surge in the popularity of association subdivisions composed of freestanding homes, which are especially prevalent in the West and Southwest. These include private gated communities created by developers in which the streets, sidewalks, other common areas like parks, and sometimes even the police force are privately owned and operated by a private homeowners' association organized along the lines of a condominium association. Presumably, persons who purchase freestanding homes in a gated community obtain no more tax benefits than do persons who purchase freestanding homes in an ordinary subdivision.

5.   Another explanation for the surge in popularity of owning rather than renting is the housing price bubble that started in the late 1980s and accelerated through the 1990s and 2000s. Once the bubble burst, it was clear that many people had unrealistic expectations that housing prices would always rise faster than inflation and in particular that they would always go up not down. (See Chapter VII.) This belief, which was widespread, no doubt encouraged many people who otherwise would have preferred to rent, to buy a condo. It also encouraged many people who already had a primary residence to buy a condominium as a second home or an investment property, in the expectation that the value would keep going up over time and they could eventually sell at a profit. Some accounts of the bursting of the housing bubble and the ensuing flood of foreclosures in 2007–08 emphasize that the problem was especially severe in communities with high percentages of condominiums.

6.   Is the phenomenon entirely demand-driven, or is it possible that it is also in part supply-driven? One contention, which relates primarily to association subdivisions, is that local governments faced with budgetary restraints prefer association subdivisions to ordinary subdivisions because more local expenditures—for new school buildings, streets, parks, and even policing—can be off-loaded to developers who agree to pay for these things as part of the price of being allowed to develop. Local officials use their discretion over zoning and over zoning and building permits to tilt the market for new construction in favor of exclusionary communities. See Steven Siegel, The Public Role in Establishing Private Residential Communities, 38 Urb. Law. 859 (2006); Hannah Wiseman, Public Communities, Private Rules, 9 Geo. L.J. 697 (2010). This of course would explain only the boom in association subdivisions, not the rising preference for condominiums over rental housing in apartment-style complexes.

7.   Can you think of other explanations besides tax benefits, housing bubbles, or local government budgetary constraints for why persons might prefer to own rather than rent the personal living space they occupy? For example, who is more likely to have discretionary control over how to remodel a kitchen or a bathroom in an apartment: a renter or an owner of a cooperative or condominium unit? Is there any reason to think that preferences regarding these sorts of individual control variables may have changed in recent decades? Could lessors respond to increased demand for custom kitchens and Jacuzzis in bathrooms by remodeling apartments to a tenant's specifications in return for a long-term lease? Why have we not seen

this response by lessors in the marketplace for housing? Alternatively, are common interest communities a device for loading up on collective amenities so as to discriminate indirectly against low-income and minority residents? Lior J. Strahilevitz, Exclusive Amenities in Residential Communities, 92 Va. L. Rev. 437 (2007).

Condos Versus Coops

Condominiums and cooperatives are alternative legal forms for accomplishing the same end: Individual ownership of living units combined with collective governance of common facilities. In the competition between these forms, the condominium is the clear winner. Coops had a significant head start of about 85 years. But once statutes were adopted in most states authorizing condominiums, and real estate professionals became comfortable with the condominium model—roughly the mid-1970s—condominiums took off and left cooperatives in the dust. New York City, the only place where significant numbers of cooperatives remain, confirms the inherent advantages of the condominium form. Real estate professionals have long perceived that condominiums command a higher price than cooperative apartments for otherwise similar units. One study finds that the typical condominium apartment sells for 8.8 percent more than an equivalent cooperative. Michael H. Schill et al., The Condominium Versus Cooperative Puzzle: An Empirical Analysis of Housing in New York, 36 J. Legal Stud. 275, 312 (2007).

Two factors appear to account for the greater appeal of the condominium. One is financing. Coops were originally financed by a blanket mortgage on the entire facility, with individual shareholders responsible for a portion of the debt. Financing was limited to each shareholder's portion of the unpaid balance on the blanket mortgage. Today, purchasers can obtain separate financing for their unit, secured by their shares in the association. But even today the common facilities are often subject to a mortgage for which all shareholders are responsible. For condominiums, each unit owner has a fee simple in her individual unit. The value of the unit includes the owner's interest as a tenant in common in the common facilities. The entire unit value is subject to financing in the same way as a free-standing home or other real estate is.

Second and more importantly, the fact that all residents bear a portion of the risk of default by any single shareholder means that cooperative boards typically impose severe financial restrictions on who can buy into a coop. Often potential purchasers must demonstrate that they have large amounts of unencumbered liquid investment assets before they are allowed to purchase. This limits the number of potential purchasers, which makes the market for coops thinner. Coop boards are also given very broad discretion to investigate the financial history and personal affairs of potential purchasers, at least ostensibly to assure themselves that the prospect is a good credit risk (although many suspect that aspirations for exclusiveness also play a role). This close scrutiny discourages some potential purchasers from trying to buy into a coop and shuts out others who try but fail to make the grade. All of which again drives down the price relative to condominiums, where a requirement of board approval for a purchase is less common and when it exists is typically much less demanding.

b. JUDICIAL REVIEW OF GOVERNANCE DISPUTES

When multi-unit facilities like high-rise apartments or shopping centers are governed by leases, questions about governance of the complex are relatively straightforward: The lessor rules over the complex like a dictator. The lessor's dictatorship, as previously noted, is constrained by market forces and by the specific promises she makes in leases with tenants. But subject to these constraints, the lessor can make decisions about management of the common areas and shared facilities unilaterally. She can, for example, decide what color of wallpaper to put in the lobby, whether to convert the furnace from heating oil to natural gas, or whether the occupants of the individual units will be allowed to keep pets.

As the Hansmann excerpt suggests, when multi-unit facilities are organized as cooperatives or condominiums, the governance questions are significantly more problematic. Now, the owners of the individual units are also, collectively, the body responsible for management of common areas and shared facilities. Two principal mechanisms are used in cooperatives and condominiums to solve ongoing governance problems. The first is contractual. The articles of incorporation or the master deed establishing the cooperative or condominium will contain a number of rules and regulations that run with the ownership of the individual interests, and hence can be said to bind any person who acquires an ownership interest in one of the individual units. The other is to establish a board of directors, homeowners' association, or similar governing body that is charged with authority to establish rules and regulations—and bring enforcement actions—against individual unit owners. The following cases explore the role of the courts in overseeing both types of mechanisms.

Nahrstedt v. Lakeside Village Condominium Association, Inc.

Supreme Court of California, 1994.
878 P.2d 1275.

■ KENNARD, JUSTICE. A homeowner in a 530-unit condominium complex sued to prevent the homeowners association from enforcing a restriction against keeping cats, dogs, and other animals in the condominium development. The owner asserted that the restriction, which was contained in the project's declaration[1] recorded by the condominium project's developer, was "unreasonable" as applied to her because she kept her three cats indoors and because her cats were "noiseless" and "created no nuisance." Agreeing with the premise underlying the owner's complaint, the Court of Appeal concluded that the homeowners association could enforce the restriction only upon proof that plaintiff's cats would be likely to interfere with the right of other homeowners "to the peaceful and quiet enjoyment of their property."

Those of us who have cats or dogs can attest to their wonderful companionship and affection. But the issue before us is not whether in the abstract pets can have a beneficial effect on humans. Rather, the narrow issue here is whether a pet restriction that is contained in the recorded declaration of a condominium complex is enforceable against the challenge of a homeowner. As we shall explain, the Legislature, in Civil Code section 1354, has required that courts enforce the covenants, conditions and restrictions contained in the recorded declaration of a common interest development "unless unreasonable."[2] * * *

I

Lakeside Village is a large condominium development in Culver City, Los Angeles County. It consists of 530 units spread throughout 12 separate 3-story buildings. The residents share common lobbies and hallways, in addition to laundry and trash facilities.

The Lakeside Village project is subject to certain covenants, conditions and restrictions (hereafter CC & R's) that were included in the developer's declaration recorded with the Los Angeles County Recorder on April 17, 1978, at the inception of the development project. Ownership of a unit includes membership in the project's homeowners association, the Lakeside Village Condominium Association (hereafter Association), the body that enforces the project's CC & R's, including the pet restriction, which provides in relevant part: "No animals (which shall mean dogs and cats), livestock, reptiles or poultry shall be kept in any unit."[3]

---

[1]   The declaration is the operative document for a common interest development, setting forth, among other things, the restrictions on the use or enjoyment of any portion of the development. (Civ.Code, §§ 1351, 1353.) In some states, the declaration is also referred to as the "master deed." (See Dulaney Towers Maintenance v. O'Brey, 418 A.2d 1233, 1235 (Md. App. 1980).)

[2]   Under Civil Code section 1354, subdivision (a) such use restrictions are "enforceable equitable servitudes, unless unreasonable."

[3]   The CC & R's permit residents to keep "domestic fish and birds."

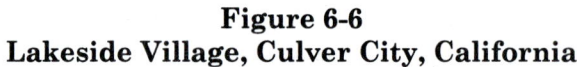

Figure 6-6
Lakeside Village, Culver City, California

Courtesy of Jack and Ginny Sher.

In January 1988, plaintiff Natore Nahrstedt purchased a Lakeside Village condominium and moved in with her three cats. When the Association learned of the cats' presence, it demanded their removal and assessed fines against Nahrstedt for each successive month that she remained in violation of the condominium project's pet restriction.

Nahrstedt then brought this lawsuit against the Association, its officers, and two of its employees, asking the trial court * * * to declare the pet restriction "unreasonable" as applied to indoor cats (such as hers) that are not allowed free run of the project's common areas. Nahrstedt also alleged she did not know of the pet restriction when she bought her condominium. * * *

The Association demurred to the complaint. In its supporting points and authorities, the Association argued that the pet restriction furthers the collective "health, happiness and peace of mind" of persons living in close proximity within the Lakeside Village condominium development, and therefore is reasonable as a matter of law. The trial court sustained the demurrer as to each cause of action and dismissed Nahrstedt's complaint. Nahrstedt appealed.

A divided Court of Appeal reversed the trial court's judgment of dismissal. In the majority's view, the complaint stated a claim for declaratory relief based on its allegations that Nahrstedt's three cats are kept inside her condominium unit and do not bother her neighbors.

According to the majority, whether a condominium use restriction is "unreasonable," as that term is used in section 1354, hinges on the facts of a particular homeowner's case. Thus, the majority reasoned, Nahrstedt would be entitled to declaratory relief if application of the pet restriction in her case would not be reasonable. * * *

On the Association's petition, we granted review to decide when a condominium owner can prevent enforcement of a use restriction that the project's developer has included in the recorded declaration of CC & R's.

II

Today, condominiums, cooperatives, and planned-unit developments with homeowners associations have become a widely accepted form of real property ownership. These ownership arrangements are known as "common interest" developments. The owner not only enjoys many of the traditional advantages associated with individual ownership of real property, but also acquires an interest in common with others in the amenities and facilities included in the project. It is this hybrid nature of property rights that largely accounts for the popularity of these new and innovative forms of ownership in the 20th century. * * *

Use restrictions are an inherent part of any common interest development and are crucial to the stable, planned environment of any shared ownership arrangement. * * * The restrictions on the use of property in any common interest development may limit activities conducted in the common areas as well as in the confines of the home itself. Commonly, use restrictions preclude alteration of building exteriors, limit the number of persons that can occupy each unit, and place limitations on—or prohibit altogether—the keeping of pets.

Restrictions on property use are not the only characteristic of common interest ownership. Ordinarily, such ownership also entails mandatory membership in an owners association, which, through an elected board of directors, is empowered to enforce any use restrictions contained in the project's declaration or master deed and to enact new rules governing the use and occupancy of property within the project. * * *

In Hidden Harbour Estates v. Basso, 393 So.2d 637 (Fla. Dist. Ct. App. 1981), the Florida court distinguished two categories of use restrictions: use restrictions set forth in the declaration or master deed of the condominium project itself, and rules promulgated by the governing board of the condominium owners association or the board's interpretation of a rule. (Id. at p. 639.) The latter category of use restrictions, the court said, should be subject to a "reasonableness" test, so as to "somewhat fetter the discretion of the board of directors." (Id. at p. 640.) Such a standard, the court explained, best assures that governing boards will "enact rules and make decisions that are reasonably related to the promotion of the health, happiness and peace of mind" of the project owners, considered collectively. (Ibid.)

By contrast, restrictions contained in the declaration or master deed of the condominium complex, the Florida court concluded, should not be evaluated under a "reasonableness" standard. (Hidden Harbour Estates v. Basso, supra, 393 So.2d at pp. 639–640.) Rather, such use restrictions are "clothed with a very strong presumption of validity" and should be upheld even if they exhibit some degree of unreasonableness. (Id. at pp. 639, 640.) Nonenforcement would be proper only if such restrictions were arbitrary or in violation of public policy or some fundamental constitutional right. (Id. at pp. 639–640.) * * *

Indeed, giving deference to use restrictions contained in a condominium project's originating documents protects the general expectations of condominium owners "that restrictions in place at the time they purchase their units will be enforceable." (Note, Judicial Review of Condominium Rulemaking, supra, 94 Harv.L.Rev. 647, 653; Ellickson, Cities and Homeowners' Associations, 130 U.Pa.L.Rev. 1519, 1526–1527 (1982) [stating that association members "unanimously consent to the provisions in the association's original documents" and courts therefore should not scrutinize such documents for "reasonableness."].) This in turn encourages the development of shared ownership housing—generally a less costly alternative to single-dwelling ownership—by attracting buyers who prefer a stable, planned environment. It also protects buyers who have paid a premium for condominium units in reliance on a particular restrictive scheme. * * *

III

In California, common interest developments are subject to the provisions of the Davis-Stirling Common Interest Development Act (hereafter Davis-Stirling Act or Act). (§ 1350 et seq.) The Act, passed into law in 1985, consolidated in one part of the Civil Code certain definitions and other substantive provisions pertaining to condominiums and other types of common interest developments. (Stats.1985, ch. 874, § 14, p. 2774.) * * *

Pertinent here is the Act's provision for the enforcement of use restrictions contained in the project's recorded declaration. That provision, subdivision (a) of section 1354, states in relevant part: "The covenants and restrictions in the declaration shall be enforceable equitable servitudes, *unless unreasonable,* and shall inure to the benefit of and bind all owners of separate interests in the development." (Italics added.)[9] To determine when a restrictive covenant included in the declaration of a common interest development cannot be enforced, we must construe section 1354. In doing so, our primary task is to ascertain legislative intent, giving the words of the statute their ordinary meaning.

---

[9]   Section 1354 also confers standing on owners of separate interests in a development and on the association to enforce the equitable servitudes, and it sets out requirements for commencing a civil action.

The words, however, must be read in context, considering the nature and purpose of the statutory enactment. * * *

As we discussed previously, recorded CC & R's are the primary means of achieving the stability and predictability so essential to the success of a shared ownership housing development. In general, then, enforcement of a common interest development's recorded CC & R's will both encourage the development of land and ensure that promises are kept, thereby fulfilling both of the policies identified by the Restatement. (See Rest., Property, § 539, com. f, p. 3230.)

When courts accord a presumption of validity to all such recorded use restrictions and measure them against deferential standards of equitable servitude law, it discourages lawsuits by owners of individual units seeking personal exemptions from the restrictions. This also promotes stability and predictability in two ways. It provides substantial assurance to prospective condominium purchasers that they may rely with confidence on the promises embodied in the project's recorded CC & R's. And it protects all owners in the planned development from unanticipated increases in association fees to fund the defense of legal challenges to recorded restrictions. * * *

Contrary to the dissent's accusations that the majority's decision "fray[s]" the "social fabric" (dis.opn., post), we are of the view that our social fabric is best preserved if courts uphold and enforce solemn written instruments that embody the expectations of the parties rather than treat them as "worthless paper" as the dissent would (dis.opn., post). Our social fabric is founded on the stability of expectation and obligation that arises from the consistent enforcement of the terms of deeds, contracts, wills, statutes, and other writings. To allow one person to escape obligations under a written instrument upsets the expectations of all the other parties governed by that instrument (here, the owners of the other 529 units) that the instrument will be uniformly and predictably enforced. * * *

Refusing to enforce the CC & R's contained in a recorded declaration, or enforcing them only after protracted litigation that would require justification of their application on a case-by-case basis, would impose great strain on the social fabric of the common interest development. It would frustrate owners who had purchased their units in reliance on the CC & R's. It would put the owners and the homeowners association in the difficult and divisive position of deciding whether particular CC & R's should be applied to a particular owner. Here, for example, deciding whether a particular animal is "confined to an owner's unit and create[s] no noise, odor, or nuisance" (dis. opn., post) is a fact-intensive determination that can only be made by examining in detail the behavior of the particular animal and the behavior of the particular owner. Homeowners associations are ill-equipped to make such investigations, and any decision they might make in a particular case could be divisive or subject to claims of partiality.

Enforcing the CC & R's contained in a recorded declaration only after protracted case-by-case litigation would impose substantial litigation costs on the owners through their homeowners association, which would have to defend not only against owners contesting the application of the CC & R's to them, but also against owners contesting any case-by-case exceptions the homeowners association might make. In short, it is difficult to imagine what could more disrupt the harmony of a common interest development than the course proposed by the dissent. * * *

V

Under the holding we adopt today, the reasonableness or unreasonableness of a condominium use restriction that the Legislature has made subject to section 1354 is to be determined *not* by reference to facts that are specific to the objecting homeowner, but by reference to the common interest development as a whole. As we have explained, when, as here, a restriction is contained in the declaration of the common interest development and is recorded with the county recorder, the restriction is presumed to be reasonable and will be enforced uniformly against all residents of the common interest development *unless* the restriction is arbitrary, imposes burdens on the use of lands it affects that substantially outweigh the restriction's benefits to the development's residents, or violates a fundamental public policy.

Accordingly, here Nahrstedt could prevent enforcement of the Lakeside Village pet restriction by proving that the restriction is arbitrary, that it is substantially more burdensome than beneficial to the affected properties, or that it violates a fundamental public policy. * * * We conclude, as a matter of law, that the recorded pet restriction of the Lakeside Village condominium development prohibiting cats or dogs but allowing some other pets is not arbitrary, but is rationally related to health, sanitation and noise concerns legitimately held by residents of a high-density condominium project such as Lakeside Village, which includes 530 units in 12 separate 3-story buildings.

Nahrstedt's complaint alleges no facts that could possibly support a finding that the burden of the restriction on the affected property is so disproportionate to its benefit that the restriction is unreasonable and should not be enforced. Also, the complaint's allegations center on Nahrstedt and her cats (that she keeps them inside her condominium unit and that they do not bother her neighbors), without any reference to the effect on the condominium development as a whole, thus rendering the allegations legally insufficient to overcome section 1354's presumption of the restriction's validity. * * *

[Reversed and remanded.]

■ ARABIAN, JUSTICE, dissenting.

"There are two means of refuge from the misery of life: music and cats."[1]

I respectfully dissent. While technical merit may commend the majority's analysis, its application to the facts presented reflects a narrow, indeed chary, view of the law that eschews the human spirit in favor of arbitrary efficiency. In my view, the resolution of this case well illustrates the conventional wisdom, and fundamental truth, of the Spanish proverb, "It is better to be a mouse in a cat's mouth than a man in a lawyer's hands."

As explained below, I find the provision known as the "pet restriction" contained in the covenants, conditions, and restrictions (CC & R's) governing the Lakeside Village project patently arbitrary and unreasonable within the meaning of Civil Code section 1354. Beyond dispute, human beings have long enjoyed an abiding and cherished association with their household animals. Given the substantial benefits derived from pet ownership, the undue burden on the use of property imposed on condominium owners who can maintain pets within the confines of their units without creating a nuisance or disturbing the quiet enjoyment of others substantially outweighs whatever meager utility the restriction may serve in the abstract. It certainly does not promote "health, happiness [or] peace of mind" commensurate with its tariff on the quality of life for those who value the companionship of animals. Worse, it contributes to the fraying of our social fabric.

* * * [T]he value of pets in daily life is a matter of common knowledge and understanding as well as extensive documentation. People of all ages, but particularly the elderly and the young, enjoy their companionship. Those who suffer from serious disease or injury and are confined to their home or bed experience a therapeutic, even spiritual, benefit from their presence. Animals provide comfort at the death of a family member or dear friend, and for the lonely can offer a reason for living when life seems to have lost its meaning. In recognition of these benefits, both Congress and the state Legislature have expressly guaranteed that elderly and handicapped persons living in public-assistance housing cannot be deprived of their pets. (12 U.S.C. § 1701r–1; Health & Saf.Code, § 19901.) Not only have children and animals always been natural companions, children learn responsibility and discipline from pet ownership while developing an important sense of kindness and protection for animals. Single adults may find certain pets can afford a feeling of security. Families benefit from the experience of sharing that having a pet encourages. While pet ownership may not be a fundamental right as such, unquestionably it is an integral aspect of our daily existence, which cannot be lightly dismissed and should not suffer unwarranted intrusion into its circle of privacy. * * *

---

[1] Albert Schweitzer.

What is gained from an uncompromising prohibition against pets that are confined to an owner's unit and create no noise, odor, or nuisance?

To the extent such animals are not seen, heard, or smelled any more than if they were not kept in the first place, there is no corresponding or concomitant benefit. Pets that remain within the four corners of their owners' condominium space can have no deleterious or offensive effect on the project's common areas or any neighboring unit. Certainly, if other owners and residents are totally *unaware* of their presence, prohibiting pets does not in any respect foster the "health, happiness [or] peace of mind" of anyone except the homeowners association's board of directors, who are thereby able to promote a form of sophisticated bigotry. In light of the substantial and disproportionate burden imposed for those who must forego virtually any and all association with pets, this lack of benefit renders a categorical ban unreasonable under Civil Code section 1354. * * *

From the statement of the facts through the conclusion, the majority's analysis gives scant acknowledgment to any of the foregoing considerations but simply takes refuge behind the "presumption of validity" now accorded *all* CC & R's irrespective of subject matter. They never objectively scrutinize defendants' blandishments of protecting "health and happiness" or realistically assess the substantial impact on affected unit owners and *their* use of *their* property. * * *

Here, such inquiry should start with an evaluation of the interest that will suffer upon enforcement of the pet restriction. In determining the "burden on the use of land," due recognition must be given to the fact that this particular "use" transcends the impersonal and mundane matters typically regulated by condominium CC & R's, such as whether someone can place a doormat in the hallway or hang a towel on the patio rail or have food in the pool area, and reaches the very quality of life of hundreds of owners and residents. Nonetheless, the majority accept uncritically the proffered justification of preserving "health and happiness" and essentially consider only one criterion to determine enforceability: was the restriction recorded in the original declaration? If so, it is "presumptively valid," unless in violation of public policy. Given the application of the law to the facts alleged and by an inversion of relative interests, it is difficult to hypothesize any CC & R's that would not pass muster. Such sanctity has not been afforded any writing save the commandments delivered to Moses on Mount Sinai, and they were set in stone, not upon worthless paper.

Moreover, unlike most conduct controlled by CC & R's, the activity at issue here is strictly confined to the owner's interior space; it does not in any manner invade other units or the common areas. Owning a home of one's own has always epitomized the American dream. More than simply embodying the notion of having "one's castle," it represents the sense of freedom and self-determination emblematic of our national character. Granted, those who live in multi-unit developments cannot exercise this freedom to the same extent possible on a large estate. But owning pets that do not disturb the quiet enjoyment of others does not reasonably come within this compromise. Nevertheless, with no demonstrated or discernible benefit, the majority arbitrarily sacrifice the dream to the tyranny of the "commonality." * * *

[T]he majority's failure to consider the real burden imposed by the pet restriction unfortunately belittles and trivializes the interest at stake here. Pet ownership substantially enhances the quality of life for those who desire it. When others are not only undisturbed by, but *completely unaware of,* the presence of pets being enjoyed by their neighbors, the balance of benefit and burden is rendered disproportionate and unreasonable, rebutting any presumption of validity. Their view, shorn of grace and guiding philosophy, is devoid of the humanity that must temper the interpretation and application of all laws, for in a civilized society that is the source of their authority. As judicial architects of the rules of life, we better serve when we construct halls of harmony rather than walls of wrath.

I would affirm the judgment of the Court of Appeal.

NOTES AND QUESTIONS

1.   Natore Nahrstedt is said to "own" her condominium unit. But in what respects, if any, does she have more rights than a lessee would have under a lease of such a unit from a lessor (other than the convenient fact that she is allowed to deduct mortgage interest from her income for federal income tax purposes)? She is restricted by all kinds of rules and regulations, and has lost any power even to say whether she gets to keep some harmless indoor cats. Apparently when she signed the deed to the property, she also signed away a good portion of the rights associated with the "Blackstonian bundle" of full ownership, including the right to keep a pet in the unit. Does this mean that she is an owner in only a qualified sense? Or is this just a reflection of the fact that part of what it means to be an owner is to be able to enter into contracts that waive or disclaim many of the traditional rights associated with being an owner?

2.   Is the majority opinion in *Nahrstedt* faithful to the controlling language of the statute that prescribes its role in reviewing covenants, conditions, and restrictions (CC&Rs)? The statute says such CC&Rs are to be enforced "unless unreasonable." The court seems to say that any restriction in the master deed is to be given a "presumption of validity" and upheld unless it produces a completely irrational result for everyone in the common interest community. Is the dissent's analysis, which seeks to show that the restriction is unreasonable as applied to Natore Nahrstedt, more faithful to what the statute says?

3.   Can *Nahrstedt*'s announced rule strictly enforcing CC&Rs in master deeds be reconciled with *Javins*' refusal to enforce certain provisions in leases such as the lessor's disclaimer of any implied warranty of

habitability? Do prospective owners of condominium units have more choices in the marketplace than prospective residential lessees do? If so, why? Are prospective owners of condominium units more likely to be represented by counsel than are prospective residential lessees? If so, why?

4.   The California Supreme Court in *Nahrstedt* also specifically disapproved of two other California court of appeals decisions that had invalidated use restrictions in condominium complexes as unreasonable. One, *Bernardo Villas Management Corp. v. Black*, 235 Cal.Rptr. 509 (Cal. Ct. App. 1987), held that a restriction prohibiting residents from keeping any "truck, camper, trailer, boat . . . or other form of recreational vehicle" in a carport could not be applied to prevent a unit owner from keeping in the carport a clean new pickup truck with a camper shell that he used for personal transportation. The second, *Portola Hills Community Assn. v. James*, 5 Cal.Rptr.2d 580 (Cal. Ct. App. 1992), refused to enforce a planned community's restriction banning satellite dishes against a homeowner who had installed a satellite dish in his backyard that was not visible to other project residents or the public. Does *Nahrstedt*'s direction that both of these restrictions should have been upheld strike you as more problematic (in one case or in both) than upholding the restriction on pets at issue in *Nahrstedt*?

5.   Some law-and-economics oriented scholars, including Robert Ellickson in the article cited by the California Supreme Court, have argued that use restrictions contained in the master deed of a complex are presumptively efficient because the developer of the project (who writes the restrictions in the master deed) will have an incentive to include only those restrictions that cause the purchase price of units to go up. Thus, the developer of the Lakeside Village complex presumably included the restriction on pets because he or she concluded that prospective purchasers would be willing to pay more for units in a complex in which pets are prohibited. Or, perhaps more realistically, developers surmise that potential purchasers will separate into (at least) two groups—those who want to live in a pet-friendly complex and those who prefer a pet-free complex. Developers will accordingly either restrict all pets or permit pets, one way or another, in new projects depending on their perceptions of which way the market is tilting at any given point in time. This process will continue so that, at any given moment, the condominium market is roughly in equilibrium with approximately the right balance of pet-friendly and pet-free options for prospective purchasers. Theoretical commentary on these issues is divided. Some authors express optimism about the ability of purchasers to get what they want. See, e.g., Ellickson, supra, 130 U. Pa. L. Rev. at 1543–44; Clayton P. Gillette, Mediating Institutions: Beyond the Public/Private Distinction: Courts, Covenants, and Communities, 61 U. Chi. L. Rev. 1375, 1363 (1994). Others are skeptical of the market's ability to deliver a large enough range of options or to protect democratic values. See, e.g., Fennell, Contracting Communities, supra; Gerald E. Frug, Cities and Homeowners Associations: A Reply, 130 U. Pa. L. Rev. 1589, 1592–96 (1982). Empirical evidence on the value of pet restrictions is mixed: An older study suggests that allowing only cats increases, whereas allowing dogs decreases, condo value. Roger E. Cannaday, Condominium Covenants: Cats, Yes; Dogs, No,

35 J. Urb. Econ. 71 (1994). But a recent larger study suggests that condo complexes with no restrictions on pets enjoy a price premium over complexes with restrictions. Zhenguo Lin, Marcus T. Allen, & Charles C. Carter, Pet Policy and Housing Prices: Evidence from the Condominium Market, 47 J. Real Estate Fin. & Econ. 109 (2013).

6. For an interesting empirical study suggesting that developers are sensitive to the potential for later political conflict, see Yoram Barzel & Tim R. Sass, The Allocation of Resources by Voting, 105 Q.J. Econ. 745 (1990). Voting rules in common-interest communities tend to track economic stakes (i.e., by unit, floor area, or by value, and not one person one vote), and the authors argue that this is a market-driven efficient result. Barzel and Sass find that with increases in group heterogeneity and higher potential for wealth transfers, decision rules require larger supermajorities. Barzel and Sass argue that harmony is easier to achieve where pecuniary benefits are at stake, rather than direct consumption benefits. They also find that decisions over amenities that will have different impacts to different units tend to be constructed upfront rather than made subject to later decisions by the association.

7. There is a growing segment of the housing market for common-interest communities that emphasizes the development of close-knit community. Examples include facets of the Sharing Economy, sometimes made possible through new technology. A longstanding movement gaining new attention is co-housing, in which privately owned units (apartments or houses) are grouped around common facilities (such as for dining and child care), and participatory democracy is emphasized. Co-housing communities vary in terms of how easily individuals can opt out of community activities. See, e.g., Mark Fenster, Community by Covenant, Process, and Design: Cohousing and the Contemporary Common Interest Community, 15 J. Land Use & Envtl. L. 3 (1999). Should courts give greater or lesser deference to rules produced by co-housing communities than those of the typical homeowners' association? See Carrie Griffin Basas, *Olmstead*'s Promise and Cohousing's Potential, 26 Ga. St. U. L. Rev. 663, 672–78 (2010) (examining cohousing with a focus on its potential for the disabled or elderly); France Svistovski, Burning Down the Housing Market: Communal Living in New York, 47 Fordham Urb. L.J. 463 (2020) (exploring impact of legal landscape in New York City on a variety of communal living arrangements).

8. Six years after *Nahrstedt* was decided, the California legislature enacted a statute making it unlawful for a common-interest development like Lakeside Village to prohibit unit owners from keeping at least one pet. California Civil Code § 1360.5 (Supp. 2001, enacted 2000). Apparently pet lovers in California have more clout with the legislature than those who wish to live in a pet-free community. Does this strike you as an appropriate subject for legislative override of covenants, conditions, and restrictions in common-interest communities? How does this affect the living options of persons who have severe allergies to cats?

9. Recently a number of states have passed laws in response to complaints that homeowners' associations were enforcing aesthetic restrictions to prevent the flying of the American flag. For example, Illinois's

recently enacted statute provides: "Notwithstanding any provision in the association's declaration, covenants, bylaws, rules, regulations, or other instruments . . . a homeowners' association . . . may not prohibit the outdoor display of the American flag or a military flag, or both, by a homeowner on that homeowner's property if the American flag is displayed in a manner consistent with . . . Title 4 of the United States Code." Act of Aug. 8, 2003, 805 Ill. Comp. Stat. 105/103.30(a). The law allows associations to adopt "reasonable rules and regulations" regarding the display of these flags. Id. Does this legislation vindicate the freedom of the homeowner? Does it trench on the freedom of homeowners' associations? Does it promote a collective interest? Or is it impermissible viewpoint discrimination, as argued in Recent Legislation, 117 Harv. L. Rev. 2047 (2004)? Should homeowners' associations be able to ban all lawn signs, including those endorsing candidates or political positions? Should homeowners' rights to express themselves be inalienable? How would these situations be resolved under the test adopted in *Nahrstedt*?

40 West 67th Street v. Pullman

New York Court of Appeal, 2003.
790 N.E.2d 1174.

■ ROSENBLATT, J. In Matter of Levandusky v. One Fifth Ave. Apt. Corp., 553 N.E.2d 1317 [N.Y. 1990], we held that the business judgment rule is the proper standard of judicial review when evaluating decisions made by residential cooperative corporations. In the case before us, defendant is a shareholder-tenant in the plaintiff cooperative building. The relationship between defendant and the cooperative, including the conditions under which a shareholder's tenancy may be terminated, is governed by the shareholder's lease agreement. The cooperative terminated defendant's tenancy in accordance with a provision in the lease that authorized it to do so based on a tenant's "objectionable" conduct.

Defendant has challenged the cooperative's action and asserts, in essence, that his tenancy may not be terminated by the court based on a review of the facts under the standard articulated in *Levandusky*. He argues that termination may rest only upon a court's independent evaluation of the reasonableness of the cooperative's action. We disagree. In reviewing the cooperative's actions, the business judgment standard governs a cooperative's decision to terminate a tenancy in accordance with the terms of the parties' agreement.

I.

Plaintiff cooperative owns the building located at 40 West 67th Street in Manhattan, which contains 38 apartments. In 1998, defendant bought into the cooperative and acquired 80 shares of stock appurtenant to his proprietary lease for apartment 7B.

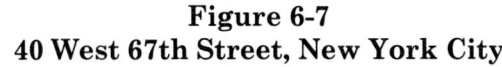

Figure 6-7
40 West 67th Street, New York City

Soon after moving in, defendant engaged in a course of behavior that, in the view of the cooperative, began as demanding, grew increasingly disruptive and ultimately became intolerable. After several points of friction between defendant and the cooperative,[1] defendant started complaining about his elderly upstairs neighbors, a retired college professor and his wife who had occupied apartment 8B for over two decades. In a stream of vituperative letters to the cooperative—16 letters in the month of October 1999 alone—he accused the couple of playing their television set and stereo at high volumes late into the night, and claimed they were running a loud and illegal bookbinding business in their apartment. Defendant further charged that the couple stored toxic chemicals in their apartment for use in their "dangerous and illegal" business. Upon investigation, the cooperative's Board determined that the couple did not possess a television set or stereo and that there was no

---

[1]   Initially, defendant sought changes in the building services, such as the installation of video surveillance, 24-hour door service and replacement of the lobby mailboxes. After investigation, the Board deemed these proposed changes inadvisable or infeasible.

evidence of a bookbinding business or any other commercial enterprise in their apartment.

Hostilities escalated, resulting in a physical altercation between defendant and the retired professor.[2] Following the altercation, defendant distributed flyers to the cooperative residents in which he referred to the professor, by name, as a potential "psychopath in our midst" and accused him of cutting defendant's telephone lines. In another flyer, defendant described the professor's wife and the wife of the Board president as having close "intimate personal relations." Defendant also claimed that the previous occupants of his apartment revealed that the upstairs couple have "historically made excessive noise." The former occupants, however, submitted an affidavit that denied making any complaints about noise from the upstairs apartment and proclaimed that defendant's assertions to the contrary were "completely false."

Furthermore, defendant made alterations to his apartment without Board approval, had construction work performed on the weekend in violation of house rules, and would not respond to Board requests to correct these conditions or to allow a mutual inspection of his apartment and the upstairs apartment belonging to the elderly couple. Finally, defendant commenced four lawsuits against the upstairs couple, the president of the cooperative and the cooperative management, and tried to commence three more.

In reaction to defendant's behavior, the cooperative called a special meeting pursuant to article III (First) (f) of the lease agreement, which provides for termination of the tenancy if the cooperative by a two-thirds vote determines that "because of objectionable conduct on the part of the Lessee * * * the tenancy of the Lessee is undesirable." The cooperative informed the share-holders that the purpose of the meeting was to determine whether defendant "engaged in repeated actions inimical to cooperative living and objectionable to the Corporation and its stockholders that make his continued tenancy undesirable."

Timely notice of the meeting was sent to all shareholders in the cooperative, including defendant. At the ensuing meeting, held in June 2000, owners of more than 75% of the outstanding shares in the cooperative were present. Defendant chose not attend. By a vote of 2,048 shares to 0, the share-holders in attendance passed a resolution declaring defendant's conduct "objectionable" and directing the Board to terminate his proprietary lease and cancel his shares. The resolution contained the findings upon which the shareholders concluded that defendant's behavior was inimical to cooperative living. Pursuant to the resolution, the Board sent defendant a notice of termination requiring him to vacate his apartment by August 31, 2000. Ignoring the notice, defendant remained in the apartment, prompting the cooperative to bring this suit

---

[2]   Defendant brought charges against the professor which resulted in the professor's arrest. Eventually, the charges were adjourned in contemplation of dismissal.

for possession and ejectment, a declaratory judgment cancelling defendant's stock, and a money judgment for use and occupancy, along with attorneys' fees and costs.

The Supreme Court * * * declined to apply the business judgment rule to sustain the shareholders' vote and the Board's issuance of the notice of termination. Instead, the court invoked RPAPL 711(1) and held that to terminate a tenancy, a cooperative must prove its claim of objectionable conduct by competent evidence to the satisfaction of the court.

Disagreeing with Supreme Court, a divided Appellate Division * * * held that *Levandusky* prohibited judicial scrutiny of actions of cooperative boards "taken in good faith and in the exercise of honest judgment in the lawful and legitimate furtherance of corporate purposes" * * * We agree with the Appellate Division majority that the business judgment rule applies and therefore affirm.

II. The *Levandusky* Business Judgment Rule

The heart of this dispute is the parties' disagreement over the proper standard of review to be applied when a cooperative exercises its agreed-upon right to terminate a tenancy based on a shareholder-tenant's objectionable conduct. In the agreement establishing the rights and duties of the parties, the cooperative reserved to itself the authority to determine whether a member's conduct was objectionable and to terminate the tenancy on that basis. The cooperative argues that its decision to do so should be reviewed in accordance with *Levandusky's* business judgment rule. Defendant contends that the business judgment rule has no application under these circumstances and that RPAPL 711 requires a court to make its own evaluation of the Board's conduct based on a judicial standard of reasonableness.

Levandusky established a standard of review analogous to the corporate business judgment rule for a shareholder-tenant challenge to a decision of a residential cooperative corporation. The business judgment rule is a common-law doctrine by which courts exercise restraint and defer to good faith decisions made by boards of directors in business settings * * * The rule has been long recognized in New York (see e.g., Flynn v. Brooklyn City R.R. Co., 53 N.E. 520 [N.Y. 1899]; Pollitz v. Wabash R.R. Co., 100 N.E. 721 [N.Y. 1912]). In *Levandusky,* the cooperative board issued a stop work order for a shareholder-tenant's renovations that violated the proprietary lease. The shareholder-tenant brought a * * * proceeding to set aside the stop work order. The Court upheld the Board's action, and concluded that the business judgment rule "best balances the individual and collective interests at stake" in the residential cooperative setting (Levandusky, 553 N.E.2d 1317).

In the context of cooperative dwellings, the business judgment rule provides that a court should defer to a cooperative board's determination "[s]o long as the board acts for the purposes of the cooperative, within the scope of its authority and in good faith" (553 N.E.2d 1317). In adopting this rule, we recognized that a cooperative board's broad powers could lead to abuse through arbitrary or malicious decision-making, unlawful discrimination or the like. However, we also aimed to avoid impairing "the purposes for which the residential community and its governing structure were formed: protection of the interest of the entire community of residents in an environment managed by the board for the common benefit" (553 N.E.2d 1317). The Court concluded that the business judgment rule best balances these competing interests and also noted that the limited judicial review afforded by the rule protects the cooperative's decisions against "undue court involvement and judicial second-guessing" (553 N.E.2d at 1323).

Although we applied the business judgment rule in *Levandusky,* we did not attempt to fix its boundaries, recognizing that this corporate concept may not necessarily comport with every situation encountered by a cooperative and its shareholder-tenants. Defendant argues that when it comes to terminations, the business judgment rule conflicts with RPAPL 711(1) and is therefore inoperative.[5] We see no such conflict. In the realm of cooperative governance and in the lease provision before us, the cooperative's determination as to the tenant's objectionable behavior stands as competent evidence necessary to sustain the cooperative's determination. If that were not so, the contract provision for termination of the lease—to which defendant agreed—would be meaningless.

We reject the cooperative's argument that RPAPL 711(1) is irrelevant to these proceedings, but conclude that the business judgment rule may be applied consistently with the statute. Procedurally, the business judgment standard will be applied across the cases, but the manner in which it presents itself varies with the form of the lawsuit. *Levandusky,* for example, was framed as a CPLR article 78 proceeding, but we applied the business judgment rule as a concurrent form of "rationality" and "reasonableness" to determine whether the decision was "arbitrary and capricious" pursuant to CPLR 7803(3) (553 N.E.2d at 1323 n.).

Similarly, the procedural vehicle driving this case is RPAPL 711(1), which requires "competent evidence" to show that a tenant is objectionable. Thus, in this context, the competent evidence that is the basis for the shareholder vote will be reviewed under the business judgment rule, which means courts will normally defer to that vote and the shareholders' stated findings as competent evidence that the tenant is indeed objectionable under the statute. As we stated in *Levandusky,* a single standard of review for cooperatives is preferable, and "we see no

---

[5]   RPAPL 711(1), in pertinent part, states: "A proceeding seeking to recover possession of real property by reason of the termination of the term fixed in the lease pursuant to a provision contained therein giving the landlord the right to terminate the time fixed for occupancy under such agreement if he deem the tenant objectionable, shall not be maintainable unless the landlord shall by competent evidence establish to the satisfaction of the court that the tenant is objectionable."

purpose in allowing the form of the action to dictate the substance of the standard by which the legitimacy of corporate action is to be measured" (553 N.E.2d 1317).

In addition, RPAPL 711 was derived from former Civil Practice Act § 1410(6), which was enacted in 1920. . . . Before that, a landlord could evict a tenant based on the landlord's sole and unfettered determination that the tenant was objectionable (see e.g. Manhattan Life Ins. Co. v. Gosford, 23 N.Y.S. 7 [N.Y. 1893]; Waitt Constr. Co. v. Loraine, 179 N.Y.S. 167 [N.Y. 1919]). By enacting former Civil Practice Act § 1410(6), the Legislature imposed on the landlord the burden of proving that the tenant was objectionable. While RPAPL 711(1) applies to the termination before us, we are satisfied that the relationships among shareholders in cooperatives are sufficiently distinct from traditional landlord-tenant relationships that the statute's "competent evidence" standard is satisfied by the application of the business judgment rule.

Despite this deferential standard, there are instances when courts should undertake review of board decisions. To trigger further judicial scrutiny, an aggrieved shareholder-tenant must make a showing that the board acted (1) outside the scope of its authority, (2) in a way that did not legitimately further the corporate purpose or (3) in bad faith.

III.

A.   The Cooperative's Scope of Authority

Pursuant to its bylaws, the cooperative was authorized (through its Board) to adopt a form of proprietary lease to be used for all shareholder-tenants. Based on this authorization, defendant and other members of the cooperative voluntarily entered into lease agreements containing the termination provision before us. The cooperative does not contend that it has the power to terminate the lease absent the termination provision.
* * *

The cooperative unfailingly followed the procedures contained in the lease when acting to terminate defendant's tenancy. In accordance with the bylaws, the Board called a special meeting, and notified all shareholder-tenants of its time, place and purpose. Defendant thus had notice and the opportunity to be heard. In accordance with the agreement, the cooperative acted on a super-majority vote after properly fashioning the issue and the question to be addressed by resolution. The resolution specified the basis for the action, setting forth a list of specific findings as to defendant's objectionable behavior. By not appearing or presenting evidence personally or by counsel, defendant failed to challenge the findings and has not otherwise satisfied us that the Board has in any way acted ultra vires. In all, defendant has failed to demonstrate that the cooperative acted outside the scope of its authority in terminating the tenancy.

B. Furthering the Corporate Purpose

Levandusky also recognizes that the business judgment rule prohibits judicial inquiry into Board actions that, presupposing good faith, are taken in legitimate furtherance of corporate purposes. Specifically, there must be a legitimate relationship between the Board's action and the welfare of the cooperative. Here, by the unanimous vote of everyone present at the meeting, the cooperative resoundingly expressed its collective will, directing the Board to terminate defendant's tenancy after finding that his behavior was more than its shareholders could bear. The Board was under a fiduciary duty to further the collective interests of the cooperative. By terminating the tenancy, the Board's action thus bore an obvious and legitimate relation to the cooperative's avowed ends.

There is, however, an additional dimension to corporate purpose that *Levandusky* contemplates, notably, the legitimacy of purpose—a feature closely related to good faith. Put differently, all the shareholders of a cooperative may agree on an objective, and the Board may pursue that objective zealously, but that does not necessarily mean the objective is lawful or legitimate. Defendant, however, has not shown that the Board's purpose was anything other than furthering the overall welfare of a cooperative that found it could no longer abide defendant's behavior.

C. Good Faith, in the Exercise of Honest Judgment

Finally, defendant has not shown the slightest indication of any bad faith, arbitrariness, favoritism, discrimination or malice on the cooperative's part, and the record reveals none. Though defendant contends that he raised sufficient facts in this regard, we agree with the Appellate Division majority that defendant has provided no factual support for his conclusory assertions that he was evicted based upon illegal or impermissible considerations. Moreover, as the Appellate Division noted, the cooperative emphasized that upon the sale of the apartment it "will 'turn over [to the defendant] all proceeds after deduction of unpaid use and occupancy, costs of sale and litigation expenses incurred in this dispute'" (742 N.Y.S.2d 264). Defendant does not contend otherwise.

Levandusky cautions that the broad powers of cooperative governance carry the potential for abuse when a board singles out a person for harmful treatment or engages in unlawful discrimination, vendetta, arbitrary decisionmaking or favoritism. We reaffirm that admonition and stress that those types of abuses are incompatible with good faith and the exercise of honest judgment. While deferential, the *Levandusky* standard should not serve as a rubber stamp for cooperative board actions, particularly those involving tenancy terminations. We note that since *Levandusky* was decided, the lower courts have in most instances deferred to the business judgment of cooperative boards but in a number of cases have withheld deference in the face of evidence that the board acted illegitimately.

The very concept of cooperative living entails a voluntary, shared control over rules, maintenance and the composition of the community. Indeed, as we observed in *Levandusky,* a shareholder-tenant voluntarily agrees to submit to the authority of a cooperative board, and consequently the board "may significantly restrict the bundle of rights a property owner normally enjoys" (553 N.E.2d 1317). When dealing, however, with termination, courts must exercise a heightened vigilance in examining whether the board's action meets the *Levandusky* test.

NOTES AND QUESTIONS

1.   Housing cooperatives are an unusual legal animal. The building is owned by an entity (usually a corporation), in which the residents own shares. The corporation then grants a lease in a particular unit to each resident, associated with the particular shares each owns. Since the cooperative is part-corporation, part-lease, you can see how the debate gets framed in *Pullman* over the standard of review of the shareholders' decision to expel Pullman. The corporation argues that the decision should be reviewed under the deferential business judgment rule that applies in shareholder suits against directors of corporations. Pullman argues that the review should be governed by the New York statute that applies to evictions of objectionable tenants under lease law.

2.   Given that residents in cooperatives are technically lessees, why isn't the standard that the New York legislature has prescribed for eviction of objectionable lessees fully applicable? Surely it cannot be the case that residents of cooperatives have a lesser interest in protecting their right to continue living in their home than do residents in rental apartments. Are commercial landlords more likely to act abusively or to seek to evict tenants for pretextual reasons? Under what circumstances might a commercial landlord have an incentive to try to terminate a lease before the end of the lease term? Does the fact that residents in a cooperative vote democratically provide additional protection against abusive eviction decisions? Or does the possibility of mob prejudice make democratic voting a more feeble form of protection than the commercial self-interest of landlords?

3.   Cooperatives and condominiums, like commercial apartments, are subject to the Fair Housing Act and other antidiscrimination laws considered in Chapter IV. See Broome v. Biondi, 17 F. Supp. 2d 211 (S.D.N.Y. 1997) (awarding $640,000 judgment against cooperative apartment for turning down an application by a mixed race couple); Fletcher v. Dakota, Inc., 948 N.Y.S.2d 263, 268 (App. Div. 2012) (holding that business judgment rule does not shield coop board against claim of intentional discrimination). But given that cooperative housing is subject to one blanket mortgage for which all residents are responsible, coops have traditionally managed to be very picky about who they agree to accept as shareholders, as long as they steer clear of violating the civil rights laws. This pickiness has carried over to rejecting many applications from famous or otherwise notorious persons, including Madonna, Billy Joel, Barbara Streisand, and Richard Nixon, perhaps on the ground that residents do not want publicity drawn to their building. Does

this local custom or culture of pickiness justify relaxing the standard of review applied to eviction of a resident? Or does it justify applying a heightened standard of review?

4.   California has joined New York in applying the business judgment rule to defer to decisions by boards of homeowners' associations, including condominiums. See Lamden v. LaJolla Shores Clubdominium Homeowners Assn., 980 P.2d 940 (Cal. 1999) (deferring to board decision not to fumigate complex for termite infestation).

Kiekel v. Four Colonies Homes Association

Court of Appeals of Kansas, 2007.
162 P.3d 57.

■ MALONE, J.: In 2004, Four Colonies Homes Association (Four Colonies) submitted a bylaw amendment to its members for approval, which placed renting restrictions on lot owners in Four Colonies' subdivision. Fifty-one percent of the lot owners present at the meeting voted in favor of the bylaw amendment. When Four Colonies attempted to enforce the bylaw against James A. Kiekel and Margaret G. Kiekel, the Kiekels filed a petition for declaratory judgment with the district court, asking the court to declare the bylaw unenforceable. Four Colonies filed a counterclaim for injunctive relief, requesting the court to enjoin the Kiekels from renting their properties. * * *

Factual and procedural background

Four Colonies is a Kansas not-for-profit corporation comprised of the property lot owners in the Four Colonies subdivision in Lenexa, Kansas. The subdivision was created in 1971 as a "condominium-type 'planned unit development'" in which individual lot owners were subject to property use restrictions pursuant to Four Colonies' Declaration of Covenants, Conditions, and Restrictions (Declaration).

The Declaration, as well as Four Colonies' Bylaws (Bylaws), were filed in the Johnson County Register of Deeds office. The Declaration includes a provision that allows it to be amended by an instrument signed by not less than 75% of the lot owners. As of 2005, the Declaration had never been formally amended pursuant to this provision. The Bylaws can be amended by a majority vote of lot owners at a meeting.

In 1997, Four Colonies proposed an amendment to the Bylaws that would have prevented owners from renting their property until the number of rental units in the subdivision was reduced to 10% of the lots, or 69 units. However, Four Colonies cancelled the vote on the amendment because it subsequently determined that the proposed bylaw was in conflict with the Declaration.

In October 2004, Four Colonies proposed another bylaw amendment that would impose various limitations on lot owners' rights to rent their property, including:

(1) a prohibition against a currently rented property being rented after any change in ownership of that property following the adoption of the By-Laws amendment; (2) a prohibition against any property not rented as of the adoption of the By-Laws amendment from being thereafter rented; (3) a requirement that all lease agreements be submitted to the Association's Board for approval every twelve months; (4) a grant of authority to the Association to terminate any lease and evict any tenant in the event a property owner fails to comply with the requirements set forth in the By-Laws amendment; and (5) a provision that the Association be entitled to recover all costs and attorney fees in terminating any lease and evicting any tenant pursuant to the terms set forth in the By-Laws amendment.

A special meeting was called to allow owners to vote on the bylaw amendment. Only 372 of the 681 lot owners (55%) attended the meeting. At the meeting, the bylaw amendment was approved with 191 (51.34%) lot owners voting in favor of the amendment and 181 (48.66%) voting against the amendment.

The Four Colonies subdivision consists of 681 property lots, including 37 duplexes, 1 tri-plex, 54 four-plexes, 1 five-plex, 23 six-plexes, 74 garden villas, and 171 free-standing homes. As of 2005, approximately 100 to 115 of the lots were being rented by their owners. Four Colonies proposed the 2004 bylaw amendment after receiving numerous complaints from lot owners about the conduct and behavior of tenants who rented property in the subdivision.

Many of these complaints were about tenants leasing from the Kiekels. Since 1988, the Kiekels have owned property lots in the subdivision but have never lived in the subdivision. As of 2005, the Kiekels, through revocable trusts, owned eight property lots in the subdivision, which they rented. Since 1999, the police have responded to the Kiekels' rental properties 15 times. Additionally, Four Colonies claimed it received 19 complaints about the Kiekels' tenants, "including parking, failing to clean up dog feces, loud and disruptive late-night parties and personal property stored or left in yards." According to Four Colonies, the Kiekels also failed to adequately maintain and repair their rental properties.

After the 2004 bylaw amendment was approved, the Kiekels received a letter from Four Colonies asking them to provide information to Four Colonies about their tenants pursuant to the bylaw. In response, the Kiekels filed a petition for declaratory judgment with the Johnson County District Court. In their petition, the Kiekels argued the 2004 bylaw amendment was void because it conflicted with the Declaration.
* * *

Four Colonies filed a counterclaim asking the district court to enjoin the Kiekels from renting their properties and to order them to sell their lots to owners who would occupy the residences. Four Colonies argued that injunctive relief was appropriate because the Kiekels were violating the Declaration's provisions that prohibited noxious activity and the commercial use of subdivision property.

In June 2005, a bench trial was held. * * * The district court denied the Kiekels' claim for declaratory relief. The district court found that the 2004 bylaw amendment was not in conflict with the Declaration and that the amendment was reasonable and enforceable. The district court also found that the Declaration authorized the board to restrict the [owners'] rental rights through a bylaw amendment. However, the district court also denied Four Colonies' counterclaim for injunctive relief based upon the evidence presented at the hearing.

The Kiekels timely appeal the district court's denial of their petition for declaratory judgment. Additionally, Four Colonies timely cross-appeals the district court's denial of its claim for injunctive relief.

Petition for declaratory judgment

* * * The district court framed the issue in this case as whether the 2004 bylaw amendment conflicted with the Declaration. The district court determined that because the bylaw amendment did not eliminate the Kiekels' right to rent their property, the bylaw amendment did not conflict with the Declaration. However, a more accurate statement of the issue is whether Four Colonies could impose a post-purchase property use restriction on lot owners through an amendment to the Bylaws. * * *

To resolve the issue at hand, this court must interpret Four Colonies' Declaration and Bylaws. The interpretation and legal effect of written instruments are matters of law, and an appellate court exercises unlimited review. McGinley v. Bank of America, N.A., 109 P.3d 1146 (Kan. 2005).

> Another well-settled rule is that covenants and agreements restricting the free use of property are strictly construed against limitations upon such use. Such restrictions will not be aided or extended by implication or enlarged by construction. Doubt will be resolved in favor of the unrestricted use of property. [Citation omitted.]

Sporn v. Overholt, 262 P.2d 828, 830 (Kan. 1953).

Examining Four Colonies' Declaration and Bylaws, it appears the intent was that the Declaration would set forth owners' fundamental ownership rights and the Bylaws would set forth enforcement and govern its procedures. This conclusion is supported by the amendment procedures included in both documents. An amendment to the Declaration requires a super-majority vote of 75% of all lot owners; whereas, an amendment to the Bylaws requires a simple-majority vote of lot owners present at a meeting. Because the Declaration defines property rights, and the Bylaws do not, it is logical that amending the Declaration would be more difficult. See 4 Thompson on Real Property

§ 36.06(a), pp. 240–41 (2d ed. 2004) (Absent "an amendment to the declaration, the enjoyment and use of the real property cannot be impaired or diminished.").

In this case, the original Declaration for the subdivision includes various restrictive covenants that impose property use restrictions on owners. These restrictions include, but are not limited to, restricting owners from using their property for commercial purposes, restricting owners from installing awnings without approval, restricting owners from erecting fences without approval, and restricting owners from having more than two household pets. Despite these restrictions, the Declaration neither expressly prohibits nor expressly permits lot owners to rent their property. The Declaration does, however, include three distinct references to lot owners' tenants. In one specific instance, the Declaration defines "resident" to include not only the owners of lots "but also the lessees and tenants of such owners." Strictly construing the Declaration, it does not place any restrictions on owners' rights to rent their property. See Sporn, 262 P. 2d at 830–31.

This conclusion is borne out by the conduct of the parties in this case. Lot owners in Four Colonies have been renting their properties since the association was created in 1971. As of 2005, approximately 100 to 115 of the lots were being rented by their owners. In 1997, Four Colonies proposed an amendment to the Bylaws that would have temporarily prevented lot owners from renting their properties, but Four Colonies withdrew the amendment because it subsequently determined that the proposed bylaw was in conflict with the Declaration.

We disagree with the district court's conclusion that the bylaw amendment did not conflict with the Declaration. The bylaw amendment essentially eliminated the right to rent property in the Four Colonies subdivision, except it contained a grandfather provision for lots that were currently being rented. More significantly, the bylaw amendment required all lease agreements to be submitted to the board of directors for approval every 12 months. The amendment further granted the board the authority to terminate any lease and evict the tenant in the event the lot owner failed to comply with the requirements set forth in the Bylaws. The bylaw amendment contained extensive property use restrictions concerning the rental of property in the Four Colonies subdivision which only could be accomplished through an amendment to the Declaration. * * *

We conclude the district court erred in finding that Four Colonies could impose rental restrictions through an amendment to the Bylaws. The Declaration could have authorized Four Colonies to restrict the owners' rental rights had more specific language been utilized. In this case, however, it is clear that the Declaration intended any property use restrictions, including restrictions on renting, to be achieved through an amendment to the Declaration. Because Four Colonies failed to properly amend the Declaration, the bylaw amendment imposing rental restrictions is void and unenforceable. Based on this determination, it is unnecessary to address the other issues the Kiekels have raised on appeal.

We sympathize with Four Colonies' desire to eliminate complaints about rental properties and to maintain an attractive neighborhood. It may be true that restricting rental rights would enhance the property values of all lots in the Four Colonies subdivision. However, to impose restrictions on owners' rights to rent their properties, Four Colonies must do so through an amendment to the Declaration. We conclude the district court erred by denying the Kiekels' petition for declaratory judgment.

Request for injunctive relief

In its cross-appeal, Four Colonies claims the district court erred in denying its counterclaim for injunctive relief. Four Colonies' request to enjoin the Kiekels from renting their property was based upon the language of the original Declaration. On appeal, Four Colonies argues the district court erred (1) in finding that the Kiekels' renting did not violate the Declaration's commercial use restriction and (2) in finding that the Kiekels' renting did not violate the Declaration's noxious activity restriction.

To obtain injunctive relief, the movant must show:

> (1) there is a reasonable probability of irreparable future injury to the movant; (2) an action at law will not provide an adequate remedy; (3) the threatened injury to the movant outweighs whatever damage the proposed injunction may cause the opposing party; and (4) the injunction, if issued, would not be adverse to the public interest.

Empire Mfg. Co. v. Empire Candle, Inc., 41 P.3d 798, 808 (Kan. 2002).

However, under the first factor, a movant does not have to independently show irreparable harm to obtain injunctive relief for the breach of a restrictive covenant. Persimmon Hill First Homes Ass'n v. Lonsdale, 75 P.3d 278, 282–83 (Kan. App. 2003). * * *

First, Four Colonies argues the Declaration's commercial use restriction prohibited the Kiekels from renting their properties. According to the Declaration, "[n]o building or structure of any sort may ever be placed, erected or used for business, professional, trade or commercial purposes on any of the property within [Four Colonies]." * * *

As we previously indicated, the Declaration neither expressly prohibits nor expressly permits lot owners to rent their property. The Declaration does, however, include three distinct references to lot owners' tenants, and in one instance the Declaration defines "resident" to include lessees and tenants on the property. It would make no sense for the Declaration to expressly refer to lessees and tenants and at the same time conclude that the rental of property violated the Declaration's commercial use restriction.

It appears that the commercial use restriction was intended to prevent lot owners from using their property as a commercial business. Just because the Kiekels earn rental income from their property, this is not the same as conducting a commercial business on the property. As long as the Kiekels' lessees use the property as a residence, there is no violation of the Declaration's commercial use restriction. Thus, the district court did not err in denying the request to enjoin the Kiekels from renting their property based upon a violation of the Declaration's commercial use restriction.

Four Colonies also argues the Declaration's noxious activity restriction prohibited the Kiekels from renting their properties. According to the Declaration, "[n]o noxious or offensive activity shall be carried on within [Four Colonies] . . ., nor shall anything ever be done which may be or become an annoyance or nuisance to the neighborhood." Four Colonies argued to the district court that the Kiekels violated this restrictive covenant by failing to maintain their property and by failing to adequately control their tenants.

In denying injunctive relief, the district court first found that although Four Colonies had shown that tenants living in the subdivision were more likely than property owners to throw disruptive parties, have unauthorized people living with them, improperly store personal property, and fail to clean up after their pets, Four Colonies had failed to prove that the Kiekels' tenants were more likely than other tenants to engage in these activities. The district court also found that Four Colonies had failed to prove that the maintenance problems associated with the Kiekels' rental properties were worse than the maintenance problems associated with other properties in the subdivision.

Additionally, the district court concluded that Four Colonies could have addressed its concerns about the maintenance of the Kiekels' properties by taking advantage of its right to restoration. According to the Bylaws, Four Colonies has a right to restore property that a lot owner has failed to maintain and to add the cost of the restoration to the owner's annual assessment. On appeal, Four Colonies argues that its right to restoration is not an adequate remedy because "there is a significant risk to paying for these repairs up front, and then hoping to recoup these costs from unit owners." However, the Bylaws allow Four Colonies to bring a legal action against an owner for the nonpayment of assessments. As such, Four Colonies has an action at law to address the maintenance problems associated with the Kiekels' property.

Four Colonies was essentially asking the district court to find that renting itself was a noxious activity. The district court recognized the general principle that an injunction is an equitable remedy. See Persimmon Hill First Homes Ass'n, 75 P. 3d at 281. The district court was especially concerned about granting the expansive remedy of enjoining the Kiekels from renting their property in order to prevent specific instances of noxious activity. Because of the broad scope of injunctive relief pursued by Four Colonies, we conclude the district court did not abuse its discretion in denying Four Colonies' claim for injunctive relief based upon a violation of the Declaration's noxious activity restriction. * * *

Affirmed in part and reversed in part.

NOTES AND QUESTIONS

1.   Here, in contrast to *Nahrstedt* and *Pullman*, the Kansas court refuses to defer to the will of the majority in the Four Colonies subdivision. It regards the right to rent to be a sufficiently important attribute of property that it cannot be prohibited unless it is proscribed with clarity in the declaration (the master deed or the CC&Rs). If the declaration is ambiguous, or contains language suggesting that renting is contemplated, renting can be prohibited only by amending the declaration. A recent Wisconsin decision reaches the opposite conclusion, finding that the bylaws can be amended to prohibit renting even though the declaration contains language implying that renting is permissible. Apple Valley Gardens Ass'n, Inc. v. MacHutta, 763 N.W.2d 126 (Wis. 2009). Which position do you regard as more sound? Protection of property rights can be invoked in support of either outcome. The Kiekels can invoke the tradition of free alienation of property in support of their position. But the homeowners' association is seeking to protect the property rights of the resident-owners in the complex—not only the value of their investment but also the quality of the community in which they live.

2.   One way of interpreting the facts in *Kiekel* is that relatively little thought was given to the implications of allowing rentals when the complex was initially created. Gradually, over time, a majority of the residents has concluded that rentals—at least on a large-scale basis—are corrosive to the community. If the only way they can change the policy is by amending the declaration, it may be impossible to stop the corrosion. Such a change requires the approval of 75 percent of all owners, and already about 16 percent are engaged in renting. One reason why renting may be toxic to a condominium association is that individual condo owners make lousy lessors. Like the Kiekels, they are not likely to live on the premises or to employ a manager on the premises. They lack much of the incentive that a full-time lessor has to screen prospective lessees or control lessee behavior in order to protect the interests of other residents, because they are not dependent on the other residents for rental income. If the consequences of allowing renting were not fully foreseeable in 1971, when Four Colonies was created, should the court be more forgiving of efforts to rein in the practice of renting units thirty years later?

3.   Restrictions on renting have also been challenged as unreasonable restraints on alienation (see Chapter V). Most courts have rejected these challenges, at least where sales are freely permitted and the rule against renting was enunciated before the owner bought into the condo complex. See Validity, Construction, and Application of Statutes, or of Condominium Association's Bylaws or Regulations, Restricting Sale, Transfer, or Lease of Condominium Units, 17 A.L.R. 4th 1247.

4.   Mixing common interest communities and leasing also creates problems for lessee. The lessee's lessor—typically an absentee owner of one or more condo units—may be hard to reach when the plumbing springs a leak or other issues arise. A call to the homeowners' association or the manager of the condo complex will likely bring a response that this is a problem for individual owners, not something the HOA can address. The lessee is also unlikely to have any voice in the affairs of the condo association, since only owners can vote for officers of the HOA. Thus, if lessees have certain preferences that diverge from those of other residents—about pool hours or parking policy—the lessees' preferences may be disregarded. And there is some evidence that HOAs have attempted to impose disproportionate costs on renters, for example by charging high "move in/move out" fees that disproportionately affect lessees, who tend to move frequently. See Jonathan D. Ross-Harrington, Property Forms in Tension: Preference Inefficiency, Rent-Seeking, and the Problem of Notice in the Modern Condominium, 28 Yale L. & Pol'y Rev. 187, 211 (2009). To top it all off, if a condo owner falls behind on his payments on a loan secured by a mortgage on the unit, the bank typically has the right to foreclose on the mortgage and put the lessee out on the street, even if she is completely current on her rent. The problems posed by these incompatibilities are not insubstantial. It is estimated that over 2.1 million condominium units in the U.S. are occupied by renters. Id. at 188.

B. SEPARATING MANAGEMENT AND NONPOSSESSORY INTERESTS IN PROPERTY

We now turn to entity property devices designed to promote nonpossessory beneficial enjoyment of assets. The principal entity devices in this category include trusts, corporations, nonprofit entities, and partnerships. Because the purpose of these organizational forms does not entail any right to possession of any particular assets, the manager is typically given greater discretion over the use and disposition of the assets than is the case with organizational forms designed for the management of a possessory interest, such as an apartment or space in a shopping center. This discretion, however, brings with it the potential for abuse. Consequently, a central concern in the design of this second category of entity property devices is what is sometimes called the "principal-agent" or "agency cost" problem. See, e.g., Michael C. Jensen & William H. Meckling, The Theory of the Firm: Managerial Behavior, Agency Costs, and Ownership Structure, 3 J. Fin. Econ. 305 (1976); see also, e.g., M.W. Lau, The Economic Structure of Trusts (2011); Robert H. Sitkoff, An Agency Costs Theory of Trust Law, 89 Cornell L. Rev. 621 (2004); Julian Velasco, Fiduciary Principles in Corporate Law, in The Oxford Handbook of Fiduciary Law 61 (Evan J. Criddle, Paul B. Miller & Robert H. Sitkoff eds., 2019). The manager (the trustee, the board of directors) is supposed to manage the property in the best interests of the beneficial owners (the trust beneficiaries, the shareholders). But it is often difficult to devise incentives that ensure that the managers do not deviate from this ideal.

1. TRUSTS

Trusts have a long and complicated history. See generally George T. Bogert, Trusts ch. 1 (6th ed. 1987). The root idea of the modern trust is grounded in the division of authority between the common-law courts and the Chancery Court, or courts of law and equity. After the Statute of Uses of 1540, the law courts recognized only rights of ownership and possession. But Chancery would recognize and enforce—through injunctions—certain equitable obligations to hold property for the benefit of a third person. The consequence was that certain assets came to have a dual personality. The legal title to the property was held in the name of one person (the "trustee"), and this person could call upon the law courts to enforce this title against third parties who entered into contracts pertaining to the property or committed torts against the property. But the beneficial use and enjoyment of the property would belong to someone else (the "beneficiary"), and Chancery would intervene to make sure that the legal title holder did not act in ways prejudicial to the equitable title of this beneficiary.

In its modern evolved form, every trust involves three legal personas plus at least one thing. See Restatement (Third) of Trusts § 3 (Am. L. Inst. 2003). The legal persona who creates the trust is known as the settlor. Typically, the settlor owns some property in fee simple or absolute title, and grants or conveys this property (without consideration, at least in return for the property so conveyed) to another legal persona, the trustee, in trust. The trustee takes legal title to the property, and is responsible for managing it, investing in it, and protecting it against third-party intrusions. The legal persona for whose benefit the trustee manages the property is known as the beneficiary. The trustee is subject to a range of legal duties, known as fiduciary duties, which constrain the trustee to manage the property in the best interests of the beneficiary. The beneficiary, however, is not actively involved in managing the property nor, in most cases, does the beneficiary have any possessory interest in the property. Instead, the beneficiary typically receives periodic distributions of income from the trust. Finally, the whole arrangement revolves around some asset or collection of assets, known as the corpus of the trust or the trust *res*. This can include land, personal property, and intellectual property rights. But in the modern world, it increasingly has come to mean stocks, bonds, and other readily-marketable intangible assets with income-earning potential.

Although the trust involves three distinct legal personas (settlor, trustee, beneficiary), it is not necessary that distinct persons play each of these roles. For example, in 401(k) retirement plans, the settlor is an individual seeking to save for her retirement, but the same person is also usually the primary beneficiary. In the case of a living trust, or even a charitable trust, it is also possible for the settlor and the trustee to be the same person. Of course, where the settlor wants the trust to endure after her death, it is necessary that the settlor appoint someone else to serve as trustee after the settlor is gone. The one thing that traditionally has been prohibited is for one person to serve both as the sole trustee and the sole beneficiary of a trust. See Restatement (Third) of Trusts § 69 (2003).

Trusts can be created by will, by inter vivos transfer of assets from a settlor to a trustee, or by a declaration of an owner that he holds property as trustee for one or more persons. Restatement (Third) of Trusts § 10 (2003). They can be created to manage the transfer of assets within a family from one generation to another, to establish instruments for charitable giving or the creation of charitable foundations, or for certain business purposes (such as where it is important to segregate assets from routine business transactions in the context of asset securitization). Putting aside its commercial applications, "[t]he normal private trust is essentially a gift, projected on the plane of time and so subjected to a management regime." John H. Langbein, Mandatory Rules in the Law of Trusts, 98 Nw. U. L. Rev. 1105, 1109 (2004) (citation omitted). Thus, trusts are interpreted on the assumption that the dominant purpose of the settlor was to benefit the beneficiaries. Under the Statute of Frauds, express trusts must be in writing. See Bogert, supra, at 49–55.

Trusts are also one area of law where the common-law forms of ownership studied in Chapter V continue to play an important role. The legal title to trust assets is nearly always held in undivided fee simple or absolute ownership. This permits the trustee to deal with these assets the way a full owner would—by buying, selling, leasing, or mortgaging the assets as market conditions dictate, in order to maximize the risk-appropriate return to the trust. The beneficial interest, however, is often carved up among several beneficiaries spread over multiple generations. In order to describe these interests, the law of trusts has borrowed the categories of the estate system. Thus, we commonly find that one beneficiary (a spouse for example) is given a life estate in trust, followed by one or more vested remainders in trust (in the children or grandchildren, for example). If children or grandchildren present more complicated contingencies, then contingent remainders or executory interests in trust can be used. This incorporation of the estate system to describe beneficial interests has no effect on the deployment of the underlying resources, since the trustee is free to deal with those resources without regard to the law of waste, the rules of contribution and accounting, or other rules that apply where legal interests are carved up using the categories of the estate system. The only function of the estate system in the law of trusts is in ascertaining which persons are to receive, in what amounts, distributions from the trust income and assets.

The fact that most of the exotic future interests studied in Chapter V exist today only as beneficial interests in trusts helps explain why these complications are tolerable from an information-gathering and enforcement perspective. If contingent remainders and executory interests were commonly encountered as in rem rights, they would greatly complicate the process of processing information about these rights, certainly for transactional and secured-lending purposes. But when these interests exist as beneficial interests in a trust, they do not complicate transactions in the underlying assets, which are typically held in fee simple by the trustee. Thus, the common use of trusts in the disposition of family wealth and pension plans permits the system of property rights to tolerate greater complexity than would be the case if all interests had to be held as legal estates.

Trusts afford settlors even greater flexibility through the use of powers of appointment. A power of appointment arises when a donor of property by will or trust creates or reserves a power in some other person to designate the recipient(s) of particular property or beneficial interests in property. The recipient of such a power can be either the trustee or one of the beneficiaries. This affords greater flexibility in carving up beneficial interests, but at the cost of greater discretion in the person exercising the power. This discretion comes in degrees because powers can be constrained by donor stipulation in various ways. See Restatement (Third) of Property: Wills and Other Donative Transfers § 17.1 (2011).

a. SPENDTHRIFT TRUSTS

Scholars sometimes debate whether the trust is a distinctive form of property, or whether it is simply a type of third-party beneficiary contract in which the settlor contracts with the trustee to manage assets for the benefit of the beneficiary. Compare Henry Hansmann & Ugo Mattei, The Functions of Trust Law: A Comparative Legal and Economic Analysis, 73 N.Y.U. L. Rev. 434 (1998) with John H. Langbein, The Contractarian Basis of the Law of Trusts, 105 Yale L.J. 625 (1995); see also Lau, Economic Structure, supra. One critical point in favor of the "property" characterization is that trust assets are generally treated as being distinct from the assets of both the settlor and the trustee, and thus cannot be reached by individual creditors of either the settlor or the trustee. More controversially, in many jurisdictions the assets of some trusts cannot be reached by the individual creditors of the beneficiaries. In jurisdictions that permit these so-called "spendthrift trusts," trust assets are cordoned off from all but those who have dealt with the trust qua trust. At least in this sense, the trust can be regarded as a distinctive type of property right.

Broadway National Bank v. Adams

Supreme Judicial Court of Massachusetts, 1882.
133 Mass. 170.

■ MORTON, C. J. The object of this bill in equity is to reach and apply in payment of the plaintiff's debt due from the defendant Adams the income of a trust fund created for his benefit by the will of his brother. The eleventh article of the will is as follows: "I give the sum of seventy-five thousand dollars to my said executors and the survivors or survivor of them, in trust to invest the same in such manner as to them may seem prudent, and to pay the net income thereof, semiannually, to my said brother Charles W. Adams, during his natural life, such payments to be made to him personally when convenient, otherwise, upon his order or receipt in writing; in either case free from the interference or control of his creditors, my intention being that the use of said income shall not be anticipated by assignment. At the decease of my said brother Charles, my will is that the net income of said seventy-five thousand dollars shall be paid to his present wife, in case she survives him, for the benefit of herself and all the children of said Charles, in equal proportions, in the manner and upon the conditions the same as herein directed to be paid him during his life, so long as she shall remain single. And my will is, that, after the decease of said Charles and the decease or second marriage of his said wife, the said seventy-five thousand dollars, together with any accrued interest or income thereon which may remain unpaid, as herein above directed, shall be divided equally among all the children of my said brother Charles, by any and all his wives, and the representatives of any deceased child or children by right of representation."

There is no room for doubt as to the intention of the testator. It is clear that, if the trustee was to pay the income to the plaintiff under an order of the court, it would be in direct violation of the intention of the testator and of the provisions of his will. The court will not compel the trustee thus to do what the will forbids him to do, unless the provisions and intention of the testator are unlawful.

The question whether the founder of a trust can secure the income of it to the object of his bounty, by providing that it shall not be alienable by him or be subject to be taken by his creditors, has not been directly adjudicated in this Commonwealth. The tendency of our decisions, however, has been in favor of such a power in the founder.

It is true that the rule of the common law is, that a man cannot attach to a grant or transfer of property, otherwise absolute, the condition that it shall not be alienated; such condition being repugnant to the nature of the estate granted. Co. Lit. 223 a; Blackstone Bank v. Davis, 38 Mass. (21 Pick.) 42 (1838).

Lord Coke gives as the reason of the rule, that "it is absurd and repugnant to reason that he, that hath no possibility to have the land revert to him, should restrain his feoffee in fee simple of all his power to alien," and that this is "against the height and puritie of a fee simple." By such a condition, the grantor undertakes to deprive the property in the hands of the grantee of one of its legal incidents and attributes, namely, its alienability, which is deemed to be against public policy. But the reasons of the rule do not apply in the case of a transfer of property in trust. By the creation of a trust like the one before us, the trust property passes to the trustee with all its incidents and attributes unimpaired. He takes the whole legal title to the property, with the power of alienation; the *cestui que trust* [beneficiary] takes the whole legal title to the accrued income at the moment it is paid over to him. Neither the principal nor the income is at any time inalienable.

The question whether the rule of the common law should be applied to equitable life estates created by will or deed, has been the subject of conflicting adjudications by different courts, as is fully shown in the able and exhaustive arguments of the counsel in this case. As is stated in *Sparhawk v. Cloon,* 125 Mass. 263 (1878), from the time of Lord Eldon the rule has prevailed in the English Court of Chancery, to the extent of holding that when the income of a trust estate is given to any person (other than a married woman) for life, the equitable estate for life is alienable by, and liable in equity to the debts of, the *cestui que trust,* and that this quality is so inseparable from the estate that no provision, however express, which does not operate as a cesser or limitation of the estate itself, can protect it from his debts.

The English rule has been adopted in several of the courts of this country.

Other courts have rejected it, and have held that the founder of a trust may secure the benefit of it to the object of his bounty, by providing that the income shall not be alienable by anticipation, nor subject to be taken for his debts.

The precise point involved in the case at bar has not been adjudicated in this Commonwealth; but the decisions of this court which we have before cited recognize the principle, that, if the intention of the founder of a trust, like the one before us, is to give to the equitable life tenant a qualified and limited, and not an absolute, estate in the income, such life tenant cannot alienate it by anticipation, and his creditors cannot reach it at law or in equity. It seems to us that this principle extends to and covers the case at bar. The founder of this trust was the absolute owner of his property. He had the entire right to dispose of it, either by an absolute gift to his brother, or by a gift with such restrictions or limitations, not repugnant to law, as he saw fit to impose. His clear intention, as shown in his will, was not to give his brother an absolute right to the income which might hereafter accrue upon the trust fund, with the power of alienating it in advance, but only the right to receive semiannually the income of the fund, which upon its payment to him, and not before, was to become his absolute property. His intentions ought to be carried out, unless they are against public policy. There is nothing in the nature or tenure of the estate given to the *cestui que trust* which should prevent this. The power of alienating in advance is not a necessary attribute or incident of such an estate or interest, so that the restraint of such alienation would introduce repugnant or inconsistent elements.

We are not able to see that it would violate any principles of sound public policy to permit a testator to give to the object of his bounty such a qualified interest in the income of a trust fund, and thus provide against the improvidence or misfortune of the beneficiary. The only ground upon which it can be held to be against public policy is, that it defrauds the creditors of the beneficiary.

It is argued that investing a man with apparent wealth tends to mislead creditors, and to induce them to give him credit. The answer is, that creditors have no right to rely upon property thus held, and to give him credit upon the basis of an estate which, by the instrument creating it, is declared to be inalienable by him, and not liable for his debts. By the exercise of proper diligence they can ascertain the nature and extent of his estate, especially in this Commonwealth, where all wills and most deeds are spread upon the public records. There is the same danger of their being misled by false appearances and induced to give credit to the equitable life tenant when the will or deed of trust provides for a cesser or limitation over, in case of an attempted alienation, or of bankruptcy or attachment, and the argument would lead to the conclusion that the English rule is equally in violation of public policy. We do not see why the founder of a trust may not directly provide that his property shall go to his beneficiary with the restriction that it shall not be alienable by anticipation, and that his creditors shall not have the right to attach it in advance, instead of indirectly reaching the same result by a provision for a cesser or a limitation over, or by giving his trustees a discretion as to paying it. He has the entire *jus disponendi,* which imports that he may give it absolutely, or may impose any restrictions or fetters not repugnant to the nature of the estate which he gives. Under our system, creditors may reach all the property of the debtor not exempted by law, but they cannot enlarge the gift of the founder of a trust and take more than he has given.

The rule of public policy which subjects a debtor's property to the payment of his debts, does not subject the property of a donor to the debts of his beneficiary, and does not give the creditor a right to complain that, in the exercise of his absolute right of disposition, the donor has not seen fit to give the property to the creditor, but has left it out of his reach.

Whether a man can settle his own property in trust for his own benefit, so as to exempt the income from alienation by him or attachment in advance by his creditors, is a different question, which we are not called upon to consider in this case. But we are of opinion that any other person, having the entire right to dispose of his property, may settle it in trust in favor of a beneficiary, and may provide that it shall not be alienated by him by anticipation, and shall not be subject to be seized by his creditors in advance of its payment to him.

It follows that, under the provisions of the will which we are considering, the income of the trust fund created for the benefit of the defendant Adams cannot be reached by attachment, either at law or in equity, before it is paid to him.

Bill dismissed.

NOTES AND QUESTIONS

1. The purpose of a spendthrift trust is to provide financial support for persons who are regarded by the settlor as being less than fully capable of managing their own financial affairs. This could be because of the beneficiary's age (young or very old), or because the beneficiary is mentally incapacitated, or because the beneficiary simply lacks experience or judgment about worldly affairs. The spendthrift trust not only provides for specialized management of the assets dedicated to the beneficiary's support, but also assures that irresponsible actions by the beneficiary will not cause the size of the trust corpus to diminish below the level the settlor has deemed appropriate to set aside for the beneficiary's financial needs.

2. A spendthrift trust, of course, does not shield money from creditors once it has been distributed to the beneficiary. What the instant decision holds, and a majority of American jurisdictions concur in this, is that the settlor may provide in the trust agreement that the interest of the beneficiary cannot be attached or garnished by the beneficiary's creditors while it is still under the management and control of the trustee. Creditors therefore will have to periodically sue the beneficiary, when they calculate that the beneficiary has received a distribution from the trust, in an attempt to recover portions of the debt.

3. Not everyone has applauded these objectives. John Chipman Gray, a professor at Harvard Law School, thought that such trusts represented the triumph of paternalism over the ethic of individual responsibility. He wrote: "If there is one sentiment, therefore, which it would seem to be the part of all in authority, and particularly of all judges, to fortify, it is the duty of keeping one's promises and paying one's debts. [Judges approving spendthrift trusts were moved] by that spirit, in short, of paternalism, which is the fundamental essence alike of spendthrift trusts and of socialism." John Chipman Gray, Restraints on the Alienation of Property iii, ix (2d ed. 1895). Note that Gray did not object to large inheritances of wealth. His objection was to inheritances coupled with spendthrift clause protection. Can you articulate why someone like Gray might regard the ability to couple inheritance with spendthrift protection as presenting a much more troubling incursion on the ethic of individual responsibility than does large inheritance standing alone?

4. One of the objections to the creation of spendthrift trusts is that creditors of the beneficiary may not have notice that the assets sustaining the beneficiary cannot be reached to satisfy the beneficiary's personal debts. This is a version of the problem of "ostensible ownership," which we consider

further in Chapter VII. The court says that this objection has little force in the context of spendthrift trusts, given that deeds to property are publicly recorded and wills are made public when they are probated. This does not cover all of the options, however, because it is also possible to create a trust while one is alive (called an inter vivos trust), and such a trust, including one having a spendthrift provision, could not be discovered by creditors by searching through records of deeds and probated wills. Also, how realistic is it to expect ordinary trade creditors (such as department stores and auto dealers) to engage in a search of property deeds and wills before extending credit to someone like Charles W. Adams?

5.   The traditional understanding has been that spendthrift clauses can be imposed only on trusts created for the benefit of others; one cannot set up a trust for oneself protected by a spendthrift provision. See, e.g., Restatement (Third) of Trusts §§ 58(2) & 60, cmt. f (2003). This understanding is beginning to break down as several states, evidently in the interest of attracting trust business, have enacted statutes permitting the creation of self-settled "asset protection trusts." See Jesse Dukeminier & Robert H. Sitkoff, Wills, Trusts, and Estates 712–24 (10th ed. 2017). If John Chipman Gray was so upset about spendthrift trusts for the benefit of others, what would he say about self-settled spendthrift trusts? If state legislatures cannot be counted on to reject such ideas, what remedy is there to stop their spread? See Symposium: Trust Law in the 21st Century: Policy, Logic, and Persuasion in the Evolving Realm of Trust Asset Protection, 27 Cardozo L. Rev. 2621 (2006); Stewart E. Sterk, Asset Protection Trusts: Trust Law's Race to the Bottom?, 85 Cornell L. Rev. 1035 (2000); Note, Dynasty Trusts and the Rule Against Perpetuities, 116 Harv. L. Rev. 2588 (2003).

b.   TRUST FIDUCIARY DUTIES

A pervasive difficulty created by the trust is making sure that the trustee follows the instructions of the settlor and exercises his managerial discretion in the interest of the beneficiaries. The settlor is often not around (indeed is often dead), and so cannot monitor the performance of the trustee. The beneficiaries may be very young, unsophisticated, or highly dispersed, making effective monitoring by the beneficiaries equally problematic. The law's solution to the monitoring problem has been to impose a series of duties on the trustee, called fiduciary duties, which are designed to ensure that the trustee acts in the best interests of the trust and the beneficiaries, rather than using the trust *res* and powers given by the trust instrument for self-enrichment. Courts enforce these fiduciary duties quite strictly. We do not have the space here to provide a complete review of all trust fiduciary duties. For overviews, see Restatement (Third) of Trusts: Prudent Investor Rule (Am. L. Inst. 1990); Bogert, supra, at 334–449; The Oxford Handbook of Fiduciary Law (Evan J. Criddle, Paul B. Miller & Robert H. Sitkoff eds., 2019). The following case is illustrative of the types of problems that can arise, and of the attitude of the courts when breaches of fiduciary duties are exposed.

Rothko v. Reis

Court of Appeals of New York, 1977.
372 N.E.2d 291.

■ COOKE, JUDGE. Mark Rothko, an abstract expressionist painter whose works through the years gained for him an international reputation of greatness, died testate on February 25, 1970. The principal asset of his estate consisted of 798 paintings of tremendous value, and the dispute underlying this appeal involves the conduct of his three executors in their disposition of these works of art. In sum, that conduct as portrayed in the record and sketched in the opinions was manifestly wrongful and indeed shocking.

Figure 6-8
Mark Rothko in his 69th Street Studio

Photograph by Hans Namuth. Courtesy of the Center for Creative Photography, University of Arizona. ©1991 Hans Namuth Estate.

[Rothko's] will was admitted to probate on April 27, 1970 and letters testamentary were issued to Bernard J. Reis, Theodoros Stamos and Morton Levine. Hastily and within a period of only about three weeks and by virtue of two contracts each dated May 21, 1970, the executors dealt with all 798 paintings.

By a contract of sale, the estate executors agreed to sell to Marlborough A.G., a Liechtenstein corporation (hereinafter MAG), 100 Rothko paintings as listed for $1,800,000, $200,000 to be paid on execution of the agreement and the balance of $1,600,000 in 12 equal interest-free installments over a 12-year period. Under the second agreement, the executors consigned to Marlborough Gallery, Inc., a domestic corporation (hereinafter MNY), "approximately 700 paintings listed on a Schedule to be prepared", the consignee to be responsible for costs covering items such as insurance, storage[,] restoration and promotion. By its provisos, MNY could sell up to 35 paintings a year from each of two groups, pre-1947 and post-1947, for 12 years at the best price obtainable but not less than the appraised estate value, and it would receive a 50% Commission on each painting sold, except for a commission of 40% on those sold to or through other dealers.

Petitioner Kate Rothko, decedent's daughter and a person entitled to share in his estate by virtue of an election under EPTL 5–3.3, instituted this proceeding to remove the executors, to enjoin MNY and MAG from disposing of the paintings, to rescind the aforesaid agreements between the executors and said corporations, for a return of the paintings still in possession of those corporations, and for damages. She was joined by the guardian of her brother Christopher Rothko, likewise interested in the estate, who answered by adopting the allegations of his sister's petition and by demanding the same relief. The Attorney-General of the State, as the representative of the ultimate beneficiaries of the Mark Rothko Foundation, Inc., a charitable corporation and the residuary legatee under decedent's will, joined in requesting relief substantially similar to that prayed for by petitioner. * * *

Following a nonjury trial covering 89 days and in a thorough opinion, the Surrogate found: that Reis was a director, secretary and treasurer of MNY, the consignee art gallery, in addition to being a coexecutor of the estate; that the testator had a 1969 inter vivos contract with MNY to sell Rothko's work at a commission of only 10% and whether that agreement survived testator's death was a problem that a fiduciary in a dual position could not have impartially faced; that Reis was in a position of serious conflict of interest with respect to the contracts of May 21, 1970 and that his dual role and planned purpose benefited the Marlborough interests to the detriment of the estate; that it was to the advantage of coexecutor Stamos as a "not-too-successful artist, financially", to curry favor with Marlborough and that the contract made by him with MNY within months after signing the estate contracts placed him in a position where his personal interests conflicted with those of the estate, especially leading to lax contract enforcement efforts by Stamos; that Stamos acted negligently and improvidently in view of his own knowledge of the conflict of interest of Reis; that the third coexecutor, Levine, while not acting in self-interest or with bad faith, nonetheless failed to exercise ordinary prudence in the performance of his assumed fiduciary obligations since he was aware of Reis' divided loyalty, believed that Stamos was also seeking personal advantage, possessed personal opinions as to the value of the paintings and yet followed the leadership of his coexecutors without investigation of essential facts or consultation with competent and disinterested appraisers, and that the business transactions of the two Marlborough corporations were admittedly controlled and directed by Francis K. Lloyd. It was concluded that the acts and failures of the three executors were clearly improper to such a substantial extent as to mandate their removal under SCPA 711 as estate fiduciaries. The Surrogate also found that MNY, MAG and Lloyd were guilty of contempt in shipping, disposing of and selling 57 paintings in violation of the temporary restraining order dated June 26, 1972 and of the injunction dated September 26, 1972; that the contracts for sale and consignment of paintings between the executors and MNY and MAG provided inadequate value to the estate, amounting to a lack of mutuality and fairness resulting from conflicts on the part of Reis and Stamos and improvidence on the part of all executors; that said contracts were voidable and were set aside by reason of violation of the duty of loyalty and improvidence of the executors, knowingly participated in and induced by MNY and MAG; that the fact that these agreements were voidable did not revive the 1969 inter vivos agreements since the parties by their conduct evinced an intent to abandon and abrogate these compacts. The Surrogate held that the present value at the time of trial of the paintings sold is the proper measure of damages as to MNY, MAG, Lloyd, Reis and Stamos. He imposed a civil fine of $3,332,000 upon MNY, MAG and Lloyd, same being the appreciated value at the time of trial of the 57 paintings sold in violation of the temporary restraining order and injunction. It was held that Levine was liable for $6,464,880 in damages, as he was not in a dual position acting for his own interest and was thus liable only for the actual value of paintings sold MNY and MAG as of the dates of sale, and that Reis, Stamos, MNY and MAG, apart from being jointly and severally liable for the same damages as Levine for negligence, were liable for the greater sum of $9,252,000 "as appreciation damages less amounts previously paid to the estate with regard to sales of paintings." * * * The liabilities were held to be congruent so that payment of the highest sum would satisfy all lesser liabilities including the civil fines and the liabilities for damages were to be reduced by payment of the fine levied or by return of any of the 57 paintings disposed of, the new fiduciary to have the option in the first instance to specify which paintings the fiduciary would accept.

The Appellate Division * * * affirmed * * *

In seeking a reversal, it is urged that an improper legal standard was applied in voiding the estate contracts of May, 1970, that the "no further inquiry" rule applies only to self-dealing and that in case of a conflict of interest, absent self-dealing, a challenged transaction must be shown to be unfair. The subject of fairness of the contracts is intertwined with the issue of whether Reis and Stamos were guilty of conflicts of interest.[2] Scott is quoted to the effect that "[a] trustee does not

---

[2]   In New York, an executor, as such, takes a qualified legal title to all personalty specifically bequeathed and an unqualified legal title to that not so bequeathed; he holds not in

necessarily incur liability merely because he has an individual interest in the transaction * * * In Bullivant v. First Nat. Bank (141 N.E. 41 (Mass. 1923)) it was held that * * * the fact that the bank was also a creditor of the corporation did not make its assent invalid, if it acted in good faith and the plan was fair" (2 Scott, Trusts, § 170.24, p. 1384 (emphasis added)), and our attention has been called to the statement in Phelan v. Middle States Oil Corp., 220 F.2d 593, 603 (2d Cir. 1955), where Judge Learned Hand found "no decisions that have applied (the no further inquiry rule) inflexibly to every occasion in which the fiduciary has been shown to have had a personal interest that might in fact have conflicted with his loyalty."

These contentions should be rejected. First, a review of the opinions of the Surrogate and the Appellate Division manifests that they did not rely solely on a "no further inquiry rule", and secondly, there is more than an adequate basis to conclude that the agreements between the Marlborough corporations and the estate were neither fair nor in the best interests of the estate. This is demonstrated, for example, by the comments of the Surrogate concerning the commissions on the consignment of the 698 paintings and those of the Appellate Division concerning the sale of the 100 paintings. The opinions under review demonstrate that neither the Surrogate nor the Appellate Division set aside the contracts by merely applying the no further inquiry rule without regard to fairness. Rather they determined, quite properly indeed, that these agreements were neither fair nor in the best interests of the estate.

To be sure, the assertions that there were no conflicts of interest on the part of Reis or Stamos indulge in sheer fantasy. Besides being a director and officer of MNY, for which there was financial remuneration, however slight, Reis, as noted by the Surrogate, had different inducements to favor the Marlborough interests, including his own aggrandizement of status and financial advantage through sales of almost one million dollars for items from his own and his family's extensive private art collection by the Marlborough interests. Similarly, Stamos benefited as an artist under contract with Marlborough and, interestingly, Marlborough purchased a Stamos painting from a third party for $4,000 during the week in May, 1970 when the estate contract negotiations were pending. The conflicts are manifest. Further, as noted in Bogert, Trusts and Trustees (2d ed.), "The duty of loyalty imposed on the fiduciary prevents him from accepting employment from a third party who is entering into a business transaction with the trust" (§ 543, subd. (S), p. 573). "While he [a trustee] is administering the trust he must refrain from placing himself in a position where his personal interest or

his own right but as a trustee for the benefit of creditors, those entitled to receive under the will and, if all is not bequeathed, those entitled to distribution under the EPTL (Blood v. Kane, 29 N.E. 994, 994–95 (N.Y 1892); see Bischoff v. Yorkville Bank, 112 N.E. 759, 760 (N.Y. 1916); Bankers Sur. Co. v. Meyer, 98 N.E. 399, 400 (N.Y. 1912); but see Restatement, Trusts 2d, § 6; Bogert, Trusts (Hornbook Series 5th ed.), p. 31).

that of a third person does or may conflict with the interest of the beneficiaries" (Bogert, Trusts (Hornbook Series 5th ed.), p. 343). Here, Reis was employed and Stamos benefited in a manner contemplated by Bogert. In short, one must strain the law rather than follow it to reach the result suggested on behalf of Reis and Stamos.

Levine contends that, having acted prudently and upon the advice of counsel, a complete defense was established. Suffice it to say, an executor who knows that his coexecutor is committing breaches of trust and not only fails to exert efforts directed towards prevention but accedes to them is legally accountable even though he was acting on the advice of counsel. When confronted with the question of whether to enter into the Marlborough contracts, Levine was acting in a business capacity, not a legal one, in which he was required as an executor primarily to employ such diligence and prudence to the care and management of the estate assets and affairs as would prudent persons of discretion and intelligence, accented by "[n]ot honesty alone, but the punctilio of an honor the most sensitive" (Meinhard v. Salmon, 164 N.E. 545, 546 (N.Y. 1928)). Alleged good faith on the part of a fiduciary forgetful of his duty is not enough. He could not close his eyes, remain passive or move with unconcern in the face of the obvious loss to be visited upon the estate by participation in those business arrangements and then shelter himself behind the claimed counsel of an attorney.

Further, there is no merit to the argument that MNY and MAG lacked notice of the breach of trust. The record amply supports the determination that they are chargeable with notice of the executors' breach of duty.

The measure of damages was the issue that divided the Appellate Division. The contention of Reis, Stamos, MNY and MAG, that the award of appreciation damages was legally erroneous and impermissible, is based on a principle that an executor authorized to sell is not liable for an increase in value if the breach consists only in selling for a figure less than that for which the executor should have sold. For example, Scott states:

> The beneficiaries are not entitled to the value of the property at the time of the decree if it was not the duty of the trustee to retain the property in the trust and the breach of trust consisted merely in selling the property for too low a price. (3 Scott, Trusts (3d ed.), § 208.3, p. 1687 (emphasis added)).

> If the trustee is guilty of a breach of trust in selling trust property for an inadequate price, he is liable for the difference between the amount he should have received and the amount which he did receive. He is not liable, however, for any subsequent rise in value of the property sold. (Id., § 208.6, pp. 1689–1690.)

A recitation of similar import appears in Comment d under Restatement, Trusts 2d (§ 205): "d. Sale for less than value. If the trustee is authorized to sell trust property, but in breach of trust he sells it for less than he should receive, he is liable for the value of the property at the time of the sale less the amount which he received. If the breach of trust consists *only* in selling it for too little, he is not chargeable with the amount of any subsequent increase in value of the property under the rule stated in Clause (c), as he would be if he were not authorized to sell the property. See § 208." (Emphasis added.) However, employment of "merely" and "only" as limiting words suggests that where the breach consists of some misfeasance, other than solely for selling "for too low a price" or "for too little", appreciation damages may be appropriate. Under Scott (§ 208.3, pp. 1686–1687) and the Restatement (§ 208), the trustee may be held liable for appreciation damages if it was his or her duty to retain the property, the theory being that the beneficiaries are entitled to be placed in the same position they would have been in had the breach not consisted of a sale of property that should have been retained. The same rule should apply where the breach of trust consists of a serious conflict of interest which is more than merely selling for too little.

The reason for allowing appreciation damages, where there is a duty to retain, and only date of sale damages, where there is authorization to sell, is policy oriented. If a trustee authorized to sell were subjected to a greater measure of damages he might be reluctant to sell (in which event he might run a risk if depreciation ensued). On the other hand, if there is a duty to retain and the trustee sells there is no policy reason to protect the trustee; he has not simply acted imprudently, he has violated an integral condition of the trust * * *

Here, the executors, though authorized to sell, did not merely err in the amount they accepted but sold to one with whom Reis and Stamos had a self-interest. * * * [S]ince the paintings cannot be returned, the estate is therefore entitled to their value at the time of the decree, i. e., appreciation damages. These are not punitive damages in a true sense, rather they are damages intended to make the estate whole. Of course, as to Reis, Stamos, MNY and MAG, these damages might be considered by some to be exemplary in a sense, in that they serve as a warning to others, but their true character is ascertained when viewed in the light of overriding policy considerations and in the realization that the sale and consignment were not merely sales below value but inherently wrongful transfers which should allow the owner to be made whole.

The decree of the Surrogate imposed appreciation damages against Reis, Stamos, MNY and MAG in the amount of $7,339,464.72 computed as $9,252,000 (86 works on canvas at $90,000 each and 54 works on paper at $28,000 each) less the aggregate amounts paid the estate under the two rescinded agreements and interest. Appellants chose not to offer evidence of "present value" * * *. Under the circumstances, it was impossible to appraise the value of the unreturned works of art with an absolute certainty and, so long as the figure arrived at had a reasonable basis of computation and was not merely speculative, possible or imaginary, the Surrogate had the right to resort to reasonable conjectures and probable estimates and to make the best approximation possible through the exercise of good judgment and common sense in arriving at that amount. This is particularly so where the conduct of wrongdoers has rendered it difficult to ascertain the damages suffered with the precision otherwise possible. Significantly, the Surrogate's factual finding as to the present value of these unreturned paintings was affirmed by the Appellate Division and, since that finding had support in the record and was not legally erroneous, it should not now be subjected to our disturbance. * * *

We have considered the other alleged errors urged by the parties, and find those arguments to be without merit. In short, we find no basis for disturbing the result reached below.

NOTES AND QUESTIONS

1.   For further background, see Lee Seldes, The Legacy of Mark Rothko (1979). Seldes regards the case as "the greatest art scandal" of the century. Bernard Reis was a close confidant of Rothko and served as his principal advisor on financial and business matters. He drafted the will that named himself, Stamos, and Levine as the executors of Rothko's estate and as directors of the Rothko Foundation. The will left no paintings to Rothko's estranged widow or his two children, Kate and Christopher. Rothko's widow, Mell, died shortly after Rothko committed suicide, leaving the two children orphans. Through their guardians and lawyers, they elected to take a forced share, equal to one-half the estate under New York law, and brought suit to rescind the sweetheart contract the executors had made with Marlborough. Seldes portrays Frank Lloyd, the director of the Marlborough Gallery, as the mastermind who induced Reis and the other executors to breach their duties to the estate. He gave Reis and Stamos retainers that put them in a conflict of interest with the estate and pushed successfully for the sweetheart contract. After the New York Court of Appeals affirmed the judgment, Lloyd was indicted for tampering with evidence, and fled to the Bahamas to avoid extradition. Nevertheless, he returned the paintings that had been spirited out of the country in violation of the injunction and paid off the judgment in full. Bernard Reis, his assets exhausted by the litigation, filed for bankruptcy.

2.   Although technically this decision involves the duties of the executors of an estate, as the court notes in footnote 2 executors act as trustees for the creditors and the beneficiaries of the estate. The court draws upon concepts of fiduciary duty, especially the duty of loyalty and the duty of prudence, developed in the context of trust management, and its conclusions would be equally applicable to the management of a family trust. See The Oxford Handbook of Fiduciary Law, supra.

3.   Would the terms of the contract with Marlborough justify a finding of breach of fiduciary duty standing on their own? Notice that Rothko entered

into a contract before his death giving Marlborough the exclusive right to sell his paintings at a 10% commission. This would tend to suggest that there was nothing inherently prejudicial to the estate in appointing Marlborough the exclusive sales agent. The executors also instructed the agent that after the initial batch of paintings was sold, sales were to be limited to 35 paintings per year. This was designed to prevent flooding the market with Rothkos and driving down the price of the paintings. The principal bone of contention seems to be that the executors agreed to a higher commission—50% as opposed to 10% under the contract with Rothko. But is it clear that the 50% commission would result in a lower net value to the estate than a 10% commission? Presumably Marlborough has a greater incentive under a 50% commission to work hard to sell the paintings at a high price. How is a court to decide whether agreeing to a 50% commission as opposed to a 10% commission is a breach of fiduciary duty? Suppose instead the estate agreed to sell all the paintings to Marlborough for $1 million dollars in cash, and several years later they are worth $5 million. Would the contract necessarily be suspect? Would anyone complain if, instead of appreciating, the value of the paintings crashed in later years?

4. Here, of course, there was more than what appears to be a one-sided contract with Marlborough. Reis was a director and officer (and had an undisclosed retainer) with the gallery and was eager to enlist Marlborough in selling art from his own collection. Stamos was also under contract with Marlborough and anxious to curry the gallery's favor. Levine was not charged with any conflict of interest but was said to have acted imprudently by not objecting to the conflicts of Reis and Stamos. Would these conflicts be enough to remove the executors and charge them with millions of dollars in damages liability if they had negotiated a highly beneficial deal for the estate? Is there any claim that any of the executors stands to profit directly from the contract with Marlborough?

5. More controversial is the court's upholding "appreciation damages" against Reis, Stamos, and Marlborough galleries (but not Levine). Assume the appraised value of a Rothko painting was $100,000 at his death, was sold by Marlborough for $200,000 at a time when it had an appraised value of $300,000 and had a value of $400,000 when the trial court entered the decree finding a breach of fiduciary duty. Because the executors were authorized to sell the paintings for the benefit of the estate, the measure of damages would ordinarily be $300,000 minus $200,000, or $100,000—that is, the difference between the appraised value at the time of the sale and the amount obtained through the sale. The court rules, however, that the damages are $400,000 minus $200,000, or $200,000—that is, the difference between the appraised value at the time of the decree and the amount actually obtained through sale. Was the award of appreciation damages in *Rothko* a disguised form of punitive damages? See Richard V. Wellman, Punitive Surcharges Against Disloyal Fiduciaries—Is *Rothko* Right?, 77 Mich. L. Rev. 95 (1978) (arguing that the damages award was excessive and that decision will cause fiduciaries to be excessively cautious in disposing of artwork and other assets with uncertain value). Or is it an indirect way of imposing a constructive trust on Reis, Stamos, and Marlborough—a "constructive constructive trust,"

as it were? In a constructive trust, a wrongdoer will be treated as holding property taken from another as if he were a trustee for the victim and must disgorge not only the amount taken but all proceeds, including appreciation, attributable to the asset—its "traceable product." Restatement Third, Restitution and Unjust Enrichment §§ 55, 59. Various presumptions, some of them looking like extreme versions of the accession principles we saw in Chapter III, may apply in favor of the victim and against the wrongdoer. In any event, it is clear that we do not want trustees to be reckless with assets held in trust. What is wrong with rules that make trustees excessively cautious?

c.   CHANGED CIRCUMSTANCES

One of the recurring problems with interests that persist over long periods of time is that conditions may change in ways that may not have been foreseeable to someone at the time the interest was created. Situations of this sort arise with particular frequency in the charitable trust context. The doctrine of cy pres traditionally operates where a settlor (who cannot be consulted) has expressed a specific charitable intent that, due to changed circumstances, is impossible or undesirable to fulfill, but where the settlor also expressed a related general charitable intent that could still be fulfilled with some judicial modification of the interests created. For example, a trust may provide that a house is to be used as a hospital in a particular town, but it turns out that the hospital in a neighboring village adequately serves the needs of the community. See In re Neher, 18 N.E.2d 625 (N.Y. 1939) (employing cy pres to allow the town to use the house for administrative purposes). The proper grounds and degree of judicial intervention remain controversial. Consider the following case.

Wilber v. Owens

Supreme Court of New Jersey, 1949.
65 A.2d 843.

■ HEHER, JUSTICE. The bill of complaint [by Charles P. Wilber, as sole acting executor of the last will of William Brokaw Bamford, deceased, against John Owens and Asbury Park National Bank & Trust Company, the Trustees of Princeton University, and others] seeks a construction of the will of William Brokaw Bamford, deceased.

The appeal is from the decretal findings that the testator had "a general charitable intent" (142 N.J.Eq. 99, 59 A.2d 570, 584) and the "trust created by" the tenth paragraph of the will "is a valid charitable trust," and also from the direction that the executor pay over the corpus of the trust to the Trustees of Princeton University "in trust to invest and reinvest the same, and to use the income in some fitting manner for scientific and philosophical research in its Department of Philosophy as said Trustees of Princeton may in their best judgment decide."

The avowed purpose of this provision of the will was the creation of a trust, to be known as the "Exton-Bamford Research Fund," and the use of "the income thereof in some fitting manner to continue and carry forward to a completion and to publish for popular understanding the results of the researches contained or outlined in" the testator's "manuscript entitled 'Random Scientific Notes seeking the Essentials in Place and Space' or by whatever future title" he "might designate them."

The learned Vice Chancellor found that the "Random Notes" are "irrational, unintelligible, and of no scientific or other value"; that "the express purpose of the trust created by" the cited paragraph of the will "is impossible of accomplishment;" that the testator had "a general charitable intent and the trust" so created "is a valid charitable trust;" and that under the doctrine of cy pres Chancery was empowered to direct the use of the trust fund "to carry out, as near as may be, the testator's general intent and purpose": hence, the provision for the use of the income for "scientific and philosophical research" by Princeton University, who was named by the testator as the ultimate trustee for the execution of the trust if those given the prior option of service should decline to accept the trust on the terms and conditions laid down in the will.

First, the insistence is that the testator did not have a general charitable intent. It is said that the testator's "purpose" cannot be "disassociated from his Notes;" that while he indicated the "thought" that "his notes would be of world benefit," his "basic and fundamental purpose, desire and intent" was simply the "completion and publication for popular understanding of the results of his researches"; and that this was "paramount and vital," and not subordinate to a general charitable intent, and a construction "severing the decedent's intent from his Random Notes" would run counter to "the express terms of the will, the testimony and the evidence, all of which deny the existence of a general charitable intent."

The testamentary expression is not to be so narrowly read. It reveals a general charitable intent. The testator's dominant purpose was the devotion of his property to uses which are charitable. He gave what he considered was the bulk of his wealth to the charitable use provided in the tenth paragraph of the will. As it turned out, the bequest was far in excess of the value of his estate. The amount thus bequeathed was $150,000; and the bequest was conditioned upon the raising of a like sum by the trustee, the whole to constitute the principal of the trust in perpetuity. But the fulfillment of the trust was not made to depend upon the provision of the additional principal. In the event that the several trustees should refuse acceptance of the trust so conditioned, the same bequest was made, first to the League of Nations and, in case of a refusal, to Princeton University, in trust "for the same purposes, but upon any satisfactory terms and conditions by which" such accepting trustee "will agree to endeavor to carry out the purposes of this bequest and trust so that the results may be of benefit to the entire world." Such trustee was authorized to do the work attending the execution of the trust by its "own staff or by assignment to scientists or other qualified workers who believe that the common good of the worthy and meritorious of all mankind is greater than that of an isolated part."

Figure 6-9
Title Page of the First of the Bamford Manuscripts

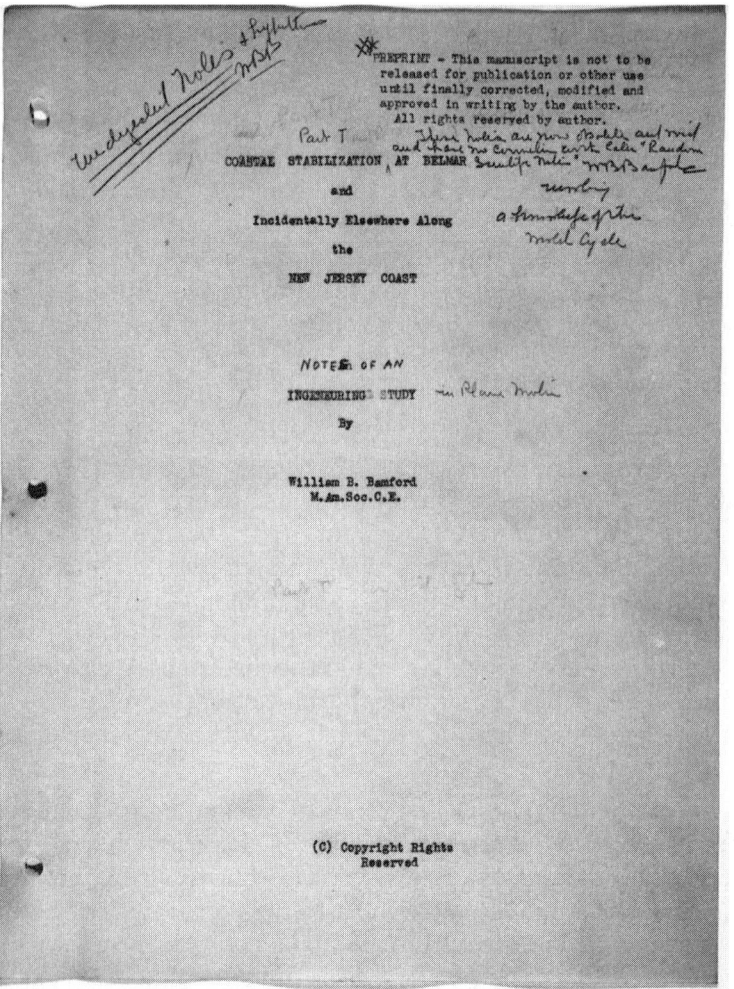

Courtesy of Princeton University Library.

Then came a series of specific and pecuniary legacies, the pecuniary legacies totaling $34,600, many of them charitable, but none to become effective until after "the provisions" of the tenth and other preceding paragraphs of the will "have been fully complied with." There was prior provision of $15,000 for the preservation of his "Random Notes" and for a scientific analysis and appraisal of the "researches" therein "outlined," to the end that such "researches" be made available "for the use and benefit of all mankind," if they "have any practical value." And, by the thirty-third paragraph of the will, the "residue" of the testator's estate was constituted a trust designated as the "Exton-Bamford Trust," to be administered by a "voluntary association" composed of designated "representative" second cousins.

This latter trust was to continue until the youngest of his second cousins attained the age of fifty years, when the corpus was to be divided equally among such of his second cousins therein mentioned as should then be living. Meanwhile, the income was to be "used and applied to promote the well being of mankind and more especially the social, physical and economic welfare and efficiency of any of my relatives who are worthy and deserving and are in special need of such assistance, or of any of my relatives who have * * * acquired special merit in their own lives through their efforts to help others beyond their ordinary duty or obligation." Authority was also given to apply such income "to the use and benefit of any worthy charitable, benevolent or educational purpose; or for the establishment and maintenance of any endowments or memorials" as may be found "to be appropriate following where reasonably possible the spirit of the various provisions of my will or of my Random Scientific Notes". In this paragraph the testator urged his kin to find "a fitting way" to "overcome the evil effects of direct inheritance of unearned property." In the event that such voluntary association should not for any reason be "set up or maintained," or if the income should not be spent by such association as provided in the will, or if all of the second cousins therein appointed to form and maintain the association should die "before the youngest one shall have attained the age of fifty years," then the residue of his estate would pass to the National Academy of Sciences at Washington, "in trust, as far as may be possible, as set forth to establish the 'Exton-Bamford Research Fund' for the purposes and under the same terms and conditions as provided" in the tenth paragraph of the will.

A general charitable intention is outstanding in these provisions. The design of the trust created by the tenth paragraph is the advancement of education and learning, and therefore it is a charitable trust. Trusts for the advancement of knowledge by research or otherwise are charitable. A gift for the benefit of an indefinite number of persons, by bringing their minds or hearts under the influence of education or religion, among other purposes, is a charity in the legal sense. A trust is charitable if the subject property is devoted to the accomplishment of purposes which are beneficial or may be supposed to be beneficial to the community. This is the prime distinction between private trusts and charitable trusts. The question is whether the accomplishment of the purpose is of such social interest to the community as to justify the dedication of the property to that purpose in perpetuity. Are the persons to benefit of a sufficiently large or indefinite class to give rise to community interest in the trust? Will the trust in operation advance the religious, educational, eleemosynary, governmental or other charitable interests of the community? Woodstown National Bank & Trust Co. v. Snelbaker, 40 A.2d 222 (N.J. Ch. 1944), affirmed, 44 A.2d 210 (N.J. 1945); Scott on Trusts, sections 348, 364, 368.

It was obviously not the testator's design to confine the trust created in paragraph ten to the mere publication of his "Random Scientific Notes" and the "results" of his "researches." He believed that the subject matter of the Notes provided the core for continued philosophic and metaphysical research that would be of inestimable benefit to mankind. The quantum of the trust fund, to run in perpetuity, is itself significant of this intention. He had evolved a social philosophy in which the economic "parasite" had no part. His worldly goods were largely inherited; and it was his belief that inherited wealth lays upon the possessor the solemn duty and responsibility of making "worthy use" of the inheritance. He had no kin nearer than first cousins; and he had determined to devote the major part of his property to the service and enrichment of his fellows. He sought to add "a small bit to the sum-total of desirable human knowledge, for the use and benefit of mankind." This we find in the "Introduction" to the first volume of his Notes. True, his Notes contributed nothing to the sum of human knowledge; and their development would not add to wisdom. Indeed, they have been termed "irrational and incoherent." Dr. Scoon said a part was understandable and a part not. Yet to the testator the text was real and vital and entirely reasonable and in keeping with his own meager understanding of the subject. No doubt, the testator's limited knowledge of the matter rendered him incapable of assessing the importance of his findings. Perhaps, he was not sufficiently tutored in the subject to voice with any degree of accuracy the thoughts that were striving for expression. But there can be no doubt of his ceaseless yearning to be of service to human kind and to use his property to that end. He conceived that his reflections and conclusions would provide the basis and the impetus for philosophic research that would in the end be socially constructive and otherwise serve the common good; but the charitable intent does not depend upon the scientific validity of his views or the depth of his understanding. We are not concerned with his philosophic or sociologic orthodoxy or rationality. Whatever the utility of his contribution, his undoubted aim was the use of his Notes as the beginning of an undertaking that would in scientific hands redound to the advantage of mankind. That was his avowed purpose. The will abounds in expressions to that effect. And in a summary or outline of his Notes, dictated shortly before his death, he declared that "The present world conditions and the critical post-war problems of world wide adjustments present a challenge to any thinking which offers promise of improved human relationships." This is an understandable commentary and a wholly rational aspiration, although the cynic would say an aspiration foredoomed. In a letter to Dr. Bowman, the President of Johns Hopkins College, written in 1935, he spoke of the trust as a means "to carry forward a research work in pure science at which I was then and still am active." And to Dr. Millikan he wrote, in the same year, of the execution of a will, still subsisting, bequeathing a trust fund of $150,000 "to carry forward a prosearch work in pure science at which I was then and still am active". But he realized that the content of his Notes might prove to be of little or no practical value. He knew the Notes were incomplete; his dominant purpose was continued research in the chosen field for the common benefit.

While the content of the Notes themselves may be wanting in scientific coherence and rationality, the ultimate aim of the testator was not irrational or absurd, and therefore the trust does not fail on this account. His was a "search for truth," not the propagation of nonsense or folly or the dissemination of absurd ideas. Even where the opinion sought to be propagated is "foolish or * * * devoid of foundation," the bequest is not necessarily void as a charitable use. Thorton v. Howe, 31 Beav. 14, 54 Eng. Rep. 1042 (Ch. 1862). In an early case in Massachusetts, the court upheld a trust to establish and maintain a school to be taught by females in which no books of instruction were to be used except spelling books and the Bible. Tainter v. Clark, 5 Allen 66 (Mass. 1862). If the general purposes for which the trust is created may reasonably be regarded as in the interest of the community, the mere fact that the members of the court and the vast majority of the people believe that the particular purpose is unwise does not serve to render the trust noncharitable. In an Irish case, upholding a trust to promote vegetarianism, Lord Justice Fitz Gibbon said that the test of beneficence is met if the "benefit" is "one which the founder believes to be of public advantage," and "his belief" is "at least rational, and not contrary either to the general law of the land, or the principles of morality." He continued: "A gift of such a character, dictated by benevolence, believed to be beneficent, devoted to an appreciably important object, and neither contra bonos mores nor contra legem, will, in my opinion, be charitable in the eye of the law, as settled by decisions which bind us. It is not for us to say that these have gone too far." In re Cranston (1898) 1 I.R. 431, 446–7.

The bequest here is for research in the sciences of philosophy and metaphysics for the ultimate good of mankind; and this is a charitable use wholly devoid of the element of illegality, immorality or absurdity, even though the matter provided by the testator as the basis for the inquiry is utterly without scientific or other value. The general purposes for which the trust was created are indubitably conducive to the common interest.

The trust does not fail because it is impossible or impracticable to carry out the particular charitable purpose. The judicial power of cy pres is invocable to effectuate the more general intention to devote the property to charitable uses. The words "cy pres" are Norman French meaning "so near" or "as near;" and the term itself suggests the limitations of the principle. Cy pres is "the doctrine of nearness or approximation." MacKenzie v. Trustees of Presbytery of Jersey City, 61 A. 1027, 1035 (N.J. 1905); Crane v. Morristown School Foundation, 187 A. 632 (N.J. 1936). Where fulfillment of the specific charitable intent cannot be had, equity will in the exercise of the power apply the property to a similar charitable purpose in accordance with the more general charitable intent. This on the theory that the testator would have so ordained if he had realized that it would be impossible to carry out the particular purpose. By this process, the intention of the testator is fulfilled as nearly as it is possible to do. We find nothing to indicate a purpose to terminate the trust here if the specific intent failed of attainment. The special intent was but a means to an end. The particular purpose was subordinate to the general charitable intention; and the decree constitutes a proper exercise of the power of cy pres. It falls within the general charitable intention and approaches as nearly as may be the particular purpose of the settlor.

Even where it is possible to carry out the particular purpose, the principle of cy pres is applicable if the fulfillment of the more specific intention would frustrate the general charitable intention of the settlor. It is then "impracticable" to carry out the particular purpose. St. James Church v. Wilson, 89 A. 519 (N.J. Ch. 1913), affirmed on this point sub nom. West v. Rector, etc., of St. James' Episcopal Church, 91 A. 101 (N.J. 1914); Restatement, Trusts, section 399, Comment M.

Where the principle is applicable, Chancery will give heed, in seeking for a charitable purpose falling within the general charitable intention, not only to the language of the trust instrument itself, but to all the circumstances tending to indicate the settlor's probable desires if he had realized that the particular purpose could not be carried out. This is according to the general canon of construction. In re Fisler's Estate, 30 A.2d 894 (N.J. 1943).

The decree is affirmed.

NOTES AND QUESTIONS

1.   The materials that William B. Bamford referred to in his will as his "Random Scientific Notes seeking the Essentials in Place and Time" now reside in a box that can be accessed through the rare book room of the Princeton University Library. The notes in the box, collected in seven spiral binders (plus appendices), are not given the title mentioned in the will (or any other title). It is, however, reasonably accurate to characterize them as "random." The earliest material chronologically, which was compiled in 1927 and appears in the first binder, is devoted to problems of beach erosion on the New Jersey coast. (See Figure 6-9.) Later volumes, to the extent they are comprehensible, build upon observations about beach movements in an effort to develop more fundamental physical laws governing the universe. In the later volumes, composed toward the end of the author's life (he died in 1945), the notes are typed or scratched in pencil on the back of various letters, advertisements, and bank statements, and include speculations about the

etymology of words and other thoughts that occurred to the author. Robert Scoon, the Stewart Professor of Philosophy at Princeton, who reviewed the notes and filed an affidavit in the case with his assessment, remarked: "The author is evidently one of a class of people, that is unfortunately well known to University Professors, who ponder current problems in solitude, jump to some general solution without subjecting themselves to the disciplines of reading the authorities or facing the criticism of other thinkers, and then appeal to us to validate their speculations." Renamed the "Exton-Bamford Fellowship Fund," as of 2017, the trust was being used to support fellowships in the Philosophy Department. https://web.archive.org/web/201310210825 21/http://giving.princeton.edu/scholarships-fellowships/fellowships/ endowed.

2.   What are the options of the court here in response to the request for construction of the will of William Brokaw Bamford? One, obviously, is to enforce paragraph ten as written, and to require that the trust "continue and carry forward" the tenets of the Random Scientific Notes. If Princeton refuses to act as trustee for this purpose, then the executor, with the court's approval, can probably designate a substitute trustee. Another option, as the decision holds, is to apply cy pres and modify the purposes of the trust created in paragraph ten so as to devote the money to something more sensible. A third option might be to declare that paragraph ten has failed because of the irrationality of the Random Notes, and that therefore the money should pass to the other pecuniary charities named in later paragraphs and ultimately to the second cousins under the residuary clause of the will, paragraph thirty-three. (Note that these residual takers apparently received nothing, because the estate ended up with less money than the decedent bequeathed in paragraph ten, which has priority over the later bequests.) If the objective is to fulfill the intentions of the donor, which of these three options do you think William Brokaw Bamford would have chosen if he were still alive? If the objective is to avoid irrationality while doing minimal violence to the provisions of the will, which would be the preferred option? Why might the court prefer the cy pres option rather than directing that the money pass under the residuary clause to the second cousins?

3.   One source of impossibility or impracticability is changed conditions. But how much do conditions have to change for a court to invoke cy pres? Bryan Mullanphy set up a trust by will in 1851, under which the income of one-third of the estate would be used "to furnish relief to all poor immigrants and travelers coming to St. Louis on their way, bona fide, to settle West." Repeated litigation beginning in 1902 sought to have cy pres applied because the number of eligible beneficiaries had dropped from an average of 1,500 per year in the period 1879 to 1896, to 387 per year by 1896, and the income far outstripped the expenses. Not until 1934 did a court apply cy pres. Even more dramatic is the story of the trusts set up by Benjamin Franklin to make start-up business loans of 60 pounds or less at 5% to young married artificers who had apprenticed in Boston or Philadelphia. Bonds in Spanish milled dollars were to be taken as security. Many aspects of the trust quickly became outmoded, including monetary amounts not indexed for

inflation and the occupational paths taken by young people. Courts applied the cy pres doctrine slowly and piecemeal over decades. For a discussion of these cases, see Lewis M. Simes, Public Policy and the Dead Hand 127–31 (1955). In a recent litigation saga, Dr. Albert C. Barnes established by his will a foundation to operate an art museum in Merion, Pennsylvania, a suburb of Philadelphia. The Barnes Foundation argued for years that the museum should be allowed to relocate to Philadelphia, where it would be visited by more people. The trust indenture also contained restrictions on how the works were to be displayed and forbidding them from being loaned out. Litigation dragged on over the course of 50 years. Dr. Barnes was considered by some to be eccentric but he clearly did not trust the Philadelphia art world to display his collection properly. See Ilana H. Eisenstein, Keeping Charity in Charitable Trust Law: The Barnes Foundation and the Case for Consideration of Public Interest in Administration of Charitable Trusts, 151 U. Pa. L. Rev. 1747 (2003). In December 2004 a suburban Philadelphia orphans' court judge ruled that the Barnes Foundation could alter its charter and move the collection to Philadelphia. In Re Barnes Foundation, 24 Fiduc. Rep. 2d 94 (2004). Further challenges by the Merion community were unsuccessful, and the museum completed the move to Philadelphia in 2012, to mixed reviews. See Allison Anna Tait, The Secret Economy of Charitable Giving, 95 B.U. L. Rev. 1663, 1698 n.227 (2015) (noting that after the move "most of the collection cannot be displayed and there are hundreds of exhibition-quality paintings in the vault.").

4.   Courts in the United States long harbored great suspicion of cy pres, stemming from abuses of related cy pres powers in England. U.S. courts are now more willing to apply cy pres to redirect property in cases in which the designated charitable purposes would be unlawful, impossible, impracticable, or wasteful. These days the courts feel increasingly free to select a substitute charitable purpose that is reasonably similar to the designated specific purpose, rather than necessarily the nearest possible one. See Uniform Trust Code § 413 (amended 2005); 2 Restatement (Third) of the Law of Trusts § 67 (2003). The new *Restatement of Trusts* reflects the more expansive approach to cy pres under which courts can redirect the use of the property not just where the designated charitable purpose becomes unlawful, impossible, or impracticable, but also when applying all of the property to the original designated purpose would be wasteful. Not surprisingly, the new *Restatement* also would give courts freedom to select a "charitable purpose that reasonably approximates the designated purpose," rather than forcing a court to discern a general charitable intent.

5.   Although the cy pres doctrine is strictly speaking limited to charitable trusts, problems involving changed circumstances can also arise under family trusts. Joseph Pulitzer, the newspaper magnate, died in 1911 leaving his newspapers in a trust to be operated by his three sons. He gave the sons broad discretion to operate and dispose of the papers, including the *St. Louis Post-Dispatch*, except for his beloved *New York World*: "I particularly enjoin upon my sons and my descendants the duty of preserving, perfecting and perpetuating 'The World' newspaper (to the maintenance and

upbuilding of which I have sacrificed my health and strength) in the same spirit in which I have striven to create and conduct it as a public institution, from motives higher than mere gain. . . ." Later, in the depths of the Great Depression, the sons petitioned the court for authority to sell the *World*. They showed that the paper had incurred heavy losses for five consecutive years, and was threatening to destroy the corpus of the trust. Without mentioning cy pres, the court agreed to permit the sale. The court noted that the law assumes that a settlor "had sufficient foresight to realize that securities bequeathed to a trustee may become so unproductive or so diminished in value as to authorize their sale where extraordinary circumstances develop or a crisis occurs. Such was the law in this state prior to the making of Mr. Pulitzer's Will. He is charged with knowledge of it." In re Pulitzer's Estate, 249 N.Y.S. 87, 93 (Sur. Ct. 1931). Ironically, although the *World* disappeared nineteen years after his death, the *Post-Dispatch*, which Pulitzer "had several times tried to sell and to which he devoted much less attention," survives to this day. W.A. Swanberg, Pulitzer 417–18 (1967).

6. Many trusts from earlier eras have provisions that discriminate on the basis of race, gender, or religion. Courts have often used cy pres to remove restrictions from gifts to schools for scholarships and other educational purposes. See, e.g., Trammell v. Elliott, 199 S.E.2d 194 (Ga. 1973) (applying cy pres to remove whites-only restriction from scholarship fund); Coffee v. William Marsh Rice University, 408 S.W.2d 269 (Tex. Civ. App. 1966) (using cy pres to remove racial restriction from organic instruments by which university was created); but cf. Trustees of University of Delaware v. Gebelein, 420 A.2d 1191 (Del. Ch. 1980) (holding administration of women-only scholarship by state university to be state action but that remedial purpose of scholarship made discrimination permissible). Recall from Chapter IV that the U.S. Supreme Court has had difficulty articulating the boundaries of state action where courts give effect to claims of one private party against another. What if a court is asked to appoint trustees to a discriminatory trust? Courts are split over whether appointing private trustees is state action. Compare In re Wilson, 452 N.E.2d 1228 (N.Y. 1983) (no) with In re Certain Scholarship Funds, 575 A.2d 1325 (N.H. 1990) (yes).

7. Although trusts are important in family wealth settlements and in transmitting property on death, they are also very important in commercial contexts. For example, trusts are commonly used in the administration of pension plans, and are used in creating separate entities to receive periodic payments like receivables or mortgage payments that can be "securitized" and sold on secondary securities markets. Overall, it has been estimated that 90% of all assets held in trust are held for commercial, rather than family, purposes. See John H. Langbein, The Secret Life of the Trust: The Trust as an Instrument of Commerce, 107 Yale L.J. 165, 177–78 (1997).

2. CORPORATIONS AND PARTNERSHIPS

Corporations and partnerships are even more important than trusts as devices for separating the management and beneficial enjoyment of assets. You will very likely take an entire course in business associations, and we have no desire to duplicate such a course here, even in part. The point of bringing up corporations and partnerships is simply to highlight that they too serve as entity property devices for separating management authority from other attributes of ownership, allowing large complexes of property to be effectively managed in ways that would be difficult if not impossible to achieve using only the common-law forms of property ownership. Placing ownership of property in a corporation or partnership is in effect an alternative to the lease, the condominium, or the trust as a mechanism for achieving integrated management of large complexes of assets.

The distinctive feature of corporations and partnerships, from a property rights perspective, is that an artificial entity is permitted to own property in its own name and right, as if it were a person. Thus, the assets of the corporation or the partnership are treated as separate and distinct from the assets of the owners or partners who form these entities. The corporation achieves this outcome by adopting a two-level ownership structure. The shareholders own the corporation. The corporation, in turn, holds title to various assets, including real and personal property, intangible property including intellectual property rights, and contract rights. The ownership interest of the shareholders gives them the right to receive dividends as periodically declared by the board of directors, and to a pro rata share of the assets upon dissolution of the corporation. Otherwise, the shareholders play only an episodic role in the management of the corporation and its assets. They elect a board of directors, and also vote on important amendments to the bylaws of the corporation and important corporate control transactions like mergers. But the day-to-day management and control of the various assets owned by the corporation is vested in the managers of the corporation, appointed by the directors. Thus, the various incidents of ownership we have studied—including the rights to exclude, to license, to destroy, and to transfer—are exercised by a large number of managers and employees, all acting in the name of the corporation. This separation of ownership and control has been familiar in corporate law since Berle and Means initially posed it as a problem. Adolf A. Berle & Gardiner C. Means, The Modern Corporation and Private Property 4–7 (1932). Their insight served as the starting point for the agency-cost theory of the firm. Berle and Means regarded separation of ownership and control as a challenge to traditional notions of property. But this separation of ownership and control can also be viewed as the way in which the exclusionary and governance strategies traditionally associated with property are accommodated to the complexities of modern business organizations. Indeed, there is an increasing awareness that the problem of defining entity property raises property-like questions of boundary placement and the information costs implicated by in rem effects. See, e.g., John Armour & Michael J. Whincop, The Proprietary Foundations of Corporate Law, 27 Oxford J. Legal Stud. 429 (2007); Edward M. Iacobucci & George G. Triantis, Economic and Legal Boundaries of Firms, 93 Va. L. Rev. 515

(2007); Joshua Getzler, Plural Ownership, Funds, and the Aggregation of Wills, 10 Theoretical Inquiries L. 241 (2009).

The relationships among the managers and employees are governed largely by contract (including the bylaws of the corporation and employment contracts). Hence corporations are often described as a "nexus of contracts." See, e.g., Frank Easterbrook & Daniel Fischel, The Economic Structure of Corporate Law 24–25 (1991); Michael C. Jensen & William H. Meckling, The Theory of the Firm: Managerial Behavior, Agency Costs, and Ownership Structure, 3 J. Fin. Econ. 305 (1976). But what gives the contracts a "nexus" is the understanding that the corporation as an entity owns the assets of the enterprise, and that the corporation as an entity is in turn owned by the shareholders. See Melvin A. Eisenberg, The Conception That the Corporation is a Nexus of Contracts, and the Dual Nature of the Firm, 24 J. Corp. L. 819 (1999); Henry E. Smith, Property as Platform: Coordinating Standards for Technological Innovation, 9 J. Competition L. & Econ. 1057, 1064–70 (2013).

For partnerships, the matter is more complicated, although practically speaking the result today is the same: entity ownership. It was not always so. Traditionally the formation of a partnership gave rise to ownership of the assets by tenancy in partnership. This operated something like a tenancy in common. Each partner was a direct owner of the assets (along with the other partners) and was entitled to a proportionate share of the earnings. Governance of the assets was by consent or by partnership agreement. Today, partnerships are everywhere regarded as having a two-level ownership structure, analogous to corporations. The partners own the partnership conceived of as an entity, and the partnership, as an entity, owns the underlying assets. This was achieved indirectly by the Uniform Partnership Act, which defined a partnership as an association of co-owners, but then proceeded to give the partnership most of the attributes of ownership. See Uniform Partnership Act (1914). The Revised Uniform Partnership Act embraces this conclusion directly, providing in that "[a] partnership is an entity." Revised Uniform Partnership Act § 201 (1997).

What are the implications of recognizing corporations and partnerships as entities with ownership rights distinct from the rights of the shareholders and partners that own these entities? Henry Hansmann and Reinier Kraakman have argued that one very important implication is that corporations and partnerships are shielded from claims of creditors of the individual shareholders or partners. The entity itself is not liable for the personal debts of its owners. Thus, if shareholder A fails to pay his debts, A's creditors cannot come after the corporation's factory. Henry Hansmann & Reinier Kraakman, The Essential Role of Organizational Law, 110 Yale L.J. 387 (2000). Moreover, Hansmann and Kraakman argue that this aspect of the law of business organizations cannot be created by contract, because it would be prohibitively costly to do so; it must be authorized legislatively, and hence can be called a rule of property.

Another implication of the entity-ownership feature of corporations and partnerships is that it permits the specialization of functions we have emphasized throughout the chapter. By placing ownership of assets in an artificial legal entity like a corporation or a partnership, assets can be subjected to a sophisticated governance regime defined by the nexus of contracts that make up the legal entity. Thus, just as the trust permits a specialization of functions between the trustee as manager of assets and the beneficiaries as recipients of earnings, so corporations and partnerships permit a similar division. The officers and employees of the entity serve as the specialized managers of a complex of assets. The benefits of this asset management—typically in the form of profits earned—are then distributed among stakeholders, most prominently through dividends paid to shareholders or shares of earnings distributed to partners, in accordance with corporate and partnership law and contractual understandings established for these purposes within the entity. (Entity law also provides for the distribution of the entity assets upon dissolution of the entity.) This specialization of functions permits larger and more complicated collections of assets to be managed effectively than would be possible if the only tools available were the common-law forms of property surveyed in Chapter V.

Also, as in the case of the trust, the corporation raises difficult problems about how to manage the managers. Like the trustees of a trust, the directors and officers of a corporation are subject to a variety of fiduciary duties. In particular, directors and officers are subject to a duty of loyalty to the corporation. This means, among other things, that they may not seek to benefit personally from business opportunities that by right belong to the corporation, nor may they take actions for their personal benefit that disadvantage the corporation. These doctrines apply to the management and acquisition of property by the corporation. See, e.g., Northeast Harbor Golf Club, Inc. v. Harris, 725 A.2d 1018 (Me. 1999) (president of golf course breached fiduciary duty by acquiring in her own name property surrounding the golf course for development). There is, needless to say, an enormous literature on whether the constraints corporate agents face are adequate. The constraints come from a variety of sources. The federal Securities and Exchange Commission regulates activities related to the issuance and transfer of corporate securities. Corporation law imposes various fiduciary duties on corporate directors and officers, and state courts entertain suits by shareholders for alleged violations of these duties. And the market provides a significant constraint, in that individual shareholders who do not approve of the conduct of the managers can sell their shares, and hence "exit" from the corporation at relatively low cost. If more shareholders exit than enter, the price of the stock falls, which may attract the attention of the board of directors or can even lead to a takeover of the corporation in order to replace the managers.

Note that business organizations come in a set list of forms somewhat reminiscent of the *numerus clausus* of forms of ownership. In addition to the sole proprietorship—where an individual owns the business assets in fee simple or absolute ownership—the principal options are the business corporation and the partnership. But there are variations, which have been expanding in number. For example, in a conventional partnership, the individual partners are liable for the debts of the partnership as an entity, in contrast to the corporation, where the shareholders have no liability for the debts of the corporation beyond the value of their shares. But recently, many states have recognized limited liability partnerships, which are like regular partnerships with the added feature of limited liability for the individual partners. This is why many law firms now sport the designation "LLP" after their name.

CHAPTER VII

SECURITY INTERESTS

A. INTRODUCTION

One of the most important attributes of property, from both an economic and legal point of view, is its role in facilitating the flow of investment capital by providing a form of security for loans. Nearly all purchases of real property are made with borrowed money using the purchased property as security for the loan; most purchases of vehicles and other types of expensive personal property are also financed with security taken in the acquired property. In addition, owners of businesses, large and small, frequently borrow money to expand or improve their operations using existing, purchased, or after-acquired property as security. Secured lending has also been proclaimed as the key to greater and more equitably distributed economic growth in developing countries. Most prominently, Hernando de Soto has argued that if informal property rights of urban squatters and rural peasants were formalized, this would allow them to use these rights as collateral for secured loans, which could then be used to finance small start-up businesses. See Hernando de Soto, The Mystery of Capital (2000). Secured lending, on this view, is the secret of economic development in the West, and if emulated elsewhere could have a transformative effect on world poverty. Although these views have been contested and exuberant mortgage lending in the United States produced a major recession in 2007–08, there is no doubt that secured lending is a central feature of mature economic systems, and a core contribution that private property makes to those systems.

Ronald J. Mann, The Concept of Collateral, in
Commercial Finance: A Transactional Approach
77–83 (2017).

The use of collateral is probably the most well-known mechanism for enhancing the likelihood that a borrower will perform as agreed in a credit transaction. Because a grant of collateral makes the likelihood of performance more secure, such a transaction commonly is referred to as a secured transaction. [I begin] with a discussion of four basic topics about such a transaction: (1) what it means for a lender to receive a grant of collateral, (2) why a lender would want to do so, (3) the source of the legal rules that govern those transactions, and (4) the extent to which parties are free to contract around them.

A.   What Is a Security Interest?

The first task for the student of secured transactions is to understand what it means for a borrower to grant collateral to a lender. Although the reference to a "grant[ing]" of collateral might suggest that the borrower identifies some particular item of property and conveys it to the lender, that is not the case. On the contrary, the borrower simply grants to the lender a right against the asset in question. The asset in question is usually referred to as the "collateral" because the lender's right against the asset provides a secondary or collateral source of repayment for the lender. Traditionally, the lender's right against the collateral has been described as a "lien."

Although the term "lien" continues to be common in transactions involving real estate, the states and Congress, through the UCC and the Bankruptcy Code, respectively, have adopted the term "security interest," reflecting the notion that the lender receives an interest in a particular asset to make the transaction more secure. See, e.g., UCC § 9–109(a)(1) (stating that UCC Article 9 applies to "a[ny] transaction, regardless of its form, that creates a security interest in personal property or fixtures by contract"); Bankruptcy Code § 101(51) ("[S]ecurity interest means lien created by an agreement."). * * *

The main continuing distinction between the terms lien and security interest relates to the voluntariness of the transaction. The term "security interest" is limited to transactions in which the borrower voluntarily grants an interest in particular property. See Bankruptcy Code § 101(51) ("[S]ecurity interest means lien created *by an agreement.*"). Thus, a borrower normally grants a security interest in personal property by executing a document called a "security agreement." See UCC § 9–102(a)(73) (defining "security agreement"). For real property, the document normally is called a mortgage or a deed of trust. See, e.g., Restatement of Mortgages § 4.1 ("A mortgage creates a security interest in real estate."). From the term "mortgage" come the common terms mortgagor (the borrower or debtor that grants the mortgage) and mortgagee (the lender, creditor, or secured party to whom the mortgage is granted).

In many contexts, however, statutes provide for the automatic creation of a lien without the consent of the borrower. For example, if a defendant does not voluntarily comply with a monetary judgment issued by a court, the plaintiff generally can obtain a "judgment lien" or a "judicial lien" to force the defendant to comply. Similarly, if a contractor provides services or materials for the construction of a building but the owner fails to pay for those services or materials, the contractor can obtain a "mechanic's lien" against the building. * * *

The most important concept in the law of secured transactions is the nature of the security interest. In substance, the security interest (or lien) is a relation between a debt and an asset that entitles the holder of the debt to certain rights with respect to the asset. Notice that the definition ties the security interest to a particular debt rather than a particular lender. Thus, if the debt is transferred from one lender to another, the security interest generally follows automatically to the new lender. In the common parlance, "the lien follows the debt."

Although the details of the relation created by a security interest are quite complicated * * * , the basic idea is a simple one. In substance, the borrower agrees that the lender has a group of special remedial rights against the collateral, such as a speedier remedy (a right to nonjudicial repossession, for example), a right to sell the collateral to satisfy the debt, or a priority in the proceeds of the asset if the borrower should become bankrupt. In some cases, the lender might take possession of the collateral (think of the pawn shop operator), but ordinarily the borrower retains possession of the collateral during the term of the loan.

The lender's rights against the collateral continue until (and only until) the debt has been repaid. Once the debt is repaid, the security interest terminates entirely, even if the borrower previously has defaulted. Although that sounds like a common-sense proposition, it has several significant consequences. The first is commonly known as the borrower's "equity of redemption." Suppose that a borrower promises to repay a debt in equal monthly installments over a period of two years, but fails to make the first six payments. If the borrower at that point tenders to the lender the entire amount owing on the debt, the borrower is said to "redeem" the collateral (hence the term "equity of redemption"). At that point, the security interest is completely discharged from the collateral, even though the borrower failed to comply with its obligations in a timely manner. It may be that the total due from the borrower is considerably larger than the amount originally borrowed (because of interest, late charges, or the like), but it is fundamental to the secured transaction that the security interest is discharged if the borrower pays that total amount at any point before the lender has sold the collateral to satisfy the debt. Traditionally, it is only at that point—when the lender has sold the collateral—that the borrower is "foreclosed" from "redeeming" the collateral; hence the classic term "foreclosure" for the lender's sale.

An important corollary of the equity of redemption is the single-repayment rule. That rule generally prohibits the creditor from retaining funds or assets with a value that exceeds the outstanding balance of the debt. Thus, if the lender sells the collateral at foreclosure, the lender cannot retain any funds that exceed the outstanding balance of the debt at that time (including, of course, previously accrued interest as well as appropriate costs and fees). The idea is that once the balance paid to the lender equals the total outstanding debt, the lien is discharged and the lender thus can have no interest in any excess funds.

B.   Why Take a Security Interest?

To understand the dynamics of secured transactions in practice, it is important to understand precisely why borrowers and lenders use secured transactions rather than guaranties or simple unsecured transactions. One obvious answer is that the grant of collateral increases the likelihood of payment by enhancing the ability of the lender to obtain repayment through forced sale of the collateral. If there is a default or the borrower files for bankruptcy, the lender knows that it will be entitled to its collateral, or at a minimum (in bankruptcy) to the value of the collateral as of the time of the bankruptcy. That result is quite different from the rights of the typical unsecured creditor, who has no claim on any particular asset and thus tends to receive little or nothing in a bankruptcy of its borrower.

From that perspective, the collateral essentially functions by allowing the borrower to precommit to sure payment. That precommitment, in turn, should lower the interest rates that the lender needs to charge for its business to be profitable. That perspective underlies all the doctrinal legal rules developed to govern secured transactions, which generally operate on the view that the lender's direct legal rights of enforcement against the collateral is the central feature of secured transactions. Hence, the legal rules tend to assume that any enhancement of the lender's enforcement rights increases the efficacy of the transactions by enhancing the likelihood of payment and thus lowering the up-front cost of credit.

Although there is a kernel of truth to that basic law-centered perspective, the reality of secured transactions suggests that a complete picture must take account of a set of more indirect and complicated motivations for the use of collateral. For one thing, in most contexts (especially in business-related transactions) it is quite uncommon—even in cases of default—for a lender to repossess a borrower's collateral or conduct a foreclosure sale to obtain payment of the debt. Furthermore, the remedy of foreclosure is a most ineffective way to obtain payment: When lenders do conduct foreclosure sales, they rarely succeed in obtaining full payment of their debts. For example, statistics on commercial real-estate loans (the area in which the best statistics are available) suggest that a typical foreclosure sale results in a loss to the lender of about 40% of its original loan amount.

Thus, it is important as you study the relevant legal rules to consider the various other indirect effects of the use of collateral in lending transactions. For present purposes, two of those effects warrant attention. The simplest arises from the leverage that the transaction gives to the lender. * * * [I]t is an unfortunate fact that the foreclosure process typically destroys considerable value. That is true because the price at which an asset is sold at an involuntary foreclosure sale held by the lender generally will be lower than the asset's value to the borrower. The asset might have some particular idiosyncratic value to the borrower; it might be a generations-old family farm, for example. Or, it might just be worth more to the borrower because of the borrower's dependence on it; think of the losses a borrower might suffer if it lost a small machine crucial to its production process.

But whatever the reason, borrowers understand that foreclosure will be a costly process that will not just take an asset from them; the process will dispose of the asset at a low cost, typically leaving the borrower liable for the remaining balance of the debt. Thus, the prospect of the destructive losses that result from a foreclosure can give the borrower an incentive far beyond a simple precommitment to payment. From the lender's perspective, that incentive helps to diminish the chances that the borrower will engage in the kinds of risky conduct that might limit the borrower's ability to repay the loan as agreed.

The use of secured transactions also works indirectly to solve a lender's concerns about excessive borrowing by its clients. For a variety of reasons starting with a desire for its clients to operate prudently, lenders typically worry that their clients will borrow excessively in the future and thus increase the risk of nonpayment of the loans that the first lender already has made. The earlier lender could (and often does) try to solve the problem by extracting a promise from its borrower that it will refrain from future borrowing (a negative-debt covenant). As a general matter, however, negative-debt covenants are quite ineffective, especially for smaller borrowers. For one thing, those covenants affect future lenders only if they know about them, and borrowers may have little incentive to tell prospective lenders about restrictions imposed by their prior lenders. More seriously, the negative-debt covenant generally can be enforced only against the borrower, not against future lenders. Thus, if a future lender makes a loan to the borrower without knowledge of the covenant of the earlier lender, the borrower will remain obligated to repay the new loan even if the new loan violated the negative-debt covenant that the borrower previously made to the earlier lender.

The public notice of a secured transaction indirectly helps to solve that problem. As you will see later, in most secured transactions, the secured creditor obtains its position only by placing a notice of the transaction in the appropriate public records (usually a "financing statement" for personal-property transactions, a "mortgage" for real-property transactions). Because future lenders are likely to discover that notice, those future lenders are likely to learn of the bank's position, which significantly diminishes the ability of the borrower to obtain excessive debt. In many contexts, that indirect effect of the security interest—to limit future borrowing—is much more important to the transaction than any of the other effects described earlier.

C. What Law Governs Security Interests?

In the context of real-estate transactions, the law of security interests (known as the law of mortgages) has had a long and checkered history, with a strong tradition of forceful judicial development, but relatively limited statutory involvement other than codifications of the rules for foreclosure sales. Indeed, efforts to codify uniform rules for real-estate security interests have been notably unsuccessful. Most obviously, not a single jurisdiction chose to enact either the Uniform Land Security Interest Act (the "ULSIA"), which the National Conference of Commissioners on Uniform State Laws ("NCCUSL") promulgated in 1985, or the Uniform Nonjudicial Foreclosure Act, promulgated in 2002.

Thus, the law of mortgages exists in a series of common law rules. As with all common law rules, there are differences between states. For the most part, however, the basic concepts are relatively uniform throughout American jurisdictions. Accordingly, after the failure of the ULSIA, the American Law Institute (the "ALI") pressed forward in the 1990's with a project to develop what is now known as the Restatement of Mortgages. (The official title is the Restatement of the Law Third: Property: Mortgages.) Adopted in 1997, the Restatement of Mortgages provides a useful and up-to-date explication of the principal rules of real estate security interests. * * *

The story is quite different for personal property security interests. In that area, there has been a strong tradition of statutory codification. During the first part of this century, the law in the area was divided into a wide variety of difficult-to-reconcile areas, ranging from chattel mortgages, to pledges, to field warehousing, to rarer devices such as the redoubtable hypothec (a predecessor to the security interest common in the civil law in Louisiana). In an effort to encourage commerce by bringing sense to the area, the ALI and NCCUSL included in the first version of the UCC an article dealing specifically with personal property security interests, Article 9; the reporter was the famous Yale professor Grant Gilmore.

All things considered, Article 9 generally is thought to be one of the most successful of the original articles of the UCC. Nevertheless, the pressures of changing commercial practices have forced periodic revisions. Most recently, in 1998 the ALI adopted a completely rewritten version of Article 9. Although it made important substantive changes in a number of areas, the core policy decisions implicit in the original statute remained untouched.

D. Mandatory and Default Rules

Much of commercial law consists of a set of background or default rules that apply only when parties fail to address the topics in their contracts. Thus, for example, UCC Article 2 establishes a complex framework of rules regarding the responsibility a buyer and seller bear for loss or damage of property during the various stages of a sales transaction. But many of those rules apply only in the absence of a contrary contract. If the parties decide in their contract to adopt a contrary rule—the buyer bears all risk of loss starting at the moment of contract—then that rule ordinarily would apply notwithstanding the more buyer-favorable rule in the UCC.

By contrast, the most fundamental precepts of the law of security interests are mandatory rules that apply notwithstanding any contrary contractual determinations of the parties. In particular, whenever parties enter into a transaction that involves a security interest or lien, the law will recast the relationship as necessary to ensure two things discussed above:

(1) If the borrower pays the entire amount secured by the collateral at any time before foreclosure, the security interest is discharged entirely, notwithstanding any prior default.

(2) If the lender takes the collateral in satisfaction of the debt, the lender almost invariably is obligated to conduct some type of foreclosure sale to determine the value of the property. That right to force a foreclosure is designed to ensure that the lender does not retain the collateral when its value exceeds the balance owed on the debt.

Those rules have a distinguished tradition, stemming from the English prohibitions on "clogging the equity of redemption." That phrase reflects the traditional description of the borrower's right to pay the debt at any time—that is, the right to pay after the due date—as the "equity of redemption." In the archaic parlance, a contractual provision limiting that right improperly "clogs" the equity of redemption, and thus is invalid.

Although the mandatory character of those concepts has an ancient lineage, their importance continues in modern transactions, as evidenced by their appearance in both the UCC and the Restatement. See UCC § 9–109(a)(1) ("[T]his article applies to a[ny] transaction, regardless of its form, that creates a security interest in personal property or fixtures by contract."); Restatement of Mortgages § 3.1(b) ("Any agreement in or created contemporaneously with a mortgage that impairs the mortgagor's [equity of redemption] is ineffective."). * * *

NOTES AND QUESTIONS

1. Security interests can be seen as another form of divided ownership. Typically, the borrower holds a fee simple (or absolute title) and enjoys all rights associated with possession, including the right to exclude others. These rights are subject to the security interest, which is a nonpossessory interest that ripens into a possessory interest under certain conditions, namely, nonrepayment of the loan. In terms of the forms of property considered in Chapters V and VI, perhaps the closest analogue is a fee simple subject to an executory limitation, with the condition that leads to forfeiture being a default on the loan. In earlier times, this parallel was even closer, in that a mortgage was an actual transfer of title to the lender/mortgagee, which would be returned upon repayment of the loan. If the borrower/mortgagor defaulted, the title would remain with the lender. As we have seen in *Harms v. Sprague* (Chapter V), this "title" theory of mortgages at common law has largely given way to a lien theory; even those states in which mortgages are cast in the form of a land conveyance treat mortgages

functionally as liens. Further, as we will discuss shortly, the harshness of the traditional conveyance approach to mortgages, under which the borrower/mortgagor would lose the property no matter how much of the loan had been paid at the time of default, has softened. After a great deal of maneuvering by parties, courts, and legislatures, a mortgagee seeking foreclosure these days must be very careful and must afford the mortgagor various opportunities to repair the situation and retain ownership of the property. In the case of personal property, the holder of the security interest can much more easily take possession of the collateral to satisfy the loan, often including by means of self-help, as we saw in *Williams v. Ford Motor Credit Co.* (Chapter IV).

2.   The mortgage or other security interest is distinct from the debt it secures. In any mortgage of real estate, the purchaser of the real estate (or someone borrowing on already-owned real estate) often signs and gives over two documents, a promissory note and the mortgage itself. The promissory note includes a promise to pay the principal with interest, a schedule of payment due dates, and a list of conditions.* For example, the note may include a condition that upon a sale of the asset or failure to make timely payment the entire balance is due immediately. The second piece of paper, the mortgage, secures the debt embodied in the promissory note. It grants the lender (the obligee of the note) a conditional property interest in the asset. The mortgagor is thus the borrower (the obligor on the note) and the owner of the asset. (For reasons we will see shortly, the mortgagor is also often the one with "equity" in the asset.) The mortgagee is the party with the security interest and who is owed the balance of the loan plus interest. In the case of personal property, a security interest is often part of a financing statement, which tends to be a separate piece of paper in addition to the note itself.

3.   For both real estate and personal property, mortgages and other security interests give their holders two rights, a "property right" and a "priority right," and it is useful to keep these distinct. Both rights relate to circumstances in which the debtor has trouble paying off the loan. In the event of a default on the loan or other breach, the *property right* gives the secured party the right to take over the property and sell it to satisfy the debt. Again, real and personal property security interests differ significantly in the level of procedural protections for the mortgagor. Process requirements often make security interests less attractive from the secured party's point of view; they can reduce the volume of lending and can lead to higher interest rates or evasions of such requirements by use of substitute devices. The history of security interests is littered with decisions over how

---

*   Many notes, such as those in the typical residential real estate transaction, provide for an "amortized" schedule of repayments. Amortization is a payment scheme for paying a predetermined sum plus interest over a fixed period of time so that the principal is eliminated at the end of the period. Usually the payments are equal in size, and each is comprised of principal and interest such that each payment's interest component is the rate-based amount of interest on the principal amount before that payment. The result is that early payments are weighted more towards interest and later ones more towards principal. As principal is paid off, the mortgagor builds up "equity" (short for "equity of redemption"), to which we turn in the next section.

to treat various installment sale contracts and special leases, as well as more modern "bankruptcy remote vehicles" used in asset securitizations.

The second right afforded by a security interest is the *priority right*. This means that where collateral is sold to satisfy the debt, the secured debt is satisfied out of the proceeds of the collateral in its order of seniority. Under the Uniform Commercial Code (UCC) as enacted in the states, a party with a security interest in personal property has priority over unsecured parties. Subject to exceptions, a secured party also has priority over other secured creditors according to the date on which it filed a financing statement or perfected its security interest, whichever is earlier. U.C.C. § 9–322. Perfection normally involves a filing of the financing statement in the prescribed place, or taking possession of the collateral. (Security interests given to finance the purchase of the property serving as security are governed by special rules. See U.C.C. §§ 9–309(1), 9–324.) Interestingly the current (revised) Article 9 gives extra priority to possession or control, U.C.C. §§ 9–313, 9–314. Likewise, to preserve maximum priority, mortgages of real property are subject to the filing requirements of the state in which the property is located. These systems vary, but all of them require some form of notice for the benefit of subsequent purchasers and lenders. Thus, a debt secured by a first mortgage on real estate is paid before a debt secured by a second mortgage, and a second mortgage takes similar priority over a third mortgage. Here "first mortgage" and "second mortgage" refer to priority rights, and this usually follows the date of their creation (and filing, as required, see Chapter VIII), but parties can agree to subordinate their debt to other debt, usually in return for a higher interest rate. And all secured debt has priority over unsecured debt. If a loan is undersecured, then it is treated according to its priority up to the amount of the security and the rest is handled as unsecured debt. Thus, if a loan with an outstanding balance of $1,000 is secured by property worth only $800, the secured party is entitled to priority (within the hierarchy of secured debt if there is other secured debt) for $800 and has an unsecured claim for $200.

4.   The property right and the priority right afforded by a security interest are most relevant for debtors in financial distress, and it often happens that such debtors wind up in bankruptcy with the security interest in place. Bankruptcy law provides a procedure to collect the assets of the debtor and do a once-and-for-all division of these assets among the various claimants. Bankruptcy is closely related to insolvency, the state of having liabilities in excess of one's assets. Sometimes a solvent debtor can choose to enter bankruptcy to effect a reorganization, for a variety of reasons. Involuntary bankruptcies, in which a creditor can force a debtor into bankruptcy, are reserved for insolvent debtors. In the case of an individual debtor, the motivation is to provide a fresh start, subject to restraints on using the mechanism by certain debtors. Many of the issues are empirical, including the reasons behind increased filings in recent years, and normative, including the proper role of stigma and the fresh start.

It is sometimes said that bankruptcy reflects a policy of trying to prevent creditors from racing to grab assets of a debtor on the brink of insolvency in an effort to satisfy themselves and leave other creditors empty-handed. See, e.g., Thomas H. Jackson, The Logic and Limits of Bankruptcy Law (1986). For example, receiving a voluntary payment from the debtor 90 days or less before the filing of a bankruptcy case may be deemed a voidable preference, allowing the bankruptcy trustee to force its return to the estate. 11 U.S.C. § 547(b). Because they enjoy a priority right, lien creditors and those with other security interests are generally in a better position in bankruptcy proceedings than are general creditors. This means they have less reason to engage in racing behavior to try to grab the assets of a creditor who is on the verge of insolvency.

B. LIENS AND THE PROBLEM OF NOTICE

Security interests present a basic informational problem that is at the heart of property: How can people figure out which assets are subject to security interests? Without any limit on security interests or requirements to register them, one would always face the problem of the potential "secret lien," a problem that preoccupied people in earlier times, and is still a live issue today. For example, when should a purchaser of an asset take the asset subject to the seller's previously given security interest in favor of a third party? In earlier times, when registries were nonexistent and commerce was simpler, possession was usually taken as the best evidence of property rights. Thus, unless the lender took actual possession of the mortgaged property or collateral, the mortgagor would appear to the rest of the world as an owner. Accordingly, many security interests, especially in earlier times, involved the lender taking possession of the asset through a bailment, an arrangement which is called a "pledge." In some ancient societies such as in Mesopotamia, lenders would even take possession of land under a type of rent-free lease in order to secure loans, an arrangement that is almost unknown in modern economies. See Robert C. Ellickson & Charles DiA. Thorland, Ancient Land Law: Mesopotamia, Egypt, Israel, 71 Chi.–Kent L. Rev. 321, 394–96 (1995). Later in the ancient world, markers on the land itself would give notice of a mortgage, as with the engraved marker-stone (called a *horos*) in ancient Athens. Id. at 397. Pledges of personal property are still common, notably in pawn shops. Where the lender takes possession as security, the security interest does not present informational problems, although the lender as bailee might exceed its rights with respect to the collateral. Often, however, a borrower wants to give security in an asset that he will continue to use, such as business equipment.

Today, security interests in which the borrower keeps possession of the collateral are very common and well accepted. But this was not always so. Possession as evidence of ownership is both a historic approach and a departure point for the more complicated schemes we will study in this Chapter and the next. Particularly in the case of personal property, courts started from a basic suspicion of non-possessory security interests. These presented a problem of "ostensible ownership," in which third parties might deal with and lend further to the borrower in the belief that his assets would be available to back those further third-party claims. In real estate, mortgages could be recorded, thus diminishing but not extinguishing a similar concern about secret liens.

Liens exist in all sorts of shapes and sizes and can be imposed as a matter of law as well as when someone takes out a loan and consents to give a security interest in return. Liens imposed as a matter of law present particularly difficult problems of notice and can be a surprise even to the owner of an asset.

Timmer v. Gray

Minnesota Court of Appeals, 1986.
395 N.W.2d 477.

■ CRIPPEN, JUDGE. Appellants Martin and Lylia Timmer sought to obtain possession of two farm discs they had purchased from Farmers Home Administration. The trial court gave possession of the discs to the Timmers, subject to an equitable lien in favor of respondent Jed Maggert, who had repaired the discs. The trial court determined that Maggert's unpaid repair bill necessitated an equitable lien in order to prevent unjust enrichment of the Timmers. We affirm.

FACTS

Terrance Heaton owned two farming discs. Heaton last used the discs in 1982 and left them in disrepair on land he rented that year from Tom Glowack. In 1984, the Farmers Home Administration (FmHA) acquired legal title to the discs pursuant to a security agreement between the FmHA and Heaton. The FmHA acquired possession of the discs when Heaton filed bankruptcy. Although the FmHA had possession, the agency chose to leave the discs on the land rented by Heaton. At this time, Tom Glowack, the landowner, permitted William Gray, a neighboring farmer, to take possession of the discs. During 1984, Gray arranged with respondent Jed Maggert to have the discs repaired. Maggert performed $857 worth of repairs on the discs, but did not receive any compensation from Gray. The discs are presently worth substantially more than the cost of repair.

On December 7, 1984, Martin and Lylia Timmer purchased the discs from the FmHA for $75. It is unclear whether Maggert completed all of his repairs prior to the sale; however, the last work was completed at about the time of the sale. The evidence does not suggest the FmHA or the Timmers had actual knowledge of Maggert's repair work at the time of the sale, nor does the evidence indicate that Maggert had any information to suggest that Gray did not own the discs.

Figure 7-1
An International Harvester 1066 and a Disk Harrow

By Daniel Christensen—Own work, CC BY 3.0, https://commons.wikimedia.org/w/in dex.php?curid=8336883.

At the time of the sale, Gray possessed a fully repaired disc and Maggert still had possession of the other disc. The Timmers brought an action for replevin and conversion. Maggert counterclaimed to recover the cost of his repair work. The trial court found the Timmers to be the rightful owners of the discs, subject to an equitable lien in favor of Maggert. The Timmers appeal that portion of the order granting Maggert an equitable lien.

ISSUE

Did the trial court err in awarding respondent an equitable lien on appellants' property based on the theory of unjust enrichment?

ANALYSIS

The trial court awarded Maggert an equitable lien based on the theory of unjust enrichment. Considerations of right and justice and various equitable maxims warrant the imposition of an equitable lien in certain instances. See Lindell v. Lindell, 185 N.W. 929, 930 (Minn. 1921). The theory of unjust enrichment is "founded on the principle that no one ought unjustly to enrich himself at the expense of another." Cady v. Bush, 166 N.W.2d 358, 361 (Minn. 1969) (quoting Heywood v. Northern Assurance Co., 158 N.W. 632, 633 (Minn. 1916)).

Actions for unjust enrichment may be based on failure of consideration, fraud, mistake, and situations where it would be morally wrong for one party to enrich himself at the expense of another. See, e.g., Anderson v. DeLisle, 352 N.W.2d 794, 796 (Minn. Ct. App. 1984) (unjust enrichment action based on considerations of moral wrongness); Cady, 166 N.W.2d at 361 (unjust enrichment action based on failure of consideration, fraud or mistake); Knox v. Knox, 25 N.W.2d 225, 229 (Minn. 1946) (unjust enrichment action based on unconscientious retention of property).

The failure of consideration, mistake and moral wrongness encompassing this case mandates imposition of an equitable lien based on the theory of unjust enrichment. The Timmers paid $75 for what they mistakenly believed to be a pair of discs in disrepair. Instead, Maggert's repair work provided the Timmers with a pair of discs worth much more. In this situation, it would be wrong to allow the Timmers to receive substantially improved property, for a nominal price, at Maggert's expense.

Our conclusion is forged in part by the fact that Maggert performed his repair work while Heaton or the FmHA owned the discs, causing the equitable lien to attach during the FmHA's possession. The personal property had been left unattended for over two years and its enrichment at the expense of an unknowing repairman is evident. An equitable lien is enforceable against any person who subsequently acquires the encumbered property, except a bona fide purchaser for value, without notice of the lien. See Minn.Stat. § 514.18, subd. 3 (1984) (mechanic's lien on personal property valid against everyone except a purchaser without notice and for value); see also Whiteside v. Rocky Mountain Fuel Co., 101 F.2d 765, 770 (10th Cir.1938).

We cannot conclude that Maggert's lien is expunged by purchasers who pay a nominal amount for property they fail to examine. The Timmers lack the status of bona fide purchasers. Payment of $75 for property worth much more constitutes a lack of value. See Nichols-Frissell Co. v. Crocker, 157 N.W. 1072, 1072 (Minn. 1916) (payment of a small sum for title examination and quit claim deed did not constitute value); see also Tremont v. General Motors Acceptance Corp., 223 N.W. 137 (Minn. 1929) (payment of over one-half the purchase price constituted the value necessary to support the contract).

Furthermore, it cannot be said that FmHA or the Timmers were without notice that the discs had been repaired. A simple inspection would have revealed Maggert's possession and improvements. Equity says if a loss is to fall on one of two innocent parties, it should fall on one who is in a better position to prevent it. Hughes v. Monnahan, 165 N.W.2d 231, 234 (Minn. 1969). We have considered Maggert's opportunities to check on ownership of the discs, but we conclude that any shortcoming of Maggert was outweighed by the Timmers' failure to prevent their loss by inspecting the property prior to purchase.

Our conclusion would differ had the Timmers inspected the discs and paid value for them. These actions would allow us to view the Timmers as innocent parties and extinguish Maggert's equitable lien. Maggert would then be left with an unjust enrichment action against earlier owners. Since this is not the scenario, an equitable lien in favor of Maggert is necessary to prevent unjustly enriching the Timmers. The litigation in this case has not addressed the question whether Timmers assert or enjoy rescission rights on their purchase of the discs.

DECISION

The trial court's order granting Maggert an equitable lien on the Timmers' discs is affirmed.

NOTES AND QUESTIONS

1.   *Timmer* involves several kinds of security interests, both voluntary and involuntary. The problem addressed by the court begins when farmer Heaton borrows money from a federal government agency, the FmHA, and in return gives the agency a security interest in some of his personal property, including the discs. When Heaton fails to repay the debt and declares bankruptcy, the FmHA is entitled to repossess the discs and sell them, in order to obtain at least partial repayment of the debt. Although the court says the FmHA "acquired possession" when Heaton failed to repay, it does not mean this literally; what it means is that the agency had the right to foreclose on its security interest and sell the discs. Actual physical possession of the discs at the time of the foreclosure, unbeknownst to the FmHA, had been transferred to farmer Gray and from Gray to Maggert, whom Gray had requested to repair the discs. There is no sign or other indication on the discs that they are subject to a security interest in favor of the FmHA, or that the debt on which the security interest is based has not been paid. Thus, when farmer Gray asks Maggert to repair the discs, neither of them, presumably, is aware of the government's security interest. When the FmHA sells the discs in partial satisfaction of the security interest to the Timmers for $75, the Timmers have never inspected the discs and are, of course, unaware of the repairs that Maggert has made, increasing the value of the discs to much more than $75.

2.   In theory, the repairs executed by Maggert could give rise to an involuntary security interest called a mechanic's lien. At common law, persons who provided repairs or performed other services on personal property were held to have a mechanic's lien, which applied as long as they retained possession of the personal property. Innkeepers and operators of warehouses would also have a lien on goods in their possession in a similar fashion. Today, mechanic's liens are almost always governed by statute. The Minnesota Mechanics' Lien statute, in effect when the principal case was decided and cited by the court, reads as follows:

M.S.A. § 514.18

Subdivision 1. Mechanics' lien on personal property.
Whoever, at the request of the owner or legal possessor of any personal property, shall store or care for or contribute * * * to its preservation, care, or to the enhancement of its value, shall have a

lien upon such property for the price or value of such storage, care, or contribution, and for any legal charges against the same paid by such person to any other person, and the right to retain possession of the property until such lien is lawfully discharged.

Subd. 2. Nonpossessory lien; notice. Notwithstanding the voluntary surrender or other loss of possession of the property on which the lien is claimed, the person entitled thereto may preserve the lien upon giving notice of the lien at any time within 60 days after the surrender or loss of possession, by filing in the appropriate filing office under the Uniform Commercial Code, Minnesota Statutes, section 336.9–501 a verified statement and notice of intention to claim a lien. The statement shall contain a description of the property upon which the lien is claimed, the work performed or materials furnished and the amount due.

Subd. 3. Priority; security; interest; foreclosure. The lien shall be valid against everyone except a purchaser or encumbrancer in good faith without notice and for value whose rights were acquired prior to the filing of the lien statement and who has filed a statement of interest in the appropriate filing office. The lien shall be considered a security interest under the Uniform Commercial Code and foreclosure thereon shall be in the manner prescribed for security interests under article 9 of the Uniform Commercial Code.

Subd. 4. Motor vehicles excluded. Subdivisions 2 and 3 shall apply to machinery, implements and tools of all kinds but shall not apply to motor vehicles.

3.   Did Jed Maggert, who repaired the discs, comply with the Mechanics' Lien statute? If not, why not? If a mechanic fails to comply with the statute, is it proper for the court to declare an "equitable lien" that performs the same function as a mechanic's lien? For a recent decision that throws out a mechanic's lien for $3.2 million of landscaping services because the landscaping company failed to comply with a confusing notice provision, see Shady Tree Farms v. Omni Financial, 14 1 Cal.Rptr.3d 112 (Cal. Ct. App. 2012).

4.   How can the court say that the Timmers did not acquire the discs as bona fide purchasers for value? The court does not suggest that the Timmers had any notice of the repairs performed by Maggert. Occasionally courts will decide that a bill of sale or deed that recites "$1 and other valuable consideration" does not establish a purchase "for value." See, e.g., Hood v. Webster, infra Chapter VIII. But the Timmers paid $75 for the discs, which was evidently the price set by the FmHA. What if the Timmers purchased the discs to add to their collection of old farm machinery in their yard, and had no intention of paying the much higher price for a fully-functioning set of repaired discs?

5.   Mechanic's liens reflect some specific policies, centering around the protection of trade creditors and the facilitation of improvement projects. Thomas Jefferson and James Madison, who wanted to promote the building

of Washington, D.C., were a driving force behind the first mechanic's lien statute, in Maryland, which embraced the District in 1791. Unlike mechanic's liens for personal property, mechanic's liens on real property are solely created by statute. Many kinds of professionals can now claim mechanic's liens, including in the case of real estate a wide variety of contractors and even design professionals. What sets them apart from many other liens on real estate is that they are frequently valid against third parties even before they are "perfected" (usually by filing), and states vary as to how long an unperfected mechanic's lien has third-party effect. For this reason, an exclusive focus on the deservingness of the potential lien holder can lead to overlooking the unfairness and information costs this imposes on other creditors and potential purchasers of assets. See Chad J. Pomeroy, Ending Surprise Liens on Real Property, 11 Nev. L.J. 139 (2010) (discerning a trend toward greater allowance of surprise liens because of concern for the lienholder and arguing against trend on fairness and information cost grounds). How easy should it be for lien creditors to get priority over other creditors?

6.   All security interests are intangible rights, and hence all present a potential problem of notice. One solution to the problem of notice is for the party holding the security interest to retain possession of the property subject to the security interest, as under the common law mechanic's lien. This is also the solution when the security interest takes the form of a pledge, as in the case of pawnshop loans. Another solution is to require actual notice of the security interest to potential interested parties, as required by some statutory mechanic's lien statutes. A third solution, as under the Minnesota Mechanics' Lien statute, is to require that security interests be publicly recorded, in some kind of public repository of information about property titles (see Chapter VIII). Which solution is best? Is there any way to provide notice of interests that are imposed as a matter of equity, such as constructive trusts or the "equitable lien" adopted in the principal case by the Minnesota appeals court?

7.   As we will see in the next Chapter, the notice problem has been partially solved through recording systems for real estate and related filing systems for security interests in personal property. Some commentators see security interests as primarily a contractual problem with few or no third-party effects, see, e.g., Alan Schwartz, A Theory of Loan Priorities, 18 J. Legal Stud. 209, 220–22, 249–59 (1989), while others see them as presenting ostensible ownership problems for such third parties, see, e.g., Jonathan C. Lipson, Secrets and Liens: The End of Notice in Commercial Finance Law, 21 Emory Bankr. Dev. J. 421 (2005). Like bailments, leases, and trusts, security interests have both a contractual and property aspect. See Thomas W. Merrill & Henry E. Smith, The Property/Contract Interface, 101 Colum. L. Rev. 773, 833–43 (2001). The Uniform Commercial Code still allows perfection of security interests by possession. UCC § 9–313(a). Such a security interest is known as a pledge. Indeed, this is the only way to create a security interest in money. As we will see in greater detail in the next Chapter, some instruments are negotiable, meaning that under a wide variety of circumstances, the current holder is entitled to payment and is

free from most defenses; money is the ultimate in negotiability in that one can get good title to cash even from a thief. Generally, the more negotiable something is, the more a security interest in it has to be by possession. Can you see why? Negotiability and ostensible ownership rules (e.g., good faith purchaser) are in part about allocating information costs, the burdens of inquiry, and the costs of errors as between affected parties to a transaction.

The "Puzzle" of Secured Debt

Secured debt has been treated by commentators as something of a "puzzle" and has been regarded with a certain degree of suspicion. The excerpt from Ronald Mann, supra, explains why lenders prefer secured rather than unsecured debt. But commentators have been puzzled about why borrowers take on secured debt as well as unsecured debt, instead of simply allowing all creditors to share pro rata in their assets. Thomas H. Jackson & Anthony T. Kronman, Secured Financing and Priority Among Creditors, 88 Yale L.J. 1143, 1146 (1979). True, the secured lender will offer a lower interest rate because of the decreased risk that it will not be repaid. But this simply *raises* the interest rate on whatever other debt the borrower will take on and lowers the value of the borrower's equity interest. At first blush, the total amount of risk remains the same, and manipulating the ratio of secured debt to unsecured debt (or debt to other equity-like interests) should not make any difference to total value under the control of a person or firm.

Some have gone further and argued that secured debt is objectionable on social policy grounds: By taking out secured debt, the borrower gets a lower interest rate, but contrary to initial appearances not all other creditors adjust their interest rates to reflect the increased risk left over for them. The clearest case is tort creditors: Tort victims have no way of avoiding interactions with tortfeasors who are loaded up with secured debt, but the secured debt may make a judgment against the tortfeasor less valuable since it will have lower priority. Perhaps other creditors are also "nonadjusting" in this way; candidates would include trade creditors. See, e.g., Lucian Arye Bebchuk & Jesse M. Fried, The Uneasy Case for the Priority of Secured Claims in Bankruptcy, 105 Yale L.J. 857, 885 (1996); Luke Sperduto, Three and A Half Rules for Tort Claims in (and Out of) Chapter 11, 95 Am. Bankr. L.J. 127 (2021). Empirical evidence is scarce. One study calls into question whether fraud on nonadjusting creditors actually occurs. See Yair Listokin, Is Secured Debt Used to Redistribute Value from Tort Claimants in Bankruptcy? An Empirical Analysis, 57 Duke L.J. 1037, 1078 (2008) (presenting results that suggest that firms do not use secured debt to exploit tort claimants). A recent empirical study finds that firms increase their use of secured debt as they approach bankruptcy. Barry E. Adler & Vedran Capkun, Debt-Equity Conflict and the Incidence of Secured Credit, 62 J.L. & Econ. 551 (2019).

More benign explanations for secured credit have also been offered. A secured creditor can specialize in monitoring a given asset, and this specialization can lower overall information costs. Debt holders must worry about the actions of the (equity) owners of the firm, because the latter will have an incentive to take risks with the firm's assets (including substituting them for riskier assets): The equity owners as holders of the residual claim will enjoy all of the upside, but will be able to force debt holders to take more downside risk. These "agency costs" can be addressed by security interests. The secured creditor specializes in monitoring the asset held as security. This reduces overall monitoring costs because it prevents duplicative monitoring of any given asset and prevents freeriding by other debt holders on these monitoring efforts. Moreover, each secured creditor can specialize in a class of asset (and a particular asset within the class as well), and need not worry about the interaction of risk from other assets with the risk from the asset in question. See, e.g., Jackson & Kronman, supra; Hideki Kanda & Saul Levmore, Explaining Creditor Priorities, 80 Va. L. Rev. 2103 (1994); Saul Levmore, Monitors and Freeriders in Commercial and Corporate Settings, 92 Yale L.J. 49 (1982); see also Henry Hansmann & Reinier Kraakman, The Essential Role of Organizational Law, 110 Yale L.J. 387, 417–23 (2000). In other words, the benefits of a security interest seem to be a special case of the internalization and information-cost benefits of property rights more generally. Bankruptcy, a subject for another course, has a slightly different effect on each of these rights.

C. REAL ESTATE MORTGAGES

Although we have seen that personal intangible property, especially intellectual property, is now more important than ever, land continues to be a convenient asset against which to borrow. The very features that make land a good candidate for centralized records—its value, fixed location, and permanence—make it a good candidate for an asset to use to secure loans, particularly long-term loans and even loans whose proceeds will be used to finance projects other than the acquisition of the real estate. The land records themselves make the functioning of mortgages smoother, although not without some bumpiness, as we will see in the next Chapter.

Some mortgages are taken on property already owned by the borrower, but many mortgages are purchase money mortgages, used to finance the acquisition of the real property used as security for the loan. (Many personal property security interests likewise are purchase money security interests, and these receive special favorable treatment under the UCC. Think of security interests in consumer goods like cars or household furniture.) In transactions involving a purchase money mortgage, the source of the financing can be the seller of the asset or a financial institution. In the case of financial institutions, the mortgages are very often bought and sold, often in packages, to other institutions.

A real estate mortgage typically secures payment on a note used to borrow the money to purchase the property. The mortgage document represents the security interest and the note contains the terms of and evidences the loan itself. The mortgage and the note are separate. In times past, courts subscribed to a title theory of mortgages, in which the borrower would transfer legal title to the lender and would only get it back upon payment of the note. These days courts treat mortgages as liens, regardless of the form that they take, even if the mortgage purports to convey legal title. One can say that if the title is "transferred" merely to secure repayment of a note, then it is treated as a lien. As we will see, because of the efforts of parties, especially mortgagees, to avoid the protections afforded by courts to mortgagors, there has been a complex history of form and substance in the area of mortgages.

Much of the terminology of mortgage law derives from the history of the courts of equity, although the meaning of the terms has in many cases changed over time. As the borrower made payments, he acquired important protections against forfeiture, especially in courts of equity (recall that equity abhors a forfeiture). One of these protections was the right to redeem the property even after a default, called the "equity of redemption." This is the source of the term "equity" to denote the stake that a homeowner has built up in the real property.

In addition to "equity," the terms "foreclosure" and "redemption" have several related meanings, because in the history of mortgage lending, legislatures, courts, and contracting parties have innovated at many points and have reacted to each other's moves. The term "foreclosure" traces back to what is also known as "strict foreclosure," a regime under which the mortgagee would have the right to be declared the owner of the premises without any sale of the premises. Between the seventeenth and nineteenth centuries, strict foreclosure gradually gave way to a system of foreclosure followed by sale, known as "judicial foreclosure" or "foreclosure by judicial sale." The mortgagee was allowed to bid for the property but the process was subject to notice and other procedural requirements to protect the mortgagor and to help ensure a fair price.

"Foreclosure" can also refer as a shorthand to "foreclosure by sale." In a fashion reminiscent of landlords with their reenter and relet clauses, mortgagees would avoid the complexities of going to the equity court and obtaining a judicial foreclosure by putting a clause in the mortgage indenture providing for an express authority in the mortgagee upon default of the mortgagor to sell the property free of the equity of redemption. This power of sale was later subjected to some of the same judicial safeguards and procedures associated with judicial foreclosure.

"Redemption" is correspondingly ambiguous. As noted it can refer to the equitable period of redemption ("equity of redemption") developed by courts of equity, and "foreclosure" originally meant foreclosure of the equity of redemption. More typically today it is a period provided for by statute during which the mortgagor has the right to redeem the property even after a foreclosure sale. The mechanics involved and the duration of the redemption period vary widely by state. A typical period would be one year after foreclosure sale. This means that the purchaser of the property at the foreclosure sale cannot be certain of retaining the property, as opposed to being forced to return it for the purchase price plus interest, for the period of one year.

Jurisdictions also differ as to whether a mortgagee can seek a deficiency judgment against the mortgagor if the mortgaged premises turn out at sale to be worth less than the outstanding note. Where personal recourse is possible according to its terms and allowed by law, a note is said to be recourse; if not, a note is nonrecourse, and the debtor can walk away from the property without further liability. In some states residential mortgages must be nonrecourse, but home equity loans (for improvements or simply access to a house's value) are permitted to be recourse.

Legislatures as well as courts have been active in the history of mortgages and foreclosures. Ever since 1820 in the aftermath of the Napoleonic Wars, legislatures have vacillated between facilitating powers of sale in good times and hedging them about with restrictions in favor of mortgagors in periods of economic distress. Often legislatures would institute or lengthen periods of redemption (whether before or after foreclosure sale) in times of widespread default, and would shorten them in flush times. Before the mortgage crisis starting in 2007, the most recent episode of wholesale legislative intervention on behalf of mortgagors took place during the Great Depression, which led a number of states to pass mortgage moratoria. The U.S. Supreme Court upheld the Minnesota moratorium in the face of Contracts Clause and Due Process challenges in *Home Building and Loan Association v. Blaisdell*, 290 U.S. 398 (1934). The Minnesota Mortgage Moratorium Law had declared that during the emergency period, mortgagors could obtain relief from foreclosure and execution sales through authorized judicial proceedings and that periods of redemption could be extended. The Court stated that "[t]he economic interests of the State may justify the exercise of its continuing and dominant protective power notwithstanding interference with contracts," id. at 437, and likened mass foreclosures stemming from the Depression to natural disasters. Whether and how to provide relief in times of widespread financial distress is a live issue today and one to which we return at the end of this Chapter.

Murphy v. Financial Development Corporation

Supreme Court of New Hampshire, 1985.
495 A.2d 1245.

■ DOUGLAS, JUSTICE. The plaintiffs brought this action seeking to set aside the foreclosure sale of their home, or, in the alternative, money damages. The Superior Court (*Bean,* J.), adopting the recommendation of a Master (*R. Peter Shapiro,* Esq.), entered a judgment for the plaintiffs in the amount of $27,000 against two of the defendants, Financial Development Corporation and Colonial Deposit Company (the lenders).

The plaintiffs purchased a house in Nashua in 1966, financing it by means of a mortgage loan. They refinanced the loan in March of 1980, executing a new promissory note and a power of sale mortgage, with Financial Development Corporation as mortgagee. The note and mortgage were later assigned to Colonial Deposit Company.

In February of 1981, the plaintiff Richard Murphy became unemployed. By September of 1981, the plaintiffs were seven months in arrears on their mortgage payments, and had also failed to pay substantial amounts in utility assessments and real estate taxes. After discussing unsuccessfully with the plaintiffs proposals for revising the payment schedule, rewriting the note, and arranging alternative financing, the lenders gave notice on October 6, 1981, of their intent to foreclose.

During the following weeks, the plaintiffs made a concerted effort to avoid foreclosure. They paid the seven months' mortgage arrearage, but failed to pay some $643.18 in costs and legal fees associated with the foreclosure proceedings. The lenders scheduled the foreclosure sale for November 10, 1981, at the site of the subject property. They complied with all of the statutory requirements for notice. See RSA 479:25.

At the plaintiffs' request, the lenders agreed to postpone the sale until December 15, 1981. They advised the plaintiffs that this would entail an additional cost of $100, and that the sale would proceed unless the lenders received payment of $743.18, as well as all mortgage payments then due, by December 15. Notice of the postponement was posted on the subject property on November 10 at the originally scheduled time of the sale, and was also posted at the Nashua City Hall and Post Office. No prospective bidders were present for the scheduled sale.

In late November, the plaintiffs paid the mortgage payment which had been due in October, but made no further payments to the lenders. An attempt by the lenders to arrange new financing for the plaintiffs through a third party failed when the plaintiffs refused to agree to pay for a new appraisal of the property. Early on the morning of December 15, 1981, the plaintiffs tried to obtain a further postponement, but were advised by the lenders' attorney that it was impossible unless the costs and legal fees were paid.

At the plaintiffs' request, the attorney called the president of Financial Development Corporation, who also refused to postpone the sale. Further calls by the plaintiffs to the lenders' offices were equally unavailing.

The sale proceeded as scheduled at 10:00 a.m. on December 15, at the site of the property. Although it had snowed the previous night, the weather was clear and warm at the time of the sale, and the roads were clear. The only parties present were the plaintiffs, a representative of the lenders, and an attorney, Morgan Hollis, who had been engaged to conduct the sale because the lenders' attorney, who lived in Dover, had been apprehensive about the weather the night before. The lenders' representative made the only bid at the sale. That bid of $27,000, roughly the amount owed on the mortgage, plus costs and fees, was accepted and the sale concluded.

Later that same day, Attorney Hollis encountered one of his clients, William Dube, a representative of the defendant Southern New Hampshire Home Traders, Inc. (Southern). On being informed of the sale, Mr. Dube contacted the lenders and offered to buy the property for $27,000. The lenders rejected the offer and made a counter offer of $40,000. Within two days a purchase price of $38,000 was agreed upon by Mr. Dube and the lenders and the sale was subsequently completed.

The plaintiffs commenced this action on February 5, 1982. The lenders moved to dismiss, arguing that any action was barred because the plaintiffs had failed to petition for an injunction prior to the sale. The master denied the motion. After hearing the evidence, he ruled for the plaintiffs, finding that the lenders had "failed to exercise good faith and due diligence in obtaining a fair price for the subject property at the foreclosure sale. . . ."

The master also ruled that Southern was a bona fide purchaser for value, and thus had acquired legal title to the house. That ruling is not at issue here. He assessed monetary damages against the lenders equal to "the difference between the fair market value of the subject property on the date of the foreclosure and the price obtained at said sale."

Having found the fair market value to be $54,000, he assessed damages accordingly at $27,000. He further ruled that "[t]he bad faith of the 'Lenders' warrants an award of legal fees." The lenders appealed.

The first issue before us is whether the master erred in denying the motion to dismiss. The lenders, in support of their argument, rely upon RSA 479:25, II, which gives a mortgagor the right to petition the superior court to enjoin a proposed foreclosure sale, and then provides: "Failure to institute such petition and complete service upon the foreclosing party, or his agent, conducting the sale prior to sale shall thereafter bar any action or right of action of the mortgagor based on the validity of the foreclosure."

If we were to construe this provision as the lenders urge us to do, it would prevent a mortgagor from challenging the validity of a sale in a case where the only claimed unfairness or illegality occurred during the sale itself—unless the mortgagor had petitioned for an injunction before any grounds existed on which the injunction could be granted. We will not construe a statute so as to produce such an illogical and unjust result.

The only reasonable construction of the language in RSA 479:25, II relied upon by the lenders is that it bars any action based on facts which the mortgagor knew or should have known soon enough to reasonably permit the filing of a petition prior to the sale.

The master could not have found that this was such an action, because the only unfairness referred to in his report involves the amount of the sale price. Thus, his denial of the lenders' motion to dismiss was proper.

The second issue before us is whether the master erred in concluding that the lenders had failed to comply with the often-repeated rule that a mortgagee executing a power of sale is bound both by the statutory procedural requirements *and* by a duty to protect the interests of the mortgagor through the exercise of good faith and due diligence. We will not overturn a master's findings and rulings "unless they are unsupported by the evidence or are erroneous as a matter of law." Summit Electric, Inc. v. Pepin Brothers Const., Inc., 427 A.2d 505, 507 (N.H. 1981).

The master found that the lenders, throughout the time prior to the sale, "did not mislead or deal unfairly with the plaintiffs." They engaged in serious efforts to avoid foreclosure through new financing, and agreed to one postponement of the sale. The basis for the master's decision was his conclusion that the lenders had failed to exercise good faith and due diligence in obtaining a fair price for the property.

This court's past decisions have not dealt consistently with the question whether the mortgagee's duty amounts to that of a fiduciary or trustee. Compare Pearson v. Gooch, 40 A. 390, 390–91 (N.H. 1897) and Merrimack Industrial Trust v. First Nat. Bank of Boston, 427 A.2d 500, 504 (N.H. 1981) (duty amounts to that of a fiduciary or trustee) with Silver v. First National Bank, 236 A.2d 493, 494–95 (N.H. 1967) and Proctor v. Bank of N.H., 464 A.2d 263, 266 (N.H. 1983) (duty does not amount to that of a fiduciary or trustee). This may be an inevitable result of the mortgagee's dual role as seller and potential buyer at the foreclosure sale, and of the conflicting interests involved.

We need not label a duty, however, in order to define it. In his role as a seller, the mortgagee's duty of good faith and due diligence is essentially that of a fiduciary. Such a view is in keeping with "[t]he 'trend . . . towards liberalizing the term [fiduciary] in order to prevent unjust enrichment.'" Lash v. Cheshire County Savings Bank, Inc., 474 A.2d 980, 981 (N.H. 1984) (quoting Cornwell v. Cornwell, 356 A.2d 683, 686 (N.H. 1976)).

A mortgagee, therefore, must exert every reasonable effort to obtain "a fair and reasonable price under the circumstances," Reconstruction Finance Corp. v. Faulkner, 143 A.2d 403, 410 (N.H. 1958), even to the extent, if necessary, of adjourning the sale or of establishing "an upset

[handwritten margin note: fair price determined case-by-case]

price below which he will not accept any offer." Lakes Region Fin. Corp. v. Goodhue Boat Yard, Inc., 382 A.2d 1108, 1111 (N.H. 1978).

What constitutes a fair price, or whether the mortgagee must establish an upset price, adjourn the sale, or make other reasonable efforts to assure a fair price, depends on the circumstances of each case. Inadequacy of price alone is not sufficient to demonstrate bad faith unless the price is so low as to shock the judicial conscience.

We must decide, in the present case, whether the evidence supports the finding of the master that the lenders failed to exercise good faith and due diligence in obtaining a fair price for the plaintiffs' property.

[handwritten margin note: bad faith req.]

We first note that "[t]he duties of good faith and due diligence are distinct. . . . One may be observed and not the other, and any inquiry as to their breach calls for a separate consideration of each." Wheeler v. Slocinski, 131 A. at 600 (N.H. 1926). In order "to constitute bad faith there must be an intentional disregard of duty or a purpose to injure." Id. at 600–01.

There is insufficient evidence in the record to support the master's finding that the lenders acted in bad faith in failing to obtain a fair price for the plaintiffs' property. The lenders complied with the statutory requirements of notice and otherwise conducted the sale in compliance with statutory provisions. The lenders postponed the sale one time and did not bid with knowledge of any immediately available subsequent purchaser. Further, there is no evidence indicating an intent on the part of the lenders to injure the mortgagor by, for example, discouraging other buyers.

There is ample evidence in the record, however, to support the master's finding that the lenders failed to exercise due diligence in obtaining a fair price. "The issue of the lack of due diligence is whether a reasonable man in the [lenders'] place would have adjourned the sale," id. at 601, or taken other measures to receive a fair price.

[handwritten margin note: equity]

In early 1980, the plaintiffs' home was appraised at $46,000. At the time of the foreclosure sale on December 15, 1981, the lenders had not had the house reappraised to take into account improvements and appreciation. The master found that a reasonable person in the place of the lenders would have realized that the plaintiffs' equity in the property was at least $19,000, the difference between the 1980 appraised value of $46,000 and the amount owed on the mortgage totaling approximately $27,000.

[handwritten margin note: ①]

At the foreclosure sale, the lenders were the only bidders. The master found that their bid of $27,000 "was sufficient to cover all monies due and did not create a deficiency balance" but "did not provide for a return of any of the plaintiffs' equity."

[handwritten margin note: lowball = bad faith; ②]

Further, the master found that the lenders "had reason to know" that "they stood to make a substantial profit on a quick turnaround sale." On the day of the sale, the lenders offered to sell the foreclosed property to William Dube for $40,000. Within two days after the foreclosure sale, they did in fact agree to sell it to Dube for $38,000. It was not necessary for the master to find that the lenders knew of a specific potential buyer before the sale in order to show lack of good faith or due diligence as the lenders contend. The fact that the lenders offered the property for sale at a price sizably above that for which they had purchased it, only a few hours before, supports the master's finding that the lenders had reason to know, at the time of the foreclosure sale, that they could make a substantial profit on a quick turnaround sale. For this reason, they should have taken more measures to ensure receiving a higher price at the sale.

While a mortgagee may not always be required to secure a portion of the mortgagor's equity, such an obligation did exist in this case. The substantial amount of equity which the plaintiffs had in their property, the knowledge of the lenders as to the appraised value of the property, and the plaintiffs' efforts to forestall foreclosure by paying the mortgage arrearage within weeks of the sale, all support the master's conclusion that the lenders had a fiduciary duty to take more reasonable steps than they did to protect the plaintiffs' equity by attempting to obtain a fair price for the property. They could have established an appropriate upset price to assure a minimum bid. They also could have postponed the auction and advertised commercially by display advertising in order to assure that bidders other than themselves would be present.

Instead, as Theodore DiStefano, an officer of both lending institutions testified, the lenders made no attempt to obtain fair market value for the property but were concerned *only* with making themselves "whole." On the facts of this case, such disregard for the interests of the mortgagors was a breach of duty by the mortgagees.

Although the lenders *did* comply with the statutory requirements of notice of the foreclosure sale, these efforts were not sufficient in this case to demonstrate due diligence. At the time of the initially scheduled sale, the extent of the lenders' efforts to publicize the sale of the property was publication of a legal notice of the mortgagees' sale at public auction on November 10, published once a week for three weeks in the Nashua Telegraph, plus postings in public places. The lenders did not advertise, publish, or otherwise give notice to the general public of postponement of the sale to December 15, 1981, other than by posting notices at the plaintiffs' house, at the post office, and at city hall. That these efforts to advertise were ineffective is evidenced by the fact that no one, other than the lenders, appeared at the sale to bid on the property. This fact allowed the lenders to purchase the property at a minimal price and then to profit substantially in a quick turnaround sale.

We recognize a need to give guidance to a trial court which must determine whether a mortgagee who has complied with the strict letter of the statutory law has nevertheless violated his additional duties of good faith and due diligence. A finding that the mortgagee had, or should have had, knowledge of his ability to get a higher price at an adjourned sale is the most conclusive evidence of such a violation. See Lakes Region Fin. Corp. v. Goodhue Boat Yard, Inc., 382 A.2d at 1111.

More generally, we are in agreement with the official Commissioners' Comment to section 3–508 of the Uniform Land Transactions Act:

> The requirement that the sale be conducted in a reasonable manner, including the advertising aspects, requires that the person conducting the sale use the ordinary methods of making buyers aware that are used when an owner is voluntarily selling his land. Thus an advertisement in the portion of a daily newspaper where these ads are placed or, in appropriate cases such as the sale of an industrial plant, a display advertisement in the financial sections of the daily newspaper may be the most reasonable method. In other cases employment of a professional real estate agent may be the more reasonable method. It is unlikely that an advertisement in a legal publication among other legal notices would qualify as a commercially reasonable method of sale advertising.

13 Uniform Laws Annotated 704 (West 1980). As discussed above, the lenders met neither of these guidelines.

While agreeing with the master that the lenders failed to exercise due diligence in this case, we find that he erred as a matter of law in awarding damages equal to "the difference between the fair market value of the subject property . . . and the price obtained at [the] sale."

Such a formula may well be the appropriate measure where *bad faith* is found. In such a case, a mortgagee's conduct amounts to more than mere negligence. Damages based upon the *fair market value,* a figure in excess of a *fair* price, will more readily induce mortgagees to perform their duties properly. A "fair" price may or may not yield a figure close to fair market value; however, it will be that price arrived at as a result of due diligence by the mortgagee.

Where, as here, however, a mortgagee fails to exercise due diligence, the proper assessment of damages is the difference between a fair price for the property and the price obtained at the foreclosure sale. We have held, where lack of due diligence has been found, that "the test is not 'fair market value' as in eminent domain cases nor is the mortgagee bound to give credit for the highest possible amount which might be obtained under different circumstances, as at an owner's sale." Silver v. First National Bank, 236 A.2d 493, 495 (N.H. 1967) (quoting Reconstruction Finance Corp. v. Faulkner, 143 A.2d 403, 410 (N.H. 1958)) (citation omitted). Accordingly, we remand to the trial court for a reassessment of damages consistent with this opinion.

Because we concluded above that there was no "bad faith or obstinate, unjust, vexatious, wanton, or oppressive conduct," on the part of the lenders, we see no reason to stray from our general rule that the prevailing litigant is not entitled to collect attorney's fees from the loser. Therefore, we reverse this part of the master's decision.

Reversed in part; affirmed in part; remanded.

■ BROCK, JUSTICE, dissenting: I agree with the majority that a mortgagee, in its role as seller at a foreclosure sale, has a fiduciary duty to the mortgagor. I also agree with the majority's more specific analysis of that duty * * *, including its references to the commissioners' comment to the U.L.T.A., as well as those to *Wheeler* and other decisions of this court.

On the record presently before us, however, I cannot see any support for the master's finding that the lenders here failed to exercise due diligence as we have defined that term. I would remand the case to the superior court for further findings of fact.

Specifically, the master made no findings regarding what an "owner . . . voluntarily selling his land" would have done that the lenders here did not do, in order to obtain a fair price. * * *

Although the report nowhere states specifically *what* the lenders should have done, its clear implication is that they should have made a higher bid at the foreclosure sale.

There is no authority for such a conclusion. The mortgagee's fiduciary duty extends only to its role as a *seller*. Once the mortgagee has exerted every reasonable effort to obtain a fair price (which may sometimes include setting an upset price and adjourning the sale if no bidder meets that price), it has no further obligation in its role as a potential buyer.

As the majority notes, a low price is not of itself sufficient to invalidate a foreclosure sale, unless the price is "so low as to shock the judicial conscience." The price here was clearly not that low. Cf. Shipp Corp., Inc. v. Charpilloz, 414 So.2d 1122, 1124 (Fla. Dist. Ct. App. 1982) (bid of $1.1 million was not grossly inadequate compared to a market value of between $2.8 and $3.2 million).

Because it is unclear whether the master applied the correct standard regarding the mortgagee's duty, and because the record as presently constituted cannot support a determination that the lenders violated that standard, I respectfully dissent.

NOTES AND QUESTIONS

1.   The duty of the mortgagee to obtain a fair price creates a right running in favor of the defaulting mortgagor. Might it create a similar right in others? In DeLellis v. Burke, 598 A.2d 203 (N.H. 1991), the New Hampshire Supreme Court declined to extend the fiduciary duty of the mortgagee recognized in *Murphy* to other creditors of the mortgagor.

2.   What is the minimum the mortgagee could have done to avoid liability here? Which is likely to be the better approach: A rule spelling out which procedures are sufficient (a safe harbor, if you will)? Or an ex post standard? Or some combination of the two? What exactly does it mean to obtain a "fair" price for property at a judicial sale? The concept of "fair market value" is well developed in the context of eminent domain: It is the value that a willing buyer would pay a willing seller for similar property in an arm's length transaction. See Chapter X, Part C. The court indicates that a "fair" price can be less than fair market value, but exactly how close it must be is left pretty vague.

3.   Even if a court sides with the mortgagor in a case like *Murphy*, mortgagors with substantial equity would be well-advised to try to sell the property themselves, if at all possible. The mortgagor is likely to get a much better price than the lender, even if spurred by the threat of *Murphy*-style litigation. Consider the Murphys. If they sell on their own, they can give clean title to the purchaser, and they should realize the fair market value. But if the property is sold by the lender through foreclosure, it will be subject to any common law or statutory rights of redemption that the Murphys have, which means it will sell at a substantial discount from its market value. The Murphys selling the house themselves thus looks like a win-win proposition: The lender gets its money back without incurring the costs of foreclosure, and the Murphys get to pocket the full amount of their equity in the house without having to spend time and money suing the lender. Given that the Murphys appear to have significant equity in the house beyond the mortgage balance, why didn't they follow this course of action once it became clear that they would otherwise lose the house? They appear to be unwilling to take action themselves, preferring to sit and watch while the mortgagee sells their home at the foreclosure sale. How unusual do you suppose this response is for a family in financial crisis? If mortgagees have a fiduciary duty to try to get a "fair" price for the property through a judicial foreclosure sale, should mortgagors have a duty not to destroy value by doing nothing to prevent property with positive equity from going to foreclosure?

4.   There are substitutes to the mortgage for providing security in the transfer of real estate. Probably the most commonly encountered substitute is the land sale contract (or installment sale contract), considered in the next case. One reason to use a substitute like the land sale contract is to avoid the many restrictions on mortgages and mortgage foreclosures imposed by legislatures and courts over the years. As *Murphy* suggests, these restrictions add to the costs and risks of using mortgages. Another reason is to provide credit to persons who present an especially high risk of default. Land sale contracts are often used to finance a purchase of real estate when the prospective purchaser is unable to obtain financing from a bank or other professional lending institution, either because credit markets are tight or the purchaser is a very poor credit risk. In these circumstances, the seller may elect to finance the sale him- or herself, by using a land sale contract.

Skendzel v. Marshall

Supreme Court of Indiana, 1973.
301 N.E.2d 641.

■ HUNTER, JUSTICE. Petitioners seek transfer to this Court as a result of an adverse ruling by the Court of Appeals. Plaintiff-respondents originally brought suit to obtain possession of certain real estate through the enforcement of a forfeiture clause in a land sale contract. Plaintiff-respondents suffered a negative judgment, from which they appealed. The Court of Appeals reversed, holding that the defendant-petitioners had breached the contract and that the plaintiff-respondents had not waived their right to [enforce] the forfeiture provisions of the contract.

In December of 1958, Mary Burkowski, as vendor, entered into a land sale contract with Charles P. Marshall and Agnes P. Marshall, as vendees. The contract provided for the sale of certain real estate for the sum of $36,000.00, payable as follows:

> $500.00, at the signing, execution and delivery of this contract, the receipt whereof is hereby acknowledged; $500.00 or more on or before the 25th day of December, 1958, and $2500.00 or more on or before the 15th day of January, 1960, and $2500.00 or more on or before the 15th day of January of each and every year thereafter until the balance of the contract has been fully paid, all without interest and all without relief from valuation and appraisement laws and with attorney fees.

The contract also contained a fairly standard section which provided for the treatment of prepayments—but which the Court of Appeals found to be of particular importance. It provided as follows:

> Should Vendees have made prepayments or paid in advance of the payments herein required, said prepayments, if any, shall at any time thereafter be applied in lieu of further principal payments required as herein stated, to the extent of such prepayments only.

The following is the forfeiture/liquidated damages provision of the land sale contract:

> It is further agreed that if any default shall be made in the payment of said purchase price or any of the covenants and/or conditions herein provided, and if any such default shall continue for 30 days, then, after the lapse of said 30 days' period, *all moneys and payments previously paid shall, at the option of the Vendor without notice or demand, be and become forfeited and be taken and retained by the Vendor as liquidated damages* and thereupon this contract shall terminate and be of no further force or effect; provided, however, that nothing herein contained shall be deemed or construed to prevent the Vendor from enforcing specific performance of this agreement in the event of any default on the part of the Vendees in complying, observing

and performing any of the conditions, covenants and terms herein contained * * * . (Emphasis added.)

The vendor, Mary Burkowski, died in 1963. The plaintiffs in this action are the assignees (under the vendor's will) of the decedent's interests in the contract. They received their assignment from the executrix of the estate of the vendor on June 27, 1968. One year after this assignment, several of the assignees filed their complaint in this action alleging that the defendants had defaulted through non-payment.

The schedule of payments made under this contract was shown by the evidence to be as follows:

Date	Amount Paid	Total of Paid Principal
12/1/1958	$ 500.00	$ 500.00
12/25/1958	500.00	1,000.00
3/26/1959	5,000.00	6,000.00
4/5/1960	2,500.00	8,500.00
5/23/1961	2,500.00	11,000.00
4/6/1962	2,500.00	13,500.00
1/15/1963	2,500.00	16,000.00
6/30/1964	2,500.00	18,500.00
2/15/1965	2,500.00	21,000.00

No payments have been made since the last one indicated above—$15,000.00 remains to be paid on the original contract price.

In response to the plaintiff's attempt to enforce the forfeiture provision, the defendants raised the affirmative defense of waiver. The applicable rule is well established and was stated by the Court of Appeals as follows:

Where a contract for the sale and purchase of land contains provisions similar to those in the contract in the case at bar, *the vendor may waive strict compliance with the provisions of the contract by accepting overdue or irregular payments*, and having so done, equity requires the vendor give specific notice of his intent that he will no longer be indulgent and that he will insist on his right of forfeiture unless the default is paid within a reasonable and specified time. (Emphasis added.) * * *

It follows that where the vendor has not waived strict compliance by acceptance of late payments, no notice is required to enforce its provisions.

In essence, the Court of Appeals found that there was no waiver because the vendors were obligated to accept prepayment, and, "the payments made, although irregular in time and amount, were prepayments on the unpaid balance through and including the payment due on January 15, 1965." (289 N.E.2d at 771.) The Court concluded that up to January 15, 1966, "the vendors waived no rights under the contract, because they were obliged to accept prepayment." (Id.) and that, "(t)he vendors could not have insisted on forfeiture prior to January 15, 1966, the date of the first missed payment." (Id.) (We believe the Court of Appeals miscalculated here; the vendors could not have insisted on forfeiture until January 16, 1968.)

If forfeiture is enforced against the defendants, they will forfeit outright the sum of $21,000, or well over one-half the original contract price, as liquidated damages *plus possession*.

Forfeitures are generally disfavored by the law. In fact, ". . . (e)quity abhors forfeitures and beyond any question has jurisdiction, which it will exercise in a proper case to grant relief against their enforcement." 30 C.J.S. Equity § 56 (1965) and cases cited therein. This jurisdiction of equity to intercede is predicated upon the fact that "the loss or injury occasioned by the default must be susceptible of exact compensation." 30 C.J.S., supra. * * *

Paragraph 17 of the contract, supra, provides that all prior payments "become forfeited and be taken and retained by the Vendor as liquidated damages." "Reasonable" liquidated damage provisions are permitted by the law. See 22 Am.Jur., 2d Damages § 212 (1965). However, the issue before this Court, is whether a $21,000 forfeiture is a "reasonable" measure of damages. If the damages are unreasonable, i.e., if they are disproportionate to the loss actually suffered, they must be characterized as penal rather then compensatory. Under the facts of this case, a $21,000 forfeiture is clearly excessive. * * *

If we apply the specific equitable principle announced above—namely, that the amount paid be considered in relation to the total contract price—we are compelled to conclude that the $21,000 forfeiture as liquidated damages is inconsistent with generally accepted principles of fairness and equity. The vendee has acquired a substantial interest in the property, which, if forfeited, would result in substantial injustice.

Under a typical conditional land contract, the vendor retains legal title until the total contract price is paid by the vendee. Payments are generally made in periodic installments. *Legal* title does not vest in the vendee until the contract terms are satisfied, but equitable title vests in the vendee at the time the contract is consummated. When the parties enter into the contract, all incidents of ownership accrue to the vendee. The vendee assumes the risk of loss and is the recipient of all appreciation in value. The vendee, as equitable owner, is responsible for taxes. The vendee has a sufficient interest in land so that upon sale of that interest, he holds a vendor's lien.

This Court has held, consistent with the above notions of equitable ownership, that a land contract, once consummated constitutes a present sale and purchase. The vendor "has, in effect, exchanged his property for the unconditional obligation of the vendee, the performance of which is secured by the retention of the legal title." Stark v. Kreyling, 188 N.E. 680, 682 (Ind. 1934). The Court, in effect, views a conditional land contract as a sale with a security interest in the form of legal title reserved by the vendor. Conceptually, therefore, the retention of the title by the vendor is the same as reserving a lien or mortgage. Realistically, vendor-vendee should be viewed as mortgagee-mortgagor. To conceive of the relationship in different terms is to pay homage to form over substance. * * *

It is also interesting to note that the drafters of the Uniform Commercial Code abandoned the distinction between a conditional sale and a security interest. Section 1–201 of the UCC (IC 1971, 26–1–1–201) (Ind.Ann.Stat. § 19–1–201 (1964 Repl.)) defines "security interest" as "an interest in personal property or fixtures which secures payment or performance of an obligation . . . retention or reservation of title by a seller of goods notwithstanding shipment or delivery to the buyer is limited in effect to a reservation of 'security interest.'" We can conceive of no rational reason why conditional sales of real estate should be treated any differently.[1]

A conditional land contract in effect creates a vendor's lien in the property to secure the unpaid balance owed under the contract. This lien is closely analogous to a mortgage—in fact, the vendor is commonly referred to as an "equitable mortgagee." In view of this characterization of the vendor as a lienholder, it is only logical that such a lien be enforced through foreclosure proceedings. Such a lien "(has) all the incidents of a mortgage" D. S. B. Johnston Land Co. v. Whipple, 234 N.W. 59, 61 (N.D. 1930), one of which is the right to foreclose. * * *

The vendor's interest clearly constitutes a "lien upon real estate" and should, therefore, be treated as one. The basic foreclosure statute—that is for mortgages executed after July 1, 1957—provides for a six-month period of redemption, commencing with the filing of the complaint. Additionally, it establishes the procedures attendant to the foreclosure sale. * * *

Forfeiture is closely akin to strict foreclosure—a remedy developed by the English courts which did not contemplate the equity of redemption. American jurisdictions, including Indiana, have, for the

---

[1]   In fact, the Commissioners on Uniform State Laws have recognized the transparency of any such distinctions. Section 3–102 of the Uniform Land Transactions Code (working draft of first tentative draft) reads as follows:

> This Article applies to security interests created by contract, including mortgage . . . land sales contract . . . and any other lien or title retention contract intended as security.

We believe this position is entirely consistent with the evolving case law in the area.

most part, rejected strict foreclosure in favor of foreclosure by judicial sale:

> The doctrine of strict foreclosure developed in England at a time when real property had, to a great extent, a fixed value; the vastly different conditions in this country, in this respect, led our courts to introduce modifications to the English rules of foreclosure. Generally, in consonance with equity's treatment of a mortgage as essentially a security for the payment of the debt, foreclosure by judicial sale supplanted strict foreclosure as the more equitable mode of effectuating the mutual rights of the mortgagor and mortgagee; and there is at the present time, in the majority of the American states, no strict foreclosure as developed by the English courts—either at law or in equity—by which a mortgagee can be adjudged absolute owner of the mortgaged property. The remedy of the mortgagee is by an action for the sale of the mortgaged premises and an application of the proceeds of such sale to the mortgage debt, and although usually called an action to foreclose, it is totally different in its character and results from a strict foreclosure. The phrase "foreclosure of a mortgage" has acquired, in general, a different meaning from that which it originally bore under the English practice and the common law imported here from England. In this country, the modern meaning of the term "foreclosure" denotes an equitable proceeding for the enforcement of a lien against property in satisfaction of a debt.

55 Am.Jur.2d, Mortgages, § 549 (1971). Guided by the above principles we are compelled to conclude that judicial foreclosure of a land sale contract is in consonance with the notions of equity developed in American jurisprudence. A forfeiture—like a strict foreclosure at common law—is often offensive to our concepts of justice and inimical to the principles of equity. This is not to suggest that a forfeiture is an inappropriate remedy for the breach of all land contracts. In the case of an abandoning, absconding vendee, forfeiture is a logical and equitable remedy. Forfeiture would also be appropriate where the vendee has paid a minimal amount on the contract at the time of default and seeks to retain possession while the vendor is paying taxes, insurance, and other upkeep in order to preserve the premises. Of course, in this latter situation, the vendee will have acquired very little, if any, equity in the property. However, a court of equity must always approach forfeitures with great caution, being forever aware of the possibility of inequitable dispossession of property and exorbitant monetary loss. We are persuaded that forfeiture may only be appropriate under circumstances in which it is found to be consonant with notions of fairness and justice under the law.

In other words, we are holding a conditional land sales contract to be in the nature of a secured transaction, the provisions of which are subject to all proper and just remedies at law and in equity.

Turning our attention to the case at hand, we find that the vendor-assignees were seeking forfeiture, including $21,000 already paid on said contract as liquidated damages and immediate possession. They were, in fact, asking for strict application of the contract terms at law which we believe would have led to unconscionable results requiring the intervention of equity. "Equity delights in justice, but that *not* by halves." (Story, Eq. Pl. § 72.) On the facts of this case, we are of the opinion that the trial court correctly refused the remedy sought by the vendor-assignees, but in so refusing it denied all remedial relief to the plaintiffs. Equity will "look upon that as done which ought to have been done." (Story, Eq.Jur. § 64(g)). Applying the foregoing maxims to the case at bar, where such parties seek unconscionable results in such an action, equity will treat the subject matter as if the final acts and relief contemplated by the parties were accomplished exactly as they should have been in the first instance. Where discretionary power is not exercised by a trial court, under the mistaken belief that it was without this power, a remand and direction by a court of review is necessary and proper. This is not an unwarranted interference with the trial court's function. Upon appeal to this Court, we have the judicial duty to *sua sponte* direct the trial court to apply appropriate equitable principles in such a case. Consistent with such above-stated rules, this Court has the undeniable authority to remand with guidelines which will give substantial relief to plaintiffs under their secured interests and will prevent the sacrifice of the vendees' equitable lien in the property.

For all of the foregoing reasons, transfer is granted and the cause is reversed and remanded with instructions to enter a judgment of foreclosure on the vendors' lien, pursuant to Trial Rule 69(C) and the mortgage foreclosure statute (IC 1971, 32–8–16–1 (Ind.Stat.Ann., § 3–1801 (1968 Repl.))) as modified by Trial Rule 69(C). Said judgment shall include an order for the payment of the unpaid principal balance due on said contract, together with interest at 8% per annum from the date of judgment. The order may also embrace any and all other proper and equitable relief that the court deems to be just, including the discretion to issue a stay of the judicial sale of the property, all pursuant to the provisions of Trial Rule 69(C). Such order shall be consistent with the principles and holdings developed within this opinion. * * *

■ PRENTICE, JUSTICE (concurring). I have some concern that our opinion herein might be viewed by some as indicating an attitude of indifference towards the rights of contract vendors. Such a view would not be a true reflection.

Because the installment sales contract, with forfeiture provisions, is a widely employed and generally accepted method of commerce in real estate in this state, it is appropriate that a vendee seeking to avoid the forfeiture, to which he agreed, be required to make a clear showing of the inequity of enforcement. In any given transaction anything short of enforcing the forfeiture provision may be a denial of equity to the vendor. It has been set forth in the majority opinion that if the vendee has little or no real equity in the premises, the court should have no hesitancy in declaring a forfeiture. It follows that if the vendee has indicated his willingness to forego his equity, if any, whether by mere abandonment of the premises, by release or deed or by a failure to make a timely assertion of his claim, he should be barred from thereafter claiming an equity.

If the court finds that forfeiture, although provided for by the terms of the contract, would be unjust, it should nevertheless grant the vendor the maximum relief consistent with equity against a defaulting vendee. In so doing, it should consider that, had the parties known that the forfeiture provision would not be enforceable, other provisions for the protection of the vendor doubtlessly would have been incorporated into the agreement. Generally, this would require that the transaction be treated as a note and mortgage with such provisions as are generally included in such documents customarily employed in the community by prudent investors. Terms customarily included in such notes and mortgages but frequently omitted from contracts include provisions for increased interest during periods of default, provision for the acceleration of the due date of the entire unpaid principal and interest upon a default continuing beyond a reasonable grace period, provisions for attorneys' fees and other expenses incidental to foreclosure, for the waiver of relief from valuation and appraisement laws and for receivers.

[handwritten margin note: If they knew it wouldn't be enforced, k would have looked different]

NOTES AND QUESTIONS

1. Do you think the court's reaction to the suit to recover possession would be different if the $21,000 paid by the Marshalls had been characterized as rent? $21,000 is nearly 60 percent of the purchase price, which seems like a lot to forfeit. But another way of looking at the situation is that the $21,000 entitled the Marshalls to remain in possession for nine years, which works out to $194 per month. Could the contract be drafted in such a way as to convert the payments to rent rather than speak of forfeitures?

2. By holding that the installment sales contract is a mortgage, *Skendzel* superimposes all the protections that legislatures and courts have afforded to mortgagors, plus any that the legislature might add later, onto the land sale contract. Is this outcome advantageous to purchasers of real estate with poor credit ratings? One way to look at the situation is to characterize mortgage foreclosure rules as a type of consumer protection law which legislatures and courts have determined should be afforded to all persons who finance the purchase of land. From this perspective, the land sale contract looks like a loophole that should be closed. Another way of looking at the situation is that the land sale contract is a type of financing device employed by sellers that comes into play primarily when purchasers cannot obtain a mortgage from a bank or other professional lender. Sellers

may be willing to finance the transaction themselves in these circumstances only if they have a very high degree of security in the event of default. If sellers under land sale contracts can get only the same heavily-regulated foreclosure rights that professional mortgagees get, then they may decline to engage in self-financing. This might leave potential purchasers with poor credit ratings with no option other than seeking financing from sub-prime mortgage lenders, where they will pay very high interest rates. (Note by the way that the land sale contract in *Skendzel* provides for no interest.)

3.   The court questions why real estate should be treated any differently from personal property in distinguishing (or not) between a conditional installment sale and a security interest. The UCC does not prohibit the use of installment sales contracts; it merely recognizes that they are a type of security interest. See U.C.C. § 2–401. And there are differences between personal property and real estate as sources of collateral. For example, the extensive self-help available to the holder of a security interest in personal property (see Williams v. Ford Motor Credit Co., Chapter IV) does not apply to the holder of a real estate mortgage, who generally must bring a judicial foreclosure action. Also, there is nothing like the equity of redemption in the personal property context. Are there nevertheless reasons to welcome the court's effort to look to the UCC for guidance?

4.   Why should parties in effect be forbidden to contract around the protections afforded under judicial foreclosure? Why is following the parties' contract here to elevate form over substance: Weren't the parties trying to achieve a different result, i.e., to bypass foreclosure? Here again the question of the parties' intent and its role is complicated. Under the UCC and the approach the court here takes toward real estate mortgages, parties will be taken to have created a security interest if that is their intent. But their intent is pigeonholed into the category of security interest. The parties are simply not allowed to contract for something like a security interest but with different features, such as a heftier remedy. This pigeonholing exercise can even crop up in a regulatory context. See FCC v. NextWave Pers. Commc'ns Inc., 537 U.S. 293 (2003) (holding that under the Bankruptcy Code the FCC could not achieve the effect of a security interest through cancellation of a broadband PCS license for failure to pay after a spectrum auction). Nevertheless, parties do sometimes, particularly with high-loan-to-value mortgages, contract for mortgage insurance, either with private companies, or one of two federal agencies, the Federal Housing Administration or the Veterans Administration. Federal regulation plays a major role in this market. See Quintin Johnstone, Private Mortgage Insurance, 39 Wake Forest L. Rev. 783 (2004).

5.   The court invokes the rule from contract law and equity that liquidated damages are enforceable only if they are a reasonable prediction of actual damages; anything in excess of this is a "penalty" and is unenforceable. This has long puzzled commentators. Why would well-informed parties mutually agree to a clause that shrinks the size of the contractual pie? Why doesn't the breacher simply "breach" the liquidated damages provision as well? See generally Michael Pressman, The Two-

Contract Approach to Liquidated Damages: A New Framework for Exploring the Penalty Clause Debate, 7 Va. L. & Bus. Rev. 652 (2013).

6.   For another case holding that a similar contractual arrangement (buyer transfers deed to lender and takes back a contract for deed that provides for a penalty-style forfeiture if there is a default) is subject to the state statute on mortgages, see Mid-State Investment Corp. v. O'Steen, 133 So.2d 455 (Fla. Dist. Ct. App. 1961). For the older approach upholding an installment land sale contract, see, e.g., Pease v. Baxter, 41 P. 899 (Wash. 1895). Notice how the efforts of mortgagees to get around procedural requirements for foreclosure associated with mortgages play a role in the dynamic identified in the following excerpt.

Carol M. Rose, *Crystals and Mud in Property Law*

40 STAN. L. REV. 577, 577–79, 583–85 (1988).

Property law, and especially the common law of property, has always been heavily laden with hard-edged doctrines that tell everyone exactly where they stand. Default on paying your loan installments? Too bad, you lose the thing you bought and your past payments as well. Forget to record your deed? Sorry, the next buyer can purchase free of your claim, and you are out on the street. Sell that house with the leak in the basement? Lucky you, you can unload the place without having to tell the buyer about such things at all.

In a sense, hard-edged rules like these—rules that I call "crystals"— are what property is all about. If, as Jeremy Bentham said long ago, property is "nothing but a basis of expectation," then crystal rules are the very stuff of property: their great advantage, or so it is commonly thought, is that they signal to all of us, in a clear and distinct language, precisely what our obligations are and how we may take care of our interests. Thus, I should inspect the property, record my deed, and make my payments if I don't want to lose my home to unexpected physical, legal, or financial impairments. I know where I stand and so does everyone else, and we can all strike bargains with each other if we want to stand somewhere else.

Economic thinkers have been telling us for at least two centuries that the more important a given kind of thing becomes for us, the more likely we are to have these hard-edged rules to manage it. We draw these ever-sharper lines around our entitlements so that we know who has what, and so that we can trade instead of getting into the confusions and disputes that would only escalate as the goods in question became scarcer and more highly valued.

At the root of these economic analyses lies the perception that it costs something to establish clear entitlements to things, and we won't bother to undertake the task of removing goods from an ownerless "commons" unless it is worth it to us to do so. What makes it worth it? Increasing scarcity of the resource, and the attendant conflicts over it. To use the example given by Harold Demsetz, one of the most notable of the modern economists telling this story, when the European demand for fur hats increased demand for (and scarcity of) fur-bearing animals among Indian hunters, the Indians developed a system of property entitlements to the animal habitat. Economic historians of the American West tell a similar story about the development of property rights in various minerals and natural resources. Easy-going, anything-goes patterns of appropriation at the outset came under pressure as competition for resources increased, and were finally superseded by much more sharply defined systems of entitlement. In effect, as our competition for a resource raises the costs of conflict about it, those conflict costs begin to outweigh the costs of taking it out of the commons and establishing clear property entitlements. We establish a system of clear entitlements so that we can barter and trade for what we want instead of fighting.

The trouble with this "scarcity story" is that things don't seem to work this way, or at least not all the time. Sometimes we seem to substitute fuzzy, ambiguous rules of decision for what seem to be perfectly clear, open and shut, demarcations of entitlements. I call this occurrence the substitution of "mud" rules for "crystal" ones.

Thus, in the examples with which I began, we find that, over time, the straightforward common law crystalline rules have been muddied repeatedly by exceptions and equitable second-guessing, to the point that the various claimants under real estate contracts, mortgages, or recorded deeds don't know quite what their rights and obligations really are. * * *

B.   Of Mortgages and Mud

Early common law mortgages were very crystalline indeed. They had the look of pawnshop transactions and were at least sometimes structured as conveyances: I borrow money from you, and at the same time I convey my land to you as security for my loan. If all goes well, I pay back my debt on the agreed "law day," and you reconvey my land back to me. But if all does not go well and I cannot pay on the appointed day, then, no matter how heartrending my excuse, I lose my land to you and, presumably, any of the previous payments I might have made. As the fifteenth century commentator Littleton airily explained, the name "mortgage" derived from the rule that, if the debtor "doth not pay, then the land which he puts in pledge . . . is gone from him for ever, and so dead."

This system had the advantage of great clarity, but it sometimes must have seemed very hard on mortgage debtors to the advantage of scoundrelly creditors. Littleton's advice about the importance of specifying the precise place and time for repayment, for example, conjures up images of a wily creditor hiding in the woods on the repayment day to frustrate repayment; presumably, the unfound creditor could keep the property. But by the seventeenth century, the intervention of courts of equity had changed things. By the eighteenth and nineteenth centuries, the equity courts were regularly giving debtors as many as three or four "enlargements" of the time in which they might pay and redeem the property before the final "foreclosure," even when the excuse was lame. One judge explained that an equity court might well grant more time even after the "final" order of "foreclosure absolute," depending on the particular circumstances.

The muddiness of this emerging judicial remedy argued against its attractiveness. Chief Justice Hale complained in 1672 that, "[b]y the growth of Equity on Equity, the Heart of the Common Law is eaten out, and legal Settlements are destroyed; . . . as far as the Line is given, Man will go; and if an hundred Years are given, Man will go so far, and we know not whither we shall go."[40] Instead of a precise and clear allocation of entitlements between the parties, the "equity of redemption" and its unpredictable foreclosure opened up vexing questions and uncertainties: How much time should the debtor have for repayment before the equitable arguments shifted to favor the creditor? What sort of excuses did the debtor need? Did it matter that the property, instead of dropping in the lap of the creditor, was sold at a foreclosure sale?

But as the courts moved towards muddiness, private parties attempted to bargain their way out of these costly uncertainties and to reinstate a crystalline pattern whereby lenders could get the property immediately upon default without the costs of foreclosure. How about a separate deal with the borrower, for example, whereby he agrees to convey an equitable interest to the lender in case of default? Nothing doing, said the courts, including the United States Supreme Court, which in 1878 stated flatly that a mortgagor could not initially bargain away his "equity of redemption."[45] Well, then, how about an arrangement whereby it looks as if the lender already owns the land, and the "borrower" only gets title if he lives up to his agreement to pay for it by a certain time? This seemed more promising: In the 1890s California courts thought it perfectly correct to hold the buyer to his word in such an arrangement, and to give him neither an extension nor a refund of past payments. By the 1960s, however, they were changing their minds about these "installment land contracts." After all, these deals really had exactly the same effect as the old-style mortgages—the defaulting buyer could lose everything if he missed a payment, even the very last payment. Human vice and error seemed to put the crystal rule in jeopardy: In a series of cases culminating with a default by a "willful but repentant" little old lady who had stopped paying when she mistakenly thought that she was being cheated, the California Supreme Court decided to treat these land contracts as mortgages in disguise.[48] It gave the borrower "relief from forfeiture"—a time to reinstate the installment contract or get back her past payments.

---

[40]   Roscarrick v. Barton, 22 Eng. Rep. 769, 770 (1672).

[45]   Peugh v. Davis, 96 U.S. 332, 337 (1878).

[48]   MacFadden v. Walker, 488 P.2d 1353 (Cal. 1971) * * *

With mortgages first and mortgage substitutes later, we see a back-and-forth pattern: crisp definition of entitlements, made fuzzy by accretions of judicial decisions, crisped up again by the parties' contractual arrangements, and once again made fuzzy by the courts. Here we see private parties apparently following the "scarcity story" in their private law arrangements: when things matter, the parties define their respective entitlements with ever sharper precision. Yet the courts seem at times unwilling to follow this story or to permit these crystalline definitions, most particularly when the rules hurt one party very badly. The cycle thus alternates between crystal and mud. * * *

NOTES AND QUESTIONS

1.   Are we destined to cycle between crystals and mud in all areas? In the area of mortgages? Rose emphasizes the role that courts have played in "muddying up" mortgage law, especially because they see disputes arise individually and ex post. On the other hand, according to some scholars, it has been legislatures responding to populist pressures during economic downturns that have provided relief from the stringency of mortgage law. See, e.g., A.H. Feller, Moratory Legislation: A Comparative Study, 46 Harv. L. Rev. 1061 (1933); Robert H. Skilton, Developments in Mortgage Law and Practice, 17 Temp. L.Q. 315 (1943); see also, e.g., Sheldon Tefft, The Myth of Strict Foreclosure, 4 U. Chi. L. Rev. 575 (1937). Interestingly, in the Colonial period and the early Republic, exemptions that had protected real property from creditors in England (in the interest of maintaining social position), were removed in favor of commercial interests, a development that led to lower interest rates, the rise of a market in land, and greater availability of capital for economic development. Claire Priest, Credit Nation: Property Laws and Institutions in Early America (2021).

2.   If some equilibrium between crystals and mud is possible, what is the optimal mix of the two? Does one's answer depend somewhat on who is expected to figure things out? What exactly does it mean for mortgage law to be "muddy?" Sometimes a contrast is drawn between rules, in which decisions are made ex ante, and standards, which give discretion ex post. See, e.g., Louis Kaplow, Rules Versus Standards: An Economic Analysis, 42 Duke L.J. 557, 568–88 (1992). At other times, emphasis is placed on the amount of information required to make a decision under a rule (minimal) versus a standard (lots). See, e.g., Frederick Schauer, Playing by the Rules (1991); Henry E. Smith, The Language of Property: Form, Context, and Audience, 55 Stan. L. Rev. 1105 (2003). Recall the discussion of minor building encroachments in Chapter IV, where one approach (*Pile v. Pedrick*) might be interpreted as laying down a bright-line rule to provide clear incentives for future actors and another (*Golden Press v. Rylands*) assesses a wider range of contextual information in order to minimize the costs from mistakes committed in the past. Is the tension between these approaches the same as the dynamic described by Rose in the context of mortgage foreclosure? How about the role of courts of equity? What role should notions of disproportionate hardship play? Why does equity abhor a forfeiture, as the saying goes? See Henry E. Smith, Equity as Meta-Law, 130 Yale L.J. 105,

1108–10 (2021) (arguing that interventions of equity can lead to stable "sedimentation").

3.   Recall the *numerus clausus* principle, which we explored in Chapter V. One aspect of the principle is that the legislature has primary responsibility for modifying the list of basic property forms. Does the history of foreclosure as described by Rose conform to this expectation? At least aspirationally, even old equity courts were supposed to exercise extra caution to avoid undoing the law and its attendant predictability where property rights are concerned. Charles Grey, The Boundaries of the Equitable Function, 20 Am. J. Legal Hist. 192 (1976). How much of the muddying here has consequences for third parties, through the in rem aspect of property? In her article, Rose finds the same cycle of crystals and mud with respect to land records, which, as we shall see in the next Chapter, present notice issues, often involving mortgages.

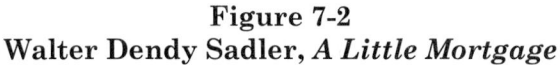

Figure 7-2
Walter Dendy Sadler, *A Little Mortgage*

Mortgages and the Financial Crisis of 2007–08

The financial crisis of 2007–08 and the deep recession that followed put a spotlight on mortgages and their significance for the economy. Mortgages played a critical role in causing the crisis and were associated with some of the most painful effects in its aftermath.

Everyone agrees that mortgages, or more accurately, the mortgage market, were central to the causes of the crisis. But the features of the mortgage market that were most critical remain a matter of controversy.

The financial meltdown was precipitated by the bursting of the U.S. housing bubble starting in 2006–07 and the steep decline in market prices for housing that followed. Many properties that had been purchased with borrowed funds secured by mortgages were "underwater," meaning the current market value of the property was less than the remaining balance owed under the mortgage indebtedness.

One reason so many loans were underwater was that, in the period leading up to the crisis, lenders had become increasingly aggressive in promoting loans with minimal down payments. Managers of financial institutions ignored reasonable ex ante estimations of risk, in part because their compensation packages promoted decisions in favor of taking on these underestimated risks. There is less agreement on why. It is doubtful that there was a sudden upsurge in "greed" or some other change in human nature in the years leading up to 2007. But there is no shortage of other more plausible candidates for factors that contributed to the mortgage mess.

Government policy did a lot to foster the climate of excessive risk-taking during the housing bubble. The faulty regulatory and policy environment had (and to a large extent still has) a housing aspect and a banking aspect. American housing policy has long been highly focused on promoting home ownership, going back to at least the 1920s. This pro-ownership policy has expressed itself in myriad ways, from the mortgage interest tax deduction to federally sponsored home mortgage insurance. In response to the widespread distress in housing markets in the Great Depression, the federal government created agencies such as the Federal National Mortgage Association (Fannie Mae). In 1968 Fannie Mae was changed from being a government agency to a nominally private but implicitly (now explicitly) federally backed enterprise (with a spin-off, the Government National Mortgage Association, or Ginnie Mae, remaining a government agency). As a government sponsored enterprise (GSE) it was later joined in 1970 by the Federal Home Loan Mortgage Corporation (Freddie Mac). The GSEs purchase mortgages, especially those insured by the Federal Housing Administration (FHA), thereby allowing banks to extend more loans. They also repackage and sell mortgages to the markets as mortgage-backed securities (MBSs, about which more below).

Starting in the early 1990s amid accusations that banks were redlining (a term referring to a practice of shunning poor and minority areas for making loans), Fannie Mae teamed up with advocacy organizations to promote more lending to minority, low- and moderate-income home purchasers. Over time this entailed a push for lower lending standards in the subprime market. See Gretchen Morgenson & Joshua Rosner, Reckless Endangerment: How Outsized Ambition, Greed, and Corruption Led to Economic Armageddon (2011). Underwriting standards became not only lax but sloppy, and allegations of predatory lending and outright fraud, notably but not exclusively by major culprits like Countrywide, ensued. See, e.g., Katherine Porter, Misbehavior and Mistake in Bankruptcy Mortgage Claims, 87 Tex. L. Rev. 121 (2008).

During the period the housing bubble was inflating, credit was indeed cheap as the Federal Reserve kept interest rates lower than its traditional rules of thumb would have indicated. One theory is that as income distribution has become more unequal in a changing economy, policy makers have found it convenient to paper over the resulting tensions with cheap credit. At the same time, major trading partners of the United States like China and Germany pursued policies promoting export-led growth; the Chinese government in particular borrowed from its own citizens to make loans to U.S. borrowers to encourage spending, further driving down interest rates. See Raghuram G. Rajan, Fault Lines: How Hidden Fractures Still Threaten the World Economy (2010). Bank regulations permitted lower capital requirements than were advisable, and encouraged overreliance on credit agency ratings (Standard and Poor's, Moody's, Fitch); see also Paul G. Mahoney, Deregulation and the Subprime Crisis, 104 Va. L. Rev. 235 (2018) (arguing that macroeconomic policy leading to interest rate risk rather than easing regulation on banking made the crisis possible). The regulatory environment made these ratings key to whether various regulated entities like pension funds could hold securities and how much, which caused great pressure on the agencies to overrate securities.

Once the bubble got going, it took on a life of its own, as is the nature of bubbles. Economists find bubbles difficult to study because they appear to involve irrational behavior. On the other hand, it can be individually rational to ride a bubble upward, especially when monetary and regulatory policy is aimed at pumping up asset markets.

Enter financial engineering, which added fuel to the fire. The first innovation in the area of mortgage financing was the collateralized debt obligation (CDO). A CDO combines property forms like the trust (Chapter V) and, in many cases, mortgages. A CDO starts with a special purpose entity (SPE), which is a limited partnership or other limited liability organization that holds mortgages and then issues bonds based on their cash flow or market value. The bonds are structured into seniority tranches. Say an SPE holds 1,000 mortgages. The highest tranche gets paid first (from the payments generated by the cream of the 1,000), the second is paid next, all the way down to the last tranche, which is an equity-like residual claim. The theory was that the underlying loans might be risky but the highest tranche would be very safe, and so eligible for the highest credit rating, and the credit rating agencies duly obliged with high ratings for the higher tranches of very dubious collections of loans. The problem was that the risk of the underlying loans was more correlated than they were being treated as being, while the possibility of a general downturn in housing (leading to correlated default) was underestimated. But the policies promoting overinvestment in housing and overly cheap credit along with the market's expectation that the GSEs were at the ready to buy a significant chunk of mortgages led lenders, investors, and home buyers all to count on rising home prices. As long as home prices kept rising, the musical chairs could continue. Global CDO issuance reached $481.6 billion by 2007 (and crashed to just $4.3 billion by 2009).

Later in the bubble, leverage increased through more esoteric devices, such as the credit default swap (CDS). A CDS can be thought of as an insurance policy, and started being used to insure CDOs. A CDS is a derivative because its value depends on or derives from the value of a referent asset, in this case, CDOs themselves. CDSs could be used to insure CDO exposure, or they could be used to take on even greater risk. CDOs remove the need for lenders or issuers of the securities to retain any interest in the loans, even indirectly, and CDSs allow one to dispense with the underlying assets altogether. Thus, CDSs could be used to create synthetic CDOs, which are like CDOs without the ownership of the underlying components of a regular CDO. Outstanding CDSs had a notional amount of $62.2 trillion by the end of 2007.

Then the bubble burst. The defaults came in waves, involving not just subprime borrowers but also so-called Alt-A loans, which dispensed with traditional documentation and allowed smaller down payments. (In what should have been a sign of things to come, Alt-A loans were colloquially referred to at the time as "liar loans.") Defaults were also precipitated as teaser rates and adjustable rate mortgages (ARMs) adjusted upward just as housing values were tanking. As long as asset values were expected to rise, the possibility of refinancing when the time came would make such loans attractive, but once the bubble burst such loans became toxic. The problems spread through the financial sector in late 2007 and 2008. After early warning signs in 2007 when some subprime lenders went bankrupt, 2008 saw even more high-profile failures of financial institutions with exposure to the mortgage market. After bailing out Bear Stearns, which had been highly exposed to CDOs and CDSs, the government refused to bail out Lehman Brothers (which had not prepared for bankruptcy, making its mess much worse), and the stock market crashed, leading to massive bailouts of financial firms and even car makers. For a variety of perspectives, see, e.g., Timothy F. Geithner, Stress Test: Reflections on Financial Crises (2014); Alan S. Blinder, After the Music Stopped: The Financial Crisis, the Response, and the Work Ahead (2013); Kenneth Ayotte & David A. Skeel, Jr., Bankruptcy or Bailouts?, 35 J. Corp. L. 469 (2010); Lucian A. Bebchuk & Holger Spamann, Regulating Bankers' Pay, 98 Geo. L.J. 247 (2010); Robert Kolb, Lessons from the Financial Crisis: Causes, Consequences, and Our Economic Future (2010); Charles Calomiris, The Subprime Turmoil: What's Old, What's New, and What's Next, 15 J. Structured Fin. 6 (Spring 2009).

Could better regulations have prevented the problem and if so what kind of regulations are needed? Regulatory failure is clearly a large part of the story of the rise and subsequent bursting of the housing bubble and the financial crisis that it provoked. Some blame the failure of the government to prevent the use of subprime and Alt-A mortgages, CDOs, and CDSs directly. But the question is which instruments should be allowed under which circumstances. Others argue that homeowners should be required to keep a certain minimal level of equity in their home. See Ryan Bubb & Prasad Krishnamurthy, Regulating Against Bubbles: How Mortgage Regulation Can Keep Main Street and Wall Street Safe—from Themselves, 163 U. Pa. L. Rev. 1539 (2015). Historically, lenders required a down payment of 20 percent of the purchase price. During the housing bubble, this was cast aside in favor of 5 percent or zero percent, or in a few cases even negative equity (taking out a mortgage larger than the appraised value of the property), which of course meant that many of these borrowers were already under water when the bubble burst. Curiously, this is one of the few reforms not incorporated or even encouraged in the Dodd-Frank Wall Street Reform and Consumer Protection Act of 2010, presumably because it would make it harder for low-income families to purchase homes (or would force higher-income families to purchase smaller homes). Not surprisingly, 5 percent down payment loans have now reappeared in the marketplace.

Rather than restricting borrowers, the post-crisis reform effort has focused on banks. Certainly, bank regulators before the crisis allowed banks to be undercapitalized given the risks they were taking on, and stiffened capital requirements are likely part of the solution. Among its many changes to the financial system, the Dodd-Frank Act increased capital requirements for institutions that present officially designated "systemic risk" (otherwise known as "too big to fail"). Faulty corporate governance regulation also contributed to the lack of shareholder oversight over banks' activities in the bubble period. And allowing financial institutions to keep many of the exotic mortgage-related securities off their balance sheets made the problem even larger than it would have been otherwise.

Another issue that emerged from the financial crisis was the contribution of complexity to systemic financial risk. When the bubble burst, investors had little knowledge of the contents of many financial instruments. This uncertainty created panic and liquidity problems. In creating complex instruments, might there be complexity externalities, along the lines that the *numerus clausus* (Chapter V) is meant to prevent in the basic property forms? Might we need a *numerus clausus* in finance? Or might it be that the common law's suspicion of secret liens has been too much watered down in financial markets, leading to instability and eventual crash? See, e.g., Jonathan C. Lipson, Secrets and Liens: The End of Notice in Commercial Finance Law, 21 Emory Bankr. Dev. J. 421 (2005); Michael Simkovic, Secret Liens and the Financial Crisis of 2008, 83 Am. Bankr. L.J. 253 (2009). If so, why did the financial industry create the complexity in the first place? In a bubble atmosphere, prospective purchasers are less concerned with complexity and secret liens, because these only become problems in bad states of the world. As long as asset prices are expected to keep rising, there appears to be no need to worry. See Kenneth Ayotte & Patrick Bolton, Covenant Lite Lending, Liquidity, and Standardization of Financial Contracts, in Research Handbook on the Economics of Property Law 174 (Kenneth Ayotte & Henry E. Smith eds., 2011); see also Xavier Freixas, Luc Laeven & José-Luis Peydró, Systemic Risk, Crises, and Macroprudential Regulation (2015); Kathryn Judge, Fragmentation Nodes: A Study in Financial Innovation, Complexity and Systemic Risk, 64 Stan. L. Rev. 657, 672 (2012); Note, The Perils of Fragmentation and Reckless Innovation, 125 Harv. L. Rev. 1799 (2012).

The painful effects of the financial crisis and recession were many, including high unemployment, slow economic growth, and a prolonged period of ultra-low interest rates, which harmed retirees dependent on earnings from savings, insurance companies, and pension funds. But one of the most significant adverse effects was the explosion of foreclosures as those who lost their jobs could not make the payments and some who found themselves with underwater mortgages simply stopped paying in order to rid themselves of what appeared to be a losing proposition. Designing a mortgage relief program is no simple task, especially if one seeks to target help to those who can avoid default without encouraging those who can pay from engaging in strategic default. The federal government's principal program, the Home Affordable Modification Program (HAMP), was minimally successful in providing relief, see Patricia A. McCoy, Barriers to Foreclosure Protection During the Financial Crisis, 55 Ariz. L. Rev. 723 (2013), and there is evidence of strategic default in response to the program, see Christopher Mayer et al., Mortgage Modification and Strategic Default: Evidence from a Legal Settlement with Countrywide, 104 Am. Econ. Rev. 2830 (2014). Proposals were advanced to have local governments condemn underwater mortgages, and retransfer them to other lenders at values reflecting the reduced market value of the property. See, e.g., Robert C. Hockett, It Takes a Village: Municipal Condemnation Proceedings and Public/Private Partnerships for Mortgage Loan Modification, Value Preservation, and Local Economic Recovery, 18 Stan. J. L. Bus. & Fin. 121 (2012). But these proposals encountered stiff resistance from the banking industry and never got off the ground. As in past financial foreclosure crises, courts were called on to provide relief as well. As we will see in the following case, foreclosures were litigated, and the sloppiness of mortgage lenders in their paperwork came back to haunt them.

U.S. Bank National Association v. Ibanez

Supreme Judicial Court of Massachusetts, 2011.
941 N.E.2d 40.

■ GANTS, J. After foreclosing on two properties and purchasing the properties back at the foreclosure sales, U.S. Bank National Association

(U.S.Bank), as trustee for the Structured Asset Securities Corporation Mortgage Pass-Through Certificates, Series 2006–Z; and Wells Fargo Bank, N.A. (Wells Fargo), as trustee for ABFC 2005–OPT 1 Trust, ABFC Asset Backed Certificates, Series 2005–OPT 1 (plaintiffs), filed separate complaints in the Land Court asking a judge to declare that they held clear title to the properties in fee simple. We agree with the judge that the plaintiffs, who were not the original mortgagees, failed to make the required showing that they were the holders of the mortgages at the time of foreclosure. As a result, they did not demonstrate that the foreclosure sales were valid to convey title to the subject properties, and their requests for a declaration of clear title were properly denied.

Procedural history. On July 5, 2007, U.S. Bank, as trustee, foreclosed on the mortgage of Antonio Ibanez, and purchased the Ibanez property at the foreclosure sale. On the same day, Wells Fargo, as trustee, foreclosed on the mortgage of Mark and Tammy LaRace, and purchased the LaRace property at that foreclosure sale.

In September and October of 2008, U.S. Bank and Wells Fargo brought separate actions in the Land Court under G.L. c. 240, § 6, which authorizes actions "to quiet or establish the title to land situated in the commonwealth or to remove a cloud from the title thereto." The two complaints sought identical relief: (1) a judgment that the right, title, and interest of the mortgagor (Ibanez or the LaRaces) in the property was extinguished by the foreclosure; (2) a declaration that there was no cloud on title arising from publication of the notice of sale in the Boston Globe; and (3) a declaration that title was vested in the plaintiff trustee in fee simple. U.S. Bank and Wells Fargo each asserted in its complaint that it had become the holder of the respective mortgage through an assignment made *after* the foreclosure sale.

In both cases, the mortgagors—Ibanez and the LaRaces—did not initially answer the complaints, and the plaintiffs moved for entry of default judgment. In their motions for entry of default judgment, the plaintiffs addressed two issues: (1) whether the Boston Globe, in which the required notices of the foreclosure sales were published, is a newspaper of "general circulation" in Springfield, the town where the foreclosed properties lay. See G.L. c. 244, § 14 (requiring publication every week for three weeks in newspaper published in town where foreclosed property lies, or of general circulation in that town); and (2) whether the plaintiffs were legally entitled to foreclose on the properties where the assignments of the mortgages to the plaintiffs were neither executed nor recorded in the registry of deeds until after the foreclosure sales. The two cases were heard together by the Land Court, along with a third case that raised the same issues.

On March 26, 2009, judgment was entered against the plaintiffs. The judge ruled that the foreclosure sales were invalid because, in violation of G.L. c. 244, § 14, the notices of the foreclosure sales named U.S. Bank (in the Ibanez foreclosure) and Wells Fargo (in the LaRace foreclosure) as the mortgage holders where they had not yet been assigned the mortgages. The judge found, based on each plaintiff's assertions in its complaint, that the plaintiffs acquired the mortgages by assignment only after the foreclosure sales and thus had no interest in the mortgages being foreclosed at the time of the publication of the notices of sale or at the time of the foreclosure sales.

The plaintiffs then moved to vacate the judgments. At a hearing on the motions on April 17, 2009, the plaintiffs conceded that each complaint alleged a postnotice, postforeclosure sale assignment of the mortgage at issue, but they now represented to the judge that documents might exist that could show a prenotice, preforeclosure sale assignment of the mortgages. The judge granted the plaintiffs leave to produce such documents, provided they were produced in the form they existed in at the time the foreclosure sale was noticed and conducted. In response, the plaintiffs submitted hundreds of pages of documents to the judge, which they claimed established that the mortgages had been assigned to them before the foreclosures. Many of these documents related to the creation of the securitized mortgage pools in which the Ibanez and LaRace mortgages were purportedly included.

The judge denied the plaintiffs' motions to vacate judgment on October 14, 2009, concluding that the newly submitted documents did not alter the conclusion that the plaintiffs were not the holders of the respective mortgages at the time of foreclosure. We granted the parties' applications for direct appellate review.

Factual background. We discuss each mortgage separately, describing when appropriate what the plaintiffs allege to have happened and what the documents in the record demonstrate.

The Ibanez mortgage. On December 1, 2005, Antonio Ibanez took out a $103,500 loan for the purchase of property at 20 Crosby Street in Springfield, secured by a mortgage to the lender, Rose Mortgage, Inc. (Rose Mortgage). The mortgage was recorded the following day. Several days later, Rose Mortgage executed an assignment of this mortgage in blank, that is, an assignment that did not specify the name of the assignee. The blank space in the assignment was at some point stamped with the name of Option One Mortgage Corporation (Option One) as the assignee, and that assignment was recorded on June 7, 2006. Before the recording, on January 23, 2006, Option One executed an assignment of the Ibanez mortgage in blank.

According to U.S. Bank, Option One assigned the Ibanez mortgage to Lehman Brothers Bank, FSB, which assigned it to Lehman Brothers Holdings Inc., which then assigned it to the Structured Asset Securities Corporation, which then assigned the mortgage, pooled with approximately 1,220 other mortgage loans, to U.S. Bank, as trustee for the Structured Asset Securities Corporation Mortgage Pass-Through Certificates, Series 2006–Z. With this last assignment, the Ibanez and other loans were pooled into a trust and converted into mortgage-backed securities that can be bought and sold by investors—a process known as securitization. * * *

According to U.S. Bank, the assignment of the Ibanez mortgage to U.S. Bank occurred pursuant to a December 1, 2006, trust agreement, which is not in the record. What is in the record is the private placement memorandum (PPM), dated December 26, 2006, a 273-page, unsigned offer of mortgage-backed securities to potential investors. * * * However, U.S. Bank did not provide the judge with any mortgage schedule identifying the Ibanez loan as among the mortgages that were assigned in the trust agreement.

On April 17, 2007, U.S. Bank filed a complaint to foreclose on the Ibanez mortgage in the Land Court * * * . In the complaint, U.S. Bank represented that it was the "owner (or assignee) and holder" of the mortgage given by Ibanez for the property. * * * In June, 2007, U.S. Bank also caused to be published in the Boston Globe the notice of the foreclosure sale required by G.L. c. 244, § 14. The notice identified U.S. Bank as the "present holder" of the mortgage.

At the foreclosure sale on July 5, 2007, the Ibanez property was purchased by U.S. Bank, as trustee for the securitization trust, for $94,350, a value significantly less than the outstanding debt and the estimated market value of the property. The foreclosure deed (from U.S. Bank, trustee, as the purported holder of the mortgage, to U.S. Bank, trustee, as the purchaser) and the statutory foreclosure affidavit were recorded on May 23, 2008. On September 2, 2008, more than one year after the sale, and more than five months after recording of the sale, American Home Mortgage Servicing, Inc., "as successor-in-interest" to Option One, which was until then the record holder of the Ibanez mortgage, executed a written assignment of that mortgage to U.S. Bank, as trustee for the securitization trust. This assignment was recorded on September 11, 2008.

[The court then summarizes the similar history of the LaRace mortgage, for which the best documentation of Wells Fargo's holding of the mortgage at the time of the foreclosure was an unexecuted purchase and sale agreement (PSA) downloaded from the Internet, and "a schedule that it represented identified the loans assigned in the PSA, which did not include property addresses, names of mortgagors, or any number that corresponds to the loan number or servicing number on the LaRace mortgage."]

Discussion. The plaintiffs brought actions under G.L. c. 240, § 6, seeking declarations that the defendant mortgagors' titles had been extinguished and that the plaintiffs were the fee simple owners of the foreclosed properties. As such, the plaintiffs bore the burden of establishing their entitlement to the relief sought. Sheriff's Meadow Found., Inc. v. Bay-Courte Edgartown, Inc., 516 N.E.2d 144 (Mass. 1987). To meet this burden, they were required "not merely to demonstrate better title . . . than the defendants possess, but . . . to prove sufficient title to succeed in [the] action." Id. * * *

Massachusetts does not require a mortgage holder to obtain judicial authorization to foreclose on a mortgaged property. See G.L. c. 183, § 21; G.L. c. 244, § 14. * * * [A] mortgage holder can foreclose on a property, as the plaintiffs did here, by exercise of the statutory power of sale, if such a power is granted by the mortgage itself.

Where a mortgage grants a mortgage holder the power of sale, as did both the Ibanez and LaRace mortgages, it includes by reference the power of sale set out in G.L. c. 183, § 21, and further regulated by G.L. c. 244, §§ 11–17C. Under G.L. c. 183, § 21, after a mortgagor defaults in the performance of the underlying note, the mortgage holder may sell the property at a public auction and convey the property to the purchaser in fee simple, "and such sale shall forever bar the mortgagor and all persons claiming under him from all right and interest in the mortgaged premises, whether at law or in equity." Even where there is a dispute as to whether the mortgagor was in default or whether the party claiming to be the mortgage holder is the true mortgage holder, the foreclosure goes forward unless the mortgagor files an action and obtains a court order enjoining the foreclosure.

Recognizing the substantial power that the statutory scheme affords to a mortgage holder to foreclose without immediate judicial oversight, we adhere to the familiar rule that "one who sells under a power [of sale] must follow strictly its terms. If he fails to do so there is no valid execution of the power, and the sale is wholly void." Moore v. Dick, 72 N.E. 967 (Mass. 1905). * * *

One of the terms of the power of sale that must be strictly adhered to is the restriction on who is entitled to foreclose. The "statutory power of sale" can be exercised by "the mortgagee or his executors, administrators, successors or assigns." G.L. c. 183, § 21. Under G.L. c. 244, § 14, "[t]he mortgagee or person having his estate in the land mortgaged, or a person authorized by the power of sale, or the attorney duly authorized by a writing under seal, or the legal guardian or conservator of such mortgagee or person acting in the name of such mortgagee or person" is empowered to exercise the statutory power of sale. Any effort to foreclose by a party lacking "jurisdiction and authority" to carry out a foreclosure under these statutes is void. * * *

For the plaintiffs to obtain the judicial declaration of clear title that they seek, they had to prove their authority to foreclose under the power of sale and show their compliance with the requirements on which this authority rests. Here, the plaintiffs were not the original mortgagees to whom the power of sale was granted; rather, they claimed the authority to foreclose as the eventual assignees of the original mortgagees. Under the plain language of G.L. c. 183, § 21, and G.L. c. 244, § 14, the plaintiffs had the authority to exercise the power of sale contained in the Ibanez and LaRace mortgages only if they were the assignees of the mortgages at the time of the notice of sale and the subsequent foreclosure sale.

The plaintiffs claim that the securitization documents they submitted establish valid assignments that made them the holders of the Ibanez and LaRace mortgages before the notice of sale and the foreclosure sale. We turn, then, to the documentation submitted by the plaintiffs to determine whether it met the requirements of a valid assignment.

Like a sale of land itself, the assignment of a mortgage is a conveyance of an interest in land that requires a writing signed by the grantor. See G.L. c. 183, § 3; Saint Patrick's Religious, Educ. & Charitable Ass'n v. Hale, 116 N.E. 407, 408 (Mass. 1917). In a "title theory state" like Massachusetts, a mortgage is a transfer of legal title in a property to secure a debt. See Faneuil Investors Group, Ltd. Partnership v. Selectmen of Dennis, 933 N.E.2d 918, 921–22 (Mass. 2010). Therefore, when a person borrows money to purchase a home and gives the lender a mortgage, the homeowner-mortgagor retains only equitable title in the home; the legal title is held by the mortgagee. Where, as here, mortgage loans are pooled together in a trust and converted into mortgage-backed securities, the underlying promissory notes serve as financial instruments generating a potential income stream for investors, but the mortgages securing these notes are still legal title to someone's home or farm and must be treated as such.

Focusing first on the Ibanez mortgage, U.S. Bank argues that it was assigned the mortgage under the trust agreement described in the PPM, but it did not submit a copy of this trust agreement to the judge. The PPM, however, described the trust agreement as an agreement to be executed in the future, so it only furnished evidence of an intent to assign mortgages to U.S. Bank, not proof of their actual assignment. Even if there were an executed trust agreement with language of present assignment, U.S. Bank did not produce the schedule of loans and mortgages that was an exhibit to that agreement, so it failed to show that the Ibanez mortgage was among the mortgages to be assigned by that agreement. Finally, even if there were an executed trust agreement with the required schedule, U.S. Bank failed to furnish any evidence that the entity assigning the mortgage—Structured Asset Securities Corporation—ever held the mortgage to be assigned. The last assignment of the mortgage on record was from Rose Mortgage to Option One; nothing was submitted to the judge indicating that Option One ever assigned the mortgage to anyone before the foreclosure sale. Thus, based on the documents submitted to the judge, Option One, not U.S. Bank, was the mortgage holder at the time of the foreclosure, and U.S. Bank did not have the authority to foreclose the mortgage.

[The court went on to conclude that in the LaRace case the documentation of the alleged completed assignment as of the date of the foreclosure notice was insufficient.]

We do not suggest that an assignment must be in recordable form at the time of the notice of sale or the subsequent foreclosure sale, although recording is likely the better practice. Where a pool of mortgages is assigned to a securitized trust, the executed agreement that assigns the pool of mortgages, with a schedule of the pooled mortgage loans that clearly and specifically identifies the mortgage at issue as among those assigned, may suffice to establish the trustee as the mortgage holder. However, there must be proof that the assignment was made by a party that itself held the mortgage. A foreclosing entity may provide a complete chain of assignments linking it to the record holder of the mortgage, or a single assignment from the record holder of the mortgage. * * *

The judge did not err in concluding that the securitization documents submitted by the plaintiffs failed to demonstrate that they were the holders of the Ibanez and LaRace mortgages, respectively, at the time of the publication of the notices and the sales. The judge, therefore, did not err in rendering judgments against the plaintiffs and in denying the plaintiffs' motions to vacate the judgments. * * *

We now turn briefly to three other arguments raised by the plaintiffs on appeal. First, the plaintiffs initially contended that the assignments in blank executed by Option One, identifying the assignor but not the assignee, not only "evidence[ ] and confirm[ ] the assignments that occurred by virtue of the securitization agreements," but "are effective assignments in their own right." But in their reply briefs they conceded that the assignments in blank did not constitute a lawful assignment of the mortgages. Their concession is appropriate. We have long held that a conveyance of real property, such as a mortgage, that does not name the assignee conveys nothing and is void; we do not regard an assignment of land in blank as giving legal title in land to the bearer of the assignment.

Second, the plaintiffs contend that, because they held the mortgage note, they had a sufficient financial interest in the mortgage to allow them to foreclose. In Massachusetts, where a note has been assigned but there is no written assignment of the mortgage underlying the note, the assignment of the note does not carry with it the assignment of the mortgage. Rather, the holder of the mortgage holds the mortgage in trust for the purchaser of the note, who has an equitable right to obtain an assignment of the mortgage, which may be accomplished by filing an action in court and obtaining an equitable order of assignment. In the absence of a valid written assignment of a mortgage or a court order of assignment, the mortgage holder remains unchanged. This common-law principle was later incorporated in the statute enacted in 1912 establishing the statutory power of sale, which grants such a power to "the mortgagee or his executors, administrators, successors or assigns," but not to a party that is the equitable beneficiary of a mortgage held by another. G.L. c. 183, § 21, inserted by St.1912, c. 502, § 6.

Third, the plaintiffs initially argued that postsale assignments were sufficient to establish their authority to foreclose, and now argue that these assignments are sufficient when taken in conjunction with the evidence of a presale assignment. They argue that the use of postsale assignments was customary in the industry, and point to Title Standard No. 58(3) issued by the Real Estate Bar Association for Massachusetts, which declares: "A title is not defective by reason of . . . [t]he recording of an Assignment of Mortgage executed either prior, or subsequent, to foreclosure where said Mortgage has been foreclosed, of record, by the Assignee." To the extent that the plaintiffs rely on this title standard for the proposition that an entity that does not hold a mortgage may foreclose on a property, and then cure the cloud on title by a later assignment of a mortgage, their reliance is misplaced, because this proposition is contrary to G.L. c. 183, § 21, and G.L. c. 244, § 14. If the plaintiffs did not have their assignments to the Ibanez and LaRace mortgages at the time of the publication of the notices and the sales, they lacked authority to foreclose under G.L. c. 183, § 21, and G.L. c. 244, § 14, and their published claims to be the present holders of the mortgages were false. Nor may a postforeclosure assignment be treated as a preforeclosure assignment simply by declaring an "effective date" that precedes the notice of sale and foreclosure, as did Option One's assignment of the LaRace mortgage to Wells Fargo. Because an assignment of a mortgage is a transfer of legal title, it becomes effective with respect to the power of sale only on the transfer; it cannot become effective before the transfer.

However, we do not disagree with Title Standard No. 58(3) that, where an assignment is confirmatory of an earlier, valid assignment made prior to the publication of notice and execution of the sale, that confirmatory assignment may be executed and recorded after the foreclosure, and doing so will not make the title defective. A valid assignment of a mortgage gives the holder of that mortgage the statutory power to sell after a default regardless whether the assignment has been recorded. * * * A confirmatory assignment, however, cannot confirm an assignment that was not validly made earlier or backdate an assignment being made for the first time. Where there is no prior valid assignment, a subsequent assignment by the mortgage holder to the note holder is not a confirmatory assignment because there is no earlier written assignment to confirm. In this case, based on the record before the judge, the plaintiffs failed to prove that they obtained valid written assignments of the Ibanez and LaRace mortgages before their foreclosures, so the postforeclosure assignments were not confirmatory of earlier valid assignments.

Finally, we reject the plaintiffs' request that our ruling be prospective in its application. A prospective ruling is only appropriate, in limited circumstances, when we make a significant change in the common law. We have not done so here. The legal principles and requirements we set forth are well established in our case law and our statutes. All that has changed is the plaintiffs' apparent failure to abide by those principles and requirements in the rush to sell mortgage-backed securities.

Conclusion. For the reasons stated, we agree with the judge that the plaintiffs did not demonstrate that they were the holders of the Ibanez and LaRace mortgages at the time that they foreclosed these properties, and therefore failed to demonstrate that they acquired fee simple title to these properties by purchasing them at the foreclosure sale.

Judgments affirmed.

■ CORDY, J. (concurring, with whom BOTSFORD, J., joins). I concur fully in the opinion of the court, and write separately only to underscore that what is surprising about these cases is not the statement of principles articulated by the court regarding title law and the law of foreclosure in Massachusetts, but rather the utter carelessness with which the plaintiff banks documented the titles to their assets. There is no dispute that the mortgagors of the properties in question had defaulted on their obligations, and that the mortgaged properties were subject to foreclosure. Before commencing such an action, however, the holder of an assigned mortgage needs to take care to ensure that his legal paperwork is in order. Although there was no apparent actual unfairness here to the mortgagors, that is not the point. Foreclosure is a powerful act with significant consequences, and Massachusetts law has always required that it proceed strictly in accord with the statutes that govern it. As the opinion of the court notes, such strict compliance is necessary because Massachusetts both is a title theory State and allows for extrajudicial foreclosure. * * *

What is more complicated, and not addressed in this opinion, because the issue was not before us, is the effect of the conduct of banks such as the plaintiffs here, on a bona fide third-party purchaser who may have relied on the foreclosure title of the bank and the confirmative assignment and affidavit of foreclosure recorded by the bank subsequent to that foreclosure but prior to the purchase by the third party, especially where the party whose property was foreclosed was in fact in violation of the mortgage covenants, had notice of the foreclosure, and took no action to contest it.

NOTES AND QUESTIONS

1.   The judges here disapproved of the banks' sloppiness and the "rush" to securitization. At the same time, the opinion is rather formalistic. Is an invocation of formalism the best way to prevent the excesses that led to the financial meltdown? Is there any claim the mortgagors were misled because of the sloppiness, or that they do not really owe the money they have failed to pay? Is the invocation of formalism here a backdoor way of declaring a mortgage moratorium, something legislatures have often done in response to widespread financial distress? Will delaying the process of completing foreclosures hasten the day when the housing market starts to recover or postpone the recovery of that market?

2.   A paper digging into the factual background of the case argues that Ibanez was part of a fraud ring in Springfield and that the appraisals at the time of mortgaging many of his properties, including the one here, were wildly high. Zachary K. Kimball, The Ibanez Property Ring: A Surprising Hidden Story Behind a Significant Foreclosure Lawsuit (September 22, 2015), http://ssrn.com/abstract=2684522. The question then becomes how the banks allowed this to happen. Does this call into question the court's approach? A law professor who was involved as an amicus in the later stages of the litigation says no: the case was not about Ibanez but about the principles that should govern foreclosures. Adam Levitin, The Ibanez Property Ring, http://www.creditslips.org/creditslips/2015/11/the-ibanez-property-ring.html. Recall the discussion of mortgage relief programs and strategic default. Are courts better at policing individual behavior, by both mortgagors and mortgagees, than at designing mortgage relief programs? If Ibanez was not the best candidate for relief, does that excuse the banks' sloppiness or merely show how widespread it really was?

3.   Recall the Rose excerpt, supra, on the alternation of mortgage law between crystals and mud, with widespread financial distress and foreclosures being largely responsible for the turn to mud. The financial crisis of 2007–08 and cases like *Ibanez*, however, seem to tell a different story. Mortgage law, through the push for widespread securitization of loans and the proliferation of innovative and hard-to-understand sub-prime mortgages, was becoming increasingly opaque (mud-like if you will) during the run-up to the crisis. One response to mass foreclosures, at least that reflected in *Ibanez*, was to demand a return to a more "crystalline" version of mortgage law, where lenders are required strictly to follow established rules. This suggests that some kind of oscillation between crystals and mud is endemic to mortgage law, but perhaps that there is no inherent connection between which set of interests—that of lenders or borrowers—is more likely to be favored by crystals or mud.

4.   The court is at pains to say that recording the mortgages would not be required in order for the assignee to be entitled to foreclose on the mortgage. But relativity of title does not save the banks either. Why not? If the answer is that the statute and the case law require it, is that a good idea? How much protection for mortgagors do the "title theory" of mortgages and the lack of recognition of equitable assignments afford? Would the conclusion the court reached here apply in a "lien theory" state? When a note is assigned, the lien is presumed to be assigned along with it. Restatement (Third) of Property: Mortgages § 5.4(a) (1997).

5.   The concurrence brings up the issue of third-party reliance. Those purchasing a property with a foreclosure in the chain of title have some reason to worry about the validity of the earlier transfer. Would the foreclosed-upon mortgagor (Ibanez or LaRace) be able to assert the invalidity of the foreclosure sale? In a follow-on case to *Ibanez, Bevilacqua v. Rodriguez*, 955 N.E.2d 884 (Mass. 2011), the Massachusetts high court held that a third-party purchaser of property foreclosed with the defects in *Ibanez*— acquisition of the mortgage after the foreclosure—could not obtain valid title.

In *Bevilacqua*, the court believed that the invalidity of the foreclosure sale was sufficiently reflected on the records to provide inquiry notice. Will that be true in all cases? We return to recording issues in the next Chapter.

6.   The transfer of mortgages raises some additional systemic issues. Rapid transfers of mortgages have been criticized, but to the extent that alienability of mortgages has the potential in a better regulatory environment to increase the volume and accessibility of lending, transfers should not be prohibited outright. What has long stood as an obstacle to transfers of mortgages is the creaky state of land records and the great expense of recording. To get around this, in 1993 mortgage lenders and related government agencies—the Mortgage Bankers Association, Fannie Mae, Freddie Mac, Ginnie Mae, the FHA, and the Department of Veteran Affairs—created the Mortgage Electronic Registrations Systems, Inc. (MERS), which mortgage lenders and title insurance companies can pay a fee to enter as members. MERS is structured as a company that serves as a trustee in a trust arrangement where legal ownership of the mortgage is with MERS and beneficial ownership is with the member financial institution. In personam transfers of mortgages can happen between members of MERS without the need to record those transfers (because MERS itself is the record owner before and afterwards—recall the material on trusts in Chapter VI). Assignments are tracked internally with a standardized and stable tracking number throughout the life of the loan, but are not recorded in the local land records, and are thus opaque to outsiders including borrowers. Whether MERS satisfies various state requirements for valid transfers (it would seem not to be a problem in Massachusetts given the relevant dictum in *Ibanez*) is sometimes an open question. Compare Landmark Nat. Bank v. Kesler, 216 P.3d 158 (Kan. 2009) (upholding trial court's denial of MERS' motion to set aside a default judgment on grounds that MERS, being an agent and not an interest holder or servicer, was not a necessary party); MERSCORP, Inc. v. Romaine, 861 N.E.2d 81 (N.Y. 2006) (requiring the County Clerk to record assignments where MERS was record holder of the mortgage) with Santarose v. Aurora Bank FSB, 2010 WL 2232819 (S.D. Tex.) (finding no substantial likelihood of success on merits of claim that MERS lacked standing to foreclose). See, e.g., Donald J. Kochan, Certainty of Title: Perspectives After the Mortgage Foreclosure Crisis on the Essential Role of Effective Recording Systems, 66 Ark. L. Rev. 267 (2013); Gerald Korngold, Legal and Policy Choices in the Aftermath of the Subprime and Mortgage Financing Crises, 60 S.C. L. Rev. 727, 741–43 (2009); Christopher L. Peterson, Foreclosure, Subprime Mortgage Lending, and the Mortgage Electronic Registration System, 78 U. Cin. L. Rev. 1359, 1374–97 (2010). Relatedly, borrowers increasingly do not deal with the original lender but with a mortgage servicer. See Christopher K. Odinet, Foreclosed: Mortgage Servicing and the Hidden Structure of Honeownership in America (2019). And MERS in turn makes it difficult to know who actually holds the debt. In any event, MERS is a symptom of the expense and delay with land records, which is one of the topics of the next Chapter.

CHAPTER VIII

TITLE RECORDS AND THE TRANSFER OF PROPERTY

We have seen in previous chapters how important it is for those who assert property rights to let others know what exactly is being asserted. The rules of first possession, for example, are designed to make clear to those who would potentially compete for a resource that the resource belongs to someone else. For ongoing ownership, markers like boundary stones and name tags serve to put others on notice of ownership claims. Starting with the ancient civilizations, written records of various sorts have also served to evidence ownership. With the collection of these records in a centralized location, those who might have some interest in the state of a property's title need only look up the information.

Title records are deeply intertwined with transfers of property. Although persons other than potential purchasers might have reason to consult title records, purchasers—broadly conceived to include lenders—are the main users of title records. By investigating the state of title through the title records, a potential purchaser (usually having employed an expert) can gain assurance at reasonable cost that he or she is acquiring what the seller claims to have for transfer.

Good title records promote transferability. The use of such a system serves the collective interest of all potential sellers, as well as the individual interests of potential buyers. As a result, most modern systems of records do more than act as repositories of information. Instead, title records (especially land records) carry with them legal effect. In many systems, achieving an in rem effect and the ability to bind third-party good faith purchasers is only possible by filing one's interests in the public records. Some systems, such as those in Australia (the "Torrens" system) and Germany, explicitly strip out invalid claims and title defects, thereby affording nearly conclusive legal title. Things are not quite so tidy in the United States, where almost all localities employ a system of recordation more like France's, but as we will see, various recording acts and doctrines make the system of land records essential to the shape and scope of property that is actually transferred from one person to another.

There is another sense in which transfer lies at the heart of a system of property records: It is the possibility of transfer that makes the state of title more difficult to establish. If each owned thing were assigned an owner who could not alienate it (with ownership going indefeasibly to the heirs or to the state upon death), property would be a lot less complicated—and a lot less useful. In the following materials we begin with some general principles for establishing a valid transfer of property designed to enhance the security of transfers. We then turn to the bedrock principle that an owner can only convey what the owner owns, and to an important exception to this principle, in favor of good faith purchasers. Finally we survey some systems of records of ownership in various resources, including most prominently land.

A. TRANSFER AND ALIENABILITY

The power to transfer is considered an important attribute of owner sovereignty. The power to transfer enhances owner autonomy, because it permits the owner to shed responsibility for things that no longer suit the owner's wants or needs, and at the same time to acquire other things that may be better suited to the owner's wants and needs. Moreover, the power to transfer affords significant control to the owner, in that the owner is allowed in effect to appoint his or her successor as the new owner of the asset—something not possible if the owner sheds responsibility by abandonment or destruction (see Chapter IV). The power to transfer also promotes the efficient allocation of resources. If the current owner is not capable of extracting the most value from a resource (as measured by the willingness of others to pay for the output generated by the use of the resource), then a transfer can be negotiated with someone else who can perhaps do better. The process does not work perfectly of course. Transaction and information costs (and lack of self-knowledge by underperforming owners) defeat many potential transfers. But over time and over a large range of things, free transferability probably generates a higher level of socially desired output than can be obtained from other methods of managing resources. Finally, voluntary transfer is undoubtedly a less conflict-prone method of hiring and firing the gatekeeper/managers of resources than other methods of changing managers. Adverse possession and eminent domain (or for that matter, might-makes-right) are other ways of changing managers, but each has a tendency to generate litigation or worse. Voluntary transfer—where both the outgoing and the incoming manager are willing volunteers in the transfer of owner sovereignty—tends to go much more smoothly.

As we saw in Chapter V, one way the law promotes transferability of property is by putting severe limits on the ability of owners to block transfers, for example by trying to create restraints on alienation or by creating contingent interests in property not certain to vest within the period of the Rule Against Perpetuities. This Chapter focuses on ways in which the law actively seeks to promote transfer of property. Paradoxically, one way the law does this is by imposing some additional constraints on what owners do when they transfer property. For example, the law requires that owners provide adequate evidence of a transfer of ownership, either by delivering the thing to the new owner or by executing an appropriate writing, and it provides powerful incentives for owners to publicly record certain kinds of major transactions in property—all in the interest of making it easier for future transactions in the property to take place. A little bit of restriction on the freedom on owners to transfer today generates a lot more transfers down the road.

Transfers of property come in two basic types: exchanges (quid pro quos), in which an owner relinquishes title to some owned thing in exchange for a reciprocal transfer of some other thing (including money); and gifts, in which an owner relinquishes title to some owned thing in favor of another person without explicitly receiving or expecting to receive something in return. The law of exchanges of property is bound up with the law of contracts and is primarily studied in courses on contracts. The law of gifts is bound up with the law of trusts and estates and is often studied in courses on these topics. Here we will consider only selected topics in these areas that bear on the sovereign owner's power to transfer her owned thing.

We begin with some rules designed to enhance the transferability of assets by imposing certain requirements necessary to establish a valid transfer of some thing. Later, we turn to registration or recording of rights.

1.   RULES DESIGNED TO ENHANCE TRANSFERABILITY

The law has long favored transferability of property. One early landmark we briefly encountered in Chapter V was the Statute Quia Emptores of 1290, which provided for the alienability of land inter vivos. Feudal property systems did permit alienability but with severe and often confusing restrictions: Substituting one tenant for another might impact the quality of the feudal services owed, especially if they were in kind, such as military service. The feudal incidents themselves were abolished with the Statute of Tenures in 1660. By the same token, livery of seisin and its system of witnesses to a public act tended to keep land transactions a local affair, in contrast to the modern systems of land records we will explore later in this Chapter. Restrictions on the dead hand like the Rule Against Perpetuities and the abolition of the fee tail were also thought to promote alienability. In eighteenth-century America the shift toward freer alienability also involved making property more available to the claims of creditors. Claire Priest, Credit Nation: Property Laws and Institutions in Early America (2021). Common property, like a village grazing field, by contrast, was and is not fully alienable: The use as a grazing commons is stable and long term, and sustainable use depends on keeping those with access relatively close-knit and not allowing transfer to potential overusers. Common property remains important today but it lay at the heart of feudal systems. Many of the restrictions designed to promote the stability of the feudal system were customary. The move from feudal to modern property systems involved a removal of many of these restrictions and a generally more skeptical attitude toward custom. As we have seen, standardization of property through the *numerus clausus* principle was in part anti-feudal and designed to promote alienability. Ask yourself as we encounter land records in this Chapter how the *numerus clausus* works together, or not, with a system of title records.

The Statute of Frauds

One doctrine designed to promote transferability requires that certain important transfers of property be memorialized by a writing. The most prominent example of such a rule, which will poke its head up from time to time in these materials (although it is primarily covered in the course in contracts), is the Statute of Frauds. Originally enacted by Parliament in 1677 under the title "An Act for Prevention of Frauds and Perjuryes," 29 Car. II, c. 3, some version of the Statute of Frauds is part of state law everywhere in the United States except in Louisiana. It contains several provisions of importance to the law of property. Section one provides that interests in land, including leases, must be "putt in Writeing and signed by the parties soe making or creating the same" or else they "shall have the force and effect of Leases or Estates at Will onely." Section two excepts from this requirement "all Leases not exceeding the terme of three years." Section three provides that no interest in land may be "assigned granted or surrendered unless it be by Deed or Note in Writeing signed by the party soe assigning granting or surrendering the same." Section four provides, in part, that "noe Action shall be brought * * * upon any Contract or Sale of Lands * * * or any Interest in or concerning them * * * unlesse the Agreement upon which such Action shall be brought or some Memorandum or Note thereof shall be in Writeing and signed by the partie to be charged therewith." In short, any conveyance of a property right in land (other than a short term lease) and any contract for the assignment, surrender, or sale of a property right in land must be in writing and signed by at least one of the parties.

There has been a longstanding debate whether the Statute of Frauds, especially as applied to contracts for sales of goods and services, prevents more frauds than it promotes. But there is not much doubt that, as applied to transfers of property rights in land, it has increased the overall security of property rights, and hence has enabled transfers of property to occur more frequently and at lower cost. Indeed, the original statute was passed as a substitute for a system of registration of rights in land, and it was widely perceived as successfully promoting greater security in land markets. See Philip Hamburger, The Conveyancing Purposes of the Statute of Frauds, 27 Am. J. Legal Hist. 354 (1983). So we see one example of a restriction on alienation—a law that interferes with the ability of owners to dispose of property by oral agreement or in an unsigned writing—which nevertheless functions to enhance the overall transferability of property. See also Anthony T. Kronman & Richard A. Posner, The Economics of Contract Law 253–67 (1979); Jason Scott Johnston, The Statute of Frauds, in The New Palgrave Dictionary of Economics and Law (Peter Newman ed., 1998).

2. The Delivery Requirement

In several contexts, the law requires that a transfer take place only if the thing being transferred or some evidence of title is delivered to the transferee. For example, whenever land or an interest in land (such as an easement) is transferred by deed (a formal writing evidencing a transfer), the transfer is deemed to have taken place only if the deed is delivered to the transferee. Thus, if the transferor makes out a deed to the transferee, informs the transferee that the deed has been signed and sealed, and then puts the deed in his safe, courts generally hold that no valid transfer has occurred. As the expression goes, the deed must be "signed, sealed, and *delivered*" before the transaction is complete.

The other prominent type of transfer that requires delivery is a gift. Here, the law requires either a deed of gift (which must be delivered) or actual delivery of the object given. What is the purpose of insisting on delivery to the recipient before the courts will recognize a valid gift?

Irons v. Smallpiece

King's Bench, 1819.
106 Eng. Rep. 467.

Trover for two colts. Plea, not guilty. The defendant was the executrix and residuary legatee of the plaintiff's father, and the plaintiff claimed the colts, under the verbal gift made to him by the testator twelve months before his death. The colts however continued to remain in possession of the father until his death. It appeared further that about six months before the father's death, the son having been to a neighboring market for the purpose of purchasing hay for the colts, and finding the price of that article very high, mentioned the circumstance to his father; and that the latter agreed to furnish the colts any hay they might want at a stipulated price, to be paid by the son. None however was furnished to them till within three or four days before the testator's death. Upon these facts, Abbott, C.J., was of opinion, that the possession of the colts never having been delivered to the plaintiff, the property therein has not vested in him by the gift; but that it continued in the testator until at the time of his death, and consequently that it passed to his executrix under the will; and the plaintiff therefore was nonsuited.

Gurney now moved to set aside this nonsuit. By the gift, the property of the colts passed to the son without any actual delivery. In Wortes v. Clifton (Roll. Rep. 61), it is laid down by Coke C.J., that, by the civil law, a gift of goods is not good without delivery; but, in our law, it is otherwise; and this is recognized in Shepherd's Touchstone, tit. Gift, 226. Here, too, from the time of the contract by the father to furnish hay for the colts at the son's expense, the father became a mere bailee, and his possession was the possession of the son; and an action might now be maintained by the defendant, in her character of executrix, upon that contract, for the price of the hay actually provided.

■ ABBOTT, C.J. I am of opinion that by the law of England, in order to transfer property by gift there must either be a deed or instrument of gift, or there must be an actual delivery of the thing to the donee. Here the gift is merely verbal, and differs from a donation mortis causa only in this respect, that the latter is subject to a condition, that if the donor live the thing shall be restored to him. Now it is a well established rule of law, that a donation mortis causa does not transfer the property without an actual delivery. The possession must be transferred, in point of fact; and the late case of Bunn v. Markham, 2 Marsh. 532, 171 Eng. Rep. 268 (Assizes 1816), where all the former authorities were considered, is a very strong authority upon that subject. There Sir G. Clifton had written upon the parcels containing the property the names of the parties for whom they were intended, and had requested his natural son to see the property should pass to the donees. It was therefore manifestly his intention that the property should pass to the donees; yet as there was no actual delivery, the Court of Common Pleas held that it was not a valid gift. I cannot distinguish that case from the present, and therefore think that this property in the colts did not pass to the son by the verbal gift; and I cannot agree that the son can be charged with the hay which was provided for these colts three or four days before the father's death; for I cannot think that that tardy supply can be referred to the contract which was made so many months before.

■ HOLROYD, J. I am also of the same opinion. In order to change the property by a gift of this description, there must be a change of possession: here there has been no change of possession. If indeed it could be made out that the son was chargeable for the hay provided for the colts, then the possession of the father might be considered as the possession of the son. Here however no hay is delivered during the long interval from the time of the contract, until within a few days of the father's death; and I cannot think that the hay so delivered is to be considered in execution of the contract made so long before, and consequently the son is not chargeable of the price of it. * * *

NOTES AND QUESTIONS

1.   *Irons* is usually cited for the proposition that delivery is a requirement for a valid gift. If this is so, then why did the judges seem to think that the result might have been different if the father had charged the son for hay shortly after the son reported that prices for hay were too high in the market? At that time, the colts still remained in the custody of the father. Does this perhaps suggest that the judges in *Irons* regarded delivery as just one piece of evidence tending to show that a valid gift has been made? Is the delivery requirement here a functional substitute for the signed writing required in other contexts by the Statute of Frauds? If so, how well does it perform the "fraud preventing" function? Courts sometimes stretch the notions of constructive and symbolic delivery where intent is clear. See, e.g., Hawkins v. Union Trust Co., 175 N.Y.S. 694 (App. Div. 1919) (holding that

delivery of letter by decedent evidencing intent to give plaintiff a disused yacht was sufficient to complete gift).

2.   Why impose restrictions on gifts that do not apply to sales? In many cultures gift-giving involves an elaborate system of quid pro quo and constitutes a major part of the economy. A classic study is Marcel Mauss, The Gift: Forms and Functions of Exchange in Archaic Societies (Ian Cunnison transl., 1954). Is a quid pro quo absent from gift-giving in our own culture? A related but not identical distinction between gifts and sales arises in tax law (because gifts are not includable in the donee's income and are not deductible to the donor). In the leading decision, the U.S. Supreme Court indicated that transferor intent was crucial—namely whether the donor made the transfer from a "detached and disinterested generosity" or "out of affection, respect, admiration, charity or like impulses." Commissioner v. Duberstein, 363 U.S. 278, 285 (1960) (citations and internal quotation marks omitted). Factfinders were instructed to discover this by applying the "mainsprings of human conduct to the totality of the facts of each case." Id. at 289. Does the common law do any better? How distinct are gifts, exchanges, and thefts anyway? See Carol M. Rose, Giving, Trading, Thieving, and Trusting: How and Why Gifts Become Exchanges, and (More Importantly) Vice Versa, 44 Fla. L. Rev. 295 (1992).

3.   When we say that an asset is inalienable, what does this mean? Quite a number of assets can be given away but not sold. They are market-inalienable. Recall the discussion of body parts and personhood in Chapter III and the excerpt from Margaret Jane Radin. Other assets, like a vote or one's entire person, cannot be transferred at all. See, e.g., Richard A. Epstein, Why Restrain Alienation?, 85 Colum. L. Rev. 970, 984–87 (1985); Lee Anne Fennell, Adjusting Alienability, 122 Harv. L. Rev. 1403, 1412 n.34, 1421–22 (2009); Susan Rose-Ackerman, Inalienability and the Theory of Property Rights, 85 Colum. L. Rev. 931 (1985). What distinguishes things that cannot be given away or sold from other things, and what distinguishes things that can be given away but not sold from things that can be either given away or sold?

4.   The opinions in *Irons* refer to gifts *causa mortis*, which means gifts in contemplation of death. Such gifts are will substitutes, and rules governing their validity developed even earlier than the law on ordinary gifts, like the one in *Irons*. A valid gift *causa mortis* requires, in addition to delivery, that the donor die after making the gift. If the donor recovers, the gift is nullified. Implementing the delivery requirement can be especially difficult when one is on her deathbed, as the following case illustrates.

Foster v. Reiss

Supreme Court of New Jersey, 1955.
112 A.2d 553.

■ VANDERBILT, C.J. On April 30, 1951 the decedent, Ethel Reiss, entered a hospital in New Brunswick where she was to undergo major surgery. Just prior to going to the operating room on May 4, 1951, she wrote the following note in her native Hungarian language to her husband, the defendant herein:

My Dearest Papa:

In the kitchen, in the bottom of the cabinet, where the blue frying pan is, under the wine bottle, there is one hundred dollars. Along side the bed in my bedroom, in the rear drawer of the small table in the corner of the drawer, where my stockings are, you will find about seventy-five dollars. In my purse there is six dollars, where the coats are. Where the coats are, in a round tin box, on the floor, where the shoes are, there is two hundred dollars. This is Dianna's. Please put it in the bank for her. This is for her schooling.

The Building Loan book is yours, and the Bank book, and also the money that is here. In the red book is my son's and sister's and my brothers address. In the letter box is also my bank book.

Give Margaret my sewing machine and anything else she may want; she deserves it as she was good to me.

God be with you. God shall watch your steps. Please look out for yourself that you do not go on a bad road. I cannot stay with you. My will is in the office of the former Lawyer Anekstein, and his successor has it. There you will find out everything.

Your Kissing, loving wife,
Ethel Reiss 1951–5–4.

She placed the note in the drawer of a table beside her bed, at the same time asking Mrs. Agnes Tekowitz, an old friend who was also confined in the hospital, to tell her husband or daughter about it—"In case my daughter come in or my husband come in, tell them they got a note over there and take the note." That afternoon, while the wife was in the operating room unconscious under the effects of ether, the defendant came to the hospital and was told about the note by the friend. He took the note from the drawer, went home, found the cash, the savings account passbook, and the building and loan book mentioned in the note, and has retained possession of them since that time.

The wife was admittedly in a coma for three days after the operation and the testimony is in dispute as to whether or not she recovered consciousness at all before her death on the ninth day. Her daughter, her son-in-law, Mrs. Waldner, an old friend and one of her executrices who visited her every day, and Mrs. Tekowitz, who was in the ward with her, said that they could not understand her and she could not understand them. The defendant, on the other hand, testified that while she was "awful poor from ether" after the operation, "the fourth, fifth and sixth days I thought she was going to get healthy again and come home. She talked just as good as I with you." The trial judge who saw the witnesses and heard the testimony found that

After the operation and until the date of her death on May 13, 1951 she was in a coma most of the time; was unable to recognize members of her family; and unable to carry on intelligent conversation * * * Mrs. Reiss was never able to talk or converse after coming out of the operation until her death.

The decedent's will gave $1 to the defendant and the residue of her estate to her children and grandchildren. The decedent's personal representatives and her trustees under a separation agreement with the defendant, brought this action to recover the cash, the passbook, and the building and loan book from the defendant, who in turn claimed ownership of them based on an alleged gift *causa mortis* from his wife. The trial court granted judgment for the plaintiffs, concluding that there had been no such gift. The Appellate Division of the Superior Court reversed, and we granted the plaintiff's petition for certification to the Appellate Division.

The doctrine of *donatio causa mortis* was borrowed by the Roman law from the Greeks, 2 Bl.Com. 514, and ultimately became a part of English and then American common law. Blackstone has said that there is a gift *causa mortis* "when a person in his last sickness, apprehending his dissolution near, delivers or causes to be delivered to another the possession of any personal goods, to keep in case of his decease." 2 Bl.Com. 514. Justinian offered this definition:

> A gift *causa mortis* is one made in expectation of death; when a person gives upon condition that, if any fatality happen to him, the receiver shall keep the article, but that if the donor should survive, or if he should change his mind, or if the donee should die first, then the donor shall have it back again. These gifts *causa mortis* are in all respects put upon the same footing as legacies. * * * To put it briefly, a gift *causa mortis* is when a person wishes that he himself should have the gift in preference to the donee, but that the donee should have it in preference to the heir. Walker's Just., at 119.

* * * There is some doubt in the New Jersey cases as to whether as a result of a gift *causa mortis* the property remains in the donor until his death, or whether the transfer is considered absolute even though it is defeasible. In any event, a gift *causa mortis* is essentially of a testamentary nature and as a practical matter the doctrine, though well established, is an invasion into the province of the statute of wills * * *

In Ward v. Turner, 2 Ves.Sr. 431, 28 Eng. Rep. 275, 279 (Ch. 1752), Lord Chancellor Hardwicke said that "it was a pity that the Statute of Frauds did not set aside all these kinds of gifts." Lord Eldon expressed the opinion that it would be an improvement of the law to strike out altogether this peculiar form of gift, but since that had not been done, he felt obliged to "examine into the subject of it." Duffield v. Elwes, 1 Bligh (N.S.) 497, 533, 4 Eng. Rep. 959, 972 (K.B. 1827). Our own Vice-Chancellor Stevenson referred to it as "that ancient legal curiosity."

Dunn v. Houghton, 51 A. 71, 78 (N.J. Ch. 1902), and then later said that such gifts are "dangerous things":

> These gifts *causa mortis* are dangerous things. The law requires, before Mr. Hitt can come into this court and claim $10,000 as an ordinary testamentary gift from Mrs. Thompson, that he should produce an instrument in writing signed by Mrs. Thompson, and also acknowledged with peculiar solemnity by her in the presence of two witnesses, who thereupon subscribed their names as witnesses. That is what Mr. Hitt would have to prove if he claimed a testamentary gift in the ordinary form of one-third of Mrs. Thompson's estate. And yet, in cases of these gifts *causa mortis*, it is possible that a fortune of a million dollars can be taken away from the heirs, the next of kin of a deceased person, by a stranger, who simply has possession of the fortune, claims that he received it by way of gift, and brings parol testimony to sustain that claim. Varick v. Hitt, 55 A. 139, 153 (N.J. Ch. 1903). * * *

The first question confronting us is whether there has been "actual, unequivocal, and complete delivery during the lifetime of the donor, wholly divesting him [her] of the possession, dominion, and control" of the property[.] * * *

Here there was no delivery of any kind whatsoever. We have already noted the requirement so amply established in our cases of "actual, unequivocal and complete delivery during the lifetime of the donor, wholly divesting her of the possession, dominion, and control" of the property. This requirement is satisfied only by delivery by the *donor*, which calls for an affirmative act on her part, not by the mere taking of possession of the property by the donee. * * *

Here we are concerned with three separate items of property—cash, a savings account represented by a bank passbook, and shares in a building and loan association represented by a book. There was no actual delivery of the cash and no delivery of the indicia of title to the savings account or the building and loan association shares. Rather, the donor set forth in an informal writing her desire to give these items to the defendant. Although the writing establishes her donative intent at the time it was written, it does not fulfill the requirement of delivery of the property, which is a separate and distinct requirement for a gift *causa mortis*. The cash, passbook, and stock book remained at the decedent's home and she made no effort to obtain them so as to effectuate a delivery to the defendant.

We disagree with the conclusion of the Appellate Division that the donee already had possession of the property, and therefore delivery was unnecessary. Assuming, but not deciding, the validity of this doctrine, we note that the house was the property of the deceased and, although defendant resided there with her, he had no knowledge of the presence of this property in the house, let alone its precise location therein; therefore it cannot be said that he had possession of the property. * * *

But it is argued that the decedent's note to her husband in the circumstances of the case was an authorization to him to take possession of the chattels mentioned therein which when coupled with his taking of possession thereof during her lifetime was in law the equivalent of the delivery required in the Roman and common law alike and by all the decisions in this State for a valid gift *causa mortis*. Without accepting this contention, it is to be noted that it has no application to the present case, because here at the time the defendant obtained her note the decedent was in the operating room under ether and, according to the finding of the trial court, supra, after the operation and until the date of her death on May 13, 1951 she was in a coma most of the time; was unable to recognize members of her family; and unable to carry on intelligent conversation * * * Mrs. Reiss was never able to talk or converse after coming out of the operation until her death.

In these circumstances the note clearly failed as an authorization to the defendant to take possession of the chattels mentioned therein, since at the time he took the note from the drawer the decedent was under ether and according to the findings of the trial court unable to transact business until the time of her death. * * *

The judgment of the Appellate Division of the Superior Court is reversed and the judgment of the Chancery Division of the Superior Court will be reinstated.

■ JACOBS, J. (with whom Wachenfeld and William J. Brennan, Jr., JJ., agree) dissenting. The decedent Ethel Reiss was fully competent when she freely wrote the longhand note which was intended to make a gift *causa mortis* to her husband Adam Reiss. On the day the note was written her husband duly received it, located the money and books in accordance with its directions, and took personal possession of them. Nine days later Mrs. Reiss died; in the meantime her husband retained his possession and there was never any suggestion of revocation of the gift. Although the honesty of the husband's claim is conceded and justice fairly cries out for the fulfillment of his wife's wishes, the majority opinion (while acknowledging that gifts *causa mortis* are valid in our State as elsewhere) holds that the absence of direct physical delivery of the donated articles requires that the gift be stricken down. I find neither reason nor persuasive authority anywhere which compels this untoward result. See Gulliver and Tilson, Classification of Gratuitous Transfers, 51 Yale L.J. 1, 2 (1941):

> One fundamental proposition is that, under a legal system recognizing the individualistic institution of private property and granting to the owner the power to determine his successors in ownership, the general philosophy of the courts should favor giving effect to an intentional exercise of that power. This is commonplace enough but it needs constant emphasis, for it may

be obscured or neglected in inordinate preoccupation with detail or dialectic. A court absorbed in purely doctrinal arguments may lose sight of the important and desirable objective of sanctioning what the transferror wanted to do, even though it is convinced that he wanted to do it.

Harlan F. Stone in his discussion of Delivery in Gifts of Personal Property, 20 Col.L.Rev. 196 (1920), points out that the rule requiring delivery is traceable to early notions of seisin as an element in the ownership of chattels as well as well as land; and he expresses the view that as the technical significance of seisin fades into the background, courts should evidence a tendency to accept other evidence in lieu of delivery as corroborative of the donative intent. See Philip Mechem, The Requirement of Delivery in Gifts of Chattels, 21 Ill.L.Rev. 341, 345 (1926). Nevertheless, the artificial requirement of delivery is still widely entrenched and is defended for modern times by Mechem (supra, at 348) as a protective device to insure deliberate and unequivocal conduct by the donor and the elimination of questionable or fraudulent claims against him. But even that defense has no applicability where, as here, the donor's wishes were freely and clearly expressed in a written instrument and the donee's ensuing possession was admittedly bona fide; under these particular circumstances every consideration of public policy would seem to point towards upholding the gift. * * *

When Ethel Reiss signed the note and arranged to have her husband receive it, she did everything that could reasonably have been expected of her to effectuate the gift *causa mortis*; and while her husband might conceivably have attempted to return the donated articles to her at the hospital for immediate redelivery to him, it would have been unnatural for him to do so. It is difficult to believe that our law would require such wholly ritualistic ceremony and I find nothing in our decisions to suggest it. The majority opinion advances the suggestion that the husband's authority to take possession of the donated articles was terminated by the wife's incapacity in the operating room and thereafter. The very reason she wrote the longhand note when she did was because she knew she would be incapacitated and wished her husband to take immediate possession, as he did. Men who enter hospitals for major surgery often execute powers of attorney to enable others to continue their business affairs during their incapacity. Any judicial doctrine which would legally terminate such power as of the inception of the incapacity would be startling indeed—it would disrupt commercial affairs and entirely without reason or purpose. * * *

NOTES AND QUESTIONS

1. As implied by this case, gifts *causa mortis* potentially override other more formal methods of disposing of property upon death—here the will giving the husband $1. (Putting aside the possible effects of the separation agreement, the husband would probably be entitled to more than

this under a forced share statute. See Chapter V.) What is the rationale for insisting on the delivery requirement in the context where the intentions of the deceased seem unequivocally clear? Is it because, as the majority's reference to the Statute of Frauds suggests, the court is worried about the possibility of fraud being perpetrated in some other case? Formalities like drawing up a new will can prevent self-interested parties from perpetrating frauds, but they can do so at the cost of defeating true transferor intent. Or, does the delivery requirement provide additional assurance that the donor adequately appreciates the potential finality of the decision she is making? Cf. Lon L. Fuller, Consideration and Form, 41 Colum. L. Rev. 799, 800–03 (1941) (describing the "cautionary" function of certain legal formalities). But why doesn't the carefully composed letter satisfy this concern?

2. The New Jersey Supreme Court has not overruled *Foster* but in a later case it adopted a position closer to that advocated by the dissent. In *Scherer v. Hyland*, 380 A.2d 698, 701–02 (N.J. 1977), a woman endorsed a settlement check in blank and placed it on the kitchen table along with a suicide note in the apartment she shared with the plaintiff and then committed suicide. The court held this satisfied the constructive delivery requirement for a valid gift *causa mortis* in light of the unambiguous evidence of donative intent and the "universally understood" act of endorsing a check, which makes it negotiable. But the delivery requirement may still be alive in New Jersey. A lower court in a more recent case, relying in part on *Foster*, held that an oral expression by the decedent to the plaintiff that she wanted her to have her wedding and engagement ring when she died was not enough where there was no attempt at delivery, "physically, constructively, or symbolically." In re Estate of Link, 746 A.2d 540, 544 (N.J. Super. Ch. 1999).

3. Does one draw any comfort from the fact that the note was in Mrs. Reiss's own hand? About half the states accept a will unattested by witnesses if it is in the testator's own hand—a so-called holographic will. The Uniform Probate Code takes this approach as well. Uniform Probate Code § 2–502(b) (formerly § 2–503). New Jersey did not permit holographic wills when *Foster* was decided, but amended its probate code in 1977 to make them enforceable. See Will of Nassano, 489 A.2d 1189, 1190–91 (N.J. Super. Ct. App. Div. 1985). Would this change the outcome on the facts of *Foster*? Note that even in jurisdictions that accept holographic wills, the court must be satisfied that the writing reflects the intentions of the deceased and was not the product of coercion.

4. What additional acts would have been required to establish delivery in this case? If Adam had retrieved the pass books and the cash, had handed them to Ethel, and she had immediately handed them back, would this be enough? What is the point of requiring such a ritual?

Gilbert v. McSpadden

Court of Civil Appeals of Texas, 1936.
91 S.W.2d 889.

■ ALEXANDER, JUSTICE. On March 19, 1927, Tom Gilbert and wife executed and acknowledged a deed conveying to Gilbert's daughter, Mrs. Conde Scroggins, and his son, B. C. Gilbert, two tracts of land in Briscoe county, and on the same day they executed and acknowledged another deed conveying to Gilbert's daughter, Mrs. Cecil McSpadden, two tracts of land, one in Hill county and the other in Freestone county. Each deed recited a consideration of $1 and love and affection. Tom Gilbert kept the deeds in his possession and continued to exercise dominion over the land. On December 19, 1931, he took the deeds from his bank box in Quitaque in Briscoe county and started to the home of his daughter, Mrs. Scroggins, in Borger for the avowed purpose of delivering the deeds to her to be recorded. He arrived at the home of his said daughter at about 8 o'clock in the evening of December 20, 1931, and retired for the night. The next morning he was found dead in bed. Shortly thereafter the children found the deeds in his grip [suitcase] in his room. They immediately took possession of the deeds and had them recorded and are now claiming title to the land by virtue of said conveyances. Mrs. Georgia Oakes Gilbert, as administratrix of the estate of Tom Gilbert, deceased, claims that the deeds were never properly delivered and that as a result said land still belongs to the estate of the deceased, Tom Gilbert, and that she as administratrix is entitled to the title and possession of the land, together with the rents that have been collected therefrom, for the purpose of paying the debts owing by said estate.

It is a well-established rule that a deed does not become effective until it is delivered. It is also well settled that in order to constitute a delivery of a deed the facts and circumstances in evidence must show an intention on the part of the grantor that the deed shall presently become operative and effective. The rule is stated in 8 R.C.L. 985, as follows: "While delivery may be by words or acts, or both combined, and manual transmission of the deed from the grantor to the grantee is not required, it is an indispensable feature of every delivery of a deed, whether absolute or conditional, that there be a parting with the possession of it, and with all power and control over it, by the grantor, for the benefit of the grantee at the time of the delivery. The dominion over the instrument must pass from the grantor with the intent that it shall pass to the grantee, if the latter will accept it. And where the proof fails to show that the grantor did any act by which he parted with the possession of the deed for the benefit of the grantee, the question of intent becomes immaterial. In other words, delivery may be effected by any act or word manifesting an unequivocal intention to surrender the instrument so as to deprive the grantor of all authority over it or of the right of recalling it; but if he does not evidence an intention to part presently and unconditionally with the deed, there is no delivery. * * * And while the rule that the grantor must part with all dominion and control over his deed does not mean that he must put it out of his physical power to procure repossession of it, nevertheless, if the deed remains within the grantor's control and liable to be recalled, there is, according to almost unanimous authority, no delivery, notwithstanding that he has parted with its immediate possession. * * * " In the case at bar there was possibly an intention to deliver the deed at some date in the future, but the grantor retained possession and control of it until his death, without having evidenced an intention that it should presently become effective. There was, therefore, no such delivery as to validate the conveyance.

The judgment is reversed and the cause remanded, with instructions to the trial court to ascertain the amount of rents due the administratrix and to render judgment in her behalf as such administratrix for the title and possession of said land, together with the rents therefrom. Said judgment, however, should be so drawn as not to bar any right that appellees may have as heirs or devisees of Tom Gilbert, deceased, to recover said land, or so much thereof as may remain in the hands of the administratrix, after said estate has been fully administered.

NOTES AND QUESTIONS

1.   As suggested by the facts of *Gilbert*, there is a good deal of overlap between cases involving delivery of deeds and those involving gifts. The decision also suggests that the deed cases, like cases involving gifts *causa mortis*, frequently involve attempts by parties of relatively modest means to devise a substitute for the formalities of the Wills Act (such as the need for witnesses or attestations). The putative grantor would often draft a deed during his or her lifetime but intend for it to take effect only after death, and rather than transmit it to the grantee or record it, would hide it in a place where it would be likely to be discovered after his or her demise. Courts reached different results in assessing whether delivery occurred in these circumstances, given often sympathetic claimants and worries that permitting this sort of activity would destabilize the law of wills. Compare Matter of Est. of Dittus, 497 N.W.2d 415, 419 (N.D. 1993) (deed invalid for want of delivery because grantor placed deed in deposit box and "retained a key to the safe-deposit box, retained the income generated by renting the property, and paid the taxes on the property" until death), with McMahon v. Dorsey, 91 N.W.2d 893, 894 (Mich. 1958) (deed valid where grantor placed deed in deposit box opened only after death but made specific statements to neighbor about transfer having occurred at an earlier point). Should the law in these cases focus more on the intention of the donor, and less on whether all "dominion and control" over the deed has passed from the donor to the donee? Or would it be a better strategy to focus on ways to make wills easier and cheaper for ordinary folks to execute? See John H. Langbein, The Nonprobate Revolution and the Future of the Law of Succession, 97 Harv. L. Rev. 1108, 1134 (1984) (describing the willingness of courts to twist facts to find pre-death delivery as the "lifetime transfer fiction"); Reid Kress Weisbord, Wills for Everyone: Helping Individuals Opt Out of Intestacy, 53

B.C. L. Rev. 877 (2012) (discussing various reform proposals). As of 2021, nineteen states have adopted the Uniform Real Property Transfer on Death Act of 2009, and it is pending in another three. The Act authorizes a grantor to execute a deed that take effect only upon the grantor's death so long as the deed is both recorded during the grantor's lifetime and explicitly testamentary on its face. See § 9.

2.   Should the delivery requirement for deeds to real property apply only to gratuitous transfers and not to arm's length sales of real property? Consider in this regard that delivery (either of the object or a writing evidencing a contract) is not required in order to make a binding contract for the sale of personal property. The Uniform Commercial Code (UCC), roughly speaking, establishes a default rule that title passes on delivery. See UCC § 2–401. But delivery is not essential to the formation of a binding contact, UCC § 2–204, and the parties are free to make alternative arrangements regarding the passage of title. What accounts for the difference? Is it because land is presumed to be unique, whereas personal property (at least in the typical case) is not? Or is the delivery requirement for deeds to land just a holdover from the past, land transactions not having been "modernized" by a reform effort like the Uniform Commercial Code? Can you think of other functions the delivery requirement might play in the context of ordinary real estate transactions that do not apply to sales of personal property?

3.   Should the requirement that the parties observe formalities like the delivery requirement be applied on categorical grounds (gifts and deeds of real property—yes; sales of personal property—no), or should formalities be required or not based on more fine-grained "situational" criteria? See Adam Hirsch, Formalizing Gratuitous and Contractual Transfers: A Situation Theory, 91 Wash. U. L. Rev. 797 (2014).

B. LAND TRANSACTIONS

Personal property gifts and sales tend to be discrete events. A land transaction is stretched out over time, and extends from negotiation, to contract execution, to closing and delivery, and finally recordation. Consider the purchase of residential real estate. The seller will usually employ a real estate agent and have the property listed. The buyer will often have a real estate agent during the search process. When the buyer is interested in a particular property, the buyer will ask her real estate agent, or possibly a lawyer, to make an offer in writing. This may be preceded or followed by negotiation. Once a written offer is accepted by the seller, it is a contract, which will govern the dealings of the seller and the buyer until the closing. The Statute of Frauds requires any contract for the sale of real estate to be in writing (and signed by the person against whom it is being enforced). The real estate broker engaged by the seller will earn a commission, a percentage of the final sales price. States vary in terms of when the broker earns this commission. The law in many states provides a default rule that the broker earns the commission when the broker finds a buyer who is "ready, willing, and able" to buy the property. In such states, if the seller chooses not to sell, the seller is still liable to the broker for the commission (unless the seller and the broker have contracted for something else).

Even though the parties have an enforceable contract for sale, the seller remains in possession, because there is more work to be done before the property can change hands. The purchaser will typically seek credit to finance the purchase (see Chapter VII) and will have the state of the title investigated. Title examination will also be accompanied by an inspection of the premises for defects and any facts that might call the seller's title into question, such as possession by a third party. As we will see, the lawyer might check the land records and any other relevant records, or hire a title expert (perhaps an employee of a title insurance company) to conduct the search. Some title companies maintain their own set of records, called "title plants." Such companies will often insure title against the types of defects that a search should uncover, but not against facts like adverse possession that such a record search would not reveal.

Title insurance policies can be issued for owners or mortgage lenders. The latter generally insist on being covered by such a policy, which is almost always required in order to make the mortgage available on the secondary market. Both owners' and mortgage lenders' policies are contracts of indemnity, but unlike most forms of insurance the policy is paid for in a single lump-sum premium. The insurance company's duty is to indemnify loss from title defects that existed as of the date the policy was issued and to defend the title against legal attacks on it (and relatedly also to cure the title defect if that is possible within the policy limits). If a title defect is found by the company and disclosed to the purchaser, it is not covered by the policy; nor are defects known to the purchaser and not disclosed to the title insurer. Only problems with the title itself are covered: survey errors, adverse possession claims, and regulatory actions by government that may lower the market value of land are excluded. Sometimes the exclusions from a title insurance policy are so extensive that the policy in effect covers only what is to be found in the land records, in which case the policy serves as a guarantee of the title company's search of the records and resulting pronouncement on the state of the title. The need for title searches and title insurance are quite characteristic of recording systems. As we will see, registration systems have a guarantee built into them: The registrar of deeds will check documents for their validity and will "purge" defects and invalid claims. Registration systems are accompanied by a guarantee fund that indemnifies title holders against errors by the registrar.

Our recording system shapes the land sale contract as well. The contract will state that the seller will provide marketable title at the closing. Marketable title is title that is free from defects and encumbrances but need not be perfect title; rather some notion of reasonableness animates this standard, such that marketable title is sometimes said to be title that is free from reasonable doubt or title that a reasonable person would accept. Nonetheless, the buyer is not expected to "purchase a lawsuit." For example, a claim of adverse possession or someone else's colorable claim to have title would make title unmarketable. An encroachment of a building like those we saw in Chapter IV would make title unmarketable (and would involve the purchase of a lawsuit), but an overhanging awning or cornice probably would not render title unmarketable. A body of case law has built up around the notion of marketable title, in cases where purchasers have tried to back out of the deal based on the failure to provide marketable title. Milton R. Friedman, Contracts and Conveyances of Real Property ch. 14 (8th ed. 2017).

At the closing, the parties will execute the necessary documents and effect the transfers. The seller will execute and deliver the deed to the buyer. The buyer will make out a check to the seller for the rest of the purchase price (or will direct her attorney to disburse funds from an escrow account into which the purchase money was deposited prior to the closing), and the buyer will often also execute a note and mortgage for the lender. After the closing the buyer finally takes possession of the property. Also after the closing, the contract is no longer operative but is said to "merge" with the deed. This means that any covenants that continue to bind the seller must be part of the deed if they are to bind at all. And if there is breach the buyer must sue on the deed, not the land sale contract. Deeds come in different varieties, depending on what sort of guarantee the seller makes to the buyer. A general warranty deed contains a covenant by the seller that he is able to, and does, convey good title to the buyer. It usually contains covenants that the seller has possession, the right to convey, that there are no encumbrances (easements, mortgages, etc.) other than those stated in the deed, that the seller will defend the buyer's title against attack from parties claiming ownership under competing chains of title, that the buyer will have quiet enjoyment, and that the seller will execute any further documents needed to provide clear title. By contrast, a quitclaim deed contains no covenants of title; such a deed conveys to the buyer whatever the seller had but contains no assurance as to what that is. A special warranty deed gives a covenant against title defects stemming from acts of the grantor and related parties, but not other defects. Again, deed covenants can be supplemented by title insurance.

Unlike most sales of personal property, real estate transactions stretch over a considerable period. While the relationship of the seller and the buyer is still governed by the purchase and sale agreement, who owns the property and for what purposes? Consider the following case.

Wood v. Donohue

Court of Appeals of Ohio, First District, 1999.
736 N.E.2d 556.

■ PAINTER, JUDGE. This case involves the ancient doctrine of equitable conversion of real estate—when a contract for the sale of real property is signed, equitable title passes to the buyer. Here, the sale involved a land installment contract. The trial court, presumably relying on the doctrine of equitable conversion, held that the buyer's equitable estate in the land was equal to the amount of the purchase money the buyer had paid as of December 18, [1984] (the date a third party determined the property had been diminished in value). While appellant Steven B. Donohue (the buyer) and appellee Betty Lou Wood (the seller) both concede that the ancient law should be applied, they differ in the manner in which it should be applied under the peculiar facts of this case.

In 1983, Donohue and his girlfriend, Vicki Schroot, entered into a land installment contract with Wood to purchase a house for $87,900. Donohue and Schroot made a down payment of $30,000 and agreed to make monthly payments for the remainder of the purchase price under a thirty-year amortization schedule, with a seven-year balloon payment. The balance of the purchase price was paid in full in 1990.

The house was located on property near the Fernald uranium processing plant in Crosby Township. In 1985, a class action was initiated against the processing plant. Wood, Donohue, and Schroot filed claims. The lawsuit was settled, with the class members receiving monies for the diminution in value of their property as of December 18, 1984. The lawsuit's filing, settlement, and "diminution date" were all *after* the execution of the land contract. The Fernald trustees awarded $9,478 as compensation for the diminished value of the property involved in this case and issued a check in 1993 to Donohue, Schroot, and Wood. However, the check was not cashed.

Wood filed a complaint against Donohue, which was later amended to include Schroot and the Fernald Settlement Fund Trustees, seeking a declaration that she was entitled to 65.41% of the settlement check and that Donohue and Schroot were entitled to the remainder. After the Fernald trustees deposited a new check in an interest-bearing escrow account, Wood dismissed them from the case.

The trial court, after a bench trial, entered judgment for Wood, awarding her 65.41% of the settlement and Donohue the remainder. The apportionment was based on the portion of the purchase money paid by Donohue as of December 18, 1984, the date chosen by the Fernald trustees to determine the diminution amount. (Schroot's counsel appeared and stated on the record before trial that Schroot was surrendering any interest she had in the award. There is, however, no order journalizing her surrender or her dismissal. Instead, the trial court ordered that Schroot take nothing from the settlement.)

Donohue appeals the trial court's decision to apportion the settlement award, contending in his sole assignment of error that the trial court erred in rendering a judgment contrary to law. In support of his assignment, Donohue argues that because he was the purchaser of the property under the land installment contract, he was entitled to the full settlement amount under the doctrine of equitable conversion.

Under the long-recognized doctrine of equitable conversion, where land is contracted to be sold, even under an executory contract, equity treats the exchange as actually taking place when the contract becomes effective. As explained by Lord Thurlow in *Fletcher v. Ashburner* [1 Bro. C.C. 497 (1779)], " '[M]oney directed to be employed in the purchase of land, and land directed to be sold and turned into money, are to be considered as that species of property into which they are directed to be converted; and this in whatever manner the direction is given, whether by will, by way of contract, marriage articles, settlement, or otherwise; and whether the money is actually deposited or only covenanted to be paid, whether the land is actually conveyed or only agreed to be conveyed, the owner of the fund, or the contracting parties, may make land money, or money land.' "

Thus, the seller, in equity, becomes the owner of the purchase money, and the purchaser becomes the owner of the property. "The interest of the vendor under a contract of purchase is a right to receive the balance of the purchase price, which is secured by his retaining the legal title." Berndt v. Lusher, 178 N.E. 14, 15 (Ohio App. 1931).

Ohio courts have analogized the seller's retention of the legal title to the property as a lien "similar to a mortgage for the unpaid purchase price; the title is kept as security for the debt. Furthermore, it is presumed that a vendor with such a lien retains the title, not the land, as security for payment of the price." Flint v. Holbrook, 608 N.E.2d 809, 814 (Ohio App. 1992).

While the concept of equitable conversion has been used predominantly to determine rights under standard sales contracts, the doctrine has also been applied in Ohio to land installment contracts. In *Blue Ash Bldg. & Loan Co.,* a case in which this court determined that the sale of mortgaged property by land installment contracts constituted a "change in ownership" within the meaning of the acceleration-of-payment clauses in mortgage agreements, we applied the doctrine of equitable conversion. We relied, in part, on the following explanation of the interest of a purchaser under a land installment contract: " 'The vendee obtains an equitable estate entitling him generally to all the incidents of ownership. The vendee has the right to use the property free from interference of the vendor and is not impeachable for waste unless the security of the vendor becomes impaired.' " Blue Ash Bldg. & Loan Co. v. Hahn, 484 N.E.2d 186, 189 (Ohio App. 1984).

We explained that "[u]ntil the vendee has performed all his obligations under the contract and has attained legal title to the property, he does not stand as sole owner of the property. However, he does stand as an equitable owner of the property with the obligations and incidents of ownership attendant to possession of the property." Id. We relied on Black's Law Dictionary to define an "equitable owner" in this manner:

> " 'One who is recognized in equity as the owner of property, because the real and beneficial use and title belong to him, although the bare legal title is vested in another, *e.g.*, a trustee for his benefit. One who has present title in land which will ripen into legal ownership upon the performance of conditions subsequent. There may therefore be two "owners" in respect of the same property, one the nominal or legal owner, the other the beneficial or equitable owner.' " Id.

We then analogized a land installment contract to the situation where a seller and purchaser have entered into a contract for the sale of land, but legal title has not yet passed, to explain, " 'The purchaser's interest under an enforceable contract is treated as real property for many purposes under the principles of equitable conversion. He is regarded in equity as the owner, with the legal title held in trust for him. His position is similar to that of a mortgagor, especially where the mortgagee holds the legal title.' " Id. We concluded that "the vendee of a land installment contract stands as an equitable owner of property sold under the contract * * * ." Id.

This conclusion is further supported by R.C. 5313.01(A), which defines a "land installment contract," as "an executory agreement * * * [in which a] vendee agrees to pay the purchase price in installment payments, while the vendor retains title to the property as security for the vendee's obligation." This "statutory language clearly describes the vendor's retention of title 'as security for the vendee's obligation' to pay the balance of the installment payments under the land contract." In re Johnson, 75 B.R. 927, 930 (Bankr. N.D. Ohio 1987).

Thus, the land contract in this case effectively transferred the ownership and equitable title of the property to Donohue. As the equitable owner, Donohue bore all losses, but also was entitled to enjoy all the benefits that might accrue.

The doctrine of equitable conversion is usually applied to determine which party bears the loss when property is damaged by an accidental occurrence after a real estate contract has been entered, but before a deed is executed. The usual scenario involves a determination of who is entitled to insurance proceeds. We see no reason not to apply that analysis to the settlement proceeds in this case. To do so seems especially equitable where the land installment contract clearly demonstrates that the parties intended for Donohue to bear any loss by providing that (1) while Wood was to maintain "hazard" insurance on the property to the extent of the remaining purchase price, Donohue was to be considered a named insured and had the obligation to pay what constituted the annual premium in monthly installments, (2) the insurance proceeds were to be used either to repair or to reconstruct the property, (3) Donohue was entitled to any excess after reconstruction or repair, and (4) if the property were a total loss, Donohue had the option to repair or reconstruct the property or to apply the proceeds to the purchase price and complete the purchase.

Under the doctrine of equitable conversion, any loss in the property's value due to an accidental occurrence fell on Donohue as owner of the equitable title. We conclude that, like insurance proceeds, the settlement money from the Fernald trustees provided to Wood was held by her as trustee for Donohue, subject to her own claims for any unpaid purchase money. Thus, under the doctrine of equitable conversion, Wood was only entitled to the proceeds to the extent that she could prove that her security interest in the unpaid purchase money had been impaired. By the time the money was paid, Wood had received the purchase money. Thus, the proceeds should have been paid to Donohue alone. Otherwise, Wood would be unfairly enriched by, in effect, recovering twice on the same property—the purchase price that she asked for and received, and damages for the diminution in value, which she did not suffer.

Accordingly, we affirm the trial court's judgment as to Schroot. We reverse the trial court's judgment as to Wood and Donohue. We enter judgment for Donohue, ordering that the entire settlement amount placed in the escrow account, plus all accrued interest, be awarded to him.

Judgment accordingly.

NOTES AND QUESTIONS

1.   The doctrine of equitable conversion is sometimes said to derive from the right of the purchaser of land to the equitable remedy of specific performance. The reasoning is that because property in land is unique and an award of damages would not make the purchaser whole, one who contracts to purchase real property is therefore entitled to an order requiring conveyance of the specific rights for which the purchaser has contracted. In the principal case, why, then, does the damages award, which consists of money rather than specific property, go to Donohue? Could one consider the damages award as deferred compensation to Wood for the sale of the property?

2.   Many equitable conversion cases involve insurance proceeds. The seller and the purchaser can contract as to who bears the risk of loss and who has the duty to insure, but the default rules vary by state. Some states apply equitable conversion and put the risk of loss on the purchaser from the moment the contract of purchase and sale was signed. Other states place the loss on the seller until the closing, and still others place the loss on whoever is in possession at the time the loss occurs. (Even in states that apply equitable conversion to risk of loss, the loss falls on the seller if he negligently caused it, say by smoking in bed.) Equitable conversion matters also in how it characterizes an interest. Thus, in a will referring to "my real property"

and "my personal property," these terms track the equitable title. So if the seller dies during the executory period, her interest in the land is considered personal property, and if the purchaser dies before closing, his interest in the land is considered real property. The real versus personal property distinction can matter for other purposes as well, for instance, where real property goes directly to the heir and personal property passes through the hands of the executor. Does all this reflect people's likely intent or expectations? Or is it carrying a legal fiction too far? How about the rule that equitable conversion applies (at the moment of death) where a will directs real estate to be sold, making the property fall under the category of personal rather than real property?

3.   Equitable conversion is equitable in the sense that it was developed by the equity courts and has been shaped by the equitable mode of reasoning. It is often associated with the equitable maxim "equity regards as done that which ought to be done." More specifically the mechanics of the doctrine involve separation of legal and equitable (beneficial) title. The legal title retained by the seller can be used to establish the seller's right to remain in possession until the purchase price is paid. It also functions as a kind of security interest should the buyer fail to come up with the funds for the purchase, in an echo of the title theory of mortgages.

4.   In *Wood v. Donohue*, if we assume that the purchase price negotiated by the parties in 1983 reflected the diminished value of the property due to its proximity to the uranium processing plant, why would Ms. Wood be unjustly enriched by receiving a portion of the settlement award? Wouldn't the settlement simply offset the lower price she received on the sale because of the location of the plant? If the settlement had been agreed upon before the parties signed the land sale contract in 1983, but the proceeds were distributed after the contract was executed, would Donohue be entitled to the settlement proceeds? Or on these facts would they belong to Wood?

NOTE ON LAND DEMARCATION

In a transfer of land, or in any assertion of ownership of land, it is essential to know exactly what land is being claimed (or is covered by a mortgage, and so on). Deeds accordingly must contain some description of the land. Likewise, as we will see, part of the keeping of land records involves identifying the land. For all these purposes, some system of land demarcation is required.

Most land demarcation systems fall into one of two broad categories. Historically the more common is the *metes and bounds* system, in which land boundaries are usually marked using monuments like rocks, trees, and other structures as well as compass directions, distances, and angles ("courses and distances," as in "start at the big stone by Lake Lemon and then proceed North 25 Degrees East for 150 rods . . ."). In some cases, metes and bounds descriptions do not provide perimeters, but rather refer to the landholdings of neighbors or other nearby features. This system prevails in the Eastern states. Mistakes in this system are easy to make. Not only do monuments like trees or fences rot away, but it is not uncommon for a description to fail to achieve closure (returning to the starting point), to have some overlap with the description of an adjacent parcel, to contain misstatements like substituting "south" for "north," and so on. For example, parts of Texas use metes and bounds for claims tracing to Spanish land grants (while the rest of the state uses a version of the rectangular survey), which can lead to some knotty litigation, as described by one court:

> None of the original monuments on the ground to Porcion 72 and none of the original monuments to the grants which surround this porcion, including the location of the Rio Grande River in 1767 can be found today. Appellant admits that all of these monuments of the original surveys have disappeared except as to the beginning point of the 1767 survey of Porcion 72 which he contends that the state appointed surveyor Byron L. Simpson has located by following the footsteps of the original surveys from the calls contained in the original field notes of 1767. * * * Insofar as a determination of the boundary lines of Porcion 72 is concerned, appellant argues and the appellees agree, that the only legal relevant inquiry is the location of such grant as surveyed by the Spanish surveyors in 1767. Surveyor Simpson has attempted to locate Porcion 72 by course and distance from where he contends the beginning point was in the original survey in the year 1767, and by such construction he locates Porcion 72 in such a manner as to create a vacancy between Porcion 72 and Los Torritos Grant to the east.

Strong v. Delhi-Taylor Oil Corp., 405 S.W.2d 351, 354 (Tex. Civ. App. 1966). In urban areas the existence of well-surveyed streets makes life easier, as in this description of a parcel in Buffalo:

> All that certain piece or parcel of land, situate in the city of Buffalo, county of Erie and state of New York, being part of lot no. 121 of the Stevens Survey, bounded and described as follows:

> Beginning at a point in the westerly line of Parkdale Avenue (formerly Tryon Place), 273 feet south of its intersection with the southerly line of Delevan Avenue; thence westerly parallel with the southerly line of West Delevan Avenue 136.62 feet; thence southerly parallel with Parkdale Avenue 30 feet; thence easterly parallel with West Delevan Avenue 136.62 feet to the said westerly line of Parkdale Avenue; thence northerly along the westerly line of Parkdale Avenue 30 feet to the point of beginning.

Mary L. Cataudella & Lawrence P. Heffernan, Real Estate Title Practice in Massachusetts ch. 3 (2010).

The other type of system is the rectangular survey. Rectangles have many advantages because of their shape, in terms of how they come together, and for their easy divisibility. From the Second Century B.C., the Romans famously used large squares of 710 meters on a side divided into 100 plots. The large squares were not uniformly oriented but fitted to the local landscape. In the United States, a rectangular survey system, which originated with the Land Ordinance of 1785, defines rectangular plots of any size, employing a systematic survey with references to latitude and longitude. Starting from the point where the Ohio River crosses the Pennsylvania border, "a north-south line—a principal meridian—was to be run and a base line westward—the geographer's line—was to be surveyed; parallel lines of longitude and latitude were to be surveyed, each to be 6 miles apart, making for townships of 36 square miles or 23,040 acres. Seven rows or ranges of townships running south from the base line and west of the principal meridian were to be surveyed. Each township was to be divided into lots of one mile square containing 640 acres." Paul W. Gates, History of Public Land Law Development 65 (1968); see also Andro Linklater, Measuring America (2002). Nearly all the land in the federal public domain—the vast preponderance of the physical space of America—was eventually surveyed and disposed of using this system. This is why rural roads in most parts of the country run along straight lines (section lines), why most farms are square in shape, and why most lots in cities are rectangular.

The diagram in Figure 8-1 illustrates the system of surveying established by the Land Ordinance of 1785. It shows how you would identify a tract of property with the following legal description: "the Northwest quarter of the Southwest quarter of Section 29, Township 3 South, Range 4 West, ___ Base and Meridian." Note that every section contains 640 acres, a quarter section 160 acres, and a quarter-quarter section (such as described here) 40 acres.

Which system is better? The rectangular survey is more expensive to set up but leads to more certain descriptions and is easier to use on an ongoing basis. Metes and bounds can be tailored to rugged terrain. For recent work suggesting that the rectangular survey adds greatly to land value, see Gary D. Libecap & Dean Lueck, Land Demarcation Systems, in Research Handbook on the Economics of Property Law 257 (Kenneth Ayotte & Henry E. Smith eds., 2011). Libecap and Lueck report on a natural experiment involving the Virginia Military District, an area of Ohio that was allocated through scrip to Revolutionary war veterans under the old Virginia system of metes and bounds. In an econometric study of counties on either side of the boundary between the VMD and the rest of Ohio (which is on the rectangular survey), they show that the rectangular survey is associated with fewer disputes, more roads, 50 percent more land transactions, and substantially greater land values persisting over more than a century. Gary D. Libecap & Dean Lueck, The Demarcation of Land and the Role of Coordinating Property Institutions, 119 J. Pol. Econ. 426 (2011).

Figure 8-1
System of Land Description Established
by the Land Ordinance of 1785

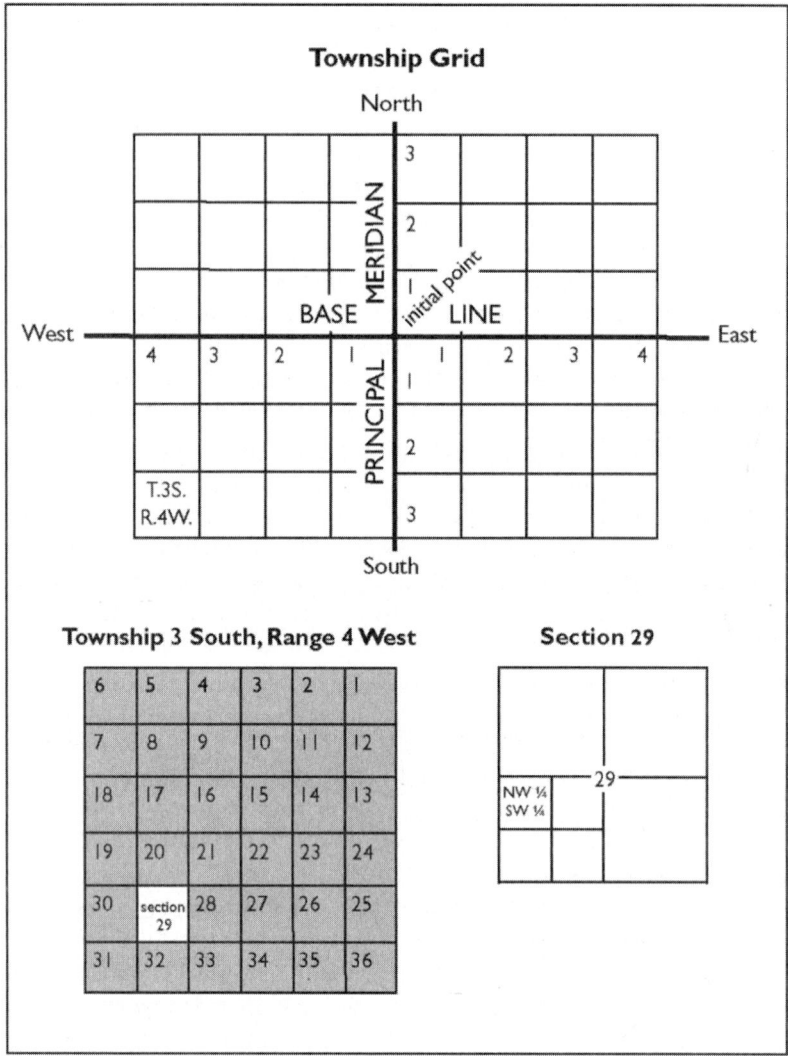

Libecap and Lueck see physical shapes as leading to economic value. Other legal institutions and community norms may be involved and even point in other directions. Libecap and Lueck do not deny that the rectangular survey also had a legal dimension, and this opens the possibility that these legal aspects or associated public investments in infrastructure may lead to the increases in land values they observe. See Benito Arruñada, Property as Sequential Exchange: The Forgotten Limits of Private Contract, 13 J. Inst. Econ. 753 (2017).

The metes and bounds system benefits from local knowledge, and it may have been uniquely suited to American colonial development. Maureen E. Brady, The Forgotten History of Metes and Bounds, 128 Yale L.J. 872 (2019).

In early New England, social and legal practices reinforced boundary upkeep and created witnesses who could attest to even the most imprecisely described boundary locations for buyers or in eventual litigation. One of these practices was "perambulation," in which neighbors and family members processed along boundaries, striking the boundary markers with sticks and branches. Children were brought along for the purpose of creating witnesses likely to be around for many years. Indeed, some anecdotes suggest that children were struck during these processions, so as to impress the boundary markers' locations more firmly into their memories. Allegra di Bonaventura, Beating the Bounds: Property and Perambulation in Early New England, 19 Yale J.L. & Human. 115 (2007). Metes and bounds descriptions, as well as the social and legal practices supporting them, may have offered other benefits to colonial society. They built social capital among existing settlers while tightly controlling entry into land markets to those who could decode markers like "where Philo Blake killed the bear." Nevertheless, as land became scarcer and the population grew, even New Englanders sought to standardize parcel descriptions—using more measurable perimeters instead of references to neighbors, for instance—and rectangular lots became more common.

What about rectangular lots might be advantageous? Is it simply a matter of reduced surveying costs? Are there other explanations for why rectangular plots of land might prove to be more productive over time? For some relevant thoughts concerning the advantages and disadvantages of laying out city streets in a grid, see Robert C. Ellickson, The Law and Economics of Street Layouts: How a Grid Pattern Benefits a Downtown, 64 Ala. L. Rev. 463 (2013), and Maureen E. Brady, The Failure of America's First City Plan, 46 Urb. Law. 507 (2014). Historically, many metes and bounds and rectangular survey systems differed not just in how land is described but also how it is allocated. In some metes and bounds systems, land was surveyed in groups of plots, but in others, settlers were given more choice about which land to claim: They could claim around rocky or marshy patches, often leaving these lower valued lands isolated and unclaimed. The rectangular system, in contrast, tended to force settlers to take quarter sections of land on an all-or-nothing basis, the bad along with the good. Today, the accuracy afforded by surveys using the rectangular system can now be replicated in a metes and bounds system using GPS technology. Does this development lead to the prediction that the differences in value identified by Libecap and Lueck will disappear in the future? If not, why not?

C. NEMO DAT

The baseline principle of our system of property regarding transfers of ownership is *nemo dat quod non habet*—"one cannot give that which one does not have." The phrase, in a closely related variant, traces back at least as far as the Digest of Justinian (Digest 50.54), which credits it to the Roman jurist Ulpian (Ad Edictum 46). In other words, if I own something because someone transferred it to me—by sale, gift, bequest, etc.—I normally have only that which the previous owner had and nothing more. This is sometimes called the "derivation" principle: The transferee's rights derive from those of the transferor. See Douglas G. Baird & Thomas H. Jackson, Cases, Problems, and Materials on Security Interests in Personal Property 3–8 (2d ed. 1987). Willingness to buy the Brooklyn Bridge is considered a symbol of gullibility because we assume everyone knows about the principle of *nemo dat* and would have to be out of their mind to think that the offeror actually has the rights to sell it. Jeanne L. Schroeder, Is Article 8 Finally Ready This Time? The Radical Reform of Secured Lending On Wall Street, 1994 Colum. Bus. L. Rev. 291, 296 & n.6.

Nemo dat is also related to the principle of "prior in time is prior in right." Here the classic problem is someone, A, who transfers his or her interest to B and then turns around, and out of mistake or deceit, transfers to C. Who owns the property? According to the *nemo dat* principle, it would be B, because A had rights to transfer when A transferred to B. Now B has the rights. When A later transfers to C, A has no rights to transfer and hence by *nemo dat* C gets nothing. Of course C could sue A, but A in such situations will often (not coincidentally) have fled the jurisdiction or be judgment-proof. There are, as we will see, situations in which C could prevail over B, but *nemo dat* and its first-in-time implications are the baseline.

Nemo dat appears to reflect an understanding that property rights are always exclusive, in the sense that two persons cannot hold the same property right at the same time. See James Y. Stern, The Essential Structure of Property Law, 115 Mich. L. Rev. 1167 (2017). Thus, if a used car dealer, perhaps out of confusion, sells the same car to three different persons, only one will end up owning the car, although the other two may have a breach of contract action against the dealer. Of course, to say that property rights are exclusive in this sense does not mean that property cannot be shared, as in a tenancy in common or joint tenancy. If A, B, and C are tenants in common, each has an interest that is exclusive against strangers, but not as against each other. But A's interest in tenancy in common cannot be held simultaneously with someone who is not a tenant in common, such as D. Is the understanding that property rights are exclusive, in this sense, another fundamental feature of property? Or can exclusivity—and *nemo dat*—be derived from the role separate legal things and associated exclusion strategies play in property law?

The *nemo dat* principle rests on a vision of a chain of transactions. Current owners must be able to trace their ownership back in time through a series of legitimate transfers (ideally) to an act of legitimate original acquisition. Later we consider ways in which the law cuts off the need for this tracing to an ultimate root of title. But the tracing itself can prove to be quite complicated, as illustrated by the following case.

Kunstsammlungen Zu Weimar v. Elicofon

United States District Court, Eastern District of New York, 1981.
536 F.Supp. 829, affirmed, 678 F.2d 1150 (2d Cir. 1982).

■ MISHLER, DISTRICT JUDGE. This action was commenced in 1969 by the Federal Republic of Germany, as the representative of the people of Germany, to recover possession from defendant Elicofon of two portraits painted by the renowned fifteenth century German artist Albrecht Duerer. The paintings disappeared from their place of safekeeping in Germany during the occupation of Germany by the Allied Forces in the summer of 1945. In 1966 the paintings were discovered in the possession of Elicofon, who had purchased them in Brooklyn, New York from an American serviceman in 1946.

By order dated March 25, 1969, this court granted the Grand Duchess of Saxony-Weimar leave to intervene as plaintiff. The Grand Duchess asserted ownership to the paintings by assignment from her husband, Grand Duke Carl August. And by order dated February 24, 1975, six years later, the Kunstsammlungen zu Weimar, a museum located in what is now the German Democratic Republic, the predecessor of which had possession of the paintings before their disappearance, and which claims to be entitled to recover them from Elicofon, was granted the right to intervene as plaintiff in this action.

Thereafter, on December 9, 1975, the original plaintiff, the Federal Republic of Germany, discontinued its claim with prejudice. And in a Memorandum of Decision and Order, dated August 24, 1978, this court dismissed the intervenor-complaint and cross-complaint of the Grand Duchess of Saxony-Weimar. Thus, the only parties remaining in the action are the plaintiff-intervenor Kunstsammlungen and the defendant Elicofon.

Presently before the court are the motions of plaintiff-intervenor Kunstsammlungen zu Weimar for summary judgment and the cross-motion of defendant Elicofon for summary judgment.

HISTORICAL SETTING & FACTS

Until 1927, the Duerer portraits which are the subject of this suit formed part of the private art collection of the Grand Duke of Saxe-Weimar-Eisenach. Under the terms of a Settlement Agreement of 1927 between the Land of Thuringia and the widow of Wilhelm Ernst, the then owner of the private collection, title to the Grand Ducal Art Collection had been transferred to the Land of Thuringia. Thuringia was created by

Figure 8-2
Albrecht Dürer, Portraits of Hans Tucher and
Felicitas Tucher, Née Rieter, 1499

(These are the portraits involved in
Kunstsammlungen zu Weimar v. Elicofon.)

Each portrait: Oil on panel, 28 × 24 cm, Schlossmuseum, Weimar.

Federal German Law of April 20, 1920 and was the legal successor to the territory of Weimar, which included as one of its seven subdivisions Saxe-Weimar-Eisenach, the territory over which the Grand Dukes formerly had presided before being ousted from power.

In 1933, Hitler assumed power in Germany. Throughout much of the period of the Third Reich, until 1943, the Duerer paintings remained on exhibit in a museum in Weimar, Thuringia, known as the Staatliche Kunstsammlungen zu Weimar, the predecessor to the Kunstsammlungen zu Weimar. But in 1943, after the commencement of World War II, Dr. Walter Scheidig, the then Director of the Staatliche, according to his account, anticipated the bombardment of Weimar and had the Duerers and other valuable items of the museum transferred to a storeroom in a wing of a nearby castle, the Schloss Schwarzburg, located in the District of Rudolstadt in the Land of Thuringia, where they remained until their disappearance in the summer of 1945.

On May 8, 1945, the Hitler Government surrendered. On June 5, 1945, the Allied Powers—the United Kingdom, the United States, the U.S.S.R. and the French Republic—issued a Declaration stating that the Allied Governments assumed supreme authority with respect to Germany, including all the powers possessed by the German Government. For the purposes of occupation, Germany was divided into four zones with one of the Four Powers assuming military authority over each zone to effect its own policy in regard to local matters and the policy of the Allied Control Council in regard to matters affecting Germany as a whole.

Under the June 1945 Declaration the Land of Thuringia was designated to be part of the Soviet Zone of Occupation. However, the American Military Forces had occupied Thuringia, with a regiment stationed at Schwarzburg Castle, since the defeat of Germany or some time before the official surrender in April or May of 1945. In accordance with the Allied plan, on July 1, 1945, the United States turned over control of Thuringia to the Soviet Armed Forces. According to Dr. Scheidig's account, the disappearance of the Duerer portraits from Schwarzburg Castle coincided in time with the departure of the American troops from the Castle.

[handwritten margin note: 1945 : Thur. in Soviet control]

Political differences and disagreement over the future of Germany developed between the Western Allies and the Soviet Union. Irreconcilable divisions prompted the Soviet Union's Commander in Chief to resign from the Allied Control Council on March 7, 1948 and the Council thereafter ceased meeting as the combined governing body of occupied Germany. On September 21, 1949, the Federal Republic of Germany was established in the former French, British and United States Zones; and on October 7, 1949, the German Democratic Republic was established in the former Soviet Zone.

On April 14, 1969, retroactive to January 1, 1969, the Minister of Culture of the German Democratic Republic, issued an order conferring juridical personality upon the former Staatliche Kunstsammlungen, which thereafter became known as the Kunstsammlungen zu Weimar, a status which under East German Law entitled the Kunstsammlungen to maintain suit for return of the Duerers. The Kunstsammlungen moved to intervene as a plaintiff in this action for return of the Duerer portraits in April 1969. In a Memorandum of Decision and Order dated September 25, 1972, we denied the motion to intervene on the ground that the Kunstsammlungen was an arm and instrumentality of the German Democratic Republic, a country not recognized by the United States at the time. On September 4, 1974, the United States extended formal recognition to the German Democratic Republic. Accordingly, by order of February 24, 1975, upon motion, we vacated our prior order and permitted the Kunstsammlungen to file its complaint. In its complaint, the Kunstsammlungen alleges that the Duerer paintings were stolen in 1945 from the Staatliche Kunstsammlungen zu Weimar and that Elicofon acquired them from the thief or his transferee and, therefore, has no right to them; and that as successor to the rights of the former Territory of Weimar and Land of Thuringia, the Kunstsammlungen is entitled to immediate possession. In his answer Elicofon denies that he holds the paintings wrongfully and on the basis of certain affirmative defenses, which are asserted in support of its motion for summary judgment, denies that the Kunstsammlungen is entitled to recover the paintings.

[handwritten margin note: US recognition of GDR opened the case back up]

SUMMARY OF ARGUMENTS

In support of its motion for summary judgment, Kunstsammlungen argues:

There exists no genuine issue of material fact as to whether Elicofon could have acquired good title. The uncontradicted account of Dr. Scheidig, Director of the Kunstsammlungen at the time the paintings disappeared, creates the irrefutable inference that the paintings were stolen in 1945 from Schwarzburg Castle. Thus, Elicofon could not have acquired good title to the Duerers even if he purchased them without knowledge of their source. * * *

A.   The Kunstsammlungen's Motion for Summary Judgment

In moving for summary judgment the movant bears the burden of showing the absence of a genuine issue as to any material fact. The Kunstsammlungen argues that the irrefutable facts in this case indicate that Elicofon could not have acquired good title to the Duerers.

According to Elicofon, he acquired the Duerer portraits in 1946 when he bought them for $450 from a young American ex-serviceman, about 25 to 30 years old, who appeared at Elicofon's Brooklyn home with about eight paintings and who told Elicofon that he had purchased the paintings in Germany. Although Elicofon learned the name of the person he has since forgotten it. Elicofon had the paintings framed and hung them on a wall in his home with others. They remained there until 1966 when a friend, Stern, having seen a pamphlet containing lists of stolen artworks, informed Elicofon of their identity. At that time Elicofon made public his possession of the Duerers which precipitated a demand by the Kunstsammlungen for their return. Elicofon maintains that he purchased the paintings in good faith, without knowledge of their source or identity.

For the purpose of its motion for summary judgment, the Kunstsammlungen accepts the truth of Elicofon's version of the manner in which he acquired the Duerers. The Kunstsammlungen argues that good faith is irrelevant.

It is a fundamental rule of law in New York that a thief or someone who acquires possession of stolen property after a theft "cannot transfer a good title even to a bona fide purchaser for value [because] [o]nly the true owner's own conduct, or the operation of law . . . can act to divest that true owner of title in his property. . . ." 3 Williston, Sales § 23–12.

The Kunstsammlungen contends that the circumstances surrounding the disappearance of the Duerers leave no question that the paintings were stolen from Schwarzburg Castle where they had been stored, and that consequently Elicofon could not have acquired title to the paintings. Elicofon claims that there does exist a question as to those facts on which the Kunstsammlungen relies to establish a theft; alternatively, he claims, such a theft does not preclude a finding that Elicofon's transferor acquired good title to the paintings in Germany.

Thus, the question on this motion is whether the facts about which there is no genuine dispute indicate that Elicofon bought the paintings from one who was incapable of conveying title.

1. The Occurrence of a Theft

On a motion for summary judgment, the moving party has the initial burden of presenting "evidence on which, taken by itself, it would be entitled to a directed verdict." Donnelly v. Guion, 467 F.2d 290, 293 (2d Cir. 1972). The facts about which the Kunstsammlungen contends there is no dispute were related by Dr. Walter Scheidig. Until 1940 Dr. Scheidig was the Deputy Director of the Kunstsammlungen zu Weimar, and from 1940 to 1967 was the Director of the museum. The facts were told by Dr. Scheidig at a deposition conducted by counsel for all parties to this action in May, 1971; in addition, various documents and letters are submitted as exhibits in support thereof. Dr. Scheidig died in 1974. [The court reviews the deposition testimony of Dr. Scheidig and concludes that there is no genuine issue of material fact as to the theft. The court then goes on to decide other issues of German law and of statutes of limitations and standing in favor of the East German art museum.] * * *

Plaintiff's motion for summary judgment is granted and defendant's cross motion for summary judgment denied. Defendant is directed to deliver the Duerers to plaintiff, the Kunstsammlungen.

Germany wins

NOTES AND QUESTIONS

1.   In its opinion affirming the district court, the Second Circuit remarked: "The search for an answer to the deceptively simple question, 'Who owns the paintings?,' involves a labyrinthian journey through 19th century German dynastic law, contemporary German property law, Allied Military Law during the post-War occupation of Germany, New York State law, and intricate conceptions of succession and sovereignty in international law." 678 F.2d at 1153. Other aspects of the dispute centered on whether the Grand Duchess of Saxony-Weimar had a claim to the paintings as being part of her ancestral private collection or whether the paintings were held as crown property. Because the court held them to be crown property, successor governments acquired all the rights of the predecessor governments; in other words, when old governments fell or one administrative unit was replaced by another, title passed from government to government under *nemo dat* as well. (The paintings now reside in the Schlossmuseum in Weimar, part of the City Palace, the traditional residence of the dukes of Saxe-Weimar and Eisenach.) How does the *nemo dat* principle figure in Justice Marshall's opinion in *Johnson v. M'Intosh*, excerpted in Chapter II?

2.   This case also illustrates that the *nemo dat* baseline forms the backdrop not only to the common law but also to German civil law. In German law, however, the good faith purchaser exception to *nemo dat* is wider than in American law, and in Germany a good faith purchaser could acquire good title from a thief. New York's choice of law provided that the law of the state where the transfer occurred should govern its validity. When

the works left the castle in Thuringia, the person living in the castle (who had been refurbishing it as a summer retreat for Hitler, and whom Dr. Scheidig suspected might have also been involved in the theft) did not have sufficient possession to be able to transfer title to a good faith purchaser under German law. And, in the alternative, if Allied Military Law applied, any such transfer was likewise void. So Elicofon's predecessor could not have achieved good title at that point. The transfer was therefore deemed to have occurred in Brooklyn, requiring the application of New York law. As stated in the case, the general rule in the United States, including New York, is that one cannot acquire good title from someone who has obtained the property other than by operation of law, such as by good faith purchase or adverse possession. Which means one cannot acquire a valid title from a thief. As we shall see, good faith purchase and adverse possession are the main exceptions to *nemo dat*.

3.   Does the adoption of *nemo dat* as the baseline rule for determining the quantum of rights obtained by transfer serve to promote the free alienation of property? If so, how? For a discussion of *nemo dat* and current and potential approaches to managing exceptions to it, see Donald J. Kochan, Dealing with Dirty Deeds: Matching Nemo Dat Preferences with Property Law Pragmatism, 64 U. Kan. L. Rev. 1 (2015).

D. The Good Faith Purchaser

The good faith purchaser doctrine represents an important exception to *nemo dat*, one that plays a central role in all the remaining materials that will be considered in this Chapter. Suppose A sells goods to B but for some reason the transaction is flawed. Let us suppose B paid for the goods with a check that bounces. B then turns around and sells the same goods to C. As long as C purchases the goods in good faith, that is, without knowledge of the flaw in the A-to-B transaction, and as long as C gives value—that is, the B-to-C transaction is not a gift—then the law will generally give C title to the goods as a good faith purchaser. The Uniform Commercial Code (UCC) recognizes both the *nemo dat* principle and the good faith purchaser exception in the following provision:

§ 2–403.

(1) A purchaser of goods acquires all title which his transferor had or had power to transfer except that a purchaser of a limited interest acquires rights only to the extent of the interest purchased. A person with voidable title has power to transfer a good title to a good faith purchaser for value. When goods have been delivered under a transaction of purchase the purchaser has such power even though

     (a)   the transferor was deceived as to the identity of the purchaser, or

     (b)   the delivery was in exchange for a check which is later dishonored, or

(c) it was agreed that the transaction was to be a "cash sale", or

(d) the delivery was procured through fraud punishable as larcenous under the criminal law.

Notice that the UCC limits the good faith purchaser doctrine to circumstances in which the transferor (B in our hypothetical) has "voidable" title. This is to be distinguished from "void" title. Property acquired by theft is a primary example of void title. Void title gives no power to create rights in another (*nemo dat* continues to apply). But voidable title gives a power to transfer to a good faith purchaser for value. Subdivisions (a) through (d) of § 2–403 describe circumstances that the UCC considers to create "voidable" title. For example, acquiring goods with a check that bounces or by means of fraud creates "voidable" title. The UCC defines "purchase" broadly to mean "taking by sale, lease, discount, negotiation, mortgage, pledge, lien, security interest, issue or reissue, gift, or any other voluntary transaction creating an interest in property." § 1–201(29). Nevertheless, those who take by gift usually cannot claim the protections of the good faith purchaser rule, because they have not purchased "for value."

Kotis v. Nowlin Jewelry, Inc.

Court of Appeals of Texas, 1992.
844 S.W.2d 920.

■ DRAUGHN, JUSTICE. Eddie Kotis appeals from a judgment declaring appellee, Nowlin Jewelry, Inc., the sole owner of a Rolex watch, and awarding appellee attorney's fees. Kotis raises fourteen points of error. We affirm.

On June 11, 1990, Steve Sitton acquired a gold ladies Rolex watch, President model, with a diamond bezel from Nowlin Jewelry by forging a check belonging to his brother and misrepresenting to Nowlin that he had his brother's authorization for the purchase. The purchase price of the watch, and the amount of the forged check, was $9,438.50. The next day, Sitton telephoned Eddie Kotis, the owner of a used car dealership, and asked Kotis if he was interested in buying a Rolex watch. Kotis indicated interest and Sitton came to the car lot. Kotis purchased the watch for $3,550.00. Kotis also called Nowlin's Jewelry that same day and spoke with Cherie Nowlin.

Ms. Nowlin told Kotis that Sitton had purchased the watch the day before. Ms. Nowlin testified that Kotis would not immediately identify himself. Because she did not have the payment information available, Ms. Nowlin asked if she could call him back. Kotis then gave his name and number. Ms. Nowlin testified that she called Kotis and told him the amount of the check and that it had not yet cleared. Kotis told Ms. Nowlin that he did not have the watch and that he did not want the watch. Ms.

Nowlin also testified that Kotis would not tell her how much Sitton was asking for the watch.

John Nowlin, the president of Nowlin's Jewelry, testified that, after this call from Kotis, Nowlin's bookkeeper began attempting to confirm whether the check had cleared. When they learned the check would not be honored by the bank, Nowlin called Kotis, but Kotis refused to talk to Nowlin. Kotis referred Nowlin to his attorney. On June 25, 1990, Kotis' attorney called Nowlin and suggested that Nowlin hire an attorney and allegedly indicated that Nowlin could buy the watch back from Kotis. Nowlin refused to repurchase the watch.

After Sitton was indicted for forgery and theft, the district court ordered Nowlin's Jewelry to hold the watch until there was an adjudication of the ownership of the watch. Nowlin then filed suit seeking a declaratory judgment that Nowlin was the sole owner of the watch. Kotis filed a counterclaim for a declaration that Kotis was a good faith purchaser of the watch and was entitled to possession and title of the watch. After a bench trial, the trial court rendered judgment declaring Nowlin the sole owner of the watch. The trial court also filed Findings of Fact and Conclusions of Law.

In point of error one, Kotis claims the trial court erred in concluding that Sitton did not receive the watch through a transaction of purchase with Nowlin, within the meaning of Tex.Bus. & Com.Code Ann. § 2.403(a). Where a party challenges a trial court's conclusions of law, we may sustain the judgment on any legal theory supported by the evidence. Incorrect conclusions of law will not require reversal if the controlling findings of facts will support a correct legal theory.

Kotis contends there is evidence that the watch is a "good" under the UCC, there was a voluntary transfer of the watch, and there was physical delivery of the watch. Thus, Kotis maintains that the transaction between Sitton and Nowlin was a transaction of purchase such that Sitton acquired the ability to transfer good title to a good faith purchaser under § 2.403.

Section 2.403 provides:

A purchaser of goods acquires all title which his transferor had or had power to transfer except that a purchaser of a limited interest acquires rights only to the extent of the interest purchased. A person with voidable title has power to transfer good title to a good faith purchaser for value. When goods have been delivered under a transaction of purchase the purchaser has such power even though

(1) the transferor was deceived as to the identity of the purchaser, or

(2) the delivery was in exchange for a check which is later dishonored, or

(3) it was agreed that the transaction was to be a "cash sale", or

(4) the delivery was procured through fraud punishable as larcenous under the criminal law.

Tex.Bus. & Com.Code Ann. § 2.403(a) (Vernon 1968).

Neither the code nor case law defines the phrase "transaction of purchase." "Purchase" is defined by the code as a "taking by sale, discount, negotiation, mortgage, pledge, lien, issue or reissue, gift or any other voluntary transaction creating an interest in property." Tex.Bus. & Com.Code Ann. § 1.201(32) (Vernon 1968). Thus, only voluntary transactions can constitute transactions of purchase.

Having found no Texas case law concerning what constitutes a transaction of purchase under § 2.403(a), we have looked to case law from other states. Based on the code definition of a purchase as a voluntary transaction, these cases reason that a thief who wrongfully takes the goods against the will of the owner is not a purchaser. See Suburban Motors, Inc. v. State Farm Mut. Automobile Ins. Co., 268 Cal.Rptr. 16, 18 (Cal. Ct. App. 1990); Charles Evans BMW, Inc. v. Williams, 395 S.E.2d 650, 651–52 (Ga. Ct. App. 1990); Inmi-Etti v. Aluisi, 492 A.2d 917, 922 (Md. Ct. Spec. App. 1985). On the other hand, a swindler who fraudulently induces the victim to deliver the goods voluntarily is a purchaser under the code. Inmi-Etti, 492 A.2d at 922; Williams, 395 S.E.2d at 652.

In this case, Nowlin's Jewelry voluntarily delivered the watch to Sitton in return for payment by check that was later discovered to be forged. Sitton did not obtain the watch against the will of the owner. Rather, Sitton fraudulently induced Nowlin's Jewelry to deliver the watch voluntarily. Thus, we agree with appellant that the trial court erred in concluding that Sitton did not receive the watch through a transaction of purchase under § 2.403(a). We sustain point of error one.

In point of error two, Kotis contends the trial court erred in concluding that, at the time Sitton sold the watch to Kotis, Sitton did not have at least voidable title to the watch. In point of error nine, Kotis challenges the trial court's conclusion that Nowlin's Jewelry had legal and equitable title at all times relevant to the lawsuit. The lack of Texas case law addressing such issues under the code again requires us to look to case law from other states to assist in our analysis.

In *Suburban Motors, Inc. v. State Farm Mut. Automobile Ins. Co.*, the California court noted that § 2.403 provides for the creation of voidable title where there is a voluntary transfer of goods. 268 Cal.Rptr. at 18. Section 2.403(a)(1)–(4) set forth the types of voluntary transactions that can give the purchaser voidable title. Where goods are stolen such that there is no voluntary transfer, only void title results. Id. at 19; Inmi-Etti, 492 A.2d at 921. Subsection (4) provides that a purchaser can obtain voidable title to the goods even if "delivery was procured through fraud

fraud, not theft
↓
voidable NOT void

punishable as larcenous under the criminal law." Tex.Bus. & Com.Code Ann. § 2.403(a)(4) (Vernon 1968). This subsection applies to cases involving acts fraudulent to the seller such as where the seller delivers the goods in return for a forged check. See Inmi-Etti, 492 A.2d at 921. Although Sitton paid Nowlin's Jewelry with a forged check, he obtained possession of the watch through a voluntary transaction of purchase and received voidable, rather than void, title to the watch. Thus, the trial court erred in concluding that Sitton received no title to the watch and in concluding that Nowlin's retained title at all relevant times. We sustain points of error two and nine.

In point of error three, Kotis claims the trial court erred in concluding that Kotis did not give sufficient value for the watch to receive protection under § 2.403, that Kotis did not take good title to the watch as a good faith purchaser, that Kotis did not receive good title to the watch, and that Kotis is not entitled to the watch under § 2.403. In points of error four through eight, Kotis challenges the trial court's findings regarding his good faith, his honesty in fact, and his actual belief, and the reasonableness of the belief, that the watch had been received unlawfully.

Good faith test (subjective)

Under § 2.403(a), a transferor with voidable title can transfer good title to a good faith purchaser. Tex.Bus. & Com.Code Ann. § 2.403(a) (Vernon 1968). Good faith means "honesty in fact in the conduct or transaction concerned." Tex.Bus. & Com.Code Ann. § 1.201(19) (Vernon 1968). The test for good faith is the actual belief of the party and not the reasonableness of that belief. La Sara Grain v. First Nat'l Bank, 673 S.W.2d 558, 563 (Tex. 1984).

Kotis was a dealer in used cars and testified that he had bought several cars from Sitton in the past and had no reason not to trust Sitton. He also testified that on June 12, 1990, Sitton called and asked Kotis if he was interested in buying a Ladies Rolex. Once Kotis indicated his interest in the watch, Sitton came to Kotis's place of business. According to Kotis, Sitton said that he had received $18,000.00 upon the sale of his house and that he had used this to purchase the watch for his girlfriend several months before. Kotis paid $3,550.00 for the watch. Kotis further testified that he then spoke to a friend, Gary Neal Martin, who also knew Sitton. Martin sagely advised Kotis to contact Nowlin's to check whether Sitton had financed the watch. Kotis testified that he called Nowlin's after buying the watch.

Cherie Nowlin testified that she received a phone call from Kotis on June 12, 1990, although Kotis did not immediately identify himself. Kotis asked if Nowlin's had sold a gold President model Rolex watch with a diamond bezel about a month before. When asked, Kotis told Ms. Nowlin that Sitton had come to Kotis' car lot and was trying to sell the watch. Ms. Nowlin testified that Kotis told her he did not want the watch because he already owned a Rolex. Ms. Nowlin told Kotis that Sitton had purchased the watch the day before. Kotis asked about the method of payment. Because Ms. Nowlin did not know, she agreed to check and call Kotis back. She called Kotis back and advised him that Sitton had paid for the watch with a check that had not yet cleared. When Ms. Nowlin asked if Kotis had the watch, Kotis said no and would not tell her how much Sitton was asking for the watch. Ms. Nowlin did advise Kotis of the amount of the check.

After these calls, the owner of Nowlin's asked his bookkeeper to call the bank regarding Sitton's check. They learned on June 15, 1990 that the check would be dishonored. John Nowlin called Kotis the next day and advised him about the dishonored check. Kotis refused to talk to Nowlin and told Nowlin to contact his attorney. Nowlin also testified that a reasonable amount to pay for a Ladies President Rolex watch with a diamond bezel in mint condition was $7,000.00–$8,000.00. Nowlin maintained that $3,500.00 was an exorbitantly low price for a watch like this.

The trier of fact is the sole judge of the credibility of the witnesses and the weight to be given their testimony. Kotis testified that he lied when he spoke with Cherie Nowlin and that he had already purchased the watch before he learned that Sitton's story was false. The judge, as the trier of fact, may not have believed Kotis when he said that he had already purchased the watch. If the judge disbelieved this part of Kotis' testimony, other facts tend to show that Kotis did not believe the transaction was lawful. For example, when Kotis spoke with Nowlin's, he initially refused to identify himself, he said that he did not have the watch and that he did not want the watch, he refused to divulge Sitton's asking price, and he later refused to talk with Nowlin and advised Nowlin to contact Kotis' attorney. Thus, there is evidence supporting the trial court's finding that Kotis did not act in good faith.

There are sufficient facts to uphold the trial court's findings even if the judge had accepted as true Kotis' testimony that, despite his statements to Nowlin's, he had already purchased the watch when he called Nowlin's. The testimony indicated that Kotis was familiar with the price of Rolex watches and that $3,550.00 was an extremely low price for a mint condition watch of this type. An unreasonably low price is evidence the buyer knows the goods are stolen. Although the test is what Kotis actually believed, we agree with appellee that we need not let this standard sanction willful disregard of suspicious facts that would lead a reasonable person to believe the transaction was unlawful. Thus, we find sufficient evidence to uphold the trial court's findings regarding Kotis' lack of status as a good faith purchaser. We overrule points of error three through eight. * * *

NOTES AND QUESTIONS

1. If Sitton had broken into the Nowlins' shop and taken the watch or ripped it out of their hands and ran off with it, he would have been a thief. In such a case he would have no title at all in the watch (void title). But

because he paid with a forged check, he had voidable title, meaning that he had the power to give good title to a good faith purchaser for value. From the point of view of someone like Kotis, why does it matter whether Sitton is a thief or a fraudster? Or is the difference what we expect of the Nowlins in terms of guarding against theft versus fraud?

2.   In this case the appellate court was called upon to review the factual determination that Kotis did not satisfy the good faith requirement. It is likely that all the judges strongly suspected Kotis knew his seller's rights to the watch were problematic. However, precisely because no one can get inside Kotis's head, and Kotis adamantly claims to be a good faith purchaser, the question becomes in part what kind of notice Kotis had of the flaw in Sitton's title. Sometimes varieties of notice are distinguished. Someone with *actual notice* knows of the relevant fact, here the fraud in the prior sale. One can lack actual notice but have a form of constructive notice called *inquiry notice*, which means that a reasonable person knowing what one does know would have engaged in further inquiry, and this further inquiry would likely have led to actual knowledge of the relevant fact. A registry, as in the case of land and a few types of personal property, is said to give a form of constructive notice called *record notice* of the relevant fact. One who has a duty to search title records will be deemed to know relevant facts disclosed by the records even if that person does not in fact inspect the records. What kind of notice, if any, did Kotis have?

3.   The proper scope of the good faith purchaser exception to *nemo dat* is a matter of controversy. The crux of the problem is that three parties are involved—the original owner, the bad actor who gains possession from the original owner in a wrongful fashion, and the innocent purchaser. Everyone agrees that the optimal solution is to force the bad actor to make everyone whole. But the problem is that the bad actor is usually gone or judgment-proof, and so we have to decide as between two comparatively innocent parties—the original owner and the innocent purchaser—who should bear the loss. One way to frame the question is to ask who as a general matter is in a better position to avoid the loss: the original owner or the potential good faith purchaser? Does the answer change depending on the situation, such that theft is covered by one rule, fraud by another, and purchases from an open street market by a third? Saul Levmore surveys a range of answers to these questions, in legal systems both ancient and modern. He hypothesizes that this is a case in which the question whether to impose the loss on the original owner or the innocent purchaser is a close one and evidence about who ought to bear the loss in any given case is hard to come by; hence we see a variety of approaches across time and space to the good faith purchaser. Saul Levmore, Variety and Uniformity in the Treatment of the Good-Faith Purchaser, 16 J. Legal Stud. 43 (1987). For example, U.S. law is less favorable to the good faith purchaser than is civil law. See also Giuseppe Dari-Mattiacci & Carmine Guerriero, Law and Culture: A Theory of Comparative Variation in Bona Fide Purchase Rules, 35 Oxford J. Legal Stud. 543 (2015) (arguing that the variation in good faith purchaser rules can be traced to deep cultural differences and, in particular, different assumptions about individual self-reliance).

Hauck v. Crawford

Supreme Court of South Dakota, 1953.
62 N.W.2d 92.

■ RUDOLPH, JUDGE. Although in form an action to quiet title, the real purpose of this action is to cancel and set aside a certain mineral deed admittedly signed by plaintiff and certain other deeds transferring the mineral rights by the grantee named in the original deed. No one has questioned the form of the action. The trial court entered judgment cancelling the deeds and defendants have appealed.

Cancellation was asked because of alleged fraud, and it was upon this basis that the trial court entered its judgment. The defendants contend, first, that there was no fraud and second, that the mineral rights were transferred to a bona fide purchaser for value and are not, therefore, subject to cancellation even though obtained by fraud in the first instance.

The facts most favorable in support of the judgment of the trial court are as follows: Plaintiff is a farmer owning and operating a farm located partly in South Dakota and partly in North Dakota. He lives on that part of the farm located in South Dakota in McPherson County. Plaintiff is 44 years old, has an 8th grade education, married and has a family. His farm consists of two sections of land which he purchased at three different times.

On May 23, 1951, while plaintiff was at a neighbor's place, three men approached him and discussed leasing plaintiff's land for oil and gas. A Mr. Crawford was the principal spokesman. Plaintiff testified that after some discussion Crawford offered 25¢ an acre for a lease. Plaintiff agreed, and one of the men apparently prepared the necessary papers on a typewriter while sitting in the back seat of the car. When the papers were prepared they were clamped to a board or pad and presented to plaintiff while in the car for signing. Printed forms were used which contained much fine print. The man who prepared the papers indicated where plaintiff should sign, and after signing in one place, partially turned the signed sheet and asked plaintiff to sign again, stating that this second sheet was a part of the lease, which plaintiff believed. Plaintiff testified that no mention was ever made of a mineral deed and to this extent is corroborated by Crawford who in response to the question, "Did you ever describe to Mr. Hauck one of the instruments as a mineral deed?", answered, "No, sir." Separate instruments were required for the land in each state. Plaintiff never received a copy of any of the instruments he signed.

It now appears that somehow plaintiff had signed a mineral deed conveying one-half the minerals in his land to D. W. Crawford. This deed was filed for record June 1, 1951, but on May 29, 1951, Crawford, the grantee, conveyed such mineral rights to the defendants White and Duncan at [Gainesville], Texas. The trial court made no finding relating to the knowledge of White and Duncan concerning the conditions under which Duncan obtained the deed, but decided the case on the basis that they were in fact bona fide purchasers for value. This statement of the facts is sufficient for our present purpose.

We are concerned with a type of fraud which the trial court, texts and decided cases refer to as "fraud in the factum" or "fraud in the execution" as distinguished from "fraud in the inducement." This type of fraud relates to misrepresentation of the contents of a document by which one is induced to sign a paper thinking that it is other than it really is. It was this type of fraud with which this court was dealing in the case of Federal Land Bank v. Houck, 4 N.W.2d 213, 218 (S.D. 1942). In this cited case we held that, as between the original parties, when a person is fraudulently induced to sign a paper believing that it is something other than it really is "the contractual knot was never tied" and such paper or instrument is not only voidable but actually void. In that case it was further held in conformity with prior holdings that "neither reason nor policy justifies the reception of a showing of negligence on the part of him who is overreached, as a countervailent or neutralizer of fraud." In other words, the perpetrator of the fraud cannot avoid his acts by a showing that the person upon whom the fraud was committed was negligent.

The Houck case, we are convinced, settles the issue of fraud. Accepting as a verity testimony of the plaintiff the misrepresentation and trickery of Crawford was complete. Crawford not only misrepresented the effect of the papers plaintiff signed, but by "manipulation of the papers" as found by the trial court tricked plaintiff into signing the deed thinking it was the lease. Under the rule of the Houck case plaintiff's negligence, if any, does not neutralize this fraud. As stated in the Houck case there was "no intention to do the act or say the words which manifest a volition to assent." It must therefore be held that as between Hauck, the grantor, and Crawford, the grantee, the deed was void.

The deed being void as distinguished from voidable it had no effect whatsoever, conveyed nothing to Crawford, and he in turn had nothing to convey to White and Duncan. As stated by Judge McCoy in the case of Highrock v. Gavin, 179 N.W. 12, 23 (S.D. 1920),

> The grantee under this void deed was as powerless to transmit title as would be the thief of stolen property. Said deed had no more force or effect than a forged deed, and, in principle, was legally analogous to a forged deed. The recording statutes furnish no protection to those who claim as innocent purchasers under a forged or otherwise void deed, where the true owner has been guilty of no negligence or acts sufficient to create an estoppel.

Throughout these proceedings appellant has contended that plaintiff is an intelligent farmer, operating a large farm, and that if he failed to detect the fact that he signed a deed such failure was due to his negligence and therefore he should not be permitted to prevail in these proceedings. We have pointed out above that plaintiff's negligence will not neutralize the fraud, or give validity to the deed, but we are convinced that this holding is not decisive as against a purchaser for value without notice. As indicated in the Highrock-Gavin case, supra, even though the deed is void if plaintiff were negligent or committed acts sufficient to create an estoppel he should bear the brunt of such negligence, rather than a bona fide purchaser.

> An "estoppel" arises when, by his conduct or acts, a party intentionally or through culpable neglect induces another to believe certain facts to exist, and such other party rightfully relies and acts on such belief so that he will be prejudiced if the former is permitted to deny the existence of such facts.

Lambert v. Bradley, 42 N.W.2d 606, 607 (S.D. 1950).

As applied to civil actions the words "culpable negligence" mean the same as actionable negligence. The action being in form an action to quiet title there was no opportunity for appellants to plead an estoppel. There being no opportunity to plead it, the defense is not waived.

As we view this case, therefore, we must revert to the issue of whether plaintiff was negligent when he affixed his signature to this deed not knowing that it was a deed he signed. On this issue the trial court made no specific determination. Whether plaintiff was negligent under all the facts and circumstances presented by this record we believe to be a question of fact which should be determined by the trial court. The question is, did plaintiff act as a person of reasonable and ordinary care, endowed with plaintiff's capacity and intelligence, would usually act under like circumstances?

We are not inclined to accept the trial court's holding that the manner in which plaintiff's signature was obtained constituted a forgery. As disclosed by the notes in 14 A.L.R. 316 and 56 A.L.R. 582, such holding is a minority view, and seems to us unsound. We believe the rule we have announced in Federal Land Bank v. Houck, supra, and in this opinion will better sustain the ends of justice. Our holding, we believe, recognizes actualities. The signature was the real signature of the plaintiff. True, plaintiff was induced to sign by a false representation, but to hold a signature thus obtained a forgery seems artificial and out of harmony with the actual facts.

The judgment appealed from is reversed.

NOTES AND QUESTIONS

1.   This case illustrates the doctrinal variability that enters into good faith purchaser doctrine, especially in the context of real property, where the UCC does not apply. How would the case be analyzed if it were a purchase of goods covered by the UCC? Real property transactions tainted by "fraud in the execution" are often held to be void whereas transactions tainted by "fraud in the inducement" are voidable, opening up the possibility that a good

faith purchaser can acquire good title. Does this approach to "void" and "voidable" make sense? Do you agree with the court's conclusion in *Hauck* that the question of Hauck's negligence is critical to whether the Texas transferees (White and Duncan) should be able to keep the mineral rights as good faith purchasers? Why should the application of the doctrine turn on Hauck's behavior, rather than Crawford's? For a proposal to make owner negligence a factor in applying good faith purchaser rules, see Alan Schwartz & Robert Scott, Rethinking the Laws of Good Faith Purchase, 111 Colum. L. Rev. 1332 (2011). For a survey of approaches to good faith purchase in various areas of law, see Stephen L. Sepinuck, The Various Standards for the Good Faith of a Purchaser, 73 Bus. Law. 581 (2018).

2.   In the "eternal triangle" of original owner, wrongdoer, and good faith purchaser for value, the dilemma usually is that the wrongdoer is absent or judgment-proof, leaving two innocent parties as potential bearers of the loss. (This would have been the situation in the *Kotis* case if Kotis had been an innocent party; Sitton's check bounced and he was presumably not good for the damages.) Here Hauck managed to drag Crawford into court. Do you think Crawford's availability had an impact on the result? Assuming Crawford still has the proceeds from the sale and is not insolvent, how should Hauck's claim against Crawford for damages come out? How adequate are damages to farmer Hauck? Note that Crawford could be sued under a constructive trust theory, under which Crawford would be deemed to hold the proceeds in trust for Hauck. Under the approach of the new *Restatement Third, Restitution and Unjust Enrichment*, Crawford, as a conscious wrongdoer, would be liable not just to return the proceeds he fraudulently acquired from Hauck but also any traceable further proceeds (say, race track winnings) he derived from them. Id. § 59.

3.   How is a subsequent purchaser supposed to know that a deed like that from Hauck to Crawford was void? Crawford and his sons apparently were on a fraud spree along the border between the Dakotas. In another case involving the Crawfords and some of the same third-party grantees (but another farming couple as victims), the North Dakota Supreme Court, after expressing some skepticism about whether there was fraud (as the trial court had found), held that the deed in question was voidable, thus allowing the good faith purchasers to acquire good title. Hoffer v. Crawford, 65 N.W.2d 625 (N.D. 1954). The North Dakota court, acknowledging the approach in the South Dakota case, endorsed a standard highly protective of good faith purchasers under which " 'the innocent purchaser should be protected unless the fraud is *clear, unequivocal, and its force undiminished by lack of care on the part of a mentally competent, defrauded grantor.*'" Id. at 631 (quoting Dixon v. Kaufman, 58 N.W.2d 797, 805 (N.D. 1953), emphasis supplied by the court in *Hoffer*). Is such a rule protecting good faith purchasers where original owners have shown lack of care in the face of fraud better than applying more discretionary notions of estoppel to owners like Hauck? Keep this question in mind when we take up land records later in this Chapter. Forgeries and frauds are but some of the "off-record risks" in the land records.

4.   Another application of "estoppel" involves the doctrine of estoppel by deed. Say A, who does not own Blackacre, gives B a deed for Blackacre. Then A acquires Blackacre. Can A prevail over B by claiming under *nemo dat* not to have conveyed anything to B? No: Under estoppel by deed, A is prevented from claiming superior title to his grantee. Under another version of the doctrine, title automatically passes to B when A finally acquires Blackacre.

E. PROVING OWNERSHIP

In this Part we consider the system of records for a variety of types of property. Even under *nemo dat* apart from its exceptions, a purchaser would like to know if the title she is being offered is valid—whether the transferor really has the rights to transfer. To the extent we move away from *nemo dat* and allow good faith purchasers to establish title by routes other than the *nemo dat* principle, we also face the question of what constitutes notice and how to provide notice in a way that is generally cost-effective. In any event, for various resources the issue is what combination of possession, markings on the asset, and records (and of what type) is most cost-effective. Moreover, when things go wrong, courts will often be faced ex post with potential unfairness in the operation of some of these systems.

Douglas Baird & Thomas Jackson, *Information, Uncertainty, and the Transfer of Property*
13 J. LEGAL STUD. 299, 302–04 (1984).

Anglo-American law assumes for the most part that an individual's interest in enjoying property that is acquired, in good faith, from someone else who appears to be the owner is not as important as recognizing the rights of the person who first owned it or who last owned it by wholly consensual transfers. Nevertheless, we shall want to ensure, even in a legal regime that conditions ownership on consensual transfer, that legal rules make it easy for prospective purchasers to investigate their chain of title. Consent, although usually a necessary condition, is rarely a sufficient one.

At one time, taking physical possession of real or tangible personal property was necessary before a person could be relatively certain that his claim was, and would remain, superior to that of others. This principle was affirmed in the case of personal property in 1601 in *Twyne's Case*. A person had purported to sell some sheep, but he had continued to take care of them, shear them, and treat them as his own. The court struck the transaction down as fraudulent, essentially on the ground that there was something wrong with selling goods but keeping possession of them. Since the transaction would have been valid had the property been physically transferred at the time of the sale, the sale itself was not at issue. Rather, the sticking point was the retention of possession. The problem with retention of possession—ostensible ownership—ultimately seems to return to a legal rule governing information as a means of reducing uncertainty. * * *

The system illustrated in *Twyne's Case* depended on a very simple legal rule and hence on minimal government intervention: to obtain priority in an asset over third-party claimants, an individual needed, in addition to the consent of the prior owner, to take physical possession of the asset. Under such a system, both *obtaining* information regarding prior claims and *disseminating* information regarding one's own claim were simple—one took possession. Between the parties to a transaction, such as a lender and the true owner, their private contract governed. But against most of the rest of the world, possession was also necessary.

Establishing ownership rights from possession, however, brings costs. A possession-based rule, for example, impedes temporal divisions of ownership of property. Under such a rule, one who acquires a remainder interest cannot easily take possession of the underlying property and ensure that his rights are superior to the rights of anyone else to whom his transferor might also try to convey the remainder interest. Moreover, a possession-based rule of title makes the tracing of claims for more than one generation difficult and hence increases the risks of a thief in the chain of title—a risk that one or the other party must bear. Certain attributes of particular kinds of property, in addition, may make such property more suitable to a system of filing claims to provide the relevant information.

Filing systems have evolved as the principal alternative to transfer rules based on possession. Public recording of interests in property may reduce the uncertainty concerning the transfer of property, because they contain virtually all relevant information, apart from that imparted by possession itself. Filing systems may also aid in the tracing of transfers over time and hence, compared to a possession-based system, reduce the risk of non-consensual transfers at the same time that they provide assurance to subsequent purchasers that they can in fact acquire good title. In short, rules of transfer that require public recordation can reduce the risks that a subsequent purchaser will not acquire good title without increasing the risk that a present owner will lose his property by theft.

Filing systems can be mixed in a variety of ways with possessory systems for determining rights to assets. * * *

Filing systems are not, however, equally suited to all kinds of property. The desirability of a particular kind of filing system turns on the type of property it is to cover. Filing systems are comparatively better than possessory systems when the property is valuable, when the property is not transferred often, and when it is important to share ownership of the property among several individuals, such as by creating a future interest or a security interest. Filing systems, moreover, are comparatively better when the property's physical use is important or when the underlying property right is abstract and unembodied. In such cases, requiring a transfer of possession as a condition of acquiring paramount rights to the asset brings with it substantial costs that do not outweigh the significant benefits of allowing one party to remain in possession despite his holding less than full ownership of the property. Filing systems, finally, will more easily accommodate *title* claims to an asset, and not just security claims, when describing the property identifies it more precisely than possessing it, when the asset has a long life, and when the property (or perhaps the debtor) is not likely to move. When these conditions hold, finding the property files and using them are comparatively easy and cost effective.

Some types of property seem better suited for one set of transfer rules than another. Real property is the paradigm of property for which a filing system of title claims is superior. One acquires ownership of Blackacre by engaging in certain public acts. This permits others who come later to discover the true owner easily, and hence facilitates consensual transfers by holders along the chain of title. As a first approximation, one has exclusive ownership of Blackacre to the extent that no one else, outside the chain of title, has engaged in those acts before, and one can learn about all such earlier acts, because notations in a filing system are both permanent and publicly accessible. * * *

The provisions requiring the recording of transfers of title to real property deal successfully with the need of potential purchasers of property for reliable information about who owns the land they wish to acquire. The recording system has the effect of reducing the uncertainty surrounding a transfer of real property without undermining the consensual nature of those transfers. And the more effective the set of rules governing the transfer of property is in increasing acquisitional certainty *and* dispositional certainty, the more valuable it is to own property in the first instance.

But not all types of property are equally suited to an informational system based on files. Money is the polar opposite of real property in that it is the best example of property that is *not* suitable for a filing system * * *

Other kinds of personal property provide intermediate cases. Recording systems that establish *title* of personal property are rare, at least when the owner is in possession of the property. The informational advantages that such a system provides do not, as a general matter, seem worth their costs. A piece of personal property is often less valuable than a piece of real property and is likely to be more frequently transferred. Moreover, a title-based recording system is much harder to organize for grain in a silo than it is for land. One has no easy way of knowing that this was the grain grown on Blackacre in one jurisdiction or on Whiteacre in another. Possession is often more reliable than description in sorting personal property. One also has no easy way of knowing in fact that the grain in the silo today was the grain that was there yesterday. Grain or its owner can easily move from one jurisdiction to another, and prospective purchasers may not know which file to check. * * *

NOTES AND QUESTIONS

1.   How critical is the practice of secured lending (see Chapter VII) to the development of filing systems for property rights? Most of the types of property that are covered by filing systems are also used as security for loans. This includes land and associated real property interests, major forms of personal property like airplanes and automobiles, and patents. Indeed, many types of personal property (such as machinery) are the subject of recording only if they are used as security for loans. On the other hand, property interests that are not often used as security for loans, like works of art, have been slower to develop registries. Does the fact that security interests are invisible help explain why registration or recording is necessary in order for secured lending to flourish? How important is taxation in explaining the development of systematic title records for property rights? If the government were to rely heavily on personal property taxes on works of fine art, would you expect a system of registration to emerge for these works? How important is it that property be difficult to alter in the development of a registration system? See Abraham Bell & Gideon Parchomovsky, Of Property and Information, 116 Colum. L. Rev. 237, 280–81 (2016).

2.   Possession and title records are meant to serve as notice to "all the world," but among that large class of persons some will need more information than others. Potential purchasers often need the most, and the title records are designed for their use—or for the experts they hire. How accessible do title records need to be? Does a potential trespasser need to look up the state of title? See, e.g., Mountain States Tel. & Tel. Co. v. Kelton, 285 P.2d 168, 170–71 (Ariz. 1955) (holding that contractor is not deemed to have constructive notice of buried cable that was subject of recorded right of way because those with no interest in the title are not bound to search title to land); Statler Mfg., Inc. v. Brown, 691 S.W.2d 445, 449–50 (Mo. Ct. App. 1985) (holding no constructive notice to contractor from properly recorded easement for aircraft right-of-way).

3.   As you read the materials in the balance of this Chapter, ask yourself whether Baird and Jackson are too optimistic about the effectiveness of the recording system for property in land. See, e.g., D. Barlow Burke, Jr., American Conveyancing Patterns: Past Improvements and Current Debates 103–04 & n.2 (1978) (noting the many risks that American recording systems give rise to and how little protection a title search provides, and citing literature); Francis S. Philbrick, Limits of Record Search and Therefore of Notice: Part I, 93 U. Pa. L. Rev. 125 (1944).

1. LAND

The keeping of land records is a practice both old and new. In the ancient Near East, records of land transactions and ownership were sometimes kept in the household—as, for example, attested by the story of Jeremiah's purchase in 587 B.C. of a field at Anathoth from his cousin

Hanamel (Jer. 32:9–15)—and sometimes in central registries. In ancient Mesopotamia and Egypt, the centralized records were probably kept for purposes like tax collection rather than to bar the claims of third parties. Robert C. Ellickson & Charles DiA. Thorland, Ancient Land Law: Mesopotamia, Egypt, Israel, 71 Chi.–Kent L. Rev. 321, 373, 380–81, 384–85 (1995).

Land records designed to cut off the contrary claims of third parties are a more recent development, which came earlier to the United States than to England. The first American recording act was the 1640 Massachusetts Bay recording statute, whose preamble states the act's purpose as "[f]or avoyding fraudulent conveyances, and that every man may know what estate or interest other men have." 6 Powell on Real Property ¶ 912 (1949) (quoting 1 Massachusetts Records at 306). In England, deeds were kept by owners and later by lawyers; concerns with privacy are thought to have delayed large-scale recording until the twentieth century. Even the major overhaul of English property in the English Land Registration Act of 1925 contained provisions for secrecy. C. Dent Bostick, Land Title Registration: An English Solution to an American Problem, 63 Ind. L.J. 55, 75–76 99–100 (1987) (arguing against these secrecy provisions for the United States). Might privacy considerations re-emerge to change land recording institutions in the near future? With the rise of computerized land recording, some firms have begun extracting and commodifying the data in land records to sell the personal and financial data these records reveal, often for targeted marketing. See Reid K. Weisbord & Stewart E. Sterk, The Commodification of Public Land Records, 97 Notre Dame L. Rev. (forthcoming), https://ssrn.com/abstract=3794846.

Land records make notice by publicizing transactions—a method in evidence in the Hebrew Bible, the Middle Assyrian Laws, and medieval English sources—less necessary and increasingly vestigial. (Recall livery of seisin and the handing over of the twig or clod of dirt in the sale of a freehold estate, see Chapter V.) Nevertheless, notice by possession has not completely died out. Consider in the following materials the role of possession in furnishing notice to third-party potential purchasers.

Benito Arruñada, *Institutional Foundations of Impersonal Exchange: Theory and Policy of Contractual Registries*
45–47, 51–52, 55–58 (2012).

Private Titling: Privacy of Claims as the Starting Point

Under the Roman Law tradition of private conveyance that was dominant in Europe until the nineteenth century, private contracts on land had *in rem* effects on third parties, even if they were kept secret. The baseline legal principle was that no one could deliver what they did not have *(nemo dat quod non habet)*, which was closely related to the principle "first in time, first in right." So, in a double sale * * * in which an owner O sells first to buyer B_1 and later to B_2, the land belongs to B_1 because when O sold to B_2, O was not the owner. In cases of conflict, the judge will allocate property and contract rights between both claimants (B_1 and B_2)—that is, will "establish title"—on the basis of evidence on possession and past transactions, whether or not these transactions had remained hidden.

This potential enforcement of adverse hidden rights made gathering all relevant consents close to impossible, hindering trade and specialization. Most transactions in land therefore gave rise, totally or partially, to contract rights and the enforcement advantage of property rights remained unfulfilled, especially with respect to abstract rights, such as mortgages. These difficulties are clear in the functioning of the two sources of evidence traditionally used to establish title under privacy: possession and the "chain of title deeds."

Reliance on Possession

First, the use of possession—that is, the fact of controlling the asset—as the basis for establishing property rights is a poor solution for durable assets, because for such assets it is often valuable to define multiple rights, at least separating ownership and possession. However, relying on possession to establish ownership makes it possible for possessors to fraudulently use their position to acquire ownership for themselves or to convey owners' rights to third parties. In such cases, owners will often end up holding a mere contract right, an *in personam* right, against the possessor committing the fraud. Understandably, under such conditions, owners will be reluctant to cede possession impersonally, for fear of losing their property. * * *

Documentary Formalization Through the Chain of Deeds

Second, some of the problems posed by possession are solved by embodying abstract rights, such as ownership and liens, and even complementary consents in the conveying contracts, which then form a series or "chain" of title documents or deeds ("chain of deeds," for brevity) that is based on what I have been calling "documentary formalization." This evidencing of rights with the chain of deeds facilitates some degree of separation of ownership and control because it is the content and possession of deeds that provide evidence of ownership. Therefore, title experts can examine the history of transactions going back to a "root of title" which is proof of ownership in itself—either because it is an original grant from the State or, more often, because of the time that has lapsed beyond the period of prescription or the statute of limitations.

This solution has also been used for a long time. For example, in the Demotic titles used in Ptolemaic Egypt between 650 and 30 BCE, the consent of affected rightholders (usually the wife and coheirs of the vendor) was stated in a specific clause (Manning 1995, 254–55). But relying on the chain of deeds also creates problems. Above all, new possibilities for error and fraudulent conveyance appear, giving rise to multiple chains of title, which leave acquirers with contract rights against the fraudulent grantor and the professionals involved in the transaction. Moreover, titles are less effective than possession in reducing the asymmetry of acquirers, as possession is observable but adverse chains of title remain private to the acquirer. Furthermore, acquirers remain fully unprotected against those hidden charges that are not voluntarily contracted, such as judgment and property tax liens. * * *

Traditional Conveyancing in England: Solicitors and the Chain of Deeds. Despite these difficulties, transactions on unregistered land in England heavily relied on the chain of deeds up until the last decades of the twentieth century. Typically, ownership was proved by possession and the whole series of deeds, which was often kept by the owner's solicitor. And mortgages were formalized by pledging the deeds with the lender. This privacy system was able to survive, despite its shortcomings, because agricultural land ownership was relatively concentrated in a few hands, which made personal transactions easier (Pottage 1998). In addition, the flaws of privacy were palliated in England by parliamentary interventions that reorganized obsolete and overly fragmented property rights (Bogart and Richardson 2009), an example of large-scale public reallocation of rights.

The English case also illustrates a constant feature of privacy regimes: to contain fraud, private conveyancing services provided by solicitors and notaries tend to develop into professional monopoly. * * *

Public Reallocation of Rights Through Judicial Purging of Titles. In a situation of systematically unclear title, of the sort that may be fostered by a privacy regime, many individuals demand that the legal system afford them greater security for their rights, especially owners who plan to make additional investments or to sell land to third parties who may be unsatisfied by personal guarantees. To fulfill this demand for greater security, legal systems often provide summary judicial procedures that aim to call on all possible claimants and solve any possible contradiction in their claims, proceeding to what * * * is a public reallocation of rights. For example, before the consolidation of recordation and registration systems, many countries in Europe resorted to special judicial procedures for clarifying title, such as the French *purge* (Cabrillac and Mouly 1997, 732) and the Spanish *purga* (Pardo Núñez 1993).

Unsatisfied demand for greater security is also behind the fake lawsuits that parties resort to with the objective of clarifying title when the law does not provide for specific summary procedures. A famous example was the English "fine," a simulated lawsuit that allowed the transaction to be entered in the books of the court and made it binding on everybody after a short period of limitation. It was used from the twelfth century until 1833 (Kolbert and Mackay 1977, 241). This type of fictitious and amicable lawsuit is found in different historical contexts, from the Bible (Ellickson and Thorland 1995, 385) to colonial

Massachusetts (Konig 1974, 160–61). Unfortunately, however, both specific purges and fake lawsuits are insecure under a privacy regime, because judges must rely on proclamations to identify all claims, given that many rights remain hidden. Therefore, their effects in many jurisdictions are not general but are limited to any identified claims.

Publicity of Claims

Whatever the palliatives applied, the costs of contracting true property *in rem* rights under a regime of pure privacy are so high that modern systems of property law have abandoned privacy in an effort to lower them. At a minimum, the law induces or requires the independent publicity of contracts, which makes them verifiable, as a prerequisite for them to attain *in rem* effects—that is, to convey property rights and not mere contract rights. If they keep their claims private, rightholders lose or risk losing *in rem* effects. Private contracts may create obligations among the conveying parties but do not bind third parties—all other rightholders and, especially, potential future buyers and lenders. Independent publicity therefore facilitates finding out which property rights are alive and which will be affected, thus making it possible to gather consents, purge titles, and reduce information asymmetries between the conveying parties. * * *

Recordation of Deeds

The next logical step in the provision of publicity is to deposit private transaction documents ("title deeds") in a public registry so that this evidence on property claims can then be used by the courts to verify them and allocate property, *in rem*, rights in case of litigation. Moreover, by making the register publicly accessible to potential acquirers, these can ascertain the quality of the sellers' title, thus reducing their information asymmetry.

After many failed attempts, such as the Statute of Enrollments issued by Henry VIII in 1535 but never enforced, and the Massachusetts 1640 Recording Act, recordation eventually started to succeed in the nineteenth century and has been used in most of the United States, part of Canada, France, and some other countries, mostly those with a French legal background. The key for its success was to switch the priority rule, because other incentives failed in convincing people to record. Historically, recordation systems thus became effective only when, in deciding on a conflict with third parties, courts determined the priority of claims from the date of recording in the public office and not from the date of the deed. This means that, instead of the conventional "first in time, first in right" rule, courts adjudicated according to the rule "first to record, first in right." For instance, in terms of a double sale * * * , the judge would give the land not to the first buyer, B_1, but to the first buyer to record the purchase.

This change in the priority rule not only protects acquirers but also avoids incomplete recording, which hampered many of the first recordation systems. The reason is that the switch in the priority rule effectively motivates acquirers such as B_1 to record from fear of losing title through a second double sale or any other granting of rights (e.g., a mortgage) by the former owner to an innocent acquirer such as B_2 (e.g., a lender) who might record his claim first. Consequently, all relevant evidence on property rights is available in the public records. From the point of view of third parties, the record, in principle, is complete * * * . Other claims may not be recorded and may well be binding for the parties who have conveyed them, but these hidden claims have no effect on third parties.[18]

Moreover, as under the privacy regime, both contractual and judicial procedures are used to remove title defects. Compared to privacy, deed recordation provides more possibilities for contracting the removal of defects, because defects are better known to buyers and insurers. The identification of rightholders also gives greater security to the summary judicial hearings that serve to identify possible adverse claims and publicly reallocate *in rem* rights. These summary hearings continue to exist today in, e.g., the French judicial *purge* and the US "quiet title" suit. In addition to purging titles directly, the existence of such a court-ordered purging possibility also reduces bargaining costs indirectly by encouraging recalcitrant claimants to reach private agreements (Cabrillac and Mouly 1997, 732–40).

However, the recording office accepts all deeds respecting certain formal requirements (mainly, the date of the contract and the names of the conveying parties), whatever their legality and their collision with preexisting property rights. In fact, the recording office is often obliged by law to file all documents fulfilling a set of formal requirements, regardless of their legal status. For example, according to Article 27201 of the California Government Code, "the county recorder shall not refuse to record any instrument, paper, or notice that is authorized or required by statute or court order to be recorded on the basis of its lack of legal sufficiency." The public record may therefore contain three kinds of deed. First, those resulting from private transactions made without previous examination. Second, those granted after an examination but without having all defects removed. Finally, those that define purged and non-contradictory property rights.

---

[18] Some important caveats are in order. First, this ideal completeness of the public record has often remained unfulfilled because of organizational and legal problems, as exemplified by the traditional problems of land records in the United States (Cross 1957; Straw 1967). Moreover, in most jurisdictions, the priority-of-recording rule applies only to innocent or good-faith acquirers for value, and judges infer that such good faith is lacking when the acquirer knew (had "notice") of the previous transactions, an aspect that is also illustrated by the different systems being applied in different states in the United States (Dukeminier and Krier 1998, 675–77; and Merrill and Smith 2007, 919–23). Finally, acquirers must usually inspect the land to find out about physical possession, as this inspection provides actual notice as to the existence of a claim or right. * * *

Transactors who record clouded titles therefore produce a negative externality for all future transactors.[20] Experts examining the title of a parcel do not know a priori which kinds of deed are recorded concerning it. For each transaction, they will thus have to examine all relevant deeds dealing with that parcel in the past, even those which may have been perfectly purged in previous transactions.

The cost of this repeated examining of deeds can be reduced with proper organization of the registry. In the short run, the easiest way to organize the information is by relying on indexes of grantors and grantees to locate the chain of transactions for a given parcel. However, this method is subject to errors, such as, for example, those caused by identical names and misspellings. * * *

Registration of Rights

Registration of rights (hereafter referred to as "registration," and often confusingly called "title registration") goes one crucial step further than recordation of deeds: instead of providing information about claims, it defines the rights. To do this, it performs a mandatory purge of claims before registering the rights. As in deed recordation, claims stemming from private transactions gain priority when transaction documents are first lodged with the registry. They are then subject, however, to substantive review by the registrar, in order to detect any potential conflict that might damage other property rights * * *. New and reallocated rights are registered only when the registrar determines that the intended transaction does not affect any other property right or that the holders of these affected rights have consented. When these conditions are met, the change in rights caused by the transaction is registered, antedating the effects of registration to the lodging date. (In a sense, any registry of rights thus contains a recording of deeds: its "lodgment" or "presentment" book is a temporary record of claims.) Otherwise, when the consent of an affected rightholder is lacking, registration is denied, and the conveying parties have to obtain the consents relevant to the originally intended transaction, restructure it to avoid damaging other rights, or desist.

NOTES AND QUESTIONS

1. One can perhaps summarize Arruñada's discussion of the differences between registration and recordation as follows. Registration resolves potential disputes about title ex ante, at the time of the transfer; recordation leaves disputes about title to be resolved ex post, once they arise. Registration confers rights in rem, in that the certificate of title is binding on third parties as well as on the parties to the transfer. Recordation by itself has no binding effect on third parties; recordation does no more than make

---

[20]   The rationale here is similar to the theory of the *numerus clausus* of property rights in Merrill and Smith (2000), who argue that the possibility that parties might invent idiosyncratic rights *in rem* would raise the information cost and thus the cost of contracting for all other participants (mainly, 26–34).

available for public inspection copies of in personam transactions (contracts, deed, liens, etc.). Under recordation, however, ex post litigation in the form of a quiet title action may draw upon records of past transactions to render judgments that have an in rem effect.

2.   In a sense, the registrar of deeds under the registration system stands in for the public of in rem duty holders. The property rights are given in rem effect precisely because the registrar has put in the ex ante effort to determine that such an effect is appropriate. Does this help explain why, according to an econometric study reported by Arruñada elsewhere, a more definitive effect given to property rights by the registration system correlates with a smaller number of forms of property the system will recognize (i.e., a stricter *numerus clausus* of property rights)? Benito Arruñada, Property Enforcement as Organized Consent, 19 J. L. Econ & Org. 401, 416–20 (2003). On one view, the *numerus clausus* is enforced in French law through the formalities required for recording interests in order to get in rem enforcement ex post. See Thomas W. Merrill & Henry E. Smith, Optimal Standardization in the Law of Property: The *Numerus Clausus* Principle, 110 Yale L.J. 1, 5 & n.8 (2000). Something similar may be true in Louisiana. See Alejandro M. Garro, The Louisiana Public Records Doctrine and the Civil Law Tradition 110–18, 150–82, 195–98 (1989).

3.   The registration system is thought to be more accurate than the recording system, but also more expensive. Among other things, it requires well-trained and non-corrupt officials to administer it. Debate about which system is better has raged for years. Compare Richard R. Powell, Registration of the Title to Land in the State of New York 69 (1938) (pro-recording); with Myres S. McDougal & John W. Brabner-Smith, Land Title Transfer: A Regression, 48 Yale L.J. 1125 (1939) (pro-registration). See also Matthew Baker et al., Optimal Title Search, 31 J. Legal Stud. 139 (2002) (the optimal title search does not include the entire record, which implies residual uncertainty). The Arruñada book excerpted above explores the evidence on this question as well as the incentives of the various actors involved in a system of land records. Note that many countries setting up land records for the first time opt for registration, but advanced countries with recordation face a somewhat different choice: whether the extra benefits of a registration system are worth the switching costs. See Joseph T. Janczyk, Land Title Systems, Scale of Operations, and Operating and Conversion Costs, 8 J. Legal Stud. 569 (1979). The benefits are likely to be less to the extent that a title insurance industry has emerged to furnish additional security of title to owners.

4.   Registration systems rely heavily on state officials and uniform administrative procedures to certify title to land. Although gross generalizations are perilous, given the many variations among registration systems, these features tend to make registration systems relatively inflexible, both in terms of how much effort officials put into any given title inquiry and in terms of the speed with which those officials generate registered deeds. Recording systems, which rely mostly on competing private actors (attorneys, title insurance companies) may be more flexible, in the sense that the resources devoted to title questions and the speed with which

title issues are resolved can be varied according to the value of the property and the urgency of completing any given transaction. Does this suggest that recording acts may have certain efficiencies overlooked in the traditional literature on tradeoffs between ex ante and ex post title determination?

2. AIRPLANES

Since the Civil Aeronautics Act of 1938, aviation law has been almost entirely federal, and it requires the registration of civil aircraft (which in turn requires proof of ownership) and the recordation of transfers of aircraft ownership as well as instruments affecting title such as security interests and leases. 49 U.S.C. § 44102(a) (2004); id. § 44107 (2004); 14 C.F.R. § 11; id. § 47.31(a) (2004). Until the conveyance or encumbrance is recorded, it is good only against (1) the transferor, and (2) third parties with actual notice. Id. § 44108(a). After recordation, an interest is good against "all persons." Id. § 44108(b). In *Philko Aviation, Inc. v. Shacket*, 462 U.S. 406, 409–11 (1983), the Supreme Court interpreted this provision as creating something like a "race-notice" system (which we discuss further, infra), thereby preempting *nemo dat*-style state laws that would permit unrecorded transfers to be valid against innocent third persons. Interestingly, while the statute speaks of "actual notice," this has been taken to include "not only knowledge that one's seller lacks good title but also knowledge of facts that would lead a reasonable person to inquire further into the seller's title." Shacket v. Philko Aviation, Inc., 841 F.2d 166, 170 (7th Cir. 1988) (Posner, J.).

Suppose that on December 1, 2004, A sells Blackcraft (the mythical prototypical airplane) to B, who then fails to file the bill of sale with the FAA. On January 15, 2005, A sells Blackcraft to C (who doesn't have notice of the earlier sale to B), who *does* file his bill of sale with the FAA. The holding in *Philko Aviation* implies that C, because he recorded first and didn't have notice, will own Blackcraft. C can rely on the lack of recordation at the time he bought Blackcraft, and the FAA registry does indeed function as a recording system from C's point of view.

3. SHIPS

Starting with the Ship Mortgage Act of 1920, federal law has provided for enforcement of mortgages on documented vessels of greater than five tons. See 46 U.S.C. § 31301 et seq. (modified and recodified in 1988). Conveyances of ships, including mortgages, are given full in rem effect against third parties only if they have been filed with the Secretary of Transportation pursuant to 46 U.S.C. § 31321. Interests which have not been filed may still be enforced against the grantor/mortgagor or his heir or devisee, or against "a person having actual notice of the sale, conveyance, mortgage, assignment or related instrument." Id. § 31321(a)(1)(C). Thus, the Ship Mortgage Act, like the FAA's registration system for airplanes, operates in practice like a "race-notice" recording act (again, see infra). The Ship Mortgage Act was designed to bring greater certainty to ship ownership, because many liens on vessels are valid without filing or possession, leading one commentator, quoting a New Orleans attorney, to observe that " '[l]iens on ships, i.e. maritime liens, are often hidden and ships acquire liens like dogs get fleas.' " Matthew J. Bauer, Marine Title Insurance, 12 Conn. Ins. L.J. 17, 23 (2005); see also Grant Gilmore & Charles L. Black, Jr., The Law of Admiralty 586–89 (2d ed. 1975). Because of these problems, a maritime title insurance industry, roughly analogous to its land-based counterpart, has arisen. See Bauer, supra.

Smaller vessels are subject to state registration schemes that operate much like automobile registration. See, e.g., Fla. Stat. Ann. § 328; Md. Code, Nat. Res., § 8–701 et seq. State vessel registration schemes vary in a fashion similar to those for auto registration. See 2 Benedict on Admiralty § 68b (7th ed. 2006).

4. AUTOMOBILES

In a way reminiscent of the federal regime for airplanes, state law provides for registration and certification of title to automobiles. Auto registration is a system under which owners have to pay a fee for the privilege of using the state's highways. Certification of title acts were passed later, at first to prevent theft. But they developed into a system for establishing the validity of ownership and security interests. To obtain a certificate of title, the owner submits an application with information including a statement of the applicant's title and each security interest in the automobile. When ownership is transferred, the owner must endorse and deliver the certificate of title to the transferee, and the transferee must then apply at the Department of Motor Vehicles for a new certificate of title within the prescribed time by presenting the endorsed certificate of title from the transferor.

States vary in what effect they give to the certification system. There are three varieties of statutes. First, "excepting" statutes provide that, when the statutory provisions on transfers of title aren't complied with, the transfer of title is invalid, except as between the two parties to the transaction. Second, "invalidating" statutes nullify a noncompliant transfer of title even as between the two parties to the transaction. Third, "nondirective" statutes provide for some penalty for noncompliance but do not affect the validity of the transfer of title. See Pamela Trimble, *Rudiger Charolais Ranches v. Van De Graaf Ranches*, and the Impact of Other State Laws on the UCC Rights of a Good Faith Purchaser, 48 Consumer Fin. L.Q. Rep. 504, 507 (1994).

The last, nondirective type, is the easiest to integrate with the Uniform Commercial Code: The UCC applies in full. Interestingly, even excepting and invalidating statutes have been held to give way to the UCC in allowing good faith purchasers in a noncomplying transaction to prevail. See, e.g., Island v. Warkenthien, 287 N.W.2d 487 (S.D. 1980); Heinrich v. Titus-Will Sales, 868 P.2d 169 (Wash. Ct. App. 1994). The net effect is to make what sound like systems analogous to Torrens-style (registration) systems for land into something like the recording systems, more equitable and oriented to the good faith purchaser. One major problem with any attempt at a definitive automobile title record is that cars can easily be taken to other jurisdictions. And a potential purchaser of an automobile has to worry that the vehicle is validly registered in another state.

Most states rely on state certificate of title acts for purposes of recording security interests in automobiles under Article 9 of the UCC (see Chapter VII). The lien is recorded on a state certificate of title, and potential transactors can ask the owner for a copy of the certificate in order to determine the status of the lien. The only potential problem arises before an application for a certificate of title is filed, but no actual case involving this gap seems to have come up. For details, see Lynn M. LoPucki & Elizabeth Warren, Secured Credit: A Systems Approach 423–38 (7th ed. 2012).

5. ART

Another type of personal property that might be considered a candidate for a registry is fine art. The ownership of art implicates two main legal problems—theft and forgeries. Owners of well-known works want to establish that they have the best rights in the work and that the work really is what it purports to be.

At present there is no central registry for title to art works. Some owners feel nervous about publicizing their ownership—at least before a theft has occurred. Until recently there have only been partial registries of stolen works.

To establish ownership of a work of art—and thereby avoid the hazards of other claims and the possibility of fakery—one has to establish the provenance of the work. Sources used include museum catalogs and records of past exhibitions. Owners and transactors often rely on *catalogues raisonnés*, which are usually compiled by an acknowledged expert and contain information on every known piece by an individual artist, including a physical description and illustration of the work, and its provenance and exhibition history. Other documentary evidence (letters, memoirs, etc.) can also be used as evidence.

Researching a provenance is not only costly, but often far less reliable than researching records in a central registry. A dramatic illustration of the problem is the famous recent forgery perpetrated by two Britons, John Drewe (*né* John Cockett) and John Myatt. Myatt forged over 200 paintings, many with acrylic paint and K-Y Jelly, and Drewe sold the works, mostly though London auction houses. But unlike most forgeries that rely on their resemblance to a master's style, Drewe forged the documents that would be used for the provenance of the works.

After getting friends to sign letters attesting to their ownership of the paintings and their authenticity, he then forged and altered correspondence and catalogs in museum libraries. (The plot was discovered only when Drewe's girlfriend called the police.) Peter Landesmann, A 20th-Century Master Scam, N.Y. Times, July 18, 1999, at SM32; Eamonn O'Neil, The Art of Deception, Scotsman, July 6, 2002, at 12. Provenance is thus like recording in being based on a history of transactions, but unlike recording, the evidence is not kept in a systematic and secure fashion. Recently, companies like Artory have begun to provide a blockchain-based service that combines aspects of provenance and chain or title in a more decentralized fashion. Because a record is no better than its starting point, Artory will only register works vetted by a "record issuer." Françoise Birnholz & Kelsey Barthold, Back to the Future: Sorting Old Law from New Technology in Blockchain Smart Contract Applications & Assessing the Need for Regulation, 89 Geo. Wash. L. Rev. Arguendo 96, 112–14 (2021). In a characteristically ironic move, the non-fungible tokens (NFTs) that make such record keeping possible are now being used in the art world to create unique digital artworks with their own scarcity value.

Figure 8-3
John Myatt in His Studio

(Motto: "In prison they called me Picasso")

Photo: Jean-Philippe Defaut/The New York Times/Redux. Today Myatt runs a business that used to be called *Genuine Fakes*. See http://www.johnmyatt.com, the official website of John Myatt, the artist "involved in the *'biggest art fraud of the 20th century'*."

6. INTELLECTUAL PROPERTY

Intellectual property is a form of personal property. But much of intellectual property law is federal law—unlike the law of personal property generally. We consider here the registration provisions for the major types of intellectual property: patent, trademark, and copyright.

In the case of patents, part of one section of the Patent Act deals with transfers and their effects against third parties:

> An assignment, grant, or conveyance shall be void as against any subsequent purchaser or mortgagee for a valuable consideration, without notice, unless it is recorded in the Patent and Trademark Office within three months from its date or prior to the date of such subsequent purchase or mortgage.

35 U.S.C. § 261. This system is like a notice recording act with a grace period. (For an explanation of the types of recording acts, see infra Part F.) Some have argued that "assignment, grant, or conveyance" includes granting a security interest. See, e.g., Raymond T. Nimmer, Revised Article 9 and Intellectual Property Asset Financing, 53 Me. L. Rev. 287, 320–22, 335–37 (2001). The Ninth Circuit has held the opposite. In re Cybernetic Services, Inc., 252 F.3d 1039, 1052 (9th Cir. 2001).

Notice that the records kept by the patent office are like registration in another respect: the Patent and Trademark Office (PTO) is called upon to evaluate the application for the patent, and those questioning its validity can under some circumstances challenge a patent's validity at the PTO. In the early nineteenth century, a system of minimal examination prevailed, which relied more on the courts to sort out which patents were actually valid. Somewhat confusingly, this system of minimal examination is called "registration" (as opposed to "examination") in the patent context. Compare F. Scott Kieff, The Case for Registering Patents and the Law and Economics of Patent-Obtaining Rules, 45 B.C. L. Rev. 55 (2003) (proposing "soft-look" registration) with Jay P. Kesan, Carrots and Sticks to Create a Better Patent System, 17 Berkeley Tech. L.J. 763, 775–76 (2002) (advocating tightened standard for granting patents at the PTO for applicants who do not elect the "enhanced prior art disclosure" option). Historically, the United States was unique in having a first-to-invent system, although this was recently changed in the Leahy-Smith America Invents Act of 2011, adopting a first-to-file system. This brings the U.S. into line with other countries and makes the patent system more like other registration regimes.

For federal trademarks, the Lanham Act sets up a similar system for the "assignment" of trademarks:

> An assignment shall be void against any subsequent purchaser for valuable consideration without notice, unless the prescribed information reporting the assignment is recorded in the United States Patent and Trademark Office within 3 months after the date of the assignment or prior to the subsequent purchase.

15 U.S.C. § 1060(a)(4). Again, this is comparable to the notice-plus-grace-period type of recording act. "Assignments" clearly include transfers of title but may not include security interests. For the complex interaction between federal intellectual property registration and (state law) Article 9, see, e.g., Nimmer, supra.

Copyrights are subject to a much looser regime. The history of copyright over the last century has been characterized by a move away from formalities. Registration is not required to claim copyright, but timely registration is advantageous for making statutory damages available when actual damages are hard to prove (and for being able to file certain infringement actions, for evidentiary purposes, etc.). But failure to register does not invalidate a copyright. 17 U.S.C. § 409–412. To comply with the Berne Convention, Congress eliminated the requirement of registration prior to suit for copyright owners from other Berne member countries.

Some recent work has examined the emergence of extralegal registries adjacent to intellectual property law in contexts where creators use informal norms and rules to regulate use rather than formal intellectual property protection. Skaters have established a registry for roller derby names, and a skater who steals a name that has been registered might be ostracized in the derby community. David Fagundes, Talk Derby to Me: Emergent Intellectual Property Norms Governing Roller Derby Pseudonyms, 90 Tex. L. Rev. 1093 (2012). Likewise, since 1946, an informal "Clown Egg Register" has operated in England that permits clowns to claim unique makeup designs by painting them on eggs. David Fagundes & Aaron Perzanowski, Clown Eggs, 94 Notre Dame L. Rev. 1313 (2019). What does the emergence of these sorts of registries suggest about the functions, benefits, and costs of recording?

7. CASH AND NEGOTIABILITY

As mentioned by Baird and Jackson, cash illustrates the good faith purchaser rule at its widest. With cash there is no duty to inquire about where it came from and whether the holder has good title. This makes cash very liquid. A thief does not obtain title to stolen cash, but one can get good title to cash even from a thief. There is not only no registry of cash, but even an original owner who could prove by using serial numbers that certain cash was his cannot recover it from a present good-faith holder.

Cash is sometimes said to be the extreme of "negotiability." A written instrument is "negotiable" when it is "capable of being transferred by delivery or indorsement when the transferee takes the instrument for value, in good faith, and without notice of conflicting title claims or defenses." Black's Law Dictionary (9th ed. 2009). Cashier's checks and bearer bonds would be examples. Negotiability is useful where the issuer is more able to bear the risk of loss or there is some special value in avoiding inquiry on the part of transferees.

Negotiability takes the good faith purchaser exception to *nemo dat* the furthest. In U.S. law, an innocent holder can acquire good title to cash and negotiable instruments even with a thief in the chain back to the original owner.

F. RECORDING ACTS

As explored in the excerpt by Arruñada, land records can be divided into recordation and registration. Nearly all localities in the United States use recordation. The key attribute of recording is that it generates, as a matter of law, constructive notice to all subsequent purchasers in the chain of title. Thus, recording acts create a powerful incentive for purchasers to file their deeds (and mortgagees their mortgages, etc.) in order to block possible good faith purchaser claims by subsequent transferees. Those interested in the state of title can examine the records, or more likely hire an expert to examine them (or a duplicate set maintained privately by the title company) and produce an "abstract" or report. From time to time, various jurisdictions in the United States have experimented with registration statutes, called Torrens Acts after the Australian law that inspired them. Most of these experiments failed, and today Minneapolis-St. Paul is the only major area still covered by a Torrens title registration system. See Kimball Foster, Certificates of Possessory Title: A Sensible Addition to Minnesota's Successful Torrens System, 40 Wm. Mitchell L. Rev. 112 (2013). As Arruñada recounts, most of the rest of the world (including Germany, Great Britain, most of the other commonwealth countries, and most developing countries) uses registration.

The first recording acts were very simple and were what we would now call the "race" type, under which the first of two property claimants to record has the better claim. These acts in effect created an exception to *nemo dat* much broader than the good faith purchaser rule, allowing any subsequent purchaser to prevail over the holder of a prior unrecorded interest. (The race statute's exception to *nemo dat* would be unavailable to anyone with respect to an interest that had been previously recorded.) This led to great unfairness in certain circumstances, as where someone knowing of a prior transaction would "purchase" the land from the grantor—who would have nothing to transfer under *nemo dat*—and then would record first. The prior purchaser was out of luck. To avoid this result, courts held that subsequent purchasers with notice of a prior conveyance would not get the protection of the statute. Marshall v. Fisk, 6 Mass. (5 Tyng) 24, 30 (1809); Farnsworth v. Childs, 4 Mass. (3 Tyng) 637, 639 (1808). Courts also developed robust doctrines of constructive notice based on possession (especially open and notorious possession), M'Mechan v. Griffing, 20 Mass. (3 Pick.) 149, 154 (1825), or even based on the publishing of the conveyance in the newspaper, Curtis v. Mundy, 44 Mass. (3 Met.) 405, 408 (1841).

In response to these developments, legislatures, with Massachusetts again in the lead, started to insert language in recording acts requiring good faith or lack of actual notice on the part of the subsequent purchaser. See 14 Powell on Real Property § 82.02[1][c][iii]. These "notice" statutes fundamentally altered the nature of the recording acts. Whereas a race statute in effect creates an exception to the good faith purchaser rule, a notice statute preserves the good faith purchaser rule in full force, with the modification that recordation provides constructive notice to subsequent purchasers. In a third variation, the race-notice statutes were adopted in the nineteenth century by several Middle Atlantic states (Maryland, New Jersey, New York, and Pennsylvania) in nearly identical language. These acts combined the features of the race statutes and the notice statutes, requiring in effect that persons be both good faith purchasers and be the first to record in order to prevail over other claimants. The Pennsylvania version spread to the Northwest Territory with the result that many of the states of the Old Northwest (e.g., Indiana, Ohio, Michigan, and Wisconsin, but not Illinois) have race-notice statutes.

Carol Rose has seen in the history of the recording acts a story of legislatures adopting "crystalline" rules followed by judicial decisions that soften the rules with various equitable defenses and qualifications, turning them into "mud." Carol Rose, Crystals and Mud in Property Law, 40 Stan. L. Rev. 577, 585–90 (1988). (The portion of this article dealing with mortgage foreclosures and redemptions is excerpted in Chapter VII.) The early history of recording acts certainly conforms to a pattern of crystals followed by mud. But it is less clear that any cycling between these poles has continued. Perhaps because the notice and race-notice statutes adopted in the nineteenth century have a built-in safety valve to prevent the worst abuses of the pure race statutes, courts were nowhere as aggressive in their construction of notice and race-notice statutes as they were of race statutes. Later in the nineteenth century, courts seem to have dropped the idea that possession by another (other than adverse possession) would itself cause subsequent purchasers to lose the protection of the recording act. To be sure, courts did make exceptions for situations of direct misrepresentation by the first purchaser to the second purchaser. See Marling v. Milwaukee Realty Co., 106 N.W. 844 (Wis. 1906); Guffey v. O'Reiley, 88 Mo. 418 (1885). As with many equitable interventions (and inventions), the protection of the good faith purchaser has morphed from a more contextual analysis to something more rule-like. See Henry E. Smith, Equity as Meta-Law, 130 Yale L.J. 105, 1094–98, 1108–10 (2021). Overall, however, it may be that we have achieved something of a stable equilibrium with respect to the understanding and application of recording acts today. (Which is not to say that application of the statutes is easy!)

Before we turn in more detail to the various types of recording acts, it is important to know how a title search does—and sometimes does not—work.

Title Search and "Chain of Title"

Recording acts require that public officials, such as the county clerk or recorder of deeds, maintain an office in which deeds and other documents affecting title may be recorded. Typically there will be a recorder's office in every county in a state. The employees who run these offices do little if any screening of the documents submitted for recordation. Thus, not only deeds and mortgages, but also judicial judgments, letters, and memoranda may be recorded. Every recording office has at least two indexes: a grantee index and a grantor index. As their names suggest, the grantee index includes, by name, all grantees referenced in the documents that have been submitted for recordation; the grantor index includes, by name, all grantors referenced in the documents that have been submitted for recordation. Grantors and grantees are arranged alphabetically, although there may be a separate index for each year. Some recorders' offices—but not all—also keep something called a tract index, in which all documents submitted for recordation are listed by the legal description of the property under the surveying system established by the Land Ordinance of 1785 (or an equivalent parcel indexing system developed for a metes and bounds state). This is extremely useful, either as a shortcut to doing a title search or as a check against the search results produced using the grantor and grantee indexes.

In jurisdictions where the search mechanism is an index by grantor and grantee, performing a title search involves tracing the series of transactions from one's would-be transferor back to a "root of title" and then tracing forward. First one looks in the grantee index for one's transferor to find the deed by which he took from his predecessor, the deed from the predecessor's predecessor, and so on. This ensures that the would-be transferor obtained his title through a chain of legitimate transfers. In many states, marketable title acts (see below) allow the search to stop at some date in the past—say 30 or 40 years ago—rather than needing to trace all the way to the sovereign or some other "root." Second, once one has gone back far enough, one repeats the process going forward in time through the grantor index. Tracing forward involves investigating what each of the people discovered in the grantee index did with the title in the relevant period. One might think that this period is the time between execution of the deed to the grantor and the date of execution of the deed from the grantor to the next link in the chain, but this would be inadequate. Instead, for each of the people in the chain, one must look in the grantor index between (i) the date of execution of the deed to that person and (ii) the date that the deed from that person to the next person *was recorded*. One is responsible for knowing what each person might have granted from the time of execution of the deed to that person but before it is recorded, and one has to check for possible transactions after that person executed a deed to another but before that deed was recorded. Anything outside the period bounded by (i) and (ii)—the period before the execution of the deed to X and after the recording of the deed from X—is said to be outside the "chain of title" and as to such matters the land records do *not* furnish constructive notice. Consequently, if something is outside the chain of title (outside the legally defined reasonable search), the good faith purchaser exception to *nemo dat* applies.

[handwritten margin note: if not btw ① and ② ↓ outside chain ↓ good faith purchaser may apply ✓]

The chain of title concept is a compromise between a more thorough but more expensive search and a less thorough but more manageable search. The mechanics are best appreciated though an example.

Example. On April 15, 2021 you are considering a purchase from D of a parcel known as Blackacre, located in the town of Springfield. You must perform a title search to ascertain the state of the title. Here is a sketch, assuming that the state only requires a title search going back 40 years. More might be required in other jurisdictions.

Running backwards in the Grantee Index:

1.   Look up D in the Grantee Index and find his grantor, C. The index refers to a deed from C to D on April 1, 2010, recorded that day.

2.   Search C backwards from April 1, 2010 until you find a reference to a deed from B, dated October 1, 2001 and recorded on April 15, 2006. *[handwritten: record-]*

3.   Search under B backwards from October 1, 2001 and find a deed from A on January 30, 1983 and recorded that day.

4.   Search A backwards to 1981. A owned Blackacre on January 1, 1966.

Running forward in the Grantor Index:

1.   Search A forward in the Grantor Index from January 1, 1981 to January 30, 1983 (deed to B).

2.   Search B forward from January 30, 1983 until *April 15, 2006* (recordation of deed to C).

3.   Search C forward from *October 1, 2001* (date of deed to C) until April 1, 2010 (deed to D).

4.   Search D forward from April 1, 2010 until the present.

Chain of Title (from the minimal search):

January 1, 1981—January 30, 1983: A owns and then conveys to B.

January 30, 1983—October 1, 2001: B owns and then conveys to C, but the deed is not recorded until April 15, 2006.

October 1, 2001—April 1, 2010: C owns and then conveys to D.

April 1, 2010—April 15, 2021: D owns.

In a recording system, the official keeping the records has a duty to accept and file records of the proper form, but has no duty to investigate the state of title. In this example, we assumed that all the recorded deeds were legitimate. This is not always so.

Types of Recording Acts

Today in the United States, there are three types of recording acts:

1.   Race. Under a race statute, as between successive grantees of interests in real property, the first to record prevails. This was the original type of statute, but now at most two states have a simple race statute. So if O sells to A and then sells to B, but B records before A, then B has title; A has only a claim against O. Race statutes create an exception to the *nemo dat* principle and a partial exception to the good faith purchaser doctrine, insofar as the first party to record wins even if she has actual notice of a prior conveyance. An example of a race statute:

> (a)   No (i) conveyance of land, or (ii) contract to convey, or (iii) option to convey, or (iv) lease of land for more than three years shall be valid to pass any property interest as against lien creditors or purchasers for a valuable consideration from the donor, bargainor or lessor but from the time of registration thereof in the county where the land lies * * *

N.C. Stat. § 47–18. See Rowe v. Walker, 441 S.E.2d 156 (N.C. Ct. App. 1994), aff'd, 455 S.E.2d 160 (N.C. 1995).

2.   Notice. Under a notice statute, as between successive grantees of an interest in real property, a subsequent purchaser for value prevails over a prior grantee only if the subsequent purchaser lacked notice of the earlier conveyance. Jurisdictions have used varied terms to differentiate among forms of notice. See, e.g., Blevins v. Johnson Cty., 746 S.W.2d 678, 683 (Tenn. 1988) (noting that state's courts consider "inquiry notice" a species of "actual notice" and citing others that treat it as a species of "constructive notice"). In general, notice may be actual or constructive. A person has actual notice of an adverse interest if that person has actual knowledge of it, while that person has constructive notice of an adverse interest if: (1) the person has implied notice of the interest, because the person has acquired knowledge of particular facts related to the interest in question that would provoke a person of common sense and prudence to make reasonable inquiries which would have led to the discovery of the adverse interest; or (b) the person has inquiry notice of the interest, because a person conducting standard due diligence with common sense and prudence would have discovered the adverse interest; or (c) the person has record notice of the interest, because a document evidencing an adverse interest is recorded in the chain of title to the property. Again, jurisdictions may vary in particulars as to how they describe these forms of notice or whether they recognize certain forms of notice at all. See Restatement (Fourth) of Property, Vol. 5, Div. IV, Ch. 3, §§ 3.1–3.2 (Am.

L. Inst. Council Draft No. 4, Sept. 24, 2021); In re Daylight Dairy Prod., Inc., 125 B.R. 1, 3 (Bankr. D. Mass. 1991) ("Massachusetts law does not recognize inquiry notice of unrecorded deeds or mortgages.").

Because recording imparts constructive notice of an interest to all others, note the incentive to record immediately in order to be protected from subsequent good faith purchasers. An example of a notice statute:

> A conveyance of an estate in fee simple, fee tail or for life, or a lease for more than seven years from the making thereof, * * * shall not be valid as against any person, except the grantor or lessor, his heirs and devisees and persons having actual notice of it, unless it * * * is recorded in the registry of deeds for the county or district in which the land to which it relates lies.

Mass. Gen. Laws Ann. Ch. 183, § 4.

3.   Race-Notice. Under a race-notice statute, as between successive grantees of an interest in real property, a subsequent purchaser for value prevails over a prior grantee only if: (1) the subsequent purchaser lacked notice of the earlier interest; and (2) the subsequent purchaser records first. This is like the race statute but solves the problem of the unscrupulous subsequent buyer under the race approach. An example of a race-notice statute:

> Every conveyance of real property or an estate for years therein, other than a lease for a term not exceeding one year, is void as against any subsequent purchaser or mortgagee of the same property, or any part thereof, in good faith and for a valuable consideration, whose conveyance is first duly recorded * * *

Cal. Civ. Code § 1214.

4.   Mixed regimes. Some states apply a race regime to mortgages but another type of recording act to conveyances in general. Compare the following two Arkansas statutes:

> Every mortgage of real estate shall be a lien on the mortgaged property from the time it is filed in the recorder's office for record, and not before. The filing shall be notice to all persons of the existence of the mortgage.

Ark. Code Ann. § 18–40–102.

> (a) Every deed, bond, or instrument of writing affecting the title, in law or equity, to any real or personal property, within this state which is, or may be, required by law to be acknowledged or proved and recorded shall be constructive notice to all persons from the time the instrument is filed for record in the office of the recorder of the proper county.
>
> (b) No deed, bond, or instrument of writing for the conveyance of any real estate, or by which the title thereto may be affected in law or equity, made or executed after December 21, 1846, shall be good or valid against a subsequent purchaser of the real

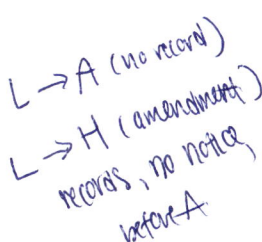

notice

estate for a valuable consideration without actual notice thereof or against any creditor of the person executing such an instrument obtaining a judgment or decree which by law may be a lien upon the real estate unless the deed, bond, or instrument, duly executed and acknowledged or proved as required by law, is filed for record in the office of the clerk and ex officio recorder of the county where the real estate is situated.

Ark. Code Ann. § 14–15–404. See also Pa. Stat. Ann. tit. 21, § 351 (race-notice statute for conveyances other than mortgages); id. § 622 (race statute for mortgages).

Some states allow a "grace period" for filing such that the bona fide purchaser prevails over the prior grantee only if the prior grantee fails to record within the grace period. See, e.g., Del. Code Ann. tit. 25, § 153 (providing for 15-day grace period).

The Shelter Rule

Finally, courts have interpreted recording acts to create an exception for certain transferees who otherwise would be barred from obtaining title because they are not good faith purchasers for value. Suppose O conveys to A, who does not record. Then O conveys to B who gives value and has no notice of the prior conveyance to A. B then records. Under a race, notice, or race-notice recording act, B should prevail over A. But what happens if B then gifts the land to C (so C is not a bona fide purchaser *for value* under the recording act), or B sells to C, even though C was aware of the prior deed to A? A literal reading of the statutes might lead one to think that C should lose to A under these circumstances, since C is not a good faith purchaser. But under what has been called the Shelter Rule, courts have held that C prevails against A. See, e.g., Jones v. Independent Title Co., 147 P.2d 542, 543 (Cal. 1944). Once B prevails against A, they have reasoned, B should be given all the attributes of ownership, including the right to make normal *nemo-dat* style transfers of the property. If the rule were otherwise, then B would have less than full ownership, because he could not give away the property or sell it to those with notice of the transfer to A.

The Shelter Rule has limits of its own: If B in our hypothetical seeks to transfer the property back to O, the original owner, the Shelter Rule does not apply; under the "original owner exception" to the Shelter Rule, O cannot shelter under B's rights. See, e.g., Chergosky v. Crosstown Bell, Inc., 463 N.W.2d 522 (Minn. 1990). It is generally thought that the opportunities for collusion in such an arrangement are too great, and precluding B from conveying B's full rights to O does not significantly curtail B's market.

Recording Doctrines Based on Chain of Title

The recording acts in conjunction with the notion of chain of title define a legally required search for one who wishes to take advantage of the protection afforded good faith purchasers under the act. If a deed or encumbrance would be revealed by the legally required search—putting it within the chain of title—then it affords constructive notice. But if the deed or encumbrance is outside that search (not in the chain of title), it does not afford constructive notice to a subsequent purchaser for value and so its holder loses out to the GFPV. As we will see, things are not so tidy in light of off-record matters that can affect the title of even a GFPV, but even the notion of chain of title and legally reasonable search can be difficult to define around the edges. Consider some perennial problems that arise when the only search mechanism is an index by grantor and grantee. (Note that these problems may be less likely to arise where there is a tract index or searchable electronic land records.)

The "Wild Deed." A wild deed is one deemed outside the chain of title because a prior conveyance in the chain was not recorded. A wild deed can arise (1) when a purported grantor records the transfer of an interest that the grantor does not in fact have or (2) when a grantee records before her grantor, as the following example illustrates. Say O grants to A, who does not record. O then grants to B, who does not record. What if then B conveys to C, and then C, A, and B record in that order? Who would win in a notice or race-notice jurisdiction, A or C? C's is a wild deed because it is not connected up to the common grantor by a continuous chain of recording, and C is sometimes said to be a "stranger to the title." Searchers of traditional records will not find the wild deed in a conventional chain of title search, because the name of the grantee, here B, would be unknown to searchers. Moreover, in the period between A's recording and B's recording, a purchaser from A would have no way of finding C's deed. See Board of Education of Minneapolis v. Hughes, 136 N.W., 1095 (Minn. 1912). The majority of courts agree that one cannot benefit from the recording act's exception to *nemo dat* if one traces one's ownership to a wild deed. For recent examples, see Salt Lake County v. Metro West Ready Mix, Inc., 89 P.3d 155 (Utah 2004); Holland v. Hattaway, 438 So.2d 456, 470 (Fla. Dist. Ct. App. 1983); see also Zimmer v. Sundell, 296 N.W. 589 (Wis. 1941). Some courts simply deny that the holder of a wild deed is a good faith purchaser, on the rationale that someone in C's position has constructive notice and could relatively easily make sure that her grantor's (B's) deed is recorded before she records (or purchases, for that matter).

Late (and Early) Recorded Deeds. Problems can arise if someone records so late that another branch of title gets started in the meantime. Consider this scenario: O sells to A and then to B, who has actual notice of the O-to-A sale. B then records and then A records. Then B sells to C, who has no actual notice of the O-to-A sale. C then records. First, C cannot take advantage of the shelter rule. (Do you see why?) Under the majority approach to this question, the chain of title concept makes C the winner. When doing a search forward, C is supposed to search O as a grantor from the time O acquired the interest until the time that B recorded. At that latter point A has not recorded yet, but it would be burdensome for C to have to search O as grantor all the way down to the present. See Morse v. Curtis, 2 N.E. 929 (Mass. 1885); see also Restatement (Fourth) of Property, Vol. 5, Div. IV, Ch. 4, § 4.4 (Am. L. Inst. Council Draft No. 4, Sept. 24, 2021). Yet some courts do go beyond the classic chain of title and require searches from each grantor in one's chain of title down to the present, which would pick up A's deed in our example. In such jurisdictions, C would have constructive notice of A's deed, and A would prevail over C. See Woods v. Garnett, 16 So. 390, 392 (Miss. 1894).

Similarly, if someone conveys land before acquiring it, the earlier conveyance is outside the chain of title of a later purchaser and so would not, even if recorded, furnish constructive notice. Thus, if O conveys Blackacre to A, then acquires Blackacre and records, and conveys it to B, A might invoke estoppel by deed. Nevertheless, most courts would hold that there being no reasonable way for B to know of A, B prevails over A. See, e.g., Sabo v. Horvath, 559 P.2d 1038, 1044 (Alaska 1976); Wheeler v. Young, 55 A. 670 (Conn. 1903); see also Restatement (Fourth) of Property, Vol. 5, Div. IV, Ch. 4, § 4.3 (Am. L. Inst. Council Draft No. 4, Sept. 24, 2021). But, as with the late recorded deed, some courts do hold that a deed like A's if recorded furnishes constructive notice to B, thereby holding B to a more stringent search. See 11 Thompson on Real Property § 92.09(c)(2)(B)(i), at 185–86 (David A. Thomas ed., 3d ed. 2015).

"Mother Hubbard" Clauses. Sometimes deeds will use a general description of a collection of lands without specifically enumerating them. For example, a deed might convey " 'all interest of whatsoever nature in all working interests and overriding royalty interest in all Oil and Gas Leases in Coffey County, Kansas, owned by them whether or not the same are specifically enumerated above . . .' " Luthi v. Evans, 576 P.2d 1064, 1067 (Kan. 1978). Such a deed is valid as between the parties, but such a deed does not impart constructive notice to subsequent purchasers. Such a description does not permit the deed to be indexed properly in a tract index, and even a subsequent purchaser who finds such a deed would have a lot of investigating to do to figure out which parcels the deed covered and what happened to them. Generally "Mother Hubbard" clauses do not on their own furnish constructive notice to subsequent purchasers. A grantee of a deed with such a clause should file in the land records an affidavit with a specific description of the lands conveyed or covered.

Restrictions on Adjacent Tracts. In a somewhat similar fashion, an owner may convey parcels while restricting retained land. This is particularly common in subdivisions. What if the developer sells Lot 1 with a reciprocal covenant that Lot 1 and adjacent Lot 2 (and perhaps other lots in the area) will be used for residential purposes only? The developer then sells Lot 2 without any such restriction. Some courts hew closely to the chain of title and emphasize the burden on the subsequent purchaser and hold that a purchaser of Lot 2 without actual notice is not bound. See, e.g., Spring Lakes v. O.F.M. Co., 467 N.E.2d 537 (Ohio 1984); Buffalo Academy of the Sacred Heart v. Boehm Bros., Inc., 196 N.E. 42 (N.Y. 1935). Other courts require searchers to look at the deeds for adjacent parcels and find constructive notice, especially if the parcels are part of the same subdivision. See Guillette v. Daly Dry Wall, 325 N.E.2d 572, 574 (Mass. 1975) (purchaser is required to look through other conveyances in the same subdivision by the same grantor); Finley v. Glenn, 154 A. 299, 301 (Pa. 1931) (purchaser is responsible for restrictions contained in conveyances from his grantor that affect the purchased parcel); see also Restatement (Fourth) of Property, Vol. 5, Div. IV, Ch. 3, § 3.2 cmt. f (Am. L. Inst. Council Draft No. 4, Sept. 24, 2021) ("[A] subsequent purchaser is charged with inquiry notice of claims or encumbrances that would be discovered by a purchaser engaging in standard due diligence, i.e., those restrictions that would be apparent based on a reasonable examination of the property. When a party argues that a purchaser is on inquiry notice by virtue of a common plan, an evaluation of the circumstances should take into account the degree of uniformity of appearance or type of use, as well as the presence or absence of other facts (such as the existence of a homeowner's association for enforcement) suggesting the property may be encumbered."). See also *Sanborn v. McLean* on the "common plan doctrine" in Chapter IX. Also in that chapter we will see how easements can arise in ways other than by grant. Such easements (by implication, necessity, estoppel) constitute yet another source of off-record risks for the prospective purchaser.

Improper Indexing. Sometimes instruments will be improperly recorded. Somewhat surprisingly, a majority of courts have held that indexing is not part of recordation and so not essential to the giving of constructive notice. A minority of courts have held that a failure to index, or sometimes incorrect indexing, can prevent the giving of constructive notice. As one Iowa court put it, without a means to locate it, a single deed in the voluminous land records "might as well be buried in the earth as in a mass of records without a clue to its whereabouts, or . . . the instrument might as well be written on a slate or copied into the Recorder's family Bible." Barney v. McCarty, 15 Iowa 510, 521 (1864); see also Restatement (Fourth) of Property, Vol. 5, Div. IV, Ch. 4, § 4.2 (Am. L. Inst. Council Draft No. 4, Sept. 24, 2021) (adopting minority approach). Variants of the same name may lead to difficulties in constructing a chain of title. As between the recorder of an improperly indexed interest and a later searcher, who can more easily deal with the problem?

All errors are not created equal. Traditionally, a reasonable searcher must search for very close variants of a name, especially if they sound alike and the differences are small, but not distant ones, especially if they begin with a different letter ("Cheffey" versus "Sheffey"). Similarly, errors in descriptions can deprive a deed of the constructive notice-giving effect, depending on how confusing they are. (The Mother Hubbard clause presents a related problem.)

PROBLEMS

In the following conveyances for value, what is the result under each type of statute? [Hint: In working though the problems, begin with the last conveyance, chronologically speaking, and then work back toward conveyances earlier in time. Once you find a party that prevails under the recording act, that party will generally prevail against all earlier claimants.]

1.   O conveys to A. O then conveys to B, who is unaware of the conveyance to A. B records immediately. Then A records.

2.   O conveys to A. O then conveys to B, who is aware of the conveyance to A. B records immediately. Then A records.

3.   O conveys to A, who does not record. Then O conveys to B, who also does not record. Then O conveys to C, who does not record. First assume that B and C are each unaware of the previous grants from O. Then consider: What if each of them *is* aware?

4.   O conveys to A. O then conveys to B, who has no knowledge of A's deed. Then A records. B then records and sells to C.

5.   O conveys to A. O then conveys to B, who has no knowledge of A's deed. Then A records. B then records and sells to O. (This is the same situation as in Problem 4, except C is replaced by O).

6.   O conveys to A. O then conveys to B who has actual notice of the deed from O to A. B records, and then A records. Then B sells to C.

7.   O conveys to A before O has any title. A immediately records. O then acquires title from X and records. O then conveys to B.

8.   O conveys to A. O then conveys to B, who does not record. B conveys to C who records immediately. A conveys to D. Then A and D both record, and finally B records.

9.   O owns adjacent parcels and sells parcel 1 to A and includes in the deed a covenant to restrict parcel 2 to residential use. Then O sells parcel 2 to B without mentioning the restriction, but mentions a subdivision plan in the deed. Is B bound by the covenant?

10.   O conveys a fee simple to A, who does not record. O then enters into a land sale contract with B, which obligates B to pay to O a down payment and make a series of payments; after the last payment is made, O will convey a deed to B in fee simple. B records the contract but finds out about the prior O-to-A deed before making the final payment. Assume O is judgment-proof.

At this point the attentive reader may be wondering whether there can be circular priorities. The answer is yes, especially in situations of mortgages and other liens, which present a classic brain-teaser. Consider the situation where O owns Blackacre and mortgages it to A for $30,000. A does not record the mortgage. O then mortgages Blackacre to B for $4000. B records but has notice of A's mortgage. O then mortgages to C for $5000, and C records. The fund for distribution (say from a foreclosure) is insufficient to satisfy all three liens. For a variety of solutions and discussion of judicial approaches, see, e.g., 4 American Law of Property § 17.33; Carville D. Benson, Jr., Circuity of Lien—A Problem in Priorities, 19 Minn. L. Rev. 139, 153 (1935); Albert Kocourek, Note, Diversities De La Ley: A First-Rate Legal Puzzle—A Problem in Priorities, 29 Ill. L. Rev. 952, 955 (1935); see also 2 Grant Gilmore, Security Interests In Personal Property 1020–46 (1965).

Electronic Land Records

Land records are increasingly computerized and even available on the Internet. The first step in migrating to electronic recordation is to scan paper title documents and organize them into a simple database, akin to a spreadsheet, with possibly the addition of a parcel identifier number. Statutes are needed in order to give electronic filing, online notice, and electronic searches legal effect, and legislatures are beginning to do so, with a majority having passed the Uniform Real Property Electronic Recording Act (URPERA). Further legal implications from computerization of land records may be on the horizon. As long as records can be searched electronically by grantor and grantee, the type of search that is cost-effective increases, which can be expected to create pressure to expand the notions of "chain of title" and constructive notice. Recall that chain of title is based on the limited search, described earlier, that is reasonable to expect a prospective purchaser to engage in. Electronic records can be expected to have an even greater impact if they allow search by tract or property location rather just by grantor and grantee. The most advanced systems are beginning to use geographic information systems (GIS) that integrate a variety of information on an interactive map. The demand for electronic record keeping is reflected in the adoption by mortgage industry participants of the Mortgage Electronic Registrations Systems, Inc. (MERS), which is unlike the public records in not being transparent (a feature which has made it the subject of ongoing litigation, see Chapter VII). On the other hand, online land records raise issues about privacy, including the handling of personal information. See, e.g., Ostergren v. Cuccinelli, 615 F.3d 263, 267–68 (4th Cir. 2010) (imperfect redaction of social security numbers from recorded documents); see also Reid K. Weisbord & Stewart Sterk, The Commodification of Public Land Records, 97 Notre Dame L. Rev. (forthcoming).

The legal status of electronic records is still being established but their principal advantage stems from their searchability. Consider again the concepts of constructive notice and chain of title in the light of electronic search of land records. The wild deed, the late (and early) recorded deed, the restriction on adjacent land, and misindexing are all easier for subsequent searchers to deal with in an electronic search, especially if search by tract is possible. Nonetheless, decisions will have to be made, most probably in passing statutes, to redraw the boundaries of the new broader notion of chain of title in some cases. Would a subsequent searcher be able to prove that, after a diligent search, she was still unable to find the earlier deed? Cases have yet to establish the required parameters of electronic search. Although overruled on other grounds, one court has endorsed an overall "diligent search" or reasonableness approach in evaluating the steps searchers should have taken and the documents searchers should have located. First Citizens Nat. Bank v. Sherwood, 817 A.2d 501, 505 (Pa. Super. Ct. 2003), rev'd on other grounds, 879 A.2d 178 (Pa. 2005). For a thorough discussion of these issues, see Emily Bayer-Pacht, The Computerization of Land Records: How Advances in Recording Systems Affect the Rationale Behind Some Existing Chain of Title Doctrines, 32 Cardozo L. Rev. 337 (2010); see also Dale A. Whitman, Are We There Yet? The Case for a Uniform Electronic Recording Act, 24 W. New Eng. L. Rev. 245 (2002); Tanya D. Marsh, Foreclosures and the Failure of the American Land Title Recording System, 111 Colum. L. Rev. Sidebar 19 (2011).

Even more speculative are the first stirrings of the use of blockchain to supplement land records and to reduce fraud. Blockchain uses a distributed digital leger protected by practically unreversible cryptographic functions to authenticate structured records ("blocks"). Pilot projects in Vermont and Cook County have been undertaken. For the promises and limits of this technology in the area of property transactions, see, e.g., Benito Arruñada, Blockchain's Struggle to Deliver Impersonal Exchange, 19 Minn. J.L. Sci. & Tech. 55 (2018); Matt Koronczak, The New "Chain" of Title: How Blockchain Will Affect Land Title Research, Recordation, and Insurance 5 Tex A&M J. Prop. L. 401 (2019). How might this lowering of information costs affect the duty to search? Would you expect the availability of online records to lead to a tightening or loosening of the *numerus clausus* and related restrictions on property forms?

Ease of search improves the usability of a recording system: Electronic search makes the recording system better as a recording system and indirectly makes rights more secure. In general, those defects of the recording system stemming from practical limitations—the lack of a tract index, the difficulty of searching under multiple spellings, and the like—are amenable to a technological solution.

Still, electronic land records do nothing directly to cut off inconsistent rights, as a registration system does. Recall that the main difference between recordation and registration is that in the latter an official (the registrar of deeds) will not only receive the transactional documents but will examine them and purge invalid or nonconforming interests, with the result of a clean and indefeasible title. In a registration system there are two sets of records, the lodgment or presentation diary (the set of incoming and as yet unexamined documents with the time of filing for priority purposes) and the definitive titles themselves (the result of the examination and purge). The presentation diary is easiest to automate, along the lines discussed earlier. In a registration system there is the further question of how far to try to automate the process of creating definitive title. Generally, this part of the process is still handled by humans. New Zealand is attempting to automate all of its Torrens system. Automating registration is likely to require even more standardization of legal interests in land, and, interestingly, New Zealand with its extreme automation of its Torrens registration system has made an effort to further standardize land transaction documents, see https://www.linz.govt.nz/land/land-registration/prepare-and-submit-your-dealing. (A recent article assessing the prospects of digitizing the Torrens Registration System used in Australia and New Zealand argues that this would make property less secure, by increasing the opportunities for fraud. Rod Thomas, Australasian Torrens Automation, Its Integrity, and the Three Proof Requirements, 2012 NZ Law Review 227 (2013).) If electronic registration causes delay, confusion, or increased incidents of fraud in the process of producing definitive title (the move from the presentation diary to clean title), a registration system can become in effect a recordation system (as it in effect is between presenting transaction documents and the issuance of clean title). For a discussion of the many issues raised by electronic registration, see Benito Arruñada, Leaky Title Syndrome?, New Zealand L.J. 115 (April 2010). How does the prospect of online land records affect the choice between registration and recordation?

Given that most modern recording acts are modifications of the good faith purchaser rule, elements of that rule continue to play an important role in the implementation of the recording acts. One important and recurring requirement that is drawn from good faith purchaser doctrine is that the recording acts only protect persons who are good faith purchasers "for value." Consider the following case.

Hood v. Webster

Court of Appeals of New York, 1936.
2 N.E.2d 43.

■ LOUGHRAN, JUDGE. Florence F. Hood owned a parcel of farm land in the town of Phelps, Ontario county. This property had been devised to her by her husband, whose will said that, should she predecease him, he wanted his estate to go to his brother, the plaintiff here. In 1918 Mrs. Hood executed a deed of the farm to the plaintiff and delivered it to his attorney as an escrow to take effect on her death. The Appellate Division has confirmed a finding of the Equity Term that this delivery was subject to no other condition. A majority of this court has come to the conclusion that the contrary of the fact so found may not be declared as matter of law on this record.

Having all along occupied the property, Mrs. Hood in 1928 granted it to the defendants (her brother and a nephew) by a deed then recorded. She died in 1933. The prior deed held as an escrow was thereupon delivered over to the plaintiff who had it recorded. In this action to annul the subsequent deed to the defendants, it has been held that on the foregoing facts the plaintiff was entitled to prevail.

On this appeal by the defendants, the parties concede that the case made by the findings depends for its solution upon the force and effect of section 291 of the Real Property Law (Consol.Laws, c. 50). It is thereby provided that every conveyance of real property not recorded "is void as against any subsequent purchaser in good faith and for a valuable consideration, from the same vendor, his heirs or devisees, of the same real property or any portion thereof, whose conveyance is first duly recorded."

Did the single circumstance that the subsequent deed to the defendants was first on record establish, in the absence of evidence to the contrary, the matters thus essential to avoid the prior deed to the plaintiff?

We think this question of burden of proof as fixed by the recording act is not for us an open one. The defendants were bound to make out by a fair preponderance of evidence the affirmative assertion of their status as purchasers in good faith and for a valuable consideration.

Brown v. Volkening, 64 N.Y. 76 (1876), and Constant v. University of Rochester, 19 N.E. 631 (N.Y. (1899)), Id., 31 N.E. 26, as read by us, are not authorities to the contrary. In those cases the court did say that the party who claimed under an unrecorded conveyance was required to prove that the subsequent record purchaser took with notice. But here, as elsewhere, it must be kept in mind that the phrase "burden of proof" may stand in one connection "for the never changing burden of establishing the proposition in issue," and in another "for the constantly changing burden of producing evidence." Thayer, Preliminary Treatise on Evidence, 353–389. In the Brown and Constant Cases the controlling factor was that substantial value had been paid for the subsequent conveyance. That fact was more than evidence of consideration. It was further the basis for the auxiliary inference that there was also good faith in the transaction, and what was said respecting the burden of proof had reference to the duty of adducing evidence to repel that inference. For the same reason, the burden of proof (in the same sense) is upon the holder of an unrecorded conveyance when a subsequent deed first recorded acknowledges receipt by the grantor of a consideration sufficient to satisfy the statute.

We have a different case here. Under their defense of purchase for value without notice the defendants offered no evidence of actual considerations given. The subsequent deed to them expressed their payment of "One Dollar and other good and valuable consideration." This recital was not enough to put them into the position of purchasers for a valuable consideration in the sense of the statute. Ten Eyck v. Whitbeck, 31 N.E. 994 (N.Y. 1892); Lehrenkrauss v. Bonnell, 92 N.E. 637 (N.Y. 1910).

no real consideration

The duty of maintaining the affirmative of the issue, and in a primary sense the burden of proof, was cast upon the defendants by the recording act. They failed to discharge that burden.

The judgment should be affirmed, with costs.

■ CRANE, CHIEF JUDGE (dissenting). I cannot agree with Brother LOUGHRAN'S view of the law nor with his conclusion on the evidence in this case. * * *

It is conceded that the holder of a prior unrecorded deed has the burden of proving the lack of good faith in the holder of a subsequent recorded deed. The burden is upon him to prove notice or such circumstances as would give notice to a reasonable man. I can see no reason for complicating this rule by shifting the burden of proof when it comes to valuable consideration. It is just as easy to prove lack of consideration in this day when parties may be witnesses and examined before trial as it is to prove notice or bad faith. We should not impair the force and efficacy of the recording statutes upon which it has become a habit and custom to rely in the transfer of real property. A deed or mortgage on record is good as against prior unrecorded deeds or incumbrances until notice or bad faith or a lack of consideration is proven. The burden of proof should rest with the person who asserts the invalidity. * * *

Naturally this burden of proof readily shifts and where fraud is shown or circumstances which cast suspicion upon the transactions the defendant—subsequent vendee—may be called upon to show or prove his good faith and the consideration. * * *

I go still further, however, and hold that the plaintiff is not entitled to recover on the evidence. Florence F. Hood was a widow of about fifty-five years of age, living alone on a small farm, which is the subject of this action. The plaintiff, William J. Hood, is her brother-in-law. She married his brother. The defendant Almon B. Farwell is her brother, and the defendant Howard A. Webster her nephew. Mrs. Hood was left by her husband with this farm and no money with the exception of a mortgage of $1,200 upon property in Nebraska. She was desirous and anxious to get enough money to live on the farm and the plaintiff proposed to give it to her during her natural life in exchange for the farm. She was brought in January of 1913 to the office of the plaintiff's lawyer, at which time she executed a deed of the farm to the plaintiff and also an agreement, which was part and parcel of one transaction, wherein the plaintiff agreed to pay her $200 a year as long as she lived. The deed was not given to the plaintiff; it was given to the lawyer to hold in escrow for no other purpose that can be imagined except to insure the plaintiff's paying the $200 a year and keeping his agreement. The delivery of the deed in escrow and the promise of the plaintiff were all one and the same transaction, and the payment of the money by the plaintiff was clearly a condition precedent to be fulfilled before he was entitled to the deed. Florence Hood lived for twenty years thereafter and died on the 29th day of January, 1933. The plaintiff broke all his promises and agreements. He never paid her a dollar, so far as this record shows. He owed her at the time of her death $4,000, not counting simple interest, and the courts below, dealing in equity, have turned over to him the farm, without requiring the plaintiff to do equity and pay to the estate the money he owes.

The agreement drawn by the plaintiff's lawyer went so far as to require Florence Hood, during all the years that she lived, to work the farm and to pay out of its produce all the taxes and upkeep, and this she did. Florence Hood repudiated the plaintiff, no doubt because of his failure to pay her any money or to keep his agreement, and in 1928 executed and delivered a deed of the farm to Howard A. Webster, her nephew, who had come to live with her and help her on the farm. This deed has been recorded and is the one which the plaintiff seeks to set aside and which the courts below have set aside in the face of the plaintiff's default. In this I think the courts were clearly in error as there is no evidence to justify the conclusion that the farm was to be given or the deed to it turned over to the plaintiff without any consideration or regard whatever to his obligations, acts, or responsibilities. Even the $1,200 mortgage on the Nebraska property was given to the plaintiff in 1913 on the understanding and agreement that he was to support and care for his sister-in-law by paying $200 a year. This apparently he still keeps or has disposed of.

When we consider that this elderly widow had nothing but a farm which had to be worked, and was in fear and dread of financial distress, there is only one possible conclusion, in my judgment, to be drawn from the execution of these instruments. Florence Hood was to give the farm to William Hood at her death in consideration for his paying to her $200 a year for her to live on; and that it was never her intention or any part of the transaction that he should have the farm for nothing or in default of his obligation. The courts below have given him the farm for nothing, so far as this record shows, instead of to the nephew who helped his aunt work the farm in order to meet taxes, upkeep, and a living.

The record is none too full, so that the conclusions which I have drawn are based entirely upon the evidence or lack of evidence which appeared on the trial. As a matter of law, therefore, on this evidence, the plaintiff failed to make out a case entitling him to equitable relief and the removal of the defendants' deed from the record.

The judgment should be reversed and the complaint dismissed, with costs in all courts. * * *

Judgment affirmed.

NOTES AND QUESTIONS

1. What kind of recording act does New York have? Who should have the burden of production on consideration and good faith? The burden of persuasion?

2. What should qualify as "consideration" in order to make someone a purchaser "for value"? The original purpose of the "value" requirement in good faith purchase doctrine was to protect reasonable reliance. Was there such reliance here? Most courts require substantial and not nominal consideration, do not require full market value to be paid, but do not allow love and affection or familial relationship to count. See Dale A. Whitman et al., The Law of Property § 11.10, at 774–75 (4th ed. 2019). Why doesn't the nephew's agreement to move onto the farm to help his widowed aunt count as "consideration"?

3. Is the majority expressing a preference for the *nemo dat* baseline? Why is it assumed that *nemo dat* favors the plaintiff? Note that, because the plaintiff's deed was only delivered into escrow, it is not prior to the nephew's deed unless the court treats it equitably as "relating back" to the time of delivery into escrow. Should equity be applied here (see the next Note)? Does the majority seem to think Mrs. Webster did something wrong? Does its decision undermine the policy of the recording act of allowing good faith purchasers to rely on the land records? As far as making the land records reliable here, who is the cheapest cost avoider? Does the fact that all of the parties here have some family connection influence the dissent? How about the majority?

4. The action to annul a recorded deed is likewise an equitable one. Because the holder of the prior unrecorded deed was seeking an equitable remedy, shouldn't an equity court have asked whether he himself had done equity—in accord with the maxim "he who seeks equity must do equity." (See Chapter IV.) If one takes the dissent's view of the facts, should the court have denied relief on that ground alone, or at least conditioned the requested annulment on his paying Mrs. Webster's estate everything he had inequitably withheld from her, with interest? Is this an example of New York courts carrying out the merger of law and equity in the wrong way?

The Limits of Title Searches

Performing the prescribed title search and applying the recording act in effect in the jurisdiction do not necessarily resolve the question of who has title. A title search that turns up a clean title is not the end of the story. There are off-record matters that may still bind (or totally deprive) a subsequent bona fide purchaser. As we have seen, forgeries and frauds can lead to claims—especially if the fraud victim is wholly blameless—that a title search might not turn up. Similar problems can arise from the incapacity of a grantor, deficiencies in the formalities in the execution of an instrument, liens (such as those for taxes) that are not required to be recorded, and other matters. See Ralph L. Straw, Jr., Off-Record Risks for Bona Fide Purchasers of Interests in Real Property, 72 Dickinson L. Rev. 35 (1967); see also Restatement (Fourth) of Property, Vol. 5, Div. IV, Ch. 5 (Am. L. Inst. Council Draft No. 4, Sept. 24, 2021) (describing forgeries, fraud, duress, undue influence, incapacitation, intoxication, minority, and legal disability as possible problems in a chain of title that may affect the rights of a subsequent bona fide purchaser).

Sometimes the recording acts fail to apply on their own terms. As we saw, most of the time this means that the *nemo dat* principle applies. In a jurisdiction with a notice statute, if O sells to A and then to B, but B has notice, then A wins by *nemo dat*. Or in a race-notice jurisdiction, if O sells to A and then to B who has no notice, and A then records before B, B fails to benefit from the recording act and A is the *nemo dat* winner. But when we add equitable interests into the mix, things can get a little more complicated. A might have a beneficial interest in Blackacre under a trust, or A might have an equitable interest in property in B's hands under a constructive trust theory (say, because B stole from A and invested the proceeds in Blackacre). Especially in the latter situation, A's interest is not likely to be recorded. Generally, where a recording act does not apply, *nemo dat* or a closely related principle *qui prior tempore potior est jure* ("prior in time is stronger in right") will decide as between the competing interests (prior legal interest beats later legal interest; prior equitable interest beats later equitable interest; and prior legal interest beats later equitable interest). But where a prior equitable interest competes with a later legal interest, the legal interest only prevails if it was acquired for value and without notice. This interplay of two equitable principles (*prior tempore*, and good faith purchase for value) in this last scenario is indirectly the source of the notice element in the recording acts themselves. See 14 Powell on Real Property § 82.02[3][c]; Ralph W. Aigler, The Operation of the Recording Acts, 22 Mich. L. Rev. 405 (1924).

As discussed earlier, the rise of electronic recording promises to ameliorate some of these problems. Despite the convenience of electronic records, problems such as forged deeds and other off-record defects remain. States differ as to whom to hold responsible in such situations. Title insurance helps manage some of these risks. Other risks, like adverse possession, are not covered by title insurance policies. When adverse possession occurs, a new chain of title is started in the adverse possessor. In the case of land, this can cause notice problems for those relying on land records, because adverse possession is not reflected in the land records, and no recording system cuts off adverse possession claims. This explains the need for surveying and physical inspection notwithstanding the cleanest of title chains as revealed by the recording system. Probably prospective owners are more able to detect such problems than are title companies, but before taking much comfort in this thought, consider the following case.

Mugaas v. Smith

Supreme Court of Washington, 1949.
206 P.2d 332.

■ HILL, JUSTICE. This is an action by Dora B. Mugaas, a widow, to quiet title to a strip of land 135 feet in length and with a maximum width of 3 1/2 feet which she claims by adverse possession, and to compel Delmar C. Smith and his wife to remove therefrom any and all buildings and encroachments. From a judgment quieting title to the strip in Mrs. Mugaas and directing the removal of any and all buildings and encroachments, the Smiths appeal.

The appellants contend that the respondent has failed to establish adverse possession of the tract in question. The character of the respondent's possession over the statutory period is one of fact, and the trial court's finding in that regard is to be given great weight and will not be overturned unless this court is convinced that the evidence preponderates against that finding. We are of the opinion that the evidence was sufficient to sustain the trial court's findings, and the conclusions based thereon, that the respondent had acquired title to the strip in question by adverse possession. The evidence would have warranted a finding that her adverse possession dated back to 1910.

holding: YES AP

The only serious questions raised by this appeal are attributable to the fact that the fence which between 1910 and 1928 clearly marked the boundary line for which respondent contends, disappeared by a process of disintegration in the years which followed, and, when appellants purchased the property in 1941 by a legal description and with a record title which included the disputed strip, there was no fence and nothing to mark the dividing line between the property of appellants and respondent, or to indicate to the appellants that the respondent was claiming title to the strip in question.

no fence showing divide

We have on several occasions approved a statement which appears in Towles v. Hamilton, 143 N.W. 935, 936 (Neb. 1913), that:

> * * * It is elementary that, where the title has become fully vested by disseisin so long continued as to bar an action, it cannot be divested by parol abandonment or relinquishment or by verbal declarations of the disseizor, nor by any other act short of what would be required in a case where his title was by deed.

✓ right but AP doesn't go away w/ lack of use

The fact that the respondent had ceased to use the strip in question in such a way that her claim of adverse possession was apparent did not divest her of the title she had acquired.

Appellants' principal contention is that we have held, in a long line of cases, that a bona fide purchaser of real property may rely upon the record title. The cases cited by appellants construe our recording statute, Rem.Rev.Stat. §§ 10596–1, 10596–2, and involve contests between those relying upon the record title and those relying upon a prior unrecorded conveyance as conveyances are defined by Rem.Rev.Stat. § 10596–1. The holdings in the cases cited give effect to that provision of § 10596–2 which states that any unrecorded conveyance " * * * is void as against any subsequent purchaser or mortgagee in good faith and for a valuable consideration from the same vendor, his heirs or devisees, of the same real property or any portion thereof whose conveyance is first duly recorded. * * * "

Appellants cite no cases, and we have found none, supporting their contention that, under a recording statute such as Rem.Rev.Stat. §§ 10596–1, 10596–2, a conveyance of the record title to a bona fide purchaser will extinguish a title acquired by adverse possession. The trial judge, in his admirable memorandum decision, quoted the following from the opinion in Ridgeway v. Holliday, 59 Mo. 444, 454 (1875):

> * * * But it is contended by the defendant that he is a purchaser for value from Voteau who appeared from the record to be the owner, and was in possession, without any notice of the prior adverse possession which passed the title to Ridgeway, or of any claim on his part to the premises; and that as against him, the defendant, Ridgeway, cannot assert his title; that to permit him to do so, would be giving to an adverse possession greater force and efficacy than is given to an unrecorded conveyance. These objections, it must be admitted, are very forcible. The registry act, however, cannot, in the nature of things, apply to a transfer of the legal title by adverse possession, and such title does not stand on the footing of one acquired and held by an unrecorded deed, and of such title, the purchaser may not expect to find any evidence in the records.

He quoted, also, the following from Schall v. Williams Valley R. Co., 35 Pa. 191, 204 (1860):

> An unrecorded paper title does not affect a purchaser without actual notice, and the learned judge pronounced a title by the statute of limitations, if unaccompanied by a continued possession, as no more than an unrecorded paper title. If this be sound doctrine, then the claimant under the statute, however he may have perfected his right, must keep his flag flying for ever, and the statute ceases to be a statute of *limitations*.
>
> The first observation we have to make on his ruling is, that titles matured under the statute of limitations, are not within the recording acts. However expedient it might be to require some public record of such titles to be kept, and however inconvenient it may be to purchasers to ascertain what titles of that sort are outstanding, still we have not as yet any legislation on the subject, and it is not competent for judicial decision to force upon

them consequences drawn from the recording acts. Those acts relate exclusively to written titles.

These cases seem to us to be directly in point, and to afford a complete answer to appellants' contention. However, appellants say that these and other cases are not applicable because legislation has been enacted, i.e., Rem.Rev.Stat. § 10577, to bring possessory titles within the recording act. That section reads as follows:

> Whenever any person, married or single, having in his or her name the legal title of record to any real estate, shall sell or dispose of the same to an actual bona fide purchaser, a deed of such real estate from the person holding such legal record title to such actual bona fide purchaser shall be sufficient to convey to and vest in such purchaser the full legal and equitable title to such real estate free and clear of any and all claims of any and all persons whatsoever not appearing of record in the auditor's office of the county in which such real estate is situated.

The appellants contend that, under this section of the statute, the full legal and equitable title is vested in them as bona fide purchasers from the record title holder, and that the title acquired by adverse possession is thereby extinguished. We again quote a sentence from the Pennsylvania decision:

> * * * If this be sound doctrine, then the claimant under the statute, however he may have perfected his right, must keep his flag flying for ever, and the statute ceases to be a statute of *limitations*.

If Rem.Rev.Stat. § 10577 has the effect claimed for it by the appellants, the only way in which a person who has acquired title by adverse possession could retain it against the purchaser of the record title is to make his possession and use of the property so continuous, so open, and so notorious as to prevent anyone from becoming a bona fide purchaser.

impractical obligation on AP

Immediately following this section in Rem.Rev.Stat., this statement appears in italics: "This section relates to community property only." It was § 1 of chapter 151 of the Laws of 1891, and the title of the act was "An Act to protect innocent purchasers of community real property." The other three sections of that act appear in Rem.Rev.Stat. as §§ 10578, 10579, and 10580; and the act in its entirety, in accordance with its title, is for the protection of innocent purchasers against undisclosed community interests. It is too clear for argument that the act never was intended to have, and could not have, constitutionally, in view of its restricted title, any such application as that for which appellants contend. * * *

N/A to this case

Appellants have placed too great a weight on too frail a reed. * * *

The judgment is affirmed.

NOTES AND QUESTIONS

1.   We encountered adverse possession in Chapter II as a mode of acquisition of property. Adverse possession can be seen as an exception to the *nemo dat* principle, in that it allows shifts in title other than by a chain of voluntary transfers. Nevertheless, recall that an adverse possessor only holds adversely against the present possessor. Thus, for example, if the present possessor holds only a life estate, the adverse possessor acquires only a life estate at the end of the statutory period. This mimics *nemo dat* in that the forced transfer from the present title owner does not transfer rights greater than the owner had.

2.   The court seems to think that if adverse possession claims are subject to the recording act, then the adverse possessor (AP) would have to maintain adverse possession forever, which would run counter to its being based on a statute of limitations and its function to wipe away stale claims. How true is this? Couldn't the AP file a quiet title action and record the judgment, thus starting a new record chain of title? Wouldn't it be desirable for the AP to do so? Does this case give the AP much incentive to give notice? The U.S. Supreme Court has upheld statutes requiring owners of dormant mineral rights periodically to re-record their interest, on pain of having the interest lapse. See Texaco, Inc. v. Short, 454 U.S. 516 (1982). Would such a lapse statute be desirable for claims based on adverse possession?

3.   If adverse possession claims were trumped by interests memorialized in recording acts, wouldn't this greatly simplify the process of ascertaining whether the transferor of any particular piece of property has good title? Or would it in fact make the process of ascertaining title even more complicated, if an adverse possessor is currently on the property and there have also been multiple transfers and recordings of title in the recent past?

4.   Many states have adopted legislation that reflects something of a compromise between reliance on recording acts and allowing claims of title outside the record based on adverse possession. So-called *marketable title acts* set a period, often 30 or 40 years, beyond which claims are deemed extinguished and searchers need not inquire further in the official records. See, e.g., Fla. Stat. Ann. §§ 712.01–.10; Mich. Comp. L. § 565.101; N.C. Gen. Stat. § 47B–2; Utah Code Ann. §§ 57–9–1 to 57–9–10. The National Conference of Commissioners on Uniform State Laws proposed a Uniform Marketable Title Act in 1977 as one section of the Uniform Simplification of Land Transfers Act, which was then made into a stand-alone model act in 1990. This act was based on an influential Michigan act, which was modeled on legislation adopted in 1950 in Ontario, Canada. See Walter E. Barnett, Marketable Title Acts—Panacea or Pandemonium?, 53 Cornell L. Rev. 45, 47, 52–60 (1967). Such a statute makes most interests unenforceable after the specified time period unless something is put in the record within that time window. The idea is to allow people to stop title searches at a given point and not have to go all the way back to the sovereign. There are exceptions (allowing continued enforcement) for interests in the nature of easements that give notice by their physical existence and for other

easements that were excepted or reserved by a recorded instrument and evidenced by something physical.

5.   Do marketable title acts represent a kind of adverse possession of claims based on adverse possession? Or do they have this function only for adverse possession claims that are no longer possessory? Suppose the statute of limitations for adverse possession is 20 years and the marketable title act prescribes a period of 40 years for title examinations. B enters A's land in 1960 and remains on the land openly, notoriously, continuously, exclusively, and adversely under a claim of right for the next 45 years. B has made no attempt to record the right to the land based on adverse possession. In 2005, A transfers to C. Can C rely on the marketable title act to extinguish B's claim of title by adverse possession? See Dale A. Whitman et al., The Law of Property § 11.12, at 797 (4th ed. 2019) (noting that "a person who is occupying the land may, under some of the acts, have possession treated as the equivalent of notice of his or her claim").

CHAPTER IX

THE LAW OF NEIGHBORS

A world in which owners simply had the basic right to exclude is one in which many problems would be left unsolved. As we have seen, not all physical invasions are severe enough to warrant giving the owner any power of veto—think of high-altitude airplane overflights. Other invasions, while significant, are closer cases in terms of whether to permit owners to exclude, or not to exclude, or to force them to allow the invasion but at a judicially determined price. The uses to which neighboring property is put can also have an impact on the value and enjoyment of land even if there is nothing in the nature of an invasion at all.

This Chapter will consider a range of legal devices to control conflicts among neighbors over incompatible uses of land. The principal devices considered are nuisance liability, servitudes (easements and covenants), and zoning. As solutions to land-use conflicts, these devices correspond roughly to tort, contract, and regulation. Each of these devices presents some special issues, but they are often functional substitutes; for example, noise problems could be controlled by the law of nuisance, by covenants negotiated by neighbors or their predecessors, or by restrictions on commercial activities through the law of zoning. Sometimes more than one device may apply to the same problem, and sometimes they complement each other.

A. NUISANCE

1. THE BASIC FRAMEWORK

Nuisance law has been termed a doctrinal "mess" and "mystery"—and even a "garbage can of law"—but the traditional starting point for nuisance is where trespass leaves off. Recall from Chapter I that relatively large intrusions of land are controlled by the law of trespass, which at least insofar as intentional intrusions are concerned, imposes a simple rule (no trespassing) subject to some exceptions (considered in Chapter IV, such as the defense of necessity and antidiscrimination laws). Lesser intrusions that go only to use and enjoyment of land are governed by the law of nuisance. In Chapter I, we encountered a nuisance case, *Hendricks v. Stalnaker*, which involved the court in a balancing of a water well and a septic system. The court found the defendant's well not to be a nuisance even though under local spacing regulations the plaintiffs were no longer able to operate a septic system on their property.

Hendricks is not unusual in claiming that the law of nuisance requires the court to balance the utility of two conflicting uses. The *Restatement of Torts*, which the court invoked, says that when a

balancing test

nontrespassory invasion of land is intentional, the question is whether the interference is substantial and unreasonable. Because an interference is intentional when the actor knows or should know that the conduct is causing harm, Restatement (Second) of Torts § 825 (1979), the reasonableness of the interference is often an issue. The reasonableness inquiry, according to the *Restatement*, calls for balancing the value of the competing landowners' activities: An activity is unreasonable if the social harm of the defendant's activity outweighs its social utility. Restatement (Second) of Torts § 826–828 (1979); William L. Prosser, Handbook of the Law of Torts § 87, at 581, § 89 at 596 (4th ed. 1971). Not all courts subscribe to the *Restatement* approach, however, and where courts do not engage in explicit balancing one must ask whether some other approach better explains the result. As we will see, one of the reasons nuisance law appears so confused is that notions of invasion—who sent what where—continue to play a role in nuisance law.

Jost v. Dairyland Power Cooperative

Supreme Court of Wisconsin, 1969.
172 N.W.2d 647.

The action is one for damages for injury to crops and loss of market value of farm lands. The plaintiffs are farmers living within, or near, the city limits of Alma, Wisconsin. Their farms are located on the bluffs overlooking the Mississippi River. In 1947 the Dairyland Power Cooperative erected a coal burning electric generating plant at Alma. It is the contention of the farmers that consumption of high-sulfur-content coal at this plant has increased from 300 tons per day in 1948 to 1,670 tons per day in 1967. There was testimony that the 1967 coal consumption resulted in discharging approximately 90 tons of sulfur-dioxide gas into the atmosphere each day. There was substantial evidence to show that the sulphur-dioxide gas, under certain atmospheric conditions, settled on the fields, causing a whitening of the alfalfa leaves and a dropping off of some of the vegetation. There was also testimony to show that the sulphur compounds resulting from the industrial pollution killed pine trees, caused screens to rust through rapidly, and made flower raising difficult or impossible. There was some testimony to show that some of the sulphur came from locomotives or from river barges, but there was testimony that the power plant was the source of most of the contamination. Defendant's witness, a farmer who was 'hit' less frequently by the sulphurous fumes, estimated his crop damage at 5 percent. There was also evidence of damage to apple trees, sumac, and wild grape, in addition to the alfalfa damage.

Each of the plaintiff farmers testified that his land had diminished in value as the result of the continuing crop loss.

Defendant offered testimony of realtors to the effect that there had been no diminution of market value. One of these witnesses was the assessor of the city of Alma. Two of the three farms were on the city's tax roll. * * *

■ HEFFERNAN, JUSTICE. [The court begins by distinguishing nuisance and negligence, the latter being based on injury stemming from a lack of due care. Although some nuisances arise from negligent behavior, a lack of due care is not required for a nuisance, and something can be a nuisance even if it is carried on according to industry standards of due care.] * * *

The jury found that Dairyland Power Cooperative produced its power in such a manner as to constitute a continuing nuisance to the plaintiffs. The following question was, however, answered "no" by the jury, "Did such nuisance cause substantial damage to their alfalfa crops and lands?" Nevertheless, the jury found the damage to the Jost alfalfa crops amounted to $250 for each of the two years, the Andrew Noll damage to $145 for each year, and the Norbert Noll damage to $145 for each year. In addition, Andrew Noll's farm was found to have sustained a $500 diminution in market value.

Appellant claims that the trial judge erred in changing the answer to the substantial damage question from "no" to "yes." It should be noted that this question posed more than one point for the jury's determination; one, did the nuisance cause the damage, and, two, was the damage substantial. The cause element of the question, however, is not argued; and all that defendant contends is that the damage, though caused by the nuisance, was not substantial and that, therefore, the court erred in changing the jury's answer. The rule is clear. A trial court may not change the jury's answer to a question unless it appears that the answer is not supported by any "credible evidence."

The damage to the alfalfa crop was undisputed. Even Danzinger, the neighboring farmer who testified, ostensibly for the defendant, estimated the crop damage at 5 percent. Moreover, the jury found the damage to the alfalfa crop alone to be not less than $200 for the least damaged of the plaintiffs. The court defined substantial damage as:

> . . . a sum, assessed by way of damages, which is worth having; opposed to nominal damages, which are assessed to satisfy a bare legal right. Substantial damages are damages which are considerable in amount and intended as a real compensation for a real injury.

The jury was properly instructed. The sums found for crop damage, though meager, are supported by the evidence. Having found such sums to be justly owing, it appears that by no rationalization can it be concluded that the sums properly payable did not constitute 'substantial damage.' In the oft-quoted case, *Pennoyer v. Allen*, 14 N.W. 609 (Wis. 1883), the court points out that only a "substantial injury" is [compensable] or protected against by law. Substantial injury is defined as "tangible" injury, or as a "discomfort perceptible to the senses of ordinary people." The Restatement, 4 Torts, p. 246, sec. 827, follows the same rationale:

> . . . where the invasion involves physical damage to tangible property, the gravity of the harm is ordinarily regarded as great even though the extent of the harm is relatively small. But where the invasion involves only personal discomfort and annoyance, the gravity of the harm is generally regarded as slight unless the invasion is substantial and continuing.' See, also, Prosser, supra, p. 599.

Here the damage was to tangible property. The damage was apparent and undisputed. * * *

We conclude that the injury was substantial as a matter of law, since under the reasoning of *Pennoyer*, supra, and the Restatement, the injury was obvious injury to tangible property. Moreover, it was, in fact, of such a nature that the jury placed more than a nominal value upon the injury done.

Defendant strenuously argues that it was prejudiced by the court's refusal to permit certain testimony, particularly testimony that tended to show that defendant had used due care in the construction and operation of its plant, and to show that the social and economic utility of the Alma plant outweighed the gravity of damage to the plaintiffs.

Defendant's contention that the evidence should have been admitted rests on two theories; one, that due care, if shown, defeats a claim for nuisance, and, two, that, if the social utility of the offending industry substantially outweighs the gravity of the harm, the plaintiffs cannot recover damages.

We can agree with neither proposition. As this court pointed out in *Bell v. Gray-Robinson Construction Co.*, 62 N.W.2d 390, 392 (Wis. 1954):

> A nuisance not rest on the degree of care used . . . but on the degree of danger existing even with the best of care. (Citing authority) To constitute a nuisance, the wrongfulness must have been in the acts themselves (*i.e.*, the consequence of the acts) rather than in the failure to use the requisite degree of care in doing them . . . .

* * * In any event it is apparent that a continued invasion of a plaintiff's interests by non-negligent conduct, when the actor knows of the nature of the injury inflicted, is an intentional tort, and the fact the hurt is administered non-negligently is not a defense to liability. See Prosser, supra, pp. 594 ff., sec. 88; Restatement, supra, p. 226, sec. 822.

It is thus apparent that the facts tending to show freedom from negligence would not have constituted a defense to plaintiffs' nuisance action. * * *

While there are some jurisdictions that permit the balancing of the utility of the offending conduct against the gravity of the injury inflicted, it is clear that the rule permitting such balancing, is not approved in Wisconsin where the action is for damages. We said in *Pennoyer v. Allen*, supra, 14 N.W. at 613:

> When such comfort and enjoyment are so impaired, and compensation is demanded, it is no defense to show that such business was conducted in a reasonable and proper manner, and with more than ordinary cleanliness, and that the odors so sent over and upon such adjacent premises were only such as were incident to the business when properly conducted. It is the interruption of such enjoyment and the destruction of such comfort that furnishes the ground of action, and it is no satisfaction to the injured party to be informed that it might have been done with more aggravation. The business is lawful; but such interruption and destruction is an invasion of private rights, and to that extent unlawful. It is not so much the manner of doing as the proximity of such a business to the adjacent occupant which causes the annoyance. A business necessarily contaminating the atmosphere to the extent indicated should be located where it will not necessarily deprive others of the enjoyment of their property, or less their comfort while enjoying the same.

In *Dolata v. Berthelet Fuel & Supply Co.*, 36 N.W.2d 97, 99 (Wis. 1949), relying on Pennoyer, this court concluded that even though a coalyard was operated properly, nevertheless, it, a socially and economically useful business, would be abated if it caused substantial damage to the adjoining plaintiff.

It appears clear that the doctrine of comparative injury is not entertained in Wisconsin in damage suits for nuisance. In *Abdella v. Smith*, 149 N.W.2d 537 (Wis. 1967), the doctrine was alluded to by a citation from Prosser. The case involved not an action for damages, but an injunction to abate the nuisance. The same problem was discussed in the earlier case of *Holman v. Mineral Point Zinc Co.*, 115 N.W. 327 (1908), where, in an action for damages occasioned by sulphurous fumes, defendant sought to rely on the theory that injury to a socially and economically useful factory by the granting of relief would outweigh the possible or actual injury to the plaintiff. This court stated, in discussing a case cited by the parties therein:

> "That was a suit to enjoin the operation of a copper smelter as a nuisance, and for damages occasioned by the destruction of timber on near-by lands. It is there held that, where an owner of property cannot use the same at all without indirectly injuriously affecting the property of another, the sound discretion of a court of equity is invoked when it is appealed to and asked to abate such use as a nuisance, and in such case the court will consider the comparative injury which will result from the granting or refusing of an injunction, and that it will not be

granted when it would cause a large loss to the defendant, while the injury to the plaintiff, if refused, will be comparatively slight and can be compensated by damages. That decision could only be applicable on the question of the abatement of the nuisance, as the right of the plaintiff to recover damages is distinctly recognized. As already stated, this is an action to abate the nuisance and for damages, and the complaint is not demurrable, if otherwise sufficient, simply because the court on final hearing might not grant all the relief that is prayed for." * * *

115 N.W. at 329.

As in *Holman*, the question of comparative injury is not before us, since this is a suit for damages, not abatement of a nuisance. Defendant nevertheless urges us to adopt the rule of the Restatement, which he contends applies the rule to damage suits for nuisance. It should be pointed out, however, that the Restatement recognizes that:

> For the purpose of determining liability for damages for private nuisance, conduct may be regarded as unreasonable even though its utility is great and the amount of harm is relatively small . . . . It may be reasonable to continue an important activity if payment is made for the harm it is causing, but unreasonable to continue it without paying." Restatement, 4 Torts, p. 224, ch. 40.

Prosser, supra, page 621, too, states:

> In an action for damages, the relative hardship upon the plaintiff and the defendant is not material, once the nuisance is found to exist.

We therefore conclude that the court properly excluded all evidence that tended to show the utility of the Dairyland Cooperative's enterprise. Whether its economic or social importance dwarfed the claim of a small farmer is of no consequence in this lawsuit. It will not be said that, because a great and socially useful enterprise will be liable in damages, an injury small by comparison should so unredressed. We know of no acceptable rule of jurisprudence that permits those who are engaged in important and desirable enterprises to injure with impunity those who are engaged in enterprises of lesser economic significance. Even the government or other entities, including public utilities, endowed with the power of eminent domain—the power to take private property in order to devote it to a purpose beneficial to the public good—are obliged to pay a fair market value for what is taken or damaged. To contend that a public utility, in the pursuit of its praiseworthy and legitimate enterprise, can, in effect, deprive others of the full use of their property without compensation, poses a theory unknown to the law of Wisconsin, and in our opinion would constitute the taking of property without due process of law.

We adhere to the rule of *Pennoyer v. Allen*. Although written in 1883, we believe it remains completely applicable under modern conditions. We conclude that injuries caused by air pollution or other nuisance must be compensated irrespective of the utility of the offending conduct as compared to the injury. Nor do we imply that a different rule should apply where the remedy sought is abatement rather than damages. That point is not considered herein. We consider that the rule of *Dolata* continues to be the law in Wisconsin where the action is for abatement.

We conclude, however, that the court erred in concluding that the evidence failed to show a diminution in the market value. The evidence was uncontradicted that the value of crops raised had diminished in value and that certain types of vegetation were dying out or had died out completely. It is clear that the nuisance has continued for several years and will continue for an indefinite period into the future.

The jury found there was a continuing nuisance. Under these circumstances, we conclude that the injury was permanent and that, as a matter of law, the market value of the land was diminished. See McCormick, Damages (hornbook series), p. 500, sec. 127. How much it was diminished we need not determine, since we are satisfied that there should be a new trial on the issue of diminution of market value only in regard to the real property of all plaintiffs.

We see no basis for the jury's conclusion that the market value of one of the farms was reduced by $500 and the value of the others not at all. Such a result—although there could have been a differential—is completely unsupported by the evidence.

We conclude that the plaintiffs are entitled to recover for the crops and damage to vegetation for the years complained of—1965 and 1966—as found by the jury, but after those years recovery cannot again be for specific items of damage on a year-by-year basis. Their avenue for compensation is for permanent and continuing nuisance as may be reflected in a diminution of market value. Of course, permitting a recovery now for a permanent loss of market value presupposes that the degree of nuisance will not increase. If such be the case, an award of damages for loss of market value is final. If, however, the level of nuisance and air pollution should be increased above the level that may now be determined by a jury, with a consequent additional injury the plaintiffs would have the right to seek additional permanent damage to compensate them for the additional diminished market value.

Judgment affirmed in part and reversed in part consistent with this opinion.

NOTES AND QUESTIONS

1. In rejecting the pure balancing approach, the court in *Jost* acknowledges that other courts and to some extent the Restatement (Second) of Torts allow the value of the respective parties' activities to factor into the

determination of reasonableness. The term "reasonable" crops up often in the common law, most prominently in the law of negligence. There it refers to an evaluation of the *defendant*'s activity, which includes both its costs and benefits. The court in *Jost* in parts of the opinion not excerpted here was adamant in keeping the two torts separate. For an argument that negligence and nuisance should both be about balancing costs and benefits of the defendant's activities, see, e.g., William M. Landes & Richard A. Posner, The Economic Structure of Tort Law, 48–50 (1987). Like the court in *Jost*, others see nuisance as distinct and based on equal right given background expectations about the use and enjoyment of land. See, e.g., Gregory C. Keating, Nuisance as a Strict Liability Wrong, 4 J. Tort L. 1 (2012).

2.   Even if it is distinct from reasonableness in negligence, pinpointing what is "reasonable" for purposes of nuisance has been hard to formulate (contributing to the "mystery" of nuisance). It is often said that the focus in nuisance is on the reasonableness of the impact on the use and enjoyment of the plaintiff's land, considering the nature of the locality (as in the next case). In older law, this analysis traveled under the banner of the maxim *sic utere tuo ut alienum non laedas,* "use what is yours so as not to injure what belongs to another," which we will encounter later. This idea is often said to be question begging, but often what it referred to was a reconciliation of presumptive but conflicting rights in the two parties—generating electricity and growing alfalfa, treating waste in septic tanks and drawing water from wells, etc. Resolving such conflicts involves a structured set of inquiries about how important uses are. For courts like *Jost*, this is not cost-benefit analysis, but turns on such factors as whether the intrusion causes physical damage to the plaintiff's property. The touchstone is the impact on the plaintiff's use and enjoyment. Courts also tend to recognize that there are some activities—such as those that are prohibited by statute or extreme interferences that would be offensive anywhere and anytime (nuisances per se) or activities done purely out of spite—that also count as nuisances. For one formulation, see Restatement (Fourth) of Property, Vol. 2, Div. I, § 7.2 (Am. L. Inst. Council Draft No. 4, Sept. 24, 2021). When all is said and done, would all-things-considered balancing be better?

3.   Is the court in *Jost* right that the value of the offending activity should never be taken into account? The court itself alluded to the possibility that hardship to the defendant might factor into whether an injunction is appropriate (more on this later). Are there any circumstances in which physical damage from an activity can fail to count as a nuisance even for purposes of damages? What if the activity brings benefits to the entire local community? Does it matter that the polluter has not made any attempt to acquire easements from surrounding landowners?

4.   Nuisance has always been called upon to handle conflicts between agricultural and residential uses. Recently, in response to worries about farms being pushed out of business through nuisance suits, every state has passed some kind of right-to-farm law that protects agricultural operations against a range of nuisance claims. A couple of states have even amended their constitutions in this direction. See generally Jonathan Morris, "One

Ought Not Have So Delicate A Nose": CAFOs, Agricultural Nuisance, and the Rise of the Right to Farm, 47 Envtl. L. 261 (2017).

5.   What would Coase say about the conflict in *Jost*? Recall that the well-versus-septic-system conflict in *Hendricks v. Stalnaker* (Chapter I) presented at first glance a fairly reciprocal problem (but did it?), which was reflected in the court's rhetoric of balancing. In rejecting balancing, the court in *Jost* sees nuisance as involving something other than reciprocal harms. Is there another sense, though, in which the court emphasizes symmetry at the level of rights? If nuisance is about reconciling conflicting presumptive rights, the process traditionally was required to be symmetric: determining which set of rights maximized mutual freedom or usefulness of land. What A could do to B would be mirrored by what B could do to A. Engaging in a very valuable use did not give one special weight in the determination of these mutual rights and duties. On the other hand, can one always formulate rights and duties as symmetric? Farmer Jost had a right in the abstract to run an electricity-generating plant, but how realistic was that? Or is the point that special solicitude for running the plant would violate prevailing norms and expectations in the locality? Consider the following case, which reflects a conflict similar to the one in *Jost*, but reflects a type of analysis that tended to prevail before the issue of whether to engage in balancing (or not) came to dominate nuisance law.

Campbell v. Seaman

Court of Appeals of New York, 1876.
63 N.Y. 568.

■ EARL, J. The plaintiffs owned about forty acres of land, situate in the village of Castleton, on the east bank of the Hudson river, and had owned it since about 1849. During the years 1857, 1858 and 1859 they built upon it an expensive dwelling-house, and during those years, and before and since, they improved the land by grading and terracing, building roads and walks through the same, and planting trees and shrubs, both ornamental and useful.

The defendant had for some years owned adjoining lands, which he had used as a brick-yard. The brick-yard is southerly of plaintiffs' dwelling-house about 1,320 feet, and southerly of their woods about 567 feet. In burning bricks defendant had made use of anthracite coal. During the burning of a kiln sulphuric acid gas is generated, which is destructive to some kinds of trees and vines. The evidence shows, and the referee found, that gas coming from defendant's kilns had, during the years 1869 and 1870, killed the foliage on plaintiff's white and yellow, pines and Norway spruce, and had, after repeated attacks, killed and destroyed from 100 to 150 valuable pine and spruce trees, and had injured their grape vines and plum trees, and he estimated plaintiff's damages from the gas during those years at $500.

This gas did not continually escape during the burning of a kiln, but only during the last two days, and was carried into and over plaintiff's land only when the wind was from the south.

It is a general rule that every person may exercise exclusive dominion over his own property, and subject it to such uses as will best subserve his private interests. Generally, no other person can say how he shall use or what he shall do with his property. But this general right of property has its exceptions and qualifications. *Sic utere tuo ut alienum non laedas** is an old maxim which has a broad application. It does not mean that one must never use his own so as to do any injury to his neighbor or his property. Such a rule could not be enforced in civilized society. Persons living in organized communities must suffer some damage, annoyance and inconvenience from each other. For these they are compensated by all the advantages of civilized society. If one lives in the city he must expect to suffer the dirt, smoke, noisome odors, noise and confusion incident to city life. As Lord Justice James beautifully said, in Salvin v. North Brancepeth Coal Co., (1874) L. R. 9 Ch. App. 705: "If some picturesque haven opens its arms to invite the commerce of the world, it is not for this court to forbid the embrace, although the fruit of it should be the sights and sounds and smells of a common seaport and ship-building town which would drive the Dryads and their masters from their ancient solitudes."

But every person is bound to make a reasonable use of his property so as to occasion no unnecessary damage or annoyance to his neighbor. If he make an unreasonable, unwarrantable or unlawful use of it, so as to produce material annoyance, inconvenience, discomfort or hurt to his neighbor, he will be guilty of a nuisance to his neighbor. And the law will hold him responsible for the consequent damage. As to what is a reasonable use of one's own property [this] cannot be defined by any certain general rules, but must depend upon the circumstances of each case. A use of property in one locality and under some circumstances may be lawful and reasonable, which, under other circumstances, would be unlawful, unreasonable and a nuisance. To constitute a nuisance, the use must be such as to produce a tangible and appreciable injury to neighboring property, or such as to render its enjoyment specially uncomfortable or inconvenient.

Within the rules thus referred to, that defendant's brick burning was a nuisance to plaintiffs cannot be doubted. Numerous cases might be cited, but it will be sufficient to cite, mainly, those where the precise question was involved in reference to brick burning. * * *

Hole v. Barlow, (1858) 140 Eng. Rep. 1113 (C.P.), * * * was an action for a nuisance arising from the burning of bricks on defendant's own land near to the plaintiff's dwelling-house, and the judge at the trial told the jury that no action lies for the reasonable use of a lawful trade in a

---

*   [Use what is yours so as not to damage what is another's.—eds.]

convenient and proper place, even though some one may suffer inconvenience from its being carried on * * * .

In *Bamford v. Turnley,* Cockburn, J., before whom the case was tried, followed *Hole v. Barlow,* and charged the jury that if they thought the spot was convenient and proper, and that the use by the defendant of his premises was, under the circumstances, a reasonable use of his own land, he would be entitled to a verdict. The jury found for the defendant, but upon the hearing in the Exchequer Chamber it was held that the instructions were erroneous, and that it was no answer in an action for a nuisance creating actual annoyance and discomfort in the enjoyment of neighboring property that the injury resulted from a reasonable use of the property, and that the act was done in a convenient place, nor that the same business had been carried on in the same locality for seventeen years. The doctrine of *Hole v. Barlow* was distinctly repudiated, and that case was in terms overruled. * * *

In this country, so far as I can ascertain, the question of nuisance from brick burning has rarely been before the courts. The only case to which our attention has been called is *Huckenstine's Appeal*, 70 Pa. 102 (1871). In that case Agnew, J., says: "Brick making is a useful and necessary employment and must be pursued near to towns and cities where bricks are chiefly used. Brick burning, an essential part of the business, is not a nuisance *per se.* (Attorney-General v. Cleaver, (1811) 34 Eng. Rep. 297, 301 (Ch.).) It, as many useful employments do, may produce some discomfort and even some injury to those near by, but it does not follow that a chancellor would enjoin therefore." He then goes on to say that the aid of an injunction is not matter of right, but of grace, and concludes that there were so many similar nuisances in the locality that it was not clear that this nuisance increased the discomfort from them, and that it was doubtful whether the plaintiff had suffered any material damage from the acts, and therefore held that an injunction ought not to issue and that the plaintiff should be left to his remedy at law. * * * Without further citation of authority I think it may safely be said that no definition of nuisance can be found in any text book or reported decision which will not embrace this case.

But the claim is made that although the brick burning in this case is a nuisance, a court of equity will not and ought not to restrain it, and the plaintiffs should be left to their remedy at law to recover damages, and this claim must now be examined.

Prior to Lord Eldon's time, injunctions were rarely issued by courts of equity. During the many years he sat upon the woolsack this remedy was resorted to with increasing frequency, and with the development of equity jurisprudence, which has taken place since his time, it is well said that the writ of injunction has become the right arm of the court. It was formerly rarely issued in the case of a nuisance until plaintiff's right had been established at law, and the doctrine which seems now to prevail in Pennsylvania, that this writ is not matter of right, but of grace, to a large extent prevailed. But now a suit at law is no longer a necessary preliminary, and the right to an injunction, in a proper case, in England and most of the States, is just as fixed and certain as the right to any other provisional remedy. The writ can rightfully be demanded to prevent irreparable injury, interminable litigation and a multiplicity of suits, and its refusal in a proper case would be error to be corrected by an appellate tribunal. It is matter of grace in no sense except that it rests in the sound discretion of the court, and that discretion is not an arbitrary one. If improperly exercised in any case either in granting or refusing it, the error is one to be corrected upon appeal. Here the remedy at law was not adequate. The mischief was substantial and, within the principle laid down in the cases above cited and others to which our attention has been called, irreparable.

The plaintiffs had built a costly mansion and had laid out their grounds and planted them with ornamental and useful trees and vines, for their comfort and enjoyment. How can one be compensated in damages for the destruction of his ornamental trees, and the flowers and vines which surrounded his home? How can a jury estimate their value in dollars and cents? The fact that trees and vines are for ornament or luxury entitles them no less to the protection of the law. Every one has the right to surround himself with articles of luxury, and he will be no less protected than one who provides himself only with articles of necessity. The law will protect a flower or a vine as well as an oak. (Cooke v. Forbes, (1867) 5 L.R. Eq. 166 (V.C.); Broadbent v. Imperial Gas Co., (1857) 44 Eng. Rep. 170 (Ch.).) These damages are irreparable too, because the trees and vines cannot be replaced, and the law will not compel a person to take money rather than the objects of beauty and utility which he places around his dwelling to gratify his taste or to promote his comfort and his health.

Here the injunction also prevents a multiplicity of suits. The injury is a recurring one, and every time the poisonous breath from defendant's brick-kiln sweeps over plaintiffs' land they have a cause of action. Unless the nuisance be restrained the litigation would be interminable. The policy of the law favors, and the peace and good order of society are best promoted by the termination of such litigations by a single suit.

The fact that this nuisance is not continual, and that the injury is only occasional, furnishes no answer to the claim for an injunction. The nuisance has occurred often enough within two years to do the plaintiffs large damage. Every time a kiln is burned some injury may be expected, unless the wind should blow the poisonous gas away from plaintiffs' lands. Nuisances causing damage less frequently have been restrained.

It matters not that the brick-yard was used before plaintiffs bought their lands or built their houses. One cannot erect a nuisance upon his land adjoining vacant lands owned by another and thus measurably control the uses to which his neighbor's land may in the future be subjected. He may make a reasonable and lawful use of his land and thus cause his neighbor some inconvenience, and probably some damage which the law would regard as *damnum absque injuria*.* But he cannot place upon his land any thing which the law would pronounce a nuisance, and thus compel his neighbor to leave his land vacant, or to use it in such way only as the neighboring nuisance will allow.

It is claimed that the plaintiffs so far acquiesced in this nuisance as to bar them from any equitable relief. I do not perceive how any acquiescence short of twenty years can bar one from complaining of a nuisance, unless his conduct has been such as to estop him. There is no proof that plaintiffs, when they bought their lands, knew that any one intended to burn any bricks upon the land now owned by defendant. From about 1840 to 1853 no bricks were burned there. Then from 1853 to 1857 bricks were burned there, and then not again until 1867. From 1857 to 1867 the brick yard was plowed and used for agricultural purposes. Before suit brought, plaintiffs objected to the brick burning. No act or omission of theirs induced the defendant to incur large expenses or to take any action which could be the basis of an estoppel against them, and therefore there was no acquiescence or laches which should bar the plaintiffs, within any rule laid down in any reported case.

It is true that if a party sleeps on his rights and allows a nuisance to go on without remonstrance or without taking measures either by suit at law or in equity to protect his rights, and allows one to go on making large expenditures about the business which constitutes the nuisance, he will sometimes be regarded as guilty of such laches as to deprive him of equitable relief. But this is not such a case.

The defendant claims a prescriptive right to burn bricks upon his land and to cause the poisonous vapors to flow over plaintiffs' lands. Assuming that defendant could acquire by lapse of time and continuous user the prescriptive right which he claims, there has not here been a continuous use and exercise of the right for twenty consecutive years. Anthracite coal was first used for burning bricks in this yard in 1834, and after six years brick burning was discontinued. It was not resumed again until about 1853, and after four years it was again discontinued, and it was not resumed again until 1867. So that anthracite coal, which caused plaintiffs' damage, had not been used in all for twenty years and certainly not continuously in burning bricks upon the yard now owned by defendant. If he could acquire the right claimed by prescription, he, and those under whom he holds, must for twenty years have caused the poisonous gases to flow over plaintiffs' land whenever they burned bricks and the wind blew from the direction of the kiln. Such a prescription neither the allegations in the answer nor the proofs upon the trial, nor the findings of the referee, warrant. The referee finds that the premises of defendant have been known and used as a brick-yard for over twenty-five years. This is not a finding that they have been used as a brick-yard

---

*   [Damage without legal injury.—eds.]

for twenty-five years continuously, or that they have caused the poisonous gases to flow over plaintiffs' land for that length of time continuously.

Where the damage to one complaining of a nuisance is small or trifling, and the damage to the one causing the nuisance will be large in case he be restrained, the courts will sometimes deny an injunction. But such is not this case; here the damage to the plaintiffs, as found by the referee, is large and substantial. It does not appear how much damage the defendant will suffer from the restraint of the injunction. He does not own the only piece of ground where bricks can be made. We know that material for brick making exists in all parts of our State, and particularly at various points along the Hudson river. An injunction need not therefore destroy defendant's business or interfere materially with the useful and necessary trade of brick making. It does not appear how valuable defendant's land is for a brick-yard, nor how expensive are his erections for brick making. I think we may infer that they are not expensive. For aught that appears, his land may be put to other use just as profitable to him. It does not appear that defendant's damage from an abatement of the nuisance will be as great as plaintiffs' damages from its continuance. Hence this is not a case within any authority to which our attention has been called, where an injunction should be denied on account of the serious consequences to the defendant.

We cannot apprehend that our decision in this case can improperly embarrass those engaged in the useful trade of brick making. Similar decisions in England, where population and human habitations are more dense, do not appear to have produced any embarrassment. In this country there can be no trouble to find places where brick can be made without damage to persons living in the vicinity. It certainly cannot be necessary to make them in the heart of a village or in the midst of a thickly settled community. * * *

It follows from these views that the judgment should be affirmed. * * *

NOTES AND QUESTIONS

1.   When the court says "[a] use of property in one locality and under some circumstances may be lawful and reasonable, which under other circumstances, would be unlawful, unreasonable and a nuisance," it is stating what is often called the "locality rule." Did the locality rule determine the result here? How do we define the locality? In one famous statement it has been said that "what would be a nuisance in *Belgrave Square* would not necessarily be so in *Bermondsey*." Sturges v. Bridgman, (1879) 11 Ch. D. 852, 855 (Eng.). (Bermondsey was an industrial district back then; today it is "quite the foodie mecca, with fancy lofts to match." Tom Dyckhoff, Let's move to: Bermondsey, London SE1, GUARDIAN, http://www.theguardian.com/money/2012/jan/13/bermondsey-london-se1-property-review. Does this make the locality rule an engine of inequality and environmental injustice? See

Allan Beever, The Law of Private Nuisance 31 (2013) (arguing against locality rule on these grounds); but see Christopher Essert, Nuisance and the Normative Boundaries of Ownership, 52 Tulsa L. Rev. 85 115–18 (2016) (arguing that locality as an aspect of the boundaries of ownership does not have inegalitarian implications). Is locality to be taken in a looser fashion (agricultural versus urban, manufacturing versus residential)? See Restatement (Fourth) of Property, Vol. 2, Div. I, Ch. 7 (Am. L. Inst. Council Draft No. 4, Sept. 24, 2021). If the locality mattered, why did this cut against the defendant? The Hudson Valley in the late nineteenth century was the largest brickmaking region, serving the fastest growing city in the world. George V. Hutton, The Great Hudson River Brick Industry 7 (2003). And Castleton in particular was known for brickmaking:

> The business of brickmaking has been a prominent industry of the town [of Schodack] for many years, and has chiefly been carried on in and near Castleton, where the soil is well adapted for its manufacture. The enterprise first assumed importance about the year 1825, and has since been carried on by various persons. The principal yard is now and has been for many years operated by Nathan N. Seaman, whose sons are now in partnership with him. Peter Niser also has a yard at Castleton. Many thousand brick are annually shipped from this point.

Nathaniel Bartlett Sylvester, History of Rensselaer Co., New York 413 (1880), available at https://archive.org/details/historyofrenssel00sylv. And yet of Castleton the same source also says that "[t]he cultivation of the rich soil of the town has always constituted its principal industry." Id. Or was the court swayed by the apparent flexibility of location and relocation within the area, as evidenced by the sporadic use of the works in question?

2. One understanding is that the locality rule relaxes the Blackstonian exclusion regime, but only tolerates invasions that reflect mutually beneficial forbearance, thus maximizing the neighbors' mutual liberty. As long as the uses in a given area are relatively uniform, each landowner gets what Richard Epstein calls "implicit in-kind compensation" in the form of an ability by the (unsuccessful) plaintiff to engage in the complained-of use as well. See, e.g., Richard A. Epstein, Nuisance Law: Corrective Justice and Its Utilitarian Constraints, 8 J. Legal Stud. 49, 88 (1979); see also J.E. Penner, Nuisance and the Character of the Neighbourhood, 5 J. Envtl. L. 1, 14–25 (1993). This live-and-let-live principle was very unlikely to extend to activities that cause physical damage to land. Why might that be? And yet, short of physical damage, if a location is particularly suited to an intense use, courts are more forgiving in the face of claims of nuisance. In a later case, *Tucker v. Mack Paving Co.*, 70 N.Y.S. 688 (App. Div. 1901), the New York Appellate Division distinguished *Campbell v. Seaman* where the defendant was engaged in mining: The operations were being conducted with reasonable care and could not be moved, unlike the brick yard in *Campbell* which could be more easily removed to a more remote area. On the question of the nature of the plaintiffs' and defendant's rights the court had this to say:

Under these circumstances we think the plaintiff has no legal ground of complaint. The protection of property is doubtless one of the great reasons for government. But it is equal protection to all which the law seeks to secure. The rule governing the rights of adjacent landowners in the use of their property seeks an adjustment of conflicting interests through a reconciliation by compromise, each surrendering something of his absolute freedom, so that both may live. To exclude the defendant from blasting to adapt its lot to the contemplated uses, at the instance of the plaintiff, would not be a compromise between conflicting rights, but an extinguishment of the right of the one for the benefit of the other. This sacrifice, we think, the law does not exact.

Id. at 692, quoting Booth v. Rome, Watertown & Ogdensburg Terminal R.R. Co., 35 N.E. 592, 596 (N.Y. 1893) (Andrews, C.J.). This sounds a lot like natural rights and Epstein's implicit in-kind compensation, but is it? Or is it balancing in favor of the "more valuable" use?

3.   Since the nineteenth century there has been a trend toward some form of balancing, at least in name, although some decisions like *Jost* have rejected even that. The reformulation of nuisance law in the *First Restatement of Torts* subsumes the locality rule into a general utilitarian balancing test. Restatement (First) of Torts §§ 822, 826 (1939). Perhaps the way for the *Restatement*'s balancing approach was paved by courts sympathetic to large employers in the Great Depression. See, e.g., Bove v. Donner-Hanna Coke Corp., 258 N.Y.S. 229 (N.Y. App. Div. 1932); Todd J. Zywicki, A Unanimity-Reinforcing Model of Efficiency in the Common Law: An Institutional Comparison of Common Law and Legislative Solutions to Large-Number Externality Problems, 46 Case W. Res. L. Rev. 961, 1020–21 (1996) (discussing Great Depression era case of Versailles Borough v. McKeesport Coal & Coke Co., 83 Pittsburgh Legal J. 379 (Pitt. Co. Ct. 1935), and noting "the poor economic conditions of the time suggested that people in the Pittsburgh area would be willing to sacrifice some amount of environmental quality for the assurance that their jobs would remain intact" and that using balancing analysis "[i]n finding for the coal company, the court did consider the community's depressed economic conditions"). Indeed, commentators have long been on the lookout for evidence of courts softening tort liability as a "subsidy" for industry. The evidence for the subsidy thesis in the nineteenth century has come in for heavy criticism. Compare Lawrence M. Friedman, A History of American Law 475 (2d. ed. 1985); Morton J. Horwitz, The Transformation of American Law, 1780–1860, at 85–89 (1977) (setting forth the subsidy thesis) with A.W. Brian Simpson, Leading Cases in the Common Law 163–94 (1995); Gary T. Schwartz, Tort Law and the Economy in Nineteenth-Century America: A Reinterpretation, 90 Yale L.J. 1717, 1735–58 (1981) (critiquing the subsidy thesis); Gary T. Schwartz, The Character of Early American Tort Law, 36 UCLA L. Rev. 641, 642–43 (1989) (arguing that courts in the nineteenth century were generous in upholding tort liability against defendants in emerging industry). Some commentators have proposed a compromise approach under which the locality would dictate the remedy available, with damages liability for

activities deemed subnormal or unneighborly in light of community standards. See, e.g., Robert C. Ellickson, Alternatives to Zoning: Covenants, Nuisance Rules, and Fines as Land Use Controls, 40 U. Chi. L. Rev. 681, 728–33 (1973); Edward Rabin, Nuisance Law: Rethinking Fundamental Assumptions, 63 Va. L. Rev. 1299, 1317–21 (1977).

4.   Pro-balancing courts, Legal Realists, and even the stray formalist have been sharply critical of the maxim *sic utere tuo ut alienum non laedas*, invoked in *Campbell* and in many other older nuisance cases. According to the critics, the maxim is empty or circular, without a substantive definition of what counts as an injury. See Lucas v. South Carolina Coastal Council, 505 U.S. 1003, 1031 (1992) (criticizing *sic utere* maxim as conclusory); Hale v. Farmers Elec. Membership Corp., 99 P.2d 454, 456 (N.M. 1940) (holding that although *sic utere* is a good moral precept, it is useless as a grounds for decision because it does not determine any right or obligation, and citing cases and commentary to this effect); Oliver Wendell Holmes, Privilege, Malice, and Intent, 8 Harv. L. Rev. 1, 3 (1894) (criticizing "hollow deductions from empty general propositions like *sic utere tuo ut alienum non laedas*, which teaches nothing but a benevolent yearning"). Do you agree that *sic utere* is inevitably vacuous? (See Note 2 after *Jost*, supra.)

5.   One problem that has called for a contextualized analysis is "coming to the nuisance." At first blush, someone who buys a parcel that is located next to an intensive use should know what they're getting into. And someone introducing a sensitive use like a residence into a district that is uniformly commercial or industrial will tend not to prevail on a nuisance claim. See, e.g., Gilbert v. Showerman, 23 Mich. 448 (1871) (Cooley, J.). But, as the opinion in *Campbell* points out, a flat rule making the plaintiff's coming to the nuisance a defense means that someone can acquire rights against neighbors simply by being first, and as we have seen this incentive structure leads to wasteful races to be first. In general, courts are reluctant to grant the defense and instead balance a number of factors, including timing, good faith and absence of spite, the public interest in the defendant's activities, and estoppel-like notions. Giving both sides an incentive to maximize joint value of the parcels is not a trivial problem. See, e.g., Robert Innes, Coming to the Nuisance: Revisiting *Spur* in a Model of Location Choice, 25 J.L. Econ. & Org. 286 (2009); Donald Wittman, First Come, First Served: An Economic Analysis of "Coming to the Nuisance," 9 J. Legal Stud. 557 (1980). Should the doctrine aim at defining optimal behavior? If so what is that? Or is the problem, again, one of reconciling conflicting presumptive rights? John C.P. Goldberg & Henry E. Smith, Wrongful Fusion: Equity and Torts, in Equity and Law: Fusion and Fission 309, 315–18 (John C.P. Goldberg, Peter Turner & Henry E. Smith eds., 2019).

6.   If we say that someone buying in the face of the nuisance has already paid a depressed price for the land, where does that leave the seller? Shouldn't the right to bring the nuisance claim be bundled with the land? (And isn't the price dependent on the legal rule here anyway, making any argument based on the "price" circular?) One might then ask, why didn't the earlier owner (the seller) sue? Perhaps because the seller was not bothered yet—for example, by not having built a house on the parcel.

7.   In some states, one can acquire an easement to commit what would otherwise be a nuisance by committing the nuisance for the statutory period for an easement by prescription. In *Campbell*, the brick yard did not acquire an easement to commit the pollution because its use of anthracite coal to make bricks had not been continuous for the statutory period of 20 years. When should the clock start ticking on the potential plaintiff? When the brick yard opens in splendid isolation? Or when the plaintiff wants to engage in a use, like building a house with a fancy garden, that the brick yard interferes with? Or at some other point? Tolling the statute of limitations until a conflict arises allows the intensive use like the brick yard to operate in the meantime, and the conflict may never arise. See Richard A. Epstein, A Clear View of The Cathedral: The Dominance of Property Rules, 106 Yale L.J. 2091, 2105 (1997).

8.   What about the reverse situation, in which the more intensive use is newer? Should it always be considered a nuisance? Courts recognize the dynamic nature of land use and are not willing to let the sensitive use preclude the entrance of more intense commercial uses for all time, as reflected in Judge Earl's embrace of Lord Justice James's remark about Dryads and the "ancient solitudes." How can courts recognize such a trend? Does the disappointed resident have reason to complain? One could say that in such situations all the landowners have a mutual right to engage in the new use, but is this cold comfort to the put-upon resident?

2.   THE NUISANCE-TRESPASS DIVIDE

On a doctrinal level, nuisance law literally picks up where trespass leaves off: A nuisance is commonly defined as a "nontrespassory" invasion of land of a certain sort. Restatement (Second) of Torts § 821D (1979). As you consider the relationship between trespass and nuisance and the many twists to nuisance law, consider what aspects of nuisance law help vindicate owners' rights to exclude and which go beyond exclusionary rights to prescribe a governance regime for particular use conflicts. Does nuisance law reinforce or challenge the view that the right to exclude is fundamental to property? To what extent does nuisance law serve to soften the hard edges of exclusion rights? Or does nuisance law exemplify the bundle-of-sticks picture of property?

Adams v. Cleveland-Cliffs Iron Company

Court of Appeals of Michigan, 1999.
602 N.W.2d 215.

■ O'CONNELL, J. Defendants appeal as of right from a jury verdict awarding damages in trespass for invasions of plaintiffs' property by intrusions of dust, noise, and vibrations. The gravamen of this appeal presents the question whether Michigan recognizes a cause of action in trespass stemming from invasions of these intangible agents. No published decision of an appellate court of this state is directly on point. Because of the importance of this issue of first impression, we will expound on it in some detail. Following a recitation of facts, we will examine the origins of the doctrines of trespass to land and nuisance, observe recent developments of those doctrines in this and other jurisdictions, and then reaffirm for this state the traditional requirements for a cause of action in trespass.

We conclude that the law of trespass in Michigan does not cover airborne particulate[s], noise, or vibrations, and that a complaint alleging damages resulting from these irritants normally sounds instead in nuisance.

heading – No trespass, but a nuisance

I.   Facts

Plaintiffs brought suit seeking damages in both trespass and nuisance, complaining of dust, noise, and vibrations emanating from the Empire Mine, which is operated by defendant Cleveland-Cliffs Iron Company and its subsidiary, defendant Empire Iron Mining Partnership.

The Empire Mine is one of the nation's largest mines, producing eight million tons of iron ore annually. The mine operates twenty-four hours a day, year round. At the time this action was commenced, all but three plaintiffs lived near the mine, in the village of Palmer in Marquette County. Cleveland-Cliffs, which also operates the nearby Tilden Mine, employs approximately 2,200 persons, making it the area's largest civilian employer.

The Empire Mine was originally dug in the 1870s, then expanded in the 1960s. A second pit was added in 1987, and a third in 1990–91.[2] The mine engages in blasting operations approximately three times a week, year round, and the extraction and processing of the iron ore generates a great deal of airborne dust. Plaintiffs complain that the blasting sends tremors through their property and that defendants' dust constantly accumulates inside and outside plaintiffs' homes. Plaintiffs assert that these emanations aggravate their need to clean and repaint their homes, replace carpets and drapes, repair cracks in all masonry, replace windows, and tend to cause plumbing leaks and broken sewer pipes.

According to the testimony, the dust from the mine is fine, gritty, oily, and difficult to clean. Some plaintiffs complained that they seldom opened their windows because of the dust, and virtually every plaintiff complained that the snow in Palmer tended to be gray or black. Evidence presented at trial indicates that the emissions from the mining operations have consistently remained within applicable air-quality standards and that the amount of particulate matter accumulating over Palmer each month amounts to less than the thickness of a sheet of

---

[2]   With each expansion, surface material, also called "overburden," consisting of soil, subsoil, and rock was blasted loose then stockpiled at the edge of the mine property. As the mine was dug deeper, waste rock was likewise blasted loose and stockpiled. The resulting mass of overburden and waste rock is unsightly and so large that residents of Palmer have nicknamed it "Mt. Palmer" and say that it causes their town to have early sunsets.

paper, but that this amount is nonetheless four times greater than what normally settles onto surrounding communities.

In addition to concerns about the dust, many plaintiffs testified that the noise and vibrations from the blasts caused them to suffer shock, nervousness, and sleeplessness. Finally, several plaintiffs asserted that these conditions diminished the value of their homes, in some cases to the point of rendering them unmarketable.

At the close of proofs, the trial court instructed the jury concerning both trespass and nuisance. The jury found that three of the plaintiffs were not entitled to recover under either theory. Concerning the remaining fifty-two plaintiffs, however, the jury was unable to agree on a verdict regarding the nuisance claim, but returned a verdict in favor of these plaintiffs with regard to the trespass claim, awarding damages totaling $599,199. The court denied defendants' posttrial motions for a new trial or judgment notwithstanding the verdict.

Figure 9-1
The Empire Mine and the Town of Palmer

Courtesy of Airphoto—Jim Wark.

The sole issue that defendants raise on appeal is the propriety of the trial court's jury instruction concerning plaintiffs' trespass claim:

> Every unauthorized intrusion onto the lands of another is a trespass upon those lands, and it gives rise to a right to recover damages for the trespass, if any damages were caused by the trespass. So a landowner who causes emissions, dust, vibration, noise from his property onto another [sic] property assumes the risk of trespass, if the dust, vibration, noise affects the

[handwritten margin note: affects property or causes invasion... not intrude?]

neighbor's property, or if he causes by his actions, damages or invasion of his neighbor's land.

So again, to repeat. A trespass is an unauthorized intrusion into the lands of another.

reminder - trespass def

* * *

II.   Trespass and Nuisance

The general concept of "property" comprises various rights—a "bundle of sticks," as it is often called—which is usually understood to include "[t]he exclusive right of possessing, enjoying, and disposing of a thing." Black's Law Dictionary (6th ed., 1990), p. 1216. As this latter characterization suggests, the right to exclude others from one's land and the right to quiet enjoyment of one's land have customarily been regarded as separate sticks in the bundle. * * * Thus, possessory rights to real property include as distinct interests the right to exclude and the right to enjoy, violations of which give rise to the distinct causes of action respectively of trespass and nuisance. Prosser & Keeton, Torts (5th ed.), § 87, p. 622.

A.   Historical Overview

"At common law, trespass was a form of action brought to recover damages for any injury to one's person or property or relationship with another." Black's Law Dictionary (6th ed.), p. 1502. This broad usage of the term "trespass" then gave way to a narrower usage, referring to intrusions upon a person's "tangible property, real or personal." Prosser & Keeton, supra at § 13, p. 67. Today, the general concept of "trespass" has been refined into several specific forms of trespass, see Black's Law Dictionary (6th ed.), pp. 1502–1504, and related doctrines known by various names. Landowners seeking damages or equitable relief in response to violations of their possessory rights to land now generally proceed under the common-law derivatives of strict liability, negligence, nuisance, or trespass to land. It is the latter two products of this evolution from the general concept of trespass that are at issue in the present case.

" '[T]respass is an invasion of the plaintiff's interest in the exclusive possession of his land, while nuisance is an interference with his use and enjoyment of it.' " Hadfield v. Oakland Co. Drain Comm'r, 422 N.W.2d 205 (Mich. 1988) (Brickley, J., joined by Riley, C.J., and Cavanagh, J.), quoting Prosser & Keeton, supra at § 87, p. 622. Historically, "[e]very unauthorized intrusion upon the private premises of another is a trespass. . . ." Giddings v. Rogalewski, 158 N.W. 951 (Mich. 1916). Because a trespass violated a landholder's right to exclude others from the premises, the landholder could recover at least nominal damages even in the absence of proof of any other injury. Id. Recovery for nuisance, however, traditionally required proof of actual and substantial injury. Further, the doctrine of nuisance customarily called for balancing the disturbance complained of against the social utility of its cause.

distinction

Traditionally, trespass required that the invasion of the land be direct or immediate and in the form of a physical, tangible object. See, e.g., Williams v. Oeder, 659 N.E.2d 379, 382 n.2 (Ohio App. 1995) (noting then abandoning those traditional requirements); Davis v. Georgia-Pacific Corp., 445 P.2d 481, 483 (Or. 1968) (abandoning the traditional requirements); Norwood v. Eastern Oregon Land Co., 5 P.2d 1057, 1061 (Or. 1931), modified 7 P.2d 996 (Or. 1932) (wrongful diversion of water onto another's land does not constitute trespass to land). Under these principles, recovery in trespass for dust, smoke, noise, and vibrations was generally unavailable because they were not considered tangible or because they came to the land via some intervening force such as wind or water. Instead, claims concerning these irritants were generally pursued under a nuisance theory.

B. Recent Trends

Plaintiffs urge this Court to hold that they are entitled to recover in trespass for invasions of their premises by intangible things without regard for how these annoyances came to their land. Plaintiffs would have us follow the example of certain courts from other jurisdictions, which have eliminated the traditional requirements for trespass of a direct intrusion by a tangible object, directing the inquiry instead toward the nature of the interest harmed. These courts have permitted recovery in trespass for indirect, intangible invasions that nonetheless interfered with exclusive possessory interests in the land. See 75 Am. Jur. 2d, Trespass, § 33, p. 33 and cases cited. See also Mercer v. Rockwell Int'l Corp., 24 F.Supp.2d 735, 743 (W.D. Ky. 1998) (allowing an action in "negligent trespass" concerning intrusions of invisible polychlorinated biphenyls [PCBs] that actually harm the property); Williams, supra (airborne particulate matter from a sand and gravel processing facility, an asphalt plant, and a concrete plant constituted trespass); Martin v. Reynolds Metals Co., 342 P.2d 790 (Or. 1959) (trespass may stem from fluoride compounds in the form of gases and particles). We agree with the characterization of cases of this sort found in Prosser & Keeton as being "in reality, examples of the tort of private nuisance or liability for harm resulting from negligence," not proper trespass cases. Prosser & Keeton, supra at § 13, pp. 71–72 (concerning "decisions finding a trespass constituted by the entry of invisible gases and microscopic particles, but only if harm results"). Accordingly, we decline plaintiffs' invitation to strip the tort of trespass to land of its distinctive accouterments and commingle its identity with other causes of action.

As stated above, the traditional view of trespass required a direct entry onto the land by a tangible object. However, recent trends have led to an erosion of these requirements. Some courts have eliminated the requirement of a direct entry onto the land. E.g., Bradley v. American Smelting & Refining Co., 709 P.2d 782, 787–88 (Wash. 1985); Borland v. Sanders Lead Co., Inc., 369 So.2d 523, 527 (Ala. 1979); Martin, supra at 797 (observing the trend without deciding whether to join it), citing

Prosser, Torts (2d ed.), p. 56; 1 Restatement, Torts, § 158, comment h. Some courts have likewise eliminated the requirement of a tangible object. E.g., Bradley, supra at 787–88; Borland, supra at 529. See also Martin, supra at 797 (trespass to land may be accomplished by "a ray of light, by an atomic particle, or by a particulate of fluoride"). In some cases the direct-and-tangible inquiry has been supplanted by an inquiry into the force and energy of the intruding agent. E.g., Bradley, supra at 788; Borland, supra at 527; Martin, supra at 793–94.

The courts that have deviated from the traditional requirements of trespass, however, have consequently found troublesome the traditional principle that at least nominal damages are presumed in cases of trespass. Thus, under the so-called modern view of·trespass, in order to avoid subjecting manufacturing plants to potential liability to every landowner on whose parcel some incidental residue of industrial activity might come to rest, these courts have grafted onto the law of trespass a requirement of actual and substantial damages. Bradley, supra at 791; Borland, supra at 529. See also Martin, supra at 795 (observing that "[t]here are adjudicated cases which have refused to find a trespass where the intrusion is clearly established but where the court has felt that the possessor's interest should not be protected"). Logically following from a requirement of substantial damages is the weighing of those damages against the social utility of the activity causing them. Martin, supra at 795 (balancing "the intrusion . . . against the socially desirable conduct of the defendant"). See also Bradley, supra at 787 ("While the strict liability origins of trespass encourage courts to eschew a balancing test in name, there is authority for denying injunctive relief if defendant has exhausted his technological opportunities for control. . . . Acknowledging technological or economic justifications for trespassory invasions does away with the historically harsh treatment of conduct interfering with another's possessory interests.").[11]

We do not welcome this redirection of trespass law toward nuisance law. The requirement that real and substantial damages be proved, and balanced against the usefulness of the offending activity, is appropriate where the issue is interference with one's use or enjoyment of one's land; applying it where a landowner has had to endure an unauthorized physical occupation of the landowner's land, however, offends traditional principles of ownership. The law should not require a property owner to justify exercising the right to exclude. To countenance the erosion of presumed damages in cases of trespass is to endanger the right of exclusion itself.

To summarize, the effects of recent trends in the law of trespass have included eliminating the requirements of a direct invasion by a tangible

_____

[11]   We are of the opinion that this kind of analysis is generally only required in a nuisance case and that it is better to preserve that aspect of traditional trespass analysis requiring no proof of actual injury because the invasion of the plaintiff's right to exclude was regarded as tortious by itself.

object, requiring proof of actual and substantial damages, and weighing the plaintiff's damages against the social utility of the operation causing them. This so-called "modern view of trespass" appears, with all its nuances and add-ons, merely to replicate traditional nuisance doctrine as recognized in Michigan. Indeed, the trends recognized or advanced by *Bradley, Borland, Martin,* and their kindred spirits have conflated nuisance with trespass to the point of rendering it difficult to delineate the difference between the two theories of recovery.

 * * * We prefer to preserve the separate identities of trespass and nuisance. * * *

III. Holding

Recovery for trespass to land in Michigan is available only upon proof of an unauthorized direct or immediate intrusion of a physical, tangible object onto land over which the plaintiff has a right of exclusive possession. Once such an intrusion is proved, the tort has been established, and the plaintiff is presumptively entitled to at least nominal damages. Where the possessor of land is menaced by noise, vibrations, or ambient dust, smoke, soot, or fumes, the possessory interest implicated is that of use and enjoyment, not exclusion, and the vehicle through which a plaintiff normally should seek a remedy is the doctrine of nuisance. To prevail in nuisance, a possessor of land must prove *significant harm* resulting from the defendant's *unreasonable interference* with the use or enjoyment of the property. Cloverleaf Car Co. v. Phillips Petroleum Co., 540 N.W.2d 297, 301–02 (Mich.App. 1995), citing Adkins, supra at 720. Thus, in nuisance, the plaintiff must prove all damages, which may be awarded only to the extent that the defendant's conduct was "unreasonable" according to a public-policy assessment of its overall value. In the present case, because the intrusions of which plaintiffs complained were intangible things, the trial court erred in allowing the jury to award damages in trespass. Instead, any award of damages would have had to proceed from plaintiffs' alternative but (as yet) unsuccessful theory of nuisance. * * *

The trial court's instruction regarding trespass, as set forth above, recognized a right to recover in trespass "if any damages were caused by the trespass" and that the agents potentially causing the damages included "emissions, dust, vibration, noise." Thus the trial court seems to have mirrored (and indeed gone beyond) the so-called modern view of trespass according to which intangible irritants could constitute trespass. This instruction thus erroneously conflated trespass with nuisance and produced the anomalous result that the jury failed to reach agreement on the nuisance claim while awarding damages for intrusions of intangible things pursuant to the trespass claim.

A. Tangible

Because noise or vibrations are clearly not tangible objects, we hold that they cannot give rise to an action in trespass in this state.[12] We further hold that dust must generally be considered intangible and thus not actionable in trespass.

We realize, of course, that dust particles are tangible objects in a strict sense that they can be touched and are comprised of physical elements. However, we agree with those authorities that have recognized, for practical purposes, that dust, along with other forms of airborne particulate, does not normally present itself as a significant physical intrusion. See anno: Recovery in trespass for injury to land caused by airborne pollutants, 2 A.L.R.4th 1054, 1055 ("[t]raditionally, an invasion of the exclusive possession of land by intangible substances, such as an airborne pollutant, was usually held by the court not to constitute a trespass"); Williams, supra, 659 N.E.2d at 382 n.2 (observing that some courts have held that a " 'tangible invasion' or 'object' " must be "more substantial than dust, gas, or fumes"), citing Bradley, supra at 787.

Dust particles do not normally occupy the land on which they settle in any meaningful sense; instead they simply become a part of the ambient circumstances of that space. If the quantity and character of the dust are such as to disturb the ambiance in ways that interfere substantially with the plaintiff's use and enjoyment of the land, then recovery in nuisance is possible.

B. Direct

"[S]ome courts have held that if an intervening force, such as wind or water, carries pollutants onto the plaintiff's land, then the entry is not 'direct.'" Williams, supra at 382, n. 2, citing Bradley, supra at 787. However, in order to avoid harsh results most courts have avoided an overly strict distinction between direct and indirect invasions, see Prosser & Keeton, supra at § 13, pp. 68–69. Still, "[t]he differentiation between direct and indirect results may not be absolutely dead." Id. at 71.

* * * We hold that the direct invasion requirement for an action in trespass to land is still alive in Michigan. The question then becomes, how strong must the connection between cause and effect be in order to satisfy this requirement?

We agree with the Restatement view that "[i]t is enough that an act is done with knowledge that it will to a substantial certainty result in the entry of the foreign matter." 1 Restatement Torts, 2d, § 158, comment i,

---

[12]   This holds even if the noise or vibrations are so intense as to shatter all glass and fell all masonry or otherwise so persistent as to drive all persons from the premises. Although such hazards would indeed infringe on a landowner's possessory interest, it is the interest in use and enjoyment of the premises, not in exclusion from them, and therefore the cause of action lies not in trespass, but in nuisance or the related doctrines of negligence or strict liability.

p. 279. Thus, a "direct or immediate" invasion for purposes of trespass is one that is accomplished by any means that the offender knew or reasonably should have known would result in the physical invasion of the plaintiff's land.[15]

C. Damages

* * * The trial court told the jury that "trespass . . . gives rise to a right to recover damages for the trespass, if any damages were caused by the trespass." This instruction would be appropriate for nuisance, or negligence, under which theories the plaintiff must prove all damages, but not for trespass. A jury instruction with respect to the latter should announce that because the violation of the right to exclude causes cognizable injury in and of itself, a plaintiff proving that violation is presumptively entitled to at least nominal damages. The jury should be further instructed that beyond the presumed damages, the plaintiff may recover any additional, actual damages proved.

* * * We hold that recovery in trespass is appropriate for any *appreciable* intrusion onto land in violation of the plaintiff's right to exclude, while recovery in nuisance is appropriate for only *substantial* and *unreasonable* interference with the plaintiff's right to quiet enjoyment.

IV. Conclusion

There is no need to reformulate the traditional law of trespass to accommodate the problems of airborne pollution, noise, or vibrations, because the doctrines of nuisance and related causes of action have always stood ready to provide remedies. Trespass in Michigan remains a distinct doctrine providing a remedy for violation of a distinct property right. A possessor of land proving a direct or immediate intrusion of a physical, tangible object onto the land is presumptively entitled to recover at least nominal damages even absent any proof of actual injury and may recover additional damages for any injuries actually proved. * * *

Reversed and remanded. We do not retain jurisdiction.

NOTES AND QUESTIONS

1. At various times four tests have, singly or in combination, been used to demarcate the boundary of trespass and nuisance: (1) whether the

---

[15]   We note that the Restatement itself presents its rule as a departure from the traditional requirement of a direct or immediate invasion. 1 Restatement Torts, 2d, § 158, comment i, pp. 278–279 ("it is not necessary that the foreign matter should be thrown directly and immediately upon the other's land"). We would, however, adopt the Restatement's formulation as a liberalization, not a rejection, of the strictest sense of the traditional requirement for a direct or immediate invasion. Accordingly, rather than reject this traditional requirement, we preserve this requirement as something akin to proximate cause, meaning "that which, in a natural and continuous sequence, unbroken by any efficient intervening cause, produces the injury and without which the accident could not have happened, if the injury be one which might be reasonably anticipated or foreseen." Black's Law Dictionary (6th ed.), p. 1225.

defendant's action giving rise to the intrusion was committed on the plaintiff's land or outside the plaintiff's land; (2) whether the harm to the plaintiff's land was direct or indirect; (3) whether the invasion was committed by tangible matter or by some intangible substance; and (4) whether the intrusion deprives the plaintiff of possession of the land, or merely of use and enjoyment of the land. See generally Thomas W. Merrill, Trespass, Nuisance, and the Costs of Determining Property Rights, 14 J. Legal Stud. 13, 26–35 (1985). Does the *Adams* court provide a helpful synthesis by holding that trespass requires an intrusion that is both "tangible" and "direct"? Would it be more straightforward simply to ask whether the intrusion displaces the plaintiff from possession of some portion of her land?

2.   Although the *Adams* court was not willing to conflate trespass and nuisance, some jurisdictions would allow trespass to apply to what would traditionally be treated as very serious nuisances. One court has justified this move by observing that "the now famous equation $E = mc^2$ has taught us that mass and energy are equivalents and that our concept of 'things' must be reframed." See Martin v. Reynolds Metals Co., 342 P.2d 790, 793 (Or. 1959). Do you agree that relativity theory renders the traditional distinction between trespass and nuisance obsolete? The cases propounding what the *Adams* court calls the "modern view of trespass" may have been motivated less by the discoveries of modern physics than by sympathy for particular plaintiffs whose actions would be barred by the comparatively short statutes of limitations that generally apply to nuisance as opposed to trespass. See Martin v. Reynolds Metals Co., supra (plaintiff's claim barred by statute of limitations if characterized as a nuisance, but not if regarded as a trespass); Borland v. Sanders Lead Co., 369 So.2d 523 (Ala. 1979) (same). Why do you suppose trespass has a relatively long statute of limitations as compared to nuisance?

3.   As noted by the court in *Adams*, courts adopting the "modern" view do not follow the simple, strict liability approach to traditionally "nontangible" invasions. For example, would the entry by a single particle not visible to the naked eye count as a trespass? Should repeated invasion by nonvisible and otherwise harmless particles give rise to an injunction? One court, in deferring the question of which approach to take to trespass made the following observation:

> We recognize that the dispersion of airborne particles, whatever their nature, may technically be considered an entry onto land creating liability for trespass irrespective of whether any damage was caused. Because the ambient environment always contains particulate matter from many sources, such a technical reading of trespass would subject countless persons and entities to automatic liability for trespass absent any demonstrated injury. Plainly, that cannot be the law—and, as far as we can tell, no jurisdiction has so held.

John Larkin, Inc. v. Marceau, 959 A.2d 551, 555 (Vt. 2008).

4.   How do we tell whether an intrusion is "substantial"? The *Adams* court states that a need to balance the plaintiff's damages against the social utility of the defendant's activity "[l]ogically follow[s]" from the requirement of substantial damages. Do you agree? Is the court claiming that we can only know if damages are substantial if they outweigh the utility of the conduct that produces them? Would physical damage to the land ever be considered anything other than substantial? What if a plant producing a desperately needed drug moves next door to a modest residential community and causes deafening noise day and night? Is that substantial injury? Is the substantiality of the harm a question of fact? Despite the court's pronouncement, courts have taken a variety of approaches to figuring out what is substantial damage.

5.   When should a "noninvasive" nuisance be actionable? Was the intrusion in *Hendricks v. Stalnaker*, excerpted in Chapter I, noninvasive? Many cases involve aesthetic blight along with noises and odors, but getting a court to recognize a purely aesthetic nuisance was once next to impossible and is still very difficult. Compare Foley v. Harris, 286 S.E.2d 186 (Va. 1982) (upholding injunction against storage of wrecked cars); Allison v. Smith, 695 P.2d 791 (Colo. Ct. App. 1984) (nuisance from storage of disused cars and other junk) with Carroll v. Hurst, 431 N.E.2d 1344, 1349 (Ill. App. Ct. 1982) (rejecting junkyard and salvage operation as nuisance because "under Illinois law, a landowner does not have a right to a pleasing view of his neighbor's land"); Ness v. Albert, 665 S.W.2d 1, 2 (Mo. Ct. App. 1983) (holding junk not to be a nuisance because aesthetic considerations are subjective); Mathewson v. Primeau, 395 P.2d 183 (Wash. 1964) (upholding injunction for odors from hog raising operation but not for aesthetic harm from a pile of junk); see generally Prosser and Keeton on Torts § 87, at 626. Nor have courts been receptive to claims of nuisance based on the identity of a land user. See Rachel D. Godsil, Race Nuisance: The Politics of Law in the Jim Crow Era, 105 Mich. L. Rev. 505, 516 (2006) (showing that courts even in the Jim Crow South routinely denied nuisance claims based on race of occupants of neighboring parcels, in contrast to their enforcement of racially restrictive covenants); see also Taja-Nia Y. Henderson & Jamila Jefferson-Jones, #LivingWhileBlack: Blackness as Nuisance, 69 Am. U.L. Rev. 863, 898 (2020) (noting that despite this history, "ideas about racial inferiority feature prominently" in the decisions denying nuisance relief). In contrast, courts have been relatively receptive to noninvasive nuisance claims based on the depressing effect of funeral homes and graveyards. Does this make sense?

Some commentators have urged a more expansive use of nuisance for noninvasive harms, on the ground that these harms are no less real than those flowing from noises and odors. See, e.g., John Copeland Nagle, Moral Nuisances, 50 Emory L.J. 265 (2001); George P. Smith & Griffin W. Fernandez, The Price of Beauty: An Economic Approach to Aesthetic Nuisance, 15 Harv. Envtl. L. Rev. 53, 53 (1991). Others would hew closer to the traditional invasion test, at least presumptively. See, e.g., Eric R. Claeys, Jefferson Meets Coase: Land-Use Torts, Law and Economics, and Natural Property Rights, 85 Notre Dame L. Rev. 1379 (2010); Richard A. Epstein,

Nuisance Law: Corrective Justice and Its Utilitarian Constraints, 8 J. Legal Stud. 49 (1979); J.E. Penner, Nuisance and the Character of the Neighbourhood, 5 J. Envtl. L. 1, 14–25 (1993); Henry E. Smith, Exclusion and Property Rules in the Law of Nuisance, 90 Va. L. Rev. 965 (2004). Consider, in this regard, Mark v. State Department of Fish and Wildlife, 974 P.2d 716 (Or. App. 1999), in which the appeals court held the plaintiff stated a cause of action in private and public nuisance against a state agency for failing to prevent public nudity in an adjacent wildlife area. Interestingly the court employed the term "invasive nudity" despite the fact that the nudists did not actually enter onto the plaintiff's land. Rather, what counted was the unavoidability of seeing the "full adult nudity" and "repeated acts of depravity, illegality and lewdness." Id. at 718. What are the grounds for considering naked adults a nuisance, but not junked cars?

6. All the foregoing questions about tangibility, substantiality, and aesthetics have been raised more recently by groups projecting messages with light onto buildings. Sometimes, the purpose is to protest, as when artist Robin Bell projected "Emoluments Welcome" over the doors of then-President Donald Trump's D.C. hotel, or when pro-life groups projected graphic images onto Planned Parenthood facilities and a nativity scene on an American Civil Liberties Union building. But light messages have also been projected as "guerrilla" advertising, for instance, when T-Mobile projected its logo and quips about service quality onto the side of Comcast's headquarters. See Maureen E. Brady, Property and Projection, 133 Harv. L. Rev. 1143, 1145 (2020). Only a few courts have considered whether or how the property torts apply to this conduct. Compare International Union of Painters & Allied Trades District Council 15 Local 159 v. Great Wash Park, LLC, No. 67453, 2016 WL 4499940 (Nev. Ct. App. Aug. 18, 2016) (deciding the plaintiff would fail under either traditional or modern theory of trespass because light is intangible and caused no damage); id. at *8 (Tao, J., concurring) (expressing the view that nuisance's "balancing of competing interests" should permit examination of whether the "intensity, duration, or other qualities of the projection were unreasonable or excessive"); Urban Phila. Liberty Tr. v. Ctr. City Organized for Responsible Dev., Nos. 171002675, 3686 EDA 2017, 2017 WL 7313667 (Pa. Ct. Com. Pl. Dec. 28, 2017) (rejecting claim that projections were a nuisance on the grounds that projections involve constitutionally protected speech and cause no significant harm). Although most projections to date have involved union messaging, advertising, or artistic displays, one can imagine others that seem more unsavory, like an angry neighbor projecting an unsightly image onto his neighbor's house. Should light projections be considered as trespasses, nuisances, or neither? Is the projection of light messaging onto buildings meaningfully different from other forms of intangible invasions?

7. What about "virtual" invasions of land? Augmented reality games that use geolocation permit developers to place virtual objects on real property that players can see through their phone screens or other technologies. Should this sort of activity ever generate nuisance or trespass liability? Several law review publications have considered that question with respect to one of the most popular augmented reality games, "Pokémon Go,"

which let users view and try to "catch" creatures on private and public property. See Donald J. Kochan, Playing with Real Property Inside Augmented Reality: Pokemon Go, Trespass, and Law's Limitations, Whittier L. Rev., Spring 2018, at 70; Ryan Mitchell, Comment, Pokemon Go-es Directly to Court: How Pokemon Go Illustrates the Issue of Virtual Trespass and the Need for Evolved Tort Laws, 49 Tex. Tech. L. Rev. 959 (2017). What about possible liability for induced trespass (which courts are reluctant to entertain)? Molly Shaffer Van Houweling, Tempting Trespass or Suggesting Sociability? Augmented Reality and the Right to Include, 51 U.C. Davis L. Rev. 731 (2017). The creators of Pokémon Go settled a large class action lawsuit filed in California in 2019, promising to give the owners of "single-family residential properties" a right of removal "within 40 meters." Eriq Gardner, "Pokemon Go" Creator Agrees to Tighter Leash on Virtual Creatures to End Class Action, Hollywood Rep. (Feb. 15, 2019, 7:23 AM), https://www.hollywoodreporter.com/thr-esq/pokemon-go-creator-agrees-tighter-leash-virtual-creatures-end-class-action-1187097.

8.   Cleveland-Cliffs announced that it will close the Empire Mine at the end of 2016, eliminating 400 jobs in the Palmer area, and the mine has been idled indefinitely. The company cited falling iron ore prices and increased imports from China as reasons. See John Barnes, End of Empire mine, "end of the life," Detroit News (May 9, 2016), www.detroitnews.com/story/news/michigan/2016/05/08/empire-mine-end-life-michigan-upper-peninsula/84126352/; Cleveland-Cliffs Inc. 2020 Form 10-K Annual Report, U.S. Securities and Exchange Commission, at 40.

Natural Intrusions

How should courts treat intrusions from neighboring property that deprive the plaintiff of some portion of his column of space but are attributable to forces of nature rather than intentional human conduct? The classic problem involves trees planted on the defendant's land that, over time, grow branches or roots that enter the plaintiff's column of space. The traditional common law rule here treats the intruding tree as a trespass, but limits the plaintiff to self-help in remediating the trespass. Thus, the plaintiff can cut off the intruding limb or root, but cannot force the defendant to perform tree surgery, or extract a payment of damages from the defendant for any injury or harm caused by the intrusion. W. Page Keeton et al., Prosser and Keeton on Torts § 57, at 391 (5th ed. 1984); Daniel J. Wisniewski, Vegetation as a Nuisance, 8 J.L. Econ. & Pol'y 931 (2012). Can you articulate a possible rationale or rationales for this unusual rule? Does limiting the plaintiff to self-help in this context promote neighborly accommodation, or foment discord? Should there be an exception if the defendant deliberately plants a fast-growing tree next to the property line in order to harass the plaintiff? What if cutting off the limb or roots causes the tree to die?

Recently, the Virginia Supreme Court departed from the common law approach by holding that intrusions of tree roots, at least in a suburban setting, should be governed by the law of nuisance. Fancher v.

Fagella, 650 S.E.2d 519 (Va. 2007). Thus, intruding tree roots and limbs can give rise to liability if they "cause actual harm" and are "unreasonable," taking into account the nature of the locality, and both damages and injunctive relief against the owner of the tree are potentially available. Limiting the scope of nuisance the court held that " 'encroaching trees and plants are not nuisances merely because they cast shade, drop leaves, flowers, or fruit, or just because they happen to encroach upon adjoining property either above or below the ground.' " Id. at 555–56 (quoting Lane v. W.J. Curry & Sons, 92 S.W.3d 355, 364 (Tenn. 2002)). Does shifting from trespass (limited to self-help) to nuisance in this context provide a better prospect of promoting neighborly accommodation? Or is it likely to produce a lot of vexatious litigation when neighbors have different preferences about vegetation? Some states relegate the intruded upon landowner to self-help, but allow an action in cases of actual or imminent harm from the offending tree. Another, less common, approach is to limit actionability to "noxious" or "artificial" vegetation. Should access to tort law turn on evaluation of these variables? Don't forget that the law of negligence may apply to trees as well.

Another issue involving intrusions of nature concerns water. It is clear that when a defendant interferes with the natural flow of a watercourse, for example by building a dam, and this causes the plaintiff's land to be inundated by water, this deprivation of possession can be regarded as a trespass. See Restatement (Second) of Torts § 158 cmt. *i*, illus. 5. Yet, for a variety of reasons, flooding another's land has always fallen in an ambiguous territory between trespass, nuisance, and strict liability. Dan B. Dobbs, The Law of Torts 106 (2000). In the famous case of *Rylands v. Fletcher*, (1868) 3 L.R.E. & I. App. 330, 339–40 (H.L.), the English House of Lords held the defendant strictly liable for flooding caused by seepage of water from a holding pond into an abandoned mining shaft, which then burst into the plaintiff's mine. But the court limited its holding by characterizing the pond as a "non-natural" use of the land. The notion seems to be that flooding will lead to more automatic liability when caused by some human manipulation of property. American courts are divided about the rule in *Rylands*. Dobbs, supra § 347, at 952.

On the other hand, if property is inundated by a natural flood, courts have traditionally allowed landowners to exercise self-help to protect themselves from the waters, even if this results in more water inundating a neighbor's land. This is the so-called "common enemy" doctrine, briefly noted in Chapter III. The common enemy doctrine obviously bears some resemblance to the common law treatment of tree limbs and roots. Again, some courts have begun to question the doctrine, and have started to apply more nuisance-like regimes in assessing landowner behavior in the face of flooding caused by forces of nature. Smith, supra, 90 Va. L. Rev. at 1017–18.

3. PROPERTY RULES, LIABILITY RULES, AND REMEDIES

Nuisance disputes raise squarely the question of whether to enjoin the offending activity or to require the one committing the nuisance to pay damages, or some combination of both. The question whether courts should issue injunctions or award damages for violations of property rights is often discussed in the scholarly literature in terms of the distinction between "property rules" and "liability rules." Credit for this distinction goes to Guido Calabresi, one of the early pioneers of law and economics who went on to become Dean of the Yale School and then a judge on the U.S. Court of Appeals for the Second Circuit, and one of his Harvard Law School students, Douglas Melamed. As we shall see, property rules do not always equate with injunctions and damages do not always implement a liability rule. Nevertheless, property rights are strongly associated with "property rule" protection, while contract rights and many rights protected by tort law are more closely associated with "liability rule" protection. In the hands of Calabresi and Melamed, however, all types of entitlements were merged together, and analyzed in terms of the degree of protection provided against takings by third parties or the state.

Guido Calabresi & A. Douglas Melamed, *Property Rules, Liability Rules, and Inalienability: One View of the Cathedral*
85 HARV. L. REV. 1089, 1090, 1092–93 (1972).

* * * The first issue which must be faced by any legal system is one we call the problem of "entitlement." Whenever a state is presented with the conflicting interests of two or more people, or two or more groups of people, it must decide which side to favor. Absent such a decision, access to goods, services, and life itself will be decided on the basis of "might makes right"—whoever is stronger or shrewder will win. Hence the fundamental thing that law does is to decide which of the conflicting parties will be entitled to prevail. The entitlement to make noise versus the entitlement to have silence, the entitlement to pollute versus the entitlement to breathe clean air, the entitlement to have children versus the entitlement to forbid them—these are the first order of legal decisions. * * *

The state not only has to decide whom to entitle, but it must also simultaneously make a series of equally difficult second order decisions. These decisions go to the manner in which entitlements are protected and to whether an individual is allowed to sell or trade the entitlement. In any given dispute, for example, the state must decide not only which side wins but also the kind of protection to grant. * * * We shall consider three types of entitlements—entitlements protected by property rules, entitlements protected by liability rules, and inalienable entitlements. * * *

An entitlement is protected by a property rule to the extent that someone who wishes to remove the entitlement from its holder must buy it from him in a voluntary transaction in which the value of the entitlement is agreed upon by the seller. It is the form of entitlement which gives rise to the least amount of state intervention: once the original entitlement is decided upon, the state does not try to decide its value. It lets each of the parties say how much the entitlement is worth to him, and gives the seller a veto if the buyer does not offer enough. Property rules involve a collective decision as to who is to be given an initial entitlement but not as to the value of the entitlement.

Whenever someone may destroy the initial entitlement if he is willing to pay an objectively determined value for it, an entitlement is protected by a liability rule. This value may be what it is thought the original holder of the entitlement would have sold it for. But the holder's complaint that he would have demanded more will not avail him once the objectively determined value is set. Obviously, liability rules involve an additional stage of state intervention: not only are entitlements protected, but their transfer or destruction is allowed on the basis of a value determined by some organ of the state rather than by the parties themselves.

An entitlement is inalienable to the extent that its transfer is not permitted between a willing buyer and a willing seller. The state intervenes not only to determine who is initially entitled and to determine the compensation that must be paid if the entitlement is taken or destroyed, but also to forbid its sale under some or all circumstances. Inalienability rules are thus quite different from property and liability rules. Unlike those rules, rules of inalienability not only "protect" the entitlement; they may also be viewed as limiting or regulating the grant of the entitlement itself.

It should be clear that most entitlements to most goods are mixed. Taney's house may be protected by a property rule in situations where Marshall wishes to purchase it, by a liability rule where the government decides to take it by eminent domain, and by a rule of inalienability in situations where Taney is drunk or incompetent. * * *

NOTES

1.   Most of the scholarship that follows Calabresi and Melamed has focused on the distinction between property rules and liability rules and has assumed that "property rule" protection means mandatory relief (an injunction or no liability) and "liability rule" means payments of monetary compensation (usually from defendant to plaintiff but occasionally the other way around). This is an oversimplification. An entitlement is protected by a "property rule" when it cannot be taken without the holder's consent. An entitlement is protected by a "liability rule" when it can be taken by what amounts to a forced sale—the holder of the entitlement has no choice but to give it up in return for an award of monetary compensation. When we find

that an entitlement is protected by a property rule, this understanding can be enforced in a variety of ways designed to preserve the principle that the entitlement cannot be taken without the holder's consent, including throwing violators of entitlements in jail or privileging entitlement holders to use self-help to deter violators. Recall that one purpose of the punitive damages award in *Jacque v. Steenberg Homes* (in Chapter I) was to make the point that entities like Steenberg Homes cannot enter real property without the owner's consent. Thus, it is inaccurate to suggest, as some of the literature does, that the court's decision to enter an injunction somehow "creates" a property rule. An injunction is an in personam order that binds a particular party to desist from certain acts or to perform certain acts. An injunction thus will often *reflect* a judicial judgment that a certain entitlement is entitled to property rule protection. But the underlying understanding of what it means to protect an entitlement with a "property rule" is grounded in an anterior understanding about the nature of the rights that persons in the position of the entitlement holder have, and in particular in the perception that all other persons have a duty to respect these rights. Analogous points can be made about entitlements protected by liability rules. In general, whether a court decides to enter an injunction or award damages is *evidence* of the court's conception of the degree of protection the entitlement should be given, but these remedial orders do not themselves define the appropriate degree of protection. See Jules L. Coleman & Jody Kraus, Rethinking the Theory of Legal Rights, 95 Yale L.J. 1335, 1345 (1986); Dale A. Nance, Guidance Rules and Enforcement Rules: A Better View of the Cathedral, 83 Va. L. Rev. 837 (1997); see also John C. Harrison, Immunity Rules, in The Legacy of Wesley Hohfeld: Edited Major Works, Select Personal Papers, and Original Commentaries (Shyam Balganesh, Ted Sichelman & Henry Smith eds., forthcoming), https://ssrn.com/abstract= 2918975 (arguing that the Calabresi and Melamed framework wrongly conflates accidents and takings); Troy A. Rule, Entitlement-Shifting Rules, 62 B.C. L. Rev. 1193 (2021) (analyzing and critiquing devices like proposed drone regulations as "entitlement-shifting" rules).

2.   The common starting point in the literature discussing property rules and liability rules is that courts have a "choice" along two dimensions. First, they can choose to assign the entitlement to either the plaintiff or the defendant. Second, they can choose to protect this entitlement with either a property rule or a liability rule. This yields four "rules," conventionally diagrammed as follows:

Figure 9-2
Calabresi & Melamed box

Mode of Protection

	Property Rule	**Liability Rule**
Plaintiff	Rule 1	Rule 2
Defendant	Rule 3	Rule 4

Assignment of Entitlement

The stock example used to illustrate these four possibilities is a nuisance dispute like the ones in *Jost v. Dairyland Power Cooperative* and *Campbell v. Seaman* where the defendant is engaged in some polluting activity and the plaintiff is a nearby farmer or resident who objects. One possible choice the court can make (Rule 1) is to award the entitlement to the plaintiff and to protect this by a property rule. This means (among other things) that the plaintiff can insist on an injunction forcing the defendant to abate the nuisance, or if this is not possible, to stop the nuisance-generating activity. *Campbell* is an example, because the plaintiff obtained an injunction.

A second choice (Rule 2) is again to award the entitlement to the plaintiff, but this time to protect the entitlement with a liability rule. This means the defendant can take the plaintiff's entitlement without the plaintiff's consent, typically upon payment of court-determined damages, which here would probably be the diminished market value of the land subject to the nuisance. *Jost* is an example of Rule 2. The famous case of *Boomer v. Atlantic Cement*, 257 N.E.2d 870 (N.Y. 1970), a staple of torts courses, is another example of Rule 2. In that case, plaintiffs sued the defendant in nuisance for dirt, smoke, and vibrations caused by their cement plant near Albany, New York. At trial, a nuisance was found, but the court awarded temporary damages (compensating for the harm that had already occurred) as opposed to an injunction. On appeal, the New York Court of Appeals changed the remedy, awarding the plaintiffs an injunction that could be vacated upon the payment of permanent damages: the net present value of all future damages suffered by the plaintiffs. In other words, although the plaintiffs were awarded the entitlement, the cement plant could continue operating by paying. *Boomer* became a famous case, in part because when it was decided the then-nascent law-and-economics movement was concerned with problems of high transaction costs and holdouts when the number of affected parties is large. A conflict between a single polluter and multiple residents was the archetypal example of a high-transaction-cost dispute in this literature. Most commentators came to agree that in such a situation, damages (liability rules) are preferable to injunctions (property rules). The facts and the remedial outcome in *Boomer* seemed to confirm this analysis. See, e.g., A. Mitchell Polinsky, Resolving Nuisance Disputes: The Simple Economics of Injunctive and Damage Remedies, 32 Stan. L. Rev. 1075, 1076 (1980). More recently, some have begun to voice doubts. See, e.g., Daniel A. Farber, Reassessing *Boomer*: Justice, Efficiency, and Nuisance Law, in Property Law and Legal Education: Essays in Honor of John E. Cribbet 7, 8–9 (Peter Hay & Michael H. Hoeflich eds., 1988); Smith, supra, 90 Va. L. Rev. at 1037–45.

A third possibility (Rule 3) would be to award the entitlement to the defendant protected by a property rule. This means the offensive activity can continue, and the plaintiff can get it abated or removed only by getting the *defendant's* consent. Airplane overflight cases (such as *Hinman v. Pacific Air Transport* in Chapter I) might be considered Rule 3 decisions: The court holds airline companies have the entitlement to use the airspace at cruising altitudes, meaning the surface owner would have to get their consent to stop them from using it. Or *Tucker v. Mack Paving Co.*, cited in Note 1 after *Campbell*, by refusing to find the defendant liable, might be thought to create a de facto "entitlement" to pollute. (Or does it? We return to this issue at the end of this Section.)

Finally, a fourth possibility (Rule 4) is that the entitlement is awarded to the defendant, but the plaintiff can force the defendant to transfer the entitlement to the plaintiff in return for a payment of money compensation. We will encounter this possibility in the next case in this Section, *Spur Industries, Inc. v. Del E. Webb Development Co.*, where the court held that the plaintiff can force the defendant to stop committing a nuisance but only upon paying compensation to the defendant for the cost that this would entail.

3.   In discussing how to assign the initial entitlement, and the choice of whether to protect that entitlement with a property rule or a liability rule, Calabresi and Melamed addressed three factors: "economic efficiency," "distributional preferences," and "other justice considerations." Subsequent commentators have tended to collapse the three factors into two: efficiency and distributive justice. Although this simplifies (oversimplifies?) matters, the decisional calculus is still quite complex. We will offer only a flavor of the type of discussion found in the literature.

4.   Much of the literature, building on Ronald Coase (Chapter I), focuses on transaction costs. The central insight is that when transaction costs are low, thereby making consensual exchange of entitlements a realistic possibility, courts should prefer property rule protection (Rules 1 and 3). This is because efficiency concerns can be satisfied by the possibility of exchange. If the plaintiff values the entitlement more than the defendant, the plaintiff will end up with the entitlement: Either the plaintiff will refuse to sell to the defendant (under Rule 1) or the plaintiff will buy the entitlement from the defendant (under Rule 3). Conversely, if the defendant values the entitlement more than the plaintiff, then the defendant will end up with the entitlement: Either the defendant will buy the entitlement from

the plaintiff (under Rule 1) or the defendant will refuse to sell to the plaintiff (under Rule 3). Either way, the entitlement ends up in the hands of the party who values it the most, in terms of being willing to pay the most for it. And the parties themselves will have made the valuation of the entitlement, ensuring that no subjective or idiosyncratic values have been overlooked by the court. Thus, the court can concentrate on distributional concerns or other justice factors. If these non-efficiency factors favor the plaintiff, use Rule 1. Under this rule, any post-decisional flow of funds will go to the plaintiff. If the non-efficiency factors favor the defendant, use Rule 3. Any post-decisional flow of funds will then go to the defendant. Recently some scholars have argued that various more complicated liability rules can be tailored to solve these other problems, and controversy continues over the relative advantages of liability rules and property rules in the low transaction cost setting. See Note 7 infra.

5.   Things get a good deal more complicated when transaction costs are high. Here, a variety of arguments about the relative merits of property rules and liability rules have been advanced, but one point of consensus is that when transaction costs are high there may be circumstances in which shifting to liability rules is preferred, at least on efficiency grounds. One argument, which originated with Calabresi and Melamed themselves, focuses on problems involving large numbers of parties on one side or another of a dispute. See 85 Harv. L. Rev. at 1106–08. Consider property rules. If the numerous side wants to buy out the singular side, it will be frustrated by free-rider problems, and if the singular side wishes to buy off the numerous side, there will tend to be hold-outs. Liability rules appear to cut through these problems, although they do present problems of their own, if plaintiffs have to organize to sue. Further, the process of assessing damages can be fraught with the same problems that would be encountered in trying to negotiate the buyout of an entitlement. Damages must be calculated by the court, and if they vary from person to person or are difficult to measure, the assessment process may also encounter analogous difficulties that render the apparent advantage of liability rules illusory. See James E. Krier & Stewart J. Schwab, Property Rules and Liability Rules: The Cathedral in Another Light, 70 N.Y.U. L. Rev. 440, 453–64 (1995).

6.   Another argument for liability rules under conditions of high transaction costs posits that courts may have more limited information than the parties about the benefits and costs of allocating entitlements. See, e.g., Polinsky, supra. Suppose, for example, that the court has good information about the plaintiff's damages, but poor information about the defendant's costs of eliminating the harm. The court is reasonably certain that the plaintiff's damages are $5,000, based on testimony about the value of the property before and after the nuisance arose. But the defendant claims that abating the nuisance will require new equipment, at a cost of tens of thousands of dollars (or even shutting down a plant, wasting a large investment and destroying jobs). The court suspects that the defendant is bluffing, and that the actual cost of eliminating the nuisance may be much less. In these circumstances, the argument goes, the court can adopt Rule 2, in effect giving the defendant the option of paying the plaintiff's damages

($5,000) or eliminating the nuisance. Now the defendant no longer has any incentive to bluff. If she can figure out a way of eliminating the nuisance for less than $5,000, she will do so. If not, she will pay the plaintiff $5,000. The result will be efficient, in the sense that the defendant will choose the lowest-cost solution for eliminating the plaintiff's injury, without any need for the court to dictate the solution or the parties to engage in exchanges of entitlements.

7.   The literature on property rules and liability rules is vast. For an overview, see Carol M. Rose, The Shadow of the Cathedral, 106 Yale L.J. 2175 (1996). The Krier and Schwab article cited above provides a particularly clear summary of the principal developments in the literature. See also, e.g., Ian Ayres, Optional Law: The Structure of Legal Entitlements (2005) (arguing for general superiority of various liability rules); Keith N. Hylton, Property Rules and Defensive Conduct in Tort Law, 4 J. Tort L. 1 (2011) (justifying property rules as obviating defensive conduct); Louis Kaplow & Steven Shavell, Property Rules Versus Liability Rules: An Economic Analysis, 109 Harv. L. Rev. 713 (1996) (arguing that liability rules are better when the parties assert incompatible demands on a resource, but property rules are better when the parties seek to make the same use of a resource); Henry E. Smith, Property and Property Rules, 79 N.Y.U. L. Rev. 1719 (2004) (defending widespread use of property rules based on information costs). Recently commentators have sought to extend the Calabresi and Melamed framework with insights from organization theory and psychology. See, e.g. Gregg P. Macey, Coasean Blind Spots: Charting the Incomplete Institutionalism, 98 Geo. L.J. 863 (2010); Jonathan Remy Nash & Stephanie M. Stern, Property Frames, 87 Wash. U. L. Rev. 449 (2010).

8.   Calabresi and Melamed also have interesting things to say about inalienability rules, which prohibit the transfer of entitlements from the original holder. Inalienability rules usually apply to persons (e.g., you cannot sell yourself into slavery), body parts (e.g., sales of organs and tissue are either prohibited or tightly regulated), cultural patrimony (e.g., you cannot sell certain kinds of Native American cultural artifacts), and so forth.

Spur Industries, Inc. v. Del E. Webb Development Co.

Supreme Court of Arizona, 1972.
494 P.2d 700.

■ CAMERON, VICE CHIEF JUSTICE. From a judgment permanently enjoining the defendant, Spur Industries, Inc., from operating a cattle feedlot near the plaintiff Del E. Webb Development Company's Sun City, Spur appeals. Webb cross-appeals. Although numerous issues are raised, we feel that it is necessary to answer only two questions. They are:

1.   Where the operation of a business, such as a cattle feedlot is lawful in the first instance, but becomes a nuisance by reason of a nearby residential area, may the feedlot operation be enjoined in an action brought by the developer of the residential area?

2.   Assuming that the nuisance may be enjoined, may the developer of a completely new town or urban area in a previously agricultural area be required to indemnify the operator of the feedlot who must move or cease operation because of the presence of the residential area created by the developer?

The facts necessary for a determination of this matter on appeal are as follows. The area in question is located in Maricopa County, Arizona, some 14 to 15 miles west of the urban area of Phoenix, on the Phoenix-Wickenburg Highway, also known as Grand Avenue. About two miles south of Grand Avenue is Olive Avenue which runs east and west. 111th Avenue runs north and south as does the Agua Fria River immediately to the west. See Exhibits A and B below.

Farming started in this area about 1911. In 1929, with the completion of the Carl Pleasant Dam, gravity flow water became available to the property located to the west of the Agua Fria River, though land to the east remained dependent upon well water for irrigation. By 1950, the only urban areas in the vicinity were the agriculturally related communities of Peoria, El Mirage, and Surprise located along Grand Avenue. Along 111th Avenue, approximately one mile south of Grand Avenue and 1 1/2 miles north of Olive Avenue, the community of Youngtown was commenced in 1954. Youngtown is a retirement community appealing primarily to senior citizens.

In 1956, Spur's predecessors in interest, H. Marion Welborn and the Northside Hay Mill and Trading Company, developed feed-lots, about 1/2 mile south of Olive Avenue, in an area between the confluence of the usually dry Agua Fria and New Rivers. The area is well suited for cattle feeding and in 1959, there were 25 cattle feeding pens or dairy operations within a 7 mile radius of the location developed by Spur's predecessors. In April and May of 1959, the Northside Hay Mill was feeding between 6,000 and 7,000 head of cattle and Welborn approximately 1,500 head on a combined area of 35 acres.

In May of 1959, Del Webb began to plan the development of an urban area to be known as Sun City. For this purpose, the Marinette and the Santa Fe Ranches, some 20,000 acres of farmland, were purchased for $15,000,000 or $750.00 per acre. This price was considerably less than the price of land located near the urban area of Phoenix, and along with the success of Youngtown was a factor influencing the decision to purchase the property in question.

Figure 9-3
Exhibits A and B

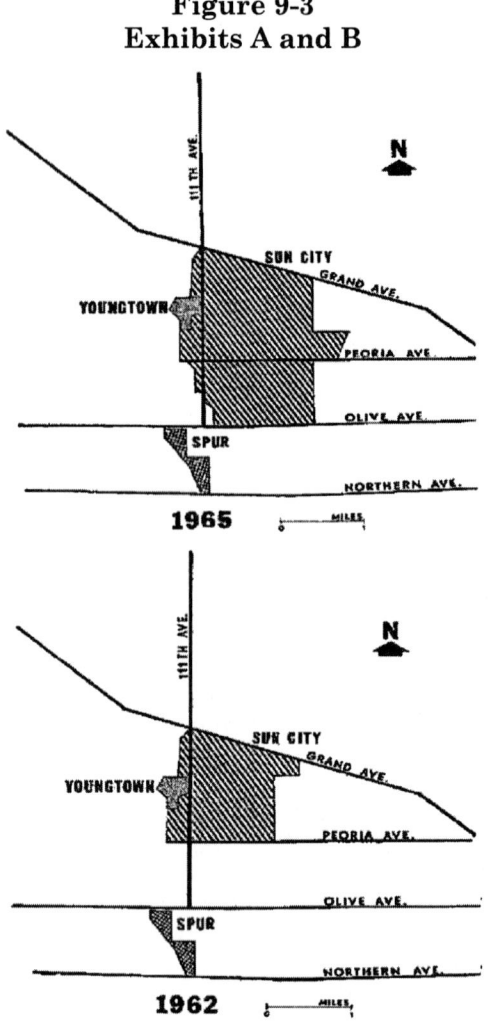

By September 1959, Del Webb had started construction of a golf course south of Grand Avenue and Spur's predecessors had started to level ground for more feedlot area. In 1960, Spur purchased the property in question and began a rebuilding and expansion program extending both to the north and south of the original facilities. By 1962, Spur's expansion program was completed and had expanded from approximately 35 acres to 114 acres. See Exhibit A[.]

Accompanied by an extensive advertising campaign, homes were first offered by Del Webb in January 1960 and the first unit to be completed was south of Grand Avenue and approximately 2 1/2 miles north of Spur. By 2 May 1960, there were 450 to 500 houses completed or under construction. At this time, Del Webb did not consider odors from the Spur feed pens a problem and Del Webb continued to develop in a southerly direction, until sales resistance became so great that the parcels were difficult if not impossible to sell. * * *

By December 1967, Del Webb's property had extended south to Olive Avenue and Spur was within 500 feet of Olive Avenue to the north. See Exhibit B above. Del Webb filed its original complaint alleging that in excess of 1,300 lots in the southwest portion were unfit for development for sale as residential lots because of the operation of the Spur feedlot.

Del Webb's suit complained that the Spur feeding operation was a public nuisance because of the flies and the odor which were drifting or being blown by the prevailing south to north wind over the southern portion of Sun City. At the time of the suit, Spur was feeding between 20,000 and 30,000 head of cattle, and the facts amply support the finding of the trial court that the feed pens had become a nuisance to the people who resided in the southern part of Del Webb's development. The testimony indicated that cattle in a commercial feedlot will produce 35 to 40 pounds of wet manure per day, per head, or over a million pounds of wet manure per day for 30,000 head of cattle, and that despite the admittedly good feedlot management and good housekeeping practices by Spur, the resulting odor and flies produced an annoying if not unhealthy situation as far as the senior citizens of southern Sun City were concerned. There is no doubt that some of the citizens of Sun City were unable to enjoy the outdoor living which Del Webb had advertised and that Del Webb was faced with sales resistance from prospective purchasers as well as strong and persistent complaints from the people who had purchased homes in that area. * * *

[N]either the citizens of Sun City nor Youngtown are represented in this lawsuit and the suit is solely between Del E. Webb Development Company and Spur Industries, Inc.

MAY SPUR BE ENJOINED?

The difference between a private nuisance and a public nuisance is generally one of degree. A private nuisance is one affecting a single individual or a definite small number of persons in the enjoyment of private rights not common to the public, while a public nuisance is one affecting the rights enjoyed by citizens as a part of the public. To constitute a public nuisance, the nuisance must affect a considerable number of people or an entire community or neighborhood. City of Phoenix v. Johnson, 75 P.2d 30 (Ariz. 1938).

Where the injury is slight, the remedy for minor inconveniences lies in an action for damages rather than in one for an injunction. Kubby v. Hammond, 198 P.2d 134 (Ariz. 1948). Moreover, some courts have held, in the "balancing of conveniences" cases, that damages may be the sole remedy. See Boomer v. Atlantic Cement Co., 257 N.E.2d 870 (N.Y. 1970), and annotation comments, 40 A.L.R.3d 601.

Thus, it would appear from the admittedly incomplete record as developed in the trial court, that, at most, residents of Youngtown would be entitled to damages rather than injunctive relief.

We have no difficulty, however, in agreeing with the conclusion of the trial court that Spur's operation was an enjoinable public nuisance as far as the people in the southern portion of Del Webb's Sun City were concerned.

§ 36–601, subsec. A reads as follows:

§ 36–601. Public nuisances dangerous to public health

A. The following conditions are specifically declared public nuisances dangerous to the public health:

1. Any condition or place in populous areas which constitutes a breeding place for flies, rodents, mosquitoes and other insects which are capable of carrying and transmitting disease-causing organisms to any person or persons.

By this statute, before an otherwise lawful (and necessary) business may be declared a public nuisance, there must be a "populous" area in which people are injured:

[I]t hardly admits a doubt that, in determining the question as to whether a lawful occupation is so conducted as to constitute a nuisance as a matter of fact, the locality and surroundings are of the first importance. A business which is not per se a public nuisance may become such by being carried on at a place where the health, comfort, or convenience of a populous neighborhood is affected. * * * What might amount to a serious nuisance in one locality by reason of the density of the population, or character of the neighborhood affected, may in another place and under different surroundings be deemed proper and unobjectionable.

MacDonald v. Perry, 255 P. 494, 497 (Ariz. 1927).

It is clear that as to the citizens of Sun City, the operation of Spur's feedlot was both a public and a private nuisance. They could have successfully maintained an action to abate the nuisance. Del Webb, having shown a special injury in the loss of sales, had a standing to bring suit to enjoin the nuisance. Engle v. Clark, 90 P.2d 994 (Ariz. 1939); City of Phoenix v. Johnson, supra. The judgment of the trial court permanently enjoining the operation of the feedlot is affirmed.

MUST DEL WEBB INDEMNIFY SPUR?

A suit to enjoin a nuisance sounds in equity and the courts have long recognized a special responsibility to the public when acting as a court of equity:

§ 104.   Where public interest is involved.

Courts of equity may, and frequently do, go much further both to give and withhold relief in furtherance of the public interest than they are accustomed to go when only private interests are involved. Accordingly, the granting or withholding of relief may properly be dependent upon considerations of public interest.

27 Am.Jur.2d, Equity, page 626.

In addition to protecting the public interest, however, courts of equity are concerned with protecting the operator of a lawfully, albeit noxious, business from the result of a knowing and willful encroachment by others near his business.

In the so-called "coming to the nuisance" cases, the courts have held that the residential landowner may not have relief if he knowingly came into a neighborhood reserved for industrial or agricultural endeavors and has been damaged thereby * * *

Were Webb the only party injured, we would feel justified in holding that the doctrine of "coming to the nuisance" would have been a bar to the relief asked by Webb, and, on the other hand, had Spur located the feedlot near the outskirts of a city and had the city grown toward the feedlot, Spur would have to suffer the cost of abating the nuisance as to those people locating within the growth pattern of the expanding city * * *

We agree, however, with the Massachusetts court that:

The law of nuisance affords no rigid rule to be applied in all instances. It is elastic. It undertakes to require only that which is fair and reasonable under all the circumstances. In a commonwealth like this, which depends for its material prosperity so largely on the continued growth and enlargement of manufacturing of diverse varieties, "extreme rights" cannot be enforced.

Stevens v. Rockport Granite Co., 104 N.E. 371, 373 (Mass. 1914).

There was no indication in the instant case at the time Spur and its predecessors located in western Maricopa County that a new city would spring up, full-blown, alongside the feeding operation and that the developer of that city would ask the court to order Spur to move because of the new city. Spur is required to move not because of any wrongdoing on the part of Spur, but because of a proper and legitimate regard of the courts for the rights and interests of the public.

Del Webb, on the other hand, is entitled to the relief prayed for (a permanent injunction), not because Webb is blameless, but because of the damage to the people who have been encouraged to purchase homes in Sun City. It does not equitably or legally follow, however, that Webb, being entitled to the injunction, is then free of any liability to Spur if Webb has in fact been the cause of the damage Spur has sustained. It does not seem harsh to require a developer, who has taken advantage of the lesser land values in a rural area as well as the availability of large tracts of land on which to build and develop a new town or city in the area, to indemnify those who are forced to leave as a result.

Having brought people to the nuisance to the foreseeable detriment of Spur, Webb must indemnify Spur for a reasonable amount of the cost of moving or shutting down. It should be noted that this relief to Spur is limited to a case wherein a developer has, with foreseeability, brought into a previously agricultural or industrial area the population which makes necessary the granting of an injunction against a lawful business and for which the business has no adequate relief.

It is therefore the decision of this court that the matter be remanded to the trial court for a hearing upon the damages sustained by the defendant Spur as a reasonable and direct result of the granting of the permanent injunction. Since the result of the appeal may appear novel and both sides have obtained a measure of relief, it is ordered that each side will bear its own costs.

Affirmed in part, reversed in part, and remanded for further proceedings consistent with this opinion.

NOTES AND QUESTIONS

1.   As noted after *Campbell v. Seaman*, coming to the nuisance is a perennial problem, and is usually handled with a multi-factor balancing test. Is coming to the nuisance like a prescriptive easement (see Note 7 after *Campbell v. Seaman*) but without the expectation that the victim of the nuisance will sue? Should the first mover simply pay low damages to owners of neighboring vacant lots (*Boomer*) and benefit from a coming to the nuisance defense if development occurs?

2.   Recall again the framework of property rules and liability rules developed by Calabresi and Melamed. This framework suggests the existence of four rules for handling nuisance disputes, based on which party is given the entitlement and whether the entitlement is protected by a property rule or liability rule. The framework thus led to the "discovery" of Rule 4, in which the polluter would have the "entitlement" to pollute, but protected only by a liability rule. See also James R. Atwood, Note, An Economic Analysis of Land Use Conflicts, 21 Stan. L. Rev. 293 (1969) (advocating injunctions with plaintiff compensating defendant in some coming to the nuisance cases). That is, one or more residents could sue to stop the pollution, but would have to pay the polluter's cost of abating or shutting down. The fact that the Arizona Supreme Court came up with something that looks very much like Rule 4 at roughly the same time Calabresi and Melamed wrote has been cited by subsequent commentators as vindicating the utility of their modeling exercise.

3.   Indeed, a number of commentators have sought to build on the remedial innovation reflected in *Spur* and Calabresi and Melamed's Rule 4. See, e.g., Ellickson, Alternatives to Zoning, supra, at 744–46 (arguing for use of Rule 4 as a second stage option for the plaintiff when a nuisance defendant opts to pay Rule 2 damages and continues the nuisance); Jeff L. Lewin, Compensated Injunctions and the Evolution of Nuisance Law, 71 Iowa L. Rev. 775, 827–31 (1986) (arguing for limited use of compensated injunctions in the interest of fairness); Edward Rabin, Nuisance Law: Rethinking

Fundamental Assumptions, 63 Va. L. Rev. 1299, 1339–46 (1977) (advocating compensated injunctions in cases of deserving plaintiffs only); see also Ian Ayres & Paul M. Goldbart, Optimal Delegation and Decoupling in the Design of Liability Rules, 100 Mich. L. Rev. 1 (2001); Saul Levmore, Unifying Remedies: Property Rules, Liability Rules, and Startling Rules, 106 Yale L.J. 2149 (1997). Others have been less enthusiastic about the possibility of Rule 4. See, e.g., Richard A. Epstein, A Clear View of *The Cathedral*: The Dominance of Property Rules, 106 Yale L.J. 2091, 2103–05 (1997) (criticizing Rule 4 as destabilizing property); Jeanne L. Schroeder, Three's a Crowd: A Feminist Critique of Calabresi and Melamed's *One View of the Cathedral*, 84 Cornell L. Rev. 394, 438 (1999) (providing feminist critique of Rule 4); Henry E. Smith, Exclusion and Property Rules in the Law of Nuisance, 90 Va. L. Rev. 965, 1007–21 (2004) (portraying Rule 4 as inconsistent with a system of basic entitlements that minimizes information costs).

4.   In fact, it appears that *Spur* has received much more attention from law review articles than from courts. Andrew Morriss reports that "*Spur* has not had much direct influence" on the law of nuisance in Arizona, and that "[t]he only reported decision from outside Arizona to consider in detail the doctrinal developments in *Spur* came in an Ohio Common Pleas Court decision rejecting *Spur* as inapplicable because of the greater amount of open space in Arizona." Andrew P. Morriss, Cattle v. Retirees: Sun City and the Battle of *Spur Industries v. Del E. Webb Development Co.*, in Property Stories 337 (Gerald Korngold & Andrew P. Morriss eds., 2d ed. 2009). What accounts for the paucity of judicial interest in the *Spur* remedy? Consider what would have happened if the conflict in *Spur* had simply been between the residents of Sun City and the feedlot. Does the court regard the senior citizens as innocent parties from whom it would not be appropriate to require payments to Spur? Would the residents have had much success in coming up with the money to purchase an injunction closing the feedlot? Given the collective-action difficulties this would have posed, how likely is it that a court would adopt such a remedy? See James E. Krier & Stewart J. Schwab, Property Rules and Liability Rules: The Cathedral in Another Light, 70 N.Y.U. L. Rev. 440, 470 (1995).

5.   More fundamentally, what is the nature of "the entitlement" under Rule 4? Does the Blackstonian package of rights ever come with a "right to pollute"? Would someone with such a "right to pollute" (in the sense of not being liable in nuisance) be able to enjoin the resident from blocking the pollution—as with fans or a wall? (Probably not.) Again, one might acquire an easement, by prescription or negotiation, to pollute and this would add to the polluter's default package of entitlements. See Henry E. Smith, Complexity and the Cathedral: Making Law and Economics More Calabresian, 48 Eur. J.L. & Econ. 43, 54–57 (2019). Does the Calabresi and Melamed framework rest on a flawed conception that whenever a court rules against a plaintiff the defendant has an entitlement that must either be purchased (Rule 3) or taken for just compensation (Rule 4) in order to achieve a different result?

Public Nuisance

Note that Del Webb brought a public nuisance action in *Spur*, whereas the other cases we have considered are private nuisance actions. Public nuisance is as old as private nuisance, but has a very different history. The original action for public nuisance was a criminal proceeding brought in local sheriffs' courts called "leets." The paradigmatic public nuisance was blocking a public highway or a navigable waterway, although actions were also brought for a miscellany of harms to community welfare such as "washing hemp or flax in streams or ponds used for watering cattle," letting animals "wander suffering from the scab," selling "unwholesome food," or catching "immature fish or hunting out of season." J.R. Spencer, Public Nuisance—A Critical Examination, 48 Cambridge L.J. 55, 60 (1989). Public nuisance entered the common law in a limited fashion pursuant to a dictum in a 1535 decision suggesting that persons who suffer "special injury" from a public nuisance like blocking a highway could sue for their individual harm in the common law courts. Anon., Y.B. Mich. 27 Hen. 8, f. 27, pl. 10 (1535). Nevertheless, most public nuisance suits continued to be brought by public officials like the attorney general (this remains true in both the U.K. and the U.S. today). Do you agree that Del Webb and his real estate development company suffered special injury—usually interpreted to mean an injury different in kind from that suffered by other members of the community—from the flies and odors emanating from the cattle feedlot?

Because public nuisance was historically regarded as a crime, an action for public nuisance in the United States requires that it be authorized by the legislature. Some states have enacted generic statutes authorizing suits for a public nuisance, without meaningfully defining the term. Others, as in the Arizona statute quoted in *Spur*, provide more specific direction about the things that qualify as a public nuisance. Over time, through a combination of piecemeal legislation and judicial extrapolations from conventional catalogues of public harms, the concept came to encompass a variety of threats to public health, safety, and comfort. These have included keeping a vicious dog, cultivating black currants (thought to cause pine blister rust), and even putting on an opera that threatens to cause a riot. See Star Opera Co. v. Hylan, 178 N.Y.S. 179 (N.Y. Sup. Ct. 1919) (refusing to enjoin officials from prohibiting the performance of a German-language opera until ratification of peace treaty with Germany, where the company's past performances had led to riotous conduct and police intervention).

Perhaps because actions by private parties pursuant to the special injury exception look very much like a tort action, William Prosser, as Reporter for the Restatement (Second) of Torts, decided in the late 1960s that public nuisance should be added to the Restatement. The result was that the Second Restatement defines a public nuisance to have many of the features of private nuisance, with its emphasis on balancing and the understanding that courts have inherent authority to declare something to be a public nuisance. See Thomas W. Merrill, Is Public Nuisance a Tort?, 4 J. Tort L. Issue 2, Article 4 (2011). This revisionism had little effect on the legal system until a coalition of state attorneys general sued the tobacco industry in the 1990s, claiming that misleading marketing of cigarettes had created a public nuisance in the form of massive health care costs borne by state governments. Although no court determined that this was a public nuisance, when the action settled for $246 billion, it stimulated (and provided seed money for) a series of similar actions seeking recovery of huge damage awards for various social ills such as lead paint residue in older buildings, injuries caused by the widespread availability of firearms, the effects of climate change, and (most recently) the marketing of slow-release opioid pills like Oxycontin said to be responsible for the opioid addiction crisis. Success in these various litigation campaigns has been mixed, but the large settlement achieved in the tobacco case and significant settlements in some of the opioid cases mean that public nuisance's role as a kind of supertort is far from over. For background, see Donald G. Gifford, Suing the Tobacco and Lead Pigment Industries (2010); Nora Freeman Engstrom & Robert L. Rabin, Pursuing Public Health Through Litigation: Lessons from Tobacco and Opioids, 73 Stan. L. Rev. 285, 301–05 (2021).

B. SERVITUDES

Nuisance law is hardly the last word on land-use conflict. Conflicts among neighbors can also be resolved by contract. Any two neighbors or even a group of neighbors can enter into a contract that commits them to certain behavior regarding the use of their land, and this will be enforced like any other bilateral contract. But such contracts would be of limited usefulness if they were binding only on the initial parties to the agreement. If one of the parties sold her land and moved away, the original deal would no longer be of any use, and the remaining party might not be able to strike a new deal with the new owner. The important contribution of property law here has been the development of doctrines that allow parties to enter into contracts that "run with the land," meaning the terms and conditions of the agreement are binding not only on the original owners but on all future owners of both the benefited and the burdened parcels. Contracts that bind successors in ownership are generically called "servitudes."

The two principal types of servitudes are easements and covenants. Very roughly speaking, an easement is functionally like a contract in which an owner agrees to waive his or her right to exclude certain kinds of intrusions by another and give the other a right to use; a covenant is a contract in which an owner agrees to abide by certain restrictions on the use of his or her land for the benefit of one or more others. Covenants are thus more of a governance mechanism and more often than easements prescribe affirmative behavior on the part of the burdened landowner.

Covenants against commercial use, for maximum building height, and even for door color have been used to control spillovers sometimes of a very subtle sort that would not fall under the law of nuisance. Appurtenant easements always run with the land. Covenants sometimes run with the land if certain conditions are met, which we will consider in some detail. Easements have always been regarded as a type of property right, the exact significance of this appellation (beyond the understanding that easements run with the land) being somewhat unclear. Covenants, even when they run with the land, are less often described as a type of property; rather they are usually spoken of as "promises respecting the use of land." Although authority on this point is scant, it appears that easements have an in rem effect, in the sense that third parties may not interfere with the performance of rights under an easement. Covenants, however, generally do not give rise to any rights against third parties (other than successors to the burdened and benefited parcels), and in this sense are more accurately thought to be in personam.

1. EASEMENTS

a. INTRODUCTION

Baseball Publishing Co. v. Bruton

Supreme Judicial Court of Massachusetts, 1938.

18 N.E.2d 362.

■ LUMMUS, JUSTICE. The plaintiff, engaged in the business of controlling locations for billboards and signs and contracting with advertisers for the exhibition of their placards and posters, obtained from the defendant on October 9, 1934, a writing signed but not sealed by the defendant whereby the defendant "in consideration of twenty-five dollars * * * agrees to give" the plaintiff "the exclusive right and privilege to maintain advertising sign one ten feet by twenty-five feet on wall of building 3003 Washington Street" in Boston, owned by the defendant, "for a period of one year with the privilege of renewal from year to year for four years more at the same consideration." It was provided that "all signs placed on the premises remain the personal property" of the plaintiff. The writing was headed "Lease No. ___." It was not to be effective until accepted by the plaintiff.

It was accepted in writing on November 10, 1934, when the plaintiff sent the defendant a check for $25, the agreed consideration for the first year. The defendant returned the check. The plaintiff nevertheless erected the contemplated sign, and maintained it until February 23, 1937, sending the defendant early in November of the years 1935 and 1936 checks for $25 which were returned. On February 23, 1937, the defendant caused the sign to be removed. On February 26, 1937, the plaintiff brought this bill for specific performance, contending that the writing was a lease. The judge ruled that the writing was a contract to give a license, but on November 2, 1937, entered a final decree for specific performance, with damages and costs. The defendant appealed. It is stipulated that on November 3, 1937, the plaintiff tendered $25 for the renewal of its right for another year beginning November 10, 1937, but the defendant refused the money.

The distinction between a lease and a license is plain, although at times it is hard to classify a particular instrument. A lease of land conveys an interest in land, requires a writing to comply with the statute of frauds though not always a seal and transfers possession. A license merely excuses acts done by one on land in possession of another that without the license would be trespasses, conveys no interest in land, and may be contracted for or given orally. A lease of a roof or a wall for advertising purposes is possible. Alfano v. Donnelly, 189 N.E. 610 (Mass. 1934). The writing in question, however, giving the plaintiff the "exclusive right and privilege to maintain advertising sign * * * on wall of building," but leaving the wall in the possession of the owner with the right to use it for all purposes not forbidden by the contract and with all the responsibilities of ownership and control, is not a lease. Gaertner v. Donnelly, Mass., 5 N.E.2d 419 (Mass. 1936); and cases cited. The fact that in one corner of the writing are found the words, "Lease No. ___," does not convert it into a lease. Those words are merely a misdescription of the writing.

Subject to the right of a licensee to be on the land of another for a reasonable time after the revocation of a license, for the purpose of removing his chattels, it is of the essence of a license that it is revocable at the will of the possessor of the land. * * * Am.Law Inst. Restatement: Torts, §§ 167–171. The revocation of a license may constitute a breach of contract, and give rise to an action for damages. But it is none the less effective to deprive the licensee of all justification for entering or remaining upon the land. * * * Compare Hurst v. Picture Theatres, Ltd., [1915] 1 K.B. 1 (Ct. App.).

If what the plaintiff bargained for and received was a license, and nothing more, then specific performance that might compel the defendant to renew the license, leaving it revocable at will, would be futile and for that reason should not be granted. 5 Williston, Contracts (Rev.Ed.) § 1442; Am.Law.Inst.Restatement: Contracts, § 377. Specific performance that might render the license irrevocable for the term of the contract would convert it into an equitable estate in land, and give the plaintiff more than the contract gave. There can be no specific performance of a contract to give a license, at least in the absence of fraud or estoppel.

The writing in the present case, however, seems to us to go beyond a mere license. It purports to give "the exclusive right and privilege to maintain" a certain sign on the defendant's wall. So far as the law permits, it should be so construed as to vest in the plaintiff the right *not a lease or license — this is an easement*

which it purports to give. That right is in the nature of an easement in gross, which, whatever may be the law elsewhere, is recognized in Massachusetts. Goodrich v. Burbank, 94 Mass. (12 Allen) 459 (1866); Carville v. Commonwealth, 78 N.E. 735 (Mass. 1906); American Telephone & Telegraph Co. of Massachusetts v. McDonald, 173 N.E. 502 (Mass. 1930); Jones v. Stevens, 177 N.E. 91 (Mass. 1931). We see no objection to treating the writing as a grant for one year and a contract to grant for four more years an easement in gross thus limited to five years. Similar writings have been so treated in other jurisdictions.

An easement, being inconsistent with seisin in the person owning it, always lay in grant and could not be created by livery of seisin. Randall v. Chase, 133 Mass. 210, 214 (1882). It is an interest in land within the statute of frauds and, apart from prescription, requires a writing for its creation. G.L.(Ter.Ed.) c. 183, § 3. Cook v. Stearns, 11 Mass. 533 (1814). Indeed, the creation of a legal freehold interest in an easement, apart from prescription, requires a deed. And differing from a lease of land for not more than seven years (Alfano v. Donnelly, 189 N.E. 610, 612 (Mass. 1934)), a grant of an easement for as short a term as five years apparently requires a deed in order to create a legal interest. Wood v. Leadbitter, 153 Eng. Rep. 351 (Ex. 1845) 13 M. & W. 838; Chadwick v. Covell, 23 N.E. 1068 (Mass. 1890); Walker Ice Co. v. American Steel & Wire Co., 70 N.E. 937 (Mass. 1904), and especially Loring, J. at 70 N.E. 937. But in equity a seal is not necessary to the creation of an easement. Since equity treats an act as done where there is a duty to do it enforceable in equity, or, as more tersely phrased, equity treats that as done which ought to be done, an enforceable unsealed contract such as the writing in this case, providing for the creation of an easement, actually creates an easement in equity.

There is no error in the final decree granting specific performance. The affirmance of this decree will not prevent an assessment of the damages as of the date of the final decree after rescript.

Interlocutory decree overruling demurrer affirmed.

Varieties of Easements

Easements are very common. They were recognized in Roman law and exist in some form in virtually all modern legal systems. What are the distinguishing features of an easement? On the one hand, an easement differs from other property rights such as a fee simple or a lease because an easement conveys the right to a particular *use* of land, as opposed to the right to *possession* of land. One can think of a possessory right as being a kind of gatekeeper right that allows the possessor to determine all of the uses to which the property will be devoted (out of a large and open-ended set of possibilities), and who will be allowed to engage in them. An easement, in contrast, is a conveyance of a right to engage in one particular use, ordinarily given to one particular person or set of persons. In terms of the bundle of sticks metaphor, a possessory right conveys a full bundle of sticks; an easement conveys just one stick out of the bundle. On the other hand, an easement differs from a mere license that permits someone to engage in a particular use of the land. A license is a waiver of the right to exclude that often arises by contract—and is (ordinarily) regarded as being revocable (see Chapter IV). An easement, however, is regarded as an irrevocable conveyance of the right to engage in a particular use of land. (It need not be indefinitely irrevocable; it can be irrevocable for a term of years, as in *Baseball Publishing*.)

Easements have always been regarded as a type of property right, even though they convey only delimited use rights. One reason for regarding easements as property is purely formal—they are created by grant rather than by contract (see the next Section for more on what this means). But there is a danger of circularity, in that one can just as easily argue that easements must be created by grant because they are property as that easements are property because they are created by grant. A more substantive reason is the feature of irrevocability. Easements have a "vested" quality that distinguishes them from gratuitous licenses and most licenses arising by contract. A third possible reason is that easements do have in rem features. Although the relationship between the grantor and grantee of an easement looks much like a bilateral exchange of promises, a valid easement also gives rise to a general duty on the part of "all the world" not to interfere with the easement. Thus, for example, if B has an easement to cross the land of A, a third party—C—would be guilty of a wrong if C attempted to block B's passage across A's land.

A basic distinction within the universe of easements is between *easements appurtenant* and *easements in gross*. An easement appurtenant is one that belongs to another parcel of land. So for example, assume Whiteacre and Blackacre are adjacent parcels of land. Whiteacre is owned by Sally and Blackacre is owned by Dan. Sally grants Dan an easement appurtenant to cross Whiteacre to reach Blackacre. Since the easement is appurtenant, it "belongs" to Blackacre, and is carved out of Whiteacre. This means that the benefit of the easement belongs to whoever happens to own Blackacre, and the burden of the easement belongs to whoever happens to own Whiteacre. The law speaks of Blackacre as being the *dominant* tract (the tract benefited or enhanced by the easement); and Whiteacre as being the *servient* tract (the tract burdened by or out of which is carved the easement). If Dan sells Blackacre to Daniella, Daniella as the owner of the dominant tract now has the right to use the right of way; Dan no longer has any rights in the easement. Similarly, if Sally sells Whiteacre to Saul, Saul is now the owner of the servient tract burdened by the easement; Sally is off the hook. Loosely speaking, an easement in gross is one that belongs to a particular grantee, as opposed to belonging to a particular tract of land. Suppose Sally grants Dan an easement in gross to fish in the pond on

Whiteacre. Now, the benefit of the easement belongs to Dan personally, not to whoever happens to be the owner of Blackacre. If Dan sells Blackacre to Daniella, the easement in gross remains with Dan; Daniella has no rights to fish in the pond unless she gets her own easement.

English courts recognized only easements appurtenant. An attempt to create an easement in gross created only a license personal to the grantee. Such a conveyance was not inheritable, i.e., would not pass on death to the heirs of the grantee, and was not transferable to a third party. American courts have been more sympathetic to easements in gross. The usual explanation is the emergence of the railroad industry in nineteenth-century America. In order to build a railroad, it was necessary to acquire the right to operate along a long narrow strip of land cutting across hundreds of separately owned parcels of property. For various reasons, many owners were willing to grant easements to railroads (or were willing to allow railroads to condemn easements), but were more reluctant to convey a fee simple in a strip of land to a railroad. But such an easement, crossing many separate parcels, would not be appurtenant to any particular tract of land; it would be in gross to the railroad enterprise. So, in order to accommodate the growth of the railroad industry, many American courts concluded that easements in gross could be created that were inheritable and transferable—provided the grant was of a commercial character. Thus, most American states permitted easements in gross for railroad or utility purposes—or for the erection of billboards, as in the *Baseball Publishing* case—whereas in England one would have to use grants of a fee simple or leases to accomplish these purposes. Although courts have been increasingly liberal about permitting parties to create inheritable and transferable easements in gross, most courts continue to hold that easements in gross for purely recreational purposes such as hunting, camping, boating, or fishing are not inheritable or transferable. See Note, The Easement in Gross Revisited: Transferability and Divisibility Since 1945, 39 Vand. L. Rev. 109 (1986).

Closely related to an easement in gross, but narrower in purpose, is something called a *profit à prendre* or "profit" for short. This is the right to enter on the land of another in order to extract something of value, such as timber, or fruit from trees, or fish or game from a lake or forest. It is also used to permit extraction of surface minerals, such as sand or gravel, although deep rock mining and oil and gas extraction are usually governed by mineral leases. Profits are very ancient and were recognized by the English common law. They are generally governed by the same rules as easements appurtenant. The grant of a profit carries with it an implied license to enter the land for purposes of carrying out the profit, and this license remains irrevocable as long as the profit continues.

Another basic distinction among easements is between *affirmative* easements and *negative* easements. Affirmative easements permit the easement holder to perform some affirmative act on the land of another.

One can think of an affirmative easement as permitting action on the servient tract that otherwise would be a trespass or an invasive nuisance. A negative easement permits the easement holder to demand that the owner of the servient tract desist from certain actions that might harm the easement holder. Virtually all easements are affirmative easements. English common law recognized only four narrow categories of negative easements: blocking sunlight from falling on windows on the dominant tenement; interfering with the flow of air in a defined channel to the dominant tenement; removing lateral support to a building on the dominant tenement; and interfering with the flow of water in an artificial stream to the dominant tenement. English law also permitted easements to be established by prescription in these four narrow areas. (See Fontainebleau Hotel Corp. v. Forty-Five Twenty-Five, Inc., infra.) American courts have been somewhat more adventuresome about permitting express negative easements outside the traditional four categories. For example, the California Supreme Court once upheld a negative easement for an unobstructed view of San Francisco Bay over a neighboring property. Petersen v. Friedman, 328 P.2d 264 (Cal. Ct. App. 1958). As a rule, however, when someone wants to impose a negative duty on a servient landowner to desist from taking action that might harm the dominant tract, lawyers today will accomplish this by drafting a covenant that runs with the land. Once running covenants were recognized in *Tulk v. Moxhay*, infra, the logical thing to do would have been to have restricted easements to affirmative easements (waivers of exclusion rights) and to have required that all negative duties imposed on servient landowners be embodied in written covenants. This is the general thrust of the way things are done, but the doctrine is not quite that tidy.

A final distinction that is sometimes of importance is between *private* easements and *public* easements. Private easements authorize specific named parties (individuals or enterprises) to use land for designated purposes. Public easements authorize the general public to use land for designated purposes. Public roads, highways, and navigable waterways are most often owned in fee simple by some governmental entity, subject (in the case of navigable water) to a trust obligation to the public (see Chapter III). But occasionally they are held as easements, in which case the public holds only a right to use the property, and the underlying owner of the underlying fee retains all other rights. Public access rights for recreational purposes, such as beaches, bike trails, and portages, are more likely to be held as public easements than are roads and highways. Sometimes the public holds negative easements, such as scenic easements, conservation easements, or historic preservation easements. These, like public easements of access, can be acquired by condemnation as well as by gift or purchase.

NOTES AND QUESTIONS

1.   Why was the common law so hostile to the creation of easements in gross? After the development of recording acts that permit the recording of property interests like easements, is there any continuing reason to disfavor easements in gross?

2.   Easements ordinarily can be subdivided. For example, if Blackacre has an easement of way over Whiteacre, and Blackacre is subdivided into four lots, absent previous agreement to the contrary each of the new lot owners will have an easement over Whiteacre. Should parties be permitted to subdivide easements in gross? Suppose the Baseball Publishing Company wants to subdivide its easement in gross in order to allow three different firms to post billboards in the space initially designated for the Baseball Publishing Company. Do you foresee any problems in permitting this to happen?

3.   How does the court in *Baseball Publishing* weigh different evidence in determining whether the agreement creates a license, lease, or easement? In a more recent decision considering whether a document created a license or an easement, the Court of Appeals of Kansas weighed five factors, none dispositive on their own: (1) the manner of creation of the right, including the existence or absence of words ordinarily used in the conveyance of real estate; (2) the nature of the right created, including whether the holder of the right can maintain or improve the burdened property; (3) the duration of the right, which if set or perpetual is more likely indicative of an easement; (4) the amount of consideration given for the right, with a more substantial amount being indicative of an easement; and (5) whether any right to revoke or terminate the right is reserved, with revocability more likely to indicate a license. Gilman v. Blocks, 235 P.3d 503 (Kan. Ct. App. 2010). In that case, similar to *Baseball Publishing*, the court disregarded frequent use of the term "license" in the agreement. Should the express term used by the parties carry more import? If not, which of these factors seems most important?

4.   Notice that *Baseball Publishing* is another illustration of the *numerus clausus* principle. The parties have an agreement that would allow the company to use the side of a building for a series of five renewable one-year terms for purposes of putting up an advertising sign. In order to ascertain the legal effect of this agreement, the court feels compelled to assign the agreement to one of several possible boxes: license, lease, or easement in gross. Should the court proceed this way, or should it just recognize a new interest ("advertising sign privileges on buildings for renewable terms") that corresponds with the apparent intentions of the parties?

b.   CREATION OF EASEMENTS

Although easements are regarded as property rights, at common law they could not be created by the quaint ceremony of livery of seisin, only by grant. To create property by grant, including an easement, the grantor must deliver to the grantee a *deed* to the property. A deed, in turn, was originally understood to mean a writing under seal. The seal was a unique mark or symbol, impressed on paper with melted wax. Over the years, the requirement of melted wax was softened, to the point where today in most jurisdictions a deed is just a piece of paper that conveys a property right—although in some jurisdictions formalities such as attestation of signatures by notaries or witnesses are still required. Because an easement is an interest in land, the Statute of Frauds also requires that easements be in writing.

The common law imposed another limitation on the creation of easements that sometimes can provide a trap for the unwary. An easement could be created by grant, of the direct A-to-B variety. Alternatively, an easement could be created by reservation to the grantor, A, in a grant to B of a possessory interest in land. Thus, if A granted Blackacre to B, A could in the deed granting Blackacre reserve to himself an easement over Blackacre, perhaps to access other land retained by the grantor. But, at common law one could not create a grant by reservation in a third party. For example, if A granted Blackacre to B, A could not in the deed to B reserve an easement in Blackacre running to C. Some modern American courts have disapproved of this rule. See, e.g., Willard v. First Church of Christ, Scientist, 498 P.2d 987 (Cal. 1972). They have reasoned that the original rationale for the rule was to prevent easements, which were created by grant rather than livery of seisin, from being used to do an end run around the rules of seisin important to the feudal system. Feudalism being dead, these courts have reasoned, the rule against creating easements in third parties by reservation should also be rejected. Can you think of other possible rationales for the rule against creating easements by reservation in third parties? If the recording system in the jurisdiction has only a grantor-grantee index, and does not have a tract index, might there be situations in which it would be hard to discover that someone like C holds an easement created by reservation in a deed between A and B?

All this sounds reasonably straightforward: If you want to create an easement, get a lawyer to put it in writing, follow whatever formalities are necessary to create a deed, and record the instrument in the local registry of deeds. Unfortunately, people seem more prone to ignore the need for writings and lawyers where easements are concerned, than they are when conveying possessory interests. There are a variety of possible reasons for this. Easements are generally of lower value (in the grand scheme of things) than possessory interests, and this may account for more rational ignorance about the requirements of the law. Also, norms of neighborly accommodation often serve as a substitute for, or a supplement to, explicit easements. People may rely on these norms, and may even feel that it is unneighborly to demand that informal understandings be formalized in legal agreements. In any event, the need for a writing is often ignored, and this has given rise to lots of litigation about issues of access to land. Courts have responded by creating a variety of doctrines that allow easements or easement-like rights to be recognized without any writing: doctrines that recognize easements by implication, necessity, prescription, or estoppel. Courts have held that when these doctrines apply, they constitute an implied exception to the requirements of the Statute of Frauds.

Schwab v. Timmons

Supreme Court of Wisconsin, 1999.
589 N.W.2d 1.

■ JON P. WILCOX, J. The petitioners, James and Katherine Schwab and Dorice McCormick (petitioners), seek review of a decision affirming the circuit court's dismissal of their declaratory judgment action requesting an easement by necessity or by implication for both ingress and egress and utilities over the properties owned by the respondents in order to gain access to their landlocked parcels located in Door County. The circuit court, as affirmed by the court of appeals, concluded that the historical circumstances in this case do not fit the typical situation from which ways of necessity are implied and that even if they did, the easement would not have survived because it was not recorded.

On appeal, the petitioners claim they are entitled to an easement by necessity or by implication over the respondents' properties; or in the alternative, they seek an expansion of the common law in this state to recognize an easement by necessity where property is landlocked due to geographical barriers and due to the actions of the common owner and grantor, in this case the United States. We conclude that the petitioners have failed to establish entitlement to an easement by implication or by necessity either because of actions by the federal government or by geographical barriers. Not only were the parcels at issue not landlocked at the time of conveyance, but the petitioners themselves created their landlocked parcels when they conveyed away their highway access. We refuse to turn 100-plus years of Wisconsin common law on its head to accommodate such actions. Accordingly, we affirm the court of appeals.

I.

The facts are not in dispute. The petitioners and the respondents all own property that is located on Green Bay in the Village of Ephraim in Door County. The properties are situated between the waters of Green Bay on the west and a bluff ranging in height from 37 to 60 feet on the east. [Figure 9-4] is a diagram of the properties (lots and parcels) involved.

Prior to 1854, the property involved was owned by the United States and was divided into three lots: Lot 2, the northernmost lot; Lot 3; and Lot 4, the southernmost lot. In 1854, the United States granted by patent Lot 4 to Ingebret Torgerson, but retained Lots 2 and 3. At the time that Lot 4 was severed from Lots 2 and 3, the United States did not retain a right-of-way through Lot 4 to get to Lots 2 and 3. At oral argument, it was explained that at the time of this conveyance by the United States, the eastern boundary of the lots extended to the east to what is now a public roadway. The lots were comprised of property both above and below the bluff with access to a public roadway from above. In 1882, the United States granted Lots 2 and 3 to Halvor Anderson.

At some point after the United States granted the lots, they were further subdivided into parcels. After 1854, Lots 2, 3, and 4 were never fully owned by one person or entity * * *

The petitioners' parcels are located in Lot 2, the northernmost lot. McCormick owns the northernmost parcel and the Schwabs own two adjacent parcels directly south of McCormick. Together the properties comprise over 1200 feet of frontage and over nine acres of property. Directly south of the Schwabs' parcels is a parcel owned by the Timmons within Lot 2, followed to the south by a parcel owned by the Lenzes, also in Lot 2; all of the remaining respondents' parcels follow sequentially to the south, located in Lots 3 and 4, with the parcel owned by Hobler being the southernmost parcel located at the southern boundary of Lot 4.

It was indicated at oral argument that the current eastern boundary line, the bluff line—which produced parcels above and below the bluff— was created at various unknown times. The Schwabs' parcels were originally purchased by James' parents in the 1940s and were later gifted to James in 1965 and 1974. At purchase, the Schwabs' parcels extended east from the waters of Green Bay to property above the bluff where there was access to a public roadway and a house. Some time after the 1974 inheritance, the Schwabs conveyed the property above the bluff to James' relatives and retained the parcel below. McCormick also inherited her parcel which originally included land above and below the bluff with highway access from above, and she conveyed the property above the bluff to a third party, retaining the parcel below.

As they currently stand, both of the petitioners' parcels are bordered by water on the east [sic] and the bluff on the west [sic]. Because their properties are between the lake and the bluff, the petitioners claim their only access is over the land to the south, owned by the respondents, for which they do not have a right-of-way.

A private road runs north from Hobler's parcel across all of the respondents' properties terminating on the Lenz parcel. Timmons also has the right to use the private road. This is the road that the petitioners are seeking to extend for their use. Negotiations for an agreement to extend the road have failed.

Figure 9-4
Map from *Schwab v. Timmons*

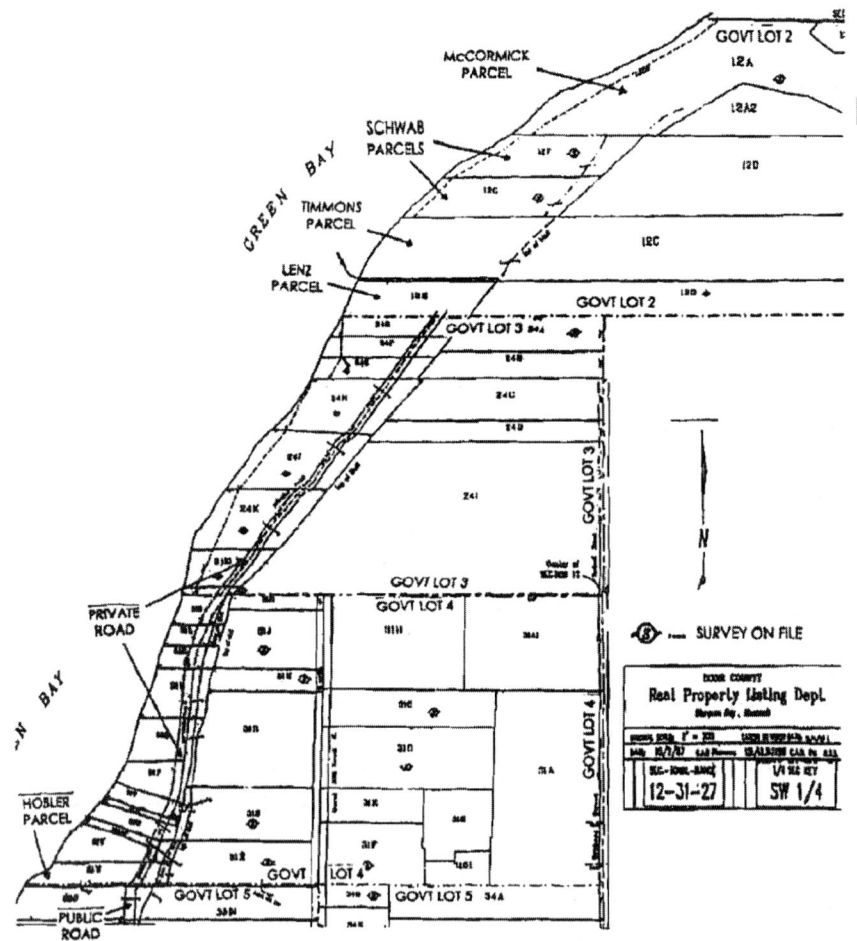

In 1988, the petitioners petitioned the Village of Ephraim, pursuant to Wis. Stat. § 80.13 (1985–86), to extend a public road—North Shore Drive—to the private road beginning at the Hobler property northward over all of the respondents' properties to McCormick's property. Section 80.13 allows a landowner to request the local government, in its discretion, to construct a public roadway at the petitioning landowners' expense. The Village of Ephraim board, however, declined the request finding that extending the road was not in the public's interest.

Consequently, the petitioners brought this declaratory judgment action seeking an easement by necessity or by implication to gain access to their land. The easement would include the perpetual right to travel, including the right for ingress, egress and for public utilities, over the now private road, which stretches over 15 of the respondents' parcels to the Lenz property, as well as the right to build a road over the Lenz and

Timmons properties up to the McCormick property. The respondents filed motions to dismiss the amended complaint.[3] * * *

III.

The petitioners claim an easement by implication or by necessity over the respondents' properties. An easement is a "liberty, privilege, or advantage in lands, without profit, and existing distinct from the ownership of the land." Stoesser v. Shore Drive Partnership, 494 N.W.2d 204 (Wis. 1993). With an easement, there are two distinct property interests—the dominant estate, which enjoys the privileges granted by an easement and the servient estate, which permits the exercise of those privileges. An easement can be used only in connection with the real estate to which it belongs.

Easements by implication and by necessity are similar, but legally distinguishable concepts. Since the early 1900s, the public policy in Wisconsin has strongly opposed the implication of covenants of conveyance, i.e., easements. Backhausen v. Mayer, 234 N.W. 904 (Wis. 1931); Miller v. Hoeschler, 105 N.W. 790 (Wis. 1905).

An easement by implication arises when there has been a "separation of title, a use before separation took place which continued so long and was so obvious or manifest as to show that it was meant to be permanent, and it must appear that the easement is necessary to the beneficial enjoyment of the land granted or retained." Bullis v. Schmidt, 93 N.W.2d 476, 478–79 (Wis. 1958) (quoting 1 Thompson, Real Property § 390 at 630 (perm. ed.)).[4] Implied easements may only be created when the necessity for the easement is "so clear and absolute that without the easement the grantee cannot enjoy the use of the property granted to him for the purposes to which similar property is customarily devoted." Bullis, 93 N.W.2d at 480 (quoting Miller, 105 N.W. at 792).

The petitioners have failed to establish a claim for an easement by implication. While a landlocked parcel may satisfy the necessity element, it is apparent from the amended complaint that the private road the petitioners seek to extend does not and has never extended to the petitioners' properties. They have failed to allege that any use by the United States was so obvious, manifest or continuous as to show that it was meant to be permanent. * * *

---

[3]   Petitioners filed their initial complaint in May 1996. They then filed an amended complaint in August 1996. * * *

[4]   The traditional elements of an implied easement are:

    (1) common ownership followed by conveyance separating the unified ownership;

    (2) before severance, the common owner used part of the property for the benefit of the other part, a use that was apparent, obvious, continuous and [permanent];

    (3) and the claimed easement is necessary and beneficial to the enjoyment of the parcel previously benefitted.

7 Thomson, Real Property § 60.03(b)(4)(i) at 426 (Thompson ed. 1994). Wisconsin courts have not specifically adopted these elements as the law of this state and we do not do so here.

An easement of necessity "arises where an owner severs a landlocked portion of his [or her] property by conveying such parcel to another." Ludke v. Egan, 274 N.W.2d 641 (Wis. 1979). To establish an easement by necessity, a party must show common ownership of the two parcels prior to severance of the landlocked parcel, and that the owner of the now landlocked parcel cannot access a public roadway from his or her own property, Ludke, 274 N.W.2d at 645. If this can be demonstrated, an easement by necessity will be implied over the land retained by the grantor. Id.

The petitioners argue that the United States ownership of all three lots prior to 1854 satisfies the common ownership requirement—a question never before addressed by this court. We conclude that we need not reach that issue because even if the United States' possession of the three lots could constitute common ownership, the petitioners have conceded that neither Lot 2, nor Lot 3 were landlocked when the United States conveyed Lot 4. Rather, at the time of conveyance, the eastern boundary of the lots was above and east of the bluff (the current boundary line). Access to a public roadway was possible above the bluff. A party may only avail himself or herself of an easement by necessity when the common owner severs *a landlocked portion* of the property and the owner of the landlocked portion cannot access a public roadway. Id. 274 N.W.2d 641. Because the United States never severed a landlocked portion of its property that was inaccessible from a public roadway, the petitioners have failed to establish the elements for an easement by necessity.

Nevertheless, petitioners insist that the property was effectively landlocked because of the geographical barriers inhibiting access. As the petitioners see it, their land was landlocked because the land to the south was owned by an individual, the land to the east and north was bordered by a cliff and rocky terrain, and the land to the west was bordered by the waters of Green Bay. * * *

Wisconsin courts have never before recognized geographical barriers alone as circumstances warranting an easement by necessity. In fact, case law suggests otherwise. This court stated in *Backhausen* that a way of necessity is not merely one of convenience, and "the law will not imply such a way where it has provided another method for obtaining the same at a reasonable expense to the landowner." Backhausen, 234 N.W. at 905.

While the petitioners have provided evidence that the cost of building a road over the bluff would cost approximately $700,000[,] an unreasonable expense, it is apparent that they consider other methods of access—a stairway, an elevator—unacceptable. Petitioners narrowly focus on vehicular access to the lake itself as the only possible way to enjoy this property. Certainly it may be more convenient for the petitioners to seek an extension of the private road to their parcels rather than travel across the property above the bluff and navigate the bluff, but that in itself does not create the right to an easement by necessity. A grantor is not landlocked when he or she has difficulty getting from his or her land to a public road as long as he or she can get from his or her land to a public road. See Ludke, 274 N.W.2d 641. See also Sicchio v. Alvey, 103 N.W.2d 544 (Wis. 1960) (Access to building at front, even though rear entry was used, does not allow for right-of-way by necessity to rear entry of store).

In this case, the petitioners had access to a public road, albeit not ideal or the most convenient access, which they sold off. Thus, the petitioners' current ownership of landlocked property resulted not from a grant of property to them but by their own acts in conveying away their highway access. They were not unwitting purchasers of landlocked property (stemming from the United States 1854 sale).

An easement by necessity only exists where an owner sells a *landlocked* parcel to another, in which case the law will recognize a way of necessity in the *grantee* over the land retained by the *grantor*. Rock Lake Estates Unit Owners Ass'n v. Township of Lake Mills, 536 N.W.2d 415, 424 (Wis. Ct. App. 1995) (citing Ludke, 274 N.W.2d at 645). The petitioners in this case are the grantors, not the grantees, and as in *Rock Lake Estates,* the conveyances which resulted in their landlocked property were made by the petitioners when they sold off the property above the bluff. We conclude that it would be contrary to this state's policy against encumbrances for this court to award an easement to the petitioners over parcels of unrelated third parties under these circumstances.

Finally, the petitioners assert that without an easement their property will be virtually useless because they will have no way to get to it. Thus, the petitioners renew their request for a "drastic" expansion of the law arguing that there is no rational basis for landlocked property. The petitioners suggest that this court set forth a "reasonable use" test that balances the equities by weighing the competing interests of the need and benefit to allow access by easement to develop otherwise useless land versus the detriment such a burden may place on other property to use an existing road. The petitioners insist that the benefit and policy towards development far outweigh any anticipated costs to the burdened property.

In order to adopt the petitioners' proposal, we would have to ignore not only long-standing precedent in this state, but also well-established public policy as illustrated in our recording and conveyance statutes. Long ago this court recognized:

> It is so easy, in conveying a defined piece of land, to express either any limitations intended to be reserved over it, or to be conveyed with it over other land, that the necessity of raising any such grant or reservation by implication is hardly apparent. Courts of equity can afford relief where the grant is not of that understood by both parties to be conveyed, or so understood by one by inducement of the other. Such rights outside the limits of one's proper title seriously derogate from the policy of both

our registry statutes and our statute against implication of [covenants] in conveyances. That policy is that a buyer of land may rely on the public records as information of all the conveyances, and upon the words of the instruments for all rights thereunder.

Miller, 105 N.W. at 792.

More recently in Kordecki v. Rizzo, 317 N.W.2d 479 (Wis. 1982), this court reiterated that a purchaser of real estate has three sources of information from which to learn of rights to the land he or she is about to purchase: (1) reviewing the chain of title; (2) searching other public records that may reveal other non-recorded rights, such as judgments or liens; and (3) inspecting the land itself. These sources may be irrelevant under the petitioners' proposal if someone with a landlocked piece of property desired a right-of-way through another person's property "in the interest of development."

The petitioners are effectively asking this court to sanction hidden easements. An easement which in this case was not created by, but was, according to petitioners, clearly intended by the United States at conveyance. * * *

The decision of the court of appeals is affirmed.

NOTES AND QUESTIONS

1.   How do you suppose the Schwabs and Ms. McCormick got to their lakefront parcels between the 1940s and when the lawsuit was filed in 1996? Note that Timmons, their neighbor immediately to the south, is said to have the right to use the private road, even though it does not extend to his parcel.

2.   In addition to refusing Schwab and McCormick access to the private road, the Supreme Court of Wisconsin refused to create an easement by necessity over the parcels that Schwab and McCormick had sold to the east, cutting off their previous access to a public road. The court found that it would be "contrary to this state's policy" to create an easement when the grantors' actions resulted in them landlocking themselves. This part of the opinion was later distinguished by *McCormick v. Schubring*, 672 N.W.2d 63, 69 (Wisc. 2003), which clarified:

[O]ur statement in *Schwab* that, "An easement by necessity only exists where an owner sells a *landlocked* parcel to another, in which case the law will recognize a way of necessity in the *grantee* over the land retained by the *grantor*," Schwab, 224 Wis.2d at 40, 589 N.W.2d 1 (emphasis in the original), should be read to further explain that an easement of necessity may traverse property that is or was held by the grantor who created the landlocked condition, but cannot traverse property of an unrelated third party. And, it should not be read to conclude that only a grantee may obtain an easement of necessity for landlocked property. This explanation is also in accord with legal treatises that have concluded that both grantees and grantors may seek an easement

of necessity, Restatement (Third) of Prop.: Creation of Servitudes
§ 2.15, and the long-standing public policy of this state that favors
utilization of land. Dillman v. Hoffman, 38 Wis. 559, 574 (1875).

Under current Wisconsin law, then, the Schwabs and McCormicks might
have been able to get an easement by necessity over the parcels to their east.
Why do you think the court was unsympathetic to this result in *Schwab*?
Which rule—the one suggested in *Schwab* or the one mentioned in the
excerpt—seems preferable? Should courts hold *grantors* to a stricter
requirement of necessity than in cases where the *grantee* is arguing for an
easement?

3.   Suppose the Schwab and McCormick parcels could be accessed from
the lake by boat during the summer months, and suppose further that the
principal use of property in Door County is for summer vacation homes.
Would this by itself suffice to defeat a claim for an easement by implication
or by necessity?

4.   The principal reason cited by the court for the hostility toward
claims of easements by implication and by necessity is that this would
"sanction hidden easements." In other words, prospective purchasers and
other persons attempting to ascertain the nature and extent of property
rights in the area would not be able to discover the existence of the easement
by searching the public records. Why couldn't the court solve this problem by
insisting that the petitioners, as a condition of obtaining the equitable relief
they seek, record the judgment granting them an easement by implication or
necessity along with the other deeds and instruments that pertain to the title
to these lots? Can you think of reasons besides problems of notice why courts
should be reluctant to recognize easements by implication or necessity?

5.   About half the states have adopted statutes that provide for
condemnation of private easements for access to landlocked or inaccessible
property. See, e.g., Sorenson v. Czinger, 852 P.2d 1124, 1127 (Wash. Ct. App.
1993), discussing Rev. Code Wash. § 8.24.010. Under these statutes, the
landlocked owner can force the servient owner(s) to convey an easement, but
must pay just compensation (fair market value) for the rights so obtained.
(Typically, these statutes also require the landlocked owner to apply to a
government official for permission and allow the owner of the proposed
servient land to object.) Is this a better solution to the problem illustrated by
the principal case than either forcing the parties to negotiate past a
stalemate (as the Wisconsin Supreme Court's decision apparently
contemplates) or granting an easement based on a balancing of costs and
benefits (as the petitioners suggest in their last-ditch argument for a
"drastic" expansion of easements by necessity)? Do rights of private
condemnation for easements of access satisfy the "public use" requirement of
the Fifth Amendment and parallel provisions of state constitutions (see
Chapter X.C)? If your answer is no, then why aren't the common-law
doctrines of easements by implication or necessity also unconstitutional?

Warsaw v. Chicago Metallic Ceilings, Inc.

Supreme Court of California, 1984.
676 P.2d 584.

■ RICHARDSON, JUSTICE. We granted a hearing in this case to consider whether one who acquires a valid prescriptive easement over another's property nonetheless may be required to compensate that person for either (1) the fair market value of the easement, or (2) the cost of removing or relocating any encroaching structures which interfere with use of the easement. We conclude that the statutes which define and validate prescriptive easements neither authorize nor contemplate an award to the underlying property owner of compensation for the reasonable value of the easement, and that under the circumstances in this case it would be improper to charge the owner of the easement with any portion of the cost of removing encroachments.

Although we disagree with the Court of Appeal's resolution of the foregoing issues, its opinion (per Compton, J.) correctly determined the other issues on appeal from the trial court's judgment declaring that plaintiffs had acquired a prescriptive easement over defendant's property. 188 Cal.Rptr. 563. Accordingly, we adopt that portion of the opinion as follows:*

This is an appeal from an equitable decree which declared that plaintiffs had acquired an easement by prescription over the property of defendant. Defendant was ordered to dismantle and relocate a structure which had been erected on its own property but which interfered with plaintiffs' use of the easement. [ ]

This action involves two contiguous parcels of real estate which front on [the west side of] Downey Road in the City of Vernon. Downey Road runs in a generally north-south direction. The two parcels are approximately 650 feet deep. Plaintiffs own the southerly parcel and defendant owns the northerly parcel. Both parcels were acquired in 1972 from a common owner.

At the time of acquisition both parcels were unimproved. Plaintiffs' arrangement with the seller was that the seller would construct on the parcel to be purchased by plaintiffs a large commercial building erected to plaintiffs' requirements. The building covered almost the entire parcel. A 40 foot wide paved driveway was laid out along the northern edge of plaintiffs' property to provide access to loading docks on the northern side of plaintiffs' building.

For its part defendant constructed on its property a substantially smaller building which ran only about one-half the depth of the northerly

---

* Brackets together, in this manner [ ], are used to indicate deletions from the opinion of the Court of Appeal; brackets enclosing material * * * are, unless otherwise indicated, used to denote insertions or additions by this court.

parcel and left vacant a strip of ground about 150 feet wide along the side of the parcel which abutted plaintiffs' property.

From the beginning it was apparent that plaintiff's 40 foot wide driveway was inadequate since the large trucks which carried material to and from plaintiffs' loading dock could not turn and position themselves at these docks without traveling onto the defendant's property. The inability of these trucks to make such use of defendant's property would destroy the commercial value of plaintiff's building.

The court found that because of the fact that the possibility of creating an easement over defendant's property was considered and rejected in the original negotiations between the seller, plaintiffs and defendant, no easement by implication was created. The trial court further found that the existence of the driveway on plaintiffs' property militated against the creation of an easement by necessity.

From 1972 until 1979 trucks and other vehicles servicing plaintiffs' facility used a portion of the vacant ground on defendant's property to enter, turn, park and leave the area of plaintiffs' loading dock. On at least two occasions during that period plaintiffs sought, unsuccessfully, to acquire an easement from defendant or to create mutual easements over plaintiffs' and defendant's property.

In 1979 defendant developed plans to construct a warehouse on the southerly portion of the property including that portion of the property being used by plaintiffs. A pad of earth was raised along the southerly portion of defendant's property approximately five feet from the property line. This grading effectively blocked plaintiffs' use of the area and plaintiffs commenced this action for injunctive and declaratory relief.

When the trial court denied plaintiffs' request for a preliminary injunction to prevent further construction, defendant proceeded to erect a building on the contested area.

After a trial on the merits, the trial court found that plaintiffs had acquired a 25 foot wide prescriptive easement over and along the southern portion of defendant's property for the full depth of the property. As noted defendant was ordered to remove that portion of the building which interfered with the described easement. Further the trial court gave defendant 90 days to accomplish the removal and purported to reserve jurisdiction to award damages for failure of defendant to comply with the mandatory injunction. This appeal ensued.

The elements necessary to establish a prescriptive easement are well settled. The party claiming such an easement must show use of the property which has been open, notorious, continuous and adverse for an uninterrupted period of five years. Whether the elements of prescription are established is a question of fact for the trial court, and the findings of the court will not be disturbed where there is substantial evidence to support them.

Further, the existence of a prescriptive easement must be shown by a definite and certain line of travel for the statutory period. "The line of travel over a roadway which is claimed by prescription may not be a shifting course, but must be certain and definite. Slight deviations from the accustomed route will not defeat an easement, but substantial changes which break the continuity of the course of travel will destroy the claim to prescriptive rights. . . . [Citations.] [M]anifestly the distance to which a roadway may be changed without destroying an easement will be determined somewhat by the character of the land over which it passes, together with the value, improvements, and purposes to which the land is adapted." (Matthiessen v. Grand, 268 P. 675, 678 (Cal. Dist. Ct. App. 1928).)

The trial court found that "the truckers using [the disputed parcel] did, in fact, follow a definite course and pattern, and while admittedly, no two truck drivers followed the exact course . . . and the traffic situation . . . varied from day to day, the deviation taken by various drivers over the seven-year period was only slight."

The evidence revealed that truck drivers who were making deliveries to or receiving goods from plaintiffs used the parcel to approach the building, swing around and back into plaintiffs' loading dock. Since the drivers varied in their abilities, the space required to complete this [maneuver] was variable. No two drivers followed precisely the same course, but all used the parcel for the same purpose—to turn their vehicles so they could enter plaintiffs' loading docks. There was substantial evidence to support the findings on this issue.

Defendant contends that there was no evidence supporting use of several hundred feet of the westerly portion of the parcel. From the trial transcript, it is difficult to discern exactly to which portion of the parcel specific bits of testimony pertain. [ ] [Our review of the record, however, discloses substantial evidence supporting the establishment of a prescriptive easement over the westerly portion at issue.]

Defendant contends that there was no substantial evidence that plaintiffs' use of the property was hostile rather than permissive. Again, we find that this contention is without merit.

The issue as to which party has the burden of proving adverse or permissive use has been the subject of much debate. However, [ ] [we agree with the view, supported by numerous authorities,] that continuous use of an easement over a long period of time without the landowner's interference is presumptive evidence of its existence and in the absence of evidence of mere permissive use it will be sufficient to sustain a judgment. (MacDonald Properties, Inc. v. Bel-Air Country Club, [140 Cal.Rptr. 367 (Cal. Ct. App. 1977), and cases cited].)

Defendant relies on evidence that plaintiffs at one time attempted to purchase the disputed parcel from the seller and at various times attempted to negotiate for an express easement. Whether the use is hostile or is merely a matter of neighborly accommodation, however, is a question of fact to be determined in light of the surrounding circumstances and the relationship between the parties.

There was evidence adduced at trial that despite plaintiffs' unsuccessful attempts to negotiate an express easement, their use of the property continued uninterrupted for approximately seven years. There was no evidence that defendant had ever expressly permitted plaintiffs to use the parcel for truck and vehicular traffic. In fact defendant's adamant refusal to negotiate on the issue is evidence that no permission was given or contemplated.

Defendant's next assignment of error is addressed to the trial court's order to remove that part of the completed structure which interferes with plaintiffs' easement. Defendant argues that a mandatory injunction may not issue to enjoin a completed act. However, there is extensive authority standing for the proposition that a court of equity may, in a proper case, issue a mandatory injunction for protection and preservation of an easement including, where appropriate, an order for removal of an obstruction already erected. The determination as to whether such remedy is appropriate is within the sound discretion of the trial court. A mandatory injunction may issue even if the cost of removal is great under certain circumstances, especially if the encroaching structure was wilfully erected with knowledge of the claimed easement.

As the court in *Morgan v. Veach*, 139 P.2d 976 (Cal. Dist. Ct. App. 1943), explained:

> An appropriate statement relative to defendants' assertion that an injunction would work an inequitable burden is in 28 Am.Jur., section 56, page 253 as follows: "In view of the drastic character of mandatory injunctions, the rule under consideration as to balancing the relative conveniences of the parties applies with special force to a prayer for such mandatory relief. Where, therefore, by innocent mistake or oversight, buildings erected . . . slightly encroach . . . and the damage to the owner of the buildings by their removal would be greatly disproportionate to the injury . . . the court may decline to order their removal. . . . But relief by way of a mandatory injunction will not be denied on the ground that the loss caused by it will be disproportionate to the good accomplished, where it appears that the defendant acted with a full knowledge of the complainant's rights and with an understanding of the consequences which might ensue. . . ."
>
> In a note in 57 A.L.R., first column, page 343, it was said: "Wilfulness on the part of the defendant in proceeding with the violation of the restriction after warning by the complainant, especially after suit is brought, is a ground for equitable relief by mandatory injunction greatly stressed by the courts." (139 P.2d at 980.)

In the case at bench, the structure to be removed was not begun until after the underlying action was filed. It was completed while the litigation was still pending. Defendant gambled on the outcome of the action and lost. The fact that its decision may have been reasonable in light of the denial of the preliminary injunction does not change the result. * * * (End of Court of Appeal opinion.)

We next consider whether defendant is entitled to any offsetting monetary relief from plaintiffs. Defendant contends that the trial court's judgment is overly harsh because it both granted plaintiffs an easement over a 16,250-square-foot parcel of defendant's property free of charge and also required defendant to incur the entire cost of relocating or reconstructing its building. Would application of equitable principles dictate that plaintiffs either pay to defendant the fair market value of the easement they acquired, or contribute a portion of the costs of relocating? We think not.

Initially, the statutory procedure for acquiring an easement by prescription quite clearly retains the traditional common law rule that such an easement may be obtained without incurring any liability to the underlying property owner. Civil Code section 1007, enacted in 1872, provides that "Occupancy for the period prescribed by the Code of Civil Procedure as sufficient to bar any action for the recovery of the property *confers a title thereto,* denominated a title by prescription, *which is sufficient against all. . . ."* (Italics added.) We have confirmed that if the requisite elements of a prescriptive use are shown, "Such use for the five-year statutory period of Code of Civil Procedure section 321 *confers a title by prescription."* (Taormino v. Denny, 463 P.2d 711, 716 (Cal. 1970) fns. omitted, italics added.)

Thus, plaintiffs herein have acquired a title by prescription which is "sufficient against all," including defendant. That being so, there is no basis in law or equity for requiring them to compensate defendant for the fair market value of the easement so acquired. To exact such a charge would entirely defeat the legitimate policies underlying the doctrines of adverse possession and prescription " 'to reduce litigation and preserve the peace by *protecting* a possession that has been maintained for a statutorily deemed sufficient period of time.' " (Italics added, Gilardi v. Hallam, 636 P.2d 588, 592 (Cal. 1981), quoting from an earlier case; see also the Restatement of Property, intro. note at pp. 2922–2923; 3 Powell, The Law of Real Property (1981 ed.) ¶ 413, pp. 34–103—34–104.) As described by Professor Powell, "Historically, prescription has had the theoretical basis of a lost grant. Its continuance has been justified because of its functional utility in helping to cause prompt termination of controversies before the possible loss of evidence and in *stabilizing* long continued property uses." (Ibid., fn. omitted, italics added.) If the doctrine of prescription is truly aimed at "protecting" and "stabilizing" a long and continuous use or possession as against the claims of an alleged "owner" of the property, then the latter's claim for damages or fair compensation for an alleged "taking" must be rejected.

The Court of Appeal recently described the rationale underlying the related adverse possession doctrine as follows: "[I]ts underlying philosophy is basically that land use has historically been favored over disuse, and that therefore he who uses land is preferred in the law to he who does not, even though the latter is the rightful owner. [Fn. omitted.] Hence our laws of real property have sanctioned certain types of otherwise unlawful taking of land belonging to someone else, while, at the same time, our laws with respect to other types of property have generally taken a contrary course. This is now largely justified on the theory that the intent is not to reward the taker or punish the person dispossessed, but to reduce litigation and preserve the peace by protecting a possession that has been maintained for a statutorily deemed sufficient period of time. . . . [¶] Quite naturally, however, dispossessing a person of his property is not easy under this theory, and it may even be asked whether the concept of adverse possession is as viable as it once was, or whether the concept always squares with modern ideals in a sophisticated, congested, peaceful society. . . . [¶] *Yet this method of obtaining land remains on the books,* and if a party proves all five of the [requisite] elements [citation], he can claim title to another's land. . . ." (Finley v. Yuba County Water Dist., 160 Cal.Rptr. 423, 427 (Cal. Ct. App. 1979), italics added.)

Similarly, the system of acquiring an interest in land by prescription "remains on the books," and any decision to alter that system by requiring the payment of compensation clearly would be a matter for the Legislature. Defendant cites no authorities indicating that the present system is unconstitutional in any respect.

Assuming that an award of compensation for the value of the easement is unavailable, may the courts nonetheless order the easement owner to contribute all or part of the cost of relocating or reconstructing an encroaching building? It is at least arguable that a court of equity could order, in an appropriate case, that the plaintiff contribute a portion of the cost of relocating an *innocent* encroachment, as a condition to an award of injunctive relief. As previously noted, it is well established that a court has discretion to balance the hardships and *deny* removal of an encroachment if it was innocently made and does not irreparably injure the plaintiff, and where the cost of removal would greatly exceed the inconvenience to the plaintiff by its continuance. If, as the foregoing cases establish, an outright denial of injunctive relief would be sustained under those circumstances, then no compelling reason exists for depriving the trial court of the *lesser* power of granting the injunction on condition that the plaintiff pay a reasonable portion of the cost of relocation. (See Collester v. Oftedahl, 48 Cal.App.2d 756, 760–61 (Cal. Dist. Ct. App. 1941) [injunctive relief conditioned upon payment of costs]; cf. Farmers Ins. Exch. v. Ruiz, 59 Cal.Rptr. 13, 17–18 (Cal. Ct. App. 1967); 2 Witkin,

Cal. Procedure (2d ed. 1970) Provisional Remedies, § 82, at p. 1520; 2 Pomeroy's Equity Jurisprudence (5th ed. 1941) § 385 et seq. ["He who seeks equity must do equity"].)

In the present case, however, it is apparent that it would be inequitable to charge plaintiffs, who lawfully perfected an easement by prescription, for the cost of removing an encroaching structure erected by defendant with prior notice of plaintiffs' claim. As previously noted, defendant's building was erected *after* plaintiffs' suit was filed and remained pending. Under similar circumstances, the courts have deemed an encroachment to be wilful and have ordered its removal despite a disproportionate hardship to the defendant. Likewise, plaintiffs should not be required to contribute to the cost of relocating encroaching structures which were erected by defendant with full knowledge of plaintiffs' claim.

The judgment is affirmed.

■ GRODIN, JUSTICE, concurring. I cannot accept the majority's attempted justification for the current law of prescriptive easements. How, in today's urban society, litigation is reduced or the peace is preserved by allowing persons situated as are these plaintiffs to acquire rights in what is concededly the land of another without a cent of payment is beyond my comprehension. I therefore agree entirely with the policy criticisms contained in Justice Reynoso's dissenting opinion.

I am persuaded, however, that if change is to come to this arcane area of the law it should come through the Legislature rather than through the courts. It is not alone the existence of Civil Code section 1007 which persuades me, for as my dissenting colleague observes that section, adopted in 1872, was early interpreted as merely fixing the time within which a right by prescription may be acquired. But, in 1965 the Legislature modified the harsh application of the prescriptive easement doctrine by adding Civil Code section 1008, which permits a property owner to avoid acquisition of an easement by the simple expedient of posting a sign.[1] Given that modification, and that degree of legislative attention, I would leave the next move to Sacramento. I therefore join in affirming the trial court's judgment.

■ REYNOSO, JUSTICE, dissenting. I respectfully dissent from that portion of the majority opinion which denies compensation of fair market value for the easement. * * *

Plaintiffs called upon the power of the trial court, acting in equity, to declare and protect a prescriptive easement. The court agreed. Yet the practical result, as indicated by the Court of Appeal opinion (per Compton, J.), is that: "A simple affirmance of the judgment would result

---

[1]   Civil Code section 1008 provides: "No use by any person or persons, no matter how long continued, of any land, shall ever ripen into an easement by prescription, if the owner of such property posts at each entrance to the property or at intervals of not more than 200 feet along the boundary a sign reading substantially as follows: 'Right to pass by permission, and subject to control, of owner: Section 1008, Civil Code.'"

in plaintiffs, who are admittedly trespassers, acquiring practical possession of a sixteen thousand two hundred fifty (16,250) square foot parcel of defendant's valuable property free of charge. . . ."

The majority argues that the result, unjust or not, is ordained by statute. I disagree. My review of the statutes cited by the majority convinces me that they have not removed from the courts the traditional power to invoke the equitable doctrines which deal with fairness. Those doctrines persuade me that plaintiffs should pay fair market value for the property interest acquired. * * *

The law of prescriptive easements and their enforcement enjoyed a long history at common law before 1872. In that year Civil Code section 1007 was enacted. It merely codified the general concept of prescriptive easement found at common law. We must look, therefore, to common law precepts to resolve the issue at hand.

At common law, the declaration of whether a prescriptive easement existed was considered an action at law. It remains so. However, the protection of the declared right was generally considered, and still is, an action in equity.

Mere citation to Civil Code section 1007 resolves nothing. The term "title by prescription," for example, describes the rights which a person acquires upon establishing a prescriptive easement. Nothing more. The case at bench assumes acquisition; the real issue deals with the conditions which the court may impose to protect that judicially declared easement. Thus, in *Taormino v. Denny*, 463 P.2d 711 (Cal. 1970), cited by the majority, our court did no more than affirm the prescriptive right over a private roadway. Not surprisingly, the parties have not cited the section before the trial court, the appellate court, or before us. Neither the trial court nor the Court of Appeal mentioned it. And no papers before us mention the code section. Yet, the section erroneously forms the basis for the majority opinion. * * *

The Court of Appeal correctly identified the nature of plaintiff's cause of action and the issue in this appeal when it wrote: "This is an appeal from an *equitable decree* which declared that plaintiffs had acquired an easement by prescription over the property of defendant." (Emphasis added.) Neither the parties nor the majority disagree with that characterization.

We come, therefore, to the power of the court in equity. Whether the trial court must order the plaintiffs to pay fair market value for the prescriptive easement, as the Court of Appeal concluded, depends on the breadth of discretion which the court in equity enjoys. Let us briefly explore the concept of equity.

Equity's origins lie in the King's extraordinary judicial power, exercised through the Chancery, to administer justice whenever "it was probable that a fair trial in the ordinary Courts would be impeded, and also whenever, . . . , the regular administration of justice was hindered."

(5 Pomeroy's Equity Jurisprudence § 31 P. 37 (1941), hereinafter Pomeroy.) The Chancellor was obliged to look only to "Honesty, Equity, and Conscience [ ]" to decide conflicts. (Id., § 35, p. 40.) Today, it is only a matter of degree that separates the early Chancellors who decided "whether reason and conscience demanded special intervention...." (Walsh on Equity, § 53, p. 282 (1930)) from the modern judges and their grants of equitable relief. (Id.) The modern judge remains the repositor of special relief; he stands in the states' stead "modifying the rigor of hard and fast rules at law where reason and conscience demand it." (Ibid.) * * *

Traditionally the courts have not imposed a condition that fair market value be paid before a prescriptive easement will be declared and protected. However, in my view, the courts do not [sic] have such power. In the case at bench that power should be exercised.

The role which the court in equity can play is seen in two disparate examples, one old and one new. First, we look to the traditional case wherein the building of one owner trespasses upon that of another. Where the law recognizes a legal wrong in such a trespass, and would normally order the removal of the encroaching building (as was done in the case at bench), the court in equity may instead order that money damages be paid by the encroaching party as a condition of protecting the encroachment, particularly where the encroachment was unintentional. (See Walsh, § 55, pp. 284–85.) Second, I cite a quite different example which does not deal with property. The courts, pursuant to their inherent equitable powers, have created several exceptions to the statutory rule (Code Civ.Proc., § 1021) which requires each party to pay his or her own attorney fees. (See Serrano v. Priest, 569 P.2d 1303, 1306–15 (Cal. 1977).) These examples simply illustrate the not too startling notion that courts of equity, in search of fairness, may (1) impose conditions before a decree protecting rights will issue, (2) grant monetary damages, and (3) extend statutory rights. I cite these only to stress that no reason abides in the history, concept or modern practice of equity which would so restrict the power of the court that it could not impose a requirement that fair market value be paid by the trespasser who is granted a prescriptive easement.

Finally, I turn to the fairness issue. By permitting the prescriptive easement in the case at bench the state, acting through the court, endorses a private action akin to eminent domain. Practically, it is the taking of property rights from defendant and giving them to plaintiff. Can it be fair to reward a wrongdoer and punish an innocent property owner?

The majority says "yes." It is fair, according to the majority, for several reasons including (1) reducing litigation, (2) protecting possession, and (3) preference for use over [disuse] of land. None of these reasons is convincing. First, no litigation was reduced. Society should not be in the business of forcing an owner of land to bring suit when a trespass has occurred. Such a policy increases litigation. Second, the possession of the easement has in fact been protected; plaintiffs are only required to pay for the easement. Third, modern society evidences a preference for planned use, not the ad hoc use of a trespasser. It is questionable that in the urban setting of the case at bench, such use by the trespasser is preferred by society.

I do not rely solely on my personal view of fairness. Rather, it is my role as a judge, as it was with the chancellor, to apply a "conception of justice in accordance with the prevailing reason and conscience of the time." (Walsh, § 53, p. 281.) (See also 5 Pomeroy, Equity Jurisprudence, § 67, p. 89; "[Equity] is so constructed . . ., that it possesses an inherent capacity of expansion, so as to keep abreast of each succeeding generation and age.") The final decree of the trial court, approved by the majority, contravenes today's basic notions of fairness and justice. A requirement that plaintiffs pay fair market value for the land use given them is the least our society expects. * * *

The suggestion of the concurring opinion that the Legislature should study this area of law bears underscoring. The statutes need to reflect today's realities. Certainly—they should at least ameliorate the harsh consequences the majority feels compelled to enforce. However, I note that the recent legislative changes referred to in the concurrence only provide a landowner relief from the *creation* of a prescriptive easement. There remains the need for an equitable avenue by which the courts may relieve a landowner subject to a prescriptive easement of an otherwise inequitable burden.

I would affirm the judgment. However, I would remand to the trial court for further proceedings to fix an amount of reasonable compensation to be paid by plaintiffs to defendant. That compensation would be the fair market value of the property interest acquired. From that compensation damages, if any, sustained by plaintiff should be subtracted.

NOTES AND QUESTIONS

1.   What is the best characterization of the state of mind of the plaintiff in *Warsaw*: good faith, bad faith, or unclear? What state of mind does the California Supreme Court seem to require to establish an easement by prescription?

2.   The opinion recites that to establish an easement by prescription, the use must be continuous and must follow a "definite course and pattern." More direct issues with the continuity requirement were raised in *United States v. Platt*, a case involving the Zuni indigenous tribe. As a part of their religious practice, every four years, a maximum of eighty members of the Zuni tribe go on a 110-mile pilgrimage on the summer solstice from their reservation in northwest New Mexico to a mountain area the tribe calls Kohlu/wala:wa in northeast Arizona. The Zuni believe that Kohlu/wala:wa is "their place of origin, the basis for their religious life, and the home of their dead." 730 F. Supp. 318, 319 (D. Ariz. 1990). In 1985, Earl Platt, the owner of eighteen to twenty miles of the land crossed during the pilgrimage,

expressed an intent to interfere with future crossings. The Arizona district court determined that, although the crossing occurs on one day once every four years, the Zuni had established an easement by prescription over Platt's land, noting that the pilgrimage extended at least back to the early twentieth century, that the route remained "consistent and relatively unchanged," that their claim to ongoing use was evidenced by their cutting down of fences in their way, and that the practice was "open visible and known to the community." Id. at 320–24. In what ways does this approach to the continuity requirement for prescriptive easements remind you of the treatment of that requirement in adverse possession cases like *Scott v. Anderson-Tully Co.* or *Howard v. Kunto* (see Chapter II)?

3.   What do you think of the idea of requiring the adverse user (AU) (or adverse possessor, AP) to pay the true owner (TO) the fair market value of the easement (or the possessory rights) obtained through prescription or adverse possession? The standard rules of prescription and adverse possession involve what Calabresi and Melamed call property rules. One day before the statute of limitations runs, the TO has the entitlement protected by a property rule. This means the TO can block the AU or AP from further using the property without the TO's consent. The day after the statute of limitations runs, the AU or AP has the entitlement, also protected by a property rule. This means that the AU or AP can now use self-help or otherwise stop the TO (or any other person) from interfering with her use right or possessory right without her consent. The innovation embraced by the California Court of Appeal, but rejected by a majority of the California Supreme Court, would mean that the passage of the statute of limitations would transform an entitlement in the TO protected by a property rule into an entitlement in the TO protected by a liability rule. In other words, the AU or AP could in effect force a transfer of use rights or possessory rights by the TO, but only upon payment of just compensation to the TO.

4.   Another way to frame the question would be to ask whether we should consider the successful AU to have been unjustly enriched, giving rise to a claim of restitution. Is there any way to tell whether the AU is unjustly enriched other than by reference to the legal entitlement? Which is what? (Consider in this regard that one who pays by mistake an unenforceable debt cannot sue to get the payment back, and promising to pay a debt that is past the statute of limitations will cause the statute to start over.) Does Justice Reynoso's invocation of traditional equity support a restitution theory? Whether or not you agree with the idea of indemnification or restitution by one claiming prescription (or adverse possession), do you think an indemnification requirement would make more sense, or less sense, in the context of an irrevocable license by estoppel, as in *Holbrook v. Taylor*, the next case?

5.   As in a number of other California cases we have considered (*Moore v. Regents of the University of California, Intel Corp. v. Hamidi, Marvin v. Marvin, Kendall v. Ernest Pestana, Nahrstedt v. Lakeside Village Condominium*) the debate among the Justices here centers on the question of institutional choice: Which institution, legislature or court, is primarily responsible for updating property law? Here all but one of the Justices thinks

the legislature must do the updating. But is the proposal here really all that radical? Why isn't the defendant simply in the position of one seeking restitution for unjust enrichment (see Chapter IV)?

Figure 9-5
Land at Issue in *Warsaw v. Chicago Metallic Ceilings*

6.   Under the liability rule regime endorsed by the Court of Appeal, what happens if the TO has abandoned the property or cannot be located to receive the payment of compensation? At what point in time would the property taken be valued—at the point of original entry or use, when the statute of limitations runs, or when the judgment awarding title to the AP (or ownership of an easement to the AU) becomes final? How would the shift from a property rule in the AU or AP to a liability rule in the TO affect the incentives of the parties to monitor for trespasses and negotiate written easements when appropriate? Would you allow compensation in all cases, or only in certain kinds of cases, e.g., where the original entry was in bad faith? For discussion of these issues, see Thomas W. Merrill, Property Rules, Liability Rules, and Adverse Possession, 79 Nw. U. L. Rev. 1123 (1985).

Holbrook v. Taylor

Supreme Court of Kentucky, 1976.
532 S.W.2d 763.

■ STERNBERG, JUSTICE. This is an action to establish a right to the use of a roadway, which is 10 to 12 feet wide and about 250 feet long, over the unenclosed, hilly woodlands of another. The claimed right to the use of the roadway is twofold: by prescription and by estoppel. Both issues are heatedly contested. The evidence is in conflict as to the nature and type of use that had been made of the roadway. The lower court determined that a right to the use of the roadway by prescription had not been established, but that it had been established by estoppel. The landowners, feeling themselves aggrieved, appeal. We will consider the two issues separately.

In *Grinestaff v. Grinestaff*, 318 S.W.2d 881 (Ky. 1958), we said that an easement may be created by express written grant, by implication, by prescription, or by estoppel. It has long been the law of this commonwealth that "(a)n easement, such as a right of way, is created when the owner of a tenement to which the right is claimed to be appurtenant, or those under whom he claims title, have openly, peaceably, continuously, and under a claim of right adverse to the owner of the soil, and with his knowledge and acquiescence, used a way over the lands of another for as much as 15 years." Flener v. Lawrence, 220 S.W. 1041 (Ky. 1920); Rominger v. City Realty Company, 324 S.W.2d 806 (Ky. 1959).

In 1942 appellants purchased the subject property. In 1944 they gave permission for a haul road to be cut for the purpose of moving coal from a newly opened mine. The roadway was so used until 1949, when the mine closed. During that time the appellants were paid a royalty for the use of the road. In 1957 appellants built a tenant house on their property and the roadway was used by them and their tenant. The tenant house burned in 1961 and was not replaced. In 1964 the appellees bought their three-acre building site, which adjoins appellants, and the following year built their residence thereon. At all times prior to 1965, the use of the haul road was by permission of appellants. There is no evidence of any probative value which would indicate that the use of the haul road during that period of time was either adverse, continuous, or uninterrupted. The trial court was fully justified, therefore, in finding that the right to the use of this easement was not established by prescription.

As to the issue on estoppel, we have long recognized that a right to the use of a roadway over the lands of another may be established by estoppel. In *Lashley Telephone Co. v. Durbin*, 228 S.W. 423 (Ky. 1921), we said:

> Though many courts hold that a licensee is conclusively presumed as a matter of law to know that a license is revocable at the pleasure of the licensor, and if he expend money in connection with his entry upon the land of the latter, he does so at his peril * * * , yet it is the established rule in this state that where a license is not a bare, naked right of entry, but includes the right to erect structures and acquire an interest in the land in the nature of an easement by the construction of improvements thereon, the licensor may not revoke the license and restore his premises to their former condition after the licensee has exercised the privilege given by the license and erected the improvements at considerable expense; * * *

In *Gibbs v. Anderson*, 156 S.W.2d 876 (Ky. 1941), Gibbs claimed the right, by estoppel, to the use of a roadway over the lands of Anderson. The lower court denied the claim. We reversed. Anderson's immediate predecessor in title admitted that he had discussed the passway with Gibbs before it was constructed and had agreed that it might be built through his land. He stood by and saw Gibbs expend considerable money in this construction. We applied the rule announced in *Lashley Telephone Co. v. Durbin*, supra, and reversed with directions that a judgment be entered granting Gibbs the right to the use of the passway.

In *McCoy v. Hoffman*, 295 S.W.2d 560 (Ky. 1956), the facts are that Hoffman had acquired the verbal consent of the landowner to build a passway over the lands of the owner to the state highway. Subsequently, the owner of the servient estate sold the property to McCoy, who at the time of the purchase was fully aware of the existence of the roadway and the use to which it was being put. McCoy challenged Hoffman's right to use the road. The lower court found that a right had been gained by prescription. In this court's consideration of the case, we affirmed, not on the theory of prescriptive right but on the basis that the owner of the servient estate was estopped. After announcing the rule for establishing a right by prescription, we went on to say:

> * * * On the other hand, the right of revocation of the license is subject to the qualification that where the licensee has exercised the privilege given him and erected improvements or made substantial expenditures on the faith or strength of the license, it becomes irrevocable and continues for so long a time as the nature of the license calls for. In effect, under this condition the license becomes in reality a grant through estoppel. * * * .

In *Akers v. Moore*, 309 S.W.2d 758 (Ky. 1958), this court again considered the right to the use of a passway by estoppel. Akers and others had used the Moore branch as a public way of ingress and egress from their property. They sued Moore and others who owned property along the branch seeking to have the court recognize their right to the use of the roadway and to order the removal of obstructions which had been placed in the roadway. The trial court found that Akers and others had acquired a prescriptive right to the use of the portion of the road lying on the left side of the creek bed, but had not acquired the right to the use of so much of the road as lay on the right side of the creek bed. Consequently, an appeal and a cross-appeal were filed. Considering the right to the use of the strip of land between the right side of the creek bed and the highway, this court found that the evidence portrayed it very rough and apparently never improved, that it ran alongside the house in which one of the protestors lived, and that by acquiescence or by express consent of at least one of the protestors the right side of the roadway was opened up so as to change the roadway from its close proximity to the Moore residence. The relocated portion of the highway had only been used as a passway for about six years before the suit was filed. The trial court found that this section of the road had not been established as a public way by estoppel. We reversed. In doing so, we stated:

> We consider the fact that the appellees, Artie Moore, et al. had stood by and acquiesced in (if in fact they had not affirmatively consented) the change being made and permitted the appellants to spend money in fixing it up to make it passable and use it for six years without objecting. Of course, the element of time was not sufficient for the acquisition of the right of way by adverse possession. But the law recognizes that one may acquire a license to use a passway or roadway where, with the knowledge of the licensor, he has in the exercise of the privilege spent money in improving the way or for other purposes connected with its use on the faith or strength of the license. Under such conditions the license becomes irrevocable and continues for so long a time as its nature calls for. This, in effect, becomes a grant through estoppel. Gibbs v. Anderson, 288 Ky. 488, 156 S.W.2d 876 (Ky. 1941); McCoy v. Hoffman, Ky., 295 S.W.2d 560 (Ky. 1956). It would be unconscionable to permit the owners of this strip of land of trivial value to revoke the license by obstructing and preventing its use.

In the present case the roadway had been used since 1944 by permission of the owners of the servient estate. The evidence is conflicting as to whether the use of the road subsequent to 1965 was by permission or by claim of right. Appellees contend that it had been used by them and others without the permission of appellants; on the other hand, it is contended by appellants that the use of the roadway at all times was by their permission. The evidence discloses that during the period of preparation for the construction of appellees' home and during the time the house was being built, appellees were permitted to use the roadway as ingress and egress for workmen, for hauling machinery and material to the building site, for construction of the dwelling, and for making improvements generally to the premises. Further, the evidence reflects that after construction of the residence, which cost $25,000, was completed, appellees continued to regularly use the roadway as they had been doing. Appellant J. S. Holbrook testified that in order for appellees to get up to their house he gave them permission to use and repair the roadway. They widened it, put in a culvert, and graveled part of it with "red dog", also known as cinders, at a cost of approximately $100. There is no other location over which a roadway could reasonably be built to provide an outlet for appellees.

No dispute had arisen between the parties at any time over the use of the roadway until the fall of 1970. Appellant J. S. Holbrook contends that he wanted to secure a writing from the appellees in order to relieve him from any responsibility for any damage that might happen to anyone on the subject road. On the other hand, Mrs. Holbrook testified that the writing was desired to avoid any claim which may be made by appellees of a right to the use of the roadway. Appellees testified that the writing was an effort to force them to purchase a small strip of land over which the roadway traversed, for the sum of $500. The dispute was not resolved and appellants erected a steel cable across the roadway to prevent its use and also constructed "no-trespassing" signs. Shortly thereafter, the suit was filed to require the removal of the obstruction and to declare the right of appellees to the use of the roadway without interference.

The use of the roadway by appellees to get to their home from the public highway, the use of the roadway to take in heavy equipment and material and supplies for construction of the residence, the general improvement of the premises, the maintenance of the roadway, and the construction by appellees of a $25,000 residence, all with the actual consent of appellants or at least with their tacit approval, clearly demonstrates the rule laid down in *Lashley Telephone Co. v. Durbin*, supra, that the license to use the subject roadway may not be revoked.

The evidence justifies the finding of the lower court that the right to the use of the roadway had been established by estoppel.

The judgment is affirmed.

NOTES AND QUESTIONS

1. By extinguishing the title of true owner (TO), adverse possession leads to the same result as a transfer of full possessory rights of ownership from the original true owner (TO) to the adverse possessor (AP), after the statute of limitations runs (provided the other elements of adverse possession are satisfied—see Chapter II). An easement by prescription mimics the transfer of an easement over the land of the TO to the adverse user (AU), after the statute of limitations runs. How does one know whether the behavior of the adverse party constitutes adverse possession or adverse use? Suppose in *Holbrook* that the appellees and their predecessors had parked vehicles overnight on the roadway. Would this transform a prescriptive easement case into an adverse possession case? Why doesn't placing the "red dog" on the driveway make this adverse possession rather than prescription?

2. Recall that the five standard elements for establishing adverse possession are that the possession must be (1) actual, (2) exclusive, (3) open and notorious, (4) continuous, and (5) adverse under a claim of right. Which of these elements are relaxed or modified in establishing an easement by prescription?

3. It would appear that prescription requires lack of permission and that estoppel requires permission, or at least acquiescence (coupled with reliance). Why? Although modern easements by prescription closely track adverse possession, this was not always the case. An older theory, now less in favor, rested prescription on the fiction of a "lost grant": The running of the prescriptive period raises an irrebuttable presumption that sometime in the past the owner of the servient land granted an easement (satisfying the statute of frauds) but that the grant was lost. See, e.g., Shellow v. Hagen,

101 N.W.2d 694, 696–97 (Wis. 1960); Romans v. Nadler, 14 N.W.2d 482, 485 (Minn. 1944); Bryant v. Foot, (1867) 2 L.R.–Q.B. 161, 181 (Eng.). Although this fiction has been much criticized, see Restatement (Third) of Property (Servitudes) § 2.17 cmt. b (2000), it does raise the question whether the acquisition of an easement by prescription should be associated with an adverse stance by the potential acquirer. Would allowing the acquisition of an easement after accommodating behavior foster neighborly behavior? How do (and should) potential servient owners protect themselves from claims of prescription or estoppel?

4.   If an encroaching user obtains an easement by prescription, this results in a perpetual easement in all respects equivalent to an easement by grant. What rights are established when the encroaching user obtains an irrevocable license by estoppel? Does an irrevocable license run with the land? Does it create rights enforceable against third parties? The court in the principal case quotes an earlier Kentucky decision, which says the interest "continues for so long as its nature calls for." What does this mean?

5.   Suppose landowner A, knowing where the lot line is, observes neighboring landowner B building a driveway over the land of owner A. Landowner B does not know he is trespassing and in fact thinks the driveway is on his own land. If landowner A simply watches the construction day after day without giving any permission, express or implied, to use his land for the driveway, and landowner B proceeds to complete the driveway, can landowner B claim an irrevocable license by estoppel?

6.   Why does the law have so many different doctrines for bailing out owners of dominant tracts of land who fail to negotiate a written grant of an easement from the owner(s) of servient tracts? Can you think of ways of reducing the number of doctrines? Would you advocate replacing them all with something like the private condemnation statutes in use in about half the states?

Fontainebleau Hotel Corp. v. Forty-Five Twenty-Five, Inc.

District Court of Appeal of Florida, Third District, 1959.
114 So.2d 357.

■ PER CURIAM. This is an interlocutory appeal from an order temporarily enjoining the appellants from continuing with the construction of a fourteen-story addition to the Fontainebleau Hotel, owned and operated by the appellants. Appellee, plaintiff below, owns the Eden Roc Hotel, which was constructed in 1955, about a year after the Fontainebleau, and adjoins the Fontainebleau on the north. Both are luxury hotels, facing the Atlantic Ocean. The proposed addition to the Fontainebleau is being constructed twenty feet from its north property line, 130 feet from the mean high water mark of the Atlantic Ocean, and 76 feet 8 inches from the ocean bulkhead line. The 14-story tower will extend 160 feet above grade in height and is 416 feet long from east to west. During the winter months, from around two o'clock in the afternoon for the remainder of the day, the shadow of the addition will extend over the cabana, swimming pool, and sunbathing areas of the Eden Roc, which are located in the southern portion of its property.

In this action, plaintiff-appellee sought to enjoin the defendants-appellants from proceeding with the construction of the addition to the Fontainebleau (it appears to have been roughly eight stories high at the time suit was filed), alleging that the construction would interfere with the light and air on the beach in front of the Eden Roc and cast a shadow of such size as to render the beach wholly unfitted for the use and enjoyment of its guests, to the irreparable injury of the plaintiff; further, that the construction of such addition on the north side of defendants' property, rather than the south side, was actuated by malice and ill will on the part of the defendants' president toward the plaintiff's president; and that the construction was in violation of a building ordinance requiring a 100-foot setback from the ocean. It was also alleged that the construction would interfere with the easements of light and air enjoyed by plaintiff and its predecessors in title for more than twenty years and "impliedly granted by virtue of the acts of the plaintiff's predecessors in title, as well as under the common law and the express recognition of such rights by virtue of Chapter 9837, Laws of Florida 1923 * * * ." Some attempt was also made to allege an easement by implication in favor of the plaintiff's property, as the dominant, and against the defendants' property, as the servient, tenement.

The defendants' answer denied the material allegations of the complaint, pleaded laches and estoppel by judgment.

The chancellor heard considerable testimony on the issues made by the complaint and the answer and, as noted, entered a temporary injunction restraining the defendants from continuing with the construction of the addition. His reason for so doing was stated by him, in a memorandum opinion, as follows:

> In granting the temporary injunction in this case the Court wishes to make several things very clear. The ruling is not based on any alleged presumptive title nor prescriptive right of the plaintiff to light and air nor is it based on any deed restrictions nor recorded plats in the title of the plaintiff nor of the defendant nor of any plat of record. It is not based on any zoning ordinance nor on any provision of the building code of the City of Miami Beach nor on the decision of any court, nisi prius or appellate. It is based solely on the proposition that no one has a right to use his property to the injury of another. In this case it is clear from the evidence that the proposed use by the Fontainebleau will materially damage the Eden Roc. There is evidence indicating that the construction of the proposed annex by the Fontainebleau is malicious or deliberate for the purpose of injuring the Eden Roc, but it is scarcely sufficient, standing alone, to afford a basis for equitable relief.

This is indeed a novel application of the maxim sic utere tuo ut alienum non laedas. This maxim does not mean that one must never use his own property in such a way as to do any injury to his neighbor. Beckman v. Marshall, 85 So.2d 552 (Fla. 1956). It means only that one must use his property so as not to injure the lawful rights of another. Cason v. Florida Power Co., 76 So. 535 (Fla. 1918). In Reaver v. Martin Theatres, 52 So.2d 682, 683 (Fla. 1951), under this maxim, it was stated that "it is well settled that a property owner may put his own property to any reasonable and lawful use, so long as he does not thereby deprive the adjoining landowner of any right of enjoyment of his property which is recognized and protected by law, and so long as his use is not such a one as the law will pronounce a nuisance." [Emphasis supplied.]

No American decision has been cited, and independent research has revealed none, in which it has been held that—in the absence of some contractual or statutory obligation—a landowner has a legal right to the free flow of light and air across the adjoining land of his neighbor. Even at common law, the landowner had no legal right, in the absence of an easement or uninterrupted use and enjoyment for a period of 20 years, to unobstructed light and air from the adjoining land. Blumberg v. Weiss, 17 A.2d 823 (N.J. 1941); 1 Am.Jur., Adjoining Landowners, § 51. And the English doctrine of "ancient lights" has been unanimously repudiated in this country. 1 Am.Jur., Adjoining Landowners, § 49, p. 533; Lynch v. Hill, 6 A.2d 614 (Del. Ch. 1939), overruling Clawson v. Primrose, 4 Del.Ch. 643 (1873).

There being, then, no legal right to the free flow of light and air from the adjoining land, it is universally held that where a structure serves a useful and beneficial purpose, it does not give rise to a cause of action, either for damages or for an injunction under the maxim sic utere tuo ut alienum non laedas, even though it causes injury to another by cutting off the light and air and interfering with the view that would otherwise be available over adjoining land in its natural state, regardless of the fact that the structure may have been erected partly for spite.

We see no reason for departing from this universal rule. If, as contended on behalf of plaintiff, public policy demands that a landowner in the Miami Beach area refrain from constructing buildings on his premises that will cast a shadow on the adjoining premises, an amendment of its comprehensive planning and zoning ordinance, applicable to the public as a whole, is the means by which such purpose should be achieved. (No opinion is expressed here as to the validity of such an ordinance, if one should be enacted pursuant to the requirements of law. Cf. City of Miami Beach v. State ex rel. Fontainebleau Hotel Corp., 108 So.2d 614, 619 (Fla. App. 1959).) But to change the universal rule—and the custom followed in this state since its inception—that adjoining landowners have an equal right under the law to build to the line of their respective tracts and to such a height as is desired by them (in the absence, of course, of building restrictions or regulations) amounts, in our opinion, to judicial legislation. As stated in Musumeci v. Leonardo, [75 A.2d 177 (R.I. 1950)], "So use your own as not to injure another's property is, indeed, a sound and salutary principle for the promotion of justice, but it may not and should not be applied so as gratuitously to confer upon an adjacent property owner incorporeal rights incidental to his ownership of land which the law does not sanction."

We have also considered whether the order here reviewed may be sustained upon any other reasoning, conformable to and consistent with the pleadings, regardless of the erroneous reasoning upon which the order was actually based. We have concluded that it cannot.

The record affirmatively shows that no statutory basis for the right sought to be enforced by plaintiff exists. The so-called Shadow Ordinance enacted by the City of Miami Beach at plaintiff's behest was held invalid in City of Miami Beach v. State ex rel. Fontainebleau Hotel Corp., supra. It also affirmatively appears that there is no possible basis for holding that plaintiff has an easement for light and air, either express or implied, across defendants' property, nor any prescriptive right thereto—even if it be assumed, arguendo, that the common-law right of prescription as to "ancient lights" is in effect in this state. And from what we have said heretofore in this opinion, it is perhaps superfluous to add that we have no desire to dissent from the unanimous holding in this country repudiating the English doctrine of ancient lights.

The only other possible basis—and, in fact, the only one insisted upon by plaintiff in its brief filed here, other than its reliance upon the law of private nuisance as expressed in the maxim *sic utere tuo ut alienum non laedas*—for the order here reviewed is the alleged violation by defendants of the setback line prescribed by ordinance. The plaintiff argues that the ordinance applicable to the Use District in which plaintiff's and defendants' properties are located, prescribing "a front yard having a depth of not less than one hundred (100) feet, measured from the ocean, * * * ," should be and has been interpreted by the City's zoning inspector as requiring a setback of 100 feet from an established ocean bulkhead line. As noted above, the addition to the Fontainebleau is set back only 76 feet 8 inches from the ocean bulkhead line, although it is 130 feet from the ocean measured from the mean high water mark.

Figure 9-6
The Fontainebleau and Eden Roc Hotels,
Miami Beach, Florida

Courtesy of The Bramson Archive, Miami, FL. The Bramson Archive, Miami, FL. The first image shows the hotels before the wall, the second image after its construction.

While the chancellor did not decide the question of whether the setback ordinance had been violated, it is our view that, even if there was such a violation, the plaintiff would have no cause of action against the defendants based on such violation. The application of simple mathematics to the sun studies filed in evidence by plaintiff in support of its claim demonstrates conclusively that to move the existing structure back some 23 feet from the ocean would make no appreciable difference in the problem which is the subject of this controversy. The construction of the 14-story addition is proceeding under a permit issued by the city pursuant to the mandate of this court in City of Miami Beach v. State ex rel. Fontainebleau Hotel Corp., supra, which permit authorizes completion of the 14-story addition according to a plan showing a 76-foot setback from the ocean bulkhead line. Moreover, the plaintiff's objection to the distance of the structure from the ocean appears to have been made for the first time in the instant suit, which was filed almost a year after the beginning of the construction of the addition, at a time when it was roughly eight stories in height, representing the expenditure by defendants of several million dollars. In these circumstances, it is our view that the plaintiff has stated no cause of action for equitable relief based on the violation of the ordinance—assuming, arguendo, that there has been a violation.

Since it affirmatively appears that the plaintiff has not established a cause of action against the defendants by reason of the structure here in question, the order granting a temporary injunction should be and it is hereby reversed with directions to dismiss the complaint.

Reversed with directions.

NOTES AND QUESTIONS

1.   The Fontainebleau, designed by architect Morris Lapidus, was the premier hotel of Miami Beach when it was constructed. It was originally owned by two partners, Ben Novack and Harry Mufson. When they had a falling out, Mufson proceeded to build the Eden Roc, immediately to the north of the Fontainebleau. Novack retaliated by ordering an addition, called the Fontainebleau Towers, on the site of the "kit kat" swimming pool, which was originally north of the main pool and hence abutted the Eden Roc property. This is the addition at issue in the principal case. When it was completed, the Towers nearly doubled the capacity of the Fontainebleau (to 1,000 rooms). Not only did the Towers cast a shadow on the Eden Roc swimming pool, Novack also ordered that the north wall of the addition, facing the Eden Roc, remain windowless and unpainted, thereby degrading the view of the Eden Roc patrons—though some sources say the wall retained some windows in Novack's own special suite, where he could look down on the shadow his structure cast. However, after Mufson was defeated in his attempt to enjoin the addition, he was able to extend the deck of the Eden Roc, with a new pool, further to the east, thereby escaping the shadow cast in the winter months by the Towers. See Seth Bramson, Miami Beach 106, 108 (2005). In 2008, the owners of the Eden Roc remodeled their hotel to build a twenty-one-story tower alongside the border with the Fontainebleau, thereby bringing the longstanding battle started by Novack and Mufson to an end. See Joseph Brown, Eden Roc Hotel Miami Beach: A New Tower that Ends the Feud, South Beach Magazine, Jan. 9, 2008, at https://www.south beachmagazine.com/eden-roc-hotel-miami-beach/.

2.   Is there a simple explanation for the conclusion in *Fontainebleau Hotel* that one cannot create an easement by prescription in the flow of sunlight across land? A prescriptive easement arises when an adverse user

repeatedly trespasses on the land of the true owner, and the true owner allows the statute of limitations for an action in trespass to run. Where is the trespass in *Fontainebleau Hotel*?

3.   Can one obtain an easement by grant for the flow of sunlight across a neighbor's property? Some jurisdictions have said yes. See, e.g., Pacifica Homeowners' Ass'n v. Wesley Palms Retirement Community, 224 Cal.Rptr. 380 (Cal. Ct. App. 1986); Pierce v. Northeast Lake Washington Sewer and Water Dist., 870 P.2d 305 (Wash. 1994). But the most common way of providing for something like the flow of sunlight across land (other than through zoning ordinances) would be through negotiation of a restrictive covenant that limits the height of the neighboring building. Interestingly, one cannot obtain a restrictive covenant by prescription. The simple explanation, again, would be that the conduct required by the typical restrictive covenant does not involve any trespass by the benefited property owner on the land of the burdened property owner. Similarly, no state's common law provides for a right to acquire an easement of light by prescription. Might some form of liability rule be applied in this context? Iowa has passed a statute that allows something like a solar easement by private eminent domain, with ex ante application to a public official and a requirement of just compensation. Iowa Code §§ 564A. See generally Sara C. Bronin, Solar Rights, 89 B.U. L. Rev. 1217 (2009); Troy A. Rule, Shadows on the Cathedral: Solar Access Laws in a Different Light, 2010 U. Ill. L. Rev. 851.

4.   But here is a complication: In England and in most American jurisdictions, one can acquire by grant an easement to commit a nuisance on the land of another. For example, if A wants to construct a smelly smelter on his land, but anticipates that this will create a nuisance for B who lives next door, A can try to acquire an easement from B permitting A to cast smelly fumes on the land of B. (Of course, A will have to pay dearly for such an easement.) Also, as noted earlier, in England, and in some American states, one can also acquire an easement by prescription to commit a nuisance. See Campbell v. Seaman, supra. Thus, if A builds a smelter that casts smelly fumes on the land of B, and the statute of limitations for B to bring a nuisance action against A runs, A can claim to have acquired an easement by prescription to create the nuisance. If one can acquire an easement by prescription to commit a nuisance on the land of a neighbor in the form of smelly fumes, why cannot one acquire an easement by prescription to be free of having the flow of sunlight blocked by a neighbor's building? Courts have generally rejected claims that blocking solar access is a nuisance. See Sher v. Leiderman, 226 Cal.Rptr. 698 (Cal. Ct. App. 1986); American Nat'l Bank & Trust Co. v. City of Chicago, 568 N.E.2d 25 (Ill. App. Ct. 1990). However, two jurisdictions have ruled to the contrary, holding that blocking sunlight can be a nuisance. See Tenn v. 889 Associates, Ltd., 500 A.2d 366 (N.H. 1985) (Souter, J.); Prah v. Maretti, 321 N.W.2d 182 (Wis. 1982). In such a jurisdiction, would *Fontainebleau Hotel* come out differently?

5.   In the case of the smelly fumes, the put-upon landowner has had its attention drawn to the adverse use. Can the same be said for someone whose neighbor claims later to have been relying on access to sunlight? If

one accepts that blocking light could be a nuisance, how should a court resolve the conflict? Can any landowner with a worthy project acquire rights over adjacent land with no notice? If not, how should nuisance law evolve in response to changing conditions?

6.   As we saw in Chapter III, many Western states employ the doctrine of prior appropriation to allocate water, and some Western states have adopted legislation providing for prior appropriation rights in solar access, N.M. Stats. §§ 47–3–1 to 42–3–5; Wyoming Stat. § 34–22–101, et seq.; see also Note, The Allocation of Sunlight: Solar Rights and the Prior Appropriation Doctrine, 47 Colo. L. Rev. 421 (1976). Does a "me first" approach to solar collectors make sense? If the plaintiff had prevailed in *Fontainebleau Hotel*, would there be a potential for a wasteful race to build? If building and maintaining a swimming pool restricts the rights of the neighboring landowner, would each of the landowners be encouraged to build more quickly than they would otherwise? Is this a situation in which first-in-time should prevail, or one where its dangers of wasteful racing are prominent?

7.   The court in *Fontainebleau Hotel* states that it does not matter whether the addition to the Fontainebleau may have been constructed partly out of spite. But pure spite can sometimes lead to greater intervention. Particularly where one landowner erects a fence solely to block light and air from a neighbor, many courts have been willing to find a nuisance and issue an injunction. See, e.g., Flaherty v. Moran, 45 N.W. 381 (Mich. 1890). Mixed motives will usually lead to no liability. See, e.g., Kuzniak v. Kozminski, 65 N.W. 275 (Mich. 1895). See also Nadav Shoked, Two Hundred Years of Spite, 110 Nw. U. L. Rev. 357 (2016). Compare in this regard *Keeble v. Hickeringill*, in Chapter II. Might the spite fence doctrine be a solution to the problem of a landowner seeking to use the *ad coelum* rule to exclude highflying airplanes?

c.   TERMINATION OF EASEMENTS

Easements may be terminated in a number of ways. The most approved method is by deed, releasing or extinguishing the easement. Easements are also terminated as a matter of law when the dominant and servient tract come under common ownership. This is said to result in a merger of the easement into the larger fee simple. A third method of termination is adverse possession or prescription. If the owner of the servient tract blocks the easement, and the owner of the dominant tract fails to object before the statute of limitations runs, then the easement will be extinguished. Finally, easements may be extinguished if prolonged nonuse gives rise to an inference that the easement has been abandoned. However, changed circumstances are generally not considered a ground for modification or termination of an easement, unless the easement is stated in terms of a particular purpose that has become obsolete. See Jon W. Bruce & James W. Ely, Jr., The Law of Easements and Licenses in Land § 9.03 (1988).

Abandonment of railroad rights-of-way has given rise to extensive litigation under the Rails-to-Trails Act, 16 U.S.C. § 1247(d), adopted in 1983. The Act provides a mechanism whereby rail lines that are scheduled to be abandoned can be taken over for public use as recreational trails. Many landowners who live next to these lines object. They argue that railroad rights-of-way were often established as easements for "railroad purposes," and when the easement ceases to be used for railroad purposes, the land should revert to them, as servient owners under these original easements. The owners argue that if the government insists on converting the easements into public recreational trails, this constitutes a taking of their property for which they are entitled to just compensation. In *Preseault v. ICC*, 494 U.S. 1 (1990), the Supreme Court upheld the constitutionality of the Rails-to-Trails Act, but also recognized that servient landowners might have a claim for a taking based on the language of the particular deeds authorizing railroad operations over their property. Later decisions have established that resolution of such a takings claim requires courts to interpret the nature of the property interest originally acquired by the railroad (easement or fee simple); the scope of the interest acquired by the railroad (unrestricted or limited to railroad purposes); and when the railroad abandoned the property. For recent decisions adjudicating specific disputes involving rails-to-trails projects, see, Samuel C. Johnson 1988 Trust v. Bayfield County Wisconsin, 649 F.3d 799 (7th Cir. 2011); Thompson v. United States, No. 09-612L, 2011 WL 4914782 (Fed. Cl. 2011); see also Marvin M. Brandt Revocable Trust v. United States, 572 U.S. 93 (2014) (holding that railroad right of way was an easement, which when abandoned was extinguished, leaving an unburdened fee simple).

d.   MISUSE OF EASEMENTS

Penn Bowling Recreation Center, Inc. v. Hot Shoppes, Inc.

United States Court of Appeals, District of Columbia Circuit, 1949.
179 F.2d 64.

■ MCALLISTER, CIRCUIT JUDGE. In 1938, the Norment Estate conveyed a portion of its real property to appellee, Hot Shoppes, Inc., and subjected a part thereof to a sixteen-foot right of way for ingress and egress. This resulted in an easement for the benefit of the balance of the unconveyed property, adjacent thereto, which was retained by the Estate, and which, by virtue of the easement, became the dominant tenement. A part of this dominant estate came into ownership of appellant, Penn Bowling Recreation Center, Inc., by mesne conveyances, in 1940, two years after the creation of the right of way.

On February 5, 1948, appellee, Hot Shoppes, erected a barrier of iron posts and cement concrete blocks within the right of way and alongside it, interfering with the full enjoyment of the easement by Penn Bowling;

and shortly thereafter, appellant filed its complaint to enjoin appellee from maintaining the structure within the right of way and interfering with the use thereof. Appellee, in its answer denied that appellant was entitled to the use of the right of way, and asked for a permanent injunction against such use by appellant, as well as for a judgment declaring it to be permanently forfeited and extinguished by abandonment. Both parties filed motions for a preliminary injunction, but before a hearing was had on these motions, appellee filed a motion for summary judgment, asking dismissal of the complaint, a permanent injunction against the use by appellant of the right of way, and a declaratory judgment declaring that it had been permanently forfeited and extinguished by abandonment. The district court granted appellee's motion for summary judgment as prayed; and from such judgment, the Penn Bowling Recreation Center appeals.

The arguments that appellee addressed to the district court on the hearing on the motion for summary judgment embraced the contentions that appellant, as owner of the dominant tenement, had forfeited and extinguished the right of way by abandonment, as the result of subjecting the servient tenement to an additional and enlarged use or servitude in connection with other premises to which the easement was not appurtenant; that it had been guilty of the misuse of the easement of the right of way by reason of having used it for the parking of motor vehicles; and that, by certain masonry constructions, appellant had, in any event, made it impossible to use the right of way for egress and ingress.

With regard to the claim that appellant had subjected the servient tenement to a burden in excess of that imposed by the original easement, it appears that after the creation of the right of way for the benefit of the dominant tenement, appellant purchased not only that tenement but other real property adjacent thereto, the latter property not being entitled to the enjoyment of the easement. Appellant then constructed a building occupying a part of the dominant tenement, as well as the additional property adjacent thereto. Not all of the dominant tenement is occupied by the building. In fact, the total of the area of that portion of the dominant tenement, together with the non-dominant property over which the building is constructed, is a smaller area than the area of the original dominant tenement. The building, thus constructed, houses a large bowling alley and restaurant. Appellant in the past has been using the right of way to bring fuel oil, food, equipment, and supplies to the building, and removing trash, garbage, and other material therefrom.

It is contended by appellant that since the area of the dominant and non-dominant land served by the easement is less than the original area of the dominant tenement, the use made by appellant of the right of way to serve the building located on the lesser area is not materially increased or excessive. It is true that where the nature and extent of the use of an easement is, by its terms, unrestricted, the use by the dominant tenement may be increased or enlarged. McCullough et al. v. Broad

Exchange Company et al., 92 N.Y.S. 533 (App. Div. N.Y. 1905). But the owner of the dominant tenement may not subject the servient tenement to use or servitude in connection with other premises to which the easement is not appurtenant. See Williams v. James, Eng. Law. Rep. (1867), 2 C.P. 577. And when an easement is being used in such a manner, an injunction will be issued to prevent such use. Appellant, therefore, may not use the easement to serve both the dominant and non-dominant property, even though the area thereof is less than the original area of the dominant tenement.

The disposition of the foregoing issue brings us to the principal legal question in the case: whether appellant's use of the right of way resulted in the forfeiture and extinguishment of the easement by abandonment, and thereby entitled appellee, on a motion for summary judgment, to a decree permanently enjoining appellant from using the right of way.

Misuse of an easement right is not sufficient to constitute a forfeiture, waiver, or abandonment of such right. The right to an easement is not lost by using it in an unauthorized manner or to an unauthorized extent, unless it is impossible to sever the increased burden so as to preserve to the owner of the dominant tenement that to which he is entitled, and impose on the servient tenement only that burden which was originally imposed upon it.

From the record before us, we are unable to ascertain what the total additional burden is that has been cast upon the servient tenement as the result of appellant's use of the right of way for ingress to, and egress from, the building which was located on part of the dominant and the non-dominant property. As has been mentioned, the building houses a bowling alley and restaurant. From affidavits on file, it appears that a soda fountain and luncheonette used in connection with the restaurant are located in that part of the building situate on the non-dominant real estate, which, of course, is not entitled to enjoyment of the easement; and it further appears that the right of way is used for the purpose of bringing supplies for the fountain and luncheonette and removing trash and garbage therefrom. It is not disclosed whether other supplies or materials brought to, or removed from, the building over the right of way are required for the use of that part of the structure located on the dominant estate or on the non-dominant property, or both. Affidavits filed by appellant indicate, however, that oil for heating purposes is delivered to the loading platform over the right of way. Whether the oil furnace is located on the dominant or non-dominant property does not appear. But it is declared on the part of Penn Bowling that if the right of way were barred to appellant, a great hardship would result in the operation of the building housing the bowling alley and other facilities, and would necessitate large and expensive alterations of its building. Appellant may well be obliged to remodel its structure in order to operate, but it would appear that this can be done and, consequently, appellee is not entitled to a decree extinguishing the easement or to a permanent injunction on the pleadings and proofs before us. Furthermore, appellant's building fronts on a public thoroughfare and changes conceivably could be made so that the non-dominant property could be served from the street. In any event, appellant can use the right of way only to serve the dominant tenement.

An authorized use and an unauthorized use may be intermingled in such a way as to justify enjoining any use until the circumstances have so changed that the authorized use may be permitted without affording opportunity for the unauthorized use, which it would be difficult to discover or prove. In such a case, the issuance of an injunction may be justified restraining any use until the building is so altered or changed that that part of it which is on the dominant tenement may enjoy the easement without permitting its enjoyment by the other part of the building having no right thereto. So where it can not be ascertained whether the easement of a right of way is being used solely for the enjoyment of the dominant tenement, or for additional property also, an injunction may be granted against further use of the easement until such time as it may be shown that only the dominant tenement is served by the easement.

Appellee claims that appellant itself has made the use of the right of way for ingress and egress impossible, by constructing adjacent to its building a wall and loading platform which occupies the space between the building and the right of way, and that, therefore, appellant can not get onto its premises from the right of way but can only come up to them. To this contention, appellant replies that the platform, which occupies a space ten feet wide, can easily be demolished and leveled off even with the right of way, and thus afford ample space for any of its trucks to park on appellant's own land for purposes of loading or unloading. If the loading dock were removed so as to permit the use of the right of way for the dominant estate, appellee's contention that appellant has made it impossible to use the easement for ingress or egress could not be sustained. This is a question, however, to be determined by the trial court after the taking of proofs in regard thereto.

Moreover, it is asserted by appellant that, in any event, in using the right of way for ingress to and egress from the dominant tenement, appellant is not required to cross over the line separating its property from the right of way, but that ingress and egress not only mean passing over the easement onto appellant's property and going from such property back over the easement, but also comprehend the coming to, and going away from, the line of the dominant tenement. On this question, we here express no opinion, as the determination of such issue is, in the first instance, for the trial court.

Appellee further complains that appellant misused the easement by parking motor vehicles on the right of way. The use of the easement for purposes of ingress and egress does not include its use for parking purposes and an injunction may issue to prevent such a use. However, it is to be said that appellant is entitled to a reasonable use and enjoyment of the easement for purposes of ingress and egress. In determining what is a reasonable use, the easement is to be construed in the light of the situation of the property and the surrounding circumstances for the purpose of giving effect to the intention of the parties. The long continued use of the right of way for the purpose of loading or unloading supplies at appellant's premises may indicate an intention of the parties that the easement might be used for that purpose. But appellant would thereby acquire no right to make any use of the easement which would unreasonably interfere with its use by appellee. Appellee has located on the premises in question its central offices and commissary, which is engaged in supplying sixteen restaurants in Washington and vicinity, and requires almost constant use of the driveway by appellee. Appellant's parking of vehicles on the right of way at a time when appellee needs its use would constitute an unlawful interference with the latter's right. The determination of these questions largely depends upon the circumstances of the case and is properly for the district court.

In accordance with the foregoing, the judgment is set aside and the case remanded to the district court for further proceedings consonant with this opinion, with the reservation of right to the appellee to apply for a temporary injunction pending final decision of the court.

NOTES AND QUESTIONS

1. What is Hot Shoppes' real complaint here? Does the court's disposition promise to achieve a resolution of the dispute? Why did the parties resort to litigation rather than working out the conflict among themselves like good neighbors?

2. Suppose Penn Bowling does not use the easement for nonappurtenant property, but simply experiences a surge in patronage that requires more intensive use of the easement. What standard should a court employ in assessing a claim of "overuse" of an easement? See Hayes v. Aquia Marina, Inc., 414 S.E.2d 820 (Va. 1992) (applying a standard of reasonableness in assessing such a claim); Bartholomew v. Staheli, 195 P.2d 824 (Cal. App. 1948) (upholding injunction against increased use of an easement where an "easement for access to a tranquil home and farm was converted into a turbulent route to reach a hilarious nudist colony"). Does it make sense to apply a rule of strict liability to claims of nonappurtenant use, while assessing other claims of overuse under a standard of reasonableness?

3. The court in this case considers only injunctive relief (a property rule) rather than damages (a liability rule). Would a liability rule provide a better mechanism for mediating conflicts over misuse of an easement? In a widely noted case that also involved the use of an easement to serve after-acquired nonappurtenant property, the court decided to award damages rather than injunctive relief. Brown v. Voss, 715 P.2d 514 (Wash. 1986); see also Lee J. Strang, Damages as the Appropriate Remedy for "Abuse" of an Easement: Moving Toward Consistency, Efficiency, and Fairness in Property Law, 15 Geo. Mason L. Rev. 933 (2008). In *Brown*, since no actual harm could

be shown (the intensity of use did not increase), only $1 in nominal damages was awarded. Is such an award likely to achieve a resolution of the issues between the parties?

2. COVENANTS

Closely related to easements are covenants or promises respecting the use of land. Easements are paradigmatically about the right to go onto land; they are abrogations of the servient owner's right to exclude. Covenants are generally about the right to insist on the use or nonuse of land; as such, they typically prescribe a more or less elaborate system of governance rules. Easements are nearly always affirmative, but covenants can be either affirmative or negative.

There is little doubt that a contract between two neighbors, A and B, respecting the way they use their respective properties can be enforced by either one against the other. Thus, if A and B promise each other to plant only red geraniums in their window boxes, and A decides instead to plant white geraniums, B can sue A for breach of contract, assuming the usual contractual formalities (consideration, etc.) are met. The difficulties arise when one of the original parties, let's say A, has transferred her interest, and the question becomes whether the promise is enforceable against A's successor when A's successor decides to plant white geraniums. Over the years, courts have developed two theories that will allow promises respecting the use of the land to run with the land. One theory asks whether the promise is enforceable against successors as an "equitable servitude." The other asks whether the promise is enforceable against successors as a "real covenant." In a throwback to the old division between common-law courts and courts of equity, often the critical factor in determining which theory applies is the nature of the relief that the plaintiff seeks. If an injunction is sought, then the matter lies in equity, and courts will generally apply the equitable servitude theory. If damages are sought, then the matter falls on the common-law side of the old division, and courts will generally apply the real covenant theory. It is important to appreciate, however, that equitable servitudes and real covenants are not two different things. They are the same thing—promises respecting the use of land—and the label that attaches in deciding whether these promises run with the land is determined by the theory for enforcing the promise against successors, not by any thing intrinsic in the nature of the promise itself.

Notwithstanding the different theories for determining whether they run with the land, all covenants share certain features in common. Covenants are less "property like" than easements and lie closer to the contract end of the property-contract spectrum. Thus, it appears that covenants impose no duties of forbearance on third parties. Moreover, one cannot acquire a covenant by prescription, implication, necessity, or estoppel. The Statute of Frauds applies, and all covenants must be in writing. Generally speaking, covenants function like "add ons" to the basic package of rights and liabilities that landowners normally have—specific modifications that originate in written contractual undertakings that relate to particular parcels of land.

a.   EQUITABLE SERVITUDES

English common law recognized only one circumstance in which covenants regarding the use of land would run to successors in interest: when either a lessor or a lessee transferred his interest in property subject to a lease (see Chapter VI). The common-law courts refused to enforce covenants between neighboring landowners as interests running with the land. This proved to be a major inconvenience in efforts to control incompatible land uses by contract. Eventually, the court of equity came to the rescue.

Tulk v. Moxhay
Court of Chancery, England, 1848.
2 Phillips 774, 41 Eng. Rep. 1143.

In the year 1808 the Plaintiff, being then the owner in fee of the vacant piece of ground in Leicester Square, as well as of several of the houses forming the Square, sold the piece of ground by the description of "Leicester Square garden or pleasure ground, with the equestrian statue then standing in the centre thereof, and the iron railing and stone work round the same," to one Elms in fee: and the deed of conveyance contained a covenant by Elms, for himself, his heirs, and assigns, with the Plaintiff, his heirs, executors, and administrators, "that Elms, his heirs, and assigns should, and would from time to time, and at all times thereafter at his and their own costs and charges, keep and maintain the said piece of ground and square garden, and the iron railing round the same in its then form, and in sufficient and proper repair as a square garden and pleasure ground, in an open state, uncovered with any buildings, in neat and ornamental order; and that it should be lawful for the inhabitants of Leicester Square, tenants of the Plaintiff, on payment of a reasonable rent for the same, to have keys at their own expense and the privilege of admission therewith at any time or times into the said square garden and pleasure ground."

The piece of land so conveyed passed by divers mesne conveyances into the hands of the Defendant, whose purchase deed contained no similar covenant with his vendor: but he admitted that he had purchased with notice of the covenant in the deed of 1808.

The Defendant having manifested an intention to alter the character of the square garden, and asserted a right, if he thought fit, to build upon it, the Plaintiff, who still remained owner of several houses in the square, filed this bill for an injunction; and an injunction was granted by the Master of the Rolls to restrain the Defendant from converting or using the piece of ground and square garden, and the iron railing round the same, to or for any other purpose than as a square garden and pleasure ground in an open state, and uncovered with buildings. * * *

■ THE LORD CHANCELLOR [Cottenham] * * * That this Court has jurisdiction to enforce a contract between the owner of land and his neighbour purchasing a part of it, that the latter shall either use or abstain from using the land purchased in a particular way, is, what I never knew disputed. Here there is no question about the contract: the owner of certain houses in the square sells the land adjoining, with a covenant from the purchaser not to use it for any other purpose than as a square garden. And it is now contended, not that the vendee could violate that contract, but that he might sell the piece of land, and that the purchaser from him may violate it without this Court having any power to interfere. If that were so, it would be impossible for an owner of land to sell part of it without incurring the risk of rendering what he retains worthless. It is said that, the covenant being one which does not run with the land, this Court cannot enforce it; but the question is, not whether the covenant runs with the land, but whether a party shall be permitted to use the land in a manner inconsistent with the contract entered into by his vendor, and with notice of which he purchased. Of course, the price would be affected by the covenant, and nothing could be more inequitable than that the original purchaser should be able to sell the property the next day for a greater price, in consideration of the assignee being allowed to escape from the liability which he had himself undertaken.

That the question does not depend upon whether the covenant runs with the land is evident from this, that if there was a mere agreement and no covenant, this Court would enforce it against a party purchasing with notice of it; for if an equity is attached to the property by the owner, no one purchasing with notice of that equity can stand in a different situation from the party from whom he purchased. * * *

With respect to the observations of Lord Brougham in *Keppell v. Bailey* (2 M. & K. 517), [39 Eng. Rep. 1042 (Ch. 1834),] he never could have meant to lay down that this Court would not enforce an equity attached to land by the owner, unless under such circumstances as would maintain an action at law. If that be the result of his observations, I can only say that I cannot coincide with it.

I think the cases cited before the Vice-Chancellor and this decision of the Master of the Rolls perfectly right, and, therefore, that this motion must be refused, with costs.

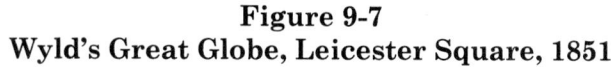

Figure 9-7
Wyld's Great Globe, Leicester Square, 1851

Source: Survey of London, Vol. 34, The Parish of St. Anne Soho (F.H.W. Sheppard ed., 1966) (illustration 43a, T.H. Shepherd).

NOTES AND QUESTIONS

1.   Leicester Square has had a long history that implicates many of the themes of this course:

> In the middle of the seventeenth century the Earl of Leicester laid out Leicester Square and built Leicester House on its north side * * * The basin [in the center] was replaced in 1748 by a gilded equestrian statue, in metal, of George I by Van Nost. [The property descended to two married Sidney sisters, one of whose shares was sold to James S. Tulk in 1772. Later, partition was had.] Meanwhile, the social status of Leicester Square had declined, and since the division of ownership the central garden had fallen on evil days * * * The enclosure became a wilderness, a receptacle for rubbish, and a last resting place for dead cats. King George lost an arm and his horse a leg.

> Both Tulk and Moxhay died in 1849. In 1851 (the year of the first International Exposition, at the Crystal Palace) Wyld, a geographer, purchased the garden from Moxhay's widow for the purpose of erecting thereon a building to contain a large model of the earth. As the Tulk family objected, Wyld made an agreement with them, which refers to the very ruinous and dilapidated condition of the garden and the iron railings, and in which Wyld was licensed to erect a globe for ten years in return for an option to the Tulks to purchase an undivided half of the garden at the end of that time for £500. The owners of the former Sidney houses on the north side of the Square refused to participate in this agreement. A vast domed structure known as "Wyld's Globe" was then erected and used for geographical and historical lectures and exhibits. In

1861 John A. Tulk, the grandson of Charles, exercised the option, so that he and Wyld became co-tenants of the garden. The Globe was taken down and the battered statue again set up, to be treated to the jokes of Punch and the pranks of idlers, who on October 17, 1866, painted the horse white with black spots and put a foolscap on the head of King George.

By this time the public authorities had become active. In 1863 a bill was introduced in Parliament for a public market in the Square, which was successfully opposed. In 1865 the Metropolitan Board of Works took possession of the garden under the Town Gardens Protection Act of 1863 (26 Vict. c.13), which empowered the Board to take charge of any grounds which had been set apart for the use of the inhabitants of a surrounding square, when the body appointed for the care of the same had neglected to keep it in proper order. John A. Tulk at once brought an action of trespass *quare clausum fregit* against the Board and won a decision that Leicester Square was not within the statute * * * Thus Tulk succeeded in keeping the Square in its desolate condition. Tulk hoped to convert the garden into building land, as Moxhay had formerly tried to do. The maintenance of billboards around the enclosure was prevented by another equity decree (unreported), probably at the suit of the north side owners. While an appeal was pending, the Metropolitan Board of Works obtained compulsory powers of acquisition by the Leicester Square Act, 1874 (27 & 38 Vict. c.10).

Before condemnation took place, Albert Grant, M.P., purchased Tulk's rights, opened negotiations with the other owners, took possession of the garden, and offered it free of cost to the Board of Works for public enjoyment. The unfortunate horse was removed in February, 1874 and replaced by a statue of Shakespeare, while the four corners of the garden were ornamented with statues of former residents of Leicester Square—Reynolds, Newton, Hogarth, and Dr. John Hunter. After Mr. Grant had laid out the park in its present form at a total expenditure of £28,000, it was handed over to the public on July 2, 1874.

Zechariah Chafee, Jr. & Sidney Post Simpson, Cases on Equity, Jurisdiction and Specific Performance 704–06, 710–11 (1934).

2.   Is the Chancellor's reasoning here circular? That one is bound to perform an obligation of which he has notice cannot be doubted, but just because one has notice does not mean that he has an obligation. Is the charge of circularity overcome by the observation that "the price would be affected by the covenant, and nothing could be more inequitable than that the original purchaser should be able to sell the property the next day for a greater price"? If the covenant is understood not to be binding on a subsequent purchaser, wouldn't this be reflected in the price?

3.   Is *Tulk v. Moxhay* consistent with the *numerus clausus*? In order to meet the understandable demand for enforcement of covenants, the court in *Tulk* was well aware that it had to limit the holding in *Keppell v. Bailey*, 39

Eng. Rep. 1042 (Ch. 1834), the leading English case holding that courts lack authority to transform contract rights into new forms of property rights. In *Keppell*, the purchasers of an iron works covenanted on behalf of themselves and their successors and assigns to purchase all limestone required by the works from a particular quarry and to ship the limestone to the works on a particular railroad. In the court's view such an arrangement was enforceable as a contract between the original parties and would not work as an unreasonable restraint on alienation, but the Court of Chancery held that this type of agreement did not fall within the recognized types of servitudes enforceable against subsequent purchasers as a property right running with the land:

> There can be no harm to allowing the fullest latitude to men in binding themselves and their representatives, that is, their assets real and personal, to answer in damages for breach of their obligations. This tends to no mischief, and is a reasonable liberty to bestow; but great detriment would arise and much confusion of rights if parties were allowed to invent new modes of holding and enjoying real property, and to impress upon their lands and tenements a peculiar character, which should follow them into all hands, however remote. Every close, every messuage, might thus be held in several fashion; and it would hardly be possible to know what rights the acquisition of any parcel conferred, or what obligations it imposed.

39 Eng. Rep. at 1049. Lord Chancellor Brougham seemed to object to "fancies," as they have been called, on the grounds that they create excessive third-party information costs. For development of this idea, see Thomas W. Merrill & Henry E. Smith, Optimal Standardization in the Law of Property: The *Numerus Clausus* Principle, 110 Yale L.J. 1 (2000). Is *Tulk* inconsistent with this view? Who needs to look out for the content of covenants? Or does notice, such as that provided by modern land records, mean that any restriction should be able to run with the land? See, e.g., Richard A. Epstein, Notice and Freedom of Contract in the Law of Servitudes, 55 S. Cal. L. Rev. 1353 (1982); see also Alfred F. Conard, Easement Novelties, 30 Cal. L. Rev. 125, 131–33 (1942). Is this an example of "equitable property," the prominent example being the trust (Chapter VI)? If so what exactly is equitable property? See Ben McFarlane, *Tulk v. Moxhay* (1848), in Landmark Cases in Equity (Charles Mitchell & Paul Mitchell eds., 2012).

4.   Given its origins in equity, it follows that general considerations of equity apply in determining whether to issue an injunction enforcing an equitable servitude. For example, in *Wrotham Park Estate Co. Ltd. v. Parkside Homes Ltd.*, [1974] 1 W.L.R. 798 (Eng.), the court declined to grant a permanent injunction against a developer who had constructed homes on land in violation of a servitude (of which the developer had notice) requiring advance permission of the layout plan by the dominant owner. The court found that the homes had already been built and were occupied, and that the dominant owner had not sought a preliminary injunction before construction started, and thus a permanent injunction requiring demolition of the homes would cause undue hardship. The developer was, however, required to pay

damages, based on a percentage of the profits earned from the development. Compare *Boomer v. Atlantic Cement*, supra, in the context of nuisance.

b. REAL COVENANTS

American courts did not consider themselves bound by the English view that covenants run to successors in interest only in the lessor-lessee context. Instead, they developed the concept of the real covenant—a covenant attached to fee simple property that, under certain circumstances analogous to the lessor-lessee doctrine of running covenants, will bind successors in an action at law. The following case applies this American invention to a subdivision that featured an early version of the common-interest communities so prevalent today (see Chapter VI).

Neponsit Property Owners' Association, Inc. v. Emigrant Industrial Savings Bank

Court of Appeals of New York, 1938.
15 N.E.2d 793.

■ LEHMAN, JUDGE. The plaintiff, as assignee of Neponsit Realty Company, has brought this action to foreclose a lien upon land which the defendant owns. The lien, it is alleged, arises from a covenant, condition or charge contained in a deed of conveyance of the land from Neponsit Realty Company to a predecessor in title of the defendant. The defendant purchased the land at a judicial sale. The referee's deed to the defendant and every deed in the defendant's chain of title since the conveyance of the land by Neponsit Realty Company purports to convey the property subject to the covenant, condition or charge contained in the original deed. * * *

It appears that in January, 1911, Neponsit Realty Company, as owner of a tract of land in Queens county, caused to be filed in the office of the clerk of the county a map of the land. The tract was developed for a strictly residential community, and Neponsit Realty Company conveyed lots in the tract to purchasers, describing such lots by reference to the filed map and to roads and streets shown thereon. In 1917, Neponsit Realty Company conveyed the land now owned by the defendant to Robert Oldner Deyer and his wife by deed which contained the covenant upon which the plaintiff's cause of action is based.

That covenant provides:

> And the party of the second part for the party of the second part and the heirs, successors and assigns of the party of the second part further covenants that the property conveyed by this deed shall be subject to an annual charge in such an amount as will be fixed by the party of the first part, its successors and assigns, not, however exceeding in any year the sum of four ($4.00) Dollars per lot 20x100 feet. The assigns of the party of

the first part may include a Property Owners' Association which may hereafter be organized for the purposes referred to in this paragraph, and in case such association is organized the sums in this paragraph provided for shall be payable to such association. The party of the second part for the party of the second part and the heirs, successors and assigns of the party of the second part covenants that they will pay this charge to the party of the first part, its successors and assigns on the first day of May in each and every year, and further covenants that said charge shall on said date in each year become a lien on the land and shall continue to be such lien until fully paid. Such charge shall be payable to the party of the first part or its successors or assigns, and shall be devoted to the maintenance of the roads, paths, parks, beach, sewers and such other public purposes as shall from time to time be determined by the party of the first part, its successors or assigns. And the party of the second part by the acceptance of this deed hereby expressly vests in the party of the first part, its successors and assigns, the right and power to bring all actions against the owner of the premises hereby conveyed or any part thereof for the collection of such charge and to enforce the aforesaid lien therefor.

These covenants shall run with the land and shall be construed as real covenants running with the land until January 31st, 1940, when they shall cease and determine.

Every subsequent deed of conveyance of the property in the defendant's chain of title, including the deed from the referee to the defendant, contained, as we have said, a provision that they were made subject to covenants and restrictions of former deeds of record.

There can be no doubt that Neponsit Realty Company intended that the covenant should run with the land and should be enforceable by a property owners association against every owner of property in the residential tract which the realty company was then developing. The language of the covenant admits of no other construction. Regardless of the intention of the parties, a covenant will run with the land and will be enforceable against a subsequent purchaser of the land at the suit of one who claims the benefit of the covenant, only if the covenant complies with certain legal requirements. These requirements rest upon ancient rules and precedents. The age-old essentials of a real covenant, aside from the form of the covenant, may be summarily formulated as follows: (1) It must appear that grantor and grantee intended that the covenant should run with the land; (2) it must appear that the covenant is one "touching" or "concerning" the land with which it runs; (3) it must appear that there is "privity of estate" between the promisee or party claiming the benefit of the covenant and the right to enforce it, and the promisor or party who rests under the burden of the covenant. Clark on Covenants and Interests Running with Land, p. 74. Although the deeds of Neponsit Realty

Company conveying lots in the tract it developed "contained a provision to the effect that the covenants ran with the land, such provision in the absence of the other legal requirements is insufficient to accomplish such a purpose." Morgan Lake Co. v. New York, N. H. & H. R. R. Co., 186 N.E. 685, 686 (N.Y. 1933). In his opinion in that case, Judge Crane posed but found it unnecessary to decide many of the questions which the court must consider in this case.

Figure 9-8

Street Scene in Neponsit Subdivision, June 2006

The covenant in this case is intended to create a charge or obligation to pay a fixed sum of money to be "devoted to the maintenance of the roads, paths, parks, beach, sewers and such other public purposes as shall from time to time be determined by the party of the first part [the grantor], its successors or assigns." It is an affirmative covenant to pay money for use in connection with, but not upon, the land which it is said is subject to the burden of the covenant. Does such a covenant "touch" or "concern" the land? These terms are not part of a statutory definition, a limitation placed by the State upon the power of the courts to enforce covenants *intended* to run with the land by the parties who entered into the covenants. Rather they are words used by courts in England in old cases to describe a limitation which the courts themselves created or to formulate a test which the courts have devised and which the courts voluntarily apply. Cf. Spencer's Case, 5 Co. Rep. 16a, 77 Eng. Rep. 72 (K.B. 1583) Coke, vol. 3, part 5, 16a; Mayor of Congleton v. Pattison, 10 East 130, 103 Eng. Rep. 725 (Ch. 1808). In truth such a description or test so formulated is too vague to be of much assistance and judges and academic scholars alike have struggled, not with entire success, to formulate a test at once more satisfactory and more accurate. "It has been found impossible to state any absolute tests to determine what covenants touch and concern land and what do not. The question is one for the court to determine in the exercise of its best judgment upon the facts of each case." Clark, op. cit. p. 76.

Even though that be true, a determination by a court in one case upon particular facts will often serve to point the way to correct decision in other cases upon analogous facts. Such guideposts may not be disregarded. It has been often said that a covenant to pay a sum of money is a personal affirmative covenant which usually does not concern or touch the land. Such statements are based upon English decisions which hold in effect that only covenants, which compel the covenanter to submit to some restriction on *the use* of his property, touch or concern the land, and that the burden of a covenant which requires the covenanter to do an affirmative act, even on his own land, for the benefit of the owner of a "dominant" estate, does not run with his land. Miller v. Clary, 103 N.E. 1114 (N.Y. 1913). In that case the court pointed out that in many jurisdictions of this country the narrow English rule has been criticized and a more liberal and flexible rule has been substituted. In this State the courts have not gone so far. We have not abandoned the historic distinction drawn by the English courts. So this court has recently said: "Subject to a few exceptions not important at this time, there is now in this state a settled rule of law that a covenant to do an affirmative act, as distinguished from a covenant merely negative in effect, does not run with the land so as to charge the burden of performance on a subsequent grantee [citing cases]. This is so though the burden of such a covenant is laid upon the very parcel which is the subject-matter of the conveyance." Guaranty Trust Co. of New York, v. New York & Queens County Ry. Co., 170 N.E. 887, 892 (N.Y. 1930), opinion by Cardozo, Ch. J.

Both in that case and in the case of Miller v. Clary, supra, the court pointed out that there were some exceptions or limitations in the application of the general rule. Some promises to pay money have been enforced, as covenants running with the land, against subsequent holders of the land who took with notice of the covenant. Cf. Greenfarb v. R. S. K. Realty Corp., 175 N.E. 649 (N.Y. 1931); Morgan Lake Co. v. New York, N. H. & H. R. R. Co., supra. It may be difficult to classify these exceptions or to formulate a test of whether a particular covenant to pay money or to perform some other act falls within the general rule that ordinarily an affirmative covenant is a personal and not a real covenant, or falls outside the limitations placed upon the general rule. At least it must "touch" or "concern" the land in a substantial degree, and though it may be inexpedient and perhaps impossible to formulate a rigid test or definition which will be entirely satisfactory or which can be applied mechanically in all cases, we should at least be able to state the problem and find a reasonable method of approach to it. It has been suggested that a covenant which runs with the land must affect the legal relations—the advantages and the burdens—of the parties to the covenant, as owners of particular parcels of land and not merely as members of the community in general, such as taxpayers or owners of other land. Clark, op. cit. p. 76. Cf. Professor Bigelow's article on The Contents of Covenants in Leases, 12 Mich.L.Rev. 639 (1914); 30 Law Quarterly Review, 319 (1914). That method of approach has the merit of realism. The test is based on the effect of the covenant rather than on technical distinctions. Does the covenant impose, on the one hand, a burden upon an interest in land, which on the other hand increases the value of a different interest in the same or related land?

Even though we accept that approach and test, it still remains true that whether a particular covenant is sufficiently connected with the use of land to run with the land, must be in many cases a question of degree. A promise to pay for something to be done in connection with the promisor's land does not differ essentially from a promise by the promisor to do the thing himself, and both promises constitute, in a substantial sense, a restriction upon the owner's right to use the land, and a burden upon the legal interest of the owner. On the other hand, a covenant to perform or pay for the performance of an affirmative act disconnected with the use of the land cannot ordinarily touch or concern the land in any substantial degree. Thus, unless we exalt technical form over substance, the distinction between covenants which run with land and covenants which are personal, must depend upon the effect of the covenant on the legal rights which otherwise would flow from ownership of land and which are connected with the land. The problem then is: Does the covenant in purpose and effect substantially alter these rights?

The opinion in Morgan Lake Co. v. New York, N. H. & H. R. R. Co., supra, foreshadowed a classification based upon substance rather than upon form. It was not the first case, however, in which this court has based its decision on the substantial effect of a covenant upon legal relations of the parties as owners of land. Perhaps the most illuminating illustration of such an approach to the problem may be drawn from the "party wall" cases in this State which are reviewed in the opinion of the court in Sebald v. Mulholland, 50 N.E. 260 (N.Y. 1898). The court there pointed out that in cases, cited in the opinion, where by covenant between owners of adjoining parcels of land, "a designated party was authorized to build a party wall, the other agreeing to pay a portion of its value when it should be used by him," the court was constrained to hold that "the agreement was a present one. The party who was to build and the one who was to pay were expressly designated, and the covenant to pay was clearly a personal one" (50 N.E. page 263). At the same time, the court also pointed out that such covenants must be distinguished from the covenants (passed upon by the court in the earlier case of Mott v. Oppenheimer, 31 N.E. 1097 (N.Y. 1892)), "by which the parties conferred, each upon the other, the authority to erect such [party] wall, and dedicated to that use a portion of each of their lots, with an agreement that, if either should build, the other might have the right to use it by paying his share of the expense" (50 N.E. page 262). In such a case, it was said by the court: "It was not and could not then be known who would build, or who was to pay when the wall was used. The agreement was wholly prospective, and its purpose was to impose upon the land of each, and not upon either personally, the burden of a future party wall, and to secure to the land, and thus to its subsequent owners, a corresponding right to the use of the wall by paying one-half of its value. * * * In that case the character of the agreement, its obvious purpose, its prospective provisions, and the situation of the lands when the agreement was made, all concurred in showing an intent that its covenants should run with the land, and clearly justified the court in so holding" (50 N.E. page 262).

Looking at the problem presented in this case from the same point of view and stressing the intent and substantial effect of the covenant rather than its form, it seems clear that the covenant may properly be said to touch and concern the land of the defendant and its burden should run with the land. True, it calls for payment of a sum of money to be expended for "public purposes" upon land other than the land conveyed by Neponsit Realty Company to plaintiff's predecessor in title. By that conveyance the grantee, however, obtained not only title to particular lots, but an easement or right of common enjoyment with other property owners in roads, beaches, public parks or spaces and improvements in the same tract. For full enjoyment in common by the defendant and other property owners of these easements or rights, the roads and public places must be maintained. In order that the burden of maintaining public improvements should rest upon the land benefited by the improvements, the grantor exacted from the grantee of the land with its appurtenant easement or right of enjoyment a covenant that the burden of paying the cost should be inseparably attached to the land which enjoys the benefit. It is plain that any distinction or definition which would exclude such a covenant from the classification of covenants which "touch" or "concern" the land would be based on form and not on substance.

Another difficulty remains. Though between the grantor and the grantee there was privity of estate, the covenant provides that its benefit shall run to the assigns of the grantor who "may include a Property Owners' Association which may hereafter be organized for the purposes referred to in this paragraph." The plaintiff has been organized to receive the sums payable by the property owners and to expend them for the benefit of such owners. Various definitions have been formulated of "privity of estate" in connection with covenants that run with the land, but none of such definitions seems to cover the relationship between the plaintiff and the defendant in this case. The plaintiff has not succeeded to the ownership of any property of the grantor. It does not appear that it ever had title to the streets or public places upon which charges which are payable to it must be expended. It does not appear that it owns any other property in the residential tract to which any easement or right of enjoyment in such property is appurtenant. It is created solely to act as the assignee of the benefit of the covenant, and it has no interest of its own in the enforcement of the covenant.

The arguments that under such circumstances the plaintiff has no right of action to enforce a covenant running with the land are all based upon a distinction between the corporate property owners association and the property owners for whose benefit the association has been formed. If that distinction may be ignored, then the basis of the arguments is destroyed. How far privity of estate in technical form is necessary to enforce in equity a restrictive covenant upon the use of land, presents an interesting question. Enforcement of such covenants rests upon equitable principles (Tulk v. Moxhay, 2 Phillips, 774, 41 Eng. Rep. 1143 (Ch. 1848); Trustees of Columbia College v. Lynch, 70 N.Y. 440 (1877); Korn v. Campbell, 85 N.E. 687 (N.Y. 1908)), and at times, at least, the violation "of the restrictive covenant may be restrained at the suit of one who owns property or for whose benefit the restriction was established, irrespective of whether there were privity either of estate or of contract between the parties, or whether an action at law were maintainable." Chesebro v. Moers, 134 N.E. 842, 843 (N.Y. 1922). The covenant in this case does not fall exactly within any classification of "restrictive" covenants, which have been enforced in this State, and no right to enforce even a restrictive covenant has been sustained in this State where the plaintiff did not own property which would benefit by such enforcement so that some of the elements of an equitable servitude are present. In some jurisdictions it has been held that no action may be maintained without such elements. But cf. VanSant v. Rose, 103 N.E. 194 (Ill. 1913). We do not attempt to decide now how far the rule of Trustees of Columbia College v. Lynch, supra, will be carried, or to formulate a definite rule as to when, or even whether, covenants in a deed will be enforced, upon equitable principles, against subsequent purchasers with notice, at the suit of a party without privity of contract or estate. Cf. Equitable Rights and Liabilities of Strangers to a Contract, by Harlan F. Stone, 18 Columbia Law Review, 291 (1918). There is no need to resort to such a rule if the courts may look behind the corporate form of the plaintiff.

The corporate plaintiff has been formed as a convenient instrument by which the property owners may advance their common interests. We do not ignore the corporate form when we recognize that the Neponsit Property Owners' Association, Inc., is acting as the agent or representative of the Neponsit property owners. As we have said in another case: when Neponsit Property Owners' Association, Inc., "was formed, the property owners were expected to, and have looked to that organization as the medium through which enjoyment of their common right might be preserved equally for all." Matter of City of New York, Public Beach, Borough of Queens, 199 N.E. 5, 9 (N.Y. 1935). Under the conditions thus presented we said: "It may be difficult, or even impossible to classify into recognized categories the nature of the interest of the membership corporation and its members in the land. The corporate entity cannot be disregarded, nor can the separate interests of the members of the corporation" (199 N.E. page 8). Only blind adherence to an ancient formula devised to meet entirely different conditions could constrain the court to hold that a corporation formed as a medium for the enjoyment of common rights of property owners owns no property which would benefit by enforcement of common rights and has no cause of action in equity to enforce the covenant upon which such common rights depend. Every reason which in other circumstances may justify the ancient formula may be urged in support of the conclusion that the formula should not be applied in this case. In substance if not in form the covenant is a restrictive covenant which touches and concerns the defendant's land, and in substance, if not in form, there is privity of estate between the plaintiff and the defendant. * * *

NOTES AND QUESTIONS

1. The action here is to foreclose a lien on the property in order to secure payment of a debt. Foreclosure was originally regarded as a proceeding in equity. Why then does the court apply the real covenant doctrine as opposed to the equitable servitude theory of *Tulk v. Moxhay*?

2. Covenants in leases run to successors of the original lessor or lessee if (1) the lessor and lessee intend that they will run; and (2) the covenant is one that "touches and concerns" the land. The court here adds a third requirement: that there be "privity of estate" between the party claiming the benefit of the covenant and the party subject to the burden of the covenant. This is obviously designed to mimic the privity of estate that exists in lease law between the lessor and a lessee in possession (see Chapter VI). But what function does the privity-of-estate requirement perform here? Would it be better to require that the party to be burdened must have notice of the covenant, as under the theory of equitable servitudes? Does privity of estate serve as a stand-in for a requirement that the benefit of the promise be appurtenant to a particular parcel of land? Does it make sense to restrict running covenants to those that benefit particular land? The English law of equitable servitudes, as it has developed since *Tulk*, limits running covenants to those appurtenant to particular interests in land. See Robert Megarry & William Wade, The Law of Real Property § 32–044, at 1352 (Charles Harpum et al. eds., 7th ed. 2008).

3. The court paraphrases with approval Professor Bigelow's definition of "touch and concern" as a promise that affects "the advantages and the burdens" of the owners of the parcels of land either benefited or burdened by the promise. How helpful is this in singling out those promises respecting land which should run? If the owner of Blackacre promises to cut the hair of the owner of Whiteacre, and the owner of Whiteacre promises in return to pay $10 a month to the owner of Blackacre, would not this affect "the advantages and the burdens" of owning either Blackacre or Whiteacre? Can you formulate a better test for giving content to what it means for a promise to touch and concern the land?

4. Now that the jurisdictions of law and equity have merged, the distinction between equitable servitudes and real covenants grounded in the nature of the relief being sought no longer makes any sense. And indeed,

there is authority suggesting that one can get damages under an equitable servitude theory and an injunction under a real covenant theory. See Joseph William Singer, Property § 6.5 (5th ed. 2017). Most parties want specific performance—an injunction—anyway (*Neponsit* is something of an exceptional case in this regard). Having these two bodies of doctrine does give plaintiffs some flexibility in choosing which path to pursue in seeking enforcement. Let us then restate the elements that must be satisfied under the two approaches to running covenants.

c.   THE REQUIREMENTS FOR COVENANTS TO RUN

The major issue with covenants is whether the benefits and burdens of the deal between the original parties will extend to successors of those parties—whether the benefits and burdens "run with the land." The traditional approaches at law and equity are set out in the American Law Institute's Restatement (First) of Property (1944). As you walk through each approach below, the following diagram may be helpful. In it, the original parties (A and B) stand in a relationship called "horizontal" privity (denoted by horizontal arrows), and successors (C1, C2, etc., and D1, D2, etc.) stand in a relationship of "vertical" privity to the original parties, respectively.

Real Covenant Theory

At law (traditionally in a damages action), for the *burden* of a promise to run to the successors in interest to the promisor, one would have to establish:

(i)   *Intent for the burden to run*. This can be by language or inferable "from the circumstances under which the promise was made." Restatement (First) of Property § 531 cmt. c. So if B covenants with A, who is allergic to peanuts, that B will not eat peanuts in the backyard, the benefit probably won't run to A's successor unless the circumstances indicate otherwise (for example, A is running an allergy clinic and sells to another allergy clinic).

(ii)   *Horizontal privity*. Traditionally a lessor-lessee relationship was required. Later this was expanded to include other relationships bonded by a strong "community of interest" between the parties. See id. § 534 cmts. a, f. This included relationships defined by a transfer of at least some interest in the benefitted or burdened land. Id. § 534(a). Many have questioned whether this requirement has real content. This requirement (or lack of it) is illustrated in the following scenario: Two neighbors sign an agreement wherein they both agree to restrict their use of their parcels to residential use and they record. Because they are not in a grantor-grantee relationship (NB: they could have done this with a straw), there is no horizontal privity and so traditionally the burden does not run. Under the Restatement (Third) of Property (about which more later), which doesn't require horizontal privity, the burden would run.

Figure 9-9
Running Covenants

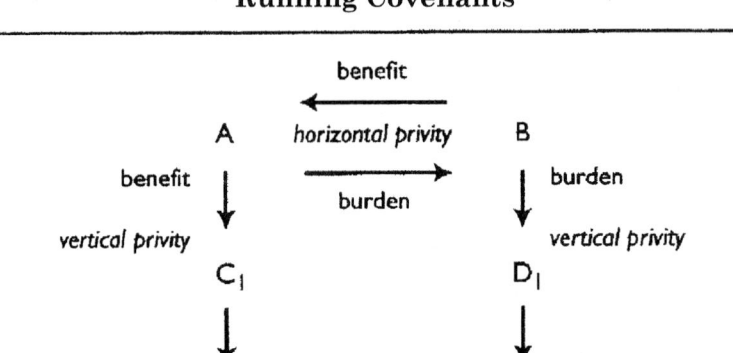

(iii) *Vertical privity.* For the burden to run at law, the successor in interest to the promisor who covenanted for the *burden* must hold the entire durational interest held by the promisor at the time she made the covenant. See id. at § 535. In a lessor-lessee situation, vertical privity would be present in assignments (where these are determined by whether the whole interest is transferred, see Chapter VI), but not in a sublease.

(iv) *Touch and concern.* The covenant must touch and concern the land, as discussed in the cases. As we will see this requirement is abandoned in the Restatement (Third) of Property, but no court has yet clearly followed this proposed approach.

At law, for the *benefit* of a promise to run, there are fewer requirements, presumably because a selling landowner would have an incentive to advertise benefits, as opposed to burdens:

(i)   *Intent for the benefit to run.*

(ii) *Vertical privity.* For the benefit to run, the successor in interest to the promisee or beneficiary need only succeed to *some estate or interest*, not necessarily an estate or interest of the same duration as was held by the promisee or beneficiary (so this is a less stringent requirement than in the case of the vertical privity required for burden to run). See id. § 547.

(iii) *Touch and concern.*

Equitable Servitude Theory

In equity, courts starting with *Tulk v. Moxhay*, supra, have been more accommodating in granting enforcement. Traditionally equity would give specific performance, which is the remedy that parties usually want in these cases. Equity was more hospitable to affirmative covenants than was the common law. And by allowing equitable enforcement of negative covenants, parties were able to expand somewhat upon the limited menu of negative easements (light, air, subjacent/lateral support, flow of artificial stream).

For the *burden* of a promise to run in equity, there must be:

(i)   *Intent.*

(ii) *Notice.* This is characteristic of equity. If the covenant is in the deed given to the successor in interest to the promisor, there is no problem enforcing it against the successor. If it is not in the deed, then actual or inquiry notice must be present. Inquiry notice is furnished by facts that would make a reasonable person inquire further and find the covenant. If the successor has neither actual nor inquiry notice, then she is considered a bona fide purchaser (like a good faith purchaser considered in Chapter VIII) and the burden cannot be enforced against her. See Restatement (First) of Property § 539. With the advent of recording acts, constructive notice through filing in the land records is another avenue for satisfying the notice requirement.

(iii) *Touch and concern* (sometimes expressed in equity as "affecting the use of the land").

For the *benefit* of a promise to run in equity, there must be:

(i)   *Intent.*

(ii) *Touch and concern* (again, with variant language).

Can you see why notice would not be required for the benefit to run in equity?

The *Third Restatement*

The American Law Institute's *Restatement (Third) of Property: Servitudes* (2000) (hereinafter "Restatement") relaxes some of these requirements. By and large, it takes a more contractarian approach to servitudes. The *Restatement* advocates abolishing the traditional property-law requirements for the running of servitudes, such as the touch and concern doctrine and the privity requirements. In place of the traditional requirements for enforcing servitudes against successors that made the running of a servitude exceptional, the *Restatement* makes enforceability the default. Broadly speaking, this would give servitudes a strongly contractarian flavor. Like the law of contracts, the *Restatement* features writing requirements and exceptions for violations of public policy, unconscionability, and the like. These exceptions are perhaps stronger than in current contract law but differ from them mostly in degree.

The *Restatement* provides for a baseline for the creation of servitudes that is grounded in contract and party intent: "A servitude is created (1) if the owner of the property to be burdened (a) enters into a contract or makes a conveyance intended to create a servitude that complies with § 2.7 (Statute of Frauds) or § 2.9 (exception to the Statute of Frauds) . . ." Restatement (Third) of Property: Servitudes § 2.1 (2000). The associated commentary makes clear the motivation for this approach:

> This Chapter's [Chapter 2, Creation of Servitudes] treatment of servitude creation reflects the basic position that servitudes are useful devices that people ought to be able to use without artificial constraints. The primary function of the law is to ascertain and give effect to the intent of the parties, not to force them into arbitrary transactional forms. If they meet minimal formal requirements, their expressed intent is effective to create a servitude, unless the transaction violates a constitutional, statutory, or public-policy norm.

Id. Introductory Note at 49.

The *Restatement* itself is, if anything, clearer in making validity conform to a contract-like rather than a property-like vision of servitudes:

> A servitude created as provided in Chapter 2 is valid unless it is illegal or unconstitutional or violates public policy.

> Servitudes that are invalid because they violate public policy include, but are not limited to:

>> (1) a servitude that is arbitrary, spiteful, or capricious;

>> (2) a servitude that unreasonably burdens a fundamental constitutional right;

>> (3) a servitude that imposes an unreasonable restraint on alienation under § 3.4 or § 3.5;

>> (4) a servitude that imposes an unreasonable restraint on trade or competition under § 3.6; and

>> (5) a servitude that is unconscionable under § 3.7.

Restatement (Third) of Property: Servitudes § 3.1 (2000). Comment a, entitled "Historical note and rationale" states:

> This section applies the modern principle of freedom of contract to creation of servitudes. The Restatement of Contracts explains the principle: "In general, parties may contract as they wish, and courts will enforce their agreements without passing on their substance. . . . The principle of freedom of contract is rooted in the notion that it is in the public interest to recognize that individuals have broad powers to order their own affairs."

Id. § 3.1 cmt. a. (footnote omitted, citing to Restatement Second, Contracts, Introductory Note to Chapter 8.). As noted earlier, this means that, as under contract law, servitudes are presumed valid. Id. ("The effect of the rule is to shift to the party claiming invalidity of a servitude the burden to establish that it is illegal or unconstitutional, or violates public policy."). Id.

As of this writing no court has clearly adopted this approach, to the annoyance of the Reporter. See Susan F. French, Symposium on Servitudes, Part II, Can Covenants Not to Sue, Covenants Against Competition and Spite Covenants Run with Land? Comparing Results Under the Touch or Concern Doctrine and the Restatement Third, Property (Servitudes), 38 Real Prop. Prob. & Tr. J. 267 (2003). Some courts have loosened the touch and concern requirement, for example by making it one factor in a reasonableness inquiry, see Davidson Bros., Inc. v. D. Katz & Sons, Inc., 579 A.2d 288 (N.J. 1990); and one court approvingly (and confusingly) cited a tentative draft of the *Restatement* in a case involving an easement in gross (easements were never required to touch and concern in order to be enforceable against successor servient landowners), Bennett v. Commissioner of Food and Agriculture, 576 N.E.2d 1365, 1367–68 (Mass. 1991). Mostly courts have ignored the *Restatement*. Note, Touch and Concern, the Restatement (Third) of Property: Servitudes, and a Proposal, 122 Harv. L. Rev. 938, 944–45 (2009). Some commentators have argued that the older doctrines serve a useful purpose in allowing courts to police servitudes more closely. See, e.g., A. Dan Tarlock, Touch and Concern is Dead, Long Live the Doctrine, 77 Neb. L. Rev. 804 (1998); Jeffrey E. Stake, Toward an Economic Understanding of Touch and Concern, 1988 Duke L.J. 925. For discussion of the policies of allowing servitudes to run, and the differences between servitudes in real, personal, and intellectual property, see Carol M. Rose, Servitudes, in Research Handbook on the Economics of Property Law 296 (Kenneth Ayotte & Henry E. Smith, eds. 2011); Molly Shaffer Van Houweling, The New Servitudes, 96 Geo. L.J. 885 (2008).

Eagle Enterprises, Inc. v. Gross

Court of Appeals of New York, 1976.
349 N.E.2d 816.

■ GABRIELLI, JUSTICE. In 1951, Orchard Hill Realties, Inc., a subdivider and developer, conveyed certain property in the subdivision of Orchard Hill in Orange County to William and Pauline Baum. The deed to the Baums contained the following provision:

> The party of the first part shall supply to the party of the second part, seasonally from May 1st to October 1st, of each year, water for domestic use only, from the well located on other property of the party of the first part, and the party of the second part agrees to take said water and to pay the party of the first part, a fee of Thirty-five ($35.00) dollars per year, for said water so supplied.

In addition, the deed also contained the following:

> It is expressly provided that the covenants herein contained shall run with the land * * * and shall bind and shall enure to the benefit of the heirs, distributees, successors, legal representatives and assigns of the respective parties hereto.

Appellant is the successor in interest of Orchard Hill Realties, Inc., and respondent, after a series of intervening conveyances, is the successor in interest of the Baums. The deed conveying title to respondent does not contain the aforementioned covenant to purchase water and, in fact, none of the deeds following the original deed to the Baums contained the mutual promises regarding water supply. While some of the deeds in the chain of title from Baum contained a provision that they were made subject to the restrictions in the deed from Orchard Hill Realties to Baum, the deed to respondents contained no such covenants, restrictions or "subject to" clause.

According to the stipulated facts, respondent has refused to accept and pay for water offered by appellant since he has constructed his own well to service what is now a year-round dwelling. Appellant, therefore, instituted this action to collect the fee specified in the covenant (contained only in the original deed to Baum) for the supply of water which, appellant contends, respondent is bound to accept. The action was styled as one "for goods sold and delivered" even though respondent did not utilize any of appellant's water. Two of the lower courts found that the covenant "ran" with the land and, hence, was binding upon respondent as successor to the Baums, but the Appellate Division reversed and held that the covenant could not be enforced against respondent. We must now decide whether the promise of the original grantees to accept and make payment for a seasonal water supply from the well of their grantor is enforceable against subsequent grantees and may be said to "run with the land". We agree with the determination of the Appellate Division and affirm its order.

Regardless of the express recital in a deed that a covenant will run with the land, a promise to do an affirmative act contained in a deed is generally not binding upon subsequent grantees of the promisor unless certain well-defined and long-established legal requisites are satisfied (Nicholson v. 300 Broadway Realty Corp., 164 N.E.2d 832, 834 (N.Y. 1959); Neponsit Prop. Owners' Assn. v. Emigrant Ind. Sav. Bank, 15 N.E.2d 793, 794–95 (N.Y. 1938); see, also, Morgan Lake Co. v. New York, New Haven & Hartford R.R. Co., 186 N.E. 685, 687 (N.Y. 1933); Miller v. Clary, 103 N.E. 1114 (N.Y. 1913); Mygatt v. Coe, 42 N.E. 17 (N.Y. 1895); 13 N.Y.Jur., Covenants and Restrictions, § 12, pp. 252–253). In the landmark Neponsit case (supra), we adopted and clarified the following test, originating in the early English decisions, for the enforceability of affirmative covenants (cf. Spencer's Case, 77 Eng. Rep. 72 (K.B. 1583)), and reaffirmed the requirements that in order for a covenant to run with the land, it must be shown that:

(1)   The original grantee and grantor must have intended that the covenant run with the land.

(2)   There must exist "privity of estate" between the party claiming the benefit of the covenant and the right to enforce it and the party upon whom the burden of the covenant is to be imposed.

(3)   The covenant must be deemed to "touch and concern" the land with which it runs.

Even though the parties to the original deed expressly state in the instrument that the covenant will run with the land, such a recital is insufficient to render the covenant enforceable against subsequent grantees if the other requirements for the running of an affirmative covenant are not met. The rule is settled that "[r]egardless of the intention of the parties, a covenant will run with the land and will be enforceable against a subsequent purchaser of the land at the suit of one who claims the benefit of the covenant, only if the covenant complies with certain legal requirements" (Neponsit, supra, 15 N.E.2d p. 795; see, also, *Morgan Lake Co. v. New York, New Haven & Hartford R.R. Co.*, supra, 262 186 N.E. p. 686). Thus, although the intention of the original parties here is clear and privity of estate exists, the covenant must still satisfy the requirement that it "touch and concern" the land.

It is this third prong of the tripartite rule which presents the obstacle to appellant's position and which was the focus of our decisions in *Neponsit* and *Nicholson v. 300 Broadway Realty Corp.* (164 N.E. 2d 832, 834, supra). *Neponsit* first sought to breathe substance and meaning into the ritualistic rubric that an affirmative covenant must "touch and concern" the land in order to be enforceable against subsequent grantees. Observing that it would be difficult to devise a rule which would operate mechanically to resolve all situations which might arise, Judge Lehman observed that "the distinction between covenants which run with land and covenants which are personal, must depend upon the effect of the covenant on the legal rights which otherwise would flow from the ownership of land and which are connected with the land" (Neponsit, 15 N.E.2d p. 796). Thus, he posed as the key question whether "the covenant in purpose and effect substantially alter[s] these rights" (15 N.E.2d p. 796). In *Nicholson*, this court reaffirmed the soundness of the reasoning in *Neponsit* as "a more realistic and pragmatic approach" (supra, 164 N.E.2d p. 835). * * *

A close examination of the covenant in the case before us leads to the conclusion that it does not substantially affect the ownership interest of landowners in the Orchard Hill subdivision. The covenant provides for the supplying of water for only six months of the year; no claim has been advanced by appellant that the lands in the subdivision would be waterless without the water it supplies. Indeed, the facts here point to the converse conclusion since respondent has obtained his own source of water. The record, based on and consisting of an agreed stipulation of facts, does not demonstrate that other property owners in the subdivision would be deprived of water from appellant or that the price of water would become prohibitive for other property owners if respondent terminated appellant's service. Thus, the agreement for the seasonal supply of water does not seem to us to relate in any significant degree to the ownership rights of respondent and the other property owners in the subdivision of Orchard Hill. The landowners in *Neponsit* received an easement in common to utilize public areas in the subdivision; this interest was in the nature of a property right attached to their respective properties. The obligation to receive water from appellant resembles a personal, contractual promise to purchase water rather than a significant interest attaching to respondent's property. It should be emphasized that the question whether a covenant is so closely related to the use of the land that it should be deemed to "run" with the land is one of degree, dependent on the particular circumstances of a case (Neponsit, supra, 15 N.E.2d p. 796). Here, the meager record before us is lacking and woefully insufficient to establish that the covenant "touches and concerns" the land, as we have interpreted that requirement.

There is an additional reason why we are reluctant to enforce this covenant for the seasonal supply of water. The affirmative covenant is disfavored in the law because of the fear that this type of obligation imposes an "undue restriction on alienation or an onerous burden in perpetuity" (*Nicholson v. 300 Broadway Realty Corp.*, 164 N.E.2d 832, 835, supra). In *Nicholson*, the covenant to supply heat was not interdicted by this concern because it was conditioned upon the continued existence of the buildings on both the promisor's and the promisee's properties. Similarly, in *Neponsit*, the original 1917 deed containing the covenant to pay an annual charge for the maintenance of public areas expressly provided for its own lapse in 1940. Here, no outside limitation has been placed on the obligation to purchase water from appellant. Thus, the covenant falls prey to the criticism that it creates a burden in perpetuity, and purports to bind all future owners, regardless of the use to which the land is put. Such a result militates strongly against its enforcement. On this ground also, we are of the opinion that the covenant should not be enforced as an exception to the general rule prohibiting the "running" of affirmative covenants. * * *

Order affirmed.

NOTES AND QUESTIONS

1. Does *Eagle Enterprises* clarify the legal meaning of "touch and concern" in any respect beyond the exposition in *Neponsit*? Why doesn't the promise to take water from the common well in return for a fee satisfy Professor Bigelow's definition—altering the advantages and burdens of owning particular tracts of land—endorsed in *Neponsit*?

2. Why did this covenant fail the touch and concern test? If there were visible pipes to bring the water to the land, would that serve as notice to

successors? What if every house had a pipe leading to the central source? Is the problem that the later deeds did not contain the covenant? What if the developer had filed a plan for the entire subdivision containing the restrictions? Does *Eagle Enterprises* suggest that touch and concern functions as a kind of changed circumstances doctrine? For discussion, see Stake, supra.

3.   What if each of the owners had also covenanted not to dig wells? Would the covenant to purchase water then touch and concern?

4.   Should servitudes on personal property run to successive owners? The running of servitudes is more of an issue in the case of land because it lasts much longer than typical personal property. The law has reflected some suspicion of servitudes on personal property, often without a clear articulation for the reasons. See Zechariah Chafee, Jr., Equitable Servitudes on Chattels, 41 Harv. L. Rev. 945 (1928). Unlike land, where servitudes address spillovers that affect identifiable neighbors, personal property servitudes often restrict use or the terms of resale of an item of personal property. Mostly the law has regulated these in terms of antitrust. See Dr. Miles Medical Co. v. Park, 220 U.S. 373 (1911), overruled on other grounds, Leegin Creative Leather Products, Inc. v. PSKS, Inc., 551 U.S. 877 (2007). The issue of servitudes on personal property has gained more prominence recently with the increased importance of intellectual property. See Glen O. Robinson, Personal Property Servitudes, 71 U. Chi. L. Rev. 1449 (2004). The arrangement in *ProCD v. Zeidenberg*, see Chapter IV, was in effect a sale of the software coupled with a servitude; the seller intended the restriction on the use of the software to bind any successor owner of the software as well. Patent owners sometimes impose single-use only restrictions that are meant to override a default license in the buyer to repair an item. Should holders of IP rights be able to contract for servitudes that will run with some property, tangible or intangible? An alternative to such servitudes would be to license the IP rights themselves and include the restrictions in the terms of the license. If so, should the result be any different?

d.   NOTICE AND THE COMMON PLAN

One of the requirements for covenants to run in equity is notice. If A personally deals with B, notice is an automatic by-product. In subdivisions, though, covenants trace back to a deal between the developer and the original purchasers, not directly between the purchasers themselves. Such a procedure saves greatly on transaction costs if what is desired is a set of interlocking identical mutual covenants. For a group of 100 parcels, the developer can substitute 100 similar covenants as part of the package on offer, as opposed to the 4,950 deals required for each parcel owner to covenant with each of the 99 others. Things can still go wrong, as in the following case.

Sanborn v. McLean

Supreme Court of Michigan, 1925.
206 N.W. 496.

■ WIEST, J. Defendant Christina McLean owns the west 35 feet of lot 86 of Green Lawn subdivision, at the northeast corner of Collingwood avenue and Second boulevard, in the city of Detroit, upon which there is a dwelling house, occupied by herself and her husband, defendant John A. McLean. The house fronts Collingwood avenue. At the rear of the lot is an alley. Mrs. McLean derived title from her husband, and, in the course of the opinion, we will speak of both as defendants. Mr. and Mrs. McLean started to erect a gasoline filling station at the rear end of their lot, and they and their contractor, William S. Weir, were enjoined by decree from doing so and bring the issues before us by appeal. Mr. Weir will not be further mentioned in the opinion.

Collingwood avenue is a high grade residence street between Woodward avenue and Hamilton boulevard, with single, double, and apartment houses, and plaintiffs, who are owners of land adjoining and in the vicinity of defendants' land, and who trace title, as do defendants, to the proprietors of the subdivision, claim that the proposed gasoline station will be a nuisance per se, is in violation of the general plan fixed for use of all lots on the street for residence purposes only, as evidenced by restrictions upon 53 of the 91 lots fronting on Collingwood avenue, and that defendants' lot is subject to a reciprocal negative easement barring a use so detrimental to the enjoyment and value of its neighbors. Defendants insist that no restrictions appear in their chain of title and they purchased without notice of any reciprocal negative easement, and deny that a gasoline station is a nuisance per se. We find no occasion to pass upon the question of nuisance, as the case can be decided under the rule of reciprocal negative easement.

This subdivision was planned strictly for residence purposes, except lots fronting Woodward avenue and Hamilton boulevard. The 91 lots on Collingwood avenue were platted in 1891, designed for and each one sold solely for residence purposes, and residences have been erected upon all of the lots. Is defendants' lot subject to a reciprocal negative easement? If the owner of two or more lots, so situated as to bear the relation, sells one with restrictions of benefit to the land retained, the servitude becomes mutual, and, during the period of restraint, the owner of the lot or lots retained can do nothing forbidden to the owner of the lot sold. For want of a better descriptive term this is styled a reciprocal negative easement. It runs with the land sold by virtue of express fastening and abides with the land retained until loosened by expiration of its period of service or by events working its destruction. It is not personal to owners, but operative upon use of the land by any owner having actual or constructive notice thereof. It is an easement passing its benefits and carrying its obligations to all purchasers of land, subject to its affirmative or negative mandates. It originates for mutual benefit and exists with vigor sufficient to work its ends. It must start with a common owner. Reciprocal negative easements are never retroactive; the very nature of their origin forbids. They arise, if at all, out of a benefit accorded land retained, by restrictions upon neighboring land sold by a common owner. Such a scheme of restriction must start with a common owner; it cannot arise and fasten upon one lot by reason of other lot owners conforming to a general plan. If a reciprocal negative easement attached to defendants' lot, it was fastened thereto while in the hands of the common owner of it and neighboring lots by way of sale of other lots with restrictions beneficial at that time to it. This leads to inquiry as to what lots, if any, were sold with restrictions by the common owner before the sale of defendants' lot. While the proofs cover another avenue, we need consider sales only on Collingwood.

December 28, 1892, Robert J. and Joseph R. McLaughlin, who were then evidently owners of the lots on Collingwood avenue, deeded lots 37 to 41 and 58 to 62, inclusive, with the following restrictions:

> No residence shall be erected upon said premises which shall cost less than $2,500, and nothing but residences shall be erected upon said premises. Said residences shall front on Helene (now Collingwood) avenue and be placed no nearer than 20 feet from the front street line.

July 24, 1893, the McLaughlins conveyed lots 17 to 21 and 78 to 82, both inclusive, and lot 98 with the same restrictions. Such restrictions were imposed for the benefit of the lands held by the grantors to carry out the scheme of a residential district, and a restrictive negative easement attached to the lots retained, and title to lot 86 was then in the McLaughlins. Defendants' title, through mesne conveyances, runs back to a deed by the McLaughlins dated September 7, 1893, without restrictions mentioned therein. Subsequent deeds to other lots were executed by the McLaughlins, some with restrictions and some without. Previous to September 7, 1893, a reciprocal negative easement had attached to lot 86 by acts of the owners, as before mentioned, and such easement is still attached and may now be enforced by plaintiffs, provided defendants, at the time of their purchase, had knowledge, actual or constructive, thereof. The plaintiffs run back with their title, as do defendants, to a common owner. This common owner, as before stated, by restrictions upon lots sold, had burdened all the lots retained with reciprocal restrictions. Defendants' lot and plaintiff Sanborn's lot, next thereto, were held by such common owner, burdened with a reciprocal negative easement, and, when later sold to separate parties, remained burdened therewith, and right to demand observance thereof passed to each purchaser with notice of the easement.

Figure 9-10
Sanborn Fire Insurance Map of Area in
Sanborn v. McLean

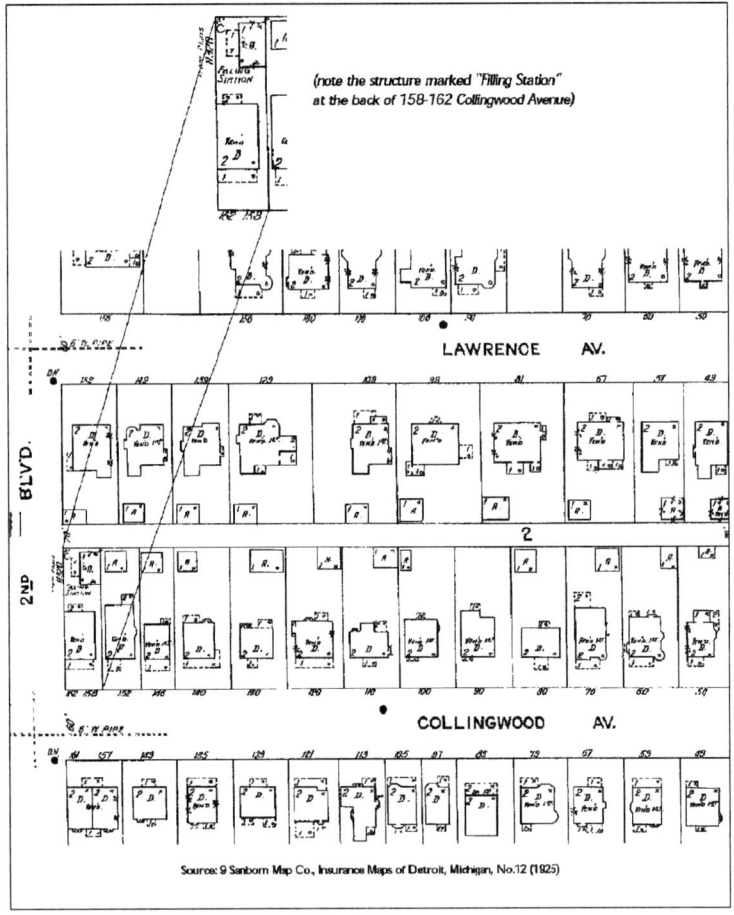

Source: 9 Sanborn Map Co., Insurance Maps of Detroit, Michigan, No. 12 (1925).

The restrictions were upon defendants' lot while it was in the hands of the common owners, and abstract of title to defendants' lot showed the common owners, and the record showed deeds of lots in the plat restricted to perfect and carry out the general plan and resulting in a reciprocal negative easement upon defendants' lot and all lots within its scope, and defendants and their predecessors in title were bound by constructive notice under our recording acts. The original plan was repeatedly declared in subsequent sales of lots by restrictions in the deeds, and, while some lots sold were not so restricted, the purchasers thereof, in every instance, observed the general plan and purpose of the restrictions in building residences. For upward of 30 years the united efforts of all persons interested have carried out the common purpose of making and keeping all the lots strictly for residences, and defendants are the first to depart therefrom.

When Mr. McLean purchased on contract in 1910 or 1911, there was a partly built dwelling house on lot 86, which he completed and now occupies. He had an abstract of title which he examined and claims he was told by the grantor that the lot was unrestricted. Considering the character of use made of all the lots open to a view of Mr. McLean when he purchased, we think, he was put thereby to inquiry, beyond asking his grantor, whether there were restrictions. He had an abstract showing the subdivision and that lot 86 had 97 companions. He could not avoid noticing the strictly uniform residence character given the lots by the expensive dwellings thereon, and the least inquiry would have quickly developed the fact that lot 86 was subjected to a reciprocal negative easement, and he could finish his house, and, like the others, enjoy the benefits of the easement. We do not say Mr. McLean should have asked his neighbors about restrictions, but we do say that with the notice he had from a view of the premises on the street, clearly indicating the residences were built and the lots occupied in strict accordance with a general plan, he was put to inquiry, and, had he inquired, he would have found of record the reason for such general conformation, and the benefits thereof serving the owners of lot 86 and the obligations running with such service and available to adjacent lot owners to prevent a departure from the general plan by an owner of lot 86.

While no case appears to be on all fours with the one at bar, the principles we have stated, and the conclusions announced, are supported by Allen v. City of Detroit, 133 N. W. 317 (Mich. 1911); McQuade v. Wilcox, 183 N. W. 771 (Mich. 1921); French v. White Star Refining Co., 201 N. W. 444 (Mich. 1924); Silberman v. Uhrlaub, 102 N. Y. S. 299 (N.Y. App. Div. 1907); Boyden v. Roberts, 111 N. W. 701 (Wis. 1907); Howland v. Andrus, 83 A. 982 (N.J. Ch. 1912).

We notice the decree in the circuit directed that the work done on the building be torn down. If the portion of the building constructed can be utilized for any purpose within the restrictions, it need not be destroyed.

With this modification, the decree in the circuit is affirmed, with costs to plaintiffs.

NOTES AND QUESTIONS

1. The court here refers to the promises as "negative reciprocal easements," but what it is talking about would more commonly be called covenants or equitable servitudes today. You will find that the terminology used by courts exhibits some variability here (as elsewhere).

2. Some courts do not go as far as the Michigan Supreme Court in recognizing the common plan doctrine. Some would not imply reciprocal negative easements at all, see, e.g., Riley v. Bear Creek Planning Comm., 551 P.2d 1213 (Cal. 1976), and others require a high proportion of the lots to have been sold with the restrictions, see, e.g., Whitton v. Clark, 151 A. 305 (Conn. 1930). The language in *Sanborn* if taken literally would imply a

restriction based on the sale of one lot with the restriction. Another variable is the degree of uniformity of the restrictions required for a court to find a common scheme or plan. See Restatement (Third) of Property: Servitudes § 2.14 (2000) (allowing common plan to be found even with some variation in restrictions). Notice that the likelihood that a purchaser will have notice is greatly increased if her individual deed makes reference to a recorded subdivision map. Restrictions incorporated in this way will satisfy even the strictest courts' standards for notice.

3.   Recall that restrictions not appearing in the land records make title searches more difficult. The restrictions on neighboring parcels here were not in the McLeans' chain of title. Instead, in the court's view, Mr. McLean had inquiry notice based on the uniformity of the neighborhood. If such uniformity could arise spontaneously, would there then be a need for covenants or for zoning (which did not exist in Detroit at the time this case arose)? Should the subsequent rise of zoning affect a court's willingness to find inquiry notice in this scenario?

e.   TERMINATION OF COVENANTS

Bolotin v. Rindge

District Court of Appeal, Second District, Division 3, California, 1964.
41 Cal.Rptr. 376.

■ FILES, JUSTICE. This is an action for declaratory relief and to quiet title against tract-wide deed restrictions which limit the use of plaintiffs' property to single family residential purposes. The trial court gave judgment declaring the restrictions to be unenforceable in part. Defendants have appealed. It is necessary to reverse the judgment because of the absence of a finding of fact on an issue which must be resolved before the controversy can be decided.

Plaintiffs own an unimproved lot situated at the northeast corner of Wilshire Boulevard and Hudson Avenue in the City of Los Angeles. This lot is a part of a tract which was subdivided by G. Allen Hancock in 1923 in the area now known as Hancock Park. Defendants are owners of other lots in the same tract. All the lots in the tract are subject to deed restrictions imposed by the original subdivider. These restrictions require, among other things, that each lot shall be used solely for single, private residences and that each residence shall front on a northsouth street. These restrictions will expire January 1, 1970. All the lots in the tract except four have been improved with single family residences. The four lots which have never been improved are the northeast and northwest corners of Wilshire and Hudson, and the two lots which are immediately north of the two corner lots.

Figure 9-11
Hudson Avenue Looking Toward
Wilshire Boulevard, 2006

As this photograph reveals, the undeveloped northeast corner lots at issue in *Bolotin* are now occupied by a substantial commercial building, as are the companion lots across the street.

There is no dispute that the Hancock Park area is one of the most desirable and expensive residential areas in the community. It is also undisputed that the character of Wilshire Boulevard has changed greatly since 1923. A stipulation of facts lists these changes in some detail. Plaintiffs' evidence also includes the testimony of a qualified real estate broker and appraiser who testified that in his opinion plaintiffs' lot was not suitable for single family residential use, that there was no commonsense use to which the property could be put so long as the deed restrictions remained, and that the highest and best use for the property would be a commercial building similar to others which have been built on Wilshire Boulevard, both east and west of the subject property. He expressed the opinion that such a development would have no adverse effect upon either the market values of the residences in the tract or upon the amenities of living there. In his opinion, a building on plaintiffs' lot would help to protect the residences from the noise of the Wilshire traffic. There is an office building on the south side of Wilshire whose parking lot is directly across the street from plaintiff's lot. The witness pointed out that the use of plaintiffs' property for a commercial building would bring the commercial influence only 100 feet closer to the defendants' residences.

Defendants produced the testimony of a real estate broker that an office building on plaintiffs' lot would make the residences in the tract much less desirable as homes. In his opinion, a commercial building would inevitably bring more traffic and more parking, and would shut out sunlight. Defendants' witness was also of the opinion that the market value of the residences would decrease if a commercial building were built on plaintiffs' lot.

The findings of fact made by the trial court consist of these two paragraphs:

> The changes in the uses of property abutting Wilshire Boulevard in the vicinity of lot 212 of tract 6388 in the City of Los Angeles and the increase of vehicular traffic on said boulevard along said lot, have resulted in said lot having no substantial value solely for single family residential purposes, but said lot has a market value in excess of $200,000.00 for business uses.

> The refusal to enforce the single family residence restriction and the prohibition of commercial use of said lot 212, contained in the deeds to said lot and adjacent lots issued in 1923 and subsequent thereto, will not have an adverse effect upon the market value of other lots in said tract or tract 7040.

The only formal conclusion of law made by the trial court was that plaintiffs are entitled to a judgment declaring that the deed restrictions are not enforceable in specified respects.

A court will declare deed restrictions to be unenforceable when, by reason of changed conditions, enforcement of the restrictions would be inequitable and oppressive, and would harass plaintiff without benefiting the adjoining owners. (Wolff v. Fallon, 284 P.2d 802 (Cal. 1955).) In that case there was a finding of fact, supported by expert testimony, that the use of the plaintiff's property for commercial purposes would not detrimentally affect the adjoining property or neighborhood. A judgment quieting title against the restrictions was affirmed.

In *Marra v. Aetna Construction Co.*, 101 P.2d 490 (Cal. 1940), at pages 492–493, the court said:

> Also well recognized is the rule that a building restriction in the nature of a servitude will not be enforced where changed conditions in the neighborhood have rendered the purpose of the restrictions obsolete. [Citations.] But, if the original purpose of the covenant can still be realized, it will be enforced even though the unrestricted use of the property would be more profitable to its owner.

In that case the evidence showed that the lot for whose benefit the restriction had been imposed was no longer being used for residential purposes, and hence the Supreme Court concluded it was no longer equitable to restrict the servient lot to residential purposes.

The difficulty in the present case is that there is no finding that the purposes of the restrictions have become obsolete, or that the enforcement of the restrictions on the plaintiffs' property will no longer benefit the defendants. The trial court's finding as to the effect upon defendants is limited to the statement that there will be no adverse effect upon market value. This is not the test.

The purpose of the deed restrictions, it seems clear enough, was to preserve the tract as a fine residential area by excluding from the tract many of the activities which might be offensive to the residents or which would create noise, traffic, congestion, or other conditions which would lessen the comfort and enjoyment of the residents. Bringing the prohibited activities into the neighborhood might or might not depreciate the market value of the homes. If the restrictions should be broken, and a commercial building erected on the Wilshire frontage, speculators might be willing to pay more for the other parcels in anticipation of future expansion of the commercial development. Thus the intrusion of an office building might increase market values even though it offended the senses of the residents and destroyed the physical conditions which had made their neighborhood a desirable one for them.

In *Miles v. Clark*, 187 P. 167 (Cal. Dist. Ct. App. 1919), at p. 172, where a decree enjoining a breach of deed restrictions was affirmed, the court said:

> The fact that apart from and surrounding the tract some business has grown up, and that the land has become more valuable in consequence, in no manner entitles defendants to be relieved of the restrictions they have created. This condition is but the natural result of the improvement of the various tracts, and the fact that the property may have become more valuable thereby for business purposes is immaterial. [Citations.] Courts in such cases are not controlled exclusively by money value, but may protect a home.

Plaintiffs have not cited any cases in which deed restrictions have been held unenforceable upon findings which were limited to the economic consequences.[1] In *Hirsch v. Hancock*, 343 P.2d 959 (Cal. Dist. Ct. App. 1959), a case which plaintiffs characterize as "strikingly similar" to this one, the court granted relief against the deed restrictions on the property at the northeast corner of Wilshire Boulevard and Rossmore

---

[1]   We note in passing that the Restatement of Property, section 537, takes the position that a promise as to the use of land is binding upon successors of the promisor only if the performance will result in benefit "in the physical use or enjoyment of the land." Comment (f) states: "*Physical use or enjoyment.* For a promise to run with the land of the promisor it is not enough that the performance of the promise operates to benefit either the promisor or the beneficiary of the promise in the use of his land but it must operate to benefit him in the physical use of his land. It must in some way make the use or enjoyment more satisfactory to his physical senses. It is not enough that the income from it is increased by virtue of it." (Accord: Daniels v. Notor, 389 Pa. 510, 133 A.2d 520.)

Since the validity of the restrictions, as such, is not in issue in the present case, it is unnecessary to consider whether section 537 is the law of California. The section is mentioned as further recognition that deed restrictions have some legally protected purpose other than economic benefit.

Avenue. The trial court in that case found that the enforcement of the restrictions would be of no substantial benefit to the owners of the other lots in the tract. That finding of fact distinguishes that case from the present one. There is no suggestion in the *Hirsch* case that the courts are concerned only with economic benefits.

* * * It is for the trial court to resolve this issue of fact.

The judgment is reversed.

NOTES AND QUESTIONS

1.   Hancock Park was developed in the 1920s as a high-end residential neighborhood. The deed restrictions on the lots included racial restrictions, minimum lot sizes of 15,000 square feet, and requirements that the lots be devoted to single-family use. See Robert C. Ellickson, Stale Real Estate Covenants (August 21, 2020), available at http://dx.doi.org/10.2139/ssrn.3678927. As Wilshire Boulevard developed into a thoroughfare, some owners of lots in Hancock Park along Wilshire opted to keep their lots vacant until 1970, when the restrictions would expire, hoping that the city might rezone to permit commercial use. This eerie stretch of land became known as the "Dead Mile," a reference to the "Miracle Mile" immediately to the west, a developed commercial strip. As of 2020, most of Hancock Park is zoned for single-family residential use and requires lots of at least 15,000 square feet, and the median value of Hancock Park homes is now around five million dollars. Id. Does this change your view of how the case should have come out, or does it suggest the court was correct in assessing that the restrictions still carried substantial value for residents? Should an analysis of changed circumstances address considerations beyond whether the restrictions still benefit the adjoining owners?

2.   The problem of changed circumstances is a general one. What is special about the covenants here is that many have an interest in their enforcement. How does this situation compare to the cy pres cases discussed in Chapter VI?

3.   How else might the problem of stability versus flexibility over time be handled? Some covenants contain sunset provisions. Sometimes the judicial doctrine of changed circumstances is applied, and in a few states covenants are time-limited by statute. See Robert C. Ellickson et al., Land Use Controls: Cases and Materials 532–36 (5th ed. 2021). Would purchasers systematically make mistakes in this area?

4.   If courts were more inclined to refuse enforcement of covenants at the edges of an area, what should happen when the owners on the new commercial-residential divide invoke changed circumstances? Might this explain the court's reluctance to intervene here?

Peckham v. Milroy

Court of Appeals of Washington, 2001.
17 P.3d 1256.

■ SWEENEY, J. A neighborhood covenant prohibits home businesses. So, the trial court enjoined Thomas Milroy's wife from operating a home day care after [a] neighbor complained.

The question before us is whether the trial court erred by enjoining the day-care business because the covenant was abandoned, or violated public policy. The trial court's findings are amply supported by the evidence here. And those findings amply support the court's conclusions of law that the covenant had not been abandoned through disuse. Nor does it violate public policy. We also agree that neither laches nor estoppel bars Mr. Peckham's claim here. We, therefore, affirm the court's summary dismissal.

FACTS

The material facts are not disputed. Spokane Terrace was platted in 1907. It includes the houses at issue here. The neighborhood is called the Spokane Terrace Addition (STA). The developer subjected some of the lots to restrictive covenants in 1955. One prohibited use of the property "for business purposes of any kind whatsoever. . . ." Clerk's Papers at 38.

Gordon Peckham moved into the STA in 1958. Thomas Milroy's parents moved into the STA in 1992. The Milroy property is subject to the restriction.

Mr. Milroy's mother fell and broke her hip in 1994. She required assistance after that. Mr. Milroy, his wife, and family decided to move into his mother's home in the STA.

They remodeled the home to accommodate the Milroy family, which included five children. They began to remodel in August 1995 and completed in December 1995. Mr. Peckham watched and photographed the construction. He complained to the county about the construction in November 1995. And he filed zoning complaints in February 1996. The Milroys moved into the home in December 1995. Mrs. Milroy obtained a day-care license and began running a day care.

The children are noisy. Mr. Peckham can hear them from inside his home. Parents of the children parked in front of Mr. Peckham's house. They walk across his yard. And they park in the alley behind his house.

Mr. Milroy's mother passed away in July 1996. He inherited the home. Mr. Peckham told Mrs. Milroy she was violating the covenants in July 1996. Mr. Peckham sued to enjoin the day-care operation in November 1997.

Several home businesses operated in the STA in violation of the restrictive covenant. These include a drapery business, a painting business, a small construction business, and a TV repair service.

Following a trial the court concluded that Mrs. Milroy's day care was a business. And that Mr. Peckham had an equitable right to enforce the covenant. The court enjoined the Milroys from operating the day care.

ANALYSIS

ABANDONMENT.

Mr. Milroy first argues the covenant prohibiting home businesses has been abandoned.

Abandonment requires proof that prior violations have eroded the general plan and enforcement is therefore inequitable. Mountain Park Homeowners Ass'n v. Tydings, 883 P.2d 1383, 1386 (Wash. 1994). A covenant is abandoned when it has been "habitually and substantially violated. . . ." Id. But a few violations do not constitute abandonment. White v. Wilhelm, 665 P.2d 407, 411 (Wash. App. 1983).

Mr. Milroy presented evidence of four home businesses in the STA. A drapery business has been run from a home in the STA since the late 1970s. A painting business was run from 1994 to 1997. A small construction and TV repair business was operated between 1963 and 1972. And a craft business has been operated from a home for the past five to six years.

The STA covers 41 blocks and includes approximately 38 to 40 lots each. The violations are neither habitual nor substantial. See Mountain Park Homeowners, supra. They comprise a very small percentage of the subdivision. A few violations do not constitute abandonment. White, supra.

Substantial evidence supports the trial court's determination that the covenant has not been abandoned.

LACHES AND ESTOPPEL.

Mr. Milroy next contends that Mr. Peckham knew Mrs. Milroy intended to operate a home day care as early as August 1995. Yet Mr. Peckham waited until November 1997 to file this action. The delay caused injury to the Milroys and was therefore unreasonable.

Laches. Laches requires: "(1) knowledge or reasonable opportunity to discover on the part of a potential plaintiff that he has a cause of action against a defendant; (2) an unreasonable delay by the plaintiff in commencing that cause of action; (3) damage to defendant resulting from the unreasonable delay." Buell v. City of Bremerton, 495 P.2d 1358, 1361 (Wash. 1972); see Valley View Indus. Park v. City of Redmond, 733 P.2d 182, 191 (Wash. 1987).

Mr. Peckham saw the Milroys remodel. But he did not know they intended to build a day-care center until after the construction started. The Milroys incurred construction expenses before Mr. Peckham knew they intended to violate the covenant.

Mr. Peckham objected to the project through early 1996. Mr. Peckham tried to enlist the aid of the county to stop the day-care operation. He told Mrs. Milroy that she was violating the covenants in July 1996.

Mr. Milroy testified that the original purpose of remodeling was to provide room for his family, not a commercial day care. Mr. Milroy stated he and his wife did not originally plan to continue the day-care service. But then they decided they needed the money. He testified the decision to operate the day care was made in late 1995, after remodeling the home.

The defense of laches requires showing all three elements. See Buell, supra. The Milroys intended to remodel for reasons other than the day care. The cost of the remodel could not, then, result from Mr. Peckham's delay in bringing this action.

The court found that Mr. Peckham did not unreasonably delay the suit. That finding is amply supported by this record.

Equitable Estoppel. Equitable estoppel requires: "(1) an admission, statement or act inconsistent with the claim asserted afterward; (2) action by the other party in reasonable reliance on that admission, statement or act; and (3) injury to that party when the first party is allowed to contradict or repudiate its admission, statement or act." Wilhelm v. Beyersdorf, 999 P.2d 54, 62 (Wash. App. 2000). Each element must be proven by clear, cogent, and convincing evidence. Id. Equitable estoppel is not favored. Robinson v. City of Seattle, 830 P.2d 318, 345 (Wash. 1992).

Mr. Milroy has not established any of the elements of equitable estoppel. Mr. Peckham made no statements and he took no actions inconsistent with his current position—the day care violates the covenant.

Mr. Milroy argues that Mr. Peckham acquiesced to the day care through his silence. Silence can lead to equitable estoppel—"[w]here a party knows what is occurring and would be expected to speak, if he wished to protect his interest, his acquiescence manifests his tacit consent." Bd. of Regents v. City of Seattle, 741 P.2d 11, 16 (Wash. 1987). Mr. Peckham was not silent. He complained to the county. He complained to Mrs. Milroy.

Neither can the Milroys show that they relied on Mr. Peckham's acquiescence. Mrs. Milroy talked to representatives of the city, county, and state about the day-care operation. She did not rely on Mr. Peckham. * * * [The court then upholds the trial court's determination that the character of the neighborhood had not changed for purposes of the doctrine of changed neighborhood conditions.]

PUBLIC POLICY.

Mr. Milroy argues that Washington public policy makes quality child care a priority. And this public policy should override restrictive covenants preventing home day care.

Mr. Milroy cites statutes which prohibit cities, towns, and counties from prohibiting home day care in residentially zoned areas. RCW 35.63.185; RCW 36.70A.450. The regulations do not, however, limit private parties from restricting land use. Restrictive covenants in residential neighborhoods are enforceable. Metzner v. Wojdyla, 886 P.2d 154, 156–57 (Wash. 1994).

If restrictive covenants that incidentally prohibit home day care should be repealed on public policy grounds, the decision should come from the Legislature—not this court. See Mut. of Enumclaw Ins. Co. v. Wiscomb, 622 P.2d 1234, 1236–37 (Wash. 1980) (determining public policy is not the judiciary's function).

Affirmed.

NOTES AND QUESTIONS

1.   We have seen abandonment and estoppel before. How are they similar or different in the context of covenants?

2.   One might ask whether covenants can be *created* by estoppel. In general, there are no covenants by estoppel, implication, or prescription. Why? Do covenants typically deal with matters as serious as those involved in easements?

3.   The Court of Appeals declined to find these covenants against public policy, but that argument met a very different response in *Taylor v. Northam*, which held that the governor of Virginia could abrogate a covenant that required the state to hold a monument to Confederate general Robert E. Lee and the land on which it stood "perpetually sacred to the monumental purpose to which it has been devoted." 862 S.E.2d 458, 461 (Va. 2021). After owners in the neighboring area sued to require the state to continue displaying the monument, the Supreme Court of Virginia found that the covenant was terminated both by changed conditions and as against public policy. In discussing changed conditions, the court noted that in the time since the covenant was drafted in 1890, both Virginia and federal courts invalidated many laws valorizing the pre-Civil-War way of life in the American South. It cited *Shelley v. Kraemer*, supra Chapter IV, and other decisions striking down devices meant to reinforce racial subordination. As for public policy, the court recited that "applicable public policy for a given time may be gathered from the enactments of the legislative branch, the expressions of the executive branch, and the opinions of this Court." Id. at 469. Even if there were not a law expressly authorizing the Governor to remove the monument, the Virginia Supreme Court would have found the state's other recent removals of monuments, the elimination of a holiday honoring Lee, and broader concerns about compelling particular government speech sufficient justifications for terminating the covenant. It rejected the

owners' argument that Virginia's public policy in favor of historic preservation supported the covenant's continued enforcement. What sources of evidence for "public policy" should courts take into account—broad public sentiment, specific legislation, or constitutional values? Cf. Skutt v. Grand Rapids, 266 N.W. 344 (Mich. 1936) (defining public policy as "community common sense and common conscience"). How should a court evaluate a covenant that purports to ban the display of flags or signage, or one that purports to restrict gun ownership? See Mazdabrook Commons Homeowners' Ass'n v. Khan, 210 N.J. 482, 486 (2012); Paul Boudreaux, Homes, Rights, and Private Communities, 20 U. Fla. J.L. & Pub. Pol. 479, 526 (2009) (observing that many common interest communities "reportedly hold restrictions against firearms in homes").

4.   Courts in different states have reached different conclusions about whether covenants that have been abrogated by the state require the payment of compensation pursuant to state or federal takings clauses (see Chapter X). See Glen O. Robinson, Explaining Contingent Rights: The Puzzle of "Obsolete" Covenants, 91 Colum. L. Rev. 546, 563 (1991). Should the government have to pay when it expressly changes public policy in a way that abrogates covenants? Several states have passed laws terminating covenants that ban solar panels, see, e.g., Ariz. Rev. Stat. Ann. § 33–439A (2007), or "accessory dwelling units" that expand housing on a particular lot, see Cal. Civ. Code § 4751 (2020).

Conservation Easements

Perhaps the fastest growing type of covenant in the United States is the conservation easement. According to one estimate, the amount of land in the United States subject to conservation easements exploded from very little in 1980 to over 56 million acres by 2015. Land Trust Alliance, 2015 National Land Trust Census Report, at http://s3. amazonaws.com/landtrustalliance.org/2015NationalLandTrustCensus Report.pdf. Conservation easements are servitudes that restrict the future development of land. The most common type of restriction prohibits subdivision and commercial development but permits existing agricultural and residential uses. Conservation easements come in a wide variety of forms, however, ranging from prohibitions on cutting timber to requiring the preservation of historic building facades.

The term "conservation easement" is something of a misnomer in that these restrictions are more accurately classified as negative covenants in gross. They are negative because they prohibit the servient landowner from engaging in certain kinds of activities; they are probably more accurately described as covenants rather than easements because they do not fit any of the traditional four categories of negative easements; and they are in gross because the power to enforce the restriction is typically given not to another landowner but to a unit of local government or a charitable land trust like the Nature Conservancy. A negative covenant in gross probably would not run with the land at common law. It could not be enforced as a real covenant, since the privity requirements would not be met. And courts generally refused to enforce covenants in gross as equitable servitudes; only appurtenant covenants were eligible for enforcement against successors with notice. See Gerald Korngold, Privately Held Conservation Servitudes: A Policy Analysis in the Context of In Gross Real Covenants and Easements, 63 Tex. L. Rev. 433, 470–79 (1984). Conservation easements therefore exist only because of legislation specifically authorizing them. Today virtually all states have enacted conservation easement laws, about half of which are based on the Uniform Conservation Easement Act promulgated in 1981. See Restatement (Third) of Property, Servitudes § 1.3, cmt. a & Statutory Note. In this sense, conservation easements are another example of a new form of property being created by legislation, consistent with the idea of the *numerus clausus*.

There appear to be multiple forces driving the rapid proliferation of conservation easements. First, many owners of land with significant aesthetic and environmental value worry about these lands succumbing to pressure for subdivision or commercial development. Of course, as long as the owners are living and hold the land in fee simple, they can reject the entreaties of developers. But many owners are apprehensive that the family farm, or woodlot, or waterfront retreat will be sold by their heirs or otherwise fall into the hands of developers after they die. A perpetual conservation easement is designed to "give peace-of-mind to current landowners worried about the future of a beloved property, whether forest or ranch, stretch of river or family farm." The Nature Conservancy, Conservation Easements: All About Conservations Easements, at http:// www.nature.org/aboutus/privatelandsconservation/conservation easements/all-about-conservation-easements.xml. In this sense, the impulse behind the movement for conservation easements is reminiscent of the aspirations of the English landed gentry to keep their country houses in the family in perpetuity.

Second, there are significant tax benefits to donating a conservation easement to a local unit of government or a charitable land trust. It is no accident that the boom in conservation easements started after the Internal Revenue Code was amended in 1976 specifically to permit tax-deductible donations of such interests. See IRC § 170(h). The instrument of donation must provide that the land is being restricted for one of several general purposes: outdoor recreation, wildlife habitat, scenic enjoyment, agricultural use, or historical importance. And the donation must be "perpetual." If these requirements are met, the landowner can deduct from her income taxes the difference between the appraised value of the land in an unrestricted state and the value of the land as restricted. Meanwhile, the landowner can continue to own the land in fee simple, pass it to heirs, or even sell it, subject to the restriction. Many states also provide that landowners are entitled to a reduction in property taxes to reflect the lower assessed value of the property after the restriction is in place. There are no reliable data on the total amount of deductions claimed for conservation easements, but according to one estimate "the charitable value of claimed donations nationwide was in the neighborhood of $20.7 billion from 2001 to 2003." Dominic P. Parker, Conservation Easements: A Closer Look at Federal Tax Policy 10 (PERC Policy Series, October 2005).

Third, many environmentalists, particularly those concerned about preserving local environmental values, have seen conservation easements as a potentially powerful tool in combating new commercial development. Traditional regulatory tools for fighting developers, such as restrictive zoning laws, encounter fierce resistance from particular landowners and developers and generate expensive litigation over regulatory takings claims (see Chapter X). Conservation easements are the product of a voluntary agreement between a landowner and a unit of local government or a land trust, and hence encounter little or no opposition. Moreover, insofar as conservation easements are financed, at least in significant part, by off-budget tax benefits given to landowners, they do not encounter the same type of public scrutiny that would be given to direct government acquisition of new parkland or nature preserves. See generally, Symposium, Perpetual Conservation Easements in the 21st Century, 2013 Utah L. Rev. 1.

The rapid emergence of conservation easements has not gone unnoticed, and is beginning to generate critical commentary. Julia Mahoney has written that the perpetual nature of conservation easements raises some of the same concerns about dead hand control we have seen in other contexts, such as the rule against restraints on alienation and the Rule against Perpetuities. See Julia D. Mahoney, Perpetual Restrictions on Land and the Problem of the Future, 88 Va. L. Rev. 739 (2002). She writes that conservation easements reflect a kind of hubris that "the ability of the present generation to predict the needs and preferences of future generations is so good that the present generation should save their descendants trouble and transaction costs by making a substantial number of land use decisions for them." Id. at 744. In addition, making easements perpetual presupposes that decisions about land use are irreversible, such that "the present generation represents nature's last or near-to-last chance, because once land is developed, it will never or almost never go back to being undeveloped." Id. at 745. This, she says, is contrary to historical experience, and reflects naiveté about "the instability of the categories of 'development' and 'preservation.' " Id.

The use of generous tax deductions to spur conservation easements has also encountered criticism as leading to abuses and poor planning. Despite safeguards in the tax code and regulations, many donors have overvalued conservation easements and taken deductions out of line with public benefits. See, e.g., Timothy Lindstrom, Income Tax Aspects of Conservation Easements, 5 Wyo. L. Rev. 1, 17–18 (2005). On the benefit side, an exposé by two reporters for the *Washington Post* reported that conservation easements have been used to generate tax deductions for real estate developers in circumstances where it is doubtful that any public benefit is created. See Joe Stephens & David B. Ottaway, Developers Find Payoff in Preservation, Washington Post, Dec. 21, 2003, at A1. For example, some developers have built homes around a golf course and have then deducted the value of a donated conservation easement in the golf course fairways. Others have pointed out the tax deduction strategy results in a pattern of expenditures that favors horse farms, trophy ranches, Nantucket cottages, and other getaways of the wealthy, which may not be the best way to allocate resources for conservation of environmentally and historically significant resources. For example, preserving land for hiking or as habitat may require the preservation of multiple contiguous parcels of land, whereas conservation easements generate only a scattershot pattern of preserved lands. Despite some subsequent efforts to address these problems by tightening requirements and improving appraisals, no broader reforms have been enacted, and abuses continue. See K. King Burnett, John D. Leshy & Nancy A. McLaughlin, Building Better Conservation Easements for America the Beautiful, Harv. Envtl. L. Rev. Online (Sept. 15, 2021) https://papers.ssrn.com/sol3/papers.cfm?abstract_id=3925094.

Finally, some traditional environmentalists have objected to conservation easements on the ground that they deprive the public of any input into the development of conservation policy. See, e.g., John D. Echeverria, Revive the Legacy of Land Use Controls, 2 Open Space 12 (Summer 2004). Conservation easements represent a strategy of providing a type of public good (e.g., environmental amenities) by private contract. This largely eliminates any role for public input or oversight into decisions about what to preserve and what sorts of public access will be provided to the resources subject to preservation controls. Since the public is paying for the conservation, both directly through tax subsidies and indirectly through foregone development opportunities, the public should have some say into the process. Instead, conservation easements are created through private negotiations between landowners and land trusts, typically with no notice to the public even after they have been created.

NOTES AND QUESTIONS

1.   Because of the voluntary nature of conservation easements, their creation is rarely accompanied by litigation. Over time, however, conflicts inevitably arise over the interpretation and enforcement of these agreements. These are usually resolved by interpreting the language of the easement or the authorizing statute. See, e.g., Ephrata Area School Dist. v. County of Lancaster, 938 A.2d 264 (Pa. 2007) (question whether consent of easement holder was required to construct a public access road across an open space easement to reach a newly constructed school); Tennessee Environmental Council, Inc. v. Bright Par 3 Assocs., L.P., No. E2003-01982-COA-R3-CV, 2004 WL 419720 (Tenn. Ct. App. 2004) (question whether

members of the public have standing to seek enforcement of a conservation easement).

2.   Although the major objections to conservation easements relate to their perpetual nature, the use of tax subsidies, and the lack of public oversight, these objections are interrelated. For example, the Internal Revenue Code provides that a donation will be deductible only if the easement is "perpetual." Why might Congress be reluctant to allow deductions for time-limited conservation easements? The IRS will allow an easement to be extinguished in the future if a change in conditions makes it "impractical or impossible" for the easement to serve its intended purpose, and if the funds acquired in extinguishing the easement are used for a conservation purpose similar to the one initially intended by the easement. Treas. Reg. § 1.170A–14(c)(2). Should a citizens' group have standing to intervene in a proceeding before the IRS to challenge either a finding that an easement had become "impractical or impossible" or the proposed use of the proceeds? See Carol Necole Brown, A Time to Preserve: A Call for Formal Private-Party Rights in Perpetual Conservation Easements, 40 Ga. L. Rev. 85 (2005) (advocating a broad right of private party standing).

3.   Would you favor imposing some time limitation on conservation easements? What about subjecting such easements to the equitable doctrine of cy pres (see Chapter VI)? See Gerald Korngold, Solving the Contentious Issues of Private Conservation Easements: Promoting Flexibility for the Future and Engaging the Public Land Use Process, 2007 Utah L. Rev. 1039; Nancy A. McLaughlin, Rethinking the Perpetual Nature of Conservation Easements, 29 Harv. Envtl. L. Rev. 421 (2005). Would these reforms reduce the incentives of persons to make donations of such easements?

C. ZONING AND OTHER LAND-USE REGULATION

These days the main source of land-use control of a public character is zoning and related land-use regulation. Zoning in the United States arose in the early twentieth century in response to the perceived inadequacies of nuisance and covenants to secure a stable regime of residential land use in a rapidly urbanizing country.

Zoning is the regulation of land uses through a general regime permitting and forbidding particular uses of land in certain locations. In a proto-zoning period in the late nineteenth and early twentieth centuries, a number of municipalities adopted ordinances prohibiting a select few uses—for example, brick making in a residential area. Modern zoning ordinances, which are far more comprehensive, date from the landmark New York Zoning Ordinance of 1916. This prescribed three zones—residence, business, and unrestricted; today New York City's zoning ordinance provides for 176 use districts. Contemporary zoning also covers matters such as lot size and shape, and building bulk and placement. There are several types of zoning, including more recently zoning that involves a contract-like deal between developers and local government. When reading the following materials ask yourself to what extent zoning is public or private law or some mixture of the two. Related to this is the question of how great an impact zoning has on owner sovereignty—and how far it should.

Zoning of the type familiar today, which governs the types of uses to which parcels may be put, took off in the 1920s. Interestingly, zoning was heavily supported by some developers, particularly those of "high class" housing. Zoning originally targeted nuisances but now commonly zoning makes fine distinctions among uses and often also restricts height, bulk, area, and exterior design. As we will see, these measures can sometimes be used to keep out those who cannot afford large lots and large houses. The earliest zoning often explicitly targeted characteristics of the user (rather than just the use), and was used to enforce racial and economic segregation. In *Buchanan v. Warley*, 245 U.S. 60 (1917), the Supreme Court struck down such schemes as violating the Fourteenth Amendment's guarantee not to be deprived of the right to dispose of property without due process of law—in that case the white seller's right to dispose of the property by selling to black people. (The lawsuit was a challenge by the local president of the NAACP, William Warley, and a white realtor friendly to the NAACP, Charles Buchanan, by having Buchanan sell to Warley on condition that Warley be able to occupy, and then having Warley breach and claim the condition as excusing performance.) The Louisville ordinance at issue in the case was designed to maintain segregation between whites and blacks and forbade any person from occupying a house on a block in which the majority of the other houses were occupied by members of the other race. See Benno C. Schmidt, Jr., Principle and Prejudice: The Supreme Court and Race in the Progressive Era, Part 1: The Heyday of Jim Crow, 82 Colum. L. Rev. 444, 498–523 (1982). We take up more subtle racial and class effects of zoning later in this Section.

Zoning ordinances and the apparatus for giving them effect are a matter of state and local law. Because local governments are creatures of their respective states, the authority to engage in zoning must come from the state. States can delegate the police power in the area of zoning to local governments. State constitutions or legislation, termed "home rule" provisions, can give some or all local governments sweeping powers to regulate, and zoning is within this broad authorization. Or the state can pass a zoning enabling act setting out the authority of local governments to act in this area.

Consider the typical zoning enabling act. Such legislation calls for a *comprehensive plan*. In many states, this requirement is in practice easy to meet, because the plan need not be in writing, or it is sometimes considered to be implicit in the *zoning* ordinance. Under the enabling act, relevant local governments—county commissions, city councils, etc.—are authorized to and expected to pass a zoning ordinance. Under such an ordinance, people can seek changes in zoning designations, but there is a danger that individually tailored adjustments will be attacked as unlawful "spot zoning." In general, it is fair to say that those envisioning the workings of zoning at the time it came into being seriously underestimated the dynamic aspect of land-use planning. Implementing change in a zoning scheme is not an easy process.

Under zoning, permits are commonly required for subdivisions, site plans, and building projects. A designated local official will be in charge of granting and denying requests for building permits, and the official will enforce the provisions of the zoning ordinance in the process of considering the request for a permit. Those dissatisfied with a denial of a permit, as well as those aggrieved by the granting of a permit, and certain other officials can appeal to a *Board of Zoning Appeals,* which can carry one of several similar sounding names and which reviews these decisions but cannot make changes in basic zoning designations themselves. Consider who is likely to have enough of a stake and low enough organizing costs to be able to mount effective opposition to a zoning decision. Developers and neighbors often fit this description, but those who might become residents in the future are much less likely to have their voices heard directly.

The Board of Zoning Appeals not only hears appeals from denials of building permits but also hears requests for *variances* (which allow for relaxation of zoning requirements in cases of undue hardship), and hears requests for *special approvals* (which go under various other names as well, such as "special exceptions," "special permits," and "conditional uses," and which permit uses only if conditions specified in the ordinance are met). The difference between a variance and a special approval is that if one satisfies criteria set forth in the zoning ordinance, one has a right to a special approval, whereas a variance is given for special hardship as determined within a broad grant of discretion to the Board under the ordinance. Aggrieved landowners can seek judicial review of the Board's decision in the regular state courts. Variances and special approvals can be termed "flexibility tools." See generally Restatement (Fourth) of Property, Vol. 7, Div. I, Ch. 6 (Am. L. Inst. Council Draft No. 3, Sept. 29, 2020).

Violators of zoning ordinances are theoretically liable for civil and criminal sanctions, although enforcement is sometimes spotty. Recall the ex ante versus ex post discussion in connection with building encroachments (see Chapter IV). Should those who have already built in violation of zoning be required to tear the offending structure down, even at great cost? Sometimes this happens. In early 2020, a New York trial court judge ordered the developers of a condominium building to remove twenty completed floors found to exceed what was permitted under zoning law, though the decision was ultimately overturned on appeal. See Stefanos Chen, Judge Orders Nearly Built Tower to Lose About 20 Floors, N.Y. Times, Feb. 14, 2020, at A25; Comm. for Environmentally Sound Dev. v. Amsterdam Ave. Redevelopment Assocs. LLC, 144 N.Y.S.3d 1 (App. Div. 2021). In Naples, Florida, a building approved by the County Commission in violation of a comprehensive plan was demolished under court order. Aisling Swift, Florida Courts Agree: If Buildings Violate Laws, They Must Be Razed, Naples Daily News, Sept. 5, 2006, https://archive.naplesnews.com/news/florida-courts-agree-if-buildings-violate-laws-they-must-be-razed-ep-405826699-330950031.html.

In the courts, the Board of Zoning Appeals is treated like a quasi-judicial administrative agency in that principles of due process and administrative law apply. Principally challenges to zoning are based on due process (substantive and procedural), the takings clause (state and/or federal), equal protection, free speech, free association, and freedom of religion. We return to some of these issues later in this Section.

Zoning comes in a number of varieties, one of which is called "Euclidean" after the scheme in the following case.

Village of Euclid v. Ambler Realty Co.

Supreme Court of the United States, 1926.
272 U.S. 365.

■ MR. JUSTICE SUTHERLAND delivered the opinion of the Court. The village of Euclid is an Ohio municipal corporation. It adjoins and practically is a suburb of the city of Cleveland. Its estimated population is between 5,000 and 10,000, and its area from 12 to 14 square miles, the greater part of which is farm lands or unimproved acreage. It lies, roughly, in the form of a parallelogram measuring approximately three and one-half miles each way. East and west it is traversed by three principal highways: Euclid Avenue, through the southerly border, St. Clair Avenue, through the central portion, and Lake Shore Boulevard, through the northerly border, in close proximity to the shore of Lake Erie. The Nickel Plate Railroad lies from 1,500 to 1,800 feet north of Euclid Avenue, and the Lake Shore Railroad 1,600 feet farther to the north. The three highways and the two railroads are substantially parallel.

Appellee is the owner of a tract of land containing 68 acres, situated in the westerly end of the village, abutting on Euclid Avenue to the south and the Nickel Plate Railroad to the north. Adjoining this tract, both on the east and on the west, there have been laid out restricted residential plats upon which residences have been erected.

On November 13, 1922, an ordinance was adopted by the village council, establishing a comprehensive zoning plan for regulating and restricting the location of trades, industries, apartment houses, two-family houses, single family houses, etc., the lot area to be built upon, the size and height of buildings, etc.

The entire area of the village is divided by the ordinance into six classes of use districts, denominated U-1 to U-6, inclusive; three classes of height districts, denominated H-1 to H-3, inclusive; and four classes of area districts, denominated A-1 to A-4, inclusive. The use districts are classified in respect of the buildings which may be erected within their respective limits, as follows: U-1 is restricted to single family dwellings, public parks, water towers and reservoirs, suburban and interurban electric railway passenger stations and rights of way, and farming, non-commercial greenhouse nurseries, and truck gardening; U-2 is extended to include two-family dwellings; U-3 is further extended to include apartment houses, hotels, churches, schools, public libraries, museums, private clubs, community center buildings, hospitals, sanitariums, public playgrounds, and recreation buildings, and a city hall and courthouse; U-4 is further extended to include banks, offices, studios, telephone exchanges, fire and police stations, restaurants, theaters and moving picture shows, retail stores and shops, sales offices, sample rooms, wholesale stores for hardware, drugs, and groceries, stations for gasoline and oil (not exceeding 1,000 gallons storage) and for ice delivery, skating rinks and dance halls, electric substations, job and newspaper printing, public garages for motor vehicles, stables and wagon sheds (not exceeding five horses, wagons or motor trucks), and distributing stations for central store and commercial enterprises; U-5 is further extended to include billboards and advertising signs (if permitted), warehouses, ice and ice cream manufacturing and cold storage plants, bottling works, milk bottling and central distribution stations, laundries, carpet cleaning, dry cleaning, and dyeing establishments, blacksmith, horseshoeing, wagon and motor vehicle repair shops, freight stations, street car barns, stables and wagon sheds (for more than five horses, wagons or motor trucks), and wholesale produce markets and salesroom; U-6 is further extended to include plants for sewage disposal and for producing gas, garbage and refuse incineration, scrap iron, junk, scrap paper, and rag storage, aviation fields, cemeteries, crematories, penal and correctional institutions, insane and feeble-minded institutions, storage of oil and gasoline (not to exceed 25,000 gallons), and manufacturing and industrial operations of any kind other than, and any public utility not included in, a class U-1, U-2, U-3, U-4, or U-5 use. There is a seventh class of uses which is prohibited altogether.

Class U-1 is the only district in which buildings are restricted to those enumerated. In the other classes the uses are cumulative-that is to say, uses in class U-2 include those enumerated in the preceding class U-1; class U-3 includes uses enumerated in the preceding classes, U-2, and U-1; and so on. In addition to the enumerated uses, the ordinance provides for accessory uses; that is, for uses customarily incident to the principal use, such as private garages. Many regulations are provided in respect of such accessory uses.

The height districts are classified as follows: In class H-1, buildings are limited to a height of two and one-half stories, or thirty-five feet; in class H-2, to 4 stories, or fifty feet; in class H-3, to eighty feet. To all of these, certain exceptions are made, as in the case of church spires, water tanks, etc.

The classification of area districts is: In A–1 districts, dwellings or apartment houses to accommodate more than one family must have at least 5,000 square feet for interior lots and at least 4,000 square feet for corner lots; in A–2 districts, the area must be at least 2,500 square feet for interior lots, and 2,000 square feet for corner lots; in A–3 districts, the limits are 1,250 and 1,000 square feet, respectively; in A–4 districts, the limits are 900 and 700 square feet, respectively. The ordinance contains, in great variety and detail, provisions in respect of width of lots, front, side, and rear yards, and other matters, including restrictions and regulations as to the use of billboards, signboards, and advertising signs.

A single family dwelling consists of a basement and not less than three rooms and a bathroom. A two-family dwelling consists of a basement and not less than four living rooms and a bathroom for each family, and is further described as a detached dwelling for the occupation of two families, one having its principal living rooms on the first floor and the other on the second floor.

Appellee's tract of land comes under U-2, U-3 and U-6. The first strip of 620 feet immediately north of Euclid Avenue falls in class U-2, the next 130 feet to the north, in U-3, and the remainder in U-6. The uses of the first 620 feet, therefore, do not include apartment houses, hotels, churches, schools, or other public and semipublic buildings, or other uses enumerated in respect of U-3 to U-6, inclusive. The uses of the next 130 feet include all of these, but exclude industries, theaters, banks, shops, and the various other uses set forth in respect of U-4 to U-6, inclusive.

Annexed to the ordinance, and made a part of it, is a zone map, showing the location and limits of the various use, height, and area districts, from which it appears that the three classes overlap one another; that is to say, for example, both U-5 and U-6 use districts are in A–4 area district, but the former is in H-2 and the latter in H-3 height districts. The plan is a complicated one, and can be better understood by an inspection of the map * * *

The lands lying between the two railroads for the entire length of the village area and extending some distance on either side to the north and south, having an average width of about 1,600 feet, are left open, with slight exceptions, for industrial and all other uses. This includes the larger part of appellee's tract. Approximately one-sixth of the area of the entire village is included in U-5 and U-6 use districts. That part of the village lying south of Euclid avenue is principally in U-1 districts. The lands lying north of Euclid Avenue and bordering on the long strip just described are included in U-1, U-2, U-3, and U-4 districts, principally in U-2.

Figure 9-12
Zoning of Properties near the Ambler Realty Tract

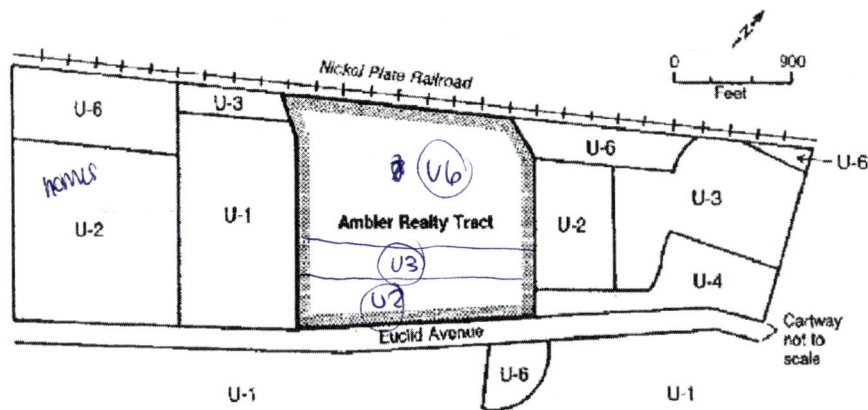

Source: Timothy Alan Fluck, *Euclid v. Ambler*: A Retrospective, 52 J. Am. Planning Ass'n 326, 329, Map 2 (Summer 1986).

The enforcement of the ordinance is entrusted to the inspector of buildings, under rules and regulations of the board of zoning appeals. Meetings of the board are public, and minutes of its proceedings are kept. It is authorized to adopt rules and regulations to carry into effect provisions of the ordinance. Decisions of the inspector of buildings may be appealed to the board by any person claiming to be adversely affected by any such decision. The board is given power in specific cases of practical difficulty or unnecessary hardship to interpret the ordinance in harmony with its general purpose and intent, so that the public health, safety and general welfare may be secure and substantial justice done. Penalties are prescribed for violations, and it is provided that the various provisions are to be regarded as independent and the holding of any provision to be unconstitutional, void or ineffective shall not affect any of the others.

The ordinance is assailed on the grounds that it is in derogation of § 1 of the Fourteenth Amendment to the Federal Constitution in that it deprives appellee of liberty and property without due process of law and denies it the equal protection of the law, and that it offends against certain provisions of the Constitution of the state of Ohio. The prayer of the bill is for an injunction restraining the enforcement of the ordinance and all attempts to impose or maintain as to appellee's property any of the restrictions, limitations or conditions. The court below held the ordinance to be unconstitutional and void, and enjoined its enforcement, 297 F. 307.

Before proceeding to a consideration of the case, it is necessary to determine the scope of the inquiry. The bill alleges that the tract of land in question is vacant and has been held for years for the purpose of selling and developing it for industrial uses, for which it is especially adapted, being immediately in the path of progressive industrial development;

*↓ market value
if used for
residential*

that for such uses it has a market value of about $10,000 per acre, but if the use be limited to residential purposes the market value is not in excess of $2,500 per acre; that the first 200 feet of the parcel back from Euclid Avenue, if unrestricted in respect of use, has a value of $150 per front foot, but if limited to residential uses, and ordinary mercantile business be excluded therefrom, its value is not in excess of $50 per front foot.

*appellee's
claims*

It is specifically averred that the ordinance attempts to restrict and control the lawful uses of appellee's land, so as to confiscate and destroy a great part of its value; that it is being enforced in accordance with its terms; that prospective buyers of land for industrial, commercial, and residential uses in the metropolitan district of Cleveland are deterred from buying any part of this land because of the existence of the ordinance and the necessity thereby entailed of conducting burdensome and expensive litigation in order to vindicate the right to use the land for lawful and legitimate purposes; that the ordinance constitutes a cloud upon the land, reduces and destroys its value, and has the effect of diverting the normal industrial, commercial, and residential development thereof to other and less favorable locations.

The record goes no farther than to show, as the lower court found, that the normal and reasonably to be expected use and development of that part of appellee's land adjoining Euclid Avenue is for general trade and commercial purposes, particularly retail stores and like establishments, and that the normal and reasonably to be expected use and development of the residue of the land is for industrial and trade purposes. Whatever injury is inflicted by the mere existence and threatened enforcement of the ordinance is due to restrictions in respect of these and similar uses, to which perhaps should be added—if not included in the foregoing—restrictions in respect of apartment houses. Specifically there is nothing in the record to suggest that any damage results from the presence in the ordinance of those restrictions relating to churches, schools, libraries, and other public and semipublic buildings.

*dismissing
arg. for those
uses*

It is neither alleged nor proved that there is or may be a demand for any part of appellee's land for any of the last-named uses, and we cannot assume the existence of facts which would justify an injunction upon this record in respect to this class of restrictions. For present purposes the provisions of the ordinance in respect of these uses may therefore be put aside as unnecessary to be considered. It is also unnecessary to consider the effect of the restrictions in respect of U-1 districts, since none of appellee's land falls within that class. * * *

Building zone laws are of modern origin. They began in this country about twenty-five years ago. Until recent years, urban life was comparatively simple; but, with the great increase and concentration of population, problems have developed, and constantly are developing, which require, and will continue to require, additional restrictions in respect of the use and occupation of private lands in urban communities.

Regulations, the wisdom, necessity, and validity of which, as applied to existing conditions, are so apparent that they are now uniformly sustained, a century ago, or even half a century ago, probably would have been rejected as arbitrary and oppressive. Such regulations are sustained, under the complex conditions of our day, for reasons analogous to those which justify traffic regulations, which, before the advent of automobiles and rapid transit street railways, would have been condemned as fatally arbitrary and unreasonable. And in this there is no inconsistency, for, while the meaning of constitutional guaranties never varies, the scope of their application must expand or contract to meet the new and different conditions which are constantly coming within the field of their operation. In a changing world it is impossible that it should be otherwise. But although a degree of elasticity is thus imparted, not to the *meaning*, but to the *application* of constitutional principles, statutes and ordinances, which, after giving due weight to the new conditions, are found clearly not to conform to the Constitution, of course, must fall.

court arg:
need to adjust scope of Const. to fit modern world

valid exercise of police power:
excercise →
→ MUST ARGUE that the zoning laws are against public welfare

The ordinance now under review, and all similar laws and regulations, must find their justification in some aspect of the police power, asserted for the public welfare. The line which in this field separates the legitimate from the illegitimate assumption of power is not capable of precise delimitation. It varies with circumstances and conditions. A regulatory zoning ordinance, which would be clearly valid as applied to the great cities, might be clearly invalid as applied to rural communities. In solving doubts, the maxim *sic utere tuo ut alienum non laedas*, which lies at the foundation of so much of the common law of nuisances, ordinarily will furnish a fairly helpful clew. And the law of nuisances, likewise, may be consulted, not for the purpose of controlling, but for the helpful aid of its analogies in the process of ascertaining the scope of, the power. Thus the question whether the power exists to forbid the erection of a building of a particular kind or for a particular use, like the question whether a particular thing is a nuisance, is to be determined, not by an abstract consideration of the building or of the thing considered apart, but by considering it in connection with the circumstances and the locality. A nuisance may be merely a right thing in the wrong place, like a pig in the parlor instead of the barnyard. If the validity of the legislative classification for zoning purposes be fairly debatable, the legislative judgment must be allowed to control.

key value:
use your prop. in a way that doesn't injure others

thus. must consider ordinances with their context

There is no serious difference of opinion in respect of the validity of laws and regulations fixing the height of buildings within reasonable limits, the character of materials and methods of construction, and the adjoining area which must be left open, in order to minimize the danger of fire or collapse, the evils of overcrowding and the like, and excluding from residential sections offensive trades, industries and structures likely to create nuisances.

generally agreed upon zoning provs.

Here, however, the exclusion is in general terms of all industrial establishments, and it may thereby happen that not only offensive or dangerous industries will be excluded, but those which are neither offensive nor dangerous will share the same fate. But this is no more than happens in respect of many practice-forbidding laws which this court has upheld, although drawn in general terms so as to include individual cases that may turn out to be innocuous in themselves. The inclusion of a reasonable margin, to insure effective enforcement, will not put upon a law, otherwise valid, the stamp of invalidity. Such laws may also find their justification in the fact that, in some fields, the bad fades into the good by such insensible degrees that the two are not capable of being readily distinguished and separated in terms of legislation. In the light of these considerations, we are not prepared to say that the end in view was not sufficient to justify the general rule of the ordinance, although some industries of an innocent character might fall within the proscribed class. It cannot be said that the ordinance in this respect "passes the bounds of reason and assumes the character of a merely arbitrary fiat." Purity Extract Co. v. Lynch, 226 U.S. 192, 204 (1912). Moreover, the restrictive provisions of the ordinance in this particular may be sustained upon the principles applicable to the broader exclusion from residential districts of all business and trade structures, presently to be discussed.

It is said that the village of Euclid is a mere suburb of the city of Cleveland; that the industrial development of that city has now reached and in some degree extended into the village, and in the obvious course of things will soon absorb the entire area for industrial enterprises; that the effect of the ordinance is to divert this natural development elsewhere, with the consequent loss of increased values to the owners of the lands within the village borders. But the village, though physically a suburb of Cleveland, is politically a separate municipality, with powers of its own and authority to govern itself as it sees fit, within the limits of the organic law of its creation and the state and federal Constitutions. Its governing authorities, presumably representing a majority of its inhabitants and voicing their will, have determined, not that industrial development shall cease at its boundaries, but that the course of such development shall proceed within definitely fixed lines. If it be a proper exercise of the police power to relegate industrial establishments to localities separated from residential sections, it is not easy to find a sufficient reason for denying the power because the effect of its exercise is to divert an industrial flow from the course which it would follow, to the injury of the residential public, if left alone, to another course where such injury will be obviated. It is not meant by this, however, to exclude the possibility of cases where the general public interest would so far outweigh the interest of the municipality that the municipality would not be allowed to stand in the way.

We find no difficulty in sustaining restrictions of the kind thus far reviewed. The serious question in the case arises over the provisions of the ordinance excluding from residential districts apartment houses, business houses, retail stores and shops, and other like establishments.

This question involves the validity of what is really the crux of the more recent zoning legislation, namely, the creation and maintenance of residential districts, from which business and trade of every sort, including hotels and apartment houses, are excluded. Upon that question this court has not thus far spoken. The decisions of the state courts are numerous and conflicting; but those which broadly sustain the power greatly outnumber those which deny it altogether or narrowly limit it, and it is very apparent that there is a constantly increasing tendency in the direction of the broader view. * * *

The matter of zoning has received much attention at the hands of commissions and experts, and the results of their investigations have been set forth in comprehensive reports. These reports which bear every evidence of painstaking consideration, concur in the view that the segregation of residential, business and industrial buildings will make it easier to provide fire apparatus suitable for the character and intensity of the development in each section; that it will increase the safety and security of home life, greatly tend to prevent street accidents, especially to children, by reducing the traffic and resulting confusion in residential sections, decrease noise and other conditions which produce or intensify nervous disorders, preserve a more favorable environment in which to rear children, etc. With particular reference to apartment houses, it is pointed out that the development of detached house sections is greatly retarded by the coming of apartment houses, which has sometimes resulted in destroying the entire section for private house purposes; that in such sections very often the apartment house is a mere parasite, constructed in order to take advantage of the open spaces and attractive surroundings created by the residential character of the district. Moreover, the coming of one apartment house is followed by others, interfering by their height and bulk with the free circulation of air and monopolizing the rays of the sun which otherwise would fall upon the smaller homes, and bringing, as their necessary accompaniments, the disturbing noises incident to increased traffic and business, and the occupation, by means of moving and parked automobiles, of larger portions of the streets, thus detracting from their safety and depriving children of the privilege of quiet and open spaces for play, enjoyed by those in more favored localities,—until, finally, the residential character of the neighborhood and its desirability as a place of detached residences are utterly destroyed. Under these circumstances, apartment houses, which in a different environment would be not only entirely unobjectionable but highly desirable, come very near to being nuisances.

If these reasons, thus summarized, do not demonstrate the wisdom or sound policy in all respects of those restrictions which we have indicated as pertinent to the inquiry, at least, the reasons are sufficiently cogent to preclude us from saying, as it must be said before the ordinance can be declared unconstitutional, that such provisions are clearly arbitrary and unreasonable, having no substantial relation to the public health, safety, morals, or general welfare.

It is true that when, if ever, the provisions set forth in the ordinance in tedious and minute detail, come to be concretely applied to particular premises, including those of the appellee, or to particular conditions, or to be considered in connection with specific complaints, some of them, or even many of them, may be found to be clearly arbitrary and unreasonable. But where the equitable remedy of injunction is sought, as it is here, not upon the ground of a present infringement or denial of a specific right, or of a particular injury in process of actual execution, but upon the broad ground that the mere existence and threatened enforcement of the ordinance, by materially and adversely affecting values and curtailing the opportunities of the market, constitute a present and irreparable injury, the court will not scrutinize its provisions, sentence by sentence, to ascertain by a process of piecemeal dissection whether there may be, here and there, provisions of a minor character, or relating to matters of administration, or not shown to contribute to the injury complained of, which, if attacked separately, might not withstand the test of constitutionality. In respect of such provisions, of which specific complaint is not made, it cannot be said that the landowner has suffered or is threatened with an injury which entitles him to challenge their constitutionality. * * *

The relief sought here is of the same character, namely, an injunction against the enforcement of any of the restrictions, limitations, or conditions of the ordinance. And the gravamen of the complaint is that a portion of the land of the appellee cannot be sold for certain enumerated uses because of the general and broad restraints of the ordinance. What would be the effect of a restraint imposed by one or more of the innumerable provisions of the ordinance, considered apart, upon the value or marketability of the lands, is neither disclosed by the bill nor by the evidence, and we are afforded no basis, apart from mere speculation, upon which to rest a conclusion that it or they would have any appreciable effect upon those matters. Under these circumstances, therefore, it is enough for us to determine, as we do, that the ordinance in its general scope and dominant features, so far as its provisions are here involved, is a valid exercise of authority, leaving other provisions to be dealt with as cases arise directly involving them.

And this is in accordance with the traditional policy of this Court. In the realm of constitutional law, especially, this Court has perceived the embarrassment which is likely to result from an attempt to formulate rules or decide questions beyond the necessities of the immediate issue. It has preferred to follow the method of a gradual approach to the general by a systematically guarded application and extension of constitutional principles to particular cases as they arise, rather than by out of hand attempts to establish general rules to which future cases must be fitted. This process applies with peculiar force to the solution of questions arising under the due process clause of the Constitution as applied to the exercise of the flexible powers of police, with which we are here concerned.

Decree reversed.

■ MR. JUSTICE VAN DEVANTER, MR. JUSTICE MCREYNOLDS, and MR. JUSTICE BUTLER dissent.

NOTES AND QUESTIONS

1. Euclid's scheme involved cumulative zoning; that is, the ordinance defined a hierarchy of uses, roughly from most sensitive and least invasive to those that are least sensitive but most objectionable to others. In any zone of a given level, one can have uses of that level or any "higher" use. Thus, as in Euclid, one could if one wished build a residence in an industrial zone but not vice versa. By contrast, in noncumulative zoning one can only have enumerated uses in any given zone. So unless it happened to be an allowable mixture, one would not be permitted to build a residence in an industrial zone. Which scheme is preferable in your view?

2. As with any scheme there is some limit as to how finegrained zoning can be, in an ex ante sense. As we saw in the case of area-wide covenants, borders between areas or zones tend to present problems. In Euclid, before the zoning, residences on the edge of the zone might be less desirable because of the prospect of nearby industry. In fact, the zoning in some sense creates the reverse "externality" at the zoning border (the actual border being within the tract that straddles the border), in that the restriction to residences makes nearby valuable industrial use less viable. Ambler wanted to use the entire tract for industrial use, but the owners of the residential tracts wanted to see industrial development nearby blocked. What would a unitary owner of all the land in the area likely want to do? Incidentally, under the pressure of wartime industrial mobilization Euclid later rezoned the entire area for industrial use and a GM plant long occupied the site after World War II. Since 1999 a portion of the by then shut-down plant was converted into a sports facility, and the area now features a mixture of commercial, industrial, and residential uses. See Ellickson et al., supra, at 112.

3. When land-use regulations are analyzed—especially under the Takings Clause, as we will see—analogies are often drawn to nuisance. Although nuisance law itself is not the primary tool of externality-control these days, it forms for better or worse a common vocabulary and possible baseline for evaluating the bads that stem from land use. *Euclid* is no exception. What do you think of Justice Sutherland's invocation of the notion of nuisance? Are apartment houses nuisances? Are duplexes (U-2) nuisances to owners of single-family homes (U-1)? For that matter, why do you think Justice Sutherland, one of the "Four Horsemen" of the pre-1937 Supreme Court, would uphold the zoning scheme here at issue in the face of the claims of a private property owner? See Barry Cushman, The Secret Lives of the Four Horsemen, 83 Va. L. Rev. 559 (1997) (arguing that the Four Horsemen were "closet liberals"). The other Horsemen (Justices Butler, McReynolds,

and Van Devanter) were in dissent in *Euclid*. For a summary of views on Sutherland's reasons, see Ellickson et al., supra, at 110.

4.   Are apartment buildings "parasites," as Justice Sutherland would have it? By contrast, the trial court in *Euclid* was highly critical of the exclusionary and class-segregating aspect of zoning. The ordinance was innovative in keeping out apartment buildings, with the result of segregation by class and race. By upholding this kind of zoning, the Supreme Court's decision made zoning an available tool for exclusion. On the background of racial zoning in the Cleveland area in this era and the attitudes of those involved in the *Euclid* case, see William M. Randle, Professors, Reformers, Bureaucrats, and Cronies: The Players in *Euclid v. Ambler*, in Zoning and the American Dream 31, 38–43 (Charles M. Haar & Jerrold S. Kayden eds., 1989).

5.   After *Euclid* and *Nectow v. City of Cambridge*, 277 U.S. 183 (1928) (striking down on due process grounds the residential designation of a parcel pursuant to zoning), the Supreme Court has had little to say about the constitutionality of zoning schemes under the Takings and Due Process Clauses. Much more happens at the state level, under state constitutions, and state courts vary greatly in how deferential they are to local zoning authorities. For example, Illinois and Pennsylvania are stricter than most about due process in the area of zoning.

6.   Zoning is not the only public tool of land-use control. Also important are subdivision controls, which regulate new subdivisions, and prescribe features of streets, utility lines, and other public infrastructure and amenities—and deal with more obvious externalities. Environmental laws and regulations can have major consequences for land use. Federal environmental laws like the Clean Water Act or Endangered Species Act can limit use of parcels. And some states require environmental impact statements for major new developments.

Nonconforming Uses

Zoning ordinances typically grandfather nonconforming uses of property in existence when a zoning scheme is enacted. For example, a commercial establishment in a residential area will be allowed to continue. Widespread intuition has it that once a use of property is established it becomes a "vested right." In contrast, before a zoning law is adopted an owner of undeveloped land has no vested right to any particular type of use, nor does the owner of property dedicated to a particular use have a vested right to switch to a different use. However poorly articulated and defended these assumptions may be, they have become established points of reference in zoning law.

Harbison v. City of Buffalo

Court of Appeals of New York, 1958.
152 N.E.2d 42.

■ FROESSEL, JUDGE. Petitioner Andrew Harbison, Sr., purchased certain real property located at 35 Cumberland Avenue in the city of Buffalo on January 5, 1924. Shortly thereafter he erected a 30-by 40-foot frame building thereon, and commenced operating a cooperage business, which, with his son, he has continued to date. The building has not been enlarged, and the volume of petitioners' business is stated to be the same now as then. The only difference is that, whereas petitioners formerly dealt mainly with wooden barrels, they now recondition, clean and paint "used" steel drums or barrels. No issue of that difference is made here. These drums, or barrels, are stacked to a height of about 10 feet in the yard, and on an average day about 600 or 700 barrels are stored there.

When petitioner Andrew Harbison, Sr., established his business in 1924, the street upon which it was located was an unpaved extension of an existing street, the city operated a dump in the area, and there was a glue factory in the vicinity. At the present time, the glue factory has gone, and there are residences adjoining both sides of petitioners' property and across the street. The change in the surrounding area is reflected by the fact that in 1924 the land was unzoned, but since 1926 (except for the period between 1949 and 1953, when it was zoned for business), the land has been zoned for residential use; and it is presently in an "R3" dwelling district.

Thus it is clear that at the time of the enactment of the first zoning ordinance affecting the premises, petitioners had an existing nonconforming use, that is, the conduct of a cooperage business in a residential zone. In 1936, under an ordinance which included the operations of petitioners in a definition of "junk dealers", petitioners applied for and received a license to carry on their business. Licenses were obtained by petitioners every year from 1936 through the fiscal year of 1956.

However, the ordinances of the City of Buffalo were amended, effective as of July 30, 1953, so as to state in chapter LXX (§ 18): "1. Continuing existing uses: Except as provided in this section, any non-conforming use of any building, structure, land or premises may be continued. Provided, however, that on premises situate in any 'R' district each use which is not a conforming use in the 'R5' district and which falls into one of the categories hereinafter enumerated shall cease or shall be changed to a conforming use within 3 years from the effective date of this amended chapter. The requirements of this subdivision for the termination of non-conforming uses shall apply in each of the following cases: * * * (d) Any junk yard'" (Defined in § 23, subd. 24.).

On November 27, 1956 the director of licenses of the City of Buffalo sent a letter to petitioners stating: "At a meeting of the Common Council under date of November 13, 1956 * * * [it] evinced its intention not to amend to modify the provisions of Chapter 18, Subdivision I of Chapter LXX of the Ordinances relation to non-conforming uses by junk yards * * * in 'R' districts. * * * you are hereby notified to discontinue the operation of your junk yard * * * at once". A subsequent application by petitioners for a wholesale junk license and one for a "drum reconditioning license" were refused on the ground that "said premises lie within an area zoned as 'R3' Dwelling District * * * and the operation of a junk yard and the outside storage of used materials is prohibited therein." Petitioners then brought this article 78 proceeding in the nature of mandamus in which they sought an order directing the city to issue a wholesale junk license to them, and the lower courts sustained them.

On this appeal, the City of Buffalo argues * * * that the ordinance, held invalid by the courts below, is a valid exercise of the police power. * * *

In the major point involved on this appeal, the city argues that the ordinance requiring the termination of petitioners' nonconforming use of the premises as a junk yard within three years of the date of said ordinance is a valid exercise of its police power. Its claim is not based on the theory of nuisance, and indeed this record contains little evidence as to the manner of operation of petitioners' business and the nature of the surrounding neighborhood. Rather, in this case, the city bases its claim largely on out-of-State decisions which have sustained ordinances requiring the termination of nonconforming uses or structures after a period of permitted continuance, where such "amortization" period was held reasonable.

When zoning ordinances are initially adopted to limit permissible uses of property, or when property is rezoned so as to prevent uses of property previously allowed, a degree of protection is constitutionally required to be given owners of property then using their premises in a manner forbidden by the ordinance. Thus we have held that, where substantial expenditures were made in the commencement of the erection of a building, a zoning ordinance may not deprive the owner of the "vested right" to complete the structure (People ex rel. Ortenberg v. Bales, 166 N.E. 339 (N.Y. 1929); see City of Buffalo v. Chadeayne, 31 N.E. 443, 443–44 (N.Y. (1892)). So, where the owner already has structures on the premises, he cannot be directed to cease using them, just as he has the right to continue a prior business carried on there.

However, where the benefit to the public has been deemed of greater moment than the detriment to the property owner, we have sustained the prohibition of continuation of prior nonconforming uses. These cases involved the prior use of property for parking lots. We have also upheld the restriction of projected uses of the property where, at the time of passage of the ordinance, there had been no substantial investment in the nonconforming use. In these cases, there is no doubt that the property owners incurred a loss in the value of their property and otherwise as a result of the fact that they were unable to carry out their prospective uses; but we held that such a deprivation was not violative of the owners' constitutional rights. In *People v. Miller*, 106 N.E.2d 34, 35 (N.Y. 1952), we explained these cases by stating that they involved situations in which the property owners would sustain only a "relatively slight and insubstantial" loss.

It should be noted that even where the zoning authorities may not prohibit a prior nonconforming use, they may adopt regulations which restrict the right of the property owner to enlarge or extend the use or to rebuild or make alterations to the structures on the property.

As these cases indicate, our approach to the problem of permissible restrictions on nonconforming uses has recognized that, while the benefit accruing to the public in terms of more complete and effective zoning does not justify the immediate destruction of substantial businesses or structures developed or built prior to the ordinance (People v. Miller, 106 N.E.2d at 35), the policy of zoning embraces the concept of the ultimate elimination of nonconforming uses, and thus the courts favor reasonable restriction of them. But, where the zoning ordinance could have required the cessation of a sand and gravel business on one year's notice, we have held it unconstitutional (Town of Somers v. Camarco, 127 N.E.2d 327 (N.Y. 1955)).

The development of the policy that nonconforming uses should be protected and their existence preserved at the stage of development existing at the time of passage of the ordinance seems to have been based upon the assumption that the ultimate ends of zoning would be accomplished as the nonconforming use terminated with time. But this has not proven to be the case, as commentators have noted that the tendency of many of these uses is to flourish capitalizing on the fact that no new use of that nature could be begun in the area. Because of this situation, communities have sought new forms of ordinances restricting nonconforming uses, and in particular have turned to provisions which require termination after a given period of time.

With the exception of a decision of the Ohio Supreme Court (which may be explained on the basis of the particular language and application of the ordinance) * * * the decisions have sustained ordinances where the time provided was held reasonable[.] * * *

A number of States and municipal bodies have adopted statutes authorizing this approach to the problem (as e. g., Ill.Ann.Stat., S.H.A., ch. 24, § 73–1; 3 Va.Code (1950), § 15–843); and the textwriters generally express the opinion that they would be constitutional if reasonable (1 Antieau on Municipal Corporation Law, § 7.03(3); Bassett on Zoning, pp. 115–116; 8 McQuillin on Municipal Corporations (3d ed.), § 25.190). Bassett, in his text on Zoning, states (p. 115) that "Several ordinances in Long Island provide (for) * * * the ousting of automobile junk yards with accessory buildings * * * the owner being given from three to six years to amortize."

Leaving aside eminent domain and nuisance, we have often stated in our decisions that the owner of land devoted to a prior nonconforming use, or on which a prior nonconforming structure exists (or has been substantially commenced), has the right to continue such use, but we have never held that this right may continue virtually in perpetuity. Now that we are for the first time squarely faced with the problem as to whether or not this right may be terminated after a reasonable period, during which the owner may have a fair opportunity to amortize his investment and to make future plans, we conclude that it may be, in accordance with the overwhelming weight of authority found in the courts of our sister States, as well as with the textwriters and commentators who have expressed themselves upon the subject.

With regard to prior nonconforming *structures*, reasonable termination periods based upon the amortized life of the structure are not, in our opinion, unconstitutional. They do not compel the immediate destruction of the improvements, but envision and allow for their normal life without extensive alterations or repairs. Such a regulation is akin to those we have sustained relating to restrictions upon the extension or substantial repair or replacement of prior nonconforming structures.

As to prior nonconforming *uses*, the closest case we have had is Town of Somers v. Camarco, 127 N.E.2d 327, supra. In that case we held that, in view of defendant's investment and the business which had been built up and carried on over the years, the provisions of the ordinance which required defendant to apply for a permit to continue its business every year, and provided further that on the termination of any approval period any structure or improvement on the premises could be ordered removed and the premises restored to their original condition as nearly as practicable, were unreasonable. There the land involved had unusual resources which made it especially suitable for the nonconforming use carried on; the improvements were necessary for the operation of the business, and the period of termination was unreasonably short. Under these circumstances the ordinance would have deprived the property owner of his "vested rights". As was pointed out in the opinion (127 N.E.2d at 328), "The courts, in order to afford stability to property owners who do have existing nonconforming uses, have imposed the test of reasonableness upon such exercise of the police powers. Therefore broad general rules and tests, such as expressed in People v. Miller, 304 N.Y. 105, 106 N.E.2d 34, must always be considered in this context."

If, therefore, a zoning ordinance provides a sufficient period of permitted nonconformity, it may further provide that at the end of such period the use must cease. This rule is analogous to that with respect to nonconforming structures. In ascertaining the reasonable period during which an owner of property must be allowed to continue a nonconforming use, a balance must be found between social harm and private injury. We cannot say that a legislative body may not in any case, after consideration of the factors involved, conclude that the termination of a use after a period of time sufficient to allow a property owner an opportunity to amortize his investment and make other plans is a valid method of solving the problem.

To enunciate a contrary rule would mean that the use of land for such purposes as a tennis court, an open air skating rink, a junk yard or a parking lot—readily transferable to another site—at the date of the enactment of a zoning ordinance vests the owner thereof with the right to utilize the land in that manner in perpetuity, regardless of the changes in the neighborhood over the course of time. In the light of our ever expanding urban communities, such a rule appears to us to constitute an unwarranted restriction upon the Legislature in dealing with what has been described as "One of the major problems in effective administration of modern zoning ordinances" (1951 Wis.L.Rev. 685). When the termination provisions are reasonable in the light of the nature of the business of the property owner, the improvements erected on the land, the character of the neighborhood, and the detriment caused the property owner, we may not hold them constitutionally invalid.

In the present case, the two lower courts have expressed the view that, "Whatever the law may be in California or Florida or other jurisdictions, in this State" no regulation infringing at any time the perpetual right of an owner to continue a prior nonconforming use is valid. Accordingly, neither court considered the question of whether the particular period prescribed by the ordinance was reasonable under the facts of this case.

Their conclusion is not in accord with the general rule applicable to protection of nonconforming uses as stated in *People v. Miller*, 106 N.E.2d 34, 35, supra. In that case we decided that where the enforcement of an ordinance requiring the termination of a prior nonconforming use caused "relatively slight and insubstantial" loss to the property owner, it would be constitutional. While it is true that the ordinance there involved did not have an "amortization" provision, nevertheless the general test enunciated is no less germane when such a provision is included in the ordinance. As previously pointed out, the period of "amortization" allowed by the ordinance is a crucial factor in determining whether the ordinance has been constitutionally applied in a given case.

Here, petitioners are engaged in the business of reconditioning barrels or used steel drums. We are told that the value of the property together with the improvements is $20,000; but there is no indication of the relative value of the land and improvements separately. It was further alleged that the improvement consists of a 30- by 40-foot frame building erected in 1924, and, in addition thereto, petitioners claim that at the insistence of the City of Buffalo, three years before the ordinance went into effect, they were obliged to install a special sewage system at a cost of $2,000 and a boiler at a cost of $700.

Material triable issues of fact thus remain, and a further hearing should adduce evidence relating to the nature of the surrounding neighborhood, the value and condition of the improvements on the premises, the nearest area to which petitioners might relocate, the cost of such relocation, as well as any other reasonable costs which bear upon the kind and amount of damages which petitioners might sustain, and whether petitioners might be able to continue operation of their business if not allowed to continue storage of barrels or steel drums outside their frame building. It is only upon such evidence that it may be ascertained whether the resultant injury to petitioners would be so substantial that the ordinance would be unconstitutional as applied to the particular facts of this case.

The order of the Appellate Division should be reversed, without costs, and the matter remanded to Special Term for a trial of the material issues and further proceedings as outlined in this opinion.

■ VAN VOORHIS, JUDGE (dissenting). The decision which is about to be rendered marks, in my view, the beginning of the end of the constitutional protection of property rights in this State in pre-existing nonconforming uses under zoning ordinances. Special Term and the Appellate Division unanimously followed the existing law in holding this amendment to the zoning ordinance of the City of Buffalo to be unconstitutional. In my view the traditional rule is right, and should not be abrogated. * * *

The phraseology of this 1953 zoning amendment is important. It reads as follows:

"§ 18. Non-conforming uses and buildings. 1. Continuing existing uses: Except as provided in this section, any non-conforming use of any building, structure, land or premises may be continued. Provided, however, that on premises situate in any 'R' district each use which is not a conforming use in the 'R5' district and which falls into one of the categories hereinafter enumerated shall cease or shall be changed to a conforming use within 3 years from the effective date of this amended chapter. The requirements of this subdivision for the termination of non-conforming uses shall apply in each of the following cases:

"(a) Any such non-conforming use involving the use of land only and not accessory to an adjacent building or structure assessed as a real estate improvement.

"(b) Any such non-conforming use involving the use of or accessory to one or more buildings or structures on the same lot, the aggregate assessed value of which improvements for tax purposes is not more than five hundred dollars ($500.00).

"(c) Any such non-conforming use consisting of a sign.

"(d) Any junk yard, auto wrecking or dismantling establishment." * * *

The plaintiffs' business [is] being confiscated, as has been mentioned, not on the basis that the improvements are assessed within

$500, but regardless of how much the improvements may be worth. It is being terminated under the language of this ordinance for the sole reason that it is classified as a junk yard. I agree with what was said by the Appellate Division (169 N.Y.S.2d 599) that "Whatever the law may be in California or Florida or other jurisdictions, in this state, the rule is as stated in People v. Miller, 304 N.Y. 105, 107, 109, 106 N.E.2d 34, 35, to wit: 'It is the law of this state that non-conforming uses or structures, in existence when a zoning ordinance is enacted, are, as a general rule, constitutionally protected and will be permitted to continue, notwithstanding the contrary provision of the ordinance.' " Not less than nine cases are cited in our opinion in People v. Miller, 106 N.E.2d 34 (N.Y. 1952), as authority for this statement (106 N.E.2d at 34). Plaintiffs' business is not a nuisance. It is not injurious to life or health or morals. The neighbors whose sensibilities are offended would have found difficulty in abating it (even if it were a nuisance) for the reason that they "came to the nuisance," in the time honored phrase, by purchasing and moving into the neighborhood while petitioners' business was in operation. Neither, in my mind, can the city abolish this business under this ordinance. Even if this case came under the clause abrogating nonconforming uses where the buildings or structures on the lot do not exceed $500 in assessed value, the ordinance would still be unconstitutional. Zoning relates to the future development of municipalities. Areas in cities that have already been developed cannot be zoned retroactively. That is the function of municipal redevelopment, which is constitutionally authorized by statutes directing payment of just compensation for property that is appropriated. It is arbitrary, in my view, to draw the line at buildings or structures valued at $500 or less. That sum is negligible in the case of large stores or factories, whereas it may represent the savings of years to small proprietors. If the line can be drawn at $500, it will soon be extended to $5,000 or perhaps to $50,000. If, in principle, the city is allowed to confiscate property without payment of just compensation, it is no answer to say that it is taking only $500. It would be a novel proposition that a municipality can take private property for a public use without compensation provided that it does not take too much. Retroactive zoning, as this clearly is, resembles slum clearance more than zoning, which is for the future. If $500 is so small an amount, then why should not the city be obliged to pay it before confiscating this use, by the same token whereby it would be required to pay just compensation in cases of slum clearance? That there is no existing statutory authority to make such a payment in this case is not justification for confiscating the prior use which is a vested right. It would be no answer to argue that the small businessman does not need to be compensated provided that he is small enough. No such rule as that can be applied in zoning administration. If any distinction of that kind were relevant, it would be more appropriate to be guided by what proportion of the businessman's assets have been invested in improvements to his property. Observing the vagaries of modern zoning, many a businessman (large or small) might properly hesitate to invest his life savings in a store or other commercial or industrial property knowing that his investment is liable to be expropriated after the enterprise has been successfully launched, if some pressure group succeeds in obtaining favorable action from a municipal legislature. That is not in the public interest. Constitutional security against such developments is infinitely more important to the public at large than the occasional presence of a nonconforming use, or the possibility that a nonconforming use may acquire some advantage by way of monopoly in the use district. * * *

In this instance, as has been said, the limitation to $500 assessed valuation in this zoning ordinance does not apply. Petitioners come under a different subdivision which outlaws after three years "Any junk yard, auto wrecking or dismantling establishment." * * *

The circumstance that this is a cooperage establishment or junk yard ought not to obscure that the principle of the decision applies to any kind of business which, due to lapse of time, has been overtaken by changes in the neighborhood. The principle of the decision applies equally to stores, shops or service organizations which are retroactively legislated out of existence by the abolition of prior nonconforming uses. If petitioners' establishment is not secure against this kind of invasion, no one else's business is better protected. The neighbors or the officials of a municipality in one year may look askance at a junk or cooperage yard, and in another year may frown upon the conduct in a particular locality of any other type of commerce or industry. The people who moved into petitioners' vicinity and now find their business offensive may not be aware that the principle of this decision unsettles their own property rights, and that it may suddenly be used against them in unexpected ways if agitation arises to legislate them out of business by a similar procedure. It makes little difference what the nature of their businesses may be. The smaller they are the more vulnerable they become to this kind of attack, which is based on the misfortune of unpopularity. Democracy depends upon respect for the individual as well as upon majority rule. The relaxation of constitutional safeguards protecting commonly accepted personal and property rights, goes hand in hand with the multiplication of pressure groups. People should not be obliged to organize to preserve rights the safeguarding of which is the proper function of law. The small manufacturer or merchant feels this acutely, since he ordinarily finds it more difficult to succeed in wielding organized power for his own protection when property rights depend upon the discretion of legislative bodies. No question is raised here concerning the good faith of the enactment or administration of this ordinance. Nevertheless petitioners find themselves confronted by the organized civil power of the municipality, set in motion by the complaints of their neighbors who wish to eliminate them from the locality in which petitioners settled first. If this part of the city is to be redeveloped, it should be done through the enactment of a statute similar in principle to slum clearance acts, whereby just compensation can be paid for private property that is confiscated for a public use. Petitioners have well-recognized legal property rights which ought to be protected in court.

Zoning, as originally conceived, related to the future development of municipalities. It was not an attempt to reconstruct the past. Cases such as Village of Euclid v. Ambler Realty Co., 272 U.S. 365 (1926), and Lincoln Trust Co. v. Williams Bldg. Corp., 128 N.E. 209 (N.Y. 1920), were decided in this frame of reference. Pre-existing nonconforming uses were uniformly excepted from the operation of zoning ordinances, and the proprietors thereof were held to have the constitutional right to continue such uses. We are now told that the protection of nonconforming uses in the beginning was a [stratagem] of city planners, "prompted by a fear that the courts would hold unconstitutional any zoning ordinance which attempted to eliminate existing nonconforming uses." (1951 Wis.L.Rev. 685; 35 Va.L.R. 352, citing Bassett on Zoning, p. 108, n. 1; also Noel, Retroactive Zoning and Nuisances, 41 Col.L.Rev. 457, 473.) The Virginia Law Review note, citing these authorities, states: "Those who led the zoning movement in its early stages adopted a lenient attitude towards nonconforming buildings. They did so because they did not wish to arouse the animosity of a large segment of property owners at a time when opposition might have jeopardized the whole success of zoning." The reasoning of these and other commentators, and of some decisions in other States, is that all zoning interferes with property rights to some degree, even in case of unused vacant land, and that now another step should be taken by eliminating pre-existing uses which were formerly held to constitute vested property rights * * *

In practice this spells confusion, instability, inability to diagnose what are legal rights, inconsistency, arbitrariness and discrimination in administrative and court decisions, and an avalanche of litigation. That Pandora's box is opened, regardless of the best possible intentions on the part of all concerned. Nor is the judgment appealed from an unwarranted interference by the courts in the province of the municipal legislature. It simply follows precedent from the beginning of zoning practice. The new rule has the additional infirmity that it opens wide new fields of discretion in administrative law without any workable standards by which it is to be guided.

The lack of any principle in applying the novel theory of "amortization" betrays a fundamental weakness in the theory. Zoning, like other public programs, is not always best administered at the hands of its enthusiasts. The existence of non-conforming uses has spoiled the symmetry in the minds of zoning experts. It has bulked so large in this context that, desirable as the elimination of nonconforming uses may be, it has sometimes been presented as though it were more important than ordinary property rights. "Many means of eliminating and controlling nonconforming uses have been proposed and tried. Among these means are retroactive zoning, amortization of nonconforming uses, abatement of nonconforming uses as nuisances, public purchase and eminent domain, prohibition of the resumption of a non-conforming use after a period of discontinuance, and refusal to provide governmental services to nonconforming users" (1951 Wis.L.Rev. 687). This Wisconsin Law Review article points out how most of these different proposals have been tried and found wanting, particularly the method by exercising the power of eminent domain which is said to have been discarded mainly for the reason that it is too expensive. The same is said at page 93 of Volume 102 of the Pennsylvania Law Review. The fault found with eminent domain is that it failed to achieve the object of destroying the owner's right in his property without paying for it. Consequently the most promising legal theory at the moment is known as "amortization". * * *

This theory to justify extinguishing nonconforming uses means less the more one thinks about it. It offers little more promise of ultimate success than the other theories which have been tried and abandoned. In the first place, the periods of time vary so widely in the cases which have been cited from different States where it has been tried, and have so little relation to the useful lives of the structures, that this theory cannot be used to reconcile these discordant decisions. Moreover the term "amortization", as thus employed, had not the same meaning which it carries in law or accounting. It is not even used by analogy. It is just a catch phrase, and the reasoning is reduced to argument by metaphor. Not only has no effort been made in the reported cases where this theory has been applied to determine what is the useful life of the structure, but almost all were decided under ordinances or statutes which prescribe the same time limit for many different kinds of improvements. This demonstrates that it is not attempted to measure the life of the particular building or type of building, and that the word "amortization" is used as an empty shibboleth. This comment applies to the ordinance at issue on this appeal. There could be no presumption that all junk yards, all auto wrecking or dismantling establishments, and all improvements assessed for tax purposes at not more than $500 will or have any tendency to depreciate to zero in three years. This shows that the ordinance in suit could not possibly have been based on the amortization theory.

Moreover this theory, if it were seriously advanced, would imply that the owner should not keep up his property by making necessary replacements to restore against the ravages of time. Such replacements would be money thrown away. The amortization theory would thus encourage owners of nonconforming uses to allow them to decay and become slums.

Although the courts of other States are divided on this question, the better reason seems to me to be on the side of the rule heretofore established in this State, wherefore I vote to affirm. * * *

Order reversed, etc.

NOTES AND QUESTIONS

1. The problem of nonconforming uses is more of an issue in older cities. The accommodation here is narrow; usually a zoning ordinance forbids a change of one nonconforming use to another. Some schemes allow a change to a "higher" nonconforming use. Originally it was thought that nonconforming uses would disappear fairly quickly as buildings aged and fell into disrepair. This did not always happen. One possible reason is that having the only use of a kind in an area is often valuable. Being the only bar in a residential neighborhood is advantageous to the bar owner. Eminent domain (taking the right to the specific use or taking ownership of the parcel) is a potential solution, but as noted in the dissent in *Harbison*, compensation must be paid. "Amortization" or phasing out the use is another solution that does not involve compensation. Some states do not allow it, see, e.g., PA Northwestern Distributors, Inc. v. Zoning Hearing Board, 584 A.2d 1372 (Pa. 1991), and others do, using a multi-factor test as in the principal case.

2. What is the difference between a use already undertaken and one only planned, or even merely potential? In terms of efficiency? Fairness? If, as Harold Demsetz argues (see Chapter III), the owner acts as a broker between the future and the present, should there be any difference between a use the owner has in mind and one she has invested in developing already? Or does an aversion to depriving an owner of an actual use reflect the psychology of ownership? Should it? Should uses that reflect personhood property in Margaret Jane Radin's sense (see Chapter III) get more protection than other uses? For an argument that the distinction between existing and future uses is not justified, see Christopher Serkin, Existing Uses and the Limits of Land Use Regulation, 84 N.Y.U. L. Rev. 1222 (2009).

3. Amortization may be prohibited or constrained by state constitutions or statutes, especially zoning enabling acts. Uncertainty sometimes lingers about whether amortization may be found to be a taking. Many of the themes here—nuisance, investment-backed uses, compensation, "blight"—will make a reappearance in Chapter X, on government forbearance and takings. Both vested rights and takings reflect a tension between stability in property rights and flexibility in government responses to new problems.

Zoning Policy

Despite its prevalence, zoning has always been very controversial. The case for zoning rests on its potential to deal with land-use externalities. For those who see rampant market failure and collective-action problems, private solutions such as covenants cannot be the entire solution. The case for the inadequacy of covenants is greatest in older neighborhoods that lack covenants that would be desired now. The transaction costs of setting up covenants to govern micro-decisions like door color would be enormous and holdout problems loom large. (By contrast, in a new development, as we have seen, developers can insert whatever package of covenants that they think will maximize profits.) Furthermore, proponents of zoning view judicial efforts to control incompatible land uses through nuisance law as inadequate as well. Particularly where land-use controls involve specific targets—such as set-backs or lot coverage—or commercial uses like gas stations that may not rise to the level of a common-law nuisance, judges are ill-equipped to supply detailed governance regimes to prescribe proper use. This problem becomes more acute when zoning and land-use planning are regarded as involving choices on an area-wide or city-wide basis. Suburban growth controls can even involve regional planning.

Zoning also can play a role in the competition of localities for residents. If localities can offer different packages of taxes and public goods, residents can sort themselves into the places that most suit them. This sort of positive interjurisdictional competition is sometimes termed the Tiebout Hypothesis ("Tiebout" is pronounced "Tee-BOWE"). Charles M. Tiebout, A Pure Theory of Local Expenditures, 64 J. Pol. Econ. 416 (1956). Essential to this type of competition is that those who do not pay can be excluded from the benefits. Bruce W. Hamilton, Zoning and Property Taxation in a System of Local Governments, 12 Urb. Stud. 205 (1975). That is, only people paying taxes will enjoy the schools, parks, etc. that those taxes fund. For those who support this type of interjurisdictional competition, zoning is viewed as a tool to prevent "fiscal freeriding," by allowing municipalities to select the types of land uses they wish to attract or avoid. Moreover, the benefits and costs from the flow of municipal services and taxes in such a model seem to be capitalized into the price of houses, which would lead one to expect homeowners to support value-maximizing packages of public goods. Homeowners can be expected to care deeply about these values, because a home is most people's single largest investment. And because it is very difficult to diversify this investment (or to insure against drops in market value), one should expect to find risk-averse behavior among homeowners (with NIMBY-ism—the not-in-my-backyard phenomenon— being its most extreme form). William A. Fischel, The Homevoter Hypothesis: How Home Values Influence Local Government Taxation, School Finance, and Land-Use Policies (2001).

The case against zoning emphasizes the flip-side of the benefits of zoning. The notion of comprehensive planning itself has its skeptics. They point to the sorry record of planning and urban renewal in the mid-to-late twentieth century, which emphasized largeness and rationalization and extreme separation of uses, leaving even the pro-planning side advocating new approaches emphasizing a greater mix of uses and consequently more vibrant street life. Zoning is subject to the limits of bureaucratic decisionmaking, including rigidity, high administrative costs, and blunt incentives, resulting in uniformity and lack of attention to widely dispersed knowledge. See Jane Jacobs, The Life and Death of Great American Cities (1961). Developers and homeowners may use the zoning process to engage in rent-seeking, restricting the supply of housing and creating local monopolies.

Requirements of large lots cause urban sprawl, raise housing costs, and promote class and racial segregation. Basically, tools to exclude those who cannot afford prescribed types of housing can be used to prevent both fiscal freeriding and to keep out those undesired by current owners.

Most U.S. cities have zoning, and the only major city not to have zoning is Houston. This case has been much studied and opponents of zoning point to it as a relatively successful example of land use without zoning. Bernard H. Siegan, Land Use Without Zoning (1972). It should be remembered, though, that Houston is not devoid of land-use regulations. In addition to widespread use of covenants, Houston also has subdivision controls, which regulate matters like lot size. Nevertheless, Houston has a greater proximity of residential and commercial uses than other cities of its size. In an econometric study on Houston, Janet Spreyer finds that after controlling for a number of factors, zoning and covenants are equally and independently effective at raising home prices over a hypothetical nuisance-only regime. Janet Furman Spreyer, The Effect of Land Use Restrictions on the Market Value of Single Family Homes in Houston, 2 J. Real Estate Fin. & Econ. 117 (1989). Another jurisdiction that has attracted a lot of attention is New Haven. Compare Andrew J. Cappel, A Walk Along Willow: Patterns of Land Use Coordination in Pre-Zoning New Haven (1870–1926), 101 Yale L.J. 617 (1991) (finding large degree of land-use coordination in one pre-zoning New Haven neighborhood) with Stephen Clowney, A Walk Along Willard: A Revised Look at Land Use Coordination in Pre-Zoning New Haven, 115 Yale L.J. 116 (2005) (finding more mixed success and failure in four pre-zoning neighborhoods in New Haven).

Recently zoning has attracted additional interest of economists using advanced statistical techniques. One problem in drawing conclusions from studies of zoning based on housing prices is that zoning may increase prices (i) because it prevents negative externalities and thereby makes housing more valuable to its current and future owners or (ii) because it causes local monopolies in the market for housing and therefore decreases welfare. Or both. Even the original interest in zoning on the part of developers of high-grade housing in the early twentieth century is consistent with either the optimistic or the pessimistic story (or, again, both). Edward Glaeser and Joseph Gyourko manage to tease these effects apart by comparing housing prices and minimum profitable production costs in localities across the United States. They find that the cost of housing in some places is quite close to the minimum profitable production cost, but in a growing number of jurisdictions especially in California and some Eastern cities, where housing prices are significantly higher than cost. This suggests that zoning and other land-use controls are the major reason for the high cost of housing in those areas and that this regulatory tax probably exceeds the externalities from new construction. The implications for the economy and society are potentially quite substantial. Edward L. Glaeser & Joseph Gyourko, The

Economic Implications of Housing Supply, 32 J. Econ. Persp. 3 (Winter 2018). In a similar paper, these authors and Raven Saks isolate the contribution of increasingly difficult regulatory approval for new building to the increase in housing costs between 1950 and 1970. Edward L. Glaeser, Joseph E. Gyourko, & Raven E. Saks, Why Have Housing Prices Gone Up?, 95 Am. Econ. Rev. 329 (2005) (Pap. & Proc.). Artificially pumped up housing prices have likely prevented labor migration and stalled income convergence between regions in the U.S. Peter Ganong & Daniel Shoag, Why Has Regional Income Convergence in the U.S. Declined?, 102 J. Urban Econ. 76 (2017).

In part as a result of these studies, several cities and states have begun trying to reduce or eliminate the single-family use districts perceived as contributing to housing unaffordability. Minneapolis, for instance, passed legislation in 2019 allowing duplexes and triplexes in any single-family area. See Emily Badger & Quoctrung Bui, Cities Start to Question an American Ideal: A House with a Yard on Every Lot, N.Y. Times (June 18, 2019), https://nyti.ms/37QtS8Z. The debate over ending single-family zoning sometimes involves broader questions about local versus state power. In late 2021, California passed a law authorizing duplexes in single-family districts that preempts more restrictive local zoning ordinances. See also John Infranca, The New State Zoning: Land Use Preemption Amid a Housing Crisis, 60 B.C. L. Rev. 823 (2019). Some critics have worried that broad preemptive legislation in this context may legitimize other forms of preemption that target innovative city policymaking. Richard C. Schragger, The Perils of Land Use Deregulation, 170 U. Pa. L. Rev. 125 (2022). Others have defended zoning for its role in constraining the pace of change, noting the possibility that deed restrictions will replace zoning with more pernicious consequences. See Christopher Serkin, A Case for Zoning, 96 Notre Dame L. Rev. 749 (2020). These arguments have met with substantial opposition on the grounds that they only serve to empower NIMBYs. See, e.g., David Schleicher, Constitutional Law for NIMBYs: A Review of 'Principles of Home Rule for the 21st Century' by the National League of Cities, 81 Ohio St. L.J. 883 (2020); David Schleicher, Exclusionary Zoning's Confused Defenders, 2021 Wis. L. Rev. 1315. Nevertheless, despite some successes for those seeking to liberalize zoning, there remains opposition, including some from organizers concerned that deregulation is a poor substitute for increased public housing subsidies and that it will contribute to gentrification. See Jenna Davis, The Double-Edged Sword of Upzoning, Brookings, July 15, 2021, https://www.brookings.edu/blog/how-we-rise/2021/07/15/the-double-edged-sword-of-upzoning/.

On a worldwide scale, land-use regulation has had a major impact on the shape of cities, with profound economic consequences. The strength of the regulatory regime tends to flatten and sometimes invert the usual sharply downward-sloping (negative exponential) population gradient. Alain Bertaud & Stephen Malpezzi, The Spatial Distribution of

Population in 48 World Cities: Implications for Economies in Transition (working paper Dec. 17, 2003); Alain Bertaud & Bertrand Renaud, Socialist Cities without Land Markets, 41 J. Urban Econ. 137 (1997). These authors present a model and empirical results, but we will consider some illustrative examples drawn from their papers. What the authors call "market cities" like Paris have the usual pattern (or one variant of it) with a low population density downtown, then rising steeply and then dropping density as one goes further out. In highly regulatory regimes housing supply is government-driven, leading sometimes to inverted density gradients; these cities include those shaped by socialism, like Moscow (see below) and cities with heavy planning like Brasilia.

High density far from the center makes development of transportation more difficult and commuting times greater, and can lead to eventual abandonment of such housing. In general, these patterns have major implications for economic development and for economies making the transition from socialism to capitalism, in particular.

Figure 9-13

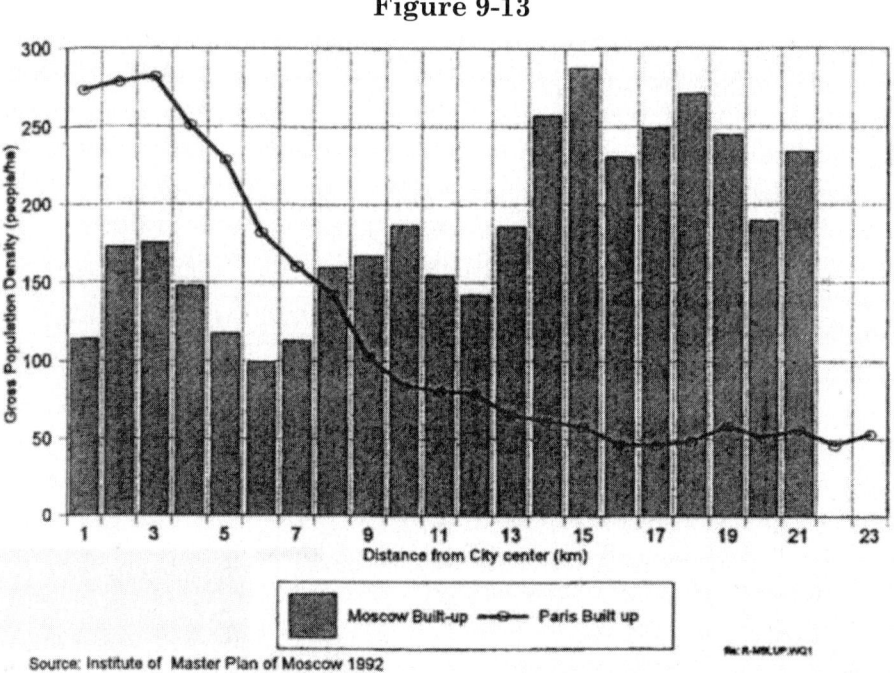

Source: Institute of Master Plan of Moscow 1992

Source: Alain Bertaud & Bertrand Renaud, Socialist Cities without Land Markets, 41 J. Urban Econ. 137, 141 (1997).

Exclusionary Zoning

We now take a closer look at one aspect of the zoning controversy— exclusionary zoning. As noted above, some accuse zoning of promoting class and race segregation, while local officials will claim that the devices in question are designed to maintain a robust tax base. Consider the following case.

Southern Burlington County N.A.A.C.P. v. Township of Mount Laurel

Supreme Court of New Jersey, 1975.
336 A.2d 713.

unlawfully exclusive zoning?

■ HALL, J. This case attacks the system of land use regulation by defendant Township of Mount Laurel on the ground that low and moderate income families are thereby unlawfully excluded from the municipality. The trial court so found, 290 A.2d 465 (N.J. Super. Law Div. 1972), and declared the township zoning ordinance totally invalid. * * *

Plaintiffs represent the minority group poor (black and Hispanic)[3] seeking such quarters. But they are not the only category of persons barred from so many municipalities by reason of restrictive land use regulations. We have reference to young and elderly couples, single persons and large, growing families not in the poverty class, but who still cannot afford the only kinds of housing realistically permitted in most places—relatively high-priced, single-family detached dwellings on sizeable lots and, in some municipalities, expensive apartments. We will, therefore, consider the case from the wider viewpoint that the effect of Mount Laurel's land use regulation has been to prevent various categories of persons from living in the township because of the limited extent of their income and resources. In this connection, we accept the representation of the municipality's counsel at oral argument that the regulatory scheme was not adopted with any desire or intent to exclude prospective residents on the obviously illegal bases of race, origin or believed social incompatibility. * * *

* * * [The township's] candid position is that, conceding its land use regulation was intended to result and has resulted in economic discrimination and exclusion of substantial segments of the area population, its policies and practices are in the best present and future fiscal interest of the municipality and its inhabitants and are legally permissible and justified. * * *

I

The Facts

Mount Laurel is a flat, sprawling township, 22 square miles, or about 14,000 acres, in area, on the west central edge of Burlington County. It is roughly triangular in shape, with its base, approximately eight miles long, extending in a northeasterly-southwesterly direction roughly parallel with and a few miles east of the Delaware River. Part of its southerly side abuts Cherry Hill in Camden County. That section of the

---

3   Plaintiffs fall into four categories: (1) present residents of the township residing in dilapidated or substandard housing; (2) former residents who were forced to move elsewhere because of the absence of suitable housing; (3) nonresidents living in central city substandard housing in the region who desire to secure decent housing and accompanying advantages within their means elsewhere; (4) three organizations representing the housing and other interests of racial minorities. * * *

township is about seven miles from the boundary line of the city of Camden and not more than 10 miles from the Benjamin Franklin Bridge crossing the river to Philadelphia.

In 1950, the township had a population of 2817, only about 600 more people than it had in 1940. It was then, as it had been for decades, primarily a rural agricultural area with no sizeable settlements or commercial or industrial enterprises. The populace generally lived in individual houses scattered along country roads. There were several pockets of poverty, with deteriorating or dilapidated housing (apparently 300 or so units of which remain today in equally poor condition). After 1950, as in so many other municipalities similarly situated, residential development and some commerce and industry began to come in. By 1960 the population had almost doubled to 5249 and by 1970 had more than doubled again to 11,221. These new residents were, of course, "outsiders" from the nearby central cities and older suburbs or from more distant places drawn here by reason of employment in the region. The township is now definitely a part of the outer ring of the South Jersey metropolitan area, which area we define as those portions of Camden, Burlington and Gloucester Counties within a semicircle having a radius of 20 miles or so from the heart of Camden city. And 65% of the township is still vacant land or in agricultural use.

The growth of the township has been spurred by the construction or improvement of main highways through or near it. * * * This highway network gives the township a most strategic location from the standpoint of transport of goods and people by truck and private car. There is no other means of transportation.

The location and nature of development has been, as usual, controlled by the local zoning enactments. The general ordinance presently in force, which was declared invalid by the trial court, was adopted in 1964. We understand that earlier enactments provided, however, basically the same scheme but were less restrictive as to residential development. The growth pattern dictated by the ordinance is typical.

Under the present ordinance, 29.2% of all the land in the township, or 4,121 acres, is zoned for industry. * * * Only industry meeting specified performance standards is permitted. The effect is to limit the use substantially to light manufacturing, research, distribution of goods, offices and the like. Some nonindustrial uses, such as agriculture, farm dwellings, motels, a harness racetrack, and certain retail sales and service establishments, are permitted in this zone. At the time of trial no more than 100 acres, mostly in the southwesterly corner along route 73 adjacent to the turnpike and I–295 interchanges, were actually occupied by industrial uses. * * * [I]t appeared clear that, as happens in the case of so many municipalities, much more land has been so zoned than the reasonable potential for industrial movement or expansion warrants. At the same time, however, the land cannot be used for residential development under the general ordinance.

The amount of land zoned for retail business use under the general ordinance is relatively small—169 acres, or 1.2% of the total. * * *

The balance of the land area, almost 10,000 acres, has been developed until recently in the conventional form of major subdivisions. The general ordinance provides for four residential zones, designated R-1, R-1D, R-2 and R-3. All permit only single-family, detached dwellings, one house per lot—the usual form of grid development. Attached townhouses, apartments (except on farms for agricultural workers) and mobile homes are not allowed anywhere in the township under the general ordinance. This dwelling development, resulting in the previously mentioned quadrupling of the population, has been largely confined to the R-1 and R-2 districts in two sections[.] * * * The result has been quite intensive development of these sections, but at a low density. The dwellings are substantial[.] * * *

A variation from conventional development has recently occurred in some parts of Mount Laurel, as in a number of other similar municipalities, by use of the land use regulation device known as "planned unit development" (PUD). This scheme differs from the traditional in that the type, density and placement of land uses and buildings, instead of being detailed and confined to specified districts by local legislation in advance, is determined by contract, or "deal," as to each development between the developer and the municipal administrative authority, under broad guidelines laid down by state enabling legislation and an implementing local ordinance. The stress is on regulation of density and permitted mixture of uses within the same area, including various kinds of living accommodations with or without commercial and industrial enterprises. The idea may be basically thought of as the creation of "new towns" in virgin territory, full-blown or in miniature, although most frequently the concept has been limited in practice, as in Mount Laurel, to residential developments of various sizes having some variety of housing and perhaps some retail establishments to serve the inhabitants. * * *

These projects, three in the southwesterly sector and one in the northeasterly sector, are very substantial and involve at least 10,000 sale and rental housing units of various types to be erected over a period of years. Their bounds were created by agreement rather than legislative specification on the zoning map, invading industrial, R-1, R-1D, R-3 and even flood plain zones. If completed as planned, they will in themselves ultimately quadruple the 1970 township population, but still leave a good part of the township undeveloped. (The record does not indicate how far development in each of the projects has progressed.) While multi-family housing in the form of rental garden, medium rise and high rise apartments and attached townhouses is for the first time provided for, as well as single-family detached dwellings for sale, it is not designed to accommodate and is beyond the financial reach of low and moderate income families, especially those with young children. The aim is quite the contrary; as with the single-family homes in the older conventional subdivisions, only persons of medium and upper income are sought as residents.

A few details will furnish sufficient documentation. Each of the resolutions of tentative approval of the projects contains a similar fact finding to the effect that the development will attract a highly educated and trained population base to support the nearby industrial parks in the township as well as the business and commercial facilities. The approvals also sharply limit the number of apartments having more than one bedroom. Further, they require that the developer must provide in its leases that no school-age children shall be permitted to occupy any one-bedroom apartment and that no more than two such children shall reside in any two-bedroom unit. The developer is also required, prior to the issuance of the first building permit, to record a covenant, running with all land on which multi-family housing is to be constructed, providing that in the event more than .3 school children per multi-family unit shall attend the township school system in any one year, the developer will pay the cost of tuition and other school expenses of all such excess numbers of children. In addition, low density, required amenities, such as central air conditioning, and specified developer contributions help to push rents and sales prices to high levels. These contributions include fire apparatus, ambulances, fire houses, and very large sums of money for educational facilities, a cultural center and the township library.

Still another restrictive land use regulation was adopted by the township through a supplement to the general zoning ordinance enacted in September 1972 creating a new zone, R-4, Planned Adult Retirement Community (PARC). * * * The extensive development requirements detailed in the ordinance make it apparent that the scheme was not designed for, and would be beyond the means of, low and moderate income retirees. * * *

All this affirmative action for the benefit of certain segments of the population is in sharp contrast to the lack of action, and indeed hostility, with respect to affording any opportunity for decent housing for the township's own poor living in substandard accommodations, found largely in the section known as Springville (R-3 zone). * * * In 1968 a private non-profit association sought to build subsidized, multi-family housing in the Springville section with funds to be granted by a higher level governmental agency. Advance municipal approval of the project was required. The Township Committee responded with a purportedly approving resolution, which found a need for "moderate" income housing in the area, but went on to specify that such housing must be constructed subject to all zoning, planning, building and other applicable ordinances and codes. This meant single-family detached dwellings on 20,000 square foot lots. (Fear was also expressed that such housing would attract low income families from outside the township.) Needless to say, such requirements killed realistic housing for this group of low and moderate income families.

The record thoroughly substantiates the findings of the trial court that over the years Mount Laurel "has acted affirmatively to control development and to attract a selective type of growth" and that "through its zoning ordinances has exhibited economic discrimination in that the poor have been deprived of adequate housing and the opportunity to secure the construction of subsidized housing, and has used federal, state, county and local finances and resources solely for the betterment of middle and upper-income persons."

There cannot be the slightest doubt that the reason for this course of conduct has been to keep down local taxes on *property* (Mount Laurel is not a high tax municipality) and that the policy was carried out without regard for non-fiscal considerations with respect to *people*, either within or without its boundaries. * * *

This policy of land use regulation for a fiscal end derives from New Jersey's tax structure, which has imposed on local real estate most of the cost of municipal and county government and of the primary and secondary education of the municipality's children. The latter expense is much the largest, so, basically, the fewer the school children, the lower the tax rate. Sizeable industrial and commercial ratables are eagerly sought and homes and the lots on which they are situate are required to be large enough, through minimum lot sizes and minimum floor areas, to have substantial value in order to produce greater tax revenues to meet school costs. Large families who cannot afford to buy large houses and must live in cheaper rental accommodations are definitely not wanted, so we find drastic bedroom restrictions for, or complete prohibition of, multi-family or other feasible housing for those of lesser income.

This pattern of land use regulation has been adopted for the same purpose in developing municipality after developing municipality. Almost every one acts solely in its own selfish and parochial interest and in effect builds a wall around itself to keep out those people or entities not adding favorably to the tax base, despite the location of the municipality or the demand for varied kinds of housing. There has been no effective intermunicipal or area planning or land use regulation. * * * One incongruous result is the picture of developing municipalities rendering it impossible for lower paid employees of industries they have eagerly sought and welcomed with open arms (and, in Mount Laurel's case, even some of its own lower paid municipal employees) to live in the community where they work. * * *

II

The Legal Issue

The legal question before us, as earlier indicated, is whether a developing municipality like Mount Laurel may validly, by a system of land use regulation, make it physically and economically impossible to provide low and moderate income housing in the municipality for the various categories of persons who need and want it and thereby, as Mount Laurel has, exclude such people from living within its confines because of the limited extent of their income and resources. Necessarily implicated are the broader questions of the right of such municipalities to limit the kinds of available housing and of any obligation to make possible a variety and choice of types of living accommodations.

We conclude that every such municipality must, by its land use regulations, presumptively make realistically possible an appropriate variety and choice of housing. More specifically, presumptively it cannot foreclose the opportunity of the classes of people mentioned for low and moderate income housing and in its regulations must affirmatively afford that opportunity, at least to the extent of the municipality's fair share of the present and prospective regional need therefor. These obligations must be met unless the particular municipality can sustain the heavy burden of demonstrating peculiar circumstances which dictate that it should not be required so to do.[10]

We reach this conclusion under state law and so do not find it necessary to consider federal constitutional grounds urged by plaintiffs. We begin with some fundamental principles as applied to the scene before us.

Land use regulation is encompassed within the state's police power. * * *

It is elementary theory that all police power enactments, no matter at what level of government, must conform to the basic state constitutional requirements of substantive due process and equal protection of the laws. These are inherent in Art. I, par. 1 of our Constitution,[11] the requirements of which may be more demanding than those of the federal Constitution. It is required that, affirmatively, a zoning regulation, like any police power enactment, must promote public health, safety, morals or the general welfare. (The last term seems broad enough to encompass the others.) Conversely, a zoning enactment which is contrary to the general welfare is invalid. * * *

* * * Frequently the decisions in this state * * * have spoken only in terms of the interest of the enacting municipality, so that it has been thought, at least in some quarters, that such was the only welfare requiring consideration. It is, of course, true that many cases have dealt

---

[10]   While, as the trial court found, Mount Laurel's actions were deliberate, we are of the view that the identical conclusion follows even when municipal conduct is not shown to be intentional, but the effect is substantially the same as if it were.

[11]   The paragraph reads:

All persons are by nature free and independent, and have certain natural and unalienable rights, among which are those of enjoying and defending life and liberty, of acquiring, possessing, and protecting property, and of pursuing and obtaining safety and happiness.

only with regulations having little, if any, outside impact where the local decision is ordinarily entitled to prevail. However, it is fundamental and not to be forgotten that the zoning power is a police power of the state and the local authority is acting only as a delegate of that power and is restricted in the same manner as is the state. So, when regulation does have a substantial external impact, the welfare of the state's citizens beyond the borders of the particular municipality cannot be disregarded and must be recognized and served. * * *

This essential was distinctly pointed out in Euclid, where Mr. Justice Sutherland specifically referred to " * * * the possibility of cases where the general public interest would so far outweigh the interest of the municipality that the municipality would not be allowed to stand in the way." (272 U.S. at 390). * * *

This brings us to the relation of housing to the concept of general welfare just discussed and the result in terms of land use regulation which that relationship mandates. There cannot be the slightest doubt that shelter, along with food, are the most basic human needs. * * *

It is plain beyond dispute that proper provision for adequate housing of all categories of people is certainly an absolute essential in promotion of the general welfare required in all local land use regulation. Further the universal and constant need for such housing is so important and of such broad public interest that the general welfare which developing municipalities like Mount Laurel must consider extends beyond their boundaries and cannot be parochially confined to the claimed good of the particular municipality. It has to follow that, broadly speaking, the presumptive obligation arises for each such municipality affirmatively to plan and provide, by its land use regulations, the reasonable opportunity for an appropriate variety and choice of housing, including, of course, low and moderate cost housing, to meet the needs, desires and resources of all categories of people who may desire to live within its boundaries. Negatively, it may not adopt regulations or policies which thwart or preclude that opportunity.

It is also entirely clear, as we pointed out earlier, that most developing municipalities, including Mount Laurel, have not met their affirmative or negative obligations, primarily for local fiscal reasons. * * *

We have spoken of this obligation of such municipalities as "presumptive." The term has two aspects, procedural and substantive. Procedurally, we think the basic importance of appropriate housing for all dictates that, when it is shown that a developing municipality in its land use regulations has not made realistically possible a variety and choice of housing, including adequate provision to afford the opportunity for low and moderate income housing or has expressly prescribed requirements or restrictions which preclude or substantially hinder it, a facial showing of violation of substantive due process or equal protection under the state constitution has been made out and the burden, and it is a heavy one, shifts to the municipality to establish a valid basis for its action or non-action. The substantive aspect of "presumptive" relates to the specifics, on the one hand, of what municipal land use regulation provisions, or the absence thereof, will evidence invalidity and shift the burden of proof and, on the other hand, of what bases and considerations will carry the municipality's burden and sustain what it has done or failed to do. Both kinds of specifics may well vary between municipalities according to peculiar circumstances.

We turn to application of these principles in appraisal of Mount Laurel's zoning ordinance, useful as well, we think, as guidelines for future application in other municipalities. * * *

[O]ur opinion is that Mount Laurel's zoning ordinance is presumptively contrary to the general welfare and outside the intended scope of the zoning power in the particulars mentioned. A facial showing of invalidity is thus established, shifting to the municipality the burden of establishing valid superseding reasons for its action and non-action. We now examine the reasons it advances.

Holding on presumption

The township's principal reason in support of its zoning plan and ordinance housing provisions, advanced especially strongly at oral argument, is the fiscal one previously adverted to, i.e., that by reason of New Jersey's tax structure which substantially finances municipal governmental and educational costs from taxes on local real property, every municipality may, by the exercise of the zoning power, allow only such uses and to such extent as will be beneficial to the local tax rate. * * *

mun.'s fiscal reason

We have previously held that a developing municipality may properly zone for and seek industrial ratables to create a better economic balance for the community *vis-a-vis* educational and governmental costs engendered by residential development, provided that such was " * * * done reasonably as part of and in furtherance of a legitimate comprehensive plan for the zoning of the entire municipality." Gruber v. Mayor and Township Committee of Raritan Township, 186 A.2d 489, 493 (N.J. 1962). We adhere to that view today. But we were not there concerned with, and did not pass upon, the validity of municipal exclusion by zoning of types of housing and kinds of people for the same local financial end. We have no hesitancy in now saying, and do so emphatically, that, considering the basic importance of the opportunity for appropriate housing for all classes of our citizenry, no municipality may exclude or limit categories of housing for that reason or purpose. While we fully recognize the increasingly heavy burden of local taxes for municipal governmental and school costs on homeowners, relief from the consequences of this tax system will have to be furnished by other branches of government. It cannot legitimately be accomplished by restricting types of housing through the zoning process in developing municipalities. * * *

By way of summary, what we have said comes down to this. As a developing municipality, Mount Laurel must, by its land use regulations, make realistically possible the opportunity for an appropriate variety and choice of housing for all categories of people who may desire to live there, of course including those of low and moderate income. It must permit multifamily housing, without bedroom or similar restrictions, as well as small dwellings on very small lots, low cost housing of other types and, in general, high density zoning, without artificial and unjustifiable minimum requirements as to lot size, building size and the like, to meet the full panoply of these needs. Certainly when a municipality zones for industry and commerce for local tax benefit purposes, it without question must zone to permit adequate housing within the means of the employees involved in such uses. (If planned unit developments are authorized, one would assume that each must include a reasonable amount of low and moderate income housing in its residential "mix," unless opportunity for such housing has already been realistically provided for elsewhere in the municipality.) The amount of land removed from residential use by allocation to industrial and commercial purposes must be reasonably related to the present and future potential for such purposes. In other words, such municipalities must zone primarily for the living welfare of people and not for the benefit of the local tax rate.[20]

* * * Frequently it might be sounder to have more of such housing, like some specialized land uses, in one municipality in a region than in another, because of greater availability of suitable land, location of employment, accessibility of public transportation or some other significant reason. But, under present New Jersey legislation, zoning must be on an individual municipal basis, rather than regionally. So long as that situation persists under the present tax structure, or in the absence of some kind of binding agreement among all the municipalities of a region, we feel that every municipality therein must bear its fair share of the regional burden. (In this respect our holding is broader than that of the trial court, which was limited to Mount Laurel-related low and moderate income housing needs.)

NJ structure

The composition of the applicable "region" will necessarily vary from situation to situation and probably no hard and fast rule will serve to furnish the answer in every case. Confinement to or within a certain county appears not to be realistic, but restriction within the boundaries of the state seem practical and advisable. (This is not to say that a developing municipality can ignore a demand for housing within its boundaries on the part of people who commute to work in another state.) Here we have already defined the region at present as "those portions of Camden, Burlington and Gloucester Counties within a semicircle having a radius of 20 miles or so from the heart of Camden City." The concept of "fair share" is coming into more general use and, through the expertise of the municipal planning adviser, the county planning boards and the state planning agency, a reasonable figure for Mount Laurel can be

---

[20]   This case does not properly present the question of whether a developing municipality may time its growth and, if so, how. * * *

determined, which can then be translated to the allocation of sufficient land therefor on the zoning map. * * *

There is no reason why developing municipalities like Mount Laurel, required by this opinion to afford the opportunity for all types of housing to meet the needs of various categories of people, may not become and remain attractive, viable communities providing good living and adequate services for all their residents in the kind of atmosphere which a democracy and free institutions demand. They can have industrial sections, commercial sections and sections for every kind of housing from low cost and multi-family to lots of more than an acre with very expensive homes. Proper planning and governmental cooperation can prevent over-intensive and too sudden development, insure against future suburban sprawl and slums and assure the preservation of open space and local beauty. We do not intend that developing municipalities shall be overwhelmed by voracious land speculators and developers if they use the powers which they have intelligently and in the broad public interest. Under our holdings today, they can be better communities for all than they previously have been.

III

The Remedy

* * * We are of the view that the trial court's judgment should be modified in certain respects. We see no reason why the entire zoning ordinance should be nullified. Therefore we declare it to be invalid only to the extent and in the particulars set forth in this opinion. The township is granted 90 days from the date hereof, or such additional time as the trial court may find it reasonable and necessary to allow, to adopt amendments to correct the deficiencies herein specified. It is the local function and responsibility, in the first instance at least, rather than the court's, to decide on the details of the same within the guidelines we have laid down. If plaintiffs desire to attack such amendments, they may do so by supplemental complaint filed in this cause within 30 days of the final adoption of the amendments.

We are not at all sure what the trial judge had in mind as ultimate action with reference to the approval of a plan for affirmative public action concerning the satisfaction of indicated housing needs and the entry of a final order requiring implementation thereof. Courts do not build housing nor do municipalities. That function is performed by private builders, various kinds of associations, or, for public housing, by special agencies created for that purpose at various levels of government. The municipal function is initially to provide the opportunity through appropriate land use regulations and we have spelled out what Mount Laurel must do in that regard. It is not appropriate at this time, particularly in view of the advanced view of zoning law as applied to housing laid down by this opinion, to deal with the matter of the further extent of judicial power in the field or to exercise any such power. The municipality should first have full opportunity to itself act without judicial supervision. We trust it will do so in the spirit we have suggested, both by appropriate zoning ordinance amendments and whatever additional action encouraging the fulfillment of its fair share of the regional need for low and moderate income housing may be indicated as necessary and advisable. (We have in mind that there is at least a moral obligation in a municipality to establish a local housing agency pursuant to state law to provide housing for its resident poor now living in dilapidated, unhealthy quarters.) * * * Should Mount Laurel not perform as we expect, further judicial action may be sought by supplemental pleading in this cause.

The judgment of the Law Division is modified as set forth herein. No costs.

NOTES AND QUESTIONS

1.   New Jersey's experience with judicial remedies for exclusionary zoning has been almost unique. After this case, developers still found it difficult to get approval for low- and moderate-income housing, in the face of the many obstacles towns could set up. In *Southern Burlington County NAACP v. Township of Mount Laurel* (*Mount Laurel II*), 456 A.2d 390 (N.J. 1983), the court sought to strengthen its approach with a "builder's remedy" (an injunction requiring a permit for a builder who has succeeded in *Mount Laurel*-type litigation) and the possibility that a court would order a revision in the zoning ordinance. The court also held that affirmative measures by municipalities, such as incentive zoning and set-asides, were within the constitutionally delegated power to zone and within the range of remedies that a court could order. More recently the New Jersey Supreme Court has upheld as constitutional New Jersey legislation that set up a Council on Affordable Housing that would decide what a municipality's fair share of low- and moderate-income housing would be, would pass on whether measures satisfy this obligation, and would approve regional agreements. Hills Development Co. v. Township of Bernards, 510 A.2d 621 (N.J. 1986) (sometimes known as "*Mount Laurel III*"). Other states have either not found any violation in exclusionary zoning or have adopted milder approaches than New Jersey's. For example, the Pennsylvania Supreme Court has adopted a "fair share" analysis but generally restricts remedies to cases in which localities try to impose blanket prohibitions on certain types of uses. See BAC, Inc. v. Board of Supervisors, 633 A.2d 144 (Pa. 1993) (holding that challenger had not met its burden where some mobile homes were allowed).

2.   Many techniques have been alleged to be implicated in exclusionary zoning. These include minimum lot sizes and restrictions or prohibition on mobile homes. What if a town has never used any of these measures but still has little low- or moderate-income housing? According to the *Mount Laurel* line of decisions, would an already developed town have an affirmative obligation to provide low- and moderate-income housing? What about an older town that is gentrifying? Like zoning in general, various techniques serve multiple purposes, potentially benign and exclusionary, and the mix can change over time. Historically, ordinances ostensibly aimed

at preserving open space were often regarded as cover for exclusionary zoning. These days for a variety of reasons, open space initiatives have gained in popularity. Does this make them less exclusionary? How should they be evaluated now? See Stephen Schmidt & Kurt Paulsen, Is Open-Space Preservation a Form of Exclusionary Zoning? The Evolution of Municipal Open-Space Policies in New Jersey, 45 Urban Aff. Rev. 92 (2009).

3.   The court cites to the *Euclid* case. Recall Justice Sutherland's nuisance analogy and characterization of apartment houses as "parasites." Also, the scheme there even limited duplexes. Was Euclid's scheme an example of exclusionary zoning?

4.   The *Mount Laurel* cases rested on the state constitution. Although the federal constitution has never been interpreted in a similar way, other federal law is relevant to the problem of exclusionary zoning. Consider the Fair Housing Act and the Civil Rights Act of 1866, supra Chapter IV. For some of the literature on racial and social exclusion, see, e.g., Charles M. Haar, Suburbs Under Siege: Race, Space, and Audacious Judges (1996); Richard Thompson Ford, The Boundaries of Race: Political Geography in Legal Action, 107 Harv. L. Rev. 1941 (1994).

5.   The type of housing at issue in *Mount Laurel* was finally unanimously approved in 1997, despite protests by opponents. For developments subsequent to *Mount Laurel* and a discussion of the effectiveness of the moves and countermoves of government and housing organizations, see Ellickson et al., supra, at 679–90. A legislative alternative to *Mount Laurel*-style cases is Massachusetts' "anti-snob zoning" act, Mass. Gen. Laws ch. 40B, §§ 20 to 23, which provides for a builder's remedy if a locality fails to achieve targets such as a housing stock with 10% affordable housing. The evidence of how much *Mount Laurel* or the Massachusetts statute has contributed to the supply of low- and moderate-income housing is mixed at best. One problem is that municipalities can keep the denominator in their housing stock low by pursuing open space initiatives with extra vigor. See William A. Fischel, The Evolution of Zoning Since the 1980s: The Persistence of Localism, in Property in Land and Other Resources (Daniel H. Cole & Elinor Ostrom eds., 2012).

CHAPTER X

GOVERNMENT FORBEARANCE AND TAKINGS

There is a longstanding debate about the relationship between government and property. Locke famously argued that property rights originate in the state of nature, and government was created to protect these rights. See John Locke, Two Treatises of Civil Government bk. II, ch. V (1690). Bentham responded bluntly that "[p]roperty and law are born together, and die together. Before laws were made there was no property; take away laws, and property ceases." Jeremy Bentham, The Theory of Legislation 113 (C.K. Ogden ed., 1931) (1802). The debate is largely philosophical; the historical record is too murky to provide a definite answer to the question whether property is "pre-political" or "post-political," at least insofar as most property rights that exist today are concerned. Whatever the role of the state in bringing property into being, there is no question that government action affects property rights in a great many important ways. As Blackstone observed, even if "[t]he original of private property is probably founded in nature," nevertheless "the method of conserving it in the present owner, and of translating it from man to man, are entirely derived from society." 1 Blackstone, Commentaries *134.

In this Chapter, we focus on the question of how much the government should forbear from interfering with, or frustrating, previously recognized property rights. This general inquiry entails several subsidiary questions: How explicit must the government's promise of forbearance be before property owners can justifiably rely upon it? What sort of reasons suffice to permit the government to break its promise of forbearance? If the government breaks its promise, and has no adequate justification for doing so, what sort of remedies should the courts give to someone who has been injured by the government's lack of forbearance?

In the United States, these questions have commonly been addressed as a matter of constitutional law. During roughly the first century after the adoption of the U.S. Constitution, the clause invoked most frequently as a basis for adjudicating claims of inadequate forbearance was the Contracts Clause of Article I, § 10, which provides that no state shall pass any law "impairing the obligation of contract." The Supreme Court held in *Fletcher v. Peck*, 10 U.S. (6 Cranch) 87 (1810), that the obligation of contract includes grants of property in land, and then ruled in *Dartmouth College v. Woodward*, 17 U.S. (4 Wheat.) 518 (1819), that it also includes corporate charters. These decisions laid the groundwork for a jurisprudence in which the Court reviewed a wide range of claims of inadequate government forbearance under the Contracts Clause. Toward the end of the nineteenth century, the action shifted toward the Due Process Clauses of the Fifth and Fourteenth Amendments, which the courts interpreted to impose certain substantive restraints on government action depriving individuals of private rights. *Lochner v. New York*, 198 U.S. 45 (1905), in which the Court invalidated a maximum hours regulation as interfering with liberty of contract, is the most famous decision of this era. But the Court also held that state interferences with the expectations of property owners could violate due process. See, e.g., Truax v. Corrigan, 257 U.S. 312 (1921); Missouri Pac. Ry. v. Nebraska, 164 U.S. 403 (1896); see Ronald J. Krotoszynski, Jr., Fundamental Property Rights, 85 Geo. L.J. 555, 561–67 (1997).

In recent decades, the dominant clause for addressing these issues has become the Takings Clause of the Fifth Amendment, which has been held to apply to the states through the Fourteenth Amendment. The Takings Clause provides: "nor shall private property be taken for public use without just compensation." This Clause functions in part to regulate the power of eminent domain, considered in Part C. But the Court has also drawn upon the Clause for the understanding that certain regulations of property can go "too far," to the point where the government must proceed by eminent domain, i.e. compensate the owner, rather than by police power regulation. This understanding, which is called the "regulatory takings" doctrine, is taken up in Part D.

Although constitutional constraints have been the focal point for discussion about the proper degree of government forbearance in interfering with property rights, government forbearance is also encouraged by nonconstitutional doctrines. In Part B we consider some of these doctrines, including the rule of construction favoring vested rights, the doctrine favoring a strong version of stare decisis in matters involving property rights, and foreign investment protection treaties. But first, we consider a classic Supreme Court decision that raises questions about government forbearance with a degree of explicitness that has rarely been matched in any subsequent decision.

A. THE GENERAL PROBLEM

Charles River Bridge v. Warren Bridge

Supreme Court of the United States, 1837.
36 U.S. (11 Pet.) 420.

■ MR. CHIEF JUSTICE TANEY delivered the opinion of the court. The questions involved in this case are of the gravest character, and the court have given to them the most anxious and deliberate consideration. * * *

It appears, from the record, that in the year 1650, the legislature of Massachusetts granted to the president of Harvard College "the liberty and power," to dispose of the ferry from Charlestown to Boston, by lease or otherwise, in the behalf, and for the behoof, of the college; and that under that grant, the college continued to hold and keep the ferry, by its lessees or agents, and to receive the profits of it, until 1785. In the last-mentioned year, a petition was presented to the legislature, by Thomas Russell and others, stating the inconvenience of the transportation by ferries, over Charles river, and the public advantages that would result from a bridge; and praying to be incorporated, for the purpose of erecting a bridge in the place where the ferry between Boston and Charlestown was then kept. Pursuant to this petition, the legislature, on the 9th of March 1785, passed an act incorporating a company, by the name of "The Proprietors of the Charles River Bridge," for the purposes mentioned in the petition. Under this charter, the company were empowered to erect a bridge, in "the place where the ferry was then kept;" certain tolls were granted, and the charter was limited to forty years from the first opening of the bridge for passengers; and from the time the toll commenced, until the expiration of this term, the company were to pay £200, annually, to Harvard College; and at the expiration of the forty years, the bridge was to be the property of the commonwealth; "saving (as the law expresses it) to the said college or university, a reasonable annual compensation, for the annual income of the ferry, which they might have received, had not the said bridge been erected."

The bridge was accordingly built, and was opened for passengers on the 17th of June 1786. In 1792, the charter was extended to seventy years from the opening of the bridge; and at the expiration of that time, it was to belong to the commonwealth. The corporation have regularly paid to the college the annual sum of £200 and have performed all of the duties imposed on them by the terms of their charter.

In 1828, the legislature of Massachusetts incorporated a company by the name of "The Proprietors of the Warren Bridge," for the purpose of erecting another bridge over Charles river. This bridge is only sixteen rods, at its commencement, on the Charlestown side, from the commencement of the bridge of the plaintiffs; and they are about fifty rods apart, at their termination on the Boston side. The travellers who pass over either bridge, proceed from Charlestown square, which receives the travel of many great public roads leading from the country; and the passengers and travellers who go to and from Boston, used to pass over the Charles River bridge, from and through this square, before the erection of the Warren bridge.

The Warren bridge, by the terms of its charter, was to be surrendered to the state, as soon as the expenses of the proprietors in building and supporting it should be reimbursed; but this period was not, in any event, to exceed six years from the time the company commenced receiving toll.

Figure 10-1
The Charles River Bridge, Built in 1785

Courtesy of Instructional Resources Corporation.

When the original bill in this case was filed, the Warren bridge had not been built; and the bill was filed, after the passage of the law, in order to obtain an injunction to prevent its erection, and for general relief. The bill, among other things, charged as a ground for relief, that the act for the erection of the Warren bridge impaired the obligation of the contract between the commonwealth and the proprietors of the Charles River bridge; and was, therefore, repugnant to the constitution of the United States. Afterwards, a supplemental bill was filed, stating that the bridge had then been so far completed, that it had been opened for travel, and that divers persons had passed over, and thus avoided the payment of the toll, which would otherwise have been received by the plaintiffs. * * * In the argument here, it was admitted, that since the filing of the supplemental bill, a sufficient amount of toll had been reserved by the proprietors of the Warren bridge to reimburse all their expenses, and that the bridge is now the property of the state, and has been made a free bridge; and that the value of the franchise granted to the proprietors of the Charles River bridge, has by this means been entirely destroyed. * * *

A good deal of evidence has been offered, to show the nature and extent of the ferry-right granted to the college; and also to show the rights claimed by the proprietors of the bridge, at different times, by virtue of their charter; and the opinions entertained by committees of the legislature, and others, upon that subject. But as these circumstances do not affect the judgment of this court, it is unnecessary to recapitulate them.

The plaintiffs in error insist, mainly, upon two grounds: 1st. That by virtue of the grant of 1650, Harvard College was entitled, in perpetuity, to the right of keeping a ferry between Charlestown and Boston; that this right was exclusive; and that the legislature had not the power to establish another ferry on the same line of travel, because it would infringe the rights of the college; and that these rights, upon the erection of the bridge in the place of the ferry, under the charter of 1785, were transferred to, and became vested in "The Proprietors of the Charles River Bridge;" and that under, and by virtue of this transfer of the ferry-right, the rights of the bridge company were as exclusive in that line of travel, as the rights of the ferry. 2d. That independently of the ferry-right, the acts of the legislature of Massachusetts, of 1785 and 1792, by their true construction, necessarily implied, that the legislature would not authorize another bridge, and especially, a free one, by the side of this, and placed in the same line of travel, whereby the franchise granted to the "Proprietors of the Charles River Bridge" should be rendered of no value; and the plaintiffs in error contend, that the grant of the ferry to the college, and of the charter to the proprietors of the bridge, are both contracts on the part of the state; and that the law authorizing the erection of the Warren bridge in 1828, impairs the obligation of one or both of these contracts.

It is very clear, that in the form in which this case comes before us (being a writ of error to a state court), the plaintiffs, in claiming under either of these rights, must place themselves on the ground of contract, and cannot support themselves upon the principle, that the law divests vested rights. It is well settled, by the decisions of this court, that a state law may be retrospective in its character, and may divest vested rights, and yet not violate the constitution of the United States, unless it also impairs the obligation of a contract. [Satterlee v. Matthewson, 27 U.S. (2 Pet.) 380 (1829); Watson v. Mercer, 33 U.S. (8 Pet.) 88 (1834)]: * * * After these solemn decisions of this court, it is apparent, that the plaintiffs in error * * * must show, that the state had entered into a contract with them, or those under whom they claim, not to establish a free bridge at the place where the Warren bridge is erected. Such, and such only, are the principles upon which the plaintiffs in error can claim relief in this case.

The nature and extent of the ferry right granted to Harvard College, in 1650, must depend upon the laws of Massachusetts; and the character and extent of this right has been elaborately discussed at the bar. But in the view which the court take of the case before them, it is not necessary to express any opinion on these questions. * * *

The fact that such a right was granted to the college, cannot, by any sound rule of construction, be used to extend the privileges of the bridge company, beyond what the words of the charter naturally and legally import. Increased population, longer experience in legislation, the different character of the corporations which owned the ferry from that which owned the bridge, might well have induced a change in the policy of the state in this respect * * *. The charter to the bridge is a written instrument which must speak for itself, and be interpreted by its own terms. * * *

Much has been said in the argument of the principles of construction by which this law is to be expounded, and what undertakings, on the part of the state, may be implied. The court think there can be no serious difficulty on that head. It is the grant of certain franchises, by the public, to a private corporation, and in a matter where the public interest is concerned. The rule of construction in such cases is well settled, both in England, and by the decisions of our own tribunals. In the case of the *Proprietors of the Stourbridge Canal v. Wheeley and others*, (1831) 109 Eng. Rep. 1336 (K.B.), the court say, "the canal having been made under an act of parliament, the rights of the plaintiffs are derived entirely from that act. This, like many other cases, is a bargain between a company of adventurers and the public, the terms of which are expressed in the statute; and the rule of construction in all such cases, is now fully established to be this—that any ambiguity in the terms of the contract, must operate against the adventurers, and in favor of the public, and the plaintiffs can claim nothing that is not clearly given them by the act." And the doctrine thus laid down is abundantly sustained by the authorities referred to in this decision. * * *

Borrowing, as we have done, our system of jurisprudence from the English law; and having adopted, in every other case, civil and criminal, its rules for the construction of statutes; is there anything in our local situation, or in the nature of our political institutions, which should lead us to depart from the principle, where corporations are concerned? * * * We think not; and it would present a singular spectacle, if, while the courts in England are restraining, within the strictest limits, the spirit of monopoly, and exclusive privileges in nature of monopolies, and confining corporations to the privileges plainly given to them in their charter; the courts of this country should be found enlarging these privileges by implication; and construing a statute more unfavorably to the public, and to the rights of community, than would be done in a like case in an English court of justice. * * *

Adopting the rule of construction above stated as the settled one, we proceed to apply it to the charter of 1785, to the proprietors of the Charles River bridge. This act of incorporation is in the usual form, and the privileges such as are commonly given to corporations of that kind. It confers on them the ordinary faculties of a corporation, for the purpose of building the bridge; and establishes certain rates of toll, which the company are authorized to take: this is the whole grant. There is no exclusive privilege given to them over the waters of Charles river, above or below their bridge; no right to erect another bridge themselves, nor to prevent other persons from erecting one, no engagement from the state, that another shall not be erected; and no undertaking not to sanction competition, nor to make improvements that may diminish the amount of its income. Upon all these subject, the charter is silent; and nothing is said in it about a line of travel, so much insisted on in the argument, in which they are to have exclusive privileges. No words are used, from which an intention to grant any of these rights can be inferred; if the plaintiff is entitled to them, it must be implied, simply, from the nature of the grant; and cannot be inferred, from the words by which the grant is made.

The relative position of the Warren bridge has already been described. It does not interrupt the passage over the Charles River bridge, nor make the way to it, or from it, less convenient. None of the faculties or franchises granted to that corporation, have been revoked by the legislature; and its right to take the tolls granted by the charter remains unaltered. In short, all the franchises and rights of property, enumerated in the charter, and there mentioned to have been granted to it, remain unimpaired. But its income is destroyed by the Warren bridge; which, being free, draws off the passengers and property which would have gone over it, and renders their franchise of no value. This is the gist of the complaint; for it is not pretended, that the erection of the Warren bridge would have done them any injury, or in any degree affected their right of property, if it had not diminished the amount of their tolls. In order, then, to entitle themselves to relief, it is necessary to show, that the legislature contracted not to do the act of which they complain; and that they impaired, or in other words, violated, that contract, by the erection of the Warren bridge. * * *

If a contract on that subject can be gathered from the charter, it must be by implication; and cannot be found in the words used. Can such an agreement be implied? The rule of construction before stated is an answer to the question: in charters of this description, no rights are taken from the public, or given to the corporation, beyond those which the words of the charter, by their natural and proper construction, purport to convey. There are no words which import such a contract as the plaintiffs in error contend for, and none can be implied[.] * * *

Indeed, the practice and usage of almost every state in the Union, old enough to have commenced the work of internal improvement, is opposed to the doctrine contended for on the part of the plaintiffs in error. Turnpike roads have been made in succession, on the same line of travel; the later ones interfering materially with the profits of the first. These corporations have, in some instances, been utterly ruined by the introduction of newer and better modes of transportation and travelling. In some cases, railroads have rendered the turnpike roads on the same line of travel so entirely useless, that the franchise of the turnpike corporation is not worth preserving. Yet in none of these cases have the corporation supposed that their privileges were invaded, or any contract violated on the part of the state. * * * The absence of any such controversy, when there must have been so many occasions to give rise to it, proves, that neither states, nor individuals, nor corporations, ever imagined that such a contract could be implied from such charters. * * *

And what would be the fruits of this doctrine of implied contracts, on the part of the states, and of property in a line of travel, by a corporation, if it would now be sanctioned by this court? To what results would it lead us? If it is to be found in the charter to this bridge, the same process of reasoning must discover it, in the various acts which have been passed, within the last forty years, for turnpike companies. And what is to be the extent of the privileges of exclusion on the different sides of the road? The counsel who have so ably argued this case, have not attempted to define it by any certain boundaries. How far must the new improvement be distant from the old one? How near may you approach, without invading its rights in the privileged line? If this court should establish the principles now contended for, what is to become of the numerous railroads established on the same line of travel with turnpike companies; and which have rendered the franchises of the turnpike corporations of no value? Let it once be understood, that such charters carry with them these implied contracts, and give this unknown and undefined property in a line of traveling; and you will soon find the old turnpike corporations awakening from their sleep, and calling upon this court to put down the improvements which have taken their place. The millions of property which have been invested in railroads and canals, upon lines of travel which had been before occupied by turnpike corporations, will be put in jeopardy. We shall be thrown back to the improvements of the last century, and obliged to stand still, until the claims of the old turnpike corporations shall be satisfied; and they shall consent to permit these states to avail themselves of the lights of modern science, and to partake of the benefit of those improvements which are now adding to the wealth and prosperity, and the convenience and comfort, of every other part of the civilized world. Nor is this all. This court will find itself compelled to fix, by some arbitrary rule, the width of this new kind of property in a line of travel; for if such a right of property exists, we have no lights to guide us in marking out its extent, unless, indeed, we * * * are prepared to decide that when a turnpike road from one town to another, had been made, no railroad or canal, between these two points, could afterwards be established. This court are not prepared to sanction principles which must lead to such results. * * *

The judgment of the supreme judicial court of the commonwealth of Massachusetts, dismissing the plaintiffs' bill, must, therefore, be affirmed, with costs.

■ MR. JUSTICE McLEAN. [omitted].

■ MR. JUSTICE STORY, dissenting. * * * [B]efore we can properly enter upon the consideration of this subject, a preliminary inquiry is presented, as to the proper rules of interpretation applicable to the charter. * * *

It is a well-known rule in the construction of private grants, if the meaning of the words be doubtful, to construe them most strongly against the grantor. But it is said, that an opposite rule prevails in cases of grants by the king; for, where there is any doubt, the construction is made most favorably for the king, and against the grantee. The rule is not disputed; but it is a rule of very limited application. To what cases does it apply? * * *

[T]his doctrine in relation to the king's prerogative of having a construction in his own favor, is exclusively confined to cases of mere *donation*, flowing from the bounty of the crown. Whenever the grant is upon a valuable consideration, the rule of construction ceases; and the grant is expounded exactly as it would be in the case of a private grant—favorably to the grantee. Why is this rule adopted? Plainly, because the grant is a contract, and is to be interpreted according to its fair meaning. It would be to the dishonor of the government, that it should pocket a fair consideration, and then quibble as to the obscurities and implications of its own contract. * * *

But it has been argued, and the argument has been pressed in every form which ingenuity could suggest, that if grants of this nature are to be construed liberally, as conferring any exclusive rights on the grantees, it will interpose an effectual barrier against all general improvements of the country. * * * For my own part, I can conceive of no surer plan to arrest all public improvements, founded on private capital and enterprise, than to make the outlay of that capital uncertain and questionable, both as to security and as to productiveness. No man will hazard his capital in any enterprise, in which, if there be a loss, it must be borne exclusively by himself; and if there be success, he has not the slightest security of enjoying the rewards of that success, for a single moment. If the government means to invite its citizens to enlarge the public comforts and conveniences, to establish bridges, or turnpikes, or canals, or railroads, there must be some pledge, that the property will be safe; that the enjoyment will be co-extensive with the grant; and that success will not be the signal of a general combination to overthrow its rights and to take away its profits. The very agitation of a question of this sort is sufficient to alarm every stockholder in every public enterprise of this sort, throughout the whole country. Already, in my native state, the legislature has found it necessary expressly to concede the exclusive privilege here contended against; in order to insure the accomplishment of a railroad for the benefit of the public. And yet, we are told, that all such exclusive grants are to the detriment of the public. * * *

I go further, and maintain, not only that it is not a case for strict construction; but that the charter, upon its very face, by its terms, and for its professed objects, demands from the court, upon undeniable principles of law, a favorable construction for the grantees. * * * [T]hey are to take upon themselves the chances of success; and if the enterprise fails, the loss is exclusively their own. Nor let any man imagine, that there was not, at the time when this charter was granted, much solid ground for doubting success. In order to entertain a just view of this subject, we must go back to that period of general bankruptcy, and distress and difficulty. The constitution of the United States was not only not then in existence, but it was not then even dreamed of. The union of the states was crumbling into ruins, under the old confederation. Agriculture, manufactures and commerce were at their lowest ebb. There was infinite danger to all the states, from local interests and jealousies, and from the apparent impossibility of a much longer adherence to that shadow of a government, the continental congress. And even four years afterwards, when every evil had been greatly aggravated, and civil war was added to other calamities, the constitution of the United States was all but shipwrecked, in passing through the state conventions; it was adopted by very slender majorities. These are historical facts, which required no coloring to give them effect, and admitted of no concealment, to seduce men into schemes of future aggrandizement. I would even now put it to the common sense of every man, whether, if the constitution of the United States had not been adopted, the charter would have been worth a forty years' purchase of the tolls.

This is not all. It is well known, historically, that this was the very first bridge ever constructed, in New England, over navigable tide-waters so near the sea. The rigors of our climate, the dangers from sudden thaws and freezing, and the obstructions from ice in a rapid current, were deemed by many persons to be insuperable obstacles to the success of such a project. It was believed, that the bridge would scarcely stand a single severe winter. And I myself am old enough to know, that in regard to other arms of the sea, at much later periods, the same doubts have had a strong and depressing influence upon public enterprises. If Charles River bridge had been carried away, during the first or second season after its erection, it is far from being certain, that up to this moment, another bridge, upon such an arm of the sea, would ever have been erected in Massachusetts. I state these things, which are of public notoriety, to repel the notion that the legislature was surprised into an incautious grant, or that the reward was more than adequate to the perils. There was a full and adequate consideration, in a pecuniary sense, for the charter. But, in a more general sense, the erection of the bridge, as a matter of accommodation, has been incalculably beneficial to the public. Unless, therefore, we are wholly to disregard the declarations of the legislature, and the objects of the charter, and the historical facts of the times; and indulge in mere private speculations of profit and loss, by our present lights and experience; it seems to me, that the court is bound to come to the interpretation of this charter, with a persuasion that it was granted in furtherance, and not in derogation, of the public good. * * *

The argument of the defendants is, that the plaintiffs are to take nothing by implication. Either (say they) the exclusive grant extends only to the local limits of the bridge; or it extends the whole length of the river, or, at least, up to old Cambridge bridge. The latter construction would be absurd and monstrous; and therefore, the former must be the true one. Now, I utterly deny the alternative involved in the dilemma. The right to build a bridge over a river, and to take toll, may well include an exclusive franchise, beyond the local limits of the bridge; and yet not extend through the whole course of the river, or even to any considerable distance on the river. There is no difficulty, in common sense, or in law, in maintaining such a doctrine. But then, it is asked, what limits can be assigned to such a franchise? The answer is obvious; the grant carries with it an exclusive franchise, to a reasonable distance on the river; so that the ordinary travel to the bridge shall not be diverted by any new bridge, to the injury or ruin of the franchise. A new bridge, which would be a nuisance to the old bridge, would be within the reach of its exclusive right. The question would not be so much as to the fact of distance, as it would be as to the fact of nuisance. There is nothing new in such expositions of incorporeal rights; and nothing new in thus administering, upon this foundation, remedies in regard thereto. The doctrine is coeval with the common law itself. Suppose, an action is brought for shutting up the ancient lights belonging to a messuage; or for diverting a water-course; or for flowing back a stream; or for erecting a nuisance near a dwelling-house; the question in such cases is not one of mere distance; of mere feet and inches, but of injury—permanent, real and substantial injury—to be decided upon all the circumstances of the case. * * *

Let us see what is the result of the narrow construction contended for by the defendants. * * * Now, I put it to the common sense of every man, whether if, at the moment of granting the charter, the legislature had said to the proprietors; you shall build the bridge; you shall bear the burdens; you shall be bound by the charges; and your sole reimbursement shall be from the tolls of forty years: and yet we will not even guaranty you any certainty of receiving any tolls; on the contrary; we reserve to ourselves the full power and authority to erect other bridges, toll or free bridges, according to our own free will and pleasure, contiguous to yours, and having the same *termini* with yours; and if you are successful, we may thus supplant you, divide, destroy your profits, and annihilate your tolls, without annihilating your burdens: if, I say, such had been the language of the legislature, is there a man living, of ordinary discretion or prudence, who would have accepted such a charter, upon such terms? I fearlessly answer, no. There would have been such a gross inadequacy of consideration, and such a total insecurity of all the rights of property, under such circumstances, that the project would have dropped still-born. And I put the question further, whether any legislature, meaning to promote a project of permanent, public utility (such as this confessedly was), would ever have dreamed of such a qualification of its own grant, when it sought to enlist private capital and private patronage to insure the accomplishment of it? * * *

[I]t is conceded, that the legislature cannot revoke or resume this grant. Why not, I pray to know? There is no negative covenant in the charter; there is no express prohibition to be found there. The reason is plain. The prohibition arises by natural, if not by necessary, implication.

It would be against the first principles of justice, to presume that the legislature reserved a right to destroy its own grant. That was the doctrine in *Fletcher* v. *Peck*, 10 U.S. (6 Cranch) 87 (1810), in this court; and in other cases turning upon the same great principle of political and constitutional duty and right. Can the legislature have power to do that indirectly, which it cannot do directly? If it cannot take away, or resume, the franchise itself, can it take away its whole substance and value? If the law will create an implication, that the legislature shall not resume its own grant, is it not equally as natural and as necessary an implication, that the legislature shall not do any act directly to prejudice its own grant, or to destroy its value? * * *

It is upon this ground, and this ground only, that we can explain the established doctrine in relation to ferries. When the crown grants a ferry from A. to B., without using any words which import it to be an exclusive ferry, why is it (as will be presently shown), that by the common law, the grant is construed to be exclusive of all other ferries between the same places or *termini;* at least, if such ferries are so near that they are injurious to the first ferry, and tend to a direct diminution of its receipts? Plainly, it must be, because from the nature of such a franchise, it can have no permanent value, unless it is exclusive; and the circumstance that during the existence of the grant, the grantee has public burdens imposed upon him, raises the implication, that nothing shall be done to the prejudice of it, while it is a subsisting franchise. * * *

In the case of a ferry, there is a public charge and duty. The owner must keep the ferry in good repair, upon the peril of an indictment. He must keep sufficient accommodations for all travellers, at all reasonable times. He must content himself with a reasonable toll. Such is the *jus publicum*. In return, the law will exclude all injurious competition, and deem every new ferry a nuisance, which subtracts from him the ordinary custom and toll. * * * The same principle applies, without a shadow of difference that I am able to perceive, to the case of a bridge; for the duties are *publici juris*, and pontage and passage are but different names for exclusive toll for transportation. * * *

Wherever any other bridge or ferry is so near, that it injures the franchise, or diminishes the toll, in a positive and essential decree, there it is a nuisance, and is actionable. It invades the franchise, and ought to be abated. But whether there be such an injury or not, is a matter, not of law, but of fact. Distance is no otherwise important than as it bears on the question of fact. All that is required, is, that there should be a sensible, positive injury. In the present case, there is no room to doubt upon this point, for the bridges are contiguous; and Warren bridge, after it was opened, took away three-fourths of the profits of the travel from Charles River bridge; and when it became free (as it now is), it necessarily took away all the tolls, or all except an unimportant and trivial amount. * * *

But it is said, if this is the law, what then is to become of turnpikes and canals? Is the legislature precluded from authorizing new turnpikes or new canals, simply because they cross the path of the old ones, and incidentally diminish their receipt of tolls? The answer is plain. Every turnpike has its local limits and local *termini;* its points of beginning and of end. No one ever imagined, that the legislature might grant a new turnpike, with exactly the same location and *termini*. That would be to rescind its first grant. The grant of a turnpike between A. and B., does not preclude the legislature from the grant of a turnpike between A. and C., even though it should incidentally intercept some of the travel; for it is not necessarily a nuisance to the former grant. The *termini* being different, the grants are or may be substantially different. But if the legislature should grant a second turnpike, substantially taking away the whole travel from the first turnpike, between the same local points; then, I say, it is a violation of the rights of the first turnpike. * * *

But then again, it is said, that all this rests upon implication, and not upon the words of the charter. I admit, that it does; but I again say, that the implication is natural and necessary. It is indispensable to the proper effect of the grant. The franchise cannot subsist without it, at least, for any valuable or practical purpose. What objection can there be to implications, if they arise from the very nature and objects of the grant? If it be indispensable to the full enjoyment of the right to take toll, that it should be exclusive within certain limits, is it not just and reasonable, that it should be so construed? * * *

To the answer already given to the objection, that, unless such a reservation of power exists, there will be a stop put to the progress of all public improvements; I wish, in this connection, to add, that there never can any such consequence follow upon the opposite doctrine. If the public exigencies and interests require that the franchise of Charles River bridge should be taken away, or impaired, it may be lawfully done, upon making due compensation to the proprietors. "Whenever," says the constitution of Massachusetts, "the public exigencies require that the property of any individual should be appropriated to public uses, he shall receive a reasonable compensation therefor;" and this franchise is property—is fixed determinate property. * * *

But it is said, that if the doctrine contended for be not true, then every grant to a corporation becomes, *ipso facto,* a monopoly or exclusive privilege. The grant of a bank, or of an insurance company, or of a manufacturing company, becomes a monopoly, and excludes all injurious competition. With the greatest deference and respect for those who press such an argument, I cannot but express my surprise that it should be urged. * * * [I]n cases of ferries and bridges, and other franchises of a like nature (as has been shown), they are affected with a *jus publicum*. Such grants are made for the public accommodation; and pontage and passage are authorized to be levied upon travellers (which can only be by public authority); and in return, the proprietors are bound to keep up all suitable accommodations for travellers, under the penalty of indictment for their neglect. * * *

It has been further argued, that even if the charter of the Charles River bridge does imply such a contract on the part of the legislature, as is contended for, it is void for want of authority in the legislature to make it * * *. But let us see what the argument is, in relation to sovereignty in general. It admits, that the sovereign power has, among its prerogatives, the right to make grants, to build bridges, to erect ferries, to lay out highways; and to create franchises for public and private purposes. If it has a right to make such grants, it follows, that the grantees have a right to take, and to hold, these franchises. It would be a solecism, to declare that the sovereign power could grant, and yet no one could have a right to take. * * *

It follows, from this view of the subject, that if the sovereign power grants any franchise, it is good and irrevocable, within the limits granted, whatever they may be; or else, in every case, the grant will be held only during pleasure; and the identical franchise may be granted to any other person, or may be revoked at the will of the sovereign. This latter doctrine is not pretended; and, indeed, is unmaintainable in our systems of free government. * * * Thus, for example, if the sovereign power should expressly grant an exclusive right to build a bridge over navigable waters, between the towns of A. and B., and should expressly contract with the grantees, that no other bridge should be built between the same towns; the grant would, upon the principles of the argument, be equally void in regard to the franchise, within the planks of the bridge, as it would be in regard to the franchise, outside of the planks of the bridge; for, in each case, it would, *pro tanto*, abridge or surrender the right of the sovereign to grant a new bridge within the local limits. I am aware, that the argument is not pressed to this extent; but it seems to me a necessary consequence flowing from it. The grant of the franchise of a bridge, twenty feet wide, to be exclusive within those limits, is certainly, if obligatory, an abridgment or surrender of the sovereign power to grant another bridge within the same limits; if we mean to say, that every grant that diminishes the things upon which that power can rightfully act, is such an abridgment. Yet the argument admits, that within the limits and planks of the bridge itself, the grant is exclusive; and cannot be recalled. There is no doubt, that there is a necessary exception in every such grant, that if it is wanted for public use, it may be taken by the sovereign power for such use, upon making compensation. Such a taking is not a violation of the contract; but it is strictly an exception, resulting from the nature and attributes of sovereignty; implied from the very terms, or at least, acting upon the subject-matter of the grant, *suo jure*. * * *

Upon the whole, my judgment is, that the act of the legislature of Massachusetts granting the charter of Warren Bridge, is an act impairing the obligation of the prior contract and grant to the proprietors of Charles River bridge; and, by the constitution of the United States, it is, therefore, utterly void. I am for reversing the decree to the state court (dismissing the bill); and for remanding the cause to the state court for further proceedings, as to law and justice shall appertain.

■ MR. JUSTICE THOMPSON. [omitted]

NOTES AND QUESTIONS

1.   For background on the case, see Stanley I. Kutler, Privilege and Creative Destruction: The Charles River Bridge Case (1971); Charles Warren, The Charles River Bridge Case, 3 Green Bag 2d 78 (1999). Tolls on the Charles River Bridge were fixed by its legislative charter of 1785 and were never adjusted. Once the original construction costs were paid off, routine operating expenses were relatively low. As population and commercial activity surged in the Boston area following the adoption of the Constitution, the bridge was soon generating enormous profits; shares in the corporation eventually increased to over 300% of their original value. The perception that the bridge shareholders were making handsome profits contributed to agitation for construction of a new "free" bridge and may also help account for the relatively unsympathetic attitude of the judiciary toward the claims of the Charles River Bridge proprietors. Kutler reports that as long as the Warren Bridge was charging tolls up through the early 1830s, the Charles River Bridge managed to remain profitable, although at a much-reduced level. Once the Warren Bridge stopped charging tolls, in 1836, the Charles River Bridge could no longer cover its operating costs and defaulted on the £200 annuity to Harvard (then worth $666). After the Supreme Court decision, the proprietors of the Charles River Bridge sold their franchise to the state for a mere $25,000. In 1847, the state eventually granted Harvard $3,333 in recognition of its lost annuities; this was the last revenue Harvard would see from its ferry monopoly. Ironically, both the buyout of the Charles River Bridge and the payment to Harvard were funded out of renewed tolls imposed by the state on both bridges.

2.   Is it a fair inference from the facts of *Charles River Bridge* that the Massachusetts legislature chartered the Warren Bridge precisely for the purpose of putting the Charles River bridge out of business? In other words, that the motive of the legislature was to expropriate the investment of the shareholders of the Charles River Bridge Company? If so, this would sharply distinguish the legislative action here from other types of governmental actions that inadvertently disadvantage existing enterprises. For example, a government decision to start chartering railroads might put turnpike roads or river barges out of business, even if the railroad does not operate along a directly parallel line. But is it possible for a court to distinguish among different types of governmental actions based on the motivations of the legislature? What if the motivations are mixed or ambiguous? Would it be unseemly or perhaps even violate principles of separation of powers for courts to take evidence on or speculate about the motivations of the legislature? On the other hand, is it possible for judges not to be influenced by inferences of legislative motivation in passing on the constitutionality of laws that are enacted?

3.   Corporate charters and franchises were often viewed in the nineteenth century as a type of special privilege or monopoly that served to enrich a well-connected rentier class at the expense of the common people. The Second Bank of the United States, which Taney, serving as Attorney General, had shut down on orders from President Jackson, was a great symbol for those holding this political perspective. *Charles River Bridge* was also a contest over political symbols—the Proprietors of the Warren Bridge represented the anti-monopoly, anti-privilege views of the Jacksonian Democrats, whereas the Proprietors of the Charles River Bridge represented the pro-property rights, pro-internal improvement ideology of the Whigs like Joseph Story and Daniel Webster (who argued the cause for the Proprietors of the Charles River Bridge).

4.   The principal case involves a corporate charter or franchise, which all Justices agreed should be considered a constitutionally protected right. But the doctrine of strict construction has also been applied to government grants of more conventional property rights. For example, in Watt v. Western Nuclear, Inc., 462 U.S. 36 (1983), certain Homesteading Acts granting land to settlers had reserved to the government "all the coal and other minerals" in those lands. The question was whether the reservation of "other minerals" included gravel. The Court held that the gravel belonged to the United States, relying in part on "the established rule that land grants are construed favorably to the Government, that nothing passes except what is conveyed in clear language, and that if there are doubts they are resolved for the Government, not against it." Id. (quoting United States v. Union Pac. R.R. Co., 353 U.S. 112, 116 (1957)). (Recall also that the public trust doctrine, discussed in Chapter III, sometimes functions as a rule of construction protecting public rights against alienation.) Do you agree that the same considerations cited by Chief Justice Taney for construing corporate charters favorably to the government also require that courts construe land grants to settlers favorably to the government? For example, do considerations about the need to facilitate the development of new technology and prevent monopoly apply with the same force to grants of land to homesteaders? Another problem here is that the incidents associated with conventional grants of property like land are typically not spelled out in the grant, but are defined by common law (although in *Western Nuclear* the reservation was written in the grant, albeit in ambiguous terms). How, if at all, does one apply the doctrine of strict construction to property rights, the incidents of which are defined by common law?

5.   Is Taney's proposed accommodation between change and reliance only a temporary one? In effect, the principle of strict construction is just a default rule, around which future charter promoters and legislatures are free to contract. If the response to the decision is simply to require that all charters be made explicitly exclusive, as Story suggests it will be, then what exactly has been accomplished by the holding in the case? Will the new generation of charters at least be clearer and less subject to disputes and litigation? In *Bridge Proprietors v. Hoboken Co.*, 68 U.S. (1 Wall.) 116 (1863), the Court considered a 99-year charter that expressly barred "any other bridge" from being built near the plaintiff's bridge. The Court held that the

charter was not impaired when the state permitted a railroad bridge to be constructed nearby, because the word "bridge" did not clearly encompass a railroad bridge.

6.   Taney and Story are acutely aware of the technological dynamism of the American economy, discussing how ferries have been superseded by bridges and turnpikes by railroads. When an old-technology enterprise that enjoys some kind of government charter is being displaced by a new-technology enterprise that also enjoys some kind of government support, how does one distinguish between the impact of a change in government policy and a change in technology? In *Market Street Ry. Co. v. Railroad Comm'n*, 324 U.S. 548 (1945), the Court was faced with the claim by a street railway company that a state regulatory commission was driving it out of business. But the Court concluded that the real problem was competition from new technology, in the form of bus companies. Today, local wire-line telephone companies have lost market share to wireless and internet-based communication technologies. Their loss of business is partly due to government policy and partly due to new technology. How can courts disentangle these causes?

7.   One modern analogue of the dispute in *Charles River Bridge* is provided by controversies over what have been called "deregulatory takings." Traditionally, public utility services like electric, gas, water, and local telephone service were thought to be natural monopolies, and so only one firm was given a franchise to serve any given area. Advances in technology and new thinking about the best method of utility regulation have led to attempts to introduce competition into these industries (with mixed success). When the government sets policy to deliberately inject competition into a market that has previously been served by a monopoly, does the incumbent monopolist have a right to block the change or demand compensation for lost revenues? Should it matter if the utility franchise explicitly confers monopoly privileges on the incumbent carrier (most do not)? For a variety of perspectives on this problem, see J. Gregory Sidak & Daniel F. Spulber, Deregulatory Takings and the Regulatory Contract (1997); William J. Baumol & Thomas W. Merrill, Deregulatory Takings, Breach of the Regulatory Contract, and the Telecommunications Act of 1996, 72 N.Y.U. L. Rev. 1037 (1997); Susan Rose-Ackerman & Jim Rossi, Disentangling Deregulatory Takings, 86 Va. L. Rev. 1435 (2000); Jim Chen, The Death of the Regulatory Compact: Adjusting Prices and Expectations in the Law of Regulated Industries, 67 Ohio St. L.J. 1265, 1295–1304 (2006).

8.   Another modern analogue is the debate over the welfare effects of granting monopolies to holders of intellectual property rights such as patents and copyrights. Compare Michele Boldrin & David K. Levine, Against Intellectual Monopoly (2008); Mark A. Lemley & Mark P. McKenna, Is Pepsi Really a Substitute for Coke? Market Definition in Antitrust and IP, 100 Geo. L.J. 2055 (2012) with Jonathan Barnett, Patent Groupthink Unravels, 34 Harv. J.L. & Tech. 419 (2021); Edmund W. Kitch, Elementary and Persistent Errors in the Economic Analysis of Intellectual Property, 53 Vand. L. Rev. 1727 (2000). As Eric Posner and Glen Weyl point out, all property rights, i.e. rights to exclude others from particular resources, create a

monopoly with respect to the particular resource in question. Eric A. Posner & E. Glen Weyl, Radical Markets: Uprooting Capitalism and Democracy for a Just Society (2018). But the welfare effect of exclusion rights depends significantly on whether there are reasonable substitutes for the monopoly in question. If A owns a car, and does not want to sell it to B, the welfare effect on B depends on whether someone else has a similar car they are willing to sell to B on reasonable terms. If there are good substitutes, the monopoly right associated with property does not pose large adverse effects on social welfare. If there are no good substitutes, some form of public intervention, in the form of antitrust law, regulation of terms of service and pricing, or compulsory licensing, may be appropriate.

Forbearance Values

The dueling opinions in *Charles River Bridge* emphasize different values in trying to determine how strictly the government should be required to forbear from interfering with existing rights. Chief Justice Taney underlines the importance of accommodating change, so as to promote competition, encourage the development of new technologies like railroads, and free the present generation from the dead hand of old monopolies. Justice Story stresses the importance of protecting reliance interests, in order to encourage investors to put capital at risk in new projects. Both sets of values are still regarded today as being important in determining the optimal level of government forbearance. But there are other values to consider as well.

Chief Justice Taney emphasizes how over-protecting existing interests can stultify economic growth by stifling competition. Today, commentators would probably also consider distributive justice as a factor that might warrant government modification of property rights. Suppose, for example, that we conclude the extension of existing intellectual property rights confers a windfall on a lucky few at the expense of higher license costs and transaction costs for the many. Should the government be allowed to rescind the legislation on the ground that the extension was distributively unjust? One general question here is how often it is necessary to interfere with specific property rights on distributive justice grounds, given the option of imposing progressive taxes which can be paid from a variety of sources. Expropriation or abolition of rights in specific property is deeply unsettling to owners and very likely discourages future investment. Ratcheting up tax rates, particularly when the increases apply only in future years, is arguably a less disruptive and more effective mechanism for achieving greater distributional equity. The contending positions are set forth in Louis Kaplow & Steven Shavell, Why the Legal System Is Less Efficient than the Income Tax in Redistributing Income, 23 J. Legal Stud. 667 (1994); Louis Kaplow & Steven Shavell, Should Legal Rules Favor the Poor? Clarifying the Role of Legal Rules and the Income Tax in Redistributing Income, 29 J. Legal Stud. 821 (2000); Ronen Avraham, David Fortus, & Kyle Logue, Revisiting the Roles of Legal Rules and Tax

Rules in Income Redistribution: A Response to Kaplow & Shavell, 89 Iowa L. Rev. 1125 (2004). Still, there may be circumstances where interfering with specific property rights or expectations is the only course available to achieving what is regarded as a more just distribution of wealth. See Lee Anne Fennell & Richard H. McAdams, The Distributive Deficit in Law and Economics, 100 Minn. L. Rev. 1051 (2016); Zachary Liscow, Reducing Inequity on the Cheap: When Legal Rule Design Should Incorporate Equity as Well as Efficiency, 123 Yale L.J. 2478 (2014).

Justice Story also invokes economic growth, but he takes the perspective of those who have investment capital available for new undertakings. Is Justice Story's concern about protecting reliance interests focused on the level of return to investments or on uncertainty regarding the level of return to investments? Both are obviously relevant to any entrepreneur thinking about making an investment in a new enterprise. But there is reason to think that uncertainty is a particular concern where government forbearance is at issue. If the government engages in random acts of expropriation, this may not change the expected level of return for other investments very much (on an ex ante basis). But it is likely to raise grave concerns about the future course of government behavior and may have a disproportionate impact on discouraging new investment. (We consider at the end of Part B whether private insurance may be a solution to the problem of uncertainty about government behavior and policy.) Today, commentators would probably also emphasize another factor: A weak commitment on the part of government to forbear from interfering with property may encourage some people to spend time and money on efforts to secure legislation interfering with other people's property and may in turn cause other people to spend time and money to head off such legislation in order to protect their property from interference. Economists often refer to this kind of jockeying for government favor as "rent-seeking," with the implication that this kind of competition is a dead-weight loss to society. The issue is extremely complicated, however, as sometimes competition for the recognition or modification of property rights can lead to policy changes that benefit society. Determining the optimal level of political agitation for change in policy regarding property is therefore an almost impossible task, although it may be possible to identify some measures— like laws that seize A's property and transfer it to B without any change in the anticipated use of the resources—as being presumptively unjustified.

What we are calling forbearance can be seen as an aspect of the rule of law. Lon Fuller set out a famous list of criteria for the rule of law, including generality, clarity, non-contradiction, constancy, and non-retroactivity. See Lon L. Fuller, The Morality of Law 33–91 (2d ed. 1969). How are these criteria related to forbearance? Notice that these criteria are very similar to the possible advantages of legislatures over courts in altering the menu of property rights—the *numerus clausus* as a principle of institutional choice. Thomas W. Merrill & Henry E. Smith, Optimal Standardization in the Law of Property: The *Numerus Clausus* Principle, 110 Yale L.J. 1, 58–68 (2000). Would that choice be less plausible in the absence of the devices explored in this Chapter? There are many versions of the rule of law, and how to promote the rule of law—and what exactly to promote—have been controversial topics in law and development. See Private Law and the Rule of Law (Lisa M. Austin & Dennis Klimchuk eds., 2014); Brian Z. Tamanaha, On the Rule of Law: History, Politics, Theory (2004).

Recently, a number of scholars have attempted to determine empirically what kind of impact government forbearance has on the general level of economic activity in different countries. See, e.g., Daron Acemoglu, Simon Johnson & James Robinson, The Colonial Origins of Comparative Development: An Empirical Investigation, 91 Am. Econ. Rev. 1369 (2001); Kevin E. Davis & Michael J. Trebilcock, The Relationship Between Law and Development: Optimists and Skeptics, 56 Am. J. Comp. L. 895 (2008); Simon Johnson, John McMillan & Christopher Woodruff, Property Rights and Finance, 92 Am. Econ. Rev. 1335 (2002); Terra Lawson-Remer, Property Insecurity, 38 Brooklyn J. Int'l L. 145 (2012); Paul G. Mahoney, The Common Law and Economic Growth: Hayek Might Be Right, 30 J. Legal Stud. 503 (2001). These studies adopt a variety of measures of forbearance, although government commitment to pay just compensation when property is taken is one common yardstick. Whatever measures are used, virtually all these studies find a positive correlation between what we are calling forbearance and rates of aggregate economic growth. In any event, the law and development literature provides at least some empirical support for Justice Story's concerns, if not for his particular application of those concerns in *Charles River Bridge*.

Legislative Entrenchment

Another way to consider the problem in *Charles River Bridge* is to ask: To what extent should one legislature be able to tie the hands of a subsequent legislature? We live in a democracy, and a central tenet of democracy is majority rule. Ordinarily, majority rule is understood to mean rule by the current majority. Thus, if last year's duly-elected legislature enacts a particular measure, such as "no vehicles in the park," it is understood that this year's duly-elected legislature can adopt a different measure, such as "vehicles in the park are okay." We might think it incompatible with democracy for last year's legislature to enact a statute that says: "No vehicles in the park, and this rule cannot be repealed." If such a statute were enforced to block today's legislature from repealing the rule against vehicles in the park, this would seem like a type of dead hand control: A previous legislature, elected by a previous majority, is overriding the preferences of today's legislature, elected by today's majority, in violation of the general principle of majority rule. Commentators have taken a variety of positions on whether legislative entrenchment is permissible or desirable. For further discussion, see David Dana & Susan P. Koniak, Bargaining in the Shadow of Democracy, 148 U. Pa. L. Rev. 473 (1999); Julian Eule, Temporal Limits on the Legislative Mandate: Entrenchment and Retroactivity, 1987 Am. B. Found. Res. J. 379; Michael J. Klarman, Majoritarian Judicial Review: The Entrenchment Problem, 85 Geo. L.J. 491 (1997); John O. McGinnis & Michael B. Rappaport, Symmetric Entrenchment: A Constitutional and Normative Theory, 89 Va. L. Rev. 385 (2003); Eric A. Posner & Adrian Vermeule, Legislative Entrenchment: A Reappraisal, 111 Yale L.J. 1665 (2002); John C. Roberts & Erwin Chemerinsky, Entrenchment of Ordinary Legislation: A Reply to Professors Posner and Vermeule, 91 Cal. L. Rev. 1773 (2003); Stewart E. Sterk, Retrenchment on Entrenchment, 71 Geo. Wash. L. Rev. 231 (2003).

The proposition that government should be required to forbear from interfering with property presupposes that at least some legislative entrenchment is permissible. In particular, the hands of future legislatures must be tied insofar as they seek to repudiate promises, express or implied, to forbear from interfering with property rights. But while modern commentators often embrace extreme positions (never entrench, entrench whenever you like), notice that both Chief Justice Taney and Justice Story adopt more nuanced views. Justice Taney is relatively hostile to legislative entrenchment, but even he believes that an express promise by the legislature to make a charter exclusive would be binding on a successor legislature and would be enforced under the Contracts Clause. Justice Story is more sympathetic to entrenchment, but even he acknowledges that a future legislature can get rid of a corporate charter using the power of eminent domain. So it is likely that in practice the legal system will take up a position between the polar extremes staked out by the commentators. The critical issues are what sort of doctrines will be used to impose a limited degree of entrenchment, and what kinds of circumstances will justify departures from entrenchment.

B. OTHER SOURCES OF GOVERNMENT FORBEARANCE

The Contracts Clause, U.S. Const. art. I § 10, which prohibits states from enacting laws "impairing the obligation of contract," is encountered less frequently today than it was when the Supreme Court decided *Charles River Bridge*. But there are multiple sources of constraint on governments that can act as a brake on actions that upset expectations associated with property. In this Part we consider briefly constraints associated with procedural due process, the doctrine of vested rights (and the associated canon of interpretation disfavoring retroactive laws), the strong version of stare decisis associated with property rights, and international investment treaties, which typically include provisions protecting investors against certain types of government interference with investment property.

1. DUE PROCESS

The Fifth Amendment to the Constitution provides that no person shall "be deprived of life, liberty, or property, without due process of law." U.S. Const. amend V. This language binds the federal government. In 1868 the Fourteenth Amendment was adopted, extending the same language to state governments (and local governmental authorities that derive their powers from the states). U.S. Const. amend. XIV. Commentators and (some) judges have pointed out that "due process of law" sounds like a requirement of procedural regularity. See, e.g., Frank H. Easterbrook, Substance and Due Process, 1982 Sup. Ct. Rev. 85. Nevertheless, "due process of law" has long been understood as providing both procedural and substantive protection for property rights. The substantive protections include a requirement that courts give extra scrutiny to retroactive legislation affecting property, see, e.g., Usery v. Turner Elkhorn Mining Co., 428 U.S. 1, 16–18 (1976), and protections against excessive penalties and civil damages awards, see, e.g., BMW of North America, Inc. v. Gore, 517 U.S. 559 (1996). The core procedural protections are a requirement of notice and an opportunity to contest the legality of government deprivations of property before they occur. See, e.g., Jones v. Flowers, 547 U.S. 220 (2006) (state must take measures reasonably designed to provide notice to owner before seizing home for nonpayment of taxes); United States v. James Daniel Good Real Property, 510 U.S. 43 (1993) (state must afford owner an opportunity to contest legality of forfeiture proceeding before seizing property).

Somewhat surprisingly, however, it was not until the 1970s that the Supreme Court began to attend to the question of what sorts of interests are encompassed within the term "property" in the Due Process Clauses of the Fifth and Fourteenth Amendments. The decision that brought the question to the fore was *Goldberg v. Kelly*, 397 U.S. 254 (1970), where the Court—without explicitly so deciding—assumed that the right to receive future welfare benefits was a form of "property" protected by procedural due process. *Goldberg* cited favorably to the work of Yale Law School professor Charles Reich. See id. at 262 n.8 (citing Charles Reich, Individual Rights and Social Welfare: The Emerging Legal Issues, 74 Yale L.J. 1245 (1965) and Charles Reich, The New Property, 73 Yale L.J. 733 (1964)). Reich's visionary scholarship did not focus on the question how the word "property" should be defined for conventional legal purposes, including implementation of the due process clauses. He offered a much more far-reaching thesis about the function of property in a world in which government plays a larger role in everyday life than had been the case before the advent of the modern administrative state. In the modern world of the activist state, Reich argued, it is imperative radically to *expand* the concept of property in order to protect individuals against majoritarian tyranny. A brief excerpt from his leading article advancing this thesis follows.

Charles A. Reich, *The New Property*
73 YALE L.J. 733, 733, 768–74, 779, 782–87 (1964).

The institution called property guards the troubled boundary between individual man and the state. It is not the only guardian; many other institutions, laws, and practices serve as well. But in a society that chiefly values material well-being, the power to control a particular portion of that well-being is the very foundation of individuality.

One of the most important developments in the United States during the past decade has been the emergence of government as a major source of wealth. Government is a gigantic syphon. It draws in revenue and power, and pours forth wealth: money, benefits, services, contracts, franchises, and licenses. Government has always had this function. But while in early times it was minor, today's distribution of largess is on a vast, imperial scale.

The valuables dispensed by government take many forms, but they all share one characteristic. They are steadily taking the place of traditional forms of wealth—forms which are held as private property. Social insurance substitutes for savings; a government contract replaces a businessman's customers and goodwill. The wealth of more and more Americans depends upon a relationship to government. Increasingly, Americans live on government largess—allocated by government on its own terms, and held by recipients subject to conditions which express "the public interest."

The growth of government largess, accompanied by a distinctive system of law, is having profound consequences. It affects the underpinnings of individualism and independence. It influences the workings of the Bill of Rights. It has an impact on the power of private interests, in their relation to each other and to government. It is helping to create a new society. * * *

The characteristics of the public interest state are varied, but there is an underlying philosophy that unites them. This is the doctrine that the wealth that flows from government is held by its recipients conditionally, subject to confiscation in the interest of the paramount state. This philosophy is epitomized in the most important of all judicial decisions concerning government largess, the case of *Flemming v. Nestor*.[175]

Ephram Nestor, an alien, came to this country in 1913, and after a long working life became eligible in 1955 for old-age benefits under the Social Security Act. From 1936 to 1955 Nestor and his employers had contributed payments to the government which went into a special old-

---

[175]   363 U.S. 603 (1960).

age and survivors insurance trust fund. From 1933 to 1939 Nestor was a member of the Communist Party. Long after his membership ceased, Congress passed a law retroactively making such membership cause for deportation, and a second law, also retroactive, making such deportation for having been a member of the Party grounds for loss of retirement benefits. In 1956 Nestor was deported, leaving his wife here. Soon after his deportation, payment of benefits to Nestor's wife was terminated.

In a five to four decision, the Supreme Court held that cutting off Nestor's retirement insurance, although based on conduct completely lawful at the time, was not unconstitutional. Specifically, it was not a taking of property without due process of law; Nestor's benefits were not an "accrued property right."[176] The Court recognized that each worker's benefits flow "from the contributions he made to the national economy while actively employed," but it held that his interest is "noncontractual" and "cannot be soundly analogized to that of the holder of an annuity."[177] The Court continued:

> To engraft upon the Social Security system a concept of "accrued property rights" would deprive it of the flexibility and boldness in adjustment of ever-changing conditions which it demands . . . It was doubtless out of an awareness of the need for such flexibility that Congress included . . . a clause expressly reserving to it "[t]he right to alter, amend or repeal any provision" of the Act. . . . That provision makes express what is implicit in the institutional needs of the program.[178]

The Court stated further that, in any case where Congress "modified" social security rights, the Court should interfere only if the action is "utterly lacking in rational justification."[179] This, the Court said, "is not the case here." As the Court saw it, it might be deemed reasonable for Congress to limit payments to those living in this country; moreover, the Court thought it would not have been "irrational for Congress to have concluded that the public purse should not be utilized to contribute to the support of those deported on the grounds specified in the statute."[180]

The implications of *Flemming v. Nestor* are profound. No form of government largess is more personal or individual than an old age pension. No form is more clearly earned by the recipient, who, together with his employer, contributes to the Social Security fund during the years of his employment. No form is more obviously a compulsory substitute for private property; the tax on wage earner and employer might readily have gone to higher pay and higher private savings instead. No form is more relied on, and more often thought of as property. No form is more vital to the independence and dignity of the individual.

---

[176] Id. at 608.
[177] Id. at 609–10.
[178] Id. at 610–11.
[179] Id. at 611.
[180] Id. at 612.

Yet under the philosophy of Congress and the Court, a man or woman, after a lifetime of work, has no rights which may not be taken away to serve some public policy. The Court makes no effort to balance the interests at stake. The public policy that justifies cutting off benefits need not even be an important one or a wise one—so long as it is not utterly irrational, the Court will not interfere. In any clash between individual rights and public policy, the latter is automatically held to be superior.

The philosophy of *Flemming v. Nestor* * * * resembles the philosophy of feudal tenure. Wealth is not "owned," or "vested" in the holders. Instead, it is held conditionally, the conditions being ones which seek to ensure the fulfillment of obligations imposed by the state. Just as the feudal system linked lord and vassal through a system of mutual dependence, obligation, and loyalty, so government largess binds man to the state. And, it may be added, loyalty or fealty to the state is often one of the essential conditions of modem tenure. In the many decisions taking away government largess for refusal to sign loyalty oaths, belonging to "subversive" organizations, or other similar grounds, there is more than a suggestion of the condition of fealty demanded in older times. * * *

Property is a legal institution the essence of which is the creation and protection of certain private rights in wealth of any kind. The institution performs many different functions. One of these functions is to draw a boundary between public and private power. Property draws a circle around the activities of each private individual or organization. Within that circle, the owner has a greater degree of freedom than without. Outside, he must justify or explain his actions, and show his authority. Within, he is master, and the state must explain and justify any interference. It is as if property shifted the burden of proof; outside, the individual has the burden; inside, the burden is on government to demonstrate that something the owner wishes to do should not be done.

Thus, property performs the function of maintaining independence, dignity and pluralism in society by creating zones within which the majority has to yield to the owner. Whim, caprice, irrationality and "antisocial" activities are given the protection of law; the owner may do what all or most of his neighbors decry. The Bill of Rights also serves this function, but while the Bill of Rights comes into play only at extraordinary moments of conflict or crisis, property affords day-to-day protection in the ordinary affairs of life. Indeed, in the final analysis the Bill of Rights depends upon the existence of private property. Political rights presuppose that individuals and private groups have the will and the means to act independently. But so long as individuals are motivated largely by self-interest, their well-being must first be independent. Civil liberties must have a basis in property, or bills of rights will not preserve them.

Property is not a natural right but a deliberate construction by society. If such an institution did not exist, it would be necessary to create it, in order to have the kind of society we wish. The majority cannot be expected, on specific issues, to yield its power to a minority. Only if the minority's will is established as a general principle can it keep the majority at bay in a given instance. Like the Bill of Rights, property represents a general, long range protection of individual and private interests, created by the majority for the ultimate good of all. * * *

From the individual's point of view, it is not any particular kind of power, but all kinds of power, that are to be feared. This is the lesson of the public interest state. The mere fact that power is derived from the majority does not necessarily make it less oppressive. Liberty is more than the right to do what the majority wants, or to do what is "reasonable." Liberty is the right to defy the majority, and to do what is unreasonable. The great error of the public interest state is that it assumes an identity between the public interest and the interest of the majority.

The reform, then, has not done away with the importance of private property. More than ever the individual needs to possess, in whatever form, a small but sovereign island of his own. * * *

The most clearly defined problem posed by government largess is the way it can be used to apply pressure against the exercise of constitutional rights. A first principle should be that government must have no power to "buy up" rights guaranteed by the Constitution. It should not be able to impose any condition on largess that would be invalid if imposed on something other than a "gratuity." * * *

Beyond the limits deriving from the Constitution, what limits should be imposed on governmental power over largess? Such limits, whatever they may be, must be largely self-imposed and self-policed by legislatures; the Constitution sets only a bare minimum of limitations on legislative policy. * * *

[P]rocedure offers a valuable means for restraining arbitrary action. * * * The grant, denial, revocation, and administration of all types of government largess should be subject to scrupulous observance of fair procedures. Action should be open to hearing and contest, and based upon a record subject to judicial review. The denial of any form of privilege or benefit on the basis of undisclosed reasons should no longer be tolerated. Nor should the same person sit as legislator, prosecutor, judge and jury, combining all the functions of government in such a way as to make fairness virtually impossible. There is no justification for the survival of arbitrary methods where valuable rights are at stake. * * *

Eventually those forms of largess which are closely linked to status must be deemed to be held as of right. * * * Confiscation, if used at all, should be the ultimate, not the most common and convenient penalty. The presumption should be that the professional man will keep his license, and the welfare recipient his pension. These interests should be "vested." If revocation is necessary, not by reason of the fault of the individual holder, but by reason of overriding demands of public policy, perhaps payment of just compensation would be appropriate. The individual should not bear the entire loss for a remedy primarily intended to benefit the community.

The concept of right is most urgently needed with respect to benefits like unemployment compensation, public assistance, and old age insurance. These benefits are based upon a recognition that misfortune and deprivation are often caused by forces far beyond the control of the individual, such as technological change, variations in demand for goods, depressions, or wars. The aim of these benefits is to preserve the self-sufficiency of the individual, to rehabilitate him where necessary, and to allow him to be a valuable member of a family and a community; in theory they represent part of the individual's rightful share in the commonwealth. Only by making such benefits into rights can the welfare state achieve its goal of providing a secure minimum basis for individual well-being and dignity in a society where each man cannot be wholly the master of his own destiny. * * *

If the individual is to survive in a collective society, he must have protection against its ruthless pressures. There must be sanctuaries or enclaves where no majority can reach. To shelter the solitary human spirit does not merely make possible the fulfillment of individuals; it also gives society the power to change, to grow, and to regenerate, and hence to endure. These were the objects which property sought to achieve, and can no longer achieve. The challenge of the future will be to construct, for the society that is coming, institutions and laws to carry on this work. Just as the Homestead Act was a deliberate effort to foster individual values at an earlier time, so we must try to build an economic basis for liberty today—a Homestead Act for rootless twentieth century man. We must create a new property.

NOTES AND QUESTIONS

1.   Reich sounds a theme that plays an increasingly prominent role in theorizing about property—its role in promoting individual autonomy. See, e.g., Hanoch Dagan, A Liberal Theory of Property (2021); Gregory S. Alexander, The Complex Core of Property, 94 Cornell L. Rev. 1063 (2009). Reich's focus is on the importance of property in shielding individuals from explicit or implicit coercion by the government. In this respect, his thesis is about the importance of government forbearance. Others have argued that widely dispersed private property ownership is vital to the formation of political parties, dissident organizations, and a free press. See, e.g., Milton Friedman, Capitalism and Freedom 7–21 (1962); Richard Pipes, Property and Freedom 209–81 (1999). Reich notes that when wealth takes the form of government "largesse"—government jobs, transfer payments, and licenses and permits—not only are the means to resist government eroded, but the affirmative opportunities for government manipulation and control of individual beliefs and practices are greatly enhanced, by conditioning the receipt of largesse on conformity to government-approved behavior. His proposed solution, that government largesse should be treated more like

conventional private property, in order to provide a source of security in individuals that would promote autonomy and liberty, was equally innovative.

2. Does Reich exaggerate the extent to which government has taken over (or is about to take over) the functions previously served by private property? Would the size of the government's budget be a good proxy for how much government largesse has displaced traditional property, or can government achieve the same effect through regulatory mandates and exceptions? Is the problem that governments do not face competition? In some contexts, state and local governments compete for residents and businesses. On the local level this idea is associated with the Tiebout Hypothesis we encountered in Chapter IX in connection with zoning. Does the federal government face increasing competition from abroad?

3. Does Reich provide a persuasive account of how government "largesse" is going to be transformed into a right that the government cannot manipulate in order to induce individual conformity? He urges courts to enforce constitutional rights (to free speech, for example) when the government tries to condition receipt of government largesse on forgoing the exercise of constitutional rights, and he urges courts to strictly enforce procedural limitations on the termination of government entitlements. In these respects his counsel was, on the whole, very successful, as courts moved strongly to support these positions in the years after the publication of his article. But he was cautious about advocating strict judicial review of legislation qualifying or eliminating largesse, and in this respect his caution has also characterized the judicial attitude going forward. The Court has never recognized anything like a "takings" claim for a government reduction in benefits or employment opportunities. More broadly, can one say that there is a right to exclude others or the government from interfering with government largesse? Does this mean the analogy to property breaks down? For example, owners of private property can use self-help to protect their assets against intrusions or depredations. There is no obvious "self-help" remedy for those who are dependent on government largesse. Does this mean that the aspiration to transform largesse into a kind of "new property" is doomed to failure? Or is group action though politics the main avenue of self-help to protect government largesse? If so, does this reduce the new property to the playing out of politics? For an effort to revive Reich's vision in a modern progressive vein, see David A. Super, A New New Property, 113 Colum. L. Rev. 1773 (2013).

4. Reich acknowledges that property performs many functions, but his focus throughout is on property's role in promoting individual autonomy. In other words, his vision of why property is valuable is largely a "consumerist" one rather than a "producerist" one. Property is regarded as important because it promotes individual freedom in the way we organize our private lives; its role as a means of organizing resources for production is ignored. In practice, are these roles more closely linked than Reich acknowledges?

5. Whether or not it was inspired by Reich's writing, the Supreme Court's decision in *Goldberg* unleashed a "due process revolution," as lower

courts began requiring that claimants holding a variety of government "entitlements" critical to their wellbeing be given hearings before such entitlements were terminated. See Henry J. Friendly, "Some Kind of Hearing," 123 U. Pa. L. Rev. 1267, 1273 (1975). Perhaps taken aback, the Court quickly perceived that it was necessary to provide clearer guidance about when different types of government benefits should be regarded as "property" sufficient to trigger due process protection. The effort to provide that guidance came in the following landmark decisions.

Board of Regents v. Roth

Supreme Court of the United States, 1972.
408 U.S. 564.

■ MR. JUSTICE STEWART delivered the opinion of the Court. In 1968 the respondent, David Roth, was hired for his first teaching job as assistant professor of political science at Wisconsin State University-Oshkosh. He was hired for a fixed term of one academic year. The notice of his faculty appointment specified that his employment would begin on September 1, 1968, and would end on June 30, 1969. The respondent completed that term. But he was informed that he would not be rehired for the next academic year.

The respondent had no tenure rights to continued employment. Under Wisconsin statutory law a state university teacher can acquire tenure as a "permanent" employee only after four years of year-to-year employment. Having acquired tenure, a teacher is entitled to continued employment "during efficiency and good behavior." A relatively new teacher without tenure, however, is under Wisconsin law entitled to nothing beyond his one-year appointment. There are no statutory or administrative standards defining eligibility for re-employment. State law thus clearly leaves the decision whether to rehire a nontenured teacher for another year to the unfettered discretion of university officials.

The procedural protection afforded a Wisconsin State University teacher before he is separated from the University corresponds to his job security. As a matter of statutory law, a tenured teacher cannot be "discharged except for cause upon written charges" and pursuant to certain procedures. A nontenured teacher, similarly, is protected to some extent during his one-year term. Rules promulgated by the Board of Regents provide that a nontenured teacher "dismissed" before the end of the year may have some opportunity for review of the "dismissal." But the Rules provide no real protection for a nontenured teacher who simply is not re-employed for the next year. He must be informed by February 1 "concerning retention or non-retention for the ensuing year." But "no reason for non-retention need be given. No review or appeal is provided in such case."

In conformance with these Rules, the President of Wisconsin State University-Oshkosh informed the respondent before February 1, 1969, that he would not be rehired for the 1969–1970 academic year. He gave the respondent no reason for the decision and no opportunity to challenge it at any sort of hearing.

The respondent then brought this action in Federal District Court alleging that the decision not to rehire him for the next year infringed his Fourteenth Amendment rights. He attacked the decision both in substance and procedure. First, he alleged that the true reason for the decision was to punish him for certain statements critical of the University administration, and that it therefore violated his right to freedom of speech. Second, he alleged that the failure of University officials to give him notice of any reason for nonretention and an opportunity for a hearing violated his right to procedural due process of law.

The District Court granted summary judgment for the respondent on the procedural issue, ordering the University officials to provide him with reasons and a hearing. The Court of Appeals, with one judge dissenting, affirmed this partial summary judgment. We granted certiorari. The only question presented to us at this stage in the case is whether the respondent had a constitutional right to a statement of reasons and a hearing on the University's decision not to rehire him for another year. We hold that he did not.

I

The requirements of procedural due process apply only to the deprivation of interests encompassed by the Fourteenth Amendment's protection of liberty and property. When protected interests are implicated, the right to some kind of prior hearing is paramount. But the range of interests protected by procedural due process is not infinite.

The District Court decided that procedural due process guarantees apply in this case by assessing and balancing the weights of the particular interests involved. It concluded that the respondent's interest in re-employment at Wisconsin State University-Oshkosh outweighed the University's interest in denying him re-employment summarily. Undeniably, the respondent's re-employment prospects were of major concern to him—concern that we surely cannot say was insignificant. And a weighing process has long been a part of any determination of the form of hearing required in particular situations by procedural due process. But, to determine whether due process requirements apply in the first place, we must look not to the "weight" but to the nature of the interest at stake. We must look to see if the interest is within the Fourteenth Amendment's protection of liberty and property.

"Liberty" and "property" are broad and majestic terms. They are among the "[g]reat [constitutional] concepts . . . purposely left to gather meaning from experience. . . . [T]hey relate to the whole domain of social and economic fact, and the statesmen who founded this Nation knew too well that only a stagnant society remains unchanged." National Mutual

Ins. Co. v. Tidewater Transfer Co., 337 U.S. 582, 646 (1949) (Frankfurter, J., dissenting). For that reason, the Court has fully and finally rejected the wooden distinction between "rights" and "privileges" that once seemed to govern the applicability of procedural due process rights.[9] The Court has also made clear that the property interests protected by procedural due process extend well beyond actual ownership of real estate, chattels, or money. By the same token, the Court has required due process protection for deprivations of liberty beyond the sort of formal constraints imposed by the criminal process.

Yet, while the Court has eschewed rigid or formalistic limitations on the protection of procedural due process, it has at the same time observed certain boundaries. For the words "liberty" and "property" in the Due Process Clause of the Fourteenth Amendment must be given some meaning.

II

"While this court has not attempted to define with exactness the liberty ... guaranteed [by the Fourteenth Amendment], the term has received much consideration and some of the included things have been definitely stated. Without doubt, it denotes not merely freedom from bodily restraint but also the right of the individual to contract, to engage in any of the common occupations of life, to acquire useful knowledge, to marry, establish a home and bring up children, to worship God according to the dictates of his own conscience, and generally to enjoy those privileges long recognized ... as essential to the orderly pursuit of happiness by free men." Meyer v. Nebraska, 262 U.S. 390, 399 (1923). In a Constitution for a free people, there can be no doubt that the meaning of "liberty" must be broad indeed. See, e.g., Bolling v. Sharpe, 347 U.S. 497, 499–500 (1954); Stanley v. Illinois, 405 U.S. 645 (1972).

There might be cases in which a State refused to re-employ a person under such circumstances that interests in liberty would be implicated. But this is not such a case.

The State, in declining to rehire the respondent, did not make any charge against him that might seriously damage his standing and associations in his community. It did not base the nonrenewal of his contract on a charge, for example, that he had been guilty of dishonesty, or immorality. Had it done so, this would be a different case. For "[w]here a person's good name, reputation, honor, or integrity is at stake because of what the government is doing to him, notice and an opportunity to be heard are essential." Wisconsin v. Constantineau, 400 U.S. 433, 437 (1971). In such a case, due process would accord an opportunity to refute the charge before University officials. In the present case, however, there is no suggestion whatever that the respondent's "good name, reputation, honor, or integrity" is at stake.

---

[9]   Graham v. Richardson, 403 U.S. 365, 374.

Similarly, there is no suggestion that the State, in declining to re-employ the respondent, imposed on him a stigma or other disability that foreclosed his freedom to take advantage of other employment opportunities. The State, for example, did not invoke any regulations to bar the respondent from all other public employment in state universities. Had it done so, this, again, would be a different case. * * *

To be sure, the respondent has alleged that the nonrenewal of his contract was based on his exercise of his right to freedom of speech. But this allegation is not now before us. The District Court stayed proceedings on this issue, and the respondent has yet to prove that the decision not to rehire him was, in fact, based on his free speech activities.

Hence, on the record before us, all that clearly appears is that the respondent was not rehired for one year at one university. It stretches the concept too far to suggest that a person is deprived of "liberty" when he simply is not rehired in one job but remains as free as before to seek another.

III

The Fourteenth Amendment's procedural protection of property is a safeguard of the security of interests that a person has already acquired in specific benefits. These interests—property interests—may take many forms.

Thus, the Court has held that a person receiving welfare benefits under statutory and administrative standards defining eligibility for them has an interest in continued receipt of those benefits that is safeguarded by procedural due process. Goldberg v. Kelly, 397 U.S. 254 (1970). See Flemming v. Nestor, 363 U.S. 603, 611 (1960). Similarly, in the area of public employment, the Court has held that a public college professor dismissed from an office held under tenure provisions, Slochower v. Board of Education, 350 U.S. 551 (1956), and college professors and staff members dismissed during the terms of their contracts, Wieman v. Updegraff, 344 U.S. 183 (1952), have interests in continued employment that are safeguarded by due process. Only last year, the Court held that this principle "proscribing summary dismissal from public employment without hearing or inquiry required by due process" also applied to a teacher recently hired without tenure or a formal contract, but nonetheless with a clearly implied promise of continued employment. Connell v. Higginbotham, 403 U.S. 207, 208 (1971).

Certain attributes of "property" interests protected by procedural due process emerge from these decisions. To have a property interest in a benefit, a person clearly must have more than an abstract need or desire for it. He must have more than a unilateral expectation of it. He must, instead, have a legitimate claim of entitlement to it. It is a purpose of the ancient institution of property to protect those claims upon which people rely in their daily lives, reliance that must not be arbitrarily undermined. It is a purpose of the constitutional right to a hearing to provide an opportunity for a person to vindicate those claims.

Property interests, of course, are not created by the Constitution. Rather they are created and their dimensions are defined by existing rules or understandings that stem from an independent source such as state law—rules or understandings that secure certain benefits and that support claims of entitlement to those benefits. Thus, the welfare recipients in *Goldberg v. Kelly*, supra, had a claim of entitlement to welfare payments that was grounded in the statute defining eligibility for them. The recipients had not yet shown that they were, in fact, within the statutory terms of eligibility. But we held that they had a right to a hearing at which they might attempt to do so.

Just as the welfare recipients' "property" interest in welfare payments was created and defined by statutory terms, so the respondent's "property" interest in employment at Wisconsin State University-Oshkosh was created and defined by the terms of his appointment. Those terms secured his interest in employment up to June 30, 1969. But the important fact in this case is that they specifically provided that the respondent's employment was to terminate on June 30. They did not provide for contract renewal absent "sufficient cause." Indeed, they made no provision for renewal whatsoever.

Thus, the terms of the respondent's appointment secured absolutely no interest in re-employment for the next year. They supported absolutely no possible claim of entitlement to re-employment. Nor, significantly, was there any state statute or University rule or policy that secured his interest in re-employment or that created any legitimate claim to it. In these circumstances, the respondent surely had an abstract concern in being rehired, but he did not have a property interest sufficient to require the University authorities to give him a hearing when they declined to renew his contract of employment.

IV

Our analysis of the respondent's constitutional rights in this case in no way indicates a view that an opportunity for a hearing or a statement of reasons for nonretention would, or would not, be appropriate or wise in public colleges and universities. For it is a written Constitution that we apply. Our role is confined to interpretation of that Constitution.

We must conclude that the summary judgment for the respondent should not have been granted, since the respondent has not shown that he was deprived of liberty or property protected by the Fourteenth Amendment. The judgment of the Court of Appeals, accordingly, is reversed and the case is remanded for further proceedings consistent with this opinion. It is so ordered. Reversed and remanded.

■ [Dissenting opinions by JUSTICE DOUGLAS and JUSTICE MARSHALL are omitted.]

Perry v. Sindermann

Supreme Court of the United States, 1972.
408 U.S. 593.

■ MR. JUSTICE STEWART delivered the opinion of the Court. From 1959 to 1969 the respondent, Robert Sindermann, was a teacher in the state college system of the State of Texas. After teaching for two years at the University of Texas and for four years at San Antonio Junior College, he became a professor of Government and Social Science at Odessa Junior College in 1965. He was employed at the college for four successive years, under a series of one-year contracts. He was successful enough to be appointed, for a time, the cochairman of his department.

During the 1968–1969 academic year, however, controversy arose between the respondent and the college administration. The respondent was elected president of the Texas Junior College Teachers Association. In this capacity, he left his teaching duties on several occasions to testify before committees of the Texas Legislature, and he became involved in public disagreements with the policies of the college's Board of Regents. In particular, he aligned himself with a group advocating the elevation of the college to four-year status—a change opposed by the Regents. And, on one occasion, a newspaper advertisement appeared over his name that was highly critical of the Regents.

Finally, in May 1969, the respondent's one-year employment contract terminated and the Board of Regents voted not to offer him a new contract for the next academic year. The Regents issued a press release setting forth allegations of the respondent's insubordination. But they provided him no official statement of the reasons for the nonrenewal of his contract. And they allowed him no opportunity for a hearing to challenge the basis of the nonrenewal. * * *

[T]he Court of Appeals held that, despite the respondent's lack of tenure, the failure to allow him an opportunity for a hearing would violate the constitutional guarantee of procedural due process if the respondent could show that he had an "expectancy" of re-employment. * * *

The respondent's lack of formal contractual or tenure security in continued employment at Odessa Junior College * * * is highly relevant to his procedural due process claim. But it may not be entirely dispositive.

We have held today in *Board of Regents* v. *Roth* that the Constitution does not require opportunity for a hearing before the nonrenewal of a nontenured teacher's contract, unless he can show that the decision not to rehire him somehow deprived him of an interest in "liberty" or that he had a "property" interest in continued employment, despite the lack of tenure or a formal contract. In *Roth* the teacher had not made a showing on either point to justify summary judgment in his favor.

Similarly, the respondent here has yet to show that he has been deprived of an interest that could invoke procedural due process protection. As in *Roth*, the mere showing that he was not rehired in one particular job, without more, did not amount to a showing of a loss of liberty. Nor did it amount to a showing of a loss of property.

But the respondent's allegations—which we must construe most favorably to the respondent at this stage of the litigation—do raise a genuine issue as to his interest in continued employment at Odessa Junior College. He alleged that this interest, though not secured by a formal contractual tenure provision, was secured by a no less binding understanding fostered by the college administration. In particular, the respondent alleged that the college had a *de facto* tenure program, and that he had tenure under that program. He claimed that he and others legitimately relied upon an unusual provision that had been in the college's official Faculty Guide for many years * * *.

Moreover, the respondent claimed legitimate reliance upon guidelines promulgated by the Coordinating Board of the Texas College and University System that provided that a person, like himself, who had been employed as a teacher in the state college and university system for seven years or more has some form of job tenure. Thus, the respondent offered to prove that a teacher with his long period of service at this particular State College had no less a "property" interest in continued employment than a formally tenured teacher at other colleges, and had no less a procedural due process right to a statement of reasons and a hearing before college officials upon their decision not to retain him.

We have made clear in *Roth, supra*, that "property" interests subject to procedural due process protection are not limited by a few rigid, technical forms. Rather, "property" denotes a broad range of interests that are secured by "existing rules or understandings." A person's interest in a benefit is a "property" interest for due process purposes if there are such rules or mutually explicit understandings that support his claim of entitlement to the benefit and that he may invoke at a hearing.

A written contract with an explicit tenure provision clearly is evidence of a formal understanding that supports a teacher's claim of entitlement to continued employment unless sufficient "cause" is shown. Yet absence of such an explicit contractual provision may not always foreclose the possibility that a teacher has a "property" interest in re-employment. For example, the law of contracts in most, if not all, jurisdictions long has employed a process by which agreements, though not formalized in writing, may be "implied." 3 A. Corbin on Contracts §§ 561–572A (1960). Explicit contractual provisions may be supplemented by other agreements implied from "the promisor's words and conduct in the light of the surrounding circumstances." Id., at § 562. And, "the meaning of [the promisor's] words and acts is found by relating them to the usage of the past." Ibid.

A teacher, like the respondent, who has held his position for a number of years, might be able to show from the circumstances of this service—and from other relevant facts—that he has a legitimate claim of entitlement to job tenure. Just as this Court has found there to be a "common law of a particular industry or of a particular plant" that may supplement a collective-bargaining agreement, United Steelworkers v. Warrior & Gulf Nav. Co., 363 U.S. 574, 579 (1960), so there may be an unwritten "common law" in a particular university that certain employees shall have the equivalent of tenure. This is particularly likely in a college or university, like Odessa Junior College, that has no explicit tenure system even for senior members of its faculty, but that nonetheless may have created such a system in practice. See C. Byse & L. Joughin, Tenure in American Higher Education 17–28 (1959).[7]

In this case, the respondent has alleged the existence of rules and understandings, promulgated and fostered by state officials, that may justify his legitimate claim of entitlement to continued employment absent "sufficient cause." We disagree with the Court of Appeals insofar as it held that a mere subjective "expectancy" is protected by procedural due process, but we agree that the respondent must be given an opportunity to prove the legitimacy of his claim of such entitlement in light of "the policies and practices of the institution." Proof of such a property interest would not, of course, entitle him to reinstatement. But such proof would obligate college officials to grant a hearing at his request, where he could be informed of the grounds for his nonretention and challenge their sufficiency. * * *

■ [Concurring and dissenting opinions of CHIEF JUSTICE BURGER and JUSTICES DOUGLAS, BRENNAN and MARSHALL omitted.]

NOTES AND QUESTIONS

1.   Whatever else one makes of these decisions, do they tend to confirm Charles Reich's insight that threats to terminate government largesse—here efforts to terminate public university teachers after they have taken controversial political positions—can be used to punish dissidents and induce conformity to officially-favored viewpoints? On remand from the decision in Roth, a jury concluded that Wisconsin State University-Oshkosh had declined to renew Roth's employment contract in retaliation for his exercise of First Amendment rights. He was awarded $6,746 in damages. The issue of reinstatement was not pressed, since Roth had found new employment teaching political science at Purdue. See Chronicle of Higher Education, Nov. 26, 1973, p. 3 col. 1. Sindermann settled his case with the

---

[7]   We do not now hold that the respondent has any such legitimate claim of entitlement to job tenure. For "property interests . . . are not created by the Constitution. Rather, they are created and their dimensions are defined by existing rules or understandings that stem from an independent source such as state law. . . ." *Board of Regents* v. *Roth, supra*, at 577. If it is the law of Texas that a teacher in the respondent's position has no contractual or other claim to job tenure, the respondent's claim would be defeated.

Texas Regents, declining an offer of reinstatement and accepting a payment of $48,000 instead. Odessa American, Nov. 12, 1972 p. 1 col. 1.

2.   *Roth* and *Sindermann* were apparently designed to legitimize the due process revolution sparked by *Goldberg v. Kelly* (and by Reich's advocacy of a "new property"?), by reconciling it with the language of the Constitution and broad constitutional traditions. In the years after these decisions, the Court recognized due process "property" interests in a wide variety of government entitlements. These included rights to a public education, Goss v. Lopez, 419 U.S. 565 (1975); utility services, Memphis Light, Gas & Water Div. v. Craft, 436 U.S. 1 (1978); a horse trainer's license, Barry v. Barchi, 443 U.S. 55 (1979); and a cause of action against discrimination, Logan v. Zimmerman Brush Co., 455 U.S. 422, 430 (1982). More recently, the Court has adopted a more cautious attitude, and the expansion of due process rights appears to have halted. See generally Richard J. Pierce, Jr., The Due Process Counterrevolution of the 1990s?, 96 Colum. L. Rev. 1973 (1996). See, for example, Town of Castle Rock v. Gonzales, 545 U.S. 748 (2005), where the Court held a judicial restraining order against a woman's ex-husband did not give rise to a protected "property" right, even though the order had a warning printed on it in large caps indicating that enforcement was mandatory. The police failed to heed her repeated reports that the ex-husband had violated the order and taken their three children, whom he ultimately murdered. The Court declined to read the warning on the restraining order literally and remarked that the order did not "resemble any traditional conception of property." Id. at 766.

3.   Do you agree with the Court in *Roth* that the language of the Due Process Clauses requires a threshold determination that the claimant has an interest in either "liberty" or "property" (or, presumably, "life") at stake? This aspect of *Roth* reflects an important change in the law:

> Prior to *Roth*, Supreme Court definitions of 'liberty' and 'property' had amounted to taking the words 'life, liberty, and property' as a unitary concept embracing all interests valued by sensible men. After *Roth*, however, each word of the clause must be examined separately; so examined, we find that they do not embrace the full range of state conduct having serious impact upon individual interests.

Henry Paul Monaghan, Of "Liberty" and "Property," 62 Cornell L. Rev. 405, 409 (1977). Did the Framers of the Constitution intend this kind of careful parsing of each word as a threshold condition applying due process? Consider that the words chosen by the Framers appear to describe the three types of punishment the state is likely to mete out for violation of a crime—execution (life), imprisonment (liberty), or fines and forfeitures (property)—and that the Clause appears in the Fifth Amendment, which is largely concerned with criminal procedure. (But not exclusively—it also contains the Takings Clause!) This might suggest the Framers understood these words collectively to embrace any action by the state that would constitute a "punishment" or "sanction" directed against an individual. Consider also the Declaration of Independence, which refers to "Life, Liberty and the pursuit of Happiness" as a general phrase descriptive of inalienable human rights. What are the pros and cons of having a very broad and general threshold trigger for due process protection ("all interests valued by sensible men") as opposed to three more narrowly defined triggers with strong common-law connotations?

4.   Notice that the Court in *Roth* seemed to prescribe different methodologies for ascertaining whether an interest is "liberty" as opposed to "property." The methodology for ascertaining liberty is not discussed in any detail, other than to quote a long list of rights from Meyer v. Nebraska, 262 U.S. 390, 399 (1923), a case holding that parents have a substantive due process right to teach their children German. In discussing the methodology for identifying property rights, however, the Court notes that property rights are "not created by the Constitution." Does this imply that the Court views liberty as being created by the Constitution, whereas property is created by statutes, common-law decisions, and other types of subconstitutional law? In later decisions, some Justices would quarrel with the notion that liberty is created by the Constitution, insisting that liberties are "inalienable rights" that are recognized by but not created by the Constitution. See Sandin v. Conner, 515 U.S. 472, 489 (1995) (Ginsburg, J., dissenting); Meachum v. Fano, 427 U.S. 215, 230 (1976) (Stevens, J., dissenting). On this view, liberty is a "natural right" that exists independently of the Constitution; the significance of the Due Process Clauses is that they recognize this right and provide that it may not be taken without due process. Why cannot "property" also be regarded as an inalienable or natural right? Is there something about property that would make it more problematic to attempt to develop a "list" of inalienable property rights, analogous to the list of liberties set forth in *Meyer* and endorsed in *Roth*? In this regard, reconsider the material in Chapter III about different values subject to ownership, and how the scope of property rights has changed over time. By the way, what happened to "life" in the *Roth* discussion? What do you suppose the *Roth* Court would say about the proper method for ascertaining the meaning of "life"?

5.   When the Court announces that property rights are "not created by the Constitution" but rather "are created and their dimensions are defined by existing rules and understandings" such as those grounded in state law, does the Court mean that courts should look to state law to determine what the state regards to be property? Or does it mean only that courts should look to state law to see what sorts of interests are recognized and protected and should then independently determine as a matter of federal constitutional law whether these interests are property? See Monaghan, Of "Liberty" and "Property," supra; Thomas W. Merrill, The Landscape of Constitutional Property, 86 Va. L. Rev. 885, 916–42 (2000). The question is closely related to the more general issue, considered in Chapter I, whether "property" has some essentialist meaning, or should be considered as merely a contingent bundle of rights. If the Court understands that "property" has some distinctive federal constitutional meaning, did it provide adequate guidance in spelling out that meaning?

6.   The Court proclaims that it has rejected the "wooden distinction" between "rights" and "privileges" in determining the scope of the Due Process Clause. But how, if at all, does the rights/privileges distinction differ from the entitlements/unilateral-expectancies distinction adopted by the Court in

its place? Is it because "entitlements" are grounded in law? But aren't the "rights" that were juxtaposed to "privileges" also grounded in law, such as the common law? The Court doesn't seem to mean that entitlements must be grounded in written law; *Sindermann* clearly holds that entitlements can also be implied as a matter of common law. Is the shift in locution from rights/privileges to entitlements/expectancies merely a verbal cover for the fact that the Court has shifted the boundary of property for due process purposes to include various types of contractual or programmatic government benefits previously thought to be excluded?

7.   Is the Court's approach to defining property—looking to settled expectations rooted in objective sources like state statutory and common law—broadly consistent with the understanding of "property" reflected in *Charles River Bridge*? Recall that all the Justices in that case appeared to accept the idea that a corporate franchise to operate a toll bridge is a type of "property" entitled to constitutional protection. A corporate franchise or charter is a type of "entitlement" that did not exist at common law, but is purely the creature of legislation. In this sense, it is not too fanciful to describe corporate charters as a kind of "new property," analogous to the new property rights given due process protection in *Goldberg* and *Roth*. See Kenneth J. Vandevelde, The New Property of the Nineteenth Century: The Development of the Modern Concept of Property, 29 Buff. L. Rev. 325 (1980). Or does this overlook one potentially critical difference? Corporate charters and franchises, like common-law property, include the right to exclude others from certain assets; the government entitlements recognized to be property in *Goldberg* and *Roth* do not confer any right to exclude, but are more like contractual promises to a future stream of payments. Did the Court push the concept of "property" one step too far in *Roth*?

8.   Recall the case of Ephram Nestor, discussed in the excerpt from Charles Reich, who was stripped of his Social Security benefits when Congress passed a statute retroactively eliminating benefits for aliens who had been members of the Communist Party. See Flemming v. Nestor, 363 U.S. 603 (1960). The decisions in *Goldberg, Roth,* and *Sindermann,* stimulated hope among many that the Supreme Court would grant substantive constitutional protection under the takings or due process clauses to government "largesse" like Social Security and disability benefits. Such was not to be. The Court drew the line at procedural due process protection for the "new property," and steadfastly refused to give more than rational basis review to legislation eliminating or reducing government entitlements. See Bowen v. Gilliard, 483 U.S. 587, 605 (1987); Bowen v. Public Agencies Opposed to Social Security Entrapment, 477 U.S. 41 (1986); Richardson v. Belcher, 404 U.S. 78, 81–84 (1971). Although it is not unlikely that *Flemming v. Nestor* would come out differently today if challenged under the First Amendment, the Court's conclusion that Social Security benefits are not "property" for substantive constitutional purposes seems well entrenched. Does it make sense to say that government entitlements are "property" for procedural due process purposes but not for purposes of the Takings Clause or substantive due process?

9.   Consider procedural due process as yet another general strategy for resolving the government forbearance puzzle debated in *Charles River Bridge*. Implicit in the strategy is the principle of legality—that the government may deprive persons of property only in accordance with principles of law previously laid down. A central purpose of requiring notice and an opportunity for a hearing before any deprivation occurs is to give the owner a chance to show that the government lacks legal justification for its action. In effect, the government must forbear from interfering with previously recognized property rights unless it has a clear legal and factual justification for doing so. See John Harrison, Substantive Due Process and the Constitutional Text, 83 Va. L. Rev. 493, 497 (1997). Of course, this strategy does not provide full protection against frustration of expectations. If the government recognizes property at T_1, then changes the law at T_2 in such a way as to authorize the property to be taken, and then gives the owner a hearing at T_3 in order to challenge the legality of the taking, the hearing will show that the government deprivation has been legally authorized at T_2. This is a point of time before the proposed taking, and thus satisfies the principle of legality, even though it is also a point in time after T_1, and thus may frustrate expectations formed at T_1. Still, if one of the lessons of *Charles River Bridge* is the need for some compromise between accommodating change and protecting expectations, doesn't the procedural due process strategy provide a kind of accommodation? As a compromise, does it lean too far toward accommodating change or toward protecting expectations? Does the answer depend on the nature of the government promise in question?

2.   VESTED RIGHTS AND THE CANON DISFAVORING RETROACTIVE LAWS

Recall that Chief Justice Taney, in *Charles River Bridge*, remarks that "[i]t is well settled, by the decisions of this court, that a state law may be retrospective in its character, and may divest vested rights, and yet not violate the constitution of the United States, unless it also impairs the obligation of a contract." This was arguably accurate when it was written in 1837. There was no *federal* constitutional protection against impairment of "vested rights" by state governments other than the Contracts Clause of Article I, § 10; consequently, any federal constitutional claim that a state had impaired vested rights had to be characterized as an impairment of contract. The doctrine of substantive due process and the regulatory takings doctrine developed somewhat later, and there was no basis for applying either doctrine as a matter of federal constitutional law to the states until the Fourteenth Amendment was adopted in 1868. See Barron v. Baltimore, 32 U.S. 243 (1833) (original Takings Clause of Fifth Amendment does not apply to the states). This does not mean that state courts applying state constitutional law were similarly limited in their efforts to protect vested rights. Protection of vested rights was arguably the single most important theme of American constitutional law in the early decades of the Republic. See Edward S. Corwin, The Basic Doctrine of American

Constitutional Law, 12 Mich. L. Rev. 247 (1914); see also Gordon S. Wood, The Origins of Vested Rights in the Early Republic, 85 Va. L. Rev. 1421 (1999). If federal courts were confined largely to the Contracts Clause, state courts applied a variety of doctrines to reinforce government forbearance from interfering with so-called vested rights, including the insistence that legislation had to be prospective and general, restrictive definitions of the police power, and natural rights theories. Corwin, supra, at 255–76.

What exactly was included in the concept of "vested rights"? We have encountered this concept before. Recall from Chapter V that property law distinguishes between vested and nonvested future interests and that certain consequences follow from this; for example, nonvested future interests are subject to the Rule against Perpetuities and vested interests are not. We noted there that "vesting" is ambiguous because sometimes it means vested in interest and sometimes it means vested in possession. Recall too from Chapter IX that many state courts in the context of zoning have treated established uses of property as vested, in the sense that a zoning law cannot be enacted that would have the effect of making an existing nonconforming use unlawful.

In constitutional law as it developed in the nineteenth century, vested rights came to be understood as including, paradigmatically, private rights of property previously acquired. As Professor Woolhandler has explained,

> That private rights [were] involved [was] understood to mean that legislatures [could] not make such laws retroactive. Thus, while state legislatures could relax the requirements for adverse possession in the future, they could not provide that past acts meeting the new requirements had already effected the transfer of property; likewise, while state legislatures could change their inheritance laws prospectively, they could not declare that property that had already descended to A now belonged instead to B. Retroactive laws of this sort were often said either to deprive people of property without "due process of law" or to cross the line between "legislative" and "judicial" power. These two formulations drew on the same idea: the process that was considered "due" for an authoritative disposition of core private rights involved "judicial" application of the standing laws, and the separation of powers kept legislatures from supplying this process.

Ann Woolhandler, Public Rights, Private Rights, and Statutory Retroactivity, 94 Geo. L.J. 1015, 1024–25 (2006). See also Corwin, supra, at 275 (concluding that the core interest encompassed by the doctrine of vested rights was the right "of one who had *already* acquired some title of control over some particular piece of property, in the physical sense, to continue in that control").

Over time, the concept of "vested rights" gradually lost its allure as a basis for constitutional protection of property rights. This was due in significant part to persistent academic criticism. The Legal Realists in particular savaged the vested rights doctrine in the early decades of the twentieth century. See generally James L. Kainen, The Historical Framework for Reviving Constitutional Protection for Property and Contract Rights, 79 Cornell L. Rev. 87, 103–11 (1993). Three especially telling points were advanced in that era.

First, the vested rights doctrine assumed that interests were either vested or not vested, when in fact legal interests came with different degrees of expectation about how secure they were against legal change. The classic example was provided by the repeal of married women's dower rights. Dower was the right of a widow to a life estate in one-third of the real property of which her husband was seized during the marriage. Modification of dower rights was often a matter of controversy in the nineteenth century, see Kainen, supra, at 105–06. Dower has now been replaced in all states by some form of gender-neutral spousal share. See Chapter V on the Married Women's Property Acts. Before the legislation, at what point in time would a woman's expectation of receiving dower be strong enough to be regarded as a "vested" right? Before marriage? After marriage? After the acquisition of real property during marriage? After the death of the husband? There is no clearly correct answer to this question, and it seemed artificial to insist that there was a single condition or set of circumstances that defined when the interest became vested.

Second, the vested rights doctrine was prone to circularity. This was because whether an interest was regarded as "vested" was in part a function of whether courts found legislative interference with the interest to be a violation of the Constitution. Thus, critics maintained that the identification of an interest as "vested" often simply begged the question; courts enjoined legislation interfering with vested rights or required the state to compensate for taking vested rights, but the right was regarded as vested—of high security—because the court deemed it to be immune from legislative abrogation or deemed its taking to require compensation.

Third, and perhaps most importantly, the concept of vested rights was not embodied in the language of the U.S. Constitution nor did it appear in most state constitutions. As courts were challenged to justify their authority to intercede to protect property rights against popularly enacted legislation, they found it increasingly desirable to rest their decisions on specific constitutional clauses, like the Contracts Clause and the Takings Clause, rather than on the more amorphous concept of vested rights. The U.S. Supreme Court led the way. After a few early decisions that flirted with the idea of protecting vested rights as a matter of natural law, see Calder v. Bull, 3 U.S. (3 Dall.) 386 (1798); Fletcher v. Peck, 10 U.S. (6 Cranch) 87 (1810), the Court after the second decade of the nineteenth century consistently identified some specific textual authority for its interventions (recall again Chief Justice Taney's comments in *Charles River Bridge*). State supreme courts clung to the idea of vested rights much longer, but gradually followed the example of the U.S. Supreme Court.

Yet notwithstanding its general demise as a doctrine of constitutional law, the doctrine of vested rights reemerged as a canon of construction for interpreting legislation that arguably frustrates the expectations of owners of established property rights. The most complete modern discussion of the canon that statutes should be interpreted as applying only prospectively unless Congress clearly intends the contrary is found in the following decision.

Landgraf v. USI Film Products

Supreme Court of the United States, 1994.
511 U.S. 244.

■ JUSTICE STEVENS delivered the opinion of the Court. [The Civil Rights Act of 1991 imposed new types of liability on employers who engage in certain types of discrimination. At issue was whether the new Act applied to cases that were pending but not finally adjudicated on the effective date of the new Act. The Act said that it would "take effect upon enactment" and did not specifically address whether it would apply retroactively to conduct that took place or litigation that was commenced before enactment. The Court held that the Act should be interpreted to apply only to future conduct. Its decision includes the following discussion:]

[T]he presumption against retroactive legislation is deeply rooted in our jurisprudence, and embodies a legal doctrine centuries older than our Republic. Elementary considerations of fairness dictate that individuals should have an opportunity to know what the law is and to conform their conduct accordingly; settled expectations should not be lightly disrupted. For that reason, the "principle that the legal effect of conduct should ordinarily be assessed under the law that existed when the conduct took place has timeless and universal appeal." Kaiser Aluminum & Chem. Corp. v. Bonjorno, 494 U.S. 827, 855 (1990) (Scalia, J. concurring). In a free, dynamic society, creativity in both commercial and artistic endeavors is fostered by a rule of law that gives people confidence about the legal consequences of their actions.

It is therefore not surprising that the antiretroactivity principle finds expression in several provisions of our Constitution. [The Court briefly discusses the Ex Post Facto Clause, the Contracts Clause, the Takings Clause, the Bill of Attainder Clause, and the Due Process Clause.] * * * These provisions demonstrate that retroactive statutes raise particular concerns. The Legislature's unmatched powers allow it to sweep away settled expectations suddenly and without individualized consideration. Its responsivity to political pressures poses a risk that it may be tempted to use retroactive legislation as a means of retribution against unpopular groups or individuals. * * *

The Constitution's restrictions, of course, are of limited scope. Absent a violation of one of those specific provisions, the potential unfairness of retroactive civil legislation is not a sufficient reason for a court to fail to give a statute its intended scope. Retroactivity provisions often serve entirely benign and legitimate purposes, whether to respond to emergencies, to correct mistakes, to prevent circumvention of a new statute in the interval immediately preceding its passage, or simply to give comprehensive effect to a new law Congress considers salutary. However, a requirement that Congress first make its intention clear helps ensure that Congress itself has determined that the benefits of retroactivity outweigh the potential for disruption or unfairness.

While statutory retroactivity has long been disfavored, deciding when a statute operates "retroactively" is not always a simple or mechanical task. Sitting on Circuit, Justice Story offered an influential definition in *Society for Propagation of the Gospel v. Wheeler,* 22 F.Cas. 756 (No. 13,156) (CCNH 1814), a case construing a provision of the New Hampshire Constitution that broadly prohibits "retrospective" laws both criminal and civil. Justice Story first rejected the notion that the provision bars only explicitly retroactive legislation, *i.e.,* "statutes . . . enacted to take effect from a time anterior to their passage." Id., at 767. Such a construction, he concluded, would be "utterly subversive of all the objects" of the prohibition. Ibid. Instead, the ban on retrospective legislation embraced "all statutes, which, though operating only from their passage, affect vested rights and past transactions." Ibid. "Upon principle," Justice Story elaborated, "every statute, which takes away or impairs vested rights acquired under existing laws, or creates a new obligation, imposes a new duty, or attaches a new disability, in respect to transactions or considerations already past, must be deemed retrospective. . . ." Ibid. (citing Calder v. Bull, 3 Dall. 386 (1798), and Dash v. Van Kleeck, 7 Johns. 477 (N.Y. 1811)).

Though the formulas have varied, similar functional conceptions of legislative "retroactivity" have found voice in this Court's decisions and elsewhere.

A statute does not operate "retrospectively" merely because it is applied in a case arising from conduct antedating the statute's enactment, or upsets expectations based in prior law. Rather, the court must ask whether the new provision attaches new legal consequences to events completed before its enactment. The conclusion that a particular rule operates "retroactively" comes at the end of a process of judgment concerning the nature and extent of the change in the law and the degree of connection between the operation of the new rule and a relevant past event. Any test of retroactivity will leave room for disagreement in hard cases, and is unlikely to classify the enormous variety of legal changes with perfect philosophical clarity. However, retroactivity is a matter on which judges tend to have "sound . . . instinct[s]," see Danforth v. Groton Water Co., 59 N.E. 1033, 1034 (Mass. 1901) (Holmes, J.), and familiar considerations of fair notice, reasonable reliance, and settled expectations offer sound guidance.

Since the early days of this Court, we have declined to give retroactive effect to statutes burdening private rights unless Congress had made clear its intent. * * * The largest category of cases in which we have applied the presumption against statutory retroactivity has involved new provisions affecting contractual or property rights, matters in which predictability and stability are of prime importance. The presumption has not, however, been limited to such cases. * * *

The presumption against statutory retroactivity had special force in the era in which courts tended to view legislative interference with property and contract rights circumspectly. In this century, legislation has come to supply the dominant means of legal ordering, and circumspection has given way to greater deference to legislative judgments. See Usery v. Turner Elkhorn Mining Co., 428 U.S., at 15–16; Home Building & Loan Assn. v. Blaisdell, 290 U.S. 398, 436–444 (1934). But while the *constitutional* impediments to retroactive civil legislation are now modest, prospectivity remains the appropriate default rule. Because it accords with widely held intuitions about how statutes ordinarily operate, a presumption against retroactivity will generally coincide with legislative and public expectations. Requiring clear intent assures that Congress itself has affirmatively considered the potential unfairness of retroactive application and determined that it is an acceptable price to pay for the countervailing benefits. Such a requirement allocates to Congress responsibility for fundamental policy judgments concerning the proper temporal reach of statutes, and has the additional virtue of giving legislators a predictable background rule against which to legislate. * * *

When a case implicates a federal statute enacted after the events in suit, the court's first task is to determine whether Congress has expressly prescribed the statute's proper reach. If Congress has done so, of course, there is no need to resort to judicial default rules. When, however, the statute contains no such express command, the court must determine whether the new statute would have retroactive effect, *i.e.,* whether it would impair rights a party possessed when he acted, increase a party's liability for past conduct, or impose new duties with respect to transactions already completed. If the statute would operate retroactively, our traditional presumption teaches that it does not govern absent clear congressional intent favoring such a result. * * *

■ JUSTICE SCALIA, with whom JUSTICE KENNEDY and JUSTICE THOMAS join, concurring in the judgment. I of course agree with the Court that there exists a judicial presumption, of great antiquity, that a legislative enactment affecting substantive rights does not apply retroactively absent *clear statement* to the contrary. * * * [But I disagree] with the

Court's analysis of * * * the meaning of retroactivity. * * * The critical issue, I think, is not whether the rule affects "vested rights," or governs substance or procedure, but rather what is the relevant activity that the rule regulates. Absent clear statement otherwise, only such relevant activity which occurs *after* the effective date of the statute is covered. Most statutes are meant to regulate primary conduct, and hence will not be applied in trials involving conduct that occurred before their effective date. But other statutes have a different purpose and therefore a different relevant retroactivity event. A new rule of evidence governing expert testimony, for example, is aimed at regulating the conduct of trial, and the event relevant to retroactivity of the rule is introduction of the testimony. Even though it is a procedural rule, it would unquestionably not be applied to *testimony already taken*—reversing a case on appeal, for example, because the new rule had not been applied at a trial which antedated the statute. * * *

[S]tatutes eliminating previously available forms of prospective relief provide [a] challenge to the Court's approach. Courts traditionally withhold requested injunctions that are not authorized by then-current law, even if they were authorized at the time suit commenced and at the time the primary conduct sought to be enjoined was first engaged in. See, e.g., American Steel Foundries v. Tri-City Central Trades Council, 257 U.S. 184 (1921); Duplex Printing Press Co. v. Deering, 254 U.S. 443, 464 (1921). The reason, which has nothing to do with whether it is possible to have a vested right to prospective relief, is that "obviously, this form of relief operates only *in futuro*," ibid. Since the purpose of prospective relief is to affect the future rather than remedy the past, the relevant time for judging its retroactivity is the very moment at which it is ordered.[3]

[Dissenting opinions omitted.]

NOTES AND QUESTIONS

1.   Recall from Chapter V that the common law also contains constructional rules favoring the protection of vested rights. For example, if a remainder can be interpreted as being either vested or contingent, courts favor the vested interpretation. This saves the remainder from possible invalidation under the Rule against Perpetuities, and from other doctrines like the Destructibility of Contingent Remainders. Similarly, courts developed rules for construing defeasible fees so as to make it less likely that the grantee would experience a forfeiture. A constructional rule similar to *Landgraf* also applies in the administrative law context. See Bowen v. Georgetown University Hospital, 488 U.S. 204 (1988) (holding that a federal

---

[3]   A focus on the relevant retroactivity event also explains why the presumption against retroactivity is not violated by interpreting a statute to alter the future legal effect of past transactions—so-called secondary retroactivity. * * * A new ban on gambling applies to existing casinos and casinos under construction, even though it "attaches a new disability" to those past investments. The relevant retroactivity event is the primary activity of gambling, not the primary activity of constructing casinos.

administrative agency may promulgate rules with retroactive effect only if clearly authorized to do so by Congress).

2.   The clear intent rule of *Landgraf*, together with the various common-law rules favoring the preservation of vested rights, represents yet another strategy for reaching an accommodation between the forces of change and the need to protect reliance interests. What are the advantages and disadvantages of this strategy, relative to other strategies, such as the rule of strict construction of charters, the requirement of due process hearings before property is taken, and the requirement of compensation for takings of property? Suppose A owns Blackacre and builds a waste recycling plant on it. At the time the plant is constructed, waste recycling is a lawful use. After the plant is up and running, the legislature adopts a statute that says: "All recycling plants are hereby prohibited. This statute takes effect upon enactment." Does the canon of interpretation in *Landgraf* provide any protection for A's investment in the recycling plant?

3.   Is the clear intent rule of *Landgraf* consistent with the rule of strict construction of *Charles River Bridge*? The rule of strict construction is designed to minimize the creation of vested rights. The clear statement rule is designed to minimize the frustration of vested rights. So working in tandem, they do not directly conflict. But is the rationale for the clear statement rule, as set forth in *Landgraf*, more in keeping with the general position of Chief Justice Taney or Justice Story as to where the balance of accommodation should be struck between change and reliance?

Academic Perspectives on Retroactivity

Issues about the optimal policy toward legal retroactivity come up in many contexts, but nowhere more than in taxation, where the issue is often described in terms of "transition policy." A prototypical example of a change in tax law arguably requiring transition relief would be repealing the tax exemption from a previously tax-exempt class of bonds. Academic commentators have come to widely varying conclusions at different times about the wisdom of worrying about retroactivity and providing transition relief, such as paying damages or providing for some kind of grandfathering of existing arrangements (e.g., allowing existing tax-exempt bonds to continue to remain tax-exempt and applying the change only to newly issued bonds).

The idea with the longest history—extending back to Justice Story and beyond—is that the government should provide transition relief in order to internalize the harm of a taking or other new measure that defeats settled expectations. See Daniel E. Troy, Retroactive Legislation (1998); Richard A. Epstein, Beware of Legal Transitions: A Presumptive Voice for the Reliance Interest, 13 J. Contemp. Legal Issues 69 (2003). In the commentary on retroactivity, this "Old School" has been challenged by (what else?) a "New School," which argues that transition relief is inappropriate because of actions that owners can take to foresee and mitigate a taking or other retroactive law. See, e.g., Michael J. Graetz, Legal Transitions: The Case of Retroactivity in Income Tax Revision, 126

U. Pa. L. Rev. 47, 65 (1977); Louis Kaplow, An Economic Analysis of Legal Transitions, 99 Harv. L. Rev. 511 (1986). These scholars tend to emphasize the need for flexibility and the benefits of public-regarding projects. (Recall Chief Justice Taney's arguments about changed conditions and the need to accommodate new technology in *Charles River Bridge*.) They also analogize government-created risk to market-created risk, the latter of which we normally assume parties can deal with on their own, through insurance or diversification.

More recently in what is sometimes termed a "New New School" (or is it "New Old School"?), some have proposed that transition relief may be appropriate when government is making a commitment upon which it is desirable for people to rely. Sometimes the government may want to make a specific commitment to forbear from change or to provide transition relief. It might want to do this in order to avoid having to pay a premium to induce persons to take certain actions (given the risk of future governmental changes in policy) or to obviate wasteful anticipatory private efforts at trying to avoid being bitten by change. See, e.g., Daniel Shaviro, When Rules Change: An Economic and Political Analysis of Transition Relief and Retroactivity (2000); Kyle D. Logue, Tax Transitions, Opportunistic Retroactivity, and the Benefits of Government Precommitment, 94 Mich. L. Rev. 1129 (1996). Other times, the government may want to avoid all transition relief in order to force people to anticipate desirable change. An example would be a polluter who may face new regulations restricting effluent about which the polluter has had good information. See Saul Levmore, Changes, Anticipations, and Reparations, 99 Colum. L. Rev. 1657, 1661–86 (1999); see also Michael Doran, Legislative Compromise and Tax Transition Policy, 74 U. Chi. L. Rev. 545 (2007); Saul Levmore, Retroactive Taxation, 3 New Palgrave Dictionary of Economics and the Law 340 (1998); Kyle D. Logue, If Taxpayers Can't Be Fooled, Maybe Congress Can: A Public Choice Perspective on the Tax Transition Debate, 67 U. Chi. L. Rev. 1507 (2000) (book review); Jonathan S. Masur & Jonathan R. Nash, The Institutional Dynamics of Transition Relief, 85 N.Y.U. L. Rev. 391 (2010); Richard L. Revesz & Allison L. Westfahl Kong, Regulatory Change and Optimal Transition Relief, 105 Nw. U. L. Rev. 1581 (2011). The general issue then becomes: When if at all is it desirable for government to make general commitments to provide transition relief, or should government commitments of transition relief be channeled into formal contracts limited to specific situations?

3. STARE DECISIS

Another general legal doctrine that promotes government forbearance is stare decisis—the practice of "standing by what has been decided." Courts have long said that the duty to follow precedent carries special force where property rights are involved. As the Court put it in *Payne v. Tennessee*, 501 U.S. 808, 828 (1991), "[c]onsiderations in favor of *stare decisis* are at their acme in cases involving property and contract rights, where reliance interests are involved." In contrast, the Court continued, "stare decisis carries comparatively less weight in cases 'involving procedural and evidentiary rules.' " Id. As the following excerpt suggests, this distinction is well supported by . . . precedent!

Thomas R. Lee, *Stare Decisis in Historical Perspective: From the Founding Era to the Rehnquist Court*

52 VAND. L. REV. 645, 687–92, 694–96, 699, 702 (1999).

IV. Rules of Property and Reliance Interests

Chief Justice Rehnquist's opinion for the Court in *Payne v. Tennessee* relied extensively on the notion of a sliding stare decisis scale on commercial reliance grounds. In abandoning the previously held view that the Eighth Amendment precluded victim-impact evidence in capital cases, Rehnquist asserted that "[c]onsiderations in favor of stare decisis are at their acme in cases involving property and contract rights, where reliance interests are involved." Because the question in *Payne* "involve[ed] procedural and evidentiary rules," Rehnquist concluded that considerations in favor of stare decisis were at a minimum, and error correction was more freely available. * * *

A. Rules of Property in the Founding Era

History provides ample support for Chief Justice Rehnquist's side of the *Payne* debate. Blackstone's explication of error correction drew no express distinction between commercial cases and other decisions, but the distinction had already taken hold in the English courts. One early English statement appeared in *Morecock v. Dickins*, a 1768 case in the High Court of Chancery.[222] The issue in that case was whether Dickins, the holder of a legal mortgage on property, should be considered to have received constructive notice of a prior equitable mortgage held by Morecock, by virtue of Morecock's registration of the deed. Counsel for Morecock argued that registration should serve as constructive notice. Although Lord Camden indicated his inclination to agree with this argument on its merits, he refused to abandon settled precedent on the point:

> If this was a new point, it might admit of difficulty; but the determination in *Bedford v. Bacchus* seems to have settled it, and it would be mischievous to disturb it. . . . Much property has been settled, and conveyances have proceeded upon the ground of that determination. . . . A thousand neglects to search have been occasioned by that determination, and therefore I cannot take upon me to alter it. If this was a new case, I should have

---

[222] Morecock v. Dickins, 27 Eng. Rep. 440 (Ch. 1768).

my doubts; but the point is closed by that determination, which has been acquiesced in ever since.

The commercial reliance interests in *Morecock* were unmistakable. "A thousand neglects to search" the registries had been premised on the proposition that registration of an equitable mortgage was not constructive notice to a legal mortgagee, and thus Lord Camden preserved the precedent despite his doubts about its merits.

The converse position was also recognized in the English courts of the founding era. In *Robinson v. Bland*, the court determined, among other things, to abandon the general rule limiting a prevailing plaintiff in a breach of contract suit to interest accruing to "the day that the writ is sued out."[227] The general rule was abandoned as certainly unreasonable, and replaced with a new standard awarding interest accruing "down to the time of the last act done by the Court, to liquidate the demand." Judge Wilmot's opinion offered a reliance-based justification for the court's correction of this error:

> Where an error is established and has taken root, upon which any rule of property depends, it ought to be adhered to by the Judges, till the Legislature thinks proper to alter it: lest the new determination should have a retrospect, and shake many questions already settled: but the reforming erroneous points of practice can have no such bad consequences; and therefore they may be altered at pleasure, when found to be absurd or inconvenient.

Thus, Judge Wilmot conceived of a bifurcated stare decisis standard that is reminiscent of that offered by Chief Justice Rehnquist in *Payne*. A decision establishing "any rule of property" must be retained, Wilmot says, even when in error. But error in "points of practice" is a different matter. A change of course on such issues does not affect reliance interests, and thus the courts may abandon precedents of this nature with fewer misgivings.

James Kent's conception of stare decisis similarly recognized the increased importance of stability as to rules of property. * * * He recognized that the policy of stability and certainty was more important in certain areas of the law than in others. When decisions "create a practical rule of property," Kent explained, they should be adhered to even when subsequent judges "may feel the hardship, or not perceive the reasonableness, of the rule."[232]

B. Rules of Property in the Supreme Court

Although the dominant stare decisis question addressed by the Marshall Court was the extent of the Court's power to abandon precedent on the basis of its correctness, several Marshall Court decisions

---

[227]   Robinson v. Bland, 96 Eng. Rep. 141, 142 (K.B. 1760).

[232]   [1 James Kent, Commentaries on American Law *478 (O.W. Holmes, Jr. ed., 14th ed., Boston, Little Brown 7 Co. 1896).] * * *

acknowledged the notion of enhanced deference to property rules in the context of yielding to purportedly erroneous decisions of the state courts. In addition, the Marshall Court adverted to a similar approach in the context of suggesting that some deference was owed to a legislative construction of the Constitution, especially where property rights were implicated. Otherwise, the application and development of the rule of property standard in the Supreme Court occurred in the Taney era.

Indeed, the Taney Court's principal contribution to the stare decisis dialogue was to consider whether the Court's power of error correction varied depending on the extent of property and contract rights at stake. * * *

Chief Justice Taney [emphasized] the rule of property theme in his opinion for the Court in *The Propeller Genesee Chief v. Fitzhugh*.[262] *The Genesee Chief* presented the question whether the federal courts' admiralty jurisdiction extended to a suit arising out of a collision on Lake Ontario. Presumably, the federal courts would have lacked jurisdiction under the Court's earlier pronouncement as to the scope of Article III's Admiralty Clause in *The Steam-Boat Thomas Jefferson*.[264] Justice Story's opinion for the Court in *The Thomas Jefferson* had held that admiralty under Article III extended only to cases where the voyage at issue "was substantially performed, or to be performed, upon the sea, or upon waters within the ebb and flow of the tide." Because the Missouri River voyage in *The Thomas Jefferson* "not only in its commencement and termination, but in all its intermediate progress, was several hundreds of miles above the ebb and flow of the tide," Story's opinion held that any exercise of admiralty jurisdiction in the case was beyond that authorized by Article III.

Chief Justice Taney's opinion in *The Genesee Chief* candidly overruled *The Thomas Jefferson* and adopted a new test for admiralty jurisdiction. Taney argued that the *Thomas Jefferson* test would undermine the goal of "a perfect equality in the rights and the privileges of the citizens of the different states," in that the benefits of "safety and convenience of commerce, and the speedy decision of controversies" presented by the admiralty courts would be reserved only for "states bordering on the Atlantic." Moreover, Taney asserted that the "ebb and flow" test was "arbitrary, without any foundation in reason" in that "there is certainly nothing in the ebb and flow of the tide that makes the waters peculiarly suitable for admiralty jurisdiction, nor any thing in the absence of a tide that renders it unfit." Thus, even though the ebb and flow test concededly was the prevailing standard in England at the time of the framing of the Constitution, Chief Justice Taney rejected it as "purely artificial and arbitrary as well as unjust." Accordingly, Taney concluded that the admiralty jurisdiction properly turned on whether the

---

[262]   The Propeller Genesee Chief v. Fitzhugh, 53 U.S. (12 How.) 443 (1851).

[264]   The Steam-Boat Thomas Jefferson, 23 U.S. (10 Wheat.) 428 (1825).

waters at issue are navigable, and not on whether they are within the ebb and flow of the tide.

Despite the conviction of Taney's disdain for the rationale and correctness of *The Thomas Jefferson*, he expressly admitted to a certain degree of angst in overruling the case: "It is the decision in the case of the *Thomas Jefferson* which mainly embarrasses the court in the present inquiry. We are sensible of the great weight to which it is entitled." Having noted the general importance of adherence to precedent, however, Taney emphasized that "[t]he case of the *Thomas Jefferson* did not decide any question of property, or lay down any rule by which the right of property should be determined." Taney explained that if *The Thomas Jefferson* had established a rule of property, stare decisis would have demanded adherence to that decision:

> If it had, we should have felt ourselves bound to follow it notwithstanding the opinion we have expressed. For every one would suppose that after the decision of this court, in a matter of that kind, he might safely enter into contracts, upon the faith that rights thus acquired would not be disturbed. In such a case, stare decisis is the safe and established rule of judicial policy and should always be adhered to. . . . But the decision referred to has no relation to rights of property. It was a question of jurisdiction only, and the judgment we now give can disturb no rights of property nor interfere with any contracts heretofore made. . . . And as we are convinced that the former decision was founded in error, and that the error, if not corrected, must produce serious public as well as private inconvenience and loss, it becomes our duty not to perpetuate it.[273] * * *

C.   Rules of Property and Reliance Interests:
A Comparative Analysis

By the founding era, English courts and American commentators had embraced the notion of an enhanced rule of stare decisis in cases involving rules of property. That principle also dominated the Court's treatment of precedent during the Taney era. Indeed, on closer scrutiny even the apparent anomalies noted above disappear. The extent of the Taney Court's willingness to correct apparently erroneous precedent turned entirely on whether a change of course would "disturb . . . rights of property . . . or interfere with any contracts heretofore made." * * *

By the Taney era, then, the Court had settled on a bifurcated stare decisis standard comparable to that advocated by Chief Justice Rehnquist in *Payne*.

---

[273]   [The Propeller Genesee Chief,] at 458–59. * * *

NOTES AND QUESTIONS

1.   As Lee suggests, the idea that respect for precedent is especially important where property rights are concerned has very old roots. Note that before the merger of law and equity, one of the maxims of equity was to forbear from undoing the common law (and its predictability) with respect to property. See Charles Grey, The Boundaries of the Equitable Function, 20 Am. J. Legal Hist. 192 (1976).

2.   Notwithstanding its ancient roots, is the principle of respect for precedent honored more in the breach? We have considered a number of cases in this book where courts have either explicitly or implicitly overruled earlier decisions. Some examples: Pardee v. Camden Lumber Co., Chapter I, overruling a decision prohibiting injunctive relief for cutting timber on land; *Oregon ex rel. Thornton v. Hay*, Chapter III, recognizing for the first time a customary public right to use beach property in coastal Oregon; *Higday v. Nickolaus*, Chapter III, arguably departing from Missouri law in adopting a rule of reasonable use for groundwater rights; *Berg v. Wiley*, Chapter IV, adopting for the first time a rule prohibiting self-help in the recovery of real property; *Shelley v. Kraemer*, Chapter IX, disregarding prior decisional law suggesting that enforcement of racial covenants did not violate the Fourteenth Amendment; *Javins v. First National Realty*, Chapter VI, adopting an implied warranty of habitability for residential leases; *Sommer v. Kridel*, Chapter VI, adopting a duty to mitigate damages when a tenant abandons; *Kendall v. Ernest Pestana*, Chapter VI, overruling prior caselaw allowing a landlord to withhold consent to assignment of a lease for any or no reason at all; *Tulk v. Moxhay*, Chapter IX, permitting equitable servitudes to run with the land, contrary to prior decisions limiting running covenants to landlord-tenant relations. Do these decisions support the proposition, reflected in the Lee excerpt and endorsed in *Payne*, that courts will generally avoid "disturbing rules of property" whereas they are more inclined to overrule rules of evidence and procedure? Do these cases suggest that a neat division of "property rules" and other kinds of rules is difficult or even infeasible? Or are cases reproduced in property casebooks likely to contain an unrepresentative sample of decisions in terms of stare decisis, insofar as they include a disproportionate percentage of controversial or pathbreaking decisions?

3.   Note that the strong rule of stare decisis in property is designed to encourage forbearance by a different branch of government than the one usually of concern in this connection: the courts. Is unanticipated change in the rules a greater cause for concern when it comes from the courts, or a lesser concern? One factor here is that rule changes by courts are nearly always retroactive, in that they apply to the parties in the case where the change is announced. See Harper v. Virginia Dept. of Taxation, 509 U.S. 86 (1993). Another factor is that courts are usually regarded as more independent than legislatures, and hence less likely to succumb to pressure from the public or particular interest groups to interfere with established property rights. Which factor is more important in determining how much weight we should give to the need for forbearance by courts? See, e.g., Ronald A. Cass, Judging: Norms and Incentives of Retrospective Decisionmaking, 75

B.U. L. Rev. 941 (1995); Einer R. Elhauge, Does Interest Group Theory Justify More Intrusive Judicial Review?, 101 Yale L.J. 31 (1991); William N. Eskridge, Jr., Politics Without Romance: Implications of Public Choice Theory for Statutory Interpretation, 74 Va. L. Rev. 275 (1988).

4. FOREIGN INVESTMENT TREATIES

Government forbearance is increasingly an issue in international law. Specifically, developed nations like the United States frequently negotiate foreign investment treaties which include among their provisions agreements by the host nation to forbear from interfering with capital projects owned or financed by firms in the developed nation. The most famous of the foreign investment protection regimes was contained in Chapter 11 of the North American Free Trade Agreement or NAFTA, entered into by the United States, Canada, and Mexico. This has been superseded by the passage of the United-States-Mexican-Canada Agreement (USMCA), but the investor-protection provisions of NAFTA have been copied to one degree or another in numerous bilateral and multilateral investor protection treaties.

A basic purpose of these investor protection treaties is to provide assurances to private investors that if they commit significant capital to projects in another country they will not encounter discriminatory treatment or attempts by the host country to expropriate the investment after it has been made. In order to provide these assurances, the treaties commit the signatory countries to binding arbitration with disgruntled foreign investors. The arbitrators are given authority take evidence and review the dispute, and if they find the host country has committed a violation, they can order the host country to pay damages.

Perhaps the most controversial decision rendered by an arbitration panel established by NAFTA was Metalclad Corp. v. United Mexican States, Arbitration Panel, International Centre for Settlement of Investment Disputes, 2000, Case No. ARB(AF)/97/1, 40 I.L.M. 36, 40 I.L.M. 36 (2001), 2001 WL 313693. Metalclad, a U.S. corporation, formed a Mexican subsidiary, COTERIN, to purchase land in Guadalcazar, Mexico, for the purpose of constructing a hazardous waste disposal site. Before Metalclad purchased the property, the Federal Government of Mexico and the Mexican State of San Luis Potosi informed Metalclad that they would issue all the necessary permits. Construction of the facility began in May 1994, and was completed in March 1995. Demonstrators disrupted a planned open house or "inauguration" of the site. Later that year, Metalclad was informed that the Guadalcazar municipal authorities had, without notice to Metalclad, denied a construction permit for the facility. Subsequent efforts to resolve the impasse though litigation in the Mexican courts failed to achieve a resolution. Metalclad then initiated an arbitration proceeding against the Mexican government under Chapter 11 of NAFTA.

The arbitration panel found that the Mexican government had denied Metalclad "fair and equitable treatment" under NAFTA, in violation of Article 1105, by promising that all necessary permits had been issued and then allowing municipal authorities to insist on a building permit, which was denied. The panel found that the building permit was not justified by Article 1114, which allows the host country to ensure that investment activity is undertaken in a manner sensitive to environmental concerns. This was because federal permits had been issued indicating that the project satisfied all environmental requirements, and the local building permit was denied without reference to any defects in the facility that might indicate environmental concerns. Because the action of the municipal authorities violated the "fair and equal treatment" requirement, the panel found that it was "tantamount to expropriation" under Article 1110 of NAFTA. The panel ordered Mexico to pay Metalclad $16,685,000 in damages. Mexico brought an action alleging that the panel had acted beyond the scope of its authority, which was tried, as required by the treaty, in a Canadian court. United Mexican States v. Metalclad Corp., 89 B.C. L. R. 3d 359 (2001). The court upheld the award, with modifications, and Mexico paid up.

Some commentators have condemned decisions like *Metalclad* for offering foreign investors more protection against a lack of government forbearance than domestic investors receive. Compare Vicki Been & Joel C. Beauvais, The Global Fifth Amendment? NAFTA's Investment Protections and the Misguided Quest for an International "Regulatory Takings" Doctrine, 78 N.Y.U. L. Rev. 30, 59 (2003) (decrying *Metalclad* for suggesting "that Article 1110 may be interpreted to require compensation in several circumstances in which the Fifth Amendment has never before been applied") with Guillermo Aguilar Alvarez & William W. Park, The New Face of Investment Arbitration: NAFTA Chapter 11, 28 Yale J. Int'l L. 365, 366 (2003) (arguing that "arbitration under investment treaties such as NAFTA will enhance the type of asset protection that facilitates wealth-creating cross-border capital flows, bringing net gains for both host state and foreign investor") and Charles S. Brower & Stephan W. Schill, Is Arbitration a Threat or a Boon to the Legitimacy of International Investment Law?, 9 Chi. J. Int'l L. 471 (2009) (arguing in favor of a system of arbitration as promoting international investment).

Metalclad would likely come out differently if it arose today under the USMCA. The new treaty clarifies that "fair and equitable treatment" means only that the host country must comply with the requirements of customary international law and does not impose any more exacting requirement. The treaty also includes a list of regulatory actions that do not constitute indirect expropriation, including non-discriminatory actions that protect the environment. See Jerry L. Lai, A Tale of Two Treaties: A Study of NAFTA and the USMCA's Investor-State Dispute

Settlement Mechanisms, 35 Emory Int'l L. Rev. 259, 262–65 (2021). Perhaps most notably, the USMCA no longer allows arbitration panels to find that host nations have committed acts that are "tantamount" to expropriation; only actual expropriation is actionable.

NOTES AND QUESTIONS

1.   Should liability under NAFTA Chapter 11 or the USMCA apply to circumstances in which foreign investors suffer discrimination or differential regulatory burdens relative to domestic investors? Consider the saga of the Keystone XL Pipeline, designed to transfer oil from Canada to refineries on the Gulf Coast in the United States. When the Obama Administration denied a permit allowing the pipeline to cross the border into the United States, the Canadian firm planning to build the pipeline sued the United States for $15 billion in damages for violating NAFTA. See Todd Tucker, TransCanada is suing the U.S. over Obama's rejection of the Keystone XL pipeline. The U.S. might lose, Wash. Post (Jan. 8, 2016), http://www.washingtonpost.com/news/monkey-cage/wp/2016/01/08/transcanada-i. The action was dropped when the Trump Administration reversed the decision and issued the required permit. The Biden Administration promptly reversed the decision once again, and now TransCanada has renewed its action demanding $15 billion in damages from the U.S. under NAFTA. The pipeline has become a primary political symbol for those concerned about climate change and opposed to further petrochemical exploration and development. Did the fact that it was a Canadian project, or that it was to transport Canadian oil, contribute to the hostility? Note that the Obama and Biden Administrations were able to block the project only because it crossed an international border; a purely domestic pipeline (say from North Dakota to Louisiana) would not have been subject to the same approval requirement. Is this enough to establish discrimination or differential treatment?

2.   What would Chief Justice Taney, author of the majority opinion in *Charles River Bridge*, say about the decision of the arbitration panel in the *Metalclad* case? Did the Mexican government promise Metalclad with sufficient clarity that the company would be allowed to build a hazardous waste disposal facility without a local building permit?

Political Risk Insurance

One of the charges Been and Beauvais level against the *Metalclad* decision is that the need for compensation as ex post insurance for the risk of legal and regulatory change is obviated in part by the availability of ex ante insurance against political risk. 78 N.Y.U. L. Rev. at 38. This raises an important question about all the devices to encourage government forbearance we have considered: Can and should they be replaced by the purchase of insurance by persons anxious about the possible risk to their property from future changes in government policy? We expect property owners to purchase insurance against fires, floods, and theft. Why not require them to purchase insurance against government expropriation or other changes in government policy that destroy or devalue property rights?

The possibility of relying on insurance to compensate for takings of property or changes in government regulatory policy that adversely affect property has been discussed by a variety of scholars. See, e.g., Jonathan S. Masur & Jonathan Remy Nash, The Institutional Dynamics of Transition Relief, 85 N.Y.U. L. Rev. 391, 406–28 (2010); Steve P. Calandrillo, Eminent Domain Economics: Should "Just Compensation" Be Abolished, and Would "Takings Insurance" Work Instead?, 60 Ohio St. L.J. 451 (2003); Louis Kaplow, An Economic Analysis of Legal Transitions, 99 Harv. L. Rev. 511 (1986); Lawrence Blume & Daniel L. Rubinfeld, Compensation for Takings: An Economic Analysis, 72 Cal. L. Rev. 569 (1984). These authors pose the question: Are takings and other types of risks of adverse government action adequately addressed by political risk insurance that would spread these risks over time and across multiple owners? Early commentators recognized that private insurance would face two difficulties in this context. One is the problem of *adverse selection*: Those people who face the greatest likelihood of having their property taken or regulated may be ones most likely to purchase insurance, which would increase the costs of claims. Blume & Rubinfeld, supra, at 595–96. Another problem is *moral hazard*: Once persons have insurance, they may not put up much resistance to having their property taken or regulated, which would also increase the cost of claims. Id. at 594. More recently commentators have observed that private insurance typically requires a large set of experiential data that insurers can use to predict the size and frequency of losses and thus set a price for insurance; takings and other types of adverse government action, in contrast, occur relatively infrequently and have hard-to-predict effects on property owners. Masur & Nash, supra, at 421–26. Given these difficulties, most commentators have concluded that the government probably must step in and provide insurance (in the form of ex post compensation for takings) for persons unable to self-insure or purchase private insurance. In theory, however, if these problems could somehow be overcome, private insurance would do the trick just fine.

The political risks faced by overseas investors provide an interesting test of the proposition that insurance can provide a substitute for government forbearance. Political risk insurance has been available to U.S. firms investing overseas since 1971, when Congress created the Overseas Private Investment Corporation (OPIC), a semi-public corporation capitalized by the federal government and backed by the full faith and credit of the federal government. For many years, political risk insurance was available only through OPIC and a similar agency of the World Bank. Commentators suggested that political risk insurance was not available without government subsidy, or perhaps that government-supported insurance has an inherent advantage over private insurers because the government-backed insurers can intervene with host countries to reduce the incidence of loss. See Maura B. Perry, A Model for Efficient Foreign Aid: The Case for the Political Risk Insurance Activities of the Overseas Private Investment Corporation, 36 Va. J. Int'l L. 511 (1996).

Interestingly, however, the private insurance industry has recently made significant inroads into the political risk insurance market, to the point where private insurance now accounts for 48% of the market. See Jennifer M. DeLeonardo, Are Public and Private Political Risk Insurance Two of a Kind? Suggestions for a New Direction for Government Coverage, 45 Va. J. Int'l L. 737, 745 (2005). DeLeonardo cites a number of factors that may account for the new viability of private political risk insurance, including improved information about political risks in developing countries and rising demand for such insurance after 9/11. But one of the most important reasons she cites is the emergence of bilateral investment treaties, with their prohibitions on expropriation and their provisions for mandatory dispute settlement through arbitration. Id. at 757–59. These treaty commitments, she argues, function as a warranty of forbearance by the host country and offer a type of co-insurance (payable by the host country) for any investment losses. "By putting private source insurers more on par with public source insurers in terms of obtaining payments after settling claims, the U.S. government may have enabled private source insurers to offer products that more closely resemble public source [political risk insurance]." Id. at 759–60.

If DeLeonardo is correct that private, non-subsidized political risk insurance becomes viable only if host governments make credible commitments to forbear from interfering with property, then this suggests that private insurance cannot be a perfect substitute for other legal mechanisms to promote forbearance. To the contrary, it appears that legal mechanisms (such as a right to compensation) may be a precondition to the development of a functioning insurance market—at least a private market not subsidized by taxpayers. Evidently, these other mechanisms reduce the risk of government expropriation or interference to the point where private insurance can handle the residual (uncompensated) risk. So perhaps insurance is not the complete answer to political risk after all. See also William A. Fischel & Perry Shapiro, Takings, Insurance, and Michelman: Comments on Economic Interpretations of Just Compensation Law, 17 J. Legal Stud. 269 (1988) (arguing that insurance only evens out the timing and variance of losses but does not eliminate the demoralization caused by expropriations and other government interferences).

C. THE POWER OF EMINENT DOMAIN

"[N]or shall private property be taken for public use without just compensation."

—U.S. Const., amend. V.

The power of eminent domain presents the starkest confrontation between private property and government forbearance. When the government exercises the power of eminent domain, it "condemns" property, meaning the government compels a transfer of the property in return for monetary compensation determined by a government entity, typically a court. Eminent domain actions are regarded as "in rem," meaning the condemning authority proceeds against the property being taken, not against the owner or owners personally. That is why eminent domain cases often have names like United States v. 564.54 Acres of Land, 441 U.S. 506 (1979) or 275.81 Acres of Land, More or Less, Situated in Stonycreek Township, Somerset County, Pennsylvania, 2014 WL 1248205 (W.D. Pa. 2014). Eminent domain is deeply unsettling to property owners, especially if the condemnation involves the forced exchange of a fee simple or long-term lease which forms the basis for the condemnee's home or business. Recent experience suggests that takings of property by eminent domain are likely to encounter more resistance from property owners than is regulation of the uses of property, by zoning for example.

When does the government—or an entity exercising a delegated power of eminent domain—seek to condemn property? As a matter of practice, it is clear that eminent domain is used as an alternative to the purchase of some recognized interest in property, like a fee simple, a lease, or an easement. In theory, eminent domain could be used to acquire almost anything, like a pleasant view from a window or an individual's labor. (The military draft represents a forced acquisition of individual labor—and potentially life—but the government power of military conscription is viewed as distinct from eminent domain and does not include a just compensation requirement.) In nearly every case in which eminent domain is used, the government or other condemning authority starts by offering to purchase some exchangeable interest in property, like a fee simple, a lease or an easement. Often, the condemning authority will reach an agreement with the owner about a price, and the interest will be transferred at this price voluntarily. But if the condemning authority and the owner cannot agree on a price, the condemning authority will file an action in court to compel a transfer of the property. If the court is satisfied that the legal requirements for the use of eminent domain have been met, the court will direct a forced exchange of the relevant interest in property and determine the price the condemning authority must pay. Bear in mind, however, that even if the condemning authority reaches an agreement with the owner about a price, the bargaining between the condemning authority and the owner will take place under the shadow of eminent domain. Cf. Goldberg et al., Bargaining in the Shadow of Eminent Domain: Valuing and Apportioning Condemnation Awards Between Landlord and Tenant, 34 UCLA L. Rev. 1083 (1987). The owner will know that if push comes to shove, the condemning authority can force a transfer of the property and some government entity (usually a court) will determine the price. This unquestionably increases the condemning authority's bargaining power relative to that of the owner.

Who may exercise the power of eminent domain? The Supreme Court has held that the power of eminent domain is an inherent attribute of political sovereignty. PennEast Pipeline Co., LLC v. New Jersey, 141 S. Ct. 2244, 2254–55 (2021). Thus, the federal government can exercise the power of eminent domain, even though that power is not expressly mentioned in the Constitution and it was not until 1876 that the Court recognized a federal power of eminent domain. Kohl v. United States, 91 U.S. 367, 372 (1876). Before then, when the federal government wanted to engage in a forced exchange of property, it generally asked the relevant state to exercise the power of eminent domain, and then to transfer the property to the federal government. Compare William Baude, Rethinking the Federal Eminent Domain Power, 122 Yale L.J. 1738, 1761–77 (2013) (expressing skepticism about whether the federal government was originally thought to have the power of eminent domain) with Christian R. Bursett, The Messy History of the Federal Eminent Domain Power: A Response to William Baude, 4 Cal. L. Rev. Circuit 187 (2013) (maintaining that the evidence on this point is mixed). Each of the states, as part of their reserved sovereign powers not delegated to the federal government, also has the power of eminent domain.

Courts have long held that the power of eminent domain can be delegated by the sovereign (the federal government or the states) to other entities. This must be done by statute. States have commonly delegated the power of eminent domain to subordinate governmental bodies like counties and cities, as well as to state agencies like highway departments and redevelopment authorities. In the nineteenth century it was common for states to delegate eminent domain authority to corporations chartered to construct canals, turnpikes, and railroads, and it became an accepted understanding that these common carriers could be given such a delegated power of eminent domain. The federal government can also delegate its eminent domain authority. For example, the Court in *PennEast Pipeline*, supra, recently upheld the power of a private interstate pipeline company to condemn state-owned land, pursuant to a delegated power adopted in the Federal Power Act in 1947. Nevertheless, it is important to remember that only a political sovereign has inherent authority to engage in takings by eminent domain; anyone else claiming such a power must show that it has been delegated by statute.

The use of eminent domain authority is directly constrained by the Takings Clause of the Fifth Amendment (quoted above). This provision originally applied only to the federal government, Barron v. Baltimore, 32 U.S. (7 Pet.) 243 (1833), and because the federal government rarely exercised a power of eminent domain before 1876, the constitutional constraint was rarely invoked. The Court eventually held that similar principles apply to the states under the Due Process Clause of the Fourteenth Amendment. Chicago, Burlington & Quincy R.R. Co. v. Chicago, 166 U.S. 226, 238–39 (1897). Today, the Takings Clause is understood to be directly incorporated under the Fourteenth Amendment, Penn Central Transp. Co. v. City of New York, 438 U.S. 104, 122 (1978), so the same constraints apply to both the federal government and the states as a matter of federal constitutional law. Similarly worded clauses appear in the state constitutions of nearly all the states. These federal and state takings clauses directly constrain the use of eminent domain by the government. They have also been held to limit the power of government to adopt regulations of property that have an impact functionally equivalent to the exercise of eminent domain—the so-called regulatory takings doctrine. In both contexts, decisions of the United States Supreme Court have sought to define limits on the ability of government to rearrange property rights or to restrict the uses of property rights in the name of some public interest.

The Takings Clause is a fitting subject to conclude our study of property, because the Court, in applying the words of the Clause in different contexts, has drawn upon numerous themes and issues covered throughout the course. These include questions about how we define "property," how far property may be unbundled into discrete rights for purposes of legal analysis, how far claims of owner sovereignty should give way to concerns about public or community interests, the distinction between trespass and nuisance, the difference between possessory rights and servitudes, and—perhaps most centrally—how important it is that the government forbear from frustrating settled expectations about property.

We start this Part with takings by eminent domain. Because eminent domain trumps ordinary property rights, the power has always been viewed with some suspicion in America. Exercises of eminent domain authority must satisfy both statutory and constitutional requirements. Statutory requirements vary, but typically the condemning authority must show that it has been delegated the power of eminent domain by the legislature and that the delegated power is broad enough to encompass the proposed project. Some states require that the exercise of eminent domain be shown to be "necessary" to complete the project, and some states require that the condemning authority show it has made a good faith effort to acquire the property by voluntary exchange before invoking eminent domain. In many states, some types of projects, such as urban renewal or economic development takings, may include additional statutory requirements, such as a finding that the property in question is "blighted." The principal constitutional requirements are that the project be a "public use" and that the condemning authority has offered the property owner "just compensation." The Due Process Clauses of the Fifth and Fourteenth Amendments also presumably require notice and an opportunity for a hearing on the issue of government authority before property is seized, although surprisingly there is some contrary authority in state courts. See Rhode Island Economic Development Corp. v. The Parking Company, 892 A.2d 87 (R.I. 2006) (reaffirming state precedent holding that due process does not require notice or a hearing before property is taken under expedited "quick take" eminent domain procedures).

1. THE PUBLIC USE REQUIREMENT

One potentially significant constitutional limitation on the power of eminent domain is that it must be deployed for a "public use." There has been much debate about what this means. From the mid-nineteenth century through the early decades of the twentieth, a number of state courts (mostly applying state constitutional provisions) held that public use means actual "use by the public." See Philip Nichols, Jr., The Meaning of Public Use in the Law of Eminent Domain, 20 B.U. L. Rev. 615, 633 (1940). Under this understanding, property could be taken for highways or parks or railroads that would be used by the public. But it could not be taken for a private home or factory. This restrictive view has never gained favor with the U.S. Supreme Court, however, which by the time it got around to being clear on the subject has always construed the public use requirement in the Fifth Amendment of the U.S. Constitution to mean public advantage or benefit. See Berman v. Parker, 348 U.S. 26, 33 (1954); Rindge Co. v. Los Angeles County, 262 U.S. 700, 707 (1923). Under this broader interpretation, eminent domain can be used for any project that has some public interest rationale. The U.S. Supreme Court has also said that courts should give great deference to legislative bodies in their determinations of what sorts of projects satisfy the U.S. Constitution's public use requirement. Hawaii Housing Authority v. Midkiff, 467 U.S. 229, 241–43 (1984).

Given the Supreme Court's broad interpretation of the "public use" language in the Fifth Amendment and its deferential standard of review, federal courts have almost never invalidated a taking of property for failing the public use requirement. State courts applying takings clauses in state constitutions are somewhat more likely to say that some purposes—like a condemnation to create a private access road or to acquire a parking lot for a commercial enterprise—are not public uses. Surveys of appellate decisions in the fifty years after *Berman* have found that state courts presented with public use challenges (nearly always under state constitutions) invalidated about one of six takings challenged on this ground. See Thomas W. Merrill, The Economics of Public Use, 72 Cornell L. Rev. 61, 101 (1986); Corey J. Wilk, The Struggle over the Public Use Clause: Survey of Holdings and Trends, 1986–2003, 39 Real

Prop. Prob. & Tr. J. 251, 262 (2004). Still, eminent domain has been used in recent years for projects that many observers have found unsettling. Perhaps the most controversial decision was *Poletown Neighborhood Council v. City of Detroit*, 304 N.W.2d 455 (Mich. 1981), which upheld the condemnation of 465 acres of property in and near Detroit, Michigan for retransfer to General Motors for an auto assembly plant. The "public use" was said to be the preservation of jobs that would otherwise leave the city, contributing to a declining industrial and population base. In another case, the California Supreme Court left the door open for the City to argue that eminent domain could be used to condemn the Oakland Raiders professional football team, in order to keep it from leaving the City of Oakland. See City of Oakland v. Oakland Raiders, 646 P.2d 835, 843–44 (Cal. 1982).

At the beginning of the twenty-first century, criticisms of the use of eminent domain for economic development purposes began to mount. A number of lower court decisions invalidated exercises of eminent domain as a means of acquiring real estate for particular commercial entities. See, e.g., Southwestern Ill. Dev. Auth. v. National City Env., L.L.C., 768 N.E.2d 1 (Ill. 2002) (invalidating condemnation of recycling center for re-transfer to an auto race track for use as a parking lot); 99 Cents Only Stores v. Lancaster Redevelopment Agency, 237 F. Supp. 2d 1123 (C.D. Cal. 2001), appeal dismissed as moot, 60 Fed. Appx. 123 (9th Cir. 2003) (invalidating condemnation of lease in shopping center for retransfer to another store for expansion); Casino Reinvestment Development Authority v. Banin, 727 A.2d 102 (N.J. Super. 1998) (invalidating condemnation of land for future expansion of a commercial casino). Perhaps most dramatically, the Michigan Supreme Court overruled its decision in *Poletown*, holding that property cannot be condemned and retransferred to a commercial entity when the sole rationale is economic development. See County of Wayne v. Hathcock, 684 N.W.2d 765 (Mich. 2004). The Institute for Justice, a public interest law firm devoted to protecting private property rights, published a study collecting thousands of instances of property being condemned for retransfer to commercial entities throughout the nation. Dana Berliner, Public Power, Private Gain (2003). The Institute then convinced the U.S. Supreme Court to review one of the cases it had brought on behalf of objecting landowners in order to revisit the question of the meaning of public use. The upshot was the following intensely controversial decision.

Kelo v. City of New London, Connecticut
Supreme Court of the United States, 2005.
545 U.S. 469.

■ JUSTICE STEVENS delivered the opinion of the Court. In 2000, the city of New London approved a development plan that, in the words of the Supreme Court of Connecticut, was "projected to create in excess of 1,000 jobs, to increase tax and other revenues, and to revitalize an economically

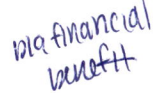

b/g financial benefit

distressed city, including its downtown and waterfront areas." 843 A.2d 500, 507 (Conn. 2004). In assembling the land needed for this project, the city's development agent has purchased property from willing sellers and proposes to use the power of eminent domain to acquire the remainder of the property from unwilling owners in exchange for just compensation. The question presented is whether the city's proposed disposition of this property qualifies as a "public use" within the meaning of the Takings Clause of the Fifth Amendment to the Constitution.

I

The city of New London (hereinafter City) sits at the junction of the Thames River and the Long Island Sound in southeastern Connecticut. Decades of economic decline led a state agency in 1990 to designate the City a "distressed municipality." In 1996, the Federal Government closed the Naval Undersea Warfare Center, which had been located in the Fort Trumbull area of the City and had employed over 1,500 people. In 1998, the City's unemployment rate was nearly double that of the State, and its population of just under 24,000 residents was at its lowest since 1920.

These conditions prompted state and local officials to target New London, and particularly its Fort Trumbull area, for economic revitalization. To this end, respondent New London Development Corporation (NLDC), a private nonprofit entity established some years earlier to assist the City in planning economic development, was reactivated. In January 1998, the State authorized a $5.35 million bond issue to support the NLDC's planning activities and a $10 million bond issue toward the creation of a Fort Trumbull State Park. In February, the pharmaceutical company Pfizer Inc. announced that it would build a $300 million research facility on a site immediately adjacent to Fort Trumbull; local planners hoped that Pfizer would draw new business to the area, thereby serving as a catalyst to the area's rejuvenation. After receiving initial approval from the city council, the NLDC continued its planning activities and held a series of neighborhood meetings to educate the public about the process. In May, the city council authorized the NLDC to formally submit its plans to the relevant state agencies for review. Upon obtaining state-level approval, the NLDC finalized an integrated development plan focused on 90 acres of the Fort Trumbull area.

The Fort Trumbull area is situated on a peninsula that juts into the Thames River. The area comprises approximately 115 privately owned properties, as well as the 32 acres of land formerly occupied by the naval facility (Trumbull State Park now occupies 18 of those 32 acres). The development plan encompasses seven parcels. Parcel 1 is designated for a waterfront conference hotel at the center of a "small urban village" that will include restaurants and shopping. This parcel will also have marinas for both recreational and commercial uses. A pedestrian "riverwalk" will originate here and continue down the coast, connecting the waterfront areas of the development. Parcel 2 will be the site of approximately 80 new residences organized into an urban neighborhood and linked by public walkway to the remainder of the development, including the state park. This parcel also includes space reserved for a new U.S. Coast Guard Museum. Parcel 3, which is located immediately north of the Pfizer facility, will contain at least 90,000 square feet of research and development office space. Parcel 4A is a 2.4-acre site that will be used either to support the adjacent state park, by providing parking or retail services for visitors, or to support the nearby marina. Parcel 4B will include a renovated marina, as well as the final stretch of the riverwalk. Parcels 5, 6, and 7 will provide land for office and retail space, parking, and water-dependent commercial uses.

The NLDC intended the development plan to capitalize on the arrival of the Pfizer facility and the new commerce it was expected to attract. In addition to creating jobs, generating tax revenue, and helping to "build momentum for the revitalization of downtown New London," the plan was also designed to make the City more attractive and to create leisure and recreational opportunities on the waterfront and in the park.

The city council approved the plan in January 2000, and designated the NLDC as its development agent in charge of implementation. See Conn. Gen.Stat. § 8–188 (2005). The city council also authorized the NLDC to purchase property or to acquire property by exercising eminent domain in the City's name. § 8–193. The NLDC successfully negotiated the purchase of most of the real estate in the 90-acre area, but its negotiations with petitioners failed. As a consequence, in November 2000, the NLDC initiated the condemnation proceedings that gave rise to this case.

II

Petitioner Susette Kelo has lived in the Fort Trumbull area since 1997. She has made extensive improvements to her house, which she prizes for its water view. Petitioner Wilhelmina Dery was born in her Fort Trumbull house in 1918 and has lived there her entire life. Her husband Charles (also a petitioner) has lived in the house since they married some 60 years ago. In all, the nine petitioners own 15 properties in Fort Trumbull—4 in parcel 3 of the development plan and 11 in parcel 4A. Ten of the parcels are occupied by the owner or a family member; the other five are held as investment properties. There is no allegation that any of these properties is blighted or otherwise in poor condition; rather, they were condemned only because they happen to be located in the development area.

In December 2000, petitioners brought this action in the New London Superior Court. They claimed, among other things, that the taking of their properties would violate the "public use" restriction in the Fifth Amendment. After a 7-day bench trial, the Superior Court granted a permanent restraining order prohibiting the taking of the properties located in parcel 4A (park or marina support). It, however, denied petitioners relief as to the properties located in parcel 3 (office space).[4]

Figure 10-2
Susette Kelo in Front of Her House

Photo by Isaac Reese, 2004 © Institute for Justice.

After the Superior Court ruled, both sides took appeals to the Supreme Court of Connecticut. That court held, over a dissent, that all of the City's proposed takings were valid. * * *

We granted certiorari to determine whether a city's decision to take property for the purpose of economic development satisfies the "public use" requirement of the Fifth Amendment.

III

Two polar propositions are perfectly clear. On the one hand, it has long been accepted that the sovereign may not take the property of *A* for the sole purpose of transferring it to another private party *B*, even though *A* is paid just compensation. On the other hand, it is equally clear that a State may transfer property from one private party to another if future "use by the public" is the purpose of the taking; the condemnation of land for a railroad with common-carrier duties is a familiar example. Neither

---

[4]　While this litigation was pending before the Superior Court, the NLDC announced that it would lease some of the parcels to private developers in exchange for their agreement to develop the land according to the terms of the development plan. Specifically, the NLDC was negotiating a 99-year ground lease with Corcoran Jennison, a developer selected from a group of applicants. The negotiations contemplated a nominal rent of $1 per year, but no agreement had yet been signed. See 843 A.2d 500, 509–10, 540 (Conn. 2004).

of these propositions, however, determines the disposition of this case.
* * *

Figure 10-3
The Kelo House and Its Surroundings

Photograph by Tim Martin. Courtesy The Day Publishing Co., New London, Connecticut.

The disposition of this case therefore turns on the question whether the City's development plan serves a "public purpose." Without exception, our cases have defined that concept broadly, reflecting our longstanding policy of deference to legislative judgments in this field.

In Berman v. Parker, 348 U.S. 26 (1954), this Court upheld a redevelopment plan targeting a blighted area of Washington, D.C., in which most of the housing for the area's 5,000 inhabitants was beyond repair. Under the plan, the area would be condemned and part of it utilized for the construction of streets, schools, and other public facilities. The remainder of the land would be leased or sold to private parties for the purpose of redevelopment, including the construction of low-cost housing.

The owner of a department store located in the area challenged the condemnation, pointing out that his store was not itself blighted and arguing that the creation of a "better balanced, more attractive community" was not a valid public use. Id., at 31. Writing for a unanimous Court, Justice Douglas refused to evaluate this claim in isolation, deferring instead to the legislative and agency judgment that the area "must be planned as a whole" for the plan to be successful. Id., at 34. The Court explained that "community redevelopment programs need not, by force of the Constitution, be on a piecemeal basis—lot by lot, building by building." Id., at 35. The public use underlying the taking was unequivocally affirmed:

We do not sit to determine whether a particular housing project is or is not desirable. The concept of the public welfare is broad and inclusive. . . . The values it represents are spiritual as well as physical, aesthetic as well as monetary. It is within the power of the legislature to determine that the community should be beautiful as well as healthy, spacious as well as clean, well-balanced as well as carefully patrolled. In the present case, the Congress and its authorized agencies have made determinations that take into account a wide variety of values. It is not for us to reappraise them. If those who govern the District of Columbia decide that the Nation's Capital should be beautiful as well as sanitary, there is nothing in the Fifth Amendment that stands in the way. Id., at 33.

In *Hawaii Housing Authority v. Midkiff*, 467 U.S. 229 (1984), the Court considered a Hawaii statute whereby fee title was taken from lessors and transferred to lessees (for just compensation) in order to reduce the concentration of land ownership. We unanimously upheld the statute and rejected the Ninth Circuit's view that it was "a naked attempt on the part of the state of Hawaii to take the property of A and transfer it to B solely for B's private use and benefit." Id., at 235 (internal quotation marks omitted). Reaffirming *Berman's* deferential approach to legislative judgments in this field, we concluded that the State's purpose of eliminating the "social and economic evils of a land oligopoly" qualified as a valid public use. 467 U.S., at 241–242. Our opinion also rejected the contention that the mere fact that the State immediately transferred the properties to private individuals upon condemnation somehow diminished the public character of the taking. "[I]t is only the taking's purpose, and not its mechanics," we explained, that matters in determining public use. Id., at 244. * * *

Viewed as a whole, our jurisprudence has recognized that the needs of society have varied between different parts of the Nation, just as they have evolved over time in response to changed circumstances. * * * For more than a century, our public use jurisprudence has wisely eschewed rigid formulas and intrusive scrutiny in favor of affording legislatures broad latitude in determining what public needs justify the use of the takings power.

IV

Those who govern the City were not confronted with the need to remove blight in the Fort Trumbull area, but their determination that the area was sufficiently distressed to justify a program of economic rejuvenation is entitled to our deference. The City has carefully formulated an economic development plan that it believes will provide appreciable benefits to the community, including—but by no means limited to—new jobs and increased tax revenue. As with other exercises in urban planning and development, the City is endeavoring to coordinate a variety of commercial, residential, and recreational uses of land, with the hope that they will form a whole greater than the sum of its parts. To effectuate this plan, the City has invoked a state statute that specifically authorizes the use of eminent domain to promote economic development. Given the comprehensive character of the plan, the thorough deliberation that preceded its adoption, and the limited scope of our review, it is appropriate for us, as it was in *Berman,* to resolve the challenges of the individual owners, not on a piecemeal basis, but rather in light of the entire plan. Because that plan unquestionably serves a public purpose, the takings challenged here satisfy the public use requirement of the Fifth Amendment.

To avoid this result, petitioners urge us to adopt a new bright-line rule that economic development does not qualify as a public use. Putting aside the unpersuasive suggestion that the City's plan will provide only purely economic benefits, neither precedent nor logic supports petitioners' proposal. Promoting economic development is a traditional and long accepted function of government. There is, moreover, no principled way of distinguishing economic development from the other public purposes that we have recognized. * * * [I]n *Berman,* we endorsed the purpose of transforming a blighted area into a "well-balanced" community through redevelopment, 348 U.S., at 33;[13] in *Midkiff,* we upheld the interest in breaking up a land oligopoly that "created artificial deterrents to the normal functioning of the State's residential land market," 467 U.S., at 242; and in [Ruckelshaus v. Monsanto Co., 467 U.S. 986 (1984)], we accepted Congress' purpose of eliminating a "significant barrier to entry in the pesticide market," 467 U.S., at 1014–1015. It would be incongruous to hold that the City's interest in the economic benefits to be derived from the development of the Fort Trumbull area has less of a public character than any of those other interests. Clearly, there is no basis for exempting economic development from our traditionally broad understanding of public purpose.

Petitioners contend that using eminent domain for economic development impermissibly blurs the boundary between public and private takings. Again, our cases foreclose this objection. Quite simply, the government's pursuit of a public purpose will often benefit individual private parties. For example, in *Midkiff,* the forced transfer of property conferred a direct and significant benefit on those lessees who were previously unable to purchase their homes. In *Monsanto,* we recognized

---

[13]   It is a misreading of *Berman* to suggest that the only public use upheld in that case was the initial removal of blight. See Reply Brief for Petitioners 8. The public use described in *Berman* extended beyond that to encompass the purpose of *developing* that area to create conditions that would prevent a reversion to blight in the future. See 348 U.S., at 34–35 ("It was not enough, [the experts] believed, to remove existing buildings that were insanitary or unsightly. It was important to redesign the whole area so as to eliminate the conditions that cause slums. . . . The entire area needed redesigning so that a balanced, integrated plan could be developed for the region, including not only new homes, but also schools, churches, parks, streets, and shopping centers. In this way it was hoped that the cycle of decay of the area could be controlled and the birth of future slums prevented"). Had the public use in *Berman* been defined more narrowly, it would have been difficult to justify the taking of the plaintiff's nonblighted department store.

that the "most direct beneficiaries" of the data-sharing provisions were the subsequent pesticide applicants, but benefiting them in this way was necessary to promoting competition in the pesticide market. 467 U.S., at 1014. The owner of the department store in *Berman* objected to "taking from one businessman for the benefit of another businessman," 348 U.S., at 33, referring to the fact that under the redevelopment plan land would be leased or sold to private developers for redevelopment. Our rejection of that contention has particular relevance to the instant case: "The public end may be as well or better served through an agency of private enterprise than through a department of government—or so the Congress might conclude. We cannot say that public ownership is the sole method of promoting the public purposes of community redevelopment projects." Id., at 34.[16]

It is further argued that without a bright-line rule nothing would stop a city from transferring citizen *A*'s property to citizen *B* for the sole reason that citizen *B* will put the property to a more productive use and thus pay more taxes. Such a one-to-one transfer of property, executed outside the confines of an integrated development plan, is not presented in this case. While such an unusual exercise of government power would certainly raise a suspicion that a private purpose was afoot,[17] the hypothetical cases posited by petitioners can be confronted if and when they arise.[18] They do not warrant the crafting of an artificial restriction on the concept of public use.

Alternatively, petitioners maintain that for takings of this kind we should require a "reasonable certainty" that the expected public benefits will actually accrue. Such a rule, however, would represent an even greater departure from our precedent. "When the legislature's purpose is legitimate and its means are not irrational, our cases make clear that empirical debates over the wisdom of takings—no less than debates over the wisdom of other kinds of socioeconomic legislation—are not to be carried out in the federal courts." Midkiff, 467 U.S., at 242. * * * The disadvantages of a heightened form of review are especially pronounced

---

[16]   Nor do our cases support Justice O'CONNOR's novel theory that the government may only take property and transfer it to private parties when the initial taking eliminates some "harmful property use." There was nothing "harmful" about the nonblighted department store at issue in Berman, 348 U.S. 26; see also n. 13, supra; nothing "harmful" about the lands at issue in the mining and agriculture cases, see, e.g., Strickley, 200 U.S. 527; and certainly nothing "harmful" about the trade secrets owned by the pesticide manufacturers in *Monsanto*, 467 U.S. 986. In each case, the public purpose we upheld depended on a private party's *future* use of the concededly nonharmful property that was taken. By focusing on a property's future use, as opposed to its past use, our cases are faithful to the text of the Takings Clause. See U.S. Const., Amdt. 5. ("[N]or shall private property be taken for public use, without just compensation"). * * *

[17]   Courts have viewed such aberrations with a skeptical eye. See, e.g., 99 Cents Only Stores v. Lancaster Redevelopment Agency, 237 F.Supp.2d 1123 (C.D. Cal. 2001); cf. Cincinnati v. Vester, 281 U.S. 439, 448 (1930) (taking invalid under state eminent domain statute for lack of a reasoned explanation). These types of takings may also implicate other constitutional guarantees. See Village of Willowbrook v. Olech, 528 U.S. 562 (2000) (*per curiam*).

[18]   Cf. Panhandle Oil Co. v. Mississippi ex rel. Knox, 277 U.S. 218, 223 (1928) (Holmes, J., dissenting) ("The power to tax is not the power to destroy while this Court sits").

in this type of case. Orderly implementation of a comprehensive redevelopment plan obviously requires that the legal rights of all interested parties be established before new construction can be commenced. A constitutional rule that required postponement of the judicial approval of every condemnation until the likelihood of success of the plan had been assured would unquestionably impose a significant impediment to the successful consummation of many such plans.

Just as we decline to second-guess the City's considered judgments about the efficacy of its development plan, we also decline to second-guess the City's determinations as to what lands it needs to acquire in order to effectuate the project. "It is not for the courts to oversee the choice of the boundary line nor to sit in review on the size of a particular project area. Once the question of the public purpose has been decided, the amount and character of land to be taken for the project and the need for a particular tract to complete the integrated plan rests in the discretion of the legislative branch." Berman, 348 U.S., at 35–36.

In affirming the City's authority to take petitioners' properties, we do not minimize the hardship that condemnations may entail, notwithstanding the payment of just compensation. We emphasize that nothing in our opinion precludes any State from placing further restrictions on its exercise of the takings power. Indeed, many States already impose "public use" requirements that are stricter than the federal baseline. Some of these requirements have been established as a matter of state constitutional law,[22] while others are expressed in state eminent domain statutes that carefully limit the grounds upon which takings may be exercised.[23] As the submissions of the parties and their *amici* make clear, the necessity and wisdom of using eminent domain to promote economic development are certainly matters of legitimate public debate.[24] This Court's authority, however, extends only to determining whether the City's proposed condemnations are for a "public use" within the meaning of the Fifth Amendment to the Federal Constitution. Because over a century of our case law interpreting that provision dictates an affirmative answer to that question, we may not grant petitioners the relief that they seek.

---

[22]   See, e.g., County of Wayne v. Hathcock, 684 N.W.2d 765 (Mich. 2004).

[23]   Under California law, for instance, a city may only take land for economic development purposes in blighted areas. Cal. Health & Safety Code Ann. §§ 33030–33037 (West 1997). See, e.g., Redevelopment Agency of Chula Vista v. Rados Bros., 115 Cal.Rptr.2d 234 (Cal. Ct. App. 2001).

[24]   For example, some argue that the need for eminent domain has been greatly exaggerated because private developers can use numerous techniques, including secret negotiations or precommitment strategies, to overcome holdout problems and assemble lands for genuinely profitable projects. See Brief for Jane Jacobs as *Amicus Curiae* 13–15; see also Brief for John Norquist as *Amicus Curiae*. Others argue to the contrary, urging that the need for eminent domain is especially great with regard to older, small cities like New London, where centuries of development have created an extreme overdivision of land and thus a real market impediment to land assembly. See Brief for Connecticut Conference for Municipalities et al. as *Amici Curiae* 13, 21; see also Brief for National League of Cities et al. as *Amici Curiae*.

The judgment of the Supreme Court of Connecticut is affirmed.

It is so ordered.

■ JUSTICE KENNEDY, concurring. I join the opinion for the Court and add these further observations. * * *

A court applying rational-basis review under the Public Use Clause should strike down a taking that, by a clear showing, is intended to favor a particular private party, with only incidental or pretextual public benefits, just as a court applying rational-basis review under the Equal Protection Clause must strike down a government classification that is clearly intended to injure a particular class of private parties, with only incidental or pretextual public justifications. See Cleburne v. Cleburne Living Center, Inc., 473 U.S. 432, 446–447, 450 (1985); Department of Agriculture v. Moreno, 413 U.S. 528, 533–536 (1973). * * *

A court confronted with a plausible accusation of impermissible favoritism to private parties should treat the objection as a serious one and review the record to see if it has merit, though with the presumption that the government's actions were reasonable and intended to serve a public purpose. Here, the trial court conducted a careful and extensive inquiry into "whether, in fact, the development plan is of primary benefit to . . . the developer [*i.e.,* Corcoran Jennison], and private businesses which may eventually locate in the plan area [*e.g.,* Pfizer], and in that regard, only of incidental benefit to the city." The trial court considered testimony from government officials and corporate officers; documentary evidence of communications between these parties; respondents' awareness of New London's depressed economic condition and evidence corroborating the validity of this concern; the substantial commitment of public funds by the State to the development project before most of the private beneficiaries were known; evidence that respondents reviewed a variety of development plans and chose a private developer from a group of applicants rather than picking out a particular transferee beforehand; and the fact that the other private beneficiaries of the project are still unknown because the office space proposed to be built has not yet been rented.

The trial court concluded, based on these findings, that benefiting Pfizer was not "the primary motivation or effect of this development plan"; instead, "the primary motivation for [respondents] was to take advantage of Pfizer's presence." Likewise, the trial court concluded that "[t]here is nothing in the record to indicate that . . . [respondents] were motivated by a desire to aid [other] particular private entities." Even the dissenting justices on the Connecticut Supreme Court agreed that respondents' development plan was intended to revitalize the local economy, not to serve the interests of Pfizer, Corcoran Jennison, or any other private party. 843 A.2d 500, 595 (Conn. 2004) (Zarella, J., concurring in part and dissenting in part). This case, then, survives the meaningful rational basis review that in my view is required under the Public Use Clause. * * *

■ JUSTICE O'CONNOR, with whom THE CHIEF JUSTICE, JUSTICE SCALIA, and JUSTICE THOMAS join, dissenting. Over two centuries ago, just after the Bill of Rights was ratified, Justice Chase wrote:

> An ACT of the Legislature (for I cannot call it a law) contrary to the great first principles of the social compact, cannot be considered a rightful exercise of legislative authority. . . . A few instances will suffice to explain what I mean. . . . [A] law that takes property from A. and gives it to B: It is against all reason and justice, for a people to entrust a Legislature with SUCH powers; and, therefore, it cannot be presumed that they have done it. Calder v. Bull, 3 Dall. 386, 388 (1798) (emphasis deleted).

Today the Court abandons this long-held, basic limitation on government power. Under the banner of economic development, all private property is now vulnerable to being taken and transferred to another private owner, so long as it might be upgraded—*i.e.,* given to an owner who will use it in a way that the legislature deems more beneficial to the public—in the process. To reason, as the Court does, that the incidental public benefits resulting from the subsequent ordinary use of private property render economic development takings "for public use" is to wash out any distinction between private and public use of property— and thereby effectively to delete the words "for public use" from the Takings Clause of the Fifth Amendment. * * *

II

* * * [W]e have read the Fifth Amendment's language to impose two distinct conditions on the exercise of eminent domain: "the taking must be for a 'public use' and 'just compensation' must be paid to the owner." Brown v. Legal Foundation of Wash., 538 U.S. 216, 231–232 (2003).

These two limitations serve to protect "the security of Property," which Alexander Hamilton described to the Philadelphia Convention as one of the "great obj[ects] of Gov[ernment]." 1 Records of the Federal Convention of 1787, p. 302 (M. Farrand ed. 1934). Together they ensure stable property ownership by providing safeguards against excessive, unpredictable, or unfair use of the government's eminent domain power—particularly against those owners who, for whatever reasons, may be unable to protect themselves in the political process against the majority's will.

While the Takings Clause presupposes that government can take private property without the owner's consent, the just compensation requirement spreads the cost of condemnations and thus "prevents the public from loading upon one individual more than his just share of the burdens of government." Monongahela Nav. Co. v. United States, 148 U.S. 312, 325 (1893); see also Armstrong v. United States, 364 U.S. 40, 49 (1960). The public use requirement, in turn, imposes a more basic limitation, circumscribing the very scope of the eminent domain power:

Government may compel an individual to forfeit her property for the *public's* use, but not for the benefit of another private person. This requirement promotes fairness as well as security.

Where is the line between "public" and "private" property use? We give considerable deference to legislatures' determinations about what governmental activities will advantage the public. But were the political branches the sole arbiters of the public-private distinction, the Public Use Clause would amount to little more than hortatory fluff. An external, judicial check on how the public use requirement is interpreted, however limited, is necessary if this constraint on government power is to retain any meaning. See Cincinnati v. Vester, 281 U.S. 439, 446 (1930) ("It is well established that . . . the question [of] what is a public use is a judicial one").

Our cases have generally identified three categories of takings that comply with the public use requirement, though it is in the nature of things that the boundaries between these categories are not always firm. Two are relatively straightforward and uncontroversial. First, the sovereign may transfer private property to public ownership—such as for a road, a hospital, or a military base. Second, the sovereign may transfer private property to private parties, often common carriers, who make the property available for the public's use—such as with a railroad, a public utility, or a stadium. But "public ownership" and "use-by-the-public" are sometimes too constricting and impractical ways to define the scope of the Public Use Clause. Thus we have allowed that, in certain circumstances and to meet certain exigencies, takings that serve a public purpose also satisfy the Constitution even if the property is destined for subsequent private use. See, e.g., Berman v. Parker, 348 U.S. 26 (1954); Hawaii Housing Authority v. Midkiff, 467 U.S. 229 (1984).

This case returns us for the first time in over 20 years to the hard question of when a purportedly "public purpose" taking meets the public use requirement. It presents an issue of first impression: Are economic development takings constitutional? I would hold that they are not. * * *

In [*Berman* and *Midkiff*] we emphasized the importance of deferring to legislative judgments about public purpose. Because courts are ill-equipped to evaluate the efficacy of proposed legislative initiatives, we rejected as unworkable the idea of courts' " 'deciding on what is and is not a governmental function and . . . invalidating legislation on the basis of their view on that question at the moment of decision, a practice which has proved impracticable in other fields.' " Id., at 240–241 (quoting United States ex rel. TVA v. Welch, 327 U.S. 546, 552 (1946)); see Berman, supra, at 32 ("[T]he legislature, not the judiciary, is the main guardian of the public needs to be served by social legislation"). Likewise, we recognized our inability to evaluate whether, in a given case, eminent domain is a necessary means by which to pursue the legislature's ends. Midkiff, supra, at 242; Berman, supra, at 103.

Yet for all the emphasis on deference, *Berman* and *Midkiff* hewed to a bedrock principle without which our public use jurisprudence would collapse: "A purely private taking could not withstand the scrutiny of the public use requirement; it would serve no legitimate purpose of government and would thus be void." Midkiff, supra, at 245. To protect that principle, those decisions reserved "a role for courts to play in reviewing a legislature's judgment of what constitutes a public use . . . [though] the Court in *Berman* made clear that it is 'an extremely narrow' one." Midkiff, supra, at 240 (quoting Berman, supra, at 32).

The Court's holdings in *Berman* and *Midkiff* were true to the principle underlying the Public Use Clause. In both those cases, the extraordinary, precondemnation use of the targeted property inflicted affirmative harm on society—in *Berman* through blight resulting from extreme poverty and in *Midkiff* through oligopoly resulting from extreme wealth. And in both cases, the relevant legislative body had found that eliminating the existing property use was necessary to remedy the harm. Berman, supra, at 28–29; Midkiff, supra, at 232. Thus a public purpose was realized when the harmful use was eliminated. Because each taking *directly* achieved a public benefit, it did not matter that the property was turned over to private use. Here, in contrast, New London does not claim that Susette Kelo's and Wilhelmina Dery's well-maintained homes are the source of any social harm. Indeed, it could not so claim without adopting the absurd argument that any single-family home that might be razed to make way for an apartment building, or any church that might be replaced with a retail store, or any small business that might be more lucrative if it were instead part of a national franchise, is inherently harmful to society and thus within the government's power to condemn.

In moving away from our decisions sanctioning the condemnation of harmful property use, the Court today significantly expands the meaning of public use. It holds that the sovereign may take private property currently put to ordinary private use, and give it over for new, ordinary private use, so long as the new use is predicted to generate some secondary benefit for the public—such as increased tax revenue, more jobs, maybe even aesthetic pleasure. But nearly any lawful use of real private property can be said to generate some incidental benefit to the public. Thus, if predicted (or even guaranteed) positive side-effects are enough to render transfer from one private party to another constitutional, then the words "for public use" do not realistically exclude *any* takings, and thus do not exert any constraint on the eminent domain power.

There is a sense in which this troubling result follows from errant language in *Berman* and *Midkiff*. In discussing whether takings within a blighted neighborhood were for a public use, *Berman* began by observing: "We deal, in other words, with what traditionally has been known as the police power." 348 U.S., at 32. From there it declared that "[o]nce the object is within the authority of Congress, the right to realize it through the exercise of eminent domain is clear." *Id.,* at 33. Following up, we said in *Midkiff* that "[t]he 'public use' requirement is coterminous with the scope of a sovereign's police powers." 467 U.S., at 240. This language was unnecessary to the specific holdings of those decisions. *Berman* and *Midkiff* simply did not put such language to the constitutional test, because the takings in those cases were within the police power but also for "public use" for the reasons I have described. The case before us now demonstrates why, when deciding if a taking's purpose is constitutional, the police power and "public use" cannot always be equated. The Court protests that it does not sanction the bare transfer from A to B for B's benefit. It suggests two limitations on what can be taken after today's decision. First, it maintains a role for courts in ferreting out takings whose sole purpose is to bestow a benefit on the private transferee—without detailing how courts are to conduct that complicated inquiry. For his part, Justice KENNEDY suggests that courts may divine illicit purpose by a careful review of the record and the process by which a legislature arrived at the decision to take—without specifying what courts should look for in a case with different facts, how they will know if they have found it, and what to do if they do not. Whatever the details of Justice KENNEDY's as-yet-undisclosed test, it is difficult to envision anyone but the "stupid staff[er]" failing it. See Lucas v. South Carolina Coastal Council, 505 U.S. 1003, 1025–1026, n. 12 (1992). The trouble with economic development takings is that private benefit and incidental public benefit are, by definition, merged and mutually reinforcing. In this case, for example, any boon for Pfizer or the plan's developer is difficult to disaggregate from the promised public gains in taxes and jobs.

Even if there were a practical way to isolate the motives behind a given taking, the gesture toward a purpose test is theoretically flawed. If it is true that incidental public benefits from new private use are enough to ensure the "public purpose" in a taking, why should it matter, as far as the Fifth Amendment is concerned, what inspired the taking in the first place? How much the government does or does not desire to benefit a favored private party has no bearing on whether an economic development taking will or will not generate secondary benefit for the public. And whatever the reason for a given condemnation, the effect is the same from the constitutional perspective—private property is forcibly relinquished to new private ownership.

A second proposed limitation is implicit in the Court's opinion. The logic of today's decision is that eminent domain may only be used to upgrade—not downgrade—property. At best this makes the Public Use Clause redundant with the Due Process Clause, which already prohibits irrational government action. The Court rightfully admits, however, that the judiciary cannot get bogged down in predictive judgments about whether the public will actually be better off after a property transfer. In any event, this constraint has no realistic import. For who among us can say she already makes the most productive or attractive possible use of her property? The specter of condemnation hangs over all property. Nothing is to prevent the State from replacing any Motel 6 with a Ritz-Carlton, any home with a shopping mall, or any farm with a factory. Cf. Institute for Justice, D. Berliner, Public Power, Private Gain: A Five-Year, State-by-State Report Examining the Abuse of Eminent Domain (2003) (collecting accounts of economic development takings).

The Court also puts special emphasis on facts peculiar to this case: The NLDC's plan is the product of a relatively careful deliberative process; it proposes to use eminent domain for a multipart, integrated plan rather than for isolated property transfer; it promises an array of incidental benefits (even aesthetic ones), not just increased tax revenue; it comes on the heels of a legislative determination that New London is a depressed municipality. Justice KENNEDY, too, takes great comfort in these facts. But none has legal significance to blunt the force of today's holding. If legislative prognostications about the secondary public benefits of a new use can legitimate a taking, there is nothing in the Court's rule or in Justice KENNEDY's gloss on that rule to prohibit property transfers generated with less care, that are less comprehensive, that happen to result from less elaborate process, whose only projected advantage is the incidence of higher taxes, or that hope to transform an already prosperous city into an even more prosperous one.

Finally, in a coda, the Court suggests that property owners should turn to the States, who may or may not choose to impose appropriate limits on economic development takings. This is an abdication of our responsibility. States play many important functions in our system of dual sovereignty, but compensating for our refusal to enforce properly the Federal Constitution (and a provision meant to curtail state action, no less) is not among them.

   * * *

It was possible after *Berman* and *Midkiff* to imagine unconstitutional transfers from A to B. Those decisions endorsed government intervention when private property use had veered to such an extreme that the public was suffering as a consequence. Today nearly all real property is susceptible to condemnation on the Court's theory. * * *

Any property may now be taken for the benefit of another private party, but the fallout from this decision will not be random. The beneficiaries are likely to be those citizens with disproportionate influence and power in the political process, including large corporations and development firms. As for the victims, the government now has license to transfer property from those with fewer resources to those with more. The Founders cannot have intended this perverse result. "[T]hat alone is a *just* government," wrote James Madison, "which *impartially* secures to every man, whatever is his *own*." For the National Gazette,

Property, (Mar. 29, 1792), reprinted in 14 Papers of James Madison 266 (R. Rutland et al. eds. 1983).

I would hold that the takings in both Parcel 3 and Parcel 4A are unconstitutional, reverse the judgment of the Supreme Court of Connecticut, and remand for further proceedings.

■ JUSTICE THOMAS, dissenting. * * * Today's decision is simply the latest in a string of our cases construing the Public Use Clause to be a virtual nullity, without the slightest nod to its original meaning. In my view, the Public Use Clause, originally understood, is a meaningful limit on the government's eminent domain power. Our cases have strayed from the Clause's original meaning, and I would reconsider them.

I

* * * Though one component of the protection provided by the Takings Clause is that the government can take private property only if it provides "just compensation" for the taking, the Takings Clause also prohibits the government from taking property except "for public use." Were it otherwise, the Takings Clause would either be meaningless or empty. If the Public Use Clause served no function other than to state that the government may take property through its eminent domain power—for public or private uses—then it would be surplusage. * * * Alternatively, the Clause could distinguish those takings that require compensation from those that do not. That interpretation, however, "would permit private property to be taken or appropriated for private use without any compensation whatever." Cole v. La Grange, 113 U.S. 1, 8 (1885) (interpreting same language in the Missouri Public Use Clause). In other words, the Clause would require the government to compensate for takings done "for public use," leaving it free to take property for purely private uses without the payment of compensation. This would contradict a bedrock principle well established by the time of the founding: that all takings required the payment of compensation. 1 Blackstone 135; 2 J. Kent, Commentaries on American Law 275 (1827) (hereinafter Kent); J. Madison, for the National Property Gazette, (Mar. 27, 1792), in 14 Papers of James Madison 266, 267 (R. Rutland et al. eds. 1983) (arguing that no property "shall be taken *directly* even for public use without indemnification to the owner"). The Public Use Clause, like the Just Compensation Clause, is therefore an express limit on the government's power of eminent domain.

The most natural reading of the Clause is that it allows the government to take property only if the government owns, or the public has a legal right to use, the property, as opposed to taking it for any public purpose or necessity whatsoever. At the time of the founding, dictionaries primarily defined the noun "use" as "[t]he act of employing any thing to any purpose." 2 S. Johnson, A Dictionary of the English Language 2194 (4th ed. 1773). The term "use," moreover, "is from the Latin *utor,* which means 'to use, make use of, avail one's self of, employ, apply, enjoy, etc.'" J. Lewis, Law of Eminent Domain § 165, p. 224, n. 4

(1888) (hereinafter Lewis). When the government takes property and gives it to a private individual, and the public has no right to use the property, it strains language to say that the public is "employing" the property, regardless of the incidental benefits that might accrue to the public from the private use. The term "public use," then, means that either the government or its citizens as a whole must actually "employ" the taken property. See id., at 223 (reviewing founding-era dictionaries). * * *

Tellingly, the phrase "public use" contrasts with the very different phrase "general Welfare" used elsewhere in the Constitution. See ibid. ("Congress shall have Power To . . . provide for the common Defence and general Welfare of the United States"); preamble (Constitution established "to promote the general Welfare"). The Framers would have used some such broader term if they had meant the Public Use Clause to have a similarly sweeping scope. * * *

II

Early American eminent domain practice largely bears out this understanding of the Public Use Clause. This practice concerns state limits on eminent domain power, not the Fifth Amendment, since it was not until the late 19th century that the Federal Government began to use the power of eminent domain, and since the Takings Clause did not even arguably limit state power until after the passage of the Fourteenth Amendment. See Note, The Public Use Limitation on Eminent Domain: An Advance Requiem, 58 Yale L.J. 599, 599–600, and nn. 3–4 (1949); Barron ex rel. Tiernan v. Mayor of Baltimore, 7 Pet. 243, 250–251 (1833) (holding the Takings Clause inapplicable to the States of its own force). Nevertheless, several early state constitutions at the time of the founding likewise limited the power of eminent domain to "public uses." Their practices therefore shed light on the original meaning of the same words contained in the Public Use Clause.

States employed the eminent domain power to provide quintessentially public goods, such as public roads, toll roads, ferries, canals, railroads, and public parks. Lewis §§ 166, 168–171, 175, at 227– 228, 234–241, 243. Though use of the eminent domain power was sparse at the time of the founding, many States did have so-called Mill Acts, which authorized the owners of grist mills operated by water power to flood upstream lands with the payment of compensation to the upstream landowner. See, e.g., id., § 178, at 245–246; Head v. Amoskeag Mfg. Co., 113 U.S. 9, 16–19, and n. 2 (1885). Those early grist mills "were regulated by law and compelled to serve the public for a stipulated toll and in regular order," and therefore were actually used by the public. Lewis § 178, at 246, and n. 3; see also Head, supra, at 18–19. They were common carriers—quasi-public entities. These were "public uses" in the fullest sense of the word, because the public could legally use and benefit from them equally. See Public Use Limitations 903 (common-carrier status traditionally afforded to "private beneficiaries of a state franchise or another form of state monopoly, or to companies that operated in conditions of natural monopoly").

To be sure, some early state legislatures tested the limits of their state-law eminent domain power. Some States enacted statutes allowing the taking of property for the purpose of building private roads. See Lewis § 167, at 230. These statutes were mixed; some required the private landowner to keep the road open to the public, and others did not. *See id.*, § 167, at 230–234. Later in the 19th century, moreover, the Mill Acts were employed to grant rights to private manufacturing plants, in addition to grist mills that had common-carrier duties. See, e.g., M. Horwitz, The Transformation of American Law 1780–1860, pp. 51–52 (1977).

These early uses of the eminent domain power are often cited as evidence for the broad "public purpose" interpretation of the Public Use Clause, but in fact the constitutionality of these exercises of eminent domain power under state public use restrictions was a hotly contested question in state courts throughout the 19th and into the 20th century. Some courts construed those clauses to authorize takings for public purposes, but others adhered to the natural meaning of "public use." As noted above, the earliest Mill Acts were applied to entities with duties to remain open to the public, and their later extension is not deeply probative of whether that subsequent practice is consistent with the original meaning of the Public Use Clause. See McIntyre v. Ohio Elections Comm'n, 514 U.S. 334, 370 (1995) (Thomas, J., concurring in judgment). At the time of the founding, "[b]usiness corporations were only beginning to upset the old corporate model, in which the raison d'être of chartered associations was their service to the public," Horwitz, supra, at 49–50, so it was natural to those who framed the first Public Use Clauses to think of mills as inherently public entities. The disagreement among state courts, and state legislatures' attempts to circumvent public use limits on their eminent domain power, cannot obscure that the Public Use Clause is most naturally read to authorize takings for public use only if the government or the public actually uses the taken property. * * *

IV

The consequences of today's decision are not difficult to predict, and promise to be harmful. So-called "urban renewal" programs provide some compensation for the properties they take, but no compensation is possible for the subjective value of these lands to the individuals displaced and the indignity inflicted by uprooting them from their homes. Allowing the government to take property solely for public purposes is bad enough, but extending the concept of public purpose to encompass any economically beneficial goal guarantees that these losses will fall disproportionately on poor communities. Those communities are not only systematically less likely to put their lands to the highest and best social use, but are also the least politically powerful. If ever there were justification for intrusive judicial review of constitutional provisions that protect "discrete and insular minorities," United States v. Carolene Products Co., 304 U.S. 144, 152, n. 4 (1938), surely that principle would apply with great force to the powerless groups and individuals the Public Use Clause protects. The deferential standard this Court has adopted for the Public Use Clause is therefore deeply perverse. It encourages "those citizens with disproportionate influence and power in the political process, including large corporations and development firms" to victimize the weak. Ante, (O'Connor, J., dissenting).

Those incentives have made the legacy of this Court's "public purpose" test an unhappy one. In the 1950's, no doubt emboldened in part by the expansive understanding of "public use" this Court adopted in *Berman,* cities "rushed to draw plans" for downtown development. B. Frieden & L. Sagalyn, Downtown, Inc. How America Rebuilds Cities 17 (1989). "Of all the families displaced by urban renewal from 1949 through 1963, 63 percent of those whose race was known were nonwhite, and of these families, 56 percent of nonwhites and 38 percent of whites had incomes low enough to qualify for public housing, which, however, was seldom available to them." Id., at 28. Public works projects in the 1950's and 1960's destroyed predominantly minority communities in St. Paul, Minnesota, and Baltimore, Maryland. Id., at 28–29. In 1981, urban planners in Detroit, Michigan, uprooted the largely "lower-income and elderly" Poletown neighborhood for the benefit of the General Motors Corporation. J. Wylie, Poletown: Community Betrayed 58 (1989). Urban renewal projects have long been associated with the displacement of blacks; "[i]n cities across the country, urban renewal came to be known as 'Negro removal.'" Pritchett, The "Public Menace" of Blight: Urban Renewal and the Private Uses of Eminent Domain, 21 Yale L. & Pol'y Rev. 1, 47 (2003). Over 97 percent of the individuals forcibly removed from their homes by the "slum-clearance" project upheld by this Court in *Berman* were black. 348 U.S., at 30. Regrettably, the predictable consequence of the Court's decision will be to exacerbate these effects. * * *

NOTES AND QUESTIONS

1. The decision in *Kelo* provoked a storm of protest, as Internet bloggers, editorial writers, and politicians across the country condemned the decision as a threat to property rights. The U.S. House of Representatives passed a resolution expressing its "grave disapproval" of the decision, and legislation was introduced in both Houses of Congress and in virtually every state to discourage or prohibit the use of eminent domain for economic development. According to a recent count, 44 states have adopted new laws or ballot measures in response to the *Kelo* decision. See Dana Berliner, Looking Back Ten Years After *Kelo,* 125 Yale L.J. Forum 82 (2015). The responses are highly diverse, ranging from broad amendments to state constitutions prohibiting any use of eminent domain that yields a "private use" (New Hampshire) or a transfer to a "private party" (Nevada), to

relatively minor adjustments in eminent domain procedures. See generally, Ilya Somin, The Grasping Hand: *Kelo v. City of New London* and the Limits of Eminent Domain 141–64 (2015). After *Kelo*, or more accurately, after the political backlash to *Kelo*, many state supreme courts began to rule on state constitutional grounds that eminent domain cannot be used for economic development purposes. See, e.g., Norwood v. Horney, 853 N.E.2d 1115 (Ohio 2006) (holding that under the Ohio Constitution property cannot be condemned solely for economic development); Board of County Comm'rs of Muskogee County v. Lowery, 136 P.3d 639, 653–54 (Okla. 2006) (holding that economic development is not a public purpose under Oklahoma law); Benson v. State, 710 N.W.2d 131, 146 (S.D. 2006) (concluding that public use is better understood to require actual use by the government or the public rather than public purpose). The New York courts, in contrast, have adhered to a broad conception of public use that includes some economic development projects. See Kaur v. New York State Urban Dev. Corp., 15 N.Y.3d 235, 933 N.E.2d 721 (2010) (upholding finding of blight in use of eminent domain to create Columbia University's new West Harlem campus); Develop Don't Destroy (Brooklyn) v. Urban Dev. Corp., 874 N.Y.S.2d 414 (N.Y. App. Div. 2009) (upholding use of eminent domain in creating the Atlantic Yards redevelopment project in Brooklyn). See generally Somin, supra at 181–203. Overall, the judicial response to *Kelo* is consistent with the pre-*Kelo* historical pattern: more deference to public use determinations by federal courts than by state courts, and significant state variation in the enforcement of the public use limitation. See Lynda J. Oswald, The Role of Deference in Judicial Review of Public Use Determinations, 39 B.C. Envtl. Aff. L. Rev. 243 (2012) (providing a comparative study). What accounts for this disuniformity?

     2.   What was it about *Kelo* that generated the profound backlash? Was it the media accounts of the facts of the case, which were repeatedly characterized as involving a taking of occupied (and nonblighted) residential homes to satisfy the demands of the Pfizer Corporation? Was it the rhetoric of Justice O'Connor's dissent, with its apocalyptic vision of a world in which every home is up for grabs if coveted by some real estate developer? Was it because the public has become increasingly skeptical of government efforts to intervene in the economy in order to promote economic growth or job creation? For a close analysis of the public response to *Kelo*, suggesting that contextual variables such as the pre-existing use of the property and the identity of the project beneficiary make a large difference in public attitudes toward eminent domain, see Janice Nadler et al., Government Takings of Private Property 286–309, in Public Opinion and Constitutional Controversy (Nathaniel Persily et al. eds., 2008).

     3.   For further details about the homeowners in *Kelo* and the aftermath of the decision, see Jeff Benedict, Little Pink House: A True Story of Defiance and Courage (2009). Once the Court's mandate issued, the judgment of condemnation became final, and legal title to the properties passed to the City of New London. Nevertheless, a number of residents, including Susette Kelo and the Derys, refused to vacate their properties. In September 2005, the New London Development Corporation served the

former owners with eviction notices informing them that if they did not vacate they would be held liable for rent for holding over in buildings now owned by the City. This triggered a new round of public outcry. Connecticut Governor Jodi Rell ordered the Corporation to rescind the eviction notices, on pain of losing any further state redevelopment aid. The Governor then appointed a mediator to try to reach a compromise between the City and the former owners. Aided by a legal opinion from the state attorney general that the City could use redevelopment funds to negotiate settlements in amounts larger than the values set in the condemnation proceedings, the former owners gradually began to settle. In March 2006, Wilhelmina Dery died at the age of 89, in the same room in which she was born. Her family settled shortly thereafter. Finally, only two former owners, Susette Kelo and Michael Cristofaro, remained intransigent. The City Council voted in June 2006 to commence eviction proceedings against them. The Governor sought to broker a last minute compromise, which the City rebuffed. The City combined its tough stance with sweetened settlement offers, which Kelo and Cristofaro accepted before any eviction could take place. The settlement with Kelo included an agreement by the City to pay to move her house to a new location, and forgive all claims of unpaid rents and taxes. One source reported the value of her settlement at $442,000, compared to the appraised value of her home of $123,000 in 2000. See Our View: Eminent Domain Ends Badly for Those Involved, Norwich Bulletin, August 29, 2006, at 7A. The house was moved in 2008. Ms. Kelo eventually decided to use her settlement money to purchase another home on the opposite side of the Thames River. Given the negative publicity about the decision, the economic recession starting in 2008, and a sharp downturn in the real estate market, the developer slated to receive the property for $1 per year, Corcoran Jennison (see footnote 4, supra), abandoned the project. Pfizer closed the research facility it had built adjacent to the site, as a cost-saving measure. Today, the Fort Trumbull Redevelopment site consists of 90 acres of bare ground, with no prospect of generating additional jobs or tax revenues in the foreseeable future. Is this sad ending attributable to a misguided use of eminent domain for economic development, a misguided assault on use of eminent domain for economic development, or just bad timing?

4.   In its most complete discussion of the public use requirement prior to *Kelo*, the Supreme Court had said that the public use requirement was "coterminous with the scope of the sovereign's police powers," and that courts should review exercises of eminent domain only to assure that they are "rationally related to a conceivable public purpose." Hawaii Housing Auth. v. Midkiff, 467 U.S. 229, 240, 242–43 (1984). (Interestingly, the Court's unanimous opinion in *Midkiff* was written by Justice O'Connor.) Courts understood this to mean that the Fifth Amendment's public use language required only the most deferential type of "rationality review," under which legislation is upheld as long as the court can conceive of a legitimate purpose the legislature might have harbored and a rational person might believe that the taking would achieve this purpose. Does *Kelo* reaffirm this highly deferential position, or does the Court suggest a more demanding standard of review?

5.   Note that the majority does not quote the line in *Berman* and *Midkiff* about eminent domain being coterminous with the police power, and Justice O'Connor, in her dissent, says "[t]his language was unnecessary to the specific holding" in *Midkiff* and "the police power and 'public use' cannot always be equated." The point the Court seemed to be making in *Berman* and *Midkiff* when it uttered these words was that the government could use the power of eminent domain to achieve any purpose within the permissible ends of government. Since government at all levels does all kinds of things to try to promote economic development, from regulating the money supply to providing tax incentives for new business investment to mandating that all children receive an education that allows them to be productive members of the workforce, the "coterminous powers" idea would seem to compel the conclusion that eminent domain can be used for economic development. Has the Court now embraced the notion that the power of eminent domain is narrower, in terms of the purposes for which it can be used, than the police power or the power to tax and spend? What is the justification for confining the power of eminent domain—which always requires the payment of just compensation—to a narrower sphere than the power to regulate or tax property—neither of which requires the payment of compensation?

6.   None of the opinions in *Kelo* discusses the holdout problem, which most commentators today regard as an important justification for the power of eminent domain. See Ilya Somin, The Grasping Hand, supra at 90–99; Richard A. Posner, The Supreme Court 2004 Term, Foreword: A Political Court, 119 Harv. L. Rev. 31, 83–94 (2005); see also James E. Krier, The Takings-Puzzle Puzzle, 38 Wm. & Mary L. Rev. 1143 (1997). Did the New London redevelopment face a holdout problem? The NLDRC acquired about 100 parcels in the 90-acre site through voluntary negotiations but had reached an impasse with the nine owners of the last 15 parcels. Could it have built around these pockets of resistance? The answer is not clear, because it was not the focus of the judicial inquiry in the lower courts. One explanation for the need to acquire all parcels is that this would make the re-transfer to a developer more appealing, since the developer could then work on the equivalent of a greenfield site rather than have to make costly adjustments to accommodate existing structures. But this argument is just a matter of costs. As the Institute for Justice has noted in some of its public statements, the plan also called for the preservation of one structure—the Italian Dramatic Club—a private club patronized by many of the city's leading figures. So the project could have proceeded without the nonconsenting parcels, provided the City was prepared to offer additional subsidies to the developer. Another explanation is that much of the area is below the 100-year floodplain, and thus had to be re-graded in order to make it eligible for new development. Whether this could be accomplished without moving or at least jacking up existing structures is doubtful. Some type of coercion of the nonconsenting owners, whether through the use of eminent domain or the police power, may thus have been necessary to complete the project. Should courts pay more attention to the severity of the holdout problem in determining whether exercises of eminent domain are for a "public use"?

7.   Does Justice O'Connor's dissenting opinion offer a normatively justifiable theory of what "public use" means? Her opinion acknowledges that public use has been defined to mean public purpose, and that property can be condemned and retransferred to another private owner if there is a valid public purpose. But, she insists, when public use is defined to mean public purpose, the purpose must be to rectify some "precondemnation use of the targeted property [that inflicts] affirmative harm on society." What is the constitutional theory that would justify restricting eminent domain to the rectification of undesirable conditions inherent in property or in the pattern of ownership of property, as opposed to the provision of public goods or positive externalities not attainable under the current pattern of ownership of property? What might Ronald Coase, see Chapter I, say about this distinction? Is this bad-prevention versus good-promotion distinction just a way to draw a line in the sand in order to avoid the slippery slopes Justice O'Connor perceives ahead if condemnation is permitted for economic development or other types of general public goods? If so, why draw the line at the bad/good distinction rather than someplace else, such as the no-pretext formulation of the majority?

8.   Would restricting eminent domain for economic development to cases involving blighted property protect minority and low-income neighborhoods, as Justice O'Connor implies? Or would minority and low-income neighborhoods be more likely to be targeted under a regime that requires a determination of "blight," as Justice Thomas argues? For evidence that traditional urban renewal programs, which typically begin with a determination that a neighborhood is blighted, disproportionately affect poor and minority neighborhoods, see Wendell E. Pritchett, The Public Menace of Blight: Urban Renewal and the Private Uses of Eminent Domain, 21 Yale L. & Pol'y Rev. 1 (2003).

9.   Many of the post-*Kelo* statutes and newly-restrictive state court decisions prohibit the use of eminent domain for "economic development." What does this mean? Does it mean that economic development cannot be *a* purpose of condemnation? If so, then nearly all takings would be unconstitutional, since nearly all takings for highways or utility easements are motivated in part by a desire to encourage economic development. Does it mean that economic development cannot be the *sole* purpose of condemnation? But was economic development the sole purpose of the taking in New London? Would it be relatively easy to evade such a restriction, by tacking a public walkway or small park onto condemnation projects otherwise designed to further some commercial development?

10.   Both Justice O'Connor and Justice Thomas argue that the words "for public use" would be meaningless unless they are understood to restrict the scope of the power of eminent domain. But why would these words be meaningless if they were understood to be a synonym for eminent domain? In other words, is it possible the Fifth Amendment can be read to say: Nor shall private property be taken *by eminent domain* without just compensation? This would not be a trivial provision: It would mandate just compensation whenever the government takes property by eminent domain (or by other processes tantamount to eminent domain), as opposed to in some

other way, such as by committing a tort or by taxation. See Matthew P. Harrington, "Public Use" and the Original Understanding of the So-Called "Takings" Clause, 53 Hastings L.J. 1245 (2002); Daniel B. Kelly, The "Public Use" Requirement in Eminent Domain Law: A Rationale Based on Secret Purchases and Private Influence, 92 Cornell L. Rev. 1, 8 (2006). As long as we are looking closely at the language of the Fifth Amendment, why would the Framers put the word "without" before "just compensation," rather than before "public use," if public use were understood to be a restriction on the scope of the power of eminent domain? On the other hand, if the public use language does not imply any restriction, would this mean that a taking from A to give to B would pass muster as long as compensation was provided? Or are there some purpose-related limits implicit in "tak[ing] for public use"/eminent domain after all?

11.   The actual drafting history of the Takings Clause is very thin. See David A. Dana & Thomas W. Merrill, Property: Takings ch. 2 (2002). Blackstone, on whom Justice Thomas relies, did not argue that eminent domain could be exercised only for public uses. Blackstone thought the power of condemnation required the constructive consent of the property owner, which could be obtained only through the approval of the legislature. 1 William Blackstone, Commentaries *135 (1768). The public use or public purpose requirement appears to have entered American law through the influence of natural rights jurists such as Grotius, Pufendorf, and Vattel. Dana & Merrill, supra, at 19–22. These writers were the ones who first used the word "eminent domain," and this term, along with the movement to restrict eminent domain to actual public uses, entered American law in the 1830s. The debate over the original understanding of "for public use" thus may boil down to whether one thinks the Framers were more influenced by Blackstone and Locke (who would require the consent of the legislature) or by continental thinkers like Grotius (who would require a public use or purpose).

2.   JUST COMPENSATION

The other significant constitutional limitation on eminent domain is that the condemning authority must pay "just compensation." The following case discusses several difficult issues that arise in attempting to fix a "just" price on property when the owner and the condemning authority have not been able to negotiate a value acceptable to both sides.

United States v. Miller

Supreme Court of the United States, 1943.
317 U.S. 369.

■ MR. JUSTICE ROBERTS delivered the opinion of the Court. This case presents important questions respecting standards for valuing property taken for public use. * * *

The United States condemned a strip across the respondents' lands for tracks of the Central Pacific Railroad, relocation of which was necessary on account of the prospective flooding of the old right-of-way by waters to be impounded by [the creation of a federally-funded dam] in California. * * *

In his report for the fiscal year ending June 30, 1937, the Secretary of the Interior stated that Shasta, California, had been selected for the site of the Sacramento River dam. Its construction involved relocation of some thirty miles of the line of the railroad.

Portions of respondents' lands were required for the relocated right-of-way. Alternate routes were surveyed by March 1936 and staked at intervals of 100 feet. Prior to the authorization of the project, the area of which respondents' tracts form a part was largely uncleared brush land. In the years 1936 and 1937 certain parcels were purchased with the intention of subdividing them and, in 1937, subdivisions were plotted and there grew up a settlement known as Boomtown, in which the respondents' lands lie. Two of the respondents were realtors interested in developing the neighborhood. By December 1938 the town had been built up for business and residential purposes.

December 14, 1938, the United States filed in the District Court for Northern California a complaint in eminent domain against the respondents and others whose lands were needed for the relocation of the railroad. On that day the Government also filed a declaration of taking. In this declaration the estimate of just compensation to be paid for a tract belonging to three of the respondents as co-tenants was estimated at $2,550 and that sum was deposited in court. On the application of these owners the court directed the Clerk to pay each of them one-third of the deposit, or $850, on account of the compensation they were entitled to receive.

The action in eminent domain was tried to a jury. The respondents offered opinion evidence as to the fair market value of the tracts involved and also as to severance damage to lots of which portions were taken. Each witness was asked to state his opinion as to market value of the land taken as at December 14, 1938, the date of the filing of the complaint. Government counsel objected to the form of the question on the ground that, as the United States was definitely committed to the project August 26, 1937, the respondents were not entitled to have included in an estimate of value, as of the date the lands were taken, any increment of value due to the Government's authorization of, and commitment to, the project. The trial court sustained the objection and required the question to be reframed so as to call for market value at the date of the taking, excluding therefrom any increment of value accruing after August 26, 1937, due to the authorization of the project. Under stress of the ruling, and over objection and exception, questions calling for opinion evidence were phrased to comply with the court's decision. The jury rendered verdicts in favor of various respondents.

The three respondents who had received $850 each on account of compensation were awarded less than the total paid them. The court entered judgment that title to the lands was in the United States and judgment in favor of respondents respectively for the amounts awarded them. Judgment was entered against the three respondents and in favor of the United States for the amounts they had received in excess of the verdicts with interest. They moved to set aside the money judgments against them on the ground that the court had no jurisdiction to enter them. The motions were overruled. All of the respondents appealed * * *

The Circuit Court of Appeals reversed the judgment holding, by a divided court, that the trial judge erred in his rulings and in his charge, and unanimously that the District Court was without jurisdiction to award the United States a judgment for amounts overpaid. A majority of the court were of opinion the witnesses should have been asked to state the fair market value of the lands as of the date of taking without qualification, and the judge should have charged that this value measured the compensation to which the respondents were entitled.

1.   The Fifth Amendment of the Constitution provides that private property shall not be taken for public use without just compensation. Such compensation means the full and perfect equivalent in money of the property taken. The owner is to be put in as good position pecuniarily as he would have occupied if his property had not been taken.

It is conceivable that an owner's indemnity should be measured in various ways depending upon the circumstances of each case and that no general formula should be used for the purpose. In an effort, however, to find some practical standard, the courts early adopted, and have retained, the concept of market value. The owner has been said to be entitled to the "value", the "market value", and the "fair market value" of what is taken. The term "fair" hardly adds anything to the phrase "market value", which denotes what "it fairly may be believed that a purchaser in fair market conditions would have given", or, more concisely, "market value fairly determined."

Respondents correctly say that value is to be ascertained as of the date of taking. But they insist that no element which goes to make up value as at that moment is to be discarded or eliminated. We think the proposition is too broadly stated. Where, for any reason, property has no market resort must be had to other data to ascertain its value; and, even in the ordinary case, assessment of market value involves the use of assumptions, which make it unlikely that the appraisal will reflect true value with nicety. It is usually said that market value is what a willing buyer would pay in cash to a willing seller. Where the property taken, and that in its vicinity, has not in fact been sold within recent times, or in significant amounts, the application of this concept involves, at best, a guess by informed persons.

Again, strict adherence to the criterion of market value may involve inclusion of elements which, though they affect such value, must in fairness be eliminated in a condemnation case, as where the formula is attempted to be applied as between an owner who may not want to part with his land because of its special adaptability to his own use, and a taker who needs the land because of its peculiar fitness for the taker's purposes. These elements must be disregarded by the fact finding body in arriving at "fair" market value.

Since the owner is to receive no more than indemnity for his loss, his award cannot be enhanced by any gain to the taker. Thus although the market value of the property is to be fixed with due consideration of all its available uses, its special value to the condemnor as distinguished from others who may or may not possess the power to condemn, must be excluded as an element of market value. The district judge so charged the jury and no question is made as to the correctness of the instruction.

can't consider special value to taker in MV

There is, however, another possible element of market value, which is the bone of contention here. Should the owner have the benefit of any increment of value added to the property taken by the action of the public authority in previously condemning adjacent lands? If so, were the lands in question so situate as to entitle respondents to the benefit of this increment?

Courts have to adopt working rules in order to do substantial justice in eminent domain proceedings. One of these is that a parcel of land which has been used and treated as an entity shall be so considered in assessing compensation for the taking of part or all of it.

This has begotten subsidiary rules. If only a portion of a single tract is taken the owner's compensation for that taking includes any element of value arising out of the relation of the part taken to the entire tract. Such damage is often, though somewhat loosely, spoken of as severance damage. On the other hand, if the taking has in fact benefited the remainder the benefit may be set off against the value of the land taken.

As respects other property of the owner consisting of separate tracts adjoining that affected by the taking, the Constitution has never been construed as requiring payment of consequential damages; and unless the legislature so provides, as it may, benefits are not assessed against such neighboring tracts for increase in their value.

If a distinct tract is condemned, in whole or in part, other lands in the neighborhood may increase in market value due to the proximity of the public improvement erected on the land taken. Should the Government, at a later date, determine to take these other lands, it must pay their market value as enhanced by this factor of proximity. If, however, the public project from the beginning included the taking of certain tracts but only one of them is taken in the first instance, the owner of the other tracts should not be allowed an increased value for his lands which are ultimately to be taken any more than the owner of the tract first condemned is entitled to be allowed an increased market value because adjacent lands not immediately taken increased in value due to the projected improvement.

how to handle nearby plots of land
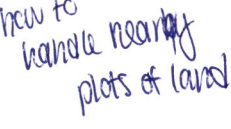

The question then is whether the respondents' lands were probably within the scope of the project from the time the Government was committed to it. If they were not, but were merely adjacent lands, the subsequent enlargement of the project to include them ought not to deprive the respondents of the value added in the meantime by the proximity of the improvement. If, on the other hand, they were, the Government ought not to pay any increase in value arising from the known fact that the lands probably would be condemned. The owners ought not to gain by speculating on probable increase in value due to the Government's activities.

In which category do the lands in question fall? The project, from the date of its final and definite authorization in August 1937, included the relocation of the railroad right-of-way, and one probable route was marked out over the respondents' lands. This being so, it was proper to tell the jury that the respondents were entitled to no increase in value arising after August 1937 because of the likelihood of the taking of their property. If their lands were probably to be taken for public use, in order to complete the project in its entirety, any increase in value due to that fact could only arise from speculation by them, or by possible purchasers from them, as to what the Government would be compelled to pay as compensation. * * *

2. We think the court below erred in holding the District Court without power to enter a judgment against three of the respondents to whom payments in excess of the jury's verdicts had been made out of the funds deposited with the Court.

Examination of the Act of February 26, 1931, discloses that the declaration of taking is to be filed in the proceeding for condemnation at its inception or at any later time. When the declaration is filed the amount of estimated compensation is to be deposited with the court to be paid as the court may order "for or on account" of the just compensation to be awarded the owners. Thus the acquisition by the Government of title and immediate right to possession, and the deposit of the estimated compensation, occur as steps in the main proceeding.

The purpose of the statute is twofold. First, to give the Government immediate possession of the property and to relieve it of the burden of interest accruing on the sum deposited from the date of taking to the date of judgment in the eminent domain proceeding. Secondly, to give the former owner, if his title is clear, immediate cash compensation to the extent of the Government's estimate of the value of the property. The Act recognizes that there may be an error in the estimate and appropriately provides that, if the judgment ultimately awarded shall be in excess of the amount deposited, the owner shall recover the excess with interest. But there is no correlative provision for repayment of any excess by the owner to the United States. The necessary result is, so the respondents say, that any sum paid them in excess of the jury's award is their property, which the United States may not recover.

All the provisions of the Act taken together require a contrary conclusion. The payment is of estimated compensation; it is intended as a provisional and not a final settlement with the owner; it is a payment "on account of" compensation and not a final settlement of the amount due. To hold otherwise would defeat the policy of the statute and work injustice; would be to encourage federal officials to underestimate the value of the property with the result that the Government would be saddled with interest on a larger sum from date of taking to final award, and would be to deny the owner the immediate use of cash approximating the value of his land.

Respondents assert that whatever the substantive right of the United States to repayment of the surplus, the District Court in rendering judgment against them deprived them of property without due process of law. We think the contention is unsound.

The District Court was dealing with money deposited in its chancery to be disbursed under its direction in connection with an action pending before it. The situation is like that in which litigants deposit money as security or to await the outcome of litigation. Notwithstanding the fact that the court released the fund to the respondents, the parties were still before it and it did not lose control of the fund but retained jurisdiction to deal with its retention or repayment as justice might require.

Denial of notice and hearing is asserted. But, while it is true that the court included the judgment of restitution in its general judgment in the condemnation proceedings without notice to the parties or hearing, the respondents made motions to set aside the judgment against them, and the court heard and acted on the motions. The respondents had full opportunity to urge any meritorious reasons why judgment of restitution should not be entered against them. We think they were entitled to no more. * * *

The judgment of the Circuit Court of Appeals is reversed and that of the District Court affirmed.

NOTES AND QUESTIONS

1.   The idea of "fair market value" as the measure of just compensation is inherently paradoxical. Eminent domain is typically used when negotiations for a market transaction break down, so by definition there is no "market value" in the sense of an arm's length negotiated price for the property in question. Instead, fair market value refers to a hypothetical price—a guess about what the property would have fetched if it had followed the path of voluntary as opposed to compelled exchange. Real estate appraisers have developed a variety of approaches for estimating fair market value. The most common are (1) examining recent transactions in which the property in question was sold, and adjusting for general changes in market prices in the area since the date of those transactions; (2) examining recent transactions of other parcels of property in the area similar to the property in question, and adjusting for differences in size, location, and quality of

improvements; (3) estimating the rental value of the property in question, and capitalizing this to reach a purchase price using a rate of return commonly used as a benchmark for real estate investments in the area; (4) determining the replacement cost of the land and improvements taken, and adjusting downward to reflect depreciation due to age and wear and tear. See 4 Julius L. Sackman, Nichols on Eminent Domain § 12.02 (3d ed. 2005); 1 Lewis Orgel, Valuation Under the Law of Eminent Domain §§ 136–38, 176–87 (James C. Bonbright ed., 2d ed. 1953); 2 id. §§ 188–89.

2.   In economic terms, the *Miller* Court can be read as saying that the owner should be awarded the *opportunity cost* of having his land taken away. The opportunity cost is the highest and best use of the land *other than* the use proposed by the condemning authority. See, e.g., Armen A. Alchian, Cost, in 3 International Encyclopedia of the Social Sciences 404, 404 (David L. Sills ed., 1968) ("[T]he cost of an event is the highest-valued opportunity necessarily forsaken."). Thus, suppose the property is currently being used as a farm, the highest and best use would be a suburban subdivision, and the government proposes to take the land for a highway. On condemnation, the government must pay the value the land would obtain if sold for development as a subdivision, the highest and best economic use (other than as a highway). What might be the justification for basing compensation awards on opportunity cost rather than existing use? See generally Katrina M. Wyman, The Measure of Just Compensation, 41 U.C. Davis L. Rev. 239 (2007).

3.   The *Miller* Court also concludes that just compensation means that the owner is not entitled to an award based on the after-condemnation value of property in the area. Thus, for example, if the current use is "uncleared brush land," and the government proposes to use the property to relocate a railroad displaced by a government-built reservoir, the value should be based on the highest and best use of uncleared brush land, not the value of land next to a government reservoir. The intuition behind this, presumably, is that awarding the condemnee the value of land next to a reservoir would confer a windfall on the condemnee. The condemnee has done nothing to create this enhanced value—it is a product of the resources that will be expended by the government in building the dam, which will be paid for by the taxpayers. Valuing condemned property on a post-condemnation basis would also be partially self-defeating, insofar as the public benefits of the taking would be capitalized in the land values and transferred to the condemnee.

4.   The issue in *Miller* is trickier. Suppose the government builds the reservoir, paying for the land according to its pre-reservoir value. Then, one year later, the government decides to build a highway around the edge of the reservoir. What is the proper valuation of the land taken for the highway— uncleared brush land in the middle of nowhere or land in the vicinity of a reservoir? Here it seems clear that, under the opportunity-cost approach, the proper value is the value of land in the vicinity of a reservoir. See Christopher Serkin, The Meaning of Value: Assessing Just Compensation for Regulatory Takings, 99 Nw. U. L. Rev. 677, 688–89 (2005). But doesn't this also confer a windfall on the condemnee? Perhaps it does, if we focus on the original cost

of the land to the condemnee, and the fact that the newly-enhanced value of the land is largely attributable to the resources the government expended in creating the reservoir. Yet there is a strong efficiency argument for awarding the condemnee the current value of the land: We want the government to select a route for the highway that takes into account all the costs of building the highway, including the costs of land. Perhaps there is a better route for the highway farther away from the reservoir, one that goes through cheaper land that has fewer alternative uses. Pricing the land at its current opportunity cost sends the right signals on highway location to the government. Note too that if the condemnee had sold the land between the time the reservoir was built and the highway project was announced, the condemnee would have obtained a price that reflects the value of land in the vicinity of a reservoir, not the price of uncleared brush land in the middle of nowhere. So in this sense there is no windfall. Do you see now why the critical issue in *Miller* is whether the substitute right-of-way for the railroad was part of the scope of original project, as opposed to being a separate project that arose after the reservoir was built?

5.   Ordinarily, as the Court notes, the temporal reference point for determining fair market value is the date at which title transfers. Does the Court inject an element of indeterminacy into the rules for determining just compensation by departing from this reference point in determining whether the respondents' property was part of a single government project? For these purposes, the Court says that the temporal reference point is "the time the Government was committed to" the project. Isn't it likely that the government's "commitment" to a project like a major reservoir solidifies gradually over time, making the Court's test inherently problematic? Why was the Court willing to subject eminent domain to the added administrative costs of its "committed to the project" test? Was it simply a dislike of rewarding land speculators? Or is there a more substantive reason for moving the temporal reference point for the scope of the project to an earlier point in time than the transfer of title? See Serkin, The Meaning of Value, supra, at 696–99.

6.   Another objection to the fair-market-value formula is that it provides no recovery for the subjective value that owners attach to their property. Most people attach some premium above market value to property they own. Otherwise, they would sell for market value. The premium may be based on the fact that they are psychologically attached to the property, or they like the neighborhood, or they have made special modifications to the property to suit their particular needs, or simply because they want to avoid the inconvenience of moving. Under the fair-market-value standard, no compensation is expressly given for this subjective premium above market value. Many commentators therefore have assumed that the fair market value measure results in systematic undercompensation of property owners, especially where the property is occupied by a residence or a functioning business. Does the problem of uncompensated subjective value suggest that condemnation of certain kinds of property likely to have high subjective value should be off limits or subject to a higher standard of review under the public use requirement? See Margaret Jane Radin, Property and

Personhood, 34 Stan L. Rev. 957, 1007–12 (1982) (excerpted in Chapter III). Would private residential homes be included in this category? What about a small business or farm that has been in the same family for many years?

7.   A less drastic proposal for dealing with the problem of subjective value would be to pay a bonus above fair market value at least in certain categories of takings. See, e.g., Robert C. Ellickson, Alternatives to Zoning: Covenants, Nuisance Rules, and Fines as Land Use Controls, 40 U. Chi. L. Rev. 681, 736–37 (1973). Some of the Mill Acts mentioned in *Kelo* (footnote 8, omitted in the excerpt) provided for such bonus compensation. See Head v. Amoskeag Mfg. Co., 113 U.S. 9 (1885) (quoting New Hampshire Mill Act, providing that compensation be set at 150% of appraised value). And in the aftermath of *Kelo*, some states have passed statutes mandating higher compensation of 125% or 150% of fair market value depending on various defined circumstances, mainly residential use. See Wyman, 41 U.C. Davis L. Rev. at 257 & n.61. But would such a system of bonus compensation create a risk of overcompensating property owners who, for whatever reason, do not attach much subjective value to their holdings? The federal government and many states have partially responded to the undercompensation problem by enacting relocation acts, which give persons whose property is condemned additional monies for some transitional expenses like moving costs. See Uniform Relocation Assistance Act of 1970, 42 U.S.C. 4601 et seq. A recent study suggests that property owners, aided by generous interpretations of federal and state relocation acts, often receive substantial premiums above fair market value, especially where takings are politically controversial. See Nicole Stelle Garnett, The Neglected Political Economy of Eminent Domain, 105 Mich. L. Rev. 101 (2006). Does this suggest that caution is in order before mandating additional awards of bonus compensation?

8.   The reasons for sticking to fair market value and denying any compensation for assembly gain or subjective values are several. The reason mentioned most often in the cases is the difficulty of valuing things like psychological attachment or consequential damages like lost business good will. Including such increments of value would therefore increase the administrative costs of eminent domain proceedings. See, e.g., United States v. 564.54 Acres of Land, 441 U.S. 506, 516–17 (1979) (declining to award replacement cost in condemnation of a summer camp). Another reason harkens back to the public use issue again. We presume eminent domain will be used only for public projects like highways and schools that provide public goods that benefit everyone in the community. These sorts of projects arguably deserve public subsidies, and one form the subsidies can take is by providing less than full indemnification to those whose property is condemned to make way for the project. So there is a linkage between the public use limitation and incomplete compensation for takings. See Thomas W. Merrill, Incomplete Compensation for Takings, 11 N.Y.U. Envtl. L.J. 110 (2002). The stronger the public use limit, the stronger the case for incomplete compensation. Does it follow that a weak public use justification, like the one upheld in *Kelo*, should be coupled with a more complete measure of just compensation? For an argument to this effect, see James E. Krier & Christopher Serkin, Public Ruses, 2004 Mich. St. L. Rev. 859.

9. In an important article, Brian Angelo Lee, Just Undercompensation: The Idiosyncratic Premium in Eminent Domain, 113 Colum. L. Rev. 593 (2013), argues that the concern about uncompensated subjective value is overstated. Lee points out that many of the values not expressly compensated in eminent domain, such as moving costs, attorneys' fees, neighborhood amenities, and even the psychological attachment to property associated with longstanding occupancy, are taken into account by owners in deciding whether to sell voluntarily. Owners will sell voluntarily only when all the costs of relocating are exceeded by the benefits of the price they obtain when they sell. Thus, insofar as fair market value is based on data about previous sales of the property, sales of comparable properties, or even the capitalization of market rents, the standard measure of compensation will capture these sorts of costs. Lee argues that commentary about just compensation should shift from "subjective value" to the question whether it is fair to compensate for "idiosyncratic value," that is, for costs (including psychological costs) associated with relocation that are idiosyncratically high relative to those of the average owner of comparable property. Lee is surely correct that fair market value captures indirectly many of the costs of relocation that are not expressly compensated. But is there reason to think that the set of owners who decide to sell voluntarily may, on average, value the costs of relocation at a lower level than owners who do not want to relocate? If so, does it remain the case that fair market value undercompensates those who do not want to move, even if to a more qualified degree than is often assumed?

The Flight 93 Case

A version of *Miller's* holding that condemned property should be valued when the government becomes committed to the project, as opposed to when title formally changes hands, was recently presented in a case in which the federal government condemned land in rural Pennsylvania as a memorial for the victims who died on Flight 93 on September 11, 2001. Flight 93 was the fourth airplane commandeered by hijackers on 9/11, who were evidently targeting either the White House or the Capitol building in Washington, D.C., for a suicide attack similar to the ones that brought down the World Trade Center towers and struck the Pentagon. The terror attack was foiled when passengers on the plane attempted to take over the cockpit, which resulted in the plane crashing in an empty field near Shanksville, Pennsylvania. All persons on the plane were killed, but the bravery of the passengers likely averted more widespread death and destruction. The passengers were regarded as national heroes.

The land on which the plane crashed was owned by a family corporation called Svonavec, Inc. It had once been strip-mined, but had no active use at the time of the crash other than as the site of some oil and gas leases. Once the debris from the crash was cleared and the FBI completed its investigation, people began driving to the site to pay their respects to the victims. Svonavec constructed a temporary viewing area on the property. Eventually between 117,000 and 167,000 people traveled to the site each year. In 2002, Congress enacted legislation establishing the site as a national memorial, to be administered by the National Park Service. Svonavec, Inc. nevertheless continued to operate a private memorial on the site for several more years. Eventually, the government instituted an eminent domain proceeding, which resulted in a formal transfer of title to the government on September 2, 2009.

There was no issue in the case about whether the taking was a legitimate public use. The fact that the memorial would be constructed and operated by the National Park Service and would be open to the public meant the taking satisfied the public use requirement under even the most restrictive understanding of that term (government ownership or actual use by the public). Interestingly, the Supreme Court's first case dealing with public use involved a condemnation of the site of the Gettysburg Civil War battlefield as a memorial to the fallen. United States v. Gettysburg Elec. R. Co., 160 U.S. 668, 682 (1896) (holding that the taking "touches the heart, and comes home to the imagination of every citizen, and greatly tends to enhance his love and respect for those institutions for which these heroic sacrifices were made.").

The most difficult legal issue in the Flight 93 case involved the proper date for undertaking the valuation, a question the trial court called "the scope of the project rule." The district judge ruled that the proper date was 2002, when Congress authorized a national memorial. Consequently, any evidence about possible value that emerged between 2002 and 2009, when title formally transferred to the government, could not be considered. 275.81 Acres of Land, More or Less, Situated in Stonycreek Township, Somerset County, Pennsylvania, 2014 WL 1248205 (W.D. Pa. 2014).

Even so, the parties submitted wildly different proposed valuations. Svonavec hired Randall Bell as an expert witness, who had made a reputation proposing valuations for memorials at other disaster sites, including the destruction of the World Trade Center towers and the bombing of the federal building in Oklahoma City. He testified that the highest and best use of the property would be for a private memorial and museum. Adopting a method based on capitalization of expected profits, including a generous estimate of annual visitation, significant revenues for admission charges and sales of souvenirs, and a low discount rate (reflecting low risk of failure for such a project), he proposed that the fair market value of the land was $23.3 million. The government's expert witness countered that the economic success of any private memorial was too speculative to be taken into account. He testified that the highest and best use was as bare land, and looking to sales of comparative land in the area proposed a value of $610,000.

The district court judge appointed a three-person commission, consisting of real estate appraisers, to recommend a fair market value. The commission largely adopted the views and methods of Mr. Bell. It concluded that the highest and best use of the land in 2002 would be as a private memorial park. Neither a comparable sales approach nor an approach based on the reproduction cost was feasible, since the property, as the site of an infamous airplane crash, was utterly unique. The commission nevertheless adjusted downward Mr. Bell's estimate of the probable number of annual visitors, reduced his proposed admissions charge, decided that a private memorial would not include a museum that sold souvenirs, and raised the discount rate to reflect higher risk. After making these and other adjustments, the commission proposed a value of $1,535,000, which the district court accepted.

The Constitution requires the payment of "just compensation." If the rationale of *Miller* is that compensation should be determined in such a manner as to avoid an unjustified windfall to the owner, why is it "just" to compensate Svonavec, Inc. for the added value created by the fortuity that a plane crashed on its land? Surely, Svonavec did nothing to generate this extra value. If the value of Svonavec's land the day before the plane crashed was $610,000, based on sales of comparable land, why is the corporation entitled to an extra $925,000 after the crash? Should the principle of the *Miller* decision be extended to exclude from the determination of market value not only any increment in value created by the government's proposed taking, but also any other fortuitous event for which the owner can claim no responsibility? Or is Svonavec's entitlement to the windfall simply a function of the general principle of accession, which automatically awards unanticipated increments in value to the owner of the relevant asset, in this case land? Recall in this connection *Goddard v. Winchell* (Chapter II), awarding a meteorite to the owner of the land on which it falls.

Partial Takings

Miller discusses another problem: how to determine just compensation when the government takes a *portion* of a parcel rather than the whole thing. Here, the established rule is that the landowner is entitled to the fair market value of what is taken plus so-called "severance damages" for any loss in value to the part that is not taken. 4A Julius L. Sackman, Nichols on Eminent Domain § 14A.03 (3d ed. 2005). For example, if the government condemns a 200-foot strip of land across an owner's property for a highway, the owner is entitled to the fair market value of the 200-foot strip of land. In addition, if the highway diminishes the value of the remaining land—perhaps by making access to the remaining land more difficult—the owner will be entitled to severance damages reflecting the reduced market value of the land not taken.

As the Court observes, many jurisdictions, including the federal government, will also make adjustments for any offsetting benefits that the taking creates for the portion of the property that is not taken. To continue with the example, if the partial taking for a highway results in an increase in the value of the land not taken—perhaps because the highest and best use of the remaining land is now for commercial uses like gas stations and motels given the proximity of the highway—then the government is entitled to subtract the increase in value of the remaining land from the compensation it must pay for the strip of land taken.

The practice of subtracting offsetting benefits became controversial during the railroad construction boom in the nineteenth century. The problem was one of horizontal equity. The introduction of the railroad would raise the value of all land in the vicinity of the railroad. But if only the landowners whose land was taken for the railroad right-of-way were charged for offsetting benefits, they could end up getting nothing for the strip of land taken, while everyone whose land was not taken would get the benefit of the higher land values without giving up anything in return. Many states responded to this situation by developing a distinction between "general" offsetting benefits and "special" offsetting benefits. General benefits, like the increased value of all land in the community due to the arrival of the railroad, were not subject to offset. Only special benefits—those that inured to the particular owner who suffered a partial taking—were eligible for offset. The distinction between general and special benefits, however, proved to be difficult to apply in many circumstances. More recently, a trend of sorts has emerged in which state courts have rejected the general/special distinction as unworkable, and instead have adopted a simple rule in partial takings cases that compares the fair market value of the property before the taking to the fair market value of the property after the taking, awarding the difference (if any) to the condemnee. See Borough of Harvey Cedars v. Karan, 70 A.3d 524 (N.J. 2013) (reviewing history, adopting the before-and-after test, and reducing compensation for a partial taking of beachfront property to install a dune providing enhanced protection against storm surges). The before-and-after approach is easy to apply, and automatically incorporates all benefits and detriments to the owner in determining compensation for a partial taking. But does it solve the horizontal equity problem that led to the general/special distinction?

The rules for partial takings apply only to those who experience a partial taking of their property. Those whose property is not subject to a partial taking but whose property values are affected by the exercise of eminent domain, such as neighbors, are not eligible for severance damages, nor are they charged for offsetting benefits. As *Miller* observes, the rules also apply only when a partial taking affects a single parcel. If a landowner owns two different parcels, any damage that a taking on one parcel does to the second parcel is not compensated (nor are offsetting benefits to the second parcel recouped). What is the rationale for limiting severance damages and offsetting benefits to the "single parcel" subject to a partial taking, rather than applying these rules more generally to all parcels affected by the exercise of eminent domain?

The Treatment of Assembly Gain

The Court in *Miller* observes: "Since the owner is to receive no more than indemnity for his loss, his award cannot be enhanced by any gain to the taker. Thus although the market value of the property is to be fixed with due consideration of all its available uses, its special value to the condemnor as distinguished from others who may or may not possess the power to condemn, must be excluded as an element of market value." This is a longstanding principle of just compensation law. See, e.g., City of New York v. Sage, 239 U.S. 57 (1915). But in certain circumstances it raises questions about whether it is consistent with what is "just." Indeed, this principle may be responsible in significant part for what the Institute of Justice (which represented the plaintiffs in the *Kelo* case) has called "eminent domain abuse," i.e., the use of eminent domain to acquire large development sites in urban areas which are then transferred at bargain prices to private entities for a development project.

The basic problem can be illustrated by a simple example. Suppose the condemnor (the government or an entity like a redevelopment corporation) proposes to condemn ten contiguous parcels of land in order to create one large parcel of land. Each of the ten parcels is exactly one-acre in size, and each has a fair market value before the condemnation of $100,000. The aggregate compensation payable to the ten owners of the ten parcels is therefore $1,000,000. After the condemnation, however, the ten-acre site has a fair market value (without regard to its proposed use) of $2,000,000. Why is that possible? It is because ten-acre sites, especially in highly developed urban areas, are scarce relative to smaller parcels. And because they are scarce, they command a higher market value on a per-acre basis under standard valuation techniques used by real estate appraisers (comparable sales, prior sales, or capitalization of future rents or profits). In effect, the assembly of ten separate parcels into one large parcel has produces an "assembly gain" that doubles the value of each parcel on a per-parcel basis. Yet under the principle stated in *Miller*, this assembly gain is captured by the condemnor not by the condemnees.

The allocation of 100 percent of the assembly gain to the condemnor may be justifiable when the taking is for a conventional public use, such as a new public school or a municipal office building. But it is more troublesome if the properties are taken with the intent to transfer the assembled parcel to a for-profit corporation for construction of a shopping center or a "big box" retail store. It appears that what happens in many of these condemn-and-retransfer schemes is that the condemning authority (e.g., a redevelopment corporation) transfers the assembled parcel to the transferee at the price paid to the individual condemnees ($100,000 per parcel as in the example above). As a consequence, the transferee gets the assembled parcel at a substantial discount relative to what it would have to pay if it acquired such a large parcel without using eminent domain ($1,000,000 rather than $2,000,000, in the example). In other words, the *Miller* principle that the condemnor captures any gain from the taking constitutes a subsidy to the use of eminent domain, which without other limiting principles can lead to over-use of eminent domain.

There are many potential solutions to the potential over-use of eminent domain reflected in condemn-and-retransfer situations. One, of course, would be to restrict or eliminate the use of the eminent domain for such projects (see the Notes and Questions following the *Kelo* case). Another would be to require the transferees in such schemes to pay the fair market value of the fully assembled parcel, rather than a price based on the aggregate of the compensation paid to the individual owners of the pre-assembled parcels. This would at least eliminate the subsidy to the transferees, which should reduce their incentive to lobby for the use of eminent domain to facilitate such projects. But if the local government or the redevelopment corporation can pocket the assembly gain, this would not eliminate the incentive of local officials to promote such schemes. A third potential solution would be to require that the assembly gain be shared with the owners of the individual parcels taken for assembly. But this would present complex problems about the appropriate sharing principle (100%, 50% or what?) and about whether sharing would be required for all exercises of eminent domain, including highways and power lines, or would be limited to some subset of condemnations, such as those for "economic development" (however defined). These complexities would almost certainly require legislation in order to implement any such reform.

A variation on the assembly gain issue is presented when the government condemns a single parcel that is legally subdivided into two or more lesser interests in property. The most common situation is when property is legally subdivided between a lessor and lessee. But it can also occur when property is subject to a present possessory interest (like a life estate) and a future interest (like a remainder) or is a fee simple subject to an easement. Here the courts have adopted a rule that is subtly different from the *Miller* rule about the assembly gain created by combining multiple physically separate parcels. The dominant rule (followed by the federal government and most states) is that the condemnor pays the fair market value of an undivided fee simple or what is called the "unit fee" for short. See generally Victor P. Goldberg et al., Bargaining in the Shadow of Eminent Domain: Valuing and Apportioning Condemnation Awards Between Landlord and Tenant, 34 U.C.L.A. L. Rev. 1083 (1987). Thus, if the property is leased (or divided between present and future interests or between a fee simple and an easement), the condemnor pays the fair market value of what the property would be worth without the legal division into separate interests. Once this award is deposited with the court, the court then apportions the compensation between the respective interest holders. For example, if the property is divided between a tenant who holds a 99-year ground lease developed by a commercial office building and a landlord who has a reversion in the land that will come into possession in 99 years, the tenant will get virtually the entire award, and the landlord will get close to nothing. Conversely, if the property is divided between a tenant who rents a house under a year-to-year periodic lease with an adjustment clause that adjusts the rent to market rates annually, and a landlord who has a reversion, the landlord will get virtually the entire award and the tenant will get close to nothing (can you see why?).

Interestingly, the unit fee rule (unlike the physical assembly rule) generally operates to award any "assembly gain" created by wiping out the separate legal interests created by divided ownership to the condemnees, rather than the condemnor. To illustrate, suppose the land is divided between a fee simple and a conservation easement held by a non-profit land preservation foundation (see Chapter IX). The conservation easement requires that the land be maintained in perpetuity for agricultural use. As restricted to such use, the market value of the land is $50,000. But if the land is taken for a highway project, under the unit fee rule the government will pay the value of an unrestricted fee simple, which may be much higher, if the highest and best use of the parcel (in economic terms) is, say, for a residential subdivision. Suppose the higher value is $100,000. By wiping out the conservation easement, the condemnation generates an additional $50,000 in value, which is deposited with the court and must be apportioned between the owner of the fee and the land preservation foundation. (Presumably the additional $50,000 would be paid to the foundation, which has lost the entire benefit of the restriction.)

On occasion, the unit fee rule can generate what appear to be unjust results. Consider, for example, City of Milwaukee Post No. 2874 Veterans of Foreign Wars v. Redevelopment Authority of the City of Milwaukee, 768 N.W.2d 749 (Wis. 2009). The VFW owned some land in downtown Milwaukee which it used as its headquarters and a social club. It agreed to convey the property to a company for construction of a high-rise hotel. In return, the company agreed to lease a large space on the ground floor of the hotel for the VFW to use as its headquarters and a social club, for a term of 99-years (renewable) at a rent of $1 per year. The company also agreed to provide all utilities, perform periodic maintenance, and pay all taxes for the VFW space. Over time, the hotel fell into disrepair. It was transferred to two different universities for use as a student dormitory. But the deterioration of the living areas above the ground floor became so serious, and the repair cost became so great, that the use of the building as a dormitory was eventually abandoned. The Milwaukee Redevelopment Authority brought an action to condemn the property, tear the hotel down, and resell the land for some more promising use. Based on expert testimony, the court agreed that the unit value of the land and building was zero (actually it was negative, since the costs of rehabilitation or demolition of the building exceeded its potential rental value). The VFW presented testimony that the value of a rent-free, cost-free ground floor space for 99-years (renewable) was $1,800,000. The Wisconsin Supreme Court, over a dissent, nevertheless declined to depart from the unit fee rule, which it characterized as settled. A unit fee value of zero divided by anything is zero, so the decision left the VFW without any facility for its activities and without any compensation. The dissent argued that this result was fundamentally unjust, and that the VFW's interest should have been valued separately from the rest of the property.

If a rule (like the unit fee rule) generally produces desirable results—in terms of simplifying valuation proceedings, creating incentives for parties to anticipate the proper allocation of condemnation awards by contract, and awarding any assembly gain to condemnees—when if ever should courts recognize an exception to the rule? In part, this is yet another version of the perennial debate between rules and standards. Should separate valuation be permitted in any case in which one of the condemnees would obtain more under separate valuation than under apportionment of the award for an undivided fee? Or would this introduce an element of gamesmanship into eminent domain proceedings that would not be worth the additional complexity and cost it would generate? Should the Milwaukee Redevelopment Corporation have compensated the VFW for the fair market value of its sweetheart lease, followed by a suit against the current owner of the hotel for restitution? The argument would be that the current owner was unjustly enriched by having the redevelopment authority take a negative value asset off its hands. What if the current owner is insolvent or cannot generate the funds to reimburse the government for compensating the VFW for the loss of its headquarters and social club?

Quick Take Statutes

The condemnation in *Miller* occurred pursuant to the federal version of what are called "quick take" statutes. These statutes, which also exist in a majority of states, are designed to streamline eminent domain proceedings by transferring title to the condemning authority before all contested issues raised by the condemnation have been resolved. See Goodwill Community Chapel v. General Motors Corp., 503 N.W.2d 705, 707 (Mich. Ct. App. 1993); 6 Julius L. Sackman, Nichols on Eminent Domain § 24.10 (3d ed. 2005). In the early years, title to property acquired by eminent domain did not pass to the condemning authority until all issues, including the amount of compensation to be paid, had been resolved. The result was that condemnation proceedings frequently were long, drawn-out affairs, which increased the costs of using eminent domain. This also gave property owners an incentive to contest as many issues as possible, since the more issues they raised in the pre-condemnation hearing, the longer the condemning authority would have to wait to gain possession of the property.

Governments eventually responded by enacting quick take statutes. These statutes generally provide that if the government deposits with the court the estimated value of the property, and the court is satisfied that the government has legal authority to condemn and that the project is for a public use, then the government can obtain title to the property before a final judgment fixing the amount of compensation is reached. As soon as the title transfers, the condemned party must move out. The condemnee collects the money deposited with the court, and then, as the respondents did in *Miller*, can continue to litigate the question of whether the compensation is adequate. If the government's estimate reflected in the money deposited with the court is too low, then the government must make up the difference (with interest) once a final judgment is entered. *Miller* holds that if the government's estimate turns out to be too high, the government is entitled to sue to get the money back. (Note that this is another example of the principle of restitution.)

The Supreme Court rejected due process challenges to early statutes that allowed the government to take title to property before the amount of compensation owed was finally determined. See, e.g., Bragg v. Weaver, 251 U.S. 57 (1919); Sweet v. Rechel, 159 U.S. 380, 395 (1895). Thus, it is settled that quick take procedures are constitutional, provided the government deposits a fair estimate of just compensation with the court before title passes and the taking is otherwise legally justified. But what if the condemnation is not legally justified, for example because the public use requirement is not met? Shouldn't property owners be entitled to a hearing to challenge the statutory authority for the condemnation and the government's assertion of a public use before title passes, even in the quick take situation? The Supreme Court has not addressed this question directly. See 6 Julius L. Sackman, Nichols on Eminent Domain § 24.10[2] (3d ed. 2005); Nicole Stelle Garnett, The Public-Use Question as a Takings Problem, 71 Geo. Wash. L. Rev. 934, 970–74 (2003). Arguably, the scope of the public use requirement should be inversely related to the due process entitlement to a prior hearing. The broader the understanding of public use, the less the need for a prior hearing to determine if the taking is warranted. Thus, if state courts and legislatures respond to *Kelo* by narrowing the scope of permissible uses of eminent domain, this should increase the rationale for due process hearings before title transfers. In *Norwood v. Horney*, 853 N.E.2d 1115 (Ohio 2006), the Ohio Supreme Court, in the course of narrowing the meaning of public use as a matter of Ohio law, also held that an Ohio quick take statute prohibiting judicial stays pending appeal to challenge a public use determination violated state separation of powers doctrine. Could this be a harbinger of things to come? Courts in Rhode Island and Maryland have also substantially curbed quick take condemnations in recent years. See Rhode Island Econ. Dev. Corp v. The Parking Co., 892 A.2d 87, 107 (R.I. 2006); Mayor of Baltimore v. Valsamaki, 916 A.2d 324, 356 (Md. 2007).

The use of quick take authority has become an issue in the on-going controversy about construction of a fence along the southern border of the United States with Mexico. When construction of a border fence was originally proposed (with bipartisan support) in 2005, Congress enacted a statute that directed the fence be built with the utmost speed. Indeed, the statute authorizing the fence delegated authority to the Secretary of Homeland Security to "waive all legal requirements such Secretary, in the Secretary's sole discretion, determines necessary to ensure expeditious construction of [the fence]." P.L. No. 109–13, § 102, 119 Stat. 302, 206 (2005) (codified as amended at 8 U.S.C. § 1103 note (2006). Congress nevertheless recognized that the Secretary could not waive the Takings Clause, so it provided that courts would have jurisdiction to hear claims "alleging a violation of the Constitution of the United States." Id. § 102(c)(2)(A). Given existing federal quick take authority, this meant that the government could take the required land without a hearing and settle the matter of compensation after the fence was built. The Obama Administration concluded that a border fence was not needed, and funding for construction was allowed to lapse. When President Trump demanded that construction of "the wall" resume, the border fence became a matter of intense partisan controversy. Congress refused to appropriate funds to resume construction of the fence, and the President responded by diverting funds from other military appropriations to allow construction to go forward. Opponents countered, in part, by proposing legislation that would strip the Trump Administration of legal authority to use quick take procedures to acquire the necessary property rights. See Eminent Domain Just Compensation Act, H.R. 440, 116th Cong. (2019) (preventing the federal government from obtaining title to land for construction of a fence "until a final judgment has been issued in a condemnation proceeding initiated under judicial process").

Like other forms of American litigation, nearly all condemnation actions settle before trial. Curtis J. Berger & Patrick J. Rohan, The Nassau County Study: An Empirical Look Into the Practices of Condemnation, 67 Colum. L. Rev. 430, 458 n.60 (1967); Yun-chien Chang, An Empirical Study of Court-Adjudicated Takings Compensation in New York City: 1990–2003, 8 J. Empirical Legal. Stud. 384 (2011). Most persons whose property is slated for a taking agree to sell without the government having to file an eminent domain action. Of course, the amount they receive in the negotiated sale is affected by the shadow cast by a possible eminent domain action. Even if a voluntary transfer is not reached, and the government files a condemnation proceeding, most persons settle with the government, usually after some preliminary legal skirmishing, rather than going to trial. In most cases that go to trial, the amount of compensation will be fixed at some level between the government's figure and the owner's figure. Yun-chien Chang, An Empirical Study of Compensation Paid in Eminent Domain Settlements: New York City, 1990–2002, 39 J. Legal Stud. 201 (2010) (finding in a large-scale study of New York condemnations that more than 50 percent of awards were for less than fair market value, 40 percent for more than FMV, and less than 10 percent for FMV; that extreme awards of less than

50 percent or more than 150 percent of FMV were common and due to inaccuracies in the appraisal methods; and that compensation levels were not correlated with other factors); see also Yun-chien Chang, Private Property and Takings Compensation (2013). Both sides know this and can save legal fees by reaching a settlement that approximates what the court would determine after a trial. From this perspective, the main significance of quick take statutes is that they alter the relative bargaining power of the government and the individual property owner. By allowing the government to take title to the property before this issue is resolved, the government's bargaining power relative to that of the owner is significantly enhanced. To the extent that due process concerns require modifications in quick take procedures, the balance of power will shift back somewhat to property owners.

D. REGULATORY TAKINGS

We turn to the most debated (but not the most litigated) issue presented by the Takings Clause, which generally goes by the name of regulatory takings. This arises when the government takes action other than a formal exercise of eminent domain, and the property owner contends that the effect of the action is such that the government should pay compensation to owner, as if the government had proceeded by eminent domain. In other words, the owner claims the government should have used eminent domain—with its requirement of just compensation—but did not. Better terms might be "inverse condemnation" or "implicit takings." The term "regulatory takings" may imply that the issue arises only when the government regulates the use of property in a way that severely affects its value. While this is often the basis for a claim, whether the government has engaged in action that is functionally equivalent to an exercise of eminent domain can also arise in contexts that do not involve use regulations, such as government-authorized invasions or appropriations of property. (See Cedar Point Nursery v. Hassid, excerpted and discussed infra.) Nevertheless, the phrase "regulatory taking" is conventionally used to describe every type of implicit taking, so we adhere to that terminology in these materials.

1. FOUNDATIONS

Virtually everything about the regulatory takings doctrine is controversial, including its origins. There is little evidence that regulations of property—even quite severe ones—were thought to require compensation in the colonial era or at the time of the adoption of the Constitution. See John F. Hart, Colonial Land Use Law and its Significance for Modern Takings Doctrine, 109 Harv. L. Rev. 1252 (1996); William Michael Treanor, The Original Understanding of the Takings Clause and the Political Process, 95 Colum. L. Rev. 782 (1995). Some claim the regulatory takings doctrine can be traced in state court decisions decided in the middle of the nineteenth century. See Kris W.

Kobach, The Origins of Regulatory Takings: Setting the Record Straight, 1996 Utah L. Rev. 1211. But most observers would agree that the Supreme Court's 1922 decision in *Mahon*, excerpted here, is where the modern doctrine began to take shape.

Pennsylvania Coal Co. v. Mahon

Supreme Court of the United States, 1922.
260 U.S. 393.

■ MR. JUSTICE HOLMES delivered the opinion of the Court. This is a bill in equity brought by the defendants in error to prevent the Pennsylvania Coal Company from mining under their property in such way as to remove the supports and cause a subsidence of the surface and of their house. The bill sets out a deed executed by the Coal Company in 1878, under which the plaintiffs claim. The deed conveys the surface but in express terms reserves the right to remove all the coal under the same and the grantee takes the premises with the risk and waives all claim for damages that may arise from mining out the coal. But the plaintiffs say that whatever may have been the Coal Company's rights, they were taken away by an Act of Pennsylvania, approved May 27, 1921 (P. L. 1198), commonly known there as the Kohler Act. * * *

The statute forbids the mining of anthracite coal in such way as to cause the subsidence of, among other things, any structure used as a human habitation, with certain exceptions, including among them land where the surface is owned by the owner of the underlying coal and is distant more than one hundred and fifty feet from any improved property belonging to any other person. As applied to this case the statute is admitted to destroy previously existing rights of property and contract. The question is whether the police power can be stretched so far.

Government hardly could go on if to some extent values incident to property could not be diminished without paying for every such change in the general law. As long recognized some values are enjoyed under an implied limitation and must yield to the police power. But obviously the implied limitation must have its limits or the contract and due process clauses are gone. One fact for consideration in determining such limits is the extent of the diminution. When it reaches a certain magnitude, in most if not in all cases there must be an exercise of eminent domain and compensation to sustain the act. So the question depends upon the particular facts. The greatest weight is given to the judgment of the legislature but it always is open to interested parties to contend that the legislature has gone beyond its constitutional power.

This is the case of a single private house. No doubt there is a public interest even in this * * *. But usually in ordinary private affairs the public interest does not warrant much of this kind of interference. A source of damage to such a house is not a public nuisance even if similar damage is inflicted on others in different places. The damage is not common or public. Wesson v. Washburn Iron Co., 95 Mass. (13 Allen) 95, 103 (1866). The extent of the public interest is shown by the statute to be limited, since the statute ordinarily does not apply to land when the surface is owned by the owner of the coal. Furthermore, it is not justified as a protection of personal safety. That could be provided for by notice. Indeed the very foundation of this bill is that the defendant gave timely notice of its intent to mine under the house. On the other hand the extent of the taking is great. It purports to abolish what is recognized in Pennsylvania as an estate in land—a very valuable estate—and what is declared by the Court below to be a contract hitherto binding the plaintiffs. If we were called upon to deal with the plaintiffs' position alone we should think it clear that the statute does not disclose a public interest sufficient to warrant so extensive a destruction of the defendant's constitutionally protected rights.

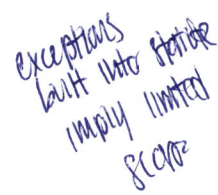

But the case has been treated as one in which the general validity of the act should be discussed. The Attorney General of the State, the City of Scranton and the representatives of other extensive interests were allowed to take part in the argument below and have submitted their contentions here. It seems, therefore, to be our duty to go farther in the statement of our opinion, in order that it may be known at once, and that further suits should not be brought in vain.

It is our opinion that the act cannot be sustained as an exercise of the police power, so far as it affects the mining of coal under streets or cities in places where the right to mine such coal has been reserved. As said in a Pennsylvania case, "For practical purposes, the right to coal consists in the right to mine it." Commonwealth v. Clearview Coal Co., 100 A. 820, 821 (Pa. 1917). What makes the right to mine coal valuable is that it can be exercised with profit. To make it commercially impracticable to mine certain coal has very nearly the same effect for constitutional purposes as appropriating or destroying it. This we think that we are warranted in assuming that the statute does.

It is true that in Plymouth Coal Co. v. Pennsylvania, 232 U.S. 531 (1914), it was held competent for the legislature to require a pillar of coal to be left along the line of adjoining property, that with the pillar on the other side of the line would be a barrier sufficient for the safety of the employees of either mine in case the other should be abandoned and allowed to fill with water. But that was a requirement for the safety of employees invited into the mine, and secured an average reciprocity of advantage that has been recognized as a justification of various laws.

The rights of the public in a street purchased or laid out by eminent domain are those that it has paid for. If in any case its representatives have been so short sighted as to acquire only surface rights without the right of support we see no more authority for supplying the latter without compensation than there was for taking the right of way in the first place and refusing to pay for it because the public wanted it very much. The protection of private property in the Fifth Amendment presupposes that it is wanted for public use, but provides that it shall not be taken for such use without compensation. A similar assumption is made in the decisions upon the Fourteenth Amendment. Hairston v. Danville & Western Ry. Co., 208 U.S. 598, 605 (1908). When this seemingly absolute protection is found to be qualified by the police power, the natural tendency of human nature is to extend the qualification more and more until at last private property disappears. But that cannot be accomplished in this way under the Constitution of the United States.

The general rule at least is that while property may be regulated to a certain extent, if regulation goes too far it will be recognized as a taking. It may be doubted how far exceptional cases, like the blowing up of a house to stop a conflagration, go—and if they go beyond the general rule, whether they do not stand as much upon tradition as upon principle. Bowditch v. Boston, 101 U.S. 16 (1879). In general it is not plain that a man's misfortunes or necessities will justify his shifting the damages to his neighbor's shoulders. Spade v. Lynn & Boston Ry. Co., 52 N.E. 747, 747 (Mass. 1899). We are in danger of forgetting that a strong public desire to improve the public condition is not enough to warrant achieving the desire by a shorter cut than the constitutional way of paying for the change. As we already have said this is a question of degree—and therefore cannot be disposed of by general propositions. But we regard this as going beyond any of the cases decided by this Court. The late decisions upon laws dealing with the congestion of Washington and New York, caused by the war, dealt with laws intended to meet a temporary emergency and providing for compensation determined to be reasonable by an impartial board. They were to the verge of the law but fell far short of the present act. Block v. Hirsh, 256 U.S. 135 (1921); Marcus Brown Holding Co. v. Feldman, 256 U.S. 170 (1921); Levy Leasing Co. v. Siegel, 258 U.S. 242 (1922).

We assume, of course, that the statute was passed upon the conviction that an exigency existed that would warrant it, and we assume that an exigency exists that would warrant the exercise of eminent domain. But the question at bottom is upon whom the loss of the changes desired should fall. So far as private persons or communities have seen fit to take the risk of acquiring only surface rights, we cannot see that the fact that their risk has become a danger warrants the giving to them greater rights than they bought.

Decree reversed.

■ MR. JUSTICE BRANDEIS dissenting. The Kohler Act prohibits, under certain conditions, the mining of anthracite coal within the limits of a city in such a manner or to such an extent "as to cause the * * * subsidence of * * * any dwelling or other structure used as a human habitation, or any factory, store, or other industrial or mercantile establishment in which human labor is employed." Act Pa. May 27, 1921, § 1 (P. L. 1198). Coal in place is land, and the right of the owner to use his land is not absolute. He may not so use it as to create a public nuisance, and uses, once harmless, may, owing to changed conditions, seriously threaten the public welfare. Whenever they do, the Legislature has power to prohibit such uses without paying compensation; and the power to prohibit extends alike to the manner, the character and the purpose of the use. Are we justified in declaring that the Legislature of Pennsylvania has, in restricting the right to mine anthracite, exercised this power so arbitrarily as to violate the Fourteenth Amendment?

Every restriction upon the use of property imposed in the exercise of the police power deprives the owner of some right theretofore enjoyed, and is, in that sense, an abridgment by the state of rights in property without making compensation. But restriction imposed to protect the public health, safety or morals from dangers threatened is not a taking. The restriction here in question is merely the prohibition of a noxious use. The property so restricted remains in the possession of its owner. The state does not appropriate it or make any use of it. The state merely prevents the owner from making a use which interferes with paramount rights of the public. Whenever the use prohibited ceases to be noxious— as it may because of further change in local or social conditions—the restriction will have to be removed and the owner will again be free to enjoy his property as heretofore.

The restriction upon the use of this property cannot, of course, be lawfully imposed, unless its purpose is to protect the public. But the purpose of a restriction does not cease to be public, because incidentally some private persons may thereby receive gratuitously valuable special benefits. Thus, owners of low buildings may obtain, through statutory restrictions upon the height of neighboring structures, benefits equivalent to an easement of light and air. Welch v. Swasey, 214 U.S. 91 (1909). Compare Lindsley v. Natural Carbonic Gas Co., 220 U.S. 61 (1911); Walls v. Midland Carbon Co., 254 U.S. 300 (1920). Furthermore, a restriction, though imposed for a public purpose, will not be lawful, unless the restriction is an appropriate means to the public end. But to keep coal in place is surely an appropriate means of preventing subsidence of the surface; and ordinarily it is the only available means. Restriction upon use does not become inappropriate as a means, merely because it deprives the owner of the only use to which the property can then be profitably put. The liquor and the oleomargarine cases settled that. Mugler v. Kansas, 123 U.S. 623, 668, 669 (1887); Powell v. Pennsylvania, 127 U.S. 678 (1888); see also Hadacheck v. Los Angeles, 239 U.S. 394 (1915); Pierce Oil Corporation v. City of Hope, 248 U.S. 498 (1919). Nor is a restriction imposed through exercise of the police power inappropriate as a means, merely because the same end might be effected through exercise of the power of eminent domain, or otherwise at public expense. Every restriction upon the height of buildings might be secured through acquiring by eminent domain the right of each owner to build above the limiting height; but it is settled that the state need not resort to that power. Compare Laurel Hill Cemetery v. San Francisco, 216 U.S.

358 (1910); Missouri Pacific Railway Co. v. Omaha, 235 U.S. 121 (1914). If by mining anthracite coal the owner would necessarily unloose poisonous gases, I suppose no one would doubt the power of the state to prevent the mining, without buying his coal fields. And why may not the state, likewise, without paying compensation, prohibit one from digging so deep or excavating so near the surface, as to expose the community to like dangers? In the latter case, as in the former, carrying on the business would be a public nuisance.

It is said that one fact for consideration in determining whether the limits of the police power have been exceeded is the extent of the resulting diminution in value, and that here the restriction destroys existing rights of property and contract. But values are relative. If we are to consider the value of the coal kept in place by the restriction, we should compare it with the value of all other parts of the land. That is, with the value not of the coal alone, but with the value of the whole property. The rights of an owner as against the public are not increased by dividing the interests in his property into surface and subsoil. The sum of the rights in the parts can not be greater than the rights in the whole. The estate of an owner in land is grandiloquently described as extending *ab orco usque ad coelum*. But I suppose no one would contend that by selling his interest above 100 feet from the surface he could prevent the state from limiting, by the police power, the height of structures in a city. And why should a sale of underground rights bar the state's power? For aught that appears the value of the coal kept in place by the restriction may be negligible as compared with the value of the whole property, or even as compared with that part of it which is represented by the coal remaining in place and which may be extracted despite the statute. * * *

Nor can existing contracts between private individuals preclude exercise of the police power. "One whose rights, such as they are, are subject to state restriction cannot remove them from the power of the state by making a contract about them." Hudson Water Co. v. McCarter, 209 U.S. 349, 357 (1908); Knoxville Water Co. v. Knoxville, 189 U.S. 434, 438 (1903); Rast v. Van Deman & Lewis Co., 240 U.S. 342 (1916). The fact that this suit is brought by a private person is, of course, immaterial. To protect the community through invoking the aid, as litigant, of interested private citizens is not a novelty in our law. That it may be done in Pennsylvania was decided by its Supreme Court in this case. And it is for a state to say how its public policy shall be enforced.

This case involves only mining which causes subsidence of a dwelling house. But the Kohler Act contains provisions in addition to that quoted above; and as to these, also, an opinion is expressed. These provisions deal with mining under cities to such an extent as to cause subsidence of—

(a) Any public building or any structure customarily used by the public as a place of resort, assemblage, or amusement, including, but not limited to, churches, schools, hospitals, theaters, hotels, and railroad stations.

(b) Any street, road, bridge, or other public passageway, dedicated to public use or habitually used by the public.

(c) Any track, roadbed, right of way, pipe, conduit, wire, or other facility, used in the service of the public by any municipal corporation or public service company as defined by the Public Service Law, section 1.

A prohibition of mining which causes subsidence of such structures and facilities is obviously enacted for a public purpose; and it seems, likewise, clear that mere notice of intention to mine would not in this connection secure the public safety. Yet it is said that these provisions of the act cannot be sustained as an exercise of the police power where the right to mine such coal has been reserved. The conclusion seems to rest upon the assumption that in order to justify such exercise of the police power there must be "an average reciprocity of advantage" as between the owner of the property restricted and the rest of the community; and that here such reciprocity is absent. Reciprocity of advantage is an important consideration, and may even be an essential, where the state's power is exercised for the purpose of conferring benefits upon the property of a neighborhood, as in drainage projects (Wurts v. Hoagland, 114 U.S. 606 (1885); Fallbrook Irrigation District v. Bradley, 164 U.S. 112 (1896)); or upon adjoining owners, as by party wall provisions (Jackman v. Rosenbaum Co., 260 U.S. 22 (1922)). But where the police power is exercised, not to confer benefits upon property owners but to protect the public from detriment and danger, there is in my opinion, no room for considering reciprocity of advantage. There was no reciprocal advantage to the owner prohibited from using his oil tanks in 248 U.S. 498; his brickyard, in 239 U.S. 394, his livery stable, in 237 U.S. 171; his billiard hall, in 225 U.S. 623; his margarine factory, in 127 U.S. 678; his brewery, in 123 U.S. 623; unless it be the advantage of living and doing business in a civilized community. That reciprocal advantage is given by the act to the coal operators.

NOTES AND QUESTIONS

1. The factual circumstances underlying *Mahon* have been much investigated by scholars. See, e.g., William Fischel, Regulatory Takings: Law, Economics, and Politics 25–47 (1995); Carol M. Rose, *Mahon* Reconstructed: Why the Takings Issue is Still a Muddle, 57 S. Cal. L. Rev. 561 (1984); Robert Brauneis, "The Foundations of Our 'Regulatory Takings' Jurisprudence": The Myth and Meaning of Justice Holmes's Opinion in *Pennsylvania Coal Co. v. Mahon*, 106 Yale L.J. 613 (1996); Stewart E. Sterk, The Federalist Dimension of Regulatory Takings Jurisprudence, 114 Yale L.J. 203, 208–210 (2004). Fischel reports that the practice among anthracite mining companies in eastern Pennsylvania was to provide compensation to surface owners if their property was damaged by subsidence, even if the

surface owner (or her predecessor in title) had waived the support right. The litigation in *Mahon* was motivated not by a desire to end this practice, but by the objections of the companies to another statute, the Fowler Act, which required them to contribute to a fund to provide compensation to surface owners whose property was damaged by mining activity of *other* companies which had gone bankrupt. Even after their victory in the Supreme Court, the mining companies continued to pay compensation for subsidence damage caused by their own operations. Why do you suppose they did that?

2.   In a reprise of *Mahon*, the Supreme Court in *Keystone Bituminous Coal Assn. v. DeBenedictis*, 480 U.S. 470 (1987), considered a similar Pennsylvania statute that made coal companies responsible for subsidence damage caused by mining bituminous coal. Applying the approach initially adopted in *Penn Central Transportation Co. v. City of New York*, the next case you will read, the Court upheld this statute against a takings claim. Although the Court purported to distinguish *Mahon* rather than overrule it, there is little doubt that *Mahon* can no longer be considered good law with respect to the question whether anti-subsidence laws give rise to a takings claim.

3.   *Mahon* is still a very important decision, however, because it is generally regarded as the source of the regulatory takings doctrine—the idea that some exercises of the police power "go too far" and hence must be pursued through an exercise of eminent domain. A proper exercise of the police power—the power to regulate crimes, public nuisances, and other activities that threaten the public health, safety, morals, or welfare—does not require that compensation be paid to those who must comply with the relevant regulations. The power of eminent domain, in contrast, can be exercised only if the government pays just compensation for property taken. *Mahon* can be read as recognizing that there must be some limit or boundary on the scope of the police power, or else the state could simply use the police power to acquire property for public use—but without having to pay just compensation. The regulatory takings doctrine recognized by the decision is, from this perspective, simply a boundary-maintenance or anti-circumvention principle designed to preserve the basic distinction between two basic powers of sovereign government. Few would quarrel with the general proposition that as long as we recognize these two powers, and as long as they have very different consequences in terms of the government's duty of compensation, *some* kind of judicial policing is necessary in order to preserve the integrity of the boundary between them. (By the way, since only the states are thought to exercise a general police power, whereas the federal government is said to exercise only enumerated powers, what is it that the power of eminent domain is being juxtaposed against when the federal government is alleged to have engaged in a regulatory taking?)

4.   From this humble and rather uncontroversial foundation, however, the doctrine of *Pennsylvania Coal v. Mahon* has grown into something much more controversial. The regulatory takings doctrine today is the most powerful substantive constitutional constraint on governmental interference with property rights. Other doctrines, such as the Contracts Clause and the doctrine of substantive due process, served this function in the past. With

the passage of time, however, the Court has come to apply these other limits in a deferential fashion, at least insofar as they are used to protect property rights. The regulatory takings doctrine, especially after 1986 when William Rehnquist became Chief Justice of the United States, emerged from the shadow of these other doctrines to become the more important constraint on government.

5.   One highly significant difference among these doctrines is that the Contracts Clause and substantive due process mark boundaries beyond which the power of government may not extend. Hence, when these limits are violated, the proper remedy is to enjoin the government action in question. The regulatory takings doctrine, in contrast, requires only that the government pay "just compensation" when it adopts a regulation that goes too far and hence represents the kind of measure that should have been accomplished by eminent domain. The proper remedy for a violation of the regulatory takings doctrine, consequently, is an award of damages from the government equal to the "just compensation" that would have been paid if the government had condemned the property using the power of eminent domain. In that sense, regulatory takings adopts a "liability rule" rather than a "property rule" approach to protecting property rights. See Calabresi & Melamed, in Chapter IX; see also Abraham Bell & Gideon Parchomovsky, Pliability Rules, 101 Mich. L. Rev. 1, 59–64 (2002).

6.   Note that the support right or "support estate" at issue in *Mahon* was, at least in functional terms, a covenant or servitude that ran with two other estates in land—the surface estate and the mineral estate. At common law, surface owners enjoy a right of subjacent support, which prohibits other persons (including owners of subjacent mineral rights) from excavating underneath the surface in such a way as to damage buildings or endanger persons and activities on the surface. (But if those buildings or activities require more support than the land in its natural state would provide, then one in need of extra support has to negotiate for a servitude for the extra support.) In *Mahon*, the surface owners—the Mahons' predecessors in interest—had signed a deed conveying the mineral rights to the coal company that included a covenant *waiving* these common-law rights of subjacent support. The waiver was in effect a servitude running with the land. The Kohler Act, in functional terms, reinstated the common-law support rights, wiping out the covenant or servitude the parties had negotiated. How important is it to the Court's decision that this particular waiver or covenant has a property-like name: the "support estate" (sometimes referred to in Pennsylvania cases as the "third estate")? How important is it to the Court's decision that this particular covenant was explicitly negotiated and exchanged (presumably for consideration) between the parties?

7.   In considering the broad run of cases, it seems reasonably clear that it is not considered a taking for the government to impose the functional equivalent of a servitude on parties who conceivably could have agreed to one as a matter of voluntary negotiation. See, e.g., Penn Central, infra (upholding historic preservation order); Gorieb v. Fox, 274 U.S. 603 (1927) (upholding open space restriction imposed by ordinance); Welch v. Swasey,

214 U.S. 91 (1909) (upholding height restriction on buildings imposed by ordinance). Why should it be permissible for the government to impose servitudes on property owners without compensation, but a taking for government to abrogate servitudes held by property owners without compensation? Should it be regarded as a regulatory taking for a court to abrogate restrictive covenants limiting houses in a subdivision to single-family occupancy under the changed circumstances doctrine (see Chapter IX)? Did the Supreme Court, when it declared racially restrictive covenants unenforceable in *Shelley v. Kraemer* (see Chapter IV), commit a regulatory taking? The Supreme Court has entertained but so far not come to any definitive conclusion on the possibility of a judicial taking. See Stop the Beach Renourishment, infra; see generally Barton H. Thompson, Jr., Judicial Takings, 76 Va. L. Rev. 1449 (1990).

8.   A careful reading of the opinions in *Mahon* will reveal that Justices Holmes and Brandeis (who more often agreed with each other on constitutional questions), did not really disagree about the factors to be considered in deciding whether a police regulation "goes too far" and must be regarded as an exercise of eminent domain. Both agreed that the diminution in value caused by the regulation, the need to protect the public against nuisance-like harms, and reciprocity of advantage among property owners are relevant factors to be considered. See if you can articulate the reasons that caused the two Justices to disagree about how each of these factors should be applied to the Kohler Act. Are the disagreements based on differences about the characterization of each factor, about the proper institution to determine the relevance of each factor, or about the presumed importance of each factor in this case?

9.   One specific ground for disagreement concerns the proper unit of property against which to measure the effect of the regulation. Justice Holmes appears to assume that the correct unit of analysis is the pillars of coal that must be left in place to support the surface. On this view, the regulation "takes" (or at least prevents the economic use of) the entire property right. Justice Brandeis, in contrast, argues that the appropriate unit of analysis is "the whole property" of the coal company. From this perspective, the regulation takes only a fraction of the property right. Which perspective is better? Under the Holmes approach, how narrowly should the "property" be defined? Can the conception of "property" be sliced finer and finer, until the definition of property coincides exactly with the interest affected by the regulation? Under the Brandeis approach, how far should the "whole property" of the company extend? To all its rights in the particular column of space in which the complaining surface owner resides? To all rights, mineral and surface, in the immediate area? To all assets on the company's balance sheet?

10.   How would you explain the understanding that "blowing up a house to stop a conflagration" is not regarded as a taking requiring the payment of compensation? Is this understanding consistent with Justice Holmes's emphasis on diminution in value, reciprocity of advantage, and whether the government action has taken a recognized property right? The rule has been traced to the Great London Fire of 1666, where the Lord Mayor of London

hesitated to order the destruction of the Inns of Court without the consent of the judges, with the result that the fire spread disastrously. See Respublica v. Sparhawk, 1 Dall. 357, 363 (Pa. 1788). Does this provide any hints about the rationale for the rule?

Miller v. Schoene

Supreme Court of the United States, 1928.
276 U.S. 272.

■ MR. JUSTICE STONE delivered the opinion of the Court. Acting under the Cedar Rust Act of Virginia, Acts Va. 1914, c. 36, as amended by Acts Va. 1920, c. 260, now embodied in Va. Code (1924) as sections 885 to 893, defendant in error, the state entomologist, ordered the plaintiffs in error to cut down a large number of ornamental red cedar trees growing on their property, as a means of preventing the communication of a rust or plant disease with which they were infected to the apple orchards in the vicinity. The plaintiffs in error appealed from the order to the circuit court of Shenandoah county which, after a hearing and a consideration of evidence, affirmed the order and allowed to plaintiffs in error $100 to cover the expense of removal of the cedars. Neither the judgment of the court nor the statute as interpreted allows compensation for the value of the standing cedars or the decrease in the market value of the realty caused by their destruction whether considered as ornamental trees or otherwise. But they save to plaintiffs in error the privilege of using the trees when felled. On appeal the Supreme Court of Appeals of Virginia affirmed the judgment. Both in the circuit court and the Supreme Court of Appeals plaintiffs in error challenged the constitutionality of the statute under the due process clause of the Fourteenth Amendment and the case is properly here on writ of error.

The Virginia statute presents a comprehensive scheme for the condemnation and destruction of red cedar trees infected by cedar rust. By section 1 it is declared to be unlawful for any person to "own, plant or keep alive and standing" on his premises any red cedar tree which is or may be the source or "host plant" of the communicable plant disease known as cedar rust, and any such tree growing within a certain radius of any apple orchard is declared to be a public nuisance, subject to destruction. Section 2 makes it the duty of the state entomologist, "upon the request in writing of ten or more reputable freeholders of any county or magisterial district, to make a preliminary investigation of the locality * * * to ascertain if any cedar tree or trees * * * are the source of, harbor or constitute the host plant for the said disease * * * and constitute a menace to the health of any apple orchard in said locality, and that said cedar tree or trees exist within a radius of two miles of any apple orchard in said locality." If affirmative findings are so made, he is required to direct the owner in writing to destroy the trees and, in his notice, to furnish a statement of the "fact found to exist whereby it is deemed necessary or proper to destroy" the trees and to call attention to the law under which it is proposed to destroy them. Section 5 authorizes the state entomologist to destroy the trees if the owner, after being notified, fails to do so. Section 7 furnishes a mode of appealing from the order of the entomologist to the circuit court of the county, which is authorized to "hear the objections" and "pass upon all questions involved," the procedure followed in the present case.

As shown by the evidence and as recognized in other cases involving the validity of this statute, Bowman v. Virginia State Entomologist, 105 S.E. 141 (Va. 1920); Kelleher v. Schoene 14 F.2d 341 (W.D. Va. 1926), cedar rust is an infectious plant disease in the form of a fungoid organism which is destructive of the fruit and foliage of the apple, but without effect on the value of the cedar. Its life cycle has two phases which are passed alternately as a growth on red cedar and on apple trees. It is communicated by spores from one to the other over a radius of at least two miles. It appears not to be communicable between trees of the same species, but only from one species to the other, and other plants seem not to be appreciably affected by it. The only practicable method of controlling the disease and protecting apple trees from its ravages is the destruction of all red cedar trees, subject to the infection, located within two miles of apple orchards.

The red cedar, aside from its ornamental use, has occasional use and value as lumber. It is indigenous to Virginia, is not cultivated or dealt in commercially on any substantial scale, and its value throughout the state is shown to be small as compared with that of the apple orchards of the state. Apple growing is one of the principal agricultural pursuits in Virginia. The apple is used there and exported in large quantities. Many millions of dollars are invested in the orchards, which furnish employment for a large portion of the population, and have induced the development of attendant railroad and cold storage facilities.

On the evidence we may accept the conclusion of the Supreme Court of Appeals that the state was under the necessity of making a choice between the preservation of one class of property and that of the other wherever both existed in dangerous proximity. It would have been none the less a choice if, instead of enacting the present statute, the state, by doing nothing, had permitted serious injury to the apple orchards within its borders to go on unchecked. When forced to such a choice the state does not exceed its constitutional powers by deciding upon the destruction of one class of property in order to save another which, in the judgment of the legislature, is of greater value to the public. It will not do to say that the case is merely one of a conflict of two private interests and that the misfortune of apple growers may not be shifted to cedar owners by ordering the destruction of their property; for it is obvious that there may be, and that here there is, a preponderant public concern in the preservation of the one interest over the other. And where the public interest is involved preferment of that interest over the property interest of the individual, to the extent even of its destruction, is one of the distinguishing characteristics of every exercise of the police power which affects property. Mugler v. Kansas, 123 U.S. 623 (1887); Hadacheck v. Los Angeles, 239 U.S. 394 (1915); Village of Euclid v. Ambler Realty Co., 272 U.S. 365 (1926); Northwestern Fertilizer Co. v. Hyde Park, 97 U.S. 659 (1878); Northwestern Laundry v. Des Moines, 239 U.S. 486 (1916); Lawton v. Steele, 152 U.S. 133 (1894); Sligh v. Kirkwood, 237 U.S. 52 (1915); Reinman v. Little Rock, 237 U.S. 171 (1915).

We need not weigh with nicety the question whether the infected cedars constitute a nuisance according to the common law; or whether they may be so declared by statute. See Hadacheck v. Los Angeles, supra, 411. For where, as here, the choice is unavoidable, we cannot say that its exercise, controlled by considerations of social policy which are not unreasonable, involves any denial of due process. The injury to property here is no more serious, nor the public interest less, than in Hadacheck v. Los Angeles, supra, Northwestern Laundry v. Des Moines, supra, Reinman v. Little Rock, supra, or Sligh v. Kirkwood, supra.

[The Court then considered and rejected the contention that the right of "ten or more reputable freeholders" to trigger an investigation was fatal. The freeholders] do not determine the action of the state entomologist. They merely request him to conduct an investigation. In him is vested the discretion to decide, after investigation, whether or not conditions are such that the other provisions of the statute shall be brought into action; and his determination is subject to judicial review. The property of plaintiffs in error is not subjected to the possibly arbitrary and irresponsible action of a group of private citizens. * * *

Affirmed.

NOTES AND QUESTIONS

1. Recall the excerpt in Chapter I where Ronald Coase claims that in cases of incompatible land uses we should not ask which use is inflicting harm on the other. Rather, he says, the problem is a "reciprocal" one: "The real question that has to be decided is: Should A be allowed to harm B or should B be allowed to harm A? The problem is to avoid the more serious harm." Whatever you think about this claim in the context of classic nuisances like air or water pollution, is this an apt characterization of the situation in *Miller v. Schoene*, where rust spores spread by leaping alternatively from cedar trees to apple trees? Does it follow that the legislature would have been equally justified in ordering the destruction of apple trees in order to halt the spread of the disease? Several authors have argued that *Miller v. Schoene* undermines the notion of state action (versus inaction) and the public/private distinction, because, in Justice Stone's words, a decision by Virginia not to have cedars cut would have been "none the less a choice." See, e.g., Louis M. Seidman & Mark V. Tushnet, Remnants of Belief: Contemporary Constitutional Issues 27 (1996); Warren Samuels, Interrelations Between Legal and Economic Processes, 14 J.L. & Econ. 435

(1971); see also Barbara H. Fried, The Progressive Assault on Laissez-Faire: Robert Hale and the First Law and Economics Movement (1998).

2.   Recent research by William Fischel casts doubt on the "reciprocal" view of *Miller v. Schoene* and raises some new questions. Fischel finds that there was a widespread and well-accepted custom that in situations where a fungus leaps from species to species of plant in its life cycle, the more commercially significant plant always prevails. He terms this norm "prices make rights." The custom clearly applied to parasite-ridden trees and other crops. Would it be a good idea to apply this notion more generally? (Does this notion in fact apply more generally?) This would be the shortest of short cuts to the result in *Kelo*, supra, since presumably it would allow any taking of property that would increase the size of the social pie. But wouldn't it also confirm Justice O'Connor's warnings about every Motel 6 being vulnerable to replacement by a Ritz-Carlton? At any rate, the more-valuable-plant-wins norm was an established background principle when *Miller* was decided. The 1914 legislation in question in *Miller* passed the Virginia House of Delegates 88 to 0 with one Dr. Caspar Otto Miller, the cedar-owning plaintiff in this case, casting a yes vote. It also turns out that apple growers, who procured the legislation after a nasty bout of cedar-apple rust, had no objection to compensating cedar owners. In fact, the initial version of the law provided for compensation. But because some owners of cedar trees which were more valuable as cut wood than as standing trees made spurious claims for compensation, the compensation provision was repealed. For more on the case and the ins and outs of cedar-apple rust, see William A. Fischel, The Law and Economics of Cedar-Apple Rust: State Action and Just Compensation in *Miller v. Schoene*, 3 Rev. L. & Econ. 133 (2007); see also Henry E. Smith, Community and Custom in Property, 10 Theoretical Inquiries L. 173, 206–09 (2008) (offering a narrower interpretation of the customary background in *Miller v. Schoene*).

3.   The Court defers to the judgment of the Virginia legislature that apple trees are of greater significance to the state economy than cedar trees, because apples are an important commercial product whereas cedar trees are used mostly for ornamental purposes. This kind of reason is enough to save the statute from condemnation on substantive due process or equal protection grounds. See, e.g., Williamson v. Lee Optical Co., 348 U.S. 483 (1955). But does this answer the question whether the owners of cedar trees should be compensated in full for their losses? Compare James Buchanan, Politics, Property, and the Law: An Alternative Interpretation of *Miller et al. v. Schoene*, 15 J.L. & Econ. 439 (1972) (arguing in favor of compensation in *Miller* on political economy grounds) with Samuels, supra, at 439, 445–48 (regarding Virginia statute as reallocation of tree owners' property rights). Recall that in unintentional combination cases like *Wetherbee v. Green* (Chapter II), courts give the thing to the party who has supplied greater value to the final good, but award damages to the other party. Does this suggest that although the apple tree owners have a better claim to keep their trees, they (or the state) should be required to compensate the owners of cedar trees?

4.   Although *Miller v. Schoene* was decided only six years after *Pennsylvania Coal v. Mahon*, most of the factors addressed by Justice Holmes in the earlier decision play no role here. Diminution in value is barely mentioned, likewise reciprocity of advantage or whether the law destroys a distinct property right. Would consideration of these factors strengthen the case in favor of compensation for the owners of the cedar trees? Why do you suppose they were ignored? The Court does mention a number of decisions upholding regulations of "noxious uses," including *Mugler v. Kansas*, 123 U.S. 623 (1887) (distillery); *Northwestern Fertilizing Co. v. Hyde Park*, 97 U.S. 659 (1878) (fertilizer plant); *Reinman v. Little Rock*, 237 U.S. 171 (1915) (livery stable); and *Hadacheck v. Sebastian*, 239 U.S. 394 (1915) (brick yard). But the Court insists an activity need not be a nuisance at common law in order to be subject to destruction at the direction of the state without any compensation. What then is the basis for the decision? Are the conflagration cases, mentioned in *Pennsylvania Coal* and discussed briefly in Note 10 after that case, relevant here? Is the appearance of cedar rust an emergency that requires immediate destruction of property in order to prevent a catastrophe for the entire community?

5.   In the spring of 2011, the Mississippi River rose to dangerously high levels, threatening to overflow a levee protecting the city of Cairo, Illinois. To protect Cairo from being flooded, the U.S. Army Corps of Engineers decided to open a hole in the levee further downstream, flooding some 130,000 acres of farmland in Missouri. A federal court refused to enjoin the Corps from taking this action, *Missouri ex rel. Koster v. U.S. Army Corps of Engineers*, 2011 WL 1630339 (E.D. Mo.), but noted that the question whether the owners of the farmland would be entitled to compensation was not presented. Interestingly, it appears that under an earlier version of the same flood control plan the federal government had acquired, in some cases by condemnation, flowage easements that allowed the Army Corps to flood the farmland in an emergency. See Story v. Marsh, 732 F.2d 1375, 1384 (8th Cir. 1984). Given the statement in *Miller v. Schoene* that the government is free to destroy one class of property in order to save another which is of greater value, why might the federal government decide to purchase or condemn flowage easements rather than rely on its power to regulate? Does this judgment suggest that *Miller v. Schoene* was wrongly decided? Or should the decision whether to compensate in the destroy-one-to-save-another context be left to government discretion?

Academic Perspectives on Regulatory Takings

The regulatory takings doctrine, not surprisingly, has generated considerable academic commentary seeking to develop a more systematic account of the purposes and proper implementation of the doctrine. Broadly speaking, academic "takings" theories fall into three categories.

One type of theory, which is doctrinal in nature, attempts to define more precisely the distinction between governmental powers, and in particular the distinction between the power of eminent domain and the police power. *Pennsylvania Coal* can be read as saying that it is necessary to draw a line between these powers, because eminent domain requires that compensation be paid whereas the police power does not. This creates a temptation for the government to evade its obligation to compensate by characterizing measures that should proceed by eminent domain (or voluntary purchase of property) as a police power regulation. Thus, we need an anti-circumvention doctrine that prevents the government from skirting its obligation to pay just compensation in appropriate circumstances.

Professor Joseph Sax of Berkeley Law School made notable contributions to this school of thought. His first attempt to characterize the boundary line between the police power and eminent domain drew a distinction between actions taken by the government when acting in an "enterprise" capacity, where compensation was required, and actions taken in "mediating" between incompatible uses of property, where no compensation was required. Joseph L. Sax, Takings and the Police Power, 74 Yale L.J. 36 (1964). Later, he modified the theory by arguing that any government action that seeks to regulate externalities associated with the use of property should be regarded as a noncompensable police power measure. Joseph L. Sax, Takings, Private Property and Public Rights, 81 Yale L.J. 149 (1971). A less conceptual approach to distinguishing among governmental powers posits that courts should start with ideal-typical situations governed by one power or the other, and then reason by analogy from the settled understandings in fitting novel situations into the picture. See David A. Dana & Thomas W. Merrill, Property: Takings 86–164 (2002). This approach can be particularized even further by observing that the power of eminent domain is invariably used to acquire interests that are "actually recognized as traded in a market in the community in which it is located." Steven J. Eagle, Regulatory Takings § 7.7(e)(5) (4th ed. 2009); see Thomas W. Merrill, The Eagle Theory, 9 Brigham-Kanner Prop. Rts. J. 17 (2020). For example, if the government adopts a regulation that has the effect of causing a compulsory transfer of a leasehold or an easement in gross—interests that are exchanged in the relevant local community and are sometimes acquired using eminent domain—the regulation would be declared a regulatory taking. But if the regulation does not conform to an interest that is tradeable on a stand-alone basis, such as a regulation requiring the use of certain building materials or imposing a restriction on the height in which buildings can be constructed, it would be regarded a police measure that does not require any payment of compensation, because it does not correspond to any interest traded on a stand-alone basis or acquired by eminent domain. Of course, which interests are traded on a stand-alone basis is partly a function of which interests are legally recognized. If the states are given discretion to define or redefine which interests are legally recognized, they may be able to influence the outcome of regulatory takings controversies, at least in close cases. Still, a blatant attempt by a state to declare a commonly exchanged type of right "not property" would presumably be seen as an attempt to evade the Constitution, and would be disregarded by the courts.

Note that it is implicit in each of these doctrinal approaches that government powers do not overlap. Either the action is an exercise of eminent domain or an exercise of the police power; it cannot be both. Likewise, either the action is an exercise of the power of taxation or an exercise of eminent domain; it cannot be both.

A second type of academic theory focuses on the impact of the government action on the property owner and posits that the regulatory takings doctrine is designed to redress actions that have an unfair distributional impact for the owner. This approach draws inspiration from the statement in *Armstrong v. United States*, 364 U.S. 40, 49 (1960), that the government should not "forc[e] some people alone to bear public burdens which, in all fairness and justice, should be borne by the public as a whole." Of course, different people have different ideas about what makes for unfair distribution.

One notable theory grounded in distributional concerns, which is probably the most famous article ever written about the takings problem, is Frank I. Michelman, Property, Utility, and Fairness: Comments on the Ethical Foundations of "Just Compensation" Law, 80 Harv. L. Rev. 1165 (1967). Michelman sought to derive rules of thumb for assessing takings claims from utilitarian social theory and John Rawls's theory of justice. He developed the concept of "demoralization costs," which he defined as the psychological pain incurred by owners and their sympathizers from government action that reduces the value of their property, plus the foregone investment caused by the fear of such reductions in value. He argued that whenever demoralization costs would be higher than what he called "settlement costs"—the costs of paying compensation and administering a compensation system—then the government should pay compensation to owners for its actions. A very different conception of unfair distribution was articulated some years later by Richard Epstein in Takings: Private Property and the Power of Eminent Domain (1985). Epstein argued that all government actions that disturb the existing distribution of wealth are constitutionally problematic. Thus, unless the government is redressing a wrong committed by an owner, for example the commission of a nuisance, or can show that its action provides "implicit in kind compensation" to all owners, compensation is always required. Both the Michelman and Epstein theories imply that very general government regulations can qualify as takings. Another approach grounded in distributional concerns would limit the scope of protection to measures that "single out" a relatively small number of owners for uniquely severe burdens while providing general benefits to everyone else. See, e.g., Saul Levmore, Takings, Torts, and Special Interests, 77 Va. L. Rev. 1333, 1344–45 (1991). Measures having a general impact on significant numbers of owners, on this view, would not require compensation because they would be presumed to be subject to effective control by the political process. Other efforts to systematize regulatory takings law from a distributional perspective include Andrea L. Peterson, The Takings Clause: In Search of Underlying Principles Part I—A Critique of Current Takings Clause Doctrine, 77 Cal. L. Rev. 1299 (1989) and Nestor M. Davison, The Problem of Equality in Takings, 102 Nw. U. L. Rev. 1, 24–27 (2008).

One implication of the various distributional theories is that the judiciary must develop a comprehensive understanding about when redistribution from A to B, or from A to many Bs, or from many As to B, is just. In other words, in order to decide takings cases we need a theory of distributive justice, or perhaps more accurately, a theory about when a system of adversarial litigation can be used to rectify departures from what a theory of distributive justice would indicate is just. This is a tall order for judges—especially since commentators cannot agree among themselves about a theory of distributive justice or about the proper role of the courts in addressing deviations from what a theory of distributive justice would require. Note further that under the various distributional theories it does not matter what sort of power the government is exercising in determining whether it has committed a taking. A government tax that has a sufficiently idiosyncratic distributional effect might be condemned as a taking. See, e.g., Eric Kades, Drawing the Line Between Taxes and Takings: The Continuous Burdens Principle and Its Broader Application, 97 Nw. U. L. Rev. 189, 223–24 (2002); Eduardo Moisés Peñalver, Regulatory Taxings, 104 Colum. L. Rev. 2182 (2004); Abraham Bell & Gideon Parchomovsky, The Uselessness of Public Use, 106 Colum. L. Rev. 1412, 1432 (2006). Similarly, an exercise of the police power can be condemned as a taking if it violates whatever norm we adopt for identifying troublesome redistributions. Conceptual distinctions grounded in history are irrelevant on this view. The task is to derive doctrinal rules and standards directly from abstract principles about just distribution and the institutional capacities of courts.

A third type of academic theory focuses on the government, and how a compensation requirement might improve the functioning of the government. One theme here is that compensation may improve the efficiency of government by requiring the government to "internalize" the costs its regulations impose on property owners. If the government can impose regulations without regard to the costs imposed on owners, it may suffer from the "fiscal illusion" that these regulations are costless, with the result that the government will engage in excessive regulation. In contrast, if the government must compensate for losses incurred by owners, the government will impose only those regulations that yield more in benefits to society than the costs imposed on owners. See, e.g., Jack L. Knetsch & Thomas E. Borcherding, Expropriation of Private Property and the Basis for Compensation, 29 U. Toronto L.J. 237, 242–44 (1979). The cost internalization argument has widespread appeal among skeptics about government regulation, as illustrated by legislative initiatives proposed in many states that would require government to pay compensation for any decline in property values above a certain threshold attributable to government regulation.

The cost internalization argument has its strong critics, however. One objection is that cost internalization works both ways. The government should have an incentive not to impose unnecessary costs on property owners, but property owners should also have an incentive not to impose unnecessary costs on everyone else, by polluting for example. Thus, requiring that the government compensate owners for every regulation that reduces the value of the owner's property would undermine the effectiveness of government efforts to stop property owners from imposing harms on others. See Louis Kaplow, An Economic Analysis of Legal Transitions, 99 Harv. L. Rev. 509 (1986); Lawrence Blume et al., The Taking of Land: When Should Compensation be Paid?, 99 Q.J. Econ. 71, 90–91 (1984). This objection suggests that the cost internalization argument is contingent on who is in greater need of cost internalization: the government or the property owner. As such, the idea may simply re-frame the debate about where to draw the line between compensable and noncompensable government action without providing a clear answer. It is also fair to question whether government agents respond systematically to incentives for cost internalization, given that taxpayers rather than government officials ultimately foot the bill. Daryl J. Levinson, Making Governments Pay: Markets, Politics, and the Allocation of Constitutional Costs, 67 U. Chi. L. Rev. 345 (2000); see also Yun-chien Chang, Empire Building and Fiscal Illusion? An Empirical Study of Government Official Behaviors in Takings, 6 J. Empirical Legal Stud. 541 (2009) (presenting empirical study suggesting that Taiwanese officials respond more to political than to economic considerations in determining compensation for condemnations).

Another strand of academic thought that focuses on government behavior adopts something of the opposite concern—that the government will *under-regulate* unless it is required to compensate property owners. The argument here is that property owners who do not receive compensation when the government regulates them in a way that significantly affects their property values will form a powerful lobby that can block the regulation. Compensation neutralizes intense opposition to government policies that promote the general welfare. Daniel Farber, Economic Analysis and Just Compensation, 12 Int'l Rev. L. & Econ. 125 (1992); Glynn S. Lunney, Jr., A Critical Reexamination of the Takings Jurisprudence, 90 Mich. L. Rev. 1892, 1954–63 (1992). Compensation on this view is like pork barrel spending or earmarks that buy off opposition and make government regulation that promotes the general welfare possible.

Which if any of these theories supports the outcomes in *Pennsylvania Coal* and *Miller v. Schoene*? Which suggests that either or both of these cases were wrongly decided? Consider how these various theories may have influenced the Court in the following landmark decision that effectively re-wrote regulatory takings law.

2.   THE "AD HOC" APPROACH

Penn Central Transportation Company v. City of New York

Supreme Court of the United States, 1978.
438 U.S. 104.

■ MR. JUSTICE BRENNAN delivered the opinion of the Court. The question presented is whether a city may, as part of a comprehensive program to preserve historic landmarks and historic districts, place restrictions on the development of individual historic landmarks—in addition to those imposed by applicable zoning ordinances—without effecting a "taking" requiring the payment of "just compensation." * * *

I

A

Over the past 50 years, all 50 States and over 500 municipalities have enacted laws to encourage or require the preservation of buildings and areas with historic or aesthetic importance. These nationwide legislative efforts have been precipitated by two concerns. The first is recognition that, in recent years, large numbers of historic structures, landmarks, and areas have been destroyed without adequate consideration of either the values represented therein or the possibility of preserving the destroyed properties for use in economically productive ways. The second is a widely shared belief that structures with special historic, cultural, or architectural significance enhance the quality of life for all. * * *

New York City, responding to similar concerns and acting pursuant to a New York State enabling Act, adopted its Landmarks Preservation Law in 1965. See N.Y.C. Admin. Code, ch. 8–A, § 205–1.0 et seq. (1976). * * *

The New York City law is typical of many urban landmark laws in that its primary method of achieving its goals is not by acquisitions of historic properties, but rather by involving public entities in land-use decisions affecting these properties * * * While the law does place special restrictions on landmark properties as a necessary feature to the attainment of its larger objectives, the major theme of the law is to ensure the owners of any such properties both a "reasonable return" on their investments and maximum latitude to use their parcels for purposes not inconsistent with the preservation goals.

The operation of the law can be briefly summarized. The primary responsibility for administering the law is vested in the Landmarks Preservation Commission (Commission), a broad based, 11-member agency assisted by a technical staff. The Commission first performs the function, critical to any landmark preservation effort, of identifying properties and areas that have "a special character or special historical or aesthetic interest or value as part of the development, heritage or cultural characteristics of the city, state or nation." If the Commission determines, after giving all interested parties an opportunity to be heard, that a building or area satisfies the ordinance's criteria, it will designate a building to be a "landmark," situated on a particular "landmark site," or will designate an area to be a "historic district." After the Commission makes a designation, New York City's Board of Estimate, after considering the relationship of the designated property "to the master plan, the zoning resolution, projected public improvements and any plans for the renewal of the area involved," may modify or disapprove the designation, and the owner may seek judicial review of the final designation decision. Thus far, 31 historic districts and over 400 individual landmarks have been finally designated, and the process is a continuing one.

Final designation as a landmark results in restrictions upon the property owner's options concerning use of the landmark site. First, the law imposes a duty upon the owner to keep the exterior features of the building "in good repair" to assure that the law's objectives not be defeated by the landmark's falling into a state of irremediable disrepair. Second, the Commission must approve in advance any proposal to alter the exterior architectural features of the landmark or to construct any exterior improvement on the landmark site, thus ensuring that decisions concerning construction on the landmark site are made with due consideration of both the public interest in the maintenance of the structure and the landowner's interest in use of the property. * * *

Although the designation of a landmark and landmark site restricts the owner's control over the parcel, designation also enhances the economic position of the landmark owner in one significant respect. Under New York City's zoning laws, owners of real property who have not developed their property to the full extent permitted by the applicable zoning laws are allowed to transfer development rights to contiguous parcels on the same city block. See New York City, Zoning Resolution Art. I, ch. 2, § 12–10 (1978) (definition of "zoning lot"). A 1968 ordinance gave the owners of landmark sites additional opportunities to transfer development rights to other parcels. Subject to a restriction that the floor area of the transferee lot may not be increased by more than 20% above its authorized level, the ordinance permitted transfers from a landmark parcel to property across the street or across a street intersection. In 1969, * * * [t]he class of recipient lots was expanded to include lots "across a street and opposite to another lot or lots which except for the intervention of streets or street intersections f[or]m a series extending to the lot occupied by the landmark building [, provided that] all lots [are] in the same ownership." New York City Zoning Resolution 74–79 (emphasis deleted). In addition, the 1969 amendment permits, in highly commercialized areas like midtown Manhattan, the transfer of all unused development rights to a single parcel. Ibid.

B

This case involves the application of New York City's Landmarks Preservation Law to Grand Central Terminal (Terminal). The Terminal, which is owned by the Penn Central Transportation Co. and its affiliates (Penn Central), is one of New York City's most famous buildings. Opened in 1913, it is regarded not only as providing an ingenious engineering solution to the problems presented by urban railroad stations, but also as a magnificent example of the French beaux-arts style.

The Terminal is located in midtown Manhattan. Its south facade faces 42d Street and that street's intersection with Park Avenue. At street level, the Terminal is bounded on the west by Vanderbilt Avenue, on the east by the Commodore Hotel, and on the north by the Pan-American Building. Although a 20-story office tower, to have been located above the Terminal, was part of the original design, the planned tower was never constructed. The Terminal itself is an eight-story structure which Penn Central uses as a railroad station and in which it rents space not needed for railroad purposes to a variety of commercial interests. The Terminal is one of a number of properties owned by appellant Penn Central in this area of midtown Manhattan. The others include the Barclay, Biltmore, Commodore, Roosevelt, and Waldorf-Astoria Hotels, the Pan-American Building and other office buildings along Park Avenue, and the Yale Club. At least eight of these are eligible to be recipients of development rights afforded the Terminal by virtue of landmark designation.

On August 2, 1967, following a public hearing, the Commission designated the Terminal a "landmark" and designated the "city tax block" it occupies a "landmark site." The Board of Estimate confirmed this action on September 21, 1967. Although appellant Penn Central had opposed the designation before the Commission, it did not seek judicial review of the final designation decision.

On January 22, 1968, appellant Penn Central, to increase its income, entered into a renewable 50-year lease and sublease agreement with appellant UGP Properties, Inc. (UGP), a wholly owned subsidiary of Union General Properties, Ltd., a United Kingdom corporation. Under the terms of the agreement, UGP was to construct a multistory office building above the Terminal. UGP promised to pay Penn Central $1 million annually during construction and at least $3 million annually thereafter. The rentals would be offset in part by a loss of some $700,000 to $1 million in net rentals presently received from concessionaires displaced by the new building.

Appellants UGP and Penn Central then applied to the Commission for permission to construct an office building atop the Terminal. Two separate plans, both designed by architect Marcel Breuer and both apparently satisfying the terms of the applicable zoning ordinance, were submitted to the Commission for approval. The first, Breuer I, provided for the construction of a 55-story office building, to be cantilevered above the existing facade and to rest on the roof of the Terminal. The second, Breuer II Revised, called for tearing down a portion of the Terminal that included the 42d Street facade, stripping off some of the remaining features of the Terminal's facade, and constructing a 53-story office building. * * * After four days of hearings at which over 80 witnesses testified, the Commission denied this application as to both proposals.

The Commission's reasons for rejecting certificates respecting Breuer II Revised are summarized in the following statement: "To protect a Landmark, one does not tear it down. To perpetuate its architectural features, one does not strip them off." Record 2255. Breuer I, which would have preserved the existing vertical facades of the present structure, received more sympathetic consideration. The Commission first focused on the effect that the proposed tower would have on one desirable feature created by the present structure and its surroundings: the dramatic view of the Terminal from Park Avenue South. Although appellants had contended that the Pan-American Building had already destroyed the silhouette of the south facade and that one additional tower could do no further damage and might even provide a better background for the facade, the Commission disagreed, stating that it found the majestic approach from the south to be still unique in the city and that a 55-story tower atop the Terminal would be far more detrimental to its south facade than the Pan-American Building 375 feet away. Moreover, the Commission found that from closer vantage points the Pan Am Building and the other towers were largely cut off from view, which would not be the case of the mass on top of the Terminal planned under Breuer I. * * *

Appellants did not seek judicial review of the denial of either certificate. * * * Instead, appellants filed suit in New York Supreme Court, Trial Term, claiming, *inter alia*, that the application of the Landmarks Preservation Law had "taken" their property without just compensation in violation of the Fifth and Fourteenth Amendments and arbitrarily deprived them of their property without due process of law in violation of the Fourteenth Amendment.

* * * The trial court granted * * * injunctive and declaratory relief, but severed the question of damages for a "temporary taking." * * * [The] Appellate Division, reversed. * * * The Appellate Division concluded that all appellants had succeeded in showing was that they had been deprived of the property's most profitable use, and that this showing did not establish that appellants had been unconstitutionally deprived of their property.

* * * The New York Court of Appeals affirmed. * * * We affirm.

II

The issues presented by appellants are (1) whether the restrictions imposed by New York City's law upon appellants' exploitation of the Terminal site effect a "taking" of appellants' property for a public use within the meaning of the Fifth Amendment, which of course is made applicable to the States through the Fourteenth Amendment, see Chicago, B. & Q. R. Co. v. Chicago, 166 U.S. 226, 239 (1897), and, (2), if so, whether the transferable development rights afforded appellants constitute "just compensation" within the meaning of the Fifth Amendment. We need only address the question whether a "taking" has occurred.

A

Before considering appellants' specific contentions, it will be useful to review the factors that have shaped the jurisprudence of the Fifth Amendment injunction "nor shall private property be taken for public use, without just compensation." The question of what constitutes a "taking" for purposes of the Fifth Amendment has proved to be a problem of considerable difficulty. While this Court has recognized that the "Fifth Amendment's guarantee . . . [is] designed to bar Government from forcing some people alone to bear public burdens which, in all fairness and justice, should be borne by the public as a whole," Armstrong v. United States, 364 U.S. 40, 49 (1960), this Court, quite simply, has been unable to develop any "set formula" for determining when "justice and fairness" require that economic injuries caused by public action be compensated by the government, rather than remain disproportionately concentrated on a few persons. See Goldblatt v. Hempstead, 369 U.S. 590, 594 (1962). Indeed, we have frequently observed that whether a particular restriction will be rendered invalid by the government's failure to pay for any losses proximately caused by it depends largely "upon the particular circumstances [in that] case." United States v. Central Eureka Mining Co., 357 U.S. 155, 168 (1958).

In engaging in these essentially ad hoc, factual inquiries, the Court's decisions have identified several factors that have particular significance. The economic impact of the regulation on the claimant and, particularly, the extent to which the regulation has interfered with distinct investment-backed expectations are, of course, relevant considerations. See Goldblatt v. Hempstead, supra, 369 U.S., at 594. So, too, is the character of the governmental action. A "taking" may more readily be found when the interference with property can be characterized as a physical invasion by government, see, e. g., United States v. Causby, 328 U.S. 256 (1946), than when interference arises from some public program adjusting the benefits and burdens of economic life to promote the common good.

"Government hardly could go on if to some extent values incident to property could not be diminished without paying for every such change in the general law," Pennsylvania Coal Co. v. Mahon, 260 U.S. 393, 413

(1922), and this Court has accordingly recognized, in a wide variety of contexts, that government may execute laws or programs that adversely affect recognized economic values. Exercises of the taxing power are one obvious example. A second are the decisions in which this Court has dismissed "taking" challenges on the ground that, while the challenged government action caused economic harm, it did not interfere with interests that were sufficiently bound up with the reasonable expectations of the claimant to constitute "property" for Fifth Amendment purposes. See, e. g., United States v. Willow River Power Co., 324 U.S. 499 (1945) (interest in high-water level of river for runoff for tailwaters to maintain power head is not property); United States v. Chandler-Dunbar Water Power Co., 229 U.S. 53 (1913) (no property interest can exist in navigable waters); see also Sax, Takings and the Police Power, 74 Yale L.J. 36, 61–62 (1964).

More importantly for the present case, in instances in which a state tribunal reasonably concluded that "the health, safety, morals, or general welfare" would be promoted by prohibiting particular contemplated uses of land, this Court has upheld land-use regulations that destroyed or adversely affected recognized real property interests. See Nectow v. Cambridge, 277 U.S. 183, 188 (1928). Zoning laws are, of course, the classic example, see Euclid v. Ambler Realty Co., 272 U.S. 365 (1926) (prohibition of industrial use). * * *

B

In contending that the New York City law has "taken" their property in violation of the Fifth and Fourteenth Amendments, appellants make a series of arguments, which, while tailored to the facts of this case, essentially urge that any substantial restriction imposed pursuant to a landmark law must be accompanied by just compensation if it is to be constitutional. * * *

They first observe that the airspace above the Terminal is a valuable property interest, citing *United States v. Causby*, supra. They urge that the Landmarks Law has deprived them of any gainful use of their "air rights" above the Terminal and that, irrespective of the value of the remainder of their parcel, the city has "taken" their right to this superadjacent airspace, thus entitling them to "just compensation" measured by the fair market value of these air rights.

Apart from our own disagreement with appellants' characterization of the effect of the New York City law, see infra, the submission that appellants may establish a "taking" simply by showing that they have been denied the ability to exploit a property interest that they heretofore had believed was available for development is quite simply untenable. * * * "Taking" jurisprudence does not divide a single parcel into discrete segments and attempt to determine whether rights in a particular segment have been entirely abrogated. In deciding whether a particular governmental action has effected a taking, this Court focuses rather both on the character of the action and on the nature and extent of the interference with rights in the parcel as a whole—here, the city tax block designated as the "landmark site."

Secondly, appellants, focusing on the character and impact of the New York City law, argue that it effects a "taking" because its operation has significantly diminished the value of the Terminal site. Appellants concede that the decisions sustaining other land-use regulations, which, like the New York City law, are reasonably related to the promotion of the general welfare, uniformly reject the proposition that diminution in property value, standing alone, can establish a "taking," see Euclid v. Ambler Realty Co., 272 U.S. 365 (1926) (75% diminution in value caused by zoning law); Hadacheck v. Sebastian, 239 U.S. 394 (1915) (87 1/2% diminution in value), and that the "taking" issue in these contexts is resolved by focusing on the uses the regulations permit. Appellants, moreover, also do not dispute that a showing of diminution in property value would not establish a taking if the restriction had been imposed as a result of historic-district legislation, but appellants argue that New York City's regulation of individual landmarks is fundamentally different from zoning or from historic-district legislation because the controls imposed by New York City's law apply only to individuals who own selected properties. * * *

It is true, as appellants emphasize, that both historic-district legislation and zoning laws regulate all properties within given physical communities whereas landmark laws apply only to selected parcels. But, contrary to appellants' suggestions, landmark laws are not like discriminatory, or "reverse spot," zoning: that is, a land-use decision which arbitrarily singles out a particular parcel for different, less favorable treatment than the neighboring ones. In contrast to discriminatory zoning, which is the antithesis of land-use control as part of some comprehensive plan, the New York City law embodies a comprehensive plan to preserve structures of historic or aesthetic interest wherever they might be found in the city, and as noted, over 400 landmarks and 31 historic districts have been designated pursuant to this plan. * * *

Next, appellants observe that New York City's law differs from zoning laws and historic-district ordinances in that the Landmarks Law does not impose identical or similar restrictions on all structures located in particular physical communities. It follows, they argue, that New York City's law is inherently incapable of producing the fair and equitable distribution of benefits and burdens of governmental action which is characteristic of zoning laws and historic-district legislation and which they maintain is a constitutional requirement if "just compensation" is not to be afforded. It is, of course, true that the Landmarks Law has a more severe impact on some landowners than on others, but that in itself does not mean that the law effects a "taking." Legislation designed to promote the general welfare commonly burdens some more than others. The owners of the brickyard in *Hadacheck*, of the cedar trees in *Miller v.*

Schoene, and of the gravel and sand mine in *Goldblatt v. Hempstead*, were uniquely burdened by the legislation sustained in those cases. Similarly, zoning laws often affect some property owners more severely than others but have not been held to be invalid on that account. For example, the property owner in *Euclid* who wished to use its property for industrial purposes was affected far more severely by the ordinance than its neighbors who wished to use their land for residences.

In any event, appellants' repeated suggestions that they are solely burdened and unbenefited is factually inaccurate. This contention overlooks the fact that the New York City law applies to vast numbers of structures in the city in addition to the Terminal—all the structures contained in the 31 historic districts and over 400 individual landmarks, many of which are close to the Terminal. Unless we are to reject the judgment of the New York City Council that the preservation of landmarks benefits all New York citizens and all structures, both economically and by improving the quality of life in the city as a whole—which we are unwilling to do—we cannot conclude that the owners of the Terminal have in no sense been benefited by the Landmarks Law. Doubtless appellants believe they are more burdened than benefited by the law, but that must have been true, too, of the property owners in *Miller, Hadacheck, Euclid*, and *Goldblatt*.

Appellants' final broad-based attack would have us treat the law as an instance, like that in *United States v. Causby*, in which government, acting in an enterprise capacity, has appropriated part of their property for some strictly governmental purpose. Apart from the fact that *Causby* was a case of invasion of airspace that destroyed the use of the farm beneath and this New York City law has in nowise impaired the present use of the Terminal, the Landmarks Law neither exploits appellants' parcel for city purposes nor facilitates nor arises from any entrepreneurial operations of the city. The situation is not remotely like that in *Causby* where the airspace above the property was in the flight pattern for military aircraft. The Landmarks Law's effect is simply to prohibit appellants or anyone else from occupying portions of the airspace above the Terminal, while permitting appellants to use the remainder of the parcel in a gainful fashion. * * *

C

Rejection of appellants' broad arguments is not, however, the end of our inquiry, for all we thus far have established is that the New York City law is not rendered invalid by its failure to provide "just compensation" whenever a landmark owner is restricted in the exploitation of property interests, such as air rights, to a greater extent than provided for under applicable zoning laws. We now must consider whether the interference with appellants' property is of such a magnitude that "there must be an exercise of eminent domain and compensation to sustain [it]." Pennsylvania Coal Co. v. Mahon, 260 U.S., at 413. That inquiry may be narrowed to the question of the severity of the impact of the law on appellants' parcel, and its resolution in turn requires a careful assessment of the impact of the regulation on the Terminal site.

Unlike the governmental acts in *Goldblatt, Miller, Causby, Griggs,* [369 U.S. 84 (1962),] and *Hadacheck,* the New York City law does not interfere in any way with the present uses of the Terminal. Its designation as a landmark not only permits but contemplates that appellants may continue to use the property precisely as it has been used for the past 65 years: as a railroad terminal containing office space and concessions. So the law does not interfere with what must be regarded as Penn Central's primary expectation concerning the use of the parcel. More importantly, on this record, we must regard the New York City law as permitting Penn Central not only to profit from the Terminal but also to obtain a "reasonable return" on its investment.

Appellants, moreover, exaggerate the effect of the law on their ability to make use of the air rights above the Terminal in two respects. First, it simply cannot be maintained, on this record, that appellants have been prohibited from occupying *any* portion of the airspace above the Terminal. While the Commission's actions in denying applications to construct an office building in excess of 50 stories above the Terminal may indicate that it will refuse to issue a certificate of appropriateness for any comparably sized structure, nothing the Commission has said or done suggests an intention to prohibit *any* construction above the Terminal. * * *

Second, to the extent appellants have been denied the right to build above the Terminal, it is not literally accurate to say that they have been denied *all* use of even those pre-existing air rights. Their ability to use these rights has not been abrogated; they are made transferable to at least eight parcels in the vicinity of the Terminal, one or two of which have been found suitable for the construction of new office buildings. Although appellants and others have argued that New York City's transferable development-rights program is far from ideal, the New York courts here supportably found that, at least in the case of the Terminal, the rights afforded are valuable. While these rights may well not have constituted "just compensation" if a "taking" had occurred, the rights nevertheless undoubtedly mitigate whatever financial burdens the law has imposed on appellants and, for that reason, are to be taken into account in considering the impact of regulation.

On this record, we conclude that the application of New York City's Landmarks Law has not effected a "taking" of appellants' property. The restrictions imposed are substantially related to the promotion of the general welfare and not only permit reasonable beneficial use of the landmark site but also afford appellants opportunities further to enhance not only the Terminal site proper but also other properties.

Affirmed.

■ MR. JUSTICE REHNQUIST, with whom THE CHIEF JUSTICE and MR. JUSTICE STEVENS join, dissenting. Of the over one million buildings and structures in the city of New York, appellees have singled out 400 for designation as official landmarks. The owner of a building might initially be pleased that his property has been chosen by a distinguished committee of architects, historians, and city planners for such a singular distinction. But he may well discover, as appellant Penn Central Transportation Co. did here, that the landmark designation imposes upon him a substantial cost, with little or no offsetting benefit except for the honor of the designation. The question in this case is whether the cost associated with the city of New York's desire to preserve a limited number of "landmarks" within its borders must be borne by all of its taxpayers or whether it can instead be imposed entirely on the owners of the individual properties. * * *

I

The Fifth Amendment provides in part: "nor shall private property be taken for public use, without just compensation." In a very literal sense, the actions of appellees violated this constitutional prohibition. Before the city of New York declared Grand Central Terminal to be a landmark, Penn Central could have used its "air rights" over the Terminal to build a multistory office building, at an apparent value of several million dollars per year. Today, the Terminal cannot be modified in *any* form, including the erection of additional stories, without the permission of the Landmark Preservation Commission, a permission which appellants, despite good-faith attempts, have so far been unable to obtain. Because the Taking Clause of the Fifth Amendment has not always been read literally, however, the constitutionality of appellees' actions requires a closer scrutiny of this Court's interpretation of the three key words in the Taking Clause—"property," "taken," and "just compensation."

A

Appellees do not dispute that valuable property rights have been destroyed. And the Court has frequently emphasized that the term "property" as used in the Taking Clause includes the entire "group of rights inhering in the citizen's [ownership]." United States v. General Motors Corp., 323 U.S. 373 (1945). The term is not used in the

> vulgar and untechnical sense of the physical thing with respect to which the citizen exercises rights recognized by law. [Instead, it] . . . denote[s] the *group of rights* inhering in the citizen's relation to the physical thing, as the right to possess, use and dispose of it . . . the constitutional provision is addressed to *every sort of interest* the citizen may possess. Id., at 377–378 (emphasis added).

While neighboring landowners are free to use their land and "air rights" in any way consistent with the broad boundaries of New York zoning, Penn Central, absent the permission of appellees, must forever maintain its property in its present state. The property has been thus subjected to a nonconsensual servitude not borne by any neighboring or similar properties.

B

Appellees have thus destroyed—in a literal sense, "taken"— substantial property rights of Penn Central. While the term "taken" might have been narrowly interpreted to include only physical seizures of property rights, "the construction of the phrase has not been so narrow. The courts have held that the deprivation of the former owner rather than the accretion of a right or interest to the sovereign constitutes the taking." Id., at 378. Because "not every destruction or injury to property by governmental action has been held to be a 'taking' in the constitutional sense," Armstrong v. United States, 364 U.S., at 48, however, this does not end our inquiry. But an examination of the two exceptions where the destruction of property does *not* constitute a taking demonstrates that a compensable taking has occurred here.

1

As early as 1887, the Court recognized that the government can prevent a property owner from using his property to injure others without having to compensate the owner for the value of the forbidden use.

> A prohibition simply upon the use of property for purposes that are declared, by valid legislation, to be *injurious to the health, morals, or safety of the community*, cannot, in any just sense, be deemed a taking or an appropriation of property for the public benefit. Such legislation does not disturb the owner in the control or use of his property for lawful purposes, nor restrict his right to dispose of it, but is only a declaration by the State that its use by any one, for certain forbidden purposes, is prejudicial to the public interests. . . . The power which the States have of prohibiting such use by individuals of their property as will be prejudicial to the health, the morals, or the safety of the public, is not—and, consistently with the existence and safety of organized society, cannot be—burdened with the condition that the State must compensate such individual owners for pecuniary losses they may sustain, *by reason of their not being permitted, by a noxious use of their property, to inflict injury upon the community.*

Mugler v. Kansas, 123 U.S. 623, 668–669 (1887).

Thus, there is no "taking" where a city prohibits the operation of a brickyard within a residential area, see Hadacheck v. Sebastian, 239 U.S. 394 (1915), or forbids excavation for sand and gravel below the water line, see Goldblatt v. Hempstead, 369 U.S. 590 (1962). Nor is it relevant, where the government is merely prohibiting a noxious use of property, that the government would seem to be singling out a particular property owner. Hadacheck, supra, at 413. Each of the cases cited by the Court for the proposition that legislation which severely affects some landowners but not others does not effect a "taking" involved noxious uses of property. See Hadacheck; Miller v. Schoene, 276 U.S. 272 (1928); Goldblatt.

The nuisance exception to the taking guarantee is not coterminous with the police power itself. The question is whether the forbidden use is dangerous to the safety, health, or welfare of others. * * *

Appellees are not prohibiting a nuisance. The record is clear that the proposed addition to the Grand Central Terminal would be in full compliance with zoning, height limitations, and other health and safety requirements. Instead, appellees are seeking to preserve what they believe to be an outstanding example of beaux-arts architecture. Penn Central is prevented from further developing its property basically because *too good* a job was done in designing and building it. The city of New York, because of its unadorned admiration for the design, has decided that the owners of the building must preserve it unchanged for the benefit of sightseeing New Yorkers and tourists.

Unlike land-use regulations, appellees' actions do not merely *prohibit* Penn Central from using its property in a narrow set of noxious ways. Instead, appellees have placed an *affirmative* duty on Penn Central to maintain the Terminal in its present state and in "good repair." Appellants are not free to use their property as they see fit within broad outer boundaries but must strictly adhere to their past use except where appellees conclude that alternative uses would not detract from the landmark. While Penn Central may continue to use the Terminal as it is presently designed, appellees otherwise "exercise complete dominion and control over the surface of the land," United States v. Causby, 328 U.S. 256, 262 (1946), and must compensate the owner for his loss. Ibid. "Property is taken in the constitutional sense when inroads are made upon an owner's use of it to an extent that, as between private parties, a servitude has been acquired." United States v. Dickinson, 331 U.S. 745, 748 (1947).

2

Even where the government prohibits a noninjurious use, the Court has ruled that a taking does not take place if the prohibition applies over a broad cross section of land and thereby "secure[s] an average reciprocity of advantage." Pennsylvania Coal Co. v. Mahon, 260 U.S., at 415. It is for this reason that zoning does not constitute a "taking." While zoning at times reduces *individual* property values, the burden is shared relatively evenly and it is reasonable to conclude that on the whole an individual who is harmed by one aspect of the zoning will be benefited by another.

Here, however, a multimillion dollar loss has been imposed on appellants; it is uniquely felt and is not offset by any benefits flowing from the preservation of some 400 other "landmarks" in New York City.

Appellees have imposed a substantial cost on less than one one-tenth of one percent of the buildings in New York City for the general benefit of all its people. It is exactly this imposition of general costs on a few individuals at which the "taking" protection is directed. * * * Less than 20 years ago, this Court reiterated that the

> Fifth Amendment's guarantee that private property shall not be taken for a public use without just compensation was designed to bar Government from forcing some people alone to bear public burdens which, in all fairness and justice, should be borne by the public as a whole.

Armstrong v. United States, 364 U.S., at 49.

As Mr. Justice Holmes pointed out in *Pennsylvania Coal Co. v. Mahon,* "the question at bottom" in an eminent domain case "is upon whom the loss of the changes desired should fall." 260 U.S., at 416. The benefits that appellees believe will flow from preservation of the Grand Central Terminal will accrue to all the citizens of New York City. There is no reason to believe that appellants will enjoy a substantially greater share of these benefits. If the cost of preserving Grand Central Terminal were spread evenly across the entire population of the city of New York, the burden per person would be in cents per year—a minor cost appellees would surely concede for the benefit accrued. Instead, however, appellees would impose the entire cost of several million dollars per year on Penn Central. But it is precisely this sort of discrimination that the Fifth Amendment prohibits. * * *

C

Appellees, apparently recognizing that the constraints imposed on a landmark site constitute a taking for Fifth Amendment purposes, do not leave the property owner empty-handed. As the Court notes, the property owner may theoretically "transfer" his previous right to develop the landmark property to adjacent properties if they are under his control. Appellees have coined this system "Transfer Development Rights," or TDR's.

Of all the terms used in the Taking Clause, "just compensation" has the strictest meaning. The Fifth Amendment does not allow simply an approximate compensation but requires "a full and perfect equivalent for the property taken." Monongahela Navigation Co. v. United States, 148 U.S., at 326. * * *

Because the lower courts held that there was no "taking," they did not have to reach the question of whether or not just compensation has already been awarded. * * *

[I]n other cases the Court of Appeals has noted that TDR's have an "uncertain and contingent market value" and do "not adequately preserve" the value lost when a building is declared to be a landmark. French Investing Co. v. City of New York, 350 N.E.2d 381, 383 (N.Y. 1976). On the other hand, there is evidence in the record that Penn

Central has been offered substantial amounts for its TDR's. Because the record on appeal is relatively slim, I would remand to the Court of Appeals for a determination of whether TDR's constitute a "full and perfect equivalent for the property taken."

II

Over 50 years ago, Mr. Justice Holmes, speaking for the Court, warned that the courts were "in danger of forgetting that a strong public desire to improve the public condition is not enough to warrant achieving the desire by a shorter cut than the constitutional way of paying for the change." Pennsylvania Coal Co. v. Mahon, 260 U.S., at 416. The Court's opinion in this case demonstrates that the danger thus foreseen has not abated. The city of New York is in a precarious financial state, and some may believe that the costs of landmark preservation will be more easily borne by corporations such as Penn Central than the overburdened individual taxpayers of New York. But these concerns do not allow us to ignore past precedents construing the Eminent Domain Clause to the end that the desire to improve the public condition is, indeed, achieved by a shorter cut than the constitutional way of paying for the change.

NOTES AND QUESTIONS

1. New York City's historic preservation ordinance was motivated in significant part by public outcry over the demolition of Penn Station at 34th Street between Seventh and Eighth Avenues, a grand structure with a classical colonnade matching the appearance of the Post Office building across the street. Penn Station was replaced by a nondescript structure housing a relocated Madison Square Garden, with the railroad terminal moved underground. Given this background, it is not surprising that the Landmarks Commission took a dim view of the proposal to build a modern tower on top of Grand Central Station, the only remaining grand historic rail terminal building in Manhattan. See Gideon Kanner, Making Laws and Sausage: A Quarter-century Retrospective on *Penn Central Transportation Co. v. City of New York*, 13 Wm. & Mary Bill Rts. J. 679 (2005).

2. On the occasion of the 25th anniversary of *Penn Central*, a conference was held at Fordham Law School that included a panel discussion by the lawyers who argued the case and the law clerks who assisted the Justices who wrote the opinions. See Looking Back at *Penn Central*: A Panel Discussion with the Supreme Court Litigators, 15 Fordham Envt'l L. Rev. 287 (2004). Among the interesting revelations are that Justice Stewart advised Justice Brennan's law clerk (David Carpenter) that the opinion should say as little as possible; that Justice Brennan spent one day editing the draft opinion; and that Justice Rehnquist's dissent was already written before the majority opinion circulated.

Figure 10-4
Pennsylvania Railroad Station, New York City

Pennsylvania Railroad Station. Undated. Museum of the City of New York.

Figure 10-5
Madison Square Garden, New York City, 2006

3.   Recall that both Justice Holmes and Justice Brandeis in *Mahon* seemed to believe that three factors were of primary importance in distinguishing between a police power measure and an exercise of the power of eminent domain: diminution in value, whether the measure is designed to regulate a nuisance, and reciprocity of advantage. Which of the dueling

opinions in *Penn Central* is more faithful to this doctrinal framework: Justice Brennan's majority opinion, or Justice Rehnquist's dissent?

4.   Justice Brennan's opinion stresses the "ad hoc" nature of regulatory takings inquiries and does not appear to lay down any definitive test for determining whether a regulation "goes too far." Shortly after it was decided, however, the Supreme Court recast *Penn Central* as having prescribed a "three-part" inquiry, looking to "the economic impact of the regulation, its interference with reasonable investment backed expectations, and the character of the government action." Kaiser Aetna v. United States, 444 U.S. 164, 175 (1979). Was this a misreading of *Penn Central*? Does the opinion suggest that diminution in value and investment backed expectations are separate factors, or are they a single factor: "the extent of the harm suffered by the property owner in view of the owner's investment-backed expectations"? Gary Lawson et al., "Oh Lord, Please Don't Let Me Be Misunderstood!": Rediscovering the *Mathews v. Eldridge* and *Penn Central* Frameworks, 81 Notre Dame L. Rev. 1, 47 (2005). And what exactly is encompassed by the "character of the government action"? Lower courts have advanced a host of things that might be covered by this factor, including elements emphasized in *Mahon* that do not otherwise appear in *Penn Central* (except in the dissent). See Thomas W. Merrill, The Character of the Governmental Action, 36 Vt. L. Rev. 649, 661–71 (2012). Despite these uncertainties, the Court has done little to clarify the ad hoc approach since reformulating it as a three-factor inquiry in *Kaiser Aetna*.

5.   However it is characterized, the *Penn Central* approach has not been friendly to takings claimants. Although the Court found a taking in two cases that purported to apply *Penn Central* to federal regulations in the decade after it was decided, see Kaiser Aetna v. United States, 444 U.S. 164 (1979); Hodel v. Irving, 481 U.S. 704 (1987); it has never invalidated a state regulation of property under the ad hoc standard. See Stewart E. Sterk, The Federalist Dimension of Regulatory Takings Jurisprudence, 114 Yale L.J. 203, 251–56 (2003). Empirical surveys of published opinions applying *Penn Central*, which of course include only a small subset of the universe of potential controversies, report that less than 10 percent of such cases find a taking. See Adam R. Pomeroy, *Penn Central* After 35 Years: A Three Part Balancing Test or a One Strike Rule?, 22 Fed. Cir. B.J. 677 (2013). The author also reports that courts are divided about whether *Penn Central* requires a balancing of three factors or simply means that failure to prevail on any one factor is fatal to the takings claim.

6.   Under the anti-circumvention theory, see Academic Perspectives on Regulatory Takings, supra, does *Penn Central* present a relatively straightforward question? If air rights, i.e., the right to develop the column of space above an existing structure, are bought and sold in the relevant market on a stand-alone basis, then it would seem that the government's regulation has taken an exchangeable form of "private property." For evidence of such transactions in urban areas, especially over railroad trackage rights, see Thomas W. Merrill, The Compensation Constraint and the Scope of the Takings Clause, 96 Notre Dame L. Rev. 1421, 1438 & n.59 (2021). Should the Penn Central Company have concentrated on developing

record evidence in support on the proposition that air rights are bought and sold as a discrete bundle of rights in Manhattan?

7.   Consider the exchange between the majority and the dissent over whether New York's Landmarks Preservation Law is similar to zoning. The Supreme Court had held in the *Euclid* case, excerpted in Chapter IX, that zoning is not unconstitutional on its face, but might be open to challenge in particular applications. The dueling opinions in *Penn Central* focus largely on the question whether the Landmarks Preservation Law is sufficiently general to qualify as a type of zoning measure. One difference between zoning laws and historic preservation laws is that the former generally operate ex ante, before significant development of property takes place, whereas the latter operate ex post, after a structure has been built which is subsequently determined to be too valuable to modify. Given the ex post nature of historic preservation, do such laws create a danger that they will be used in an oppressive or retaliatory fashion? In another prominent case involving New York's Landmarks Preservation Law, which upheld a landmark designation of a church on Park Avenue in the face of takings and free exercise of religion claims, the Second Circuit, speaking through Judge Winter, dropped the following footnote: "The Landmarks Law made a cameo appearance in a recent best-selling novel as a vehicle for political retaliation against a clerical official seeking to develop Church property. *See* T. Wolfe, *Bonfire of the Vanities* 569 (1987) ('Mort? You know that church, St. Timothy's? . . . Right . . . LANDMARK THE SON OF A BITCH!')." Rector of St. Bartholomew's Church v. City of New York, 914 F.2d 348, 355 n.3 (2d Cir. 1990).

8.   One way of reading *Penn Central* is that the government can abrogate an owner's right to destroy property without incurring any takings liability, at least when the financial burden is not too extreme. How important is the right to destroy in the traditional "bundle of sticks" that makes up full ownership of property? See Lior Jacob Strahilevitz, The Right to Destroy, 114 Yale L.J. 781, 794–96 (2005). Is abrogation of the right to destroy a more serious intrusion upon owner sovereignty than regulating the uses to which property can be put? The Court has also held that abrogation of the right to sell personal property is not a taking, Andrus v. Allard, 444 U.S. 51, 67–68 (1979) (Congress can abolish the right to sell eagle feathers without creating takings liability). However, the Court has suggested that elimination of the right to transmit property upon death will presumptively be regarded as a taking, Hodel v. Irving, 481 U.S. 704, 717 (1987), and has stressed in a number of cases that abrogation of the right to exclude is regarded as particularly serious for takings purposes. See Cedar Point Nursery v. Hassid (excerpted infra and cases cited). Does the Court have a principled basis for deciding which incidents of property are more central to ownership than others, such that elimination of the right is or is not regarded as likely to trigger takings liability? Or is the key point of *Penn Central* that generalizations about these things are not possible, and it all depends on context?

9.   Was it appropriate for the Court to toss in the transferable development rights or TDRs awarded to Penn Central as one factor to

balance in deciding whether the regulation was a taking? Or is Justice Rehnquist correct in assuming that the TDRs should be considered only on the question whether the company was given just compensation? In a later decision, Justice Scalia argued that "[p]utting TDRs on the taking rather than the just compensation side of the equation . . . is a clever, albeit transparent, device that seeks to take advantage of a peculiarity of our Takings Clause jurisprudence: Whereas once there *is* a taking, the Constitution requires just (*i.e.*, full) compensation. . . . [yet a] regulatory taking generally does not *occur* so long as land retains substantial (albeit not its full) value." Suitum v. Tahoe Regional Planning Agency, 520 U.S. 725, 747–48 (1997) (concurring opinion). Building on this critique, could a political jurisdiction like New York avoid all takings liability by providing that just enough partial compensation will be awarded in each case to permit the court to conclude, on balance, that no taking has been committed? In an ironic reprise of the debate over the TDRs, investors who acquired Grand Central to obtain the unused TDRs from the Penn Central Company sued the City of New York when it liberalized height restrictions for a developer in the area around the terminal, in return for developer investments in infrastructure and transit—thereby rendering the TDRs largely valueless. The case settled on undisclosed terms. See Christopher Serkin, *Penn Central Take Two*, 92 Note Dame L. Rev. 913 (2016). How would you assess a claim for a taking of the Penn Central TDR's under the ad hoc regulatory takings test of *Penn Central*?

10. Whatever you think of *Penn Central* as a matter of constitutional law, do you think the practice of denying compensation for historic preservation orders makes sense as a matter of policy? Some commentators have worried that "freezing" the exterior design of notable buildings, without providing any compensation for lost development rights, may have two unintended consequences: (1) persons who own buildings that are potential targets for historic preservation designation may rush to demolish them before they are protected; and (2) persons who are contemplating commissioning the construction of new buildings may turn down dramatic or innovative designs out of fear that they will be "rewarded" with a historic preservation designation, and hence will be locked into the building for all time. See Mendes Hershman, Critical Legal Issues in Historic Preservation, 12 Urb. Law. 19, 28 (1980); Carol M. Rose, Preservation and Community: New Directions in the Law of Historic Preservation, 33 Stan. L. Rev. 473, 500–01 (1981); see also David A. Dana, Natural Preservation and the Race to Develop, 143 U. Pa. L. Rev. 655 (1995) (considering a similar critique in the context of natural preservation law); Strahilevitz, The Right to Destroy, supra, at 817–18. Either or both of these incentive effects could work to impoverish the overall architectural quality of the community. Providing compensation for lost development rights would presumably eliminate these incentive effects (at least in part). But of course, it would also mean that there would probably be many fewer historic designations, because of the expense to the community of paying for lost development rights.

Seeking Compensation for Regulatory Takings

The earliest regulatory takings cases we have considered—*Pennsylvania Coal Co. v. Mahon*, supra, and *Miller v. Schoene*, supra—were brought under the Due Process Clause of the Fourteenth Amendment. It appears that in both cases (*Pennsylvania Coal* is explicit about this) the plaintiffs sought an injunction against the operation of the state statute because it did not provide just compensation. Neither case suggests that the plaintiffs could sue directly under the Takings Clause and ask the court to order the state government to pay compensation. Under established principles of sovereign immunity, courts had no authority to enter a judgment against a state government without its consent. The only remedy was to sue a state official in equity and ask the court to enjoin the official from enforcing a law that did not comport with the Constitution. See *Ex Parte Young*, 209 U.S. 123 (1908) (allowing an injunction against state officers who threatened to enforce a confiscatory rate order).

The *Penn Central* Court cast the regulatory takings doctrine as resting on the incorporation of the Takings Clause into the Fourteenth Amendment. This was foreshadowed many years earlier in *Chicago, B. & Q. R. Co. v. Chicago*, 166 U.S. 226, 239 (1897). But the first explicit invocation of the incorporation doctrine in the context of the Takings Clause occurred in *Penn Central*. Bradley C. Karkkainen, The Police Power Revisited: Phantom Incorporation and the Roots of the Takings "Muddle," 90 Minn. L. Rev. 826, 844–82 (2006). One effect of this was to direct attention to the text of the Takings Clause, which provides for one remedy for its violation—the payment of just compensation ("nor shall private property be taken for public use without just compensation"). As the Court came to recognize that the exclusive remedy for a taking is compensation, this touched off a number of difficulties within regulatory takings doctrine.

One issue that took on prominence in the 1970s and 1980s concerned a California Supreme Court rule that the only remedy for a state or local law found to be a regulatory taking was an injunction against the future enforcement of the law. Real estate developers complained that the rule was unconstitutional because it deprived them of just compensation for the period in which they were litigating the regulatory taking issue. After several false starts, the Court agreed with the developers in *First English Evangelical Lutheran Church of Glendale v. Los Angeles County,* 482 U.S. 304 (1987). The Court held that the failure to provide compensation for the period before the injunction was entered was a temporary taking and required the payment of just compensation for the loss of development rights during this period. Although there was language in a footnote suggesting that sovereign immunity was no barrier to this result, id. at 316 n.9, this was at most dicta. The defendant in the case was a county, which (unlike the state government) does not enjoy sovereign immunity. The Court later clarified that property owners could sue counties and other local government entities for just compensation in federal court under 42 U.S.C. § 1983. City of Monterey v. Del Monte Dunes at Monterey, 526 U.S. 687 (1999). But § 1983 suits seeking damages against state governments are barred by sovereign immunity.

Another development based on the compensation remedy had a significant impact on the ability of property owners to bring regulatory takings claims in federal court, even against a county or local government entity under § 1983. In *Williamson County Regional Planning Comm. v. Hamilton Bank of Johnson City*, 473 U.S. 172, 195 (1985), the Court held that since compensation is the exclusive remedy for a regulatory taking, a property owner cannot bring a taking claim under federal law until the owner has sought and been denied compensation under state provisions for obtaining compensation. Standing alone, this seemed only to promise more delay (which would give rise to compensation for a temporary taking if the owner was ultimately successful). But in *San Remo Hotel, L. P. v. City and County of San Francisco*, 545 U.S. 323 (2005), the Court held that any issues resolved in state court proceedings seeking compensation must be given preclusive effect in a subsequent federal court proceeding. This created what was called the "*Williamson County* trap": The federal Constitution creates an action for a regulatory taking, and federal courts ordinarily stand ready to vindicate federal constitutional rights; but under *Williamson County* regulatory takings claims against any state entity will ordinarily go no further than state court (except for the rare case in which the Supreme Court agrees to review the state court judgment).

Property rights advocates were upset by the *Williamson County* trap, and in *Knick v. Township of Scott*, 139 S. Ct. 2162 (2019), they persuaded the Court to overrule this aspect of *Williamson County*. Writing for a bare majority of five, Chief Justice Roberts recharacterized the nature of right established by the Takings Clause. It was not, he wrote, the denial of *compensation* for a taking of property, as *Williamson County* suggested. Rather it was a *taking of property* unaccompanied by a promise of compensation. "If a local government takes private property without paying for it, that government has violated the Fifth Amendment—just as the Takings Clause says—without regard to subsequent state court proceedings. And the property owner may sue the government at that time in federal court for the 'deprivation' of a right secured by the Constitution.' 42 U.S.C. § 1983." 139 S. Ct. at 2162.

Knick opens the door to the filing of regulatory takings claims against local governments directly in federal court under § 1983. This still leaves the question whether regulatory takings claims can be filed against a State and its agencies consistent with state sovereign immunity. In *PennEast Pipeline Co., LLC v. New Jersey*, 141 S. Ct. 2244 (2021), the Court held that sovereign immunity is no barrier to an action in federal court by a private pipeline company to condemn state-owned lands or interests in lands. It may seem odd that that states cannot invoke sovereign immunity to resist a taking of their own land, but can invoke sovereign immunity to bar a suit for compensation when they take *someone else's* land. Perhaps by some alchemy of precedent, *PennEast* will lead to an abrogation of sovereign immunity when a state takes, as well as when it resists a taking. But only time will tell.

3. PERMANENT PHYSICAL OCCUPATIONS

Loretto v. Teleprompter Manhattan CATV Corp.
Supreme Court of the United States, 1982.
458 U.S. 419.

■ JUSTICE MARSHALL delivered the opinion of the Court. This case presents the question whether a minor but permanent physical occupation of an owner's property authorized by government constitutes a "taking" of property for which just compensation is due under the Fifth and Fourteenth Amendments of the Constitution. * * * The New York Court of Appeals ruled that this appropriation does not amount to a taking. Because we conclude that such a physical occupation of property is a taking, we reverse.

I

[When cable television first came to New York City, cable companies induced landlords to permit cable wires to be installed on the roof and down the side of their buildings by offering landlords 5% of the gross revenues obtained from selling cable TV subscriptions to tenants living at the property. Later, New York enacted a statute prohibiting landlords from interfering with cable installations or demanding payments from either tenants or cable companies. A state regulatory commission ruled that landlords were entitled to a one-time payment of $1 as compensation for permitting such installations. Jean Loretto, who owned a small rental building on the upper West Side of Manhattan, filed a class action alleging that the cable mandate was a taking of her property. The installation at her building, in addition to wires suspended above the roof and running down the side of the building, consisted of two small silver boxes and screws or nails securing the wire to the roof at two-foot intervals.]

Figure 10-6
303 West 105th Street, New York City, in 2006

II

The Court of Appeals determined that § 828 serves the legitimate public purpose of "rapid development of and maximum penetration by a means of communication which has important educational and community aspects," and thus is within the State's police power. We have no reason to question that determination. It is a separate question, however, whether an otherwise valid regulation so frustrates property rights that compensation must be paid. See Penn Central Transportation Co. v. New York City, 438 U.S. 104, 127–128 (1978). We conclude that a permanent physical occupation authorized by government is a taking without regard to the public interests that it may serve. Our constitutional history confirms the rule, recent cases do not question it, and the purposes of the Takings Clause compel its retention.

A

In *Penn Central Transportation Co. v. New York City*, supra, the Court surveyed some of the general principles governing the Takings Clause. The Court noted that no "set formula" existed to determine, in all cases, whether compensation is constitutionally due for a government restriction of property. Ordinarily, the Court must engage in "essentially ad hoc, factual inquiries." Id., at 124. But the inquiry is not standardless. The economic impact of the regulation, especially the degree of interference with investment-backed expectations, is of particular significance. "So, too, is the character of the governmental action. A 'taking' may more readily be found when the interference with property can be characterized as a physical invasion by government, than when interference arises from some public program adjusting the benefits and burdens of economic life to promote the common good." Ibid. (citation omitted).

As *Penn Central* affirms, the Court has often upheld substantial regulation of an owner's use of his own property where deemed necessary to promote the public interest. At the same time, we have long considered a physical intrusion by government to be a property restriction of an unusually serious character for purposes of the Takings Clause. Our cases further establish that when the physical intrusion reaches the extreme form of a permanent physical occupation, a taking has occurred. In such a case, "the character of the government action" not only is an important factor in resolving whether the action works a taking but also is determinative.

When faced with a constitutional challenge to a permanent physical occupation of real property, this Court has invariably found a taking. As early as 1872, in *Pumpelly v. Green Bay Co.*, 13 Wall. (80 U.S.) 166, this Court held that the defendant's construction, pursuant to state authority, of a dam which permanently flooded plaintiff's property constituted a taking. A unanimous Court stated, without qualification, that "where real estate is actually invaded by superinduced additions of water, earth, sand, or other material, or by having any artificial structure placed on it, so as to effectually destroy or impair its usefulness, it is a taking, within the meaning of the Constitution." Id., 13 Wall. (80 U.S.) at 181. * * *

More recent cases confirm the distinction between a permanent physical occupation, a physical invasion short of an occupation, and a regulation that merely restricts the use of property. In United States v. Causby, 328 U.S. 256 (1946), the Court ruled that frequent flights immediately above a landowner's property constituted a taking, comparing such overflights to the quintessential form of a taking:

> If, by reason of the frequency and altitude of the flights, respondents could not use this land for any purpose, their loss would be complete. It would be as complete as if the United States had entered upon the surface of the land and taken exclusive possession of it. Id., at 261 (footnote omitted).

As the Court further explained,

> We would not doubt that, if the United States erected an
> elevated railway over respondents' land at the precise altitude
> where its planes now fly, there would be a partial taking, even
> though none of the supports of the structure rested on the land.
> The reason is that there would be an intrusion so immediate and
> direct as to subtract from the owner's full enjoyment of the
> property and to limit his exploitation of it. Id., at 264–265.

The Court concluded that the damages to the respondents "were not
merely consequential. They were the product of a direct invasion of
respondents' domain." Id., at 265–266. See also Griggs v. Allegheny
County, 369 U.S. 84 (1962). * * *

Although this Court's most recent cases have not addressed the
precise issue before us, they have emphasized that physical *invasion*
cases are special and have not repudiated the rule that any permanent
physical *occupation* is a taking. The cases state or imply that a physical
invasion is subject to a balancing process, but they do not suggest that a
permanent physical occupation would ever be exempt from the Takings
Clause. * * *

In short, when the "character of the governmental action," Penn
Central, 438 U.S., at 124, is a permanent physical occupation of property,
our cases uniformly have found a taking to the extent of the occupation,
without regard to whether the action achieves an important public
benefit or has only minimal economic impact on the owner.

B

The historical rule that a permanent physical occupation of another's
property is a taking has more than tradition to commend it. Such an
appropriation is perhaps the most serious form of invasion of an owner's
property interests. To borrow a metaphor, cf. Andrus v. Allard, 444 U.S.
51, 65–66 (1979), the government does not simply take a single "strand"
from the "bundle" of property rights: it chops through the bundle, taking
a slice of every strand.

Property rights in a physical thing have been described as the rights
"to possess, use and dispose of it." United States v. General Motors Corp.,
323 U.S. 373, 378 (1945). To the extent that the government permanently
occupies physical property, it effectively destroys *each* of these rights.
First, the owner has no right to possess the occupied space himself, and
also has no power to exclude the occupier from possession and use of the
space. The power to exclude has traditionally been considered one of the
most treasured strands in an owner's bundle of property rights.[12] See

---

[12]   The permanence and absolute exclusivity of a physical occupation distinguish it from
temporary limitations on the right to exclude. Not every physical *invasion* is a taking. As
PruneYard Shopping Center v. Robins, 447 U.S. 74 (1980); *Kaiser Aetna v. United States*, 444
U.S. 164 (1979), and the intermittent flooding cases reveal, such temporary limitations are
subject to a more complex balancing process to determine whether they are a taking. The

Kaiser Aetna, 444 U.S., at 179–180; see also Restatement of Property § 7 (1936). Second, the permanent physical occupation of property forever denies the owner any power to control the use of the property; he not only cannot exclude others, but can make no nonpossessory use of the property. Although deprivation of the right to use and obtain a profit from property is not, in every case, independently sufficient to establish a taking, see Andrus v. Allard, supra, at 66, it is clearly relevant. Finally, even though the owner may retain the bare legal right to dispose of the occupied space by transfer or sale, the permanent occupation of that space by a stranger will ordinarily empty the right of any value, since the purchaser will also be unable to make any use of the property.

Moreover, an owner suffers a special kind of injury when a *stranger* directly invades and occupies the owner's property. As Part II–A, supra, indicates, property law has long protected an owner's expectation that he will be relatively undisturbed at least in the possession of his property. To require, as well, that the owner permit another to exercise complete dominion literally adds insult to injury. See Michelman, Property, Utility, and Fairness: Comments on the Ethical Foundations of "Just Compensation" Law, 80 Harv.L.Rev. 1165, 1228, and n. 110 (1967). Furthermore, such an occupation is qualitatively more severe than a regulation of the *use* of property, even a regulation that imposes affirmative duties on the owner, since the owner may have no control over the timing, extent, or nature of the invasion.

The traditional rule also avoids otherwise difficult line-drawing problems. Few would disagree that if the State required landlords to permit third parties to install swimming pools on the landlords' rooftops for the convenience of the tenants, the requirement would be a taking. If the cable installation here occupied as much space, again, few would disagree that the occupation would be a taking. But constitutional protection for the rights of private property cannot be made to depend on the size of the area permanently occupied. Indeed, it is possible that in the future, additional cable installations that more significantly restrict a landlord's use of the roof of his building will be made. Section 828 requires a landlord to permit such multiple installations.

Finally, whether a permanent physical occupation has occurred presents relatively few problems of proof. The placement of a fixed structure on land or real property is an obvious fact that will rarely be subject to dispute. Once the fact of occupation is shown, of course, a court should consider the *extent* of the occupation as one relevant factor in

---

rationale is evident: they do not absolutely dispossess the owner of his rights to use, and exclude others from, his property.

The dissent objects that the distinction between a permanent physical occupation and a temporary invasion will not always be clear. This objection is overstated, and in any event is irrelevant to the critical point that a permanent physical occupation *is* unquestionably a taking. In the antitrust area, similarly, this Court has not declined to apply a *per se* rule simply because a court must, at the boundary of the rule, apply the rule of reason and engage in a more complex balancing analysis.

determining the compensation due. For that reason, moreover, there is less need to consider the extent of the occupation in determining whether there is a taking in the first instance.

C

Teleprompter's cable installation on appellant's building constitutes a taking under the traditional test. The installation involved a direct physical attachment of plates, boxes, wires, bolts, and screws to the building, completely occupying space immediately above and upon the roof and along the building's exterior wall.[16] * * *

Appellees raise a series of objections to application of the traditional rule here. Teleprompter notes that the law applies only to buildings used as rental property, and draws the conclusion that the law is simply a permissible regulation of the use of real property. We fail to see, however, why a physical occupation of one type of property but not another type is any less a physical occupation. Insofar as Teleprompter means to suggest that this is not a permanent physical invasion, we must differ. So long as the property remains residential and a CATV company wishes to retain the installation, the landlord must permit it.[17] * * *

Finally, we do not agree with appellees that application of the physical occupation rule will have dire consequences for the government's power to adjust landlord-tenant relationships. This Court has consistently affirmed that States have broad power to regulate housing conditions in general and the landlord-tenant relationship in particular without paying compensation for all economic injuries that such regulation entails. In none of these cases, however, did the government authorize the permanent occupation of the landlord's property by a third party. Consequently, our holding today in no way alters the analysis governing the State's power to require landlords to comply with building codes and provide utility connections, mailboxes, smoke detectors, fire extinguishers, and the like in the common area of a building. So long as these regulations do not require the landlord to suffer the physical occupation of a portion of his building by a third party, they will be analyzed under the multifactor inquiry generally applicable to

---

[16] It is constitutionally irrelevant whether appellant (or her predecessor in title) had previously occupied this space, since a "landowner owns at least as much of the space above the ground as he can occupy or use in connection with the land." United States v. Causby, supra, at 264. The dissent asserts that a taking of about one-eighth of a cubic foot of space is not of constitutional significance. The assertion appears to be factually incorrect, since it ignores the two large silver boxes that appellant identified as part of the installation. Although the record does not reveal their size, appellant states that they are approximately 18″ × 12″ × 6″, Brief for Appellant 6 n.*, and appellees do not dispute this statement. The displaced volume, then, is in excess of 1 1/2 cubic feet. In any event, these facts are not critical: whether the installation is a taking does not depend on whether the volume of space it occupies is bigger than a breadbox.

[17] It is true that the landlord could avoid the requirements of § 828 by ceasing to rent the building to tenants. But a landlord's ability to rent his property may not be conditioned on his forfeiting the right to compensation for a physical occupation.

nonpossessory governmental activity. See Penn Central Transportation Co. v. New York City, 438 U.S. 104 (1978).[19]

III

Our holding today is very narrow. We affirm the traditional rule that a permanent physical occupation of property is a taking. In such a case, the property owner entertains a historically rooted expectation of compensation, and the character of the invasion is qualitatively more intrusive than perhaps any other category of property regulation. We do not, however, question the equally substantial authority upholding a State's broad power to impose appropriate restrictions upon an owner's *use* of his property. Furthermore, our conclusion that § 828 works a taking of a portion of appellant's property does not presuppose that the fee which many landlords had obtained from Teleprompter prior to the law's enactment is a proper measure of the value of the property taken. The issue of the amount of compensation that is due, on which we express no opinion, is a matter for the state courts to consider on remand. * * *

■ JUSTICE BLACKMUN, with whom JUSTICE BRENNAN and JUSTICE WHITE join, dissenting. * * * In a curiously anachronistic decision, the Court today acknowledges its historical disavowal of set formulae in almost the same breath as it constructs a rigid *per se* takings rule: "a permanent physical occupation authorized by government is a taking without regard to the public interests that it may serve." To sustain its rule against our recent precedents, the Court erects a strained and untenable distinction between "temporary physical invasions," whose constitutionality concededly "is subject to a balancing process," and "permanent physical occupations," which are "taking[s] without regard to other factors that a court might ordinarily examine." * * *

[Section] 828 differs little from the numerous other New York statutory provisions that require landlords to install physical facilities "permanently occupying" common spaces in or on their buildings. As the Court acknowledges, the States traditionally—and constitutionally—

---

[19]   If § 828 required landlords to provide cable installation if a tenant so desires, the statute might present a different question from the question before us, since the landlord would own the installation. Ownership would give the landlord rights to the placement, manner, use, and possibly the disposition of the installation. The fact of ownership is, contrary to the dissent, not simply "incidental"; it would give a landlord (rather than a CATV company) full authority over the installation except only as government specifically limited that authority. The *landlord* would decide how to comply with applicable government regulations concerning CATV and therefore could minimize the physical, esthetic, and other effects of the installation. Moreover, if the landlord wished to repair, demolish, or construct in the area of the building where the installation is located, he need not incur the burden of obtaining the CATV company's cooperation in moving the cable. In this case, by contrast, appellant suffered injury that might have been obviated if she had owned the cable and could exercise control over its installation. The drilling and stapling that accompanied installation apparently caused physical damage to appellant's building. App. 83, 95–96, 104. Appellant, who resides in her building, further testified that the cable installation is "ugly." Id., at 99. Although § 828 provides that a landlord may require "reasonable" conditions that are "necessary" to protect the appearance of the premises and may seek indemnity for damage, these provisions are somewhat limited. Even if the provisions are effective, the inconvenience to the landlord of initiating the repairs remains a cognizable burden.

have exercised their police power "to require landlords to . . . provide utility connections, mailboxes, smoke detectors, fire extinguishers, and the like in the common area of a building." Like § 828, these provisions merely ensure tenants access to services the legislature deems important, such as water, electricity, natural light, telephones, intercommunication systems, and mail service. A landlord's dispositional rights are affected no more adversely when he sells a building to another landlord subject to § 828, than when he sells that building subject only to these other New York statutory provisions. * * *

[T]his Court long ago recognized that new social circumstances can justify legislative modification of a property owner's common-law rights, without compensation, if the legislative action serves sufficiently important public interests. See Munn v. Illinois, 94 U.S. 113, 134 (1877) ("A person has no property, no vested interest, in any rule of the common law. . . . Indeed, the great office of statutes is to remedy defects in the common law as they are developed, and to adapt it to the changes of time and circumstance"); United States v. Causby, 328 U.S., at 260–261 (In the modern world, "[c]ommon sense revolts at the idea" that legislatures cannot alter common-law ownership rights).* * *

This Court now reaches back in time for a *per se* rule that disrupts that legislative determination. Like Justice Black, I believe that "the solution of the problems precipitated by . . . technological advances and new ways of living cannot come about through the application of rigid constitutional restraints formulated and enforced by the courts." United States v. Causby, 328 U.S., at 274 (dissenting opinion). I would affirm the judgment and uphold the reasoning of the New York Court of Appeals.

NOTES AND QUESTIONS

1.   The regulation in *Loretto* seems to impose minimal harm on owners of residential rental property—indeed it probably increased the value of that property by making it more attractive to tenants. (On remand, the New York courts concluded that Ms. Loretto was entitled to only $1 in nominal compensation. Loretto v. Teleprompter Manhattan CATV Corp., 446 N.E. 2d 428 (N.Y. 1983).) Yet from the perspective of an anti-circumvention theory of regulatory takings, this was an easy case for finding a taking. All kinds of public utility companies—electric distribution companies, telephone companies, natural gas distribution companies—need to acquire easements to lay down their distribution lines. The established method of acquiring such easements, when voluntary negotiations to secure an easement break down, is to use a delegated power of eminent domain. Thus, when a new type of distribution company comes along—cable television—it seems only natural that these newcomers should also use voluntary negotiation or eminent domain to acquire easements to run their wires from building to building. A holding contrary to the one reached by the Court, suggesting that easements acquired by some utilities that impose only minor costs on servient landowners can proceed by police power regulation rather than

eminent domain, would have opened a big can of worms in an area of the law that had previously been regarded as settled. Why do you suppose the Court ignored this line of analysis and created a new per se rule for permanent physical occupations?

2.　In terms of doctrinal development, *Loretto* was significant far beyond its holding. As suggested by footnote 12 in the Court's opinion, the combination of *Penn Central* and *Loretto* suggests that regulatory takings doctrine partakes of a general "ad hoc" test, supplemented by rules of "per se" liability that apply in particular circumstances. This is similar to the approach of antitrust law, which follows a general "rule of reason" in determining whether particular restraints on trade violate the law, supplemented by "per se" rules that apply to conduct that seems to warrant liability without regard to the circumstances. See, e.g., Broadcast Music, Inc. v. Columbia Broadcasting System, Inc., 441 U.S. 1 (1979). This two-tiered structure of decisional rules was to blossom into a more complete form in *Lucas*, a case appearing later in the chapter. For overviews of the relationship between categorical and ad hoc takings tests, see Lingle v. Chevron U.S.A. Inc., 544 U.S. 528, 538–40 (2005); David A. Dana & Thomas W. Merrill, Property: Takings 86–168 (2002).

3.　Is the contrast between Justice Marshall's opinion in *Loretto* and Justice Brennan's opinion in *Penn Central* another example of the divide in property law between theories of property that stress the centrality of exclusion rights, and those that characterize property as a bundle of rights? Is *Loretto* just a reflexive transposition of a private law rule into a public law context, where it makes little sense? Or is it possible to justify the Court's rule by drawing upon some of the same reasons that justify liability without proof of harm for trespasses to land in the private law context?

4.　The right to exclude, which is given such prominence in *Loretto*, also played a role in other takings controversies decided around the same time, with mixed results. In *Kaiser Aetna v. United States*, 444 U.S. 164 (1979), the Court considered whether a federal directive to open a privately-constructed marina to the general public as part of the navigable waters of the United States was a taking. Distinguishing cases holding that regulations designed to preserve the public "navigation servitude" are not takings and stressing the importance of the right to exclude others in preserving investment-backed expectations, the Court found that the regulation was a taking. In *PruneYard Shopping Center v. Robins*, 447 U.S. 74 (1980), in contrast, the Court held that a state directive allowing persons to distribute political leaflets and information in a privately-owned shopping center was not a taking. The Court acknowledged the importance of the right to exclude, but noted that the shopping center had opened its doors to the general public (for shopping purposes), and concluded that the regulation had only a minor impact on any investment-backed expectations. Both decisions applied *Penn Central*'s ad hoc test and did not suggest any per se rule for permanent invasions or occupations.

Post-*Loretto* Developments Regarding Physical Invasions

After *Loretto*, the new per se rule for permanent physical occupations received a choppy reception. Initially, the Court interpreted the rule narrowly. In *Yee v. City of Escondido*, 503 U.S. 519 (1992), the Court held that an ordinance that took away a landlord's right to determine the identity of a replacement tenant in a mobile home park did not result in a permanent occupation, because the landlord had voluntarily chosen to lease the property in the first place. Similarly, in *FCC v. Florida Power Corp.*, 480 U.S. 245 (1987), the Court rejected the claim that a federal directive requiring utility companies to lease space on poles to cable companies at regulated rates was a permanent occupation, because the original lease arrangement had been voluntary.

The tide arguably turned when the Court began considering exactions imposed as a condition of developing property (considered more fully below). See Nollan v. California Coastal Comm., 483 U.S. 825 (1987); Dolan v. City of Tigard, 512 U.S. 374 (1994). In both decisions, the Court indicated that regulations requiring property owners to dedicate a permanent *easement of public access* would be per se takings under *Loretto*. See Nollan, 483 U.S. at 832 ("We think a 'permanent physical occupation' has occurred ... where individuals are given a permanent and continuous right to pass to and fro, so that the real property may continuously be traversed, even though no particular individual is permitted to station himself permanently on the premises.") This seemingly expanded the per se rule of *Loretto* to include permanent *rights of access*. This, of course, is characteristic of easements more generally: one can have an easement granting a permanent right of access to land even if one never uses it, and hence never occupies the land, even temporarily.

A major expansion of *Loretto* occurred in *Horne v. Department of Agriculture*, 576 U.S. 350 (2015), where the Court held that the per se rule for permanent physical occupations of real property also applies to what it called physical "appropriations" of personal property. Under New Deal-era legislation designed to prop up the prices obtained by producers of agricultural products, farmers who grow grapes for the raisin market are required to turn over their crop to government-licensed handlers. The handlers sell a portion of the crop, called free-tonnage raisins, on the open market, and give the proceeds to the producer; but the handlers hold back another portion of the crop, called reserve raisins, and dispose of them in ways that will not augment the supply of raisins in the domestic commercial market (e.g., they are sold in the foreign market). The obvious purpose of the program is to restrict the supply of raisins in the domestic market, and thereby increase the price of raisins obtained by producers.

In a suit by a producer claiming that the mandatory diversion of a portion of the crop as reserve raisins was a taking of property, the Court agreed. No one questioned that the Takings Clause applies to personal property as well as real property. The question was whether a physical appropriation of personal property by the government, analogous to a conversion, should be governed by a per se rule or the ad hoc approach of *Penn Central*. The majority opinion, by Chief Justice Roberts, held that the question was controlled by *Loretto* (576 U.S. at 361–62):

> The reserve requirement imposed by the Raisin Committee is a clear physical taking. Actual raisins are transferred from the growers to the Government. Title to the raisins passes to the Raisin Committee. The Committee's raisins must be physically segregated from free-tonnage raisins. Reserve raisins are sometimes left on the premises of handlers, but they are held "for the account" of the Government. The Committee disposes of what become its raisins as it wishes, to promote the purposes of the raisin marketing order.
>
> Raisin growers subject to the reserve requirement thus lose the entire "bundle" of property rights in the appropriated raisins—"the rights to possess, use and dispose of" them, *Loretto,* 458 U.S., at 435 (internal quotation marks omitted) * * *. The Government's "actual taking of possession and control" of the reserve raisins gives rise to a taking as clearly "as if the Government held full title and ownership," id., at 431 (internal quotation marks omitted), as it essentially does. The Government's formal demand that the Hornes turn over a percentage of their raisin crop without charge, for the Government's control and use, is "of such a unique character that it is a taking without regard to other factors that a court might ordinarily examine." Id., at 432 (citations omitted).

The Chief Justice conceded that if the government had proceeded differently, by restricting the quantity of raisins that producers could sell, this would have to be assessed under *Penn Central*'s ad hoc test. And he acknowledged that the economic impact on producers would be the same, whether the government restricted the sale of raisins or required that a portion of the crop be turned over to handlers for disposal outside the commercial market. But the functional equivalence between the two approaches ignored "the settled difference in our takings jurisprudence between appropriation and regulation. A physical taking of raisins and a regulatory limit on production may have the same economic impact on a grower. The Constitution, however, is concerned with means as well as ends." 576 U.S. at 362.

The principal dissent, by Justice Breyer, argued that even if the reserve raisin requirement could be characterized as a taking of personal property, the case should be remanded for a determination of the amount of compensation the Hornes were entitled to receive, applying the rule of offsetting benefits applied in cases of partial takings. (See Note on Partial Takings after *United States v. Miller*, supra.) He appeared to agree with the government that the benefit to producers like the Hornes from higher prices on free tonnage raisins quite likely equaled or exceeded the revenue they lost from not being able to sell the reserve raisins on the open market. The Chief Justice rejected the idea of a remand to determine the proper compensation, commenting that "this case, in litigation for more than a decade, has gone on long enough." 576 U.S. at 370.

4. EXACTIONS

One of the features of modern zoning and land-use planning is that developers must submit their plans for new subdivisions, shopping centers, and other significant real estate developments to local planning authorities for their approval before construction may begin. Under the original conception of zoning, the purpose of requiring advance approval was to ensure that the proposed development was consistent with the local zoning ordinance. As we saw in Chapter IX, in recent decades the approval process has evolved into complex negotiations between developers and local authorities over the scope, uses, and density of the proposed project. These negotiations often include what are called exactions—an agreement by the developer to donate certain property or money to the local community—as a condition of obtaining approval from authorities to proceed with the development. The justification for these exactions is that they provide resources that the community can use for public goods like new parks or schools that offset, at least in part, the burdens imposed on the community by the new development. See generally Alan A. Altshuler et & José A. Gómez-Ibáñez, Regulation for Revenue: The Political Economy of Land Use Exactions (1993).

State courts have reviewed challenges to exactions for many years, typically under state constitutional doctrines like substantive due process. In 1987, the U.S. Supreme Court took up the issue under the Takings Clause, in *Nollan v. California Coastal Comm'n*, 483 U.S. 825 (1987). The Nollans owned a dilapidated beachfront bungalow, which they wanted to replace with a larger house. The California Coastal Commission informed them that permission to undertake the development would not be granted unless they agreed to convey a lateral easement of public access along the beach behind their house. In a 5–4 decision authored by Justice Scalia, the Court declared that this exaction violated the Takings Clause. The Court assumed that the Commission could have denied the building permit outright, in the interest of ensuring "visual access" to the ocean and preventing overcrowding of beaches. But it found no nexus between these asserted public justifications and the condition the Commission wanted to impose—a lateral easement facilitating the movement of the public up and down the beach. The Court suggested that "unless the permit condition serves the same governmental purpose as the development ban, the building restriction is not a valid regulation of land but 'an out-and-out plan of extortion.'" Id. at 837 (citation omitted).

Nollan was a confusing decision because it was unclear whether the Court was advancing a general requirement that all property regulations satisfy some level of means-ends rationality, or whether it was asserting a rule unique to exactions. The following decision restated the *Nollan* holding and provided a clearer exposition of why exactions are a matter of heighten concern under the Takings Clause.

Dolan v. City of Tigard

Supreme Court of the United States, 1994.
512 U.S. 374.

■ CHIEF JUSTICE REHNQUIST delivered the opinion of the Court. Petitioner challenges the decision of the Oregon Supreme Court which held that the city of Tigard could condition the approval of her building permit on the dedication of a portion of her property for flood control and traffic improvements. We granted certiorari to resolve a question left open by our decision in *Nollan v. California Coastal Comm'n,* 483 U.S. 825 (1987), of what is the required degree of connection between the exactions imposed by the city and the projected impacts of the proposed development.

I

[The City of Tigard, Oregon, a suburb of Portland, adopted land use plans that were designed to reduce congestion in the central business district and limit flood damage that periodically occurred along the Fanno Creek. Petitioner Florence Dolan owned a plumbing and electric supply store that abutted Fanno Creek. When she sought a permit to double the size of her store and pave over the parking lot, the City Planning Commission indicated that it would grant the permit only if she agreed to dedicate a portion of her property in the 100-year floodplain of the creek as a "greenway," and further dedicate a 15-foot strip of land adjacent to the floodplain as a bicycle/pedestrian pathway. Dolan challenged the required dedications—which constituted roughly 10% of per property—as an unconstitutional taking. Oregon courts rejected the claim, and the Supreme Court granted certiorari.]

II

* * * Without question, had the city simply required petitioner to dedicate a strip of land along Fanno Creek for public use, rather than conditioning the grant of her permit to redevelop her property on such a dedication, a taking would have occurred. *Nollan, supra,* 483 U.S., at 831. Such public access would deprive petitioner of the right to exclude others, "one of the most essential sticks in the bundle of rights that are commonly characterized as property." *Kaiser Aetna v. United States,* 444 U.S. 164, 176 (1979).

On the other side of the ledger, the authority of state and local governments to engage in land use planning has been sustained against constitutional challenge as long ago as our decision in *Village of Euclid* *v. Ambler Realty Co.,* 272 U.S. 365, (1926). "Government hardly could go on if to some extent values incident to property could not be diminished without paying for every such change in the general law." Pennsylvania Coal Co. v. Mahon, 260 U.S. 393, 413 (1922). * * *

Under the well-settled doctrine of "unconstitutional conditions," the government may not require a person to give up a constitutional right—here the right to receive just compensation when property is taken for a public use—in exchange for a discretionary benefit conferred by the government where the benefit sought has little or no relationship to the property. See Perry v. Sindermann, 408 U.S. 593 (1972); Pickering v. Board of Ed. of Township High School Dist. 205, Will Cty., 391 U.S. 563, 568 (1968).

Petitioner contends that the city has forced her to choose between the building permit and her right under the Fifth Amendment to just compensation for the public easements. Petitioner does not quarrel with the city's authority to exact some forms of dedication as a condition for the grant of a building permit, but challenges the showing made by the city to justify these exactions. She argues that the city has identified "no special benefits" conferred on her, and has not identified any "special quantifiable burdens" created by her new store that would justify the particular dedications required from her which are not required from the public at large.

III

In evaluating petitioner's claim, we must first determine whether the "essential nexus" exists between the "legitimate state interest" and the permit condition exacted by the city. *Nollan,* 483 U.S., at 837. If we find that a nexus exists, we must then decide the required degree of connection between the exactions and the projected impact of the proposed development. We were not required to reach this question in *Nollan,* because we concluded that the connection did not meet even the loosest standard. *Id.,* at 838. Here, however, we must decide this question.

A

We addressed the essential nexus question in *Nollan.* The California Coastal Commission demanded a lateral public easement across the Nollans' beachfront lot in exchange for a permit to demolish an existing bungalow and replace it with a three-bedroom house. *Id.,* at 828. The public easement was designed to connect two public beaches that were separated by the Nollan's property. The Coastal Commission had asserted that the public easement condition was imposed to promote the legitimate state interest of diminishing the "blockage of the view of the ocean" caused by construction of the larger house.

We agreed that the Coastal Commission's concern with protecting visual access to the ocean constituted a legitimate public interest. *Id.,* at 835. We also agreed that the permit condition would have been constitutional "even if it consisted of the requirement that the Nollans provide a viewing spot on their property for passersby with whose sighting of the ocean their new house would interfere." *Id.,* at 836. We resolved, however, that the Coastal Commission's regulatory authority was set completely adrift from its constitutional moorings when it claimed that a nexus existed between visual access to the ocean and a permit condition requiring lateral public access along the Nollans' beachfront lot. *Id.,* at 837. How enhancing the public's ability to "traverse to and along the shorefront" served the same governmental purpose of "visual access to the ocean" from the roadway was beyond our ability to countenance. The absence of a nexus left the Coastal Commission in the position of simply trying to obtain an easement through gimmickry, which converted a valid regulation of land use into " 'an out-and-out plan of extortion.' " *Ibid.,* quoting J.E.D. Associates, Inc. v. Atkinson, 121 N.H. 581, 584, 432 A.2d 12, 14–15 (1981).

No such gimmicks are associated with the permit conditions imposed by the city in this case. Undoubtedly, the prevention of flooding along Fanno Creek and the reduction of traffic congestion in the Central Business District qualify as the type of legitimate public purposes we have upheld. It seems equally obvious that a nexus exists between preventing flooding along Fanno Creek and limiting development within the creek's 100–year floodplain. Petitioner proposes to double the size of her retail store and to pave her now-gravel parking lot, thereby expanding the impervious surface on the property and increasing the amount of storm water runoff into Fanno Creek.

The same may be said for the city's attempt to reduce traffic congestion by providing for alternative means of transportation. In theory, a pedestrian/bicycle pathway provides a useful alternative means of transportation for workers and shoppers: "Pedestrians and bicyclists occupying dedicated spaces for walking and/or bicycling ... remove potential vehicles from streets, resulting in an overall improvement in total transportation system flow" [citation omitted]. * * *

B

The second part of our analysis requires us to determine whether the degree of the exactions demanded by the city's permit conditions bears the required relationship to the projected impact of petitioner's proposed development. * * *

Since state courts have been dealing with this question a good deal longer than we have, we turn to representative decisions made by them.

In some States, very generalized statements as to the necessary connection between the required dedication and the proposed development seem to suffice. See, *e.g.,* Billings Properties, Inc. v. Yellowstone County, 144 Mont. 25, 394 P.2d 182 (1964); Jenad, Inc. v. Scarsdale, 218 N.E.2d 673 (N.Y. 1966). We think this standard is too lax to adequately protect petitioner's right to just compensation if her property is taken for a public purpose.

Other state courts require a very exacting correspondence, described as the "specifi[c] and uniquely attributable" test. The Supreme Court of Illinois first developed this test in *Pioneer Trust & Savings Bank v. Mount Prospect,* 176 N.E.2d 799, 802 (Ill. 1961). Under this standard, if the local government cannot demonstrate that its exaction is directly proportional to the specifically created need, the exaction becomes "a veiled exercise of the power of eminent domain and a confiscation of private property behind the defense of police regulations." *Id.,* at 802. We do not think the Federal Constitution requires such exacting scrutiny, given the nature of the interests involved.

A number of state courts have taken an intermediate position, requiring the municipality to show a "reasonable relationship" between the required dedication and the impact of the proposed development. Typical is the Supreme Court of Nebraska's opinion in *Simpson v. North Platte,* 292 N.W.2d 297, 301 (Neb. 1980) * * * Some form of the reasonable relationship test has been adopted in many other jurisdictions. [Citations omitted.] * * *

We think the "reasonable relationship" test adopted by a majority of the state courts is closer to the federal constitutional norm than either of those previously discussed. But we do not adopt it as such, partly because the term "reasonable relationship" seems confusingly similar to the term "rational basis" which describes the minimal level of scrutiny under the Equal Protection Clause of the Fourteenth Amendment. We think a term such as "rough proportionality" best encapsulates what we hold to be the requirement of the Fifth Amendment. No precise mathematical calculation is required, but the city must make some sort of individualized determination that the required dedication is related both in nature and extent to the impact of the proposed development. * * *

JUSTICE STEVENS' dissent [argues] that the city's conditional demands for part of petitioner's property are "a species of business regulation that heretofore warranted a strong presumption of constitutional validity." But simply denominating a governmental measure as a "business regulation" does not immunize it from constitutional challenge on the ground that it violates a provision of the Bill of Rights. * * * We see no reason why the Takings Clause of the Fifth Amendment, as much a part of the Bill of Rights as the First Amendment or Fourth Amendment, should be relegated to the status of a poor relation in these comparable circumstances. We turn now to analysis of whether the findings relied upon by the city here, first with respect to the floodplain easement, and second with respect to the pedestrian/bicycle path, satisfied these requirements.

It is axiomatic that increasing the amount of impervious surface will increase the quantity and rate of storm water flow from petitioner's property. Therefore, keeping the floodplain open and free from development would likely confine the pressures on Fanno Creek created by petitioner's development. In fact, because petitioner's property lies within the Central Business District, the CDC already required that petitioner leave 15% of it as open space and the undeveloped floodplain would have nearly satisfied that requirement. But the city demanded more—it not only wanted petitioner not to build in the floodplain, but it also wanted petitioner's property along Fanno Creek for its greenway system. The city has never said why a public greenway, as opposed to a private one, was required in the interest of flood control.

The difference to petitioner, of course, is the loss of her ability to exclude others. As we have noted, this right to exclude others is "one of the most essential sticks in the bundle of rights that are commonly characterized as property." *Kaiser Aetna,* 444 U.S., at 176. It is difficult to see why recreational visitors trampling along petitioner's floodplain easement are sufficiently related to the city's legitimate interest in reducing flooding problems along Fanno Creek, and the city has not attempted to make any individualized determination to support this part of its request. * * *

With respect to the pedestrian/bicycle pathway, we have no doubt that the city was correct in finding that the larger retail sales facility proposed by petitioner will increase traffic on the streets of the Central Business District. The city estimates that the proposed development would generate roughly 435 additional trips per day. Dedications for streets, sidewalks, and other public ways are generally reasonable exactions to avoid excessive congestion from a proposed property use. But on the record before us, the city has not met its burden of demonstrating that the additional number of vehicle and bicycle trips generated by petitioner's development reasonably relate to the city's requirement for a dedication of the pedestrian/bicycle pathway easement. The city simply found that the creation of the pathway "could offset some of the traffic demand . . . and lessen the increase in traffic congestion." * * *

No precise mathematical calculation is required, but the city must make some effort to quantify its findings in support of the dedication for the pedestrian/bicycle pathway beyond the conclusory statement that it could offset some of the traffic demand generated.

IV

Cities have long engaged in the commendable task of land use planning, made necessary by increasing urbanization, particularly in metropolitan areas such as Portland. The city's goals of reducing flooding hazards and traffic congestion, and providing for public greenways, are laudable, but there are outer limits to how this may be done. "A strong public desire to improve the public condition [will not] warrant achieving the desire by a shorter cut than the constitutional way of paying for the change." *Pennsylvania Coal,* 260 U.S., at 416.

The judgment of the Supreme Court of Oregon is reversed, and the case is remanded for further proceedings not inconsistent with this opinion.

■ JUSTICE STEVENS, with whom JUSTICE BLACKMUN and JUSTICE GINSBURG join, dissenting [omitted].

■ JUSTICE SOUTER, dissenting [omitted].

NOTES AND QUESTIONS

1.   For general commentary on the unconstitutional conditions doctrine, see Vicki Been, "Exit" as a Constraint on Land Use Exactions: Rethinking the Unconstitutional Conditions Doctrine, 91 Colum. L. Rev. 473 (1991); Mitchell N. Berman, Coercion Without Baselines: Conditions in Three Dimensions, 90 Geo. L.J. 1, 36–40 (2001); Kathleen M. Sullivan, Unconstitutional Conditions, 102 Harv. L. Rev. 1413 (1989). The doctrine has been applied with the most rigor in the First Amendment context. With respect to other constitutional rights, such as the right to trial by jury in criminal cases, the right is enforced only to the extent that courts seek to assure that waivers are "knowing and intelligent." Was the Court justified in extending a moderately robust version of the doctrine to the Takings Clause? Property is bought and sold all the time. Why not let owners in effect "sell" some property to the government in return for a benefit they value more, such as a permit to develop the property they retain? See Douglas T. Kendall & James E. Ryan, "Paying" for the Change: Using Eminent Domain to Secure Exactions and Sidestep *Nollan* and *Dolan*, 81 Va. L. Rev. 1801 (1995).

2.   In requiring that the exaction be "roughly proportionate" to the impact of the development, has the Court mandated the correct comparison in terms of what must be proportionate to what? The Court appears to understand that the value of the exaction must be proportionate to the social costs of the proposed development. In effect, the exaction is viewed as a kind of charge designed to make the owner internalize (as least partially) the social costs of the development. From a social efficiency standpoint, would it be better to compare the value of the demanded exaction in the hands of the private owner (more development or perhaps more owner autonomy) with its value in the hands of the community (more lateral beach easements, bicycle paths, wetlands, or other public goods)? One reason for requiring the government to pay just compensation when it takes property is to induce the government to make these kinds of value comparisons, taking property only when the public willingness to pay exceeds the fair market value of the property in private ownership. Should the exactions calculus try to mimic the same relevant comparison?

3.   In *Kelo v. City of New London*, supra, the Court observes that the states have adopted different approaches to the "public use" question and concludes that the federal constitutional standard should be a deferential one in order to permit the states to adopt different approaches to how the power of eminent domain is used. In *Dolan*, the Court also observes that the states have adopted different approaches to the degree of nexus required

between exactions of property and the effects of a proposed development. But now, the Court takes this variation among the states as a kind of menu of options from which to select a federal constitutional standard, which will then be imposed as a minimal requirement on all other states. Is there a justification for this difference in the assumed relationship between federal and state law with respect to these two questions about local land-use issues? Or should the Court have consistently opted in both contexts either for state variation or for minimum federal standards?

The *Koontz* Decision

The Court's most recent decision dealing with exactions is *Koontz v. St. Johns River Water Management District*, 570 U.S. 595 (2013). All Justices in the case appeared to accept the unconstitutional conditions framework established by *Nollan* and *Dolan*, and along with that framework the requirements that the exaction satisfy the "nexus" and "rough proportionality" tests. The most seriously contested issue was whether these limits apply when the exaction imposed by the government takes the form of a payment of cash as opposed to land or an easement. In *Koontz*, the government demanded the money in order to mitigate the effects of the proposed development on wetlands; it said the money would be used to enhance some wetlands on government-owned land elsewhere. Ruling in a 5–4 decision, the majority, speaking through Justice Alito, held that a demand for money to pay for such a mitigation effort is also subject to the tests of *Nollan* and *Dolan*. Justice Alito reaffirmed that taxes are not subject to challenge under the Takings Clause. Id. at 615. But he insisted that a monetary exaction is not a tax, because the exaction operates on "an identified property interest." Id. at 613, quoting Eastern Enterprises v. Apfel, 524 U.S. 498, 540 (1998) (Kennedy, J., concurring). More practically, he argued that if exactions of money were not covered by *Nollan* and *Dolan*, land use authorities could readily evade the requirements of those decisions by requiring the payment of cash, either as an alternative to demanding land or an easement or as a source of funds to acquire the desired resources.

Justice Kagan, writing for the four dissenters, acknowledged that prior decisions of the Court had held that taking a specific fund of money can be a taking. See Brown v. Legal Foundation of Washington, 538 U.S. 216 (2003) (taking by government of interest earned on client funds deposited with attorneys); Webb's Fabulous Pharmacies, Inc. v. Beckwith, 449 U.S. 155 (1980) (taking by government of interest earned on funds deposited in court in an interpleader action). But five Justices in *Eastern Enterprises* had concluded that the imposition of a general liability cannot be regarded as a taking. And in *Koontz*, the requirement to pay, although triggered by a request to develop a particular parcel of land, could be paid from any source—"a checking account, shares of stock, a wealthy uncle." Koontz, at 625. If a general liability does not create a per se taking, she argued, then it is hard to see how the unconstitutional conditions framework adopted in *Dolan* applies. Justice Kagan also complained that the majority had provided inadequate guidance for distinguishing monetary exactions from either taxes or development fees, and that this would be a source of significant confusion on the part of land use agencies and lower courts going forward.

5. ACCESS RIGHTS

Cedar Point Nursery v. Hassid

Supreme Court of the United States, 2021.
141 S.Ct 2063.

■ CHIEF JUSTICE ROBERTS delivered the opinion of the Court. A California regulation grants labor organizations a "right to take access" to an agricultural employer's property in order to solicit support for unionization. Cal. Code Regs., tit. 8, § 20900(e)(1)(C) (2020). Agricultural employers must allow union organizers onto their property for up to three hours per day, 120 days per year. The question presented is whether the access regulation constitutes a *per se* physical taking under the Fifth and Fourteenth Amendments.

I

The California Agricultural Labor Relations Act of 1975 gives agricultural employees a right to self-organization and makes it an unfair labor practice for employers to interfere with that right. Cal. Lab. Code Ann. §§ 1152, 1153(a) (West 2020). The state Agricultural Labor Relations Board has promulgated a regulation providing, in its current form, that the self-organization rights of employees include "the right of access by union organizers to the premises of an agricultural employer for the purpose of meeting and talking with employees and soliciting their support." Cal. Code Regs., tit. 8, § 20900(e). Under the regulation, a labor organization may "take access" to an agricultural employer's property for up to four 30-day periods in one calendar year. §§ 20900(e)(1)(A), (B). In order to take access, a labor organization must file a written notice with the Board and serve a copy on the employer. § 20900(e)(1)(B). Two organizers per work crew (plus one additional organizer for every 15 workers over 30 workers in a crew) may enter the employer's property for up to one hour before work, one hour during the lunch break, and one hour after work. §§ 20900(e)(3)(A)–(B), (4)(A). Organizers may not engage in disruptive conduct, but are otherwise free to meet and talk with employees as they wish. §§ 20900(e)(3)(A), (4)(C). Interference with organizers' right of access may constitute an unfair labor practice, § 20900(e)(5)(C), which can result in sanctions against the employer, see, e.g., Harry Carian Sales v. Agricultural Labor Relations Bd., 703 P.2d 27, 42 (Cal. 1985).

Cedar Point Nursery is a strawberry grower in northern California. It employs over 400 seasonal workers and around 100 full-time workers, none of whom live on the property. According to the complaint, in October

2015, at five o'clock one morning, members of the United Farm Workers entered Cedar Point's property without prior notice. The organizers moved to the nursery's trim shed, where hundreds of workers were preparing strawberry plants. Calling through bullhorns, the organizers disturbed operations, causing some workers to join the organizers in a protest and others to leave the worksite altogether. Cedar Point filed a charge against the union for taking access without giving notice. The union responded with a charge of its own, alleging that Cedar Point had committed an unfair labor practice.

Fowler Packing Company is a Fresno-based grower and shipper of table grapes and citrus. It has 1,800 to 2,500 employees in its field operations and around 500 in its packing facility. As with Cedar Point, none of Fowler's workers live on the premises. In July 2015, organizers from the United Farm Workers attempted to take access to Fowler's property, but the company blocked them from entering. The union filed an unfair labor practice charge against Fowler, which it later withdrew.

Believing that the union would likely attempt to enter their property again in the near future, the growers filed suit in Federal District Court against several Board members in their official capacity. The growers argued that the access regulation effected an unconstitutional *per se* physical taking under the Fifth and Fourteenth Amendments by appropriating without compensation an easement for union organizers to enter their property. They requested declaratory and injunctive relief prohibiting the Board from enforcing the regulation against them.

The District Court denied the growers' motion for a preliminary injunction and granted the Board's motion to dismiss. The court rejected the growers' argument that the access regulation constituted a *per se* physical taking, reasoning that it did not "allow the public to access their property in a permanent and continuous manner for whatever reason." In the court's view, the regulation was instead subject to evaluation under the multifactor balancing test of *Penn Central Transportation Co. v. New York City*, 438 U.S. 104 (1978), which the growers had made no attempt to satisfy.

A divided panel of the Court of Appeals for the Ninth Circuit affirmed. * * *

The Ninth Circuit denied rehearing en banc. Judge Ikuta dissented, joined by seven other judges. She reasoned that the access regulation appropriated from the growers a traditional form of private property—an easement in gross—and transferred that property to union organizers. The appropriation of such an easement, she concluded, constituted a *per se* physical taking under the precedents of this Court.

We granted certiorari.

II

A

* * * When the government physically acquires private property for a public use, the Takings Clause imposes a clear and categorical obligation to provide the owner with just compensation. Tahoe-Sierra Preservation Council, Inc. v. Tahoe Regional Planning Agency, 535 U.S. 302, 321 (2002). The Court's physical takings jurisprudence is "as old as the Republic." *Id.*, at 322. The government commits a physical taking when it uses its power of eminent domain to formally condemn property. See United States v. General Motors Corp., 323 U.S. 373, 374–375 (1945); United States ex rel. TVA v. Powelson, 319 U.S. 266, 270–271 (1943). The same is true when the government physically takes possession of property without acquiring title to it. See United States v. Pewee Coal Co., 341 U.S. 114, 115–117 (1951) (plurality opinion). And the government likewise effects a physical taking when it occupies property—say, by recurring flooding as a result of building a dam. See United States v. Cress, 243 U.S. 316, 327–328 (1917). These sorts of physical appropriations constitute the "clearest sort of taking," Palazzolo v. Rhode Island, 533 U.S. 606, 617 (2001), and we assess them using a simple, *per se* rule: The government must pay for what it takes. See Tahoe-Sierra, 535 U.S. at 322.

When the government, rather than appropriating private property for itself or a third party, instead imposes regulations that restrict an owner's ability to use his own property, a different standard applies. *Id.*, at 321–322. Our jurisprudence governing such use restrictions has developed more recently. Before the 20th century, the Takings Clause was understood to be limited to physical appropriations of property. See Horne v. Department of Agriculture, 576 U. S. 350, 360 (2015); Legal Tender Cases, 12 Wall. 457, 551 (1871). In Pennsylvania Coal Co. v. Mahon, 260 U.S. 393 (1922), however, the Court established the proposition that "while property may be regulated to a certain extent, if regulation goes too far it will be recognized as a taking." *Id.*, at 415. This framework now applies to use restrictions as varied as zoning ordinances, *Village of Euclid v. Ambler Realty Co.*, 272 U.S. 365, 387–388 (1926), orders barring the mining of gold, *United States v. Central Eureka Mining Co.*, 357 U.S. 155, 168 (1958), and regulations prohibiting the sale of eagle feathers, Andrus v. Allard, 444 U.S. 51, 65–66 (1979). To determine whether a use restriction effects a taking, this Court has generally applied the flexible test developed in *Penn Central*, balancing factors such as the economic impact of the regulation, its interference with reasonable investment-backed expectations, and the character of the government action. 438 U.S. at 124.

Our cases have often described use restrictions that go "too far" as "regulatory takings." See, e.g., Horne, 576 U.S. at 360; Yee v. Escondido, 503 U.S. 519, 527 (1992). But that label can mislead. Government action that physically appropriates property is no less a physical taking because it arises from a regulation. That explains why we held that an administrative reserve requirement compelling raisin growers to physically set aside a percentage of their crop for the government constituted a physical rather than a regulatory taking. Horne, 576 U.S. at 361. The essential question is not, as the Ninth Circuit seemed to think, whether the government action at issue comes garbed as a regulation (or statute, or ordinance, or miscellaneous decree). It is whether the government has physically taken property for itself or someone else—by whatever means—or has instead restricted a property owner's ability to use his own property. See Tahoe-Sierra, 535 U.S. at 321–323. Whenever a regulation results in a physical appropriation of property, a *per se* taking has occurred, and *Penn Central* has no place.

B

The access regulation appropriates a right to invade the growers' property and therefore constitutes a *per se* physical taking. The regulation grants union organizers a right to physically enter and occupy the growers' land for three hours per day, 120 days per year. Rather than restraining the growers' use of their own property, the regulation appropriates for the enjoyment of third parties the owners' right to exclude.

The right to exclude is "one of the most treasured" rights of property ownership. Loretto v. Teleprompter Manhattan CATV Corp., 458 U.S. 419, 435 (1982). According to Blackstone, the very idea of property entails "that sole and despotic dominion which one man claims and exercises over the external things of the world, in total exclusion of the right of any other individual in the universe." 2 W. Blackstone, Commentaries on the Laws of England 2 (1766). In less exuberant terms, we have stated that the right to exclude is "universally held to be a fundamental element of the property right," and is "one of the most essential sticks in the bundle of rights that are commonly characterized as property." Kaiser Aetna v. United States, 444 U.S. 164, 176, 179–180 (1979); see Dolan v. City of Tigard, 512 U.S. 374, 384, 393 (1994); Nollan v. California Coastal Comm'n, 483 U.S. 825, 831 (1987); see also Merrill, Property and the Right to Exclude, 77 Neb. L. Rev. 730 (1998) (calling the right to exclude the "*sine qua non*" of property).

Given the central importance to property ownership of the right to exclude, it comes as little surprise that the Court has long treated government-authorized physical invasions as takings requiring just compensation. The Court has often described the property interest taken as a servitude or an easement.

For example, in *United States v. Causby* we held that the invasion of private property by overflights effected a taking. 328 U.S. 256 (1946). The government frequently flew military aircraft low over the Causby farm, grazing the treetops and terrorizing the poultry. Id., at 259. The Court observed that ownership of the land extended to airspace that low, and that "invasions of it are in the same category as invasions of the surface."

Id., at 265. Because the damages suffered by the Causbys "were the product of a direct invasion of [their] domain," we held that "a servitude has been imposed upon the land." Id., at 265–266, 267; see also Portsmouth Harbor Land & Hotel Co. v. United States, 260 U.S. 327, 330 (1922) (government assertion of a right to fire coastal defense guns across private property would constitute a taking). * * *

In *Loretto* v. *Teleprompter Manhattan CATV Corp.*, we made clear that a permanent physical occupation constitutes a *per se* taking regardless whether it results in only a trivial economic loss. * * *

We reiterated that the appropriation of an easement constitutes a physical taking in *Nollan* v. *California Coastal Commission.* * * *

More recently, in *Horne* v. *Department of Agriculture*, we observed that "people still do not expect their property, real or personal, to be actually occupied or taken away." 576 U.S. at 361. The physical appropriation by the government of the raisins in that case was a *per se* taking, even if a regulatory limit with the same economic impact would not have been. Id., at 362. "The Constitution," we explained, "is concerned with means as well as ends." 576 U.S. at 362.

The upshot of this line of precedent is that government-authorized invasions of property—whether by plane, boat, cable, or beachcomber—are physical takings requiring just compensation. As in those cases, the government here has appropriated a right of access to the growers' property, allowing union organizers to traverse it at will for three hours a day, 120 days a year. The regulation appropriates a right to physically invade the growers' property—to literally "take access," as the regulation provides. It is therefore a *per se* physical taking under our precedents. Accordingly, the growers' complaint states a claim for an uncompensated taking in violation of the Fifth and Fourteenth Amendments.

C

The Ninth Circuit saw matters differently, as do the Board and the dissent. In the decision below, the Ninth Circuit took the view that the access regulation did not qualify as a *per se* taking because, although it grants a right to physically invade the growers' property, it does not allow for permanent and continuous access "24 hours a day, 365 days a year." 923 F.3d at 532 (citing *Nollan*, 483 U.S. at 832). * * *

To begin with, we have held that a physical appropriation is a taking whether it is permanent or temporary. Our cases establish that "compensation is mandated when a leasehold is taken and the government occupies property for its own purposes, even though that use is temporary." Tahoe-Sierra, 535 U.S. at 322 (citing General Motors Corp., 323 U.S. 373; United States v. Petty Motor Co., 327 U.S. 372 (1946)). The duration of an appropriation—just like the size of an appropriation, see Loretto, 458 U.S. at 436–437—bears only on the amount of compensation. See United States v. Dow, 357 U.S. 17, 26 (1958). For example, after finding a taking by physical invasion, the

Court in *Causby* remanded the case to the lower court to determine "whether the easement taken was temporary or permanent," in order to fix the compensation due. 328 U.S. at 267–268.

To be sure, *Loretto* emphasized the heightened concerns associated with "[t]he permanence and absolute exclusivity of a physical occupation" in contrast to "temporary limitations on the right to exclude," and stated that "[n]ot every physical *invasion* is a taking." 458 U.S. at 435, n. 12; see also id., at 432–435. The latter point is well taken, as we will explain. But *Nollan* clarified that appropriation of a right to physically invade property may constitute a taking "even though no particular individual is permitted to station himself permanently upon the premises." 483 U.S. at 832.

Next, we have recognized that physical invasions constitute takings even if they are intermittent as opposed to continuous. *Causby* held that overflights of private property effected a taking, even though they occurred on only 4% of takeoffs and 7% of landings at the nearby airport. 328 U.S. at 259. And while *Nollan* happened to involve a legally continuous right of access, we have no doubt that the Court would have reached the same conclusion if the easement demanded by the Commission had lasted for only 364 days per year. After all, the easement was hardly continuous as a practical matter. As Justice Brennan observed in dissent, given the shifting tides, "public passage for a portion of the year would either be impossible or would not occur on [the Nollans'] property." 483 U.S. at 854. What matters is not that the easement notionally ran round the clock, but that the government had taken a right to physically invade the Nollans' land. And when the government physically takes an interest in property, it must pay for the right to do so. See Horne, 576 U.S. at 357–358; Tahoe-Sierra, 535 U.S. at 322. The fact that a right to take access is exercised only from time to time does not make it any less a physical taking. * * *

[The Board] takes issue with the growers' premise that the access regulation appropriates an easement. In the Board's estimation, the regulation does not exact a true easement in gross under California law because the access right may not be transferred, does not burden any particular parcel of property, and may not be recorded. This, the Board says, reinforces its conclusion that the regulation does not take a constitutionally protected property interest from the growers. The dissent agrees, suggesting that the access right cannot effect a *per se* taking because it does not require the growers to grant the union organizers an easement as defined by state property law.

These arguments misconstrue our physical takings doctrine. As a general matter, it is true that the property rights protected by the Takings Clause are creatures of state law. See Phillips v. Washington Legal Foundation, 524 U.S. 156, 164 (1998); Lucas v. South Carolina Coastal Council, 505 U.S. 1003, 1030 (1992). But no one disputes that, without the access regulation, the growers would have had the right under California law to exclude union organizers from their property. See *Allred v. Harris*, 18 Cal.Rptr.2d 530, 533 (Cal. Ct. App. 1993). And no one disputes that the access regulation took that right from them. The Board cannot absolve itself of takings liability by appropriating the growers' right to exclude in a form that is a slight mismatch from state easement law. Under the Constitution, property rights "cannot be so easily manipulated." *Horne*, 576 U.S. at 365 (internal quotation marks omitted); see also *Webb's Fabulous Pharmacies, Inc. v. Beckwith*, 449 U.S. 155, 164 (1980) ("a State, by *ipse dixit*, may not transform private property into public property without compensation").

Our decisions consistently reflect this intuitive approach. We have recognized that the government can commit a physical taking either by appropriating property through a condemnation proceeding or by simply "enter[ing] into physical possession of property without authority of a court order." *Dow*, 357 U.S. at 21; see also *United States v. Clarke*, 445 U.S. 253, 256–257, and n. 3 (1980). In the latter situation, the government's intrusion does not vest it with a property interest recognized by state law, such as a fee simple or a leasehold. See *Dow*, 357 U.S. at 21. Yet we recognize a physical taking all the same. See *id.*, at 22. Any other result would allow the government to appropriate private property without just compensation so long as it avoids formal condemnation. We have never tolerated that outcome. See *Pewee Coal Co.*, 341 U.S. at 116–117. For much the same reason, in *Portsmouth*, *Causby*, and *Loretto* we never paused to consider whether the physical invasions at issue vested the intruders with formal easements according to the nuances of state property law (nor do we see how they could have). Instead, we followed our traditional rule: Because the government appropriated a right to invade, compensation was due. That same test governs here.

The Board and the dissent further contend that our decision in *PruneYard Shopping Center v. Robins*, 447 U.S. 74 (1980), establishes that the access regulation cannot qualify as a *per se* taking. * * *

* * * We disagree. Unlike the growers' properties, the PruneYard was open to the public, welcoming some 25,000 patrons a day. 447 U.S. at 77–78. Limitations on how a business generally open to the public may treat individuals on the premises are readily distinguishable from regulations granting a right to invade property closed to the public. See *Horne*, 576 U.S. at 364 (distinguishing *PruneYard* as involving "an already publicly accessible" business); *Nollan*, 483 U.S. at 832, n. 1 (same).

The Board also relies on our decision in *NLRB v. Babcock & Wilcox Co.*, [351 U.S. 105 (1956)]. But that reliance is misplaced. In *Babcock*, the National Labor Relations Board found that several employers had committed unfair labor practices under the National Labor Relations Act by preventing union organizers from distributing literature on company property. 351 U.S. at 109. We held that the statute did not require employers to allow organizers onto their property, at least outside the unusual circumstance where their employees were otherwise "beyond the reach of reasonable union efforts to communicate with them." Id., at 113; see also [Lechmere, Inc. v. NLRB, 502 U.S. 527, 540 (1992)] (employees residing off company property are presumptively not beyond the reach of the union's message). The Board contends that *Babcock*'s approach of balancing property and organizational rights should guide our analysis here. See Loretto, 458 U.S. at 434, n. 11 (discussing *Babcock* principle). But *Babcock* did not involve a takings claim. Whatever specific takings issues may be presented by the highly contingent access right we recognized under the NLRA, California's access regulation effects a *per se* physical taking under our precedents. See Tahoe-Sierra, 535 U.S. at 322.

D

In its thoughtful opinion, the dissent advances a distinctive view of property rights. The dissent encourages readers to consider the issue "through the lens of ordinary English," and contends that, so viewed, the "regulation does not *appropriate* anything." Rather, the access regulation merely "*regulates* . . . the owners' right to exclude," so it must be assessed "under *Penn Central*'s fact-intensive test." "A right to enter my woods only on certain occasions," the dissent elaborates, "is a taking only if the regulation allowing it goes 'too far.'" The dissent contends that our decisions in *Causby*, *Portsmouth*, and *Kaiser Aetna* applied just such a flexible approach, under which the Court "balanced several factors" to determine whether the physical invasions at issue effected a taking. According to the dissent, this kind of latitude toward temporary invasions is a practical necessity for governing in our complex modern world.

With respect, our own understanding of the role of property rights in our constitutional order is markedly different. In "ordinary English" "appropriation" means "*taking* as one's own," 1 Oxford English Dictionary 587 (2d ed. 1989) (emphasis added), and the regulation expressly grants to labor organizers the "right to *take* access." We cannot agree that the right to exclude is an empty formality, subject to modification at the government's pleasure. On the contrary, it is a "fundamental element of the property right," Kaiser Aetna, 444 U.S. at 179–180, that cannot be balanced away. Our cases establish that appropriations of a right to invade are *per se* physical takings, not use restrictions subject to *Penn Central*[.] * * * With regard to the complexities of modern society, we think they only reinforce the importance of safeguarding the basic property rights that help preserve individual liberty, as the Founders explained.

In the end, the dissent's permissive approach to property rights hearkens back to views expressed (in dissent) for decades. See, e.g., Nollan, 483 U.S. at 864 (Brennan, J., dissenting) ("[The Court's] reasoning is hardly suited to the complex reality of natural resource protection in the 20th century."); Loretto, 458 U.S. at 455 (Blackmun, J., dissenting) ("[T]oday's decision ... represents an archaic judicial response to a modern social problem."); Causby, 328 U.S. at 275 (Black, J., dissenting) ("Today's opinion is, I fear, an opening wedge for an unwarranted judicial interference with the power of Congress to develop solutions for new and vital national problems."). As for today's considered dissent, it concludes with "Better the devil we know ...," but its objections, to borrow from then-Justice Rehnquist's invocation of Wordsworth, "bear[ ] the sound of 'Old, unhappy, far-off things, and battles long ago,' " Kaiser Aetna, 444 U.S. at 177.

III

The Board, seconded by the dissent, warns that treating the access regulation as a *per se* physical taking will endanger a host of state and federal government activities involving entry onto private property. That fear is unfounded.

First, our holding does nothing to efface the distinction between trespass and takings. Isolated physical invasions, not undertaken pursuant to a granted right of access, are properly assessed as individual torts rather than appropriations of a property right. This basic distinction is firmly grounded in our precedent. See Portsmouth, 260 U.S. at 329–330 ("[W]hile a single act may not be enough, a continuance of them in sufficient number and for a sufficient time may prove [the intent to take property]. Every successive trespass adds to the force of the evidence."); 1 P. Nichols, The Law of Eminent Domain § 112, p. 311 (1917) ("[A] mere occasional trespass would not constitute a taking."). And lower courts have had little trouble applying it. See, e.g., Hendler v. United States, 952 F.2d 1364, 1377 (Fed. Cir. 1991) (identifying a "truckdriver parking on someone's vacant land to eat lunch" as an example of a mere trespass).

The distinction between trespass and takings accounts for our treatment of temporary government-induced flooding in *Arkansas Game and Fish Commission v. United States*, 568 U.S. 23 (2012). There we held, "simply and only," that such flooding "gains no automatic exemption from Takings Clause inspection." Id., at 38. Because this type of flooding can present complex questions of causation, we instructed lower courts evaluating takings claims based on temporary flooding to consider a range of factors including the duration of the invasion, the degree to which it was intended or foreseeable, and the character of the land at issue. Id., at 38–39. Applying those factors on remand, the Federal Circuit concluded that the government had effected a taking in the form of a temporary flowage easement. Arkansas Game and Fish Comm'n v. United States, 736 F.3d 1364, 1372 (Fed. Cir. 2013). Our approach in *Arkansas Game and Fish Commission* reflects nothing more than an application of the traditional trespass-versus-takings distinction to the unique considerations that accompany temporary flooding.

Second, many government-authorized physical invasions will not amount to takings because they are consistent with longstanding background restrictions on property rights. As we explained in *Lucas* v. *South Carolina Coastal Council*, the government does not take a property interest when it merely asserts a "pre-existing limitation upon the land owner's title." 505 U.S. at 1028–1029. For example, the government owes a landowner no compensation for requiring him to abate a nuisance on his property, because he never had a right to engage in the nuisance in the first place. See id., at 1029–1030.

These background limitations also encompass traditional common law privileges to access private property. One such privilege allowed individuals to enter property in the event of public or private necessity. See Restatement (Second) of Torts § 196 (1964) (entry to avert an imminent public disaster); § 197 (entry to avert serious harm to a person, land, or chattels); cf. Lucas, 505 U.S. at 1029, n. 16. The common law also recognized a privilege to enter property to effect an arrest or enforce the criminal law under certain circumstances. Restatement (Second) of Torts §§ 204–205. Because a property owner traditionally had no right to exclude an official engaged in a reasonable search, see, e.g., Sandford v. Nichols, 13 Mass. 286, 288 (1816), government searches that are consistent with the Fourth Amendment and state law cannot be said to take any property right from landowners. See generally Camara v. Municipal Court of City and County of San Francisco, 387 U.S. 523, 538 (1967).

Third, the government may require property owners to cede a right of access as a condition of receiving certain benefits, without causing a taking. In *Nollan*, we held that "a permit condition that serves the same legitimate police-power purpose as a refusal to issue the permit should not be found to be a taking if the refusal to issue the permit would not constitute a taking." 483 U.S. at 836. The inquiry, we later explained, is whether the permit condition bears an "essential nexus" and "rough proportionality" to the impact of the proposed use of the property. Dolan, 512 U.S. at 386, 391; see also Koontz v. St. Johns River Water Management Dist., 570 U.S. 595, 599 (2013).

Under this framework, government health and safety inspection regimes will generally not constitute takings. See, *e.g.*, Ruckelshaus v. Monsanto Co., 467 U.S. 986, 1007 (1984). When the government conditions the grant of a benefit such as a permit, license, or registration on allowing access for reasonable health and safety inspections, both the nexus and rough proportionality requirements of the constitutional conditions framework should not be difficult to satisfy. See, e.g., 7 U.S.C. § 136g(a)(1)(A) (pesticide inspections); 16 U.S.C. § 823b(a) (hydroelectric project investigations); 21 U.S.C. § 374(a)(1) (pharmaceutical inspections); 42 U.S.C. § 2201(*o*) (nuclear material inspections).

None of these considerations undermine our determination that the access regulation here gives rise to a *per se* physical taking. Unlike a mere trespass, the regulation grants a formal entitlement to physically invade the growers' land. Unlike a law enforcement search, no traditional background principle of property law requires the growers to admit union organizers onto their premises. And unlike standard health and safety inspections, the access regulation is not germane to any benefit provided to agricultural employers or any risk posed to the public. See Horne, 576 U.S. at 366 ("basic and familiar uses of property" are not a special benefit that "the Government may hold hostage, to be ransomed by the waiver of constitutional protection"). The access regulation amounts to simple appropriation of private property.

* * *

The access regulation grants labor organizations a right to invade the growers' property. It therefore constitutes a *per se* physical taking.

The judgment of the United States Court of Appeals for the Ninth Circuit is reversed, and the case is remanded for further proceedings consistent with this opinion.

■ JUSTICE KAVANAUGH, concurring.

I join the Court's opinion, which carefully adheres to constitutional text, history, and precedent. I write separately to explain that, in my view, the Court's precedent in *NLRB v. Babcock & Wilcox Co.*, 351 U.S. 105 (1956), also strongly supports today's decision.

In *Babcock*, the National Labor Relations Board argued that the National Labor Relations Act afforded union organizers a right to enter company property to communicate with employees. Several employers responded that the Board's reading of the Act would infringe their Fifth Amendment property rights. The employers contended that Congress, "even if it could constitutionally do so, has at no time shown any intention of destroying property rights secured by the *Fifth Amendment*, in protecting employees' rights of collective bargaining under the Act. Until Congress should evidence such intention by specific legislative language, our courts should not construe the Act on such dangerous constitutional grounds." Brief for Respondent in NLRB v. Babcock & Wilcox Co., O. T. 1955, No. 250, pp. 18–19.

This Court agreed with the employers' argument that the Act should be interpreted to avoid unconstitutionality. The Court reasoned that "the National Government" via the Constitution "preserves property rights," including "the right to exclude from property." Babcock, 351 U.S. at 112. Against the backdrop of the Constitution's strong protection of property rights, the Court interpreted the Act to afford access to union organizers only when "needed," ibid.—that is, when the employees live on company property and union organizers have no other reasonable means of communicating with the employees, id., at 113. See also Lechmere, Inc. v. NLRB, 502 U.S. 527, 540–541 (1992). As I read it, *Babcock* recognized that employers have a basic Fifth Amendment right to exclude from their private property, subject to a "necessity" exception similar to that noted by the Court today.

Babcock strongly supports the growers' position in today's case because the California union access regulation intrudes on the growers' property rights far more than *Babcock* allows. When this same California union access regulation was challenged on constitutional grounds before the California Supreme Court in 1976, that court upheld the regulation by a 4-to-3 vote. Agricultural Labor Rel. Bd. v. Superior Ct. of Tulare Cty., 546 P.2d 687. Justice William Clark wrote the dissent. Justice Clark stressed that "property rights are fundamental." Id., at, 546 P.2d at 712, n. 4. And he concluded that the California union access regulation "violates the rule" of *Babcock* and thus "violates the constitutional provisions protecting private property." 546 P.2d at 713. In my view, Justice Clark had it exactly right.

With those comments, I join the Court's opinion in full.

■ JUSTICE BREYER, with whom JUSTICE SOTOMAYOR and JUSTICE KAGAN join, dissenting. * * *

Does the regulation *physically appropriate* the employers' property? If so, there is no need to look further; the Government must pay the employers "just compensation." U.S. Const., Amdt. 5; see Arkansas Game and Fish Comm'n v. United States, 568 U.S. 23, 31 (2012) (" '[W]hen the government physically takes possession of an interest in property for some public purpose, it has a categorical duty to compensate the former owner' "). Or does the regulation simply *regulate* the employers' property rights? If so, then there is every need to look further; the government need pay the employers "just compensation" only if the regulation "goes too far." * * *

The Court holds that the provision's "access to organizers" requirement amounts to a physical appropriation of property. In its view, virtually every government-authorized invasion is an "appropriation." But this regulation does not "appropriate" anything; it regulates the employers' right to exclude others. At the same time, our prior cases make clear that the regulation before us allows only a *temporary* invasion of a landowner's property and that this kind of temporary invasion amounts to a taking only if it goes "too far." See, e.g., Loretto v. Teleprompter Manhattan CATV Corp., 458 U.S. 419, 434 (1982). In my view, the majority's conclusion threatens to make many ordinary forms of regulation unusually complex or impractical. And though the majority attempts to create exceptions to narrow its rule, the law's need for feasibility suggests that the majority's framework is wrong. With respect, I dissent from the majority's conclusion that the regulation is a *per se* taking.

I

* * *

A

Initially it may help to look at the legal problem—a problem of characterization—through the lens of ordinary English. The word "regulation" rather than "appropriation" fits this provision in both label and substance. It is contained in Title 8 of the California Code of Regulations. It was adopted by a state regulatory board, namely, the California Agricultural Labor Relations Board, in 1975. It is embedded in a set of related detailed regulations that describe and limit the access at issue. In addition to the hours of access just mentioned, it provides that union representatives can enter the property only "for the purpose of meeting and talking with employees and soliciting their support"; they have access only to "areas in which employees congregate before and after working" or "at such location or locations as the employees eat their lunch"; and they cannot engage in "conduct disruptive of the employer's property or agricultural operations, including injury to crops or machinery or interference with the process of boarding buses." From the employers' perspective, it restricts when and where they can exclude others from their property.

At the same time, the provision only awkwardly fits the terms "physical taking" and "physical appropriation." The "access" that it grants union organizers does not amount to any traditional property interest in land. It does not, for example, take from the employers, or provide to the organizers, any freehold estate (e.g., a fee simple, fee tail, or life estate); any concurrent estate (e.g., a joint tenancy, tenancy in common, or tenancy by the entirety); or any leasehold estate (*e.g.*, a term of years, periodic tenancy, or tenancy at will). Nor (as all now agree) does it provide the organizers with a formal easement or access resembling an easement, as the employers once argued, since it does not burden any particular parcel of property. Compare Pet. for Cert. i (asking the Court to address "whether the uncompensated appropriation of an easement that is limited in time effects a *per se* physical taking under the Fifth Amendment"), with Reply Brief 8 ("[T]he access required here does not bear *all* the hallmarks of an easement").

The majority concludes that the regulation nonetheless amounts to a physical taking of property because, the majority says, it "appropriates" a "right to invade" or a "right to exclude" others. It thereby likens this case to cases in which we have held that appropriation of property rights amounts to a physical *per se* taking.

It is important to understand, however, that, technically speaking, the majority is wrong. The regulation does not *appropriate* anything. It does not take from the owners a right to invade (whatever that might mean). It does not give the union organizations the right to exclude anyone. It does not give the government the right to exclude anyone.

What does it do? It gives union organizers the right temporarily to invade a portion of the property owners' land. It thereby limits the landowners' right to exclude certain others. The regulation *regulates* (but does not *appropriate*) the owners' right to exclude.

Why is it important to understand this technical point? Because only then can we understand the issue before us. That issue is whether a regulation that *temporarily* limits an owner's right to exclude others from property *automatically* amounts to a Fifth Amendment taking. Under our cases, it does not.

B

Our cases draw a distinction between regulations that provide permanent rights of access and regulations that provide nonpermanent rights of access. They either state or hold that the first type of regulation is a taking *per se,* but the second kind is a taking only if it goes "too far." And they make this distinction for good reason.

Consider the Court's reasoning in an important case in which the Court found a *per se* taking. In *Loretto,* the Court considered the status of a New York law that required landlords to permit cable television companies to install cable facilities on their property. 458 U.S. at 421. We held that the installation amounted to a permanent physical occupation of the property and hence to a *per se* taking. In reaching this holding we specifically said that "[n]ot every physical invasion is a taking." Id., at 435, n. 12 (emphasis deleted). We explained that the "permanence and absolute exclusivity of a physical occupation distinguish it from temporary limitations on the right to exclude." Loretto, 458 U.S. at 435, n. 12. And we provided an example of a federal statute that did *not* effect a *per se* taking—an example almost identical to the regulation before us. That statute provided " 'access . . . limited to (i) union organizers; (ii) prescribed non-working areas of the employer's premises; and (iii) the duration of the organization activity.' " Id., at 434, n. 11 (quoting Central Hardware Co. v. NLRB, 407 U.S. 539, 545 (1972)).

We also explained why permanent physical occupations are distinct from temporary limitations on the right to exclude. We said that, when the government permanently occupies property, it "does not simply take a single 'strand' from the 'bundle' of property rights: it chops through the bundle, taking a slice of every strand," "effectively destroy[ing]" "the rights 'to possess, use and dispose of it.' " Loretto, 458 U.S. at 435. We added that the property owner "ha[d] no right to possess the occupied space himself, and also ha[d] no power to exclude the occupier from possession and use of the space." Ibid. The requirement "forever denie[d] the owner any power to control the use of the property" or make any "nonpossessory use" of it. Id., at 436. It would "ordinarily empty the right" to sell or transfer the occupied space "of any value, since the purchaser w[ould] also be unable to make any use of the property." Ibid. The owner could not "exercise control" over the equipment's installation, and so could not "minimize [its] physical, esthetic, and other effects." Id., at 441,

n. 19. Thus, we concluded, a permanent physical occupation "is perhaps the most serious form of invasion of an owner's property interests." Id., at 435. * * *

As these cases have used the terms, the regulation here at issue provides access that is "temporary," not "permanent." Unlike the regulation in *Loretto*, it does not place a "fixed structure on land or real property." 458 U.S. at 437. The employers are not "forever denie[d]" "any power to control the use" of any particular portion of their property. *Id.*, at 436. And it does not totally reduce the value of any section of the property. *Ibid.* Unlike in *Nollan*, the public cannot walk over the land whenever it wishes; rather a subset of the public may enter a portion of the land three hours per day for four months per year (about 4% of the time). At bottom, the regulation here, unlike the regulations in *Loretto* and *Nollan*, is not "functionally equivalent to the classic taking in which government directly appropriates private property or ousts the owner from his domain." Lingle, 544 U.S. at 539.

At the same time, *PruneYard*'s holding that the taking was "temporary" (and hence not a *per se* taking) fits this case almost perfectly. There the regulation gave nonowners the right to enter privately owned property for the purpose of speaking generally to others, about matters of their choice, subject to reasonable time, place, and manner restrictions. 447 U.S. at 83. The regulation before us grants a far smaller group of people the right to enter landowners' property for far more limited times in order to speak about a specific subject. Employers have more power to control entry by setting work hours, lunch hours, and places of gathering. On the other hand, as the majority notes, the shopping center in *PruneYard* was open to the public generally. All these factors, however, are the stuff of which regulatory-balancing, not absolute *per se*, rules are made.

Our cases have recognized, as the majority says, that the right to exclude is a " 'fundamental element of the property right.' " For that reason, "[a] 'taking' may *more readily* be found when the interference with property can be characterized as a physical invasion by government." *Penn Central*, 438 U.S. at 124 (emphasis added); see also *Loretto*, 458 U.S. at 426 ("[W]e have long considered a physical intrusion by government to be a property restriction of an unusually serious character for purposes of the Takings Clause"). But a taking is not inevitably found just because the interference with property can be characterized as a physical invasion by the government, or, in other words, when it affects the right to exclude.

The majority refers to other cases. But those cases do not help its cause. That is because the Court in those cases (some of which preceded *Penn Central* and others of which I have discussed above) did not apply a "*per se* takings" approach. In *United States v. Causby*, 328 U.S. 256, 259 (1946), for example, the question was whether government flights over a piece of land constituted a taking. The flights amounted to 4% of the takeoffs, and 7% of the landings, at a nearby airport. See ibid. But the planes flew "in considerable numbers and rather close together." Ibid. And the flights were "so low and so frequent as to be a direct and immediate interference with the enjoyment and use of the land." Id., at 266. Taken together, those flights "destr[oyed] the use of the property as a commercial chicken farm." Id., at 259. Based in part on that economic damage, the Court found that the rule allowing these overflights went "too far." See id., at 266 (" '[I]t is the character of the invasion, not the amount of damage resulting from it, *so long as the damage is substantial*, that determines the question whether it is a taking' " (emphasis added)).

In *Portsmouth Harbor Land & Hotel Co. v. United States*, 260 U.S. 327, 329 (1922), the Court held that the Government's firing of guns across private property would be a taking only if the shots were sufficiently frequent to establish an "intent to fire across the claimants' land at will." The frequency of the projectiles itself mattered less than whether the Government acted " 'with the purpose and effect of subordinating the strip of land . . . to the right and privilege of the Government to fire projectiles directly across it for the purpose of practice or otherwise, *whenever it saw fit*, in time of peace, with the result of depriving the owner of its profitable use.' " *Ibid.* (emphasis added). Again, the Court balanced several factors—permanence, severity, and economic impact—rather than treating the mere fact of entry as dispositive. * * *

If there is ambiguity in these cases, it concerns whether the Court considered the occupation at issue to be *temporary* (requiring *Penn Central*'s "too far" analysis) or *permanent* (automatically requiring compensation). Nothing in them suggests the majority's view, namely, that compensation is automatically required for a *temporary* right of access. Nor does anything in them support the distinction that the majority gleans between "trespass" and "takings."

The majority also refers to *Nollan* as support for its claim that the "fact that a right to take access is exercised only from time to time does not make it any less a physical taking." True. Here, however, unlike in *Nollan,* the right taken is not a right to have access to the property at any time (which access different persons "exercis[e] . . . from time to time"). Rather here we have a right that does not allow access at any time. It allows access only from "time to time." And that makes all the difference. A right to enter my woods whenever you wish is a right to use that property permanently, even if you exercise that right only on occasion. A right to enter my woods only on certain occasions is not a right to use the woods permanently. In the first case one might reasonably use the term *per se* taking. It is as if my woods are yours. In the second case it is a taking only if the regulation allowing it goes "too far," considering the factors we have laid out in *Penn Central*. That is what our cases say.

Finally, the majority says that *Nollan* would have come out the same way had it involved, similar to the regulation here, access short of 365 days a year. Perhaps so. But, if so, that likely would be because the Court would have viewed the access as an "easement," and therefore an appropriation. See Nollan, 483 U.S. at 828. Or, perhaps, the Court would have viewed the regulation as going "too far." I can assume, purely for argument's sake, that that is so. But the law is clear: A regulation that provides *temporary*, not *permanent*, access to a landowner's property, and that does not amount to a taking of a traditional property interest, is not a *per se* taking. That is, it does not automatically require compensation. Rather, a court must consider whether it goes "too far."

C

The persistence of the permanent/temporary distinction that I have described is not surprising. That distinction serves an important purpose. We live together in communities. Modern life in these communities requires different kinds of regulation. Some, perhaps many, forms of regulation require access to private property (for government officials or others) for different reasons and for varying periods of time. Most such temporary-entry regulations do not go "too far." And it is impractical to compensate every property owner for any brief use of their land. As we have frequently said, "[g]overnment hardly could go on if to some extent values incident to property could not be diminished without paying for every such change in the general law." Pennsylvania Coal Co., 260 U.S. at 413. * * * Thus, the law has not, and should not, convert all temporary-access-permitting regulations into *per se* takings automatically requiring compensation.

Consider the large numbers of ordinary regulations in a host of different fields that, for a variety of purposes, permit temporary entry onto (or an "invasion of") a property owner's land. They include activities ranging from examination of food products to inspections for compliance with preschool licensing requirements. See, e.g., 29 U.S.C. § 657(a) (authorizing inspections and investigations of "any . . . workplace or environment where work is performed" during "regular working hours and at other reasonable times"); 21 U.S.C. § 606(a) (authorizing "examination and inspection of all meat food products . . . at all times, by day or night"); 42 U.S.C. § 5413(b) (authorizing inspections anywhere "manufactured homes are manufactured, stored, or held for sale" at "reasonable times and without advance notice"); Miss. Code Ann. § 49–27–63 (2012) (authorizing inspections of "coastal wetlands" "from time to time"); Mich. Comp. Laws § 208.1435(5) (2010) (authorizing inspections of any "historic resource" "at any time during the rehabilitation process"); Mont. Code Ann. § 81–22–304 (2019) (granting a "right of entry . . . [into] any premises where dairy products . . . are produced, manufactured, [or] sold" "during normal business hours"); Neb. Rev. Stat. § 43–1303(5) (2016) (authorizing visitation of "foster care facilities in order to ascertain whether the individual physical, psychological, and sociological needs of each foster child are being met"); Va. Code Ann. § 22.1–289.032(C)(8) (Cum. Supp. 2020) (authorizing "annual inspection" of "preschool programs of accredited private schools"); Cincinnati, Ohio, Municipal Code § 603–1 (2021) (authorizing entry "at any time" for any place in which "animals are slaughtered"); Dallas, Tex., Code of Ordinance § 33–5(a) (2021) (authorizing inspection of "assisted living facilit[ies]" "at reasonable times"); 6 N. Y. Rules & Regs. § 360.7 (Supp. 2020) (authorizing inspection of solid waste management facilities "at all reasonable times, locations, whether announced or unannounced"); see also Boise Cascade Corp. v. United States, 296 F.3d 1339, 1352 (Fed. Cir. 2002) (affirming an injunction requiring property owner to allow Government agents to enter its property to conduct owl surveys).

The majority tries to deal with the adverse impact of treating these, and other, temporary invasions as if they were *per se* physical takings by creating a series of exceptions from its *per se* rule. It says: (1) "Isolated physical invasions, not undertaken pursuant to a granted right of access, are properly assessed as individual torts rather than appropriations of a property right." It also would except from its *per se* rule (2) government access that is "consistent with longstanding background restrictions on property rights," including "traditional common law privileges to access private property." And it adds that (3) "the government may require property owners to cede a right of access as a condition of receiving certain benefits, without causing a taking." How well will this new system work? I suspect that the majority has substituted a new, complex legal scheme for a comparatively simpler old one.

As to the first exception, what will count as "isolated"? How is an "isolated physical invasion" different from a "temporary" invasion, sufficient under present law to invoke *Penn Central*? And where should one draw the line between trespass and takings? Imagine a school bus that stops to allow public school children to picnic on private land. Do three stops a year place the stops outside the exception? One stop every week? Buses from one school? From every school? Under current law a court would know what question to ask. The stops are temporary; no one assumes a permanent right to stop; thus the court will ask whether the school district has gone "too far." Under the majority's approach, the court must answer a new question (apparently about what counts as "isolated").

As to the second exception, a court must focus on "traditional common law privileges to access private property." Just what are they? We have said before that the government can, without paying compensation, impose a limitation on land that "inhere[s] in the title itself, in the restrictions that background principles of the State's law of property and nuisance already place upon land ownership." Lucas, 505 U.S. at 1029. But we defined a very narrow set of such background principles. See ibid., and n. 16 (abatement of nuisances and cases of " 'actual necessity' " or "to forestall other grave threats to the lives and property of others"). To these the majority adds "public or private necessity," the enforcement of criminal law "under certain circumstances," and reasonable searches. Do only those exceptions that existed in, say, 1789 count? Should courts apply those privileges as they existed at that time, when there were no union organizers? Or do we bring some exceptions (but not others) up to date, e.g., a necessity exception for preserving animal habitats?

As to the third, what is the scope of the phrase "certain benefits"? Does it include the benefit of being able to sell meat labeled "inspected" in interstate commerce? But see Horne, 576 U.S. at 366 (concluding that "[s]elling produce in interstate commerce" is "not a special governmental benefit"). What about the benefit of having electricity? Of sewage collection? Of internet accessibility? Myriad regulatory schemes based on just these sorts of benefits depend upon intermittent, temporary government entry onto private property.

Labor peace (brought about through union organizing) is one such benefit, at least in the view of elected representatives. They wrote laws that led to rules governing the organizing of agricultural workers. Many of them may well have believed that union organizing brings with it "benefits," including community health and educational benefits, higher standards of living, and (as I just said) labor peace. See, e.g., 1975 Cal. Stats. ch. 1, § 1 (stating that the purpose of the Agricultural Labor Relations Act was to "ensure peace in the agricultural fields by guaranteeing justice for all agricultural workers and stability in labor relations"). A landowner, of course, may deny the existence of these benefits, but a landowner might do the same were a regulatory statute to permit brief access to verify proper preservation of wetlands or the habitat enjoyed by an endangered species or, for that matter, the safety of inspected meat. So, if a regulation authorizing temporary access for purposes of organizing agricultural workers falls outside of the Court's exceptions and is a *per se* taking, then to what other forms of regulation does the Court's *per se* conclusion also apply?

II

Finally, I touch briefly on remedies, which the majority does not address. The Takings Clause prohibits the Government from taking private property for public use without "just compensation." U. S. Const., Amdt. 5. But the employers do not seek compensation. They seek only injunctive and declaratory relief. Indeed, they did not allege any damages. On remand, California should have the choice of foreclosing injunctive relief by providing compensation. See, *e.g.*, Knick v. Township of Scott, 139 S. Ct. 2162, 2179 (2019) ("As long as just compensation remedies are available—as they have been for nearly 150 years—injunctive relief will be foreclosed").

　　　* * *

I recognize that the Court's prior cases in this area are not easy to apply. Moreover, words such as "temporary," "permanent," or "too far" do not define themselves. But I do not believe that the Court has made matters clearer or better. Rather than adopt a new broad rule and indeterminate exceptions, I would stick with the approach that I believe the Court's case law sets forth. "Better the devil we know . . . ." A right of access such as the right at issue here, a nonpermanent right, is not automatically a "taking." It is a regulation that falls within the scope of *Penn Central*. Because the Court takes a different view, I respectfully dissent.

NOTES AND QUESTIONS

1.   *Cedar Point Nursery* takes us back to the beginnings of the course and the rival perspectives about property: one being that it is grounded in the right to exclude, the other that it is a bundle of rights. Chief Justice Roberts, writing for the majority, sees the California regulation as a violation of the right to exclude and hence as the proper subject of a per se rule. Justice Breyer, in dissent, emphasizes that the right to exclude is subject to many exceptions, and hence the California rule should be regarded as a regulation of the right to exclude governed by *Penn Central*'s ad hoc standard. But where does exclusion end and governance begin? The discussion in the opinions of *Causby* and airplane overflights underscores the difficulty. Low-level flights are subject to the right to exclude; high level flights are subject to reasonable regulation and are not a taking at all. But where exactly do we draw the line where the one principle turns into the other?

2.   *Cedar Point Nursery* is also a striking illustration of the common law nature of the Supreme Court's regulatory takings doctrine. Starting with *Loretto*'s per se rule for "permanent physical occupations," the Court borrows the understanding that a permanent right of access is also a per se taking (*Nollan* and *Dolan*), re-christens the relevant category to be "appropriations" of property rather than "occupations" (*Horne*), references older cases holding that intermittent low-level overflights and repeated firing of shells over property can be a taking (*Causby* and *Portsmouth*), distinguishes a case that involves property open to the general public (*Pruneyard*) and concludes that a regulation that permanently authorizes intermittent access to property not open to the public is subject to a per se rule. The dissent surveys the same body of precedent, concluding that intermittent access rights are a type of temporary invasion, and temporary invasions are always assessed under *Penn Central*'s ad hoc approach. Which stirring of the precedent pot is correct? By what criteria should we seek to determine which is correct?

3.   When the Court granted review in the case, the petitioners framed the issue in terms of whether the California regulation was a per se taking because it granted union organizers an easement in gross to access the growers' private land. The respondents' brief on the merits pointed out that the access right did not conform to the California law of easements, because it was not appurtenant to any specific burdened land, could not be transferred, and could not be recorded. Both the majority and the dissent appear to accept the respondents' understanding of California law on this point. Does the fact that the access right diverges from established California property forms mean, as the dissent suggests, that the regulation cannot be

regarded as a per se taking because it does not transfer a recognized property right to the union organizers? Or could the majority have reasoned that the regulation creates what is effectively a new type of easement—a permanent right of access which can be exercised at the organizers' discretion? Would the creation of a new type of easement, without compensation to the servient landowner, be a taking? Would framing the decision this way require the Court to develop a federal definition of "easement" for constitutional purposes? In a decision noted later in the chapter, *Murr v. Wisconsin*, 137 S. Ct. 1933 (2017), the Court adopted a federal constitutional definition of "parcel of land" to apply in takings cases. If "parcel" can be given a federal constitutional definition, why not "easement"? Or would the Court be better advised to avoid creating new definitions of property rights for takings purposes?

4.   How does the Court distinguish a compulsory right of intermittent access from a temporary invasion like a trespass? Is the difference that the right of access is created and authorized by enacted law, like a statute or regulation, whereas a government trespass is an "isolated" action taken by a government agent? What then about entries by government agents pursuant to statutes authorizing inspections of property in the interest of public health and safety? Near the end of its opinion, the Court suggests that these sorts of licenses authorizing entry will generally be upheld either as "background understandings" that qualify the owner's property rights, or will satisfy the nexus and rough proportionality standards the Court has developed for exactions demanded as conditions for accepting some kind of government permit or benefit (*Nollan*, *Dolan*, and *Koontz*). Should the Court have remanded the case to the lower courts to consider whether the right of access given by California to union organizers satisfies the nexus and rough proportionality tests in light of the state's interest in promoting collective bargaining by farm workers?

5.   After the majority opinion considers and responds to various objections to its extension of the *Loretto* principle, the doctrine that emerges in *Cedar Point* takes the form of a rule subject to three exceptions. The rule is not entirely clear but seems to be that any permanent right of access to enter private property not otherwise open to the public, even if intermittent, is presumptively a taking. The exceptions are for (i) isolated trespasses by government agents that are considered torts; (ii) access rights consistent with background understandings of property law, like the doctrine of necessity; and (iii) licenses that permit entry by government agents for inspections that are consistent with the nexus and rough proportionality rules of *Dolan*. Do the exceptions apply to all forms of "appropriations," including those considered in *Loretto* and *Horne*? Or are they limited to access rights like those at issue in *Cedar Point*?

6.   Are the exceptions recognized by *Cedar Point* adequately justified? The first two appear to be based on the Court's generalized sense of the common law of property, as reflected in sources like the Restatement of Torts. Why privilege the common law—or the Court's idealized conception of the common law—rather than the law of the state in question, including legislated law? (This issue is also presented by the exception for background

principles of law recognized in *Lucas v. South Carolina Coastal Comm'n*, infra.) The third exception seems to elevate the nexus and proportionality requirements to a generalized type of means-ends rationality review, more commonly associated with substantive due process. Is this a proper inquiry to inject (even in this back-handed way) into takings law? See Lingle v. Chevron U.S.A. Inc., 544 U.S. 528 (2005) (disapproving of a type of means-ends scrutiny in regulatory takings cases on the ground that this is more properly a due process test).

7.   When the Court first recognized the per se rule for permanent occupations in *Loretto*, it did so in part because the per se approach "avoids otherwise difficult line-drawing problems" and "presents relatively few problems of proof." After the extension to intermittent rights of access, are these claims still plausible? Even if the inquiry is more complex, is there still a meaningful difference between a general rule subject to exceptions (*Cedar Point*) and a general balancing test using multiple factors of undetermined weight (*Penn Central*)?

8.   The dissent notes that if California is willing to pay just compensation to the growers, the access right can continue to be enforced. How is compensation going to be determined if California wants to pursue this option? Will a study of the fair market value of different parcels work? What about a capitalization of lost earnings, as in the *Flight 93* Case, supra? For an argument that the scope of takings law is generally constrained by established techniques for determining monetary compensation, see Thomas W. Merrill, The Compensation Constraint and the Scope of the Takings Clause, 96 Notre Dame L. Rev. 1421 (2021).

9.   After *Cedar Point*, is the rule developed in *NLRB v. Babcock & Wilcox Co.*, 351 U.S. 105 (1956), as an interpretation of the National Labor Relations Act an unconstitutional taking? In *Babcock*, the Court held that labor organizers are permitted to trespass on company land to contact workers about the benefits of unionization if there is no other reasonable basis for reaching the workers (such as handing out literature on a public street or sidewalk outside a plant). Is the NLRA rule distinguishable on the ground that it entails a case-by-case consideration of circumstances, whereas the access right in *Cedar Point* is permanent and unconditional? Is the NLRA rule justified by the "background" understanding of the defense of necessity to a trespass to land? Can necessity be created by a statutory entitlement or must it be grounded in common law precedent (like the understanding that trespass is justified when escaping from an assault)? Is the NLRA rule justified because it satisfies the nexus and proportionality tests taken from the exactions cases, whereas the California regulation considered in *Cedar Point* is not "roughly proportionate" to the public interest in encouraging unionization of farm workers?

10.   After *Cedar Point*, is the approach to determining a landowner's right to exclude developed in New Jersey cases like *State v. Shack*, supra Chapter IV, an unconstitutional taking of property? Does the fact that the right of access recognized in *Shack* was developed by the New Jersey Supreme Court as a matter of common law exposition take it out from under the constitutional cloud? Or should common law decisions be treated the

same as statutes and regulations for takings purposes? For more on whether courts can commit takings by changing the common law, see Stop the Beach Renourishment, infra.

6. TOTAL LOSS OF VALUE

Lucas v. South Carolina Coastal Council
Supreme Court of the United States, 1992.
505 U.S. 1003.

■ JUSTICE SCALIA delivered the opinion of the Court. [Lucas, a real estate developer, acquired two vacant lots on the Isle of Palms, a barrier island on the coast of South Carolina, for the purpose of building and selling single-family homes on them. Before he could begin construction, South Carolina enacted the Beachfront Management Act, S.C.Code Ann. § 48–39–250 et seq. (Supp. 1990), which as implemented prohibited constructing homes on the lots.]

I

Figure 10-7
Map of the Area Involved in *Lucas*

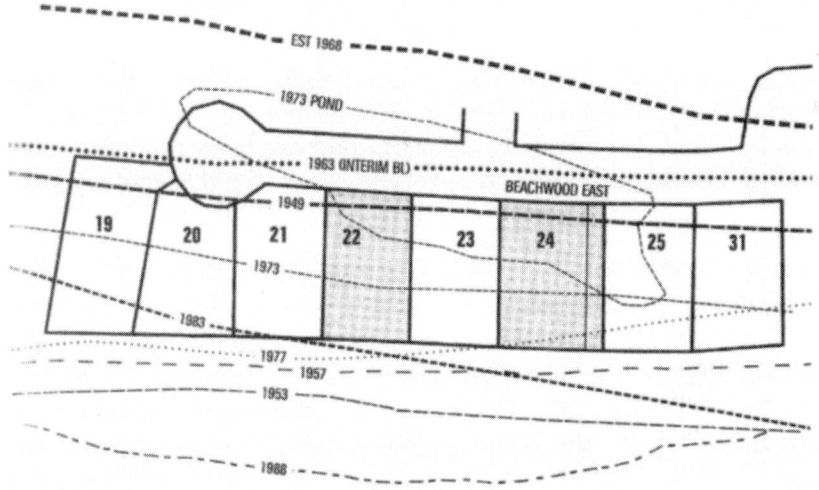

Source: Douglas R. Porter, The *Lucas* Case, Urban Land, Sept. 1992, at 27, 29. Lucas's two lots are 22 and 24 (shaded). The lines indicate the shoreline in various years and the erosion in the years immediately prior to the case.

B

Lucas promptly filed suit in the South Carolina Court of Common Pleas, contending that the Beachfront Management Act's construction bar effected a taking of his property without just compensation. Lucas did not take issue with the validity of the Act as a lawful exercise of South Carolina's police power, but contended that the Act's complete extinguishment of his property's value entitled him to compensation regardless of whether the legislature had acted in furtherance of legitimate police power objectives. Following a bench trial, the court agreed. * * * [The trial court] found that the Beachfront Management Act decreed a permanent ban on construction insofar as Lucas's lots were concerned, and that this prohibition "deprive[d] Lucas of any reasonable economic use of the lots, . . . eliminated the unrestricted right of use, and render[ed] them valueless." The court thus concluded that Lucas's properties had been "taken" by operation of the Act, and it ordered respondent to pay "just compensation" in the amount of $1,232,387.50.

The Supreme Court of South Carolina reversed. It found dispositive what it described as Lucas's concession "that the Beachfront Management Act [was] properly and validly designed to preserve . . . South Carolina's beaches." Failing an attack on the validity of the statute as such, the court believed itself bound to accept the "uncontested . . . findings" of the South Carolina Legislature that new construction in the coastal zone—such as petitioner intended—threatened this public resource. The court ruled that when a regulation respecting the use of property is designed "to prevent serious public harm," (citing, *inter alia*, Mugler v. Kansas, 123 U.S. 623 (1887)), no compensation is owing under the Takings Clause regardless of the regulation's effect on the property's value. * * *

II

As a threshold matter, we must briefly address the Council's suggestion that this case is inappropriate for plenary review. [The Court held that the case was ripe for decision, had not been rendered moot by recent legislation, and otherwise presented a justiciable controversy.]

III

A

Prior to Justice Holmes's exposition in *Pennsylvania Coal Co. v. Mahon,* 260 U.S. 393 (1922), it was generally thought that the Takings Clause reached only a "direct appropriation" of property, Legal Tender Cases, 12 Wall. 457, 551 (1871), or the functional equivalent of a "practical ouster of [the owner's] possession," Transportation Co. v. Chicago, 99 U.S. 635, 642 (1879). Justice Holmes recognized in *Mahon,* however, that if the protection against physical appropriations of private property was to be meaningfully enforced, the government's power to redefine the range of interests included in the ownership of property was necessarily constrained by constitutional limits. 260 U.S., at 414–415. If, instead, the uses of private property were subject to unbridled, uncompensated qualification under the police power, "the natural tendency of human nature [would be] to extend the qualification more and more until at last private property disappear[ed]." Id., at 415. These considerations gave birth in that case to the oft-cited maxim that, "while property may be regulated to a certain extent, if regulation goes too far it will be recognized as a taking." Ibid.

Nevertheless, our decision in *Mahon* offered little insight into when, and under what circumstances, a given regulation would be seen as going "too far" for purposes of the Fifth Amendment. In 70-odd years of succeeding "regulatory takings" jurisprudence, we have generally eschewed any " 'set formula' " for determining how far is too far, preferring to "engag[e] in . . . essentially ad hoc, factual inquiries." Penn Central Transportation Co. v. New York City, 438 U.S. 104, 124 (1978) (quoting Goldblatt v. Hempstead, 369 U.S. 590, 594 (1962)). See Epstein, Takings: Descent and Resurrection, 1987 S.Ct. Rev. 1, 4. We have, however, described at least two discrete categories of regulatory action as compensable without case-specific inquiry into the public interest advanced in support of the restraint. The first encompasses regulations that compel the property owner to suffer a physical "invasion" of his property. In general (at least with regard to permanent invasions), no matter how minute the intrusion, and no matter how weighty the public purpose behind it, we have required compensation. [Loretto v. Teleprompter Manhattan CATV Corp., 458 U.S. 419 (1982).] * * *

The second situation in which we have found categorical treatment appropriate is where regulation denies all economically beneficial or productive use of land. See Agins v. City of Tiburon, 447 U.S. 255, 260 (1980); see also Nollan v. California Coastal Comm'n, 483 U.S. 825, 834 (1987); Keystone Bituminous Coal Assn. v. DeBenedictis, 480 U.S. 470, 491–492 (1987); Hodel v. Virginia Surface Mining & Reclamation Assn., Inc., 452 U.S. 264, 295–296 (1981). As we have said on numerous occasions, the Fifth Amendment is violated when land-use regulation "does not substantially advance legitimate state interests *or denies an owner economically viable use of his land.*" Agins, supra, 447 U.S., at 260 (citations omitted) (emphasis added).[7]

---

[7]   Regrettably, the rhetorical force of our "deprivation of all economically feasible use" rule is greater than its precision, since the rule does not make clear the "property interest" against which the loss of value is to be measured. When, for example, a regulation requires a developer to leave 90% of a rural tract in its natural state, it is unclear whether we would analyze the situation as one in which the owner has been deprived of all economically beneficial use of the burdened portion of the tract, or as one in which the owner has suffered a mere diminution in value of the tract as a whole. (For an extreme—and, we think, unsupportable—view of the relevant calculus, see Penn Central Transportation Co. v. New York City, 366 N.E.2d 1271, 1276–1277 (N.Y. 1977), aff'd, 438 U.S. 104 (1978), where the state court examined the diminution in a particular parcel's value produced by a municipal ordinance in light of total value of the takings claimant's other holdings in the vicinity.) Unsurprisingly, this uncertainty regarding the composition of the denominator in our "deprivation" fraction has produced inconsistent pronouncements by the Court. Compare Pennsylvania Coal Co. v. Mahon, 260 U.S. 393, 414 (1922) (law restricting subsurface extraction of coal held to effect a taking), with Keystone Bituminous Coal Assn. v. DeBenedictis, 480 U.S. 470, 497–502 (1987) (nearly identical law held not to effect a taking); see also id., at 515–520 (REHNQUIST, C.J., dissenting); Rose, *Mahon* Reconstructed: Why the Takings Issue is Still a Muddle, 57 S.Cal.L.Rev. 561, 566–569 (1984). The answer to this difficult question may lie in how the owner's reasonable expectations have been shaped by the State's law of property—*i.e.,* whether and to what degree the State's law has accorded legal recognition and protection to the particular interest in land with respect to which the takings claimant alleges a diminution in (or elimination of) value. In any event, we

We have never set forth the justification for this rule. Perhaps it is simply, as Justice Brennan suggested, that total deprivation of beneficial use is, from the landowner's point of view, the equivalent of a physical appropriation. See San Diego Gas & Electric Co. v. San Diego, 450 U.S. 621, 652 (1981) (dissenting opinion). "[F]or what is the land but the profits thereof[?]" 1 E. Coke, Institutes, ch. 1, § 1 (1st Am. ed. 1812). Surely, at least, in the extraordinary circumstance when *no* productive or economically beneficial use of land is permitted, it is less realistic to indulge our usual assumption that the legislature is simply "adjusting the benefits and burdens of economic life," Penn Central Transportation Co., 438 U.S., at 124, in a manner that secures an "average reciprocity of advantage" to everyone concerned, Pennsylvania Coal Co. v. Mahon, 260 U.S., at 415. And the *functional* basis for permitting the government, by regulation, to affect property values without compensation—that "Government hardly could go on if to some extent values incident to property could not be diminished without paying for every such change in the general law," id., at 413—does not apply to the relatively rare situations where the government has deprived a landowner of all economically beneficial uses.

On the other side of the balance, affirmatively supporting a compensation requirement, is the fact that regulations that leave the owner of land without economically beneficial or productive options for its use—typically, as here, by requiring land to be left substantially in its natural state—carry with them a heightened risk that private property is being pressed into some form of public service under the guise of mitigating serious public harm. [citations omitted] As Justice Brennan explained: "From the government's point of view, the benefits flowing to the public from preservation of open space through regulation may be equally great as from creating a wildlife refuge through formal condemnation or increasing electricity production through a dam project that floods private property." San Diego Gas & Elec. Co., supra, 450 U.S., at 652 (dissenting opinion). The many statutes on the books, both state and federal, that provide for the use of eminent domain to impose servitudes on private scenic lands preventing developmental uses, or to acquire such lands altogether, suggest the practical equivalence in this setting of negative regulation and appropriation. [citations omitted]

B

The trial court found Lucas's two beachfront lots to have been rendered valueless by respondent's enforcement of the coastal-zone construction ban. Under Lucas's theory of the case, which rested upon our "no economically viable use" statements, that finding entitled him to compensation. Lucas believed it unnecessary to take issue with either the

---

avoid this difficulty in the present case, since the "interest in land" that Lucas has pleaded (a fee simple interest) is an estate with a rich tradition of protection at common law, and since the South Carolina Court of Common Pleas found that the Beachfront Management Act left each of Lucas's beachfront lots without economic value.

purposes behind the Beachfront Management Act, or the means chosen by the South Carolina Legislature to effectuate those purposes. The South Carolina Supreme Court, however, thought [Lucas's challenge was barred by the] long line of this Court's cases sustaining against Due Process and Takings Clause challenges the State's use of its "police powers" to enjoin a property owner from activities akin to public nuisances. See Mugler v. Kansas, 123 U.S. 623 (1887) (law prohibiting manufacture of alcoholic beverages); Hadacheck v. Sebastian, 239 U.S. 394 (1915) (law barring operation of brick mill in residential area); Miller v. Schoene, 276 U.S. 272 (1928) (order to destroy diseased cedar trees to prevent infection of nearby orchards); Goldblatt v. Hempstead, 369 U.S. 590 (1962) (law effectively preventing continued operation of quarry in residential area).

It is correct that many of our prior opinions have suggested that "harmful or noxious uses" of property may be proscribed by government regulation without the requirement of compensation. For a number of reasons, however, we think the South Carolina Supreme Court was too quick to conclude that that principle decides the present case. The "harmful or noxious uses" principle was the Court's early attempt to describe in theoretical terms why government may, consistent with the Takings Clause, affect property values by regulation without incurring an obligation to compensate—a reality we nowadays acknowledge explicitly with respect to the full scope of the State's police power. * * * "Harmful or noxious use" analysis was, in other words, simply the progenitor of our more contemporary statements that "land-use regulation does not effect a taking if it 'substantially advance[s] legitimate state interests'. . . ." Nollan, supra, 483 U.S., at 834 (quoting Agins v. Tiburon, 447 U.S., at 260); see also Penn Central Transportation Co., supra, 438 U.S., at 127; Euclid v. Ambler Realty Co., 272 U.S. 365, 387–388 (1926).

The transition from our early focus on control of "noxious" uses to our contemporary understanding of the broad realm within which government may regulate without compensation was an easy one, since the distinction between "harm-preventing" and "benefit-conferring" regulation is often in the eye of the beholder. It is quite possible, for example, to describe in *either* fashion the ecological, economic, and esthetic concerns that inspired the South Carolina Legislature in the present case. One could say that imposing a servitude on Lucas's land is necessary in order to prevent his use of it from "harming" South Carolina's ecological resources; or, instead, in order to achieve the "benefits" of an ecological preserve. [citations omitted] Whether one or the other of the competing characterizations will come to one's lips in a particular case depends primarily upon one's evaluation of the worth of competing uses of real estate. A given restraint will be seen as mitigating "harm" to the adjacent parcels or securing a "benefit" for them, depending upon the observer's evaluation of the relative importance of the use that the restraint favors. See Sax, Takings and the Police Power, 71 Yale L.J. 36, 49 (1964) ("[T]he problem [in this area] is not one of noxiousness or harm-creating activity at all; rather it is a problem of inconsistency between perfectly innocent and independently desirable uses"). Whether Lucas's construction of single-family residences on his parcels should be described as bringing "harm" to South Carolina's adjacent ecological resources thus depends principally upon whether the describer believes that the State's use interest in nurturing those resources is so important that *any* competing adjacent use must yield.

When it is understood that "prevention of harmful use" was merely our early formulation of the police power justification necessary to sustain (without compensation) *any* regulatory diminution in value; and that the distinction between regulation that "prevents harmful use" and that which "confers benefits" is difficult, if not impossible, to discern on an objective, value-free basis; it becomes self-evident that noxious-use logic cannot serve as a touchstone to distinguish regulatory "takings"— which require compensation—from regulatory deprivations that do not require compensation. *A fortiori* the legislature's recitation of a noxious-use justification cannot be the basis for departing from our categorical rule that total regulatory takings must be compensated. If it were, departure would virtually always be allowed. The South Carolina Supreme Court's approach would essentially nullify *Mahon*'s affirmation of limits to the noncompensable exercise of the police power. Our cases provide no support for this: None of them that employed the logic of "harmful use" prevention to sustain a regulation involved an allegation that the regulation wholly eliminated the value of the claimant's land. See Keystone Bituminous Coal Assn., 480 U.S., at 513–514 (Rehnquist, C.J., dissenting).

Where the State seeks to sustain regulation that deprives land of all economically beneficial use, we think it may resist compensation only if the logically antecedent inquiry into the nature of the owner's estate shows that the proscribed use interests were not part of his title to begin with. This accords, we think, with our "takings" jurisprudence, which has traditionally been guided by the understandings of our citizens regarding the content of, and the State's power over, the "bundle of rights" that they acquire when they obtain title to property. It seems to us that the property owner necessarily expects the uses of his property to be restricted, from time to time, by various measures newly enacted by the State in legitimate exercise of its police powers; "[a]s long recognized, some values are enjoyed under an implied limitation and must yield to the police power." Pennsylvania Coal Co. v. Mahon, 260 U.S., at 413. And in the case of personal property, by reason of the State's traditionally high degree of control over commercial dealings, he ought to be aware of the possibility that new regulation might even render his property economically worthless (at least if the property's only economically productive use is sale or manufacture for sale). See Andrus v. Allard, 444

U.S. 51, 66–67 (1979) (prohibition on sale of eagle feathers). In the case of land, however, we think the notion pressed by the Council that title is somehow held subject to the "implied limitation" that the State may subsequently eliminate all economically valuable use is inconsistent with the historical compact recorded in the Takings Clause that has become part of our constitutional culture.

Where "permanent physical occupation" of land is concerned, we have refused to allow the government to decree it anew (without compensation), no matter how weighty the asserted "public interests" involved, Loretto v. Teleprompter Manhattan CATV Corp., 458 U.S., at 426—though we assuredly *would* permit the government to assert a permanent easement that was a pre-existing limitation upon the landowner's title. * * * We believe similar treatment must be accorded confiscatory regulations, *i.e.,* regulations that prohibit all economically beneficial use of land: Any limitation so severe cannot be newly legislated or decreed (without compensation), but must inhere in the title itself, in the restrictions that background principles of the State's law of property and nuisance already place upon land ownership. A law or decree with such an effect must, in other words, do no more than duplicate the result that could have been achieved in the courts—by adjacent landowners (or other uniquely affected persons) under the State's law of private nuisance, or by the State under its complementary power to abate nuisances that affect the public generally, or otherwise.[16]

On this analysis, the owner of a lake-bed, for example, would not be entitled to compensation when he is denied the requisite permit to engage in a landfilling operation that would have the effect of flooding others' land. Nor the corporate owner of a nuclear generating plant, when it is directed to remove all improvements from its land upon discovery that the plant sits astride an earthquake fault. Such regulatory action may well have the effect of eliminating the land's only economically productive use, but it does not proscribe a productive use that was previously permissible under relevant property and nuisance principles. The use of these properties for what are now expressly prohibited purposes was *always* unlawful, and (subject to other constitutional limitations) it was open to the State at any point to make the implication of those background principles of nuisance and property law explicit. See Michelman, Property, Utility, and Fairness, Comments on the Ethical Foundations of "Just Compensation" Law, 80 Harv.L.Rev. 1165, 1239–1241 (1967). In light of our traditional resort to "existing rules or understandings that stem from an independent source such as state law" to define the range of interests that qualify for protection as "property" under the Fifth and Fourteenth Amendments, Board of Regents of State

---

[16]   The principal "otherwise" that we have in mind is litigation absolving the State (or private parties) of liability for the destruction of "real and personal property, in cases of actual necessity, to prevent the spreading of a fire" or to forestall other grave threats to the lives and property of others. Bowditch v. Boston, 101 U.S. 16, 18–19 (1880); see United States v. Pacific R., Co., 120 U.S. 227, 238–239 (1887).

Colleges v. Roth, 408 U.S. 564, 577 (1972); see, e.g., Ruckelshaus v. Monsanto Co., 467 U.S. 986, 1011–1012 (1984); Hughes v. Washington, 389 U.S. 290, 295 (1967) (Stewart, J., concurring), this recognition that the Takings Clause does not require compensation when an owner is barred from putting land to a use that is proscribed by those "existing rules or understandings" is surely unexceptional. When, however, a regulation that declares "off-limits" all economically productive or beneficial uses of land goes beyond what the relevant background principles would dictate, compensation must be paid to sustain it.

The "total taking" inquiry we require today will ordinarily entail (as the application of state nuisance law ordinarily entails) analysis of, among other things, the degree of harm to public lands and resources, or adjacent private property, posed by the claimant's proposed activities, see, e.g., Restatement (Second) of Torts §§ 826, 827, the social value of the claimant's activities and their suitability to the locality in question, see, e.g., id., §§ 828(a) and (b), 831, and the relative ease with which the alleged harm can be avoided through measures taken by the claimant and the government (or adjacent private landowners) alike, see, e.g., id., §§ 827(e), 828(c), 830. The fact that a particular use has long been engaged in by similarly situated owners ordinarily imports a lack of any common-law prohibition (though changed circumstances or new knowledge may make what was previously permissible no longer so, see id., § 827, Comment g.) So also does the fact that other landowners, similarly situated, are permitted to continue the use denied to the claimant.

It seems unlikely that common-law principles would have prevented the erection of any habitable or productive improvements on petitioner's land; they rarely support prohibition of the "essential use" of land, Curtin v. Benson, 222 U.S. 78, 86 (1911). The question, however, is one of state law to be dealt with on remand. We emphasize that to win its case South Carolina must do more than proffer the legislature's declaration that the uses Lucas desires are inconsistent with the public interest, or the conclusory assertion that they violate a common-law maxim such as *sic utere tuo ut alienum non laedas*. As we have said, a "State, by *ipse dixit,* may not transform private property into public property without compensation. . . ." Webb's Fabulous Pharmacies, Inc. v. Beckwith, 449 U.S. 155, 164 (1980). Instead, as it would be required to do if it sought to restrain Lucas in a common-law action for public nuisance, South Carolina must identify background principles of nuisance and property law that prohibit the uses he now intends in the circumstances in which the property is presently found. Only on this showing can the State fairly claim that, in proscribing all such beneficial uses, the Beachfront Management Act is taking nothing.[18]

---

[18]   Justice BLACKMUN decries our reliance on background nuisance principles at least in part because he believes those principles to be as manipulable as we find the "harm prevention"/"benefit conferral" dichotomy. There is no doubt some leeway in a court's

* * *

The judgment is reversed, and the case is remanded for proceedings not inconsistent with this opinion.

■ JUSTICE KENNEDY, concurring in the judgment. * * * In my view, reasonable expectations must be understood in light of the whole of our legal tradition. The common law of nuisance is too narrow a confine for the exercise of regulatory power in a complex and interdependent society. Goldblatt v. Hempstead, 369 U.S. 590, 593 (1962). The State should not be prevented from enacting new regulatory initiatives in response to changing conditions, and courts must consider all reasonable expectations whatever their source. The Takings Clause does not require a static body of state property law; it protects private expectations to ensure private investment. I agree with the Court that nuisance prevention accords with the most common expectations of property owners who face regulation, but I do not believe this can be the sole source of state authority to impose severe restrictions. Coastal property may present such unique concerns for a fragile land system that the State can go further in regulating its development and use than the common law of nuisance might otherwise permit. * * *

■ JUSTICE BLACKMUN, dissenting. Today the Court launches a missile to kill a mouse. * * *

[T]he Court justifies its new rule that the legislature may not deprive a property owner of the only economically valuable use of his land, even if the legislature finds it to be a harmful use, because such action is not part of the " 'long recognized' " "understandings of our citizens." These "understandings" permit such regulation only if the use is a nuisance under the common law. Any other course is "inconsistent with the historical compact recorded in the Takings Clause." It is not clear from the Court's opinion where our "historical compact" or "citizens' understanding" comes from, but it does not appear to be history.

The principle that the State should compensate individuals for property taken for public use was not widely established in America at the time of the Revolution.

> The colonists . . . inherited . . . a concept of property which permitted extensive regulation of the use of that property for the public benefit—regulation that could even go so far as to deny all productive use of the property to the owner if, as Coke himself stated, the regulation "extends to the public benefit . . . for this is for the public, and every one hath benefit by it." F. Bosselman, D. Callies, & J. Banta, The Taking Issue 80–81

---

interpretation of what existing state law permits—but not remotely as much, we think, as in a legislative crafting of the reasons for its confiscatory regulation. We stress that an affirmative decree eliminating all economically beneficial uses may be defended only if an *objectively reasonable application* of relevant precedents would exclude those beneficial uses in the circumstances in which the land is presently found.

(1973), quoting The Case of the King's Prerogative in Saltpetre, 12 Co.Rep. 12–13 (1606).

See also Treanor, The Origins and Original Significance of the Just Compensation Clause of the Fifth Amendment, 94 Yale L.J. 694, 697, n. 9 (1985).

Even into the 19th century, state governments often felt free to take property for roads and other public projects without paying compensation to the owners. See M. Horwitz, The Transformation of American Law, 1780–1860, pp. 63–64 (1977) (hereinafter Horwitz); Treanor, 94 Yale L.J., at 695. As one court declared in 1802, citizens "were bound to contribute as much of [land], as by the laws of the country, were deemed necessary for the public convenience." McClenachan v. Curwen, 3 Yeates 362, 373 (Pa. 1802). There was an obvious movement toward establishing the just compensation principle during the 19th century, but "there continued to be a strong current in American legal thought that regarded compensation simply as a 'bounty given . . . by the State' out of 'kindness' and not out of justice." Horwitz 65, quoting Commonwealth v. Fisher, 1 Pen. & W. 462, 465 (Pa. 1830). See also State v. Dawson, 3 Hill 100, 103 (S.C. 1836). * * *

In addition, state courts historically have been less likely to find that a government action constitutes a taking when the affected land is undeveloped. According to the South Carolina court, the power of the legislature to take unimproved land without providing compensation was sanctioned by "ancient rights and principles." Lindsay v. Commissioners, 2 S.C.L. 38, 57 (1796). "Except for Massachusetts, no colony appears to have paid compensation when it built a state-owned road across unimproved land. Legislatures provided compensation only for enclosed or improved land." Treanor, 94 Yale L.J., at 695 (footnotes omitted). This rule was followed by some States into the 1800's. See Horwitz 63–65. * * *

Nor does history indicate any common-law limit on the State's power to regulate harmful uses even to the point of destroying all economic value. Nothing in the discussions in Congress concerning the Takings Clause indicates that the Clause was limited by the common-law nuisance doctrine. Common-law courts themselves rejected such an understanding. They regularly recognized that it is "for the legislature to interpose, and by positive enactment to prohibit a use of property which would be injurious to the public." Tewksbury, 11 Metc., at 57. Chief Justice Shaw explained in upholding a regulation prohibiting construction of wharves, the existence of a taking did not depend on "whether a certain erection in tide water is a nuisance at common law or not." Alger, 7 Cush., at 104; see also State v. Paul, 5 R.I. 185, 193 (1858); Commonwealth v. Parks, 30 N.E. 174 (Mass. 1892) (Holmes, J.) ("[T]he legislature may change the common law as to nuisances, and may move the line either way, so as to make things nuisances which were not so, or to make things lawful which were nuisances").

In short, I find no clear and accepted "historical compact" or "understanding of our citizens" justifying the Court's new takings doctrine. Instead, the Court seems to treat history as a grab bag of principles, to be adopted where they support the Court's theory, and ignored where they do not. If the Court decided that the early common law provides the background principles for interpreting the Takings Clause, then regulation, as opposed to physical confiscation, would not be compensable. If the Court decided that the law of a later period provides the background principles, then regulation might be compensable, but the Court would have to confront the fact that legislatures regularly determined which uses were prohibited, independent of the common law, and independent of whether the uses were lawful when the owner purchased. What makes the Court's analysis unworkable is its attempt to package the law of two incompatible eras and peddle it as historical fact. * * *

■ JUSTICE STEVENS, dissenting. * * * In considering Lucas' claim, the generality of the Beachfront Management Act is significant. The Act does not target particular landowners, but rather regulates the use of the coastline of the entire State. See S.C. Code Ann. § 48–39–10 (Supp. 1990). Indeed, South Carolina's Act is best understood as part of a national effort to protect the coastline, one initiated by the federal Coastal Zone Management Act of 1972. Pub.L. 92–583, 86 Stat. 1280, codified as amended at 16 U.S.C. § 1451 et seq. Pursuant to the federal Act, every coastal State has implemented coastline regulations. Moreover, the Act did not single out owners of undeveloped land. The Act also prohibited owners of developed land from rebuilding if their structures were destroyed, see 1988 S.C. Acts 634, § 3, and what is equally significant, from repairing erosion control devices, such as seawalls, see S.C. Code Ann. § 48–39–290(B)(2) (Supp. 1990). In addition, in some situations, owners of developed land were required to "renouris[h] the beach . . . on a yearly basis with an amount . . . of sand . . . not . . . less than one and one-half times the yearly volume of sand lost due to erosion." 1988 S.C. Acts 634, § 3, p. 5140. In short, the South Carolina Act imposed substantial burdens on owners of developed and undeveloped land alike. This generality indicates that the Act is not an effort to expropriate owners of undeveloped land.

Admittedly, the economic impact of this regulation is dramatic and petitioner's investment-backed expectations are substantial. Yet, if anything, the costs to and expectations of the owners of developed land are even greater: I doubt, however, that the cost to owners of developed land of renourishing the beach and allowing their seawalls to deteriorate effects a taking. The costs imposed on the owners of undeveloped land, such as petitioner, differ from these costs only in degree, not in kind.

NOTES AND QUESTIONS

1.   On remand, the South Carolina Supreme Court held that the restrictions imposed by the Beachfront Management Act would not have been authorized under the South Carolina law of nuisance. Accordingly, the Act imposed a taking. The court held that the state could either abandon the law or could proceed to purchase or condemn the property. In either event, it would be liable to Mr. Lucas for having imposed a temporary taking during the time the ordinance blocked any development. Lucas v. South Carolina Coastal Council, 424 S.E.2d 484 (S.C. 1992). The case was settled when the state agreed to pay Lucas $850,000 for the two lots, plus $725,000 in interest, attorney's fees, and costs, for a total of $1,575,000. The state then turned around and sold the lots to another private developer, in order to recoup some of these expenses. See Oliver A. Houck, More Unfinished Stories: *Lucas*, *Atlanta Coalition*, and *Palila/Sweet Home*, 75 U. Colo. L. Rev. 331, 366 (2004). Does the decision to sell the lots for private development suggest, as proponents of strong takings protection might argue, that the regulation imposed an extreme burden on the landowner, and that once the state was forced to internalize this burden, it realized the regulation was not worth it? Or does the sale for private development suggest, as opponents of takings liability might argue, that states have no way to recoup the external benefits of land-use regulations, and if they have to compensate landowners for losses this will result in under-regulation of environmental harms? For a variety of views, see, e.g., Fischel, Regulatory Takings, supra, at 59–63; Vicki Been, Lucas vs. The Green Machine: Using the Takings Clause to Promote More Efficient Regulation?, in Property Stories 299 (Gerald Korngold & Andrew P. Morriss eds., 2d ed. 2009); Carol M. Rose, The Story of *Lucas*: Environmental Land Use Regulations between Developers and the Deep Blue Sea, in Environmental Law Stories 237 (Oliver A. Houck & Richard James Lazarus eds., 2005).

Figure 10-8
Lucas's Two Lots, November 1994

"View of Lucas's two lots, on either side of large square house in the center, from the edge of the ocean (looking towards northwest). Note that Lucas's lots are the only vacant lots in sight along the beach." http://www.dartmouth.edu/=wfischel/lucasessay.html. Courtesy of William A. Fischel, Department of Economics, Dartmouth College.

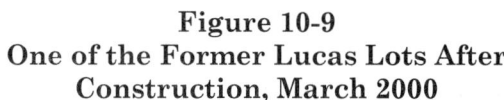

Figure 10-9
One of the Former Lucas Lots After
Construction, March 2000

"A closer view of the new, salmon-pink house. Jerry Finkel, who handled the sale of the lot for Lucas after he won his case, indicated that state officials had urged him to apply for a permit for the maximum-size house so that the state could get the highest possible price for the lot when it was sold. The house is about 5,000 square feet." http://www.dartmouth.edu/=wfischel/lucasupdate.html. Courtesy of William A. Fischel, Department of Economics, Dartmouth College.

2. *Lucas* obviously fills out the structure of categorical rules and ad hoc review that the Court began to develop in *Loretto*. The decision recognizes two per se rules of liability: for permanent physical occupations and for regulations that deprive owners of "all economically beneficial or productive use of land." What exactly is the definition of this latter category? It depends in significant part on whether one focuses on "economically beneficial" or "productive." Is an owner deprived of all "economically beneficial" use of land only when the land has a fair market value of zero? If this is what *Lucas* means, then relatively few regulations would qualify (including the regulation in *Lucas* itself if the record had been properly developed on this point; surely the land could have been sold for some positive sum of money, if only for recreational use by neighboring property owners). The principal type of regulation that would meet this definition would probably be rules requiring the remediation of hazardous wastes deposited on the land, which can render land unmarketable (this is called the "Brownfields" problem). But these rules may also fall within the nuisance

exception. Alternatively, all "productive" use of land could mean that the government has denied the owner the right to build on or otherwise economically extract value from land, as by farming. If this is what *Lucas* means, then many more regulations would fall afoul of such an understanding. For example, governments not infrequently deny development rights when development would entail destroying wetlands, or when it would eliminate the habitat of an endangered species. The Court has not clearly resolved the ambiguity but seems in more recent summaries of the *Lucas* holding to accept the zero value meaning. See, e.g., Lingle v. Chevron U.S.A. Inc., 544 U.S. 528, 538 (2005) (characterizing *Lucas* as requiring "the complete elimination of a property's value").

3.   Are there other candidates for rules of per se takings liability? Formal exercises of eminent domain clearly qualify as one. See Tahoe-Sierra, 535 U.S. at 322 ("When the government physically takes possession of an interest in property for some public purpose, it has a categorical duty to compensate the former owner, United States v. Pewee Coal Co., 341 U.S. 114, 115 (1951), regardless of whether the interest that is taken constitutes an entire parcel or merely a part thereof."). There is language in *Hodel v. Irving*, 481 U.S. 704, 717 (1987), suggesting that a complete abrogation of the right to transmit interests in land upon death might be regarded as a per se taking, although the opinion is not clear about this.

4.   If there are per se rules of takings liability, are there per se rules of nonliability? Does the nuisance regulation exception that *Lucas* recognizes for what would otherwise be per se liability for total takings constitute a per se rule of nonliability for all purposes? What if the government permanently occupies private property to abate what would be a common-law nuisance? At least one court has suggested that government occupation of property for purposes of monitoring groundwater pollution from a hazardous waste site is a permanent physical occupation that requires compensation. See Hendler v. United States, 952 F.2d 1364, 1376–77 (Fed. Cir. 1991). Do you agree? Other candidates for rules of per se nonliability include forfeitures of property used in the commission of a crime, see Bennis v. Michigan, 516 U.S. 442 (1996); regulations that implement the navigation servitude, mentioned in Chapter III, see United States v. Cherokee Nation of Oklahoma, 480 U.S. 700 (1987); and government destruction of property in order to stop the spread of fire, mentioned in *Mahon* and in footnote 16 of the Court's opinion in *Lucas*. See David A. Dana & Thomas W. Merrill, Property: Takings 110–20 (2002).

5.   More generally, what should be the standard for recognizing per se rules of takings liability or nonliability, as opposed to treating claims under *Penn Central's* ad hoc test? Both *Lucas* and *Palazzolo v. Rhode Island*, 533 U.S. 606 (2001), seem to suggest that common-law rules enter into and restrict the title to property when it is acquired, but statutory rules do not, or do so only in a more qualified fashion. What might justify privileging common-law rules over statutory rules in this fashion? Does this provide any clue as to the standard the Court may be implicitly relying upon in recognizing per se rules of liability and nonliability?

6.   Justice Scalia often sought to define constitutional rights in terms of rules rather than broad standards, see Antonin Scalia, The Rule of Law as the Law of Rules, 56 U. Chi. L. Rev. 1175 (1989), and often argued that such rules should be grounded in an objective source like the original understanding of the Framers or in well-established traditions and practices. See Antonin Scalia, A Matter of Interpretation 133–43 (1997). His effort in *Lucas* to define the police power exception in terms of established principles of nuisance law is plausibly regarded as being the product of similar impulses. If this is his objective, however, what do you make of his heavy reliance on the *Restatement (Second) of Torts* as a source for identifying existing rules of nuisance law? Recall from *Hendricks v. Stalnaker* and the notes following it in Chapter I that the *Restatement* essentially would define a nuisance in terms of a case-by-case balancing test. Such balancing tests were usually the last thing Justice Scalia wanted to see adopted in constitutional law. What then accounts for Justice Scalia's willingness to endorse the *Restatement* for purposes of defining the nuisance exception to the new per se rule of liability for total takings? For criticism of this aspect of the decision, see Lynn E. Blais, Takings, Statutes, and the Common Law: Considering Inherent Limitation on Title, 70 S. Cal. L. Rev. 1 (1996); Louise A. Halper, Why the Nuisance Knot Can't Undo the Takings Muddle, 28 Ind. L. Rev. 329 (1995). In addition to nuisance, Justice Scalia mentions in Footnote 16 the conflagration rule as part of the "otherwise" baseline of state law, under which the state can legislate or regulate without takings liability. More recently, *Cedar Point Nursery*, supra, relied on *Lucas* and the idea that certain "background principles" qualify the title to land—in that case, various privileges of entry under conditions of necessity. Should custom more generally be regarded as a source of such "background principles"? See Henry E. Smith, Community and Custom in Property, supra, at 204–06.

7.   Suppose A purchases two beachfront lots for $100,000, intending to build houses on them. The government then imposes a regulation that makes it impossible to build houses on the lots. Rather than filing a lawsuit, A sells the lots to B, for $10,000. (B may want the lots for purposes of sunbathing or may hold them on speculation that the government may change its mind someday and permit them to be built on.) Can B now file a lawsuit challenging the no-construction regulation as a regulatory taking? A problem of this form arose in *Palazzolo v. Rhode Island,* 533 U.S. 606 (2001). The Court held that B was not barred from challenging the regulation by a per se rule of nonliability. Instead, the preexisting regulation, and its impact on "reasonable investment backed expectations," was just another factor to be considered under the *Penn Central* test. Does this ignore the fact that B paid a much-reduced price for the property, in light of the prohibition reflected in the regulation? Or does focusing on B's expectations look at the problem at the wrong moment in time? See William A. Fischel & Perry Shapiro, Takings, Insurance, and Michelman: Comments on Economic Interpretations of "Just Compensation" Law, 17 J. Legal Stud. 269 (1988) (arguing that if a regulatory taking arguably occurred when A owned the land, then B should be regarded as having purchased both the land and A's cause of action for a regulatory taking). Presumably the statute of limitations for A bringing a regulatory takings claim starts to run when the regulation

is first imposed. Once the statute runs on any claim by A, does this mean the government has acquired the right to regulate by prescription, barring any subsequent takings claim by B? Or does the statute start to run again each time the land is transferred?

8.   Justice Blackmun's dissent marshals considerable evidence suggesting that regulations of the use of property were not thought to be "takings" at the time the Fifth Amendment was adopted. Does this mean that *Lucas*'s interpretation of the Takings Clause is contrary to the original understanding of the Framers? This would be ironic, because Justice Scalia, and some of the Justices who joined his opinion (most notably Justice Thomas) have frequently criticized the Court for deviating from the original understanding in its interpretation of the Constitution. See Kelo v. City of New London, supra (Thomas, J., dissenting). Or does the question of original understanding depend on the level of generality with which one describes the views of the Framers? There is no question the members of the framing generation venerated private property and regarded the protection of property to be a central task of government. See generally Jennifer Nedelsky, Private Property and the Limits of American Constitutionalism (1990). If the important "understanding" was that private property should be protected against harsh and oppressive government action, is it contrary to the original understanding to hold that regulations that go beyond traditional nuisance regulation and deny owners all economically beneficial use of property are takings? Also, since the Court here is technically applying the Fourteenth Amendment, which incorporates the Fifth Amendment's Takings Clause, is the relevant history that of the Fourteenth Amendment? See Michael B. Rappaport, Originalism and Regulatory Takings: Why the Fifth Amendment May Not Protect Against Regulatory Takings, But the Fourteenth Amendment May, 45 San Diego L. Rev. 729 (2008).

9.   If because of global warming it becomes necessary to evacuate barrier islands like the Isle of Palms and other low-lying coastal areas to avoid the effects of repeated devastation by storms and flooding, should the government be required to pay compensation to all persons whose property values are wiped out in the process? How do we distinguish between property destroyed by acts of God or nature (with or without an assist from human activity) and those wiped out by acts of government in response to these phenomena? Consider again in this connection the conflagration rule mentioned in *Mahon* and in footnote 16 of Justice Scalia's opinion in *Lucas*. Does the debate between Justice Scalia and Justice Stevens about the generality of the Beachfront Management Act—whether or not it unfairly singles out David Lucas for harsh treatment—also have a bearing on this question? See J. Peter Byrne, Rising Seas and Common Law Baselines: A Comment on Regulatory Takings Discourse Concerning Climate Change, 11 Vt. J. Envtl. L. 625 (2010).

10.   *Lucas* generated much critical scholarship in its aftermath. Some, most notably Richard Epstein, criticized the Court for not going far enough, having declined to find that a partial infringement of a property interest could also be a per se taking. See Richard A. Epstein, *Lucas v. South Carolina Coastal Council*: A Tangled Web of Expectations, 45 Stan. L. Rev.

1369 (1993). Others criticized the Court's backwards-looking approach as going too far in handcuffing modern legislatures that might want to adopt regulations protecting sensitive environmental areas. See Eric T. Freyfogle, The Owning and Taking of Sensitive Lands, 43 UCLA L. Rev. 77, 119–21 (1995). Still others questioned the precedential value of the case in light of subsequent decisions and the idiosyncratic nature of the facts (rarely is all the economic value of a property destroyed). See Richard Lazarus, Putting the Correct "Spin" on *Lucas*, 45 Stan. L. Rev. 1411, 1425 (1993); Joseph L. Sax, Property Rights and the Economy of Nature: Understanding Lucas v. South Carolina Coastal Council, 45 Stan. L. Rev. 1433 (1993).

The Denominator Problem

The denominator problem that arose in applying the diminution in value test under *Pennsylvania Coal* and *Penn Central* is also critical under the *Lucas* "total takings" test, at least if we interpret that test to mean that the regulation has deprived the owner of 100 per cent of the value of the property. For purpose of a diminution in value analysis under either *Penn Central* or *Lucas*'s total takings test, courts must do a before-and-after comparison of values. More precisely, they must compare the "numerator"—the value of the property taken by the regulation—to the "denominator"—the value of the property before the regulation.

As suggested by the dueling opinions of Justices Holmes and Brandeis in *Pennsylvania Coal*, the critical issue here concerns the definition of the "denominator." Recall that in that case, Justice Holmes appeared to assume that the denominator was the pillars of coal that had to remain in place under the regulation, but which could have been mined in the absence of the regulation. Justice Brandeis, in contrast, argued that the denominator should be the "whole property" of the coal company. In more recent opinions, the Court has generally endorsed the suggestion, made in passing in *Penn Central*, that the denominator should be the claimant's "whole parcel." See, e.g., Keystone Bituminous Coal Ass'n v. DeBenedictis, 480 U.S. 470, 498 (1987).

Footnote 7 in *Lucas* adds little to our understanding of the problem. Justice Scalia disapproved of the New York Court of Appeals decision in *Penn Central*, which had suggested that the denominator should be expressed in terms of the "total value of the takings claimant's other holdings in the vicinity." But he ultimately concluded it was unnecessary to resolve the denominator question because Lucas had a fee simple interest in real estate, and there was no question but that this was the interest that was claimed to have been taken.

Potential issues about the proper definition of the denominator continued to arise in the Court's post-*Lucas* decisions. In *Tahoe-Sierra Preservation Council, Inc. v. Tahoe Regional Planning Agency*, 535 U.S. 302 (2002), the Court considered whether a 32-month moratorium on all development of land fell within the categorical rule identified in *Lucas* for total takings of economic value. The Court held that such a moratorium should be assessed under the *Penn Central* ad hoc approach, not the categorical approach of *Lucas*. One reason Justice Stevens cited in favor of this result was that the denominator should not be defined unduly narrowly in temporal terms any more than in physical terms. His majority opinion said in part:

> * * * Petitioners seek to bring this case under the rule announced in *Lucas* by arguing that we can effectively sever a 32-month segment from the remainder of each landowner's fee simple estate, and then ask whether that segment has been taken in its entirety by the moratoria. Of course, defining the property interest taken in terms of the very regulation being challenged is circular. With property so divided, every delay would become a total ban; the moratorium and the normal permit process alike would constitute categorical takings. Petitioners' "conceptual severance" argument is unavailing because it ignores *Penn Central's* admonition that in regulatory takings cases we must focus on "the parcel as a whole." 438 U.S., at 130–131. We have consistently rejected such an approach to the "denominator" question. See Keystone, 480 U.S., at 497. See also Concrete Pipe & Products of Cal., Inc. v. Construction Laborers Pension Trust for Southern Cal., 508 U.S. 602, 644 (1993) ("To the extent that any portion of property is taken, that portion is always taken in its entirety; the relevant question, however, is whether the property taken is all, or only a portion of, the parcel in question"). * * *
>
> An interest in real property is defined by the metes and bounds that describe its geographic dimensions and the term of years that describes the temporal aspect of the owner's interest. See Restatement of Property §§ 7–9 (1936). Both dimensions must be considered if the interest is to be viewed in its entirety. Hence, a permanent deprivation of the owner's use of the entire area is a taking of "the parcel as a whole," whereas a temporary restriction that merely causes a diminution in value is not. Logically, a fee simple estate cannot be rendered valueless by a temporary prohibition on economic use, because the property will recover value as soon as the prohibition is lifted. * * *

535 U.S. at 331–32.

Another source of ambiguity concerns the exact dimensions of the "whole parcel" in any given situation. Suppose, for example, a developer owns a tract of 20 acres, which has been subdivided into 40 lots, which have not yet been developed or sold. Is the "whole parcel" the 20 acres, or is it each individual lot? Does the answer change the minute one of the lots is sold?

Many thought the Court would clarify how to define the physical dimensions of the "whole parcel" in *Murr v. Wisconsin*, 137 S. Ct. 1933 (2017). The specific question was whether a state may consider two adjacent parcels of land owned by the same owner as one parcel for zoning purposes (limiting the owner to constructing one house on the two lots), or whether each parcel must be regarded as a separate interest in property (more likely a taking as to one of the two parcels if it could not be separately developed with a house). The Court held that the determination of the relevant denominator is to be determined by a federal constitutional standard that looks to the owner's "reasonable expectations" as derived from "background customs and the whole of our legal tradition." Id. at 1945. In particular, courts should examine multiple factors, including whether the lots are considered separate or merged as a matter of state and local law, the physical characteristics of the property including whether it is subject to or likely to be subject to environmental or other regulation, and the value of the land under the challenged regulation. Id. at 1945–46. Applying these factors, the Court concluded that the proper denominator in *Murr* was the combined parcels. Having defined the whole parcel in this way, the Court held that the zoning restriction limiting the Murrs to construction of one house was neither a total taking under *Lucas* nor a taking under *Penn Central*'s ad hoc standard.

Commentators have generally been critical of *Murr*. They point out that it adds a second multi-factor test to determine the denominator which must then be applied under the *Lucas* test or *Penn Central*'s multi-factor approach. See Maureen E. Brady, *Penn Central* Squared: What the Many Factors of *Murr v. Wisconsin* Mean for Property Federalism, 166 U. Pa. L. Rev. Online 53 (2017); Nicole Stelle Garnett, From a Muddle to a Mudslide: *Murr v. Wisconsin*, 2017 Cato Sup. Ct. Rev. 131. Moreover, it is not clear that creating a new federal definition of "parcel" is required to prevent manipulation of denominators to affect the outcome of regulatory takings challenges. This concern could be addressed by applying the state law subject to an exception if the evidence suggests state law has been deliberately manipulated to affect an anticipated takings challenge, which will be uncommon given the low rate of success for regulatory takings claims. Thomas W. Merrill, Choice of Law in Takings Cases, 8 Brigham-Kanner Prop. Rights. J. 45 (2019).

Whatever the merits of *Murr*, it will undoubtedly compound the complexity and uncertainty of any regulatory takings approach that relies in whole or part on the idea of diminution in value. Diminution in value was increasingly seen as a losing argument before *Murr*, and *Murr* supplies an additional reason to avoid attempting to establish a regulatory taking by pointing to the economic impact of the regulation.

The Meaning of "Property" for Regulatory Takings Purposes

Most regulatory takings cases, like most eminent domain proceedings, involve property in land. Consequently, in most cases there is no dispute about whether the interest allegedly taken is "property." On occasion, however, regulatory takings claims present more novel types of interests, requiring the courts to determine whether the interest is "private property" protected by the Takings Clause. For the most part, the Supreme Court has sought to resolve "Is it property?" questions in the regulatory takings context by following the general precepts laid down in *Board of Regents v. Roth*, 408 U.S. 564 (1972), a procedural due process case excerpted in Part B, supra. That is, the Court has said that whether a claimant has "private property" is to be determined by looking to independent sources such as state law. As in the procedural due process context, the Court has not been very clear about whether one looks to state law for the definition of property, or only to determine the nature of the claimant's interest, with the characterization whether it is "private property" being a matter of federal constitutional law. See generally David A. Dana & Thomas W. Merrill, Property: Takings ch. IV (2002). Whatever methodology it has followed, the Court for the most part has reached what appear to be defensible conclusions about what is and is not "private property" for takings purposes. Thus, the Court has concluded that leases, trade secrets, and flowage easements are "private property," see id. at 59–60 n.89, but that the head of water in a river, a delegated power of eminent domain, and the right to receive future social security benefits are not, id. at 60 n.90.

One especially contentious issue has involved Interest on Lawyer Trust Accounts or IOLTAs. Lawyers often hold client funds for various purposes, such as advances on anticipated expenses. Under banking regulations, these funds usually cannot be deposited in interest-earning bank accounts. But they can be combined and placed in trust accounts that pay interest, provided the interest is dedicated to a charitable purpose. Many state bar associations therefore required that attorneys place such client funds in trust accounts, with the interest used to underwrite legal services to the poor. In *Phillips v. Washington Legal Foundation*, 524 U.S. 156, 163 (1998), the Court ruled 5–4 that interest earned on sums deposited in IOLTA accounts is the "private property" of the client for Takings Clause purposes, even though the interest would not exist but for the IOLTA account. In reaching this decision, the Court majority purported to follow the methodology for identifying "property" developed in *Roth*, which focuses on whether independent sources of state law recognize an interest in property. In applying this methodology, however, the Court ignored the state rules requiring the deposit of such funds in IOLTA accounts, and instead emphasized that "interest follows principal" as a matter of common law. Id. at 165–66. In this sense, the decision is consistent with *Lucas*, which insists that an owner's title is qualified by common-law nuisance rules in effect when the property is acquired, but not by statutory rules in effect when the property is acquired. Is it plausible to think that "property" is defined solely by judge-made rules of decision, and not also by state statutory law? Many forms of property, like the condominium, have been made possible only by legislation. Some kinds of property rights, like intellectual property, are almost entirely of statutory creation.

Another potentially significant decision, *Eastern Enterprises v. Apfel*, 524 U.S. 498 (1998), raised the question whether a statute that imposes a general liability on employers in the coal mining industry to fund health care benefits for retirees can be challenged under the Takings Clause. Justice O'Connor, writing for a plurality of four, answered yes; she and the Justices who joined her opinion would have invalidated the provision, which applied retroactively, as an uncompensated taking of property. Justice Kennedy concurred only in the judgment. He argued that the law did not affect any identifiable assets of the employers, and hence could not be challenged as a taking. Nevertheless, he provided the fifth vote to invalidate the law, on the ground that it violated substantive due process. Justice Breyer, writing for four dissenters, also agreed that the Takings Clause did not apply, because the law imposed only a general liability, and did not purport to take or regulate any discrete assets. Given that five Justices rejected the application of the Takings Clause, *Eastern Enterprises* suggests that "private property" for purposes of the Takings Clause refers to identifiable things or discrete assets taken by the government, but does not apply when the government simply imposes a general liability or tax that can be satisfied out of any source of wealth. The Court arguably drew back from the discrete asset requirement in *Koontz v. St. Johns River Water Management District*, supra, where the Court held that an exaction in the form of cash as a condition of permitting development would constitute a per se taking if imposed on a freestanding basis. Since the cash could be supplied from any source, this seems more like a general liability. See Thomas W. Merrill, The Landscape of Constitutional Property, 86 Va. L. Rev. 885, 974–78 (2000); Laura S. Underkuffler, *Tahoe*'s Requiem: The Death of the Scalian View of Property and Justice, 21 Const. Comment. 727, 740–46 (2004).

Another case that bears on the meaning of property for constitutional purposes is *College Savings Bank v. Florida Prepaid Postsecondary Education*, 527 U.S. 666 (1999). The issue was whether Congress could subject the states to suits for false advertising under the Lanham Act given its power to enact appropriate legislation to enforce the Due Process Clause of the Fourteenth Amendment. College Savings Bank, the plaintiff, argued that the Lanham Act could be adopted under this power, since it was designed to protect the plaintiff's "property" against deprivations by the state without due process. The Court rejected this argument on the ground that the plaintiff had no "property right" in being free from false advertising by the state. Writing for a bare majority of five, Justice Scalia wrote in part as follows:

> The hallmark of a protected property interest is the right to exclude others. That is "one of the most essential sticks in the bundle of rights that are commonly characterized as property." That is why the right that we all possess to use the public lands is not the "property" right of anyone—hence the sardonic

maxim, explaining what economists call the "tragedy of the commons," *res publica, res nullius*. The Lanham Act may well contain provisions that protect constitutionally cognizable property interests—notably, its provisions dealing with infringement of trademarks, which are the "property" of the owner because he can exclude others from using them. The Lanham Act's false advertising provisions, however, bear no relationship to any right to exclude; and Florida Prepaid's [the state agency's] alleged misrepresentations concerning its own products intruded upon no interest over which petitioner had exclusive dominion.

Id. at 673 (citations omitted).

Does this passage suggest that the Court is prepared to endorse an essentialist conception of property centered on the right to exclude others as the definition of property for federal constitutional purposes? Interestingly, the Court made no mention of *Roth* and the importance of independent sources like state law in either *Eastern Enterprises* or *College Savings Bank*. Does this mean the Court is prepared to abandon the *Roth* approach to defining property for constitutional purposes, at least insofar as it now sees the need to develop a general federal conception of what kinds of state-created interests might qualify as property? Consider also *Cedar Point Nursery*, supra, which seems to elevate the "right to exclude" to constitutional status for takings purposes.

One issue that remains unresolved is whether intellectual property rights should be regarded as "property" for Takings Clause purposes. The Supreme Court has sent mixed signals about this. In *Horne v. Department of Agriculture*, 576 U.S. 350 (2015), which held that personal property (raisins) appropriated by the government for a public use is governed by a *Loretto*-style per se rule, the Court went out of its way to quote a nineteenth-century decision which said a patent could not be appropriated by the government without just compensation. Id. at 359–60, quoting James v. Campbell, 104 U.S. 356, 358 (1882). But in *Oil States Energy Services, LLC v. Greene's Energy Group, LLC*, 138 S. Ct. 1365 (2018), the Court characterized patents as a "public franchise" that can be cancelled through an administrative process without the full evaluation of an Article III court. And in *Allen v. Cooper*, 140 S. Ct. 994, 1008 (2020), Justice Thomas, in a concurring opinion, cautioned that the Court has not resolved whether copyrights are regarded as property for constitutional purposes. For lower court decisions, see Zoltek Corp. v. United States, 442 F.3d 1345 (Fed. Cir. 2006) (per curiam) (holding patents are not protected under the Takings Clause); Jim Olive Photography v. University of Houston System, 624 S.W 3d. 764 (Tex. 2021) (declining to reach the question whether copyrights are protected property under the Takings Clause in the context of a case alleging copyright infringement by a state university). For contrasting evaluations of the historical record, see Adam Mossoff, Patents as Constitutional Private Property: The Historical Protection of Patents under the Takings Clause, 87 B.U. L. Rev. 689 (2007) (arguing that historically patents were property for purposes of the Takings Clause); Greg Reilly, Power Over the Patent Right, 95 Tulane L. Rev. 211 (2021) (contesting this reading of the history).

During the Covid pandemic a proposal was advanced to "waive" international protection for the patents of drug makers who have produced vaccines against the COVID-19 virus. The rationale for the proposal was to speed the production of these vaccines around the world, by effectively turning the vaccines into generic drugs. Would this constitute a taking of the manufacturers' patents? A federal statute, 28 U.S.C. § 1498, effectively allows the federal government to obtain a compulsory license to use any patented technology, upon a determination of just compensation. Would this be a better mechanism for speeding up production of Covid vaccines? The government could invoke its right to a compulsory license, and then authorize other drug companies to produce the patented vaccines.

7. JUDICIAL TAKINGS

Stop the Beach Renourishment, Inc. v. Florida Department of Environmental Protection

United States Supreme Court, 2010.
560 U.S. 702.

■ JUSTICE SCALIA announced the judgment of the Court and delivered the opinion of the Court with respect to Parts I, IV, and V, and an opinion with respect to Parts II and III, in which THE CHIEF JUSTICE, JUSTICE THOMAS, and JUSTICE ALITO join. We consider a claim that the decision of a State's court of last resort took property without just compensation in violation of the Takings Clause of the Fifth Amendment, as applied against the States through the Fourteenth.

I

A

Generally speaking, state law defines property interests, including property rights in navigable waters and the lands underneath them. In Florida, the State owns in trust for the public the land permanently submerged beneath navigable waters and the foreshore (the land between the low-tide line and the mean high-water line). Fla. Const., Art. X, § 11; Broward v. Mabry, 50 So. 826, 829–830 (1909). Thus, the mean high-water line (the average reach of high tide over the preceding 19 years) is the ordinary boundary between private beachfront, or littoral property, and state-owned land.

Littoral owners have, in addition to the rights of the public, certain "special rights" with regard to the water and the foreshore, Broward, 50

So., at 830, rights which Florida considers to be property, generally akin to easements, see ibid.; Thiesen v. Gulf, Florida & Alabama R. Co., 78 So. 491, 500, 507 (1918) (on rehearing). These include the right of access to the water, the right to use the water for certain purposes, the right to an unobstructed view of the water, and the right to receive accretions and relictions to the littoral property. This is generally in accord with well-established common law, although the precise property rights vary among jurisdictions.

At the center of this case is the right to accretions and relictions. Accretions are additions of alluvion (sand, sediment, or other deposits) to waterfront land; relictions are lands once covered by water that become dry when the water recedes. (For simplicity's sake, we shall refer to accretions and relictions collectively as accretions, and the process whereby they occur as accretion.) In order for an addition to dry land to qualify as an accretion, it must have occurred gradually and imperceptibly—that is, so slowly that one could not see the change occurring, though over time the difference became apparent. When, on the other hand, there is a "sudden or perceptible loss of or addition to land by the action of the water or a sudden change in the bed of a lake or the course of a stream," the change is called an avulsion.

In Florida, as at common law, the littoral owner automatically takes title to dry land added to his property by accretion; but formerly submerged land that has become dry land by avulsion continues to belong to the owner of the seabed (usually the State). Thus, regardless of whether an avulsive event exposes land previously submerged or submerges land previously exposed, the boundary between littoral property and sovereign land does not change; it remains (ordinarily) what was the mean high-water line before the event. See Bryant v. Peppe, 238 So. 2d 836, 838–839 (Fla. 1970). It follows from this that, when a new strip of land has been added to the shore by avulsion, the littoral owner has no right to subsequent accretions. Those accretions no longer add to *his* property, since the property abutting the water belongs not to him but to the State.

B

In 1961, Florida's Legislature passed the Beach and Shore Preservation Act, 1961 Fla. Laws ch. 61–246, as amended, Fla. Stat. §§ 161.011–161.45 (2007). The Act establishes procedures for "beach restoration and nourishment projects," designed to deposit sand on eroded beaches (restoration) and to maintain the deposited sand (nourishment). A local government may apply to the Department of Environmental Protection for the funds and the necessary permits to restore a beach. When the project involves placing fill on the State's submerged lands, authorization is required from the Board of Trustees of the Internal Improvement Trust Fund, which holds title to those lands.

Once a beach restoration "is determined to be undertaken," the Board sets what is called "an erosion control line." It must be set by reference to the existing mean high-water line, though in theory it can be located seaward or landward of that.[2] Much of the project work occurs seaward of the erosion-control line, as sand is dumped on what was once submerged land. The fixed erosion-control line replaces the fluctuating mean high-water line as the boundary between privately owned littoral property and state property. Once the erosion-control line is recorded, the common law ceases to increase upland property by accretion (or decrease it by erosion). Thus, when accretion to the shore moves the mean high-water line seaward, the property of beachfront landowners is not extended to that line (as the prior law provided), but remains bounded by the permanent erosion-control line. Those landowners "continue to be entitled," however, "to all common-law riparian rights" other than the right to accretions. If the beach erodes back landward of the erosion-control line over a substantial portion of the shoreline covered by the project, the Board may, on its own initiative, or must, if asked by the owners or lessees of a majority of the property affected, direct the agency responsible for maintaining the beach to return the beach to the condition contemplated by the project. If that is not done within a year, the project is canceled and the erosion-control line is null and void. Finally, by regulation, if the use of submerged land would "unreasonably infringe on riparian rights," the project cannot proceed unless the local governments show that they own or have a property interest in the upland property adjacent to the project site.

C

In 2003, the city of Destin and Walton County applied for the necessary permits to restore 6.9 miles of beach within their jurisdictions that had been eroded by several hurricanes. The project envisioned depositing along that shore sand dredged from further out. It would add about 75 feet of dry sand seaward of the mean high-water line (to be denominated the erosion-control line). The Department issued a notice of intent to award the permits, and the Board approved the erosion-control line.

The petitioner here, Stop the Beach Renourishment, Inc., is a nonprofit corporation formed by people who own beachfront property bordering the project area (we shall refer to them as the Members). It brought an administrative challenge to the proposed project, which was unsuccessful; the Department approved the permits. Petitioner then challenged that action in state court under the Florida Administrative Procedure Act. The District Court of Appeal for the First District concluded that, contrary to the Act's preservation of "all common-law riparian rights," the order had eliminated two of the Members' littoral rights: (1) the right to receive accretions to their property; and (2) the

---

[2]   We assume, as the parties agree we should, that in this case the erosion-control line is the pre-existing mean high-water line. Tr. of Oral Arg. 11–12. Respondents concede that, if the erosion-control line were established landward of that, the State would have taken property. Brief for Respondent Department et al. 15; Brief for Respondent Walton County et al. 6.

right to have the contact of their property with the water remain intact. This, it believed, would be an unconstitutional taking, which would "unreasonably infringe on riparian rights," and therefore require the showing * * * that the local governments owned or had a property interest in the upland property. It set aside the Department's final order approving the permits and remanded for that showing to be made. It also certified to the Florida Supreme Court the following question (as rephrased by the latter court):

On its face, does the Beach and Shore Preservation Act unconstitutionally deprive upland owners of littoral rights without just compensation?[3]

The Florida Supreme Court answered the certified question in the negative, and quashed the First District's remand. It faulted the Court of Appeal for not considering the doctrine of avulsion, which it concluded permitted the State to reclaim the restored beach on behalf of the public. It described the right to accretions as a future contingent interest, not a vested property right, and held that there is no littoral right to contact with the water independent of the littoral right of access, which the Act does not infringe. Petitioner sought rehearing on the ground that the Florida Supreme Court's decision itself effected a taking of the Members' littoral rights contrary to the Fifth and Fourteenth Amendments to the Federal Constitution.[4] The request for rehearing was denied. We granted certiorari.

II

A

Before coming to the parties' arguments in the present case, we discuss some general principles of our takings jurisprudence. The Takings Clause—"nor shall private property be taken for public use, without just compensation," U.S. Const., Amdt. 5—applies as fully to the taking of a landowner's riparian rights as it does to the taking of an estate in land. Moreover, though the classic taking is a transfer of property to the State or to another private party by eminent domain, the Takings Clause applies to other state actions that achieve the same thing. Thus, when the government uses its own property in such a way that it destroys private property, it has taken that property. See United States v. Causby, 328 U.S. 256, 261–262 (1946); Pumpelly v. Green Bay Co., 80 U.S. 166 (1872). Similarly, our doctrine of regulatory takings "aims to identify regulatory actions that are functionally equivalent to the classic taking."

---

[3]   The Florida Supreme Court seemingly took the question to refer to constitutionality under the Florida Constitution, which contains a clause similar to the Takings Clause of the Federal Constitution. Compare Fla. Const., Art. X, § 6, cl. (a), with U.S. Const., Amdt. 5.

[4]   We ordinarily do not consider an issue first presented to a state court in a petition for rehearing if the state court did not address it. See Adams v. Robertson, 520 U.S. 83, 89, n. 3 (1997) (per curiam). But where the state-court decision itself is claimed to constitute a violation of federal law, the state court's refusal to address that claim put forward in a petition for rehearing will not bar our review. See Brinkerhoff-Faris Trust & Sav. Co. v. Hill, 281 U.S. 673, 677–678 (1930).

Lingle v. Chevron U.S.A. Inc., 544 U.S. 528, 539 (2005). Thus, it is a taking when a state regulation forces a property owner to submit to a permanent physical occupation, Loretto v. Teleprompter Manhattan CATV Corp., 458 U.S. 419, 425–426 (1982), or deprives him of all economically beneficial use of his property, Lucas v. South Carolina Coastal Council, 505 U.S. 1003, 1019 (1992). Finally (and here we approach the situation before us), States effect a taking if they recharacterize as public property what was previously private property. See Webb's Fabulous Pharmacies, Inc. v. Beckwith, 449 U.S. 155, 163–165 (1980).

The Takings Clause (unlike, for instance, the Ex Post Facto Clauses, see Art. I, § 9, cl. 3; § 10, cl. 1) is not addressed to the action of a specific branch or branches. It is concerned simply with the act, and not with the governmental actor ("nor shall private property *be taken*" (emphasis added)). There is no textual justification for saying that the existence or the scope of a State's power to expropriate private property without just compensation varies according to the branch of government effecting the expropriation. Nor does common sense recommend such a principle. It would be absurd to allow a State to do by judicial decree what the Takings Clause forbids it to do by legislative fiat. * * *

In sum, the Takings Clause bars *the State* from taking private property without paying for it, no matter which branch is the instrument of the taking. To be sure, the manner of state action may matter: Condemnation by eminent domain, for example, is always a taking, while a legislative, executive, or judicial restriction of property use may or may not be, depending on its nature and extent. But the particular state *actor* is irrelevant. If a legislature *or a court* declares that what was once an established right of private property no longer exists, it has taken that property, no less than if the State had physically appropriated it or destroyed its value by regulation. "[A] State, by *ipse dixit*, may not transform private property into public property without compensation." [Webb's Fabulous Pharmacies, supra at 164.]

B

JUSTICE BREYER's concurrence says that we need neither (1) to decide whether the judiciary can ever effect a taking, nor (2) to establish the standard for determining whether it has done so. The second part of this is surely incompatible with JUSTICE BREYER's conclusion that the "Florida Supreme Court's decision in this case did not amount to a 'judicial taking.'" One cannot know whether a takings claim is invalid without knowing what standard it has failed to meet. Which means that JUSTICE BREYER must either (a) grapple with the artificial question of what would constitute a judicial taking if there were such a thing as a judicial taking (reminiscent of the perplexing question how much wood would a woodchuck chuck if a woodchuck could chuck wood?), or (b) answer in the negative what he considers to be the "unnecessary" constitutional question whether there is such a thing as a judicial taking. * * *

JUSTICE BREYER cannot decide that petitioner's claim fails without first deciding what a valid claim would consist of. His agreement with Part IV of our opinion necessarily implies agreement with the test for a judicial taking (elaborated in Part II-A) which Part IV applies: whether the state court has "declare[d] that what was once an established right of private property no longer exists." JUSTICE BREYER must either agree with that standard or craft one of his own. And agreeing to or crafting a *hypothetical* standard for a *hypothetical* constitutional right is sufficiently unappealing (we have eschewed that course many times in the past) that JUSTICE BREYER might as well acknowledge the right as well. Or he could avoid the need to agree with or craft a hypothetical standard by *denying* the right. But embracing a standard while being coy about the right is, well, odd; and deciding this case while addressing *neither* the standard *nor* the right is quite impossible. * * *

C

Like JUSTICE BREYER's concurrence, JUSTICE KENNEDY's concludes that the Florida Supreme Court's action here does not meet the standard for a judicial taking, while purporting not to determine what is the standard for a judicial taking, or indeed whether such a thing as a judicial taking even exists. That approach is invalid for the reasons we have discussed.* * *

III

Respondents put forward a number of arguments which contradict, to a greater or lesser degree, the principle discussed above, that the existence of a taking does not depend upon the branch of government that effects it. First, in a case claiming a judicial taking they would add to our normal takings inquiry a requirement that the court's decision have no "fair and substantial basis." This is taken from our jurisprudence dealing with the question whether a state-court decision rests upon adequate and independent state grounds, placing it beyond our jurisdiction to review. To assure that there is no "evasion" of our authority to review federal questions, we insist that the nonfederal ground of decision have "fair support." Broad River Power Co. v. South Carolina ex rel. Daniel, 281 U.S. 537, 540 (1930); see also Ward v. Board of Comm'rs of Love Cty., 253 U.S. 17, 22–23 (1920). A test designed to determine whether there has been an evasion is not obviously appropriate for determining whether there has been a taking of property. But if it is to be extended there it must mean (in the present context) that there is a "fair and substantial basis" for believing that petitioner's Members did not have a property right to future accretions which the Act would take away. This is no different, we think, from our requirement that petitioners' Members must prove the elimination of an established property right.[9]

Next, respondents argue that federal courts lack the knowledge of state law required to decide whether a judicial decision that purports merely to clarify property rights has instead taken them. But federal courts must often decide what state property rights exist in nontakings contexts, see, e.g., Board of Regents of State Colleges v. Roth, 408 U.S. 564, 577–578 (1972) (Due Process Clause). And indeed they must decide it to resolve claims that legislative or executive action has effected a taking. For example, a regulation that deprives a property owner of all economically beneficial use of his property is not a taking if the restriction "inhere[s] in the title itself, in the restrictions that background principles of the State's law of property and nuisance already place upon land ownership." Lucas, 505 U.S., at 1029. A constitutional provision that forbids the uncompensated taking of property is quite simply insusceptible of enforcement by federal courts unless they have the power to decide what property rights exist under state law.

Respondents also warn us against depriving common-law judging of needed flexibility. That argument has little appeal when directed against the enforcement of a constitutional guarantee adopted in an era when, as we said, courts had no power to "change" the common law. But in any case, courts have no peculiar need of flexibility. It is no more essential that judges be free to overrule prior cases that establish property entitlements than that state legislators be free to revise pre-existing statutes that confer property entitlements, or agency-heads pre-existing regulations that do so. And insofar as courts merely clarify and elaborate property entitlements that were previously unclear, they cannot be said to have taken an established property right. * * *

For its part, petitioner proposes an unpredictability test. Quoting Justice Stewart's concurrence in *Hughes v. Washington,* 389 U.S. 290, 296 (1967), petitioner argues that a judicial taking consists of a decision that " 'constitutes a sudden change in state law, unpredictable in terms of relevant precedents.' " The focus of petitioner's test is misdirected. What counts is not whether there is precedent for the allegedly confiscatory decision, but whether the property right allegedly taken was established. A "predictability of change" test would cover both too much and too little. Too much, because a judicial property decision need not be predictable, so long as it does not declare that what had been private property under established law no longer is. A decision that clarifies property entitlements (or the lack thereof) that were previously unclear might be difficult to predict, but it does not eliminate established

---

9   JUSTICE BREYER complains that we do not set forth "procedural limitations or canons of deference" to restrict federal-court review of state-court property decisions. * * * The test we have adopted, however (deprivation of an *established* property right), contains within itself a considerable degree of deference to state courts. A property right is not established if there is doubt about its existence; and when there is doubt we do not make our own assessment but accept the determination of the state court.

property rights. And the predictability test covers too little, because a judicial elimination of established private-property rights that is foreshadowed by dicta or even by holdings years in advance is nonetheless a taking. If, for example, a state court held in one case, to which the complaining property owner was not a party, that it had the power to limit the acreage of privately owned real estate to 100 acres, and then, in a second case, applied that principle to declare the complainant's 101st acre to be public property, the State would have taken an acre from the complainant even though the decision was predictable.

IV

We come at last to petitioner's takings attack on the decision below. * * *

Petitioner argues that the Florida Supreme Court took two of the property rights of the Members by declaring that those rights did not exist: the right to accretions, and the right to have littoral property touch the water (which petitioner distinguishes from the mere right of access to the water). Under petitioner's theory, because no prior Florida decision had said that the State's filling of submerged tidal lands could have the effect of depriving a littoral owner of contact with the water and denying him future accretions, the Florida Supreme Court's judgment in the present case abolished those two easements to which littoral property owners had been entitled. This puts the burden on the wrong party. There is no taking unless petitioner can show that, before the Florida Supreme Court's decision, littoral-property owners had rights to future accretions and contact with the water superior to the State's right to fill in its submerged land. Though some may think the question close, in our view the showing cannot be made.

Two core principles of Florida property law intersect in this case. First, the State as owner of the submerged land adjacent to littoral property has the right to fill that land, so long as it does not interfere with the rights of the public and the rights of littoral landowners. See Hayes v. Bowman, 91 So. 2d 795, 799–800 (Fla. 1957) (right to fill conveyed by State to private party); State ex rel. Buford v. Tampa, 102 So. 336, 341 (1924) (same). Second, as we described supra, if an avulsion exposes land seaward of littoral property that had previously been submerged, that land belongs to the State even if it interrupts the littoral owner's contact with the water. See Bryant, 238 So. 2d, at 837, 838–839. The issue here is whether there is an exception to this rule when the State is the cause of the avulsion. Prior law suggests there is not. In *Martin v. Busch,* 112 So. 274 (1927), the Florida Supreme Court held that when the State drained water from a lakebed belonging to the State, causing land that was formerly below the mean high-water line to become dry land, that land continued to belong to the State. 112 So., at 287; see also Bryant, supra, at 838–839 (analogizing the situation in *Martin* to an avulsion). " 'The riparian rights doctrine of accretion and reliction,' " the

Florida Supreme Court later explained, " 'does not apply to such lands.' " Bryant, supra, at 839 (quoting Martin, supra, at 112 So., at 288 (Brown, J., concurring)). This is not surprising, as there can be no accretions to land that no longer abuts the water.

Thus, Florida law as it stood before the decision below allowed the State to fill in its own seabed, and the resulting sudden exposure of previously submerged land was treated like an avulsion for purposes of ownership. The right to accretions was therefore subordinate to the State's right to fill. * * *

The Florida Supreme Court decision before us is consistent with these background principles of state property law. Cf. Lucas, 505 U.S., at 1028–1029; Scranton v. Wheeler, 179 U.S. 141, 163 (1900). It did not abolish the Members' right to future accretions, but merely held that the right was not implicated by the beach-restoration project, because the doctrine of avulsion applied. The Florida Supreme Court's opinion describes beach restoration as the reclamation by the State of the public's land, just as *Martin* had described the lake drainage in that case. Although the opinion does not cite *Martin* and is not always clear on this point, it suffices that its characterization of the littoral right to accretion is consistent with *Martin* and the other relevant principles of Florida law we have discussed.

* * * The result under Florida law may seem counter-intuitive. After all, the Members' property has been deprived of its character (and value) as oceanfront property by the State's artificial creation of an avulsion. Perhaps state-created avulsions ought to be treated differently from other avulsions insofar as the property right to accretion is concerned. But nothing in prior Florida law makes such a distinction, and *Martin* suggests, if it does not indeed hold, the contrary. Even if there might be different interpretations of *Martin* and other Florida property-law cases that would prevent this arguably odd result, we are not free to adopt them. The Takings Clause only protects property rights as they are established under state law, not as they might have been established or ought to have been established. We cannot say that the Florida Supreme Court's decision eliminated a right of accretion established under Florida law.

Petitioner also contends that the State took the Members' littoral right to have their property continually maintain contact with the water. To be clear, petitioner does not allege that the State relocated the property line, as would have happened if the erosion-control line were *landward* of the old mean high-water line (instead of identical to it). Petitioner argues instead that the Members have a separate right for the boundary of their property to be always the mean high-water line. Petitioner points to dicta in [*Board of Trustees of Internal Improvement Trust Fund v. Sand Key Assocs., Ltd.*, 512 So.2d 934 (Fla. 1987)] that refers to "the right to have the property's contact with the water remain intact," 512 So. 2d, at 936. Even there, the right was included in the definition of the right to access, ibid., which is consistent with the Florida Supreme Court's later description that "there is no independent right of contact with the water" but it "exists to preserve the upland owner's core littoral right of access to the water." Petitioner's expansive interpretation of the dictum in *Sand Key* would cause it to contradict the clear Florida law governing avulsion. One cannot say that the Florida Supreme Court contravened established property law by rejecting it.

V

Because the Florida Supreme Court's decision did not contravene the established property rights of petitioner's Members, Florida has not violated the Fifth and Fourteenth Amendments. The judgment of the Florida Supreme Court is therefore affirmed.

It is so ordered.

■ JUSTICE STEVENS took no part in the decision of this case.

■ JUSTICE KENNEDY, with whom JUSTICE SOTOMAYOR joins, concurring in part and concurring in the judgment. The Court's analysis of the principles that control ownership of the land in question, and of the rights of petitioner's members as adjacent owners, is correct in my view, leading to my joining Parts I, IV, and V of the Court's opinion. As Justice Breyer observes, however, this case does not require the Court to determine whether, or when, a judicial decision determining the rights of property owners can violate the Takings Clause of the Fifth Amendment of the United States Constitution. * * *

■ JUSTICE BREYER, with whom JUSTICE GINSBURG joins, concurring in part and concurring in the judgment. I agree that no unconstitutional taking of property occurred in this case, and I therefore join Parts I, IV, and V of today's opinion. I cannot join Parts II and III, however, for in those Parts the plurality unnecessarily addresses questions of constitutional law that are better left for another day.

* * * [I]f we were to express our views on these questions, we would invite a host of federal takings claims without the mature consideration of potential procedural or substantive legal principles that might limit federal interference in matters that are primarily the subject of state law. Property owners litigate many thousands of cases involving state property law in state courts each year. Each state-court property decision may further affect numerous nonparty property owners as well. Losing parties in many state-court cases may well believe that erroneous judicial decisions have deprived them of property rights they previously held and may consequently bring federal takings claims. And a glance at Part IV makes clear that such cases can involve state property law issues of considerable complexity. Hence, the approach the plurality would take today threatens to open the federal court doors to constitutional review of many, perhaps large numbers of, state-law cases in an area of law familiar to state, but not federal, judges. And the failure of that approach to set forth procedural limitations or canons of deference would create

the distinct possibility that federal judges would play a major role in the shaping of a matter of significant state interest—state property law.

The plurality criticizes me for my cautious approach, and states that I "cannot decide that petitioner's claim fails without first deciding what a valid claim would consist of." But, of course, courts frequently find it possible to resolve cases—even those raising constitutional questions—without specifying the precise standard under which a party wins or loses. That is simply what I would do here.

In the past, Members of this Court have warned us that, when faced with difficult constitutional questions, we should "confine ourselves to deciding only what is necessary to the disposition of the immediate case." Whitehouse v. Illinois Central R. Co., 349 U.S. 366, 373 (1955). I heed this advice here. There is no need now to decide more than what the Court decides in Parts IV and V, namely, that the Florida Supreme Court's decision in this case did not amount to a "judicial taking."

NOTES AND QUESTIONS

1. For further commentary on *Stop the Beach*, see D. Benjamin Barros, The Complexities of Judicial Takings, 45 U. Rich. L. Rev. 903 (2011); Frederick Bloom & Christopher Serkin, Suing Courts, 79 U. Chi. L. Rev. 553 (2012); Amnon Lehavi, Judicial Review of Judicial Lawmaking, 96 Minn. L. Rev. 520 (2011); Laura S. Underkuffler, Symposium: *Stop the Beach Renourishment v. Florida Department of Environmental Protection*: Judicial Takings: A Medley of Misconceptions, 61 Syracuse L. Rev. 203, 206–10 (2011). Was it possible to decide the case without determining whether there can be such a thing as a judicial taking? One possibility would be to ask whether a taking would have occurred if the Florida legislature (or executive) had by statute or regulation abrogated the right to future accretions and the right to have littoral property touch the water as part of a beach restoration program. Assume the statute provides that construction of the new beach will eliminate any right to future accretion (and liability for future erosion). A littoral owner whose property abuts the new beach would lose physical contact with the water, but would not lose any square footage of property (the boundary line would remain unchanged) and would still have the right of access to the water and an unobstructed view of the water. How would a takings claim challenging such a statute be assessed under *Loretto*? Under *Lucas*? Under the ad hoc test of either *Pennsylvania Coal* or *Penn Central*? If the answer is that the legislature would not have committed a taking under any of these tests, then could it possibly be said that the Florida Supreme Court had committed a taking in rendering a judicial judgment saying the elimination of these asserted rights did not contradict Florida property law?

2. Does *Stop the Beach* strengthen or weaken the autonomy of states in determining the content of property law? On the one hand, the opinion states in Part I that the content of property is determined by state law and can differ from one state to another. And Part IV says that established principles of state property law are immune from challenge as judicial

takings, even if they appear to be "counter-intuitive" or unjust. Thus, the Court holds that littoral owners whose property is cut off from direct contact with the water by a public beach project have no judicial takings claim, because prior Florida decisions had given the state the power to make "artificial avulsions" on submerged public land. On the other hand, Justice Scalia insists that in order to determine whether a judicial taking has occurred, federal courts must determine the content of state property law independently, without deferring to the judgment of the state judiciary in the challenged decision. In response to Justice Breyer's plea for "canons of deference" that would prevent federal courts from intruding into matters of state property law, Justice Scalia responds that federal courts must exercise independent judgment about state property law in order to give effect to the constitutional protection in the Takings Clause. Given that Parts I and IV are opinions of the Court, whereas the discussion about the need to exercise independent judgment is a plurality opinion as to which the Court was evenly divided, can it be argued that *Stop the Beach* actually enhances state autonomy over property rights?

3.   In striking the balance between protecting federal constitutional rights and preserving state court freedom in interpreting state law, the Supreme Court has most often said that it will defer to state court interpretations of state law as long as they have a "fair or substantial basis." Justice Scalia in *Stop the Beach* would adopt a different approach for judicial takings claims, asking whether the state court has eliminated an "established property right." Federal courts would exercise independent judgment in making this inquiry. But he argues in footnote 9 that the standard has deference built into it: if there is "doubt about the existence" of a right then it is not "established," and hence the state court is entitled to clarify the law without federal second-guessing. Who has the better view here? For competing perspectives, see Henry Paul Monaghan, Supreme Court Review of State-Court Determinations of State Law in Constitutional Cases, 103 Colum. L. Rev. 1919 (2003) (federal courts must exercise independent judgment as to state law issues that are "logically antecedent" to a claim of federal constitutional right); E. Brantley Webb, How to Review State Court Determination of State Law Antecedent to Federal Rights, 120 Yale L.J. 1192 (2011) (the fair or substantial basis standard has been applied most frequently by the Supreme Court in a variety of contexts and strikes the best balance between enforcement of federal rights and protection of state autonomy).

4.   Can federal courts determine if a state court has eliminated an "established property right" without having some conception—grounded in federal constitutional law—about what counts as a property right? In particular, do judicial takings claims implicate the same "conceptual severance" or "numerator/denominator" problems that have vexed regulatory takings law more generally? Suppose the Court in *Stop the Beach* had concluded that the right to future accretions was firmly established in Florida property law, and that the state supreme court had eliminated this right. Would this not then present the further question whether the right to future accretion was itself a "property right" as opposed to merely one

incident of property—one stick in the bundle of rights that belong to riparian or littoral owners? If the right to future accretion is the "property right," then its elimination sounds like a taking. But if the relevant denominator is the "whole parcel" owned by the littoral owner, then elimination of future accretions only removes one portion of the total property right, and it would be much less likely to be regarded as a taking. Given all the ink that has been spilled over this issue, in decisions like *Penn Central, Palazzolo,* and *Tahoe-Sierra,* are you surprised that Justice Scalia makes no mention of it? Is there any justification for adopting a different conception of the relevant unit of property or denominator for judicial takings purposes, as opposed to more conventional regulatory takings purposes involving legislative or executive action?

5.   Although this case is known for the Court's struggle with the possibility of judicial takings, notice that it raises issues from earlier in our study of property, from accession to the *numerus clausus.* Does the idea of a legal notion of a thing and courts' (usual) deference to legislatures in altering the list of property rights counsel against—or for—policing by federal courts for possible judicial takings?

INDEX

References are to Pages